The Renaissance

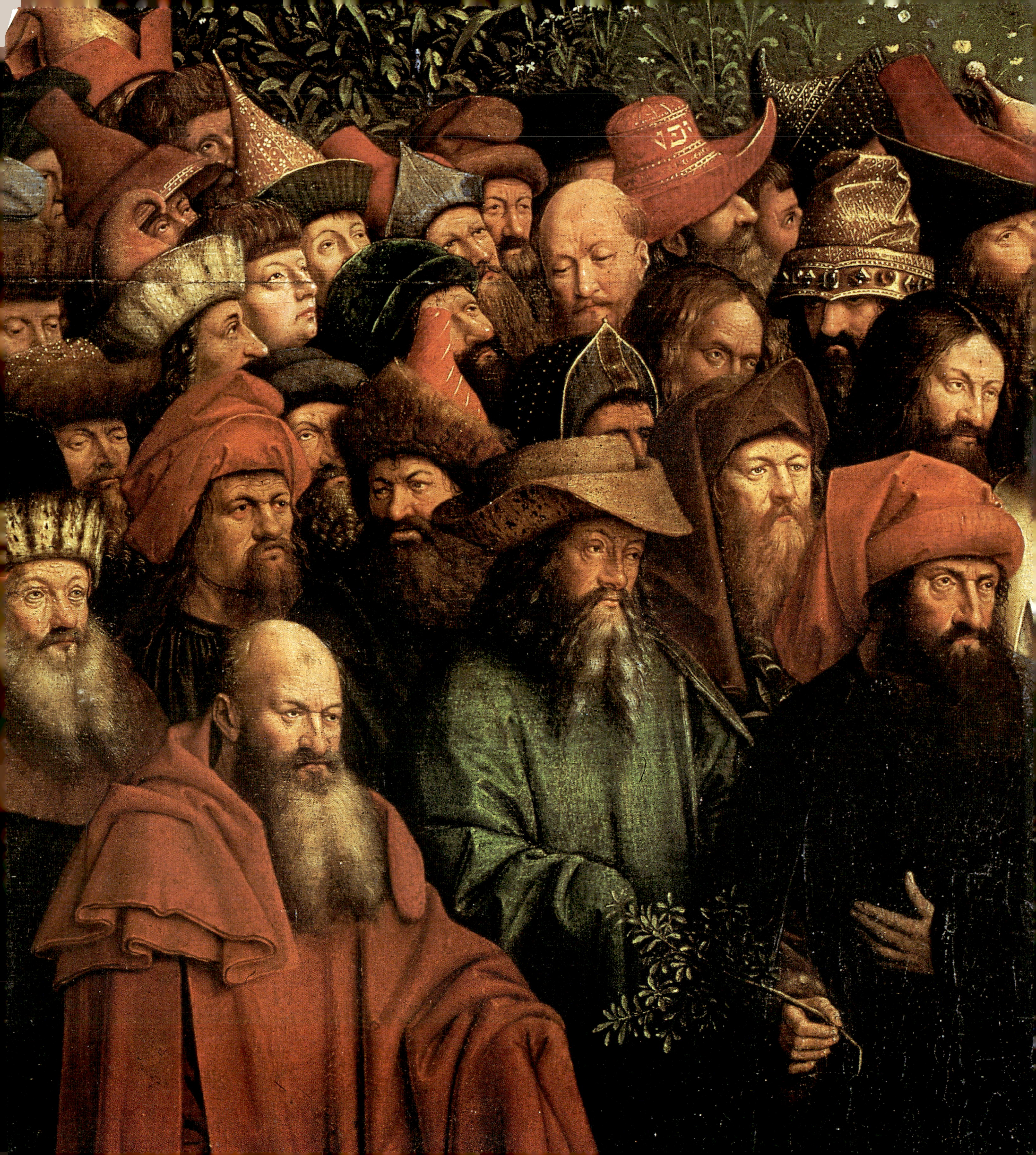

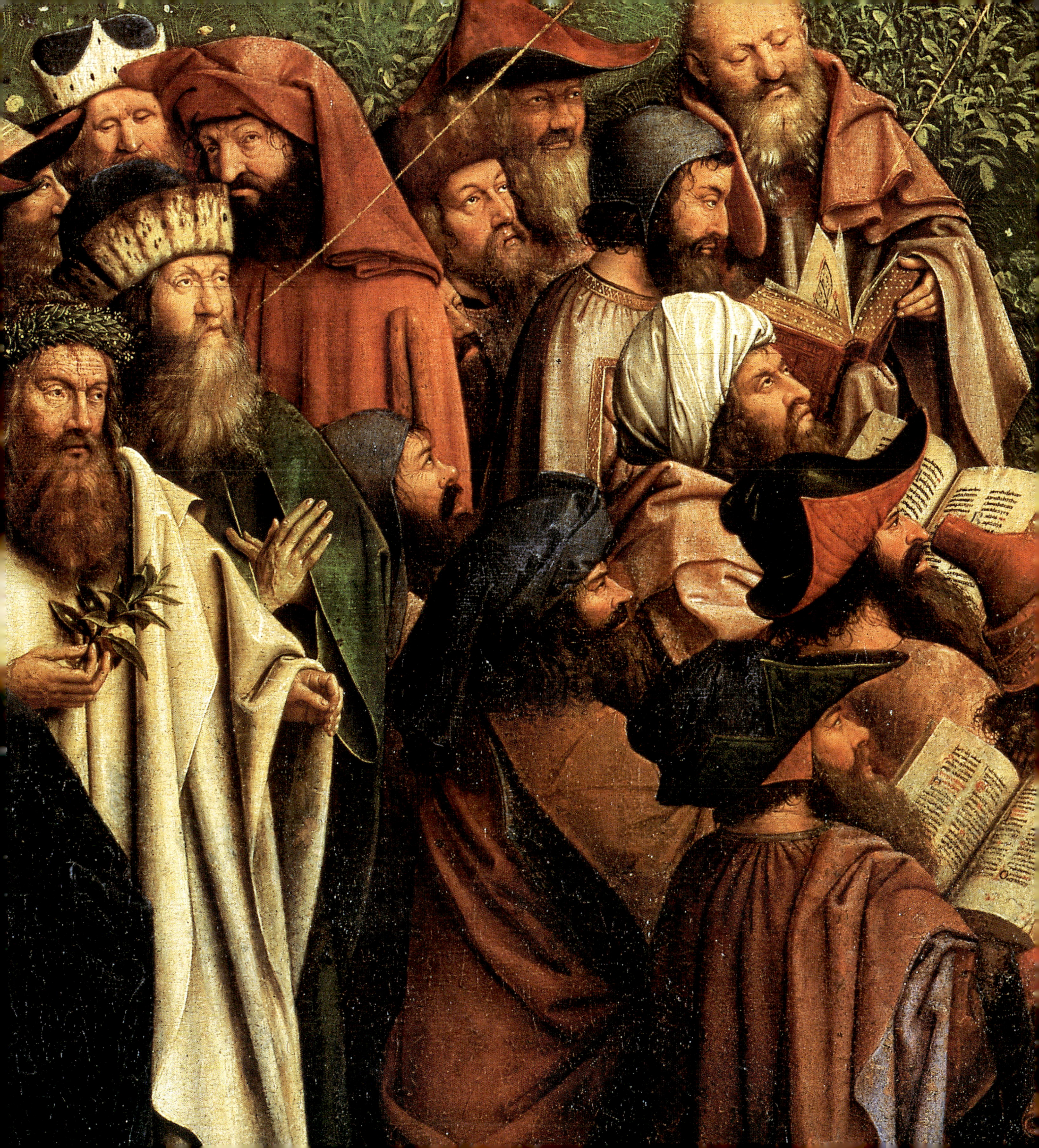

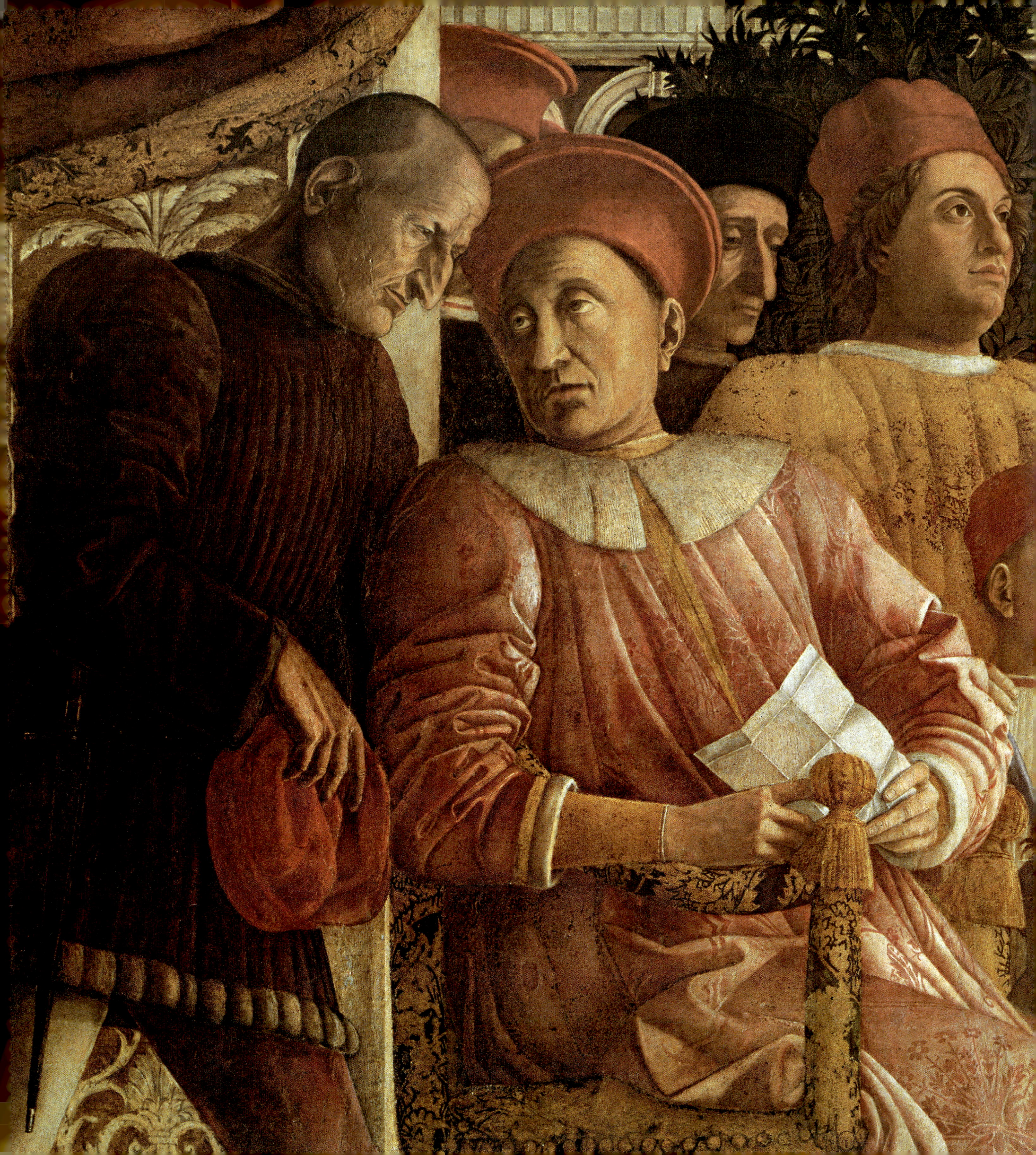

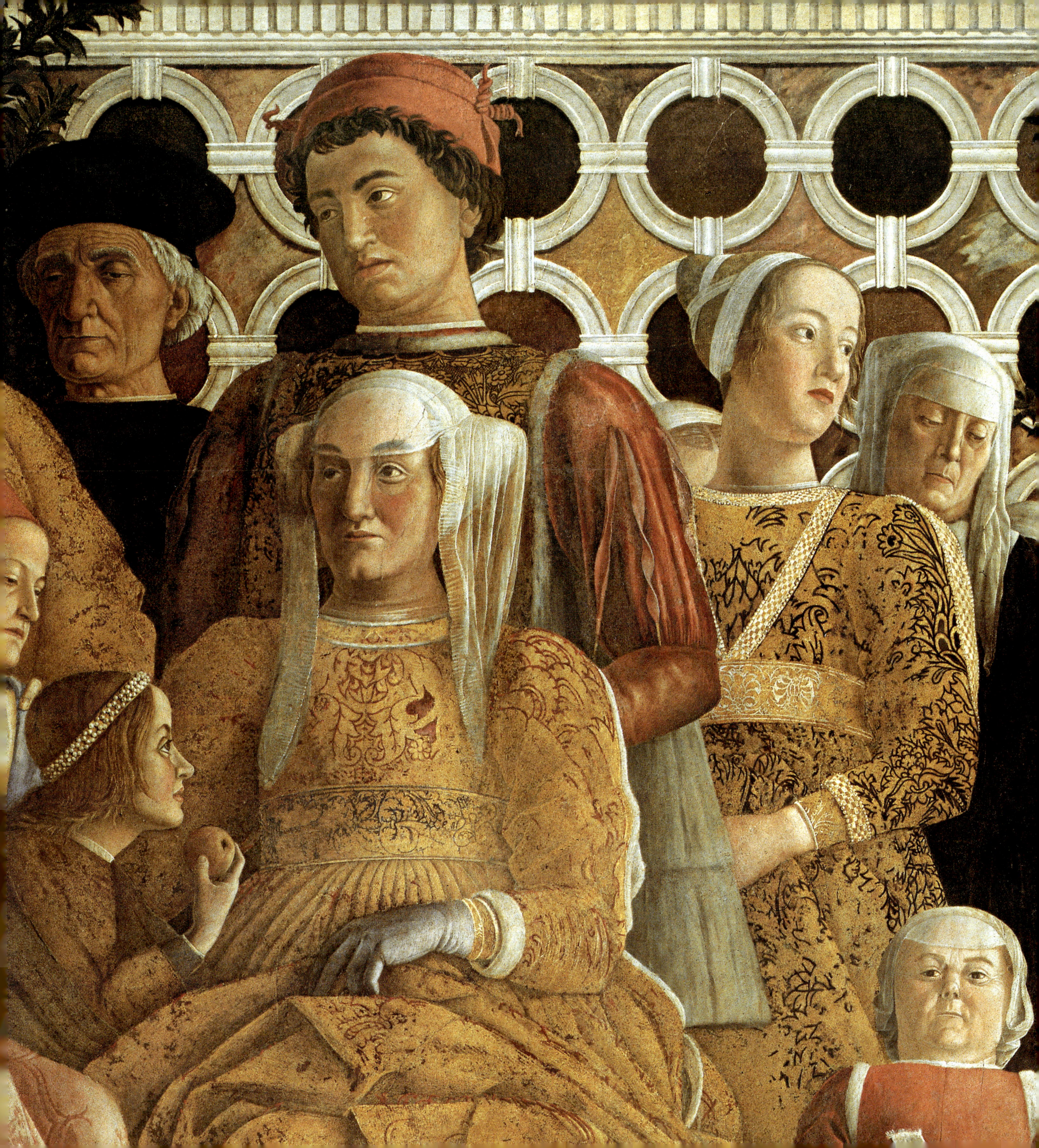

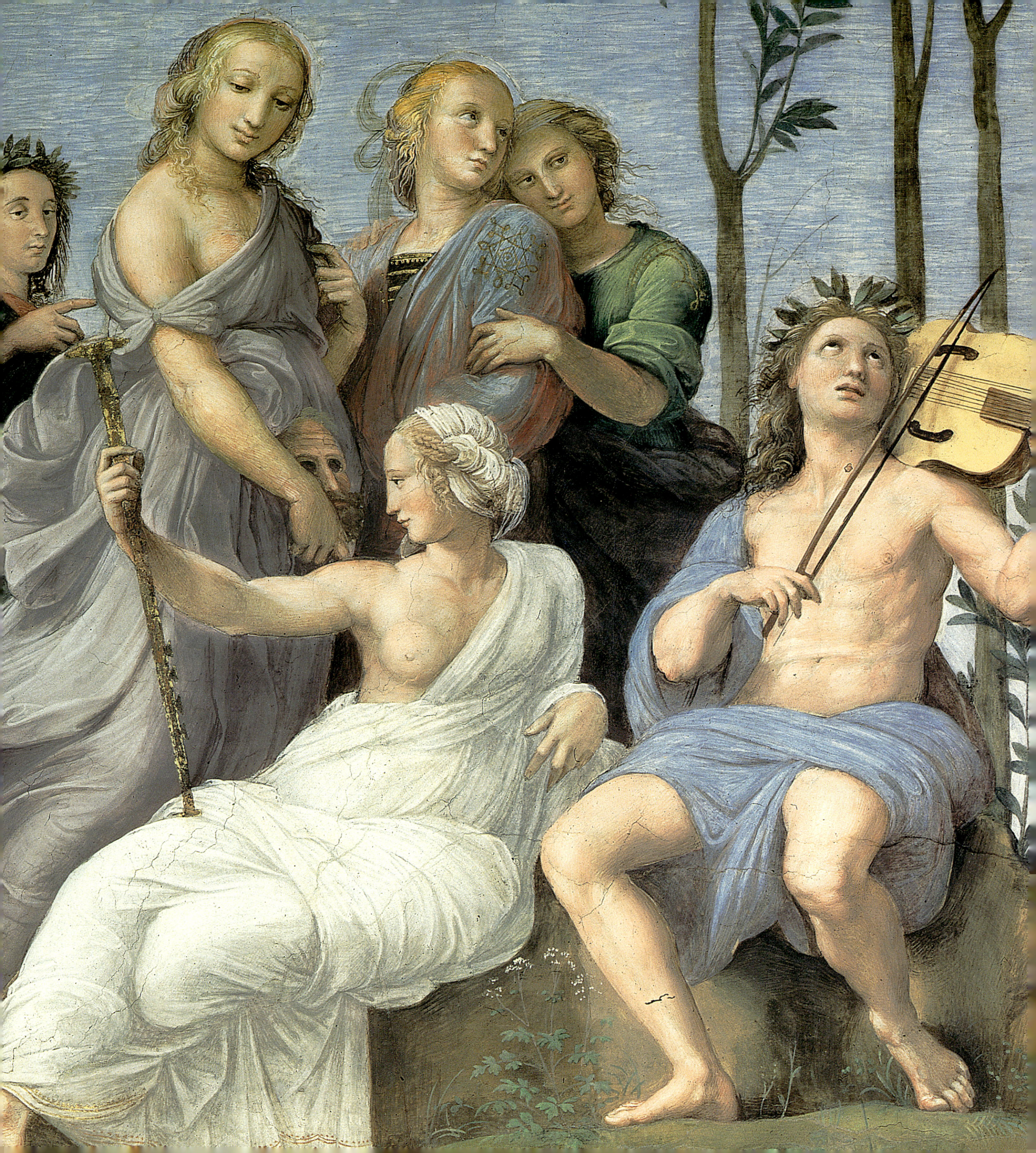

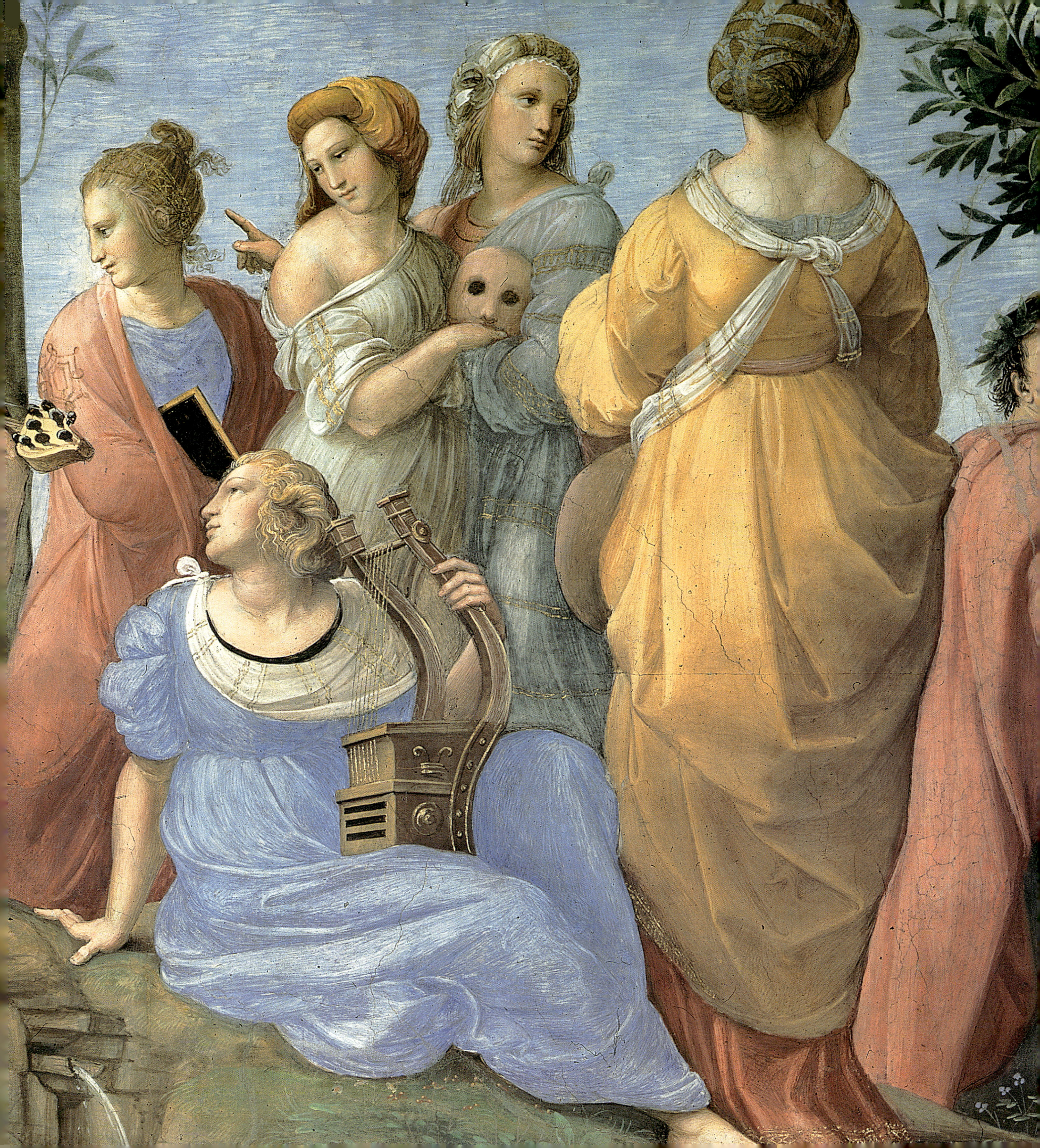

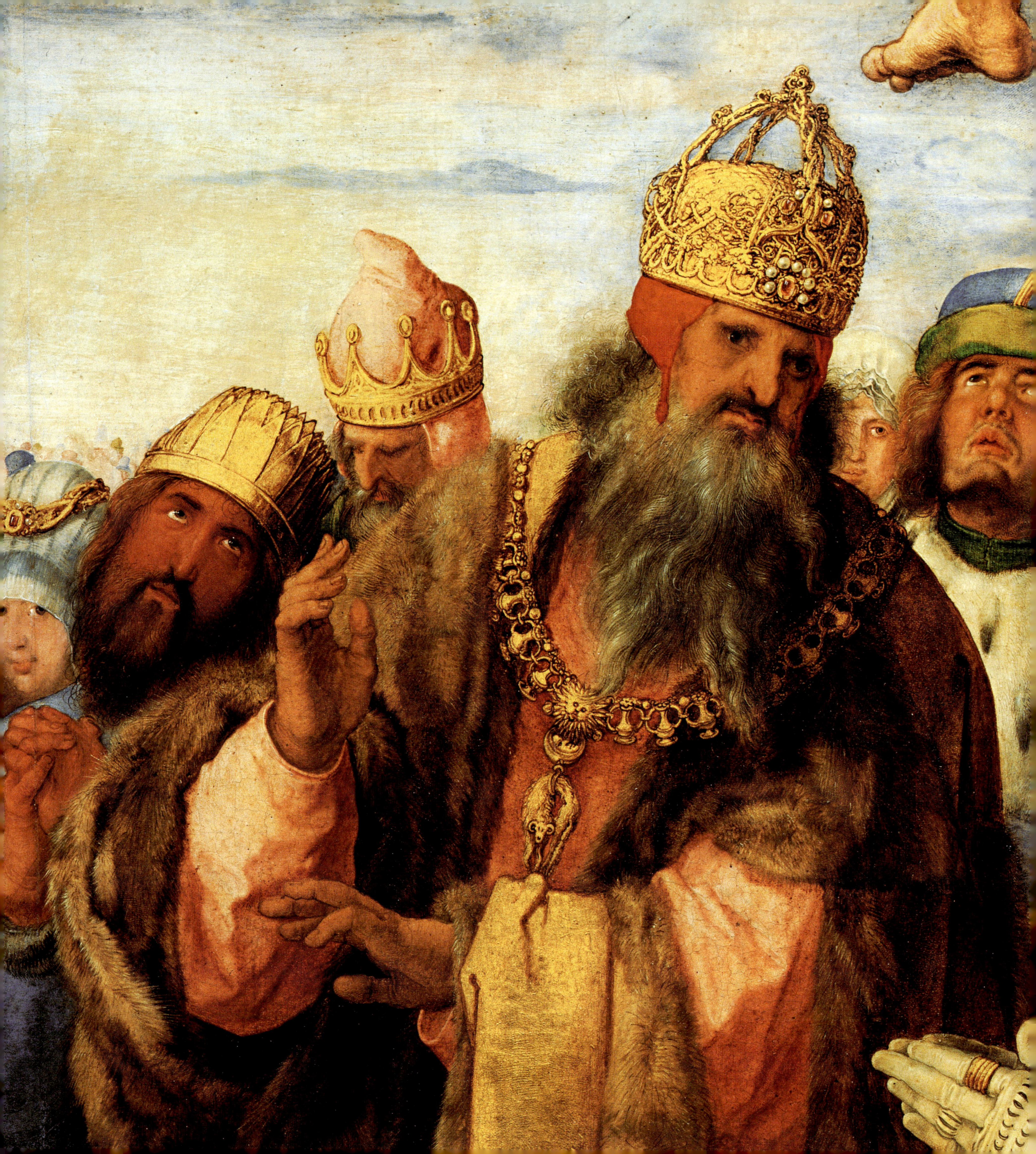

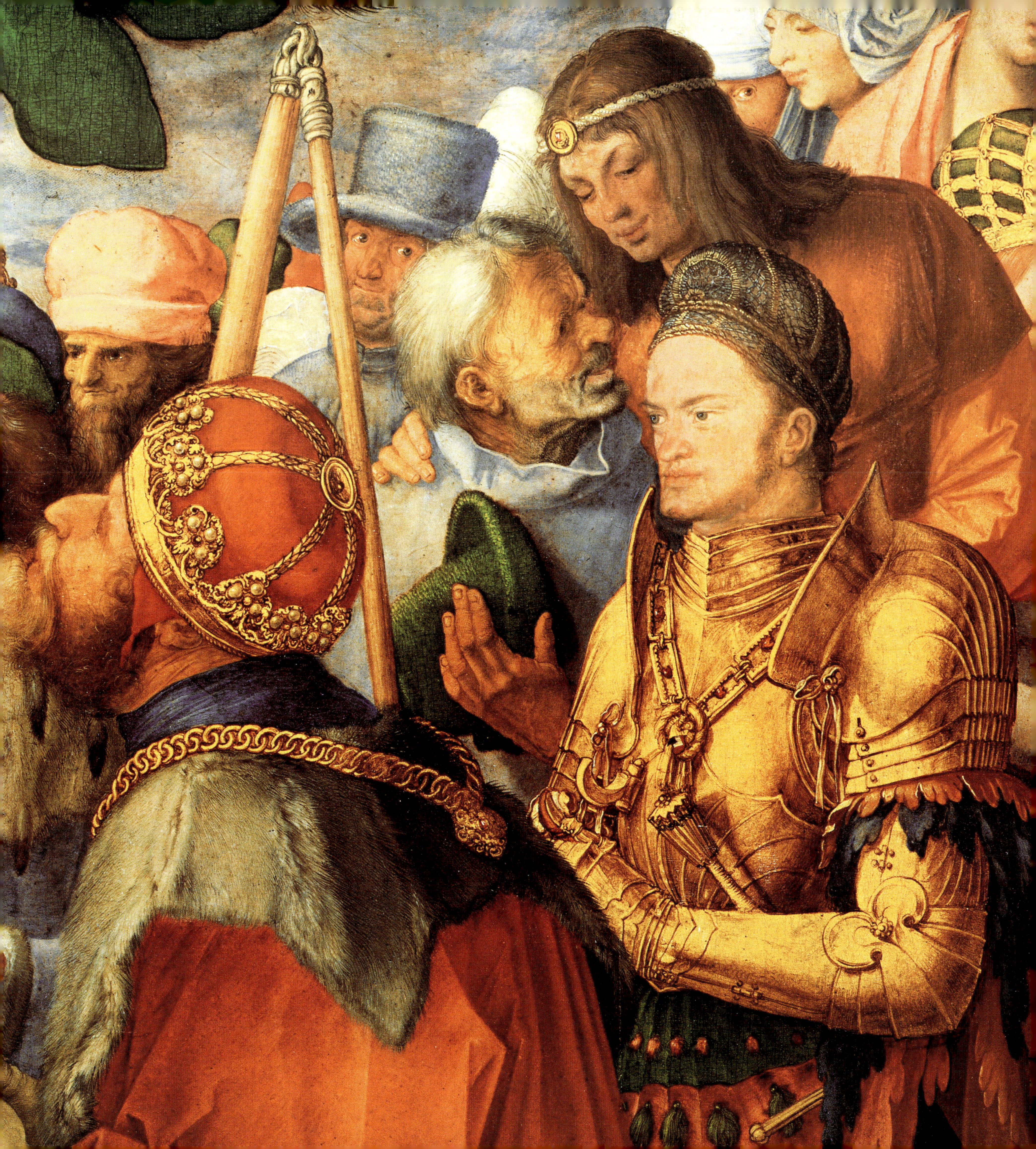

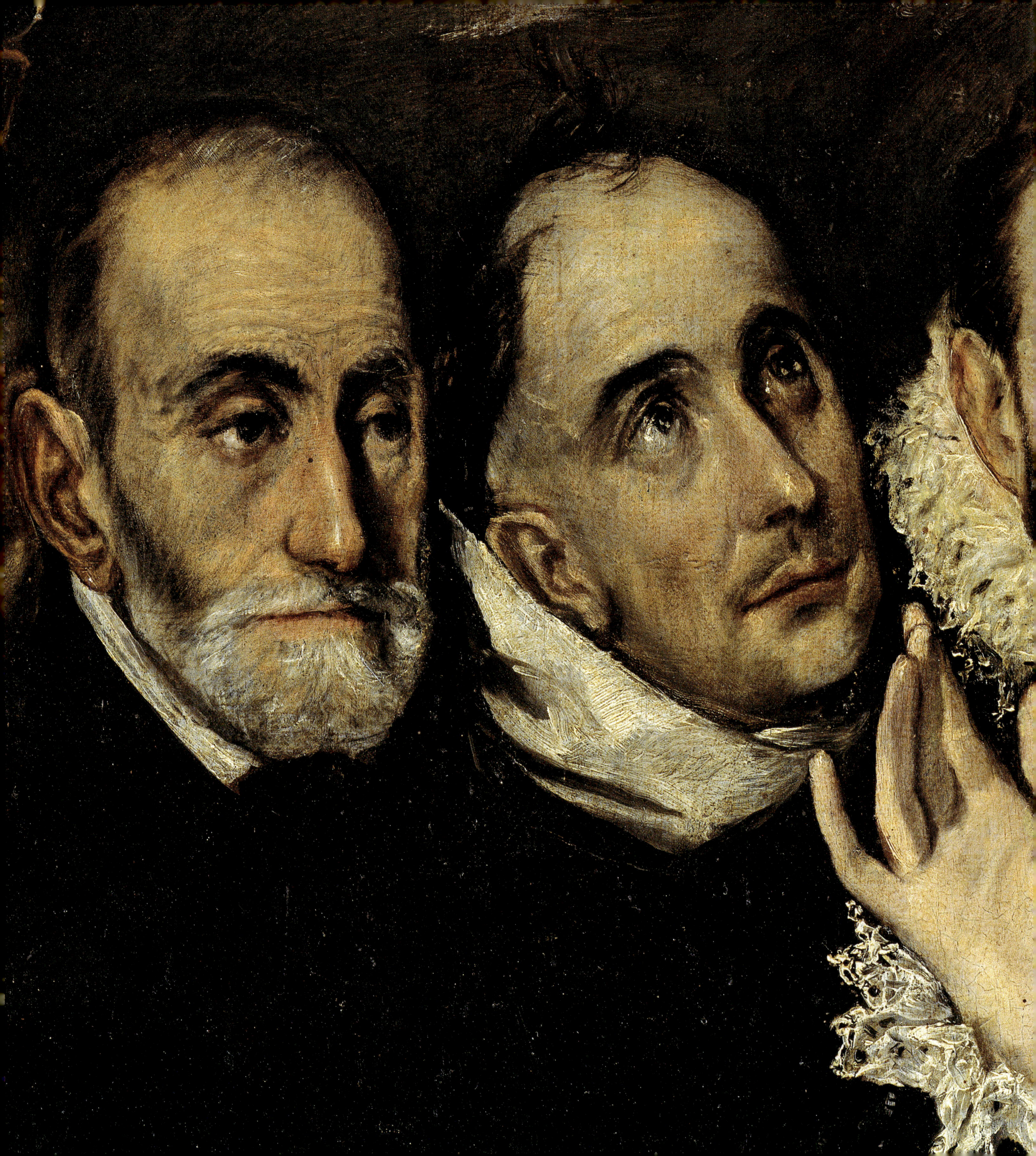

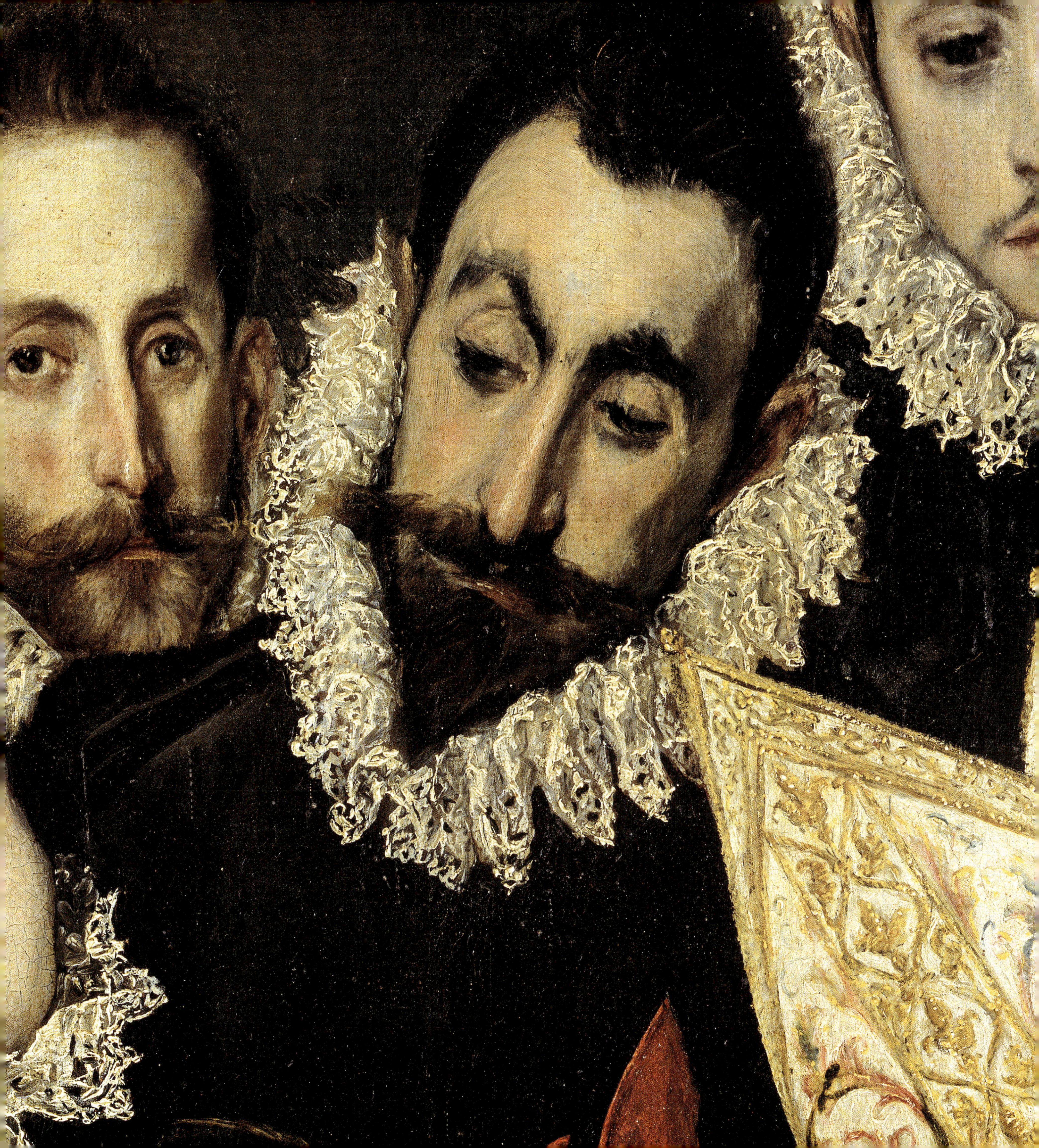

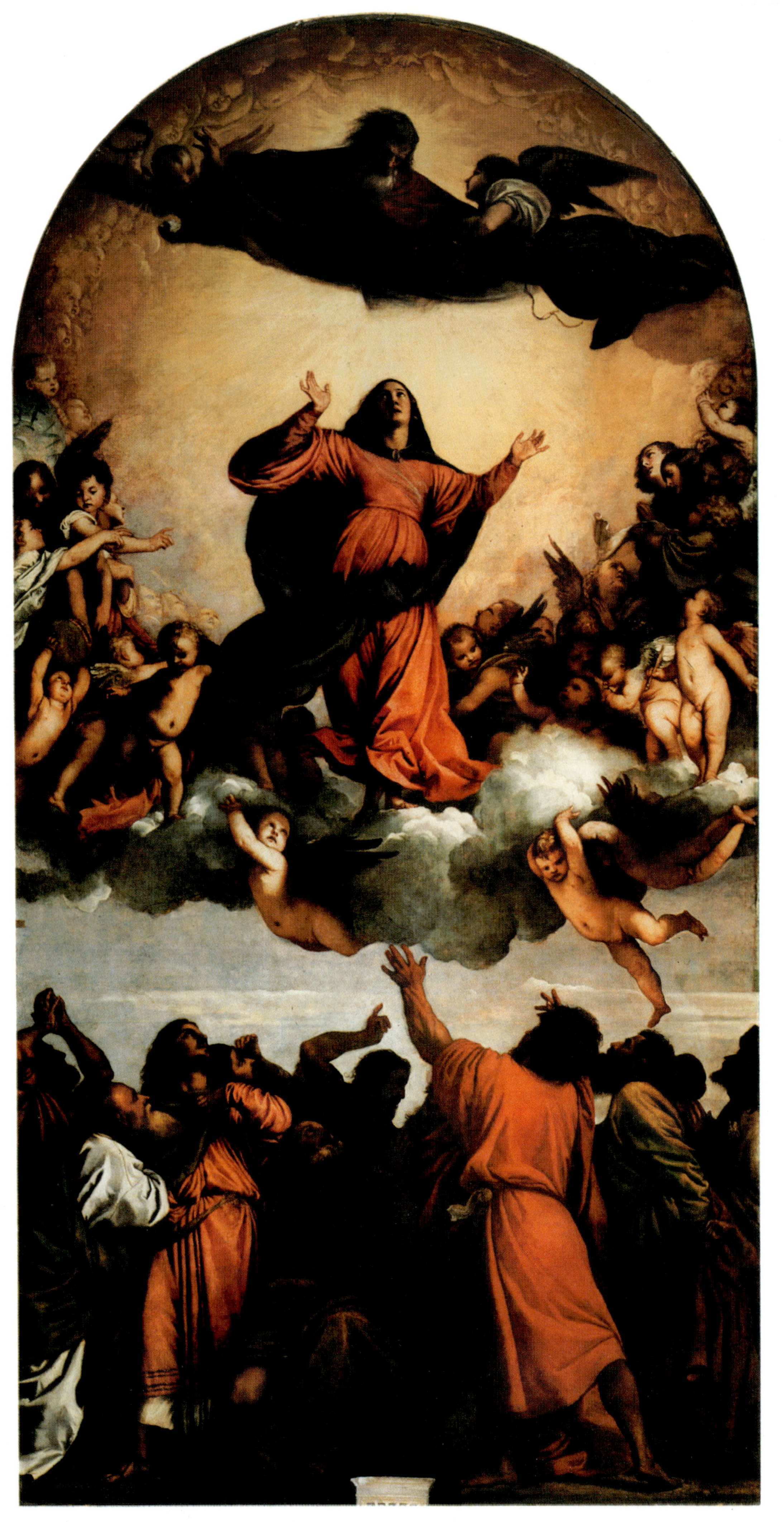

JAN VAN EYCK

MASACCIO

DONATELLO

ROGIER VAN DER WEYDEN

PIERO DELLA FRANCESCA

JEAN FOUQUET

ANTONELLO DA MESSINA

HANS MEMLING

SANDRO BOTTICELLI

HIERONYMUS BOSCH

LEONARDO DA VINCI

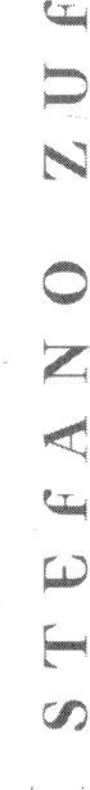

STEFANO ZUFFI

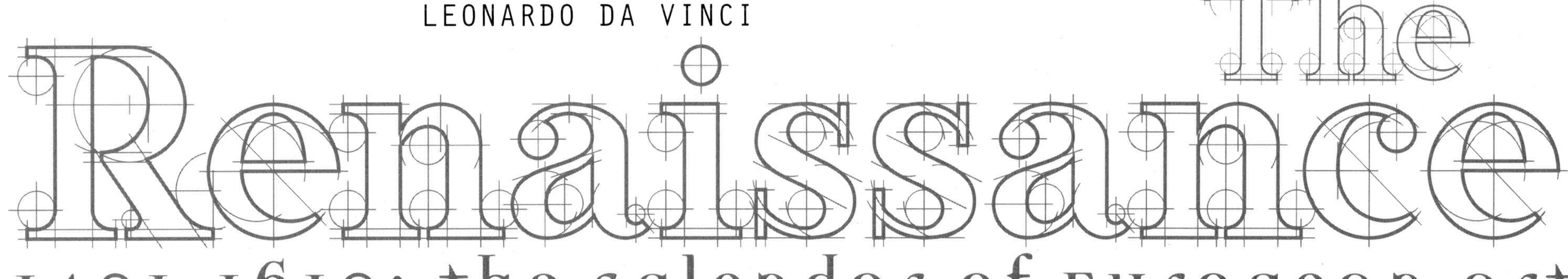

The Renaissance

1401-1610: the splendor of european art

ALBRECHT DÜRER

RAPHAEL

LUCAS CRANACH

MICHELANGELO

MATTHIS GRÜNEWALD

HANS HOLBEIN

TITIAN

PIETER BRUEGEL

PAOLO VERONESE

EL GRECO

BARNES & NOBLE BOOKS
NEW YORK

ART DIRECTOR
Giorgio Seppi

MANAGING EDITOR
Tatjana Pauli

EDITOR
Sergio Scardoni

LAYOUT
Elàstico, Milan

PICTURE RESEARCH
Lucia Impelluso, with the assistance of Carla Ingicco

TRANSLATION
Jay Hyams

© 2002 Mondadori Electa S.p. A., Milan
This edition published by Barnes & Noble, Inc. by arrangement with Mondadori
2003 Barnes & Noble Books
M 10 9 8 7 6 5 4 3 2
ISBN 0-7607-4200-6
English translation © 2003 Mondadori Electa S.p.A., Milan.
All rights reserved.
Printed and bound in Spain by Artes Gráficas Toledo, S.A.
D.L. TO: 944-2003

Contents

his book is about the European art of the fifteenth and sixteenth centuries. Those were two marvelous but also terrible centuries, periods of continuous change: political, geographical, religious, commercial, and cultural. The Renaissance began as the dream of a few intellectuals and their well-to-do patrons in the mercantile and banking cities of Tuscany and Flanders. Over the span of a few decades this "avant-garde" humanistic movement grew to become an international undertaking, shared by all the countries of Europe, from the busy cities of Germany to the courts of Italy, from the cathedrals of Spain to the monasteries of France to the Hanseatic ports and the castles of the Alps. During the fifteenth century, the Renaissance slowly spread along the rivers of Europe, from the Arno to the Rhine, from the Loire to the Tagus, from the Scheldt to the Thames, from the Vltava to the Vistula. It was a route of civilization and culture,

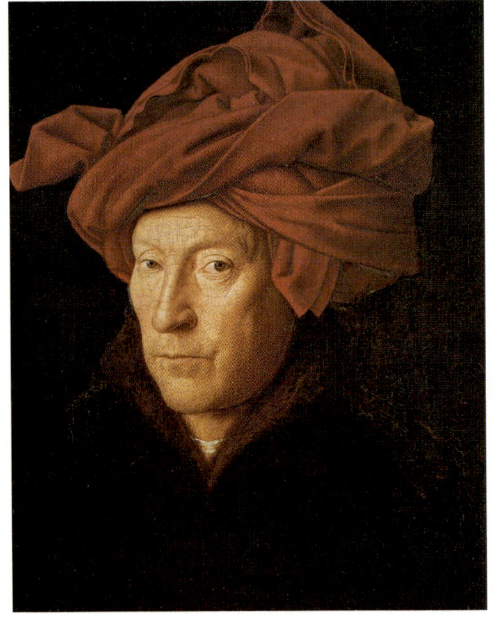

Jan van Eyck, *Man in a Red Turban*, 1433, oil on panel; National Gallery, London

which recuperated from antiquity the sense of moderation, the delight in beauty, the taste for conversation. In an unsettled Europe, divided and torn by conflicts, the sense of a common origin was beginning to make itself felt, or at least a sense of identity, of shared horizons and values.

Later, at the beginning of the sixteenth century, during its highest and most luminous stage, this ideal of a return, of a rebirth of ancient civilization, ran aground on the sharp rocks of a new world, one that had suddenly been discovered to be far larger than ever imagined and that was being bloodied by massacres carried out in the name of religion. Perhaps all along the Renaissance had been nothing but an illusion, fascinating but in the end, when it was over, bitter. Those who could do so fled the disenchantment to lose themselves in the labyrinths of mysterious gardens, in the sensuous and magical atmospheres of mannerism, in another world, a place outside time.

Introduction

Leon Battista Alberti, Tempio Malatestiano, façade, 1447–50; Rimini

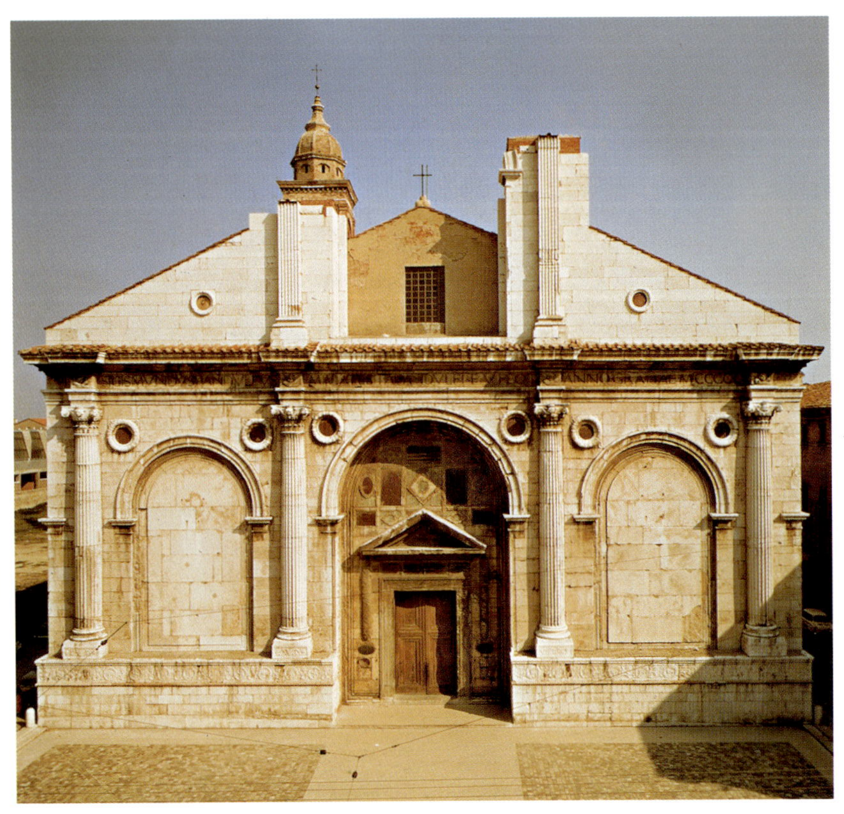

Just as the Renaissance moved toward its sunset, books about art of fundamental importance came into being. The figure of Michelangelo towers as the highest and final achievement within the complex critical construction of the most important Renaissance book on art, *The Lives of the Artists*, by Giorgio Vasari, the first edition of which appeared in 1550, the second in 1568. The long work presented a well organized series of biographies of painters, sculptors, and architects, from Cimabue and Giotto to Michelangelo. According to Vasari, art had followed an evolution, beginning from its lowest point in the Middle Ages to slowly rise through the fifteenth century, the steps of its progress marked off by conquests in the representation of nature, linear perspective, and the human body. It had reached a period of greatness with Leonardo and Raphael, but its absolute peak had been achieved by Michelangelo, after whom there could be nothing but decline: no one could ever outdo the master's sublime style, most of all in terms of the perfect representation of the most elevated subject, the human body. Vasari's particular view of the history of art, his marked preference for Tuscan masters, and the occasional inexact anecdote or detail have done nothing to diminish the fundamental value of his work. An invaluable source of information about many artists, *The Lives* is also a significant expression of the taste and culture of the Renaissance. Of course, by the time it was written the Renaissance had reached the period of its final maturation, and the symptoms of coming crisis were making themselves felt. But it was precisely those difficulties and those traumas that drove the peoples of Europe to make a further effort at growth, to once again trust in their own intelligence and ability to decide. Thus, between the end of the Renaissance and the beginning of the baroque, the age began that would bring scientific knowledge of the world, of the laws that regulate the universe, with at the same time an explosion of the most open-minded, spectacular, and grand creativity.

Looking over the entire period of the Renaissance one can clearly see the profound cultural, political, and psychological differences that run between the fifteenth and the sixteenth centuries. The fifteenth century marked a decisive step in the culture of western Europe.

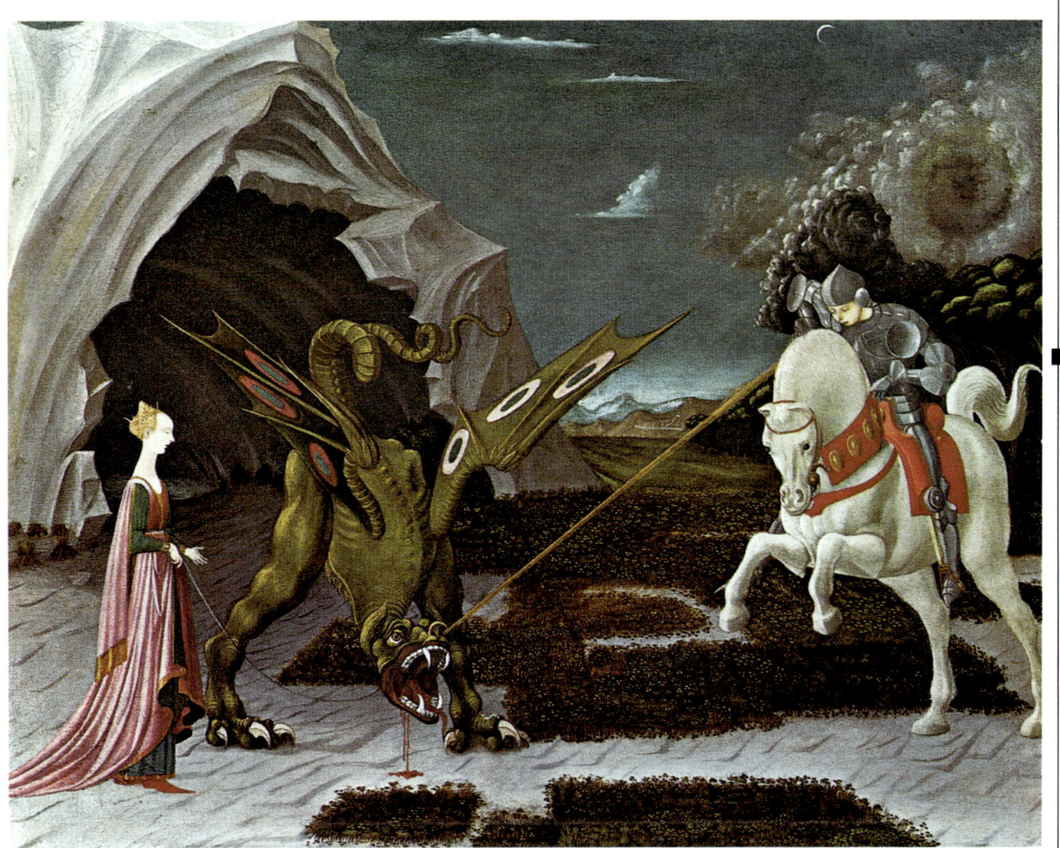

Paolo Uccello, *St. George and the Dragon*, circa 1455, tempera on canvas; National Gallery, London

The humanists, beginning with the revival of Greco-Roman civilization, set in motion the rediscovery of the values of moderation and reason, the sense of measure. It was the city Florence that first fostered the movement that would take the name of Renaissance and would later spread throughout the continent, and not as a form of nostalgia for a distant past but rather as an intensely felt involvement in the present. A succinct and highly expressive motto, exhumed from classical antiquity, perfectly summarizes the spirit of Florentine humanism: "Man is at the center of the universe." The Middle Ages had been distinguished by a constant mystical longing for God; with humanism, starting with the premises set down a century earlier by Dante and Giotto, man assumed responsibility and performed a role in history and society. The evolution of the figurative arts in Florence became the visible reflection of a more general movement of thought that came to involve every aspect of civil life in a city governed by a rich mercantile and banking middle class, an aristocratic republic, at the top of which was the Medici family. In the quiet of private studies (*studioli*), in the halls of universities, in the salons of the most refined courts, artists and men of letters brought into being one of the most profound and enduring transformations of

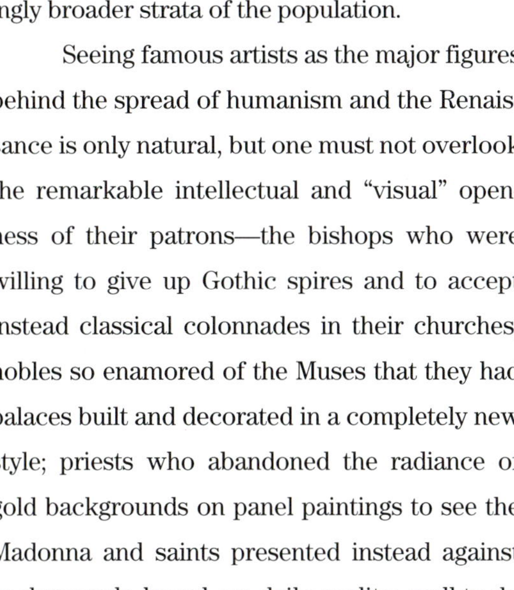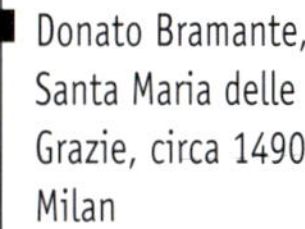

civilization. Without diminishing the intensity of his relationship with the sacred, fifteenth-century man freed himself from medieval bonds and opened himself to full knowledge of the universe, thereby also taking an active role, as a responsible protagonist, in the world and in history. The cities of Florence and Bruges, in almost the very same years, became the primary starting points for the spread of this movement, which then grew in the most varied centers, coming to involve university cities and the seats of bishops, market towns and abbeys, castles and port cities. By way of devotional images, the Renaissance then came into contact with increasingly broader strata of the population.

Donato Bramante, Santa Maria delle Grazie, circa 1490; Milan

Seeing famous artists as the major figures behind the spread of humanism and the Renaissance is only natural, but one must not overlook the remarkable intellectual and "visual" openness of their patrons—the bishops who were willing to give up Gothic spires and to accept instead classical colonnades in their churches; nobles so enamored of the Muses that they had palaces built and decorated in a completely new style; priests who abandoned the radiance of gold backgrounds on panel paintings to see the Madonna and saints presented instead against backgrounds based on daily reality; well-to-do merchants who invested part of their savings in works of art; courageous intellectuals who undertook the difficult and sometimes quite dangerous exhumation of ancient relics; the middle class who paid taxes so that their cities could be embellished with a fountain or monument; the pioneers of typography who replaced the angular Gothic scripts with clear Latin capitals. The objects we can still admire are merely a fraction of the total production of the fifteenth-century masters, and not only because of the inevitable losses caused by time by man. Renaissance nobles employed a wide variety of specialists. The "official painter" was responsible for the court's image. As might be expected, his responsibilities included the execution of portraits of the ruling family and its courtiers, the creation of fresco cycles in special rooms of the palace, the construction and decoration of altarpieces, the creation of paintings with specific dynastic value. In addition to these activities, however, there were also many "ephemeral" works: the decorations for feasts and tournaments, the arrangement of theatrical scenes, the creation of ornamental banners and hangings, the design of furniture,

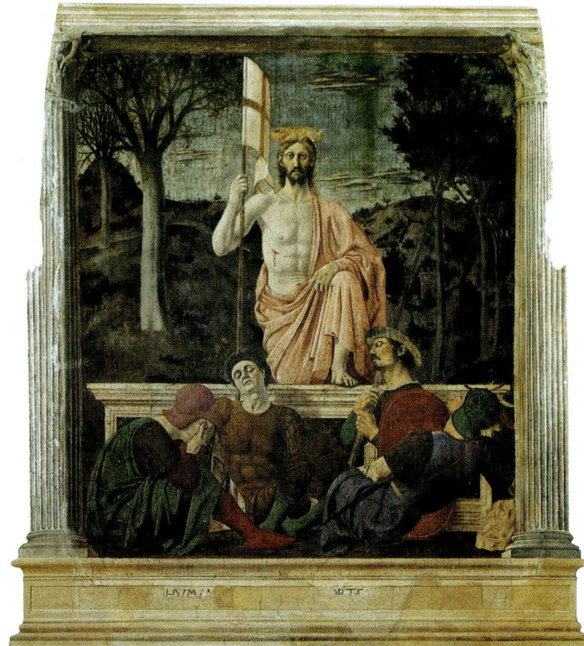

clothes, and costumes, the production and decoration of shields, armor, and heraldic devices, along with various sundry other objects. The painter was also entrusted with the "direction" of such official occasions as banquets, receptions, and the entertainment of noble guests. In anticipation of our concept of the artist, the fifteenth-century "court painter" was an all-around creative person, a designer, an advertising artist, a copywriter, in fact such a jack-of-all-trades with such a variety of responsibilities that teamwork among artists was indispensable.

By the end of the fifteenth century, humanism was no longer restricted to a few avant-garde centers and had spread throughout all of central-western Europe, from the Baltic Sea to the Mediterranean, from Poland to Portugal. Christopher Columbus's epochal voyage set a symbolic seal on a century that had had no fear of the unknown and that had made the act of discovery an extraordinary adventure. For us, the year 1492 stands as one of the pivotal dates in the history of humankind; but the Europeans of the end of the fifteenth century do not seem to have had any sense of such a radical change in their geographical, economic, and cultural horizons. The voyage of Columbus (who, as is well known, was completely unaware of having set foot on an unknown continent) had most of all symbolic value, whereas the voyages of Magellan, Vespucci, and Cabral in the years immediately after were distinguished by more direct practical outcomes. Vasco da Gama's circumnavigation of Africa (1498) and Ferdinand Magellan's voyage around the world (1517–22) opened new trade routes that finally broke the hegemony of the commercial traffic in the Mediterranean. The fact that the new continent was named for Vespucci rather than for Columbus can be interpreted as an indication of this difference.

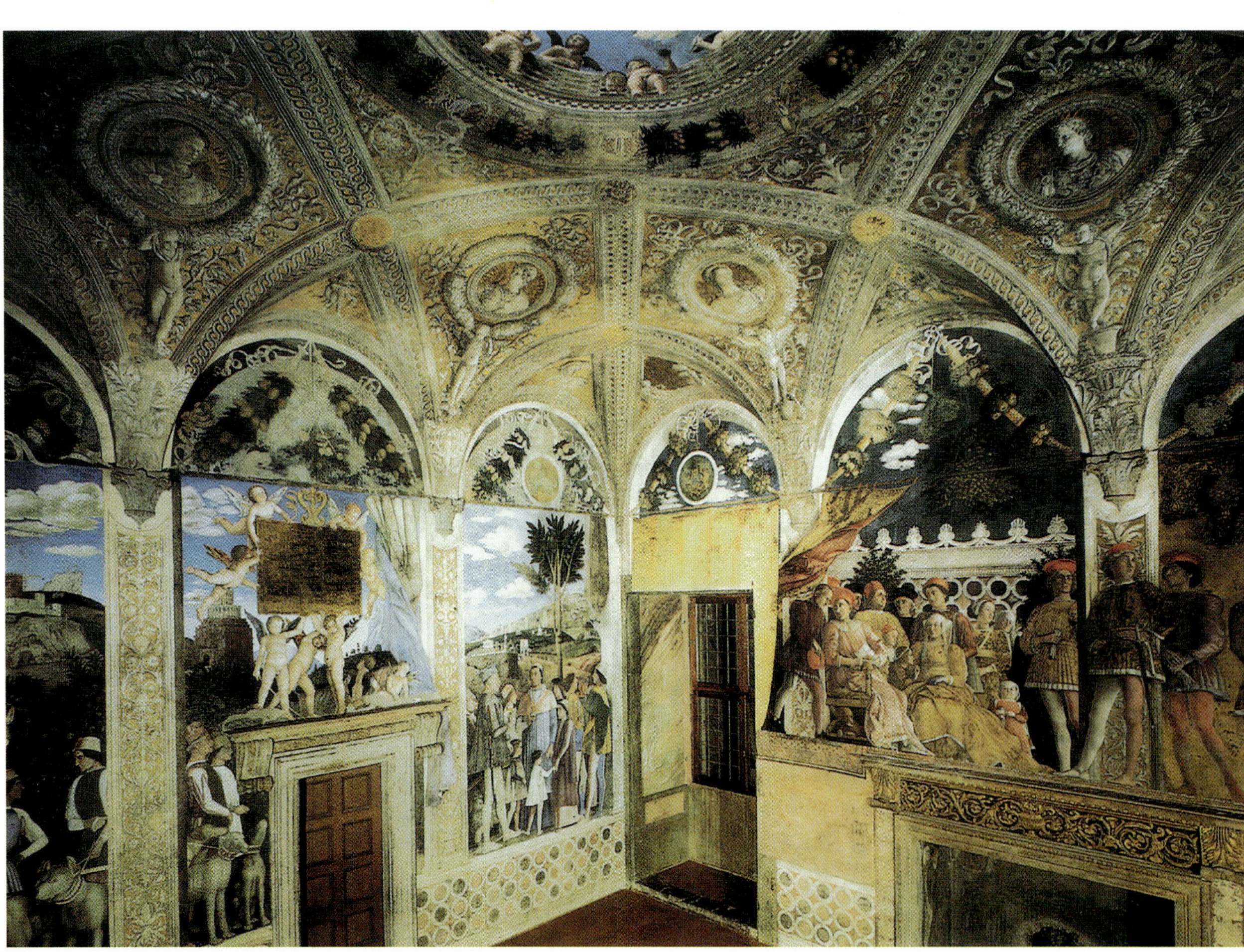

Introduction

Furthermore, in order to understand the period of history in which the overseas voyages took place it is necessary to return to that year of 1492, for the coincidences of history present other important events, most of all the expulsion of the Moors and the Jews from Spain by King Ferdinand; the premature death of Lorenzo the Magnificent in Florence; the beginning of increasingly open religious turbulence in several areas of Europe; and the spread of culture and information thanks to the first printed works, made at low cost and in large (for the time) print runs. Taken together, these very different events had the effect of breaking up the structures that had characterized the second half of the fifteenth century. The geographical discoveries can be interpreted psychologically as expressions of the desire to get free of the "old" continent, to project oneself beyond the

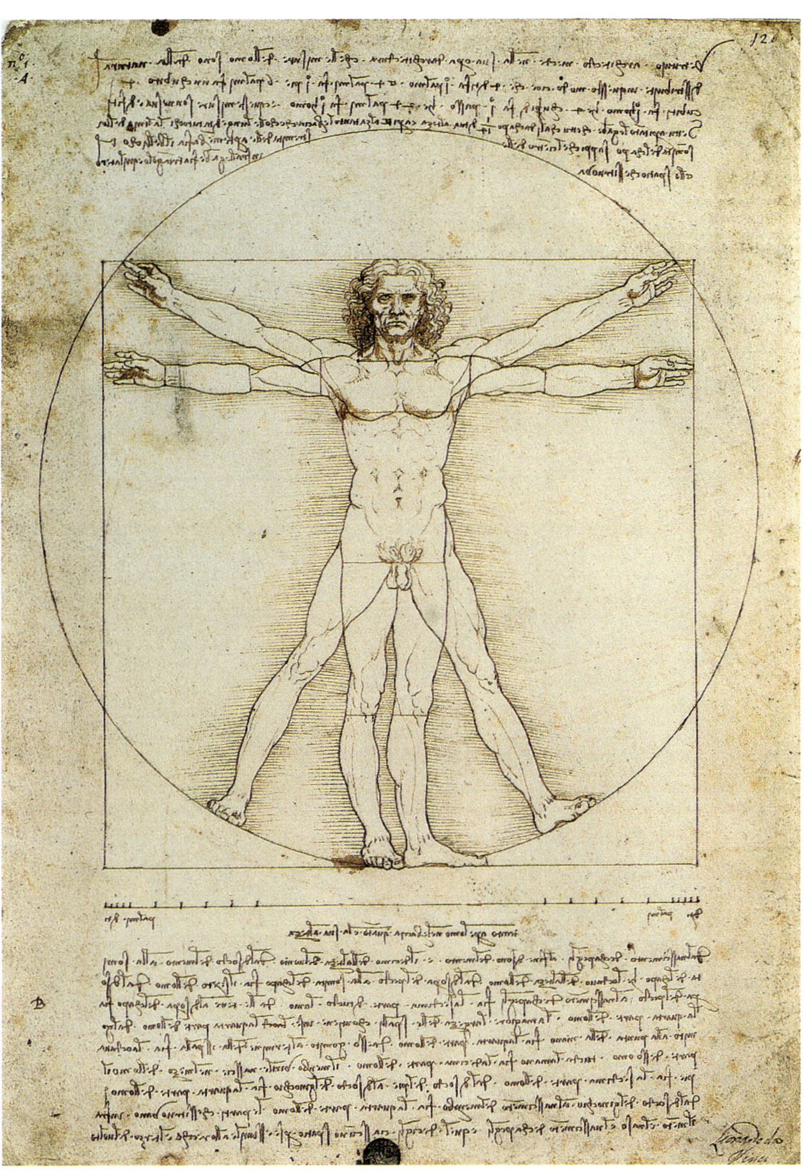

old schemes and barriers, to put oneself in a direct relationship with the world, with nature, with the mysteries of the globe. Soon enough, this individualistic longing was expressed in fierce wars that by the first half of the sixteenth century were leading to a radical change in the European situation, with the rise of the great nation states and the gradual disappearance of most of the ancient duchies and minor principalities.

In every nation of Europe, the art from the end of the fifteenth century and early years of the sixteenth seems to express this dramatic change, this anxiety about the new, this longing to establish new "borders," and not only those geographical but those of human existence. This is the period when Europe's courtly Gothic tradition began to crack apart, soon replaced by two parallel forces: the spread of the humanist culture of Italian origin to many places in many different nations, and the increasingly perceptible drive to investigate the phenomena of nature and the mysteries of the Christian religion. These contradictory drives were interpreted with an intensity verging on anguish by the leading intellectuals and artists in Europe. How could anyone hope to reconcile thorough and widespread knowledge of the classical world with the pressing desire for direct contact with nature, which so inevitably leads to rejection of the authority of the ancient texts? And how resist the desire to investigate the meaning of one's faith, perhaps doing away with canonical Latin, in order to read the Bible in one's own language?

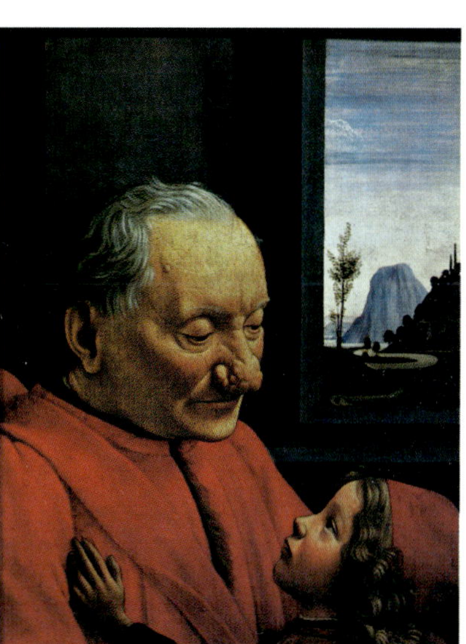

For these reasons, the period of European art and culture that coincides with the beginning of the age of geographical discoveries is one of the most complex and interesting. If fifteenth-century humanism can be considered the reflection of an epoch of meditation, stability, and the search for harmony, the immense and dramatic events of sixteenth-century art represent, with powerfully resounding fullness, a century of disturbances and wars, of troubled doubts and new impulses. It is worth noting that within the usual categories used by historians the fifteenth century still belongs to the Middle Ages, while the next century marks the beginning of the modern age.

An exemplary case is that of Leonardo da Vinci, who reached his full intellectual and artistic maturity during the closing decade of the fifteenth century. At the same time that he was making some of his best known works, Leonardo also wrote notes, drafted treatises, designed machines and inventions, drew up plans for buildings, and compiled codices and notebooks full of scientific observations in a wondrous diversity of fields, from anatomy to hydraulics, from astronomy to the flight of birds, from botany to geography. The final object of all this tireless activity was painting, which Leonardo himself considered "the most perfect of the sciences" because reproduction and study lead to the knowledge of the laws that regulate nature and the passions of humans.

Although it began twenty years later, Albrecht Dürer's career ran parallel to Leonardo's. His extraordinary figure as both artist and man of culture is emblematic of the emancipation of German painters from the almost servile state of minor artisans. During most of his career, which he dedicated to an absolute awareness of his role and intellectual stature as an artist, Dürer pursued the idea of being able to present beauty and the infinite variety of nature's manifestations through the application of a set of simple rules, within precepts based on harmonious relationships.

Here is another highly delicate point that helps in the interpretation of the most elevated artistic expressions of European artists during the period of the oceanic discoveries: the subtle anguish that entered the soul of the intellectual faced with the impossibility of getting the serene but limited certainties of classical culture, rediscovered by humanists, to coexist with the new scientific and philosophic acquisitions that were leading to an

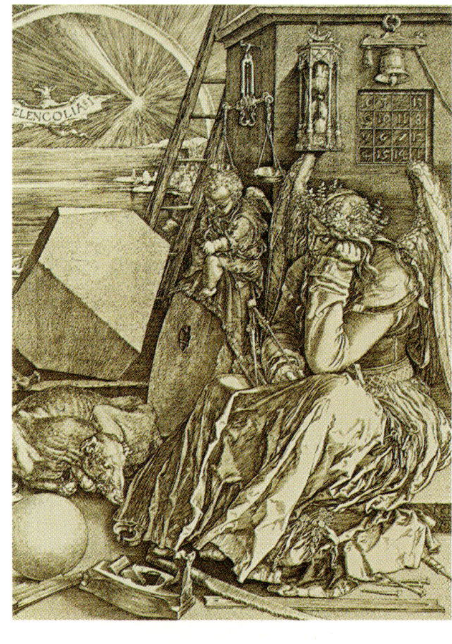

understanding of the mutability of the present and the destiny of the world. Thus, on the threshold of the Protestant Reformation, and most of all in central-northern Europe, there was a growing sense of drama, doubt, and obligation. The frightening and at the same time sublime explosion of colors and emotions in the huge Isenheim Altarpiece by Matthis Grünewald (pages 246–49), today in Colmar, is the epoch's most dramatic moment and greatest visual symbol. It is even more signif-

icant if one recalls that it was painted only a few kilometers away from Saint-Dié, the small town in Alsace where the ruling duke had formed his own humanistic society that met to discuss the arts and that numbered among its members Martin Waldseemüller. In 1507, five years before Grünewald completed his altar, that society published a map of the lands recently discovered on the far side of the Atlantic by the Spanish and Portuguese. At Waldeseemüller's suggestion those lands were named America.

A determinant factor in the circulation of ideas was the willingness of artists to travel, which they did not only to gain new ideas but also to find lucrative business. At the same time that Leonardo departed Florence at the age of thirty to work at the wealthy court of Ludovico Sforza (known as Ludovico il Moro) in Milan, other Florentines (among them Botticelli and Perugino) were leaving for Rome to fresco the walls of the Sistine Chapel. After the fall of the Sforza duchy Leonardo went to the Mantua of the Gonzagas and then to Venice before returning to bustling Florence, where he met Michelangelo, and then going to Rome (for a long stay), again to Milan, and finally to the court of Francis I of France. Raphael, having left his native Urbino and trained in the Marches and Umbria, lived in Florence from 1504 to 1508, then set off for the Rome of Pope Julius II. Dürer traveled constantly across half of Europe. He visited Venice twice, lived at the court of Emperor Maximilian I, crossed Switzerland and Alsace, went to Antwerp, while also passing through Germany, Flanders, and Holland. Not much later, Hans Holbein the Younger, after many long travels between Augsburg, Basel, and northern Italy, ended by setting himself up in London at the court of Henry VIII. Netherlandish art offers excellent examples. Such artists as Quenten Metsys, Gossart, and Jan van Scorel came by their sense of the classical, monumental, and succinct during trips to Venice and Rome; they then combined that with the inheritance of meticulous realism of the northern tradition. Thanks to these artists, the city of Antwerp wrested from Bruges the position of artistic primacy.

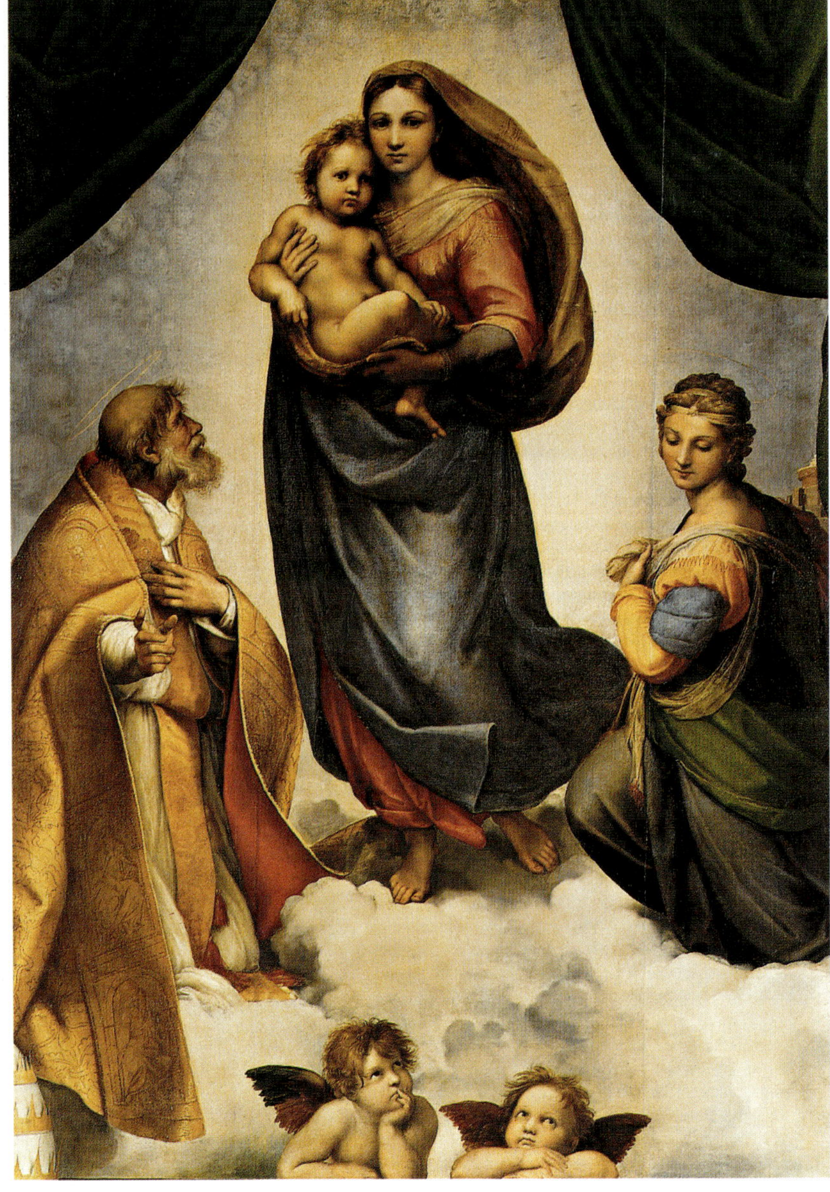

Introduction

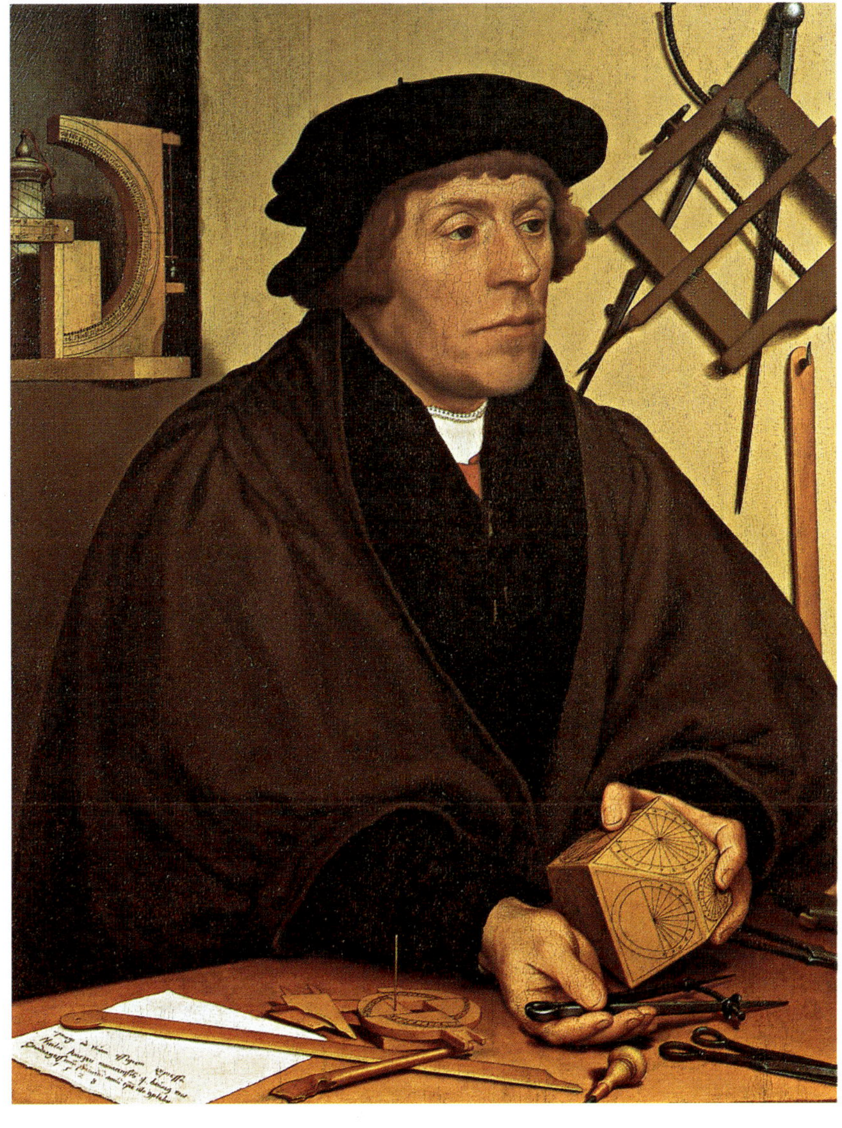

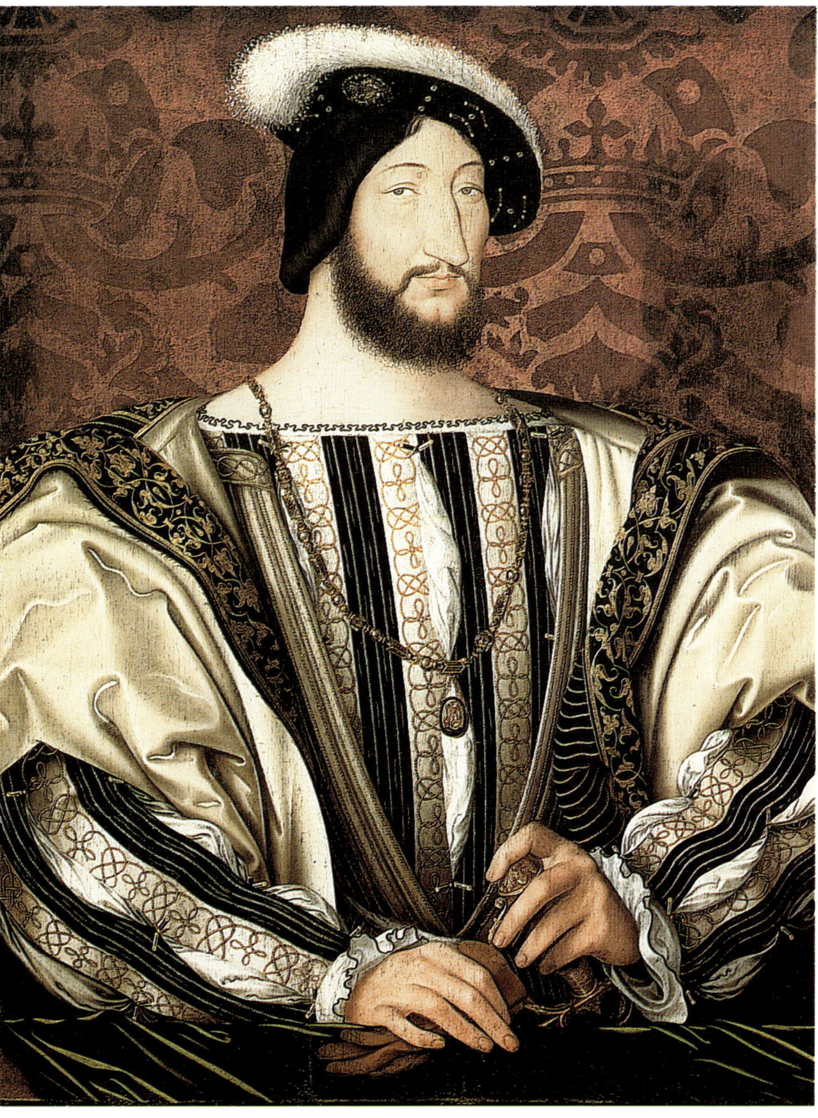

At the same time that the new Renaissance spirit was spreading, Europe was also being disturbed by a wave of intolerance for the Catholic church destined to culminate in the Reformation of Martin Luther. This agitation expressed itself in an irreverent and expressionistic current that emerges in the works of some of the greatest European artists of the sixteenth century, among them Matthis Grünewald and Hieronymus Bosch, who in ways that were often dramatic and just as often sacrilegious seem to cast doubt on the great achievements of the Renaissance.

The immense expansion of the confines of the earth with the voyages of Columbus, Vespucci, and Magellan and the profound disturbance caused by the Protestant Reformation marked the thinking of Europeans and made a decisive change in the course of history and daily life. There were particularly serious economic results for those Italian cities, such as Venice, that had based their financial fortunes on trade with the East by way of the Mediterranean Sea. The new transoceanic trade routes laid the basis for competition that would prove difficult to meet. At this point a new young ruler appeared on the confused stage of Europe, Charles V, born in the Flemish city of Ghent in 1500. Only nineteen when he took the throne, the new emperor united the crown of Spain to that of Austria, making a great "Catholic" empire that took on the task of facing the Protestant advance. Charles V had little time to devote to the elaboration of a public image. He did not possess any particular learning in terms of the figurative arts and—a not unimportant detail—was a man of rare ugliness. He thus showed great intuition in choosing Titian to be his *pintor primero*. In the more than thirty years that the relationship lasted, the Venetian painter sent dozens of masterpieces to the Spanish court, all of them distinguished by an extraordinary wealth of colors and an astonishing dynamic energy.

There is then the question of the prevalence given urban settings over those in the countryside. Fifteenth-century culture and art put great effort into the concept of an "ideal city," an urban and architectonic space constructed on the measure of man. During the sixteenth century, a period shaken to its core by historical events of universal import, this search was transformed into an overt desire for utopia. At the same time, the fascination, mystery, and respite offered by nature had been rediscovered. Writers and poets, celebrating life in the countryside, opened the way for a very particular aspect of High Renaissance culture. During the sixteenth century, and most of all in the Veneto region of northeastern Italy, the theme of the *idillio campestre* ("the country idyll") grew to great popularity as an evocation of landscapes and figures imbued with a peaceful harmony, usually with an explicit reference to music. Such feelings about nature were not restricted to Italy. An important example is the case of Germany, where masters like Albrecht Altdorfer and Lucas Cranach located religious and mythological figures in fabulous naturalistic settings of woodlands, mountain crags, and forests at sunset, achieving entrancing and evocative results. Recognizable in this phase of German art is an important precedent for the reflections on nature in the Romantic age. There is also the example of France's Francis I, who was far more interested in the construction of the residence at Fontainebleau and in châteaux along the Loire than he was in buildings in the city of Paris. Around the middle of the sixteenth century, while the concept of the "Italian garden" (a carefully designed park in which the natural elements were treated as "material" at the disposition of the architect to be combined with statues, fountains, and pathways) was taking shape in Tuscany, in the Veneto the so-called civilization of the Veneto villas was coming into existence. Faced with the crisis in Mediterranean commerce,

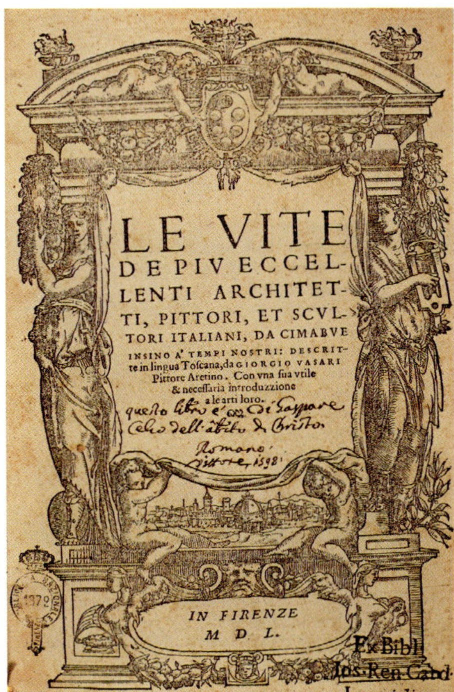

many Venetian patricians decided to invest in agricultural holdings on the mainland. Hence the popularity of villas, structures that served the double purposes of providing a pleasant country home for the owner while forming the financial and organizational center of the estate. The villas designed by Andrea Palladio stand apart, recognized as models of clarity, of classical simplicity, of perfect balance between the "functional" and the "comfortable" (to use the terms Palladio himself used in a treatise in which he presented the characteristics of his designs), they have been imitated for centuries, most of all in the Anglo-Saxon countries during the age of neoclassicism.

Cuius regio, eius religio: the ruler of a territory is free to decide the religion of the territory. With this brief formula, dictated more by weariness than by conviction, Emperor Charles V and the Protestant German princes put their names, in 1551, to the Peace of Augsburg, the final act (at least from the formal point of view) of the debilitating religious wars that had bloodied central Europe for a quarter of a century. In the city of Trent, just over the Alps, the great council called by Pope Paul III had already been active for six years, working on the solemn Catholic "response" to the internal crisis in Christianity begun by Luther. Even today the debate goes on over whether it should be called the Counter-Reformation, meaning a movement created essentially to oppose and hold back the schismatic drive of Protestantism, or instead the Catholic Reformation, meaning a movement started in response to

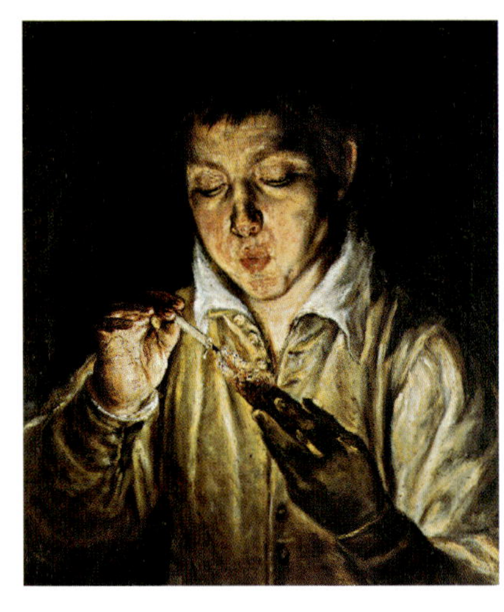

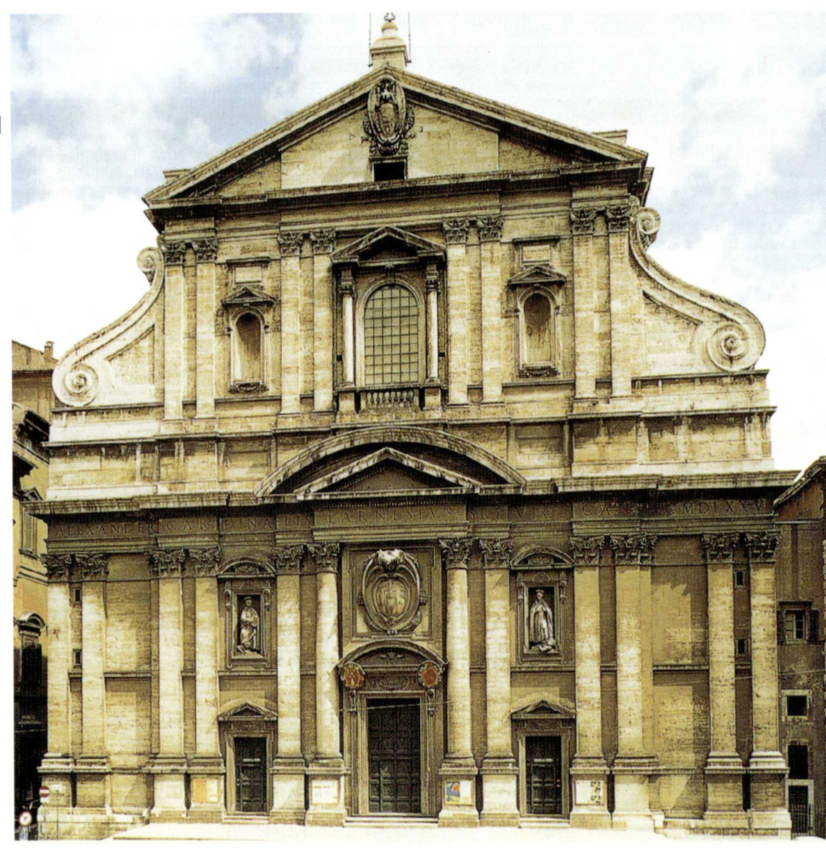

the deep need to revise the liturgy and doctrine of the church. In either case, thanks also to the creation of new, militant religious orders, culture and art left the Council of Trent radically renewed in terms of themes, methods, stimuli, and objectives. By the middle of the sixteenth century, during a period of strong internationalism of figurative and formal models, two kinds of art had clearly come into being and were coexisting, one of them profane, with a strongly aristocratic and elitist language, full of arcane symbolic references, and the other devotional, designed to awaken intense emotions among ordinary people, making reference to a simple and direct religious experience.

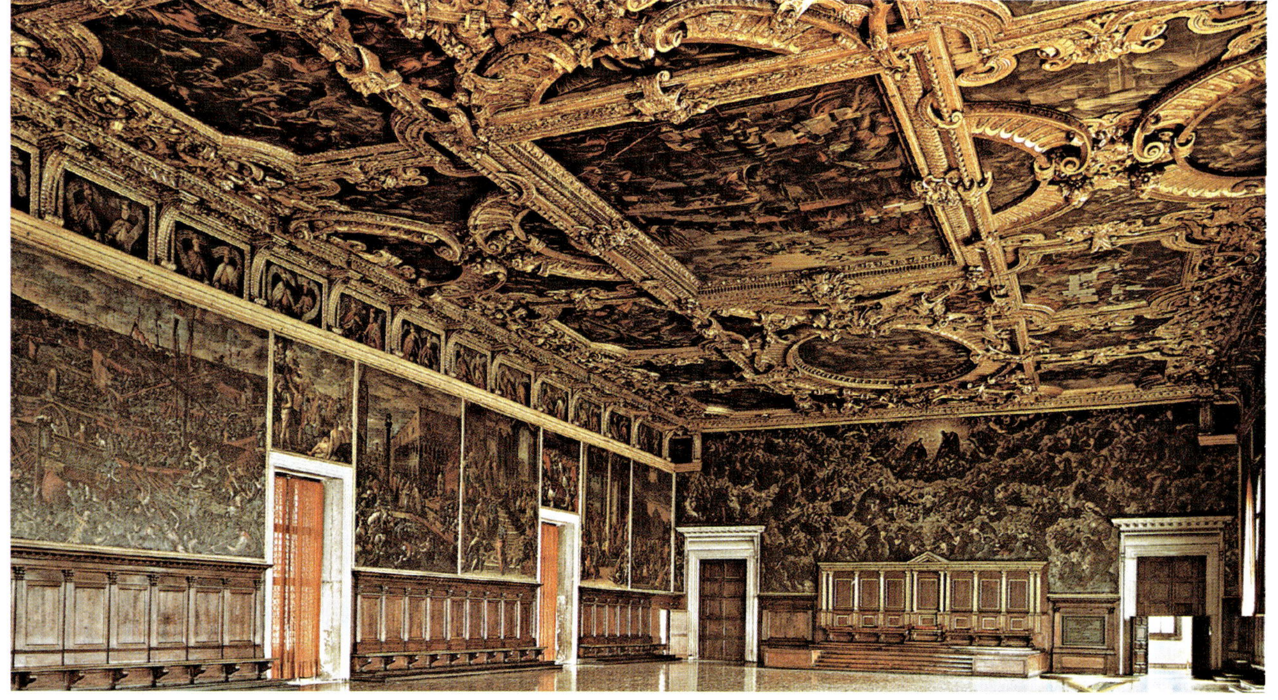

the dramatic crisis that led to the Saint Bartholomew's Day Massacre (1572). In Italy, the last great ones died, Michelangelo, Titian, Veronese, and Tintoretto. The new generations of artists had to face a completely different situation, one in which international competition was becoming increasing sharp and in which Italy was being slowly moved out of its central position. The adventure of Renaissance man, begun in the Florentine golden days of Dante and Giotto as a claim for a new role to play in the world ("You were not made to live as brutes, but to pursue virtue and knowledge"; *Inferno*, Canto XXVI), had assumed over the decades a dimension and a depth perhaps initially unforeseeable, up to the inimitable generation of the great masters born between the middle and the end of the fifteenth century. In the centuries of humanism and the Renaissance our current way of living in the world began, our ability to relate to our history and our destiny, our way of seeing the present moment as a link between a passionately studied past and a calmly faced future. The taste for beauty in every form, the love of nature, the passion for life and art are, more than any of the masterpieces by the great painters, sculptors, and architects, the true legacy of the Renaissance.

In terms of the field of painting, the council recommended a clear change in direction. Paintings were to guide the faithful, and since the faithful were often illiterate, art was to contain easily understood didactic aspects, indicating examples of Christian virtues in which the viewer could recognize him- or herself. Artists were advised to insert figures and details drawn from daily life in order to make the action seem to be located in the reality of the moment, not in some distant past. The instructions concerning sacred art of the Counter-Reformation mark a turning point and are at the basis of the movement from the Renaissance to the baroque, which had as its great protagonist, during the last decade of the century, the great Caravaggio.

The century ended on what looked like an empty stage. Following the abdication of Charles V, the great Hapsburg empire was again divided in two between Austria and Spain, and while Philip II battled against the Dutch and the English, Rudolf II moved the capital of Austria from Vienna to Prague, preparing the way for a final season of bizarre creativity. Despite the victory at Lepanto (1571), Christian Europe felt itself threatened by the advance of the Turks. France had the fortune to find a great king, Henry IV, capable of confronting

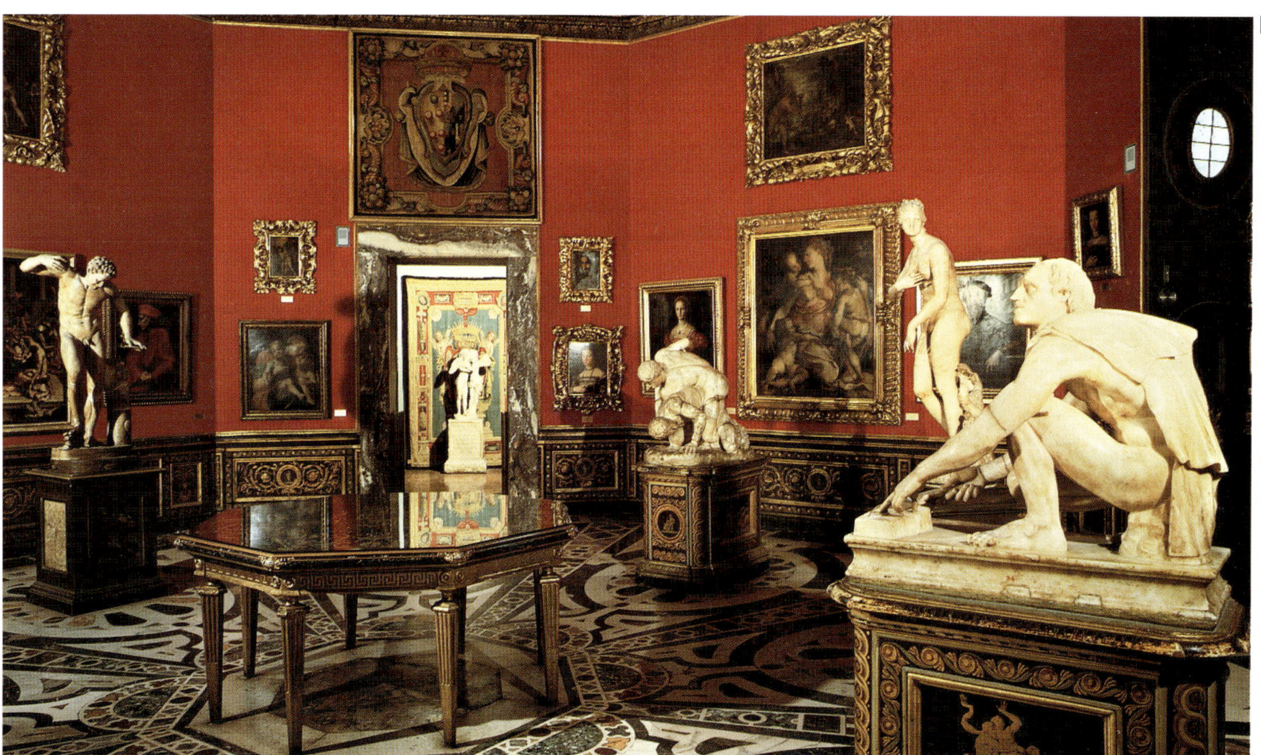

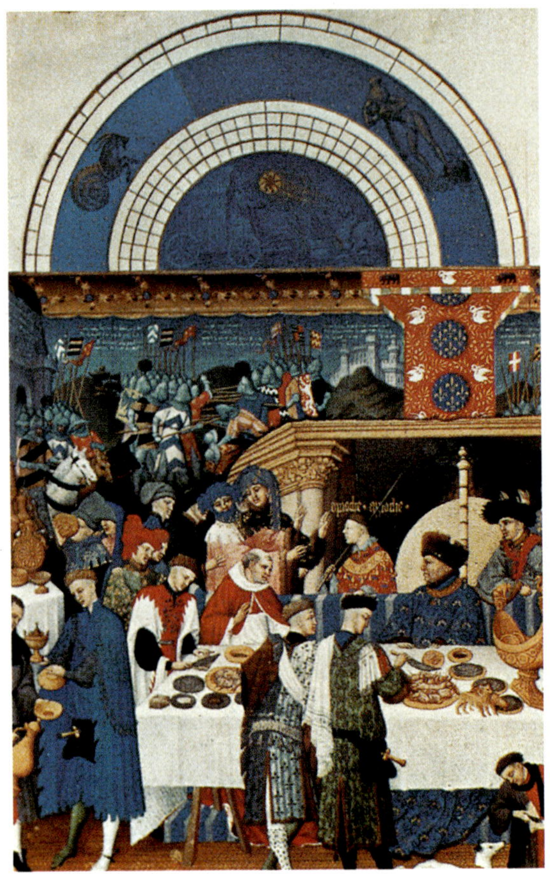

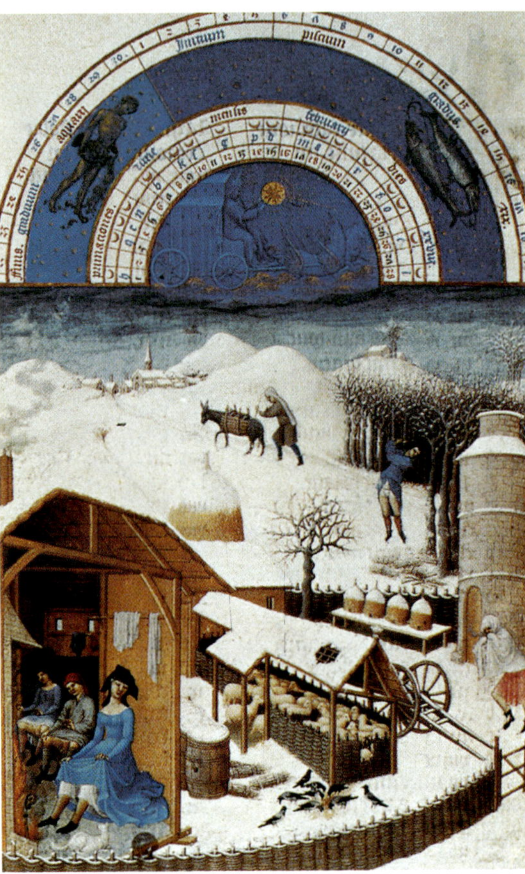

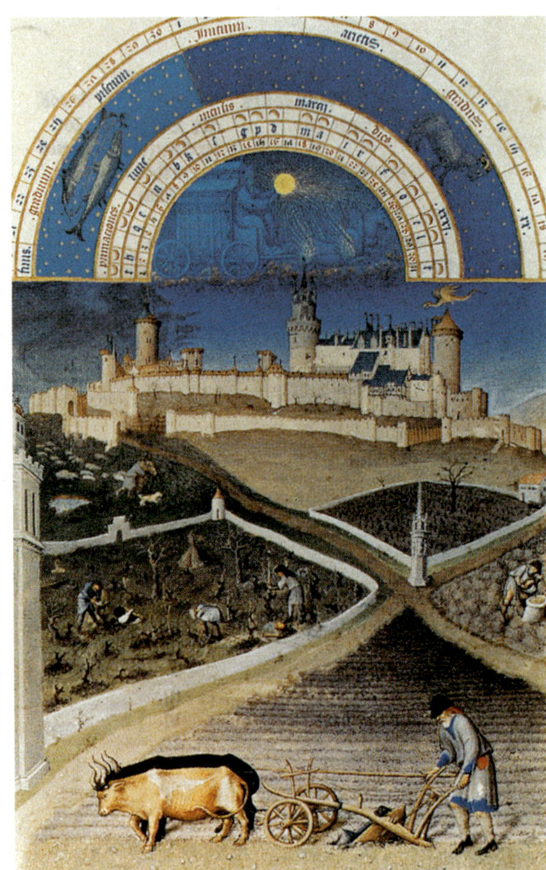

A comparison of two calendars

In choosing to use the term *Renaissance* to define not a style but an entire period of European art and culture, it is necessary to emphasize the dynamic continuity of styles, manners, expressions, and local customs that animated the fifteenth and sixteenth centuries in Europe. A visual sense of the evolution of Renaissance art over the course of the decades is offered by comparison of two series of images that are obviously closely related, having been made to serve similar functions and for similar patrons at a distance in time one from the other of about eighty years. The first

was the figurative model for the second, and the differences between the two series provide a means of measuring the changes that took place in taste and outlook between the elite courts of the late Gothic and the new cultural and social situation of the Renaissance. The fact that the two works are calendars reflects our interest here in time and its effects. Originally inserted in marvelous illuminated prayer books (one is today in loose pages, while the other has remained intact), the two series of large full-page miniatures illustrate the activities of the twelve months. In

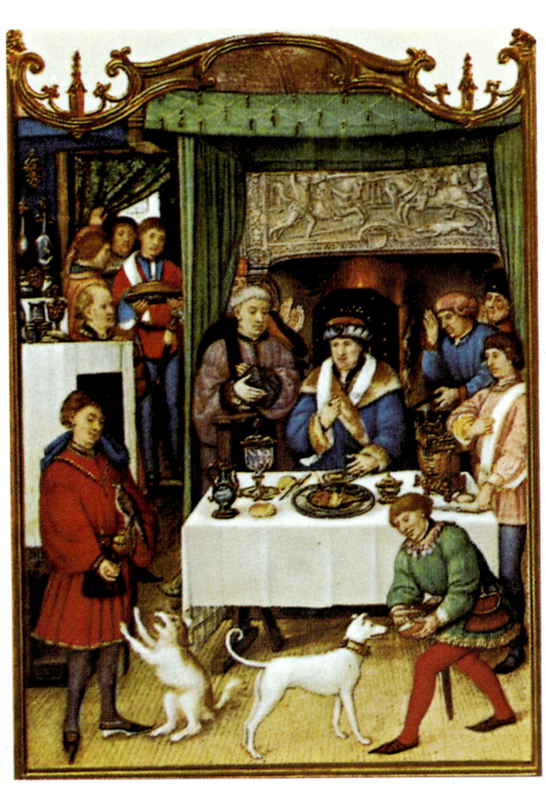

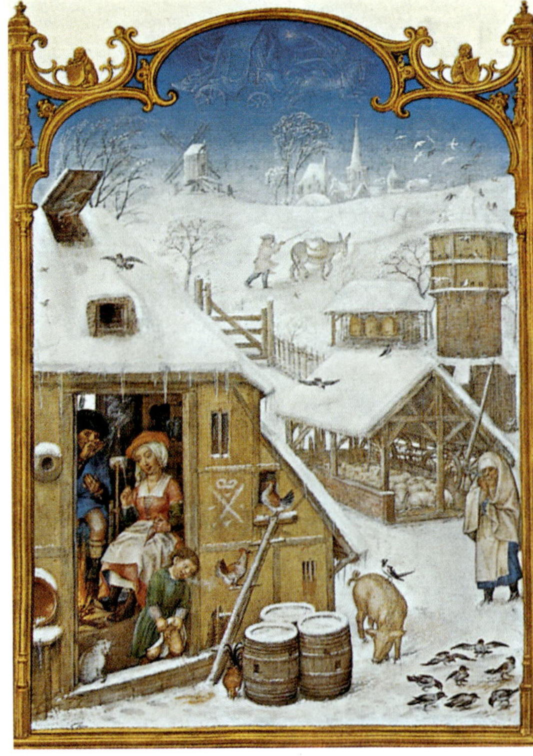

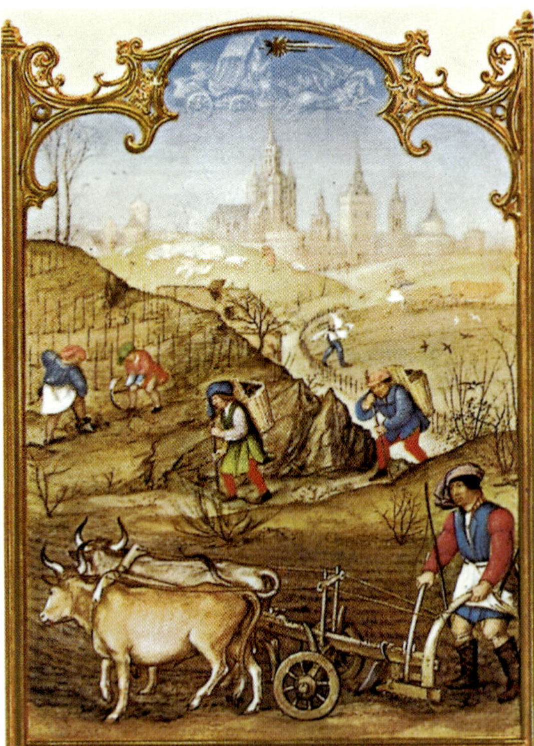

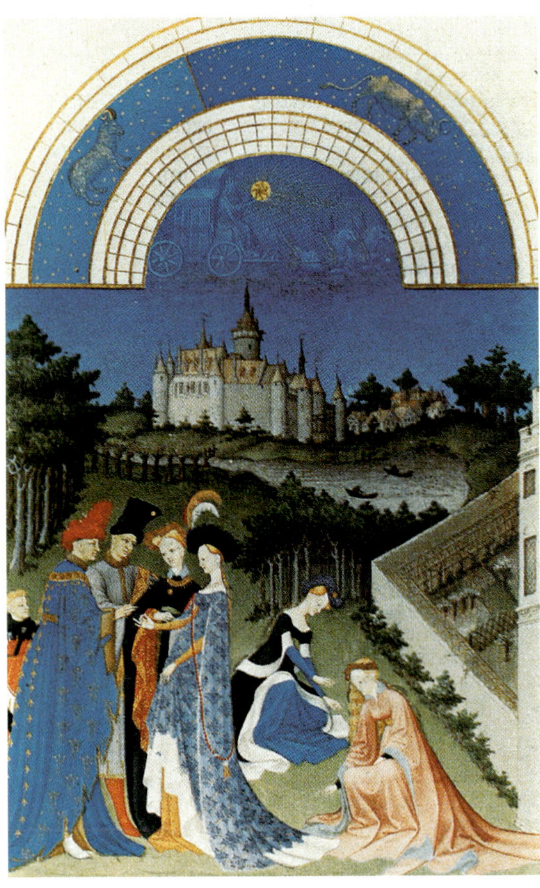 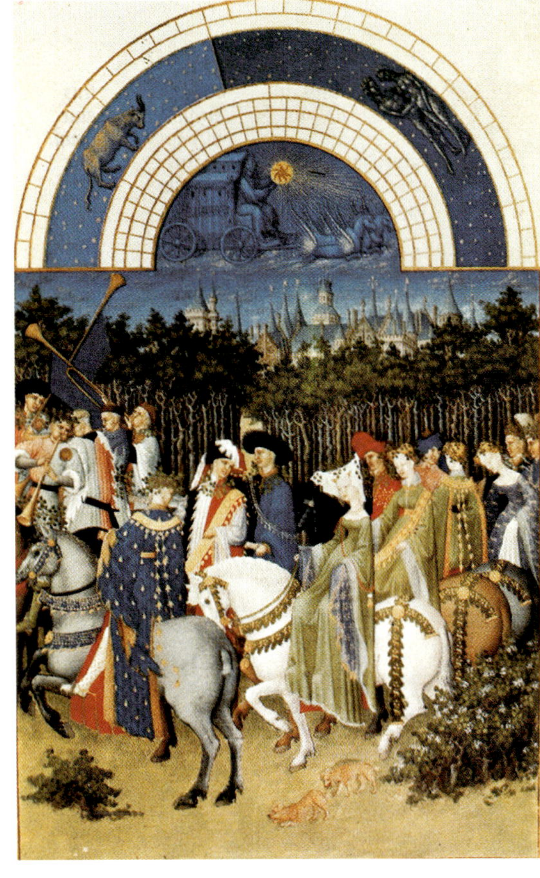 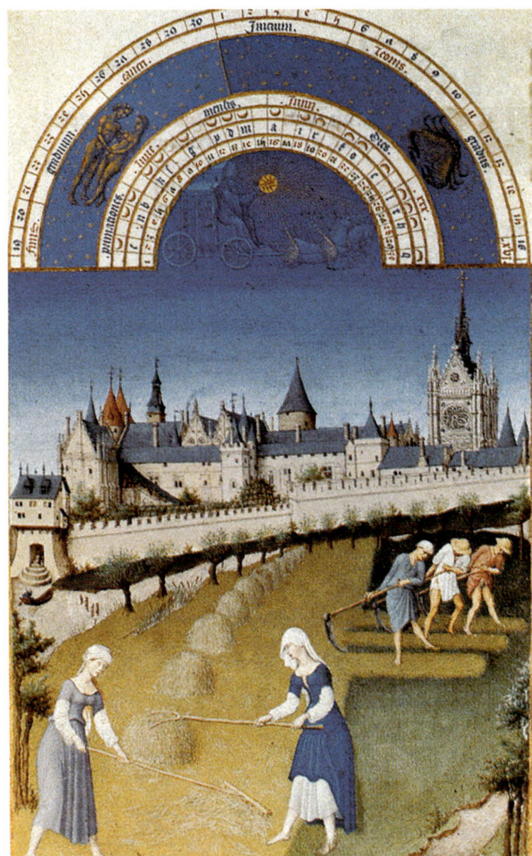

both works the passage of time is indicated by the changing seasonal labors in the fields, meaning it is directly related to the rhythms of peasant life. For this reason, given the immutable wheeling of the seasons and nature, precise points of medieval reference can be indicated. However, the nearly identical repetition of the scenes and, in contrast, the marked stylistic and cultural differences between the works, suggest the value of a closer comparison.

The first series (the top one) is from the famous *Très Riches Heures* of the duke of Berry, the illuminated pages of which are exhibited in the Musée Condé in Chantilly. This was the work of many hands, having been made by the three Limbourg brothers, Pol, Hermann, and Jean. They trained in Paris in the workshop of a goldsmith and under the tutelage of their uncle, the successful painter Jean Malouel, and around 1402 they were working in the service of Philip the Bold, duke of Burgundy. They soon became leaders of the sumptuous and elaborate figurative culture of the duchy, which spread from Dijon to embrace Flanders. After Philip the Bold's death, the Limbourgs went to the court of Jean, the duke of Berry, for whom they made this codex, which was left unfinished when all three brothers died in 1416, probably of the plague. Even if it is difficult to distinguish the contribution of each, the most skilled seems to have been Pol. The calendar is a quintessential expression of the late Gothic world. Every page includes the sign of the Zodiac, the astrological moment, and the activities of a month of the year, always against the background of the elegant castles that were the various residences of the duke of Berry. These scenes are meant to reflect the rhythms and seasonal labors

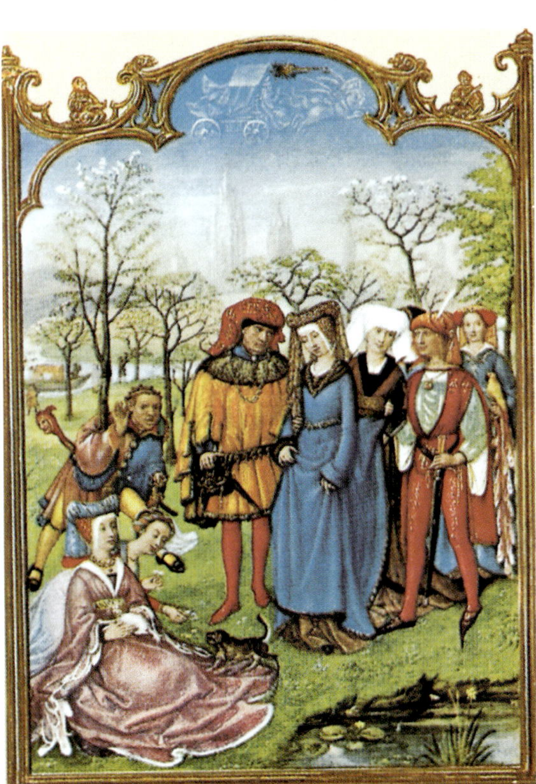 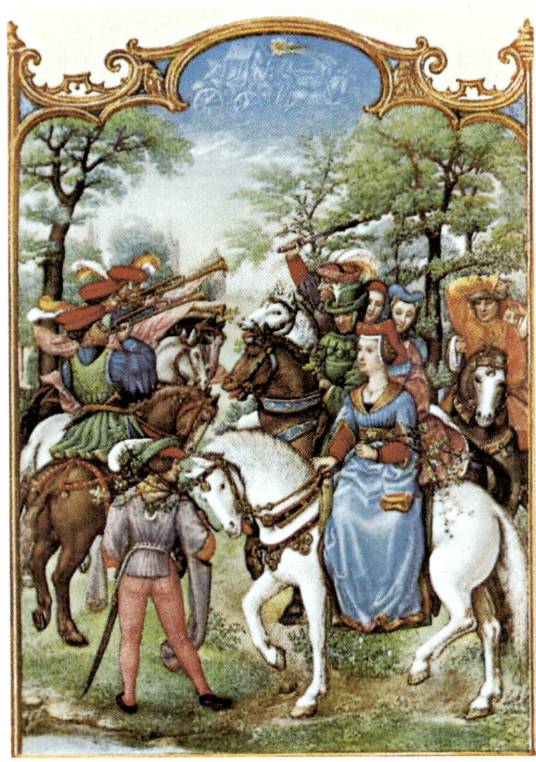 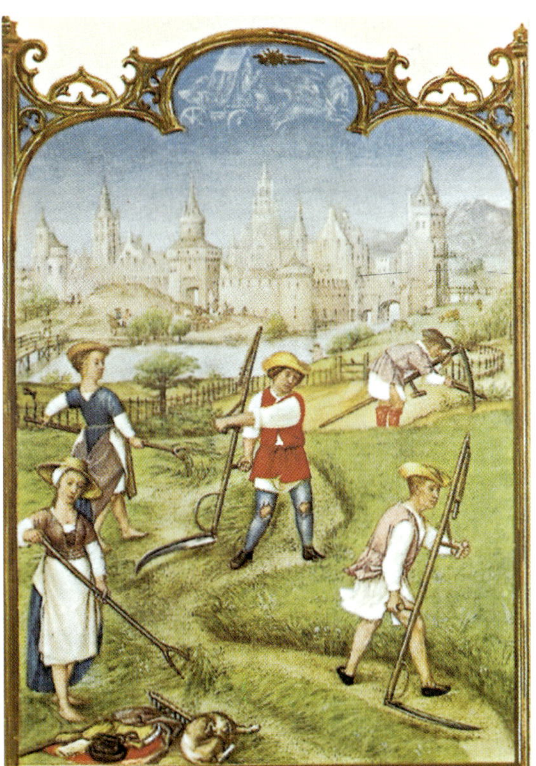

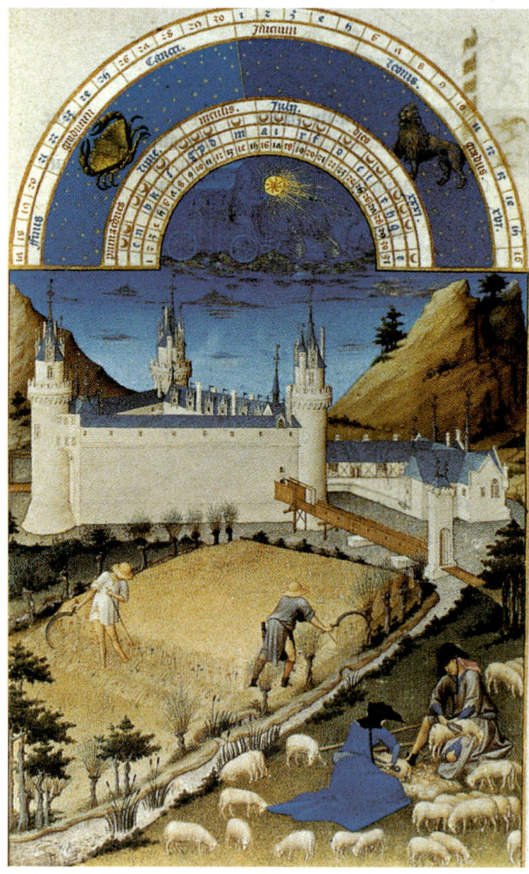 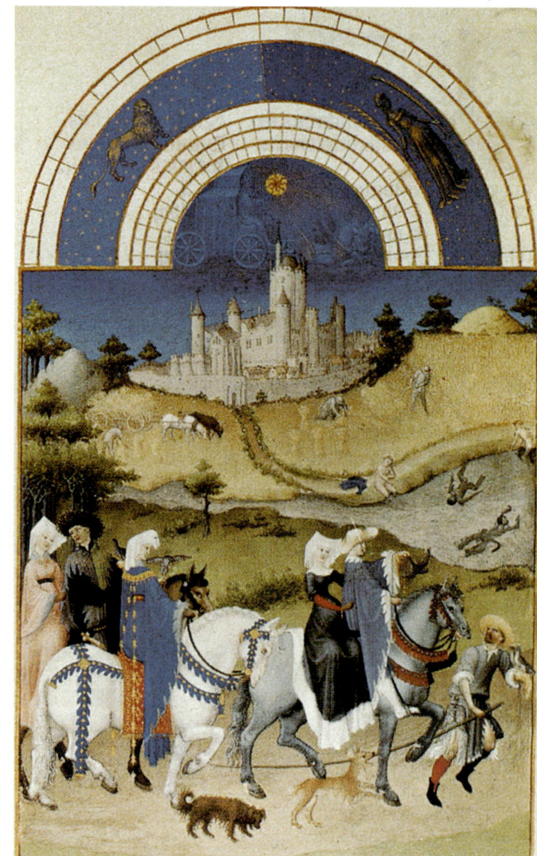 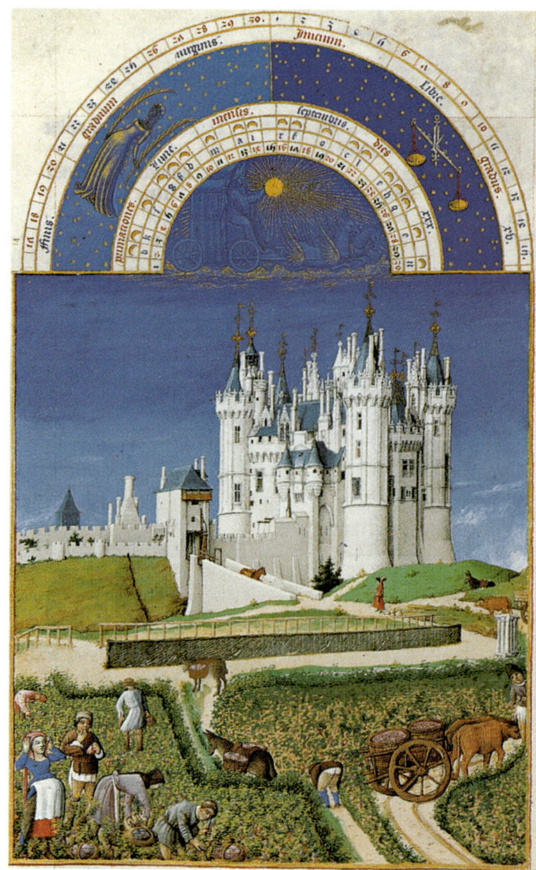

of the peasant world, yet despite the realistic details, the overall atmosphere is that of dreamy enchantment. Time must be passing, and yet everything seems suspended in a rarefied atmosphere, with the subtly elegant poses, transparency of the colors, elaborate lacy architecture. The difference between the life of the nobles and that of the peasants is made abundantly clear: on one side are the amusements of a refined society, on the other the eternal chores of the country. The world of the Limbourg miniatures took place on the thin and precious watershed of late Gothic civilization, the period J. Huizinga masterfully called "the waning of the Middle Ages." The duke of Berry's book of hours provides a precise figurative point of reference, and even after the waning of the duchy of Burgundy and the political changes that made Flanders a property of the house of Hapsburg during the last quarter of the fifteenth century, it is with us.

Standing out among the treasures of the Biblioteca Marciana in Venice is an illuminated codex known as the *Grimani Breviary*, named after the cardinal who once owned it. The precious book has a complicated history but has belonged to the city of Venice since 1592; it was made about a century before that in Bruges, probably by a group of painters and illuminators influenced by Hans Memling and by the early works of Gerard David. Because of the number and exceptional quality of its perfectly preserved miniatures, it is considered one of the most beautiful books in the world.

The breviary includes 831 parchment pages, with many full-page illustrations, all of it conceived with a majestic spirit on a truly monumental scale. Precisely who commissioned this major undertaking is unknown, the dating of the

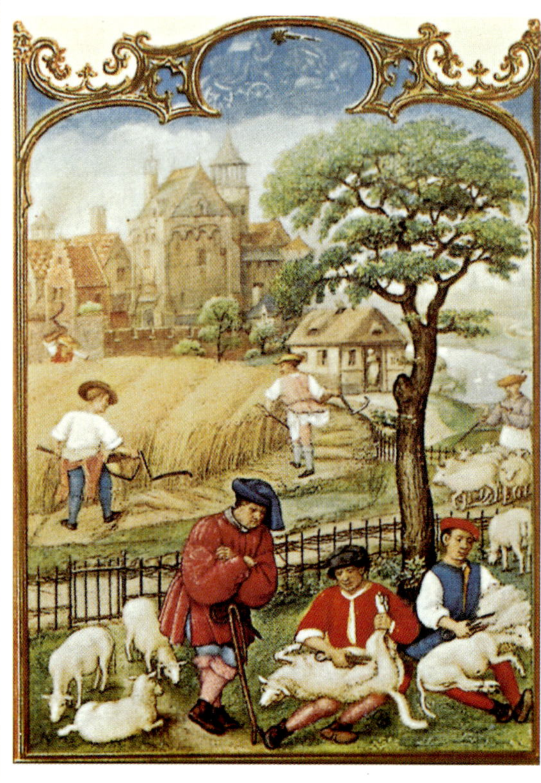 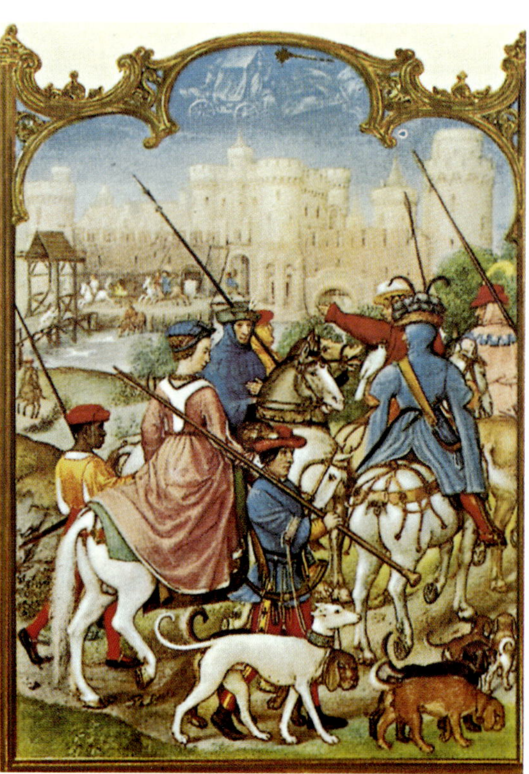 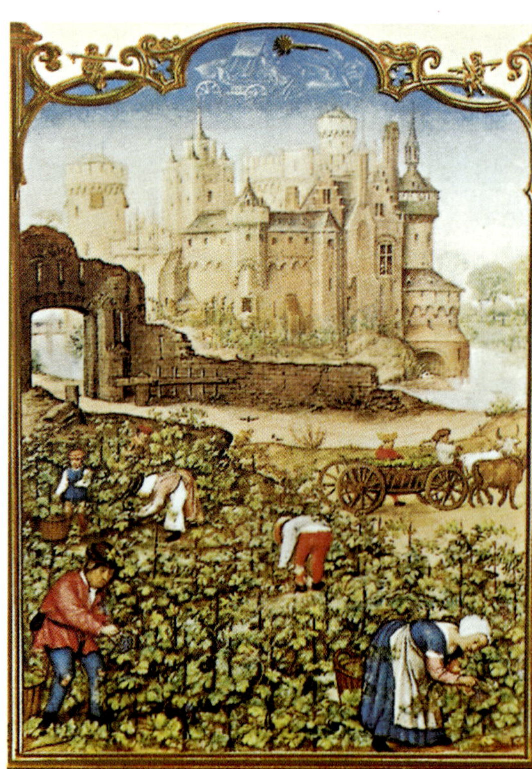

Introduction

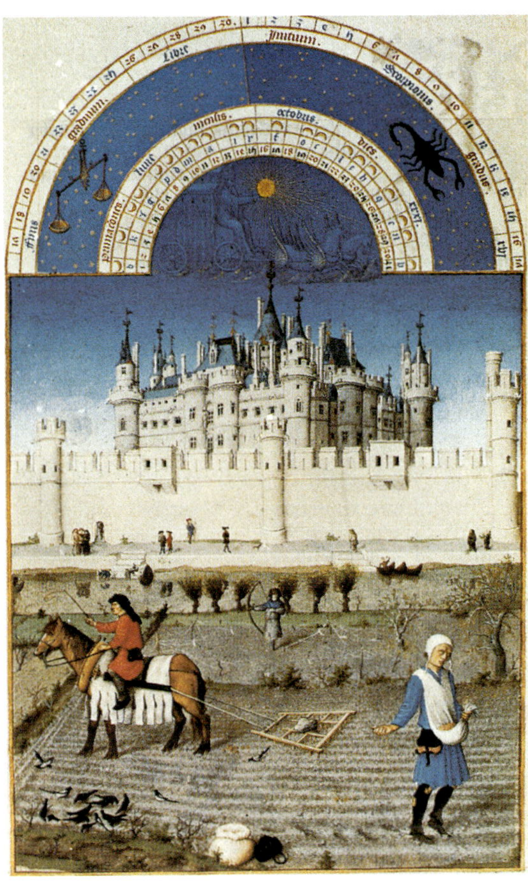 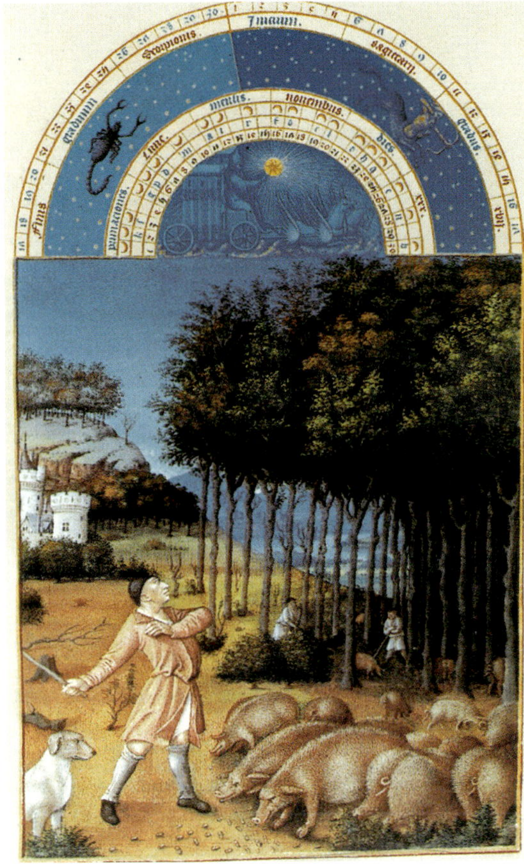 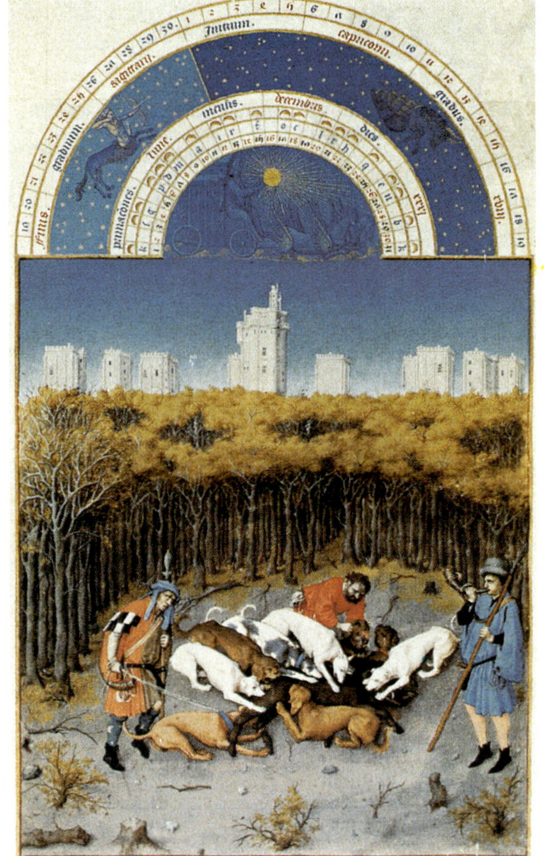

work is uncertain (its execution, which must have taken several years, probably took place around 1490), and art critics have not yet come to a conclusion concerning the identity of the various artists who made it.

Its relationship to the months illuminated by the Limbourg brothers is immediately obvious; clearly the creators of the *Grimani Breviary* wanted to make an up-to-date version of the famous early fifteenth-century prototype, and it is interesting to observe the variations. First there are the backgrounds: gone are the exclusive, enchanting castles of the duke, their place taken by lively cities, with churches, gates, palaces, bridges, and various kinds of urban activity. There is then enormous social change, for the detachment between the nobles and the peasants has diminished. The peasants assume a physical dimension, a moral stature based on the consideration of the full dignity of their work. The gesture of the barefooted peasant gathering cut hay in the month of June is no less elegant than the poses of the horseback noblewomen in the preceding month. Compared to the marvelous fables of the Limbourgs, the *Grimani Breviary* presents a new monumentality, an active and intelligent presence of man in the world; note, too, that the astrological references have become quite small, barely perceptible.

The grains inside the hourglass are, of course, all equal, but the way time passes leaves different traces. Sometimes it pours through in a ceaseless column; at others, it marks and even scratches the glass. One hundred years can pass by in a rush, almost without leaving a trace; or, as happened during the fifteenth and sixteenth centuries, the same measure of time can change the face of the world.

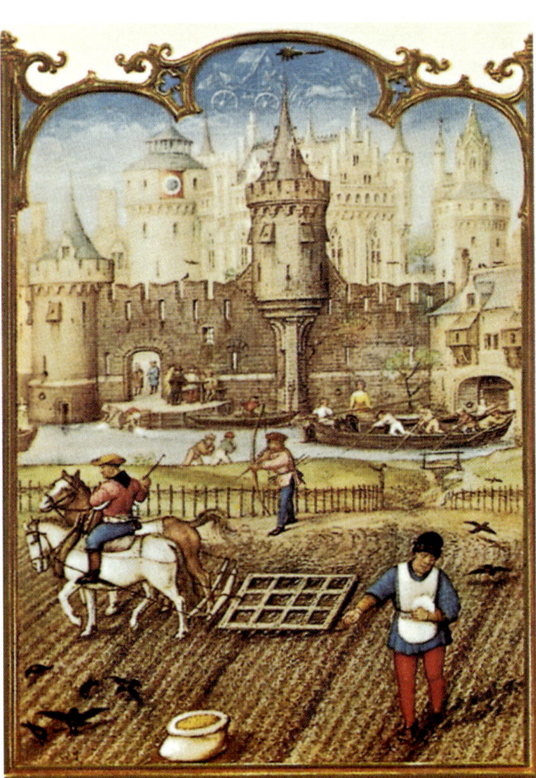 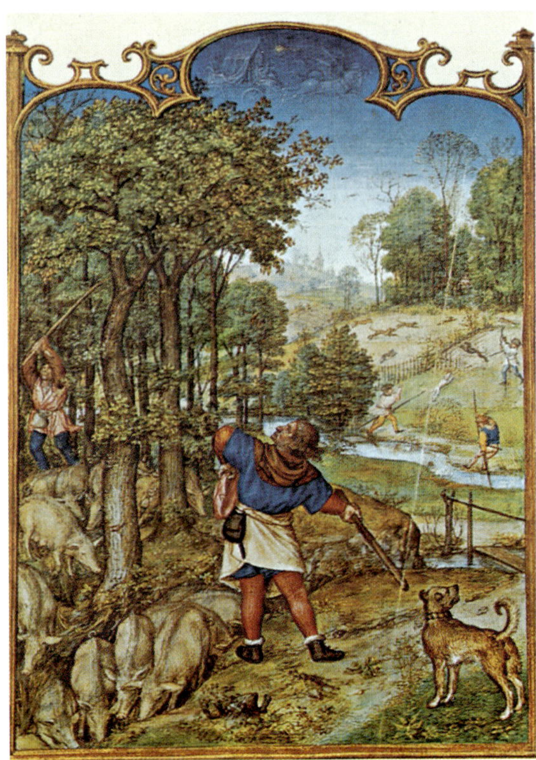 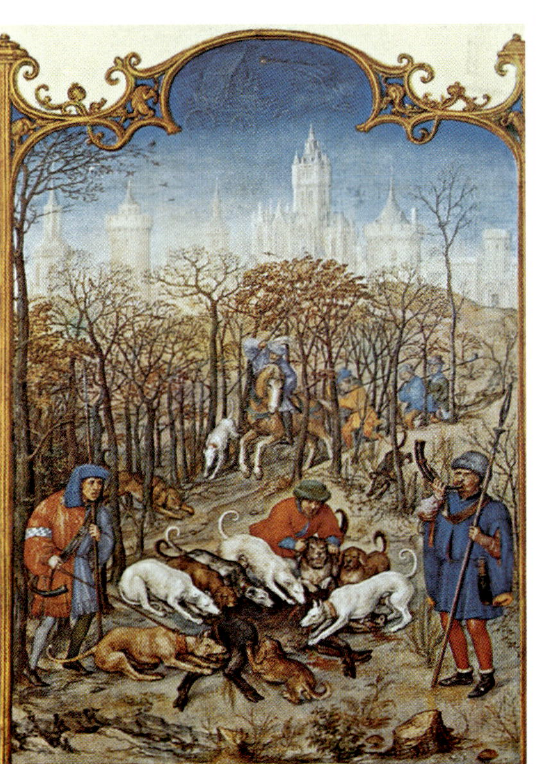

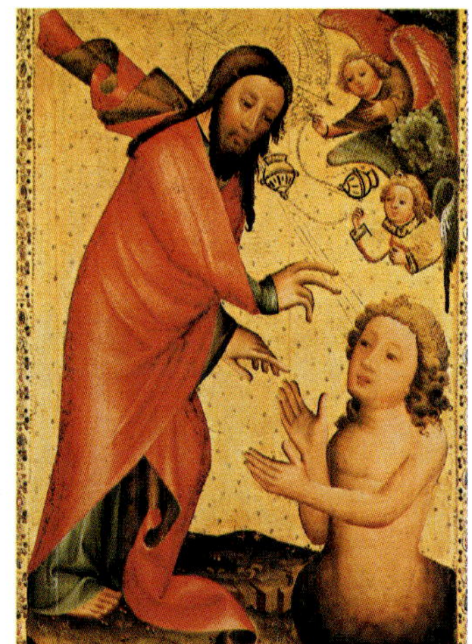

he terrible Black Death of 1348, one of the worst collective scourges of the West, left deep social, economic, and cultural scars on Europe. By then the heroic ideals of the Crusades had waned, and the international aristocracy gathered in the elegant courts of the nobility, where an elaborate, highly detailed style of art flowered. It was an art in which the stately, very human realism of Giotto was replaced by the fabulous atmospheres of chivalric romances. The effect of unreal fantasy was achieved through the well calculated balance of accurately rendered natural details (such as animals and plants) and the atmospheres of hushed, poetic beauty that were the setting. The taste for artworks and objets d'art executed with meticulous detail and made of highly valuable materials was shared by the aristocratic courts across a vast area of Europe, running from Bohemia to Catalonia, from Flanders to Burgundy, from Provence to Italy. The papal court at Avignon was of particular importance in this culture, becoming a laboratory of ornamental motifs and elegant decorative creations, which the multitude of ambassadors and visitors to the papal court then dispersed among their respective nations. The Avignon culture was distinguished by the presence of the Italian poet Francesco Petrarch, and much of its pictorial decoration was entrusted to Italian masters, among them the precursor of the courtly Gothic style, the Sienese Simone Martini, whose frescoes and panels show an exquisite decorative sensibility, with great linear grace. Another Italian personality of great importance in the papal city was the painter Matteo Giovannetti, originally from Viterbo, whose style blended close attention to nature with a vivid imagination and whose works present a lyrically transfigured reality.

These highly poetic images, immersed in an atmosphere of fantasy, were the prelude to the great creations of the courtly Gothic. By the time the popes had returned to Rome (1377), the art of Avignon had already brought about a change in the taste of European courts, all of them directed toward a new stylistic declination that would constitute the fascinating link between the medieval world and the spread of the culture of classical humanism.

In several ways, the vast and composite historical-cultural area of France became the reference point for this style. During the second half of the fourteenth century, following the French court's move to Touraine in response to the uncertainties of the Hundred Years' War, Paris experienced a certain reduction in the patronage of important works of art. This lack was in large part compensated by the rapid ascent of the duchy of Burgundy in a territory extending from Flanders to northeastern France. The dukes and their families and high dignitaries were splendid patrons of art, and their patronage was responsible for some of the most precious works of illumination, sculpture, painting, and tapestry work between the end of the fourteenth and the beginning of the fifteenth centuries.

Giving a precise definition to the borders of this "medieval autumn" style is very difficult and ultimately futile. Born in the courts of central southern Europe, the International Gothic took substantially similar forms in the various nations, in many cases holding on well past the middle of the fifteenth century. One of its fundamental traits is the mixture of diverse arts, the continuous exchange of techniques, methods, and motifs among painting, illumination, goldworking, fabrics, tapestries, and furniture, eventually coming to involve all aspects of aristocratic life. For the European courts, the production and patronage of highly refined works of art became a basic element in the "politics of image." Fine art was indispensable for acquiring visibility

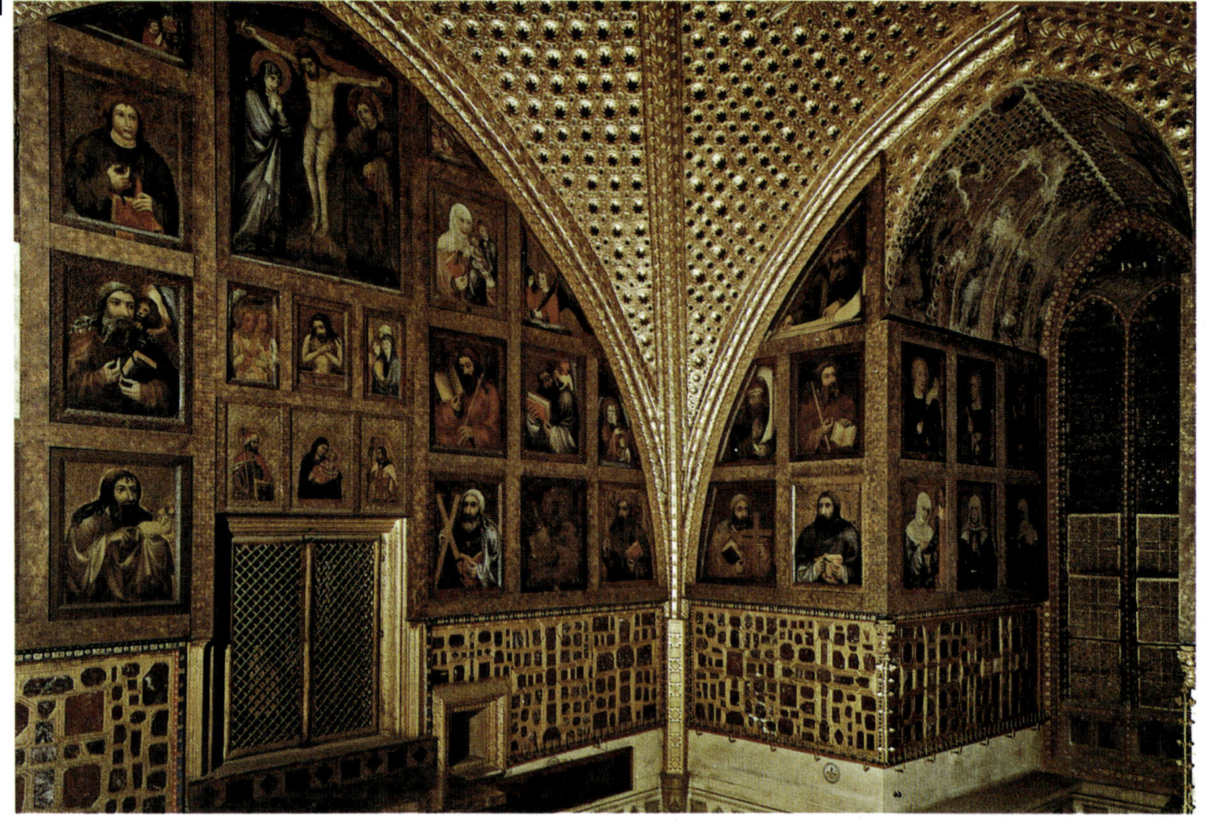

and prestige on the fluid and complicated political panorama. The most active areas were Catalonia, Burgundy, Lombardy, and Bohemia; these had the power to determine the style adopted in other courts. The image of the ruler repeated the ideals of nobility, pride, and refinement expressed by the chivalric literature, romances, and epic tales of heroic deeds of the late fourteenth century. For monumental sculpture, "public" and highly visible, spectacular solutions were preferred, and even in the case of tombs, the lord was presented in the fullness of his physical vigor. In Milan, Verona, and Naples, but also in Venice, France, and Catalonia, the portrait of the lord sitting bolt upright in the saddle of a battle charger, sheathed in parade armor, and covered with the heraldic emblems of his house became a symbol of the absolute

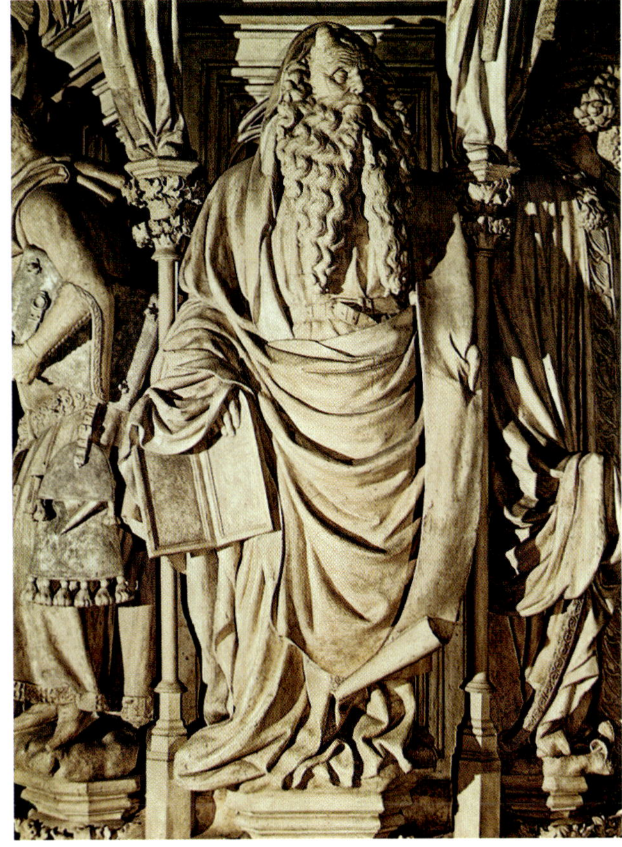

Claus Sluter, *Moses*, detail of the so-called Well of Moses, 1395–1404; charterhouse of Champmol, Dijon

creation of jewels, crowns, scepters, and other emblems of economic or royal power, works that were both sumptuous and fanciful, with the taste for the capricious line and for decoration that belongs to the most brilliant expressions of the International Gothic.

Characteristic elements of the late Gothic include, first of all, a special skill in the application and combination of the most complex artistic operations (made possible by the traditional practice of the workshop, such mixing of media was further supported by a new literary genre, the manual for artists), along with the closely related fondness for gilding and the abundant use of color. This ornamental exuberance, specifically requested by patrons, was displayed in many ways. The period saw the apogee of the illuminated page, as much for religious texts

The late Gothic world

power that is handed down after death generation after generation. The opposite of monumental sculpture was the late Gothic illumination, an example of an exquisitely "private" art, since illuminated manuscripts were made to be handled and seen by only a few select members of court. In the scenes that decorate the most precious codices the lord is shown taking pleasure in settings of daily life or in moments of amusement in his favorite occupation. The court became the ideal (and often idealized) model of a place of delights, entertainments, and refined pleasures, all of it revolving around the figure of the ruler, who constructed, or desired to imagine around himself, a sophisticated world fashioned in his image.

Art also had to reflect a sense of material wealth, far from the worries and distresses of daily life. It is therefore understandable that stylistic models came prevalently from goldworkers, who offered new and increasingly complex horizons, moving into the area of profane art and setting up new production centers. During the fourteenth and early fifteenth centuries, the goldworks of Prague competed with the Parisian ateliers for primacy in the

as for profane books; spectacular sculptural complexes, such as the royal tombs of Saint-Denis in Paris, the Arche Scaligere in Verona, certain English monuments in brass, or the immense Angevin tombs in Naples; ambitious architecture, such as the great churches built in the style of the Parler family of architects and sculptors (for example the cathedrals of Cologne, Prague, or Milan); and the beginning of the period of the immense retables in Spanish churches.

By the first decades of the fifteenth century the late Gothic was in open dialogue with the intellectual movement of humanism. The sweet, melancholy, and bloody fables of the courts blended with the university studies and the investigation of the classical world, giving life to a fascinating phenomenon.

Parisian goldsmiths, *Charles VI in Adoration of the Virgin ("The White Pony")*, 1404; Treasury of the Sanctuary, Altötting

Wilton Diptych
1397–99,
tempera on panel,
53 x 37 cm
National Gallery,
London

Hardly larger than an
illuminated manuscript,
this diptych was made
for England's Richard II,
but whether its creator
was French or English
cannot be established
with certainty. The
technique by which the
tempera was applied
recalls Italian art, but
the white gesso back-
ground and the use of
an oak panel as the
support medium are
typical of northern
European art. The
scene resembles a
stately royal ceremony;
in this, the left panel,
the king of England is
presented kneeling,
accompanied by the
three patron saints of
the royal family (St.
Edmund, Edward the
Confessor, and John the
Baptist), who present
him to the "celestial
court," painted on the
right panel (opposite).
St. Edmund bears one
of the arrows with
which he was martyred
by invading Danes in
869; the Confessor holds
a ring, symbolic of the
one that, according
to legend, he gave a
pilgrim, later revealed
to be St. John the
Evangelist. St. John
the Baptist is present
because he was Richard's
patron saint, the king
having been born on
January 6, feast day of
the baptism of Christ.

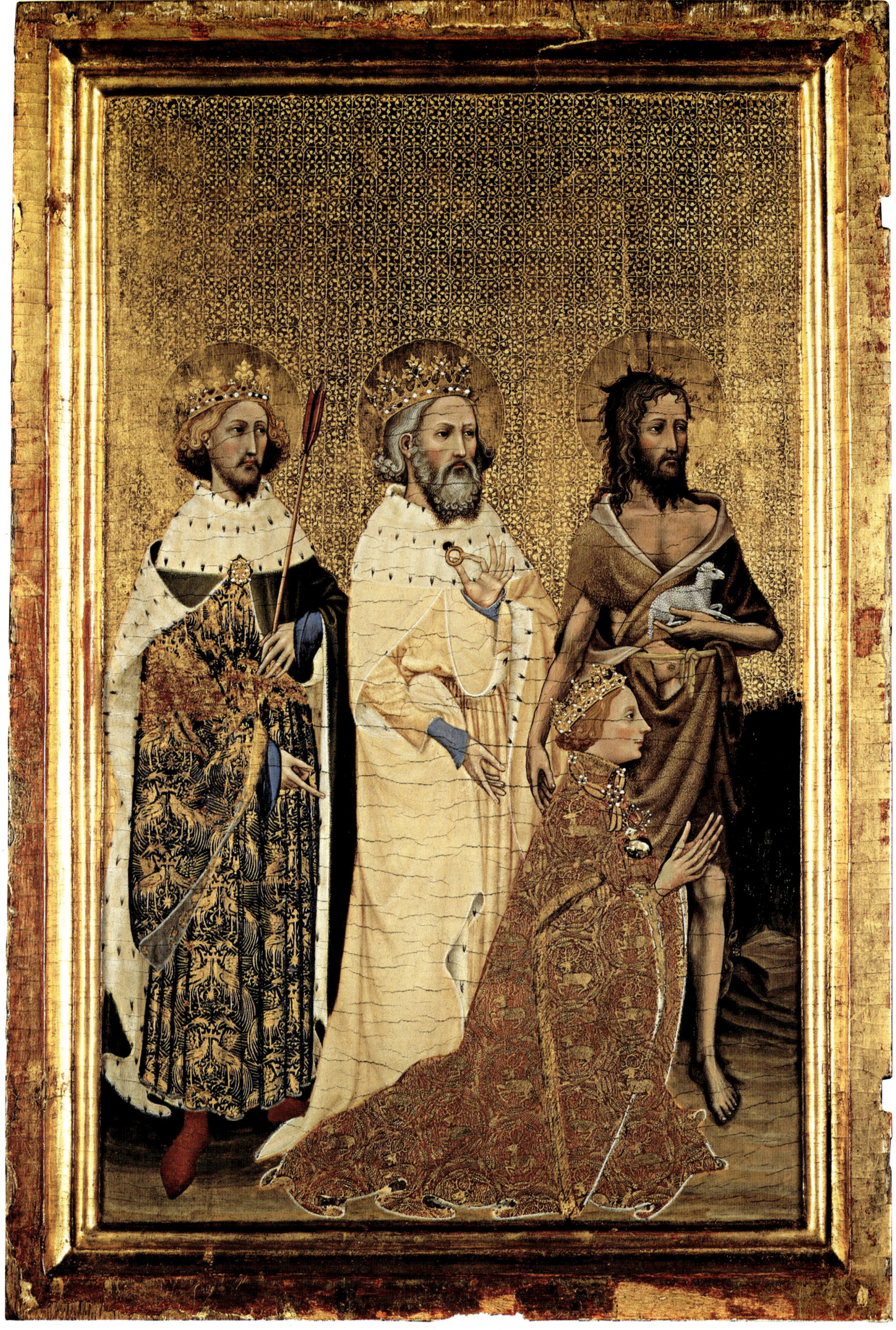

The late Gothic world

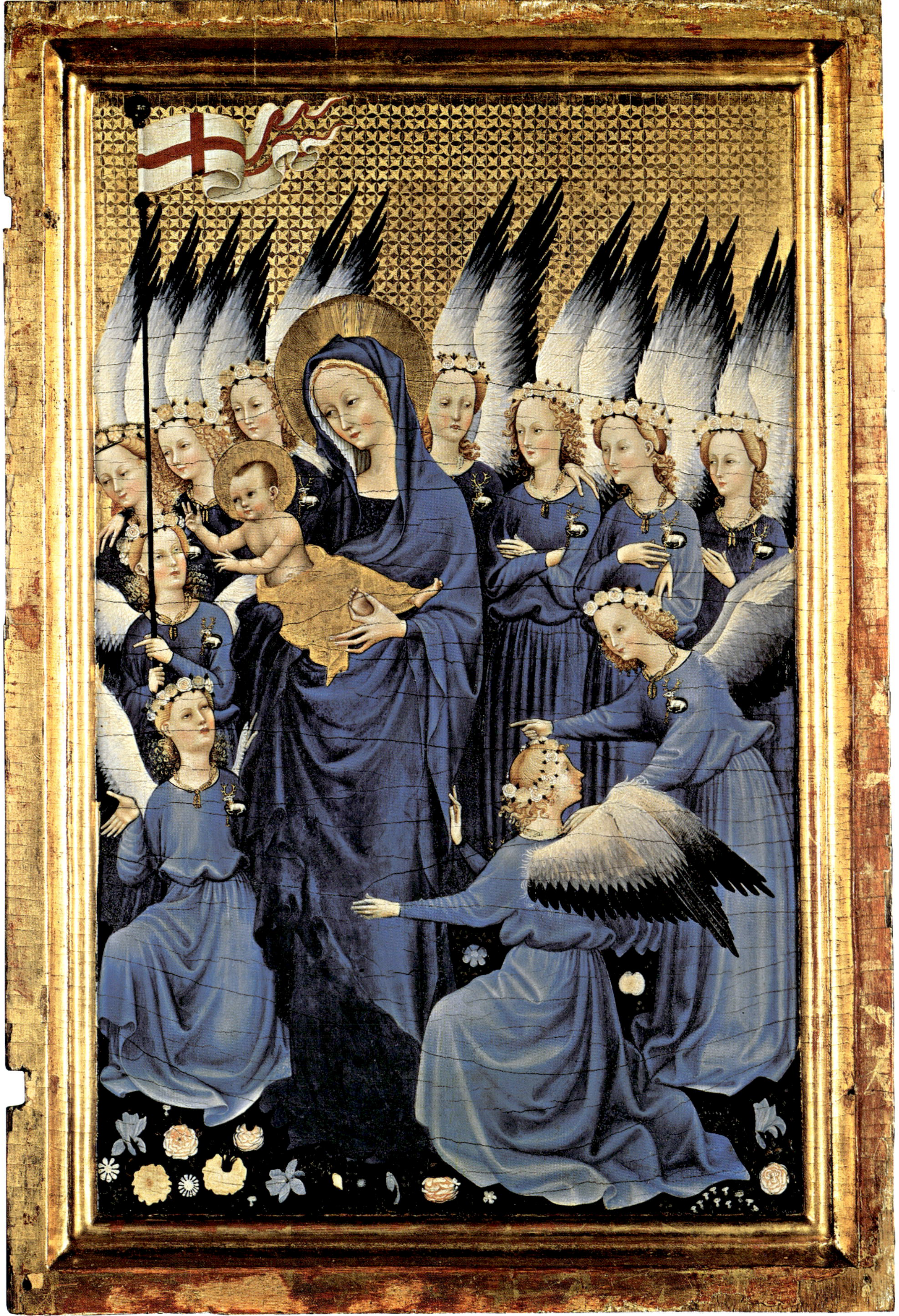

The right panel of the diptych presents the *hortus conclusus*, the enclosed flowering garden of paradise and symbol of the purity of Mary. The Madonna gazes in the direction of the kneeling donor, and the infant Christ reaches out as though to welcome the king's prayers; around them, a dense collection of symbols alludes to the royal patronage. An angel bears aloft the standard of the Resurrection, which at the same time is the flag of England. Richard, thus, is presented to the Madonna and Child to receive a sort of divine investiture. This is confirmed by the heraldic details: the angels of the celestial court wear the emblem of the king, the white deer with golden horns, and they wear necklaces of broom. The ornamental motifs on the clothes worn by Richard are composed of wreaths of this plant, inside which the deer once again appears. The *Planta genista* (broom), in fact, is one of the emblems of the royal family to which the king belonged, the Plantagenets.

The late Gothic world

These panels (today in the Bohemian art section of the Castle of Prague) are from the sumptuous decoration of the chapel of Karlstejn Castle, which, in part because of the presence on the altar of a notable work by Tommaso da Modena (circa 1350), is the most important pictorial complex from the age of Holy Roman Emperor Charles IV. Master Theodoric and his workshop made 128 panels with busts of saints, enough to completely cover the walls of the chapel. The distinctive characterizations of the gestures, dress, features, and descriptive details keep the works from becoming a parade of static devotional icons and make them instead lively images of individuals. Oddball or dreamy, distracted or smartly dressed, plump or emaciated, the busts create an unpredictable assembly of good humor, sometimes reaching the borders of caricature. The gold background with its punch decoration does not prevent a certain variety in terms of setting; and Theodoric often takes the liberty of using the frames and the area beyond as integral parts of the painted surface, thus skillfully "exiting" the rectangular perimeter of the image.

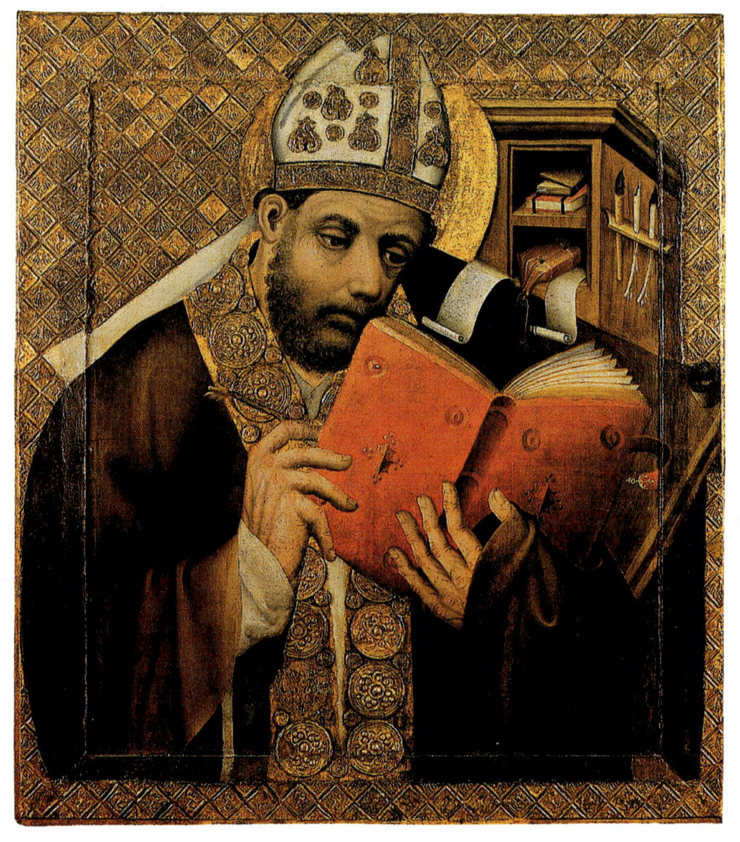

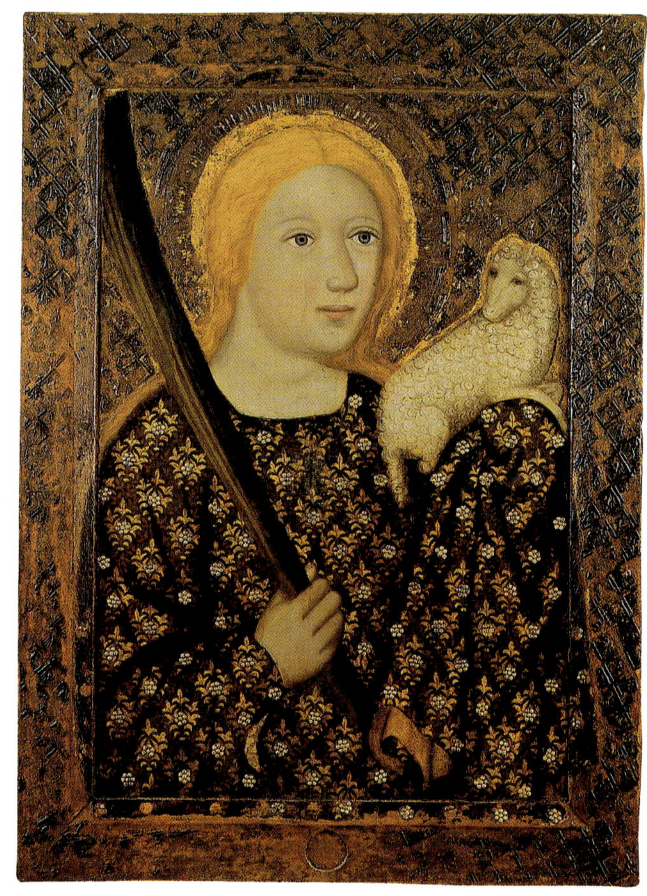

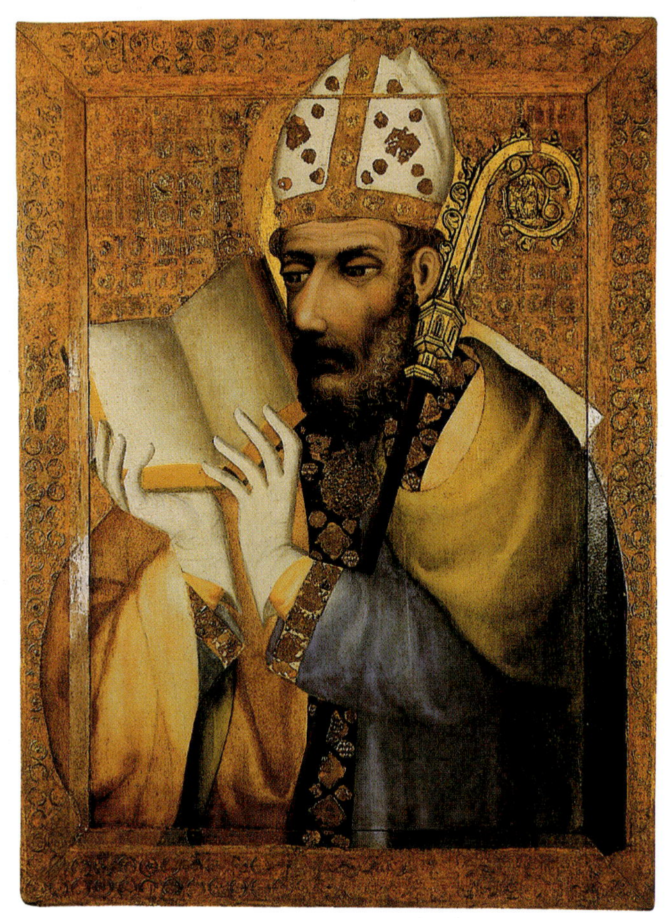

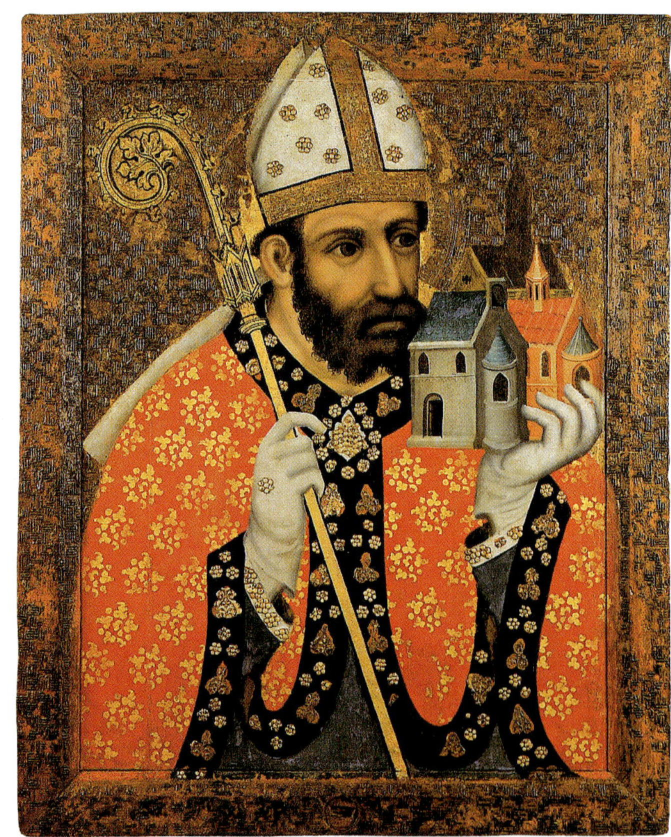

The late Gothic world

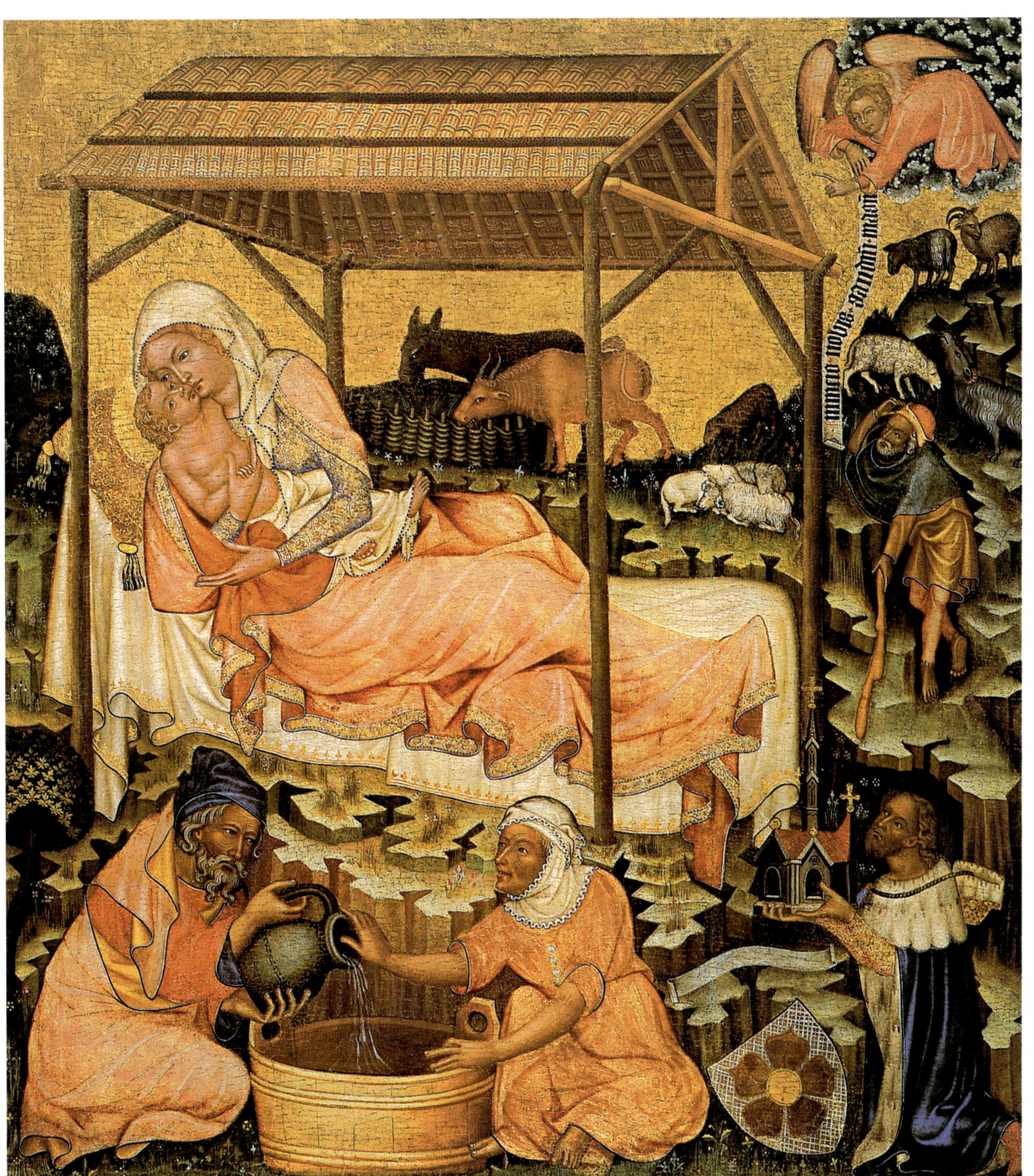

MASTER OF HOHENFURTH (OR OF VYSSI BROD)
Nativity
circa 1350
Národní Galerie, Prague

Under Charles IV (king of Bohemia, 1346–1378; Holy Roman emperor, 1355–1378), Prague became one of the most brilliant and advanced workshops in the late International Gothic. During the mid-fourteenth century Bohemian painting formed a close-knit school, full of important artistic figures; in many cases, the exact identity of these artists is unknown, but they can be recognized by stylistic differences. This period was brought to a sudden end, following the death of Charles IV, by the violent religious and political turmoil caused by John Huss. A common feature in fourteenth-century Bohemian paintings is the delicate balance between reality and fantasy, a taste for stories that blend mysticism and daily life. Another typical aspect is the "side show," and in this painting there is the minor scene involving Joseph awkwardly pouring water into the tub for the Child's bath while the midwife intervenes. Also noteworthy are the ingenuous but effective methods of indicating space, such as the elementary perspective of the hut or the jagged shapes of the rocks.

Commissioned by Louis I, duke of Anjou, these tapestries are part of a long wall hanging, five and a half meters high, originally with a length of about 150 meters. Today 70 scenes remain, about two-thirds of the original, making a length of 107 meters. Early in the 1370s, the painter and miniaturist Hennequin of Bruges made the cartoons (the large preparatory drawings in 1/1 format) used as patterns in the weaving, which was performed (1373–79) by the Parisian tapestry maker Nicolas Bataille. Hennequin reworked, adapted, and enlarged scenes of the Apocalypse from illuminated codices, combining monstrous beings with details from everyday life. By reducing the number of colors and alternating between blue or red backgrounds, he gave the tapestry intense concentration on the narrative scenes and the characters. The entire sequence was finished in about seven years, thanks to dozens of weavers busy at the same time (a skilled worker could make only about half a square meter in a year's work). Landscape backgrounds, figures, architecture, all appears on the same plane, without depth, creating a vertical "wall" from which the episodes seem to loom toward the viewer with peremptory directness.

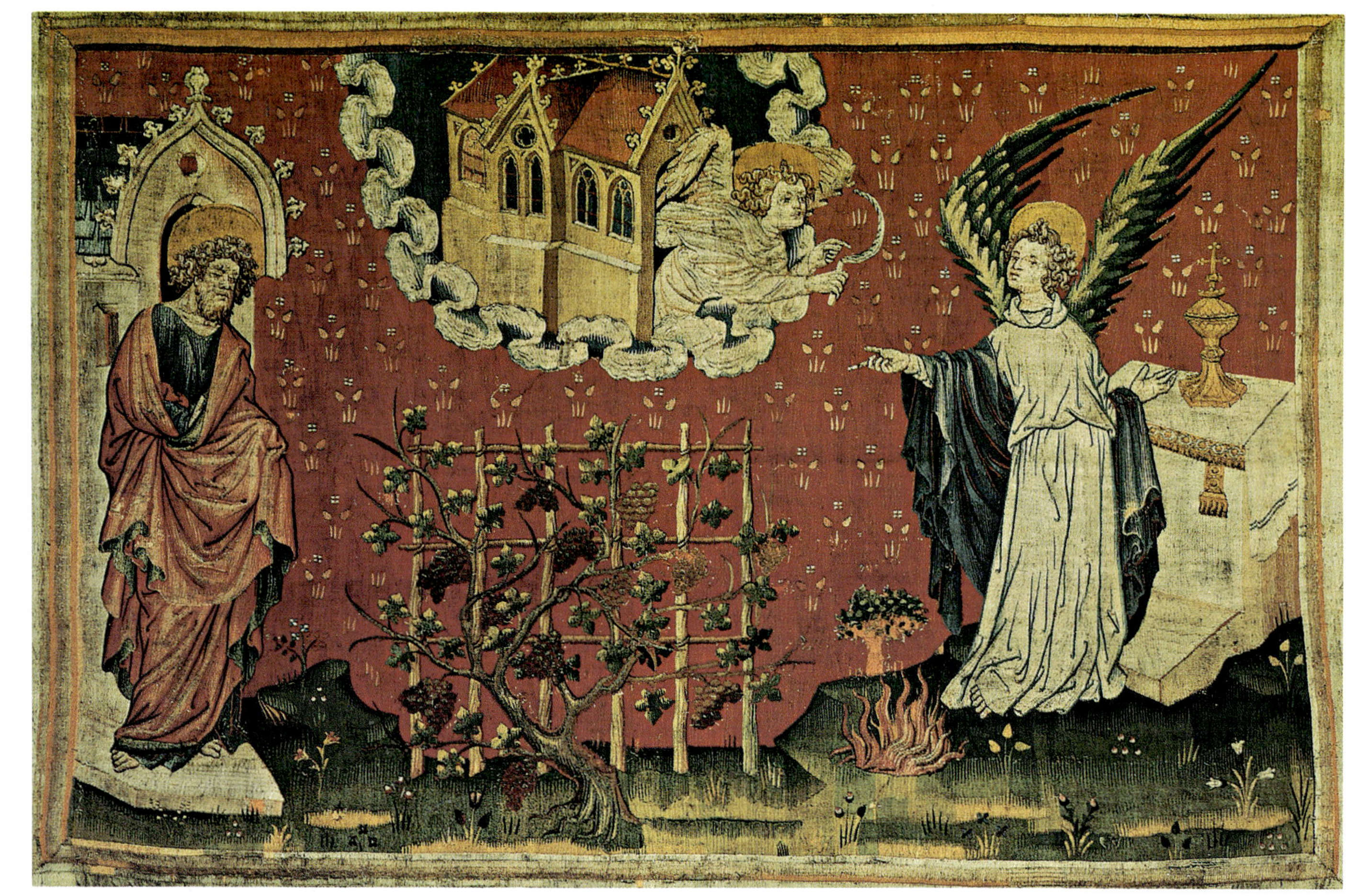

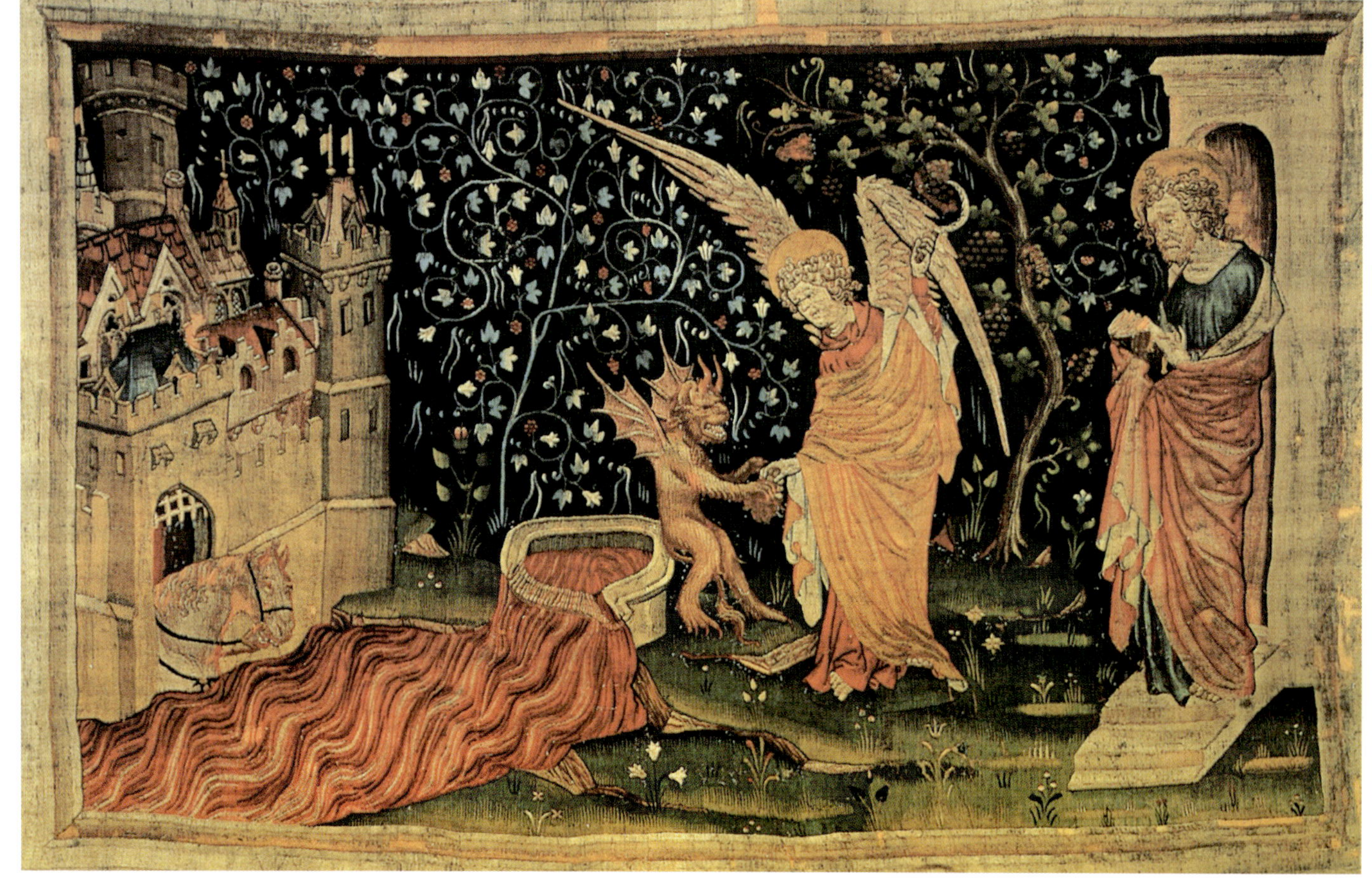

The late Gothic world

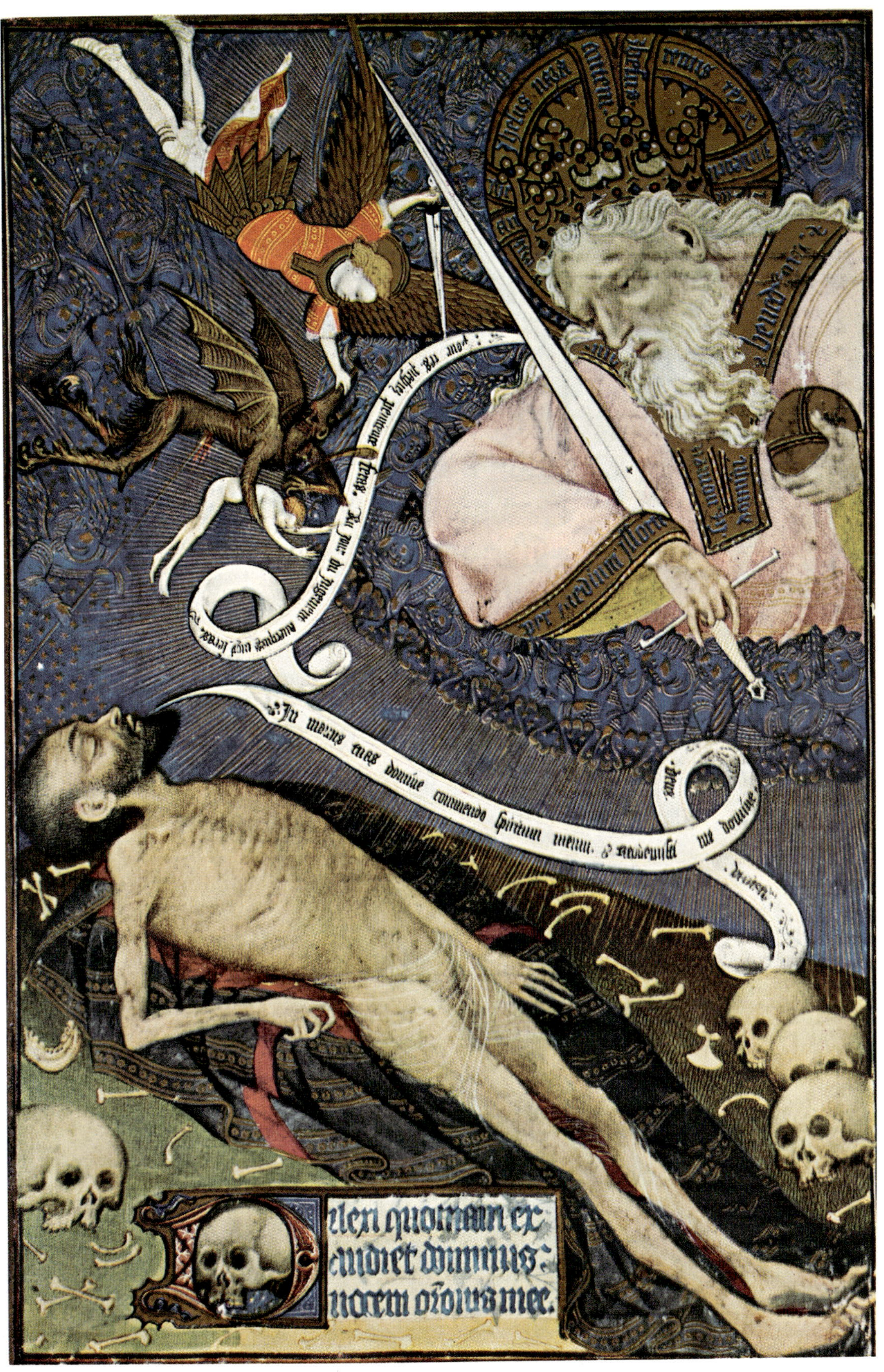

MASTER OF THE
ROHAN HOURS
**The Dead before
His Judge**
1418–25,
illuminated page
Bibliothèque Nationale,
Paris

Although it was a period of notable difficulty for the French court, shaken by the events of the ongoing war with England, and despite the recent decisive affirmation of Burgundy as the center of culture, Paris was still an artistic center of great importance. Aside from the creation of tapestries, the city was known for it many workshops specializing in the creation of exquisite luxury products, such as goldsmiths and book illuminators. Books of hours were a typical status symbol, a gift of enormous prestige. Collections of prayers and sections of holy scripture to be read at various times during the day, the books of hours often included highly elaborate illuminated images. Here a dead man addresses God (in Latin: "Into thy hands O Lord I commend my spirit"), and God responds (in French: "Do penitence for thy sins and you will be with me on judgment day"). The many macabre and gruesome details, somewhat frequent in late Gothic art, are redeemed by the marvelous naturalness of the line and the transparent clarity of the colors.

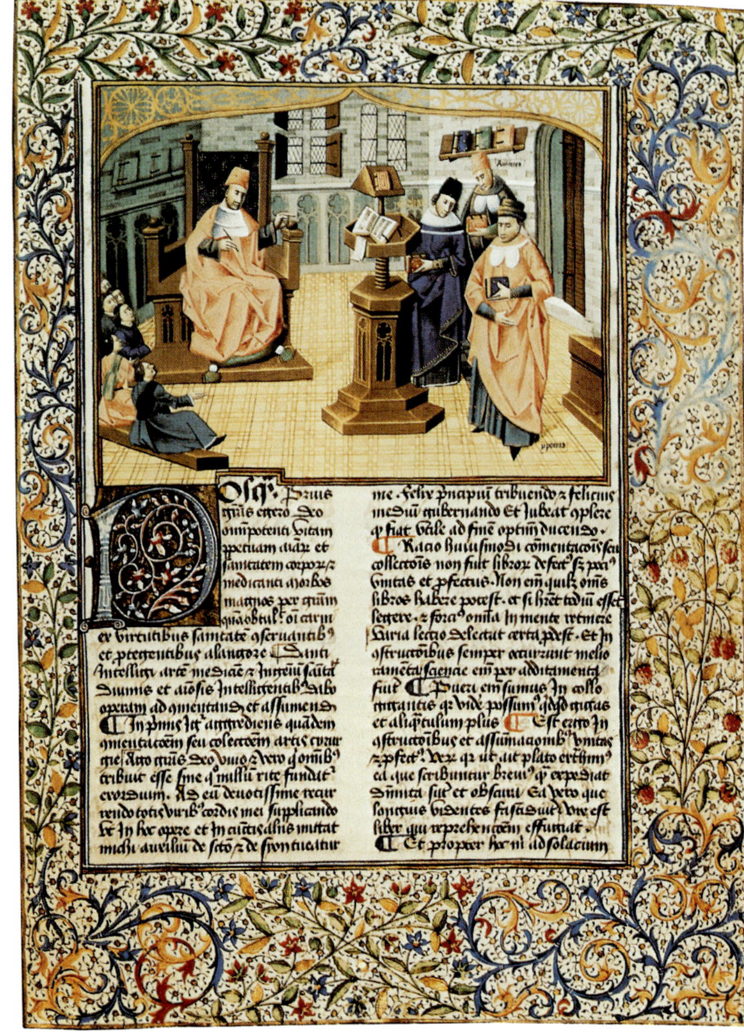

MASTER OF THE
ROHAN HOURS
The university teacher Bernard of Gordon evokes the spirits of Hippocrates, Galen, and Avicenna before his students
1418–25,
illuminated page
Bibliothèque Nationale,
Paris

The late Gothic style was most popular in the noble courts throughout Europe that were the most active and demanding patrons of artists. There was also, however, a growing demand for works of art related to universities and to the activities of scholars. The basis of the humanist culture was anchored in the "classics," here evoked within the context of a university lesson.

FOLLOWER OF
BELBELLO DA PAVIA
Ptolemy
From a codex of the Geography of Ptolemy
circa 1450,
illuminated page
Biblioteca Marciana,
Venice

Over the course of the fifteenth century the production of illuminated manuscripts on scientific subjects marked the desire of knowledge from specialists, patrons, and also bibliophiles. Although the scientists of the past are presented in a fanciful manner, the various instruments and the settings of the studiolo laboratories can be taken as meticulously accurate reflections of the true conditions of fifteenth-century researchers.

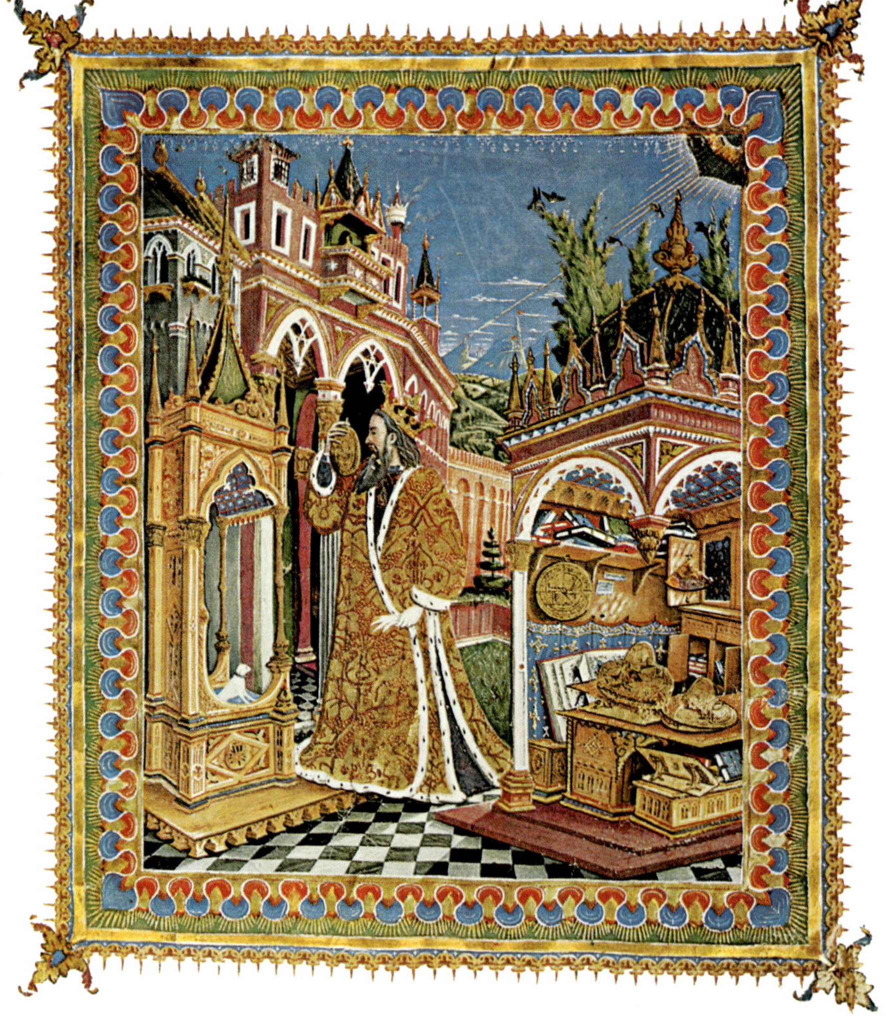

The late Gothic world

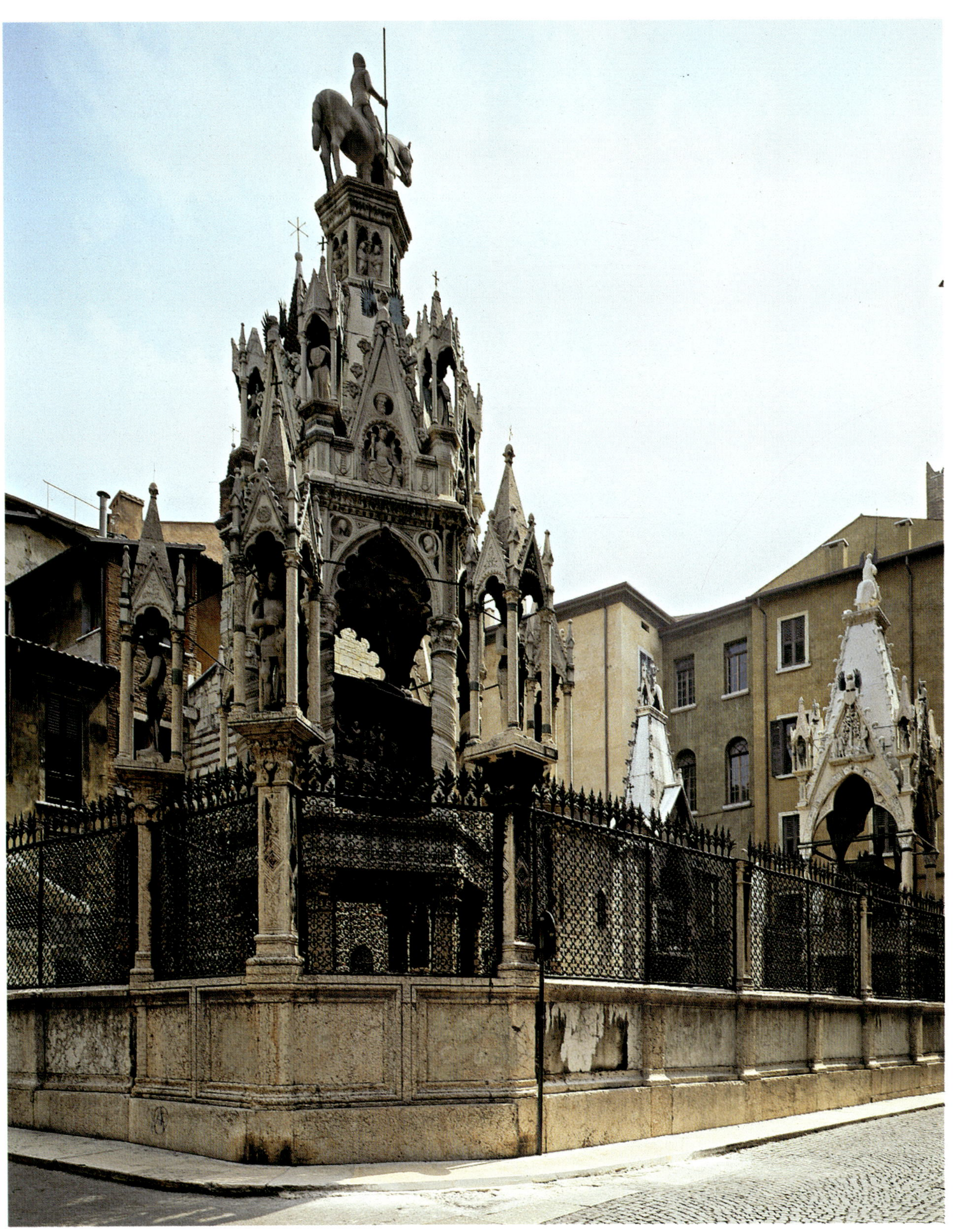

Grand dynastic tombs are a highly typical and quite widespread feature of late Gothic art, having been popular with the period's noble patrons. Most such funeral monuments and sarcophaguses are found in churches, but they were sometimes located in the open, in the middle of cities, making a striking contrast between the affirmation of worldly power and recognition of the threshold of the afterworld. Such is the case with the Arche Scaligere, spectacular marble tombs of the rulers of Verona. These include that of Cangrande I, the ruler known for the hospitality he offered the exiled Dante. These outdoor tombs were made in the fourteenth century by several groups of Veneto and Lombard sculptors. Most include open-air shrines on tiers of columns surmounted by canopies with trefoil arches. Aside from the tomb itself, there is usually an impressive equestrian statue of the ruler, dressed in armor, transmitting a sense of uninterrupted power. This complex stands in a plaza in the center of Verona and is surrounded by a wrought-iron fence; the heraldic symbol of the Scala family appears throughout the city.

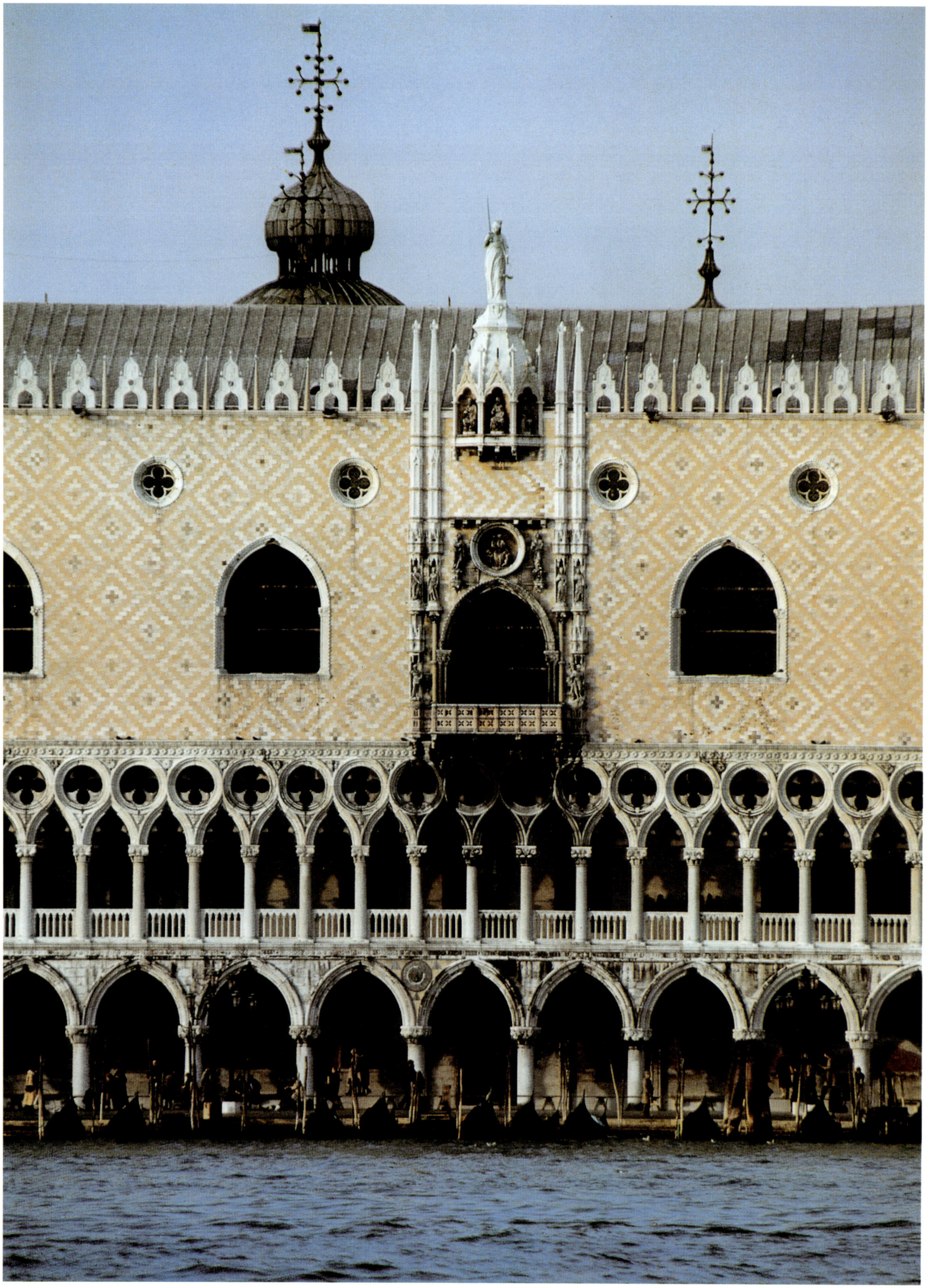

The civil architecture of Venice presents one of its most magnificent and innovative works of the late Gothic in the building that is the symbol of the Most Serene Republic of St. Mark. Rebuilt several times between 1348 and 1427, the Doge's Palace reverses the usual architectonic logic by inverting the traditional division between closed and open spaces. A loggia composed of a series of short columns with splendid carved capitals acts as the support for an airy gallery atop which rests the heaviest part of the building, such that the empty spaces are below and those full are above. The elegant geometric decoration of the upper body, with its lozenge motifs, is interrupted by large windows and by sculptural groups. Sparkling chromatic effects are achieved by the contrast between the marble surface, with its almost oriental splendor, and the airy traceried gallery. This elegant and vibrant

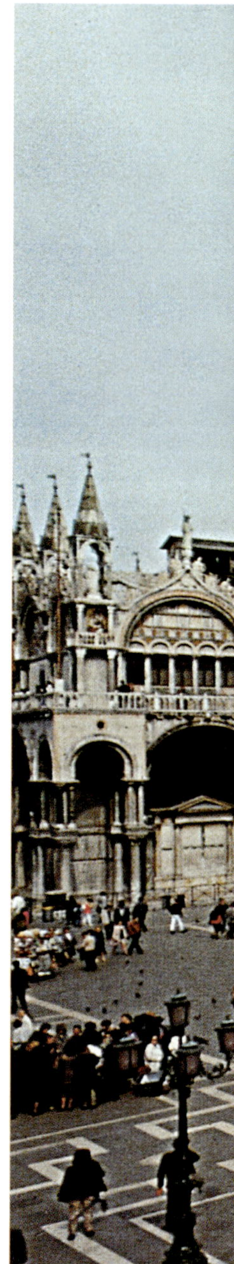

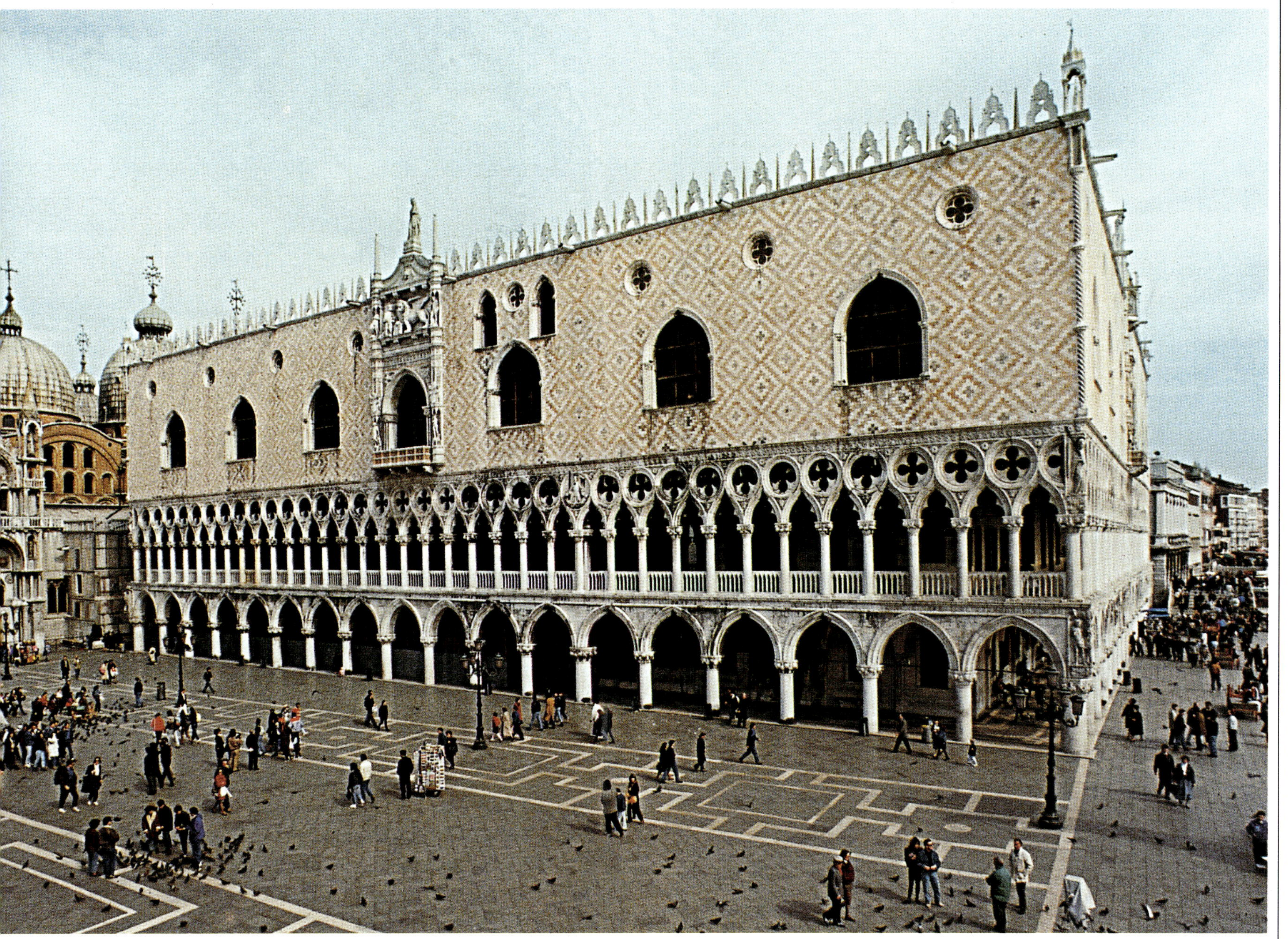

style, which perfectly matches the moving surfaces of water in the canals and the luminous atmosphere of the city, also appears in the façades of the luxurious palaces built between the fourteenth and fifteenth centuries, which make use of interwoven arches, delicate trefoils, and polychrome surfaces. Even Venetian sculpture evolved toward increasingly fanciful and decorative forms, blending influences from northern Europe with those of the Tuscan and Lombard masters active in the Doge's Palace and in the completion of the façade of St. Mark's, with its spires, pinnacles, shrines, and sculptures that are typical of late Gothic. The side of the Doge's palace facing the piazzetta was rebuilt in the first half of the fifteenth century following the stylistic modules of the side of the building made in the preceding century facing the dock. Thanks to this enlargement, the Doge's Palace extended to the basilica of St. Mark by way of the Porta della Carta (1438–42), made by the Buon workshop, father and son, which became the main entrance.

The late Gothic world

At the end of the four-teenth century the duchy of Burgundy became independent and briefly rose to become one of the most advanced and innova-tive centers of artistic creativity. Philip the Bold dedicated his attention most of all to the charterhouse (Carthusian monastery) of Champmol, commis-sioning a majestic main altar composed of an internal section in carved and gilt wood and external painted wings. The complex presents a fine example of the characteristics of Burgundian late Gothic, not only in terms of its refined elegance, impeccable technique, and use of precious materials, but also for its fondness for digression and narrative detail, the evocation of fabulous atmospheres balanced by details drawn directly from the reality of daily life.

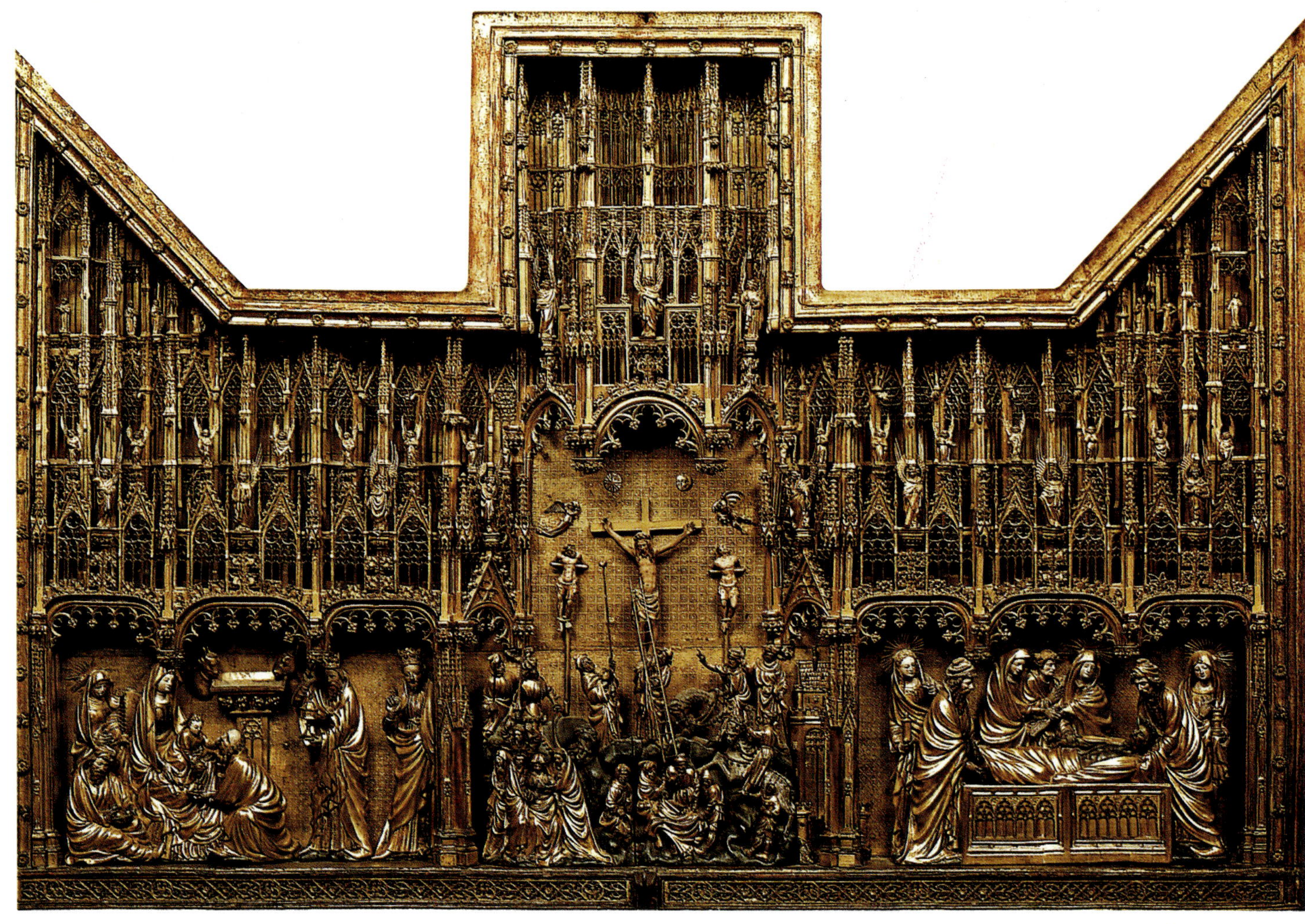

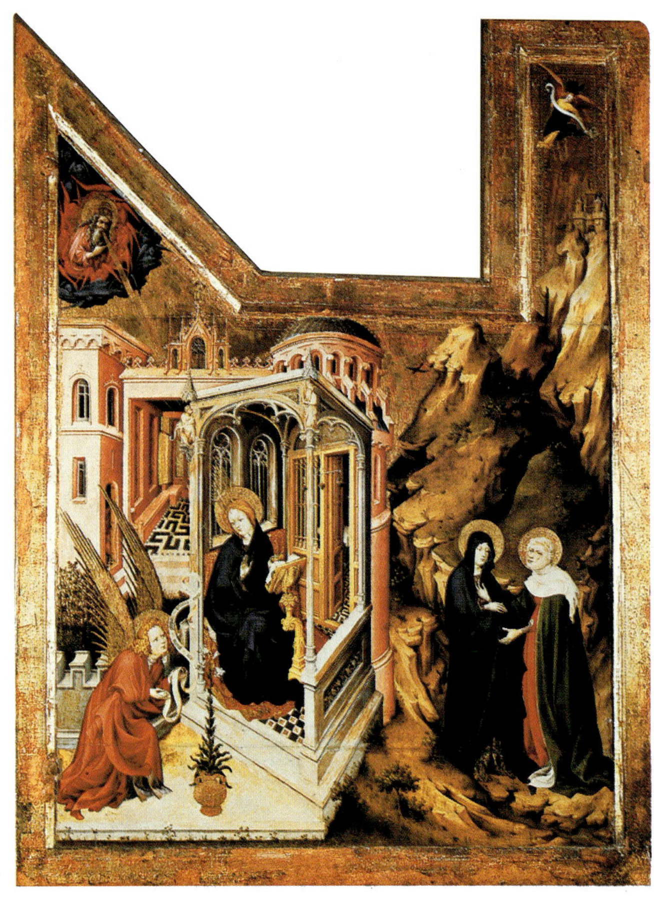

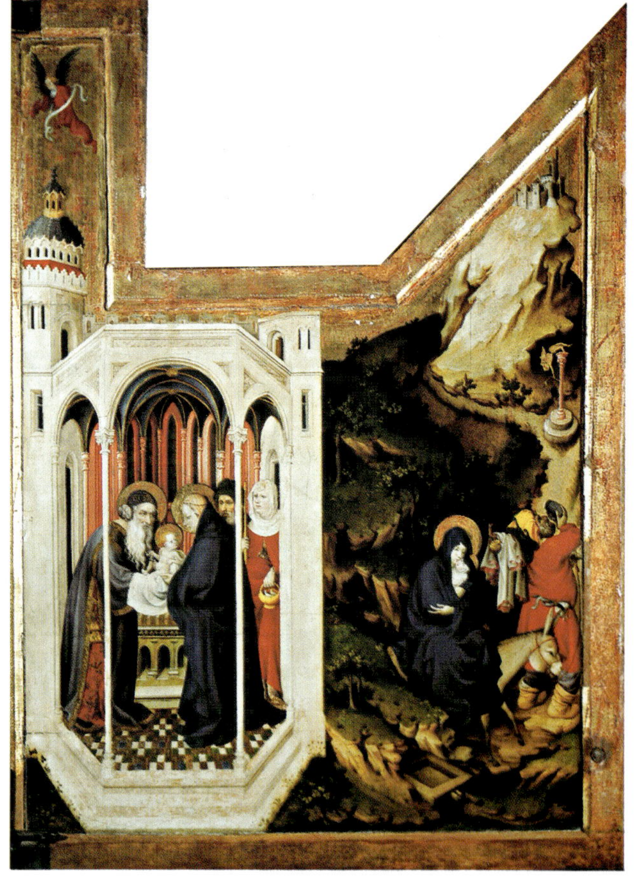

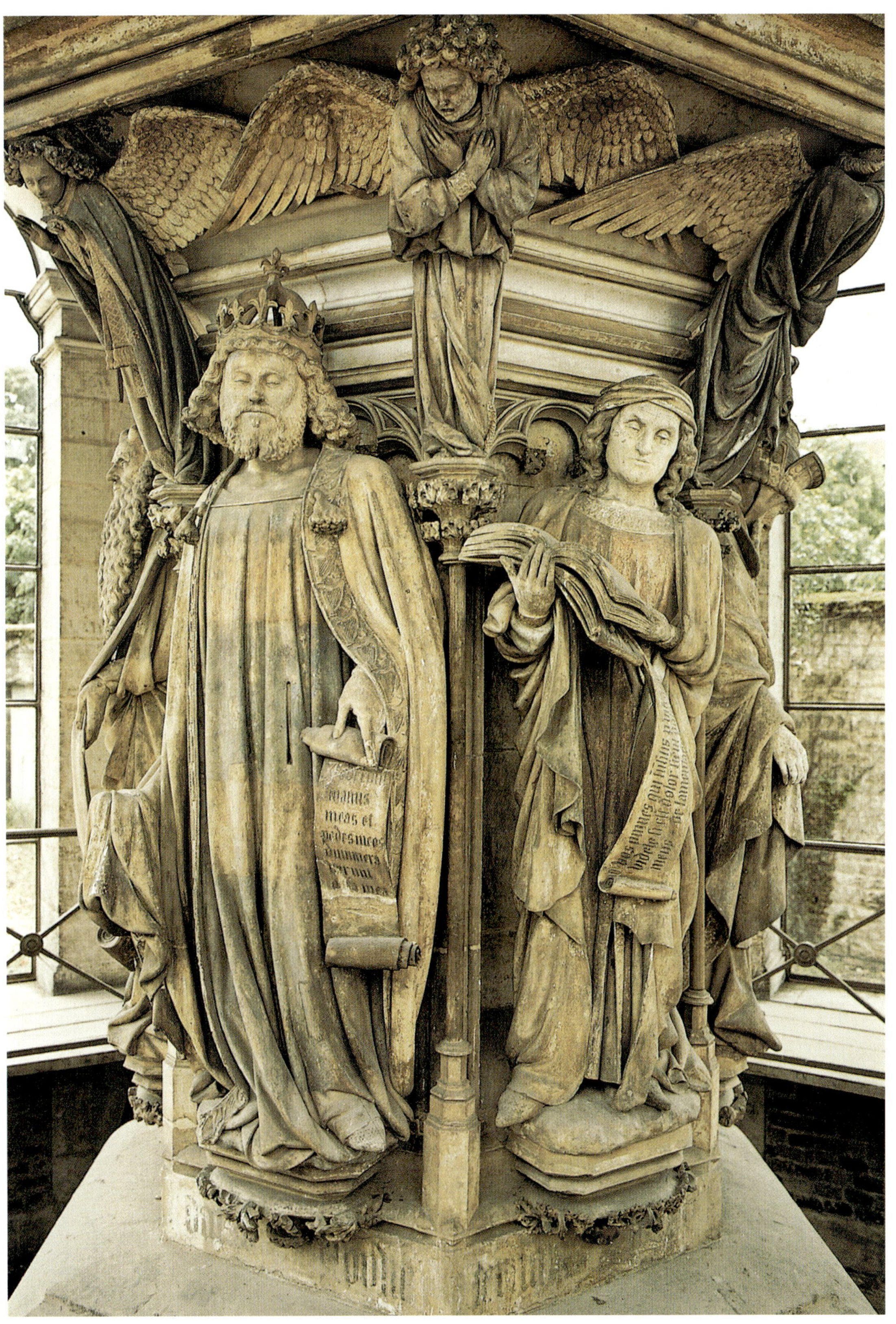

During the period of
Philip the Bold the
favored artist at the
Burgundian court was
the great Flemish sculp-
tor Claus Sluter. Most
of his activity involved
the charterhouse of
Champmol, where in
1389 he assumed the
role of artistic director.
He was thus able to
develop a revolutionary
plastic style, at once
monumental and also
realistically presented,
thanks to his extraordi-
nary skill at the physi-
cal rendering of figures,
which thus seem to
anticipate the delicate
features and psycho-
logical depth of Van
Eyck and the Flemish
portraitists. Breaking
with the taste for
refined detail, Sluter
presents synthetic
images, powerful and
monumental. The results
include the large, ani-
mated figures of the
Prophets arranged
around the so-called
Well of Moses (the base
of a giant Crucifixion,
of which the fragment
reproduced here is all
that remains), and the
simple but highly
effective figures for the
portal of the church,
with a Virgin and Child
and the kneeling figures
of the patrons with
their patron saints.
Sluter also made the
tomb of Philip the
Bold, with its dramatic
procession of hooded
figures (called *pleu-
rants*) along the border
of the sepulcher.

The late Gothic world

A youthful masterpiece by the painter, this polyptych comes from the hermitage of Valle Romita, near Fabriano. Its original appearance cannot be reconstructed because it has been mounted in a neo-Gothic frame from the end of the nineteenth century. The various panels form an anthology of motifs of International Gothic. The central scene seems to float in its heavenly gold background, while the figures are wrapped in the folds of stupendous drapery of a highly elegant design. The small angelic musicians at the bottom of the central scene rest on the celestial vault; below them is the starry sky, and between the sun and the moon can be read the painter's signature. The four saints to the sides stand on the fresh grass and flowers of paradise. Always distinguished by their sharp outlines, the figures have subtle and sweet expressions that concur in evoking the suspended atmosphere of a dream. The tone is different in the small narrative scenes above them (but perhaps originally in a predella), which are set against urban or landscape backgrounds.

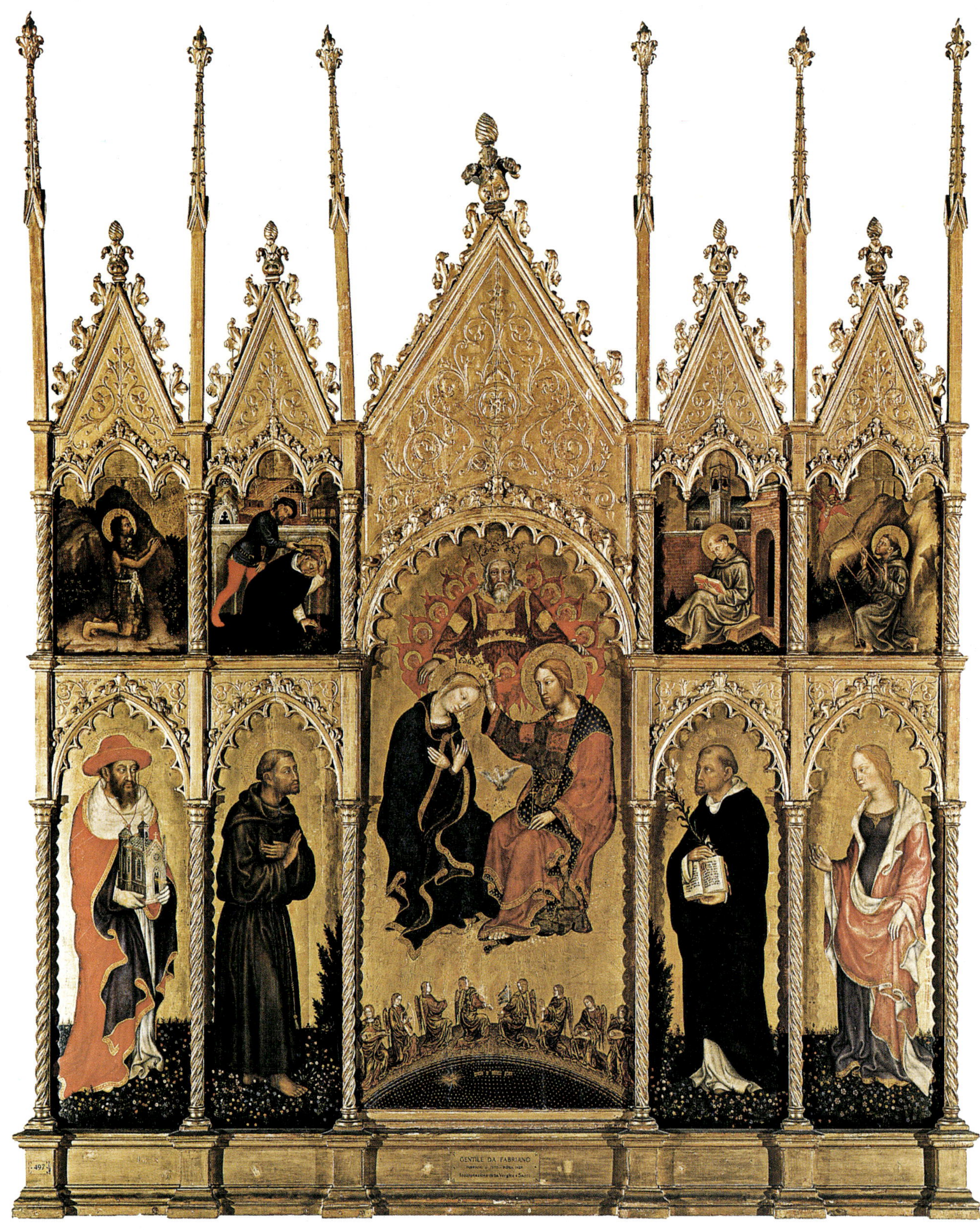

The late Gothic world

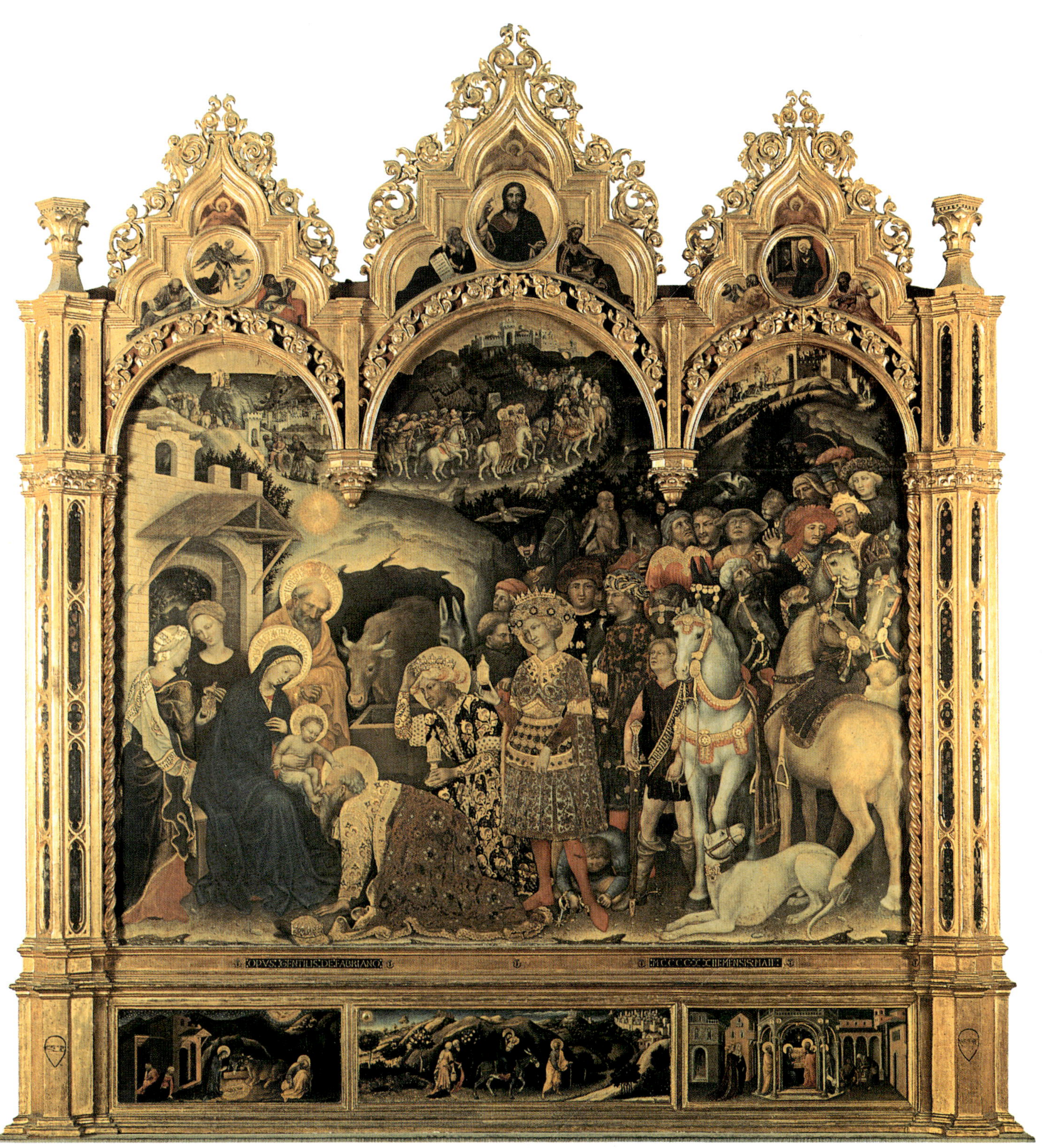

Thanks also to the frame, which is the original, we can fully appreciate this masterpiece of European painting, which appeared just before Masaccio and Van Eyck came on the scene. The painting dates to a period of transition, as indicated even by its general form: the pointed spires and curves of the frame allude to the Gothic tradition of the triptych, but the scene is organized on a landscape within a unitary space; furthermore, only by seeking out the fragments of open landscape does one realize that the painter has used a gold background. In effect, the overall impression is that of a sumptuous costume ball. In addition to the principal scene, there is the long, winding cortège, which the painter filled with minor episodes and interesting details. In a fascinating coincidence in the history of art, this absolute vertex of late Gothic painting appeared a few months before the "official" birth of humanistic painting in Florence with the beginning of the works of Masaccio and Masolino in the Brancacci Chapel of Santa Maria del Carmine on the other side of the Arno.

The late Gothic world

By the very first years of the fifteenth century, a group of young artists had begun laying the basis for a renewal of the figurative arts, carrying out and in fact often anticipating the aspirations of the humanists. Thus well in advance of the rest of Italy and Europe, Florence moved out of the Middle Ages. The creations of the Florentine architect Filippo Brunelleschi were built in accordance with a rigorous but at the same time stupendous simplicity. The revival of classical motifs and the brilliant modernization of construction techniques led to simple, linear results, with harmonious proportions and size relationships based on those of the human body. The dome of Santa Maria del Fiore is the monument-symbol of the beginning of the Renaissance. Interpreting the preexisting structures, built with great originality more than a century ear-

Lorenzo Ghiberti, detail of the eastern door, the *Gates of Paradise,* 1425–52; Baptistery, Florence

Brunelleschi and Donatello, friends from their youth, worked in perfect agreement and sometimes in direct collaboration, as in the Sagrestia Vecchia of San Lorenzo. From his first monumental statues, made for the façade and for the bell tower of the Duomo of Florence, Donatello aban-

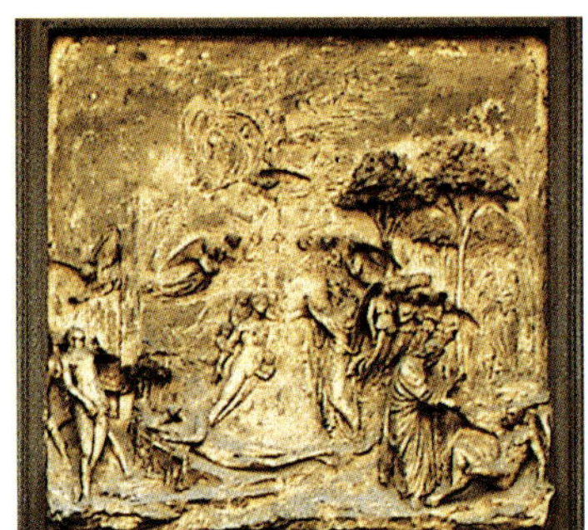

doned the elaborate drapery of the Gothic and sought a powerful means of expression. With an inexhaustible interest in reality, he presented concrete, vital figures, their gestures and features vigorously modeled and full of symbolic ideals. The *St. George* he made in 1416 for a niche in the church of

Florence and the inven

lier by Arnolfo di Cambio, Brunelleschi erected an immense structure but made it soar by way of a slightly ogival profile, obtained by way of a revolutionary feat of technical engineering: the dome is divided in segments, supported by ribs and covered by tiles.

Filippo Brunelleschi, interior of the church of San Lorenzo, 1419–60; Florence

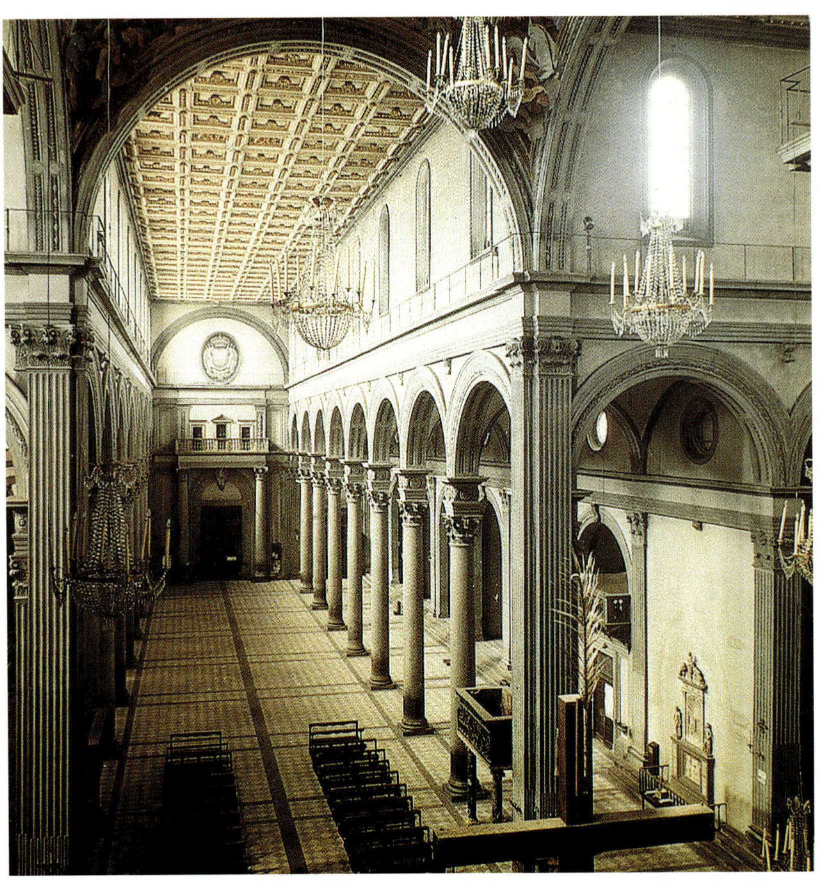

Orsanmichele (statues of the patron saints of the Florentine guilds of arts and crafts were aligned along the outer wall of the church), which belonged to the gild of armorers, became the image itself of the virtues and independence of the city's citizens, almost anticipating the *David* by Michelangelo. As an artist Donatello was deeply involved in the cultural realities of his city. He was in constant contact with his colleagues and participated in sculptures made as team projects with other masters, for which reason he played a decisive role in the development of the artistic school of Florence.

Donatello was the protagonist of a particular period of humanism, when the myth of the ancient was projected onto the present and, making itself concrete and tangible, became eternal. Donatello's sense of the classical was not an intellectual attainment but a thoroughly physical and solid experience that dated back to the years of his youth and was an unforgettable adventure. As Vasari relates, the most lively dimension of the art of Donatello remained that of the street, in dialogue with a city in full political and cultural expansion, led by a powerful financial oligarchy from out of which the Medici family was emerging in a definitive way. During the time of the sculptor, the great prophets placed in the niches of the bell tower by Giotto, interpreted as peasants with ancient wisdom, were very popular statues, the subject of local proverbs. Around Orsanmichele, *St. George* and *St. Louis*, *St. Mark* and *St. Philip*, stood out from the niches of the guilds of arts and crafts. In Piazza della Signoria, the center stage of the city's civic life, there was *Judith* cutting off the head of Holofernes, one of

Florence and the invention of the Renaissance

the most perfect monumental bronzes of the entire history of art, the symbolic emblem of the energy with which Florence was ready to oppose its enemies; below was the Mazocco, with the heraldic lion that bore the coat of arms of Florence, the fleur-de-lis. One walked, as Vasari said, among "Madonnas of marble and bronze made in low-relief, besides some scenes in marble with the most beautiful figures, marvelous in their flat-relief." And then there were the statues in the garden of the Medici house, the fountains, heraldic coats of arms on the façades of palaces, the small but sweetly moving tabernacles along the streets.

Younger than Brunelleschi and Donatello but extraordinarily precocious and inventive, Masaccio in those same years was bringing about a radical change in the course of painting. He did away with the gold and the

large perspective niche in keeping with the style of Brunelleschi. Then, once again working together with Masolino, he set off for Rome. Death took him in the first days of 1428, when he was barely twenty-six years old. Masaccio arranged every scene with solemn monumentality, every figure occupies a well defined space within a broad context, thus repeating the example of Giotto and opening the way for Michelangelo, making him a hinge for the new epoch. His conquests were rapidly carried forward by a generation of young artists. Beginning in the 1430s, masters like Fra Angelico, Paolo Uccello, and Filippo Lippi

tion of the Renaissance

rich decorations of the last stage of the Gothic to apply the new rules of perspective in sober compositions, almost bare, reduced to the essential, and for this very reason full of a grave and realistic communicative force. The frescoes of the Brancacci Chapel are one of the most sensational novelties to ever appear in the history of art. In 1424, while Florence admired the dazzling *Adoration of the Magi* made the preceding year by Gentile da Fabriano, Masolino and Masaccio began work on the frescoes in Santa Maria del Carmine. The scaffolding in the Brancacci Chapel became the podium from which Masaccio proclaimed in a deep, solemn voice (at the age of twenty-three) a new painting. Only a single year had passed since Gentile da Fabriano's crowded altarpiece scene; yet here were the clumsy feet of the Progenitors by Masaccio treading the unforgiving earth; expelled from Eden, Adam and Eve openly weep and wail. On the left wall, Masaccio painted *The Tribute Money*, a memorable turn toward the synthesis, the power, and the mute yet "awesome" flashing of the glances. Fate soon interrupted Masaccio's career, leaving him just time to make a great polyptych for Pisa (the panels of which have been dispersed among the museums of many nations) and, in Florence, the fresco of *The Trinity* in Santa Maria Novella, set within a

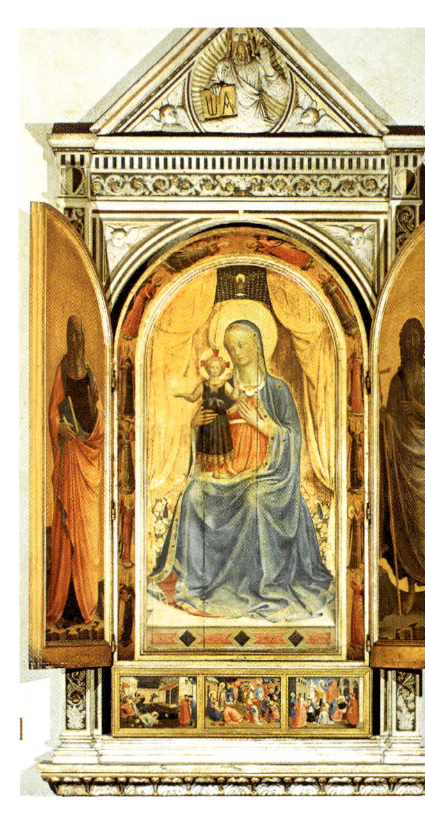

sought a personal mediation between the synthetic, almost neo-Gothic austerity of Masaccio and the taste for rich and elaborate images. Among the most important innovations were the abandonment of gold backgrounds and the passage from the multipanel polyptych to the single-field altarpiece (the "tabula quadra") in which all the figures are presented in one scene.

As had happened in politics, with the installation of the Medici dynasty, so also in art and humanistic culture the movement was toward a form of normalization. The phase of experimental efforts seemed happily over; the rules of perspective soon obtained geometric proof and scientific regulation thanks to the writing of Piero della Francesca. Leon Battista Alberti, architect and humanist, laid the theoretical basis for the arts, indicating the route for the revival of the ancient; Lorenzo Ghiberti wrote an early commentary on the history of art in Florence, once more citing Giotto as its founder. Thus, more than a century from the famous citation by Dante in his *Divine Comedy*, Giotto still maintained the "highest praise" in painting, but his fame was now rung out across a radically changed environment and had taken on a new and deeper resonance.

On August 19, 1418, Filippo Brunelleschi won the competition for the creation of the dome of the Duomo. The sprawling cathedral worksite, opened more than a century earlier by Arnolfo di Cambio, had been interrupted. No architect had succeeded in solving the problem of making a dome adequate to the Gothic mole of the Duomo and harmoniously inserted in the precious chromatic design of the white, green, and pink marble that dressed the building. Brunelleschi interpreted Arnolfo's octagonal motif in a highly original way, completing it with the insertion of elegant niched tribunes. On a powerful octagonal drum, with circular oculi, he erected the true dome. To avoid complicated and dangerous scaffolding, he designed a very high self-bearing double structure in brick, with a slightly ogival shape, highlighted and supported by powerful white ribs. Brunelleschi involved himself even in the smallest technical details of the building (from the diameter of the cables to the system of pulleys, from the shape of the mold for the bricks to the height of the risers of the stairs between the two "shells"). Crowned by a small temple and by the large sphere in copper gilt, the dome reached a total height of 107 meters.

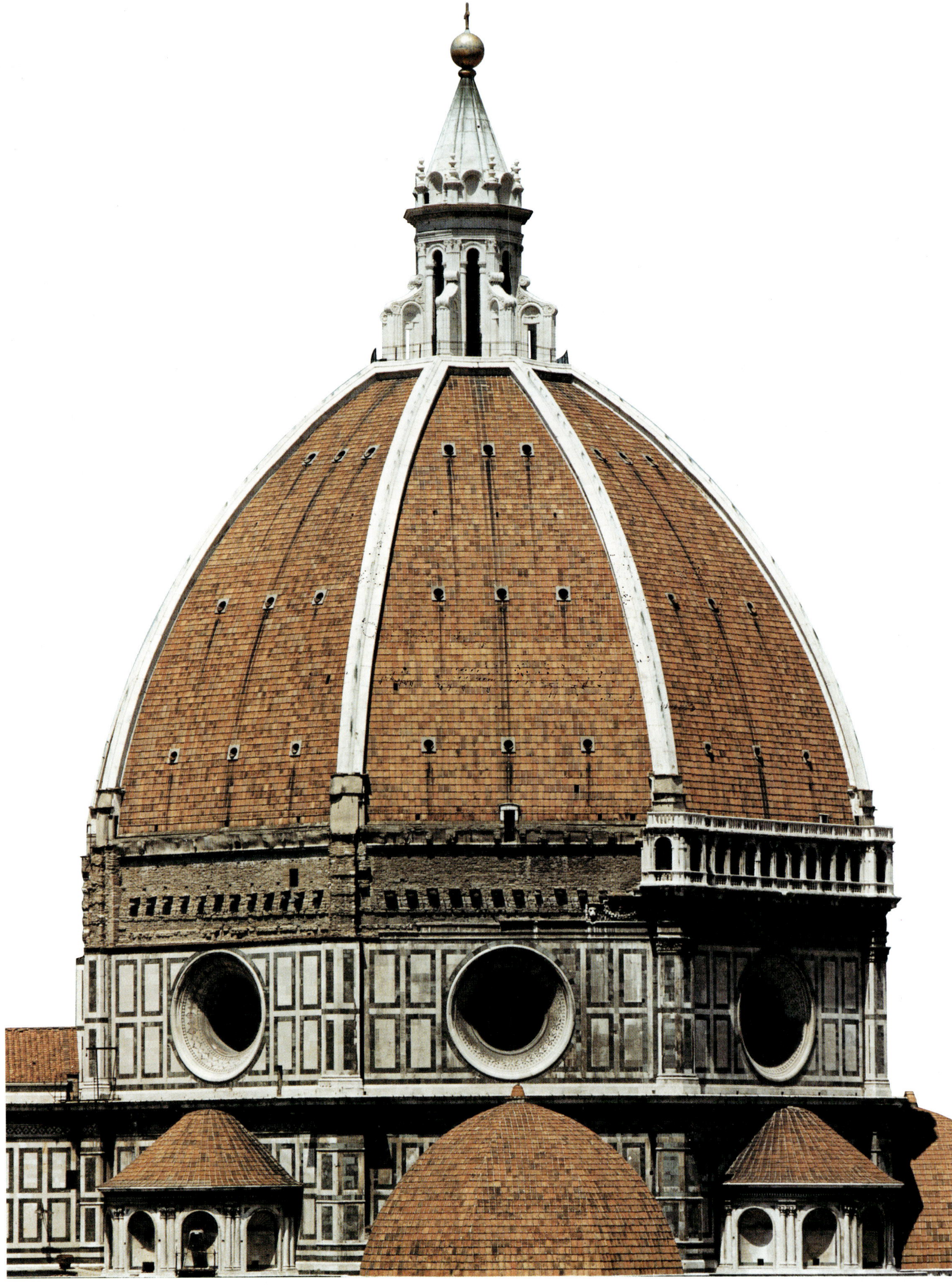

Florence and the invention of the Renaissance

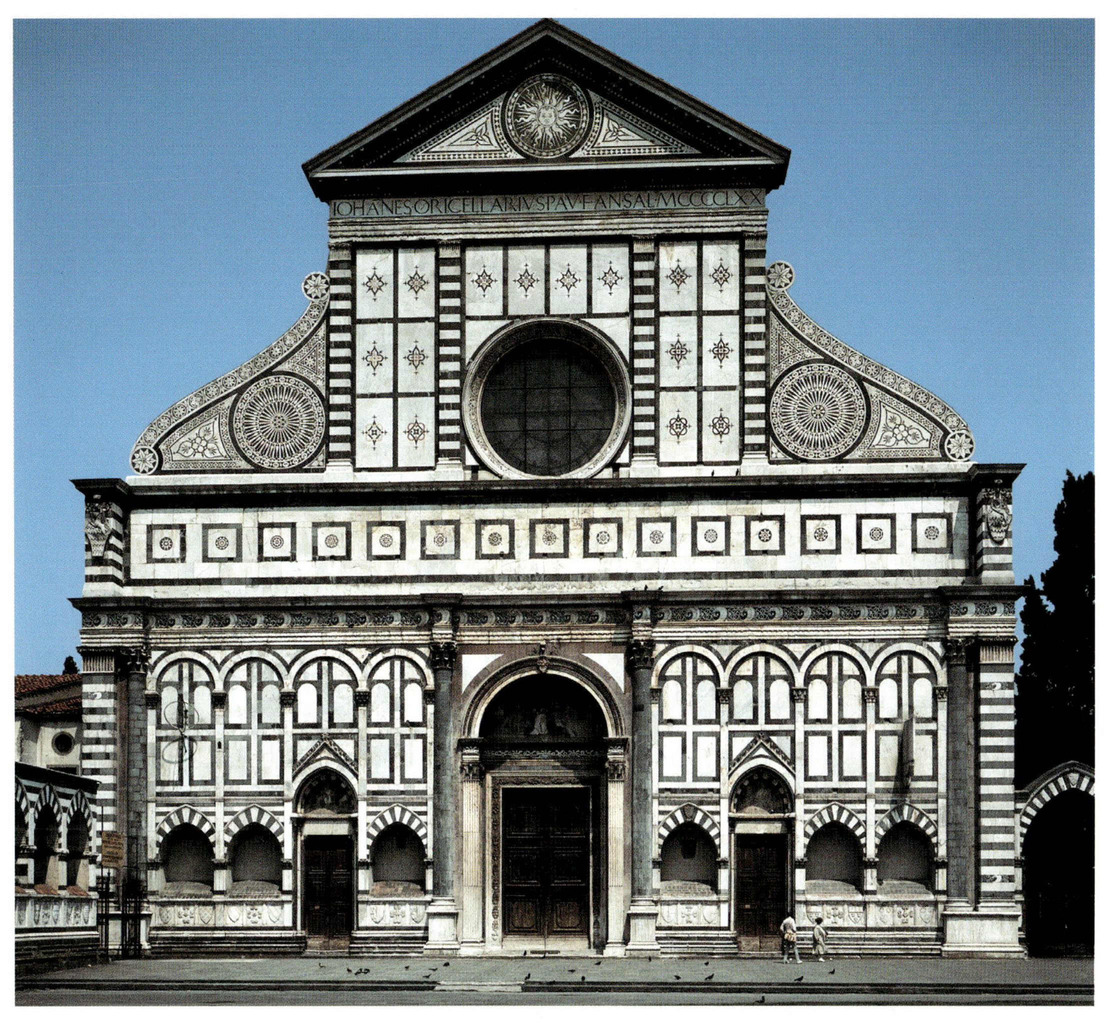

LEON BATTISTA ALBERTI
Completion of the façade of Santa Maria Novella
1456–70
Florence

Leon Battista Alberti was a perfect example of the artist-intellectual. One of the main ideas on which fifteenth-century Florentine culture was based was the search for a "divine proportion," a right way to regulate and harmonize space and within it the activities of humans. For Alberti, the proportions of the body were the point of departure for designing a world "on the measure of man," elegantly based on notions from antiquity, very much like the upper part of the façade of Santa Maria Novella, the completion of an elegant Gothic work.

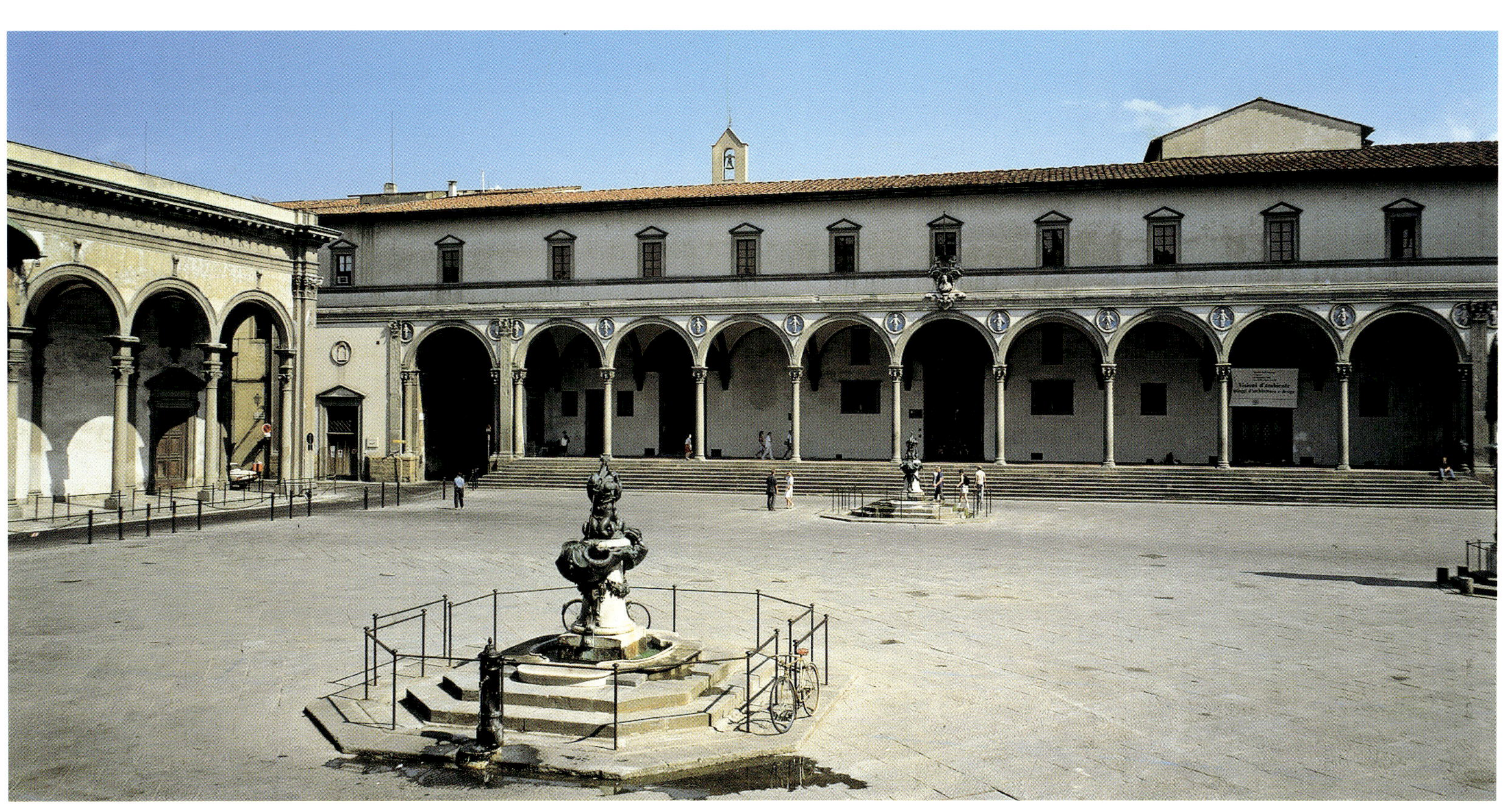

FILIPPO BRUNELLESCHI
Façade of the Ospedale degli Innocenti
1419–39
Piazza della Santissima Annunziata, Florence

The Ospedale, made to care for orphaned or abandoned children, was the most important work of social architecture by Filippo Brunelleschi. The portico with nine arches, calibrated on the base of a perfect proportional measurement, served as the model for the other buildings in the piazza, an example of urban space in an "ideal" Renaissance city.

Florence and the invention of the Renaissance

Determining the date
of the beginning of a
style or of a profound
change in culture or
civilization is always
arbitrary. But for
Florentine humanism, a
highly evocative point
of reference is offered
by 1401, the year in
which the Opera del
Duomo held a competi-
tion for the second
door of the Baptistery.
The obligatory theme
was a bas-relief in par-
tially gilt bronze with
the scene of Abraham's
Sacrifice of Isaac, to
be made within the
Gothic lobed perimeter,
already used in the
fourteenth century by
Andrea Pisano for the
first door. Following
the elimination of
seven other competi-
tors (including Jacopo
della Quercia and Nanni
di Banco), the two
finalists were Filippo
Brunelleschi and
Lorenzo Ghiberti.
Following the heated
discussions of the
judges and repeated
voting, the victory
went to Ghiberti. In
his panel, Brunelleschi
put most of his effort
into filling the space of
the frame in a harmo-
nious way. He found
room for a direct clas-
sical citation: the
figure at bottom left
repeats the motif of
the *Spinario*, a boy
pulling a thorn from
his foot.

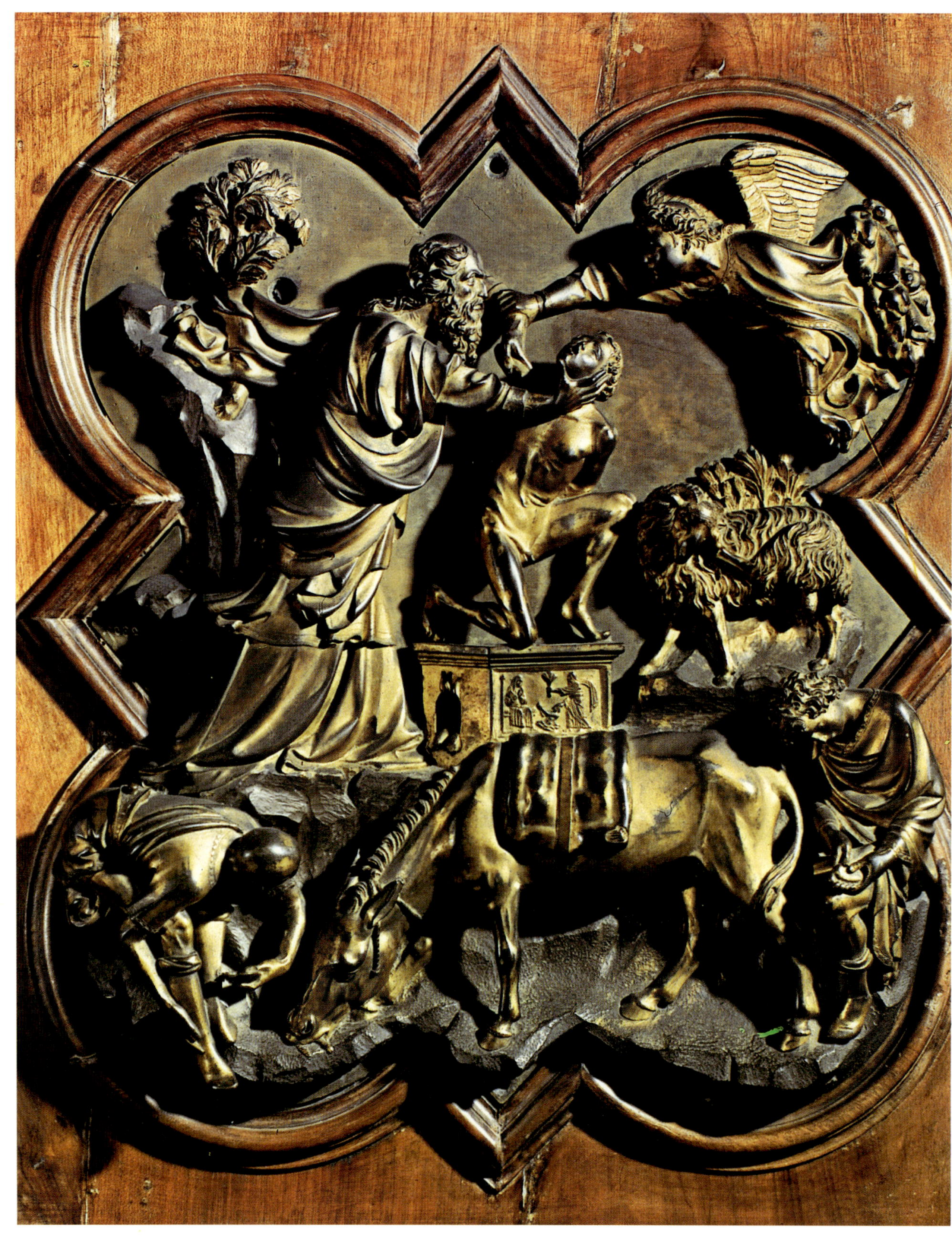

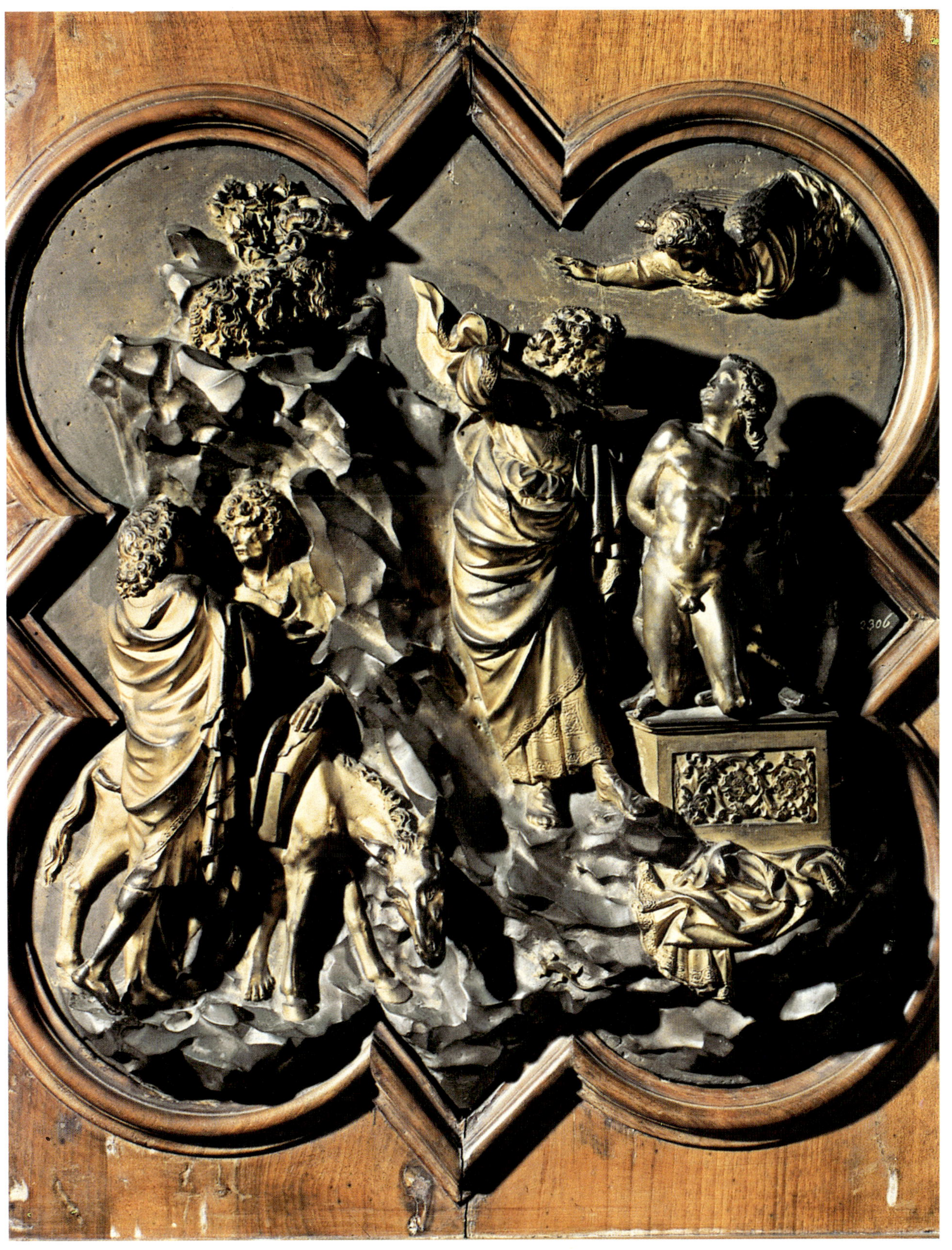

■ Lorenzo Ghiberti
**Abraham's
Sacrifice of Isaac**
1401, bronze panel
Museo Nazionale del
Bargello, Florence

The panel that won the
competition prevailed
because of the great
fluidity of the scene,
which takes place
gracefully across a
landscape that is far
more developed and
descriptive than in
Brunelleschi's version.
Also Ghiberti shows off
his classical culture,
especially in the noble
and taut figure of Isaac.
The subject, format,
and figures are the
same, but the differ-
ences between the two
versions are clear.
Brunelleschi chose a
dynamic and direct
arrangement; the angel
intervenes just in time
to stop the hand of
Abraham, with the knife
about to plunge into
the neck of a terrified
Isaac. Ghiberti pre-
ferred a quieter and
relatively less dynamic
scene, putting his effort
into the execution of
details. To the sculptural
energy of Brunelleschi,
constructed along con-
trasting lines, Ghiberti
responds with the ele-
gant accuracy of a
goldsmith, with the
attractive rhythm of a
series of curves and
undulations. It was
precisely this quality
of subtle, almost
miniaturistic creativity
that laid the basis for
Ghiberti's victory.

Florence and the invention of the Renaissance

Donatello is one of the leading figures in Vasari's *Lives of the Artists*, which emphasizes the prodigious quantity and variety of his sculptures, in a broad range of subjects, materials, and sizes: "The world remained so full of his works, that it may be affirmed right truly that no craftsman ever worked more than he did. For, delighting in every kind of work, he put his hand to anything, without considering whether it was of little or of great value." Truly few other sculptors have shown equal versatility. During the steps of his career, almost all spent in Florence but with a long stay in Padua, Donatello expressed himself in the most disparate dimensions, from the enormous equestrian monument to the small "table" bronze, and managed with equal naturalness a great variety of materials, including marble, bronze, wood, terracotta, and mixed media, resulting in an enormous variety of works. The *David* in bronze, sculpted for the garden of the Medici palace in the central period of his life, reveals remarkably smooth surfaces, indications of faultless molding. Donatello achieved a truly classical purity in the noble face of the youth, thoughtful and solitary after defeating his giant enemy.

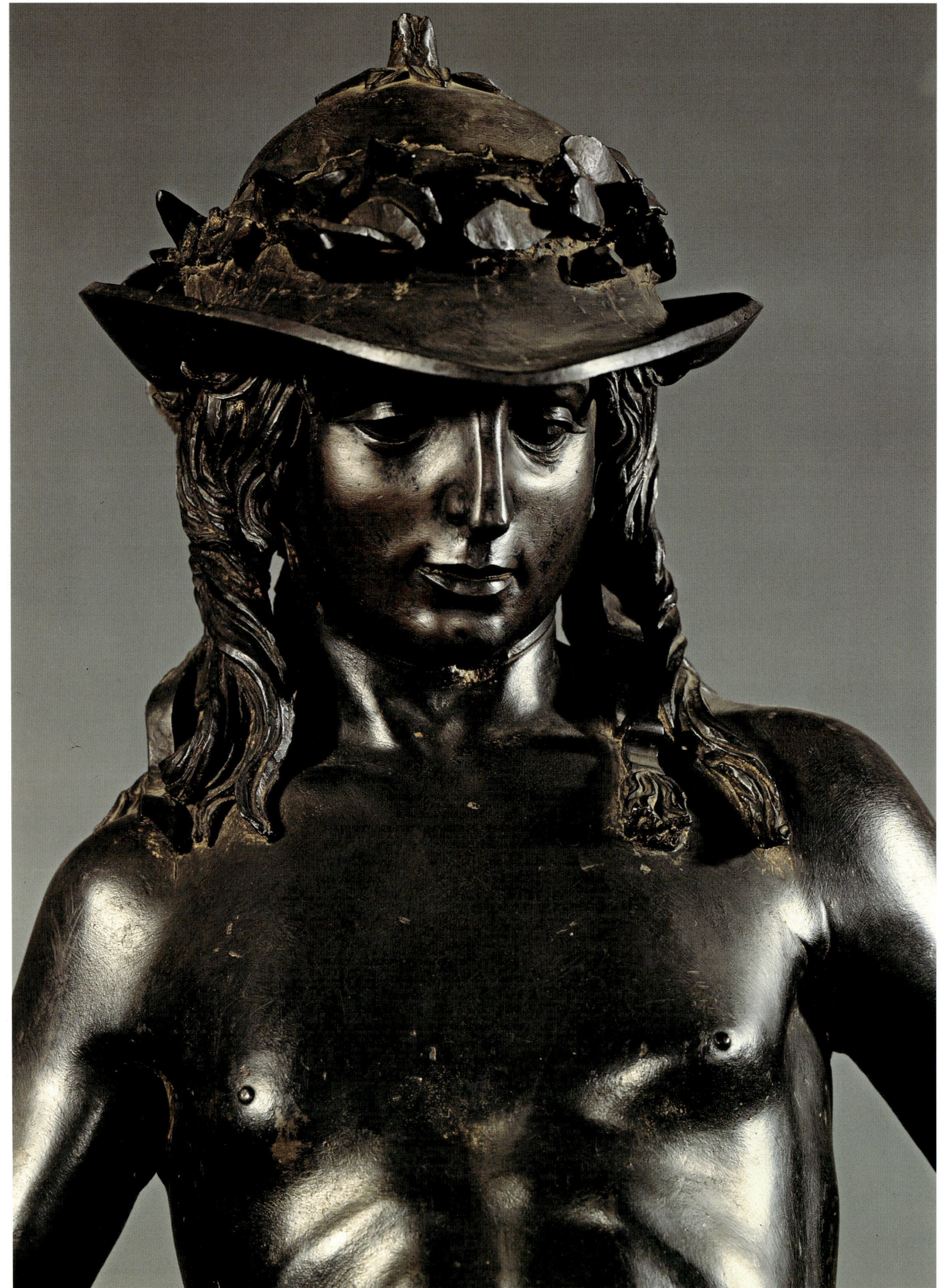

Florence and the invention of the Renaissance

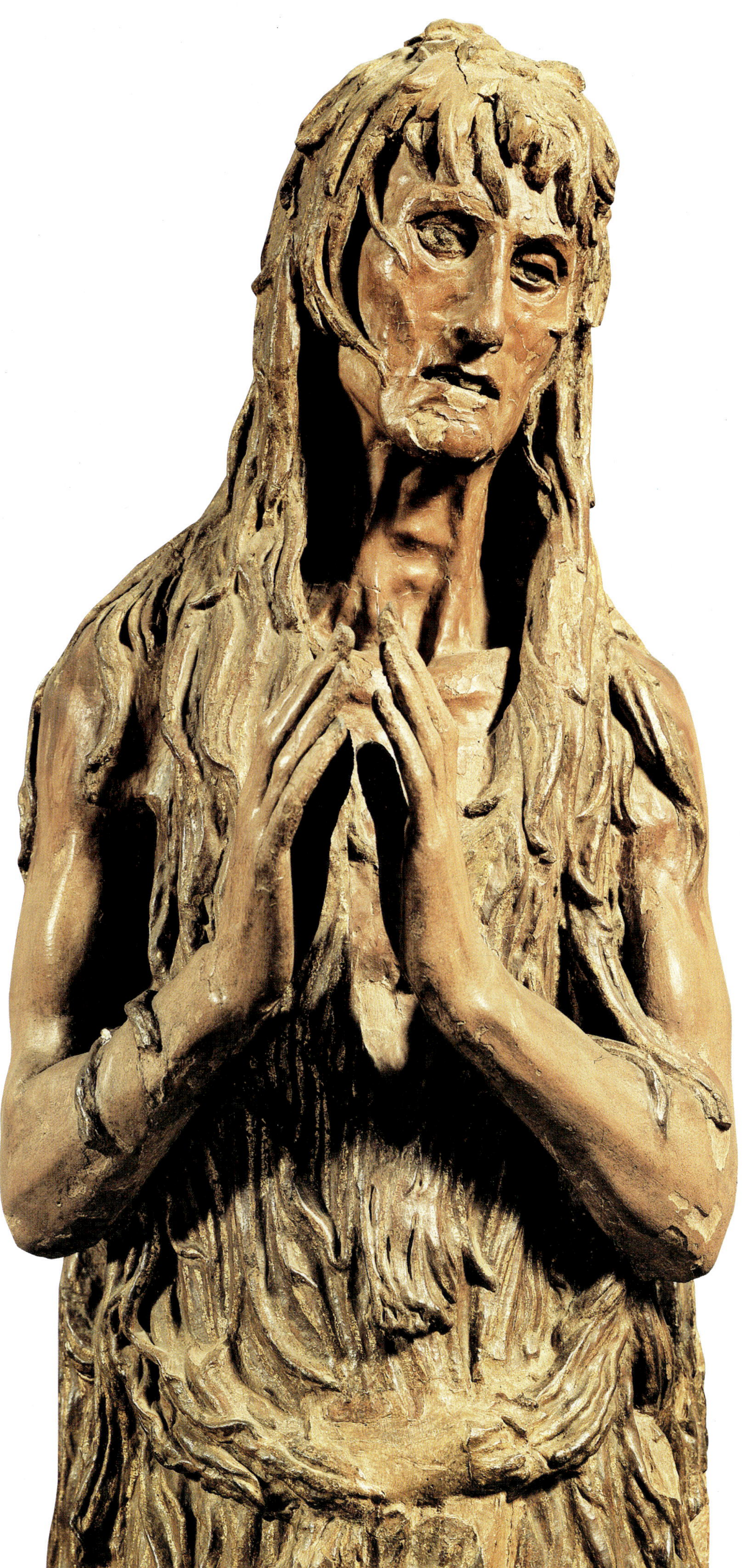

While we admire Donatello's multifaceted skills at working in so many different mediums, the variety of human and psychological situations that he took on is also astonishing, to the point that Vasari was driven to think that Michelangelo was a reborn Donatello. The *Prophets* that he carved in his youth for Florence's cathedral or the *St. George* in Orsanmichele are champions of a vigorously accepted faith; there are then the little putti that run along the choir gallery he made for the cathedral, which must rank among the Renaissance's most irreverent rascals. There are then the bronze statues of the altar in Padua, which look like they were made in a foundry in the Athens of Pericles. This Magdalene, which Donatello carved when he was nearly seventy for the Baptistery, looks like a specter devastated by penitence, by hunger, by suffering. The artist dug deeply into the grain of the wood to create a kind of parallel between the natural appearance of "bark" and the rough surface of the saint's disheveled hair and hardened skin. The toothless mouth, sunken eyes, and dramatic expression make this one of the most tragic figures of the entire fifteenth century, far distant from the humanistic ideal of "divine proportion."

Despite a few unfin-
ished details (the
façade is covered by a
simple cantilever roof),
the chapel of the Pazzi
family, built along the
right side of Santa
Croce, is ranked among
the purest examples of
humanistic architec-
ture, perfectly balanced
in its proportions and
their rhythm. The
façade, decorated by
delicate sculptures by
Desiderio da Settignano,
is composed of a portico
of Corinthian columns,
at the center of which
rises the arch of the
portal. The upper sec-
tion is divided in square
compartments, above
which rises the smooth
cylindrical drum of the
dome. Every detail is
embellished: beneath
the small dome of the
portico are glazed ter-
racottas by Luca della
Robbia, while the entry-
way has an intarsia by
Giuliano da Maiano. The
interior is composed of
a large rectangular
room with a small
square altar chapel; a
low stone bench runs
along the walls. The
pilaster strips and
lunettes are outlined
in pietra serena, and
the pale stucco walls
are enlivened by the
bright colors of the
tondos in polychrome
terracotta, also by Luca
della Robbia.

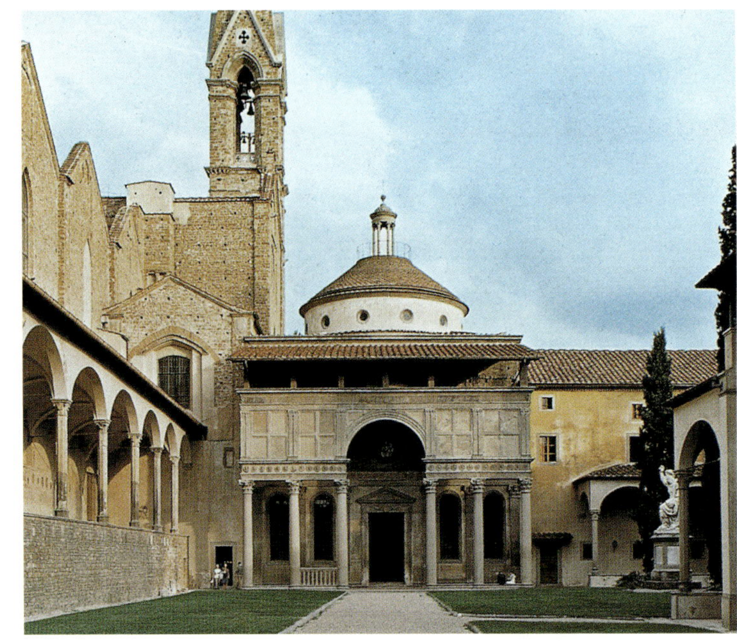

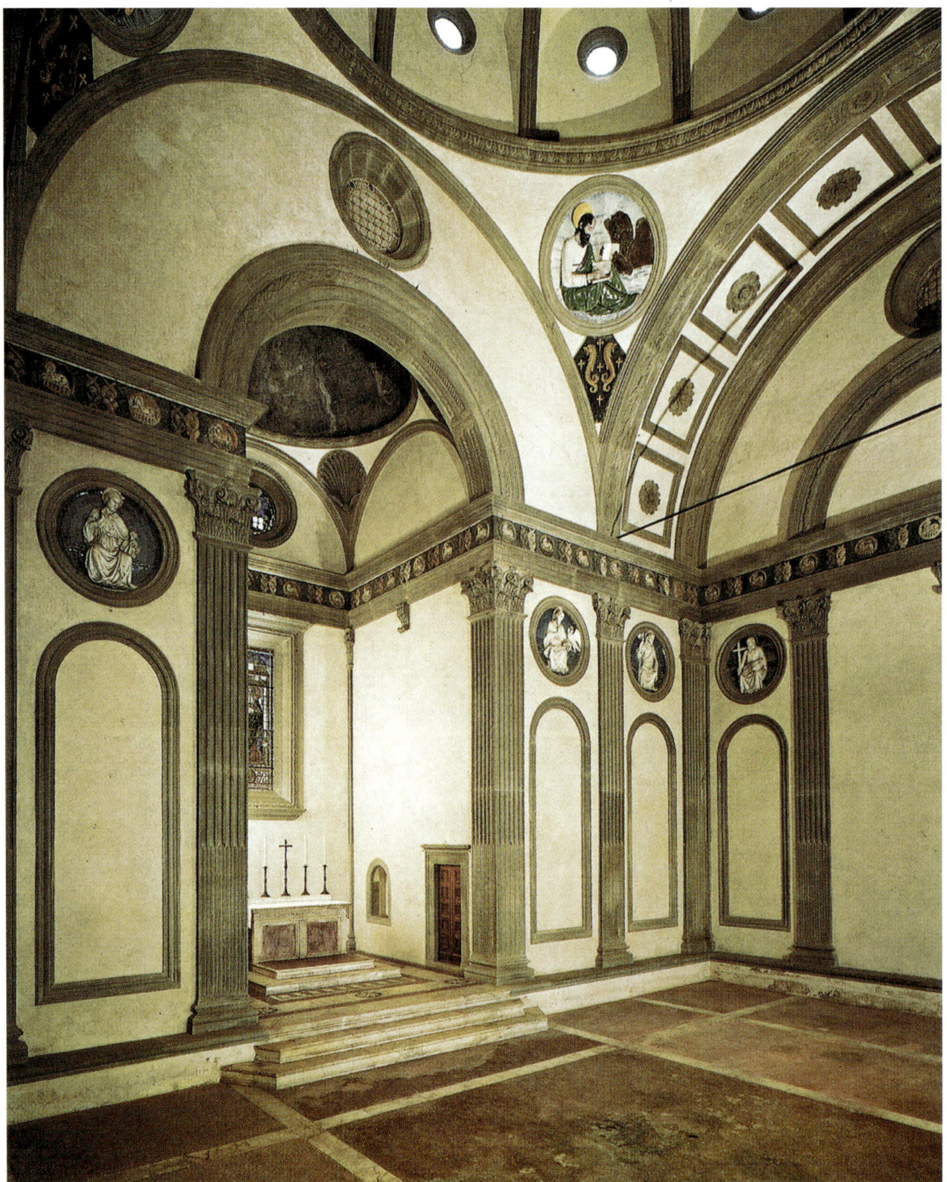

Florence and the invention of the Renaissance

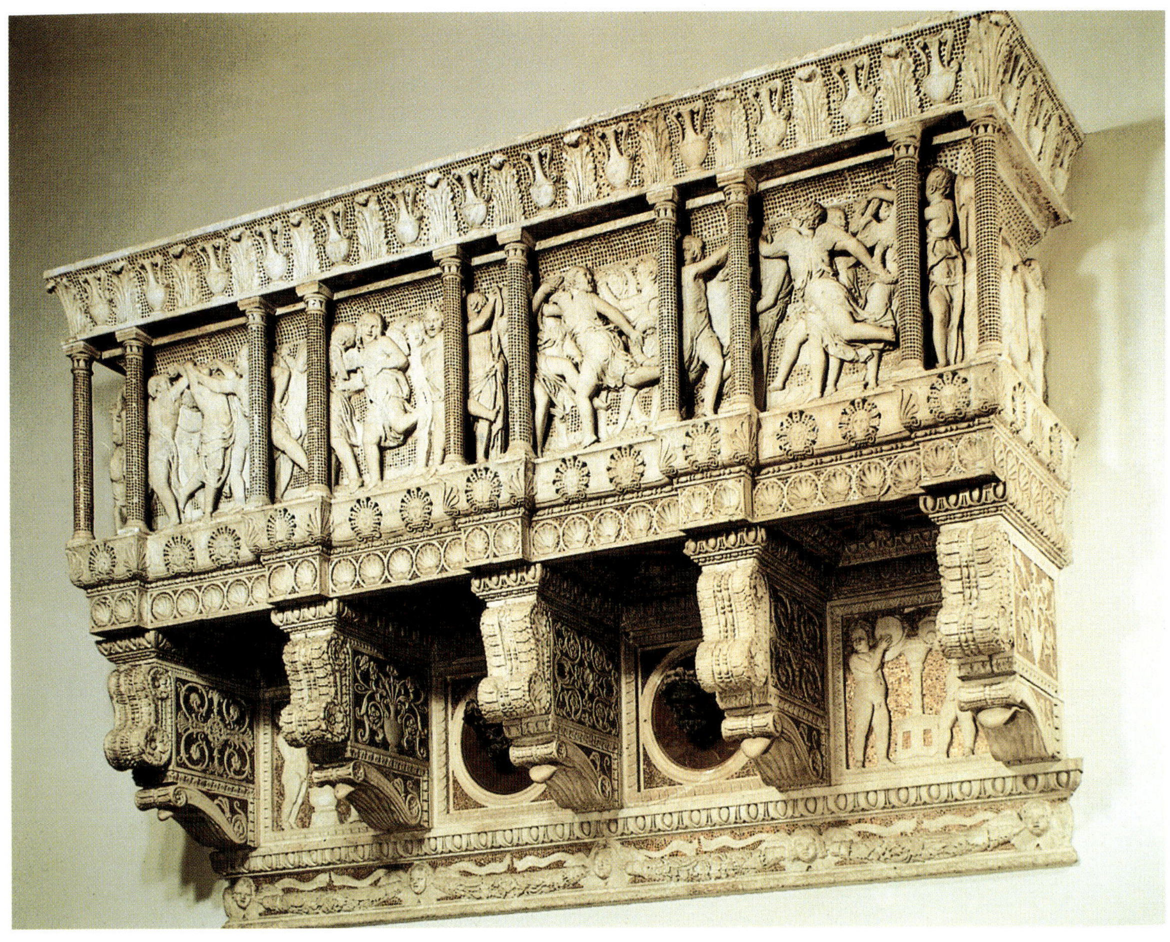

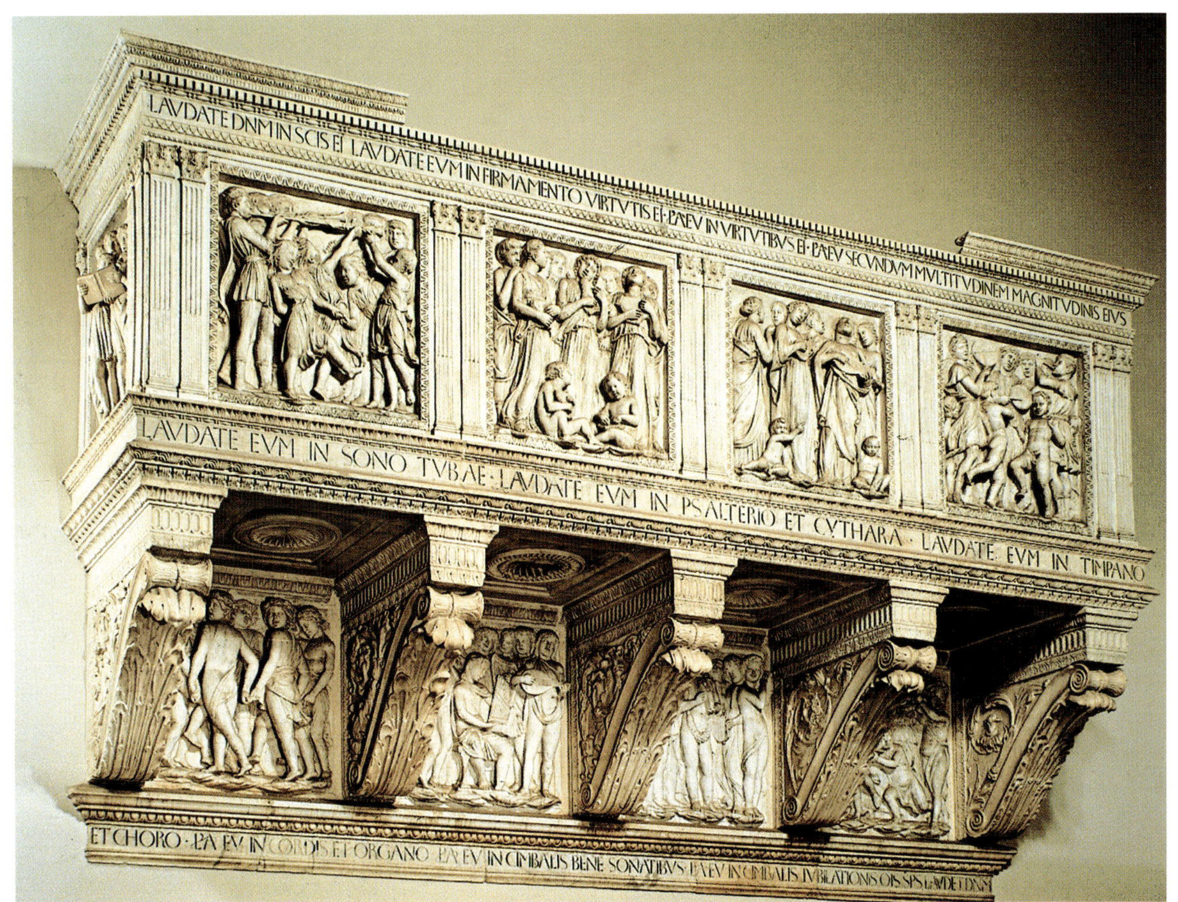

A singular habit of the Tuscan Renaissance—and one quite fortunate for posterity—was the custom of having two or more artists compete for the creation of prestigious works. The commissions to Donatello and to Luca della Robbia for small choir galleries for the Duomo of Florence would ideally date to the period between the 1401 competition between Ghiberti and Brunelleschi for the Baptistery doors and the competition, a little more than a century later, between Michelangelo and Leonardo for the battle scenes frescoed in Palazzo Vecchio. Such competitions are of great value since they make possible a comparison on equal terms between great masters. Here, Luca della Robbia presents a clear and serene structure with a broad, calm rhythm, in which squares with the figures of young singers and musicians are inserted with pleasing regularity. Donatello preferred a single, unified space, supported by pairs of densely decorated columns. Visible through the spaces between the columns are the lively antics of a gang of boys.

Florence and the invention of the Renaissance

The frescoes commissioned in 1424 by the financier Felice Brancacci for his family chapel are a milestone in the history of Italian art, the first pictorial cycle to fully abandon every legacy of the Gothic. The scenes, dedicated to the life and miracles of St. Peter, mark the arrival of the new pictorial civilization of humanism, with the development of the science of perspective. Even so, the frescoes in Santa Maria del Carmine have led a difficult life. In the beginning they were entrusted to a pair of painters with very different styles; left unfinished, they were completed several decades later (around 1480) by Filippino Lippi. Changes made to the chapel and the church (and also a serious fire) long compromised the legibility of the cycle, which seemed to be composed of dark colors, leading scholars to repeatedly insist on the "earthy" and realistic tones of Masaccio in contrast with the almost luminous tones of Masolino. Restoration work performed around 1990 brought back the

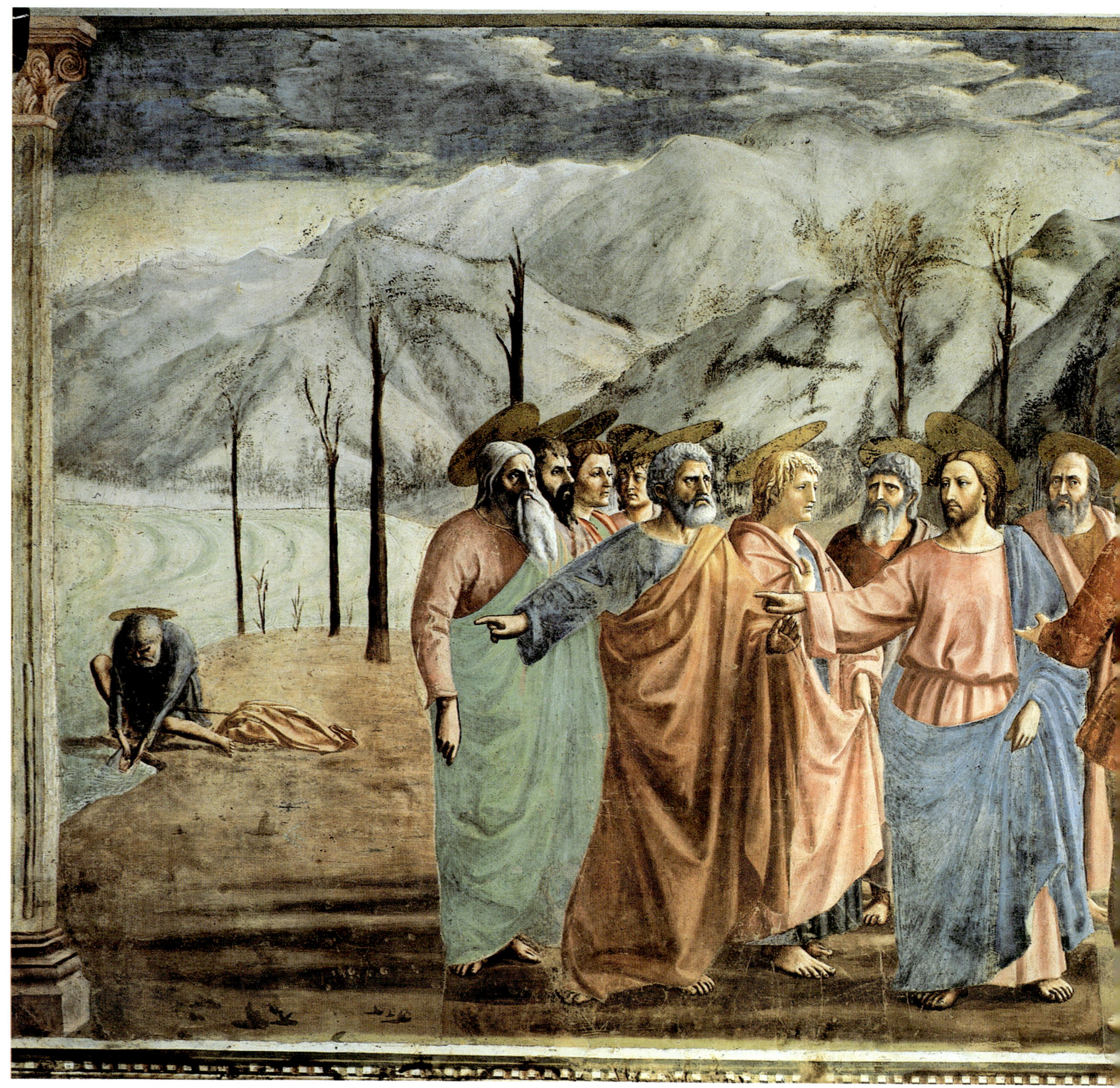

Florence and the invention of the Renaissance

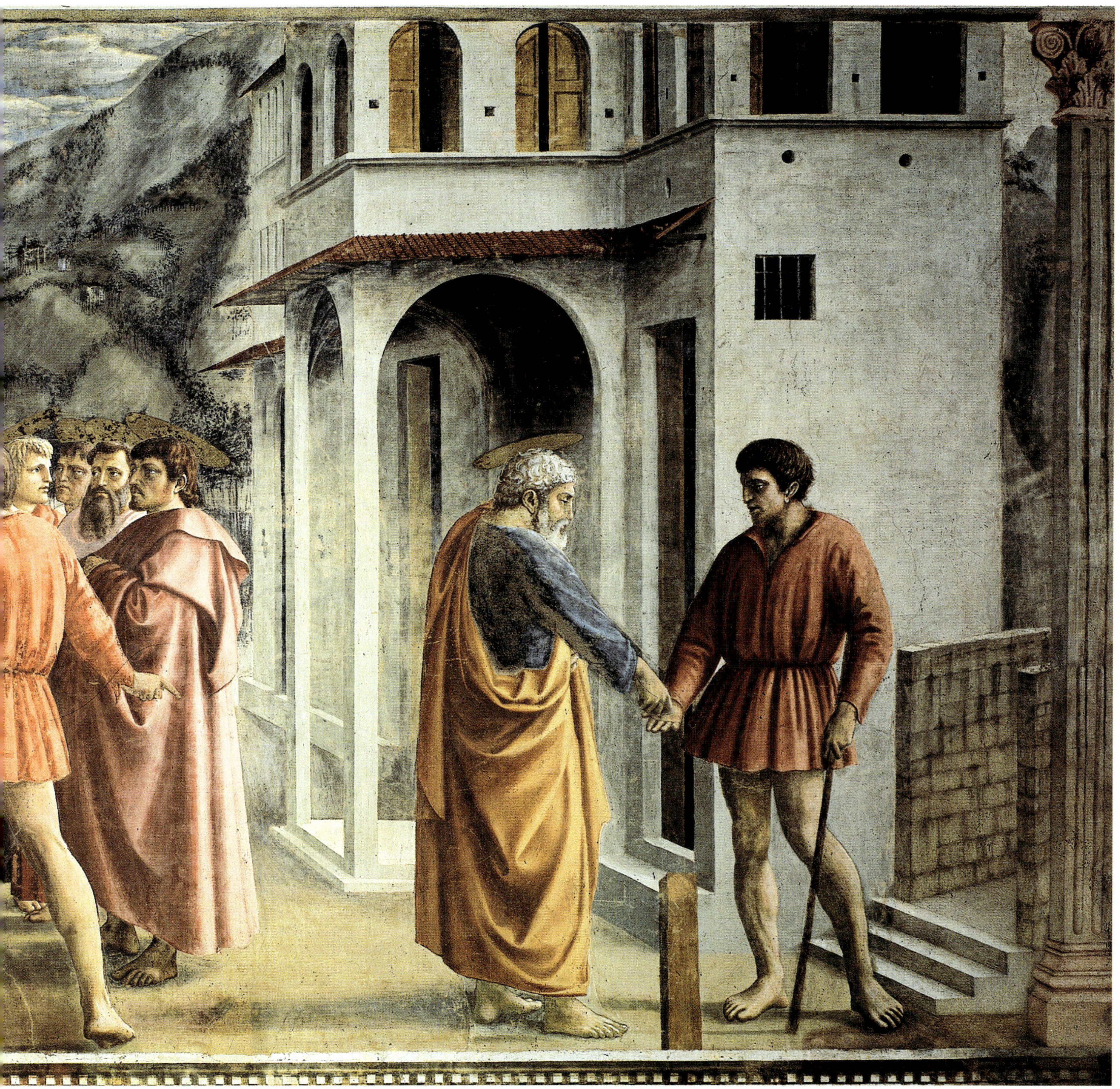

original colors, even in the areas done by Masaccio. The relationship between the two painters, far from being reducible to the transition from an "early" to a "later" style, now appears very gradual, even shaded. Even so, there is an undeniable difference between Masolino's efforts to achieve narrative fluency and Masaccio's solemnly statuesque drama, which achieves its culminating moment in the so-called human Colosseum around Christ in the *Tribute*. In this scene, the most famous and important of the cycle, Jesus Christ indicates to St. Peter how to procure the money to pay the tax for the temple. In a single landscape simplified to the essential, three different and successive moments are presented. At the center, Jesus explains to Peter that the money needed can be found in the mouth of a fish; to one side, Peter is seen with the fish, to the other he appears as he goes to the office of the tax collector to pay the tribute. Abolishing every purely decorative element, Masaccio concentrates all the compositional tension on the large group of figures, whose eloquent gestures and serious expressions add to the sense of a sculptural group.

The most peaceful scenes in the cycle of frescoes in Santa Maria del Carmine, those in which the narrative rhythm moves along without emotional jolts, were painted by Masolino. A comparison of the two artists is offered by the pairs of the Progenitors, painted symmetrically to the sides of the entrance of the chapel. In the deep green of the garden, the nudes by Masolino have the innocent purity and vigor of fine classical statuary; Adam and Eve before the fall seem to express a state of springtime, of chaste humanistic composure. Opposite this, Masaccio presents the sense of human and divine tragedy that resulted from the cruel fall from the state of grace in which Masolino's pair of Progenitors found themselves. In desperation, these nude humans are no longer admirable but rather shameful and ashamed, accentuated by the contrast between Masolino's green garden and the hard desert ground painted by Masaccio as the world outside the walls of Eden.

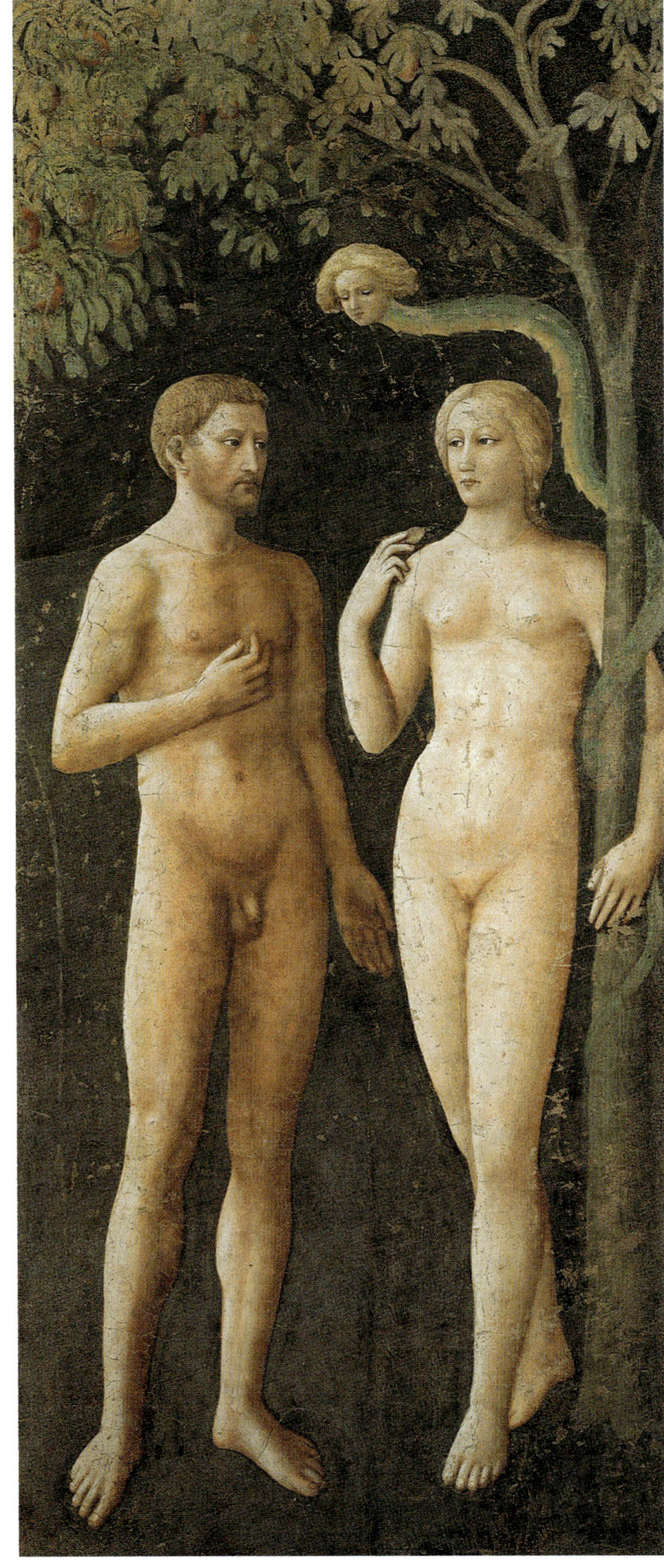

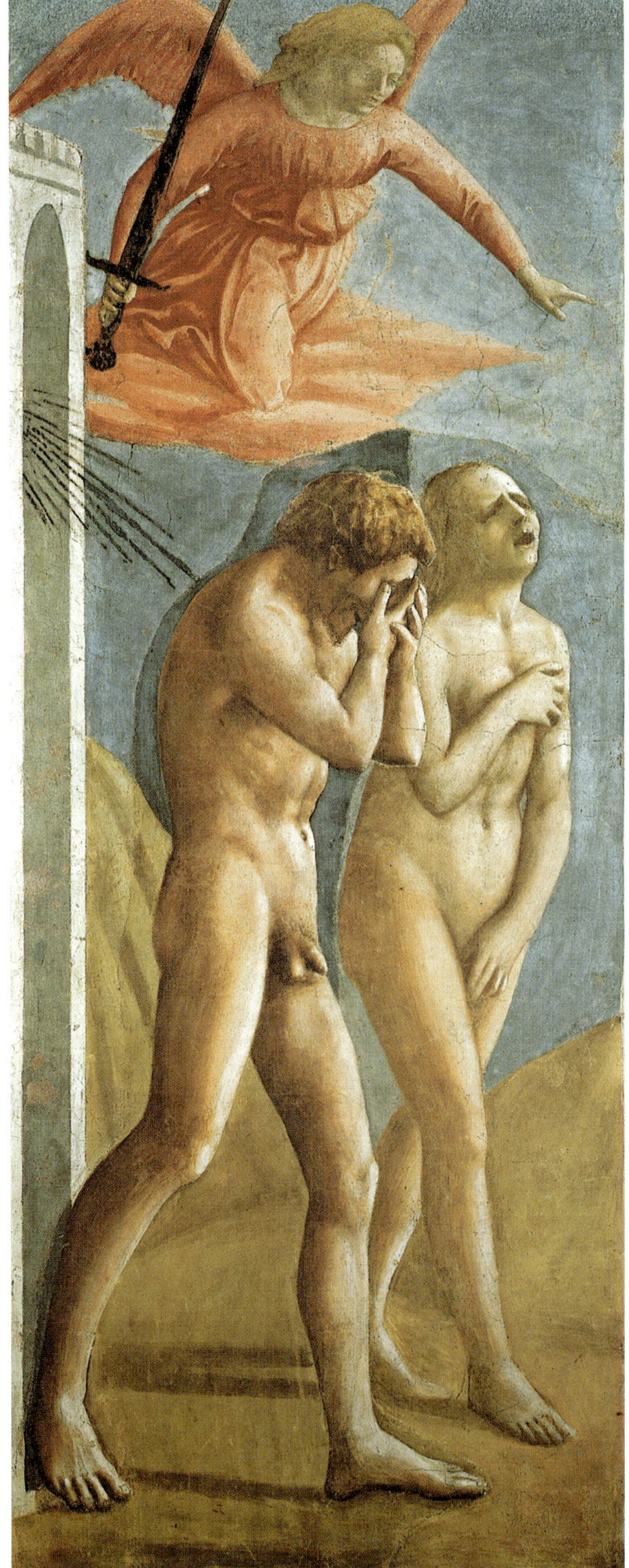

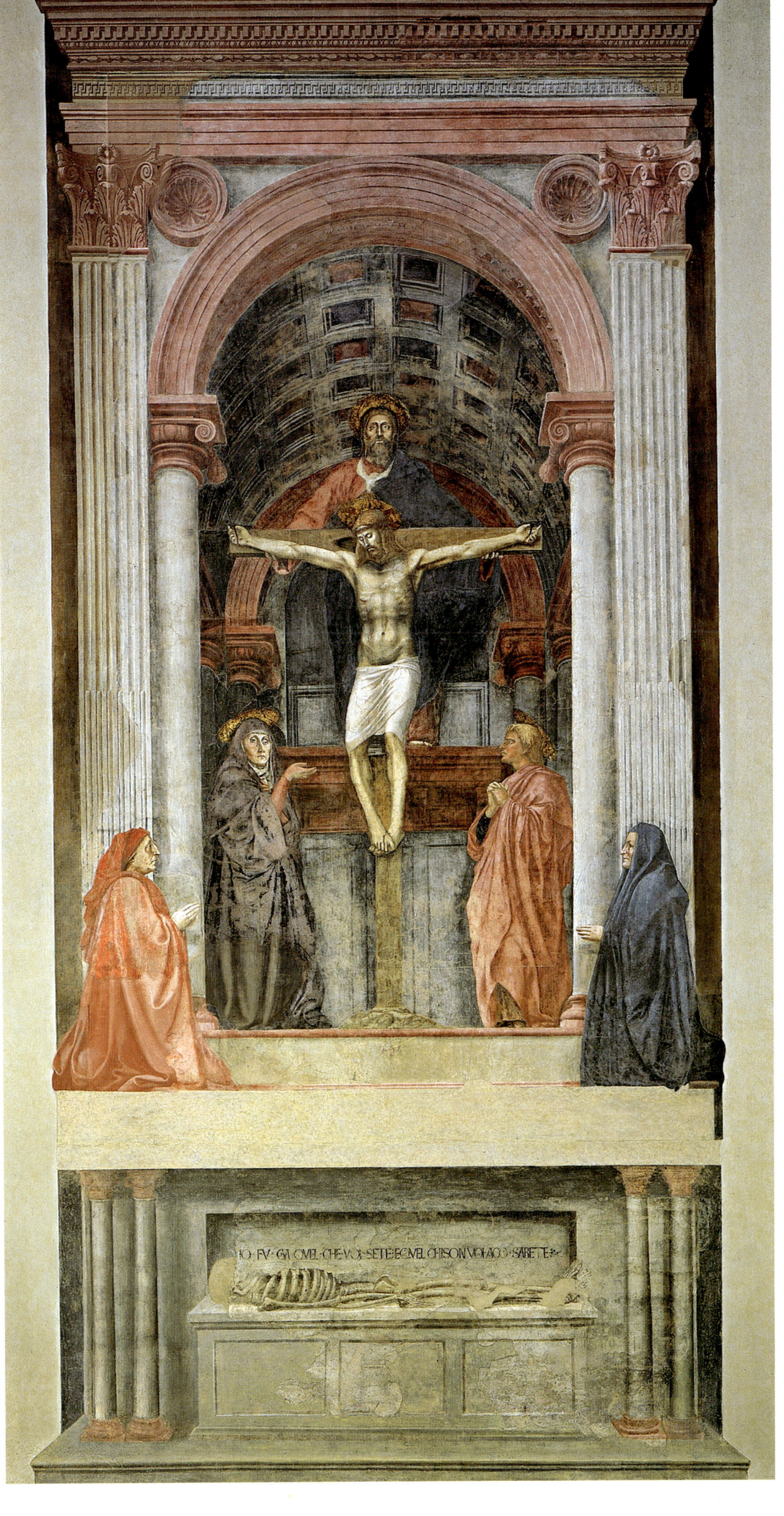

■ MASACCIO
The Trinity
circa 1426–28,
fresco,
667 x 317 cm
Santa Maria Novella,
Florence

This fresco, Masaccio's last work in Florence before his fatal trip to Rome with Masolino, is a masterpiece of perspective construction. Along the left nave of the basilica (which has no side chapels) Masaccio simulates the opening of a deep apsidal niche above an altar. The in-depth arrangement of the figures is highly accurate; the figures form a perfectly symmetrical pyramidal group scaled toward the interior of the niche while maintaining the relationships among the sizes of all the figures, with the two patrons of the work kneeling in adoration of the Trinity, which the Madonna indicates and to which St. John directs his gaze. Below, beneath the false altar, a skeleton rests on a sarcophagus bearing a grim inscription ("What you are, I once was; what I am, you will become"), symbolizing the Triumph of Death. The extraordinary architectonic background, with a coffered barrel vault framed within a pale-toned classical arch, was inspired by the innovative works of Filippo Brunelleschi, although some scholars hold that it may have been outlined by the great architect himself.

The Dominican Fra Giovanni da Fiesole, known as Fra or Beato Angelico, is usually considered a contemplative artist, capable of evoking pure, suspended, celestial atmospheres outside time. In reality, he was a painter of great breadth, fully involved in the debate of perspective and the evolution of the image, capable of taking on the most diverse techniques and sizes, from the miniature to the great cycle of frescoes. From the opening years of the 1430s, shortly after the death of Masaccio, he appears as one of the most innovative Florentine masters. The Annunciation, one of his favorite themes, is often the occasion for complex architectonic constructions in which the astonishing encounter between the angel and the Virgin takes place. In the youthful Cortona Altarpiece, the influence of Masaccio appears in the small but stupendous panels of the predella, which show an unadorned and unexpected taste for reality: like Masaccio, Fra Angelico went into the streets, mixed with the people, observed architecture, dress, and gestures to create a true image in which the episodes move along with a narrative taste so direct they have the feeling of items from the daily news.

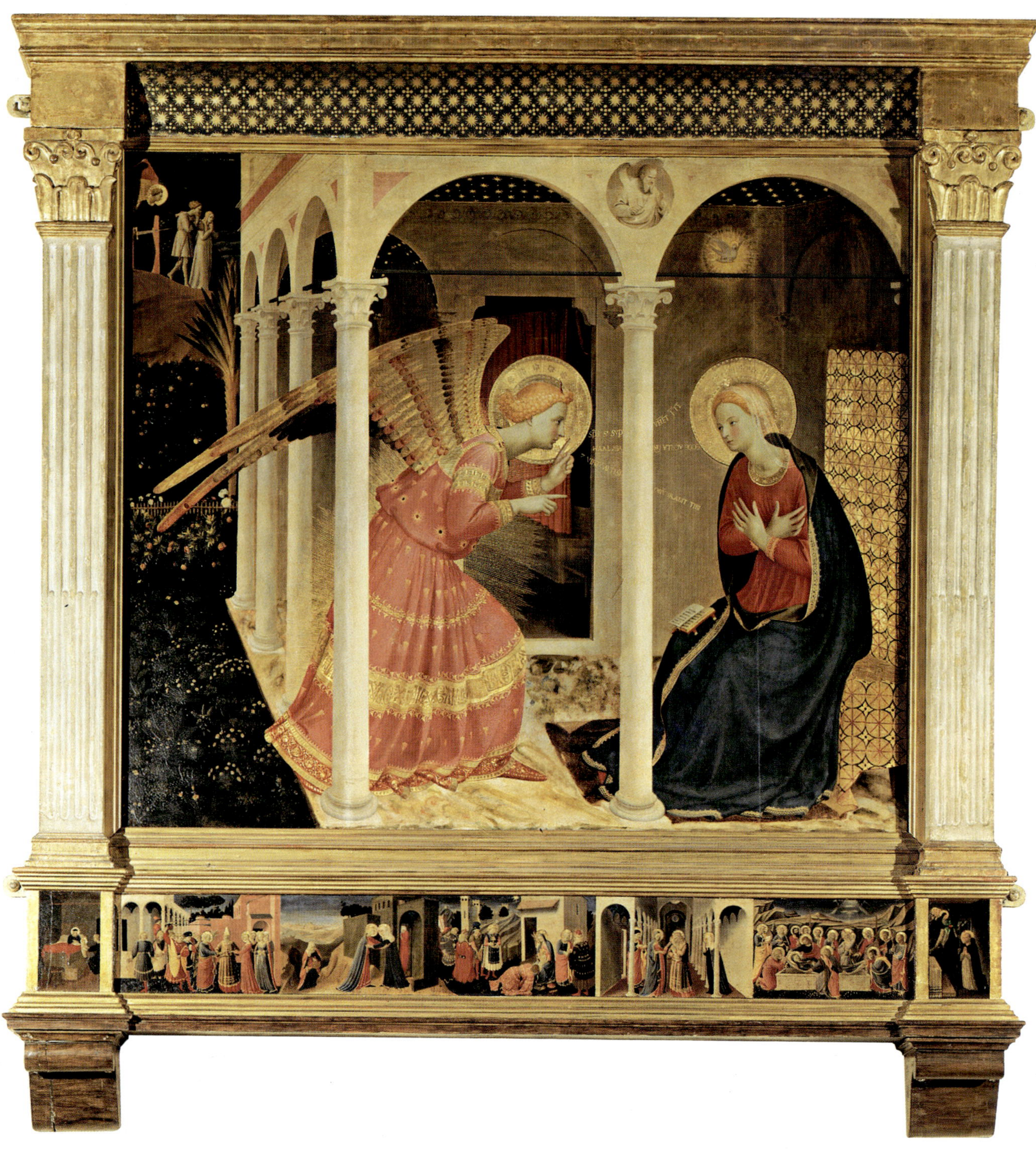

Florence and the invention of the Renaissance

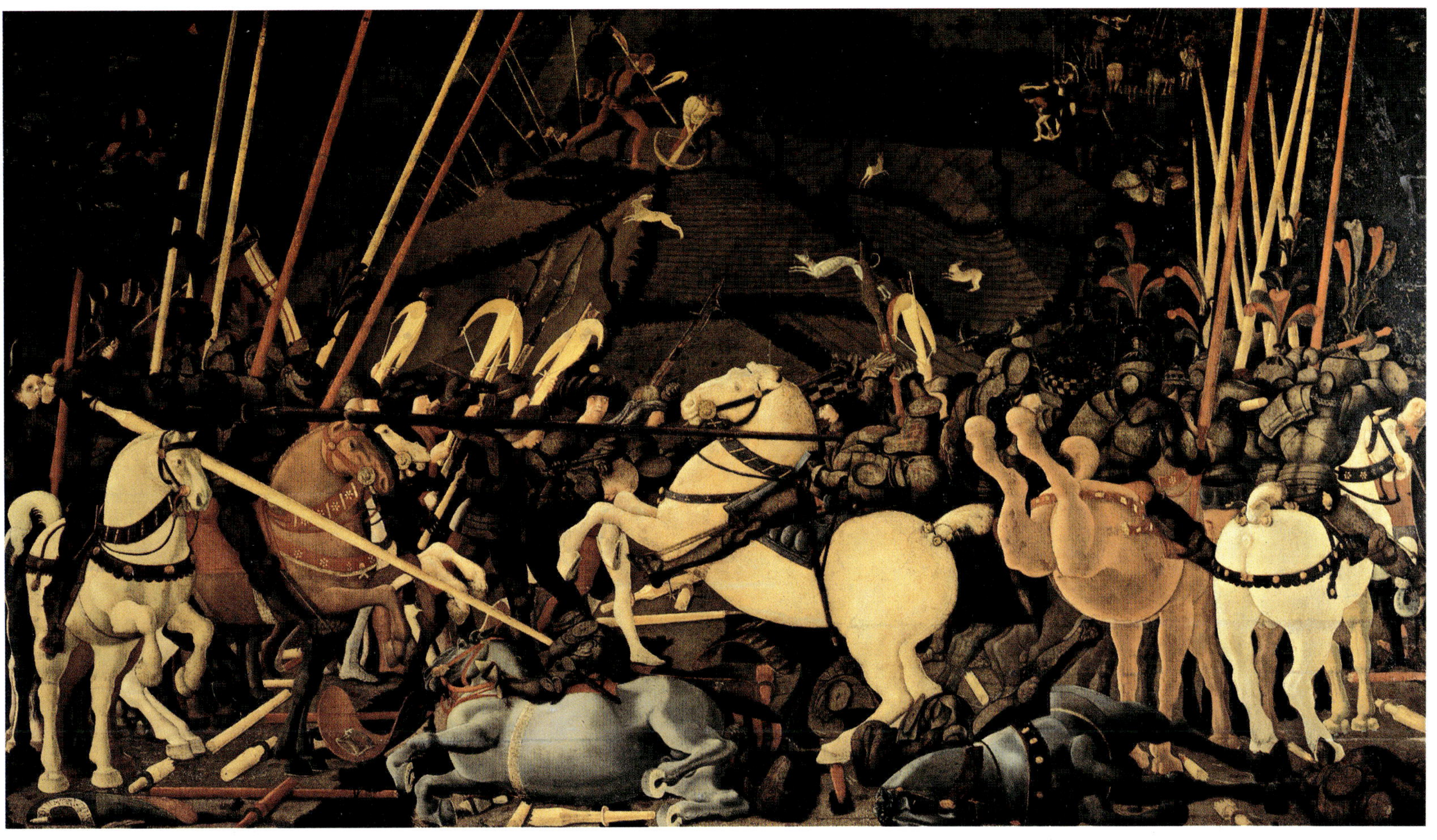

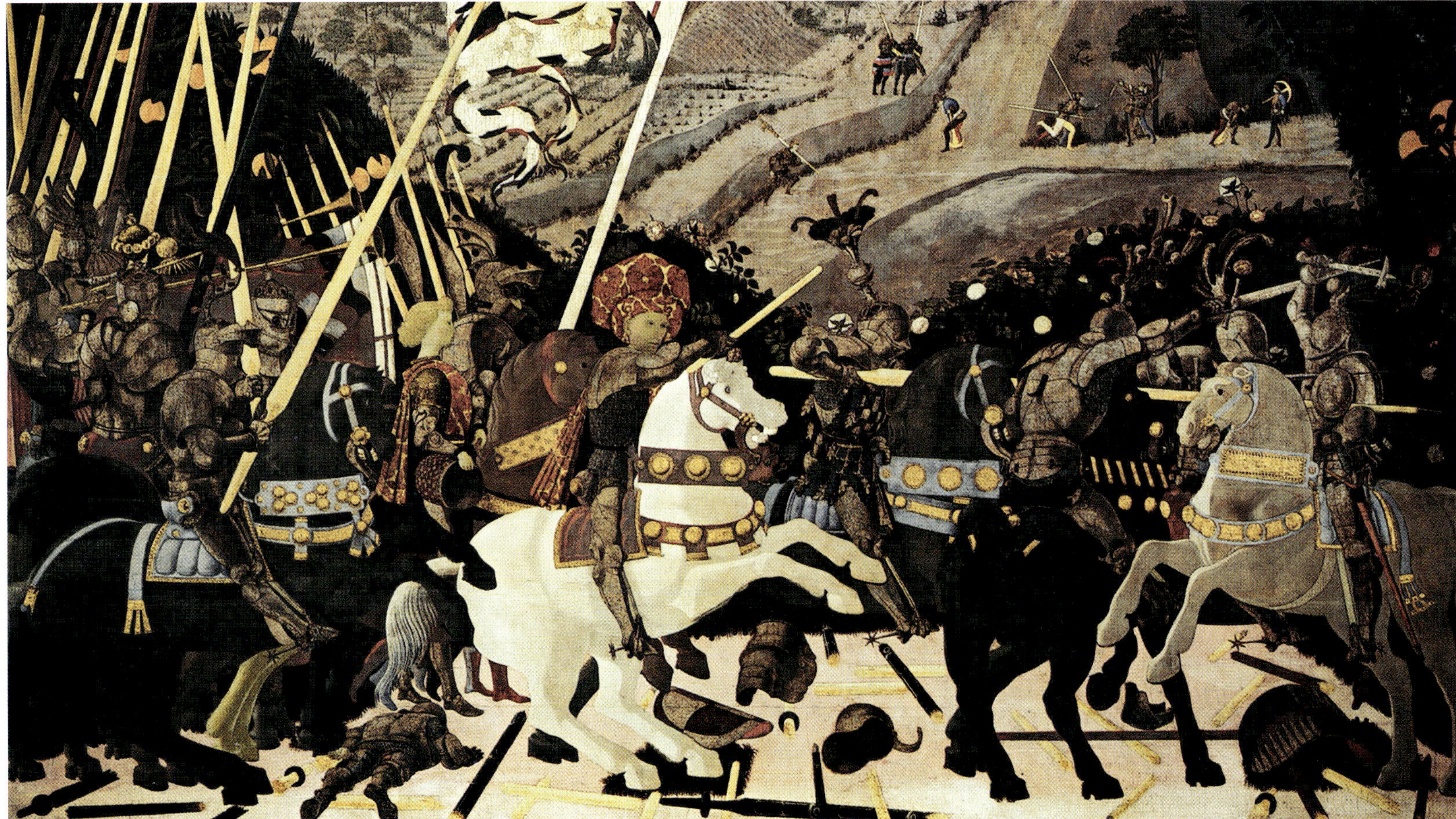

Florence and the invention of the Renaissance

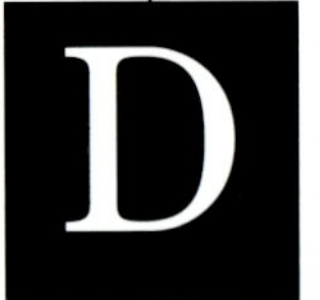

During the fifteenth century, in addition to the Italian centers of art and humanism, another great school of European Renaissance art arose in the wealthy cities of Flanders. Politically tied to the fate of the rich duchy of Burgundy, but governed in large part by groups of courageous and ambitious merchants, the main Flemish cities, such as Bruges, Ghent, Ypres, Brussels, and Louvain, experienced a period of great prosperity in the fifteenth century, supported most of all by the cloth industry. Flemish art reached international heights in the production of luxury tapestries (a technique for which the works of Tournai and Brussels enjoyed something close to a European monopoly) and in panel painting, with a highly characteristic style that blended the late Gothic taste for the sumptuous with the sense of realism, light, and perspective of the early Renaissance.

Aside from its stylistic and formal traits, Flemish painting met with great success and had a special attraction because of the use of a specific medium, oil, used as a binder for the paint. Until then, tempera had been used, which produces a less brilliant effect and does not permit the same delicacy of work. With the decline of the fourteenth-century use of gold in the background and inserts in metal, the Flemish masters used oil to apply paint in successive layers to obtain effects of transparency and atmosphere, with dramatic results of brilliance and precision in the reproduction of the surfaces of objects. It is also possible that some of these early Flemish masters experimented with the use of optical instruments, such as mirrors and lenses as aids in the minute analysis of reality and variations of light. The Flemish use of oils was enthusiastically imitated by the other European schools of painting, and by the 1570s oil was in widespread use. It became the predominant painting technique shortly after, when canvas replaced wooden panels as the support for painting.

The architecture of Flanders saw the development of a style that came to be known as "Brabant Gothic," after the Brabant region. As

The mercantile cities

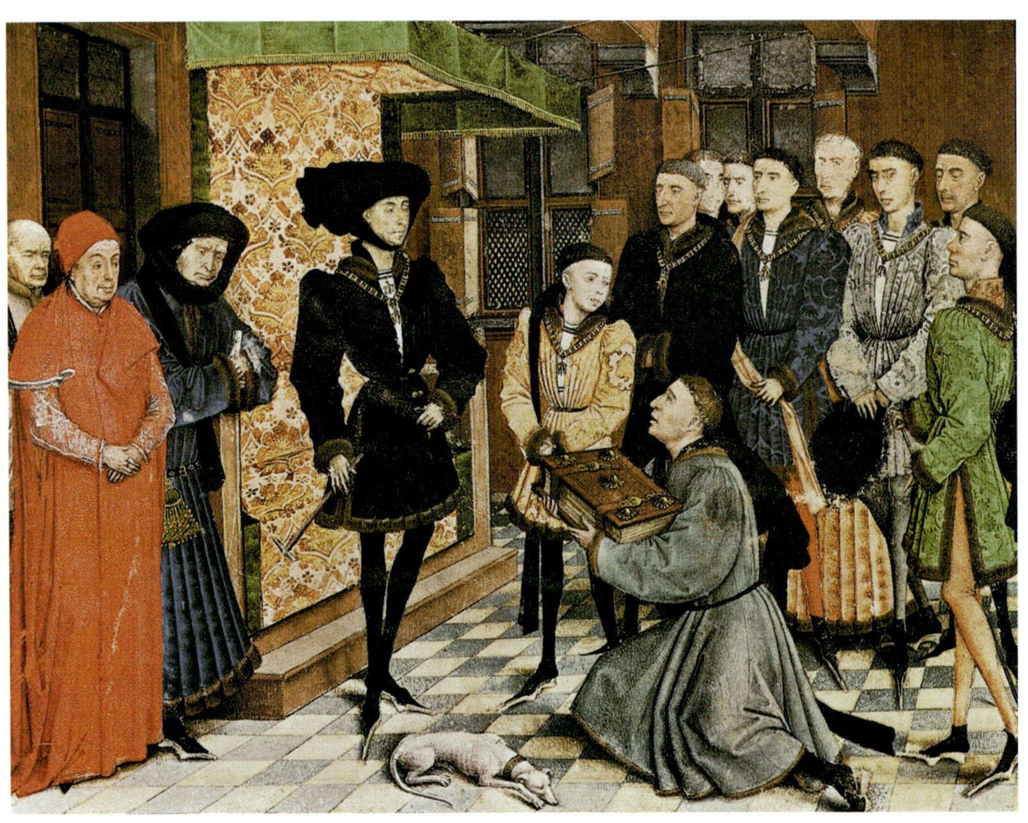

can be seen in the cathedrals of Antwerp, Brussels, and Ghent, aside from the principal church of Bruges, Flemish Gothic architecture sought spectacular effects, unexpected solutions, and very high towers. The architectonic traits of these churches, along with the important factor of the region's damp climate, prevented the creation of frescoes, which were of course quite common in Italy. In place of frescoes, Flemish religious art made use of tapestries, stained glass, complex altars made of carved wood, and, naturally, panel painting. The leading center of Flemish art was the fascinating city of Bruges, which has remained substantially intact in its monuments, its medieval urban appearance, and its rich artistic patrimony.

The leading fifteenth-century Flemish artist was Jan van Eyck, who together with his two brothers was active in Ghent and Bruges. A key figure in the history of Western art, credited with perfecting the invaluable technique of applying oil paint, Jan was a famous man, at the center of attention of artists and intellectuals, such that his reputation reached the political level. Thanks to him, the marvelous world that until then had been revealed only to the few who were fortunate enough to own Flemish and Burgundy illuminated pages moved on to the public plane of the great altar paintings. The dukes of Burgundy entrusted him with delicate diplomatic missions in various nations, and these trips gave his art a European breadth. In contact with Robert Campin and Rogier van der Weyden, Van Eyck had an extraordinary sensitivity for light, thanks to which he obtained an illusionistic rendering of materials and an analytical description of tiny details. In portraits and in religious scenes in a wide variety of sizes, there is a poetic and deeply felt sense of contemporary life, of the desire to transfer to the painted surface a small universe of objects, persons, and details investigated with light.

Van Eyck's most prestigious masterpiece is the great Ghent Altarpiece with the *Adoration of the Lamb* (completed in 1432), which is still displayed in the cathedral of Ghent, for which it was originally made. Organized like an altar with several mobile wings, some of them painted

in the Hôtel-Dieu in Beaune), Van der Weyden became a painter of international stature. On one hand, he imported the sacred scenes with large figures scaled in perspective, typical of Italian art, to Flemish art; on the other, he exported to southern Europe the taste for precious details and the technique of painting in oils. Rogier van der Weyden was in Rome in 1449–50 for the Jubilee, and he made good use of this visit to Italy. While he was in Florence he had occasion to see the works of Masaccio and Fra Angelico; in Ferrara, as a guest of the brilliant Este court, he met both Piero della Francesca and Leon Battista Alberti, encounters that may have led him to make his works even more majestic.

An attentive interpreter of human sentiments and emotions,

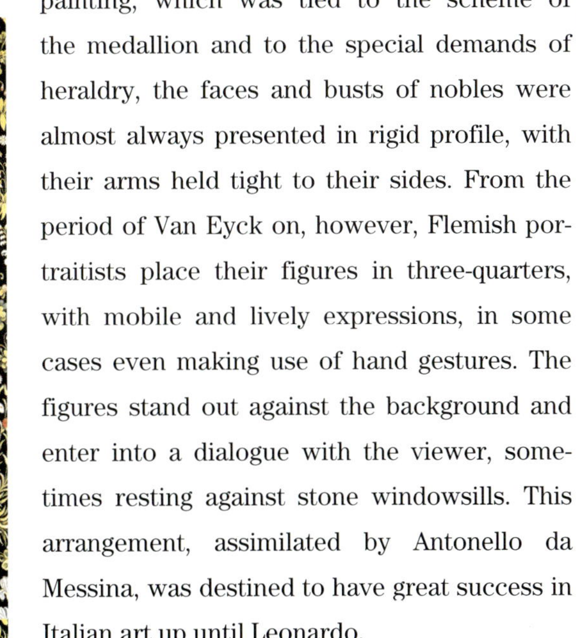

Gerard Loyet, ex-voto of Charles the Bold, 1467, gold and enamel; Treasury of the Cathedral of Saint-Paul, Liège

# of Flanders

on both sides, it is a compendium of many characteristics of Flemish art: splendidly brilliant surfaces; absolute clarity in the rendering of details; the study of anatomy; and the impeccable use of space, both in vast, open, natural panoramas and in sophisticated architectonic interiors.

Made the seat of the dukes of Burgundy in 1430, Brussels began to grow in cultural importance, with major construction worksites, such as the palaces that surround the spectacular Grand-Place, along with its own school of painting. The outstanding figure was the Walloon Rogelet de la Pasture, a student of Robert Campin and slightly younger than Jan van Eyck, who translated his name into Flemish to become Rogier van der Weyden. Working for patrons in the cities and courts of Burgundy (one of his largest and most important works is the polyptych of the *Last Judgment* preserved

Van der Weyden was also an excellent portraitist. In fact, among the many innovations that Flemish painting made to the style of European painting, portraits warrant particular attention. In the tradition of Gothic painting, which was tied to the scheme of the medallion and to the special demands of heraldry, the faces and busts of nobles were almost always presented in rigid profile, with their arms held tight to their sides. From the period of Van Eyck on, however, Flemish portraitists place their figures in three-quarters, with mobile and lively expressions, in some cases even making use of hand gestures. The figures stand out against the background and enter into a dialogue with the viewer, sometimes resting against stone windowsills. This arrangement, assimilated by Antonello da Messina, was destined to have great success in Italian art up until Leonardo.

"Millefleur" tapestry of Flemish manufacture with heraldic insignia, 1488–1501; The Cloisters Collection, Metropolitan Museum of Art, New York

ROBERT CAMPIN
**Portrait of a Man;
Portrait of a Woman**
circa 1425–30,
oil on panel,
41.7 x 27.9 cm each
National Gallery,
London

Together with Jan van Eyck, Robert Campin was one of the true founders of the modern portrait. Not only was he masterful in rendering a wide variety of physical types, expressions, ages, and subtleties of emotion, but he also enriched the symbolic depth of the portrait. In that sense his portraits of couples are particularly eloquent. Set free from the celebratory requirements of the courts of the nobility, the "middle-class" portrait thus becomes the bearer of new sentiments, with the viewer being drawn into an increasingly deep involvement in the image. Although on separate panels, these two portraits by Campin are a pair, the result of a unitary conception, and the aspects of their two personalities say much about the sentiments of this middle-class couple. The heavy-set, ruddy-faced husband seems to lean forward, claiming his space with sheer willpower; his wife seems instead to withdraw in a slight movement of submission, and her averted eyes, from within the impeccable white of her veil, give off something like a sigh.

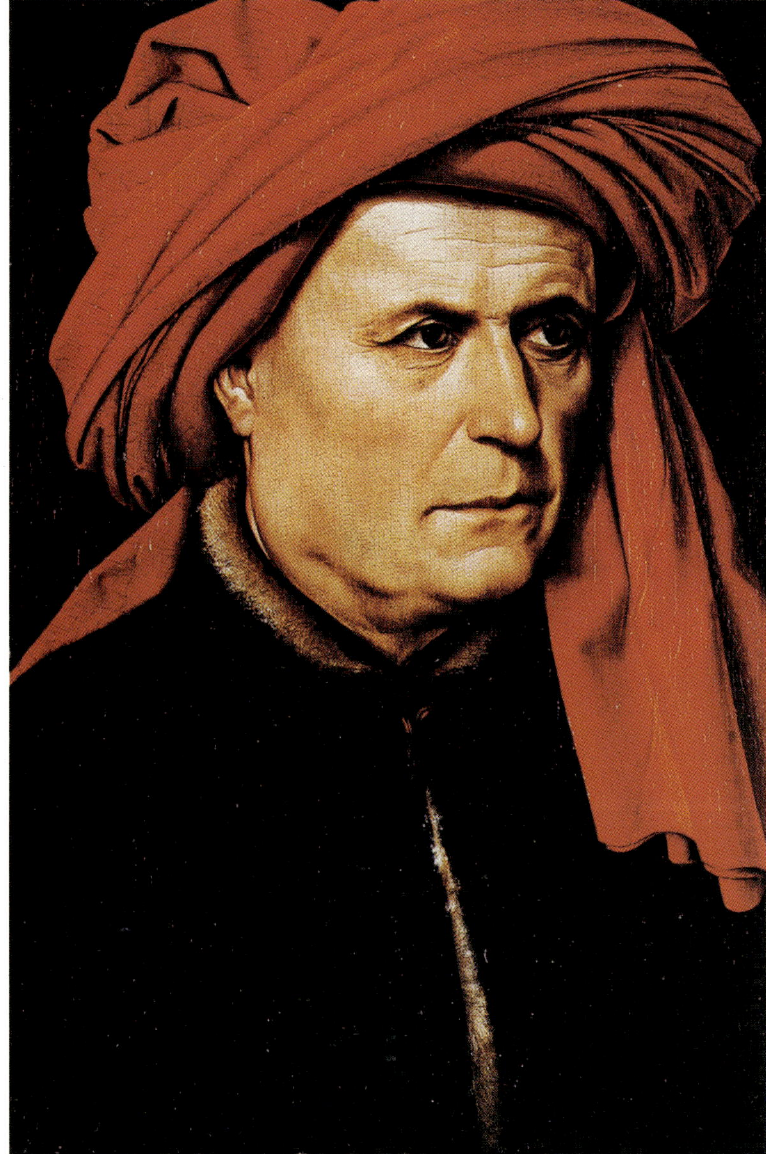

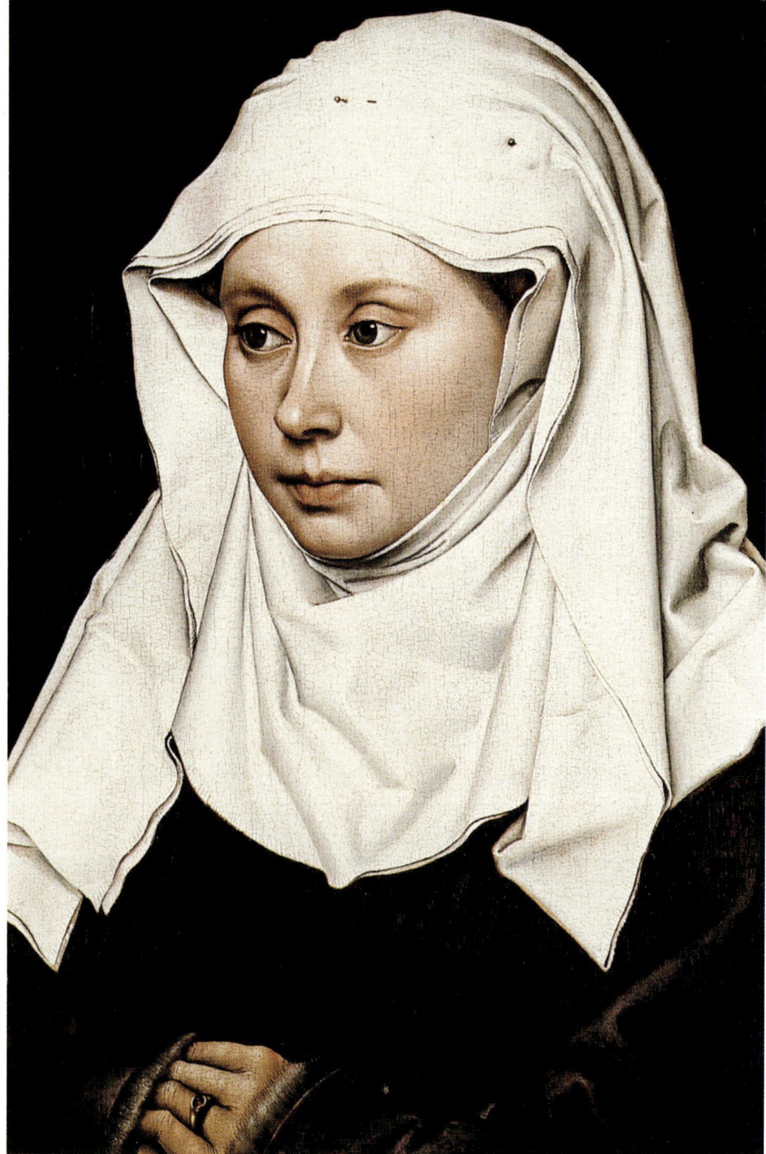

The mercantile cities of Flanders

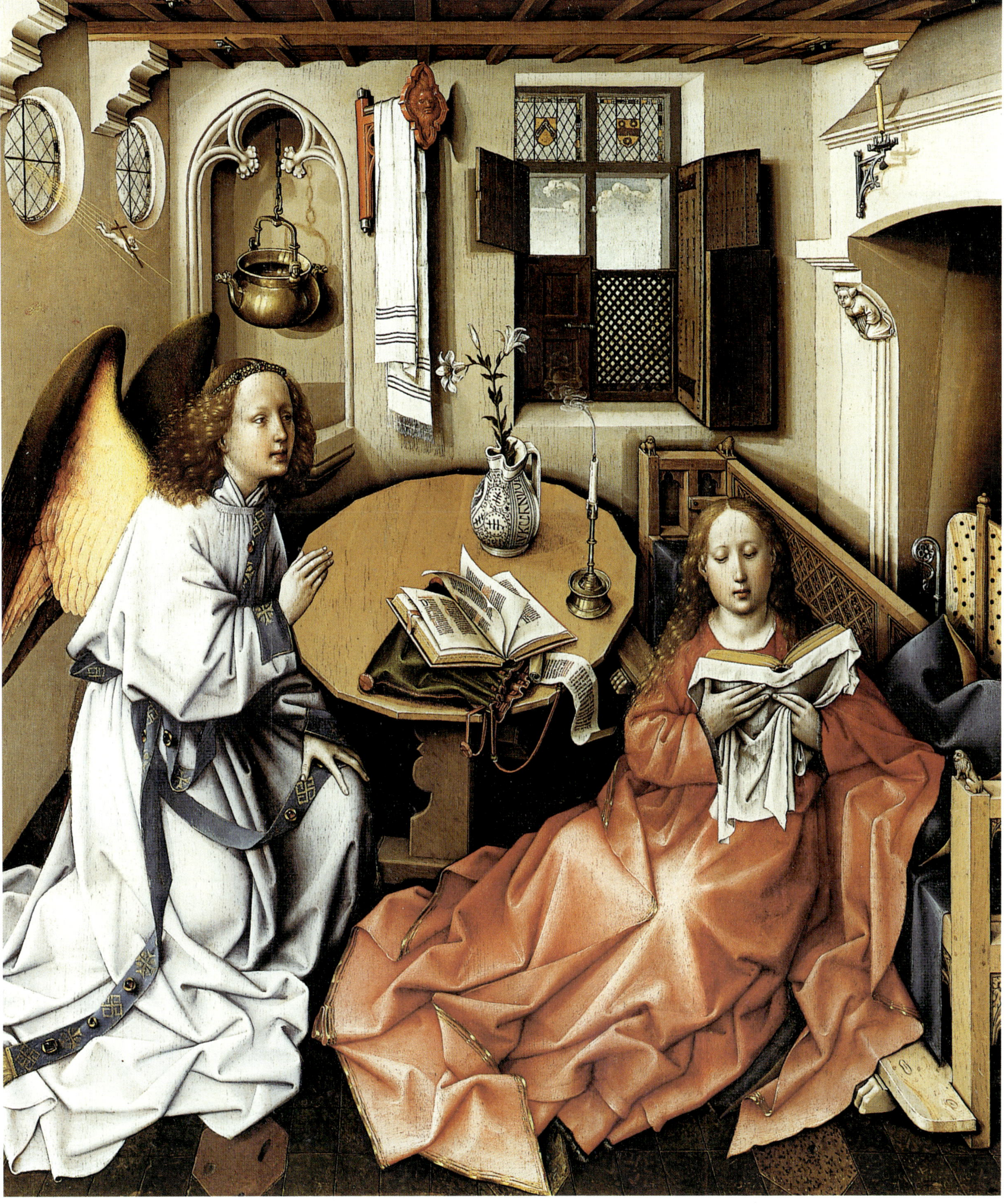

The mercantile cities of Flanders

This marvelous polyptych is composed of twelve panels, eight of which are painted on both sides, mounted on hinges so that they can be opened or closed in keeping with different periods of the liturgical year. The work was commissioned in 1425 by Jodocus Vijd of Hubert, the older of the Van Eyck brothers. Hubert died the next year, and Jan took over the work, completing it in 1432. The polyptych is the masterpiece of Flemish painting of the early fifteenth century. On the outer panels Van Eyck adopted an almost monochrome tonality, exploring the subtle variations of light on pale colors, while the interior glows with saturated, brilliant colors of a spectacular clarity. The main scene, inspired by the Apocalypse, takes place in a paradisiacal flowering garden. It is a symbolic presentation of the Eucharistic sacrifice of Christ through the figure of the Mystical Lamb. Processions of the beatified, divided into orderly, compact

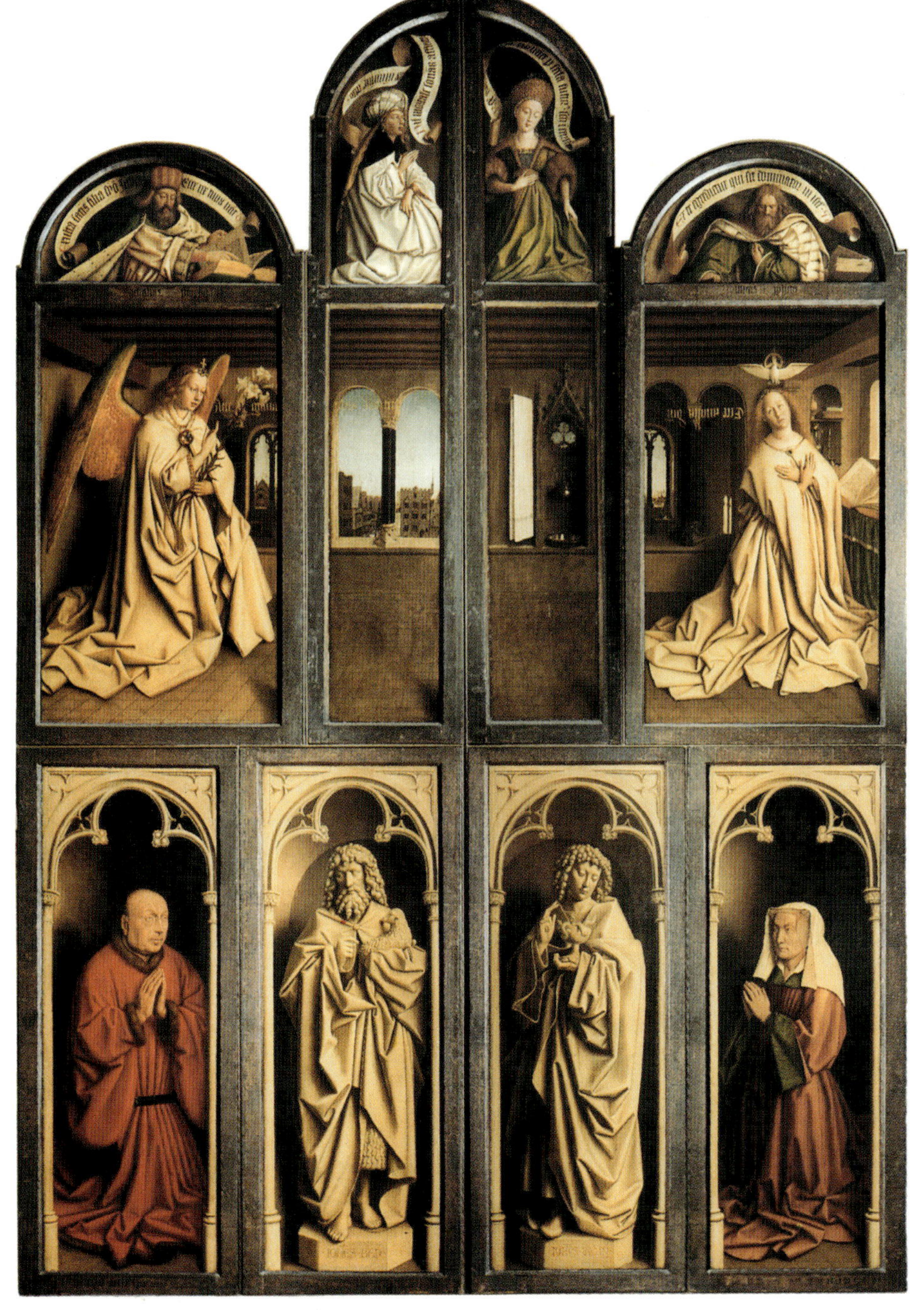

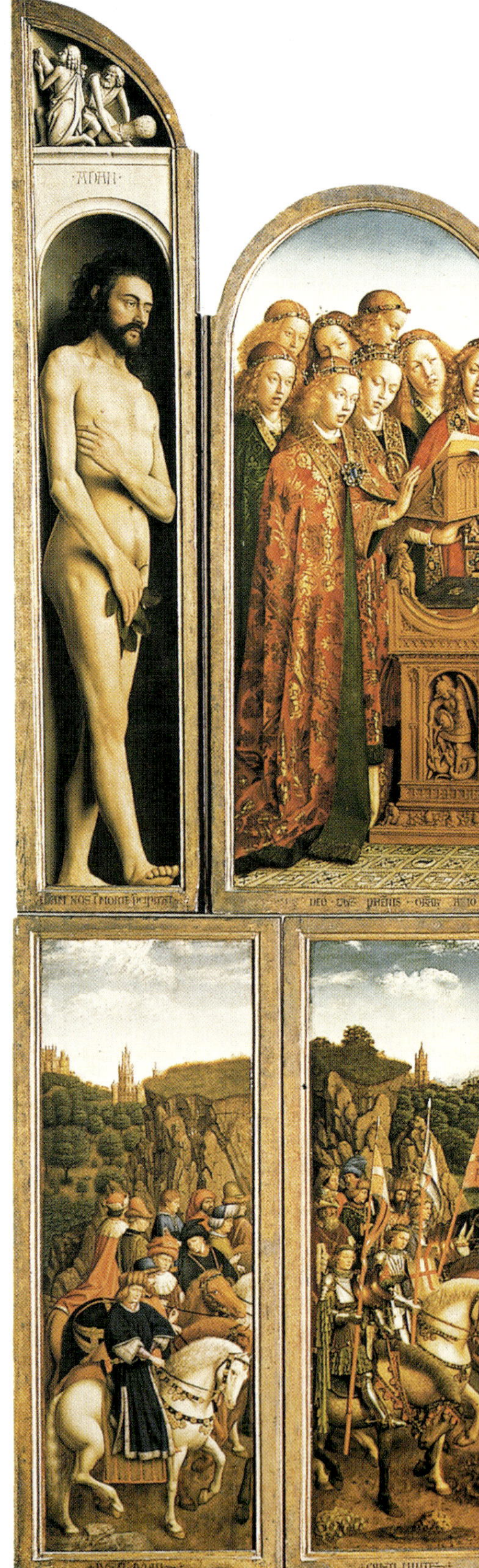

The mercantile cities of Flanders

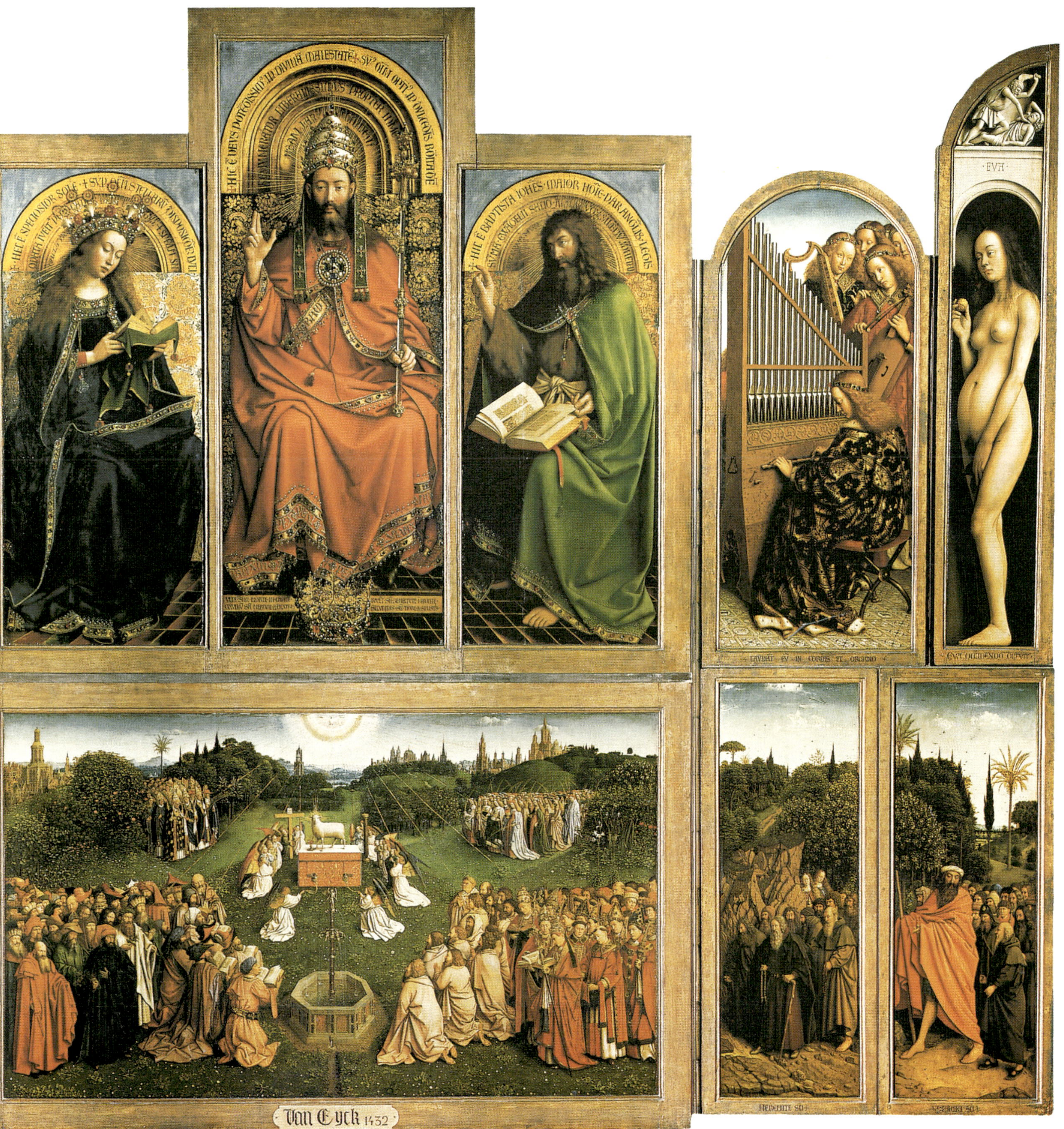

ranks, converge on the altar bearing the Lamb. In addition to the groups in the central panel (prophets, apostles, patriarchs, bishops, virgins, martyrs), those moving toward the Lamb include the just judges and soldiers of Christ, coming from the left, and the pilgrims and hermits from the right. The panels of the upper row and those on the outside illustrate the process of redemption: Adam and Eve are the origin of the story of the fate of man; Eve holds the apple of sin, and above the heads of the Progenitors are small bas-reliefs with the sacrifice of Abel and the murder of Cain. But while man falls into sin, the prophets and sibyls (the figures that appear in the curved pinnacles atop the external panels) predict future salvation. The path toward redemption begins with the Annunciation and triumphs in the central figures of John the Baptist, Mary, and God the Father. Despite the dramatic nudes of Adam and Eve, truly pioneering in their direct realism, Van Eyck does not concentrate on the human figures; unlike Masaccio and the Florentine figurative culture, he presents a multiform universe, transforming the painting into a microcosm, a complete and self-sufficient world: the human sphere and the divine harmonize and meet in the splendor of nature.

The mercantile cities of Flanders

Only rarely during the Renaissance period did the subjects of portraits submit to repeated sittings. The painters worked from sketches made from life that they then elaborated in their atelier. Very few of these preliminary drawings have survived, and one of the most important concerns *Cardinal Albergati* by Jan van Eyck. Thanks to the drawing we know that even the great Flemish portraitists, apparently so very faithful to natural reality, sought a subtle balance between absolute realism and the ability to "idealize" the figures with slight corrections to clothes, features, attitudes, expressions. Here, the passage from drawing to panel led to an image of greater severity: the face narrows, the sense of affability disappears, the neck becomes straighter, more proud, the nose assumes a more controlled size and shape. What is lost in spontaneity is made up for in solemnity and moral authority.

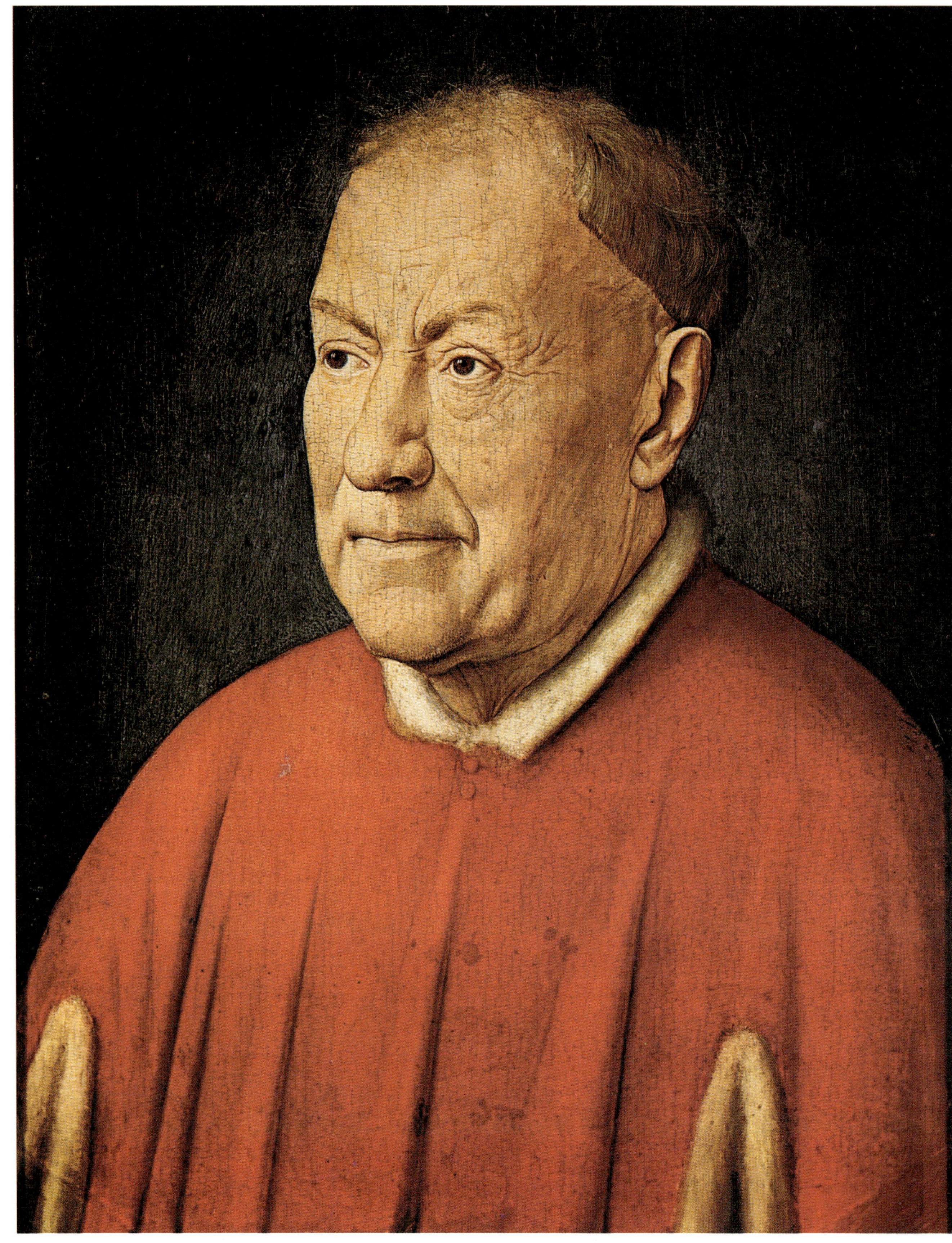

The mercantile cities of Flanders

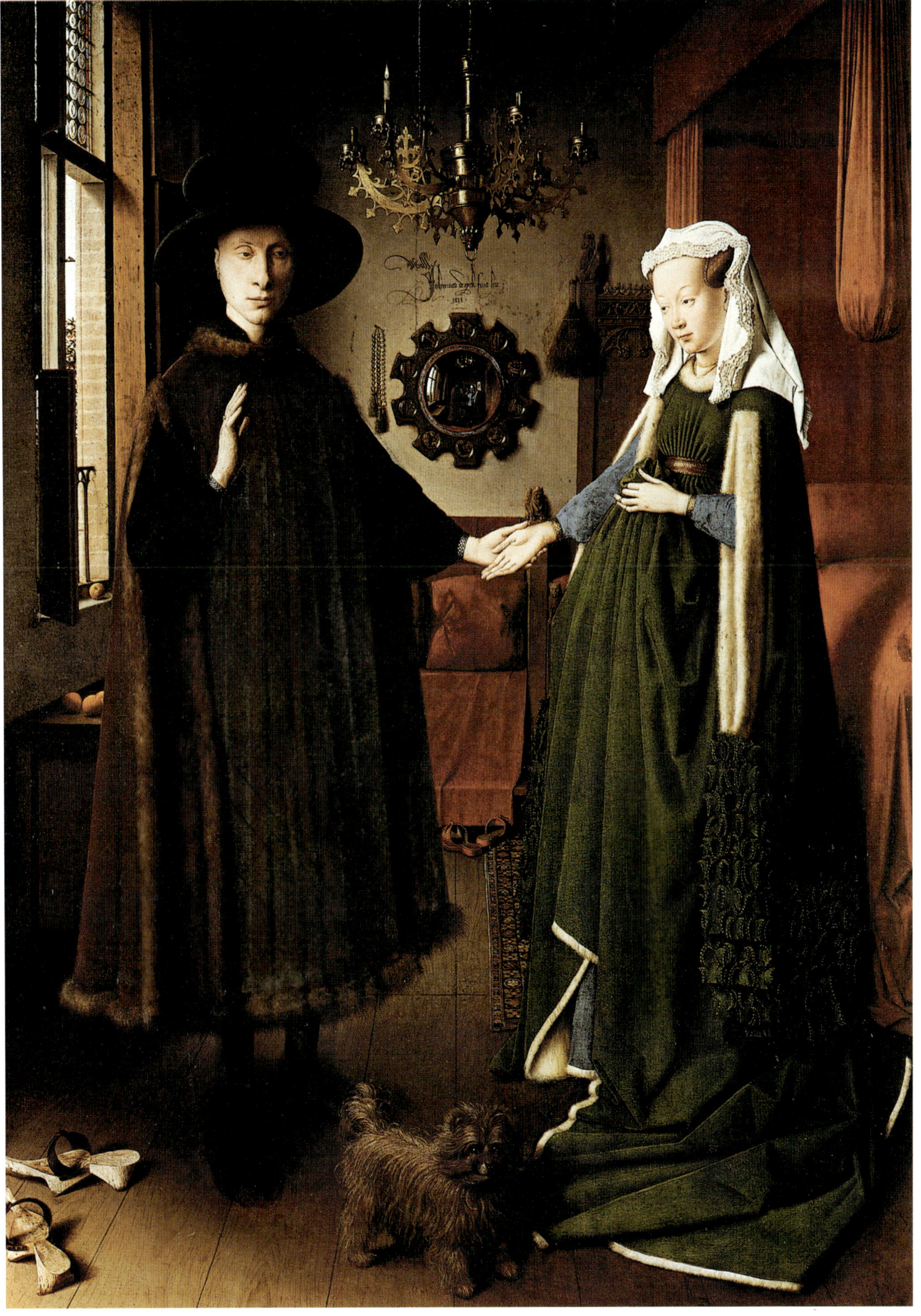

JAN VAN EYCK
The Arnolfini Couple
1434, oil on panel,
84.5 x 62.5 cm
National Gallery,
London

To recall his wedding day the Tuscan merchant Giovanni Arnolfini commissioned Van Eyck to paint a portrait of him together with his wife, Giovanna Cenami. Beginning with this idea, Van Eyck elaborates an evocative setting, played on ambivalence between descriptive realism and the symbolic value of things. The metal chandelier (true center of the composition) breaks up the volumes of the room and determines the directions of the rays of light. The orderly arrangement of the objects, the elegant clothes, the refinement of the features of the couple are indications of high social rank, while the little dog and the wooden clogs give the image a more domestic sense. With a famous expedient the painter included in the work the two witnesses of the wedding, reflected in the convex mirror behind the couple. The elaborate script above the mirror adds a further element to the play of presences and allusions: *Johannes van Eyck fuit hic*, "Jan van Eyck was here."

The mercantile cities of Flanders

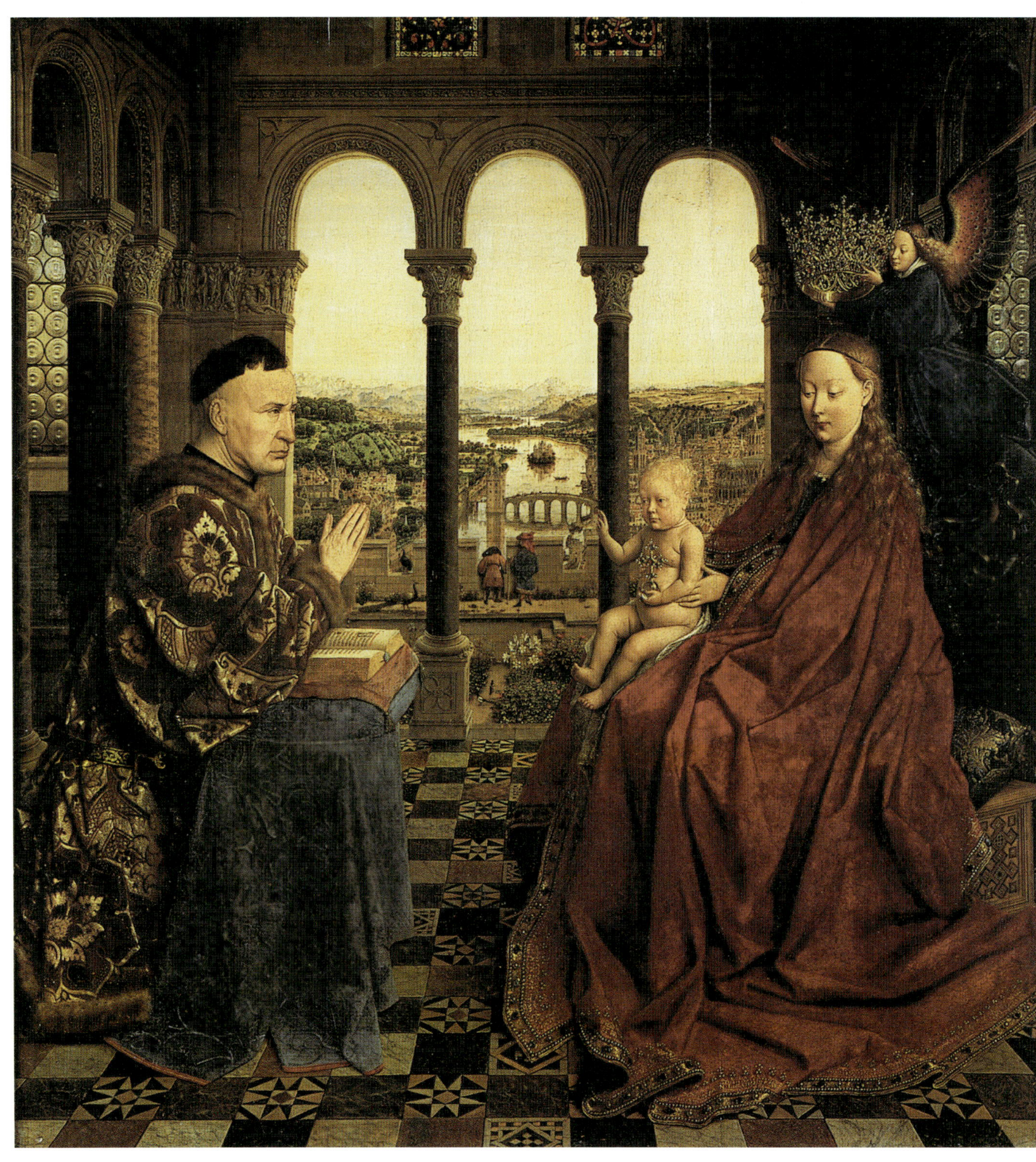

The mercantile cities of Flanders

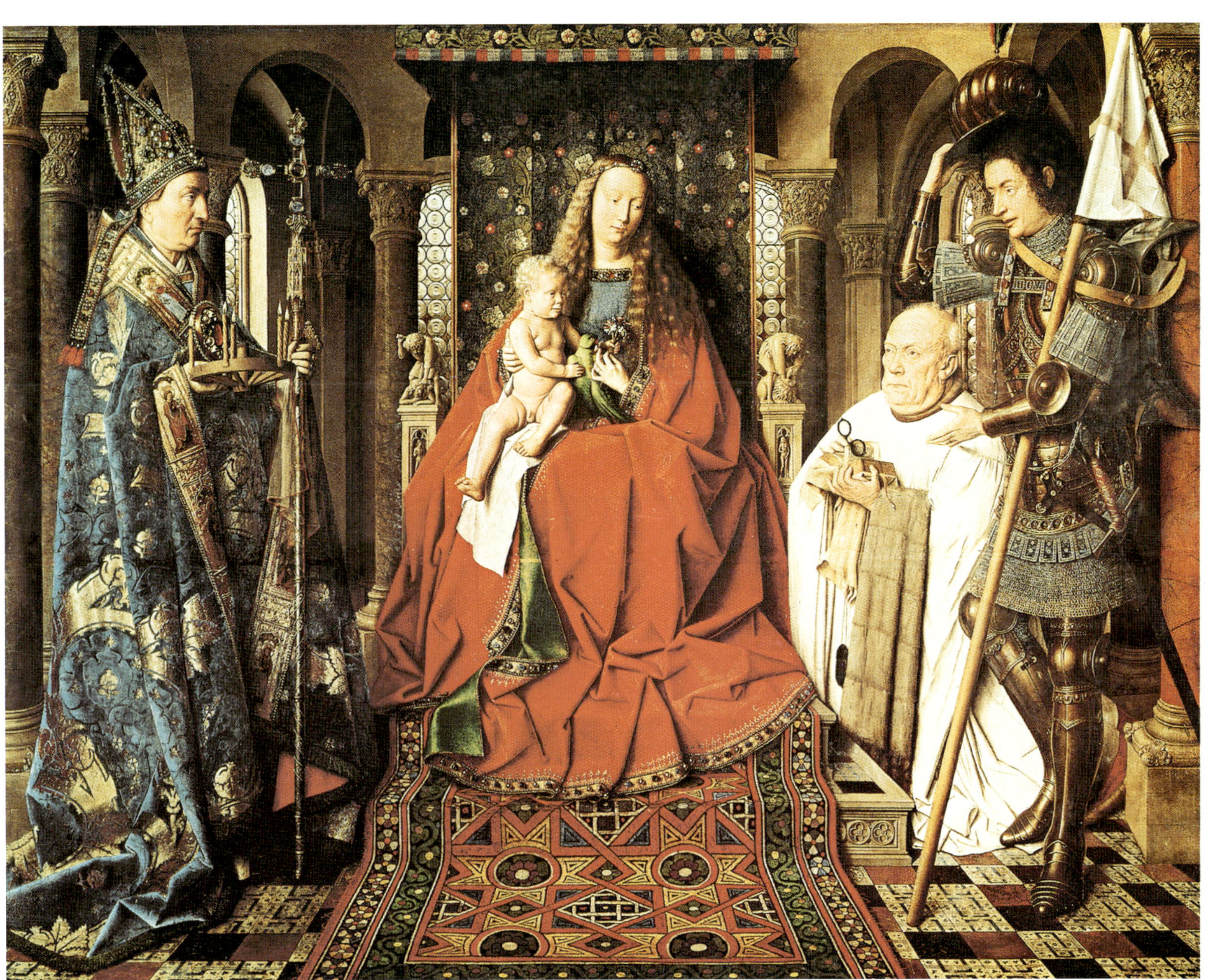

The term *sacra converzazione* ("sacred conversation") refers to paintings of the Virgin and Child flanked by saints, all of them located in the same physical space. This unusual version of a *sacra conversazione* takes place inside a Romanesque church, masterfully defined in its spatial and luministic values. The patron, dressed in a humble white tunic, is presented to the Virgin by St. George. The armored saint is presented in the same gesture of doffing his helmet as in the ex-voto of Charles the Bold (page 61). The space is pervaded by a fluid light that multiplies the infinity of descriptive details: the precious multicolored fabrics, the shining gems, the shiny armor, and naturally the portrait of the aging canon, crudely presented down to the smallest skin imperfection. Thanks to the use of oil paint, which permits the application of thin layers of transparent color, Van Eyck succeeds in capturing the effects of light falling on objects and on materials, and he does not limit himself to the presentation of atmospheric tonality or the quality of the light, but also presents its "luster," meaning the luminous sheen on objects as they react in different ways to illumination.

The mercantile cities of Flanders

Student of Robert Campin and later an important link between the founding fathers of Flemish painting and Italy, Rogier van der Weyden was gifted with a particular narrative talent. Many of his works, along the entire arc of his career, are organized in the form of a triptych or polyptych. The overall sense of the cycle, or even simply the development of an event, is thus relayed by way of the multiplicity of episodes in a sequential reading. At the same time, however, the painter never loses sight of the overall impression and makes use of interesting, sometimes highly innovative, devices. In the two triptychs reproduced here the element of continuity is the repetition of the elaborate arches that create an elegant architectonic partition. These should not be mistaken for mere decorative elements, however; the small groups of figures that decorate the intrados are iconographically related to the main scenes.

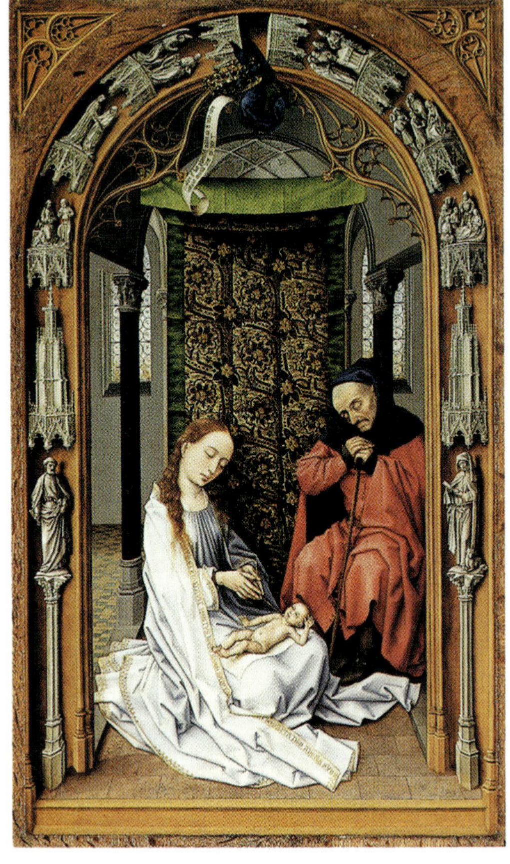
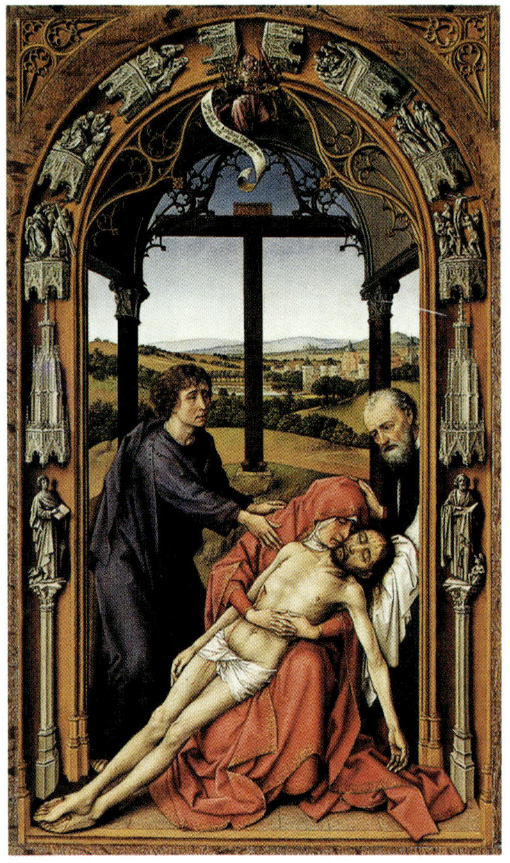
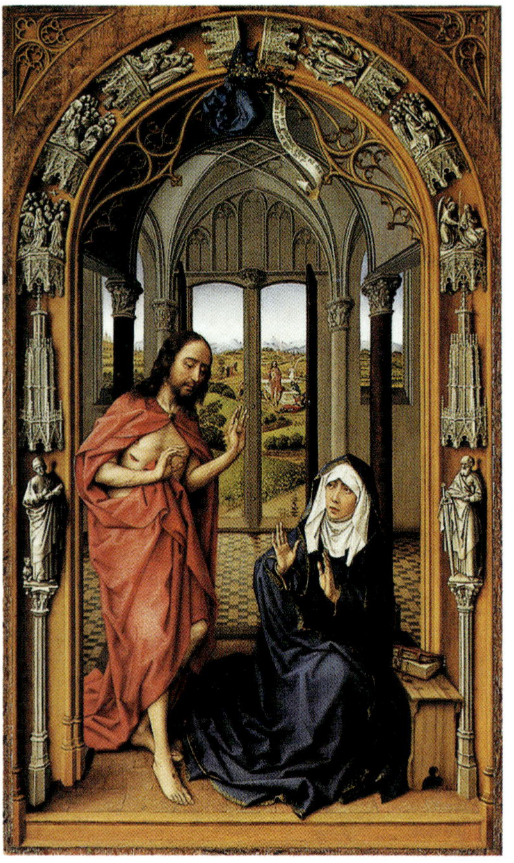
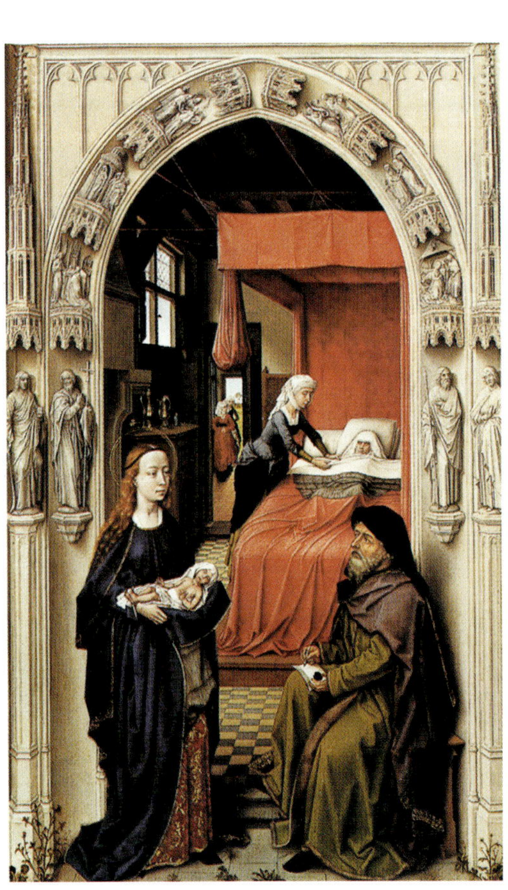
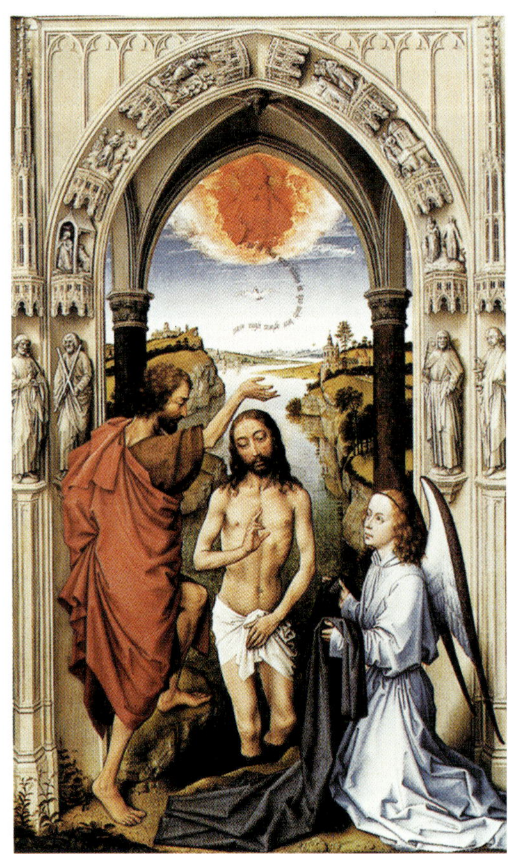
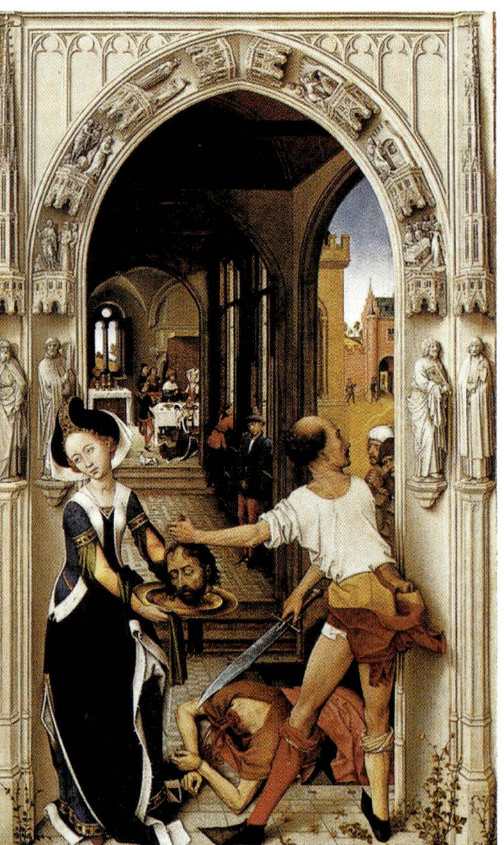

The mercantile cities of Flanders

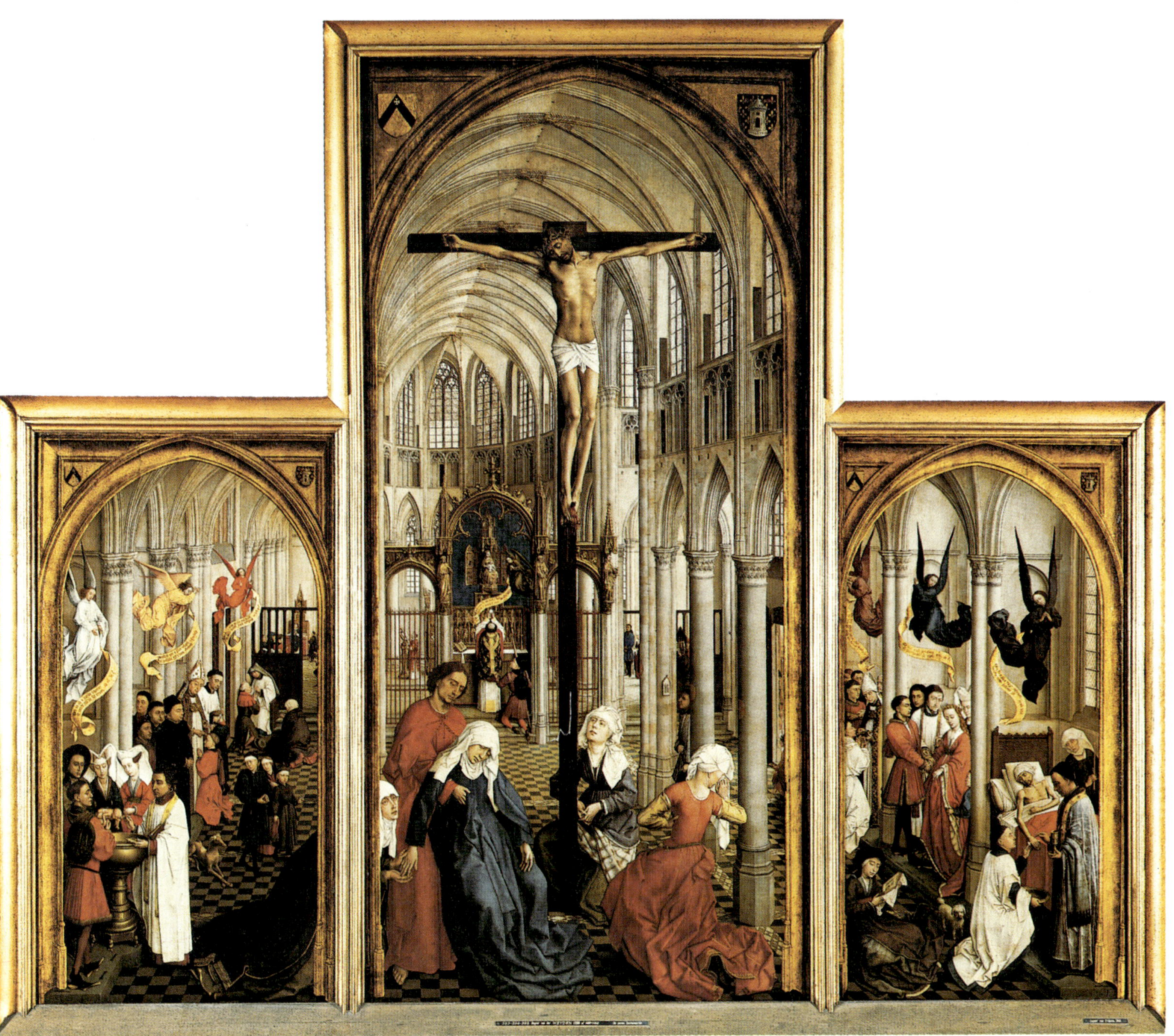

Commissioned by the
bishop of Tournai, this
triptych is one of Rogier
van der Weyden's most
powerful and original
creations. He uses a
single scene set inside
an enormous Gothic
cathedral, with the
events of the seven
sacraments distributed
between the nave and
the chapels (to the left
are baptism, confirma-
tion, and penance; to
the right are ordina-
tion, marriage, and
extreme unction; in the
center is the Eucharist).
The result is a wonder-
ful variety of situations
rendered highly legible
by the sharp details,
and despite the arrange-
ment the work has no
sense of being overly
fragmented. The dense
crowds of the side pan-
els leave room, at the
center, for a bare and
simple image, synthetic
and powerful. The cen-
tral nave of the church,
far higher than the
sides, is entirely occu-
pied by the cross of
Christ, symbol of
Eucharistic sacrifice,
while on the main altar
a priest is celebrating
the Mass. The intensity
of this section is under-
lined by the expressions
of suffering of the fig-
ures at the feet of the
cross, and the chro-
matic contrasts with
the wan light that
wraps the architecture.

In this work, one of the most dramatic paintings of the first third of the fifteenth century, Van der Weyden presents an unforgettable essay of compositional rhythm and concentration, one that was repeated and imitated many times by various Flemish and German artists of the Renaissance. Enclosing the entire scene within a sort of "box" (exactly as will be done in the next decades for statuary groups of the Deposition or the Lamentation for the Dead Christ), the painter concentrates attention on the figures and their emotions. His realism is intensely human, capable of presenting the fragility of humanity, and also the profound poetry of passion, by way of tormented gestures. Painted for a chapel of Louvain dedicated to Mary, the altarpiece is organized as a series of large, hooked curves. There is a particular eloquence in the way the line described by the lifeless body of Christ as it is lowered from the cross is repeated almost identically by the line of the Madonna as she falls in a faint. The colors, still perfect today, are of an almost indescribable beauty and intensity.

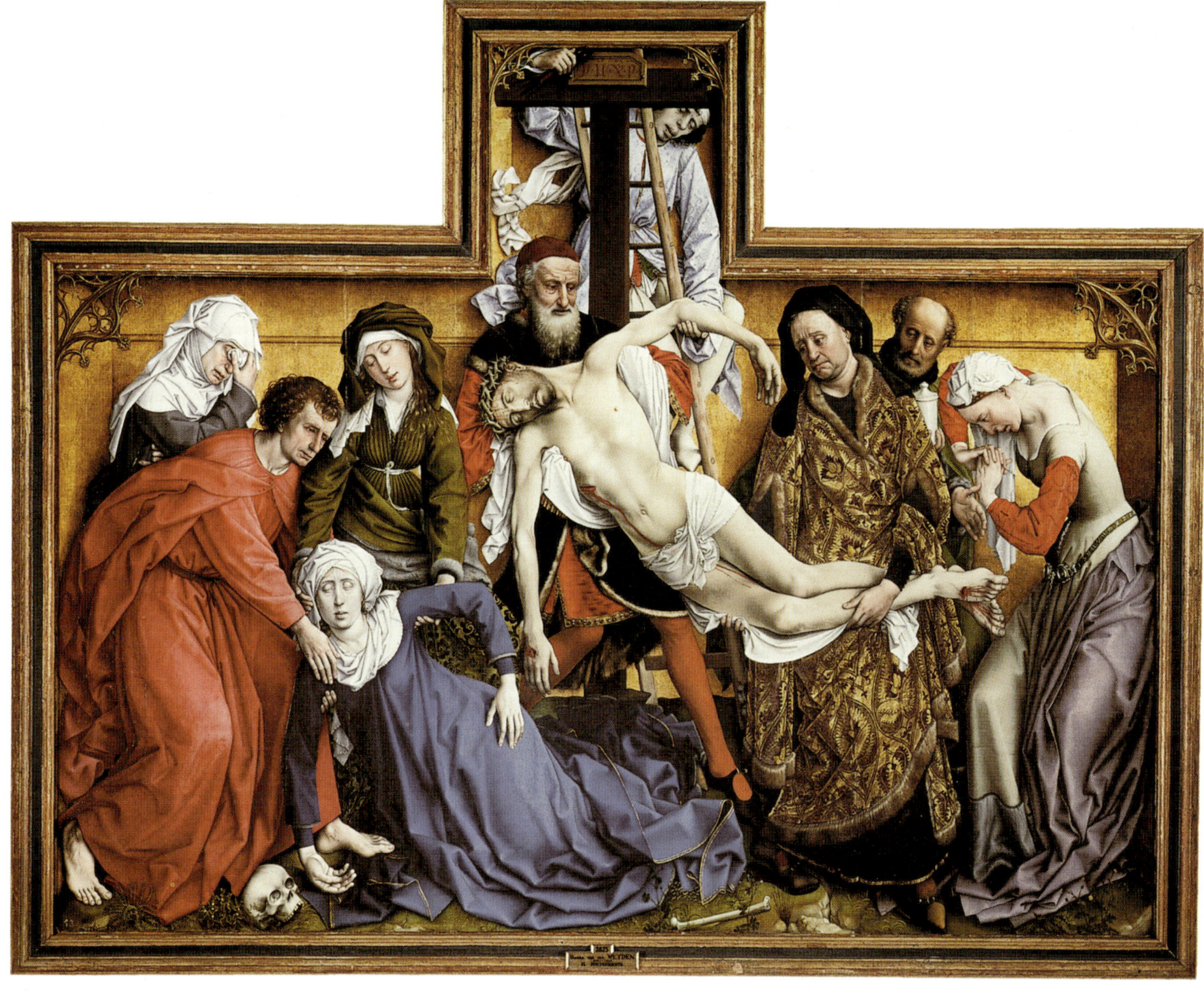

The mercantile cities of Flanders

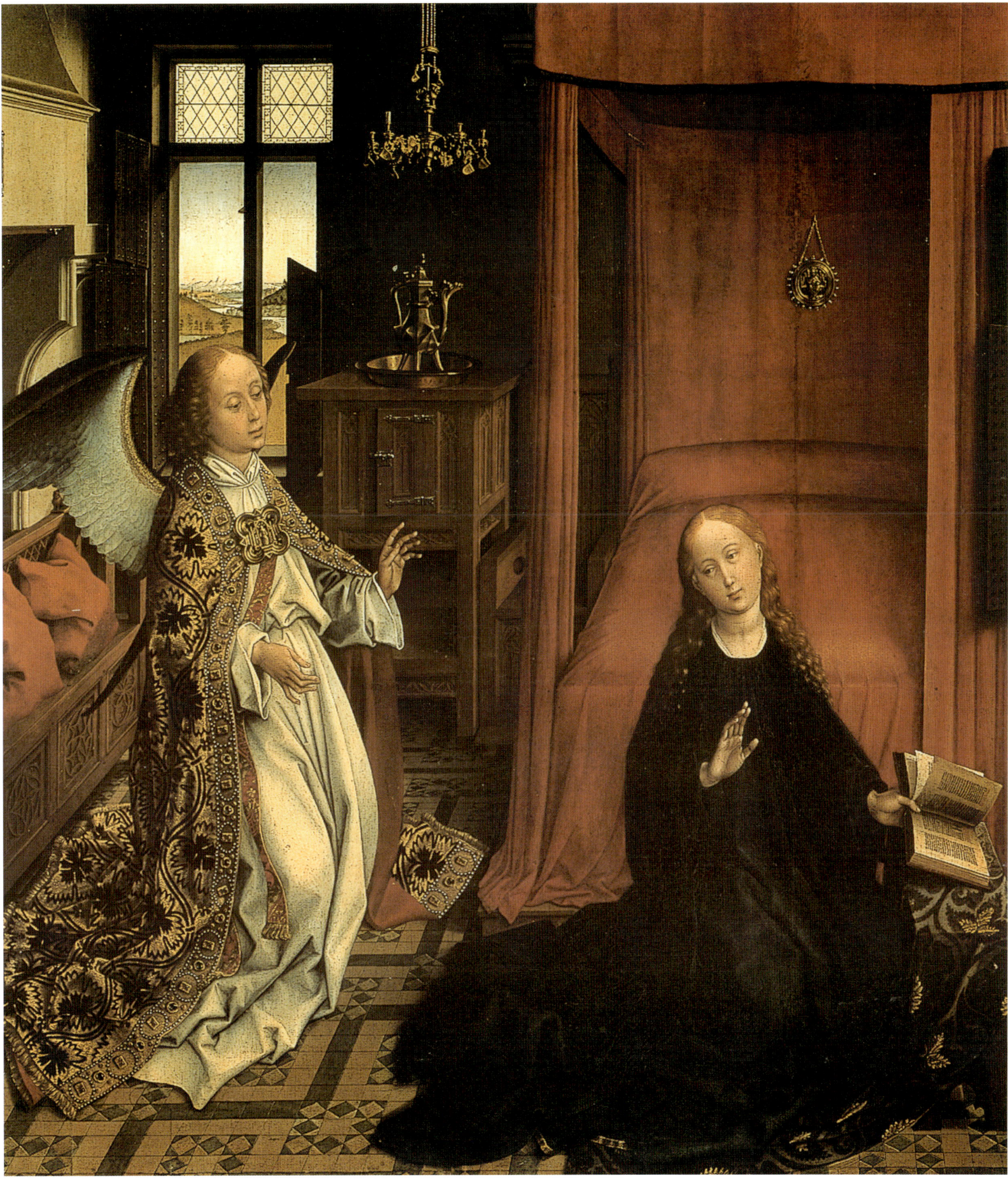

Annunciation
Central panel of the
Triptych of the
Annunciation
circa 1434,
oil on panel,
87 x 91.5 cm
Musée du Louvre, Paris

In this youthful work,
Van der Weyden reworks
ideas taken from Robert
Campin and Jan van
Eyck in light of a more
mature vision. The scene
takes place in the bed-
room of the Virgin,
which looks very much
like a middle-class
setting, as is the case
in the similar scenes
painted by his col-
leagues in the central
panel of the Mérode
Altarpiece (page 63)
and on the exterior of
the Ghent Altarpiece
(page 64). Van der
Weyden, however, reor-
ganizes the domestic
setting, arranging the
objects carefully to
keep them from inter-
fering with the figures.
The Madonna interrupts
her reading and seems
to turn toward the angel
with a natural and
spontaneous gesture.
The balance of the
composition is based
on the monumentality
of the figures, well
arranged within the
physical space of the
room and distinguished
by the sinuous shape
of their outlines. In his
magnificent brocade
cloak, the angel seems
to float above the
floor, as if the artist
wanted to emphasize
his divine nature.

**Polyptych of the
Last Judgment**
Internal panels
circa 1443–51,
oil on panel;
central panel, 212 x
101 cm, middle panels
130 x 73 cm, side pan-
els 130 x 46 cm, upper
panels 74 x 45 cm
Hôtel-Dieu, Beaune

This altarpiece, divided
in nine compartments,
is the largest work by
Van der Weyden, and
in terms of composi-
tional structure and the
accurate execution of
details, it competes with
the Ghent Altarpiece
by Jan van Eyck. The
celestial court seems to
float on the incandes-
cent cloud that culmi-
nates in the figure of
Christ the Judge. At
the center of the main
scene the Archangel
Michael weighs souls,
while the arisen men
and women, awaiting
the Last Judgment,
move around at his
feet. The composition
stands apart from the
overcrowded, halluci-
natory late medieval
versions of the same
subject. Paradise is
evoked simply with a
gilt portal, and hell is
nothing but a cliffside
licked by flames. With
an intellectual attitude
typical of nascent
humanism, the painter
does not indulge in
macabre details or in
the description of phys-
ical torments, and
emphasizes instead
the interior aspect,
the deep feelings, the
"movements of the
soul," of the figures.

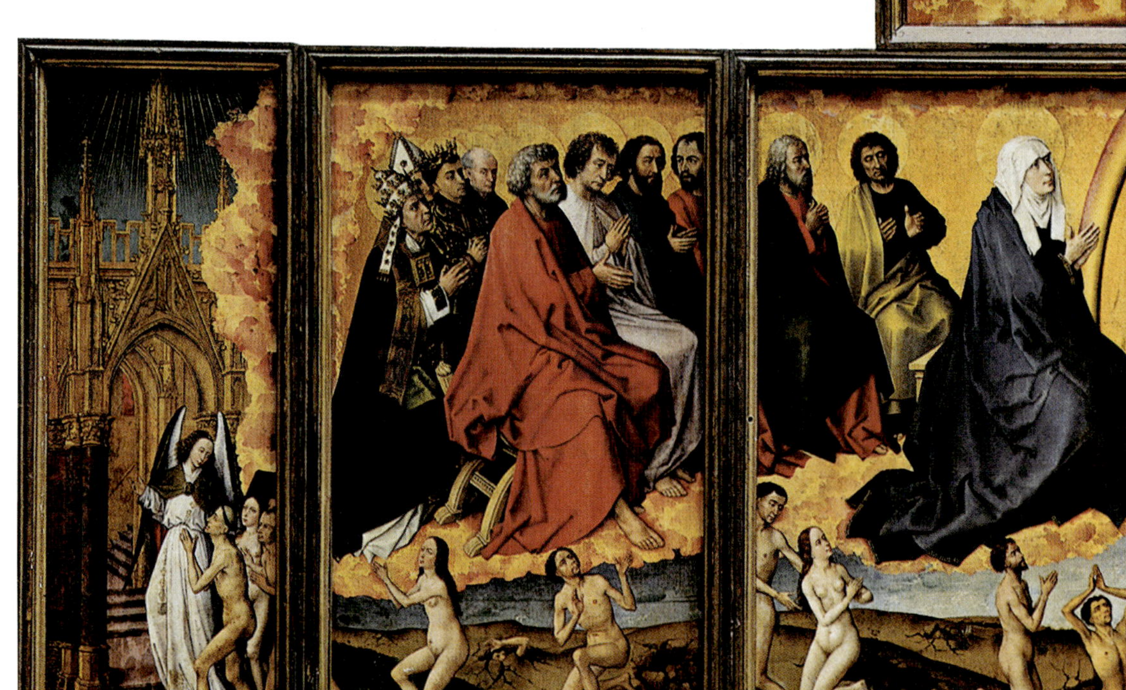

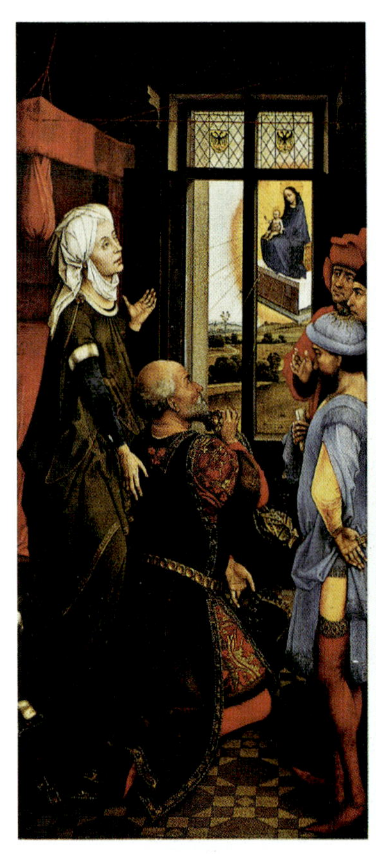

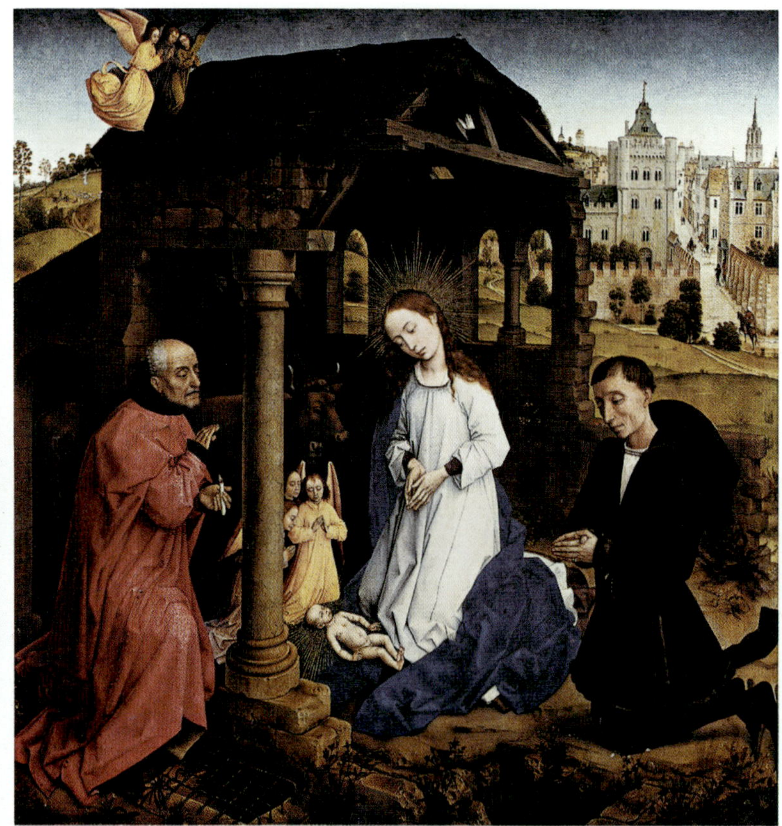

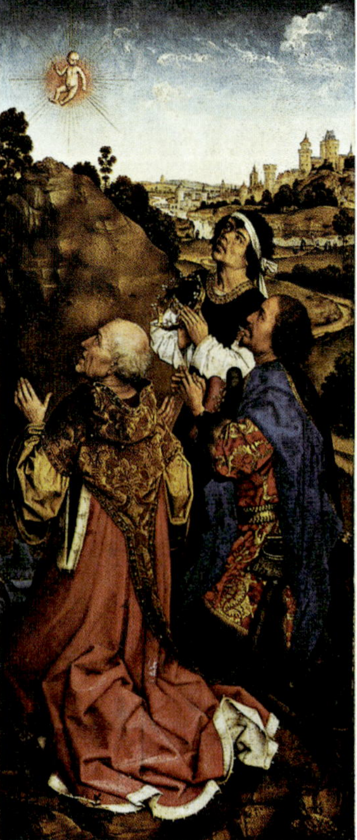

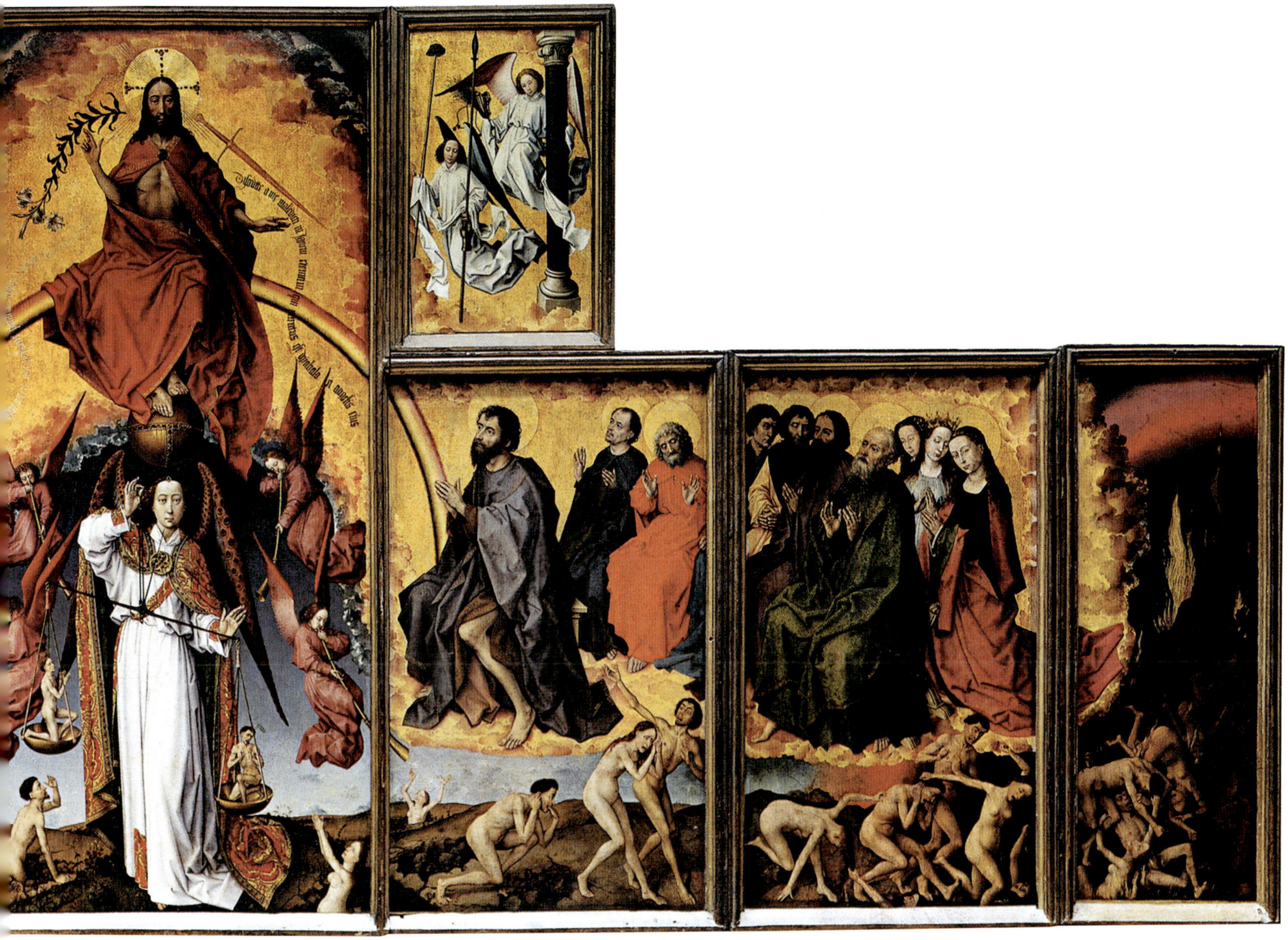

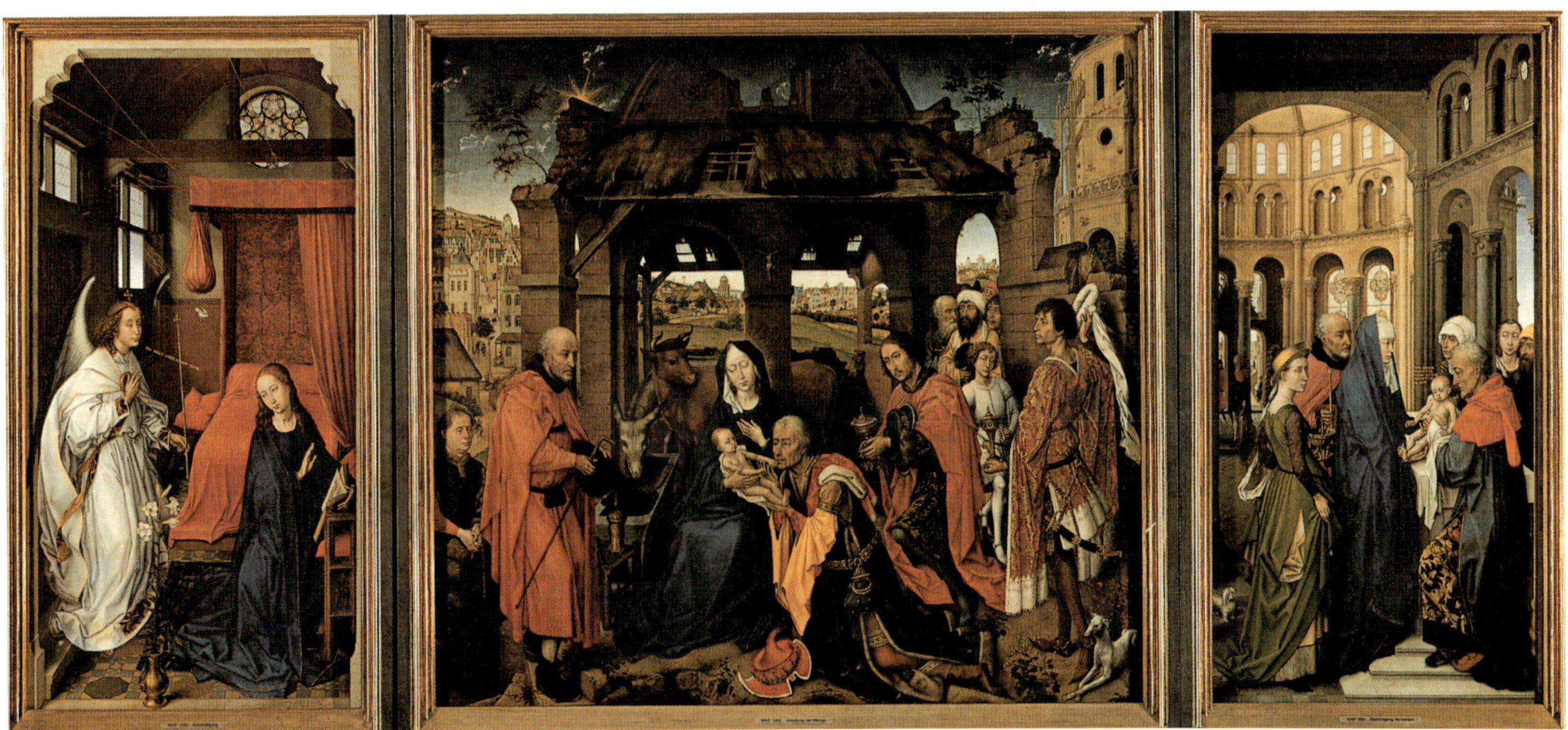

■ ROGIER VAN
DER WEYDEN
Bladelin Triptych
1445–48; oil on panel,
central panel 93.5 x
92 cm, side panels
93.5 x 41 cm
Gemäldegalerie, Berlin

The principal scene of
this triptych (*opposite
bottom*) is a Nativity
notable for its hushed
atmosphere. Mary and
the Child are doused in
a supernatural light,
while the sponsor,
Joseph, and a few small
angels assume serene
attitudes or move about
cautiously, as though to
avoid making a distur-
bance. The side panels
are more active, full of
symbolic meanings
related to the announce-
ment of the birth of
Jesus. To the left,
Emperor Augustus and
the Sibyl receive a
prophetic vision of the
Virgin; to the right, the
Magi see the figure of
the Child inside the star.

■ ROGIER VAN
DER WEYDEN
**Triptych of the
Adoration of the
Magi**
circa 1450–56, oil on
panel, central panel
139.5 x 152 cm, side
panels 139 x 72.5 cm
Alte Pinakothek,
Munich

All three panels present
festive moments, but
one already notes the
graphic and emotional
tension that was typical
of the painter's mature
works. The figures
become elongated and
more nervous, while
the faces express an
unmistakable agitation.

The mercantile cities of Flanders

A t the beginning of the fifteenth century, the vast cultural, geopolitical, and commercial area of Germany was fragmented. Nominally ruled by a centuries-old empire, it was in actuality divided up in numerous local entities, some of them enjoying great autonomy, such as the firm alliance of the Hanseatic League along the shores of the Baltic Sea. Because of this situation, and also because of the absence of a true "capital" city, several cities assumed important political, religious, and economic roles. Many different reasons were behind the growth of these numerous centers of power. The presence of a powerful bishop, the discovery and exploitation of mines, certain imperial rights, a favorable position along commercial routes, even some singular circumstance of historical events could raise a town or city to prominence. Constance and Basel, for example, became diplomatic centers at the European level because they had been sites of the two important church councils (in 1414–18 and 1431–49, respectively) that were held to repair the Great Schism and overcome the profound crisis in the role of the pope.

in German art history, *Spätgotik* ("late Gothic"), is apparently a literal translation, but it is applied to the last expressions of the style, those dating to the threshold of the sixteenth century. In the German interpretation of the International Gothic in sculpture and painting and also in illuminated manuscripts, the style includes the appearance of delicate, sinuous female figures usually immersed in the fabulous setting of a woodland or garden where the most various and marvelous adventures take place. Along the banks of the Rhine, from Lake Constance to Basel and then, following the course of the great river, to Alsace and the Black Forest, an enchanted and enchanting style came into being, a sweet and delicate art that was quite unusual for German art, which usually tends toward dramatic expressive effects.

The most important center of this "soft" style was the great and splendid city of Cologne, where a very active patrician class and dynamic religious patrons made possible the existence of numerous, thriving workshops that were in open communication with other artistic centers. The

Reliquary bust of Charlemagne, 1349; Treasury of the Cathedral, Aachen

Along the waters

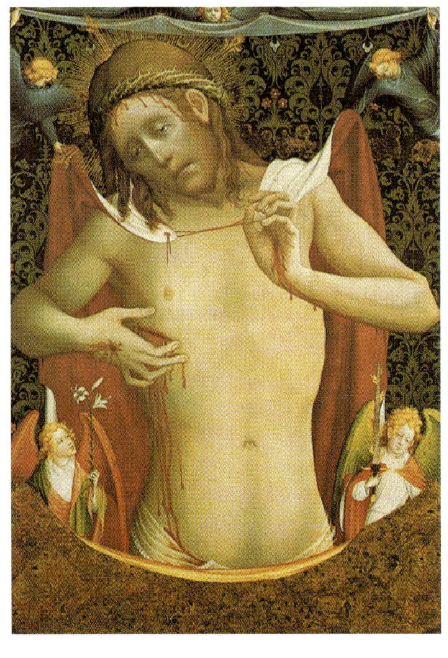

Master Francke, *Vir Dolorum (Man of Sorrows)*, 1435, panel; Kunsthalle, Hamburg

Because of this situation, fifteenth-century German art embraces a multiplicity of phenomena and tendencies that cannot always be summarized under common headings. Even so, this very polycentrism resulted in fascinating phenomena. In general, the most vital area of the entire region was the Upper Rhine, which was influenced by the nearby Franco-Flemish regions; but many of the most innovative creations came from the outer reaches of the empire, such as Bohemia and the Tyrol. In the first thirty years of the fifteenth century the style of Gothic known as International spread in Germany. However, a small linguistic distinction must be made. In the history of Italian art, "late Gothic" is applied to art of the first decades of the fifteenth century; the corresponding term

church of St. Columba in Cologne held one of the most important triptychs by Rogier van der Weyden, with the *Adoration of the Magi*, today in Munich, as its central panel. Even in an advanced center like Cologne, however, artists were ranked at the social level of "specialized artisans." Only a relatively small number of well defined historical identities is known, and many artists are known by conventional names based on their works. Even so, such artists are recognizable personalities. There is, for example, the Master of Saint Veronica, whose works blend a search for idealization with intense and sympathetic religious feelings veined with lyricism. This line of development reached its most distinctive expression in the creation of many panel paintings with a dreamy tone in which the Virgin sits in a flower garden, a genre in which Stefan Lochner, perhaps the greatest German painter before Dürer, distinguished himself. The episodes and figures of sacred history are presented as the heroes of a poetic and gentle legend that has as its final goal the garden of paradise, the song of angels, the sweetness of eternal smiles.

Trained on the banks of Lake Constance, in the elegant climate of courtly art of the Upper Rhine, Lochner traveled north along the course of

Along the waters of "Father Rhine"

the river and, making contacts as he went with the various arts schools of Alsace, Burgundy, and Flanders, finally set himself up in Cologne during the 1430s. Lochner reveals such an up-to-date awareness of developments in spatial representation that some have made out a possible contact with the Italian painting of the time, in particular with Fra Angelico. For example, the *Annunciation* he painted on the side wings of the polyptych in the cathedral of Cologne presents monumental figures placed in the correctly measured space of a domestic setting, with furnishings set in corners to exalt the scene's three dimensionality; in general, however, he preferred to align his fabulous figures against compact gilt backgrounds or in flowering gardens. Lochner died, still young, in the plague of 1451. His career reveals how the echoes of courtly culture were progressively toned down by a sincere interest in nature and the sense of reality.

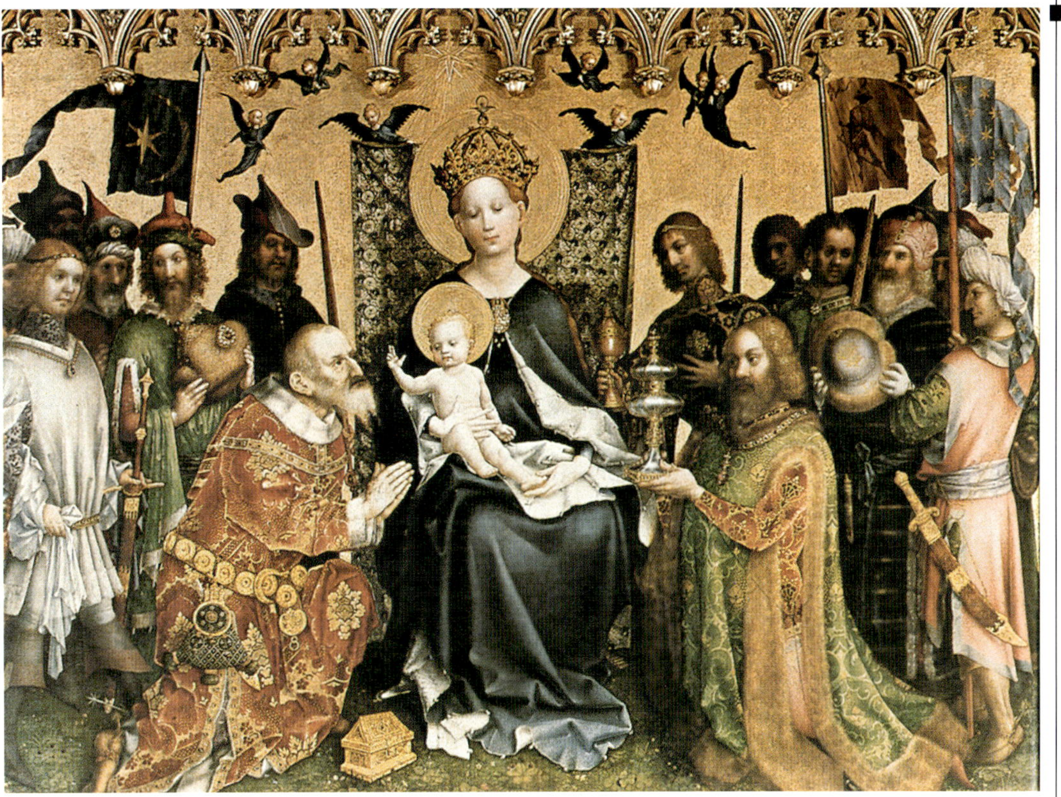

Stefan Lochner, *Adoration of the Magi*, central panel of the Altarpiece of the Patron Saints, 1440–45; Cathedral, Cologne

of "Father Rhine"

Around the middle of the century a generation of artists animated by a new sensibility toward the surrounding world appeared on the scene. Thanks also to influences from Flanders and Burgundy, the luxurious aristocratic scenes gave way to a more earthy and material vision of reality, with solid, concrete figures inserted in more coherent spatial settings in which three-dimensional perspective was beginning to make itself felt.

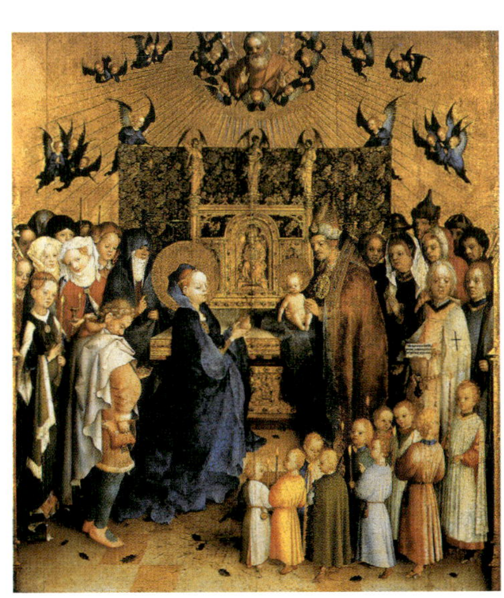

Konrad Witz, one of the great innovators in painting north of the Alps, markedly distanced himself from the lyrical, languid tones of the preceding generation of German painters, marking the passage toward painting of severe plastic energy and strong naturalism. Originally from a town in Swabia, Witz became a member of the painters' guild in Basel in 1434 and the next year was granted citizenship in that city. In the cosmopolitan climate of the city, where a church council was then being held to repair the Schism, he revealed his original personality, supported by a lively talent and a thoroughly worldly vision of reality. The clarity of light he uses, as well as his attention to detail, reveals the influence of works by contemporary Flemish artists; but in the powerful corporal reality of his figures Witz reveals knowledge of Burgundian sculpture, in particular that of Claus Sluter. Witz marks a radical change in German painting at the middle of the fifteenth century: the delicate fables of the courtly works give way to a solid, direct sense of nature, at the same time also offering scenes that can be deeply moving. The religious image moves from the rarefied atmosphere of the fable to plunge into the midst of human history and daily reality. Furthermore, the plastic, at times even brutal energy of Witz's figures constitutes an important precedent for the imminent arrival of the period of the great carved wooden altarpieces.

Stefan Lochner, *Presentation of Christ in the Temple*, 1447; Hessisches Landesmuseum, Darmstadt

Matchless example of
the "tender style," the
highly particular
interpretation of late
Gothic motifs in the
artistic centers of the
Rhineland, this dreamy
masterpiece is a
compendium of the
iconographic motifs
dear to the art of the
early fifteenth century.
The scene takes place
inside the *hortus
conclusus*, the flower-
ing garden enclosed by
a wall; all of the spring
flowers and fruit,
presented with the pre-
cision of an illuminated
herbal, are meant to
be interpreted symboli-
cally as emblems of the
virtues of the Virgin,
much like the pure
water of the fount into
which a saint dips a
golden ladle. The anony-
mous painter was not
overly concerned with

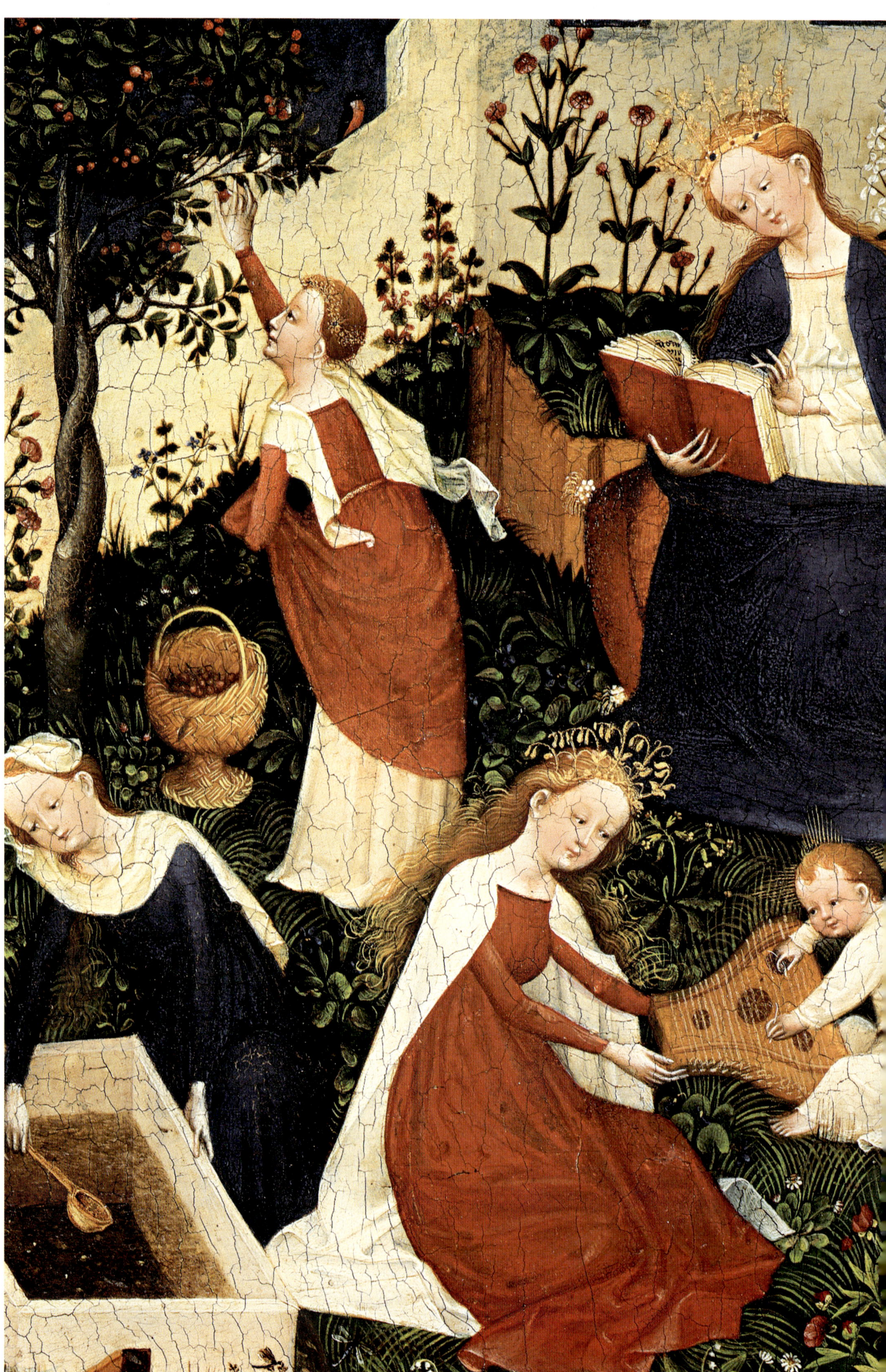

Along the waters of "Father Rhine"

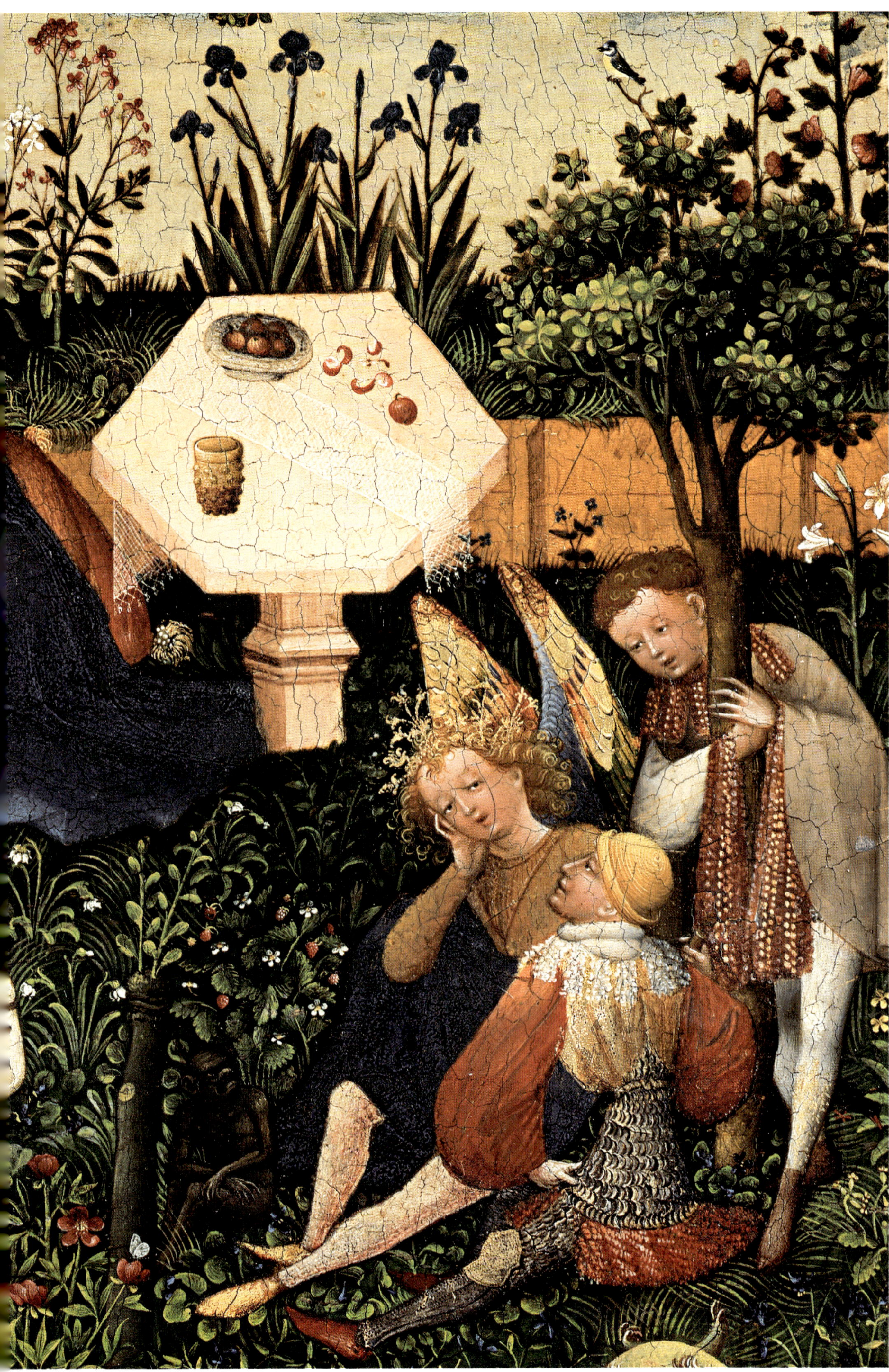

the correct presenta-
tion of perspective; the
hexagonal table beside
the Virgin Mary, for
example, seems to be
tilted forward, and all
the natural elements
are arranged in over-
lapping rows, similar
to the style character-
istic of tapestries. The
Madonna, although
wearing a crown, is
seated on a cushion
set directly on the
grass. This particular
position, common in
late Gothic art through-
out Europe, is called
the "Madonna of humil-
ity" to distinguish her
from the *Maestà*, or
"Madonna in majesty,"
which refers instead to
the Madonna seated
on a chair or throne.
Many elements in this
fabulous scene have
an intense poetry,
some because they
are presented with
miniaturistic precision,
others because of the
variety of situations
presented or the roles
played by the figures.
At the center, for
example, St. Cecilia
(patron saint of
musicians) helps the
Child play a zither.

Along the waters of "Father Rhine"

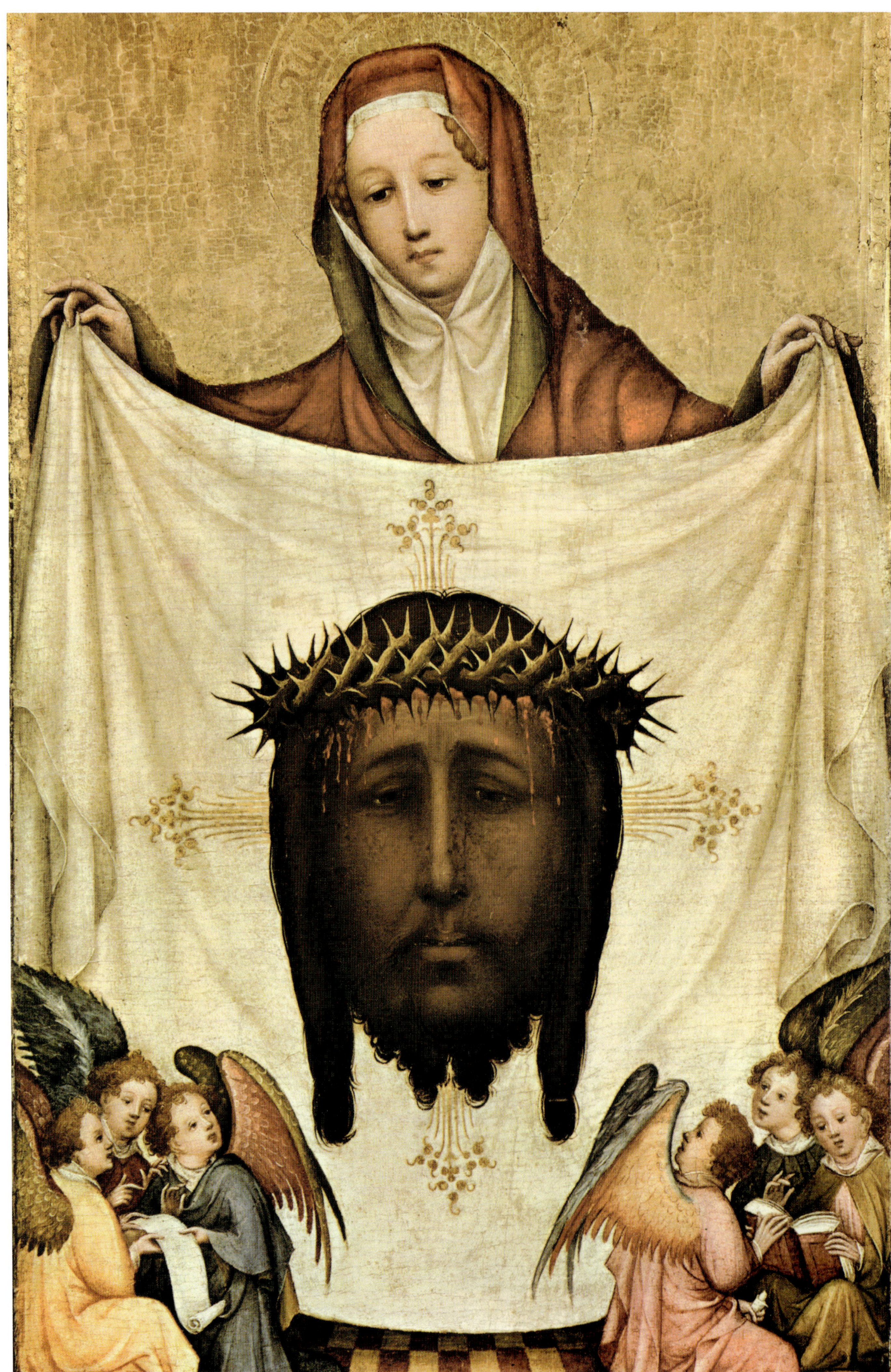

**St. Veronica with the
Sudarium of Christ**
circa 1420, panel,
78 x 48 cm
Alte Pinakothek,
Munich

An anonymous but
important artist is
named for this work,
a devotional panel
that greatly impressed
Goethe. Masters identi-
fied by the title of
their most famous work
are not at all rare in the
art of northern Europe,
where such otherwise
anonymous artists
show up throughout
the entire fifteenth
century, their charac-
ters recognized on the
basis of technical and
stylistic peculiarities
that are used to estab-
lish the dating of their
works as well as their
attribution. In this case
the work is a panel with
a simple but highly
effective layout, its
power based on the
psychological and emo-
tional responses to the
apparition of the face
of Christ and also on
the saint's humble atti-
tude, a contrast that
gives the whole a strong
lyrical sense. The sub-
tle tones of the colors,
the delicacy of the
contours, and the
preference for curving
lines strongly indicate
an artist of the early
fifteenth-century
Rhine school.

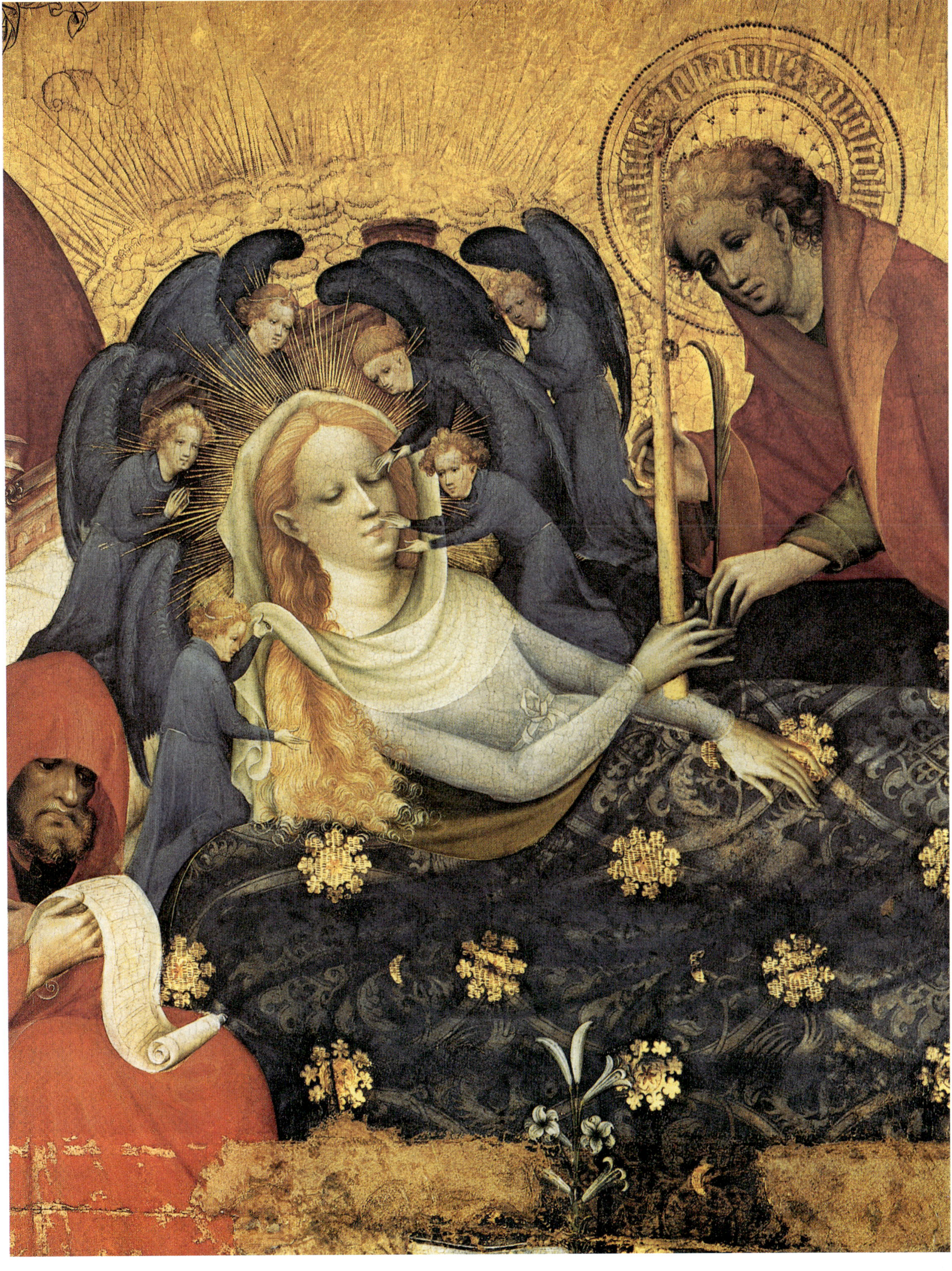

Conrad von Soest
Death of the Virgin
Detail of the Dortmund
Altarpiece with Stories
of the Virgin,
circa 1420, panel
Marienkirche,
Dortmund

An endearing aspect of
early fifteenth-century
Rhine art is the metic-
ulous, poetic, highly
delicate activity of
angels. In this case,
it is a peculiar local
interpretation of
Burgundian realism, a
style of which Conrad
von Soest was probably
personally aware. He
was originally from
Westphalia, but over
the course of his career
his works reveal a
stylistic evolution obvi-
ously related to his
personal interpretation
of Burgundian motifs.
The altar dedicated
to the Virgin, painted
for the confraternity
of the Marienkirche in
Dortmund, did not
survive intact, but it
is a work of great
fascination, a touching
image from German
painting of the early
fifteenth century.

Central panel of an altar in the parochial church of St. Lawrence in Cologne, the painting repeats the medieval iconography of the Last Judgment, enriching it with new motifs, based more on the theme of salvation than on that of the punishment of sins. At the center appears Jesus Christ seated atop two rainbows, symbol of the covenant between God and man. Beside him, the monumental figures of the Virgin and St. John intercede in favor of humanity. In the lively scene below, angels and demons fight to separate the souls of the damned from those admitted to paradise. In the grim confusion of hell, Lochner presents the dramatic struggle between diabolical monstrous beings and men of every rung of the social ladder, including a pope. On the opposite side there is the luminous scene of the crowd of the saved waiting to enter the kingdom of the heavens by way of a large portal, assisted by angels and welcomed on the threshold by a very busy St. Peter.

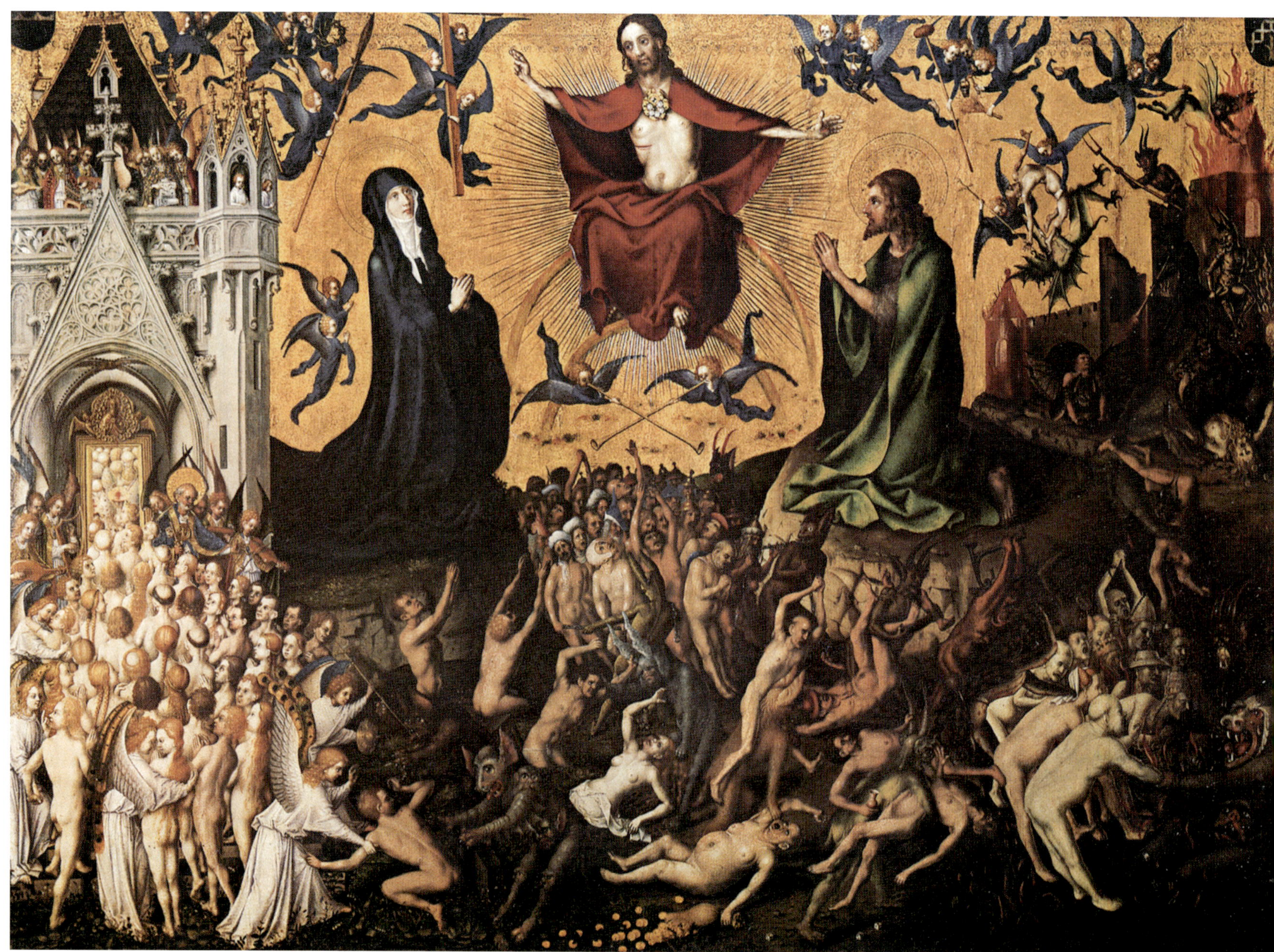

Along the waters of "Father Rhine"

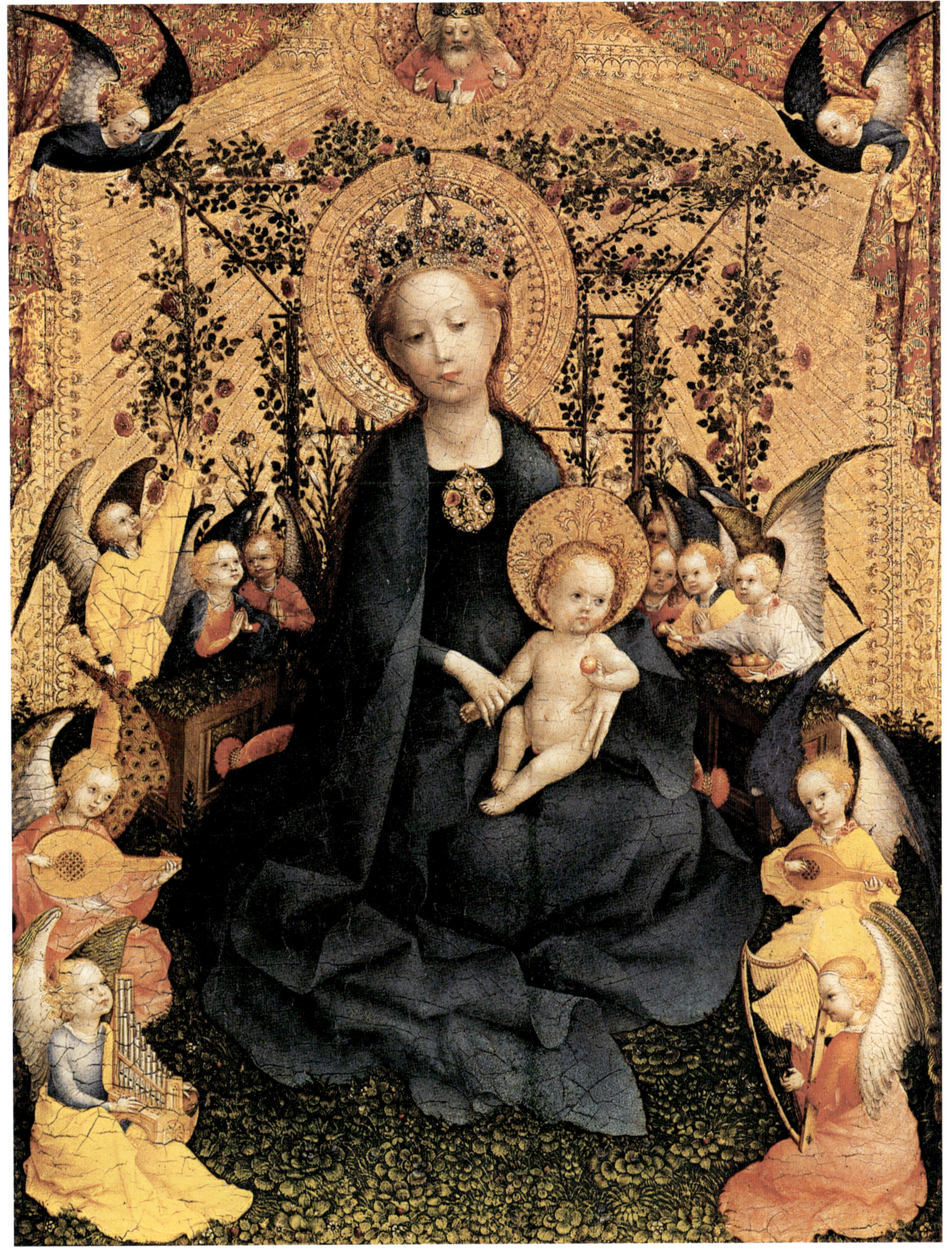

With the ever-present angels of lapis-lazuli blue, Lochner applied equal grace to majestic compositions for altars and to small panels made for domestic worship, like this delightful *Madonna of the Rose Bush*. The symbolic allusions *(Rosa Mystica* is an attribute of Mary, and the white lilies refer to purity) create a scene of amiable delicacy. In accordance with the typology of the *Madonna dell'umilità* (the "Madonna of humility"), the Virgin is seated on a cushion placed in the middle of a flowering meadow. Fresh red strawberries grow in the grass. There are four musician angels, while another seven, behind the Madonna, gather roses and apples. Above, two blue angels hold up an ornate brocade tent, almost the theater curtain for this celestial vision. Lochner varies the size of the figures notably: directly above the Virgin, in a somewhat reduced size, are the dove of the Holy Spirit and God the Father.

During the fifteenth century, the western and southern regions of Germany were enriched by notable artistic personalities. The large city of Cologne, on the banks of the Rhine, was the most lively artistic center. The anonymous Master of the Life of the Virgin is named for a cycle of panels originally dedicated to the church of St. Ursula in Cologne. Each of the scenes is the occasion for a realistic description of rooms, clothes, and objects; each is thus a small world presented with Flemish precision (making critics imagine that the artist trained in the circle of Rogier van der Weyden or Dieric Bouts), but with the typical amiability of the "sweet style" of the Rhine.

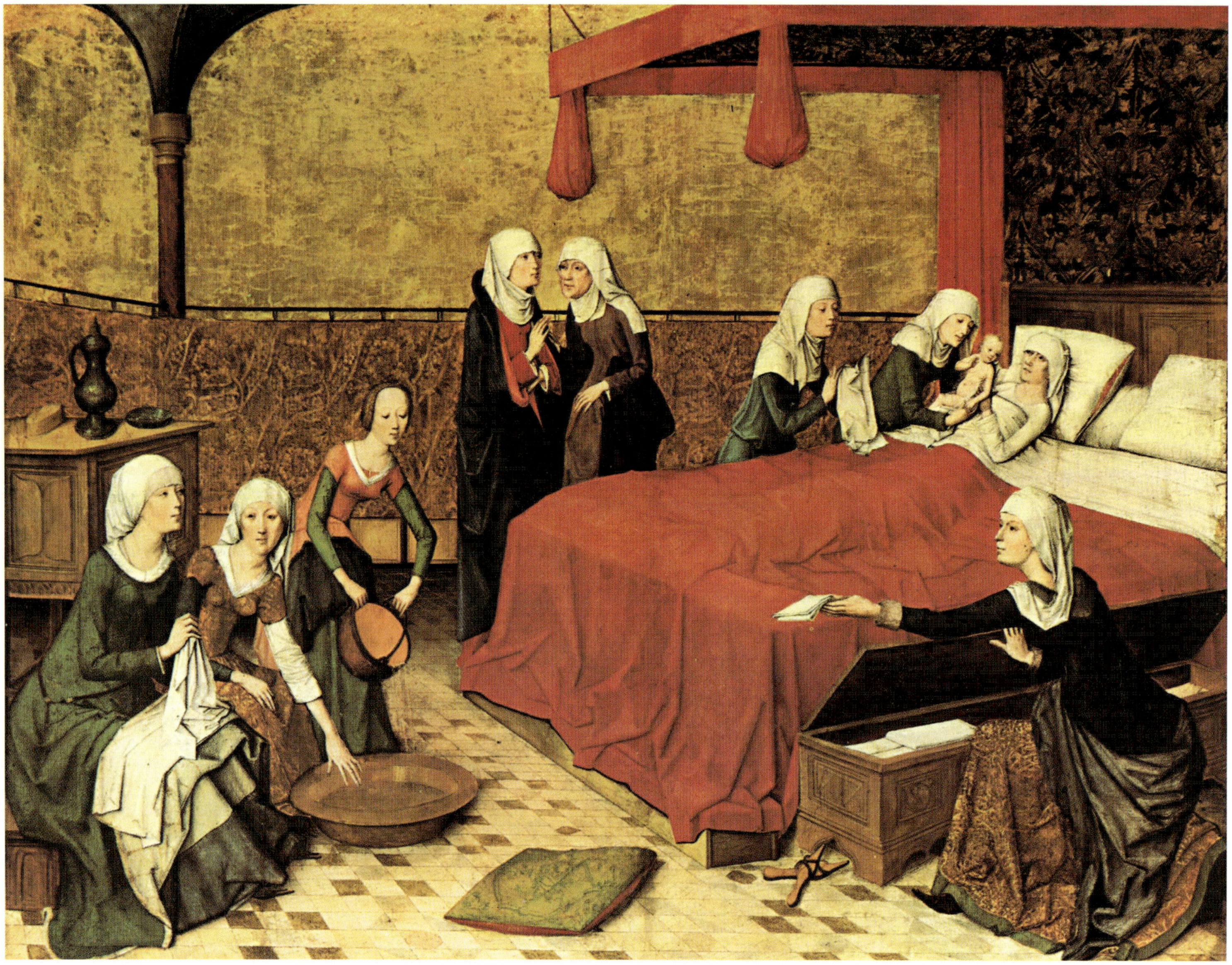

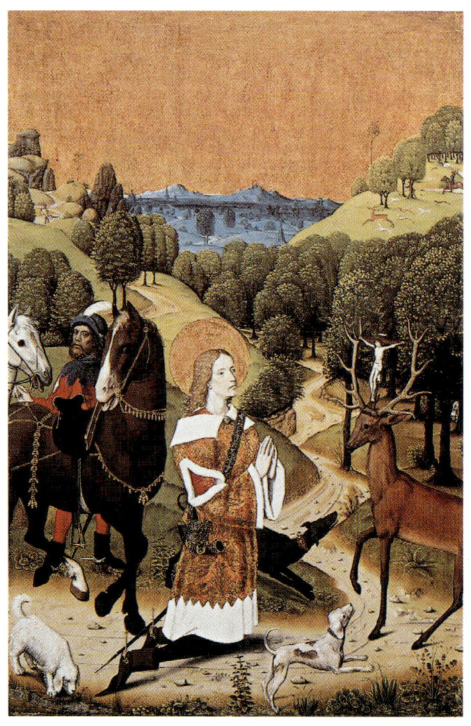

Along the waters of "Father Rhine"

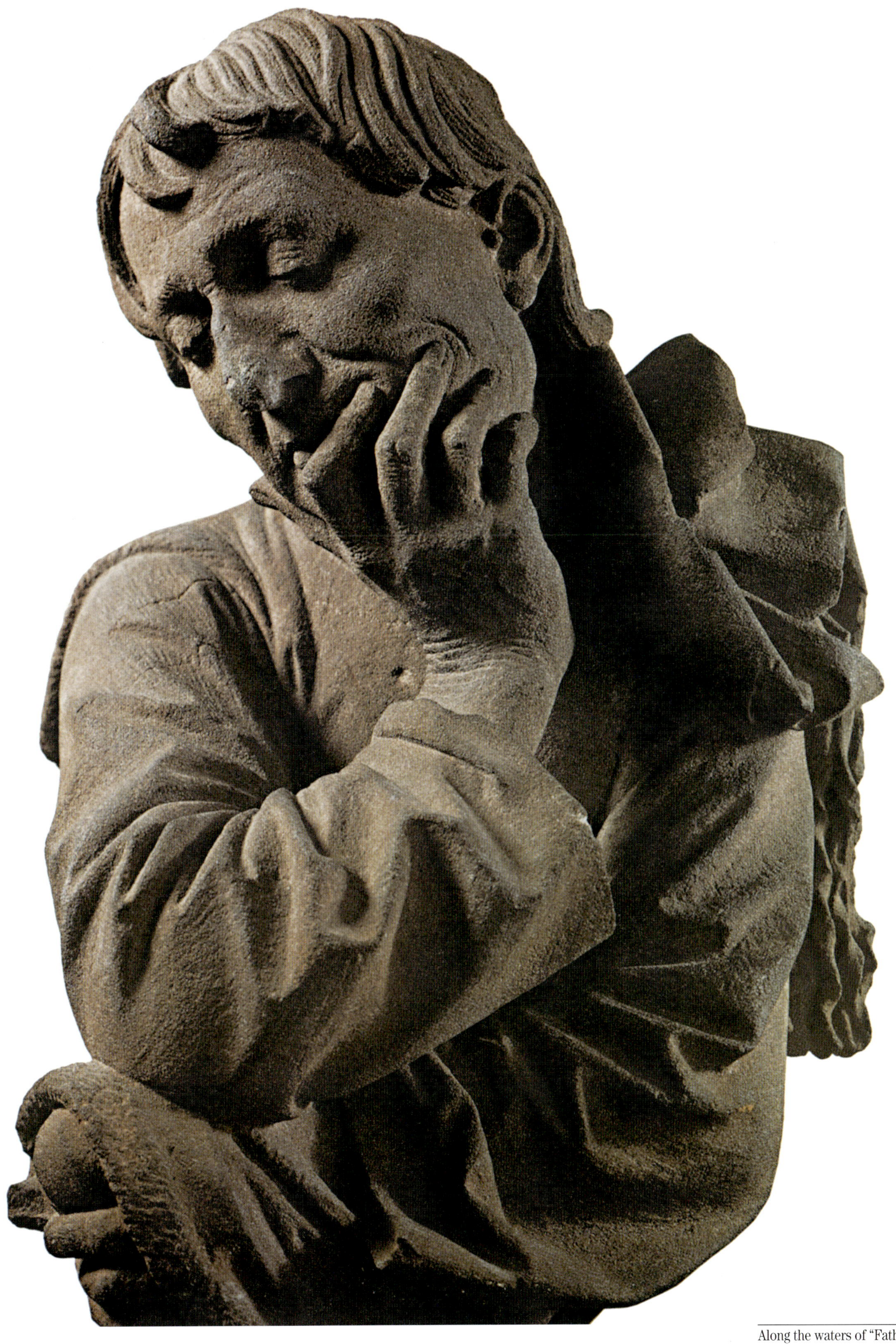

The enormous worksite of the cathedral of Strasbourg reached the height of its activity during the fifteenth century. In 1439, the peak of the tower reached 142 meters in height, becoming the tallest in Gothic Europe. Opened in 1176, the worksite was officially closed only in 1778, becoming, over the centuries, an international point of encounter and comparison. Throughout the entire fifteenth century German, French, Swiss and also Dutch and Italian artists were kept busy on the site of the enormous collective undertaking, a daring project directed beyond the human dimension. Here was the exact antithesis of the sober, measured, crystal clear, "signed by the artist" architecture being built in Florence by Filippo Brunelleschi during the same years. Among the works of art made to decorate the exterior of the cathedral (much of them today kept in the contiguous museum), the male busts by Nicolaus Gerhaert provide the fascinating testimony of an artist fascinated by human features and psychology.

Along the waters of "Father Rhine"

The St. Peter Altarpiece, commissioned by the bishop of Geneva François de Mies, is the most integral work by Konrad Witz, one of the great innovators in painting north of the Alps. Rooted in the intense social life of Basel, Witz distanced himself sharply from the dreamy lyricism of the "tender style" of his German colleagues. With a sure sense of volume, emphasized by the use of angular objects, architecture, and figures, he gave his images the sense of robust reliefs, even doing without expressions of dynamism and action. The first of these two panels is a good example. Despite the fact that the event shown is full of tension and excitement, the drama is dulled in a static, frozen vision. In the *Adoration of the Magi,* the luminous and chromatic effects concur in giving plasticity to the figures and accentuate their physical presence, as noted in the extraordinary detail of the shadow of the Madonna and Child cast on the corner of the house.

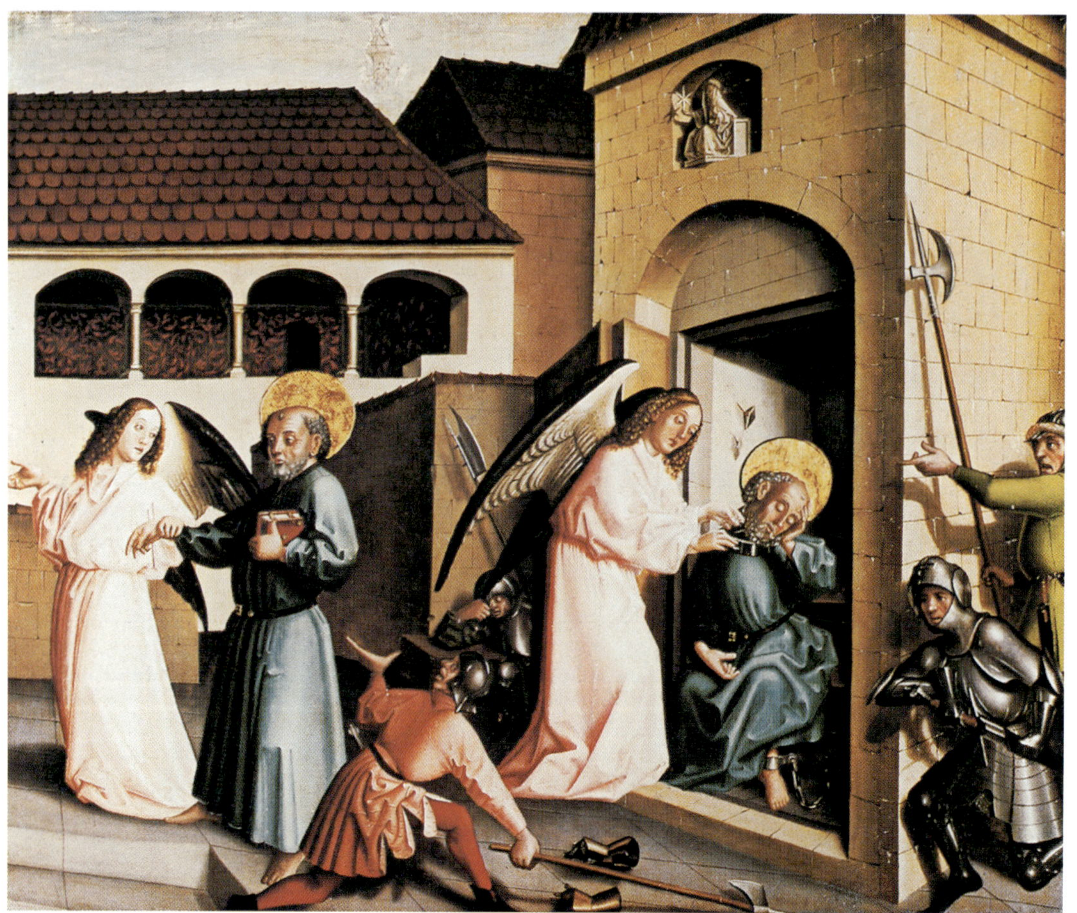

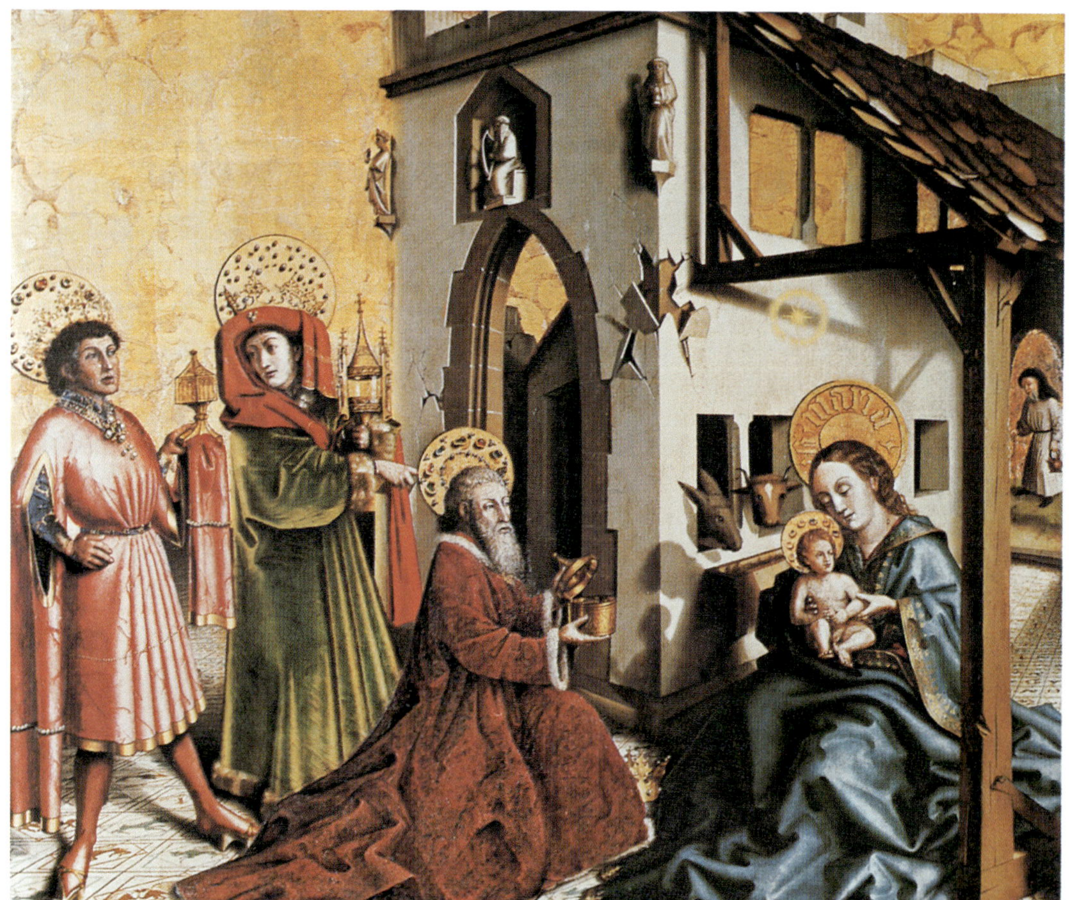

Along the waters of "Father Rhine"

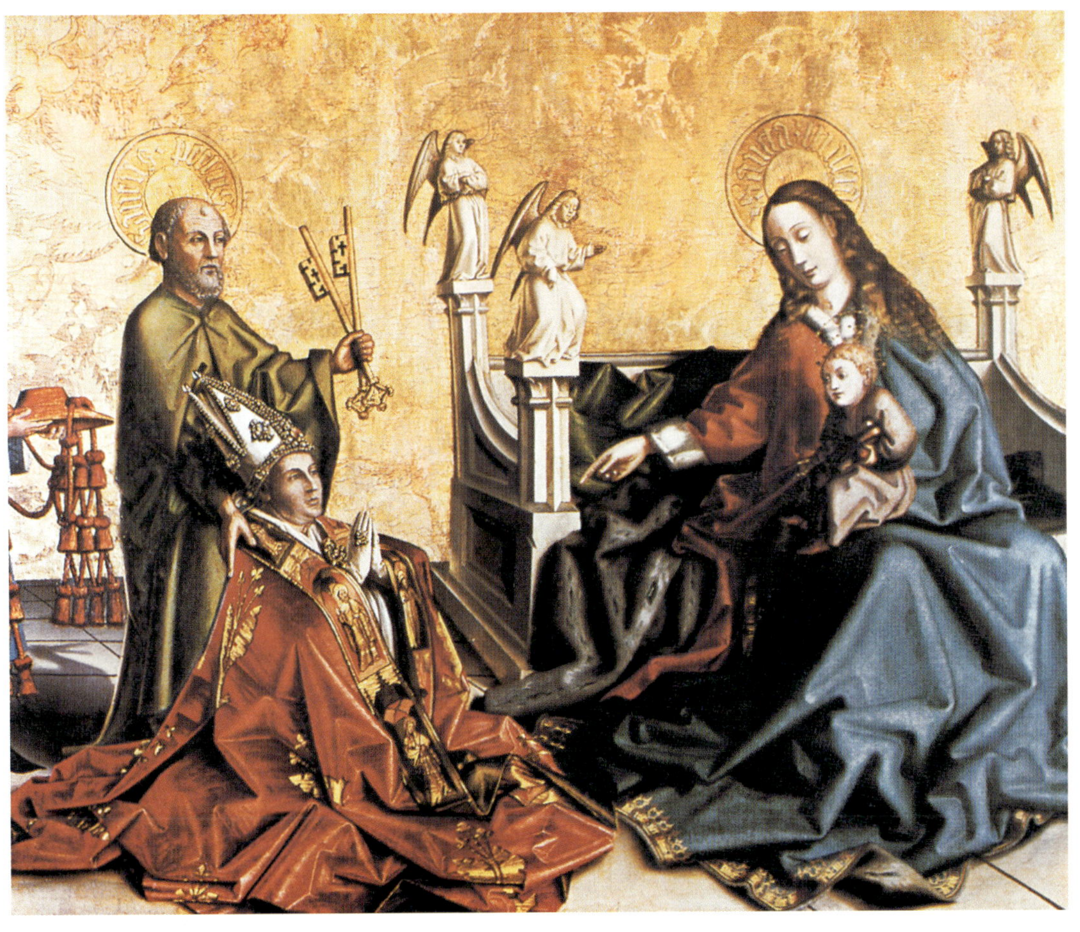

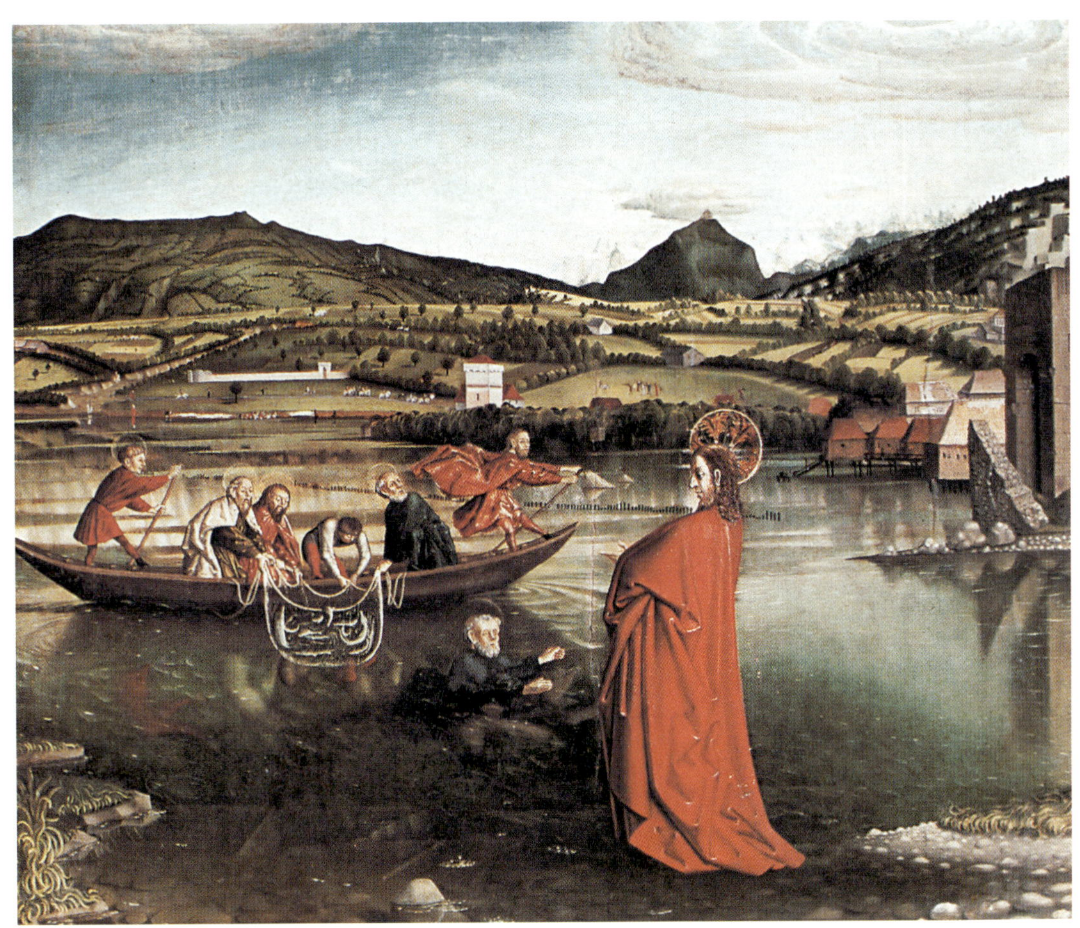

Along the waters of "Father Rhine"

MASTER OF THE SAINT
BARTHOLOMEW ALTAR
**Crucifixion Altarpiece:
external panels with
Saints Peter and Paul
and the Annunciation**
panels, 107 x 34 cm
each
Internal panels with
the Crucifixion between
Saints John the Baptist
and Cecilia and Alexis
and Agnes
panels; central panel
107 x 80 cm, side
panels 107 x 34 cm
circa 1500,
Wallraf-Richartz
Museum, Cologne

The mystery that still
surrounds the identity
of the artist does not
diminish his greatness,
a fascinating figure who
forms a link between
the Rhine tradition and
the Flemish figurative
culture near the close
of the fifteenth cen-
tury. Tied to the city
of Cologne and to the
lawyer Peter Rinck,
who commissioned this
work, the artist was so
active with the mona-
stery of the charter-
house of Cologne that
some art historians
have hypothesized
that he was himself a
Carthusian monk. At
his ease in works of
medium to small format
as well as with altar-
pieces, this anonymous
but easily recognizable
master possessed a

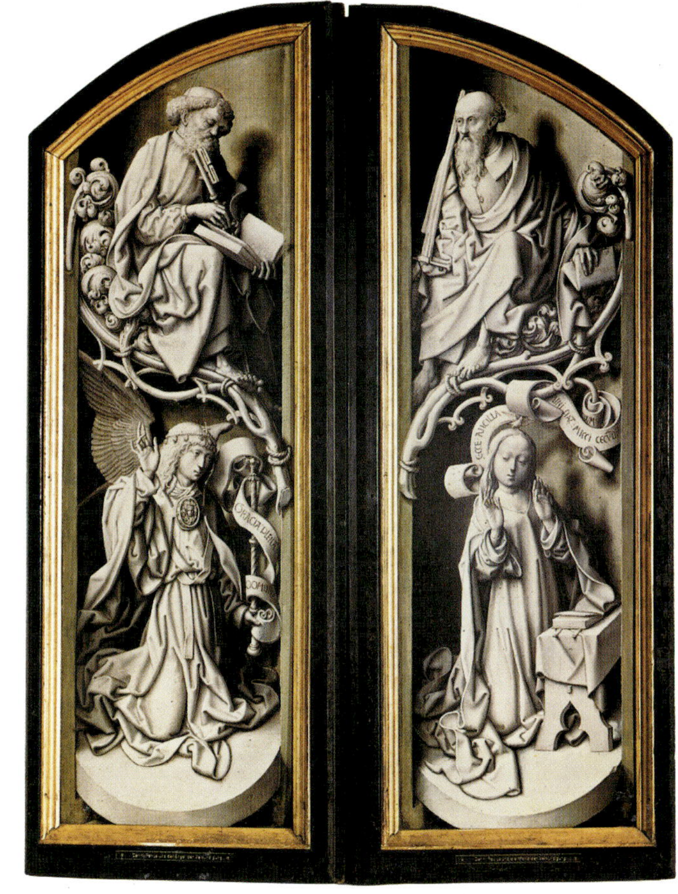

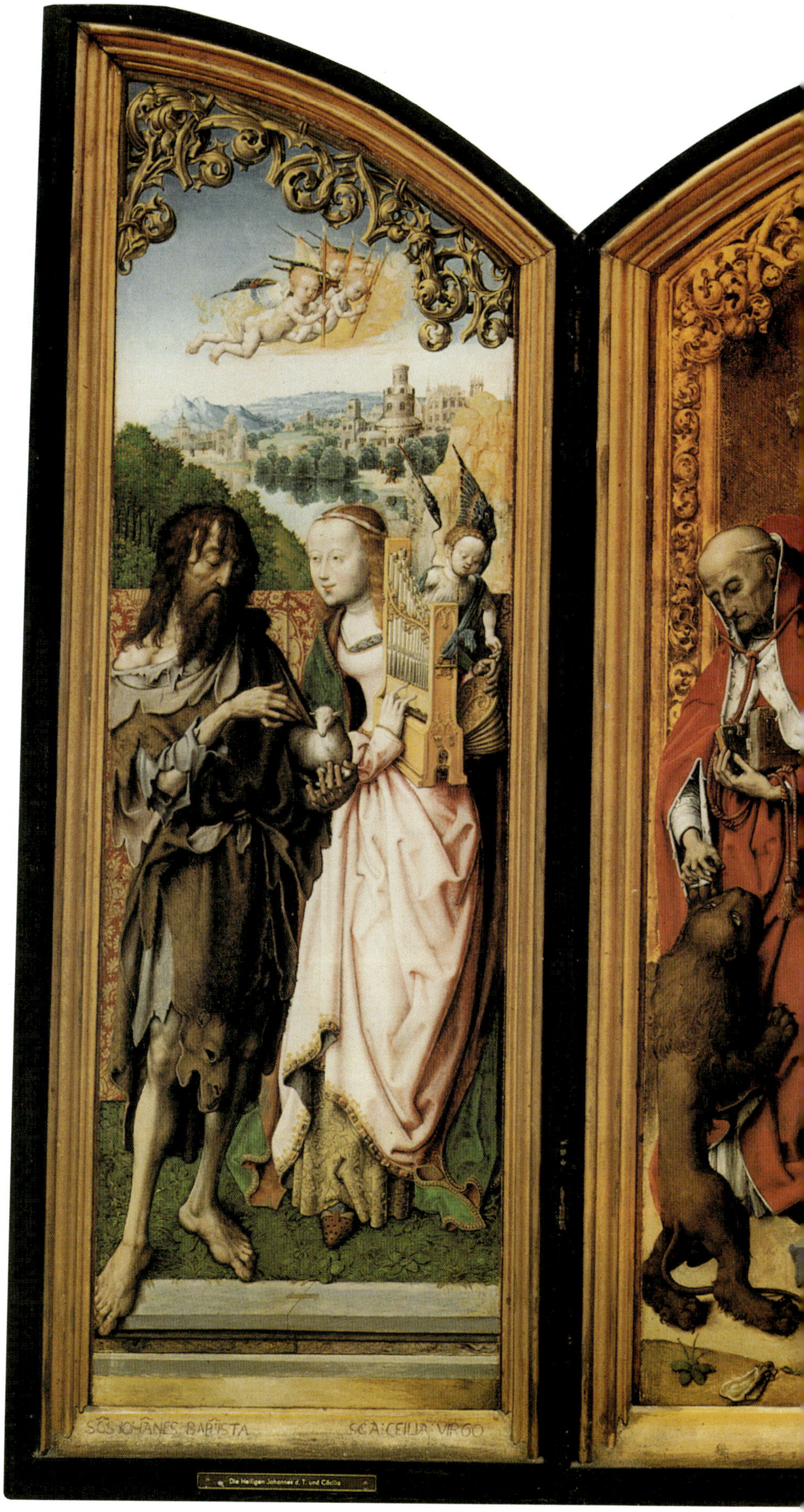

Along the waters of "Father Rhine"

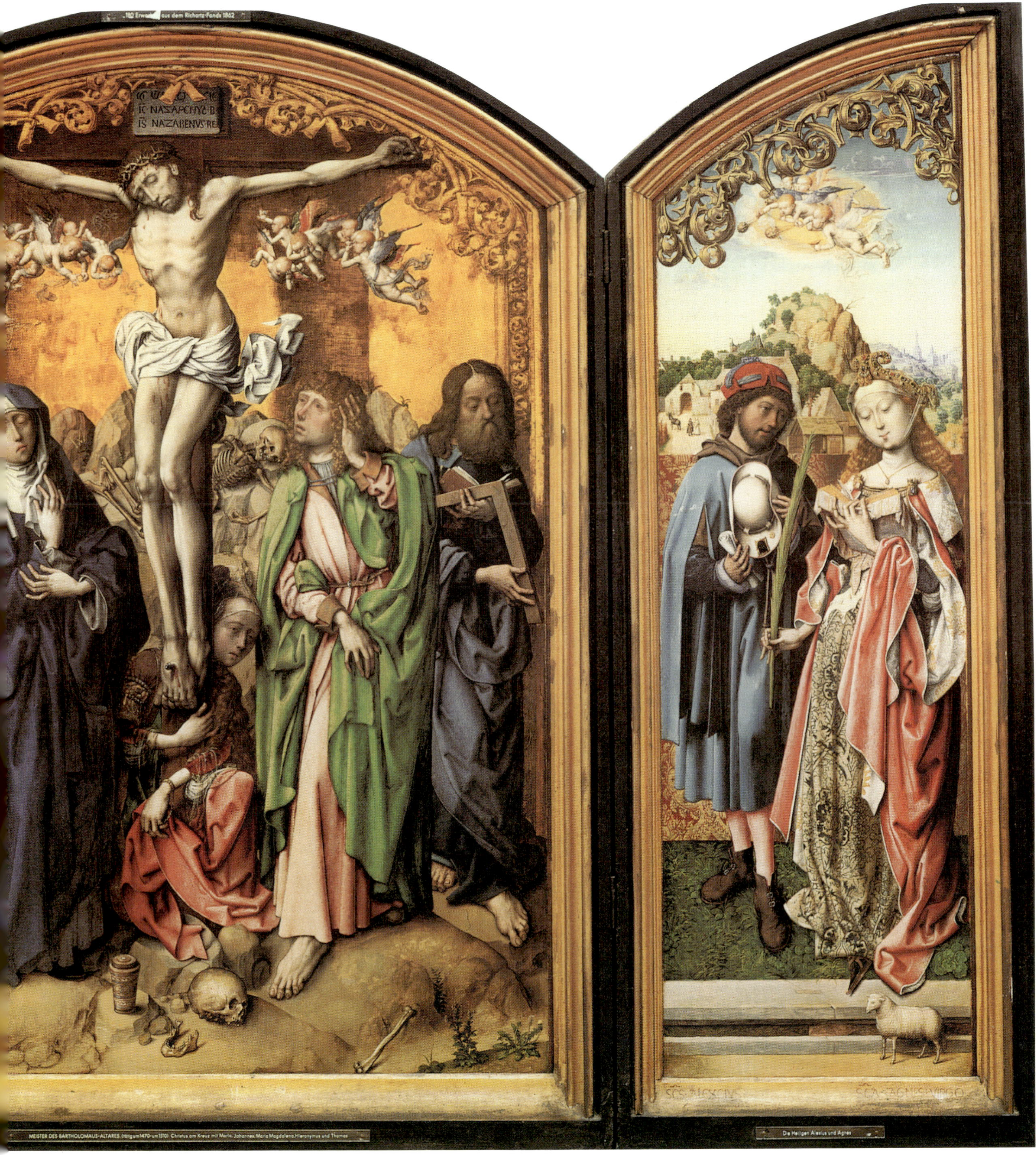

fluid and vigorous style with which he sought to create works of great breadth. Although his compositions sometimes have a monumental layout, achieved through the use of perspective skills unknown to his predecessors, they are still tied to the northern tradition in their precise rendering of details and precious materials, such as fabrics and jewels, along with their deeply felt religious sensibility. In the Crucifixion Altarpiece (a medium-size triptych, just over one meter high), the realism and the rendering of details give dramatic intensity to the Crucifixion that is visible when the side wings are opened. The unknown artist's spatial and plastic sensibility are particularly clear in the scenes painted in grisaille on the outer doors of the altar. The figures stand out against the neutral background, their bodies modeled by the sharp light, which chisels their profiles and makes them emerge from the niche almost as though they were true statues, to the point of creating, using purely pictorial means, the illusion of a sculpted altar.

By then, the popes had been gone for many years. All that remained in the palace at Avignon were frescoes, memories, harsh words and regrets, vain wishes. The kings of France, busy with that never-ending war against the English, kept moving their court in the search for a place with tranquility. Thus was Provence rejuvenated to become a splendid artistic center, source of works of art and figurative models. The old pilgrimage routes had long since become well-worn commercial roadways, and these, together with easy access to the traffic in trade goods and culture along the Mediterranean, made Avignon and the other cities of Provence centers in a dense network of relationships and intersections; from the Côte d'Azur to the Rhone valley, the French Midi experienced a splendid artistic season. The nearness of Burgundy justified the prevalent Flemish matrix, as borne out by the arrival in the region of the Master of the Aix Annunciation, perhaps identifiable as

from within which independent interpretations of established models began to take shape. The presence of colossal works of painting and sculpture can be a surprise for the visitor to Spanish cathedrals: polyptychs made of numerous overlapping levels, articulated and majestic, occupy the altars and are tall enough to cover the architecture. The making of these retables flourished during a lively historical and artistic period in Spain, the same years in which that country was moving toward territorial and religious reunification, achieved near the very end of the century by the "Catholic kings" Ferdinand of Aragon and Isabella of Castile. The Spanish retables show a local reading, often full of great originality, of various artistic influences. The presence of Jan van Eyck in Spain in 1428 indicates that attention was being paid to Flemish painting, but there was no lack of contacts with the Italian treatment of space, most of all along the Mediterranean routes leading to Naples. Furthermore, many of the leading Spanish painters were tireless travelers. The Catalan Jaime Baço (Jacomart) visited Naples and Rome; the Andalusian Bartolomé Bermejo trained in Flanders and made many trips to Aragon and Catalonia; Pedro Berruguete moved to Urbino in 1474 and became a leader in the court of

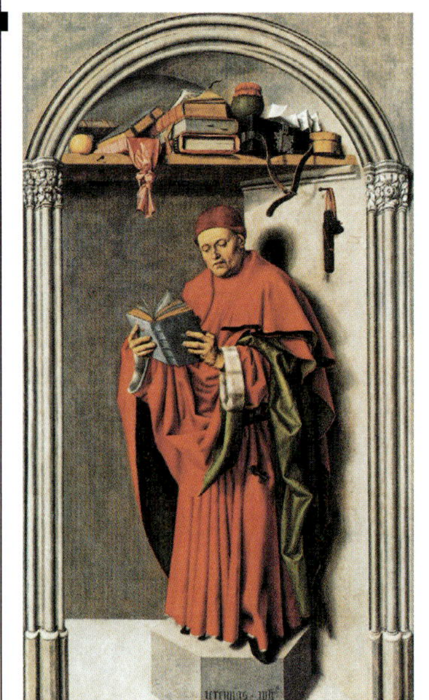

Barthélemy d'Eyck, *The Prophet Jeremiah*, right compartment of the Triptych of the Annunciation of Aix-en-Provence, 1443–45; Musées Royaux des Beaux-Arts, Brussels

Southern routes: Provence, the King

Niccolò Colantonio, *St. Francis of Assisi Giving the Rule to the First and Second Franciscan Orders*, 1444–46; Museo di Capodimonte, Naples

Barthélemy, brother of Hubert and Jan van Eyck. He is a key figure in any understanding of the stylistic exchanges among Flanders, Provence, Burgundy, and the Italian art centers. In the Midi, the fineness of the Flemish was united with the monumental style of Italian painting and, most of all, with that sense of abundant solar luminosity, so very different from the analytical light of the north. The compositions grow larger and assume a singular, characteristic appearance in which courtly pomp is mixed with sentiments drawn from the ordinary people.

Around the middle of the fifteenth century, the Mediterranean area became the site of intersecting cultural and artistic dynamics,

Federico da Montefeltro. Even so, Spain remained tenaciously—and brilliantly—anchored to the Gothic tradition, and the Gothic went through a period of magnificent opulence in fifteenth-century Spain. The final unification of Spanish territory, which began in 1469 with the marriage of Ferdinand of Aragon to Isabella of Castile, marked an important turning point in the history of Spanish painting. If one had to name a single painter whose career could summarize the traits and developments of European painting in the middle of the fifteenth century, without doubt the name would be that of Antonello da Messina. No other artist of the time was capable of striking a similar balance between the analytical sense of Flemish art and the stately

Southern routes: Catalonia, Provence, the Kingdom of Naples

monumentality of Italian painting, between the application of the humanistic rules of perspective and the atmospheric sense of light and color, between the vivacity of backgrounds and the passionate vitality of figures. This is the result of a particularly dynamic career, during which Antonello visited many important artistic centers, taking part in lively reciprocal exchanges of ideas. In substance, Antonello da Messina demonstrated a ceaseless capacity to easily absorb the artistic novelties of the cities he visited, but at the same time he himself made important contributions that led to innovations in the local schools. A fundamental artist to understanding the "Mediterranean routes" that became interwoven in international painting at the middle of the fifteenth century, Antonello followed an exemplary pictorial and existential route that brought him into dialogues with the great Flemish and Provençal masters and into contact with Piero della Francesca; he also performed a determinant role in the development of the Venetian school. After early activity in Sicily, perhaps

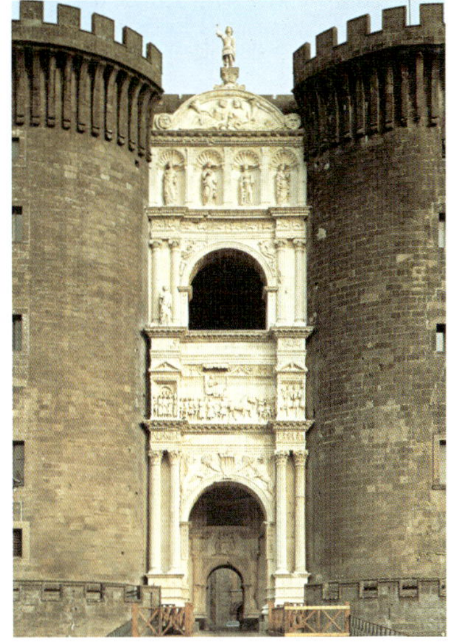

Triumphal Arch of Alfonso V of Aragon, 1452–58; Castelnuovo (Maschio Angioino), Naples

navigators in the exploration of new continents and new trade routes. The king's name is today applied to the final, sumptuous, and fantastic period of Gothic, which took place on that far tip of Europe: Manueline. From their narrow strip of land, the Portuguese looked out toward the horizon of the ocean and, during the period of Manuel, they went far beyond the borders of the known world in search of new routes to the Indies. In 1497–99 Vasco da Gama made his epochal voyage, rounding the Cape of Good Hope and sailing across the Indian Ocean to Calicut; in 1500 Cabral took part in the *descubrimiento* of fabulous Brazil (believed by many to be the Earthly Paradise lost with the sin of Adam and Eve); between 1519 and 1522 Ferdinand Magellan made his trip around the world, including a 38-day struggle to round Cape Horn. These oceanic adventures left a deep mark on the soul, culture, and art of Portugal. Marine motifs multiply everywhere: nets, hawsers, masts, oars, terrestrial globes, portolanos, instruments of measurement,

Catalonia, dom of Naples

alongside a Burgundian painter, he got his artistic training in the cosmopolitan setting of Naples around 1450 and, most of all, in contact with Flemish art and with Niccolò Colantonio. From his earliest works he revealed the ability to combine in innovative ways the attention to the smallest naturalistic details with a broad spatial breadth. Alternating trips with stays and activity in Sicily, Antonello went through a rapid and independent evolution that was expressed through new versions of the theme of the Crucifixion and a series of penetrating male portraits of figures that have remained nameless and for that very reason are wrapped in fascinating mystery. After having climbed the boot of Italy, coming into contact with Piero della Francesca in Rome and in Urbino, he reached the height of his career with the magnificent works he painted in Venice in 1475–76, a decisive moment for local painting, for Antonello's methods were quickly absorbed by Giovanni Bellini.

The great period of Portuguese art coincides with the reign of King Manuel I (1495–1521) and with the undertakings of that nation's great

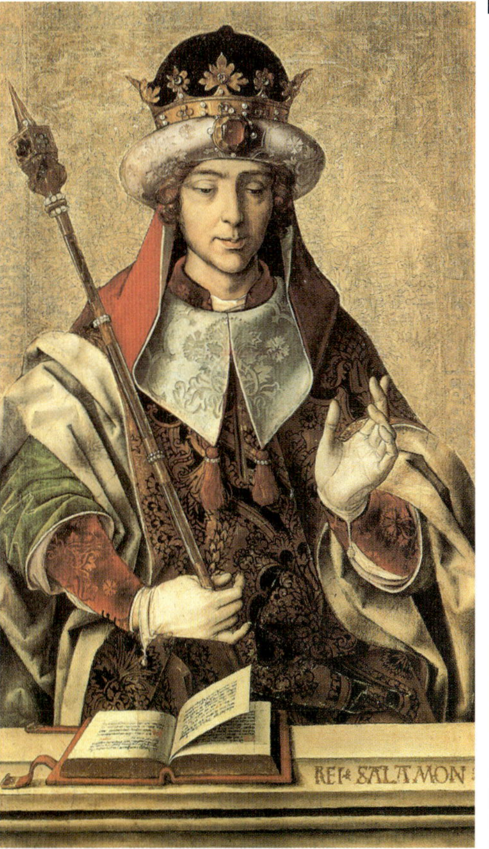

Pedro Berruguete, *Solomon,* panel from the Life of the Virgin Altarpiece; Parish Museum of St. Eulalia, Paredes de Nava (Palencia)

rudders, ship models, sails, astrolabes and sextants entered the repertory of decorative sculpture and *azulejos*, the colorful ceramics that became the most typical ornamental style in Portugal and in its overseas lands. The decoration of new buildings was connected to the development of a painting school distinct from Spanish painting of the period and tied, as though by way of their shared marine vocation, to Antwerp. The splendid Manueline period came to a sudden end with the king's death, leaving the impression of something unfinished, much like the chapel of the monastery of Batalha, which was left without a roof.

Annunciation
1443–45
oil on panel,
155 x 176 cm
Sainte-Marie-Madeleine,
Aix-en-Provence

This *Annunciation*, which
earned Barthélemy
d'Eyck the name of
Master of the Aix
Annunciation, was
painted for the chapel
of Pierre Corpici in the
cathedral of Saint-
Sauveur in Aix. It was
part of a triptych that
was later disassembled;
the central part is still
in Aix, in the church of
Sainte-Marie-Madeleine.
The principal scene,
located at the end of a
series of arches in a
church, has extraordi-
nary power and
originality for the
equilibrium of the
masses, the symbolic
use of light, and the
skillful control of
space. The figure of the
angel occupies the left
area of the painting,
marked off by two
columns and topped by
the figure of God the
Father. From God's
hand, raised in bless-
ing, rays of light travel
through the piercing
in a rose window to
illuminate the face of
Mary, kneeling in the
right area of the paint-
ing, which is far larger
than the left. In fact
the church opens in
two long naves that, by
extending the space,
give prominence to the
figure of the Virgin
and emphasize her
symbolic role as Mother
of the Church.

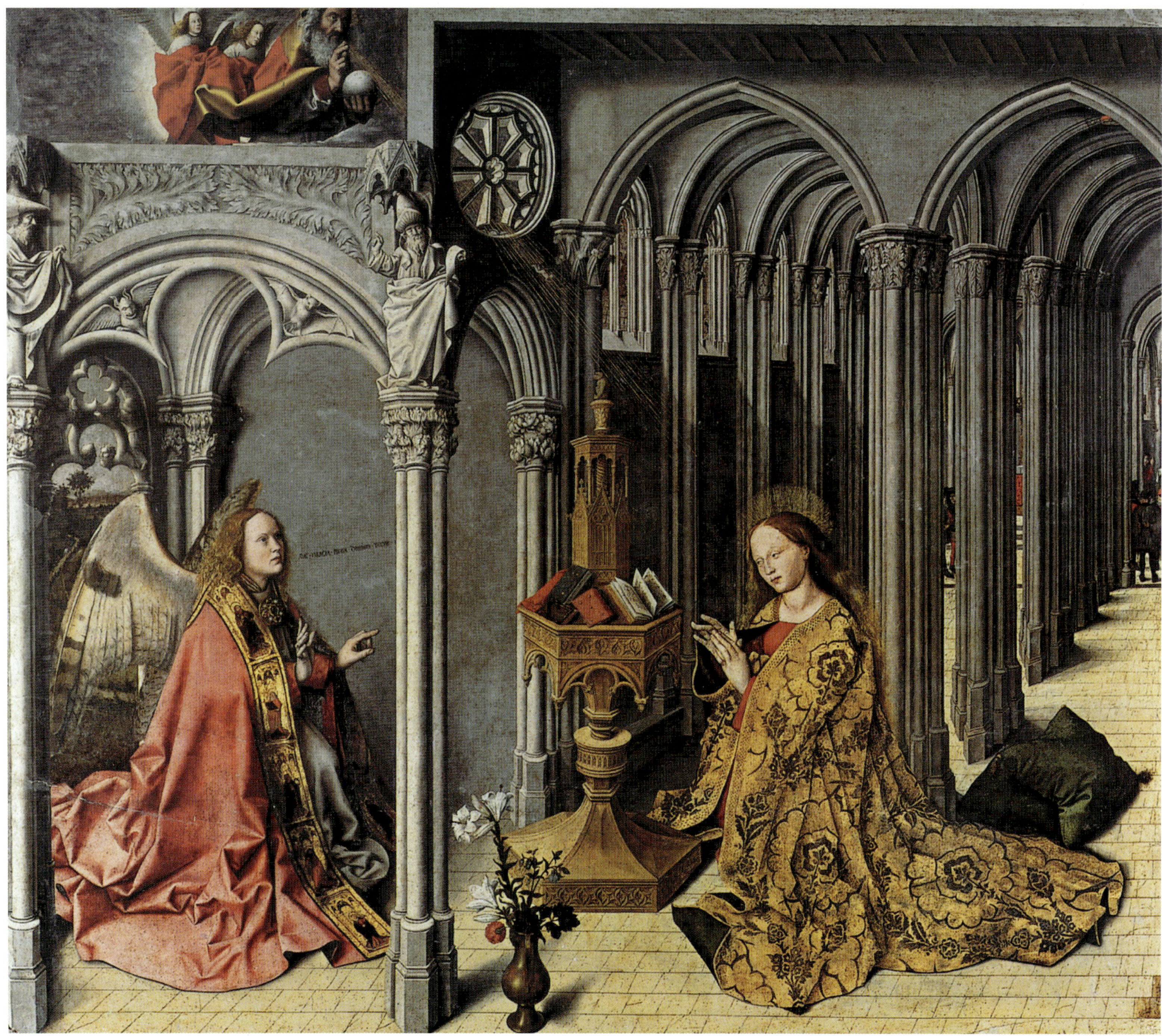

Southern routes: Catalonia, Provence, the Kingdom of Naples

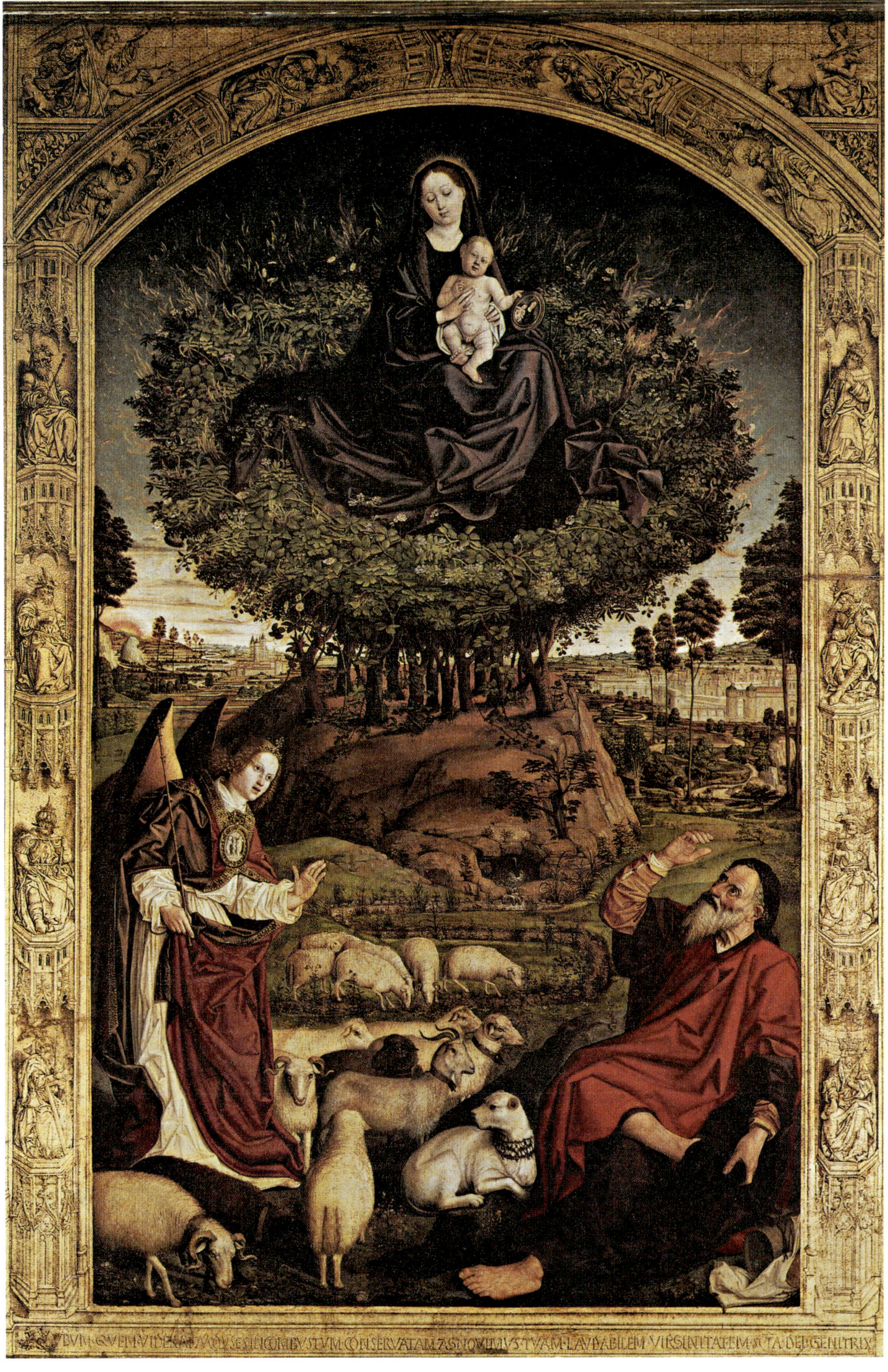

■ NICOLAS FROMENT
The Burning Bush
1475–76, panel,
305 x 225 cm
Saint-Sauveur,
Aix-en-Provence

The contemporary presence of works and artists of singular importance made Provence one of the most lively territories of art in the later fifteenth century. During his stay at the court of René of Anjou, Froment developed a personal reworking of the northern language. The central scene of the triptych of the *Burning Bush* presents the biblical episode of Moses taking his shoes off before the miraculous apparition of a bush that burns without being consumed. In Christian exegesis, the burning bush was interpreted as a prefiguration of the Immaculate Conception and the virginity of Mary. The monumentality of the composition, the vast landscape inserted in the background, and the skillful use of light, particularly how it wraps around the figures in the foreground, denote the Italian influence that was so decisive in the formation of the Avignon school.

Southern routes: Catalonia, Provence, the Kingdom of Naples

Few doubts linger among critics, by now almost unanimous in attributing this large and dramatic *Pietà*, from Villeneuve-lés-Avignon to Quarton. In any case, this is the high point, almost the emblem itself, of French painting of the mid fifteenth century, in the phase of passage from the Gothic to the Renaissance style. Basing himself on monumental sculpture, Quarton constructs a solid block of figures, pausing on the features and emotions with intense clarity. Despite the Gothic use of a punched-gold background, the work presents a monumental drama previously unknown in French art.

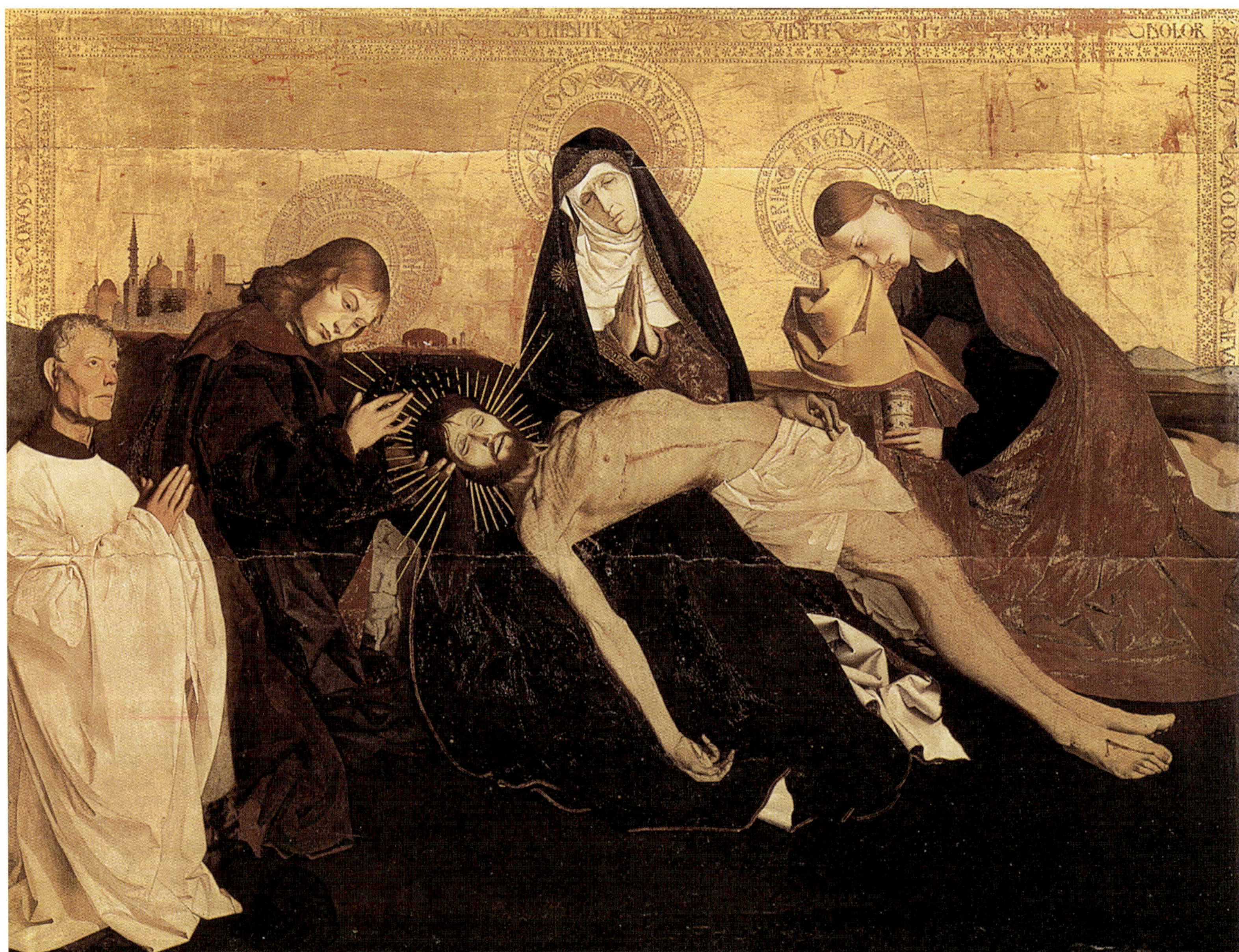

Southern routes: Catalonia, Provence, the Kingdom of Naples

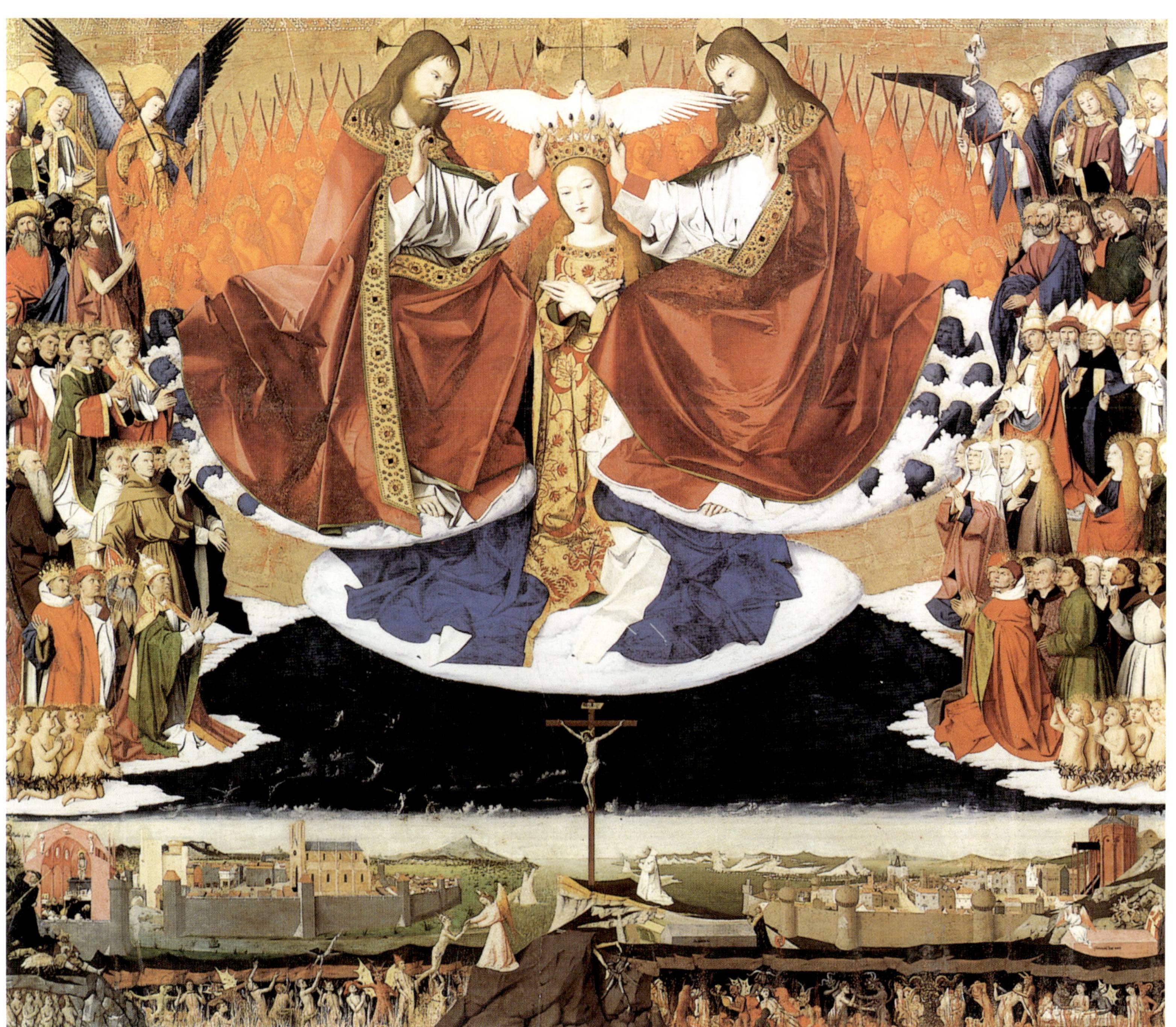

The panel presents paradise, the earth, and hell on three different levels. The center of the composition is the figure of Mary, seated in clouds and surrounded by the blessed of paradise while being crowned by the Holy Trinity. The Father and Son are purposefully identical; the dove represents the Holy Sprit. The grand central vision contrasts with the lower scenes, which seem almost isolated. Against the background of an infinite panorama beyond the skies is earth, where, to the right, Rome can be recognized by the church of St. Peter. At the lowest level is hell. To the extreme left of the painting the souls of the dead await divine judgment. At the center of the scene the blessed are welcomed by an angel and sent on to paradise. The damned twist and scream, menaced by frightening devils. The brilliant colors seem even brighter because of the study of the light, almost zenithal, which illuminates the entire composition.

Southern routes: Catalonia, Provence, the Kingdom of Naples

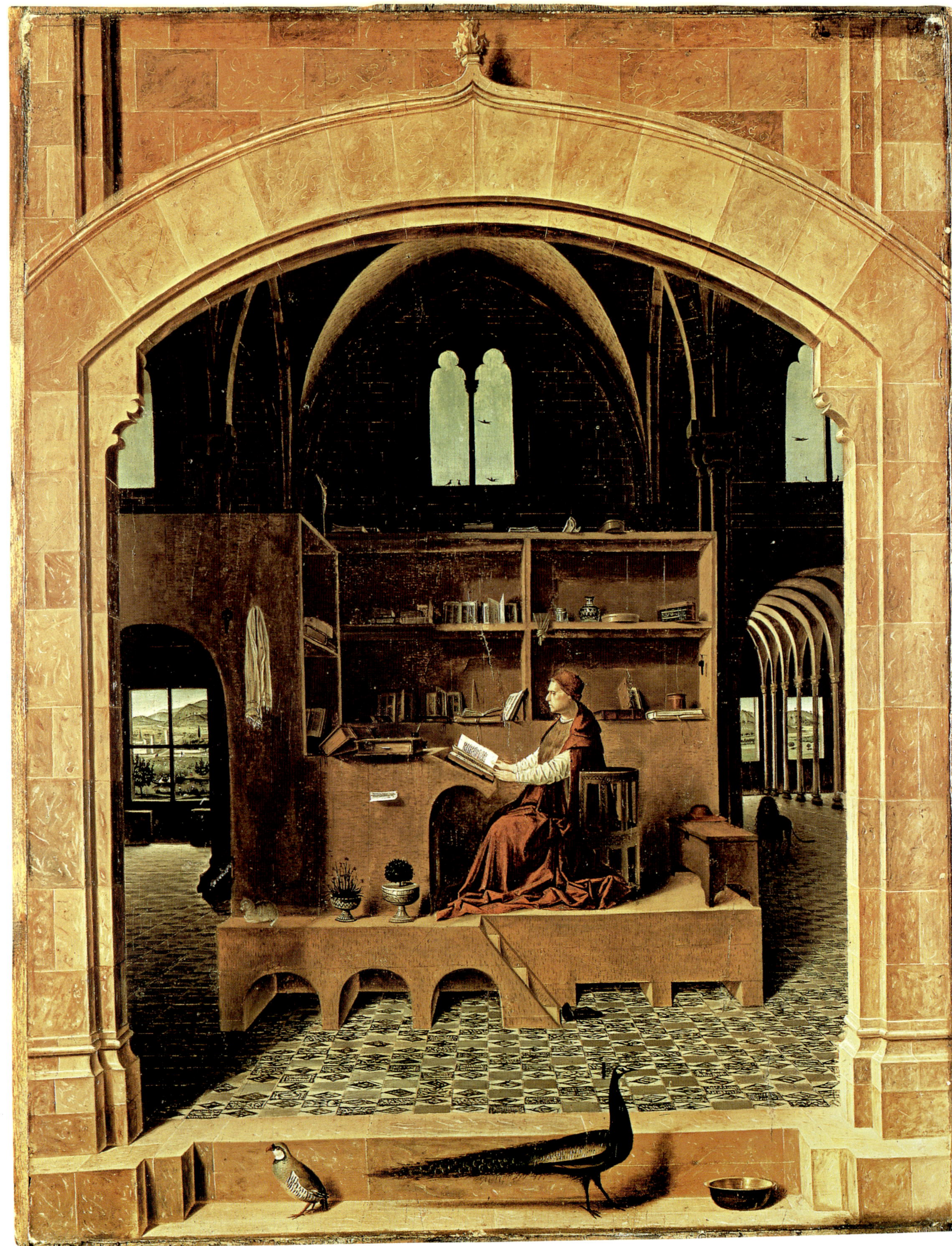

Southern routes: Catalonia, Provence, the Kingdom of Naples

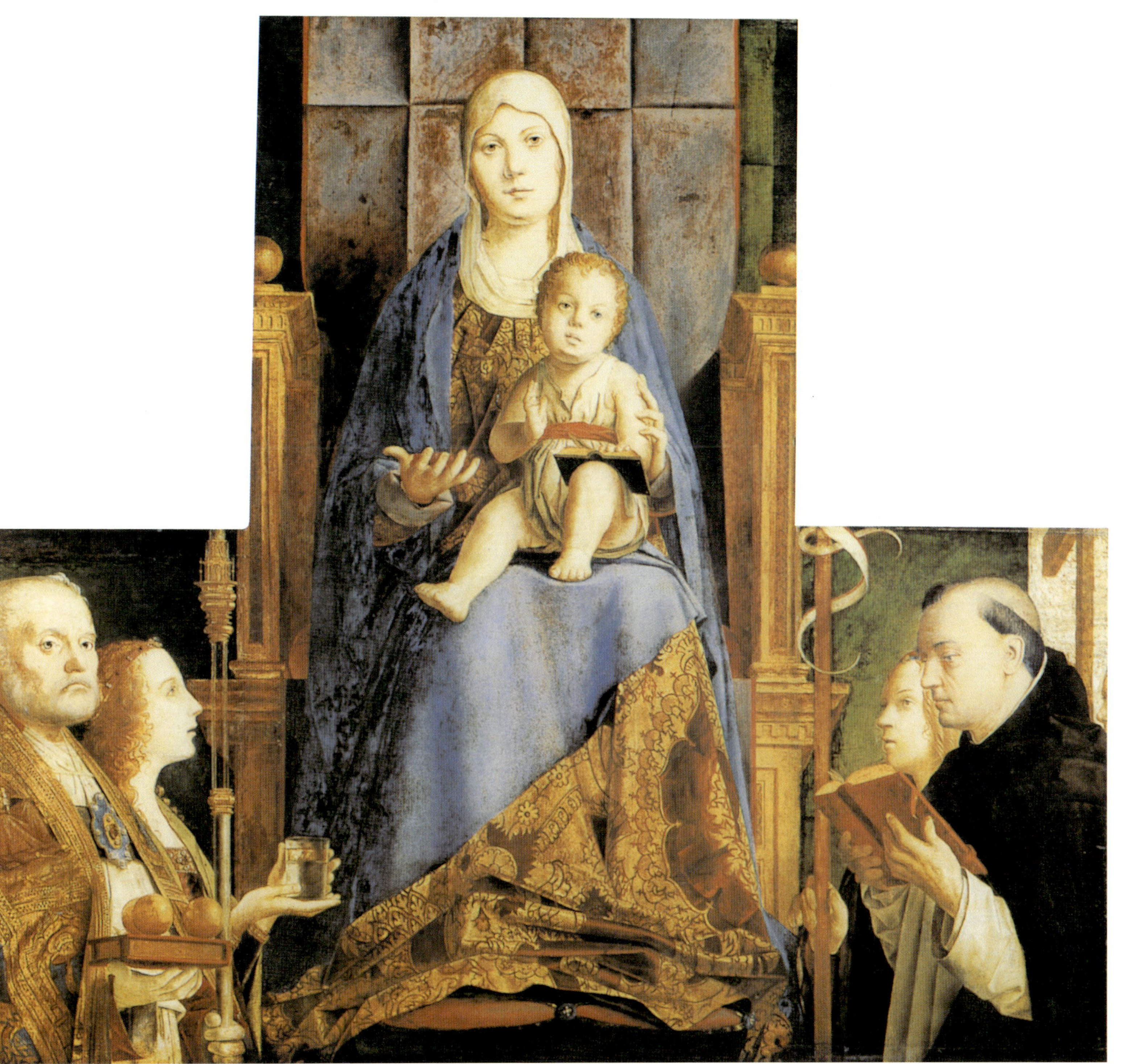

ANTONELLO
DA MESSINA
**Madonna and Child
Enthroned and Saints
Nicholas of Bari,
Anastasia, Ursula,
and Dominic**
Surviving fragments
of the San Cassiano
Altarpiece
1475–76;
central panel 115 x
64 cm, side panels
56 x 35 cm
Kunsthistorisches
Museum, Vienna

The three fragments,
united to form a cen-
tral group of figures,
are the remains of an
enormous altarpiece
that Antonello painted
during a stay in Venice
in the later period of
his career. During that
time in Venice, while
consolidating the char-
acteristics of his style
Antonello also increased
his taste for color and
light, opening the way
for the tonalism of
Giovanni Bellini. An
original version of the
model of the fifteenth-
century *sacra conver-
sazione,* this altarpiece
presents the high
throne of the Virgin
surrounded by pairs of
saints within a broad
Renaissance apse. The
regular symmetry, with
the figures inscribed
within the lines of a
triangle at the center
of the composition, is
once again brightened
by the delicacy of the
light, the attention
to detail, the subtle
psychological insight
that gives a sense of
Antonello's great skill
as a portraitist.

Southern routes: Catalonia, Provence, the Kingdom of Naples

Portrait of a Man
1470–75,
oil on panel,
35.5 x 25.5 cm
National Gallery,
London

All of Antonello's portraits present the same arrangement, one so closely associated with Van Eyck that some critics have hypothesized a stay in Flanders by Antonello: the figure stands half-bust behind a narrow wall or sill, turned three-quarters, against a neutral and almost always dark background. However, unlike most of the people painted by Flemish artists, the unknown men portrayed by Antonello look at the viewer, instituting a new relationship between the person portrayed and the person viewing the work. Antonello thus achieves an extraordinary synthesis between the two main painting schools of the time, a balance between the Flemish analytical approach and the stately monumentality of Italian painting, between the application of the humanistic rules of perspective and the sense of atmosphere, light, and color, between the vivacity of the backgrounds and the vitality of the figures. The young man in this portrait belongs to the intriguing gallery of "unknowns" painted by Antonello, although the hypothesis has been recently advanced, difficult to verify, that this is the painter's colleague Hans Memling.

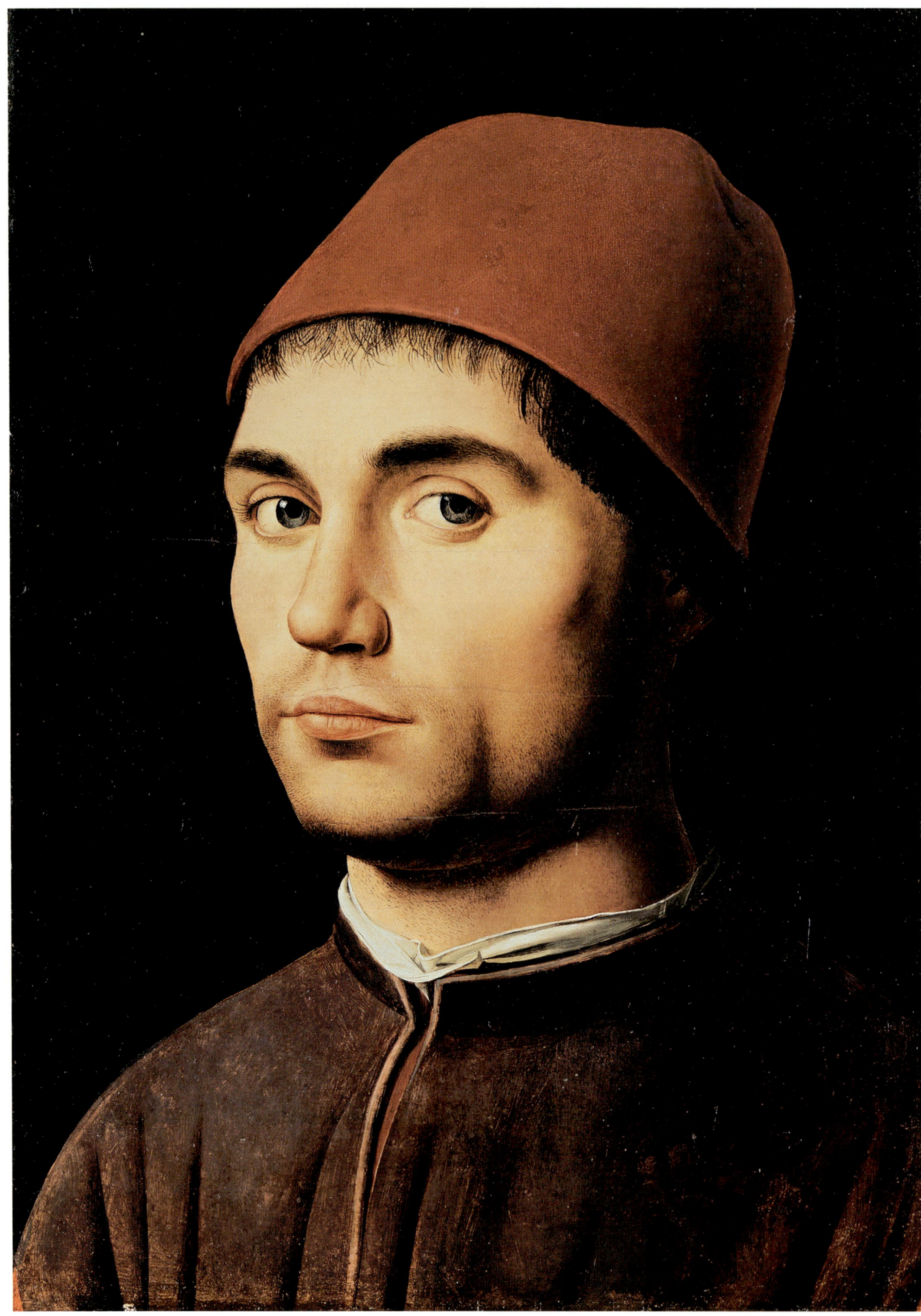

Southern routes: Catalonia, Provence, the Kingdom of Naples

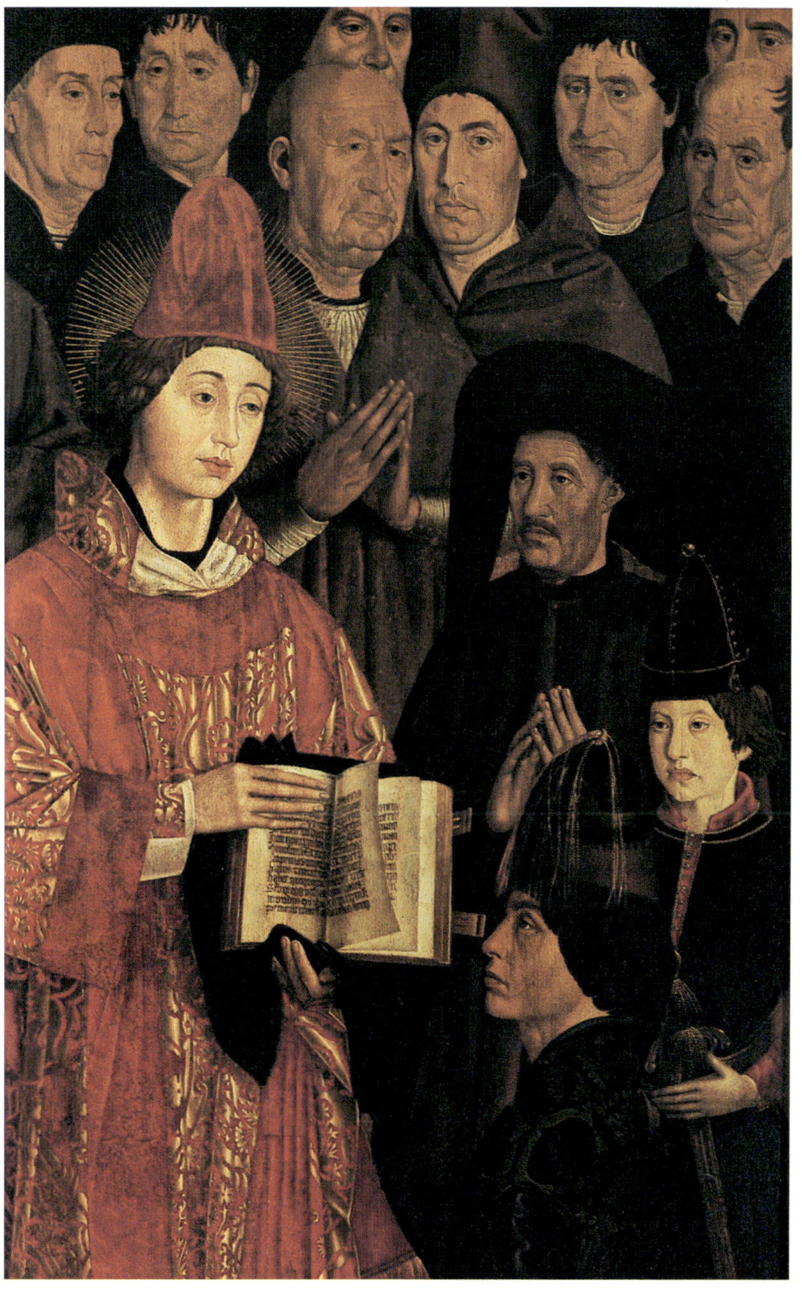

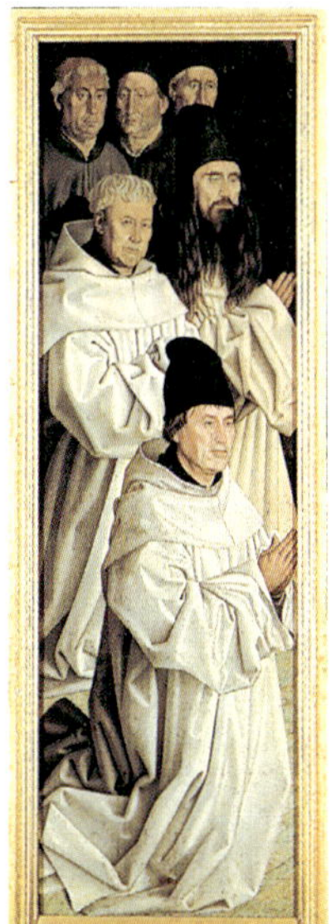
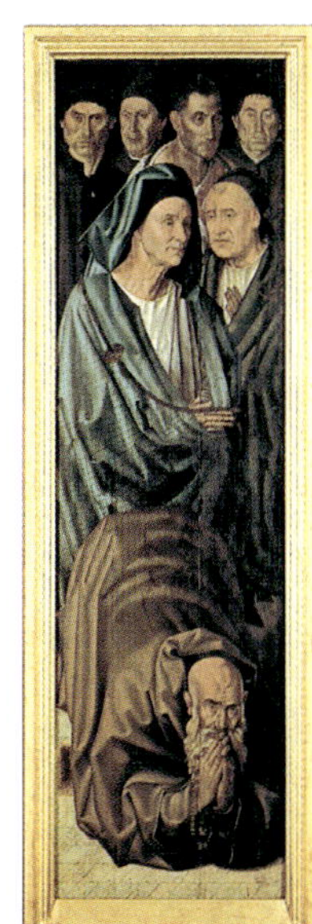
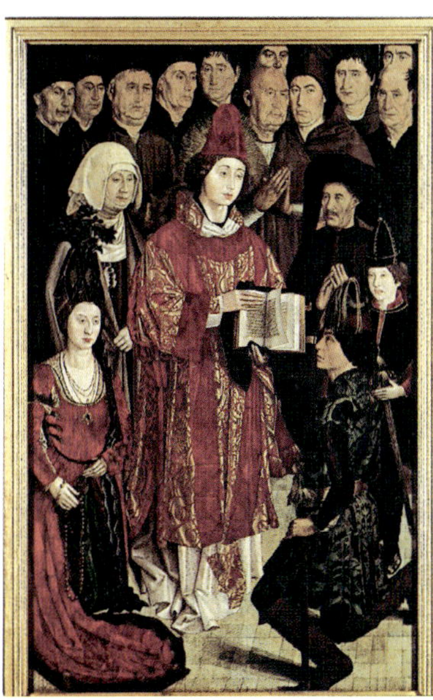
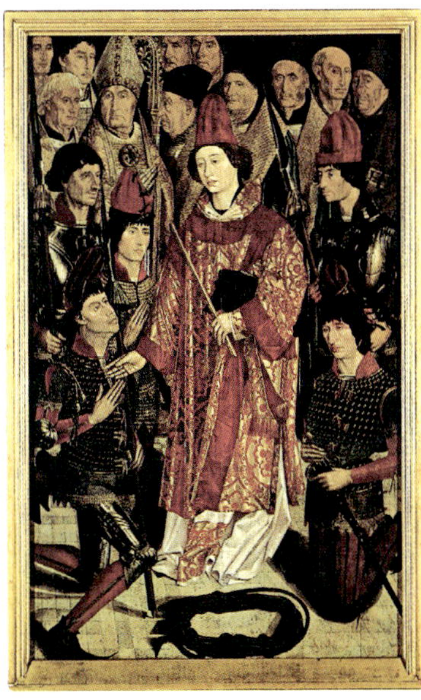
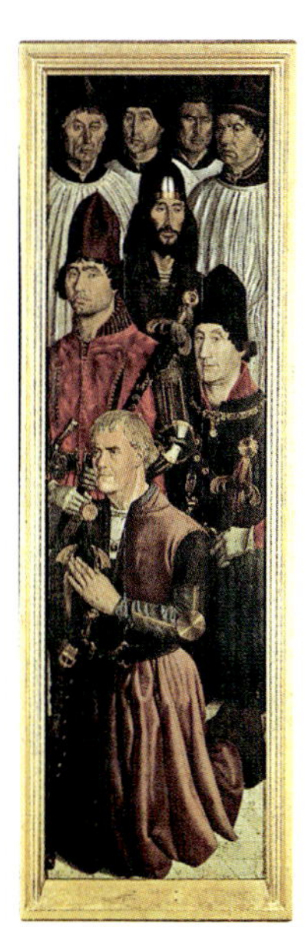
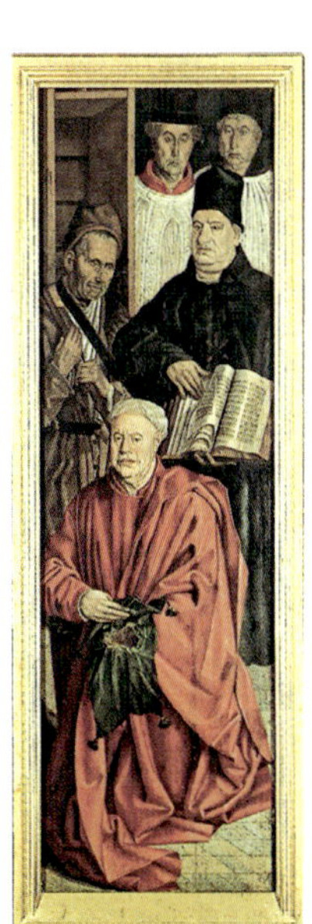

Southern routes: Catalonia, Provence, the Kingdom of Naples

**Federico da
Montefeltro with
His Son Guidobaldo**
1476, oil on panel,
134 x 75.5 cm
Galleria Nazionale delle
Marche, Urbino

Driven by a strong
desire to travel and
learn from other artistic
settings, Berruguete
had a fundamental
experience in Urbino, at
the court of Federico da
Montefeltro. Involved
in the creation of the
portraits of *Famous
Men* in the duke's
studiolo, designed and
in part made by Justus
of Ghent, Berruguete
distinguished himself
from the Flemish
master by using the
constructive and per-
spective functions of
space and by scaling
the surfaces to
accentuate the monu-
mentality of the
half-bust figures, their
well characterized
faces wrapped in ample
drapery. In this
extraordinary portrait
of the duke busy read-
ing, flanked by his son
and heir Guidobaldo,
northern realism blends
with the monumental-
ity of Melozzo da Forlì
and the rigor of Piero
della Francesca. After
making the realistic
hands of the duke in
the Montefeltro
Altarpiece by Piero
(today in Milan)
Berruguete remained
in Urbino until
1482, the year of the
duke's death.

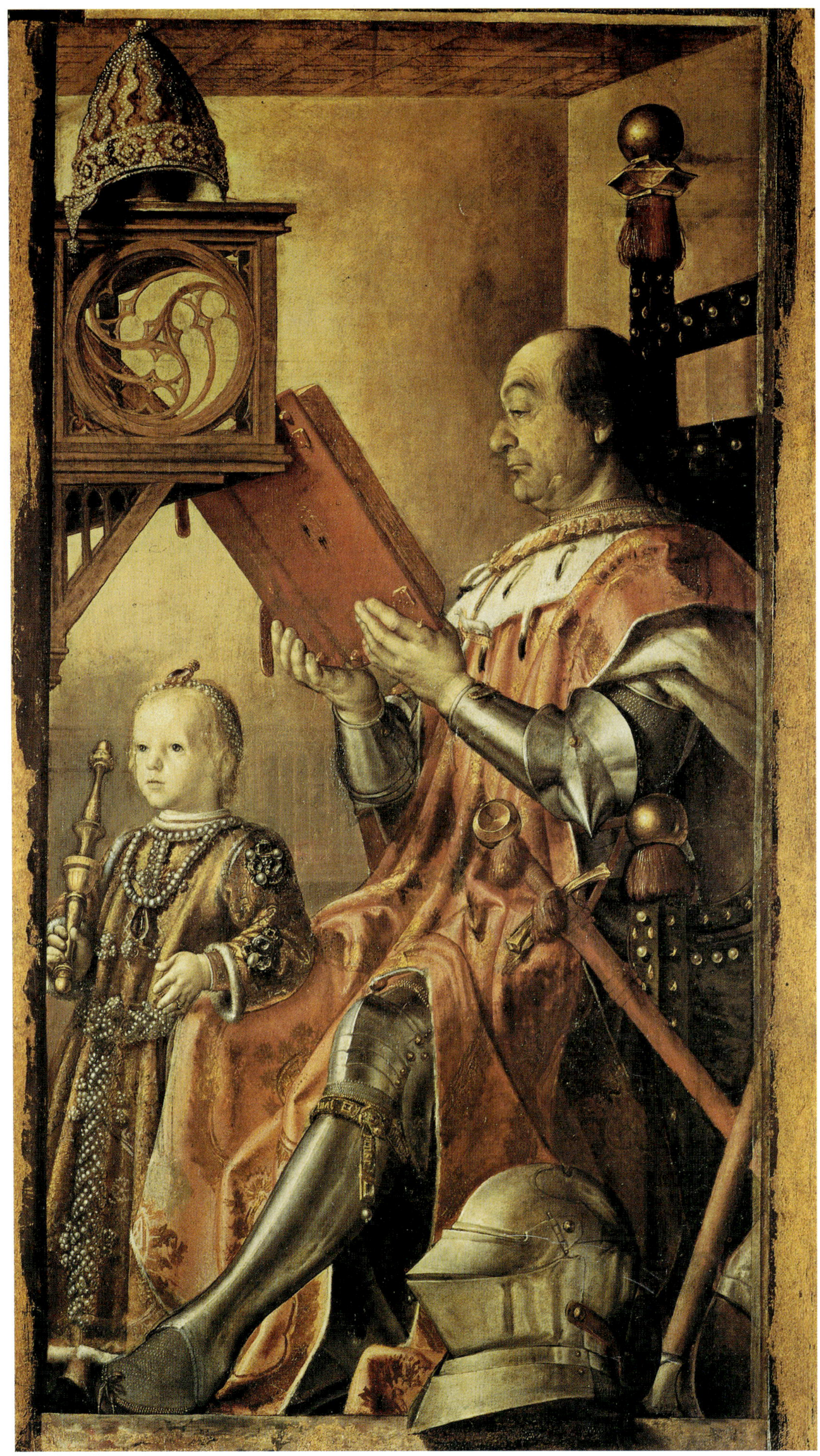

Southern routes: Catalonia, Provence, the Kingdom of Naples

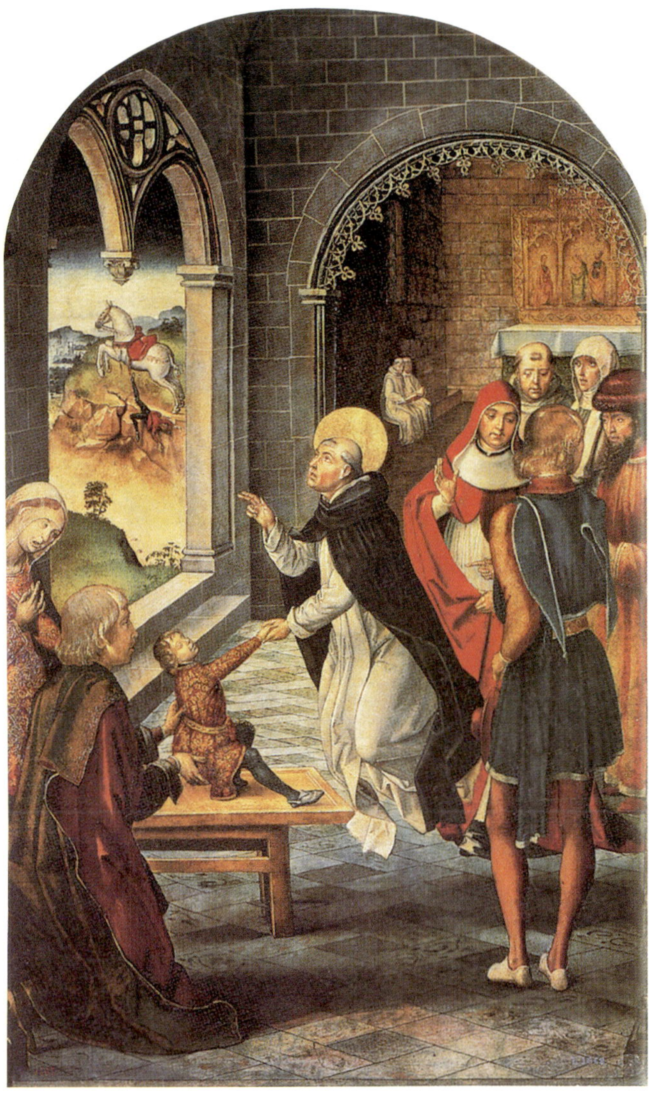

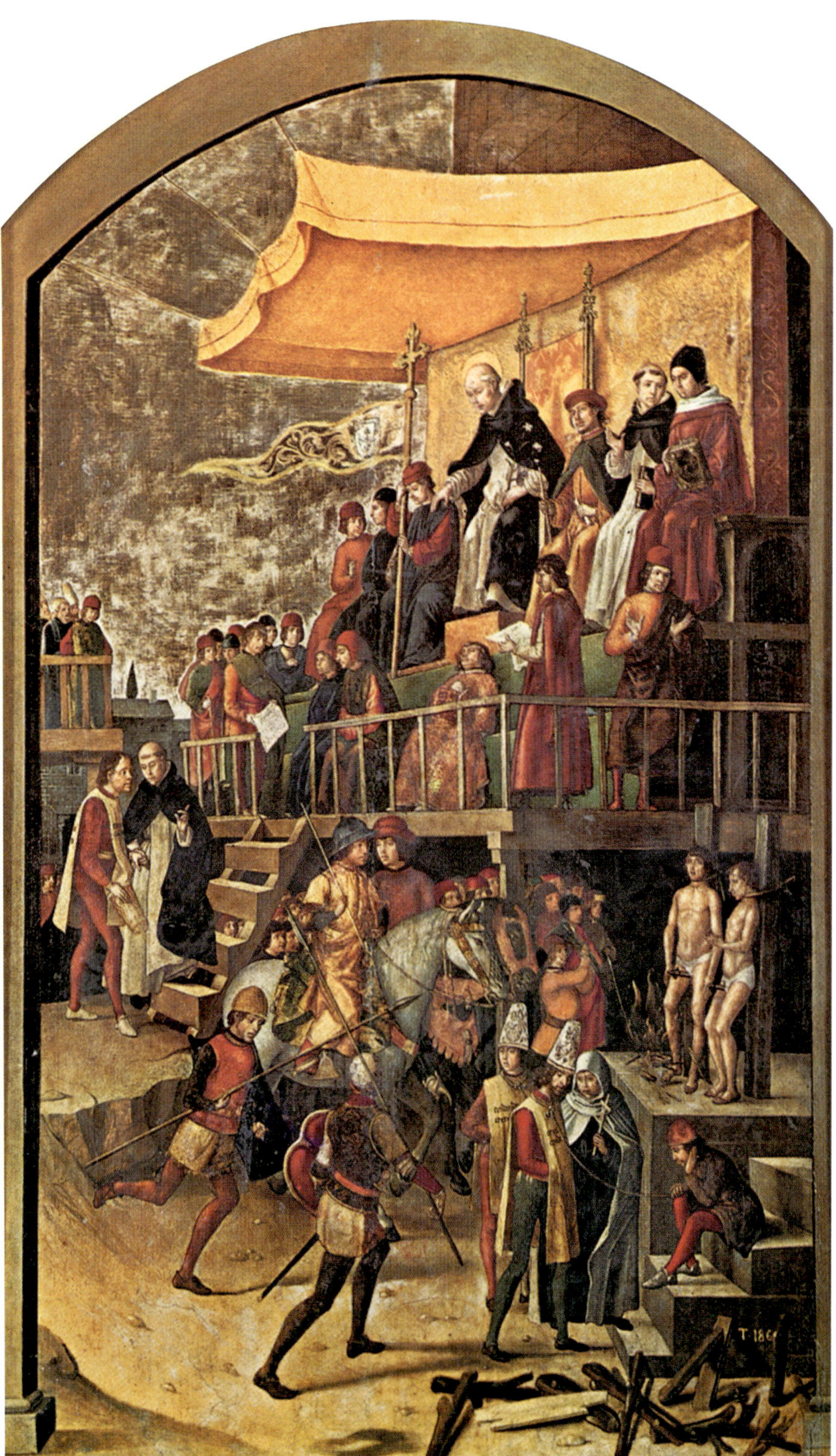

■ PEDRO BERRUGUETE
**St. Dominic Revives
a Child and Burning
of the Heretics
(Auto-da-fé)**
tempera and oil on
panel, circa 1495,
122 x 83 cm and
154 x 92 cm
Museo del Prado, Madrid

The two panels were part of a large retable dedicated to the life of St. Dominic, originally in the convent of San Tomás in Ávila and today disassembled and held in various museums. Both paintings reveal knowledge of perspective and a narrative style, characterized by a strong Flemish-style realism: the studied light effects, however, lead back to the memory of Piero della Francesca and Luca Signorelli, met during a long stay in Italy. In the crude scene of the auto-da-fé (pronouncement of judgment by the tribune of the Inquisition) Berruguete presents the reprieve being granted to the Albigensian heretic Raymond, while his companions, who have not recanted, are prepared for execution. The painting must be seen against the background of the political, historical and religious situation of Spain at the end of the fifteenth century, at the end of the *Reconquista*.

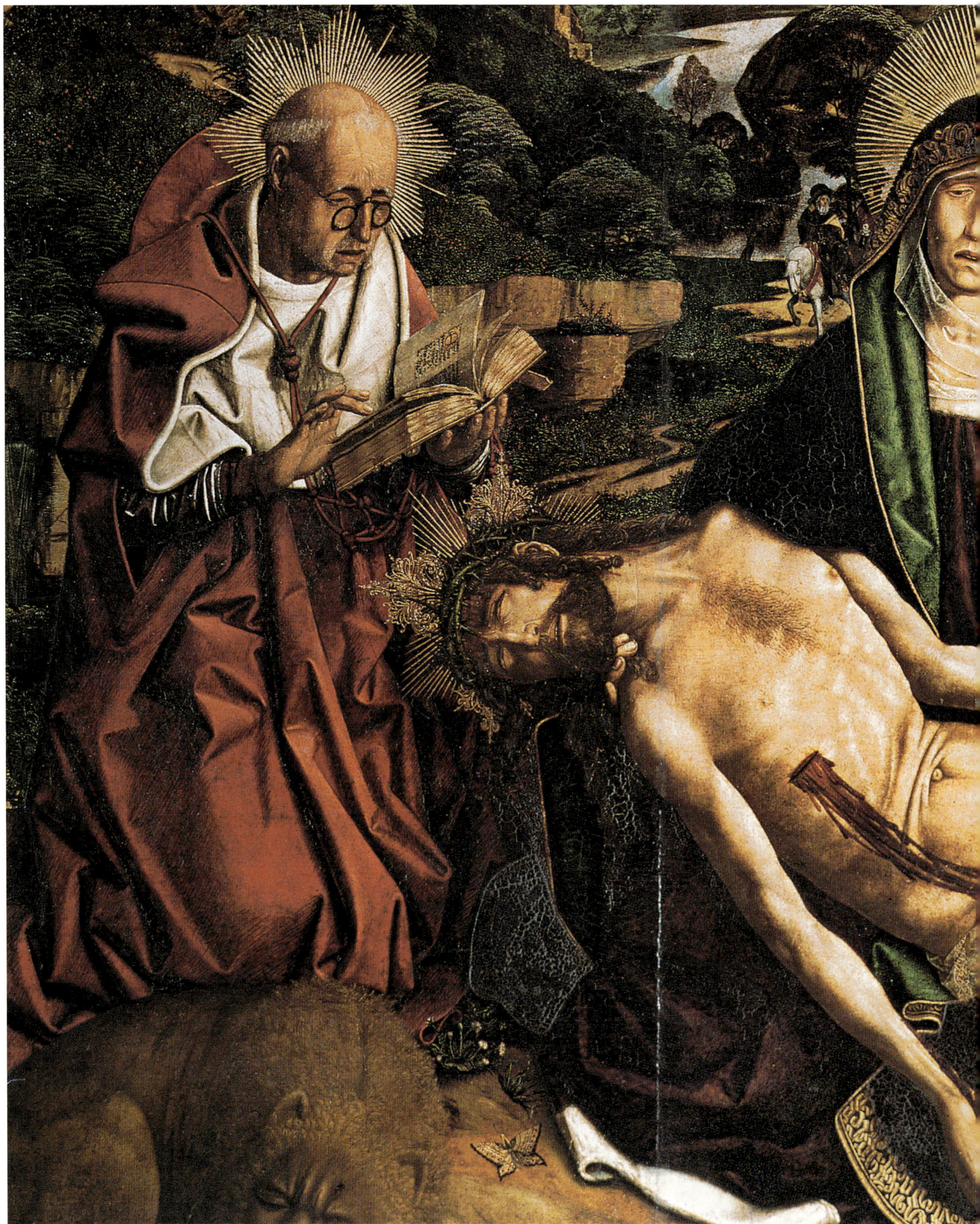

Commissioned by the canon Lluís Desplá for his private chapel in the cathedral of Barcelona, this is one of the great masterpieces of Catalan painting. The scene takes place against the background of a vast landscape. As is characteristic of the iconography of the *Pietà*, the sorrowful Madonna holds the body of her dead son in her lap. Bermejo portrays the sponsor of the work, kneeling to the right of the Virgin; to the left is St. Jerome (prototype of the intellectual ecclesiastic), intently reading, his lion at his feet. The expression on the canon's face, his eyes staring into emptiness, and even his pose clearly indicate his emotional and very immediate involvement in the drama. His

Southern routes: Catalonia, Provence, the Kingdom of Naples

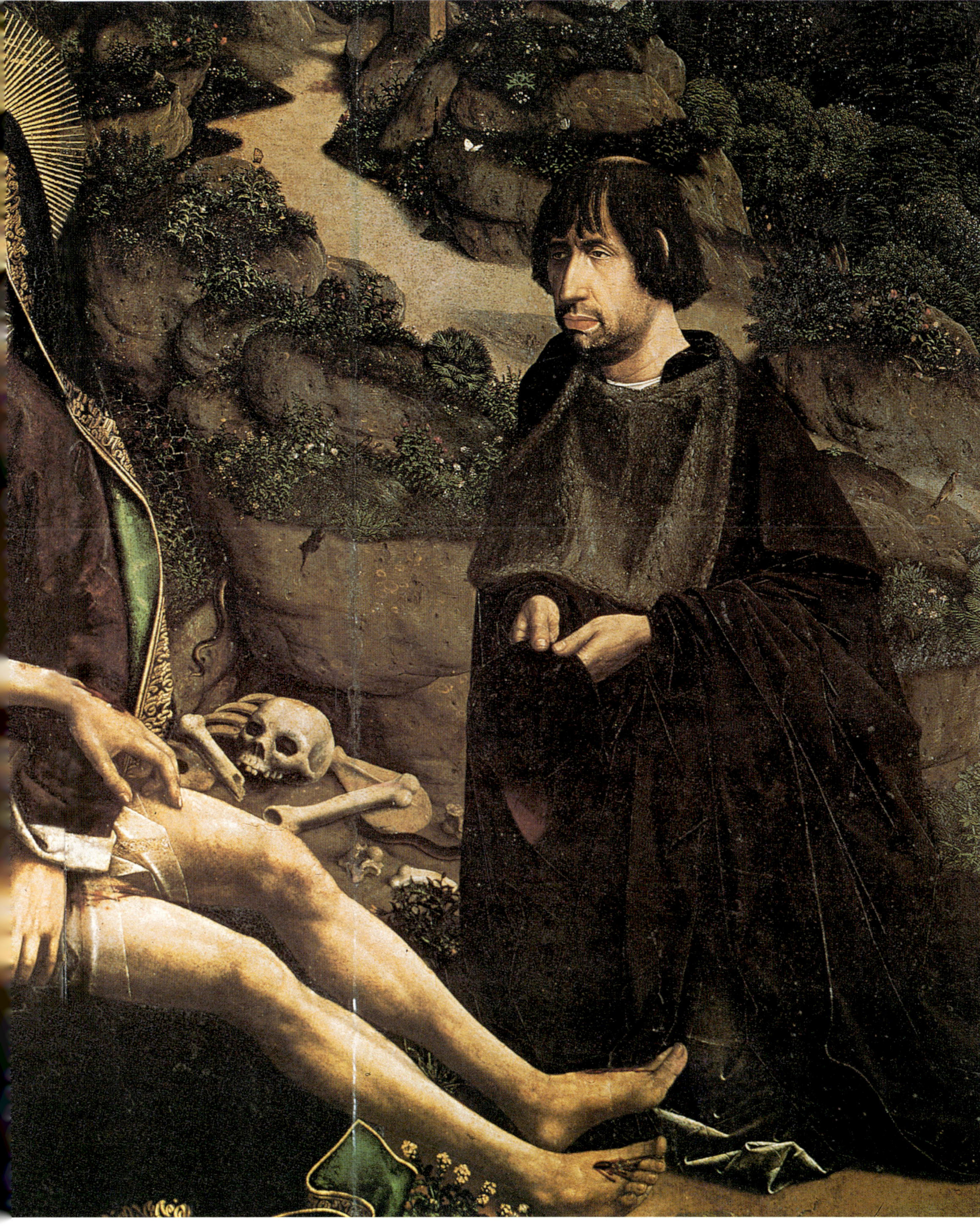

Southern routes: Catalonia, Provence, the Kingdom of Naples

he plurality of Italian artistic centers in the fifteenth century had no equal among the other nations of Europe and was indeed a special characteristic of Italian culture during the Renaissance. There were five principal states in Italy during the fifteenth century: Milan, Venice, Florence, Rome, and Naples. All around these were minor states that maintained their independence through alliances with neighbors or because of some particular strategic, political, or economic advantage. In many cases, the rulers of minor cities, like the leaders of the dynasties that ruled the major centers, used the creation of large-scale artistic and cultural undertakings to celebrate their prestige. Until the middle of the fifteenth century, the advances made in the study of perspective and the principles of humanistic art were applied almost exclusively in Florence; throughout the rest of the peninsula the late Gothic continued to hold sway, contrasting the rigors of Florentine art with the last expressions of luxurious ornamentation and ostentation, which extended even to the selection of the materials used, such as gold backgrounds in painting or the even more costly "ultramarine" blue obtained from lapis lazuli. The visits to other cities made by great Florentine artists stimulated the more widespread acquisition of humanistic

continuous flow of ideas and solutions that interwove, confronted one another, overlapped, and blended in a situation that remained polycentric, varied, competitive, and changeable, until at least the period of the Peace of Lodi (1454, a date that coincides with the year of the death of Pisanello).

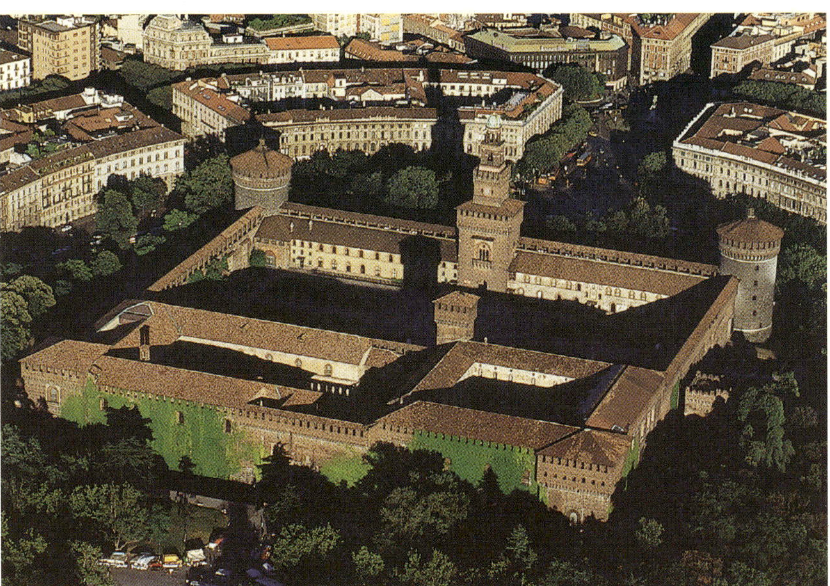

The courts of fifteenth-

taste, but these Tuscan contributions were applied over strong local styles, leading to a great variety of highly original interpretations. In Florence, the masters of the early fifteenth century concentrated their efforts on the human figure and on the idea of the "ideal city," with its pure architectonic forms, but many of the court artists in other cities held firmly to their fondness for the world of nature, creating vivid portrayals of animals and plants, costumes and landscapes, sentiments and affections. The task of achieving a synthesis of the two points of view would have to await the arrival, near the end of the century, of a truly universal genius: Leonardo da Vinci.

The case of Pisanello offers a clearer understanding of the subtleties and shadings in this period of art history. Always on the move among Verona, Mantua, Ferrara, Venice, Milan, Rome, and Naples, Pisanello helped change the taste of the noble courts from Gothic to an ornate, elaborate, and romantic humanism. There was no sudden cut-off, nor any wide division between the two currents, but rather a

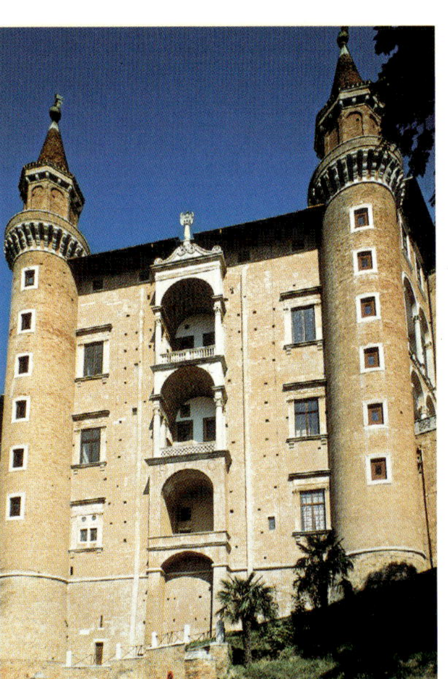

Pisanello was the champion of an art complementary to the humanistic line. It was an art in which the overflow of emotions, the urge to present the tiniest detail, flights of fancy and of feeling, and a sense of luxury and prestige that extended to the materials used in the work of art had the upper hand over intellectual control. So here then are the hares, dogs, ducks, and quail moving off the notebook pages on which they were sketched to scamper among the hooves of the enormous horses, caparisoned like circus elephants, to peek out from behind the thin columns of impossible pavilions, to hide in the shadows of forests where miracles occur, to listen curiously to an angel's announcement or to sway, blinded by the gold, amid the grass of secret gardens. The general change in Italian culture in the humanistic sense took place around the middle of the fifteenth century, when Donatello spent a decade working in the learned and advanced university city of Padua, where he created such admirable works as the equestrian monument of Gattamelata and the bronze statues on the altar of the basilica of San Antonio (the Santo) in Padua. The artistic school that took form in the shadow of these masterpieces eventually gave exceptional fruit. Although almost none of these painters stayed in Padua, each of them gave life to new humanistic ferment in other Italian regions. Such was the case with Mantegna in Verona and Mantua, with Carlo Crivelli in the Marches, Cosimo Tura in Ferrara, Michael Pacher in the Tyrol, Vincenzo Foppa in Lombardy, as well as others. The more advanced artistic schools mixed with the more traditional areas, laying the basis for a dialogue between the "center" and the "periphery" that became a general aspect of the development of all Italian art.

The operation performed by the Estes in Ferrara is an example of the passage from the Gothic culture to that of humanism. Around the first aristocratic and cultural institutions, which started at the end of the fourteenth century, grew and developed the "first modern city of Europe" up to

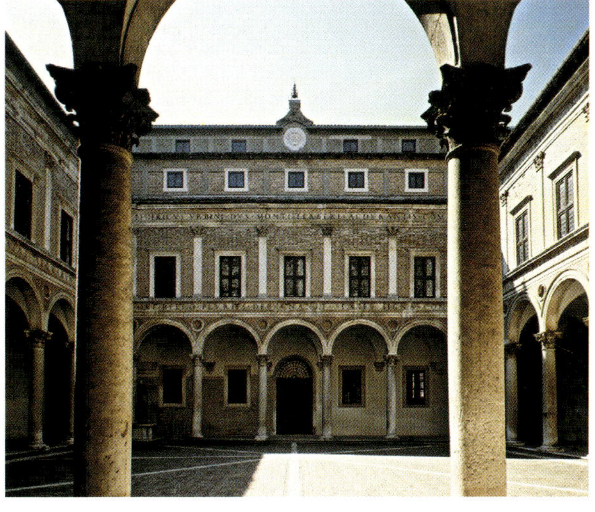

solutions. Most famous of all are the frescoes of the so-called Camera degli Sposi ("bridal chamber"), where Mantegna portrayed the Gonzaga court and, in a daring perspective artifice, "broke through" the ceiling of the room, creating a simulated circular opening, an illusionistic oculus, with a balustrade from which a small crowd of figures peers down into the room. The Camera degli Sposi in the Ducal Palace in Mantua marks an epochal turn in the style of the Italian noble courts, which passed from the elaborate late Gothic ornamentation to a more stately humanistic and intellectual image. The most integral and fascinating example of a fifteenth-century court is the residence of the duke of Urbino, created by Federico da Montefeltro, the main animator of the height of that city's arts. The duke had painters, architects, writers, and mathematicians come to Urbino. The family palace was radically reworked and enlarged in a Renaissance form, while the rooms of the palace were

Francesco di Giorgio Martini, courtyard of Ducal Palace, 1466–79; Urbino

century Italy

the creation of the Addizione Erculea, the expansion of the city by way of the construction of a Renaissance quarter, requested by Ercole d'Este and built by Biagio Rossetti. Painting was a fundamental component of the Ferrara Renaissance culture. The dukes called figures such as Rogier van der Weyden and Piero della Francesca, aside from painters of various provenance, also from Siena and even from Hungary; Lionello d'Este posed as model for a painting contest between Jacopo Bellini and Pisanello; the best talent of the place, Cosimo Tura, was sent to Padua to study at the expense of the Estes. From this rich laboratory flowered the bizarre plant of the Ferrara school of Tura, Cossa, and De Roberti. The frescoes of the Salone dei Mesi (Hall of Months) in Palazzo Schifanoia, a collective effort by the Ferrara masters around 1470, offer one of the most indicative images of the art and life of a fifteenth-century court. It is an indivisible blend of wholesome and delightful daily life and literary allegory, of arcane horoscopes and portraits of an immediate humanity.

Pisanello's position as painter for the Gonzaga court in Mantua was taken up in 1460 by the Paduan Andrea Mantegna. Thanks to him, the small Lombard court became a highly advanced laboratory of artistic Renaissance

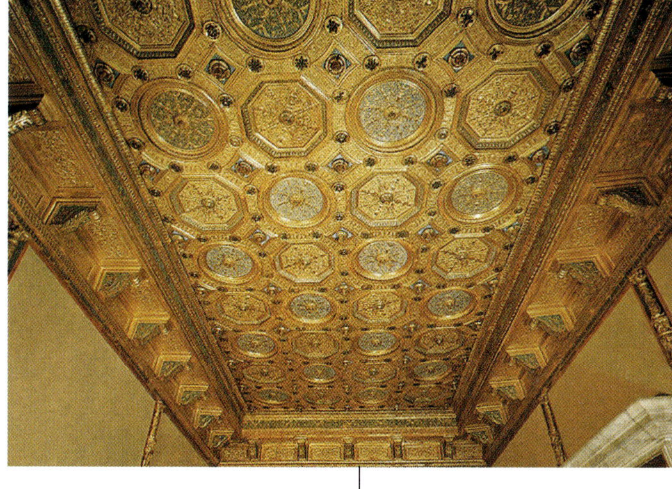

used for discussion of the form of an "ideal city," of perspective, of the history and moral inheritance of the *Famous Men*. Standing out among the painters were the Florentine Paolo Uccello, the Fleming Justus of Ghent, and the Spaniard Pedro Berruguete; these and others transformed the Urbino court into an advanced laboratory of new ideas. The most important artist, however, was Piero della Francesca, who in Urbino reached an unmatched balance between the adoption of severe geometric rules and monumental and serene breadth in painting. The climate of the Montefeltro court proved ideal for further developments, and two of the principal exponents of the High Renaissance got their beginnings in Urbino: Donato Bramante and Raphael.

A similar situation, although later, is presented by the Sforza family in Milan, who invigorated the city's art school, and with it the city's artistic standing, through the innovative contributions of Bramante and Leonardo, while also spreading open the fan of cultural references to take in Flanders and the Kingdom of Naples.

Carved and gilt ceiling of the *studiolo* of Isabella d'Este, circa 1522; Ducal Palace, Mantua

The courts of fifteenth-century Italy

Pisanello's superb drawings form an important part of his artistic creation and are probably the richest and most prestigious such works before Leonardo da Vinci. With a keen sense of the classical, he created some of the first "antique-style" nudes of humanism together with images of great eroticism; at the same time, in other drawings and studies, he presented costumes and hairstyles that were more outlandish, extravagant, multicolored, and outrageous than even the most opulent of courts could have imagined. He made almost maniacal studies of nature, plants and animals, and went on to paint fabulous landscapes in which those very same plants and animals take part as active players, almost as though they could suddenly begin to speak, becoming either very strange helpers or nasty dangers to the heroes and heroines of the fable.

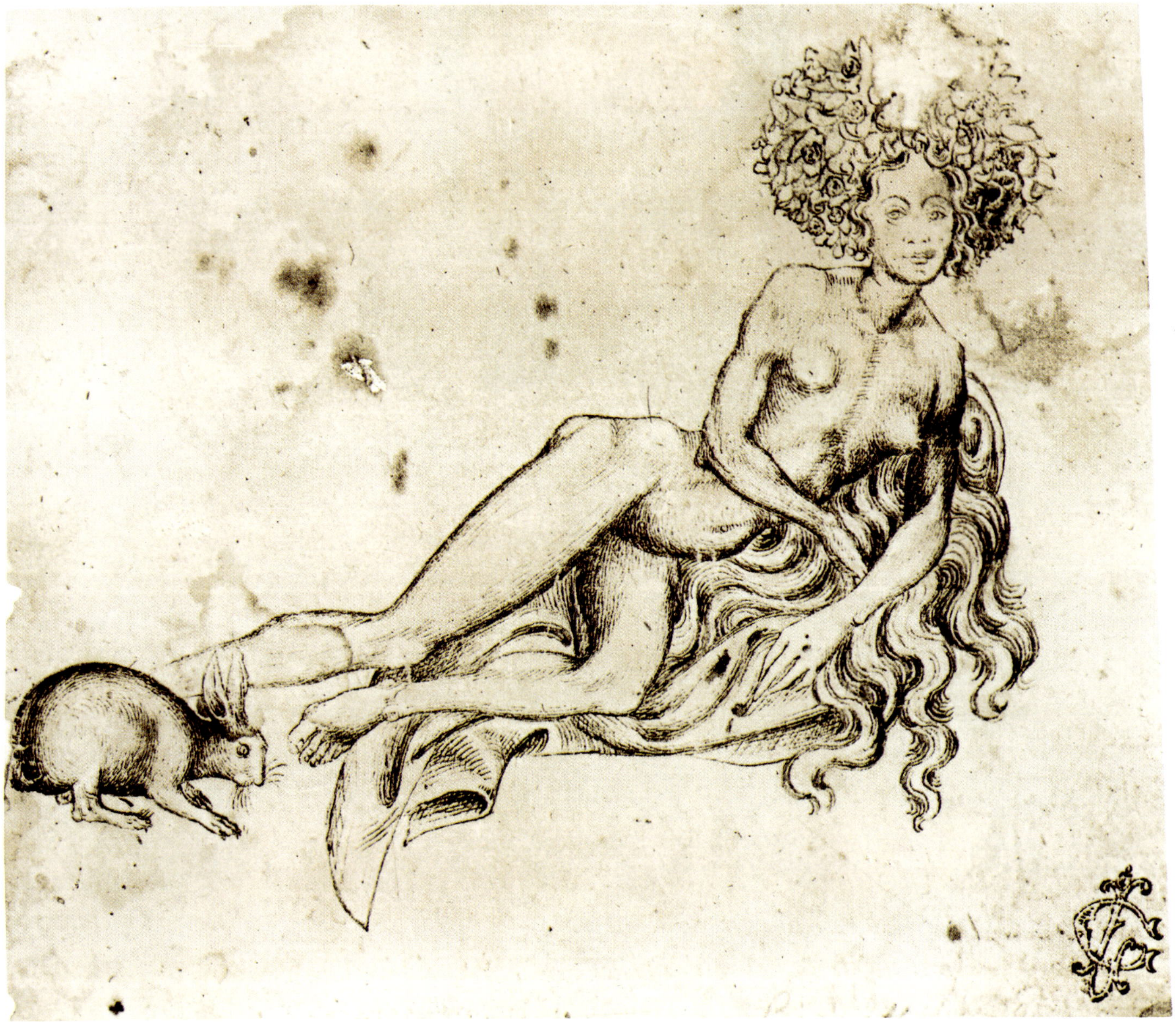

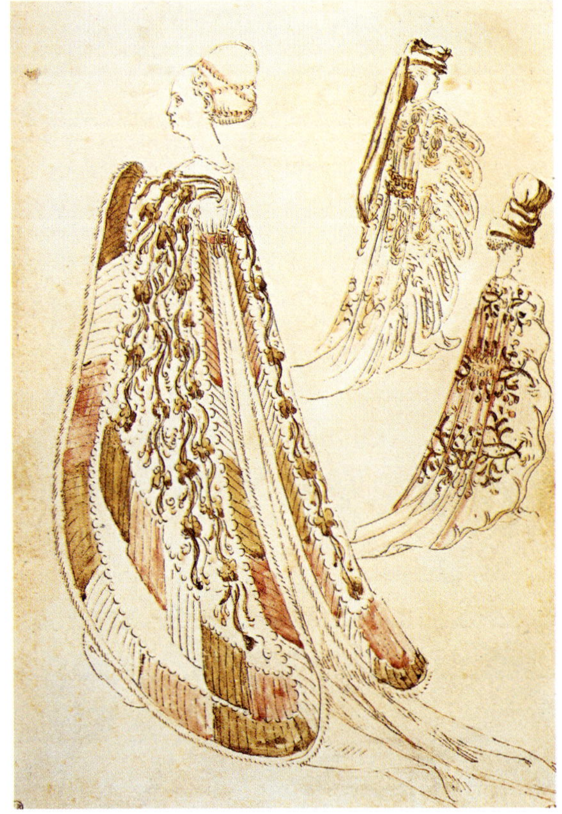

The courts of fifteenth-century Italy

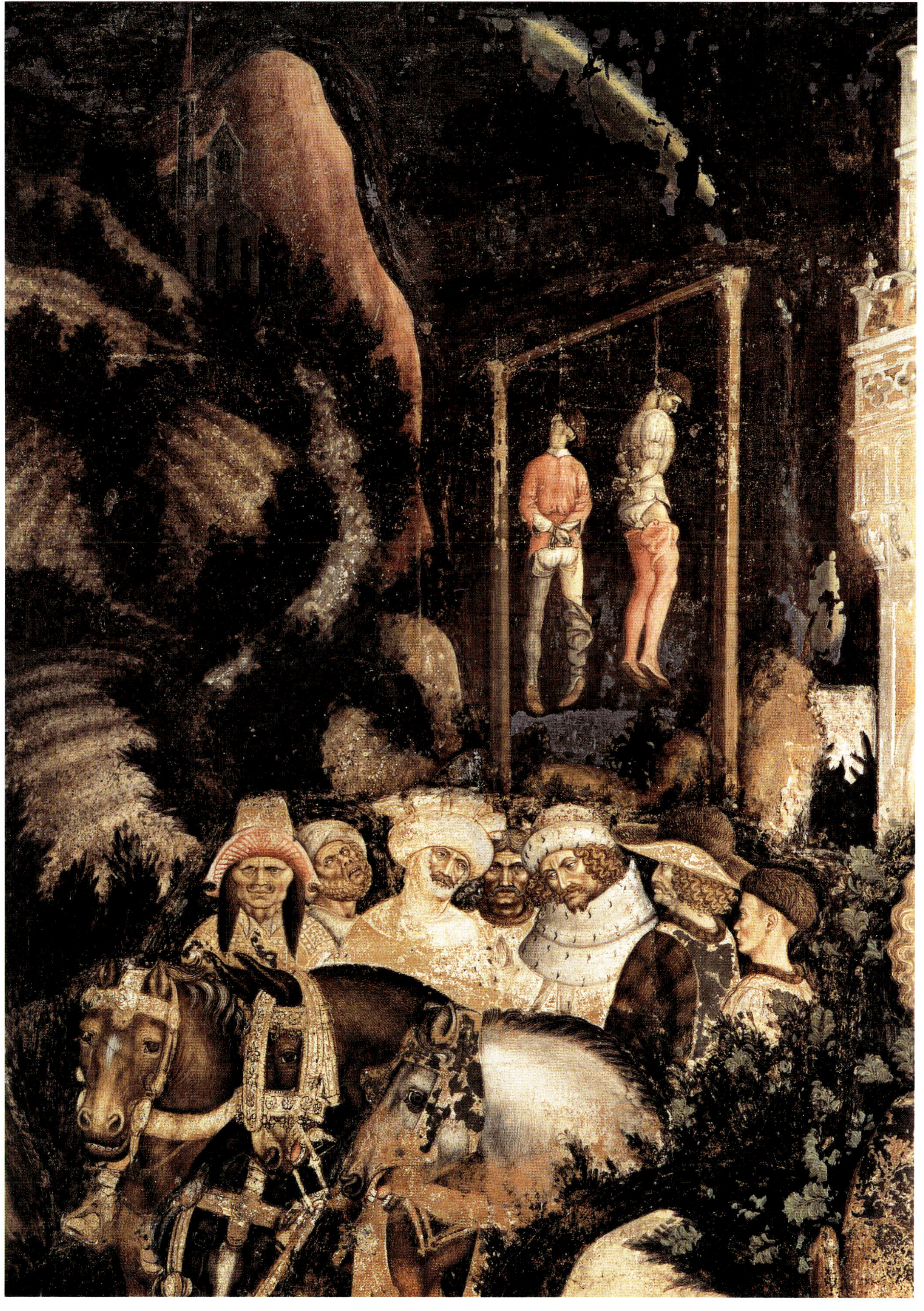

The courts of fifteenth-century Italy

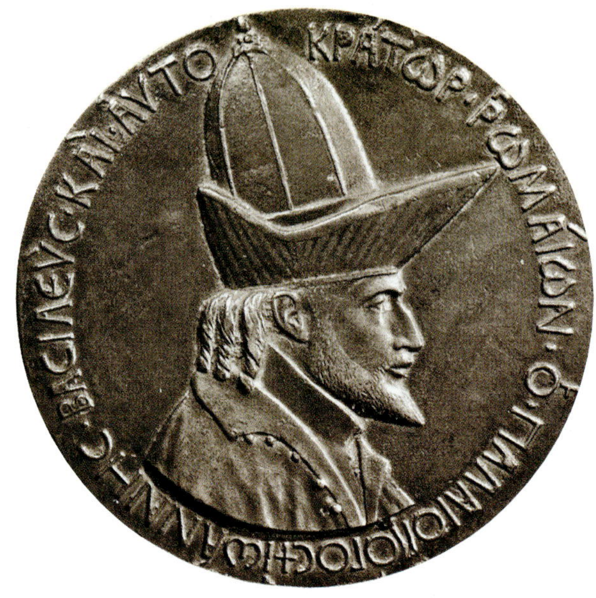

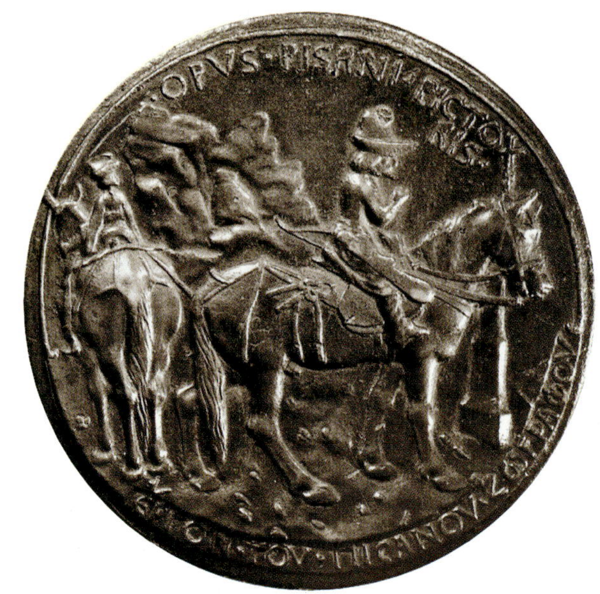

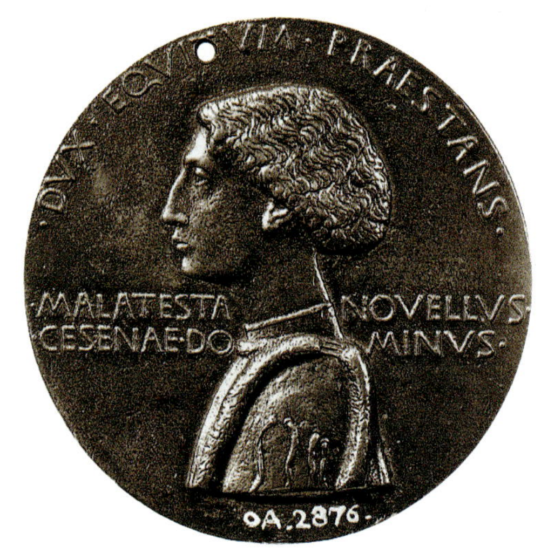

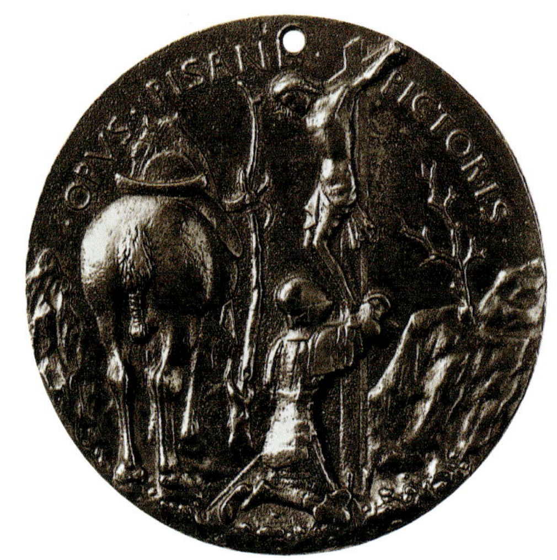

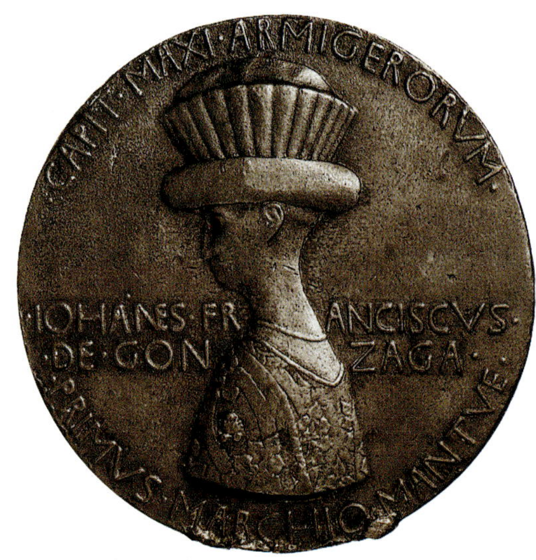

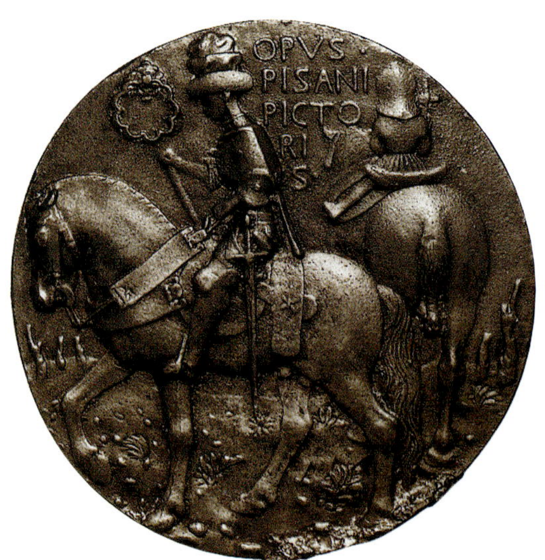

The courts of fifteenth-century Italy

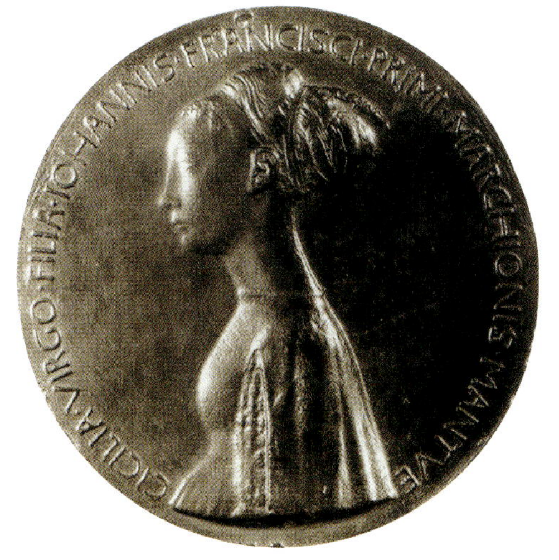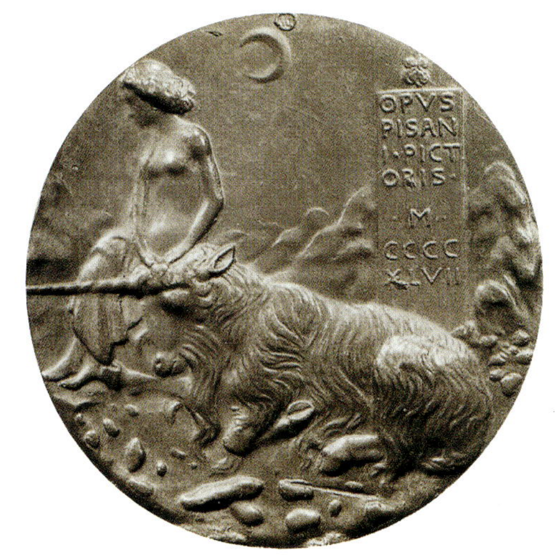

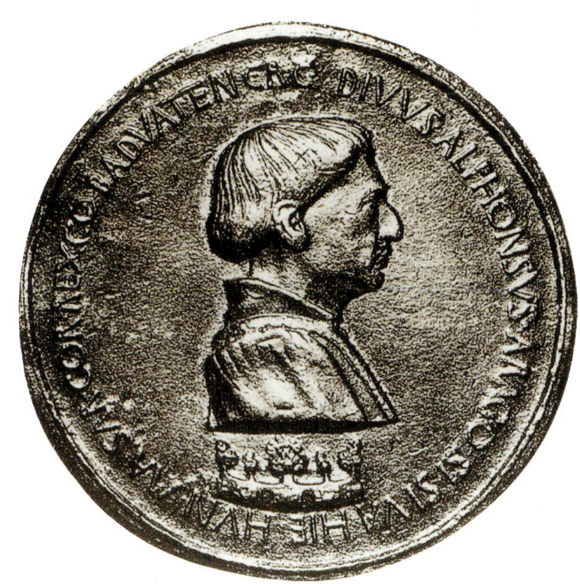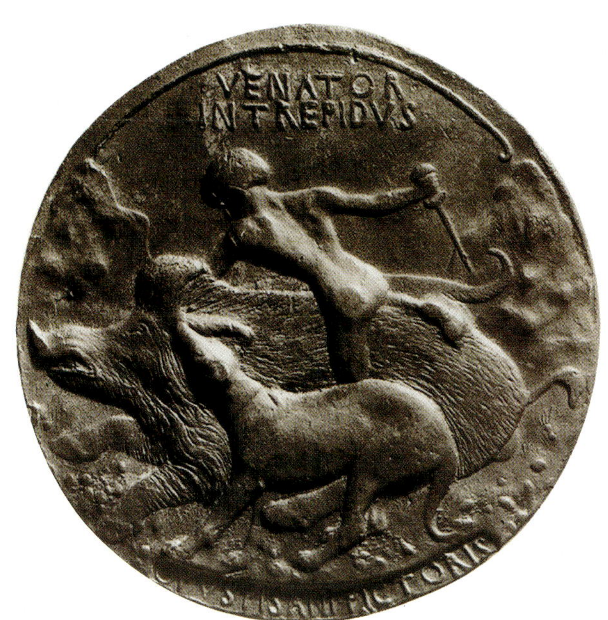

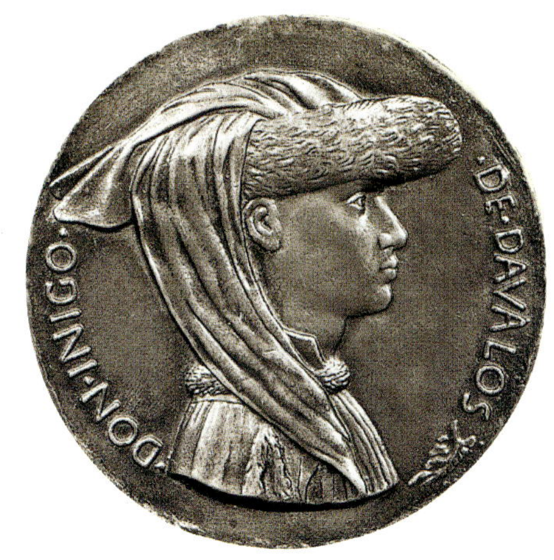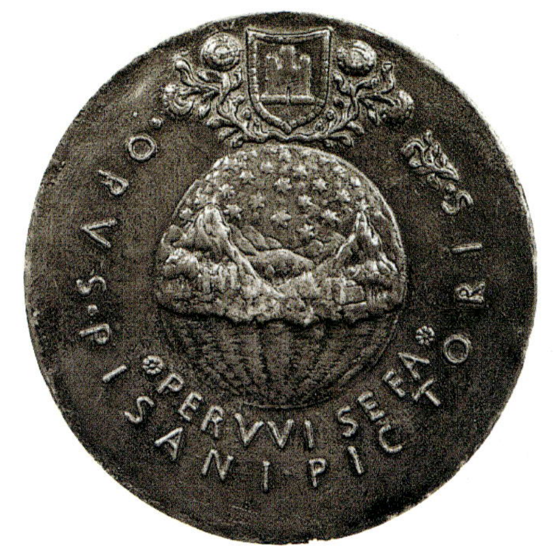

The courts of fifteenth-century Italy

The humanistic culture
was fond of making
evocative parallels
between the present
and ancient times,
using references to
classical myths and
symbols to communi-
cate feelings, actions,
and meanings. An
example of this is the
operation carried out in
the frescoes of Palazzo
Schifanoia in Ferrara,
the Estes's "pleasure
palace" on the outskirts
of the city. The activi-
ties that take place
during the months of
the year are represented
in a mixture of realism
(the architecture,
clothes, and figures)
and classical citations.
The cycle was made by
various artists under
the direction of Cosimo

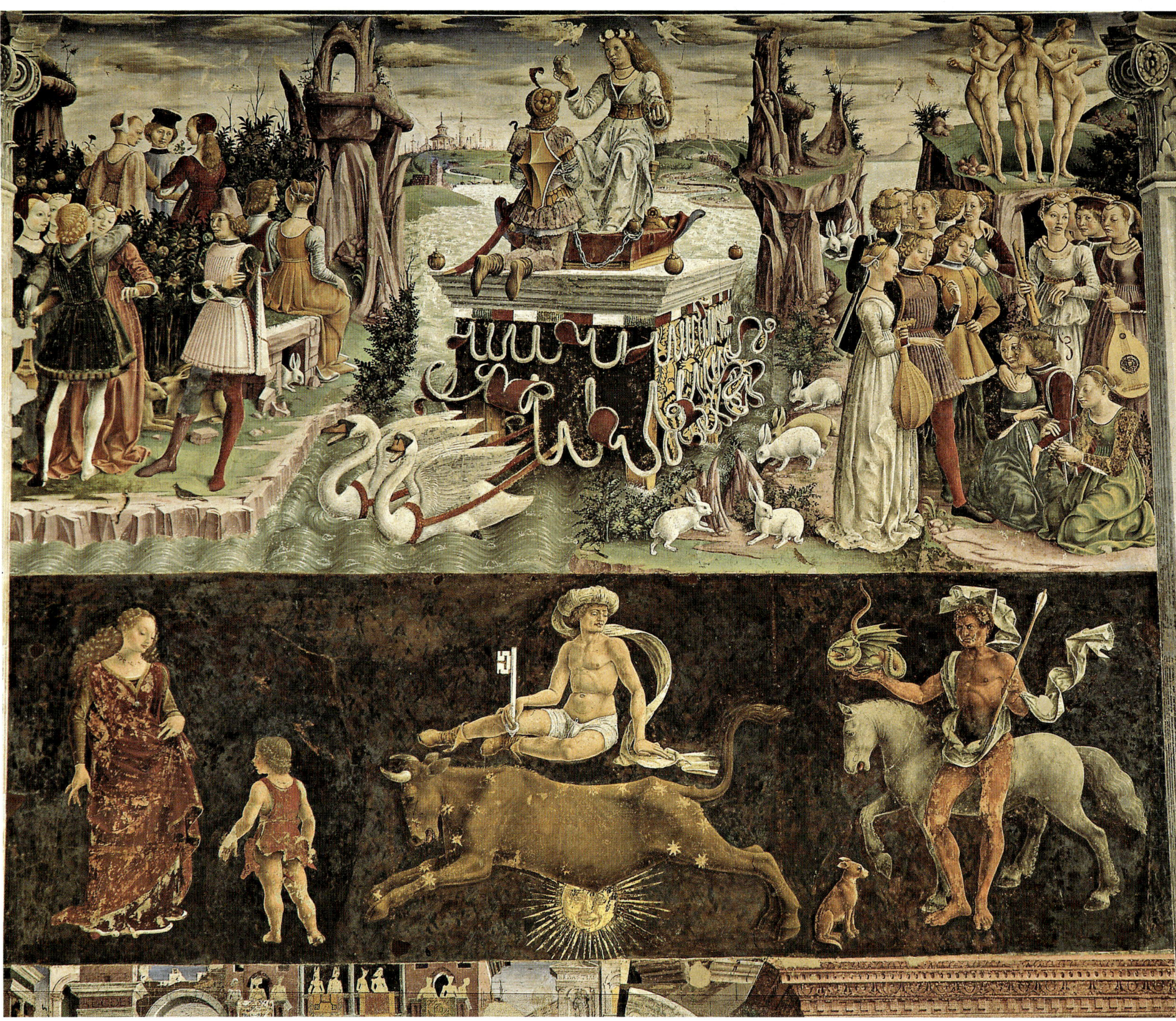

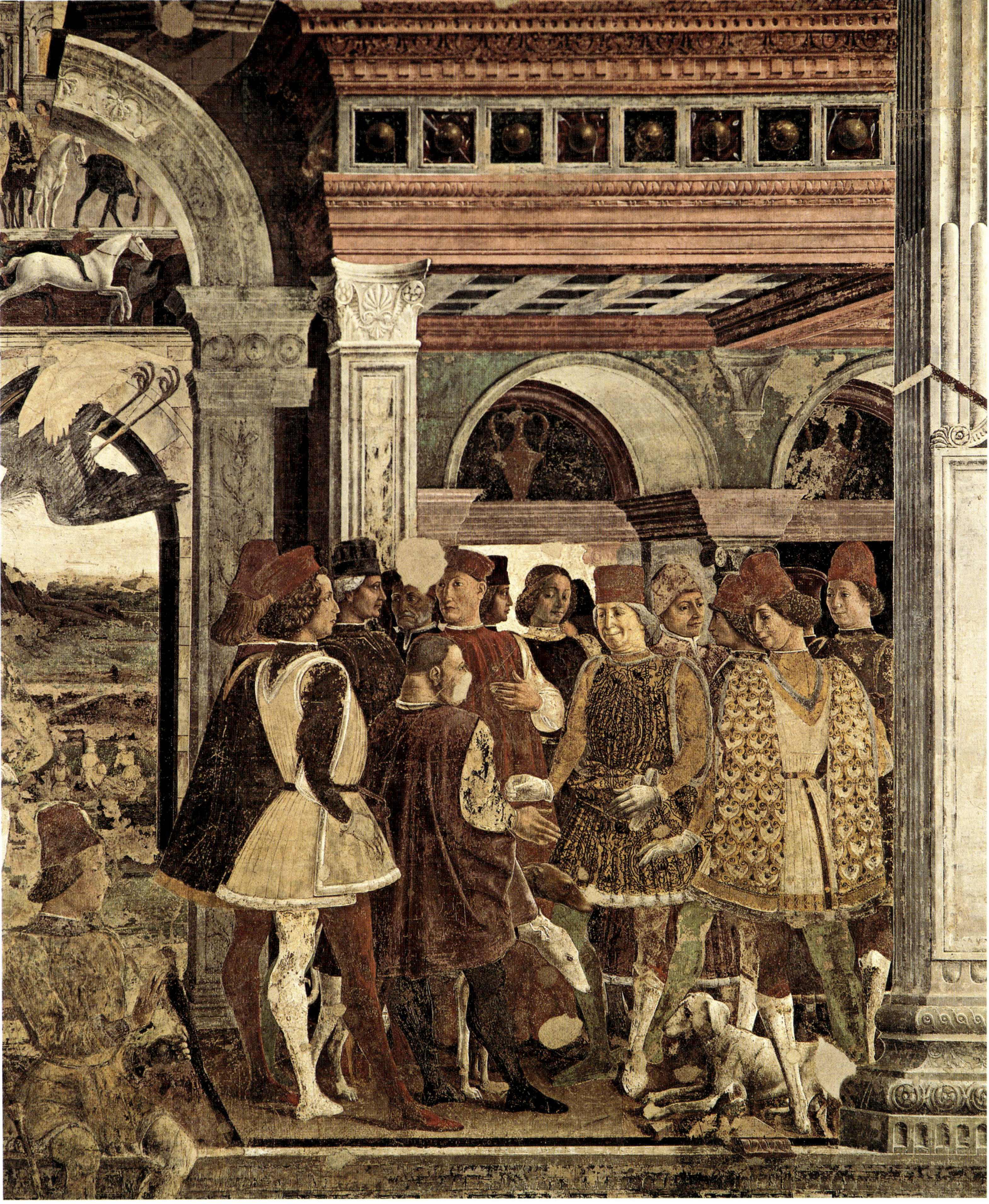

Tura and is, sadly, in a poor condition; one of the best preserved portions is the month of April. The triumph of Venus, goddess of love, is presented in a luminous spring landscape; kneeling before her is a chained Mars, god of war. All around, in fresh green fields, boys and girls experience love: they stand together and speak and sing before touching and, finally, kissing. White rabbits, traditional symbol of amorous union, abound. The taste for precious details and for the amusing description of small, secondary episodes, such as the youths embracing behind the bushes or the pensive boy who has failed to find a companion, still belong to the taste of noble courts, precisely like that of Ferrara. In this sense, in terms of their many and varied themes that interweave and take place on different levels of narration, the frescoes in the Schifanoia Palace can be compared to the chivalric poems composed for the Estes by Boiardo, Ariosto, and Tasso.

The courts of fifteenth-century Italy

Typical creations of the
figurative civilization
of the Italian fifteenth
century, these paint-
ings are works that
exist between art and
mathematics, painting
and geometry, poetic
invention and proof of
a theorem. Much like
such enigmatic, fasci-
nating panels showing
the arrangements of
silent cityscapes,
the Urbino palace of
Federico da Montefeltro
began, in 1465, to
recreate the marvel of

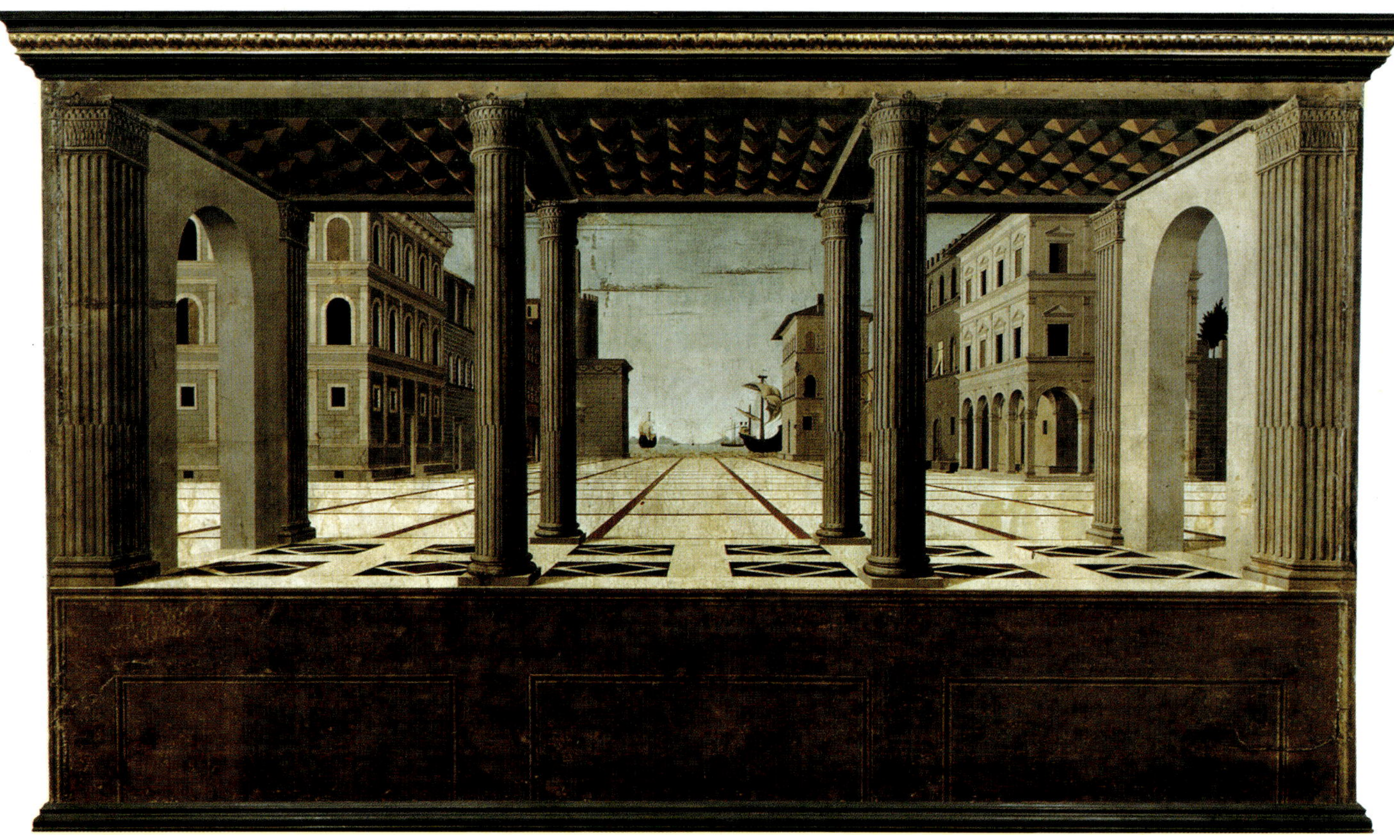

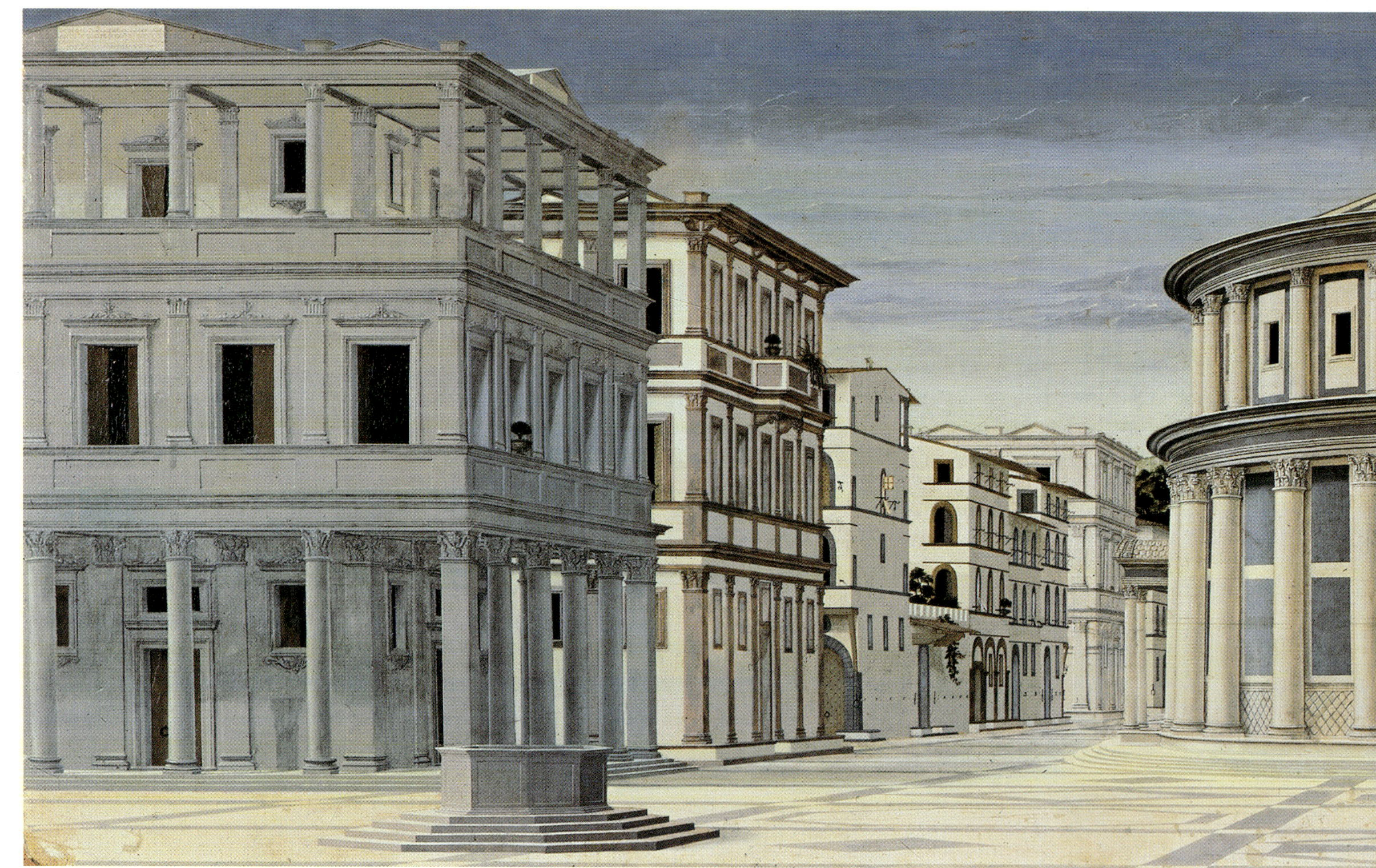

The courts of fifteenth-century Italy

an "ideal city" of the Renaissance, in which the "divine proportion" regulated every thing, measuring itself with the breath of nature, while the convergence of intellectuals and artists from many different nations gave the debate an international tone. The Montefeltro rulers transformed Urbino from the modest center of a small dukedom among the hills to a "city in the form of a palace." Every street, every house, every small angle was part of a quiet harmony in which the elegance of the proportions, the rhythm of the architecture, and the relationship between the city and the countryside flowed with spontaneous naturalness while at the same time presenting a stupendous example of a purely rational conception.

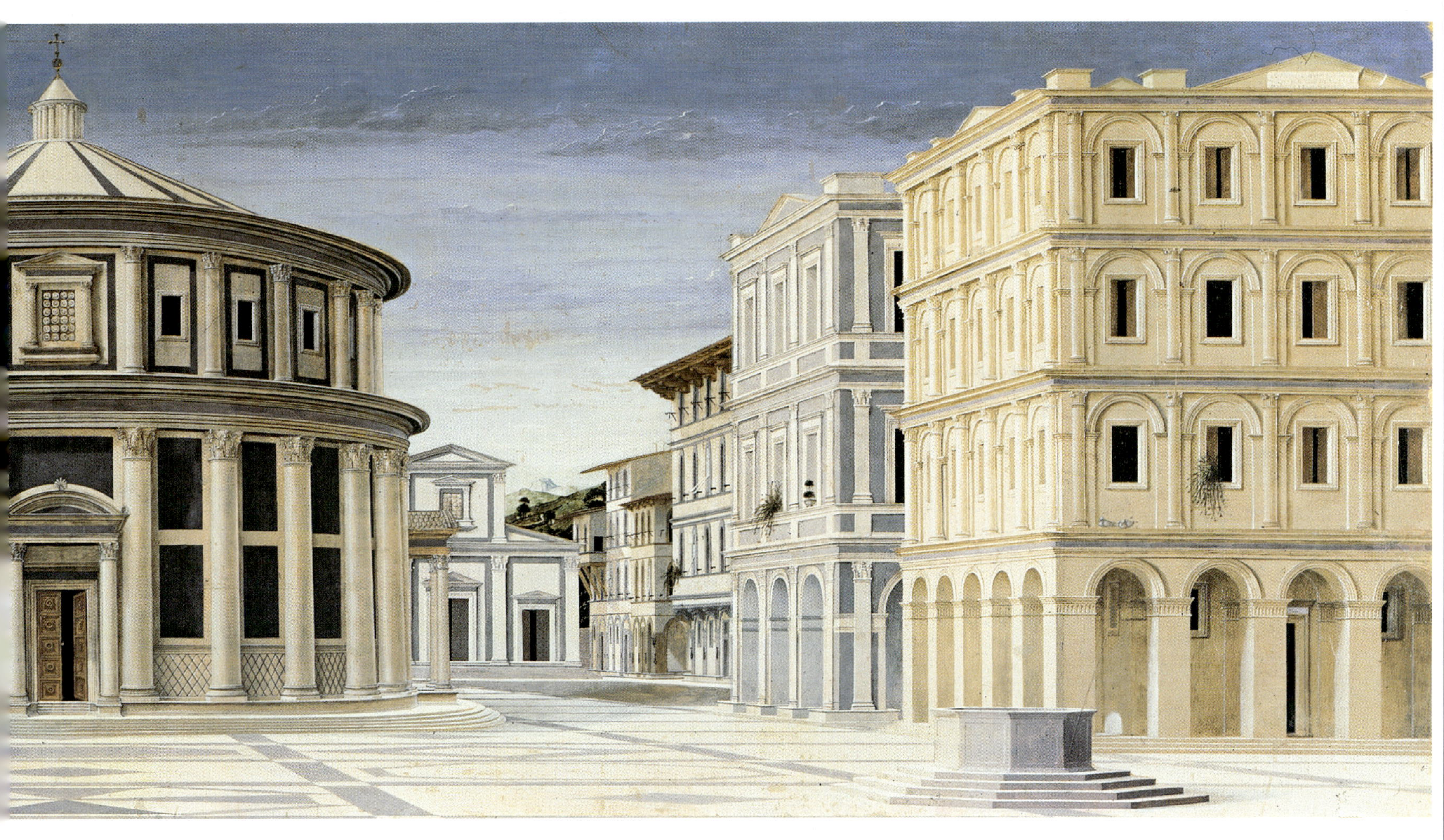

The courts of fifteenth-century Italy

The incomparable wooden intarsia of the *studiolo* of the duke of Urbino present a symbolic rendition of his history. After years passed wearing a suit of armor, a lover of peace as only true men of war can be, the duke was finally able to remove his breastplate. Now it was time for the Muses. There on the shelves were the instruments of knowledge and art: the astrolabe and the lute, the book and the armillary sphere. Looking down from above were the faces of *Famous Men*, ancient writers and thinkers far off in time but present in the silence of this minuscule heart of the great realm, this tiny space created among the great halls.

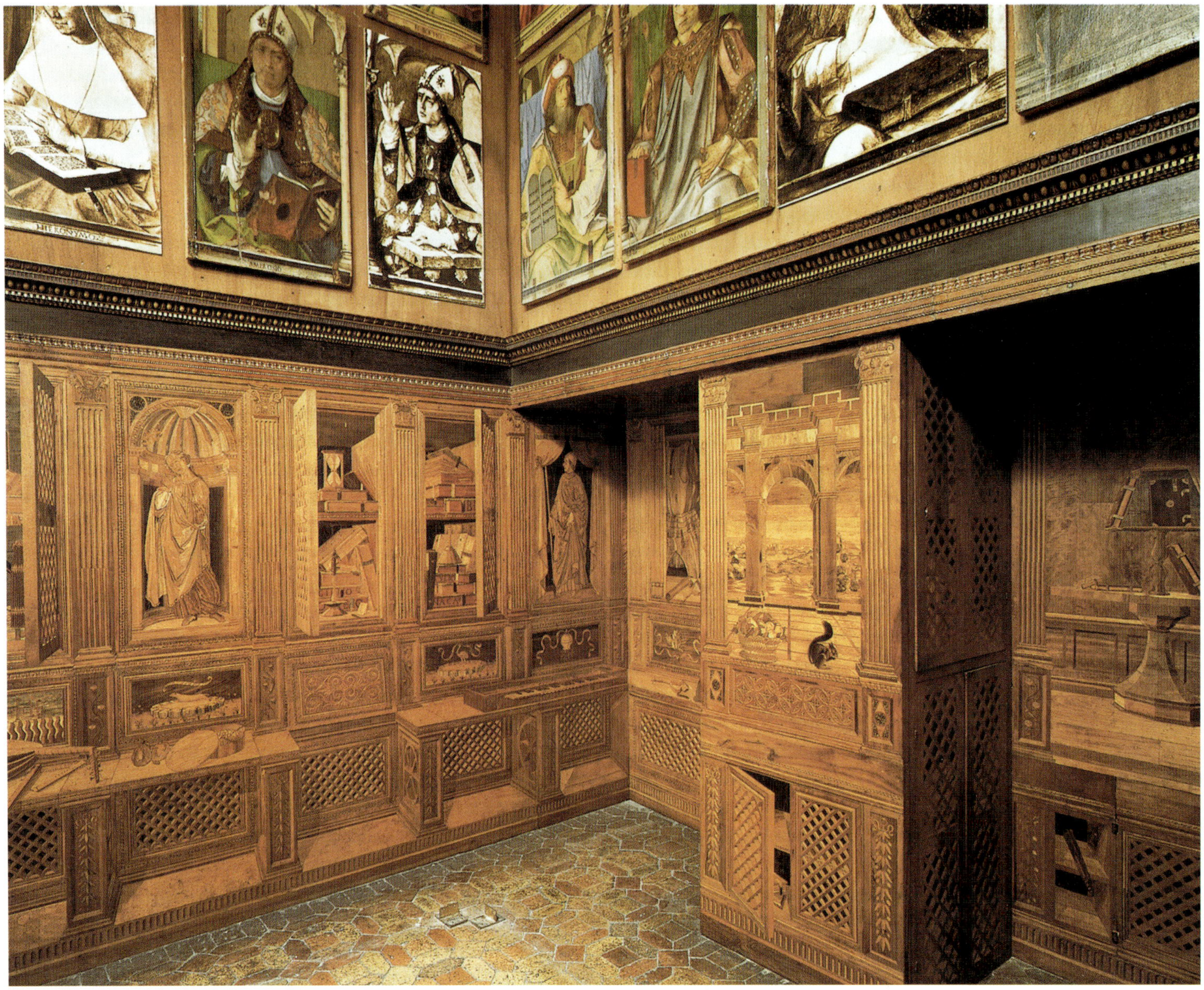

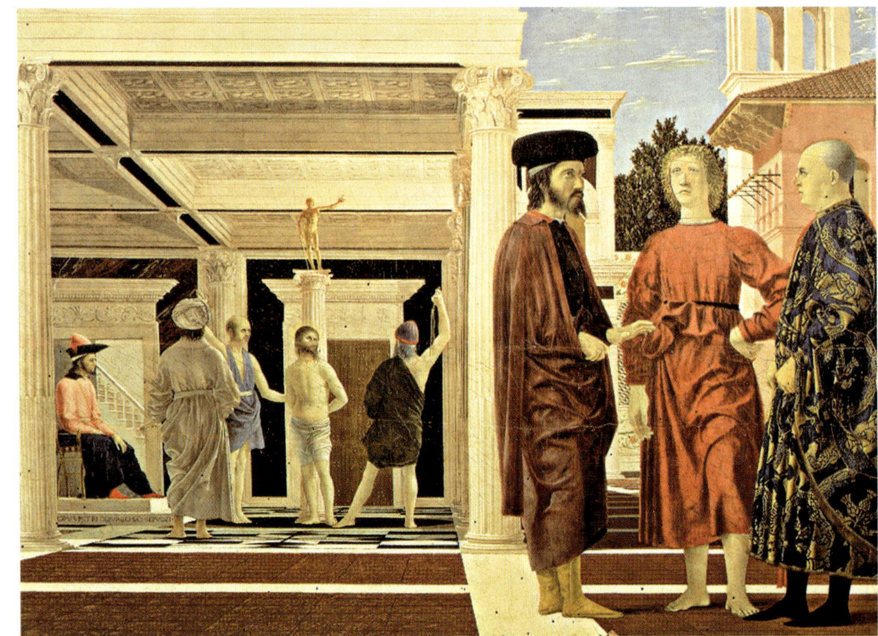

In this famous panel, the space is measured off on the basis of a strict geometric grid, while the natural light emphasizes the values of the perspective; but the whole, as in the three figures on the right, has an enigmatic sense.

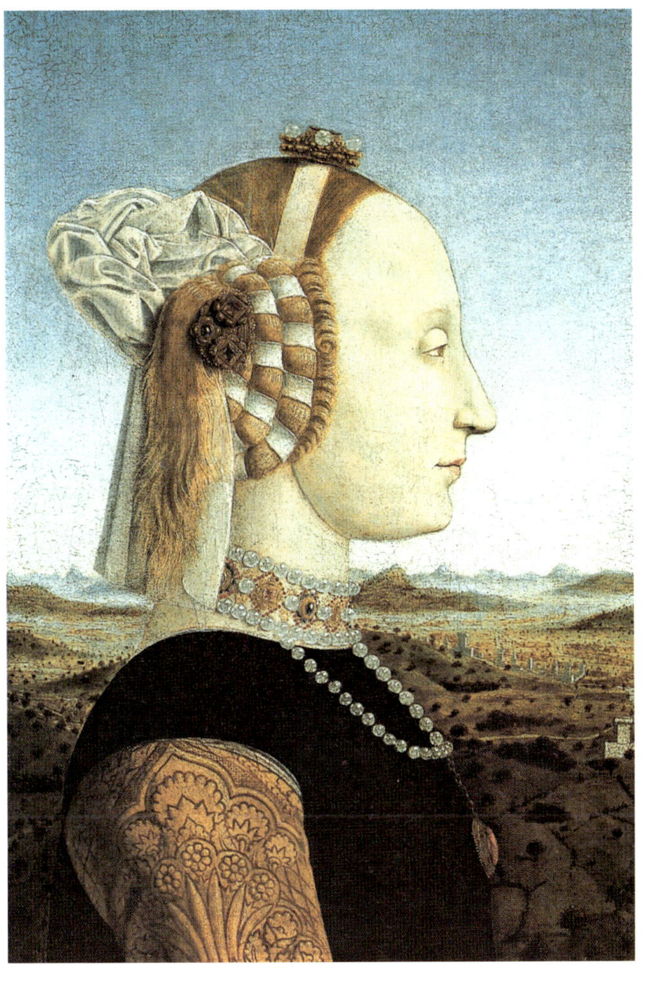
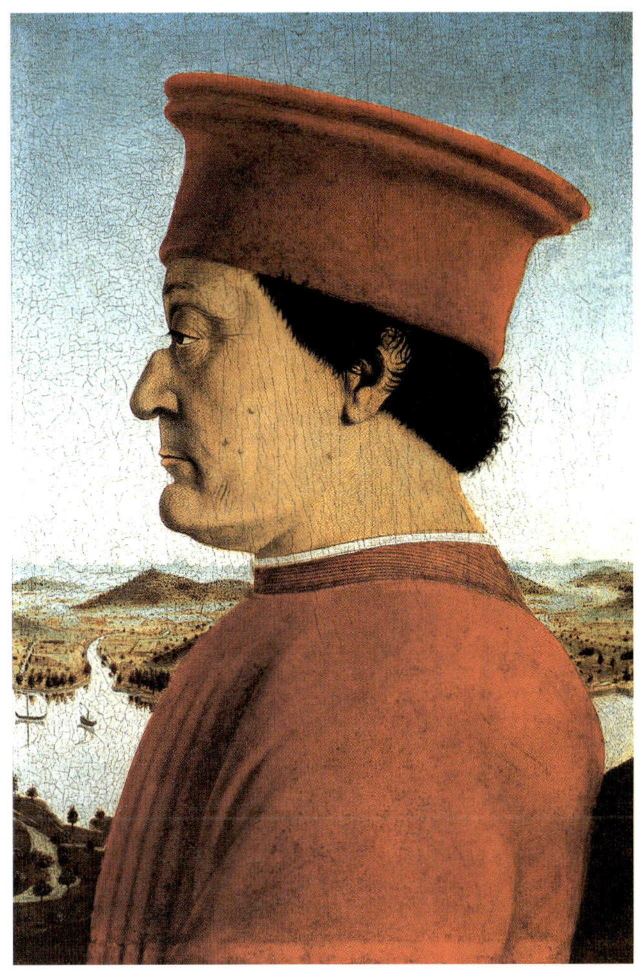

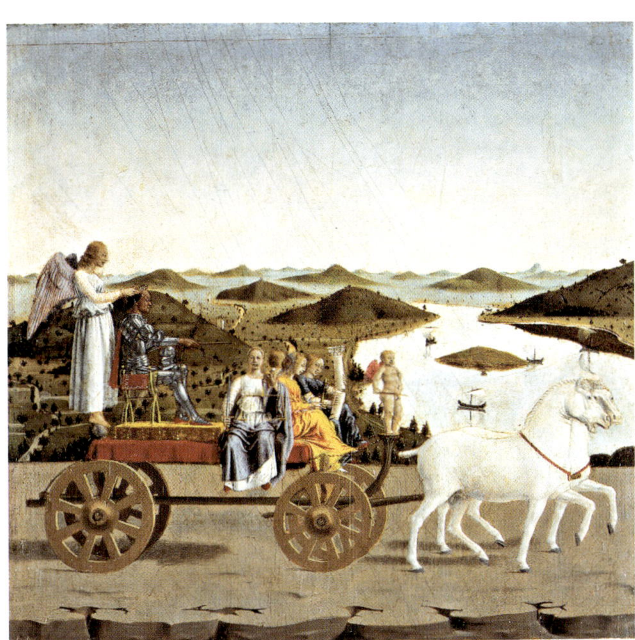

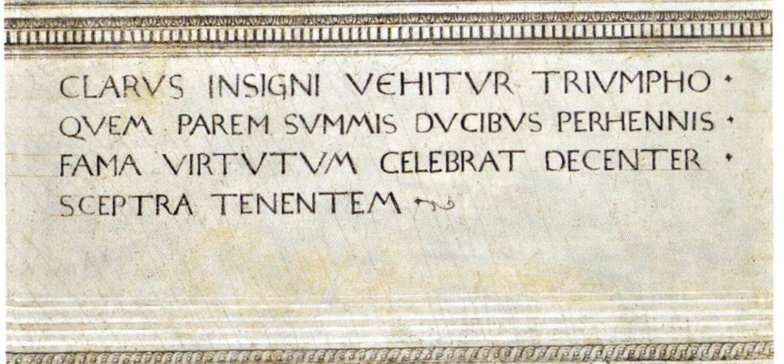

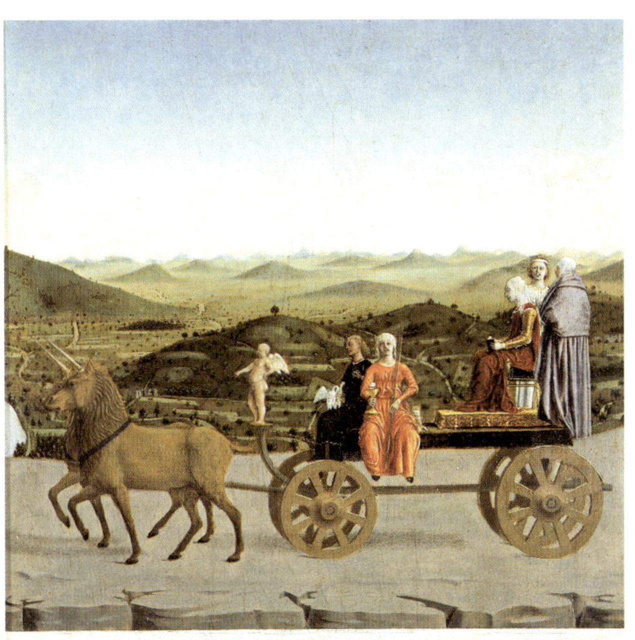

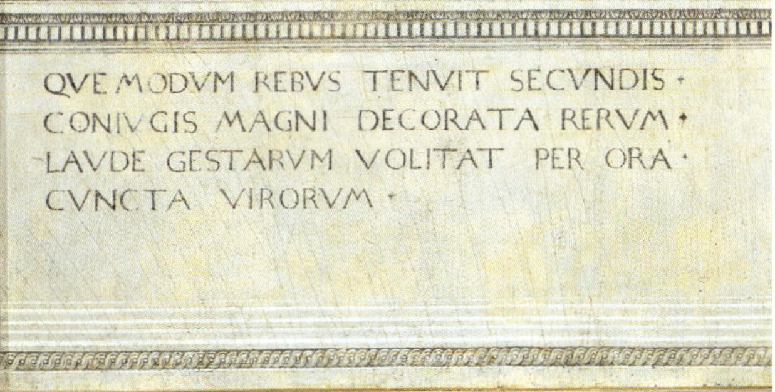

■ PIERO DELLA FRANCESCA
Urbino Diptych
On the obverse, portraits of Battista Sforza and Federico da Montefeltro; on the reverse, allegorical triumphs of the dukes, 1465–70, tempera and oil on panel, 47 x 33 cm each
Galleria degli Uffizi, Florence

The profiles of the rulers stand out against the hilly background of Montefeltro; a landscape that reappears on the reverse of the panels, which present the allegorical triumphs of the Urbino rulers. The simplification of the volumes (Battista Sforza alludes to the circle, Federico is inscribed in a square) contrasts with the minute details of the painting, comparable to Flemish art. Despite his not overly attractive appearance, Federico had his personal image multiplied, as if the palace of Urbino (built in the image and resemblance of his intellectual spirit) were an immense mirror in which he was everywhere being reflected. He is a constant presence accompanying the visitor, thanks not only to paintings, including his official portraits with the heir Guidobaldo, but also in the wooden intarsias in the enchanting *studiolo*, in the sculpture located in on the stairs, in the decorative friezes, in the repetition of his coat of arms and his monogram.

PIERO DELLA FRANCESCA
Montefeltro Altarpiece
circa 1472–74, tempera and oil on panel, 251 x 172 cm
Pinacoteca di Brera, Milan

This altarpiece was originally in the church of San Bernardino in Urbino, conceived as the funeral chapel for Duke Federico da Montefeltro. The great painter's two souls can be said to meet in this work. On one hand there are the theories of geometry, Piero himself being the author of an important treatise on perspective; on the other is the artist as creator, driven to the fashioning of an ideal image. The scene is located inside a Renaissance structure whose proportions are carefully measured in relation to the figures. The light models the figures with silent clarity, giving the group the sense of a celestial court, arranged following a precise hierarchical order. The Madonna, at the center, is seated on a folding chair; to her sides are six saints; behind are four angels, recognizable by the tips of their wings visible over their shoulders; the armored duke kneels in the act of devotion. The ostrich egg (allusion to both to the birth of Jesus and the Montefeltro coat of arms) suspended on a chain from the seashell inside the apse contributes to giving the scene its impressive sense of depth.

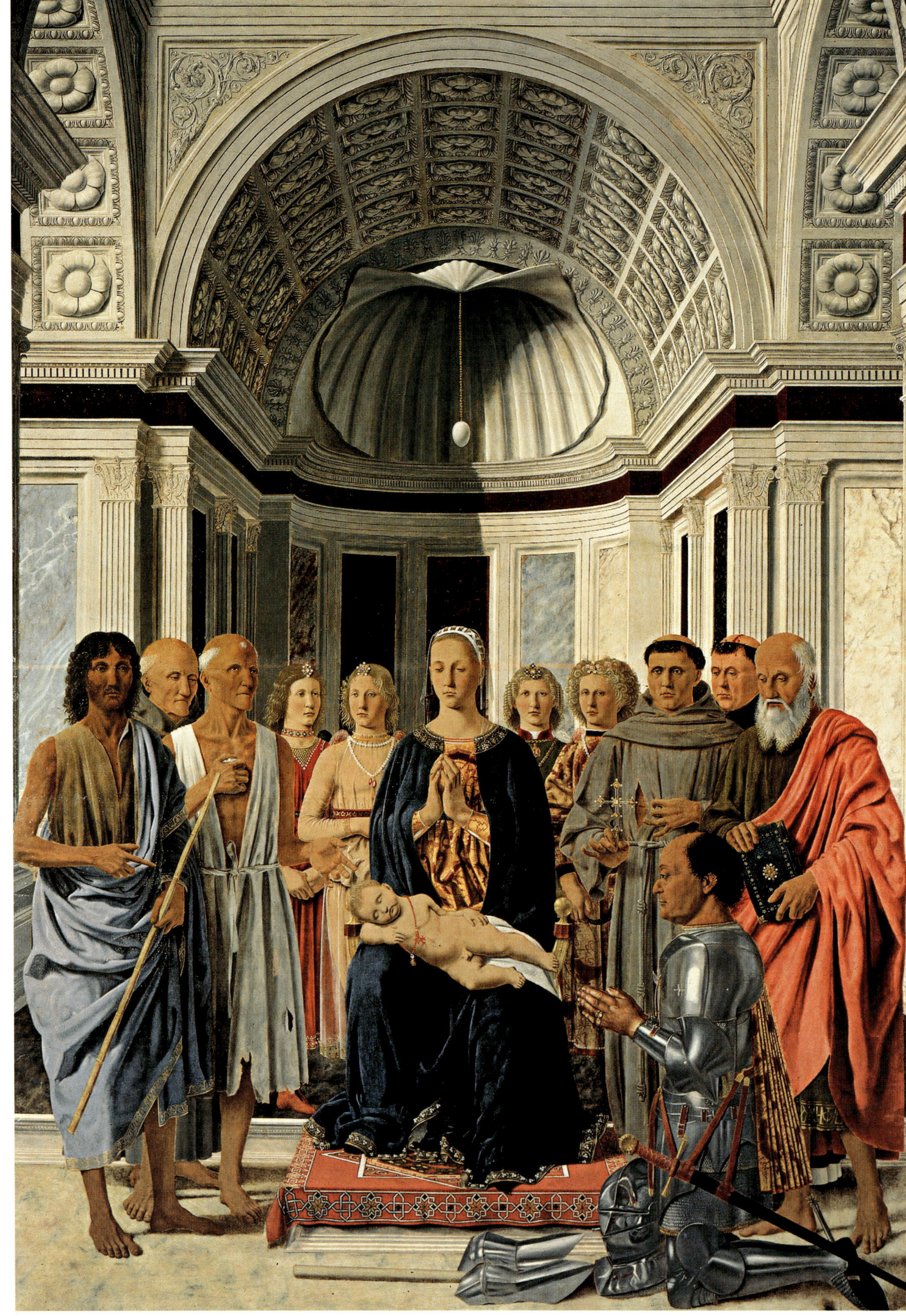

The courts of fifteenth-century Italy

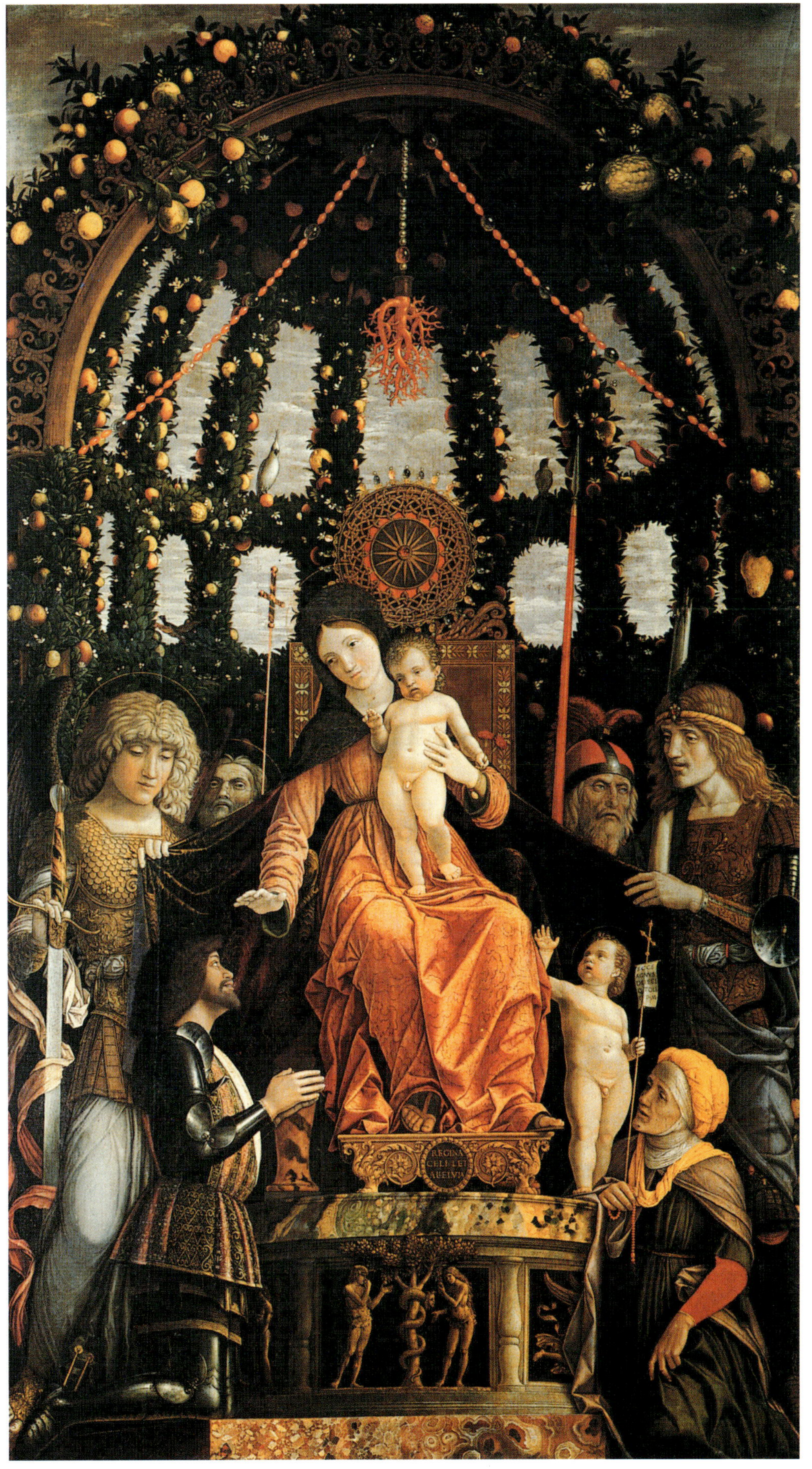

This altarpiece, with its majestic layout, was made to celebrate the battle of Fornovo (1495), at which Francesco Gonzaga ended French king Charles VIII's conquest of northern Italy. In truth, it was no more than a partial victory, but it evidently pleased the Mantuan nobleman to be—or to be seen as—the "liberator" of Italy. In an ironic twist, following the dispersion of the Gonzaga collection, the painting ended up the Louvre. Mantegna ingeniously changes the usual perspective scheme of an altarpiece, placing behind the Madonna not an architectonic background but an enormous, curving pergola, a sort of natural apse with leaves, fruit, flowers, and birds. While maintaining its sense of solemn stateliness, the scene is given lightness and atmosphere by being opened in the back to a sky across which clouds are rushing. The enormous branch of coral that hangs at the center of the composition had a symbolic value of protection and good omens.

The decoration of the so-called Camera degli Sposi is the most famous example of profane painting at the Italian courts of the Renaissance: the precious details of the late Gothic give way to scenes of great breadth supported by solid perspective and a dedication to natural observation. Two sides of the room are covered by a painted curtain that is pulled aside to reveal scenes of the Gonzagas. At the entrance, on a wall measured off with painted columns and classical motifs, a landscape full of references to Roman monuments hosts the *Meeting of the Marchese Ludovico and His Cardinal Son*, accompanied by a cortège of pages with decked-out horses and hounds; this is followed on the next wall by the *Court of the Gonzagas*, in which Mantegna demonstrates notable skills as a portraitist, varying his technique to reproduce the pink cheeks of girls, the severe faces of the older people, the smile of a dwarf.

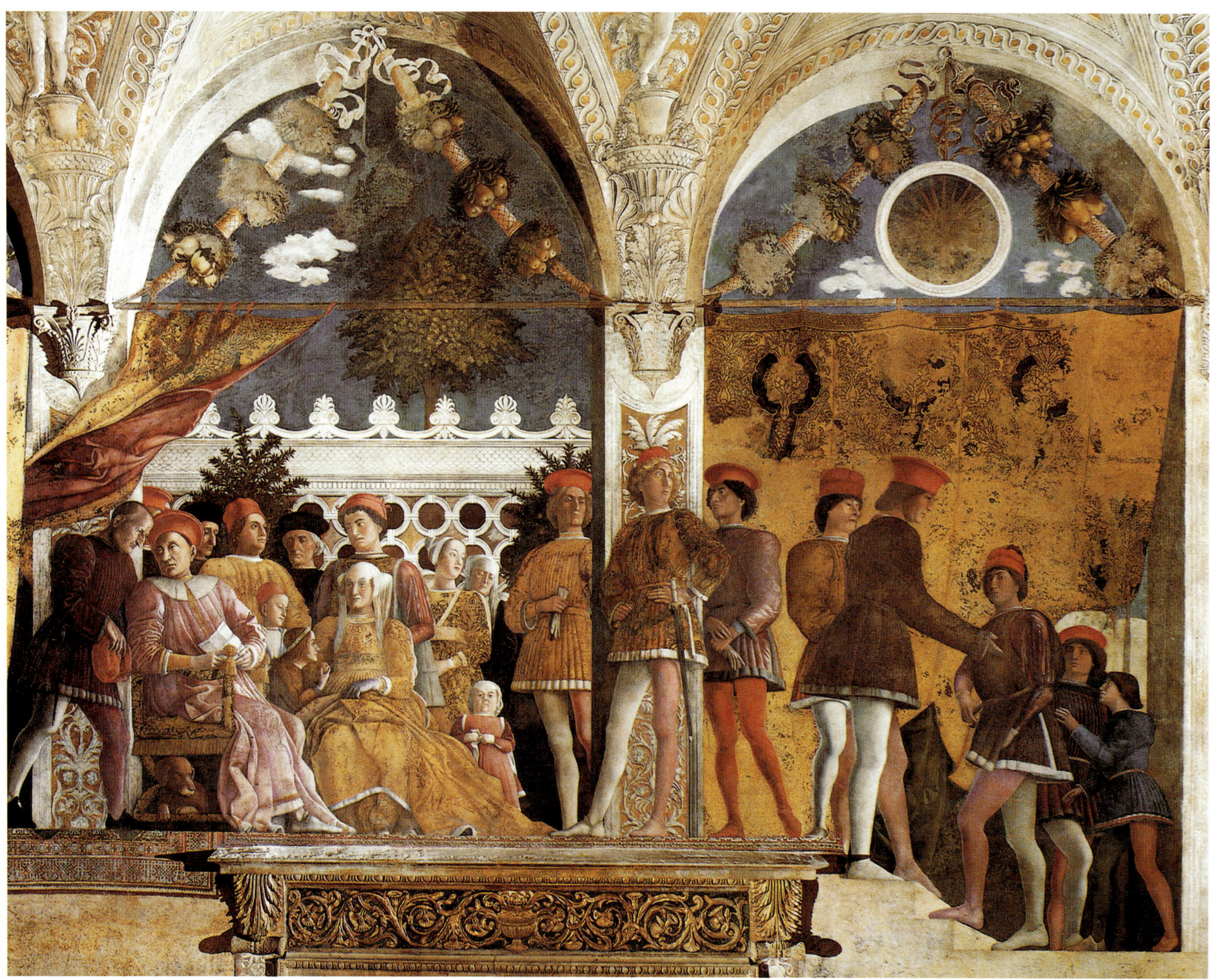

The courts of fifteenth-century Italy

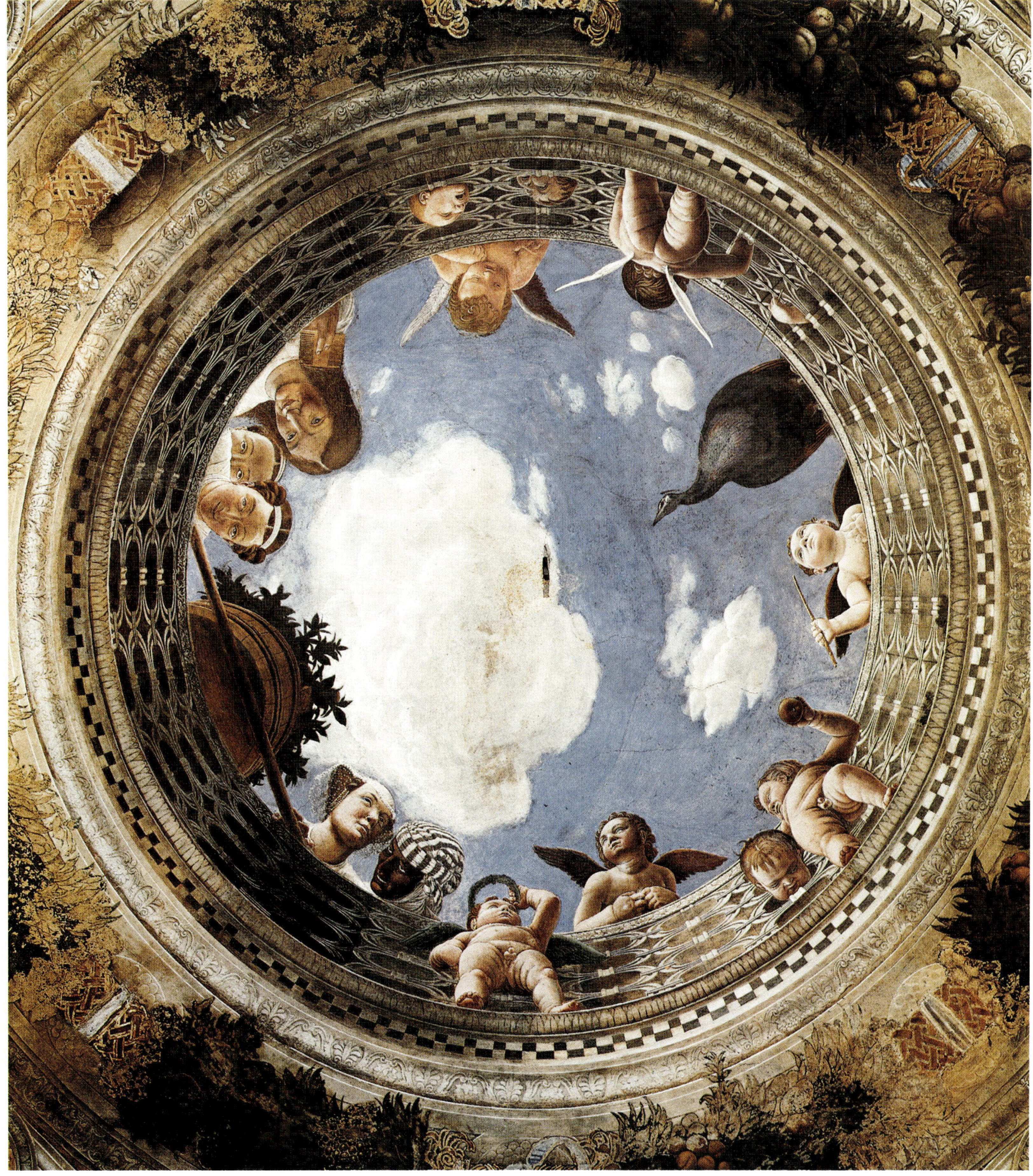

At the middle of the
vault of the *camera
picta* ("painted room")
is a circular oculus with
which Mantegna illu-
sionistically opened
the ceiling, creating a
false balustrade over
which various women
and putti, along with
an ostrich, are pre-
sented looking down
in steep perspective,
behind them a blue sky
crossed by clouds. This
daring work of illusion-
istic cunning became
an example for artists
of later generations,
first among them
Correggio in the fres-
coes of Parma. The
other parts of the vault
simulate a partition in
decorative stucco parti-
tions bearing busts of
Roman emperors.

Commissioned by Isabella d'Este to decorate her private *studiolo*, a jewel case of masterpieces inspired by classical subjects, these two canvases belong to the painter's later period. The first presents the Greek divinities related to Mount Parnassus in a natural landscape. The center is occupied by the dance of the nine Muses, inspired by Apollo playing the lyre. Above them, standing atop a sort of natural bridge-alcove, are the adulterous lovers Mars and Venus; beside them a small Cupid mocks Vulcan, Venus's husband, who swears against his faithless wife. At the far right is the god Mercury with the winged-horse Pegasus, beside Castalia, the mythical spring sacred to the Muses. The second painting is one of Mantegna's last works. Even denser with literary and moral references, it presents Athena, goddess of wisdom, bursting into the garden of the virtues to drive off a small crowd of brats, each of whom symbolizes a vice. Humanized trees and animated clouds add further fascination.

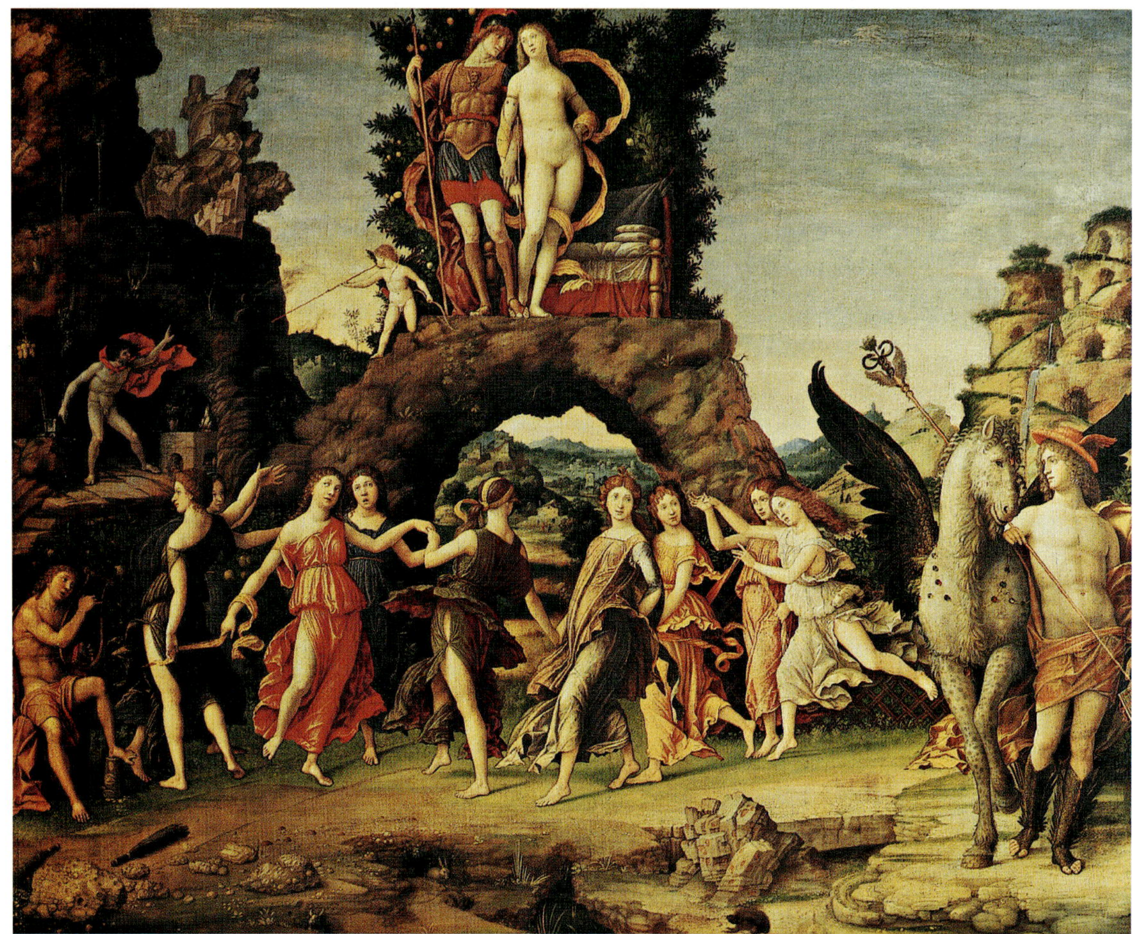

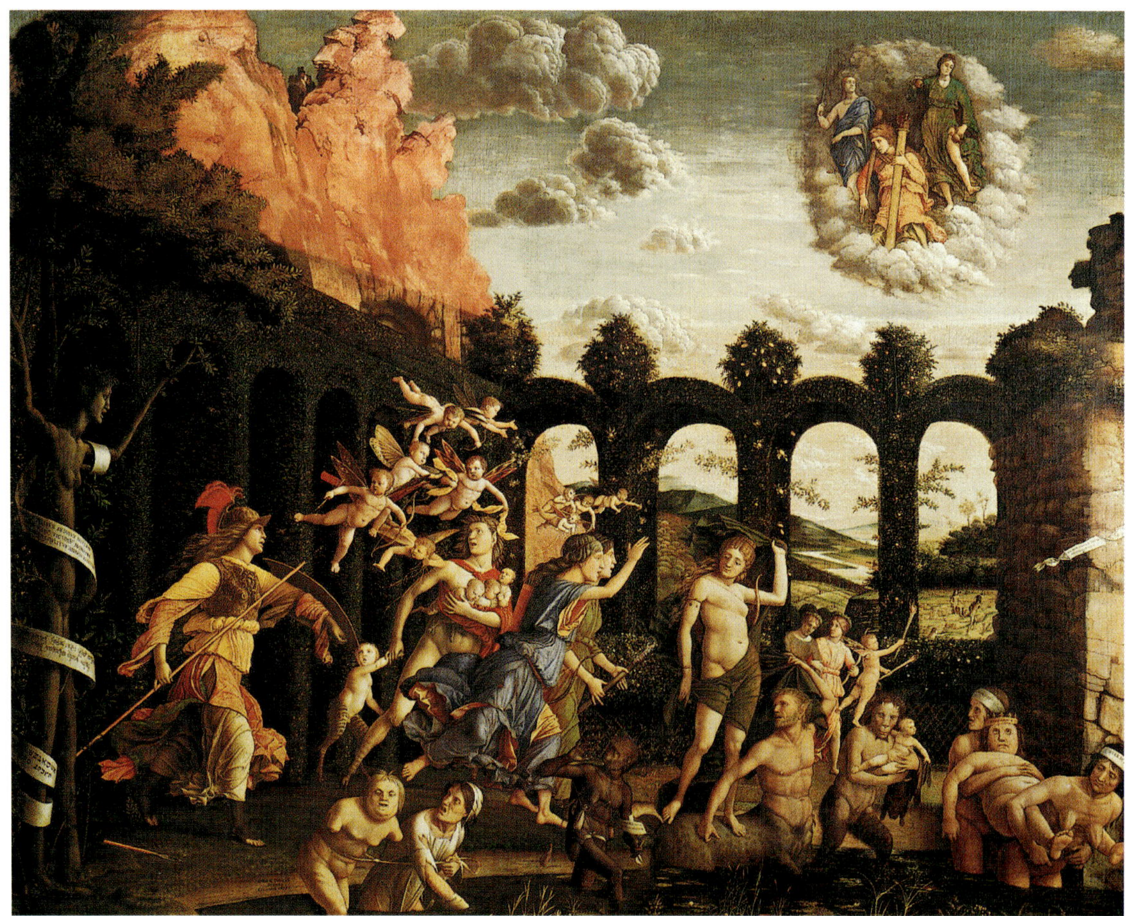

The courts of fifteenth-century Italy

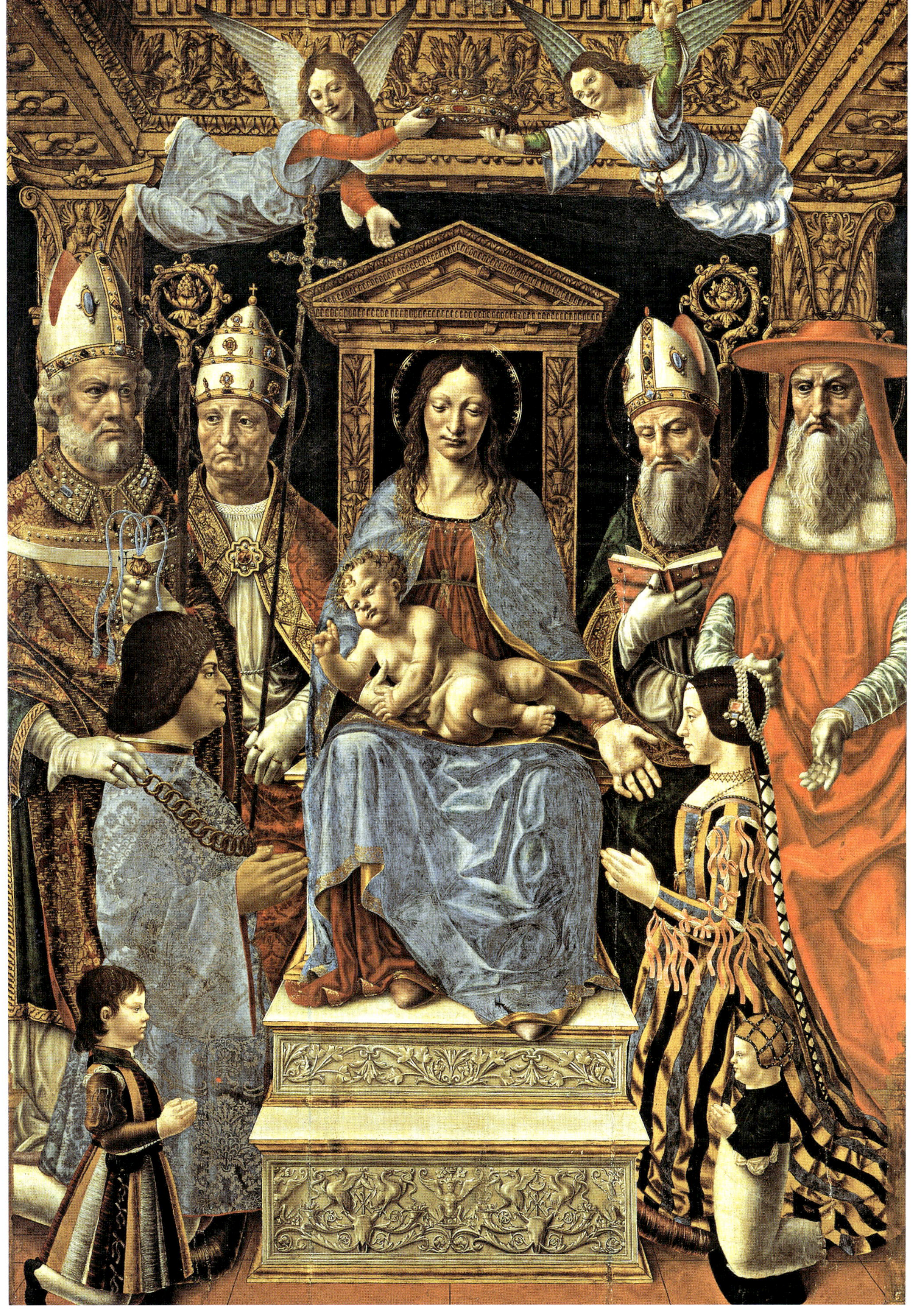

In 1494 Ludovico il Moro, hoping to have himself portrayed with his family in an altarpiece of notable importance, destined for the church of Sant'Ambrogia ad Nemus, turned to a painter who has unfortunately remained unknown and is conventionally called the Master of the Pala Sforzesca. By then Leonardo da Vinci had been living at the court in Milan for twelve years, and it was precisely around 1494 that he began preparatory work on the *Last Supper*. The Sforzesca Altarpiece marks a very important episode in the artistic history of Milan at the end of the fifteenth century, since the painter the duke chose exhibits a great many heterogeneous references. The Lombard tradition is joined to a clear effort at up-to-date humanism, leaving little room for the precious details of courtly taste. The duke and his family members, kneeling in profile, are placed in a sumptuous court of the Madonna, in the presence of four Doctors of the Church: a flood of gold, elegant clothes, shiny jewels, and luxurious ornaments wraps everything, almost impeding the recognition of the many references to Leonardo.

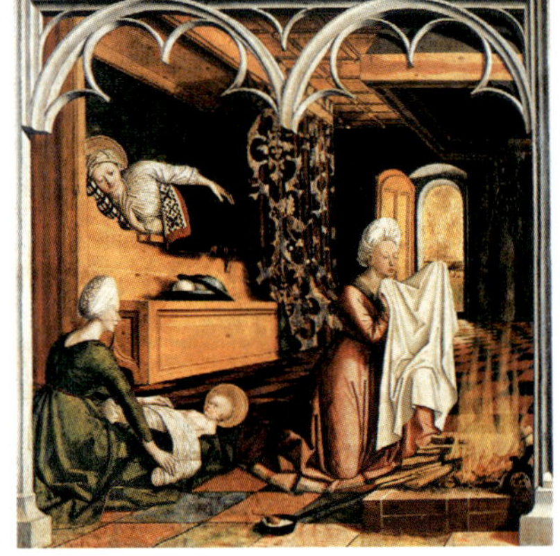

T he Jubilee Year 1450 was an important occasion for the development of European art because many leading artists from different national schools converged on Rome. The most interesting developments are presented by the case of Piero della Francesca, thanks to whom the passage was made from the age of the "pioneers" to that of the diffusion of the humanistic acquisitions over an increasingly vast territory.

Piero occupies a central position in fifteenth-century Italian and European art. Member of the second generation of humanist painters, he achieved full concord between art and geometry, between the calculated application of the rules of linear perspective and poetic expression. Piero got his artistic training in Florence, but all of his later career took place in the "provinces" (Sansepolcro, Arezzo, Rimini, Ferrara, Urbino, Perugia), so that he made a contribution of fundamental importance to the spread of humanist art to places outside Florence, just as Donatello, in exactly in those same years, was doing in Padua. In 1452 Piero began work on what would prove to be the most important undertaking of his career, the *Legend of the True Cross*

One of the key figures in the spread of humanistic motifs north of the Alps was the Frenchman Jean Fouquet. Royal portraitist beginning in the 1440s, after early activity related to the Burgundy school, Fouquet made a long trip to Italy, visiting Rome, Naples, and Florence, entering in contact with the perspective artists (Fra Angelico, Domenico Veneziano, Piero della Francesca) and studying ancient monuments. Back at the French court he achieved an effective combination of the naturalistic accuracy of the Flemings with the spatial monumentality and the clarity of light absorbed in Italy. Versatile painter, matchless creator of illuminations, Fouquet parted with the Gothic tradition to formulate a new figurative language, the highest pictorial expression of humanism in France. Fouquet is one of the major miniaturists of art history. Characteristic traits of his work are the compositional matching of images, the ability to present settings, natural details, and costumes in fascinating detail, and finally the precious technique of dusting with gold, which gives clothing an extraordinary luminosity.

Also in France, but in the Midi, Enguerrand Quarton was the greatest

The spread of from Tuscany

in Arezzo, one of the most important works of the European Renaissance because of the variety of its narrative situations, the monumentality of its figures, the faultless calculation of its spaces, and the intensity of its expressions. Piero did most of his work in the 1460s in Urbino, at the court of Federico da Montefeltro. Aside from several masterpieces, this period of his career was marked by many encounters with international artists, such as Pedro Berruguete and Justus of Ghent, and by the writing of treatises on geometry, perspective, and algebra. Because of failing eyesight he was forced to quit painting around the mid-1470s. By a singular coincidence, the artist who symbolized the intellectual world of the fifteenth century died on the same day as the discovery of the New World, October 12, 1492.

and most original among the Provençal masters of the fifteenth century. He represents a point of convergence among Flemish precision, Mediterranean light, and the compositional rigor of Piero della Francesca. Active in Avignon, he was the author of magnificent works that display a declaredly humanistic monumentality despite the persistence of the use of gold backgrounds.

To live in a border area and to prove oneself capable of making different artistic cultures harmonize are important conditions to becoming the vehicle for the diffusion of ideas and methods. This is proved by the activity of the two leading masters of German painting of the second half of the fifteenth century. Neither of the two was completely "German": Martin Schongauer was an Alsatian from Colmar, tied to a setting permeated by Flemish and Burgundian influences; Michael Pacher was a Tyrolean from Brunico with an up-to-date humanistic knowledge of perspective thanks to years spent in Padua working alongside Donatello and Mantegna. By way of different but parallel routes these two artists led German art toward the renewal of the Renaissance. Schongauer, author of delicate Madonnas and of harmonious religious scenes, was a pioneer of engraving. His prints immediately became widespread in Europe, one of the most famous of them being copied by the young Michelangelo. To a sweetness of sentiments reminiscent of the late Gothic, Schongauer added a meticulous attention in the rendering of drapery and facial expressions. From the lively artistic Alsatian center he kept in contact with various religious institutions, among them the Convent of the Antonites of Isenheim, which later saw the work of Matthis Grünewald.

In the artistic and cultural panorama of Alpine Europe at the end of the fifteenth century Michael Pacher made a cultural and poetic operation of great courage. His Tyrolean origins and his activity, concentrated between Bolzano, Bressanone (Brixen), Innsbruck, and Salzburg, offered him the opportunity of achieving a valid mediation between Italian art and the Germanic world. Many of the altarpieces Pacher caved and painted have been broken up and dispersed or, in some cases, irreparably destroyed, but it is nonetheless possible to recognize his twin powers: on the one hand a perfect knowledge of humanism and perspective, which he learned in Padua beside such masters as Donatello, Filippo Lippi, and Mantegna; and on the other, knowledgeable references to the world of the fables of the Alpine passes region. Thus in Pacher's paintings we find buildings presented in depth with harmonious perspective, but the architecture is still Gothic, with fancifully branching vaults, spires, and jutting balconies; the figures are rendered with perfect anatomical proportions but have the shaded features and intense expressions of northern art; the compositions have the well-balanced monumental breadth of the works being made in Florence during the same period, but they are brightened by the cool light and enameled colors of the last period of the Gothic in Europe. Legends of saints and episodes from the gospels, transferred to the daily life of the towns and mountains of the Tyrol, become expressions of a passionate and heartfelt human story. Even so, Pacher was not fortunate. His death coincided with the affirmation of a new European genius, capable of joining the German world to that of Italy: Dürer, a star whose brightness soon obscured the fame of Pacher.

humanism through Europe

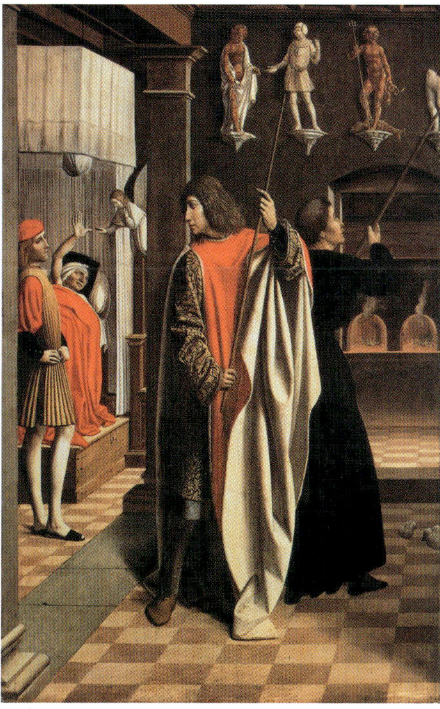

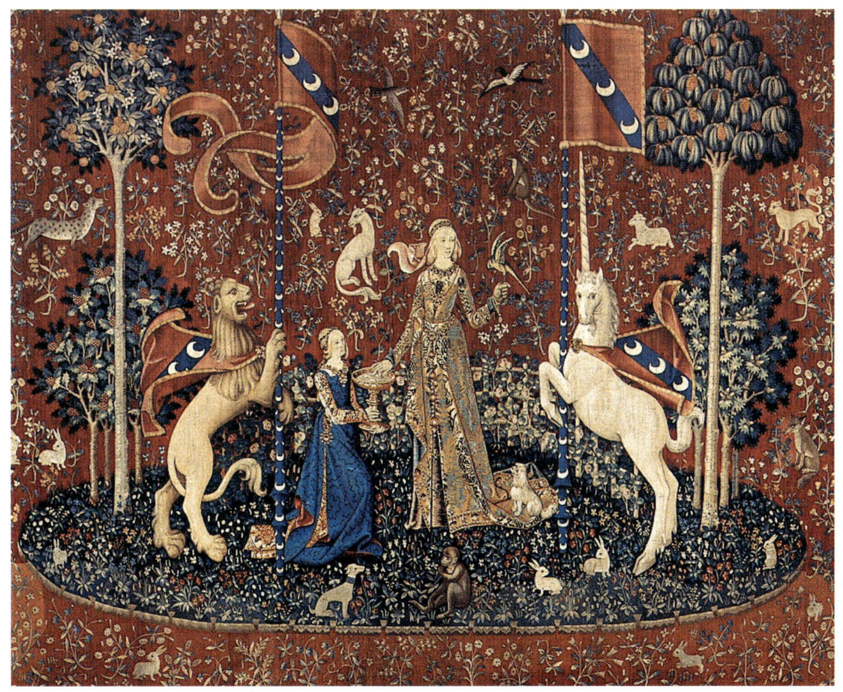

The movement in concentric circles of humanism reached the borders of the European continent, up to Lisbon. Illustrious precursor of the Portuguese school, Nuño Gonçalves is one of the most mysterious painters of the European fifteenth century. He probably died precisely in that all-important year of 1492, renowned as the beginning of the period of geographical discoveries. Celebrated by antique writers, Gonçalves left few documented traces, and apart from a few controversial attributions his name is tied to a single, although extraordinary, polyptych, dedicated to the cult of the reliquaries of St. Vincent. The crowded scene includes about sixty figures, presented with such impressive energy that it is a kind of "group portrait" of Portuguese society. There was greater resistance to humanism in Spain, busy with the difficult operation of driving out the Moors in the *Reconquista*, which ended with the surrender of Granada in that same famous 1492. After that date, and under the aegis of the *reyes catolicos*, cultural and artistic ties between Spain and Italian masters became increasingly frequent.

The spread of humanism from Tuscany through Europe

The Queen of Sheba in Adoration of the Wood and Meeting of Solomon and the Queen of Sheba
1455, fresco
San Francesco, Arezzo

This chapter is dedicated to the painting in northern Europe, but it must open with Piero della Francesca, since after the middle of the fifteenth century the pictorial works and treatises by that Tuscan master had become the common point of reference for the renewal of European art by way of humanism. The frescoes by Piero in Arezzo are an exemplary monument of the concept of balanced proportions, of measurement, order, and stateliness. This scene, inspired by the thirteenth-century *Golden Legend,* is part of the complicated story of the legend concerning the wood of the True Cross, from the death of Adam to Constantine. The painter does not present the scenes in their proper order, preferring a rhythmic structure, creating symmetry among

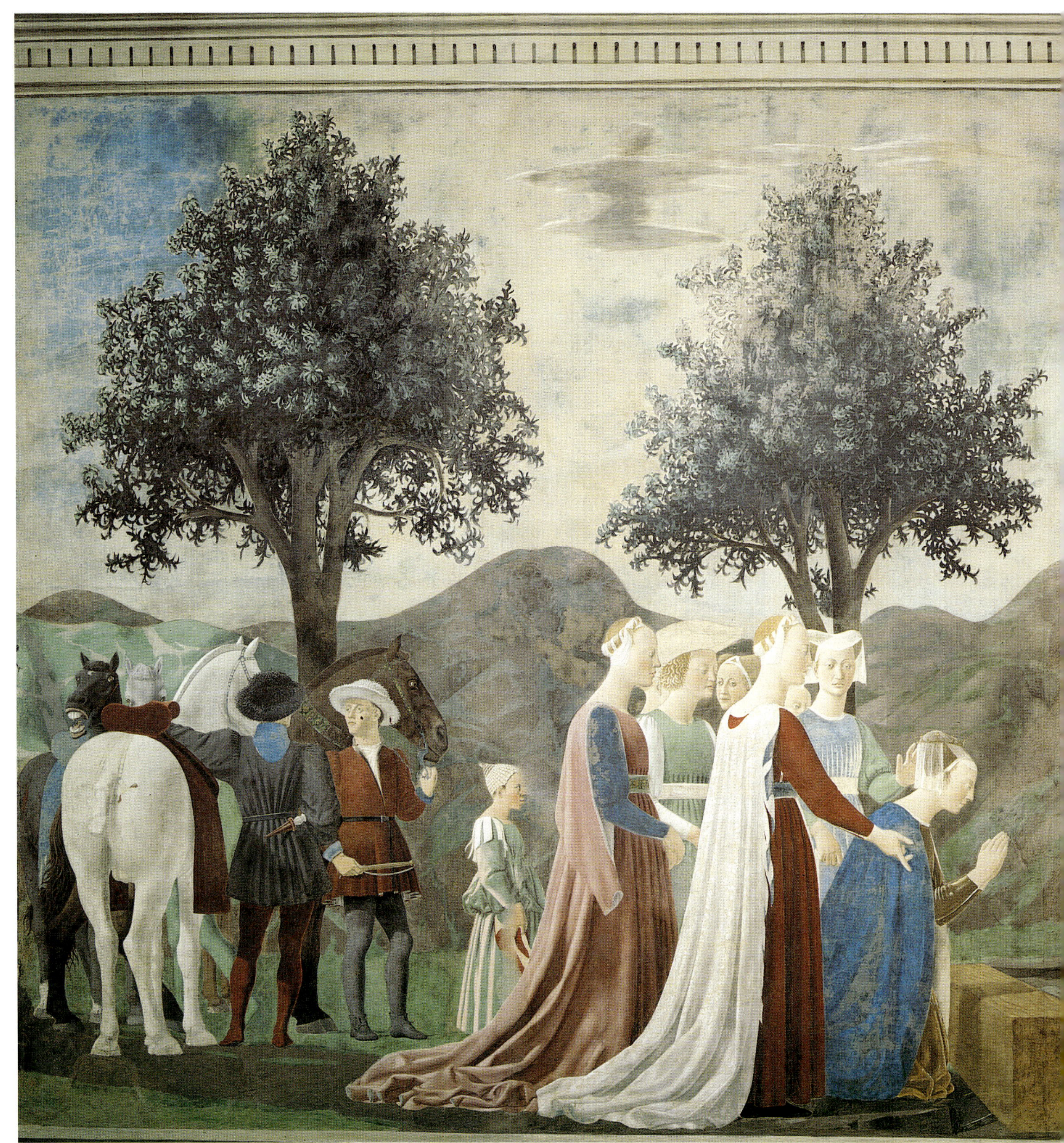

The spread of humanism from Tuscany through Europe

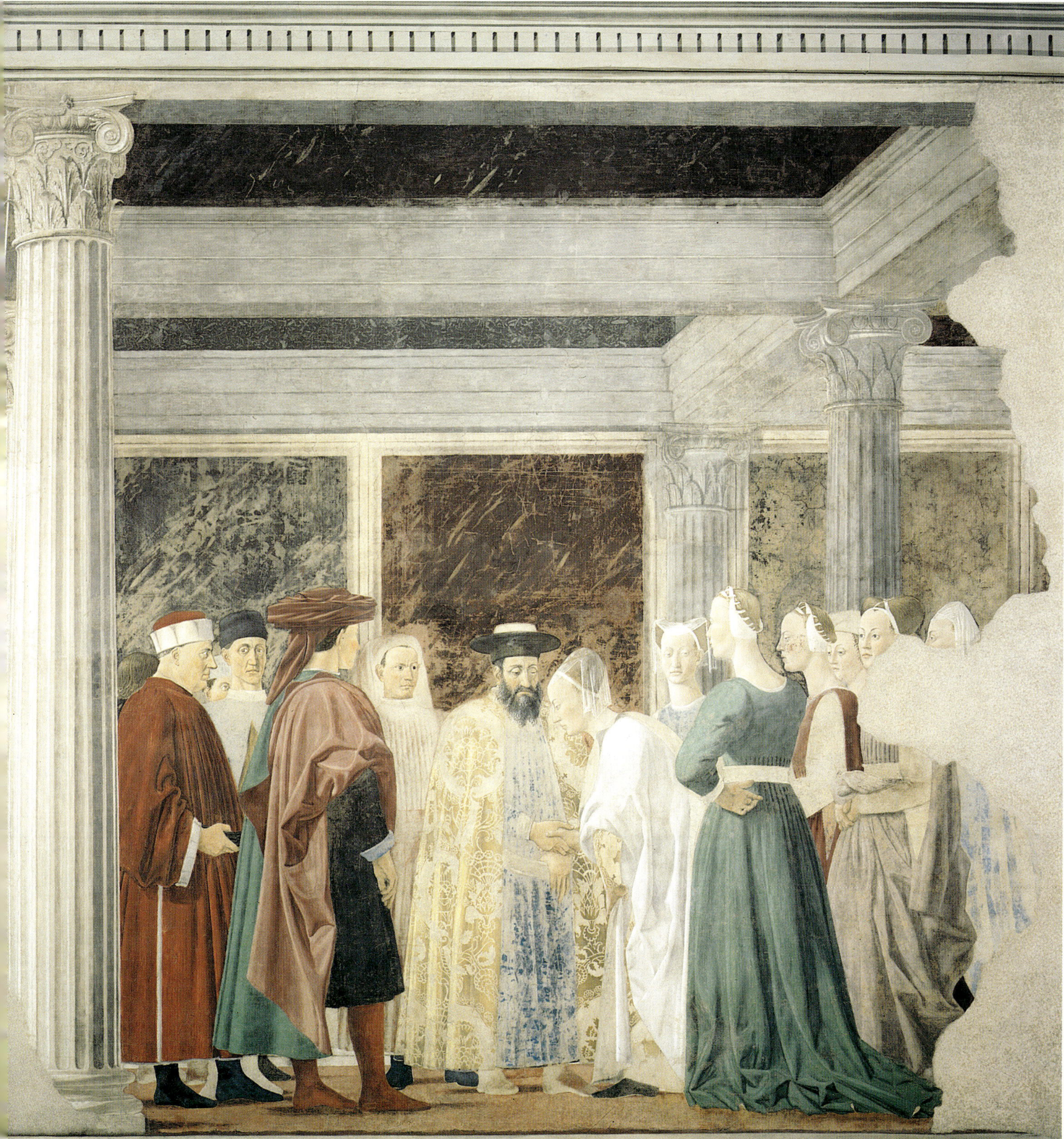

the walls. Therefore moments of great ritual solemnity alternate with confused battles, passages of lyrical contemplation are balanced by scenes of lively narration. All the scenes are dominated by the master's overarching control; the episodes and the pauses between them are presented in accordance with a cadence based on mathematical logic. The greatness of Piero della Francesca consists in his having been able to kindle a spark of life, of emotion, tenderness, or terror within this situation with its rigorous intellectual control. The world of sentiments did nothing to undermine the geometric purity of invention but instead warmed it, gave it a soul of memorable intensity. The scene of the Queen of Sheba greeting Solomon is based on the group of the apostles in the *Payment of the Tribute* by Masaccio, repeated in an even more monumental scale and inserted against architecture of absolute classical measure.

The spread of humanism from Tuscany through Europe

Jacques Coeur, rich merchant, agent of Charles VIII, king of France, and generous art patron, was the protagonist of the magnificent artistic season in Bourges at the middle of the fifteenth century. Among the artists working for him was a master of Flemish culture, probably Jacob de Littemont, who created frescoes in Coeur's splendid palace and also made this extraordinary stained-glass *Annunciation*. This is a profoundly innovative work, since for the first time the spaces of the large Gothic window are not divided in small independent squares but are considered as a grand unitary whole, organized in perspective with strong monumental impact. The sudden arrest of Jacques Coeur in 1451 (charged with poisoning one of the king's former mistresses) brought an end to this brilliant situation.

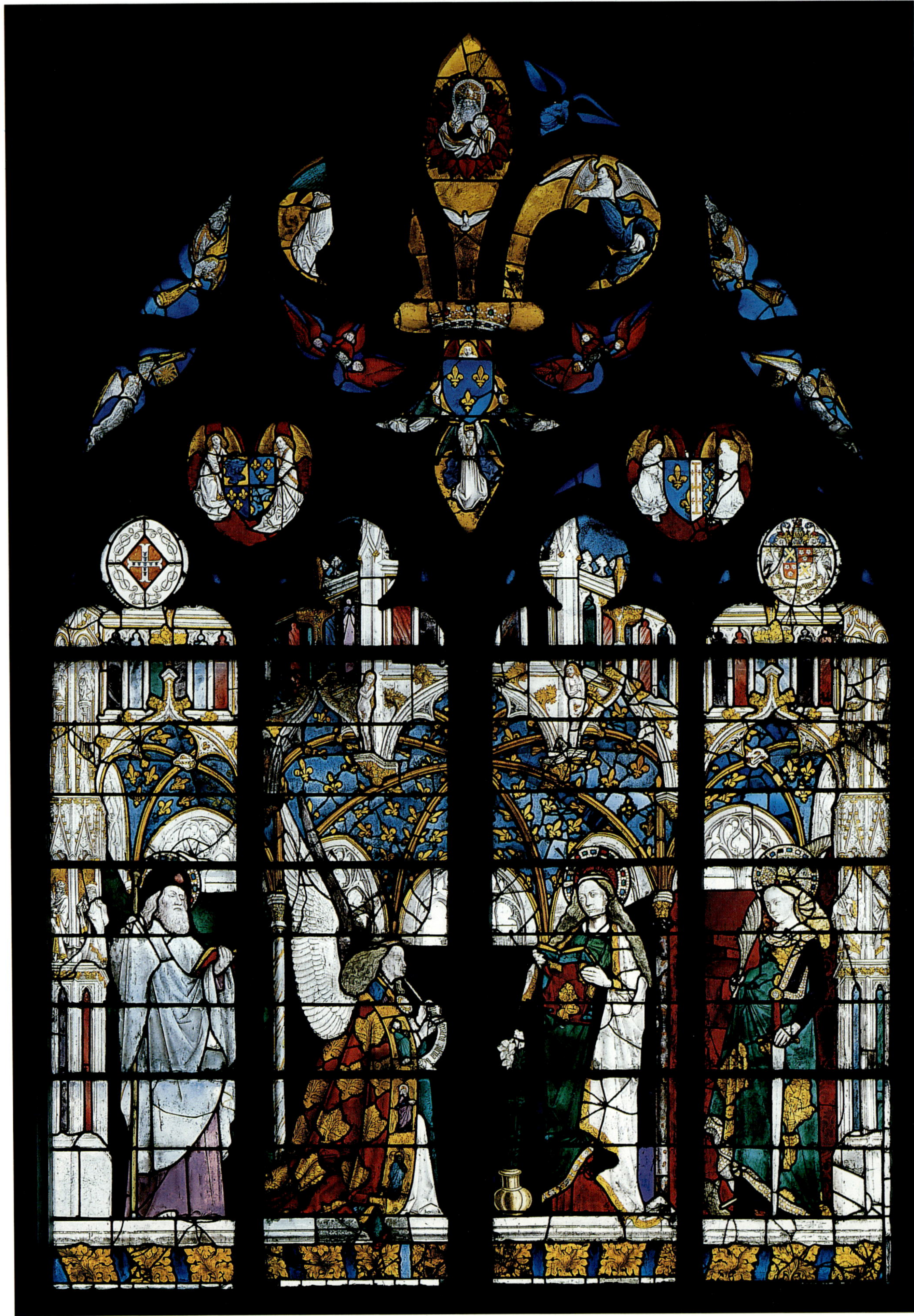

The spread of humanism from Tuscany through Europe

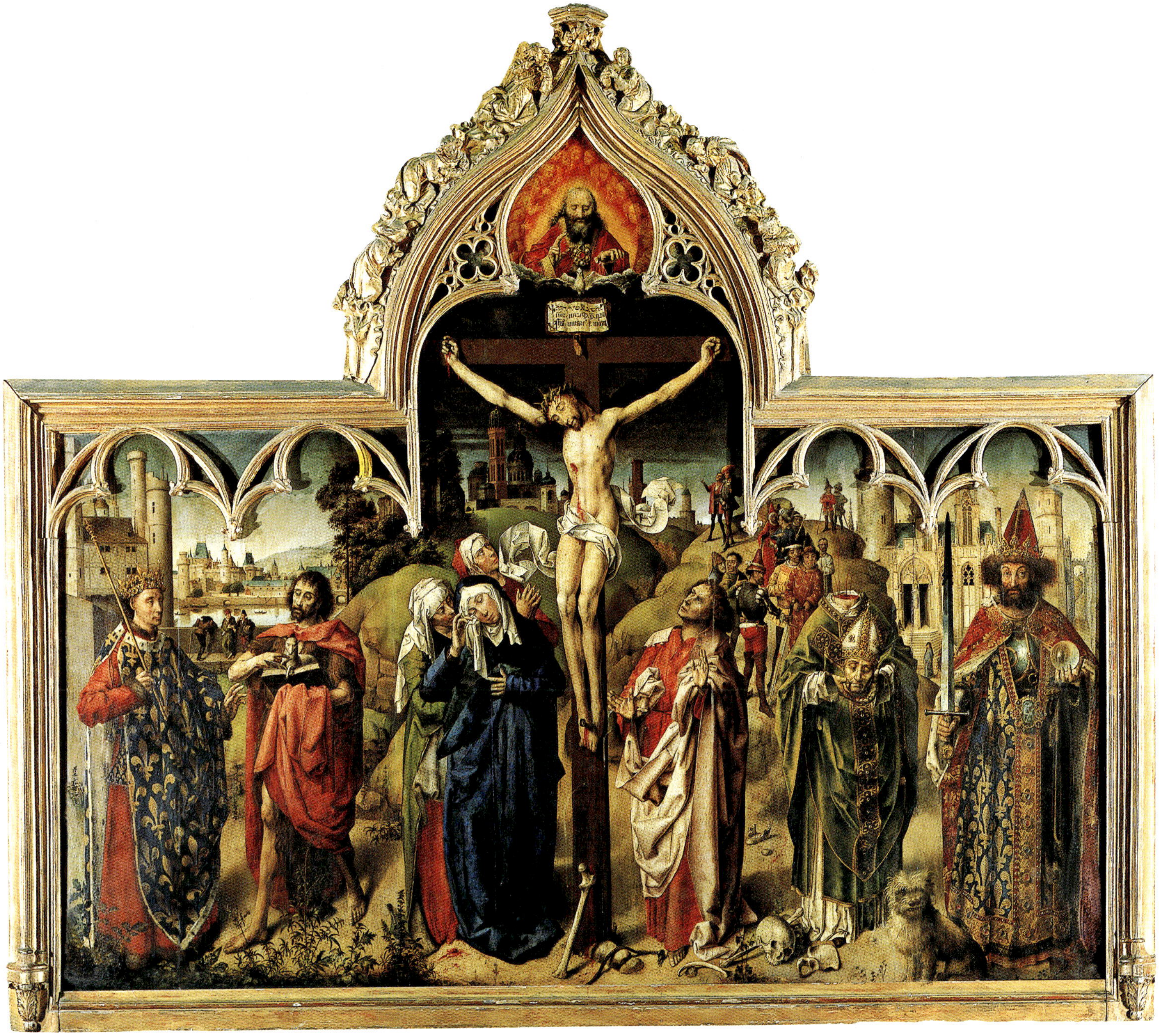

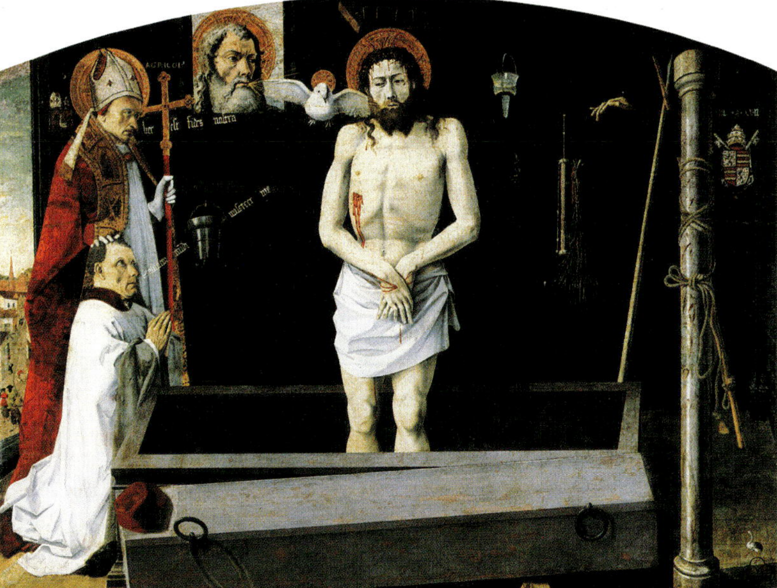

The spread of humanism from Tuscany through Europe

Jean Fouquet
**Melun Diptych:
Étienne Chevalier
with St. Stephen**
circa 1450, panel,
93 x 85 cm
Gemäldegalerie, Berlin
**Melun Diptych:
Madonna and Child**
circa 1450, panel,
91 x 81 cm
Musées Royaux des
Beaux-Arts,
Antwerp

In the left wing, the patron of the diptych, treasurer to the king of France Étienne Chevalier, protected by St. Stephen, his patron saint, kneels with sober composure. His physical volume expands within the folds of the red cloak and is exalted by the marble gallery in perspective. To the right is an unusual image of a nursing Madonna (of a type called the *Madonna del Latte* in Italy) against the compact background of a rank of red and deep blue angels, angels of the day and those of the night. The sculptural form of the Virgin, her breast rendered as a perfect orb, suggest Fouquet's possible tie to sculpture. Her face, bathed in a pure light, seems almost carved from ivory. She is wrapped in intense, direct light that exalts the purity of forms and the essentiality of the volumes, recalling Piero della Francesca. The rendering of the gems of the throne and the crown, presented in the tiniest details, is derived instead from the northern European figurative culture.

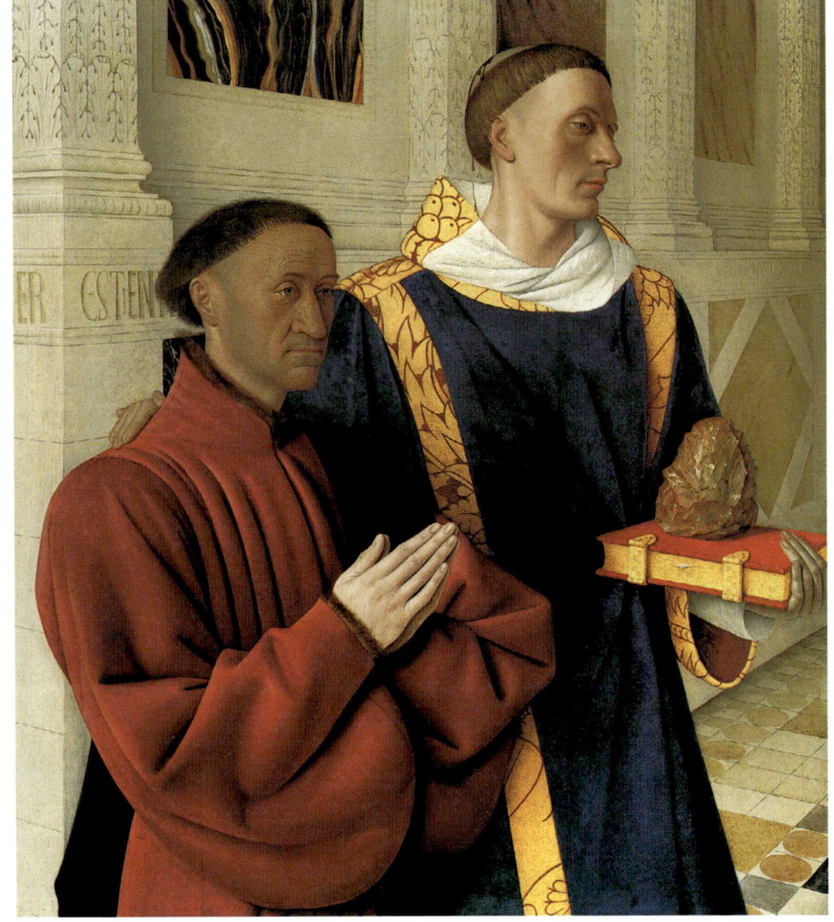

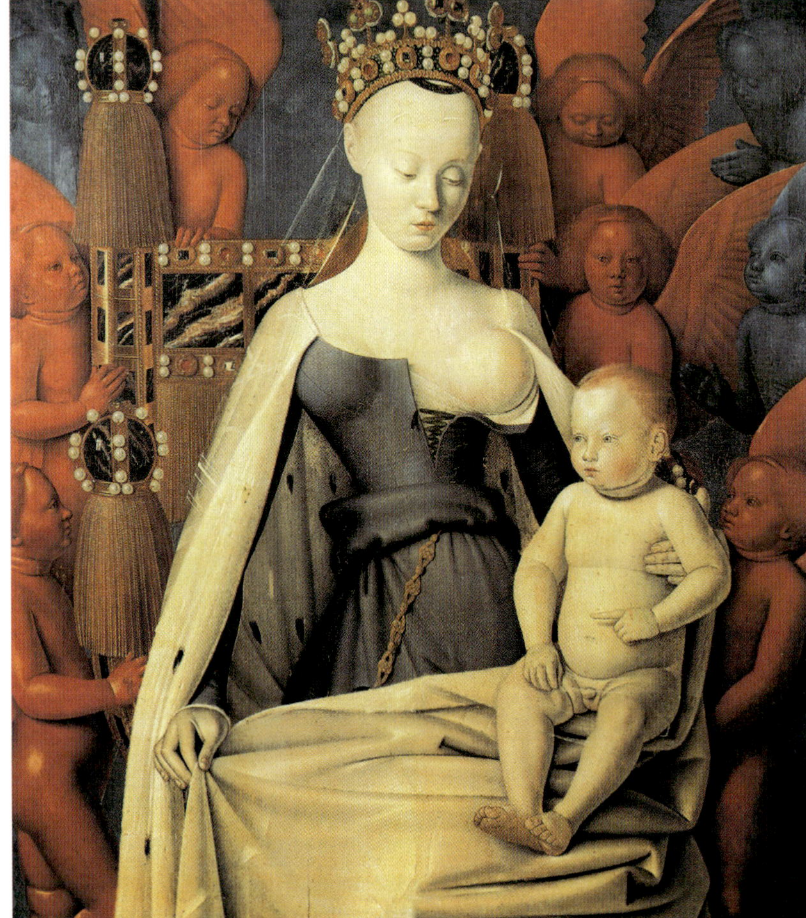

The spread of humanism from Tuscany through Europe

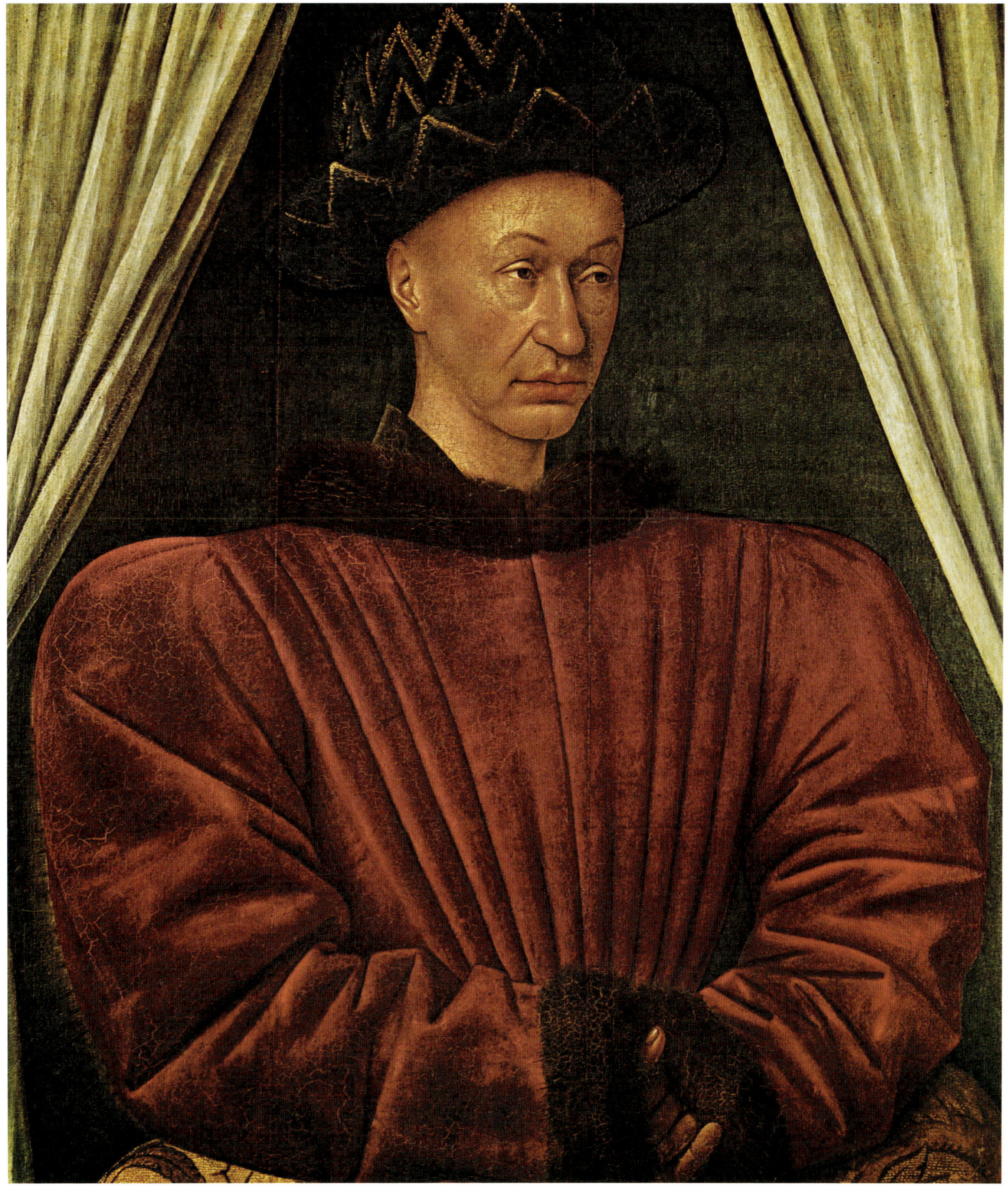

The spread of humanism from Tuscany through Europe

This work, made for the cathedral of Moulins, was commissioned by Peter II, duke of Bourbon, and his wife, Anne of Beaujeu, daughter of the king of France, Louis XI. The patrons are meticulously portrayed on the side panels, together with their daughter Suzanne and their patron saints. The thoroughly Flemish realism and the taste for description of details in the side panels contrasts with this central scene, still late Gothic in its composition but "reformed" in its search of geometries and balanced proportions. The scene is dominated by the figure of the Virgin and Child, encircled by a large multicolored halo, almost a mystical aureole; the Virgin rests her feet on a crescent moon, following an iconography typical of the Immaculate Conception. She is surrounded by a choir of angels, two of which hold a crown above her head. The light of the circle radiates outward to these adolescent angels, whose bright faces are pervaded by absorbed, dreamy expressions.

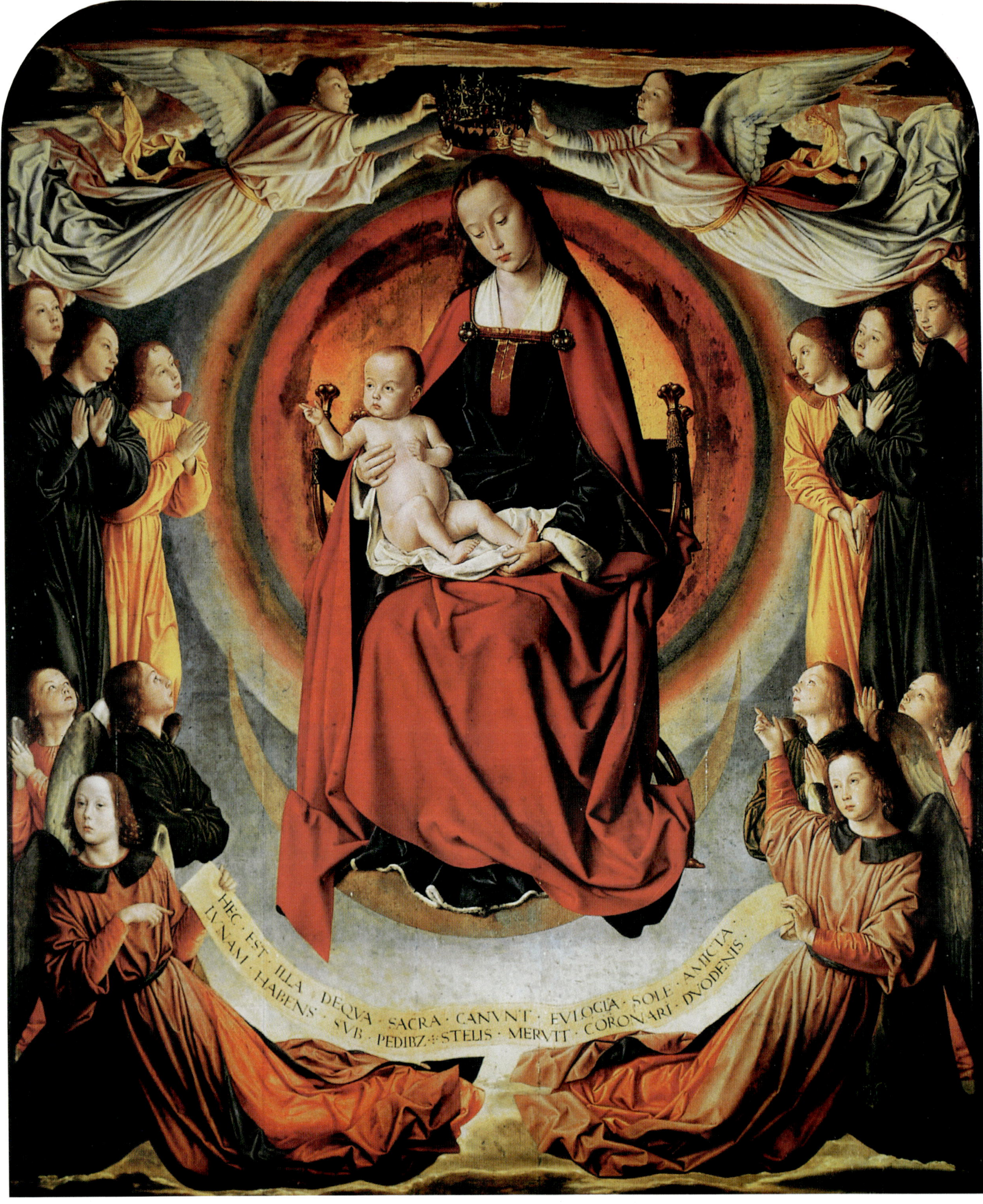

The spread of humanism from Tuscany through Europe

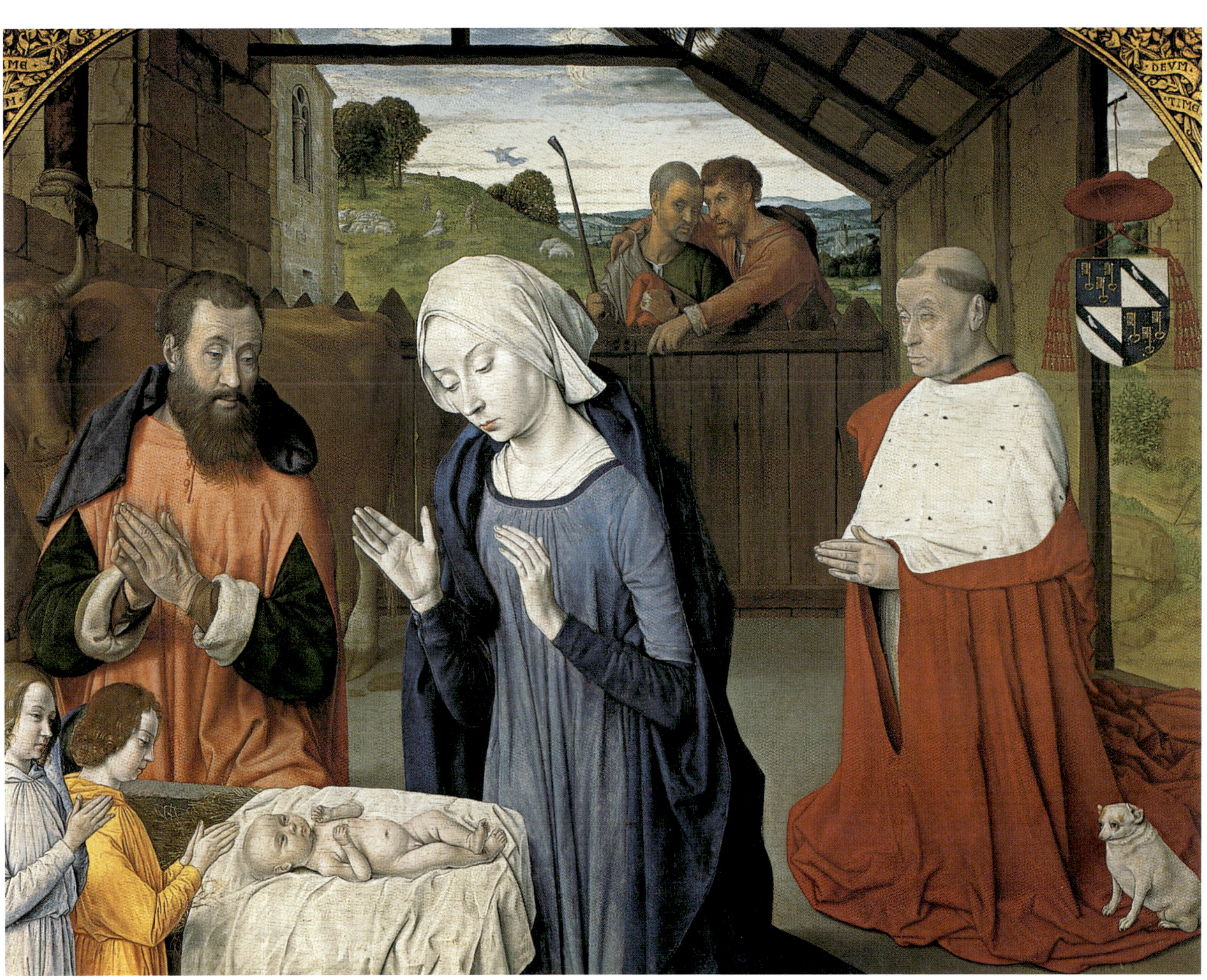

■ MASTER OF MOULINS
Nativity
circa 1480,
panel, 55 x 71 cm
Musée Rolin, Autun

Made for Cardinal Jean Rolin, this panel exudes a sense of absorption and meditation, the sort of melancholy severity that is the unmistakable sign of the art of the Master of Moulins. On the other hand, the pale coloring of the Virgin, accentuated by the cold chromatic tones of the clothes, recalls the style of the last works of Hugo van der Goes.

The spread of humanism from Tuscany through Europe

Around the year 1500, in parallel with the new energy in the kingdom of France, Paris went through an important cultural period. By then the city's university was open to the ideas of humanism, and the increasingly frequent visits to the city of the royal court led to new artistic and architectural undertakings. From the painting point of view, the Flemish influence continued to prevail in central France, following the analytic tradition of Memling, Hugo van der Goes, and Gerard David. A convincing example of this is the brilliant panels that illustrate the complex, romantic tale of St. Giles, probably made for the church of Saint-Leu-Saint-Gilles by an anonymous artist who now takes his name from this work.

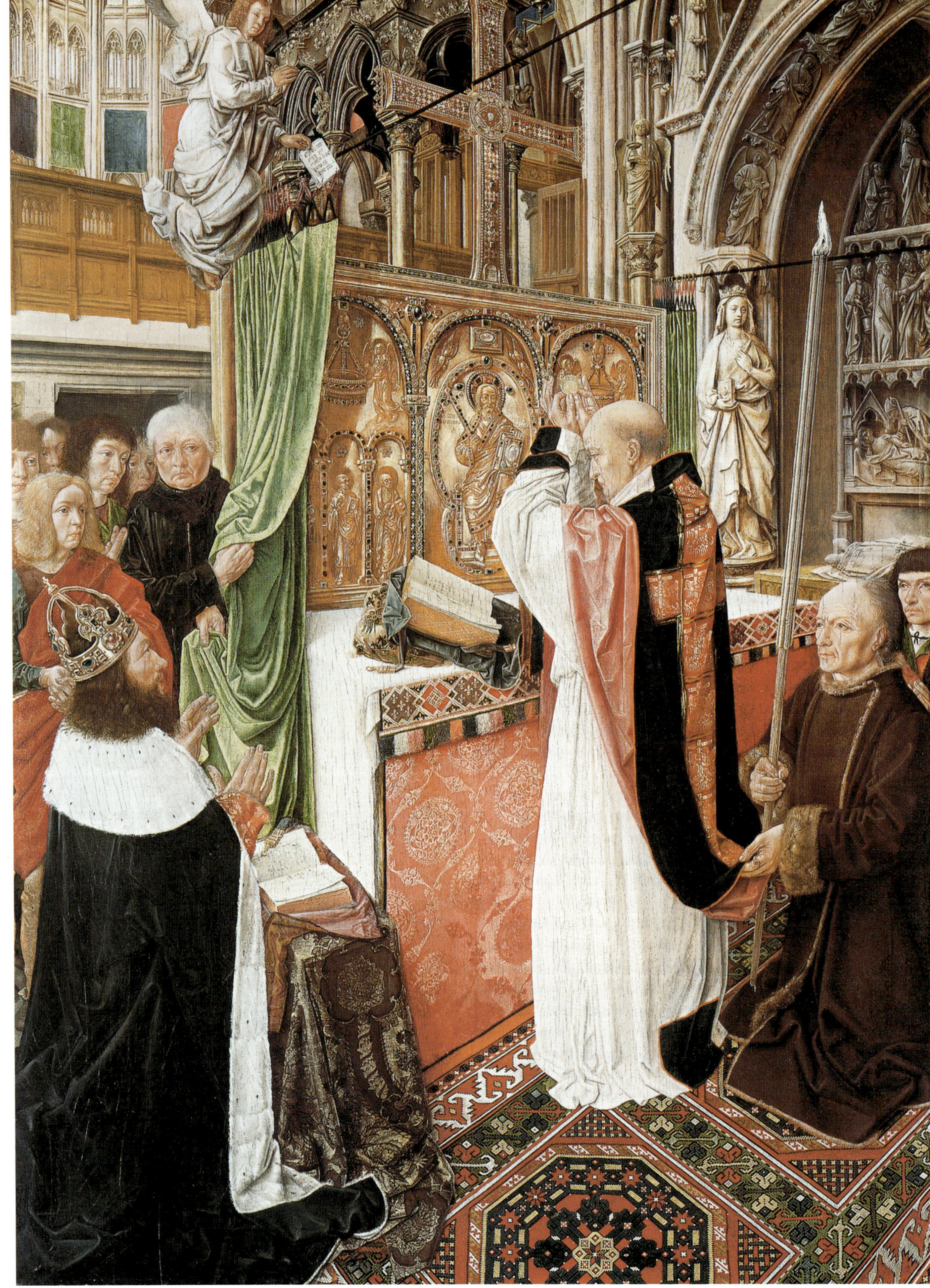

The spread of humanism from Tuscany through Europe

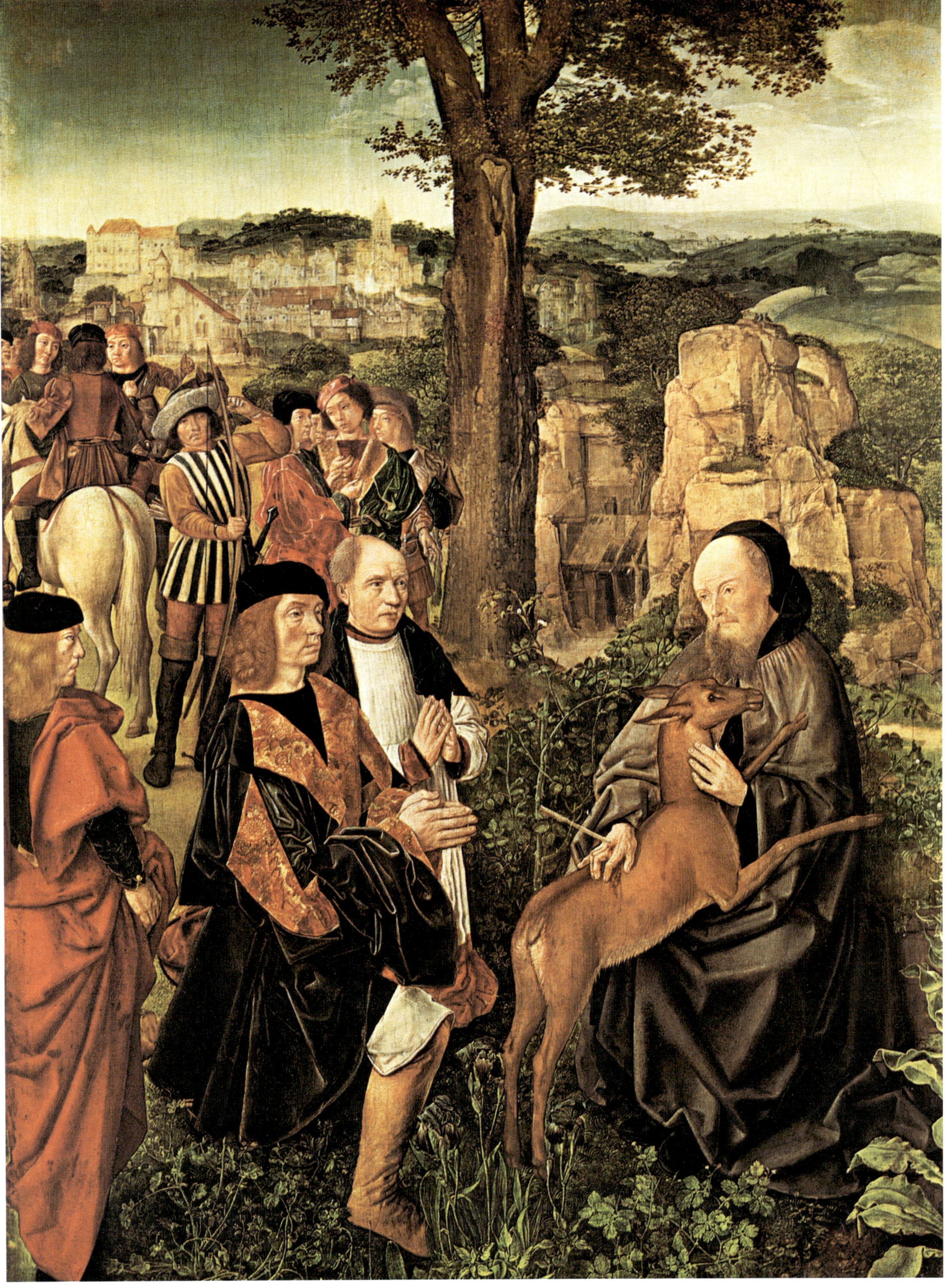

The spread of humanism from Tuscany through Europe

The work was originally in Novacella (Neustift) Abbey, near Bressanone. Despite the dispersion and destruction of many Pacher altarpieces, it is still possible to recognize the artist's style, mixing on the one hand perfect humanistic culture and perspective, absorbed in Padua alongside Donatello, Filippo Lippi, and Mantegna, and on the other a firm tie to the still Gothic world of Alpine forests and towns. In Pacher's paintings buildings are presented in depth with harmonious perspective, but the architecture is still Gothic, with branching vaults, spires, and jutting balconies; figures are rendered with perfect anatomical proportions but have the shaded features and intense expressions of northern art; the compositions have the well-balanced monumental breadth of works being made in Florence during the same period, but are brightened by the cool light and enameled colors of the late Gothic in Europe. Legends of saints and episodes from the Gospels, transferred to the daily life of the towns and mountains of the Tyrol, become expressions of a passionate and heartfelt human story.

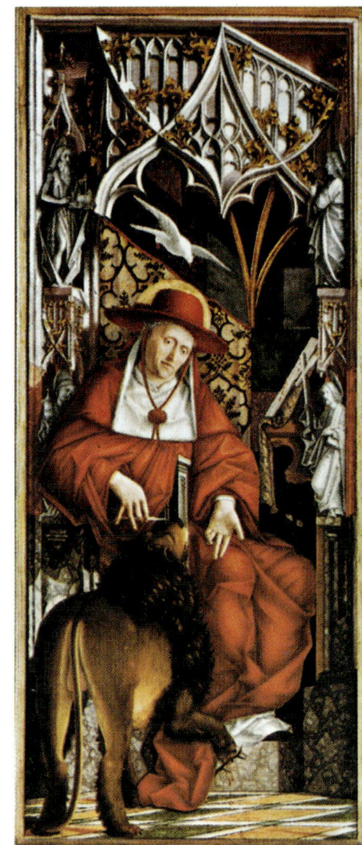
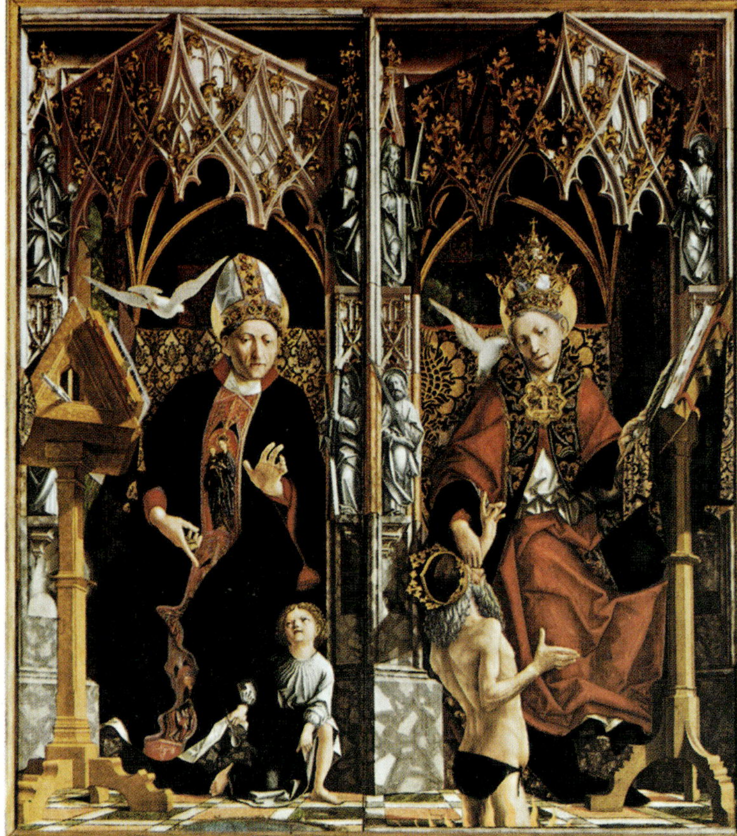
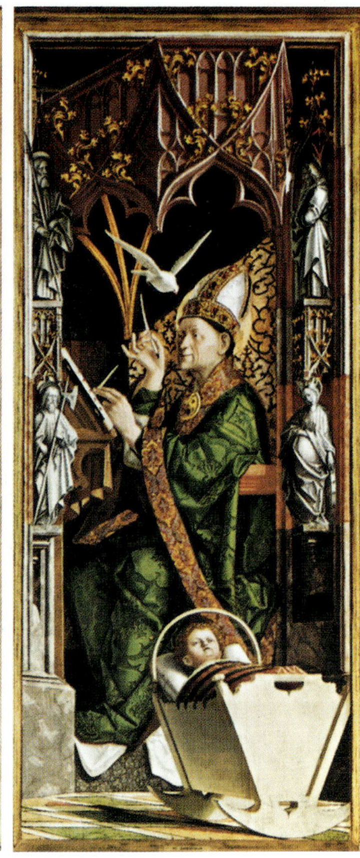

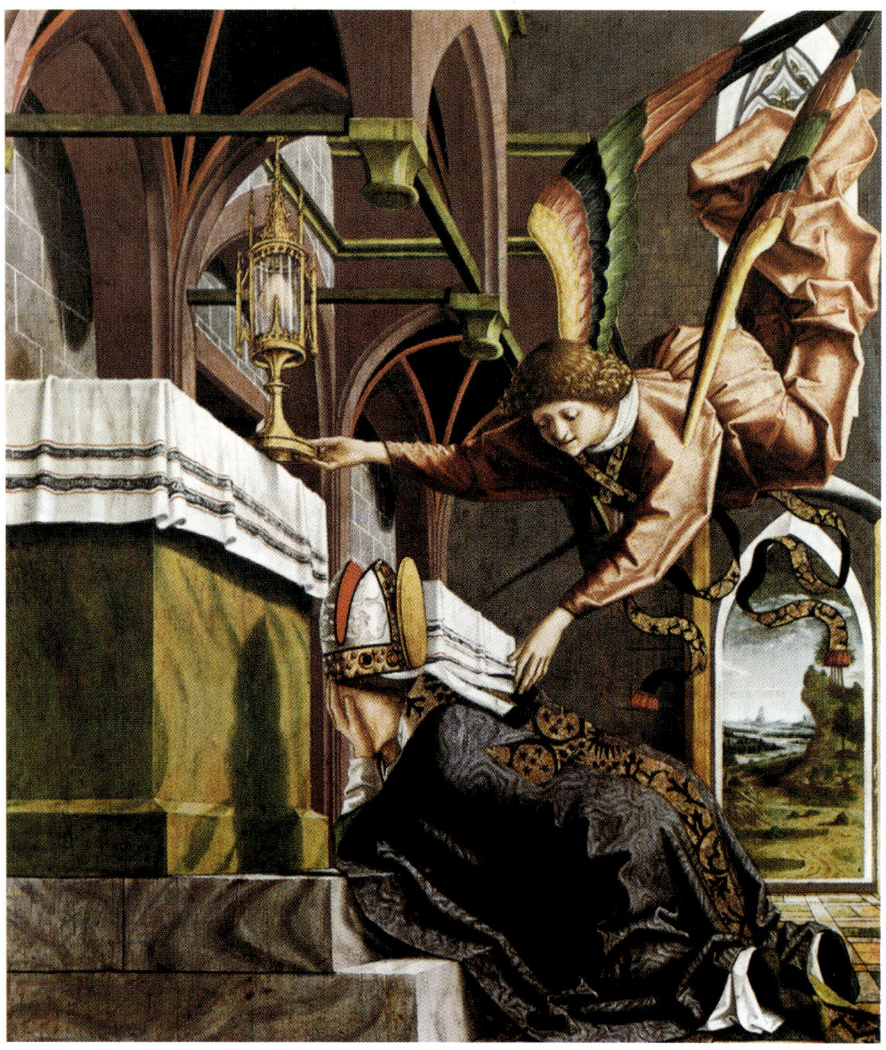

The spread of humanism from Tuscany through Europe

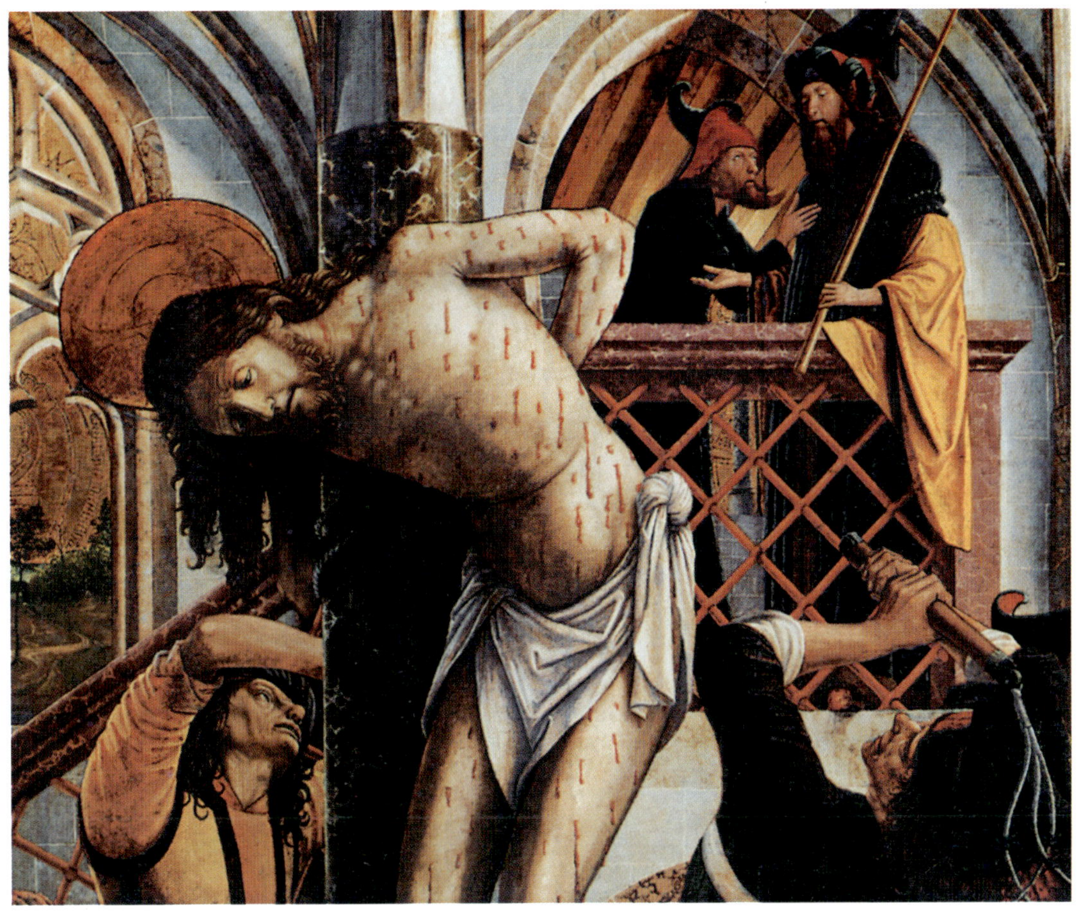

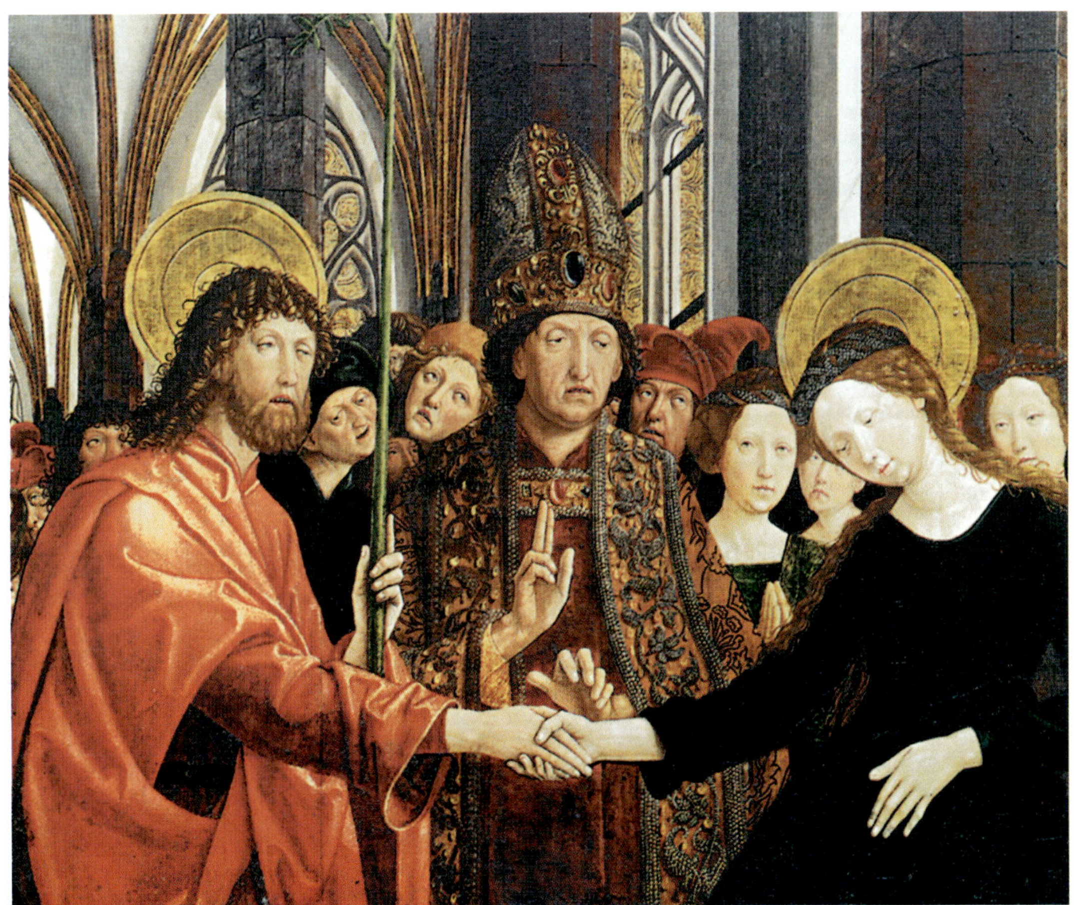

MICHAEL PACHER
**Flagellation of
Christ and Marriage
of the Virgin**
Panels from the main
altar of the parish
church of Salzburg
circa 1495–98,
panels, 113 x
139.5 cm each
Österreichische Galerie,
Vienna

The Salzburg altar,
which includes a cen-
tral part in carved wood
and painted side panels,
was Michael Pacher's
last artistic undertak-
ing. Dismembered and
partially destroyed at
the beginning of the
eighteenth century, it
can be reconstructed
only in a fragmentary
way today. On the
basis of the surviving
panels it is possible to
follow the evolution of
the artist, who took
care to give the scenes
an accurate perspective
control. The two panels
here were originally on
the opposite faces of
the same opening. The
space in the images is
not measured off using
rows of columns but
instead by the arrange-
ment of the figures.
The scenes are more
peaceful and despite
their dramatic contents
transmit a sense of
intimate greatness that
is accentuated by the
use of warm colors.

Still in the church for which it was made, the *Virgin of the Rose Bower*, the only dated painted work by Martin Schongauer, is a precious testimony of his long activity in Alsace, even if unfortunately it has been mutilated on all sides, the result of being inserted in an elaborate carved frame. The solemnly mystical effect is obtained thanks to the unusual physical presence of the Virgin, who seems to stand out from the background as though it were an elaborate tapestry picture of plants, flowers, and birds described with masterful and with great naturalistic sensibility. The angels in flight, the Virgin's thoughtful pose, the Child's twisting body, and even the climbing flowers, which sometimes seem to extend beyond the borders of the painting, create a subtle rhythm, favored by the nervous and mobile line that distinguishes the painting.

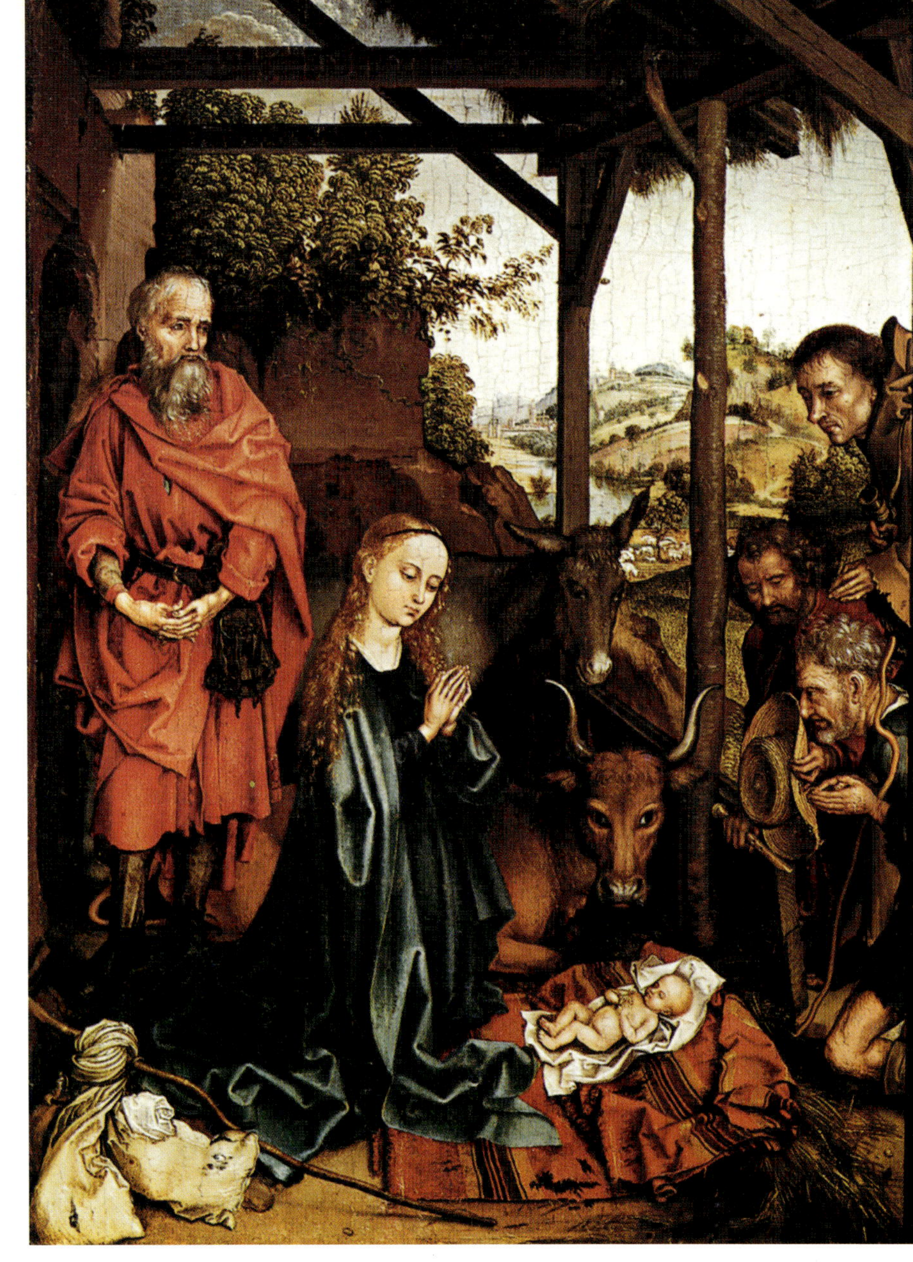

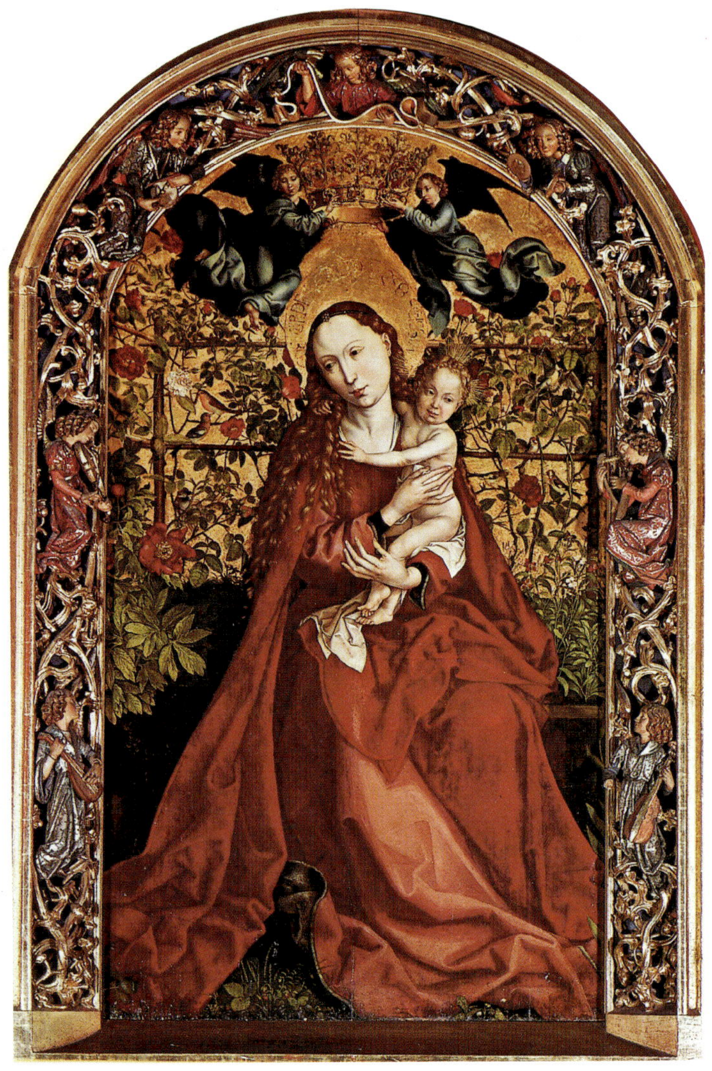

The spread of humanism from Tuscany through Europe

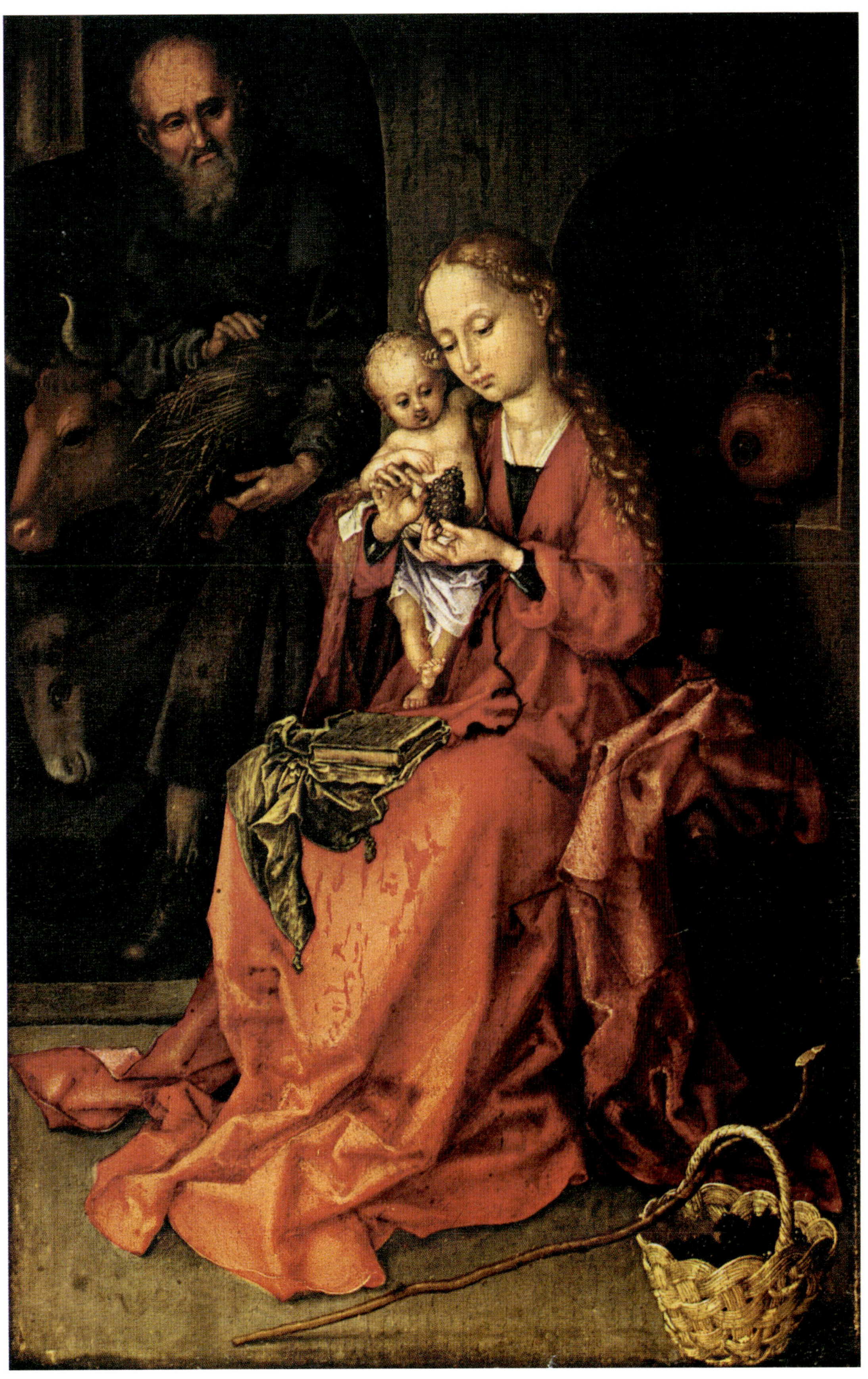

MARTIN SCHONGAUER
The Holy Family
1475–80, oil on panel,
26 x 17 cm
Kunsthistorisches
Museum, Vienna

This typical devotional work follows a format and theme dear to Schongauer, perfectly at ease in the small size and in the intimacy in which the subject is presented. The extreme formal simplification has reduced the setting to only a few elements. All attention is directed on the Holy Family and on the daily objects that shine out of the half darkness. However, in this domestic setting, so apparently bare and humble, one senses, as through a silent force, the intense presence of the divine.

The spread of humanism from Tuscany through Europe

During the course of the fifteenth century the Holy Roman Empire embraced a truly vast territory that included parts of what are today Austria and Switzerland. When the Hapsburg dynasty succeeded that of the Luxemburgs in 1437–38, the empire's area of influence expanded, although only temporarily, to include Bohemia and Hungary. Even so, during this period Germany was still not a great European power in the modern sense, like France or England. The emperors exercised effective power only over their heredity domains and those they acquired through a canny strategy of marriage, which led in 1477 to the marriage of Maximilian I to Mary of Burgundy. The remaining territory was broken up into principalities that depended only nominally on the central power; there were then the imperial cities in possession of a particular statute giving them a degree of independence.

During this period German artists were struggling to change their social standing, most of all to free themselves from the status of artisans. The second half of the century was an epoch in transition between a still Gothic sensibility and the new demands of the Renaissance. It was during this "waning of the Middle Ages" that the concept the artist had of himself began to change. Artists no longer felt they were fully represented by something as impersonal as a city tradition or membership in a local guild.

To satisfy increasingly demanding and diversified patrons artists endeavored to create personal, independent styles, to present themselves as "signatures" that differentiated them from their competitors. Thus the period on the threshold of the sixteenth century saw a flowering of different artistic styles and a multiplication in the number of centers of artistic production, out of which various exceptional personalities emerged. In terms of the history of German art, the outstanding feature of this period was the creation of great winged altarpieces, marvelous complexes that were combinations of painting and sculpture. The changing style of these works traces the gradual passage from the Gothic to a timid Renaissance up to the threshold of the radical transformation wrought by the Protestant Reformation. The altarpieces in limewood, widespread principally in central southern Germany and in the Alpine region, began going through a dynamic development beginning in the 1570s, in parallel with the evolution of other parts of church furnishings (pulpits, tabernacles, portals, carved tombs), most of all choir stalls and other large-scale complexes of wood carving. The largest and most complicated altarpieces had mobile wings that could be opened or closed according to the period of the liturgical year. Highly detailed contracts (some of which have survived) were drawn up for these works, often specifying the various tasks to be performed by sculptors and painters, although the workshop of the carvers usually saw to the presence of gilders and decorators. The polychrome decoration of the fully round statues and the wings was a fascinating aspect of these works, but its preservation always presents extremely delicate problems. Restoration that involves repainting and new gilding risks giving the sculptures an unpleasant sense of falsity; on the other hand, being overly cautious can deny the work much of its original appearance. Polychrome decoration long remained an indispensable element in German sculpture, not only in wood but also in stone. Only after the middle of the fifteenth century, with the vibrant figures that Jörg Syrlin inserted in the choir of the cathedral of Ulm and with the arrival of the ingenious Tilman Riemenschnieder, did supporters appear for the decision to leave the wood unpainted, revealing the limewood's natural colors and grain.

In the beginning, in keeping with the Gothic tradition, the figures were presented in a simple sequence, but later, beginning with the mas-

Salzburg Master, *Pietà,* circa 1400; Bayerisches Nationalmuseum, Munich

Veit Stoss, *Christ Crowned with Thorns* circa 1507; St. Sebaldus, Nuremberg

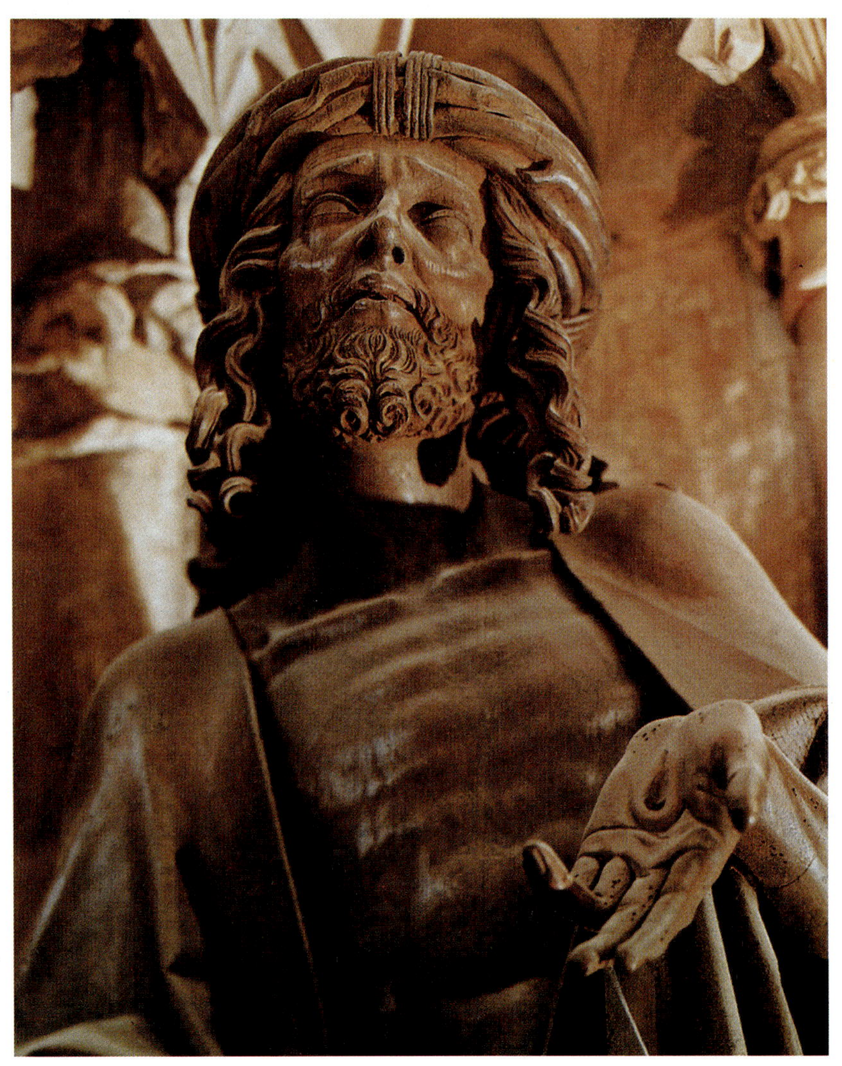

The great German altars

terpieces by Michael Pacher, the narrative scenes assumed a spectacular animation. The most spectacular German altarpiece of the fifteenth century is not in Germany, however, but in Poland. Its creator was Veit Stoss, one of the sculptors trained in the flourishing Nuremberg school, the main center of German art in the decades between the fifteenth and sixteenth centuries. Accused of forgery, he had been branded on both cheeks and expelled from the city. In 1477 he moved to Cracow and began working on the immense St. Mary Altarpiece with its main scene of *The Death of the Virgin*, for the church of St. Mary, facing the market square. It took him twelve years to complete but was well worth the effort. Using the preferred limewood Stoss laid out the most colossal version of the fifteenth-century

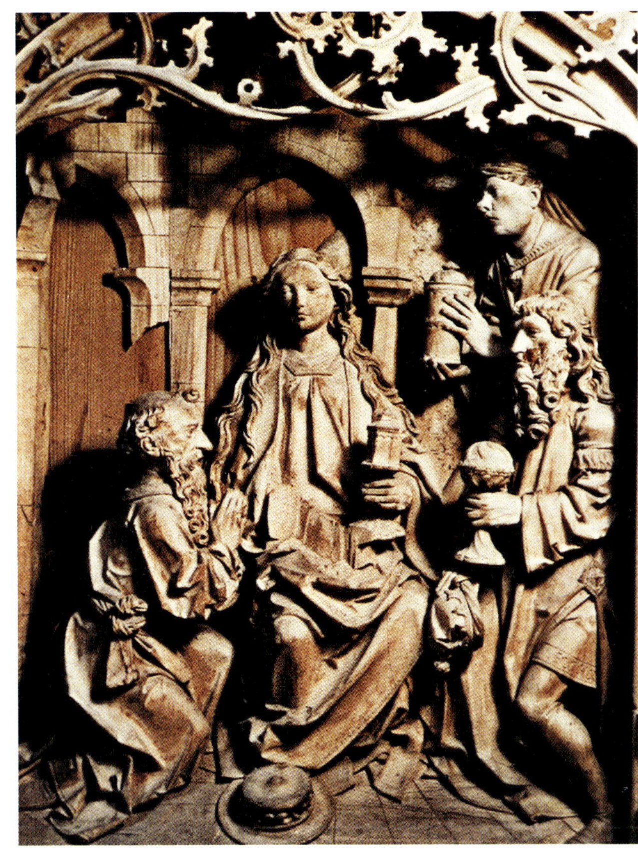

unforgettable spectacle. Stoss spent many years in Cracow. In 1492, he sculpted mottled red marble instead of wood for the tomb of King Casimir IV Jagellon, with its pierced baldachin of curved arches, made for the cathedral of Cracow. After the conclusion of this masterpiece, Stoss found himself pardoned and returned to Nuremberg, where he made important sculptures in a situation already effected by the activity of Dürer.

Stoss was primarily a specialist in wooden sculpture, but Tilman Riemenschneider, the greatest German sculptor of the Renaissance, used a variety of materials (alabaster, sandstone, stone), but he reached the heights of his expression with the creation of great winged altarpieces, crowning the German tradition in this particular genre. Born around 1460, Riemenschneider

The great German altars

Theatrum Sacrum. It is striking to think of what it must have been like during religious rites, in the light of candles under the vault of the Gothic church crowded with people in prayer. The large carved wings of the polyptych were slowly opened, with a creaking that must have given those present shivers: in the central compartment appeared the stately figures of the apostles, Herculean giants—larger than life-size figures—intent on caring for the wonderfully delicate Virgin, who seems to slip into a tranquil swoon amid a swirling wash of curling beards, flowing hair, bare muscles, and beer-master double chins. Copiously applied gold, deep blues, lively colors: it was an

had quite an adventurous career, with moments of great fame (such as the creation of the imperial tombs in the cathedral of Bamberg) alternating with periods of obscurity. When already quite old he sided with the peasants during the Peasants' Revolt of 1524–25. He was arrested, imprisoned, probably tortured, and lost much of his fortune. After this experience he produced no more important works, and he died in Würzburg in 1531. Although he was active within the Gothic tradition of winged altars, Riemenschneider presented daring innovations, beginning with his abandonment of the usual gilding and painting with bright tints to instead exalt the natural color of the wood and, as a result, to emphasize the purely sculptural qualities of the work instead of the painting. Furthermore, in his largest and most integral works, those in Rothenburg-ob-der-Tauber and Creglingen-am-Tauber, Riemenschneider adopted the expedient of "piercing" the background of the scene by means of openings or windows, thereby adding a new luminous animation. Over all his faces spreads an unmistakable atmosphere of noble melancholy tinged with foreboding.

A perfect example of
the integration of
painting and sculpture,
a work conceived and
made in a single work-
shop, this is the only
winged altarpiece by
Pacher that has reached
us practically intact
and that is still visible
in the site for which it
was made. Also still in
existence is the highly
detailed contract for
its creation, signed
December 13, 1471,
the many clauses of
which establish even
the expenses of trans-
porting the various
parts of the colossal
complex made in pine-
wood, which includes

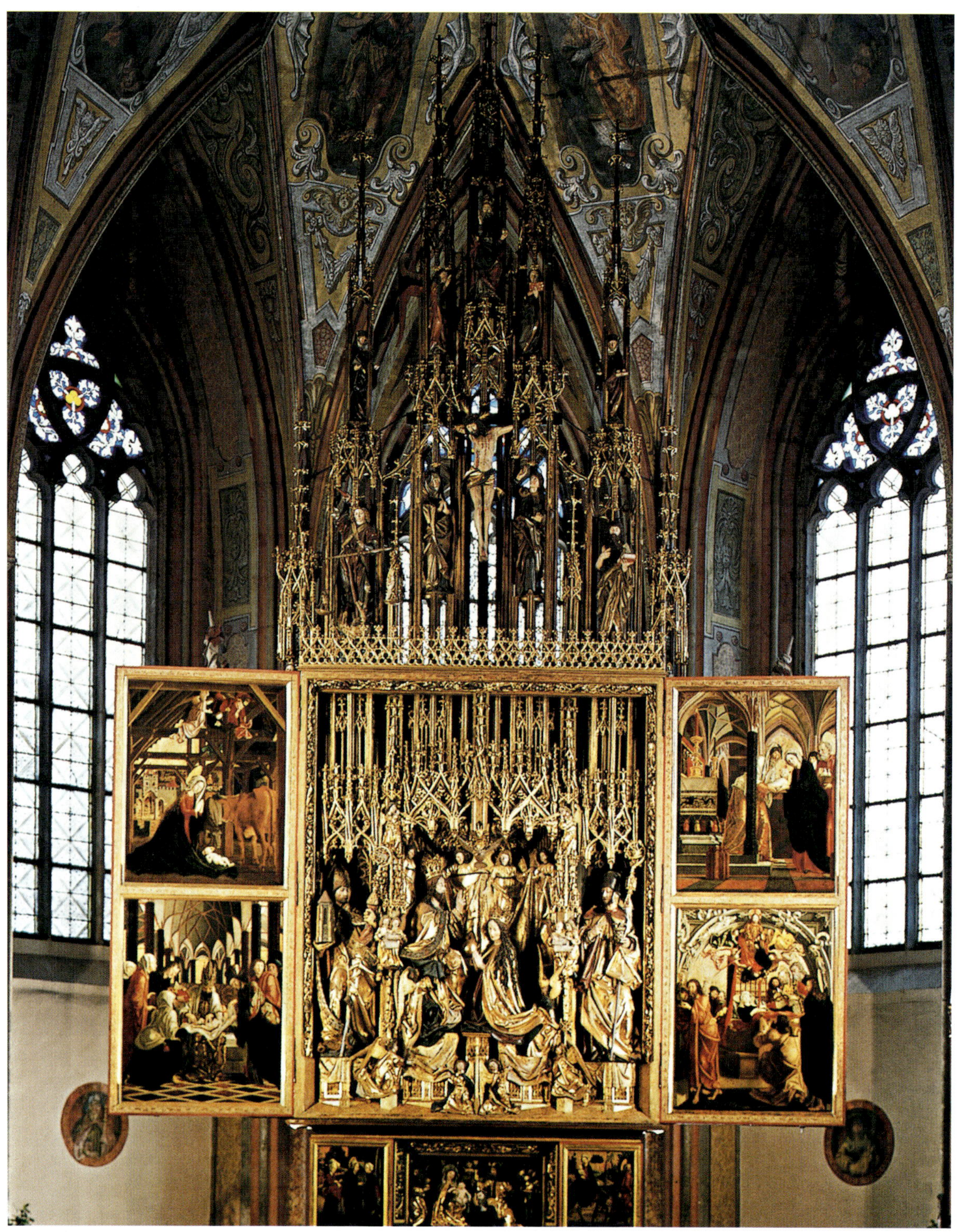

terpieces by Michael Pacher, the narrative scenes assumed a spectacular animation. The most spectacular German altarpiece of the fifteenth century is not in Germany, however, but in Poland. Its creator was Veit Stoss, one of the sculptors trained in the flourishing Nuremberg school, the main center of German art in the decades between the fifteenth and sixteenth centuries. Accused of forgery, he had been branded on both cheeks and expelled from the city. In 1477 he moved to Cracow and began working on the immense St. Mary Altarpiece with its main scene of *The Death of the Virgin*, for the church of St. Mary, facing the market square. It took him twelve years to complete but was well worth the effort. Using the preferred limewood Stoss laid out the most colossal version of the fifteenth-century

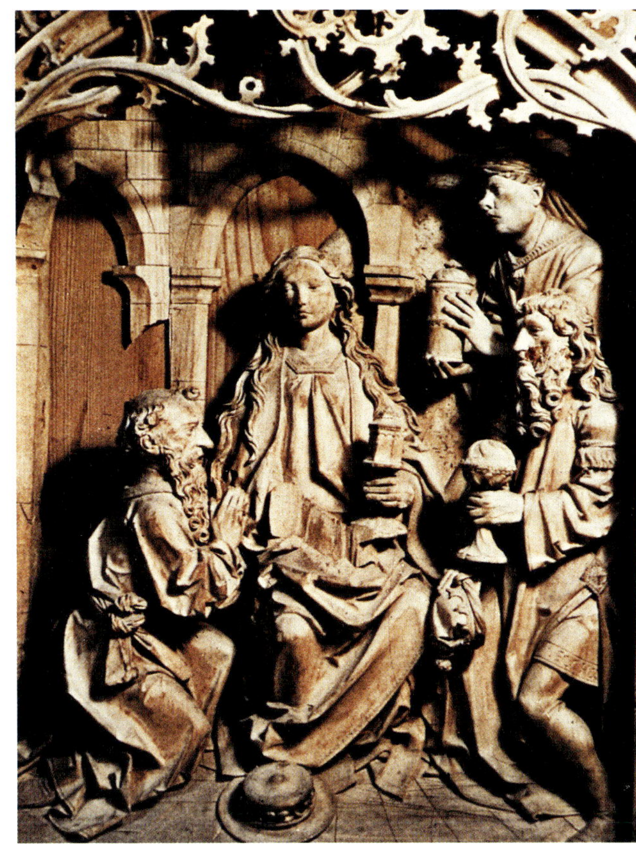

unforgettable spectacle. Stoss spent many years in Cracow. In 1492, he sculpted mottled red marble instead of wood for the tomb of King Casimir IV Jagellon, with its pierced baldachin of curved arches, made for the cathedral of Cracow. After the conclusion of this masterpiece, Stoss found himself pardoned and returned to Nuremberg, where he made important sculptures in a situation already effected by the activity of Dürer.

Stoss was primarily a specialist in wooden sculpture, but Tilman Riemenschneider, the greatest German sculptor of the Renaissance, used a variety of materials (alabaster, sandstone, stone), but he reached the heights of his expression with the creation of great winged altarpieces, crowning the German tradition in this particular genre. Born around 1460, Riemenschneider

The great German altars

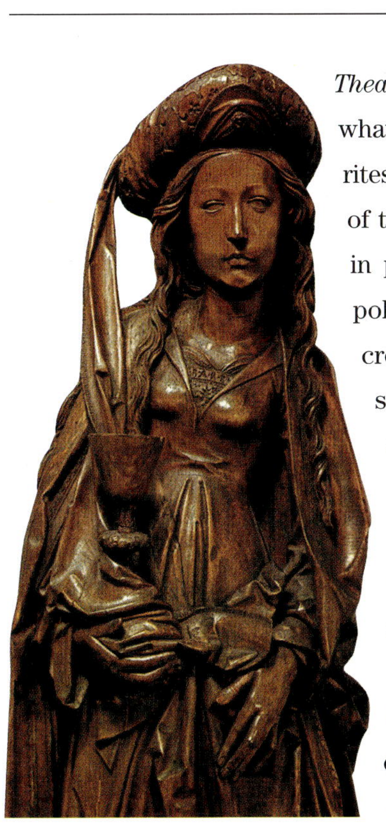

Theatrum Sacrum. It is striking to think of what it must have been like during religious rites, in the light of candles under the vault of the Gothic church crowded with people in prayer. The large carved wings of the polyptych were slowly opened, with a creaking that must have given those present shivers: in the central compartment appeared the stately figures of the apostles, Herculean giants—larger than life-size figures—intent on caring for the wonderfully delicate Virgin, who seems to slip into a tranquil swoon amid a swirling wash of curling beards, flowing hair, bare muscles, and beer-master double chins. Copiously applied gold, deep blues, lively colors: it was an

had quite an adventurous career, with moments of great fame (such as the creation of the imperial tombs in the cathedral of Bamberg) alternating with periods of obscurity. When already quite old he sided with the peasants during the Peasants' Revolt of 1524–25. He was arrested, imprisoned, probably tortured, and lost much of his fortune. After this experience he produced no more important works, and he died in Würzburg in 1531. Although he was active within the Gothic tradition of winged altars, Riemenschneider presented daring innovations, beginning with his abandonment of the usual gilding and painting with bright tints to instead exalt the natural color of the wood and, as a result, to emphasize the purely sculptural qualities of the work instead of the painting. Furthermore, in his largest and most integral works, those in Rothenburg-ob-der-Tauber and Creglingen-am-Tauber, Riemenschneider adopted the expedient of "piercing" the background of the scene by means of openings or windows, thereby adding a new luminous animation. Over all his faces spreads an unmistakable atmosphere of noble melancholy tinged with foreboding.

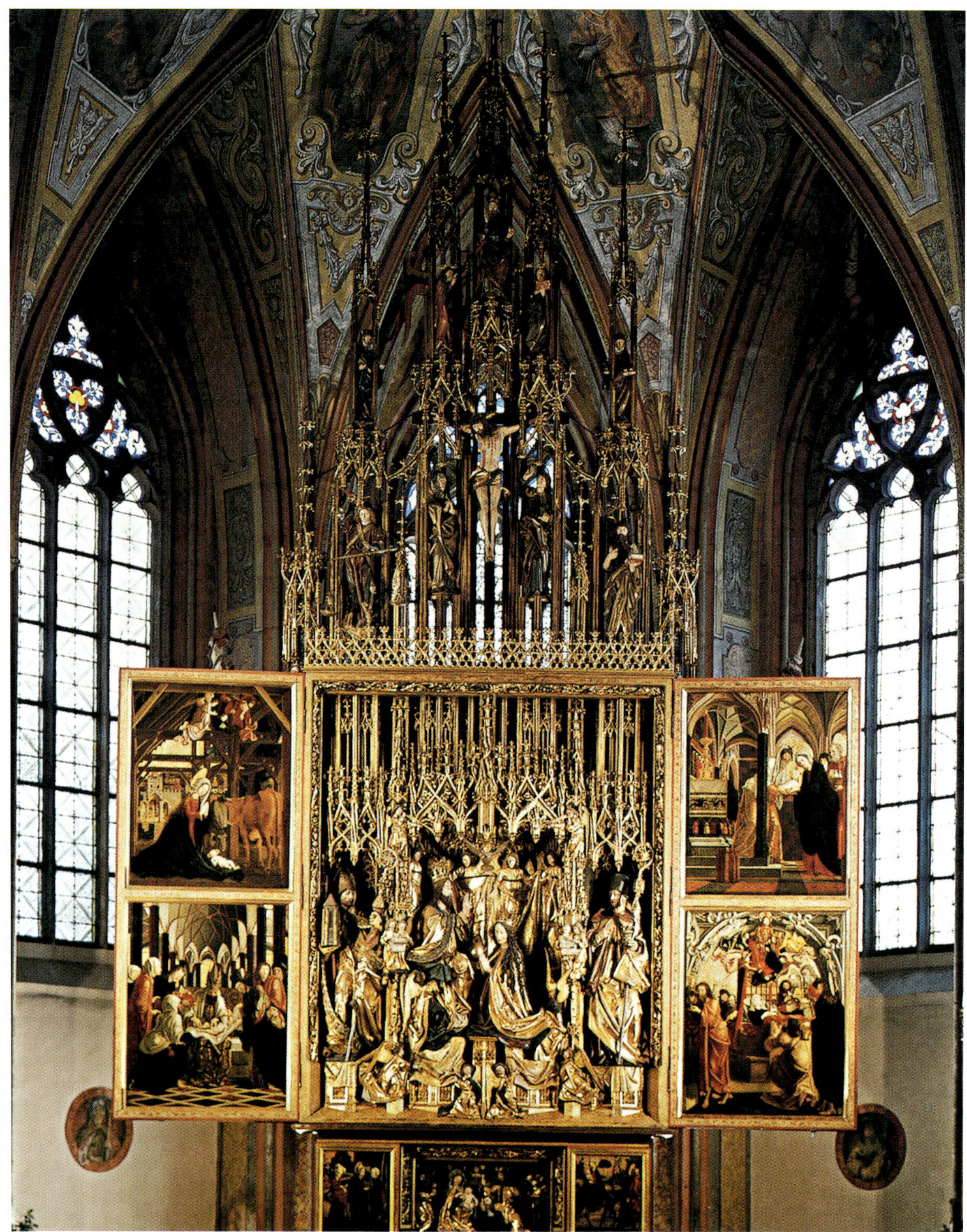

The great German altars

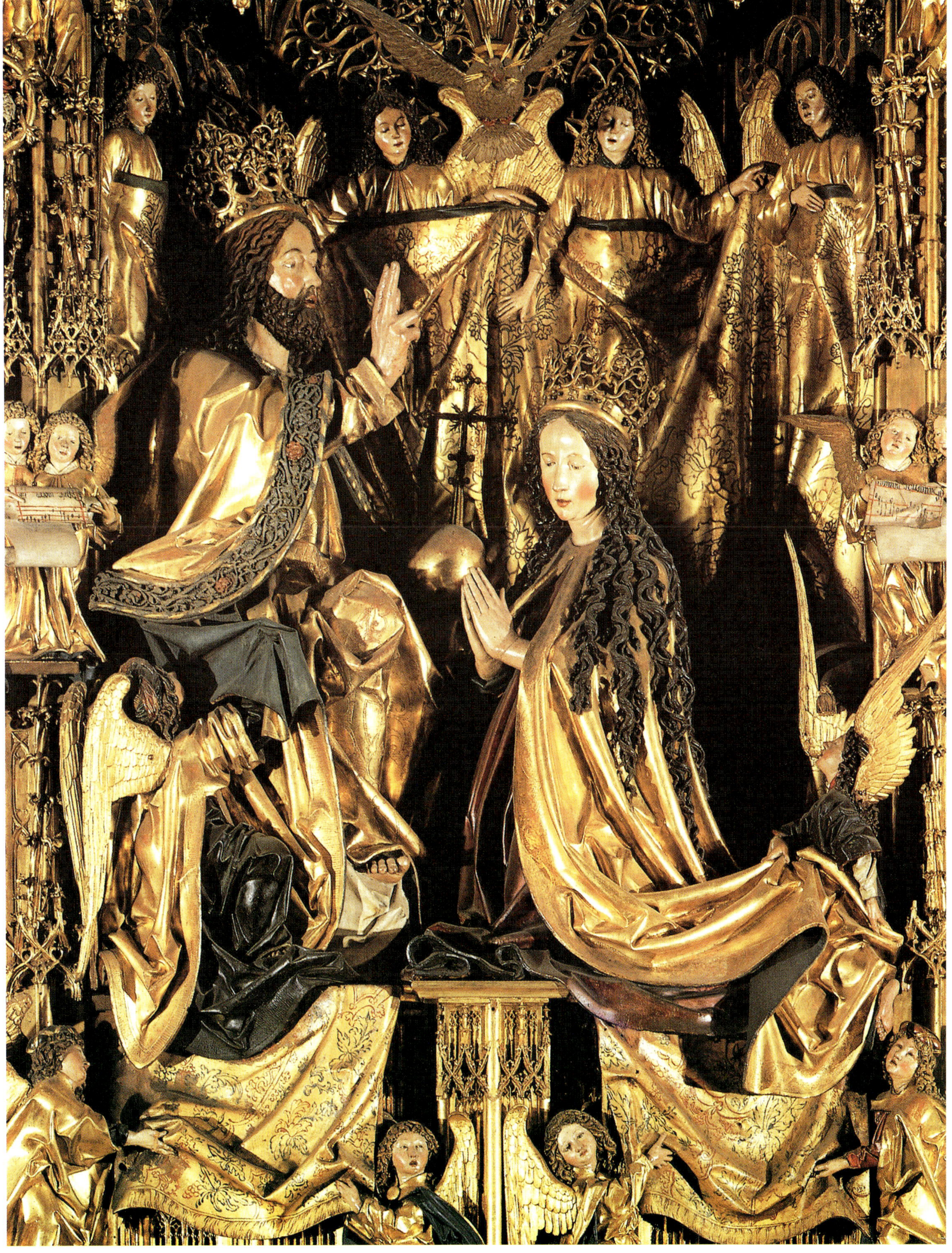

fully 16 painted compartments and an enormously ornate crowning piece, a true prodigy of creative and technical skills. The enormous spired top is centered on the carved shrine with the *Coronation of the Virgin* amid ranks of angels. The dense flowing of the drapery and cloaks and the polychrome decoration of the wooden sculptures give the scene—which was usually kept closed inside its painted doors, being opened to the faithful only on principal dates of the liturgical calendar—an aura of supernatural splendor that contrasts sharply with the solidly realistic scenes in the winged side panels. Pacher's double talent, his skills as a wood sculptor being equal to his skills as a painter, is made exuberantly clear in this work.

The great German altars

The spectacular complex of stalls of the cathedral of Ulm is one of the most impressive creations of Gothic art in Germany. The overall structure repeats traditional models, with stalls surmounted by traceried baldachins, but the idea of using half-figures of people, of great expressive effect and great involvement, to decorate the ends of the stalls is completely innovative. Even more surprising is that these are not busts of saints but "presences" of evocative characters, such as ancient sibyls and poets, thinkers and scientists from the classical world. Syrlin puts the natural color of the wood in splendid evidence, avoiding all polychrome decoration or gilding. The choir of the cathedral of Ulm had a decisive influence on the training of the young Tilman Riemenschneider.

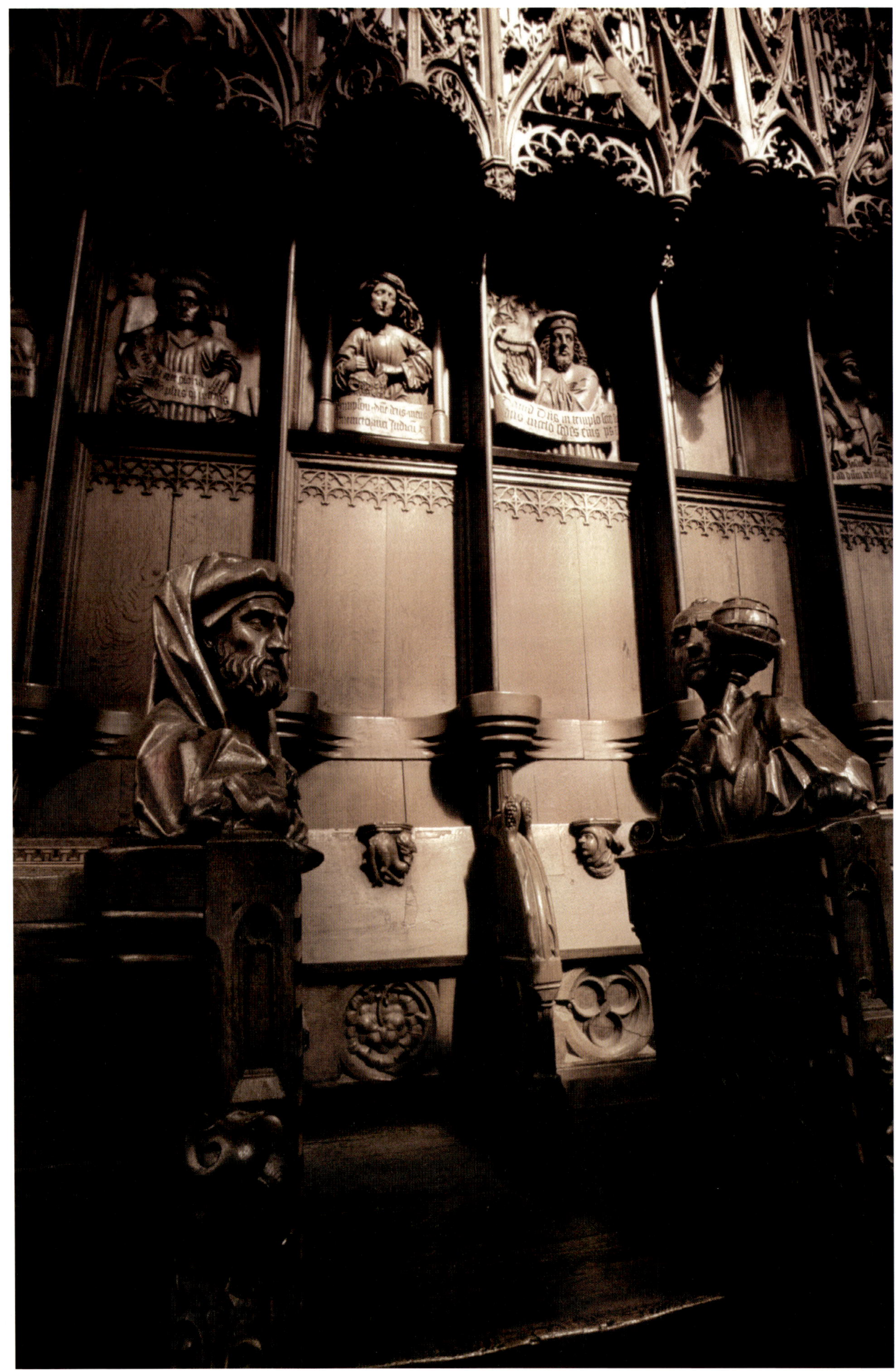

The great German altars

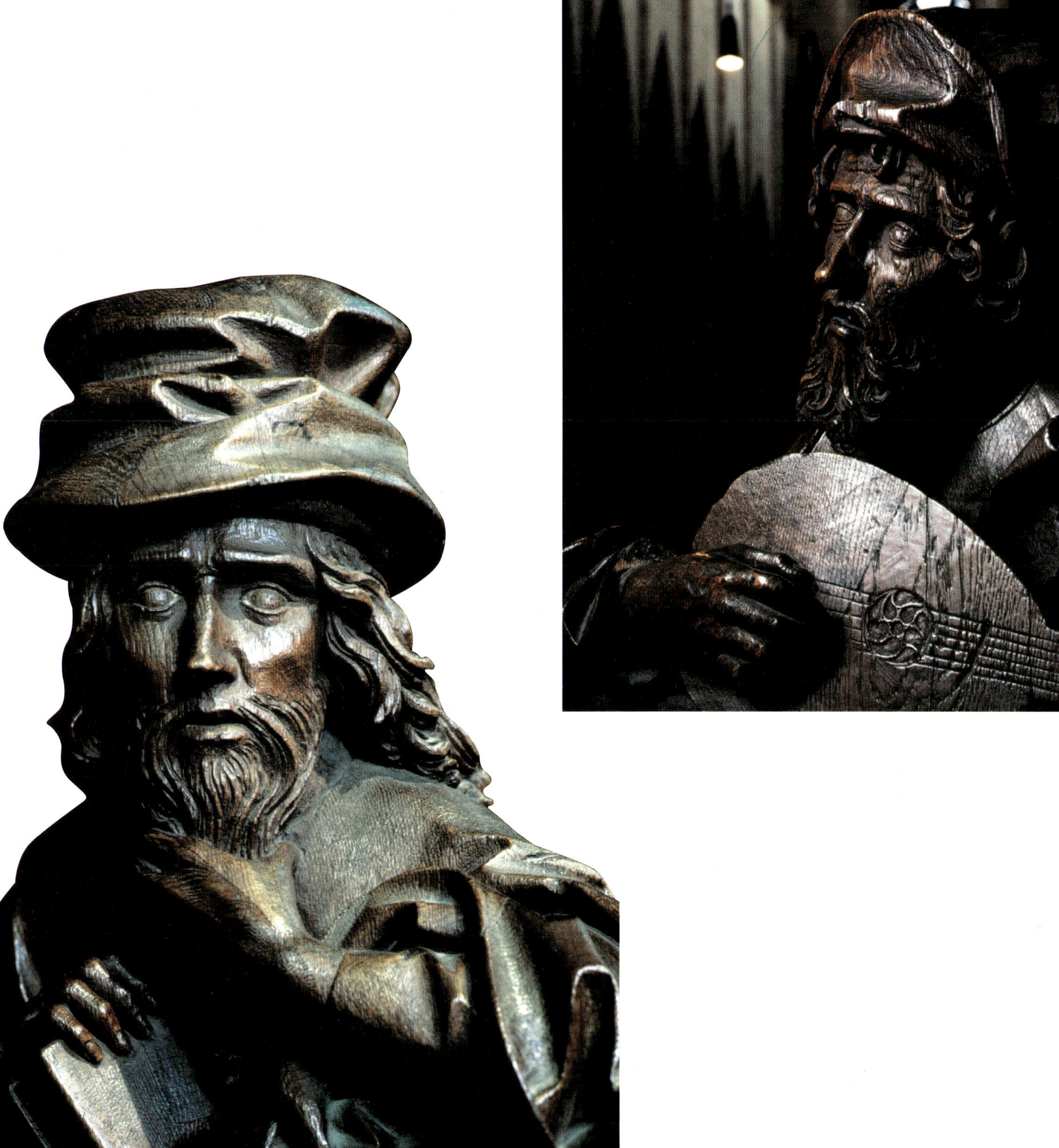

The great German altars

Expelled from the city
of Nuremberg, Veit
Stoss made his epochal
masterpiece in Cracow.
A more accurate title
for the carved scene on
the immense altar of
the *Death of the Virgin*
would be the "fainting
of the Virgin." Drawing
on his original training
as a painter, Stoss lav-
ishly applied the paint,
but it is the majestic
plastic and dynamic
scene of the enormous
carved figures that has
the prevailing impact.
The intense characteri-
zation of the emotions,
the careful and almost
theatrical arrangement
of the bodies and ges-
tures, the dynamism
given clothes, hair,
beards, and arms give
the work an irresistible
and compelling life.

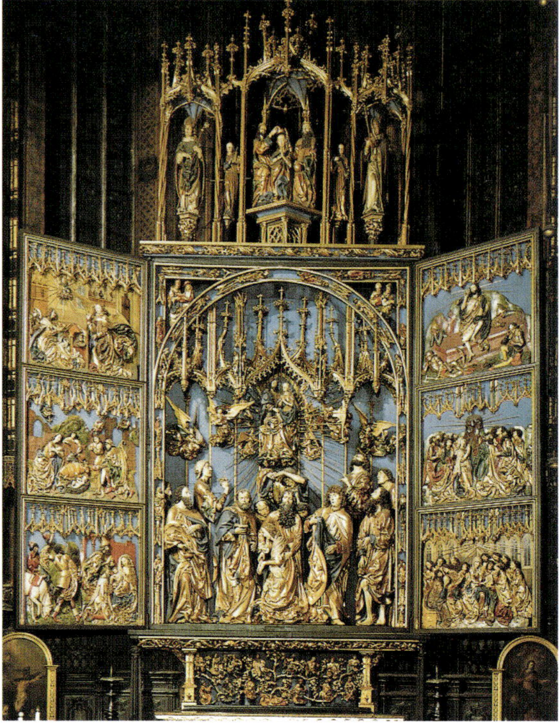

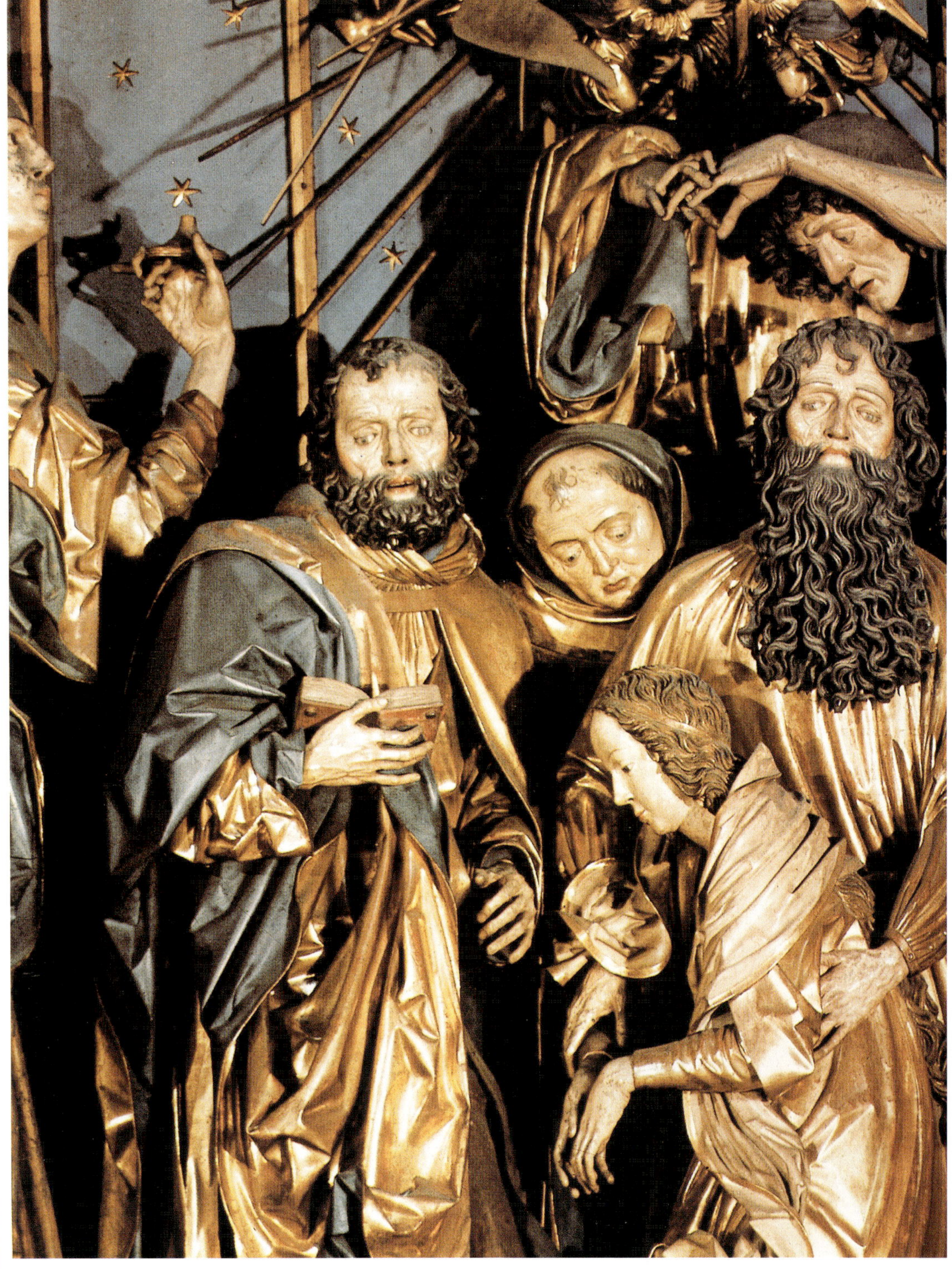

The great German altars

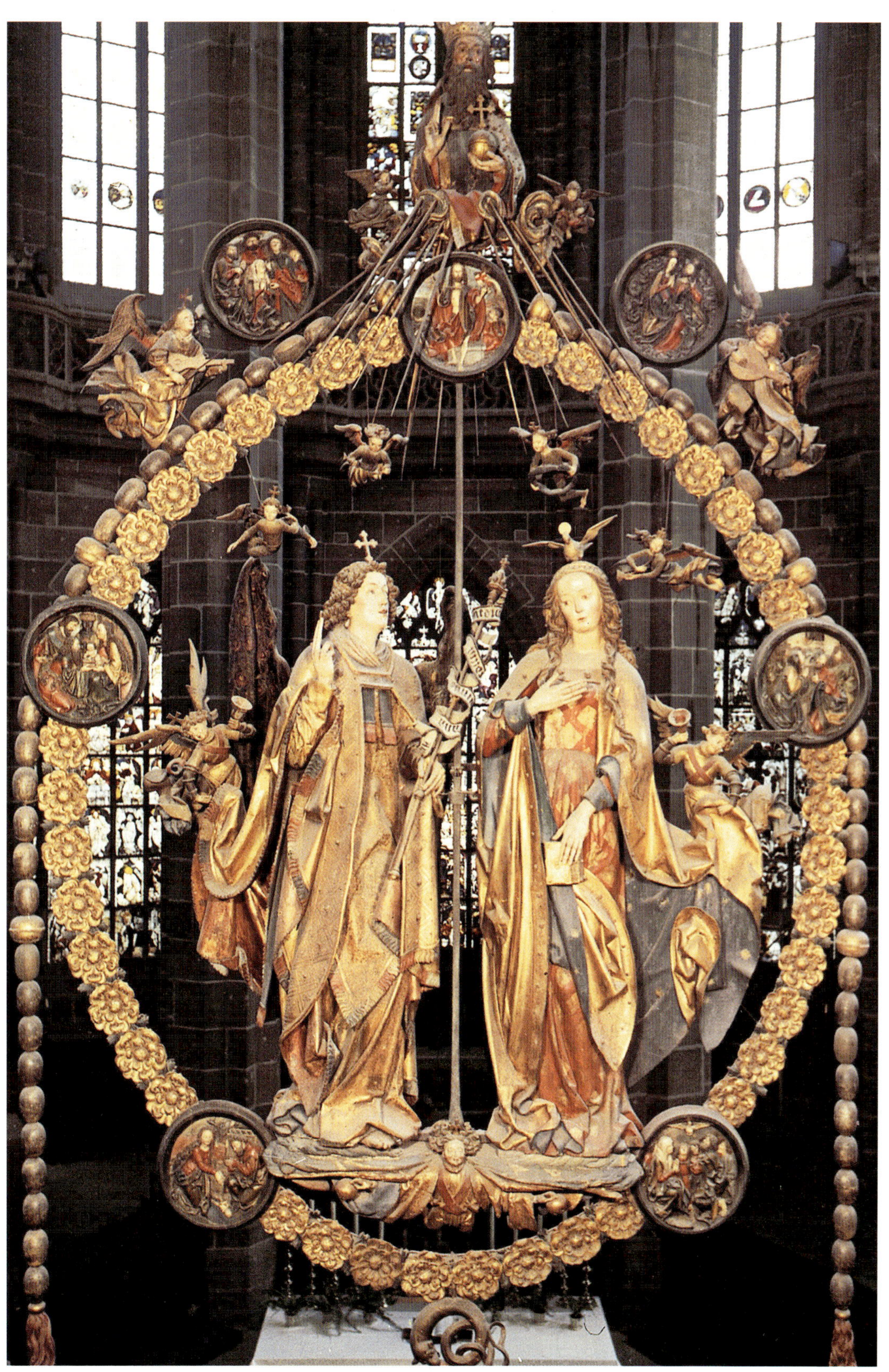

This *Annunciation*, surrounded by a halo of angels and symbols, was Stoss's last gilt and colored wood group. Without giving up on fantasy, in fact exalting it with unequaled majesty, he leaves behind every trace of the Gothic in the carving of wood.

Probably commissioned
by a Florentine mer-
chant, this small group
is an impressive exam-
ple of the virtuosic
technique in wood-
working. While reaching
an inventive apex in
the treatment of folds
and ripples—the bil-
lowing drapery of the
angel seems to antici-
pate the baroque—
Stoss was deciding to
give up the use of
paint and gilding. His
last wooden altarpiece,
made between 1520
and 1523 and today
in the cathedral of
Bamberg, is unpainted.

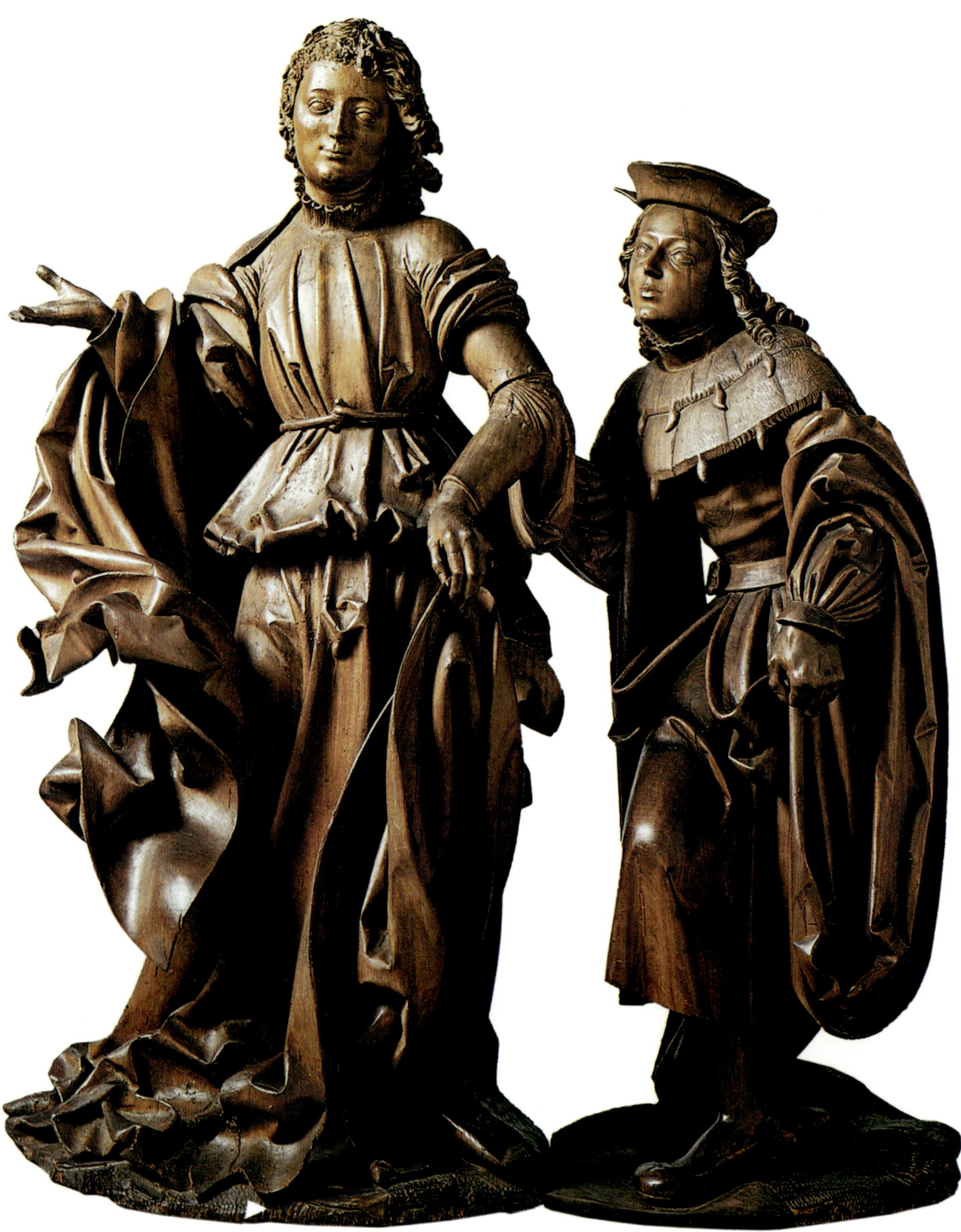

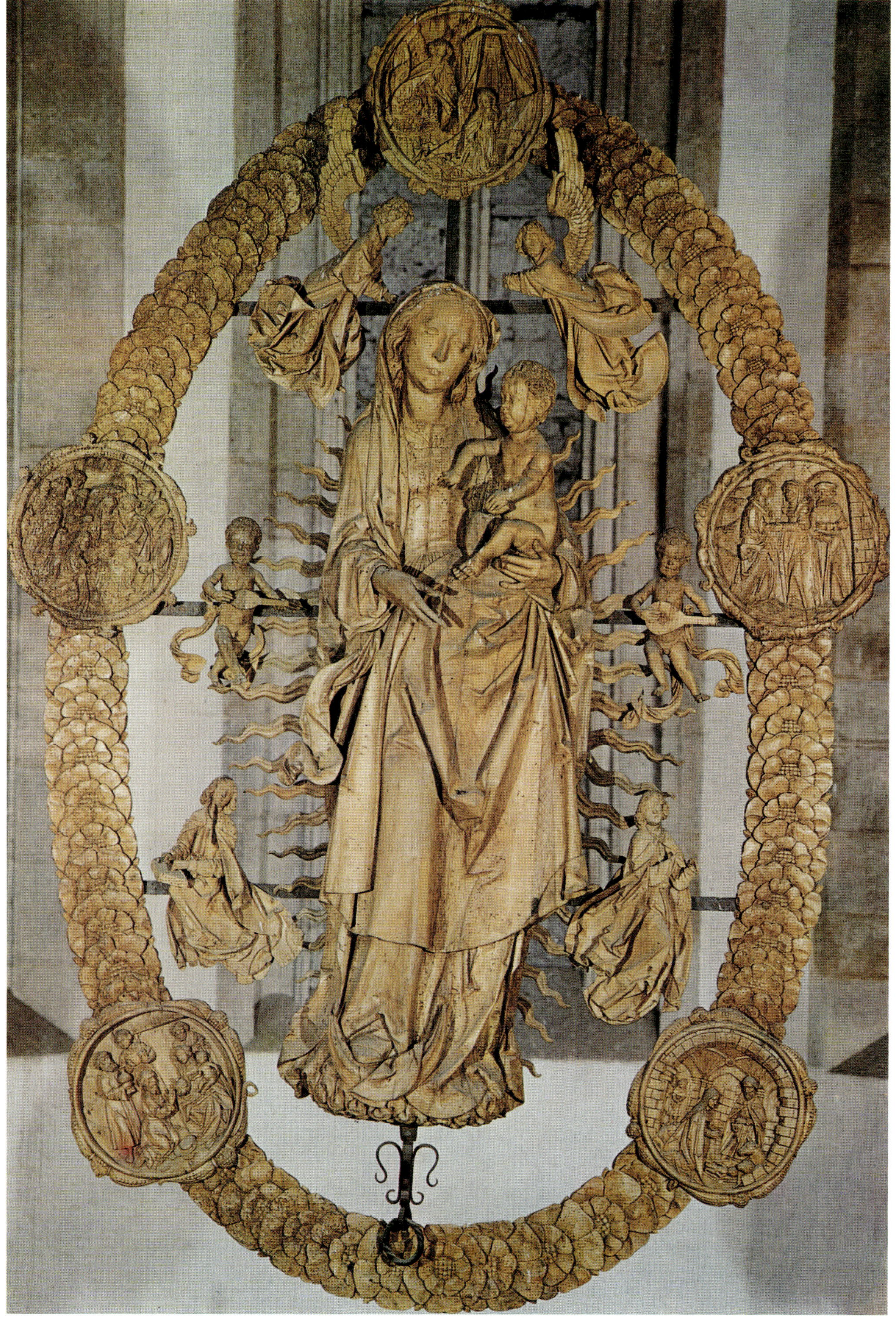

■ TILMAN
RIEMENSCHNEIDER
**Madonna
of the Rosary**
1524
Parish church, Volkach

The comparison from
a distance of the two
greatest German masters
of wood sculpture, Stoss
and Riemenschneider,
reaches moments of
fascinating intensity.
This *Madonna of the
Rosary* can be compared
to the *Annunciation*
carved by Veit Stoss in
Nuremberg. Both are
pieces of sculpture
made to be hung in the
choir of a church, the
central figures sur-
rounded by a sort of
large halo bearing
inserted carved tondi,
in this case presenting
the mysteries of the
rosary. But while Stoss
interprets the wooden
group as images of
great popular celebra-
tion, Riemenschneider
gives his figures a
reflective character,
often a kind of sorrow-
ful foreboding or noble
melancholy. With
extreme elegance,
Riemenschneider
avoids his colleague's
explosive expressions
of technical virtuosity,
preferring to concen-
trate on an emotional
and precious treatment
of the anatomic details,
brought to light by
the warm colors of
the wood.

Created to emotionally
involve the faithful,
almost like wooden
translations of miracle
plays, the great wooden
winged altarpieces
preserve intact their
fascination in those
cases, somewhat rare,
in which they are still
in their original loca-
tion. In some cases
these are small provin-
cial churches, many
with humble exteriors
that belie the presence
of these spectacular
altarpieces. An evocative
example is the modest
church in Creglingen-
am-Tauber, a short dis-
tance from Rothenburg-
ob-der-Tauber, which
preserves other sculp-
tural works of notable
quality besides this
masterpiece by
Riemenschneider.

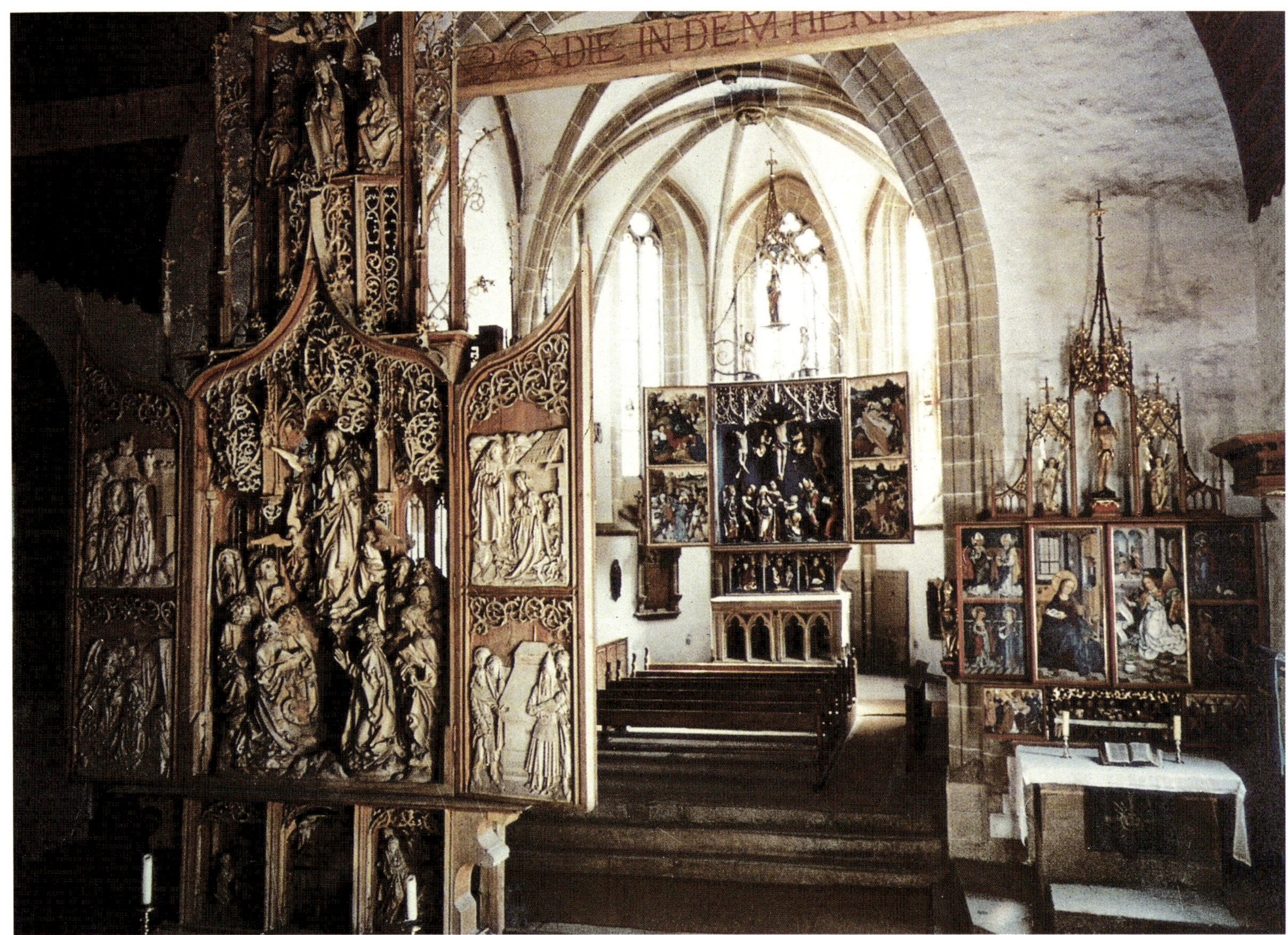

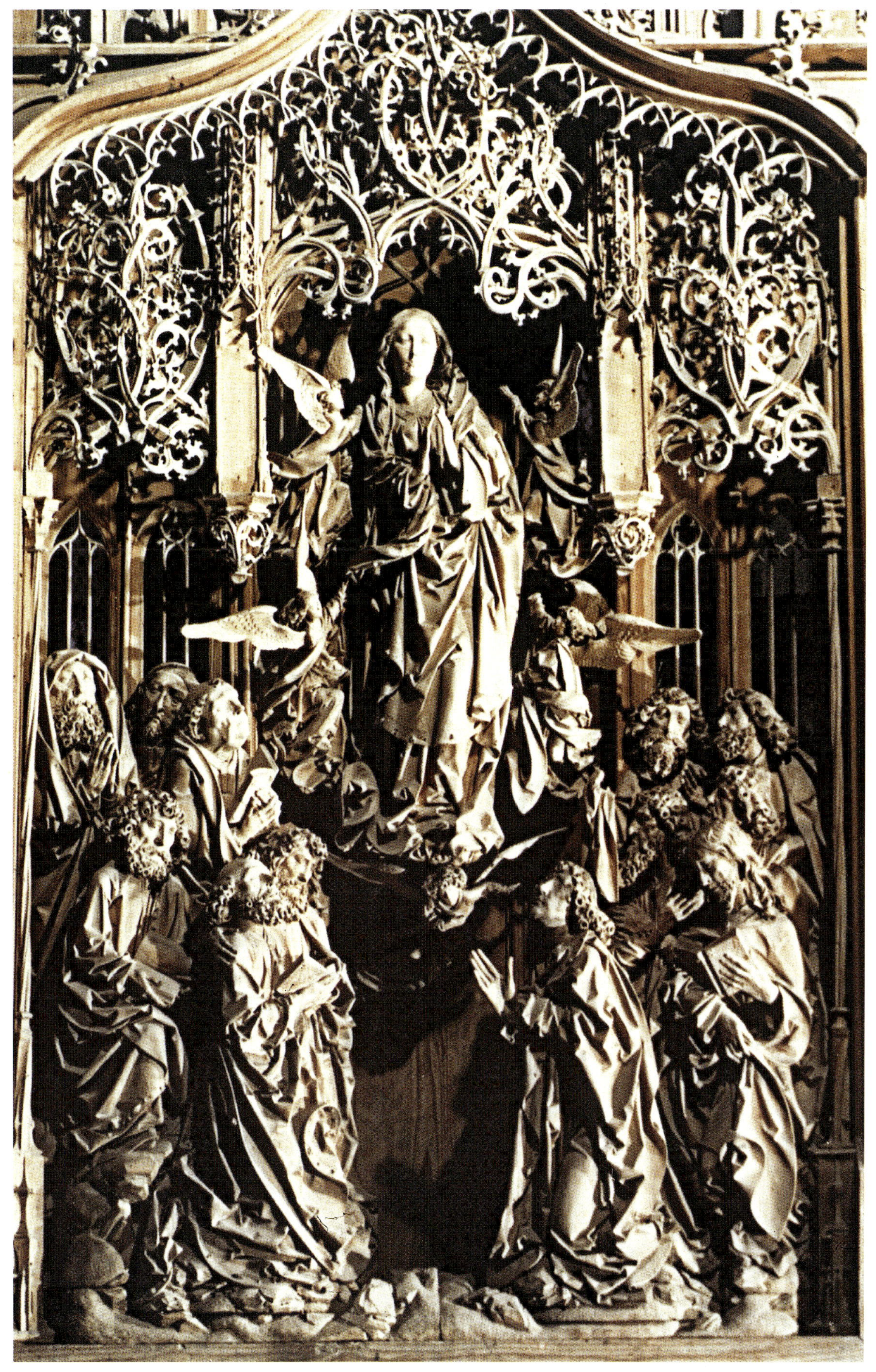

The great German altars

All that is known of the creator of this altarpiece is the initials H.L. This is the last large wooden winged altarpiece of German art. Begun in 1523, it was completed in 1526, by which time the followers of Thomas Müntzer had been exterminated, and the blood of 100,000 peasants, massacred without pity, had been spilled on the fields of the Black Forest, in Swabia, and in Thuringia. From Nuremberg, Dürer invoked the use of reason, appealing to the authority of Erasmus and Melanchthon to put an end to the excesses of Luther and to save the art threatened by the iconoclasm of the most ardent Protestants. The Breisach Altarpiece is apparently related to a long tradition, although in this case the customary layout is crushed by the visionary power of the scene and the figures. The altarpiece is dedicated to the Coronation of the Virgin, a subject held heretical by the Protestants. The episode takes place in a crowded sky, shaken by vortices, amid thick clouds and insistent presence of angels. In the middle of this Mary almost disappears amid the dense folds of a heavy cloak; her face peering out seems flustered and has the roundish look of a

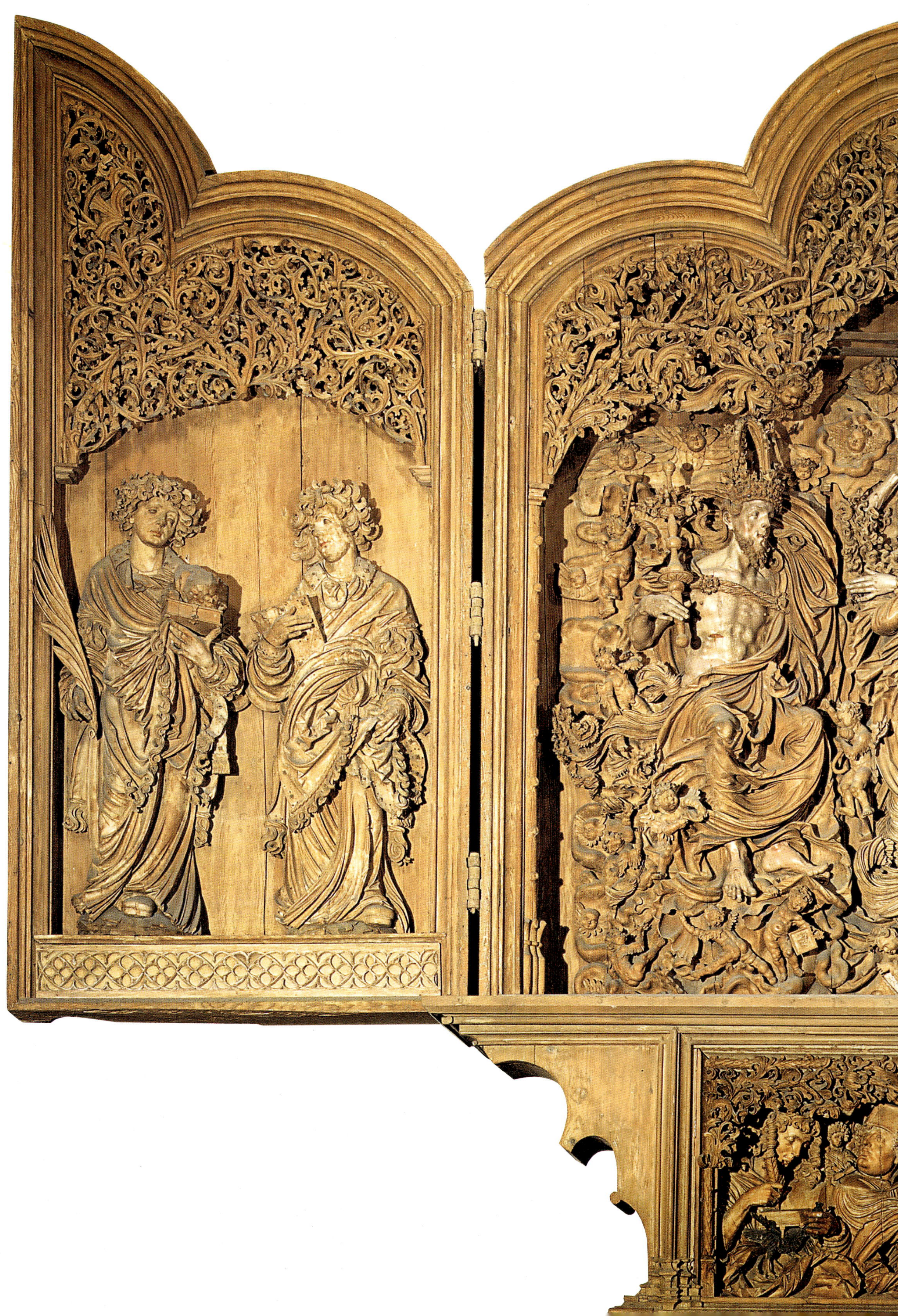

The great German altars

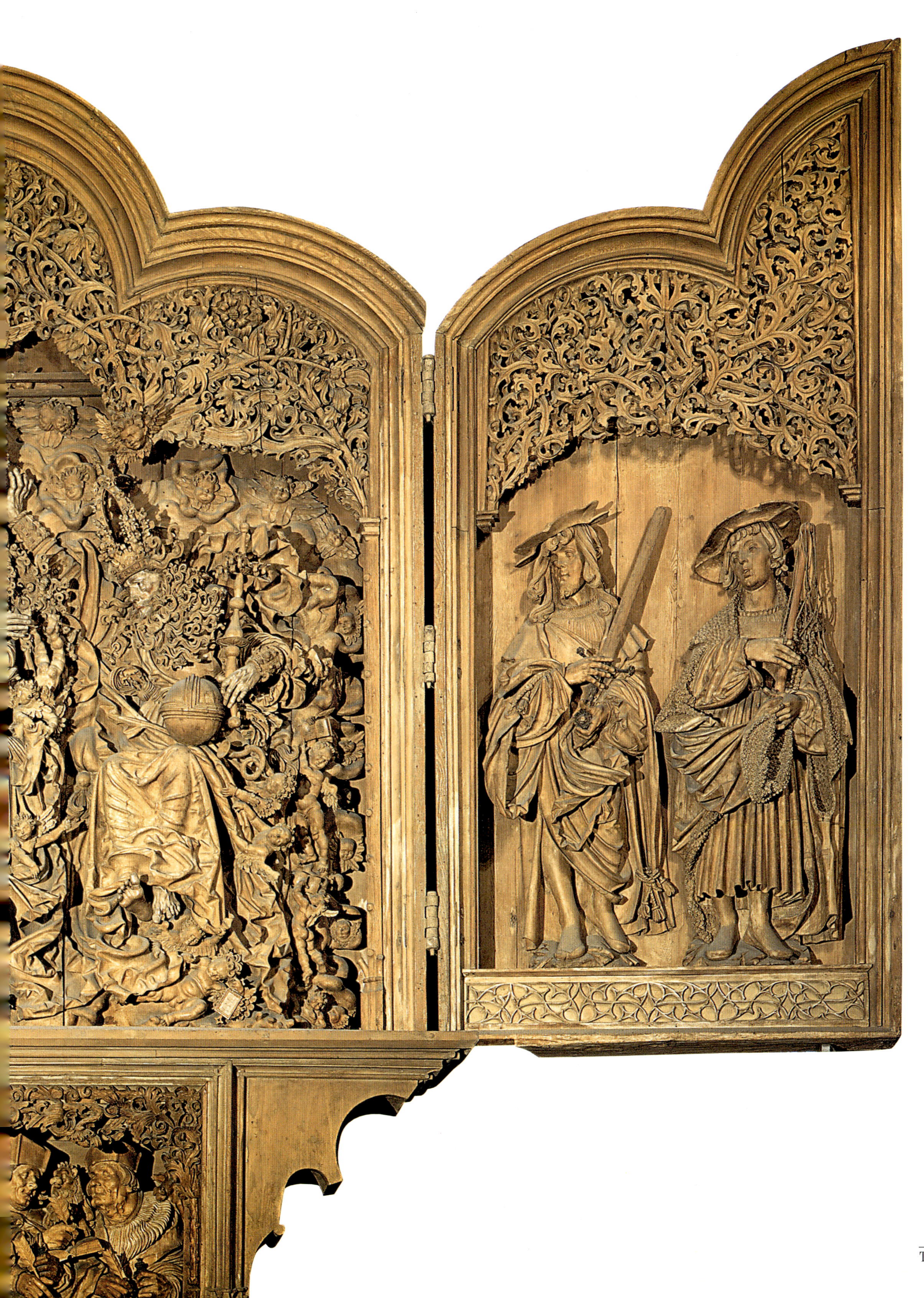

peasant girl; to the side of the Virgin, two disturbing figures awkwardly hold the crown; to the left is a half-naked Christ burdened by drapery that engulfs his extended arm; to the right is a God the Father as twisted as an ancient tree, his face tormented by wrinkles and furrows, oppressed by an impossible crown that can no longer contain his hair, which flies upward like twisting flames. He also has the most remarkable beard in all of art history, spreading outward in thousands of curls like the tentacles of a dozen enraged octopi. A few touches of color (the lips, eyes, the occasional marginal detail) do little to alter the natural blond tones of the wood. The *horror vacui* of the central compartment eases up in the doors, each of which bears a pair of saints. But again, there is a kind of feverish tension and a sort of uncontrolled extravagance. To the left, the sad curls of St. Stephen, with the giant hand that holds the book and atop it the stone of his martyrdom, shade the desperation of his eyes; he and his companion, St. Lawrence, wear classical togas that seem more like fur-lined coats. To the right, Gervasius and Protasius, dressed and decked out like casual champions of the *jeunesse dorée* of the epoch, barely manage to hold their oversize sword and whip, while their huge mantles are fastened by cords as sturdy as ship's rigging.

The great German altars

Under Philip the Good's rule (1419–67) the duchy of Burgundy grew to include Flemish lands: Flanders, Artois, the Brabant, Hainaut, Limburg, and, to the north, Holland and Zeeland. Thus the area of Burgundy corresponded to today's Belgium and parts of southern Holland and northern France. The duchy of Burgundy, perhaps the richest and most elegant state in late Gothic Europe, became an inexhaustible source of artistic ideas. With the death of Philip the Good, however, the commercial and political fortunes of Flanders began to wane, and growing international tensions endangered the stability of the region. The new duke, Charles the Bold, sought to further extend the holdings of the duchy of Burgundy, attracting the hostility of France's Louis XI and provoking a ruinous war that cost him his life during the siege of Nancy (1477). Charles's daughter and heiress, Mary of Burgundy, married the powerful Maximilian of Austria, future Holy Roman emperor. At her death, in 1482,

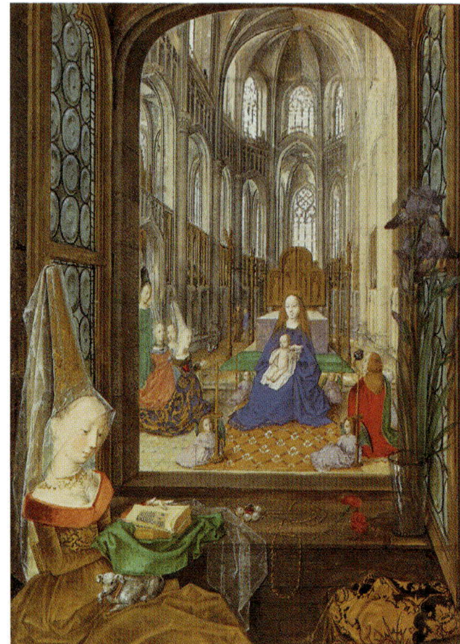

Flemish masters and represented the point of full maturation of the school of Bruges. Born in Germany, Memling trained in Cologne, where he admired the delicate works of Stefan Lochner. He went to Brussels, where became the most trusted collaborator of Van der Weyden. At the death of his master (1464) Memling set himself up in Bruges, where he spent thirty years of intense activity. Gifted with a perfect technique and a flawless sense of delicacy and measure, he was not a great experimenter. Indeed, from his youth to his maturity his works do not reveal any particular variation and present an exemplary and enduring model for late-fifteenth-century Flemish painting. His elegant paintings are without dramatic accents but present reassuring beauty, with graceful figures that inhabit a symmetrical and orderly space dominated by an imperturbable atmosphere, very different from the active realism of the masters of the preceding generation. It is precisely this progressive distancing from the

Flanders in the late

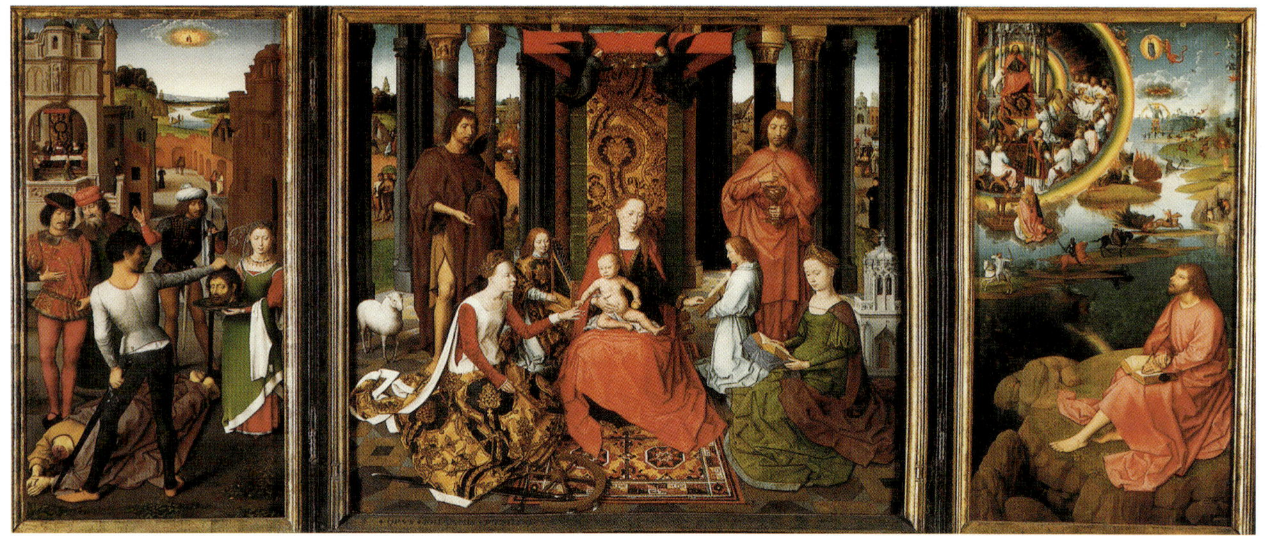

facts of life and history that makes Memling's painting emblematic of a changing season, in a city that was slowly withdrawing from the center of events.

Although there are no indications that Memling traveled, he enjoyed Europe-wide fame. He maintained intense contacts with Florentine patrons, agents of the Medici Bank in Bruges. A famous example is the *Last Judgment* that he painted for Agnolo Tani but that ended up instead in Danzig (Gdańsk); for the Portinari family he made a triptych and several portraits.

In the field of portraiture Memling developed the format of the three-quarter bust located in a landscape, destined to have a wide following in Flemish and also Italian art. His religious works are touching, among them several appealing and original panels in which several episodes are

Flanders fell prey to the conflicting aims of the Hapsburgs and the French. Maximilian was accepted as regent by most of the territories of the duchy, except for Flanders, which aligned with France and England, creating the premise for a struggle that lasted ten years and weakened the rebellious cities of Bruges, Ypres, and Ghent.

None of this constant conflict appears in the works of the artists active in Bruges. Hans Memling belonged to the second generation of located in a single architectonic or naturalistic setting. The glories of Bruges and, more in general, of the ducal patrons, encouraged other Flemish cities to "invest" in art. Tournai, for example, remained the principal center of the production of precious tapestries. Dieric Bouts worked permanently in Louvain, an ambitious city that aspired to rival the more famous Brussels and Bruges. Nominated official painter to the city, Bouts created works in which the individual scenes are elevated in a dimension outside time, while the narration seems suspended in a fascinating ritual. Of particular importance are the two large winged altarpieces he made for Louvain, the Holy Sacrament of the Eucharist and the Last Supper. However, beside these paintings of vast breadth he also created devotional images that put the accent on the humanity of the sacred figures.

A very different universe appears in the works of Hugo van der Goes. This artist, active in Ghent, was at first influenced by the smooth, silent beauty of the creations of Van Eyck. His pictorial career, however, was affected by tormented human events, with an intimate and heartfelt religious vision dominated by the awareness of sin, which eventually led

inspiration that led him to conceive images of great immediacy. Whether his works are meditative or are marked by a dramatic intensity in the narration, the element they share is an interpretation of the sacred event as something extremely actual and comprehensible, thus sometimes creating authentic poetry.

The last great master of fifteenth-century Flemish painting was Gerard David, who can be taken as an important connection between the generation of the "Flemish primitives" and the ranks of those artists who already fully belonged to the history of the fifteenth century. David was the most important painter in Bruges between the two centuries, and he cautiously managed his career, intuiting the economic and social changes taking place. He saw clearly that Bruges was rapidly losing its importance (the port was silting up), while the economic and political center of gravity shifted to Antwerp, at the mouth of the Scheldt River. David reworked the stimuli of the art of

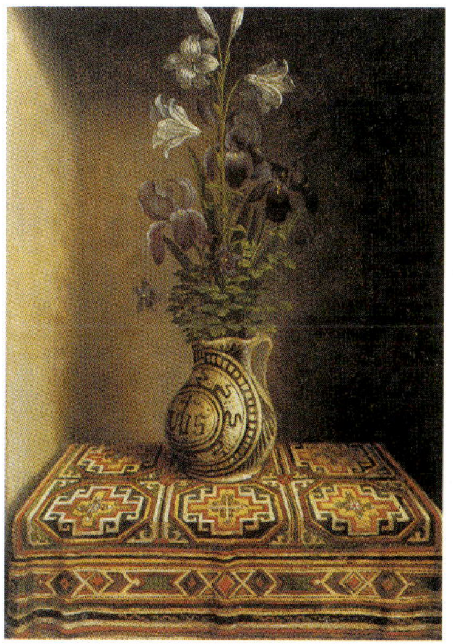

Hans Memling, *Still Life with Pitcher and Flowers on a Rug,* circa 1485-90; Thyssen-Bornemisza Collection, Madrid

fifteenth century

him to become a lay brother in the Augustinian monastery of Roode Kloster, where he lived until his death, at times on the brink of insanity. He progressively distanced himself from the stately and quiet representation of the surrounding world, overturning the canons of Flemish naturalism in strongly expressive and tense works in which even the space itself seems to disintegrate, denouncing the artificial nature of painted images compared to the natural world.

Geertgen tot Sint Jans is the most important painter of the Low Countries of the north. He was active far from the limelight of the lively Flemish cities, in his native Haarlem, which in those years had its own growing school of painting. After his first youthful works he found a natural

Van Eyck and Memling in a noble language, supported by a classical conception of forms and space that revealed his debt to Italian art. He also revived the traditional themes of Flemish painting thanks to a skilled coloristic sense of great refinement. His vision is always based on an interest in the natural fact and in the atmospheric effects of light. David's figures are no longer placed before nature as a backdrop, but are integral parts of the landscape, which sometimes breaks completely free of its role as setting for the narrative to become an evocative locale in which to abandon oneself to meditation.

With these works David heralded the great period of the landscapes of Patinir and projected his own art far beyond the borders of his century.

Gerard David, *Baptism of Christ,* circa 1515; Kunsthistorisches Museum, Vienna

Flanders in the late fifteenth century

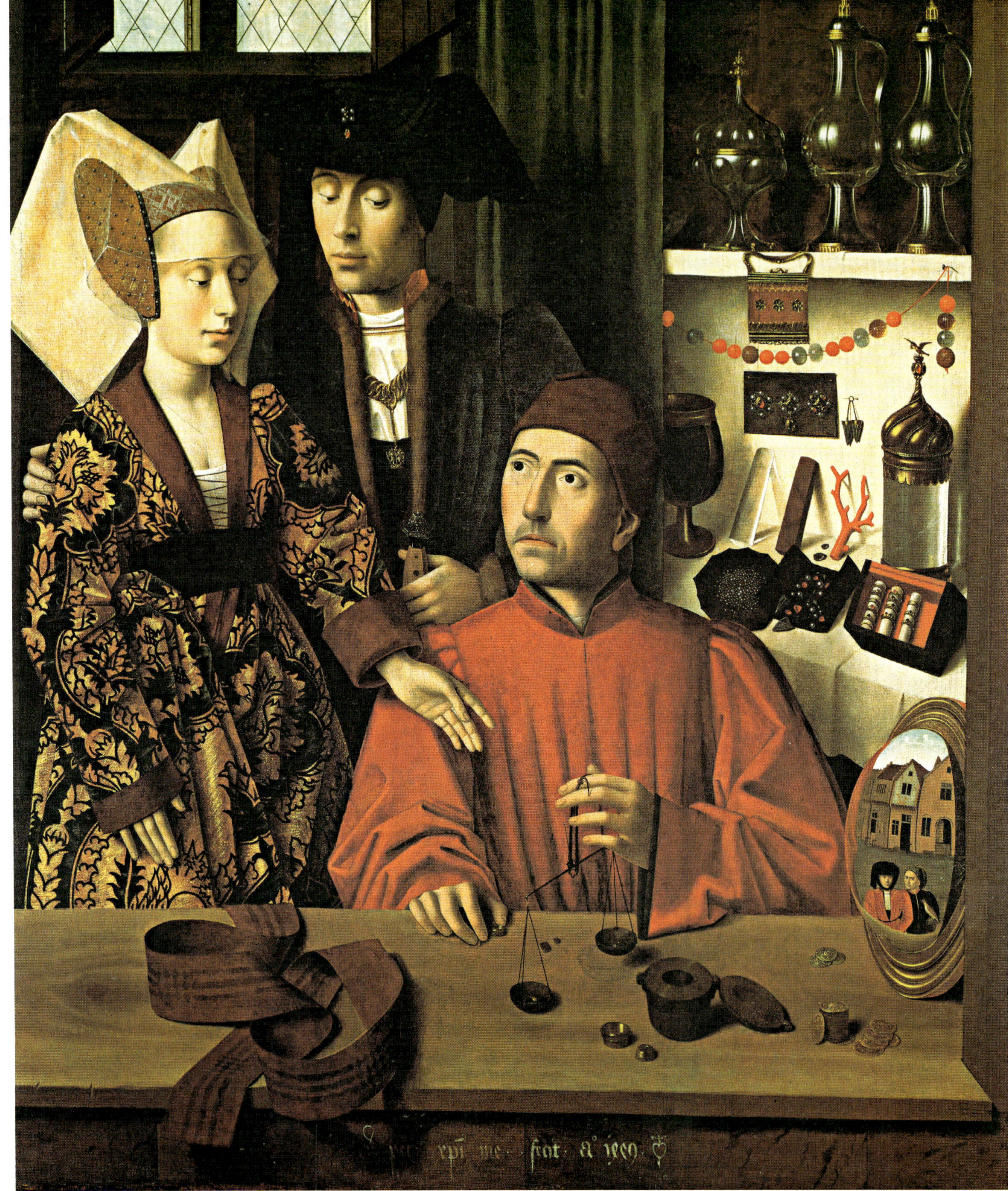

Flanders in the late fifteenth century

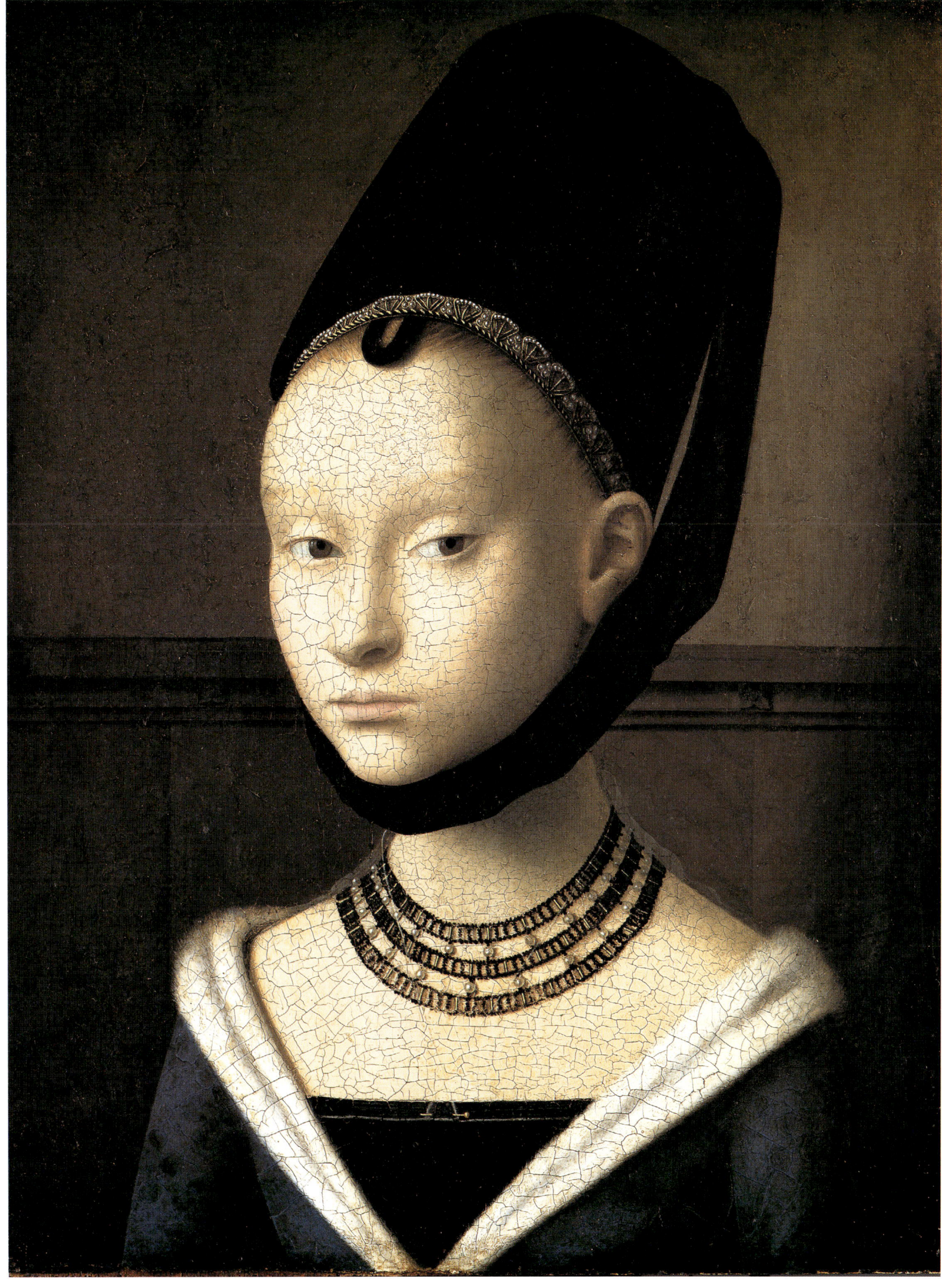

Like the other great Flemish masters of the first half of the fifteenth century (Van Eyck, Robert Campin, Van der Weyden), Petrus Christus worked in two very different genres. His paintings of religious subjects are full of descriptive details, investigated and almost enumerated by the clear, diffuse light; his portraits, instead, are almost always set against a neutral background, limiting as far as possible the description of any surrounding elements. The sitters are modeled by close light, as if they were looking out of a niche, which makes their features and emotions seem to gradually emerge into the light.

Flanders in the late fifteenth century

The arrival in Florence of this work was one of the salient artistic events in the evolution of the style of the Tuscan masters in the age of Lorenzo the Magnificent. One of the masterpieces of Flemish painting of the late fifteenth century, made for the church of St. Edigio, it was commissioned by Tommaso Portinari, representative of the Medici bank in Bruges. The triptych presents *the Adoration of the Shepherds* in its central scene; the side panels bear portraits of the kneeling members of the Portinari family, with oversize figures of saints behind them. Two related episodes are presented in the backgrounds of the side panels: to the left, Joseph and Mary make their entry into Bethlehem, where Jesus will be born; to the right, the Magi, en route to Bethlehem, stop to ask directions. The scenes are set in an open and profound landscape,

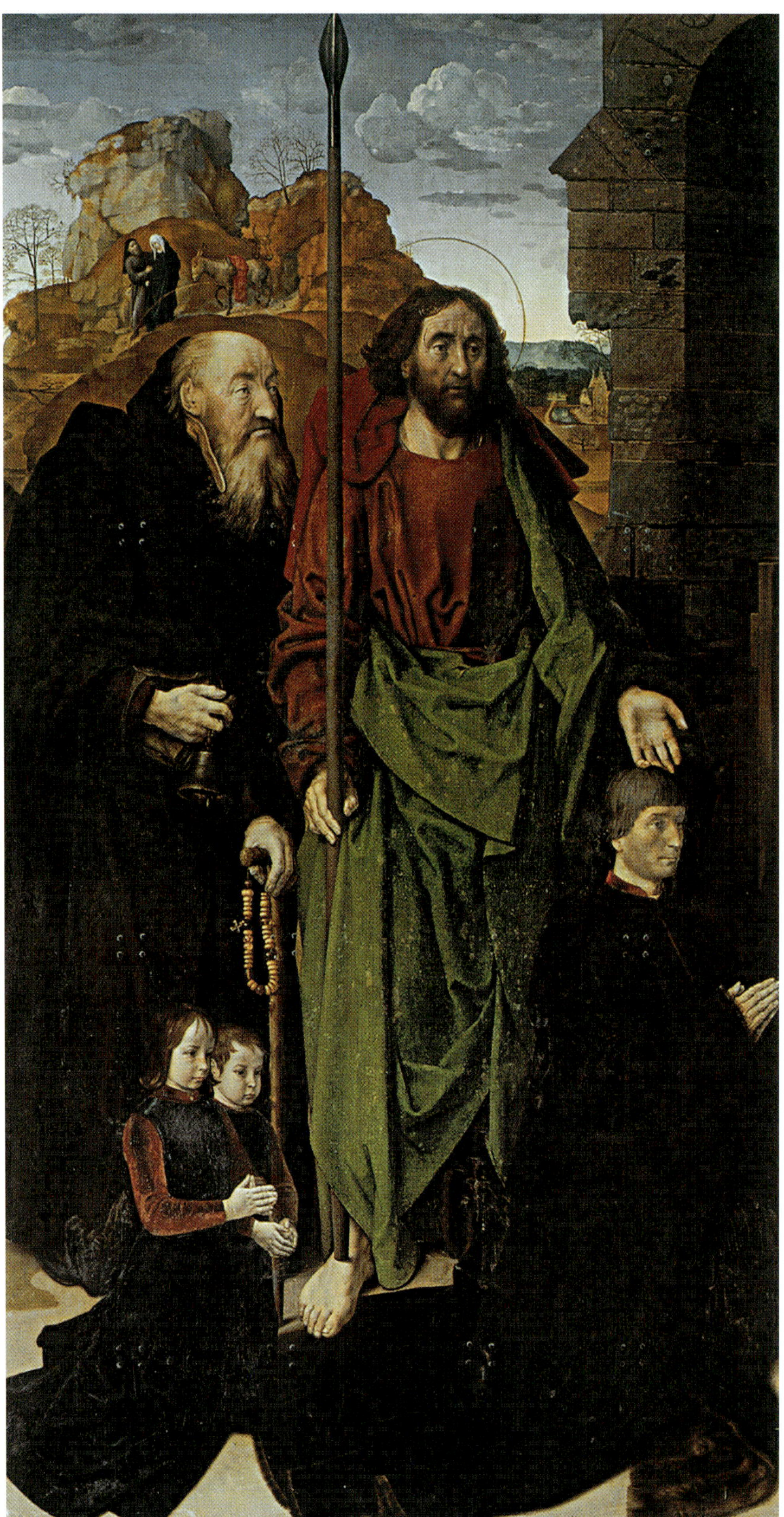

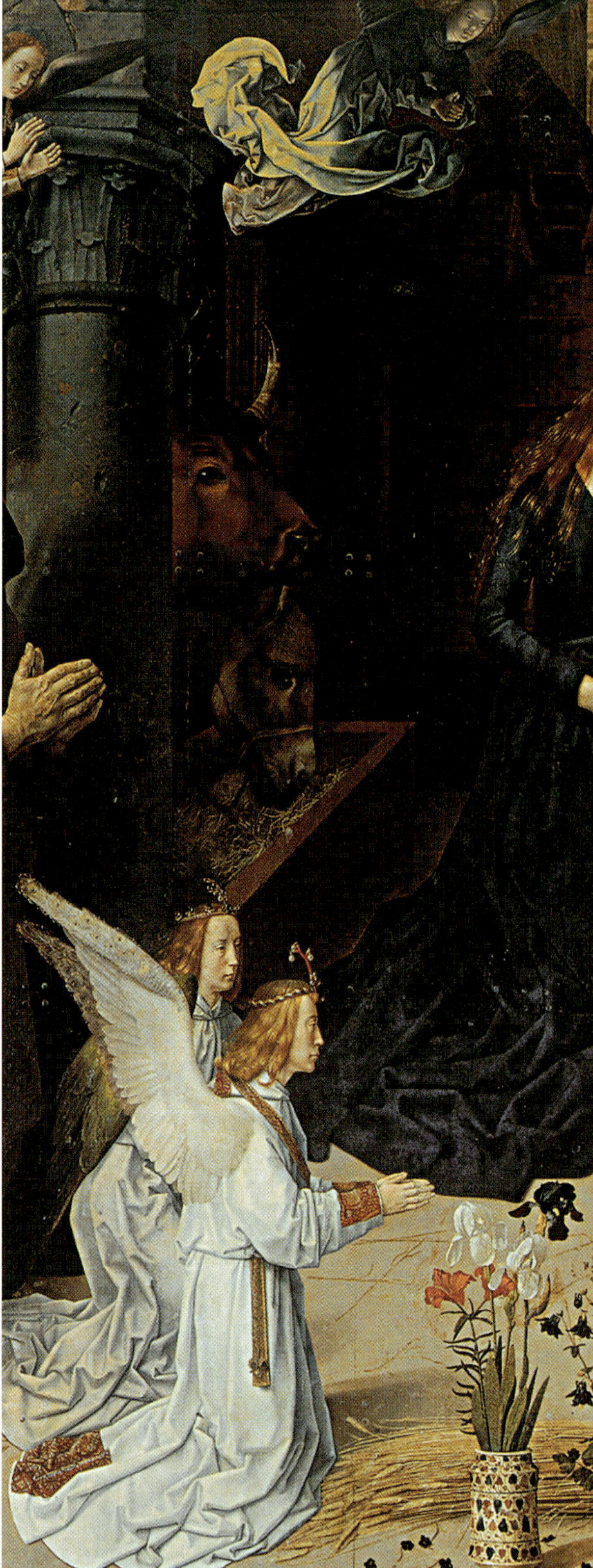

Flanders in the late fifteenth century

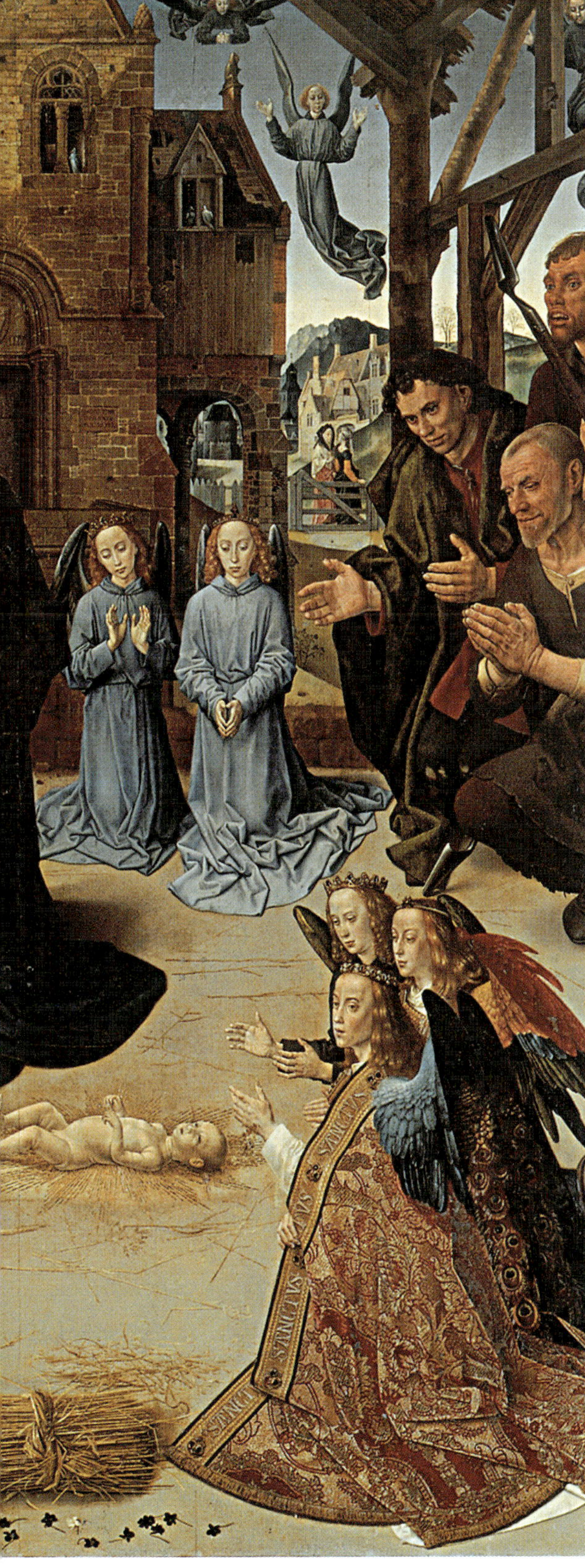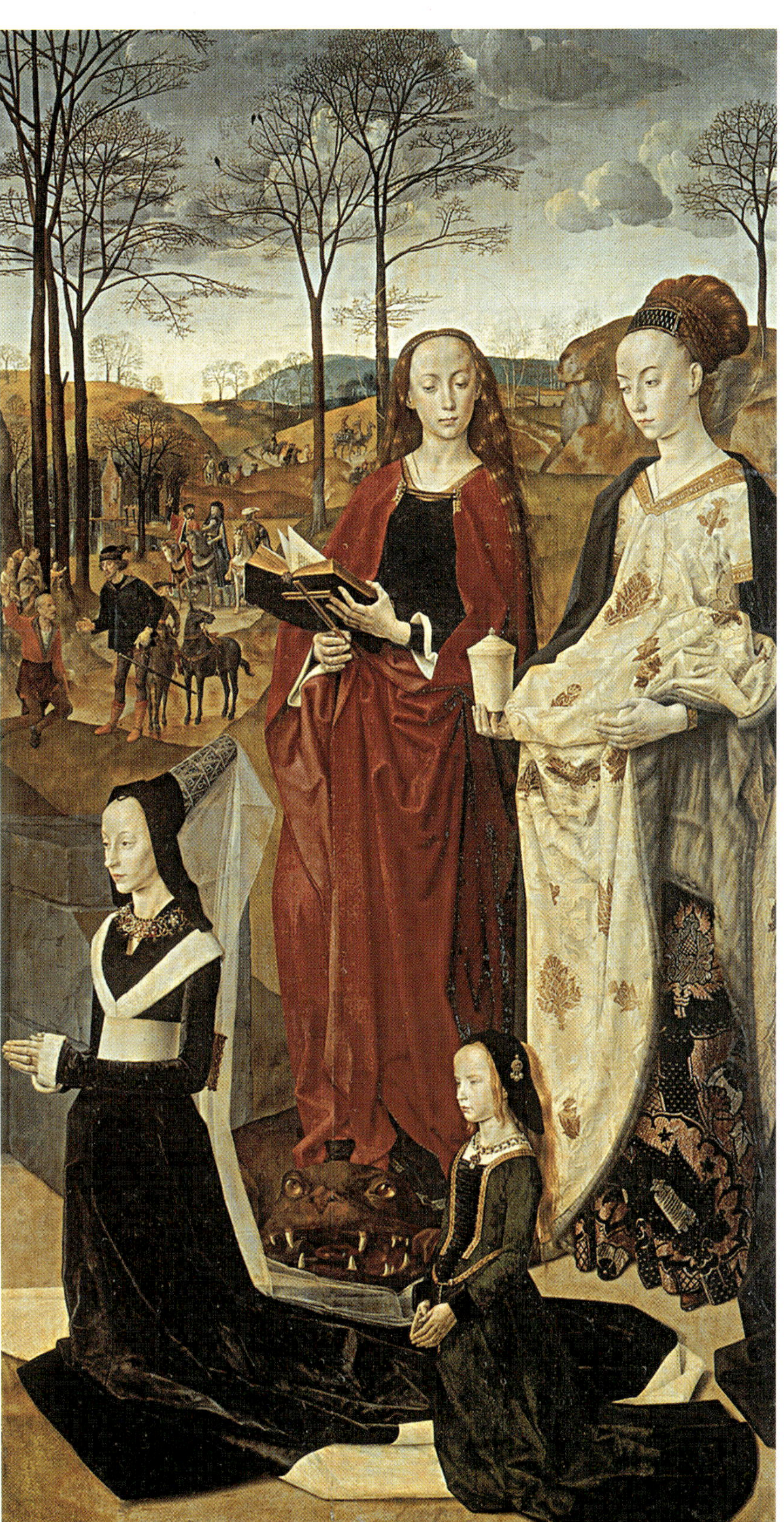

quite innovative in Flemish art, in which variations in the tones of color are used to suggest space without the use of particular geometric definition, in the manner of the landscapes of Jan van Eyck. As is typical of the tormented psychology of Van der Goes, the central panel does not present the joy of the Nativity, and instead seems to prefigure the sad destiny of the Child and his Passion. The different proportions of the figures, the description of the innumerable details, the warm tones of the reds and the cool tones of the blues amplify the tension that pervades the scene. The Child is placed on the ground, laid across some straw; left to himself, he reveals all his fragility. The faces of the Madonna and the angels are absorbed, even troubled; only the three shepherds to the right participate with pleased animation. In the foreground, the artist presents an admirable example of a still life, composed of a bundle of straw and two vases of flowers, symbolic allusions to the future sorrows of the Virgin.

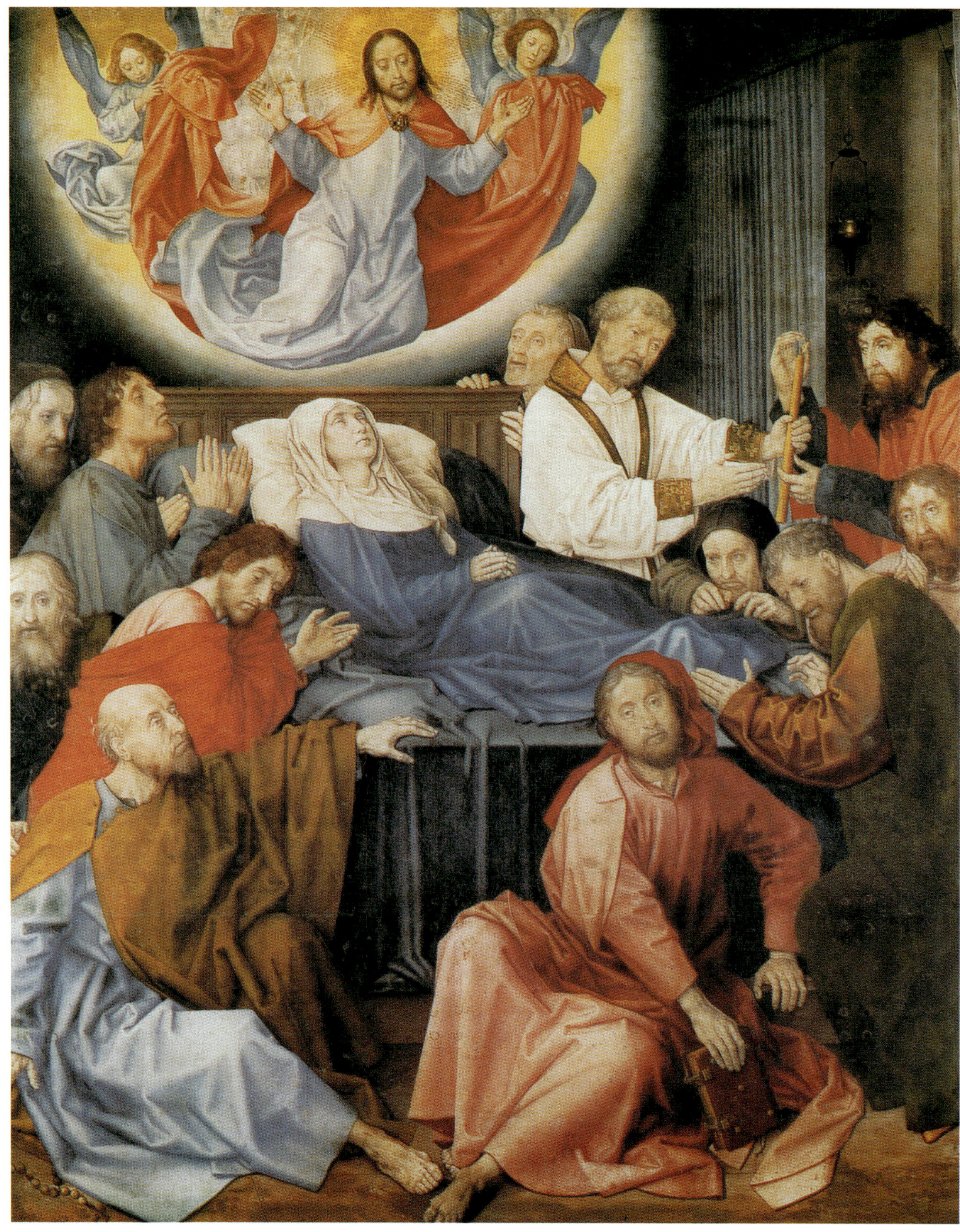

Flanders in the late fifteenth century

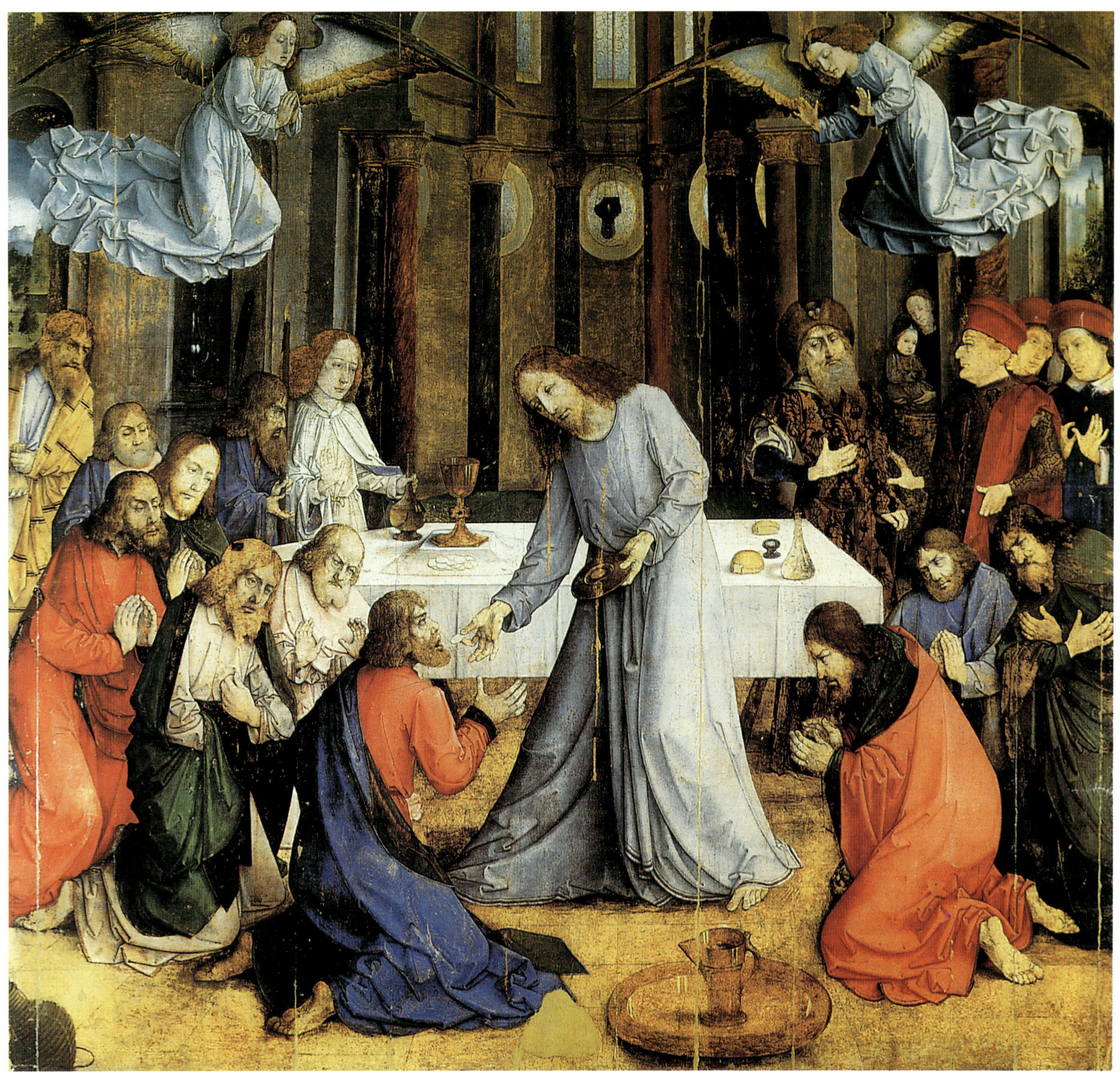

Flanders in the late fifteenth century

The artist here uses a biblical episode to present a young well-to-do woman of Bruges stepping from a bath. The furnishings of the room are presented with clarity, every detail emphasizing the comfort of this domestic setting. The tub is covered by elaborate drapes, and a servant offers a bathrobe to the young girl, who, with a distracted air, slips a foot into a slipper. This extraordinary painting, one of the first life-size realistic nudes of the Renaissance, must be studied slowly to understand the quiet rhythm of the gestures, the light, the details.

These portraits present a husband and wife of Tuscan origin, members of a celebrated family of bankers and art patrons. While the face of Tommaso Portinari, director of the Bruges branch of the Medici bank, seems imperturbable, that of his young wife seems touched by an almost imperceptible shiver, as though she were giving the ghost of a smile.

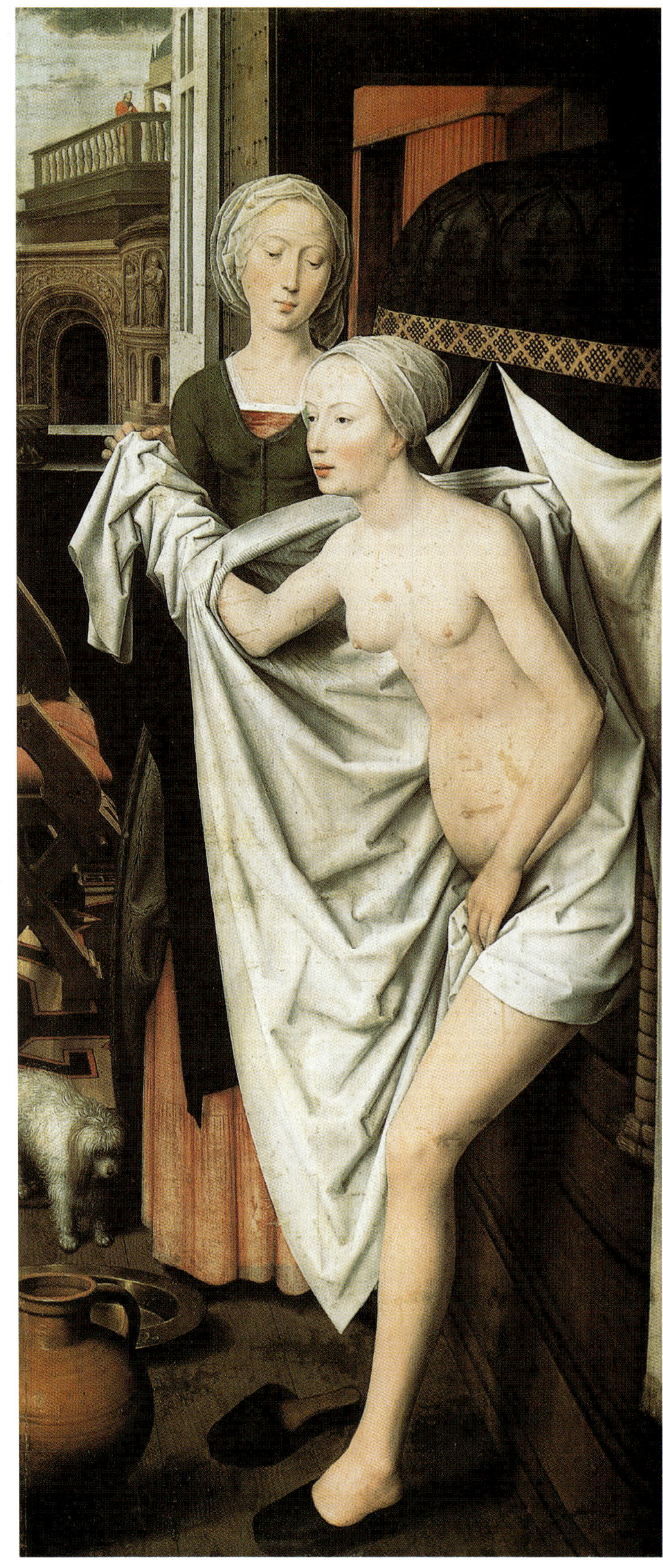

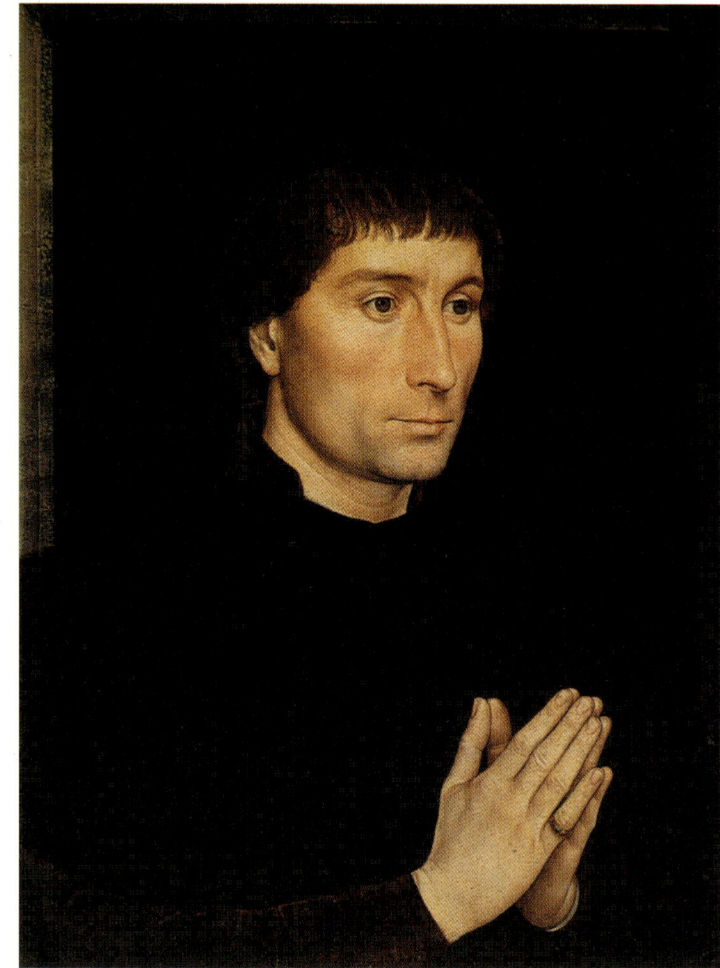

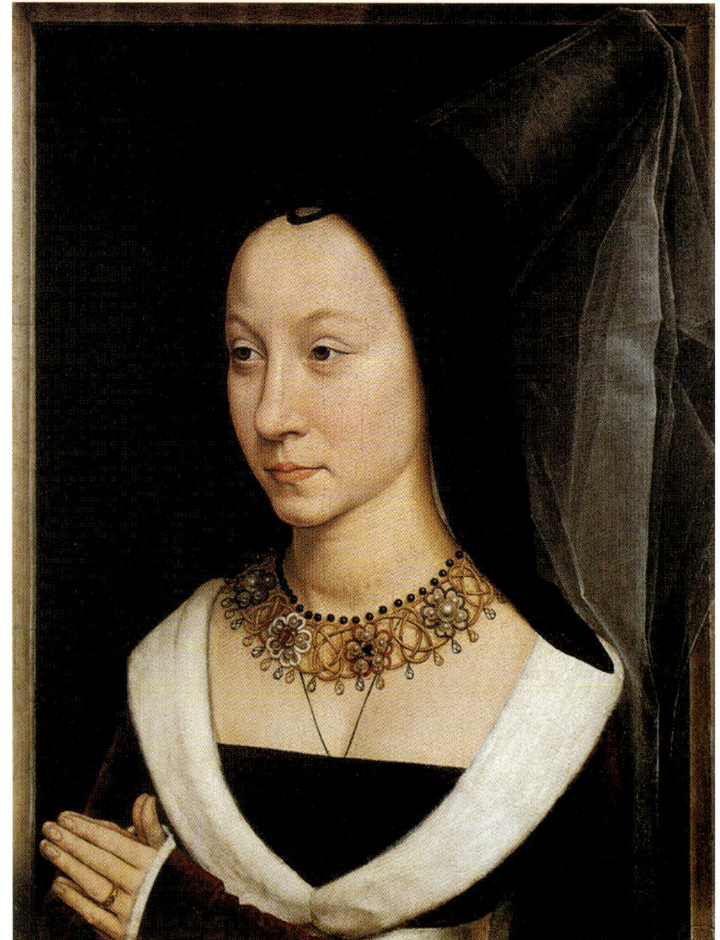

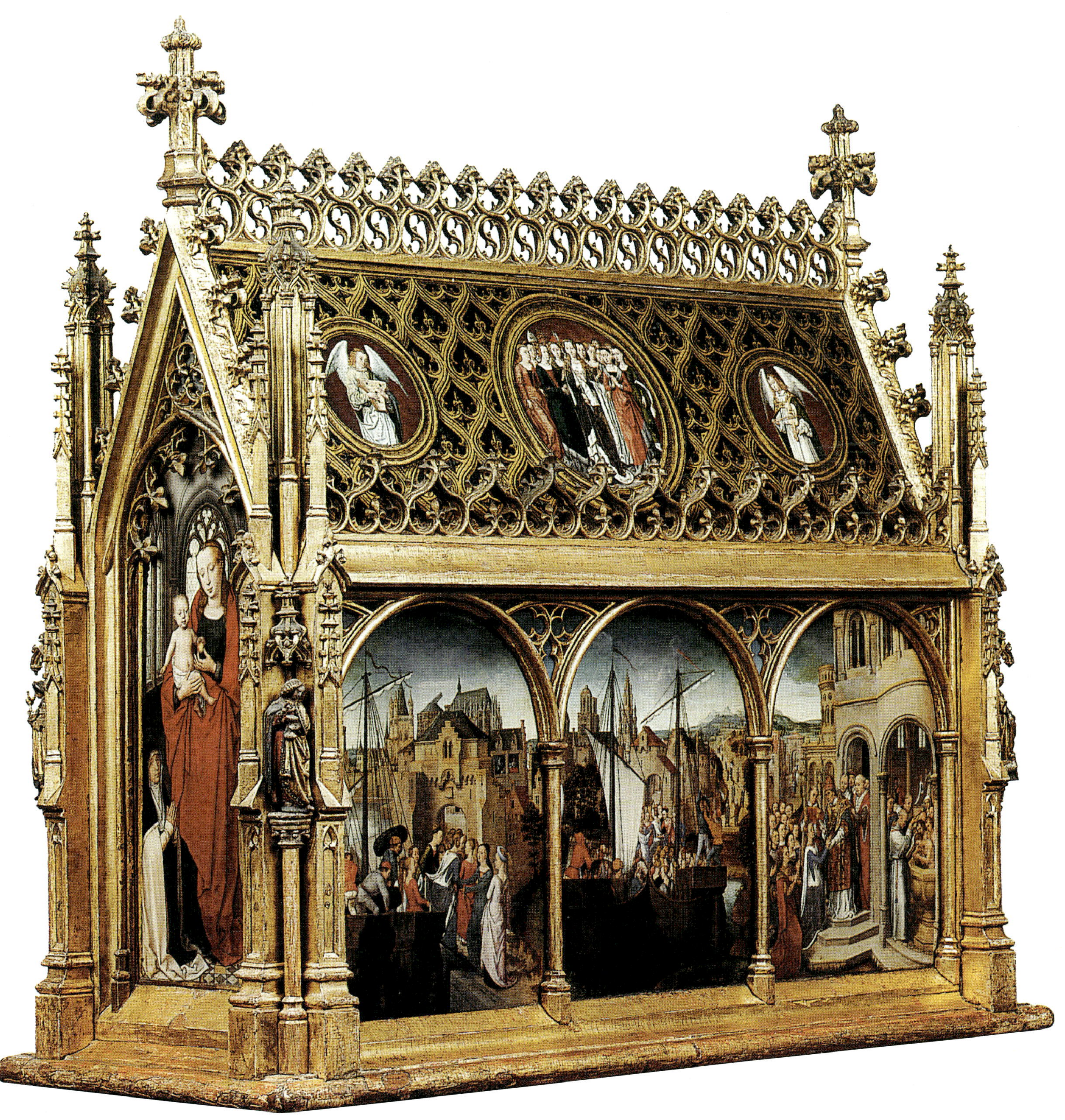

Flanders in the late fifteenth century

Painted in Bruges for
the Tuscan banker
Jacopo Tani, director of
the Flemish branch of
the Medici bank, this
triptych (one of the
outstanding master-
pieces of the European
fifteenth century) was
sent to Florence by
ship in 1473; off the
English coast, the ship
carrying the work was
attacked by the Baltic
pirate Paul Benecke.
Requests from the
Medici and Pope Pius II
for its return were all
in vain, but in fact
since its original theft
the work has attracted
the covetous desires of
kings and dictators:
Napoleon had it shipped
off to the Louvre,
Goering had it taken
to Thuringia, the Red
Army hauled it off to
the Hermitage; but
every time it eventually
has made its way back
to Gdańsk. The work is
the product of an artist
who had reached full
maturity, and it presents
all the characteristics
of Flemish painting of
the second half of the
fifteenth century: the
inexhaustible analysis
of details, the precious

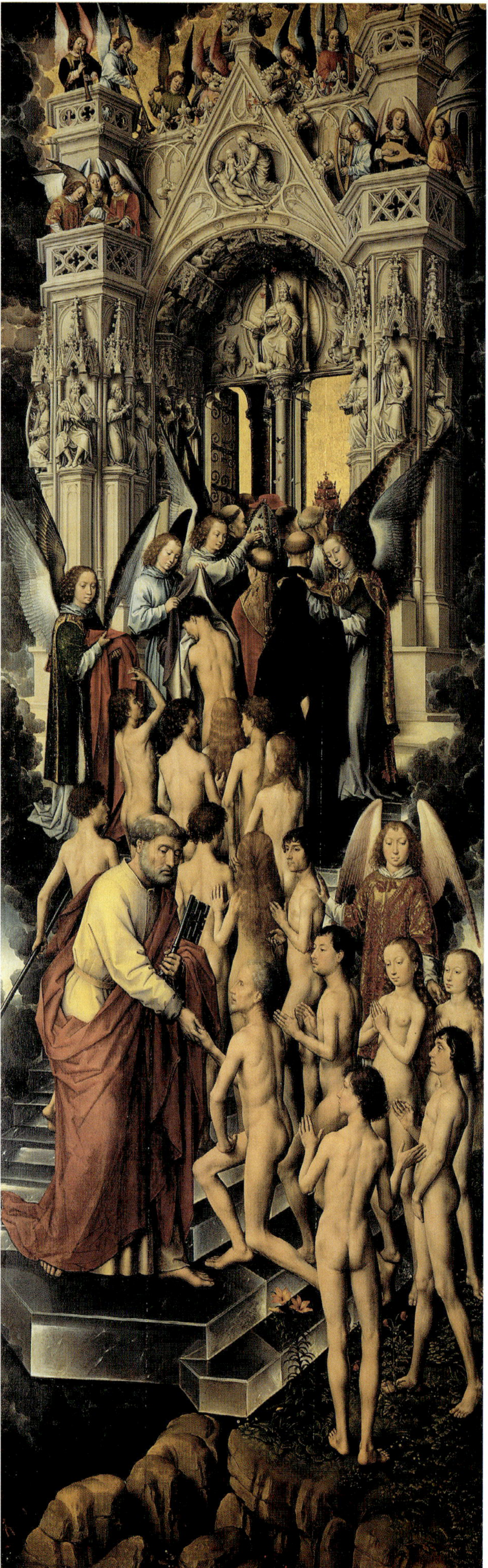

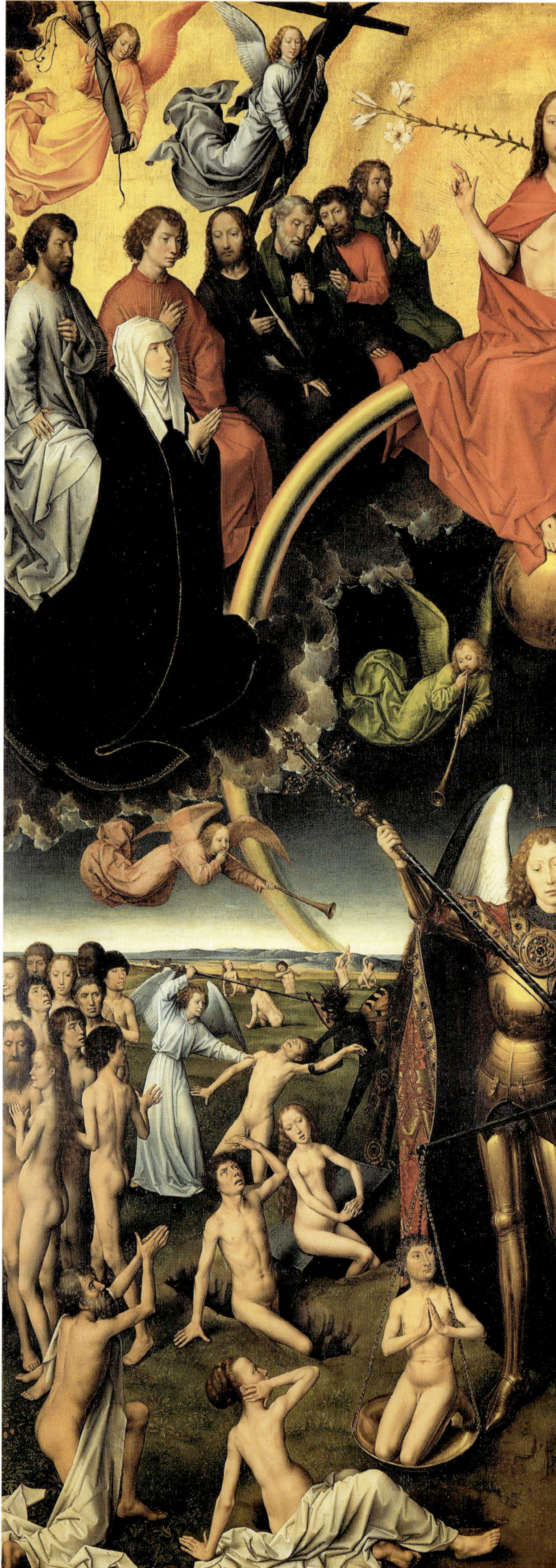

Flanders in the late fifteenth century

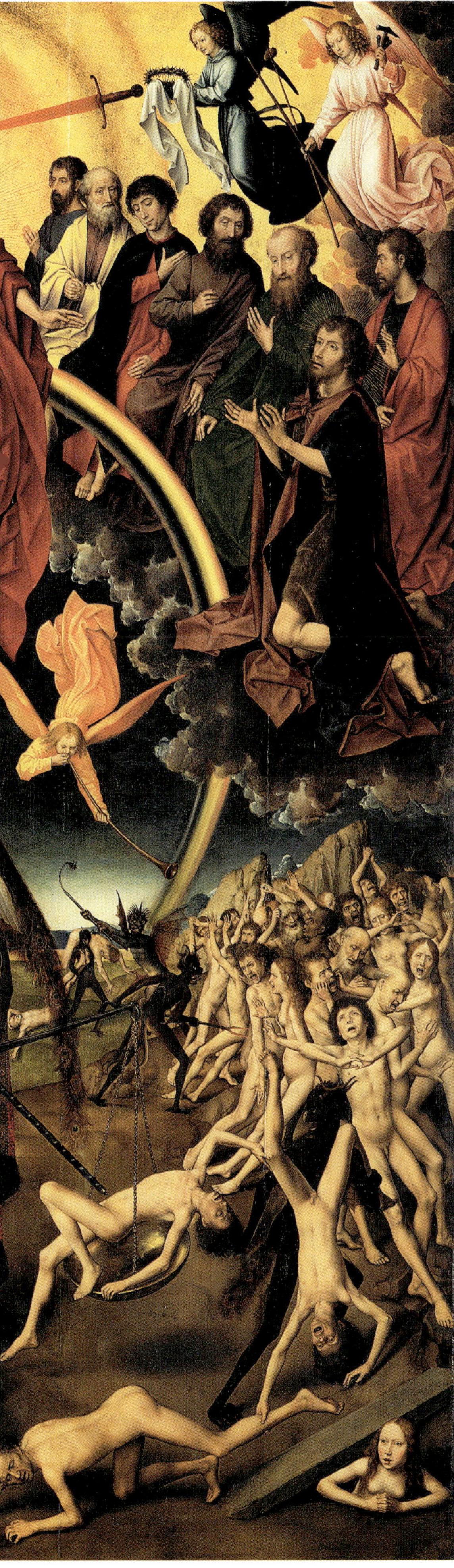

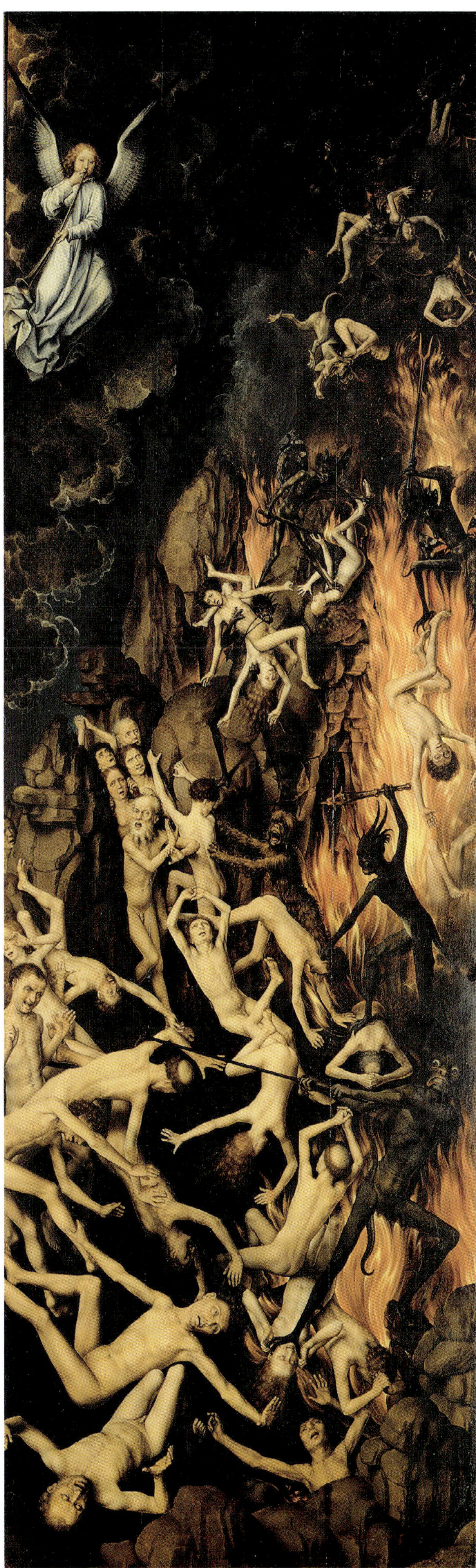

technique, the chaste nudes, and the excellence of the portraits, noticeable most of all on the back of the external doors, where the donors appear. The central panel with the *Last Judgment* is dominated by the figure of St. Michael, intent on weighing and dividing the souls. All around him, on an earth rendered barren and inhospitable, in the thickening of the final cataclysm that will cancel the world, a battle rages between angels and demons who grab at the emaciated, terrorized, defenseless arisen. One side panel shows the fires of hell, on the other the drama calms, the tensed bodies relax, the faces grow serene as Memling offers one of the most beautiful images of paradise that has ever been painted. Trembling with emotion, the blessed approach a crystal stairway suspended in the sky. Above the elaborate portal to the empyrean an angelic orchestra plays. St. Peter affectionately helps the blessed up the transparent stairs. Near the portal their naked bodies are dressed in elegant nuptial clothes prepared by angels. The door opens: on the other side we can just make out the glow of a light that never dims.

Flanders in the late fifteenth century

The internal panel of
the triptych confirms
Gerard David's adhesion
to the Flemish tradi-
tion. The homage to
the Child Jesus is
immersed in a serene
atmosphere. Among
the figures assembled
in the stone manger
the two donors stand
out, elevated to the
same level as their
patron saints. The com-
posure of the figures
increases the solem-
nity, while the scene
is enlivened by a few
anecdotal details, such
as the basket with
cloths in the foreground
and the shepherds at
the window with their
flock in the background.
The principal scene
does not break with
the standard canon,
and the true surprise
comes in the external

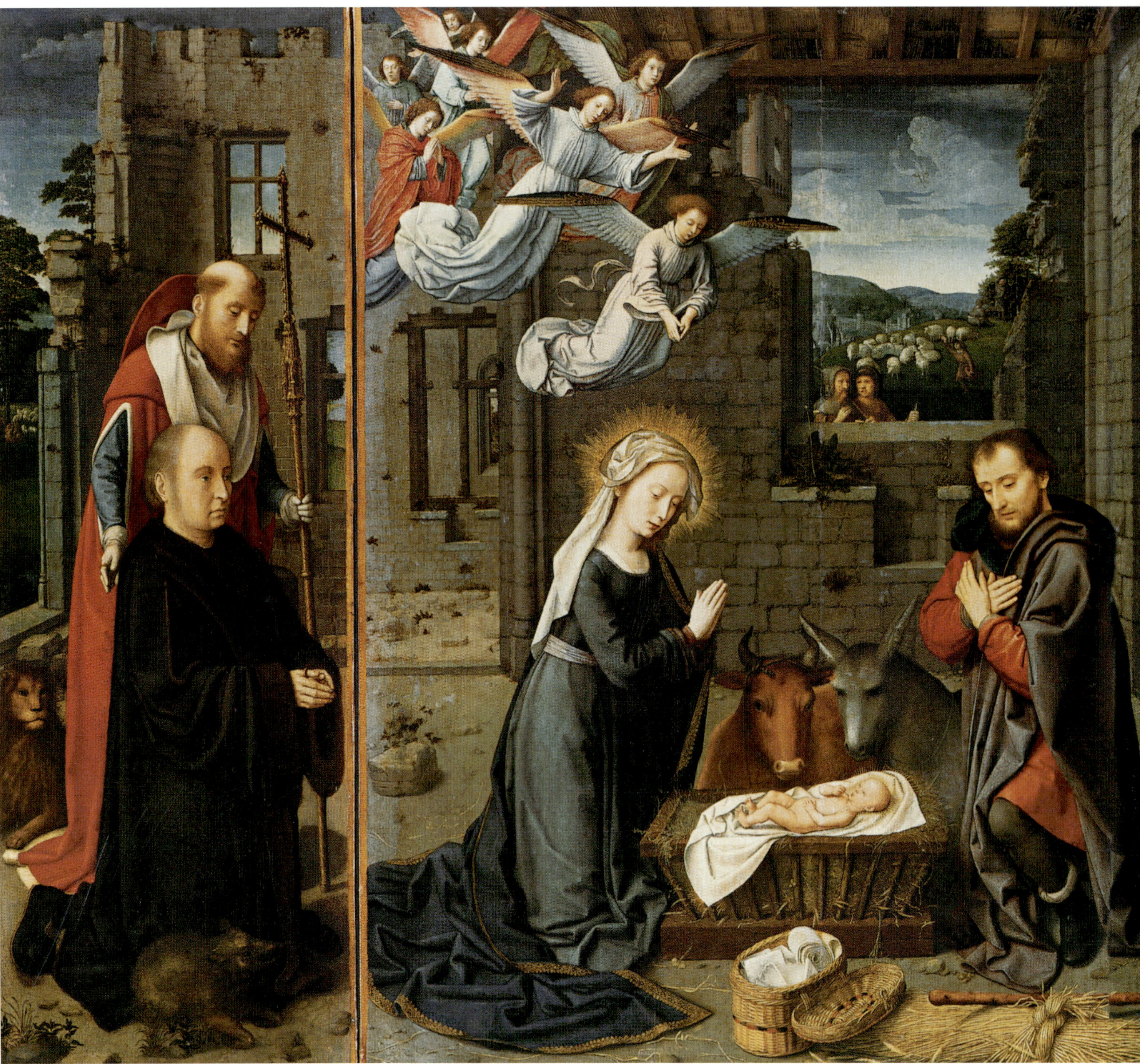

Flanders in the late fifteenth century

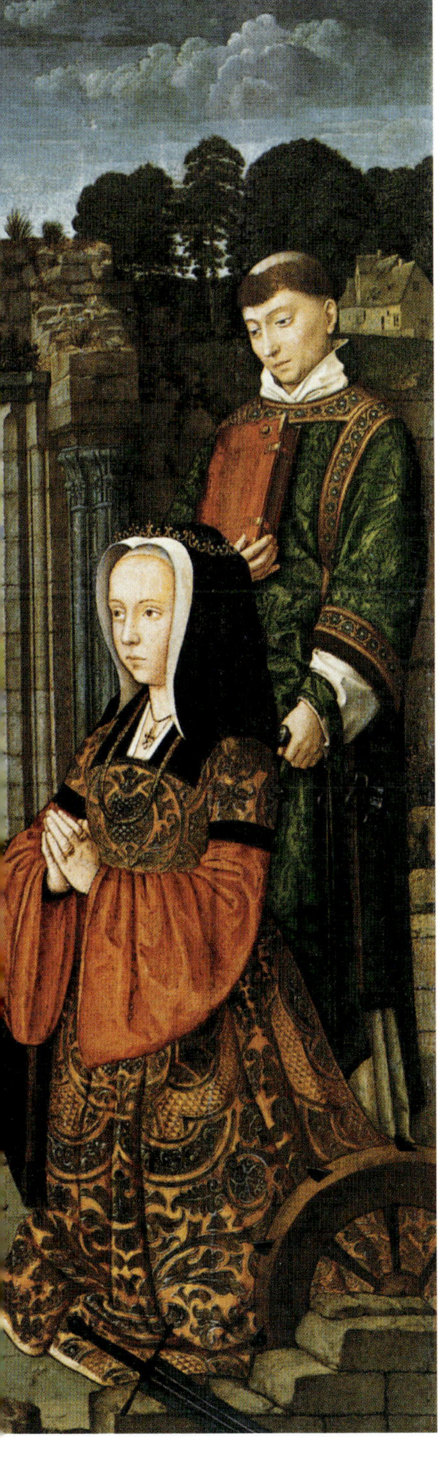

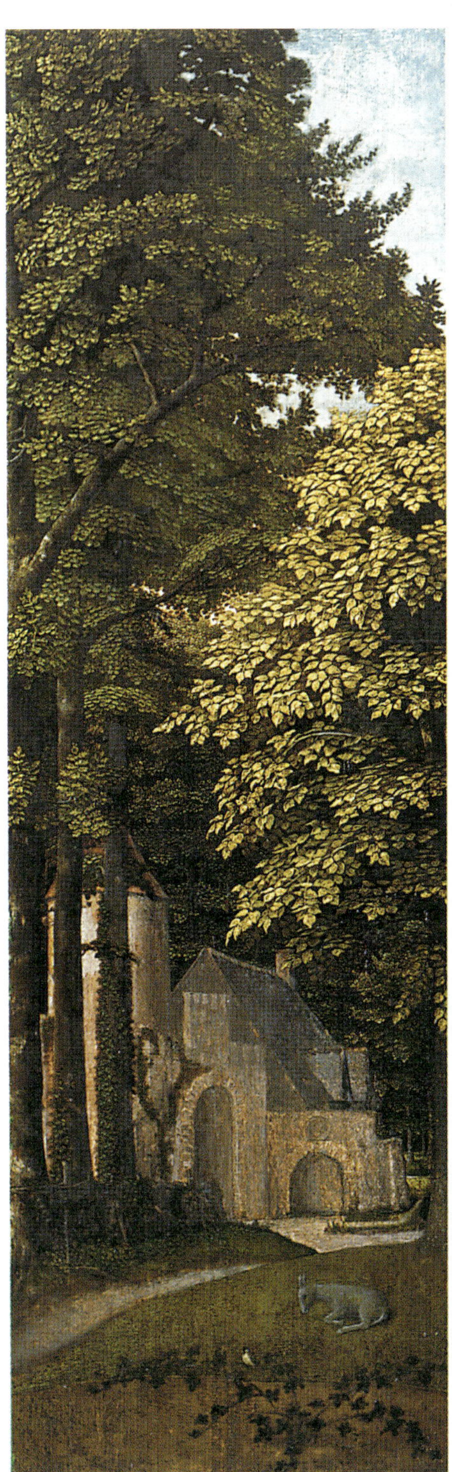

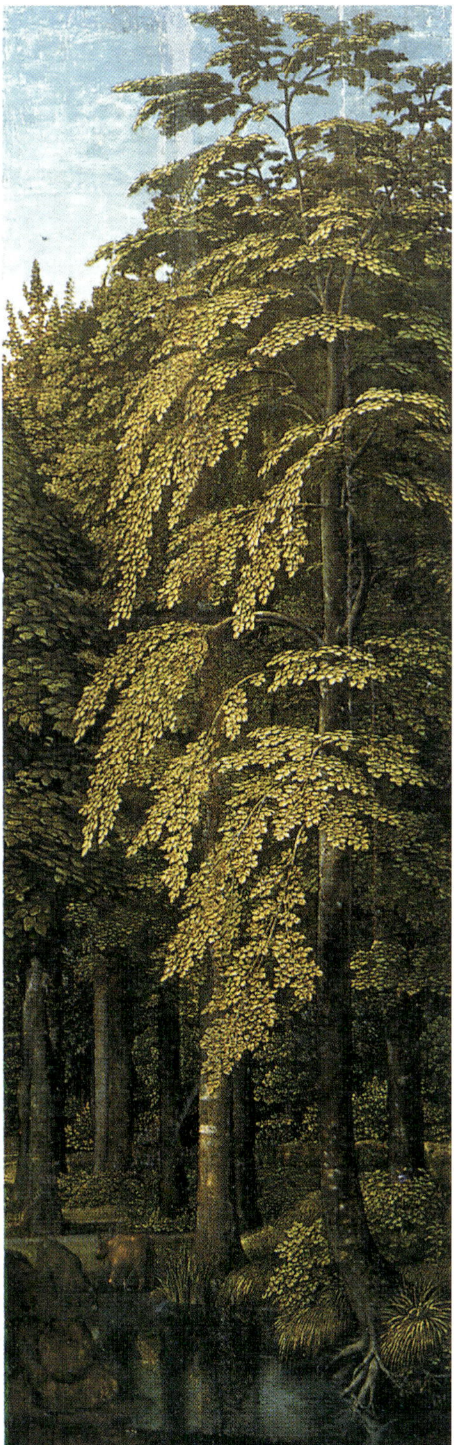

panels, which constitute a figurative document of exceptional value. Having presented the patrons of the work on the inside, David presents neither ordinary people nor saints on the external panels, nothing but a woodland without figures except for the tiny shapes of cattle grazing and a donkey resting near a stone building. In parallel with what was happening in the Danubian school of southern Germany, the landscape begins to assume a preponderant role, with the exclusion of every human presence. The naturalistic presentation of the forest is supported by a highly refined atmospheric rendering that almost gives the scene a cosmic breadth, perhaps an echo of David's knowledge of Leonardo. Of course, a landscape can have deep religious significance, introducing the faithful to a vision of the Nativity, as if the artist invited us on a pilgrimage through the woods and up to the presence of Christ. (From Dante on, "the dark wood" has been a standard metaphor for the journey of life and for the contrast between the darkness of reason and the light of knowledge.)

Gerard David created touching interpretations of the standard motifs of religious painting, translating them in the pleasant tones of a humble but also poetic ordinariness. The intimate nature of such scenes assumes an extraordinary natural-ness thanks to a soft, shaded brushstroke based on earth tones that sweeten the forms. These aspects of David's work present the evolution (not traumatic but progressive) he operated on the fifteenth-century tradition of Flemish painting, with the gradual abandon-ment of the graphic and pungent definition of details and the adoption of landscapes presented in tones that shade gradually, with-out doubt tied to the work of Leonardo.

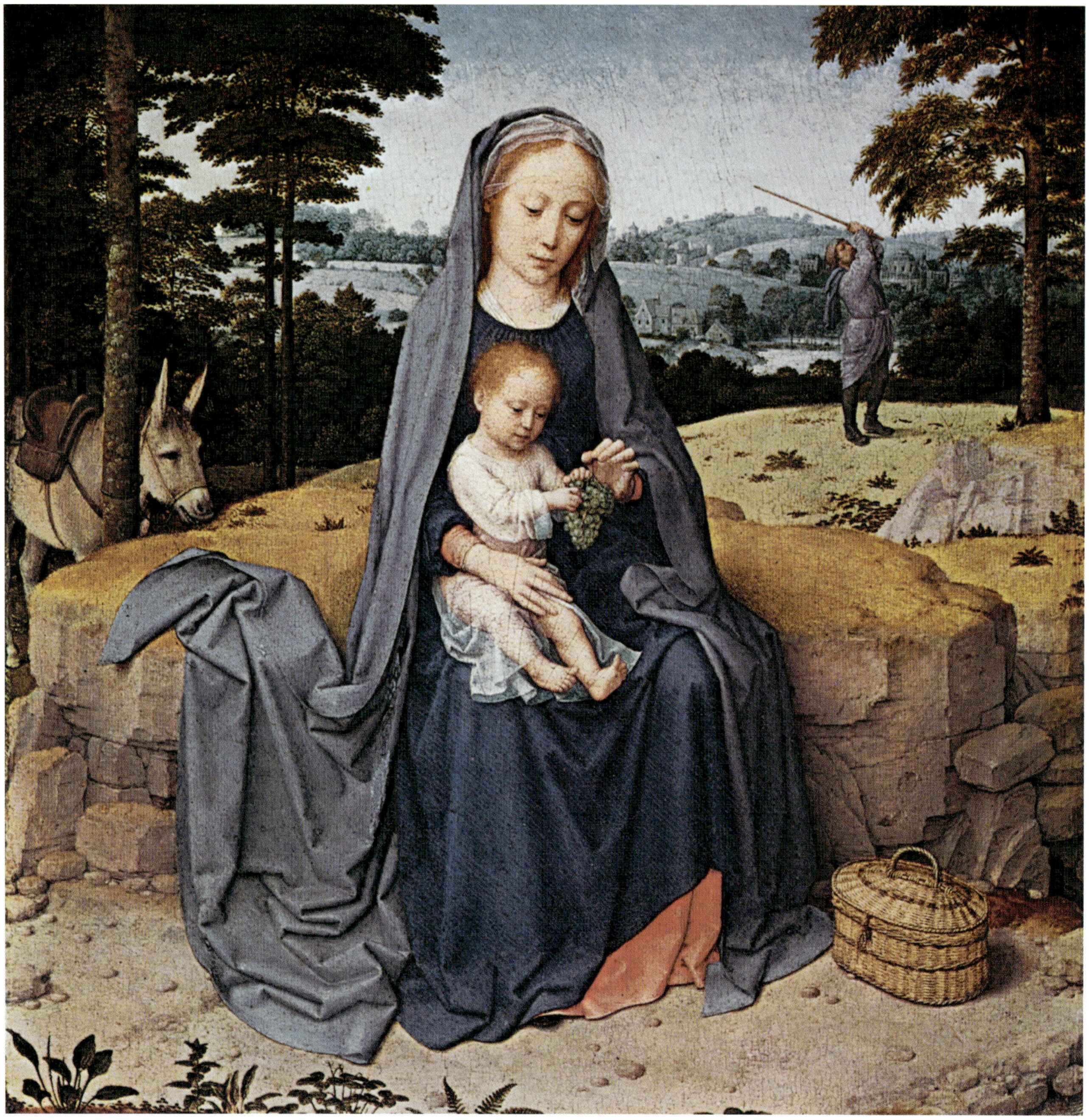

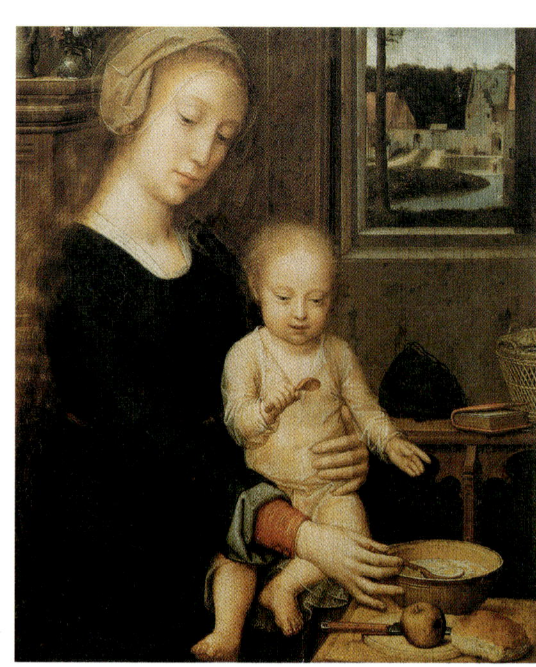

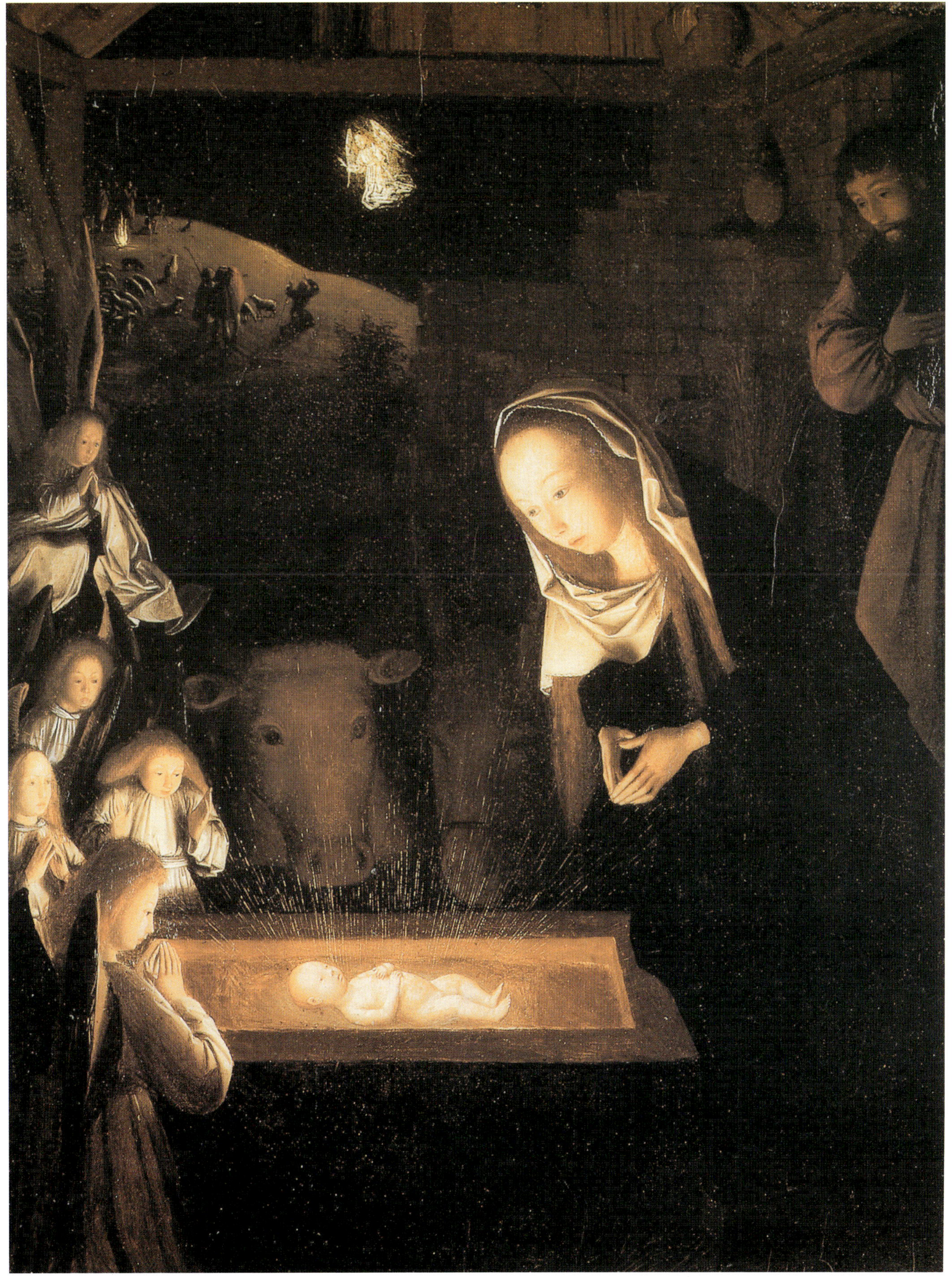

Donatello died in Florence in 1466, leaving the dramatic bronze panels for the pulpits of San Lorenzo unfinished. With him the generation of the "pioneers" lost its last champion. Young artists no longer confronted the task of elaborating new forms but were called on instead to give those forms the consistency and fullness of a school that would guide the entire world and become the visible image of civilization based on human reality. There was thus the return of an elegant art, pleasing, full of details and precious touches. An important impetus was given by the arrival of Flemish paintings, sent to Italy by the various representatives of the Medici Bank; members of the Arnolfini, Tani, or Portinari families were patrons of Jan van Eyck, Hans Memling, and Hugo van der Goes, and it was for them that those artists made many of their masterpieces. The Medici dynasty, having survived the bloody plot organized by the rival Pazzi family (April 26, 1478), consolidated its control of the city under the guidance of Lorenzo the Magnificent. Florentine art entered a new phase. The taste for graphic linearism took hold,

meant action, movement, "the movement of the soul" projected onto the cosmos, onto the landscape, onto nature. Around 1480, when his colleagues and contemporaries (they were all around thirty years old) took off for Rome, called to fresco the walls of the Sistine Chapel, Leonardo, excluded, had to content himself with a commission in a small church outside the city. This is the *Adoration of the Magi*, a work that would remain not only unfinished but also unheeded in terms of its charge of violent action and emotion, which overwhelms and involves both the painter and the viewer. In this climate, in 1482, Leonardo moved to Milan and the court of Ludovico il Moro and there began a period of research and investigation into various fields of intellect and art of which the *Last Supper* in Santa Maria delle Grazie can be taken as a sort of compendium. In 1492, when Columbus discovered America and Piero della Francesca died in Sansepolcro, Lorenzo the Magnificent also died. The preaching of the prior of the convent of San Marco, the Dominican friar Girolamo Savonarola, was exercising increasing influence not only on the spiritual life of Florence but also on the city's

Donatello, *Judith and Holofernes,* 1453; Palazzo Vecchio, Florence

Florence in the late

along with the clear and brilliant application of color, gallant controlled gestures, very often just slightly indicated. New names came to the fore: the Pollaiuolo brothers, the very young Perugino, Domenico Ghirlandaio, Filippino Lippi (son of Filippo), and most of all Sandro Botticelli, whose mythological paintings mark, during the period of Lorenzo the Magnificent, the conquest of a new height of mind and full freedom of thought. While Botticelli painted for the Medici, Ghirlandaio made cycles of frescoes for the Sassetti family in Santa Trinita, for the Tornabuoni in Santa Maria Novella, for the Vespucci in Ognissanti; Filippino Lippi completed the frescoes for the Brancacci Chapel, left unfinished at the death of Masaccio; Perugino created his most beautiful works. In the Orti Laurenziani, Lorenzo the Magnificent's garden, which served as a literary and art academy, the young Michelangelo was welcomed.

The one who rebelled against that high level of conformity was Leonardo da Vinci. To him, painting

politics, eventually leading to the exile of Piero de' Medici and the installation of a republic. The epilogue of the story was tragic: excommunicated by the pope, the friar was hanged, his body then burned in a pyre set up in Piazza della Signoria on May 23, 1498. The political and territorial equilibrium established with such difficulty by the Peace of Lodi (1454) was beginning to come apart; the armies of Charles VIII crossed into Italy. The kingdom of Naples fell, the duchy of Milan capitulated in 1499, and in coming years even Venice and Rome suffered humiliating defeats. The Tuscan masters were thus the first Italians to experience situations and sentiments that a few years later were to involve, to one degree or another, almost all of Italy.

The Florentine art of the time of Savonarola experienced the hard consequences of the repudiation of the Neoplatonic doctrines—with their exaltation of human values and the search for ideal, and substantially profane, beauty—on which the culture of Florentine humanism had until then been based. The "bonfires of the vanities"

Andrea del Verrocchio, *Woman Holding a Nosegay,* circa 1475–80; Museo del Bargello, Florence

Florence in the late fifteenth century

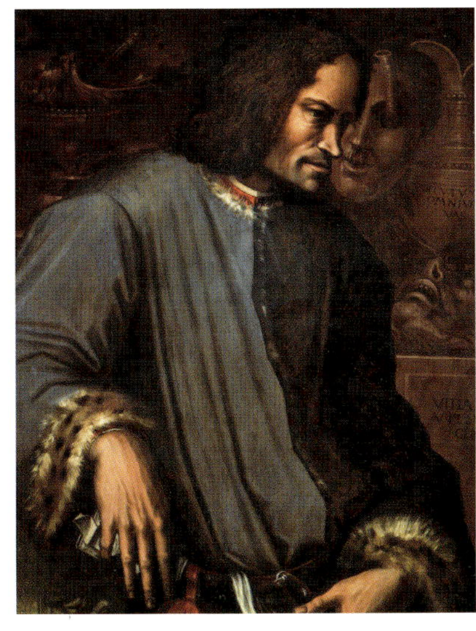

(the public pyres on which luxury objects, works of secular art, and overly provocative clothing were burnt) and the climate of austere moral rigor favored painting that was devotional and quiet, well represented by the works of Perugino and Lorenzo di Credi. On the opposite side were the painters who were profoundly, almost sorrowfully, affected by the break caused by the abrupt end of the golden age under Lorenzo. A striking example is the sudden shift in the art of Botticelli, one of the artists most intimately affected by Savonarola's preaching and also one of those most affected materially by Savonarola's measures. The intellectual uneasiness that had been present in all of his work like a subtle shiver now assumed a sharper, more dramatic tone. Giorgio Vasari saw these particular circumstances as the moment of change in Renaissance art, with the beginning of a new style

On the opposite end was Leonardo da Vinci, in those same years passionately studying the world of nature, immersing himself in the infinite spaces of oceans and the universe, facing the supreme mystery of the human "machine." Convinced that painting is "the most perfect of all the sciences," Leonardo placed no limits on the human mind's ability to know and represent the world, through the fog, the smoke, the shaded distances of unforgettable landscapes. Hypercritical, perfectionist, never completely satisfied with a result, Leonardo was indifferent to the time required for the execution of a work. In a Renaissance that still assessed the work of artists on the basis of the hours of work required and gave preference to the activity of workshops, Leonardo was the first to resolutely stress the intellectual quality of the work of the artist and affirmed, "I say to painters that no one should ever imitate the style of another," precisely during the period when Perugino's students were perfecting their methods of reproducing the style of their overly busy master. Thus, when looking at a face, Leonardo sought to know and bring to light the passions of the person, the steadfast individuality, the true vital essence, not merely the outward appearance. Vasari was no doubt right when he stated that Leonardo gave painting "movement and breath."

fifteenth century

called the "modern manner." An understanding of this passage is offered by comparison of the works of Perugino with those of Leonardo, both of whom trained together under Andrea del Verrocchio. For several decades, before and after 1500, Perugino was the most acclaimed and imitated painter in Italy, so busy that he had to keep open two workshops simultaneously, one in Florence, the other in Perugia. His works were in great demand along most of the length of the peninsula, from Rome to Venice, from the duchy of Milan to the kingdom of Naples, from Umbria to Mantua, ultimately constituting a sort of common language for late fifteenth-century painting. His was an elegant and entertaining style, with dreamy poses enveloped in an atmosphere of "sweetness and color united" (Vasari) that exalted the sweet melancholy, the indefinite psychology, the presence of luminous but indistinct landscapes, with lazy, restful rhythms. Calling to mind one of his compositions in detail is almost impossible, and perhaps useless since his figures are almost interchangeable, with the static but sharply rendered architectonic and natural spaces of absolute purity described with extreme precision but all the same practically anonymous.

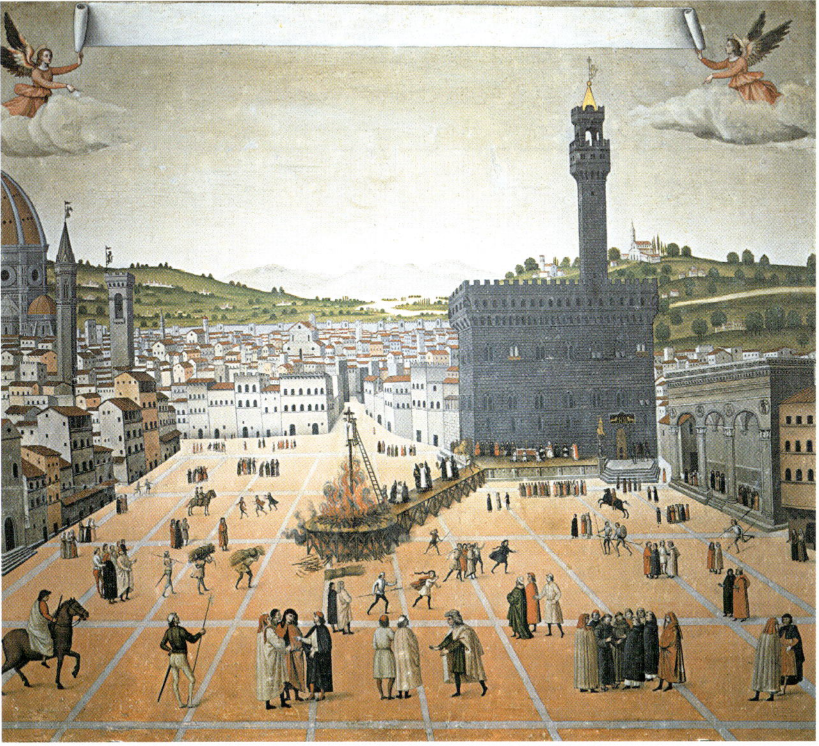

Florence in the late fifteenth century

For many reasons, both symbolic and celebratory, the *Adoration of the Magi* is a particularly frequent motif in the Florentine art of the fifteenth century. Many of the changes that took place in Tuscan painting during the early Renaissance could be illustrated simply by comparing various successive versions of this one theme, for they form an uninterrupted chain stretching from the courtly Gothic of Gentile da Fabriano to the expressive experimentalism of Leonardo da Vinci and Filippino Lippo. The presence of many paintings of the Magi kings in Florence is also a reflection of the public policy of the Medici family rulers. Florence's ruling family wished to present itself "democratically" as the leaders of a republic, not as noble tyrants ruling a dominion. The image of the Magi as a solid, united, and unanimous group moving along the same road symbolized the

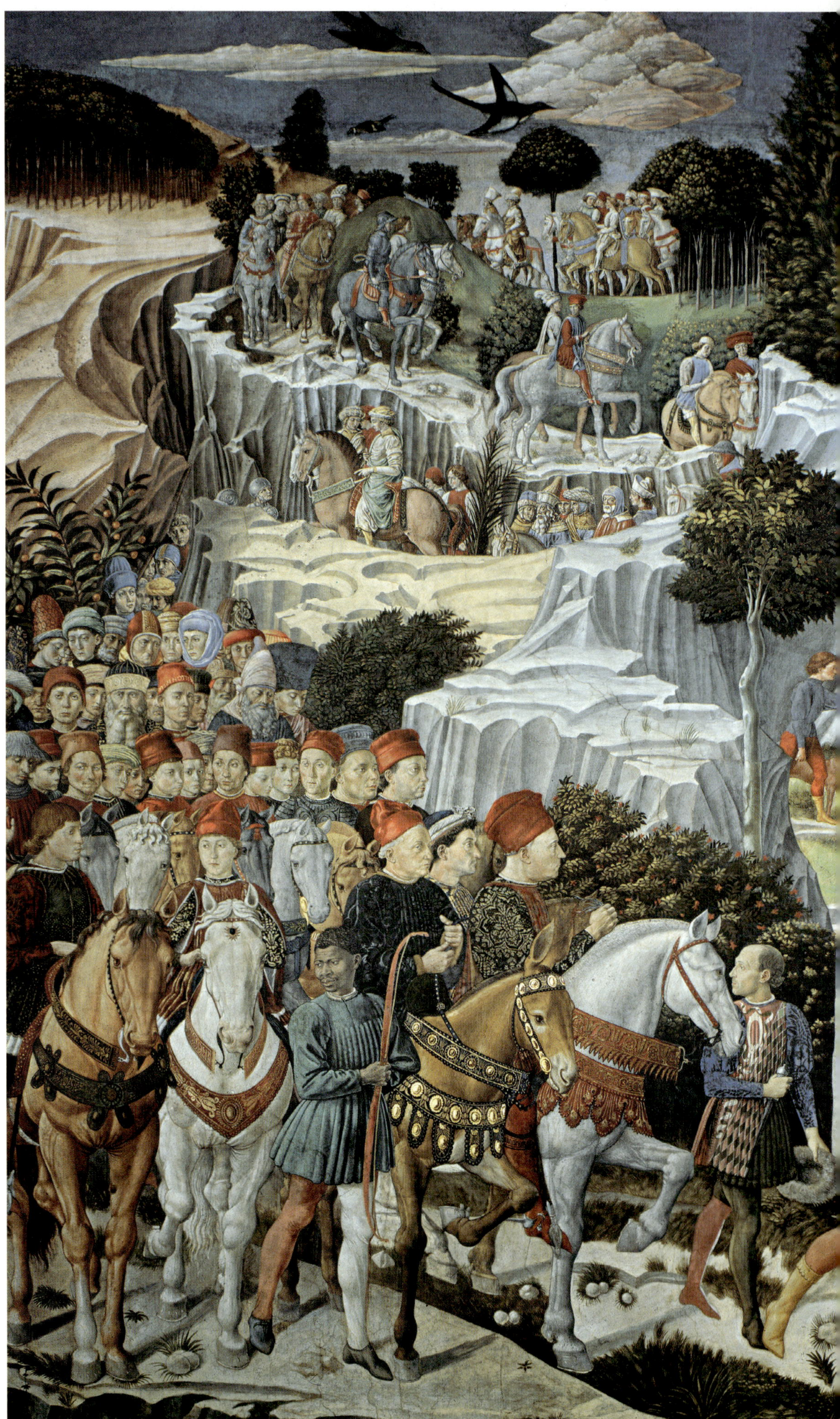

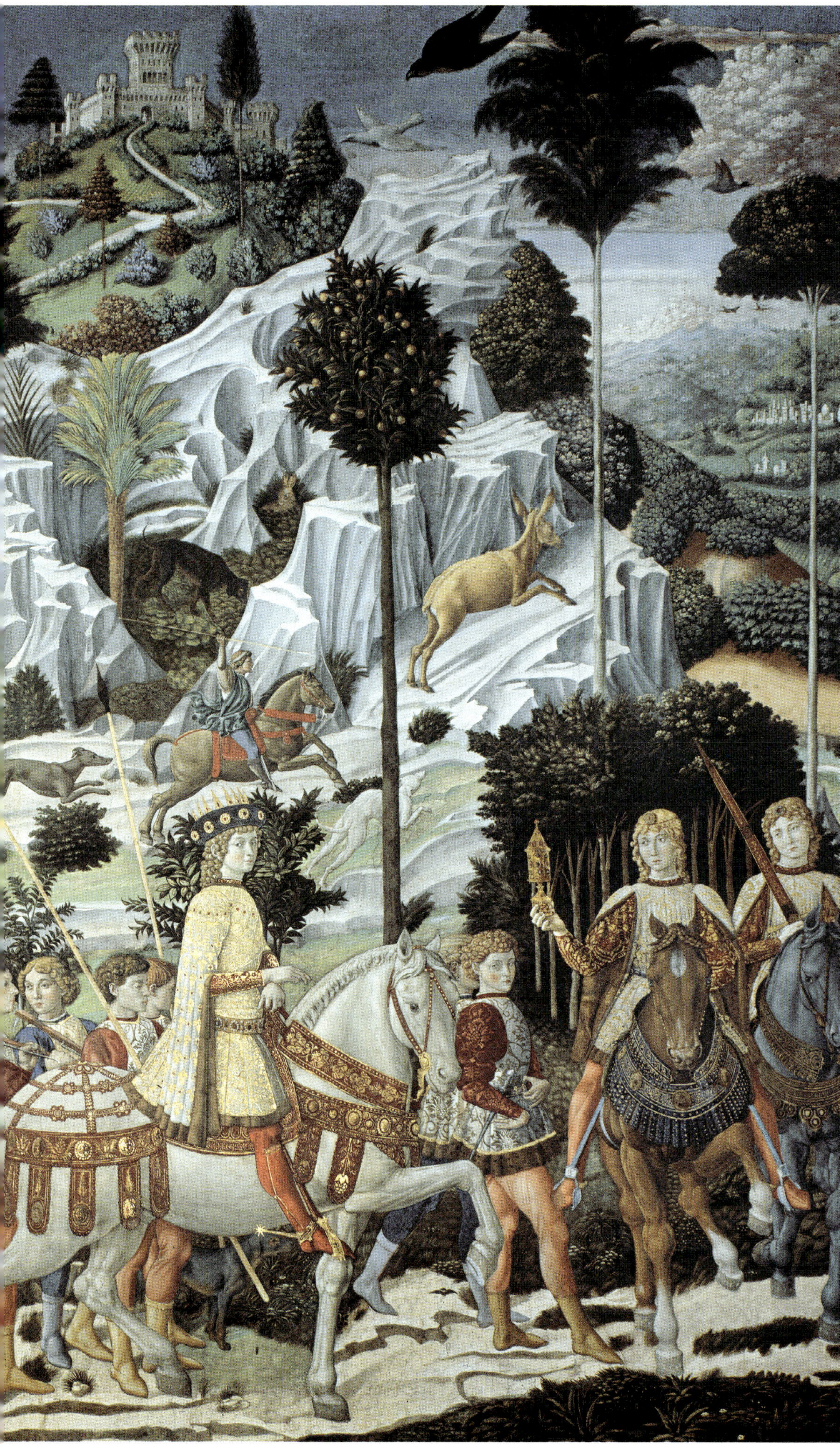

"good government" of the Medici. Furthermore, the richness of the costumes, splendor of the horses, festive atmosphere, and overall sense of well-being expressed by the cortège reflected similar, spectacular public ceremonies of the time, favoring a further identification with the members of the Medici entourage, a daring superimposition between the sacred story and an item from the daily news. Benozzo Gozzoli dresses various members of the Medici family in decidedly sumptuous banquet costumes; even so, they are accurately and individually portrayed in this work, which was displayed in the small but elegant chapel of the new family palace built in Via Larga. For the occasion, Cosimo the Elder's choice of artist appears significant. From among the many painters active in Florence, the founder of the Medici dynasty chose Benozzo Gozzoli, already a highly trusted collaborator of Fra Angelico, one of the least "modern" or experimental painters. With exaggerating in the use of perspective, Gozzoli provided his patrons with a scene of spectacular and truly princely splendor.

**Martyrdom of
St. Sebastian**
1475, tempera on panel,
292 x 203 cm
National Gallery,
London

Hercules and Antaeus
circa 1475, bronze
Museo Nazionale
del Bargello,
Florence

The art of Antonio del
Pollaiuolo (sometimes
assisted by his brother
Piero) offers certain
singular characteristics
in terms of the Tuscan
figurative culture in
the later fifteenth
century. On the one
hand, the activity of
his workshop confirms
the many talents of
Florentine artists,
capable of taking on
painting as well as
sculpture and treating
each with the same
level of skill; on the
other hand, however,
in place of the progres-
sive affirmation of an
elegant style, linear and
precious, that shows
up in the work of other
artists, Antonio del
Pollaiuolo made works
expressing the energy
of resolute plastic forms.

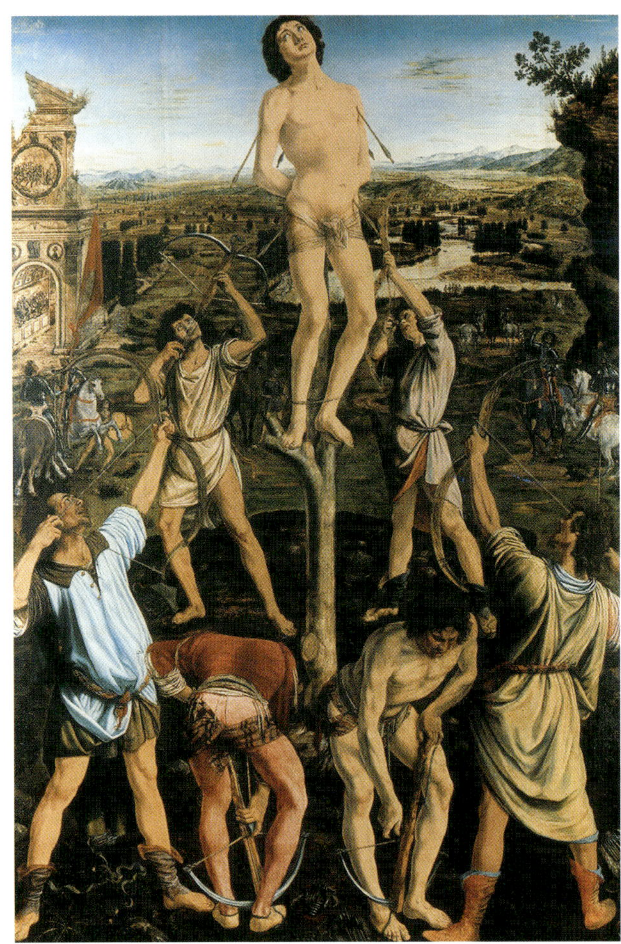

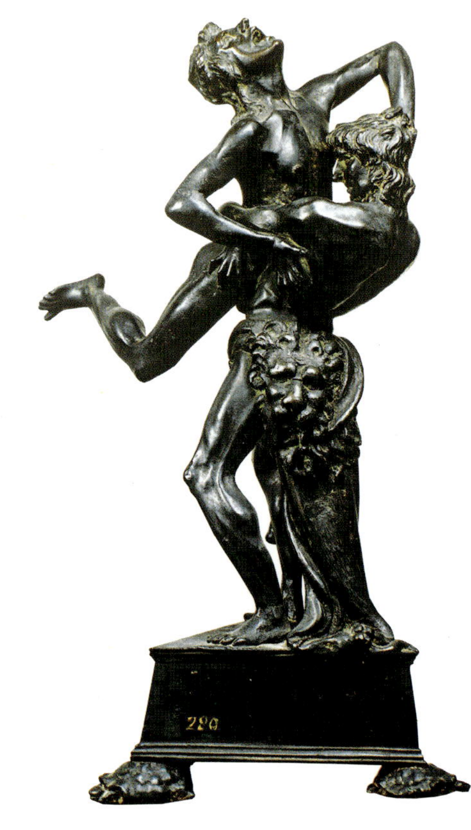

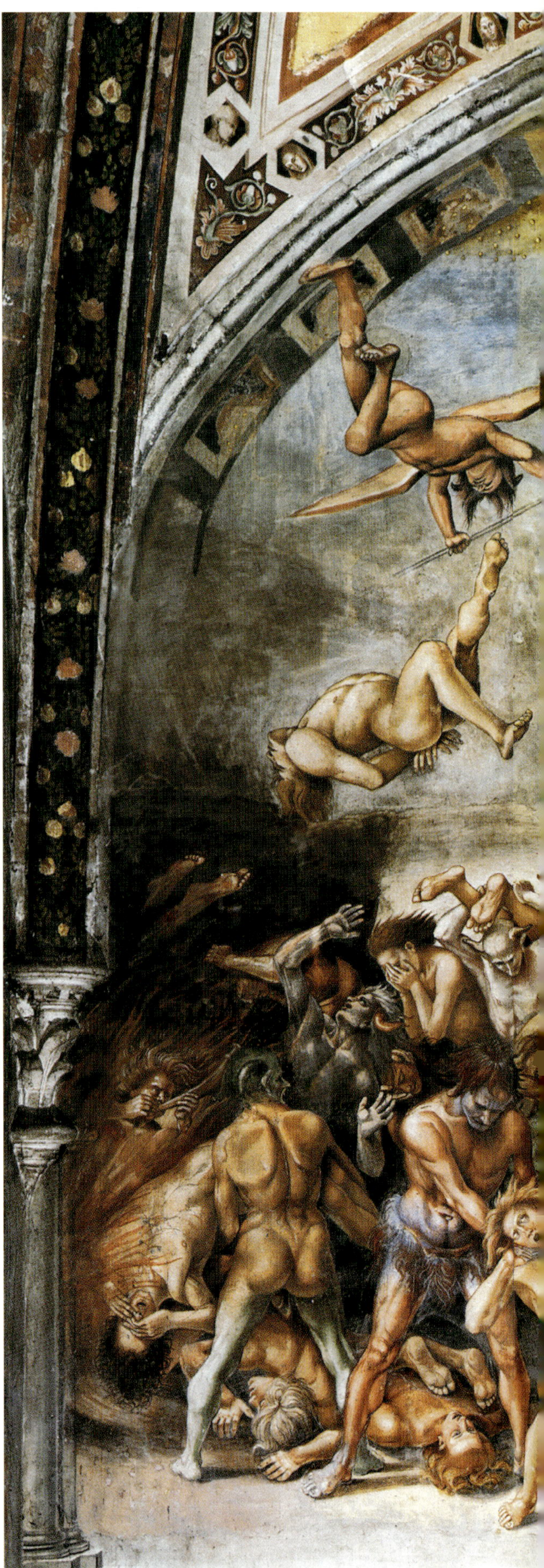

Florence in the late fifteenth century

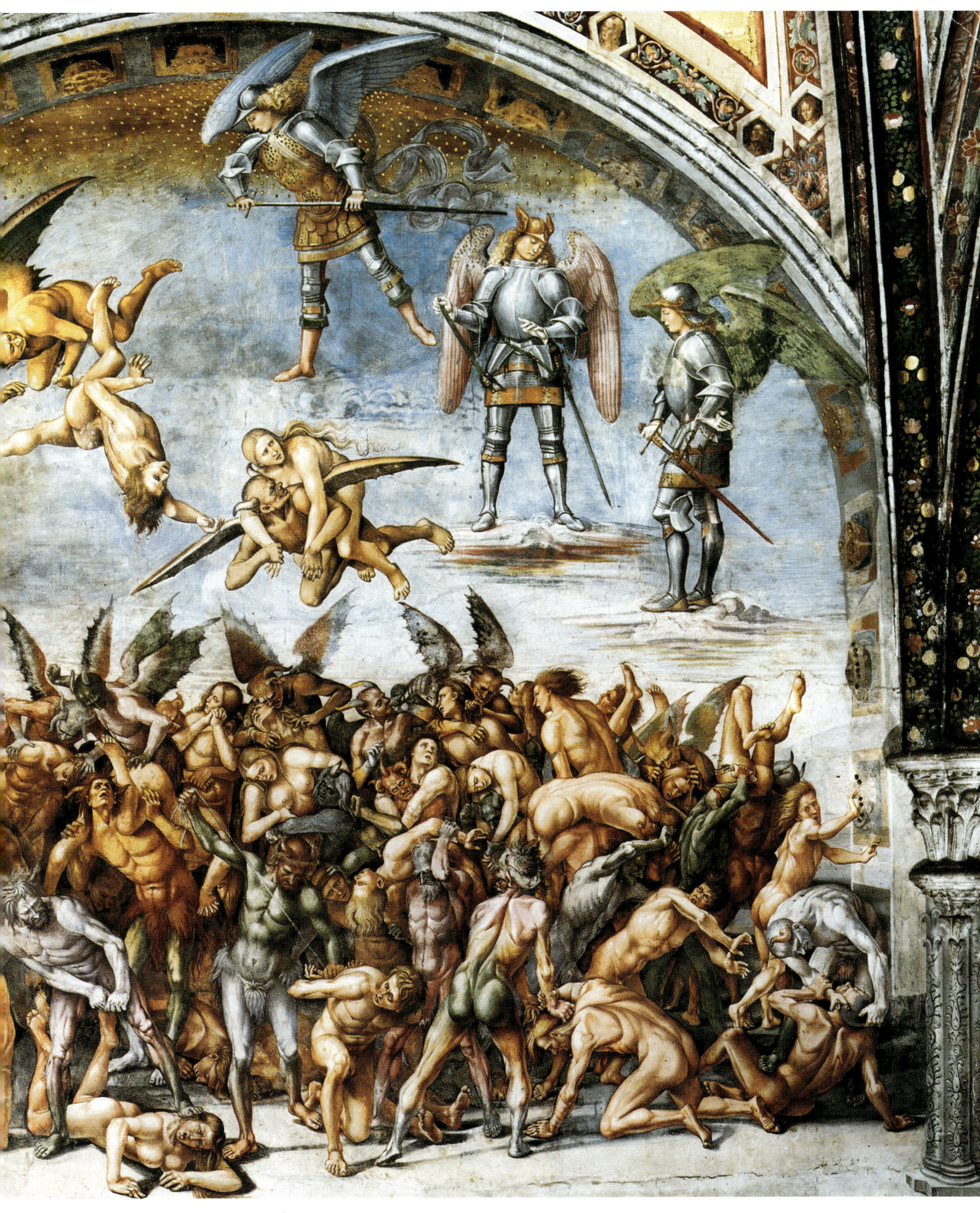

Luca Signorelli's absolute masterpiece, and also one of the most important and dramatic works of the High Renaissance, these frescoes illustrate events of the Apocalypse: *The Last Judgment, Appearance of the Anti-Christ, Resurrection of the Flesh*, and *The Damned*. The cycle had been started fifty years earlier by Fra Angelico, but he had painted only part of the vault. In what may be the most visionary cycle in all of late fifteenth-century Italian painting, Signorelli fully applied his narrative power in the large lunettes along the walls with enormous heaps of nudes that almost seem to anticipate Michelangelo. In a departure with earlier presentations of similar scenes, the devils are not recognizable by their monstrous or animallike features, but rather for their unnatural colors and their profoundly striking musculature.

Florence in the late fifteenth century

SANDRO BOTTICELLI
**Madonna of the
Magnificat**
1483–85,
tempera on panel,
118 cm in diameter
Galleria degli Uffizi

The Virgin and Child
is the most frequent
theme in the production
of Sandro Botticelli,
and he created dozens
of variations. The title
of this work is based
on the first word of the
famous prayer that the
Virgin is writing, dipping
her pen in an inkwell
held by an angel. The
decision to place the
figures in front of a
circular window empha-
sizes the strong virtu-
osity of the composi-
tion. Botticelli was one
of the masters most
interested in resolving
the difficulties pre-
sented by the tondo:
here he simulates the
effect of a curved mir-
ror, going so far as
to deform the figures
slightly, suddenly cut-
ting off the head of the
angel at the far left
and opening a view of
a distant landscape in
a position not com-
pletely symmetrical.
This experimentalism
helps maintain the
sense of tension and
sustains the exquisite,
meticulous application
of the line and the
enamel colors.

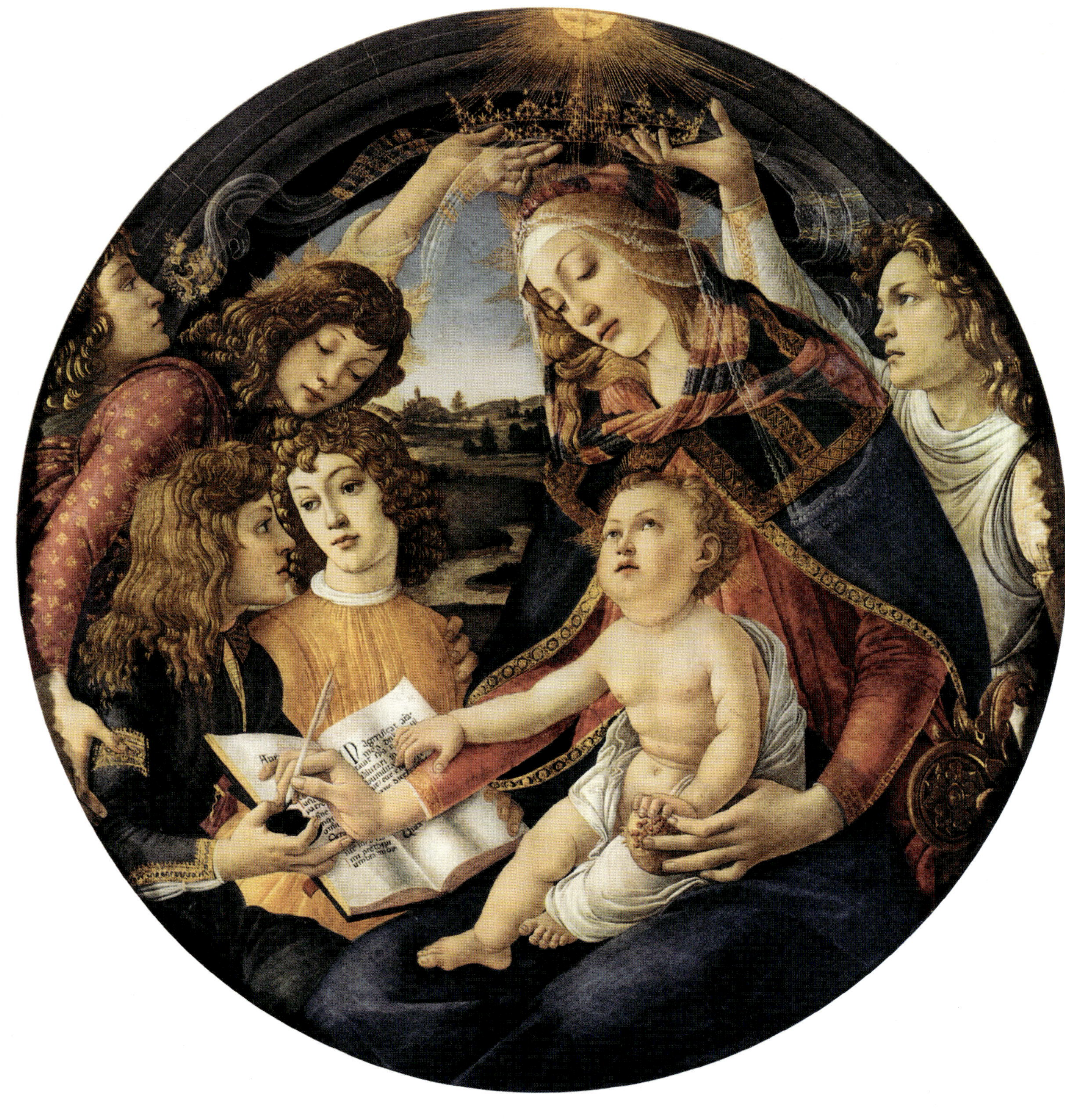

Florence in the late fifteenth century

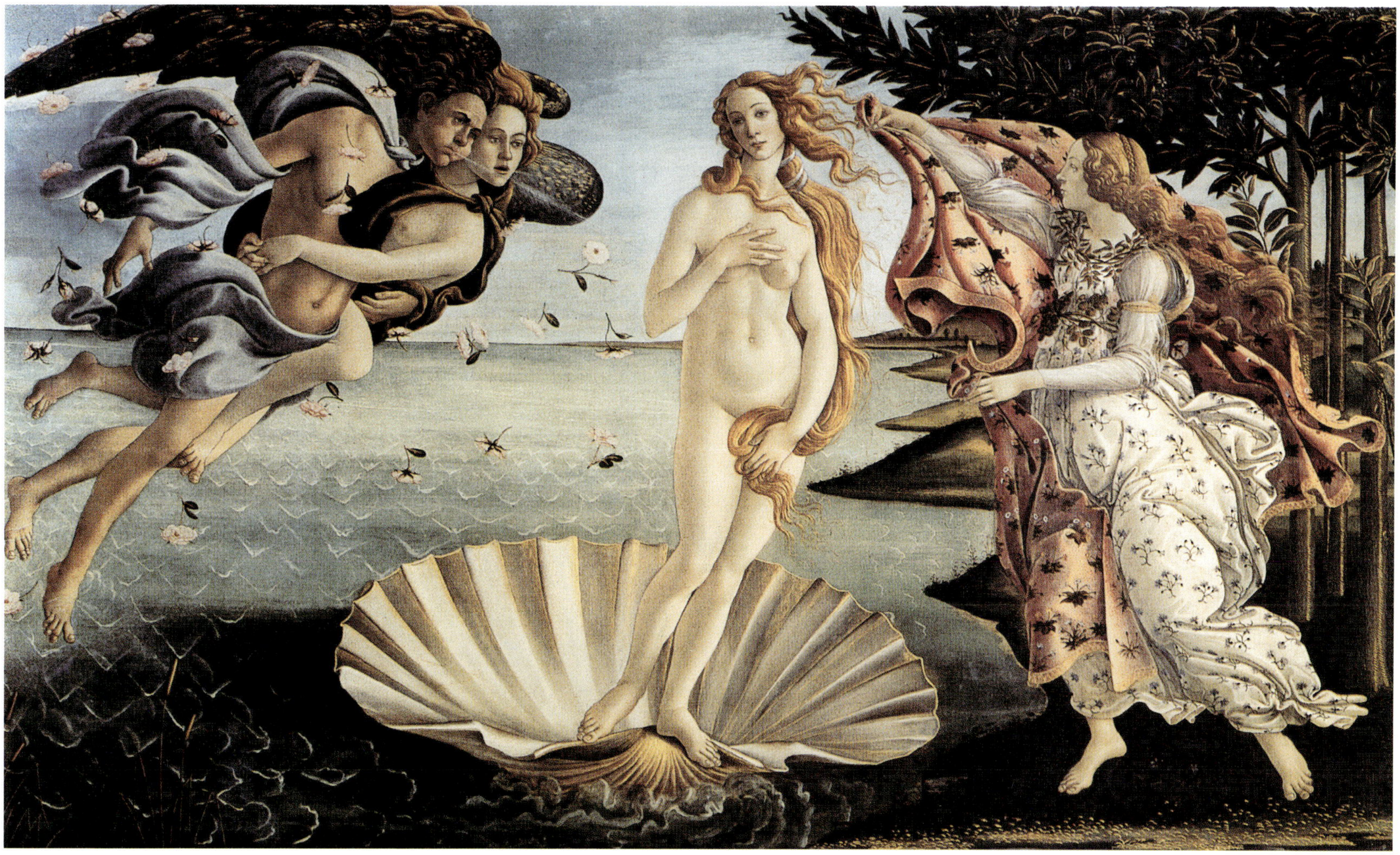

Sandro Botticelli's great mythological paintings are related to the high point of the Neoplatonic circle associated with the Medici in Florence and were in fact made under the direction of Marsilio Ficino for the Medici villa in Castello. Their primary intended audience was the young Lorenzo di Pierfrancesco de' Medici, cousin of Lorenzo the Magnificent, and they were meant to serve didactic purposes, most of all encouraging virtue along with a taste for beauty. In addition to the two enormous scenes in the Uffizi—the so-called *Spring* and *The Birth of Venus*—there are two other smaller works, *Pallas Subduing a Centaur*, also in the Uffizi, and this panel of *Venus and Mars*. The interpretation of the many details is still the subject of scholarly debate, but the overall meaning is the harmony between humans and the world achieved through the triumph of love and reason, intelligence and beauty, over the brute forces and the use of weapons.

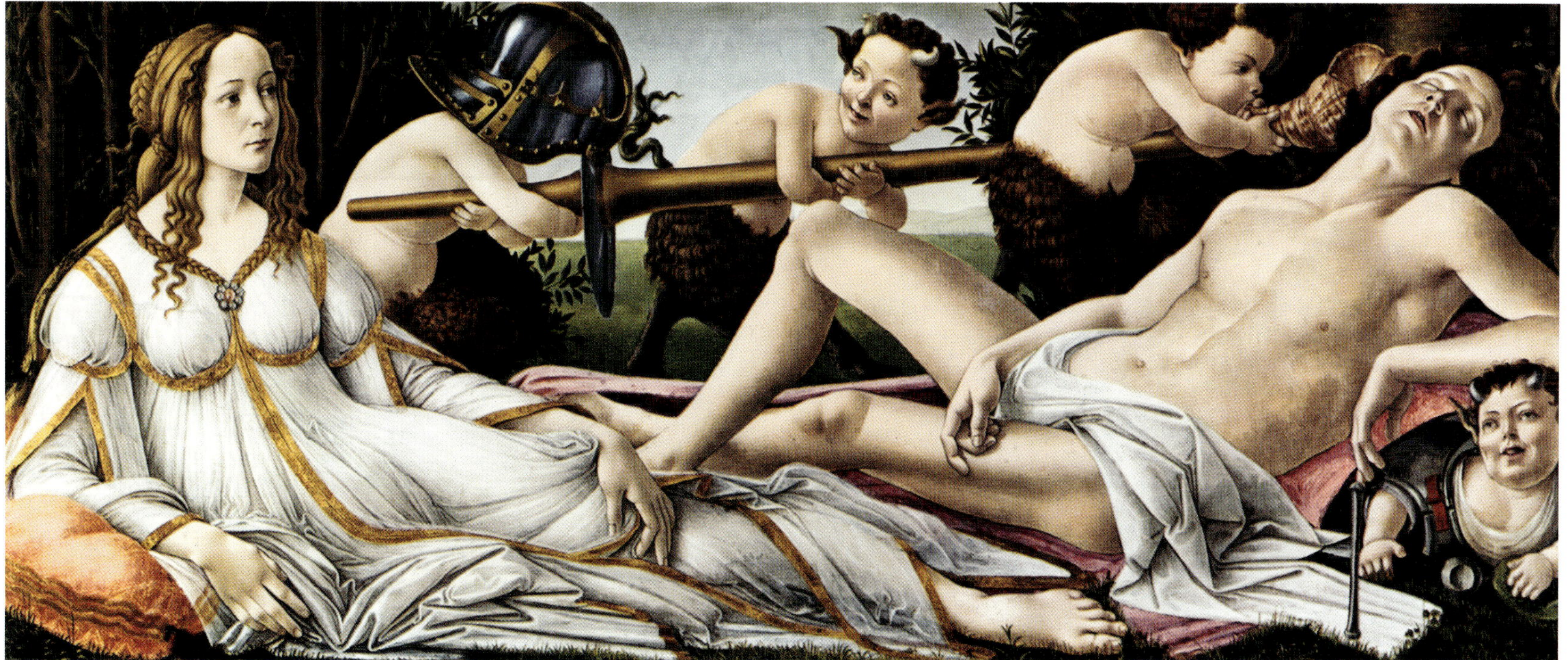

Florence in the late fifteenth century

Many expert and
exhaustive attempts
have been made to
interpret the hidden
meaning or the poetic,
philosophical, or moral
key that might unlock
and reveal the true
meaning of this famous
allegory, which was
made to inspire virtue
in a young man, the
promising heir of the
Medici family. All the
figures of the panel are
aligned along a single
plane, without depth,
against the background
of a wood, much as in
a Flemish tapestry. The
usual reading of the
work goes from right
to left and begins with
the impetuous Zephyr,
who pursues his beloved
Clori in the woods. In
the embrace of the
spring wind Clori is

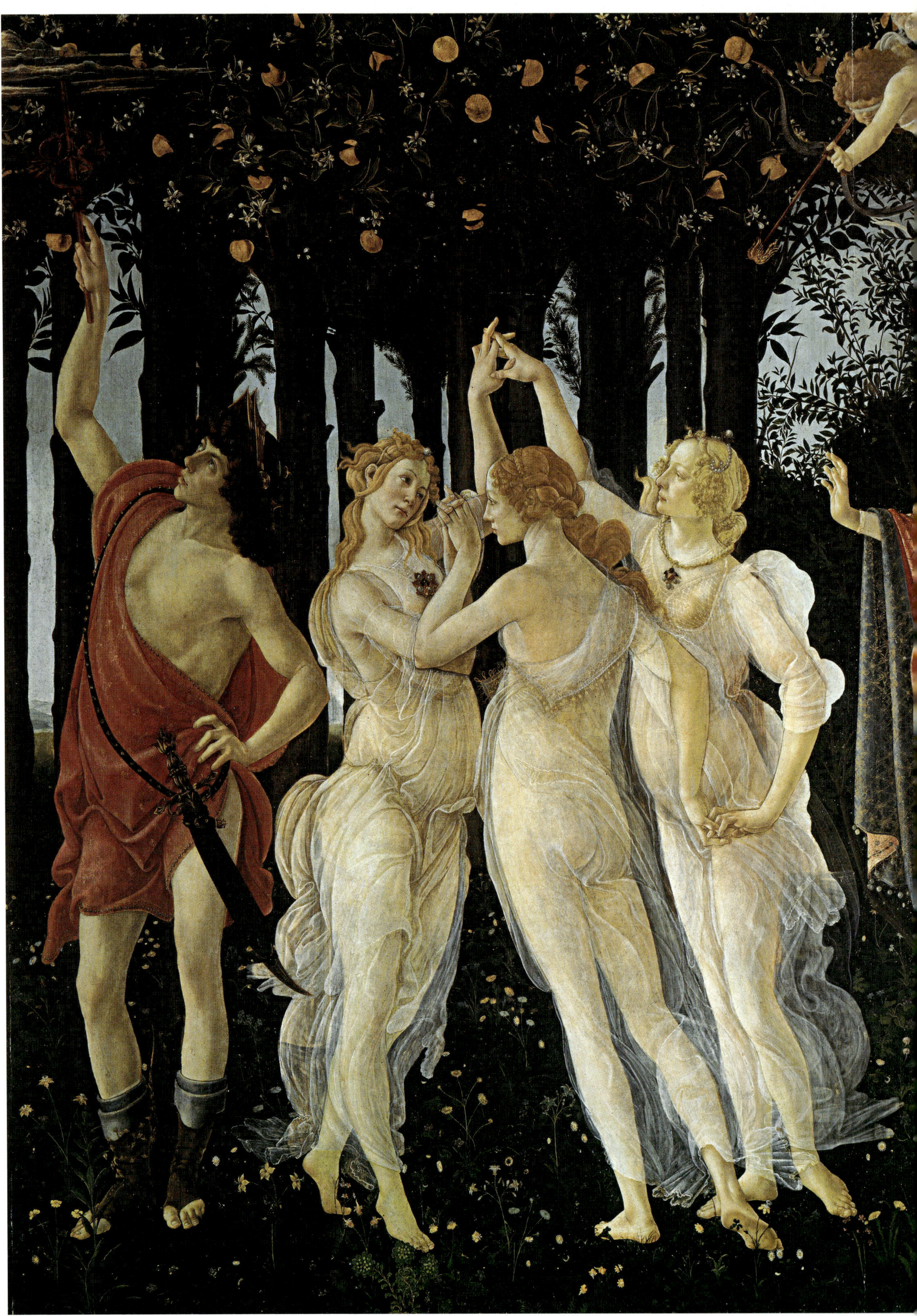

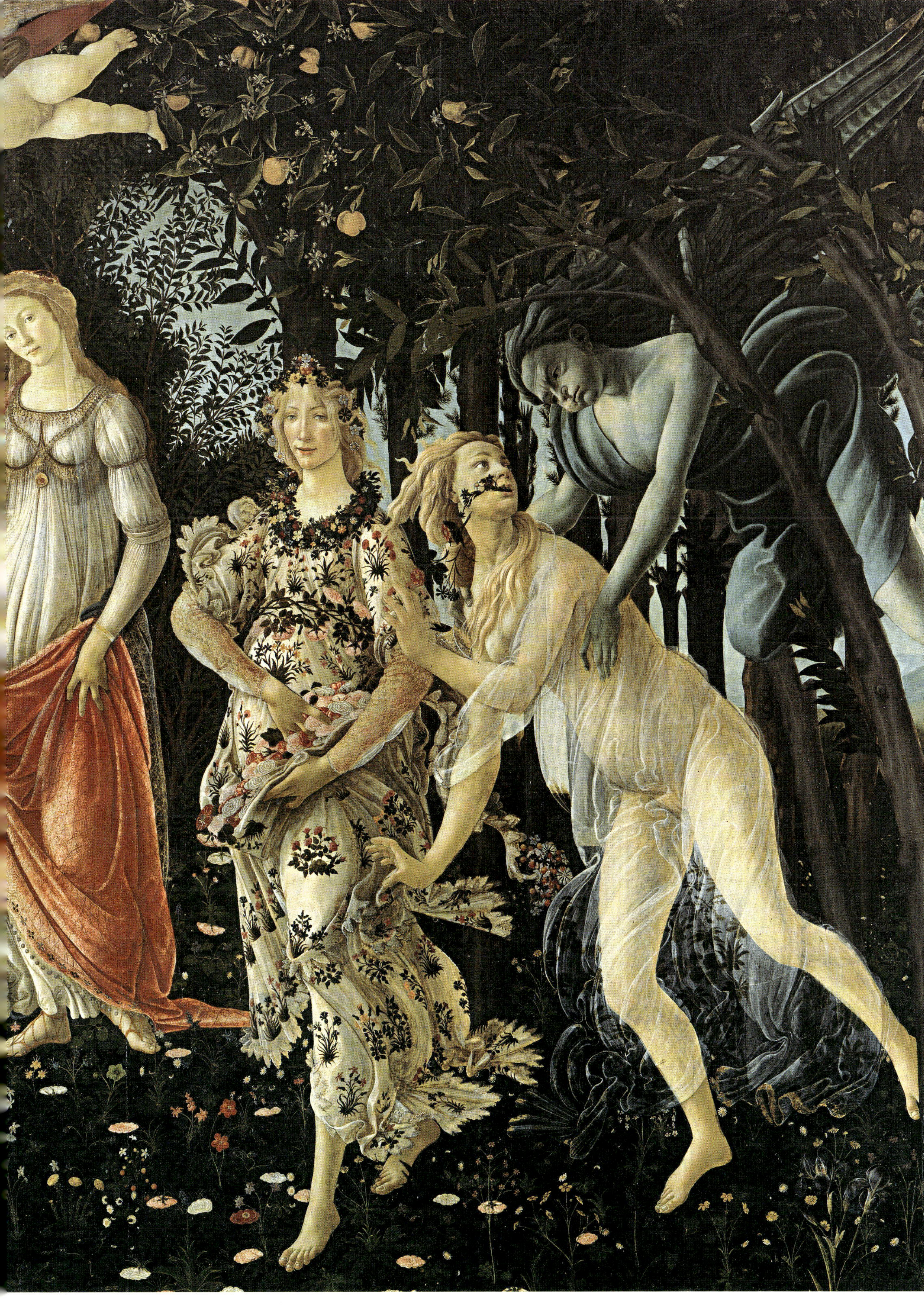

transformed into Flora, who strews the world with flowers. In fact the fabulous botanical world of *Spring* numbers about 150 species of flowers, presented with the minute precision of an herbal. The small Cupid in the air at the center of the painting is about to unleash one of his arrows. Below him the luminous figure of Venus, with a cheering gesture, stands out from the green of a large bush that is projected against a pale sky; this sequence of pale-dark-pale recalls the first Florentine works of Leonardo. Still moving left, there is then the group of the three Graces, wonderfully entwined in a dance posture, they are the image itself of serenity and concord. Finally, at the far left, Mercury uses his caduceus to clear clouds from the sky.

Commissioned by
Giovanni del Lama
(recognizable in the
middle of the group
beside the wall to the
right, turned toward
the spectator), the
panel constitutes a
somewhat cloying cele-
bration of the Medici
family, and more in
general of its group of
political and cultural
power. All the most
illustrious members of
the ruling house are
portrayed, beginning
with the elderly Cosimo,
kneeling before the
Holy Family, and his
son Piero the Gottoso,
in the red cloak at the
center of the scene.
Also shown are the
young Lorenzo, along-
side the humanists
Angelo Poliziano and
Pico della Mirandola.
Botticelli found room
even for himself,
standing at the far
right, wrapped in a
yellow-gold mantle.

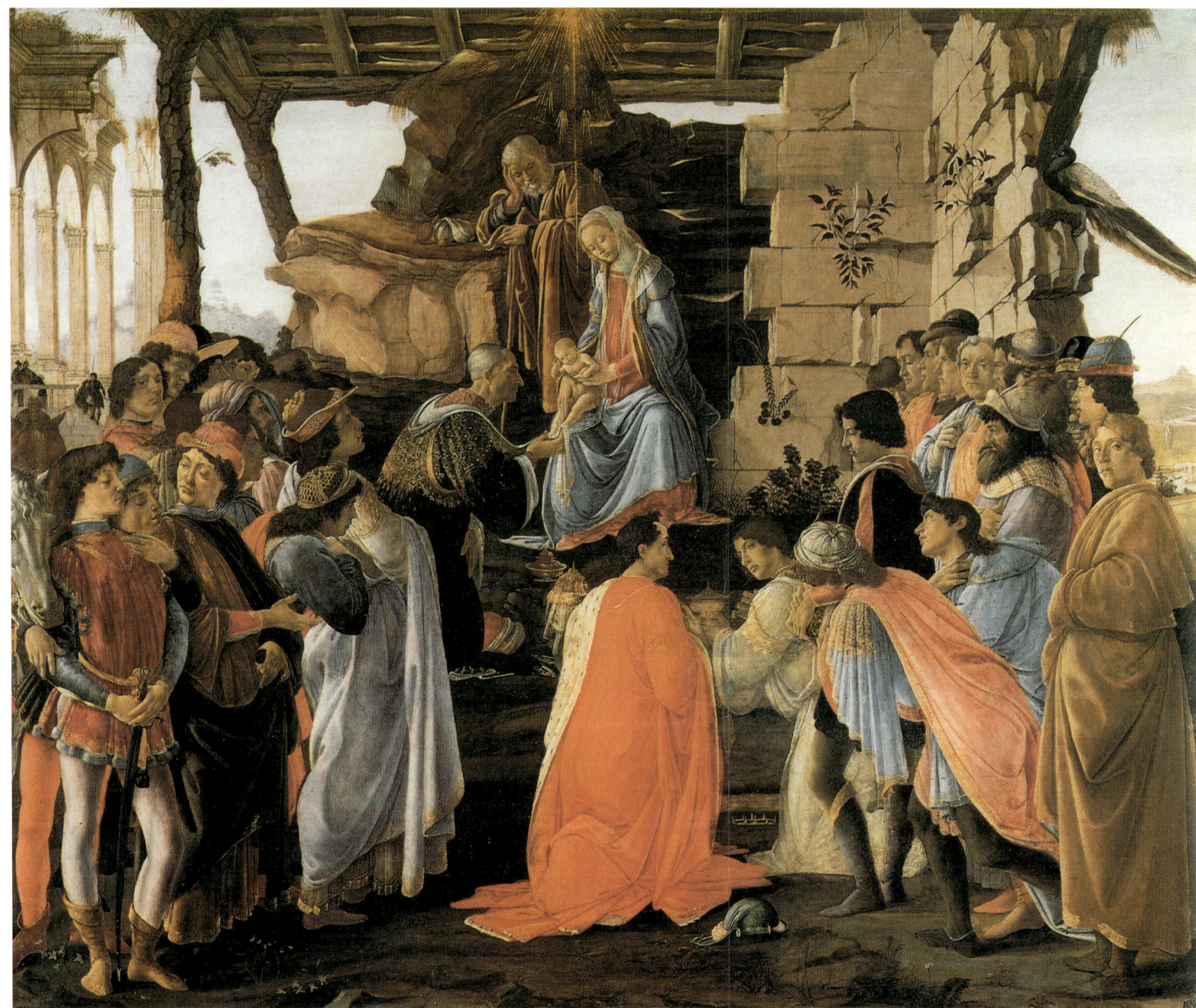

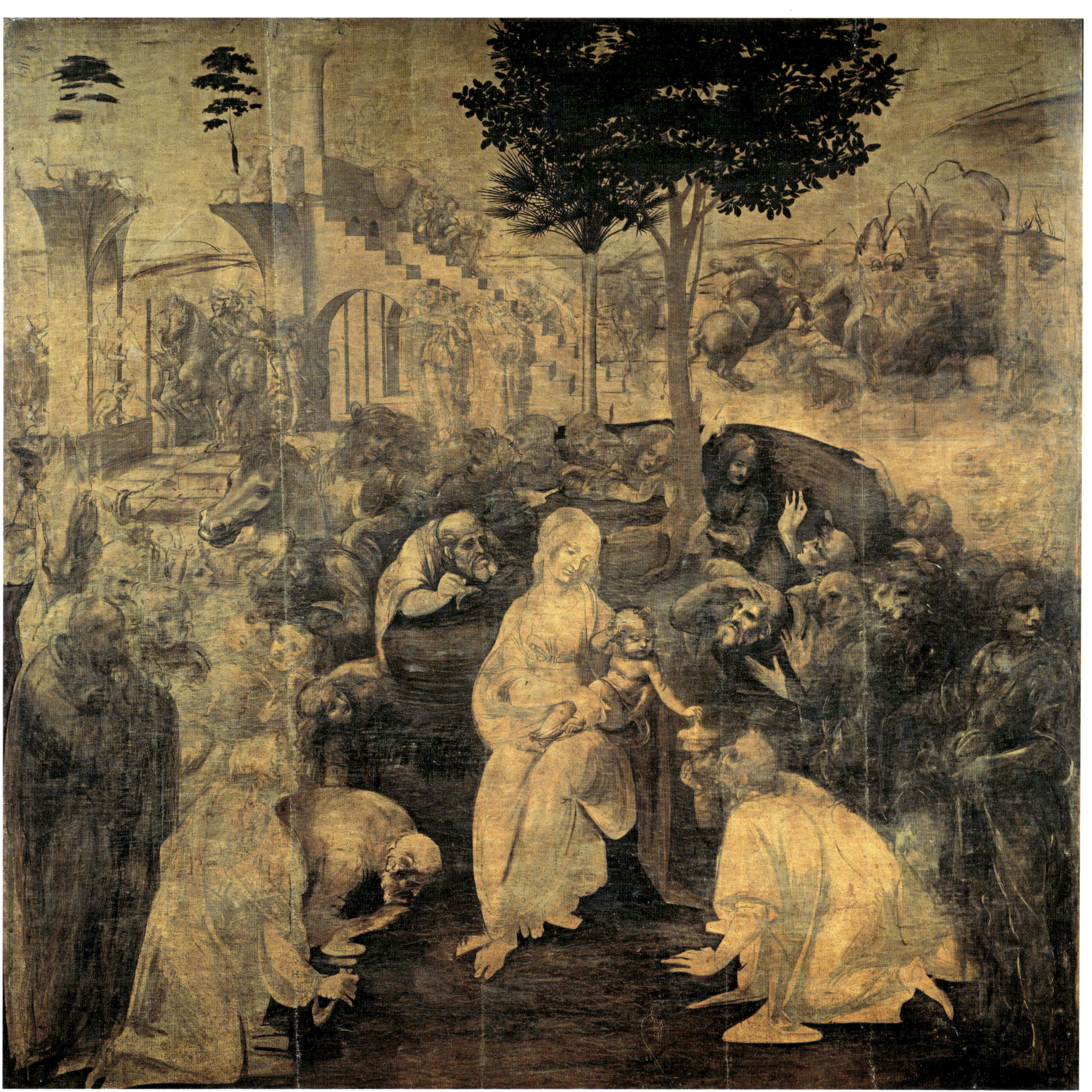

Early on, Leonardo da Vinci found himself on a collision course with the artistic school of Florence; his investigation of movement and expression, his taste for discovery, his desire to give image to feelings isolated him from his colleagues, such as Perugino, Botticelli, Ghirlandaio, who were moving toward a modulated, highly elegant linear style. When, just after 1480, those artists set off for Rome to fresco the walls of the Sistine Chapel, Leonardo, left behind in Florence, went to work on this *Adoration of the Magi*, destined for a small church in the countryside and left as a large graphic sketch, with only a few touches of paint, a work that would remain not only unfinished but also unheeded in terms of its load of violent action and emotion, which overwhelms and involves both the painter and the viewer. Leonardo gave the scene a rotary motion, hinged on the central figures of the Virgin and Child. All around is a passionately agitated crowd of figures, among whom is it not easy to distinguish which (or even how many) are the Magi.

Leonardo da Vinci made
his artistic debut around
the age of twenty as
the restless collabora-
tor of Verrocchio, and
when he went out on
his own he showed an
immediate predisposi-
tion for portraiture and
for the investigation of
nature by way of his
art. This painting openly
rivals the sculpted
busts made in the
workshop of his master,
Verrocchio, and some
of its appeal lies in its
acute naturalistic
details. The dark, spiny
juniper bush behind the
girl creates an effective
contrast with the pale
sky and also alludes to
the girl's name (Italian
ginepro: Ginevra).
Recent studies and
reconstructions have
established that the
painting was originally
larger and included the
girl's arms, in fact
much like Verrocchio's
*Woman Holding
a Nosegay.*

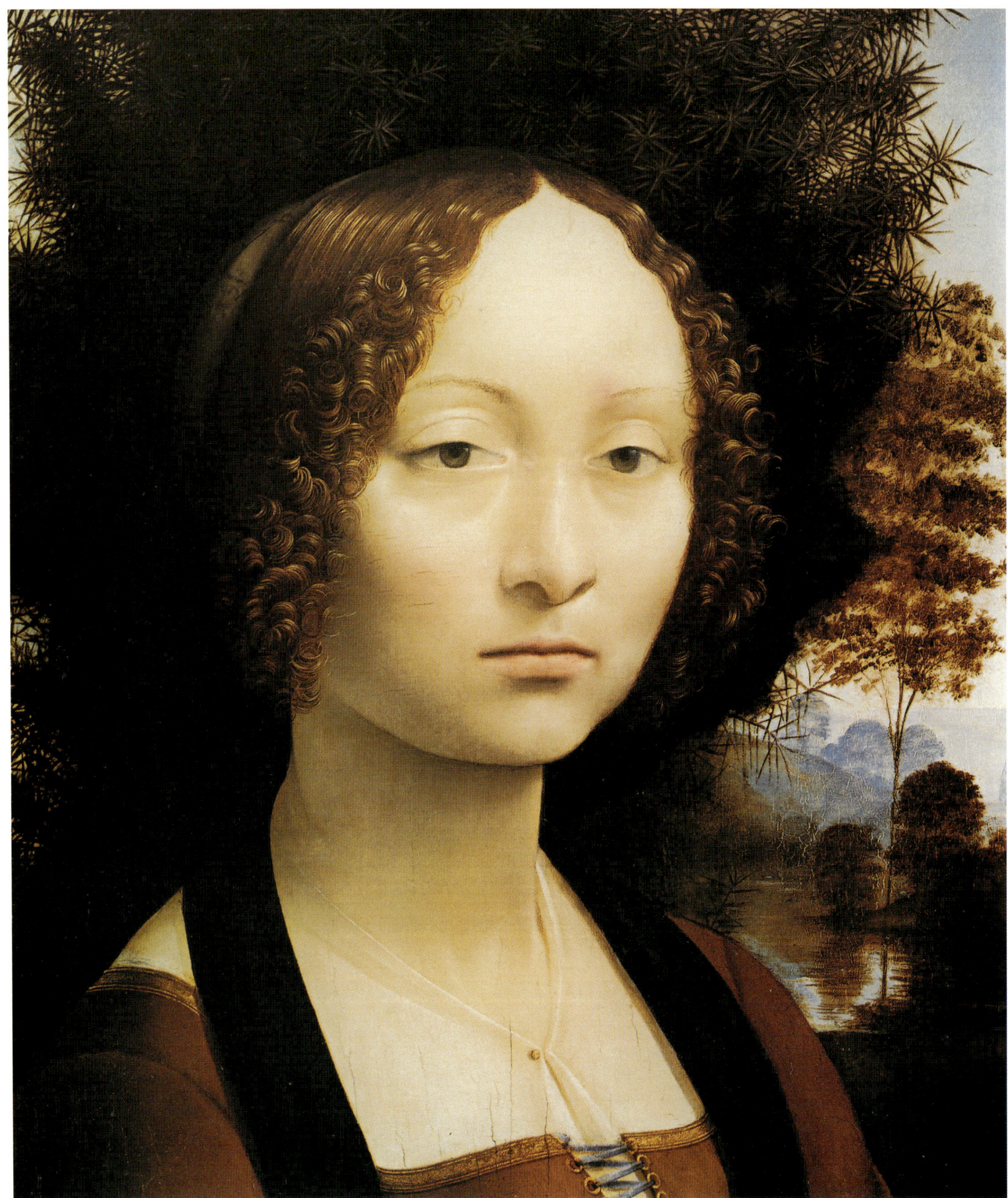

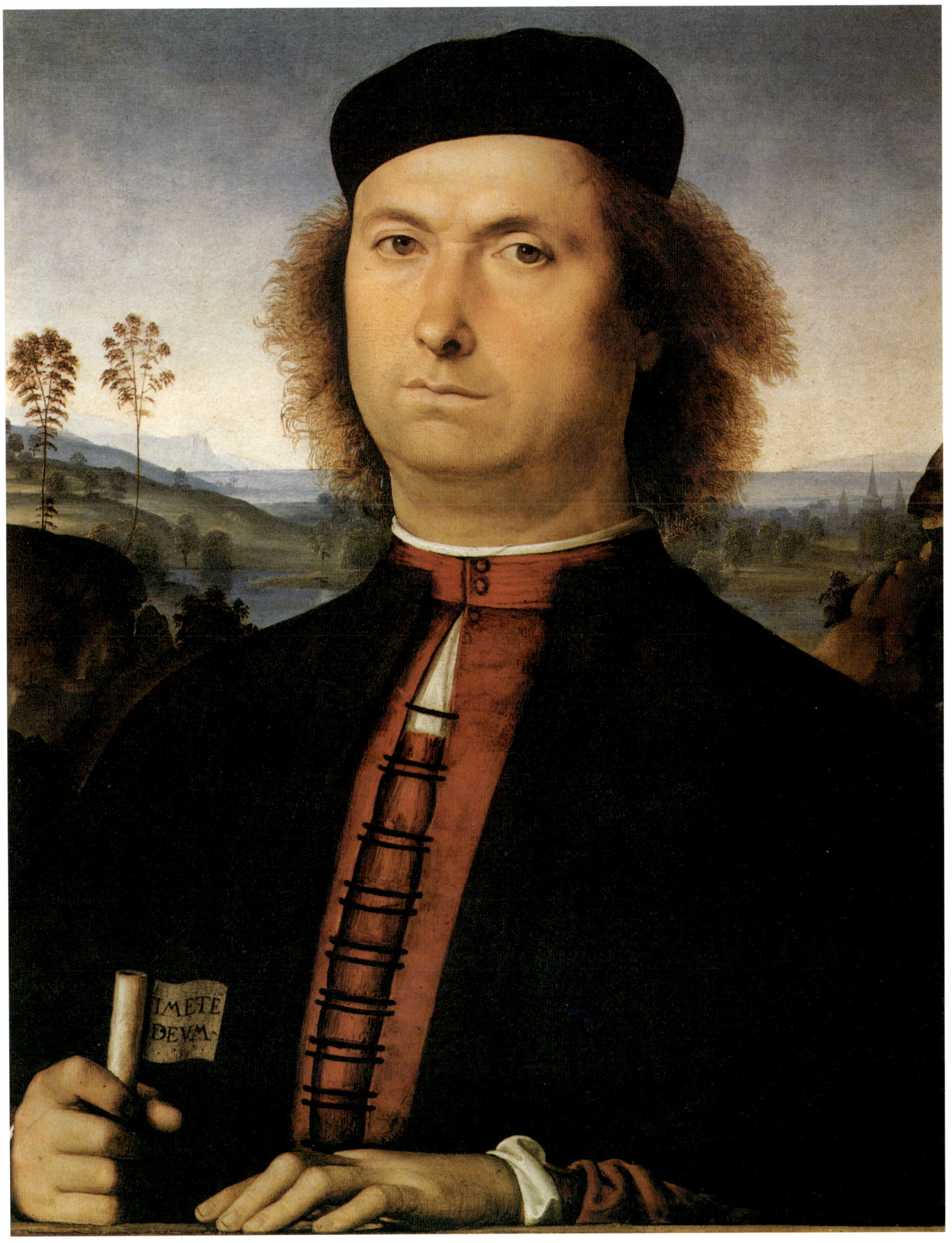

■ PERUGINO
Portrait of Francesco delle Opere
1494, oil on panel,
52 x 44 cm
Galleria degli Uffizi,
Florence

Perugino made few portraits, but they are all notable, and this is recognized as the masterpiece. The bust, hands, and face of the figure stand out with unusual vigor against the extensive background panorama (perhaps a view of Lake Trasimeno). The old lesson on volumes that Perugino had learned as a young apprentice from Piero della Francesca here returns, but it is joined to a new sensibility for light. The low sill behind which the man stands emphasizes the sense of his detachment from the viewer, while the highly accurate rendering of his features, following the trend in Florentine portraiture of the time, from Ghirlandaio to Botticelli, keeps the figure from being fully immersed in the luministic and meteorological atmosphere of the landscape, the very kind of integration between figure and nature that was about to take place in the painting of the Veneto region of northeastern Italy.

Florence in the late fifteenth century

Set inside a vast Gothic
structure in the middle
of Florence, between
the plazas of the Duomo
and the Signoria, the
church of Orsanmichele
presents an absolute
singularity: along its
exterior is a series of
niches dedicated to the
sixteen "arts," the pro-
fessional guilds into
which the productive
forces of the city were
divided. Every niche
has the statue of the
patron saint of the
guild. Many of these
are absolute master-
pieces of Renaissance
sculpture, beginning
with the *St. George* by
Donatello (replaced by
a copy for reasons of
preservation). This
group of *Christ and the
Doubting Thomas*, one
of the outstanding
works by Andrea del
Verrocchio, stands in
a niche that had previ-
ously held a work
by Donatello and
Michelozzo.

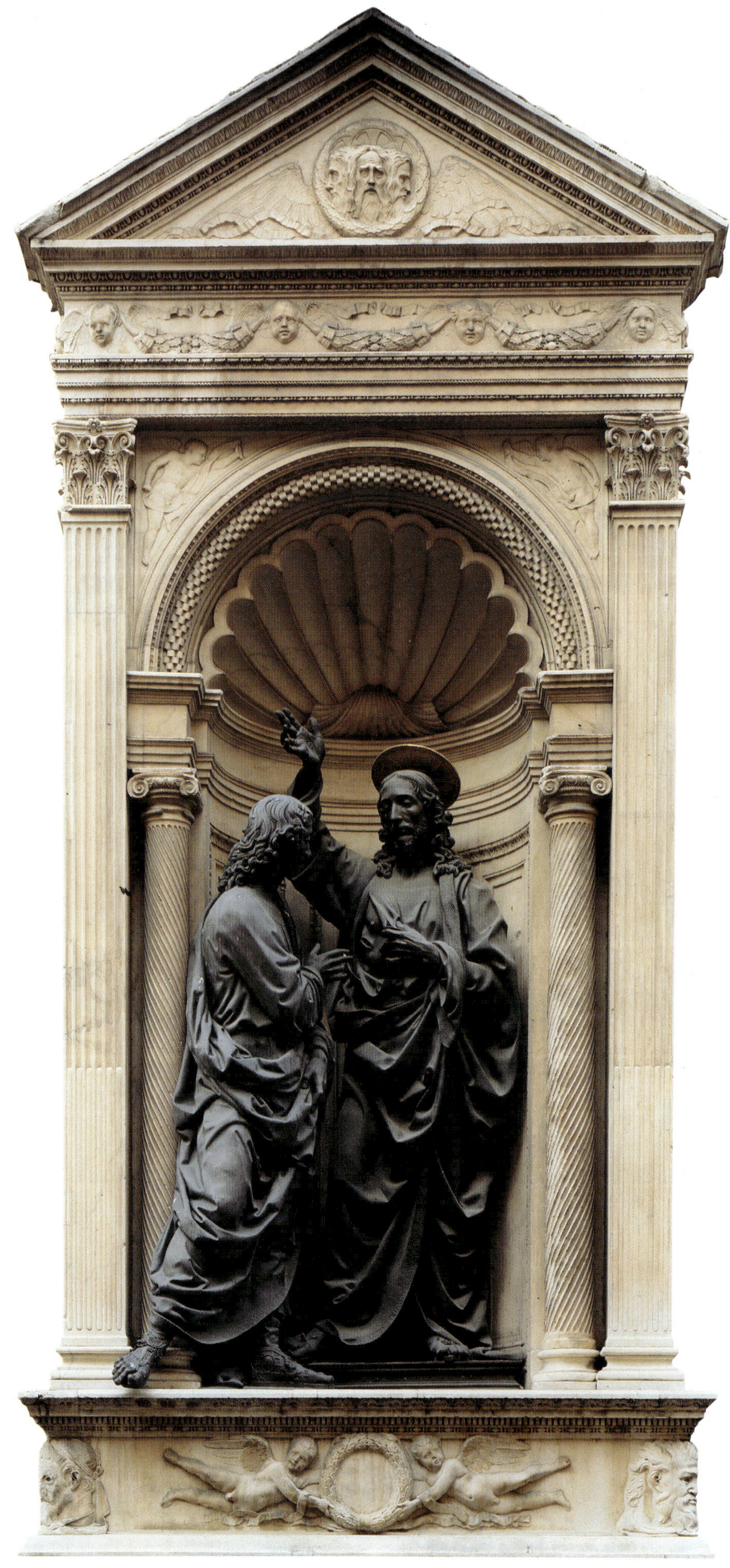

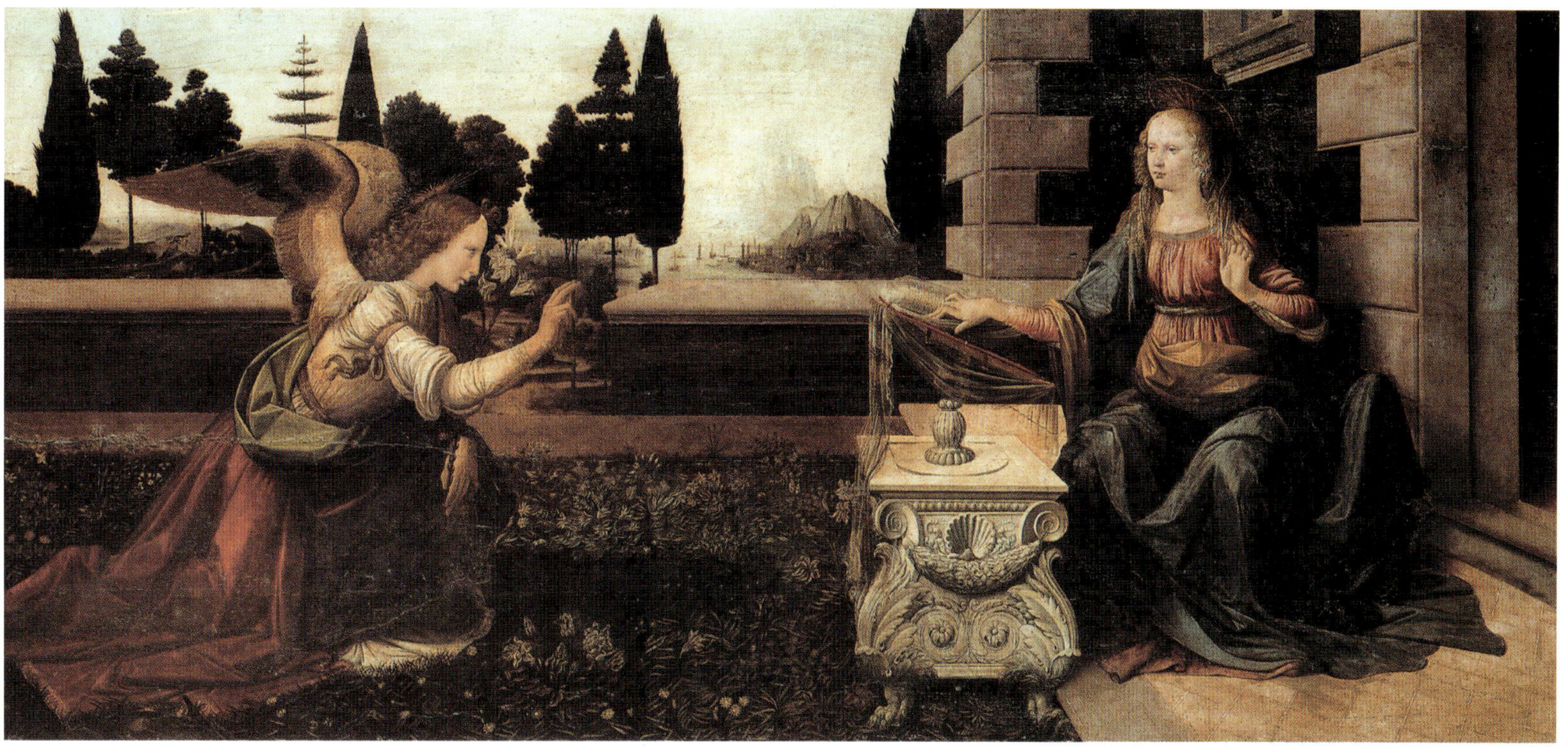

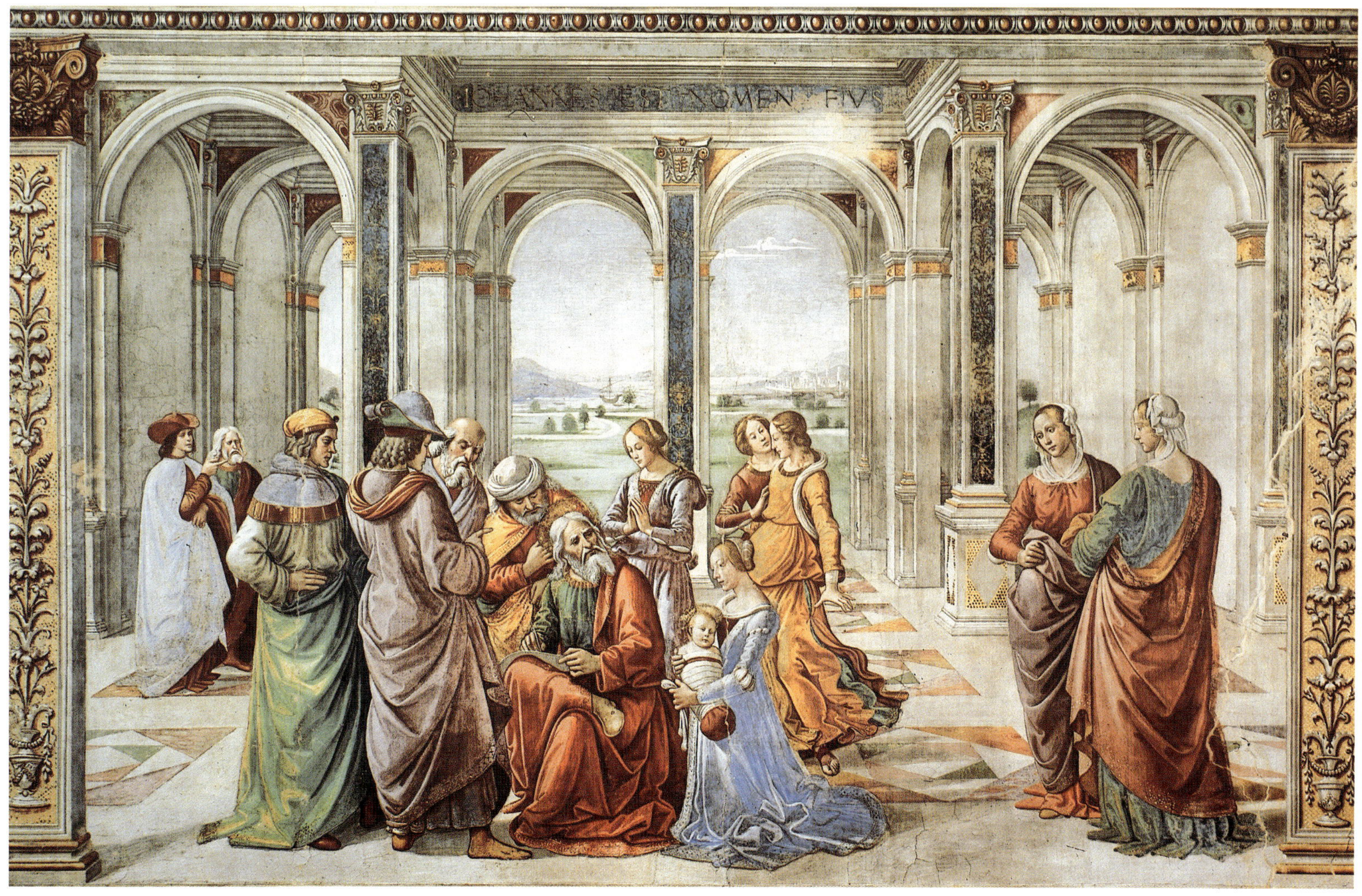

Florence in the late fifteenth century

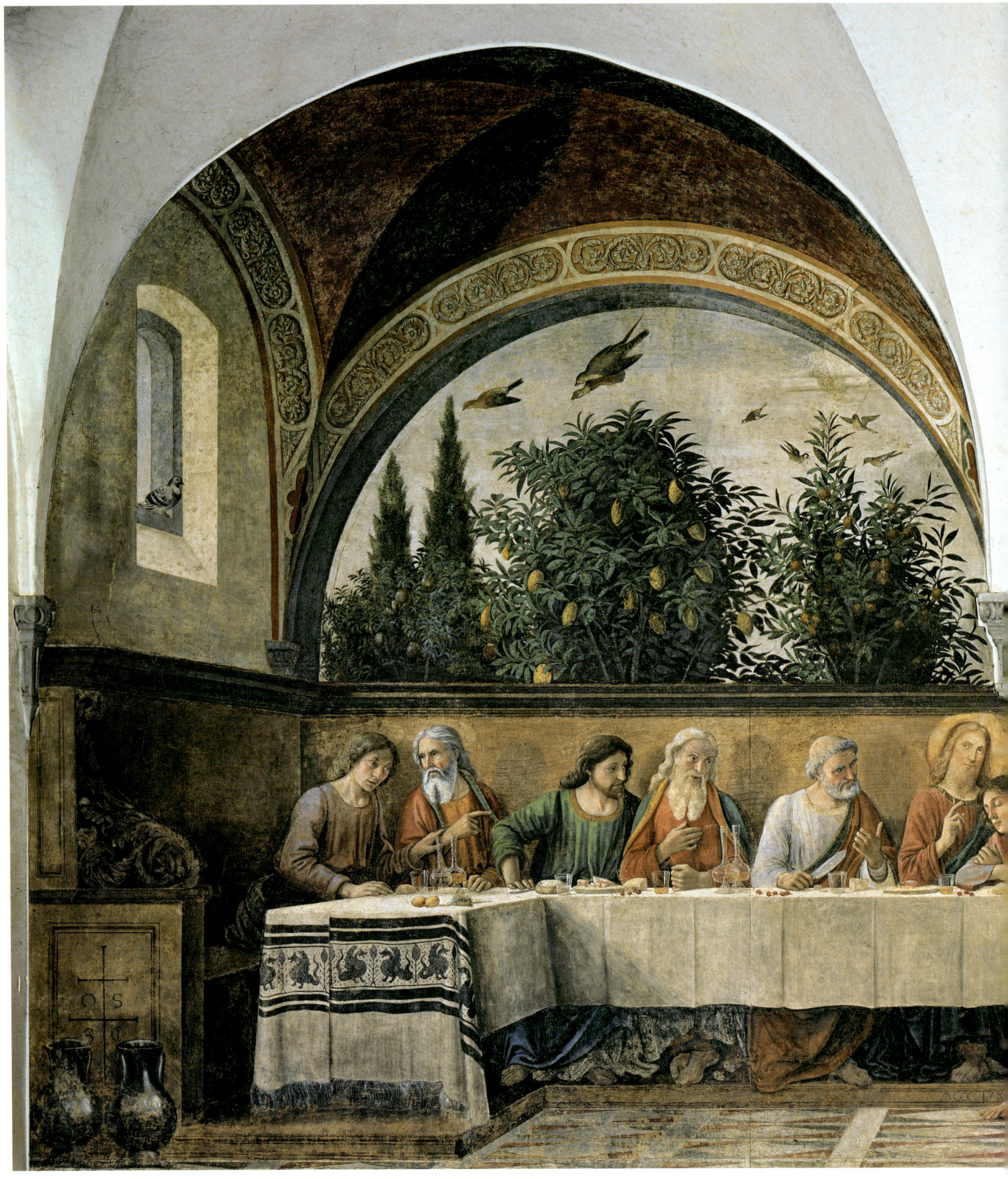

Florence in the late fifteenth century

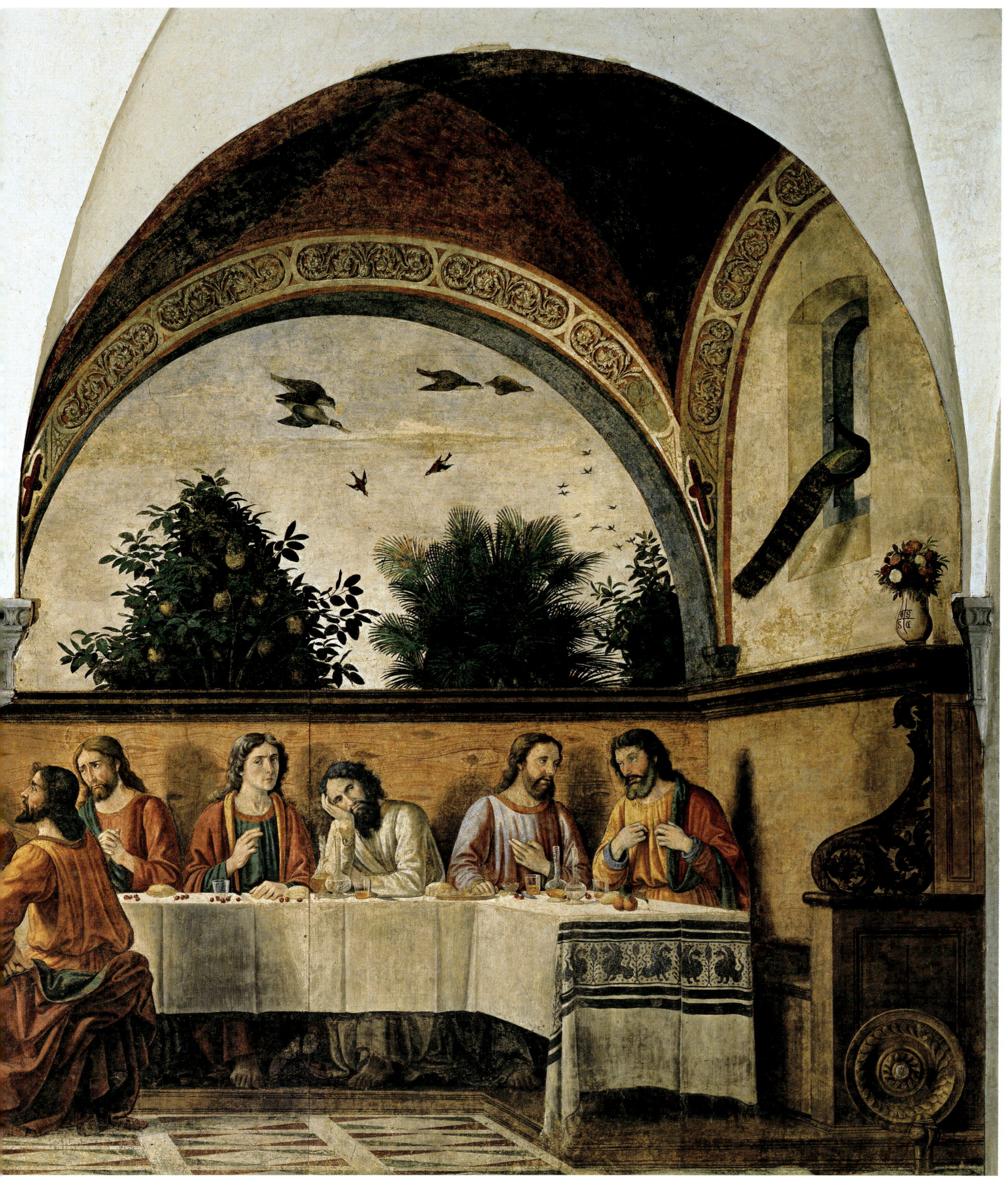

Florence in the late fifteenth century

The execution of this work began around 1494 and ended in 1497—a decidedly long time, but one that reflects the meticulous care Leonardo gave to each of his works. Leonardo made use of the entire wall, reserving the lunettes at the top for the heraldic celebration of his patron, Ludovico il Moro, duke of Milan, with coats of arms and garlands of leaves and fruits. He thus provided himself with a long rectangle in which to locate the episode of the *Last Supper,* a theme related to the setting, a convent's refectory. Leonardo spent a long time studying the overall composition and the individual figures; he then sought out a new technique for painting on walls; then he began actually working on the wall. Leonardo, most of all in the period of his

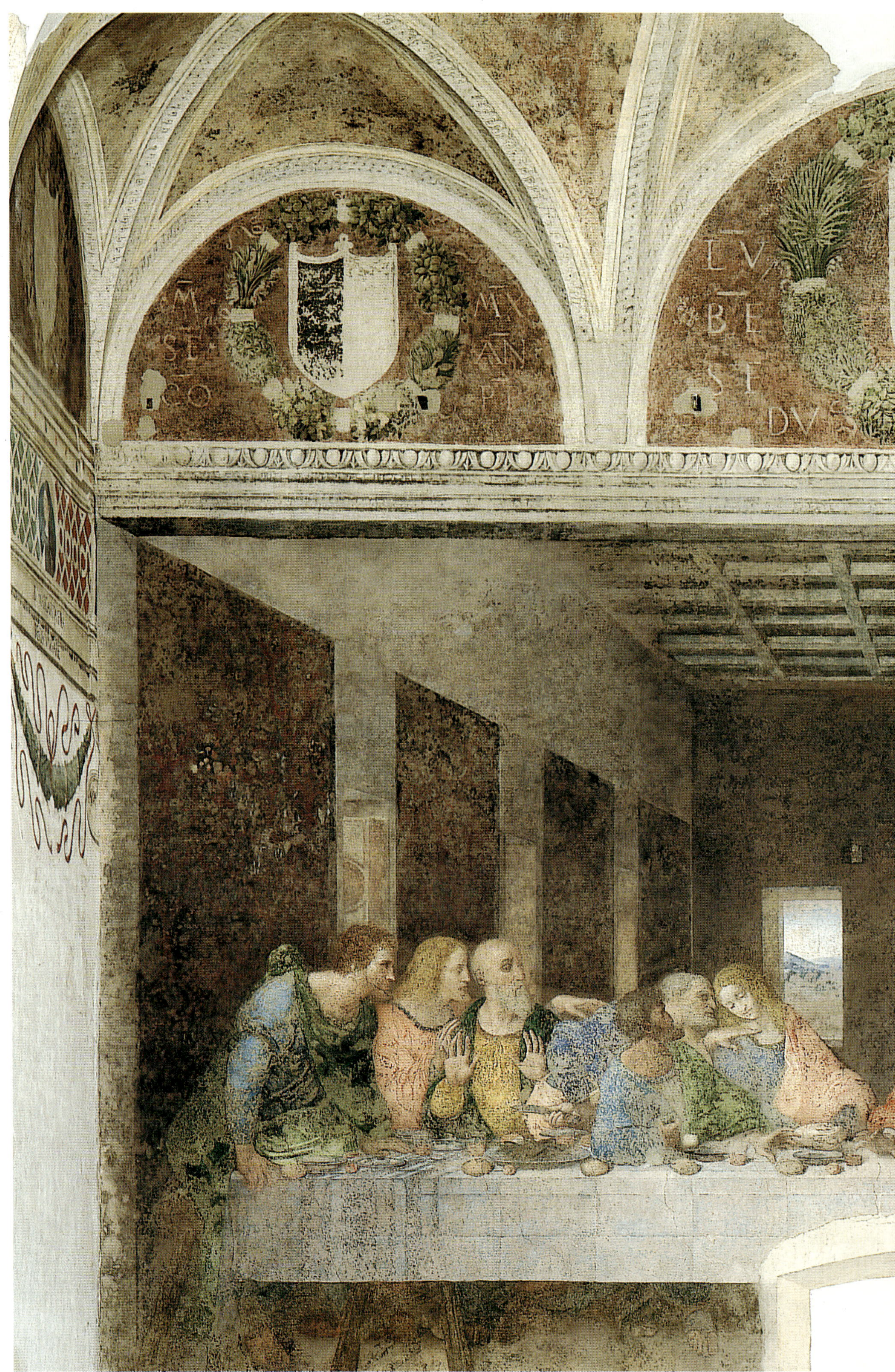

Florence in the late fifteenth century

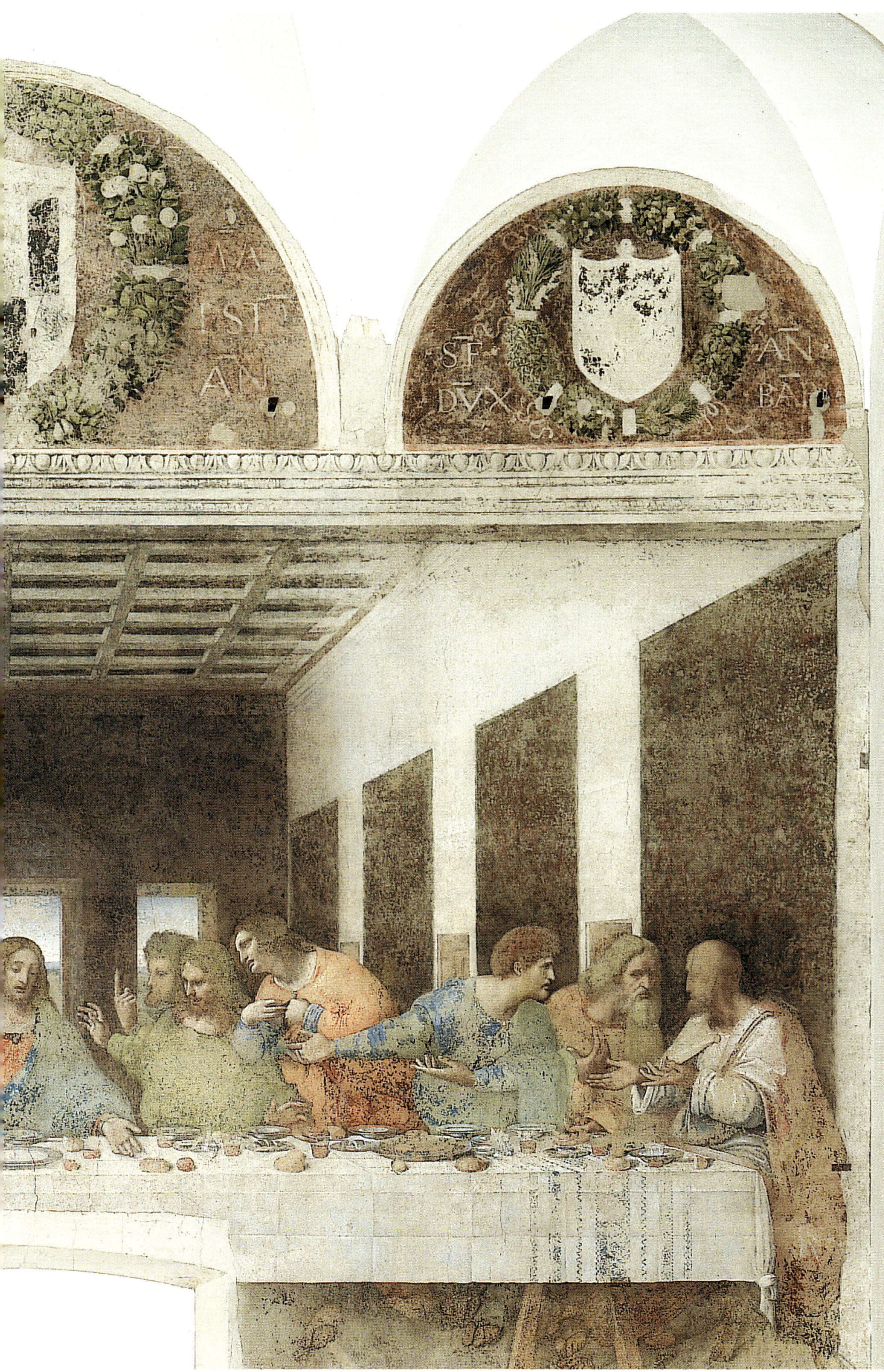

youth in Florence, had had many opportunities to study other versions of the theme, many of them quite prestigious, and in his version he introduced notable innovations in the layout of the scene. For the first time in art history, all thirteen figures are arranged along the same side of a rectangular table. The simplicity of the table set on trestles contrasts with the setting, a vast, ornate hall presented in perspective, its walls adorned with tapestries, its ceiling coffered, with three large windows in the back that letting in a pale light. Jesus occupies the center of the composition, with the apostles divided symmetrically around him, in four groups of three each. The absolute geometric regularity of the structure makes the expressive violence of the figures even more dramatic. Jesus has just spoken the phrase, "One of you will betray me," and the apostles are responding in a true storm of emotions: fear, dismay, incredulity, anguish, perplexity, resignation, sorrow.

For quite a long time, Rome was left out of the extraordinary vitality of the fifteenth century in Italy. During the first half of the century, following the period of residence in Avignon the popes' primary concern was to strengthen the church in terms of its literally doctrinal aspects; only when that had been accomplished could they turn their attention to the reanimation of the city, which had reached the lowest population level in its history. There had been a few undertakings in the 1420s, such as the activity of Gentile da Fabriano and then Pisanello in San Giovanni in Laterano, and there was Cardinal Branda di Castiglione's patronage of Masolino and Masaccio, the latter of whom died in Rome in 1428 while painting the frescoes in San Clemente. These works had set the stage for the large and systematic plan for the rebirth of the Eternal City, which was destined in less than a century's time to reassume its role as the guiding light of western civilization.

organic affirmation of the figurative culture of Tuscan origin, based on perspective, on the monumentality of the figures, and on the correct application of light. The Jubilee Year of 1450 was the occasion for the coming to Rome of such major international artists as Jean Fouquet and Rogier van der Weyden, to whom were added Piero della Francesca and perhaps Antonello da Messina.

With the name Pius II, a refined Sienese humanistic poet, Enea Silvio Piccolomini, sat on the throne of St. Peter from 1458 to 1464; but the definitive affirmation of Rome as the great center of Renaissance art and culture took place during the long papacy (1471–84) of Sixtus IV. Among his first acts was the organization of a great library in large frescoed rooms, entrusting its direction to celebrated humanists and its pictorial decoration to Melozzo da Forlì; later, around 1480, he had the Sistine Chapel built to serve as the seat of the conclave and of other important pontifical cere-

The rebirth of Rome

When he returned to Rome in 1420, Pope Martin V—whose election to pope at the Council of Constance had put an end to the Great Schism—became the first "restorer" of the pontifical seat in Rome. Beginning with the works he promoted, the popes concentrated most of their attention on two monumental areas, the Lateran and, on the opposite side of the Tiber River, the Vatican. It was there that the papal residence was transferred, and the area surrounding the basilica of St. Peter's, once an outer area, was gradually transformed into a massive worksite, a swirling laboratory of architecture and decoration: the great bronze wings of the main door, a work by Antonio Averulino, called Filarete, later a famous architect serving the Sforzas in Milan, remain as an important testimonial of this phase. The frescoes made in the Vatican by Fra Angelico around 1450, during the period of Pope Nicholas V, constitute the first

monies. He gave the goldsmith and sculptor Antonio del Pollaiuolo the job of creating his impressive sepulchral monument in bronze, preserved in the Treasury of St. Peter's.

The structure of the Sistine Chapel is very simple and, at least from the exterior, by no means striking. It is a large rectangular hall with a finely designed marble mosaic floor, divided about halfway by an elegant marble screen. The pope concentrated his attention on the frescoes along the walls, in which biblical episodes related to the figure of Moses and scenes from the Gospel that have Christ as their protagonist are compared, following a precise system of correspondences between the Old and New Testaments. In order to have this work with its complex iconography completed in a reasonably short time, the pope summoned to Rome all the leading artists then active in Florence:

Botticelli, Perugino, Ghirlandaio, Cosimo Rosselli, Luca Signorelli, and other artists of the same generation, all tied to a fluent rhythmic elegance based on the absolute control of design and decorative effect. The huge panels were laid out in accordance with a sense of great monumentality, with frequent citations of classical architecture, such as Roman triumphal arches and centrally planned structures. The gestures are neither forced nor violent, and the sequence of episodes follows a quiet and secure rhythm.

The results were extraordinary. The artists chosen by Pope Sixtus IV for the group undertaking (the painters had to follow general guidelines to achieve homogeneity in the style and size of the figures, but the hands of the various masters can be distinguished, with prominence going to Perugino and Botticelli) established the stylistic traits of Italian painting of the late fifteenth century and made the Sistine Chapel, even before Michelangelo's activity, a precise point of reference in Renaissance painting. In fact, while Botticelli returned to Florence, where he became the leading artistic figure of the age of Lorenzo the Magnificent, Perugino multiplied his activity in many regions, receiving commissions for works from all over Italy. In Rome, even after the departure of the first group of Florentine masters, the taste for large-scale decorative effects remained prevalent. In the last decade of the fourteenth century, during the controversial pontificate of Alexander VI, the Umbrian artist Bernardino Pinturicchio was very active, author among other works of the imaginative, elaborate frescoes in the papal apartment in the Vatican, filled with ornamental motifs of various origin, mythological themes, gilding, and "antique-style" decorations. At the end of the fifteen century, Rome was again the goal of young Florentine artists, such as Filippino Lippo and, most of all, Michelangelo Buronarroti. Inserted in a climate of enthusiastic rediscovery of the classical past, Michelangelo began to sculpt his first large-scale marble groups, directing his career toward sculpture. This was the period in which systematic campaigns of excavations and the research of the ruins of ancient palaces of the Roman empire were undertaken. The archaeological research, often conducted personally by important artists and architects, led to the acquisition of new and more accurate material to study in terms of classical architecture and

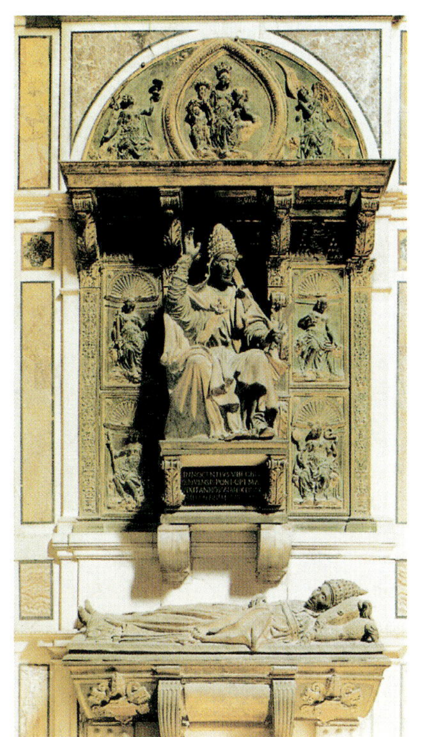

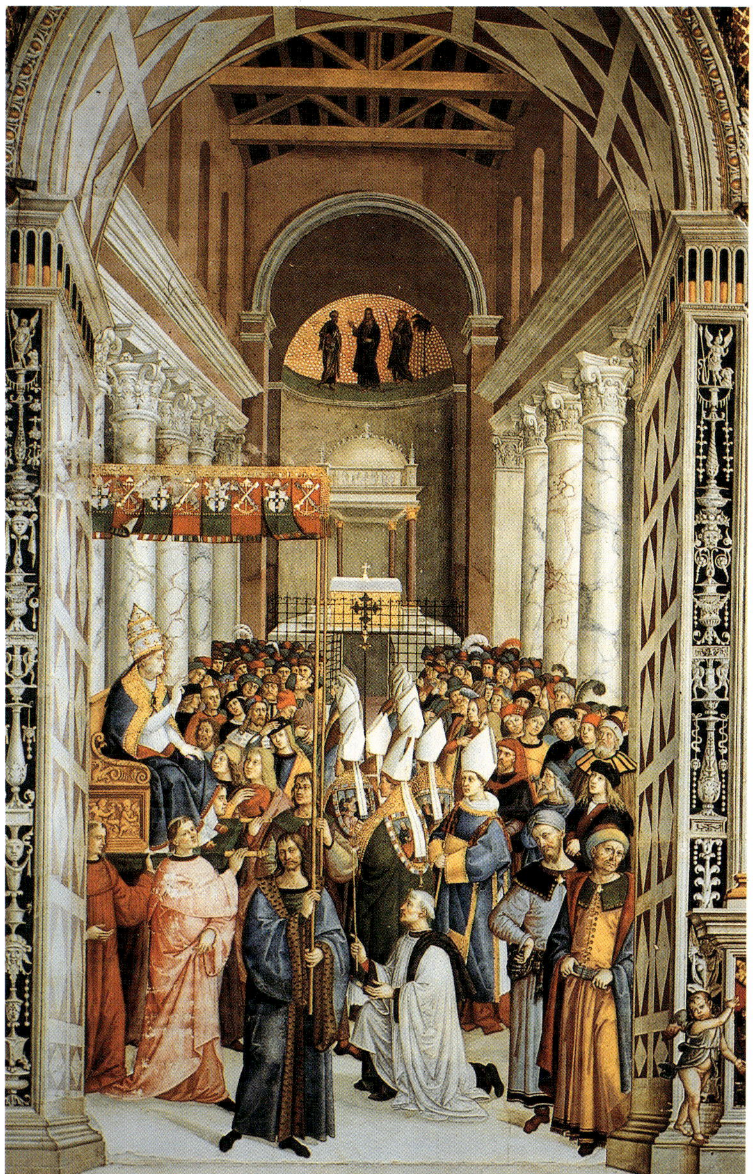

sculpture (the discovery of the dramatic Hellenistic group of the *Laocoön* was full of consequences for art). These efforts also included the discovery of ornamental stuccos and frescoes, most of all in Nero's Domus Aurea (Golden House). The motifs and architectural elements of these works immediately became models for the decoration of noble villas and palaces, in particular the decorative style that is called grotesque. Thus began, even if still in an embryonic stage, the age of Renaissance classicism, the extraordinary apotheosis of which came during the age of Julius II thanks to the architecture of Donato Bramante and the decorative undertakings of Raphael and his school.

At the beginning of the sixteenth century Rome presented an appearance completely changed from that of the beginning of the fifteenth. Thanks to the patronage of the most powerful cardinals, new churches and great palaces arose in strategic points, and the historic center of the city was about to become an immense workshop of innovative architectonic and urbanistic ideas, a state that would be characteristic of Rome's appearance for almost two centuries.

The rebirth of Rome

The articulated mass of the Vatican palaces is the result of enlargements and embellishments carried out by various popes over the course of centuries. On returning to Rome from Avignon in 1377, Gregory XI decided to move the papal see from the Lateran Palace to the Vatican, but the true architectonic history of the complex, which was gradually transformed into a grandiose abode, did not really begin until the reign of Nicholas V (1447–55). In 1473 Sixtus IV built the chapel that bears his name (the Sistine), while the small palace on the hill of the Belvedere dates to the pontificate of Innocent VIII (1484–92); Donato Bramante later joined it to the rest of the complex by way of the colossal architectonic structure of the Cortile del Belvedere. Bramante also built the loggias of the Cortile di San Damaso, completed and sumptuously decorated by Raphael. Various new buildings were later added to the

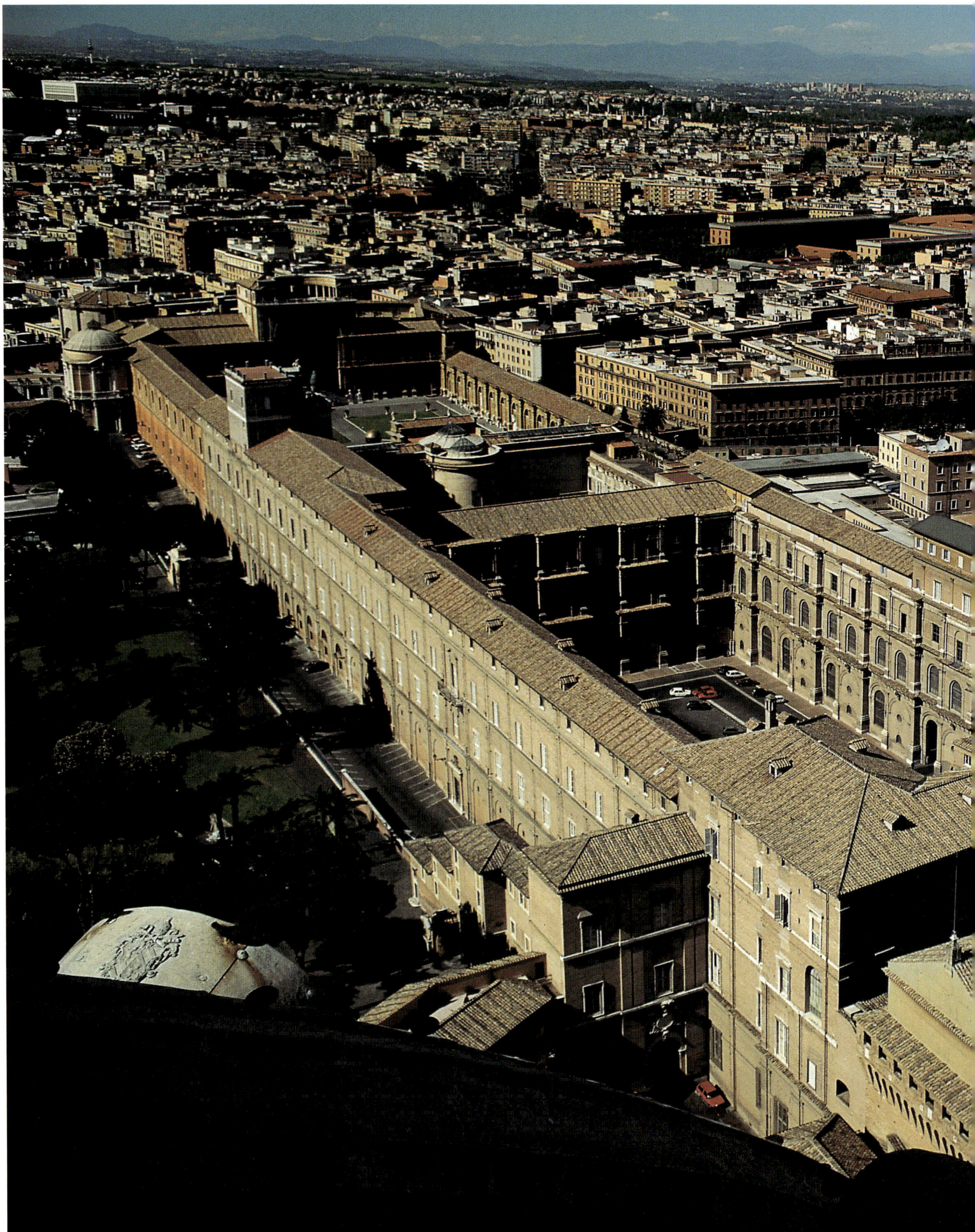

The rebirth of Rome

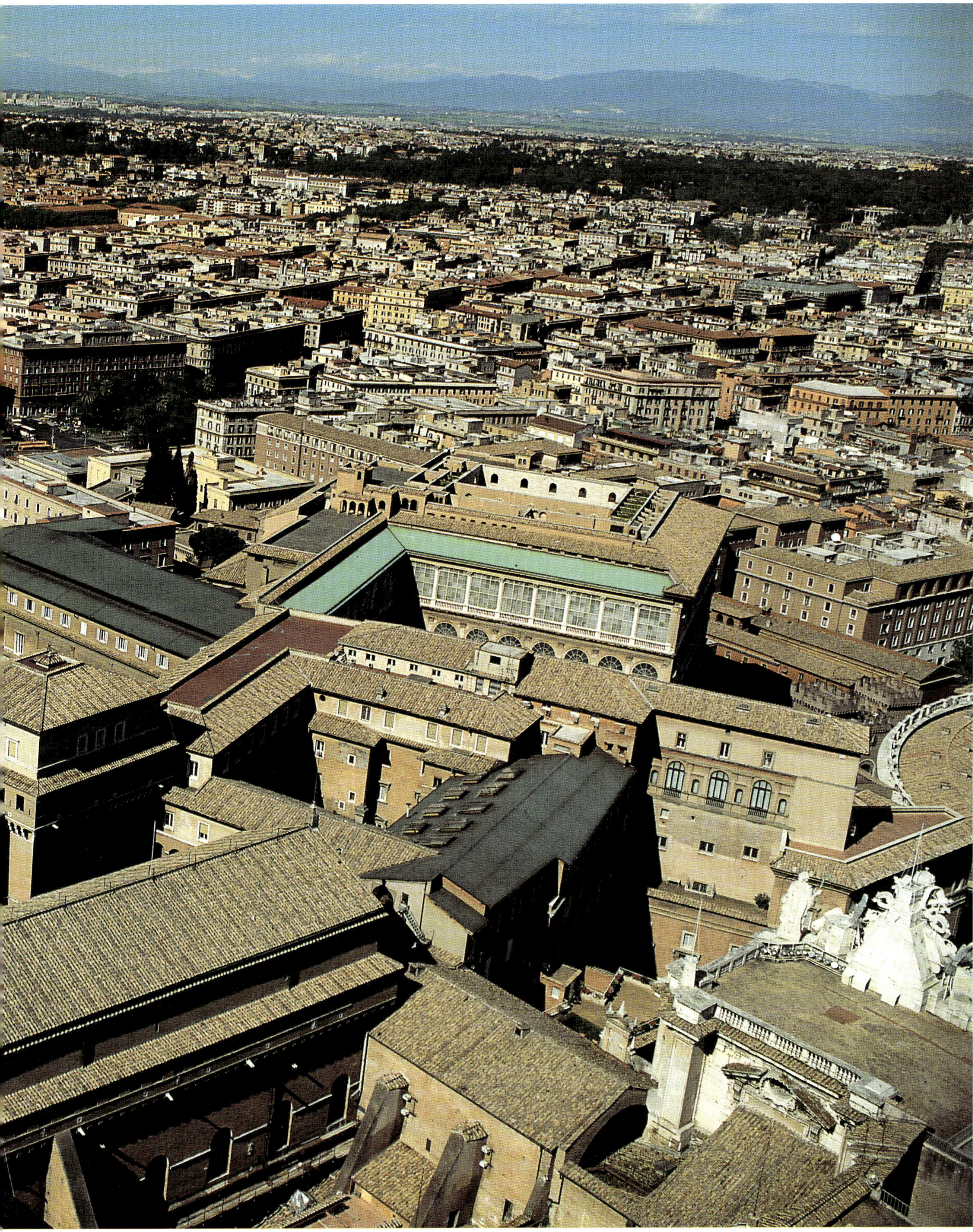

many-winged grand palace, including the Pauline Chapel by Antonio da Sangallo, the enlargements by Pirro Ligorio, the library by Domenico Fontana, and the Scala Regia designed by Bernini. At the end of the eighteenth century some of the palaces were transformed into a museum to hold the famous papal archaeological and pictorial collection. This view, taken from atop the dome of St. Peter's, gives a sense of the overall layout, based on the succession of three different courtyards: the large rectangle of the Cortile del Belvedere, the narrower space of the courtyard of the library—closed between the transversal structure of the Salone Sistino and the Braccio Nuovo ("new arm"), made by Raffaele Stern (1817–22) and recognizable by the presence of a large apsidal hall, and finally the Cortile della Pigna, with the enormous semicircular courtyard said to be "by Bramante." The rectangular body in the foreground is the Sistine Chapel.

The rebirth of Rome

Fra Angelico, who arrived in Rome in 1446, was the most important artist involved in the first phase of work on the Vatican palaces. Nicholas V charged him with the decoration of several rooms, unfortunately lost, and of his private chapel, with the *Stories of Saints Steven and Lawrence*, a masterpiece of the painter and ideal manifesto of Nicholas's Christian humanism. The well-calibrated gestures of the figures create a sense of classical and stately composure that is found in the entire cycle, making it the most important pictorial event just before the Jubilee of 1450. St. Lawrence's act of distributing alms to the poor is a reference to the Church, symbolized by the church nave in the background, which was seen as the dispenser of grace on the faithful, symbolized by the mendicants who crowd with dignity around the Roman deacon. Benozzo Gozzoli probably contributed to the execution of this scene as well as to others in the cycle.

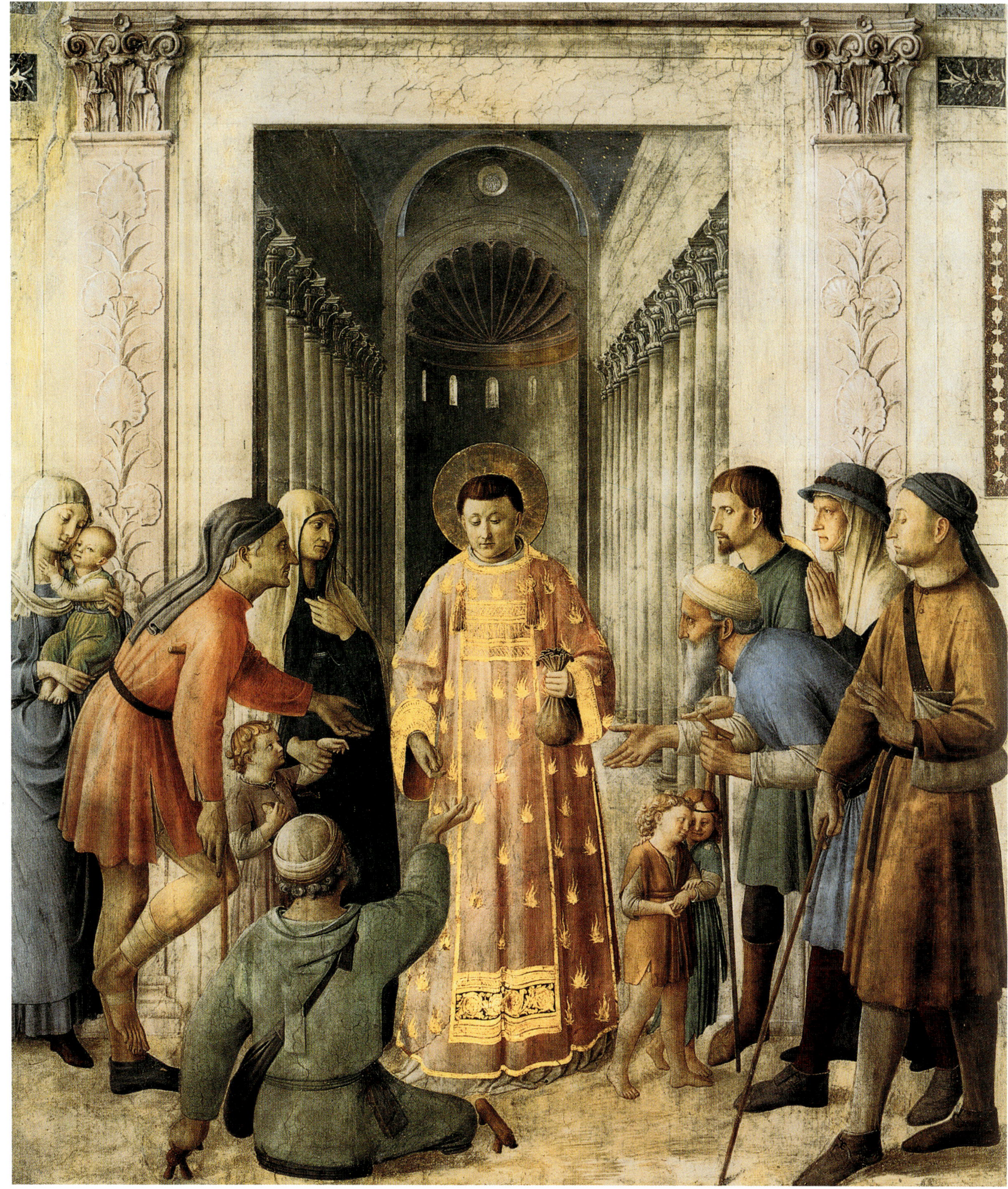

The rebirth of Rome

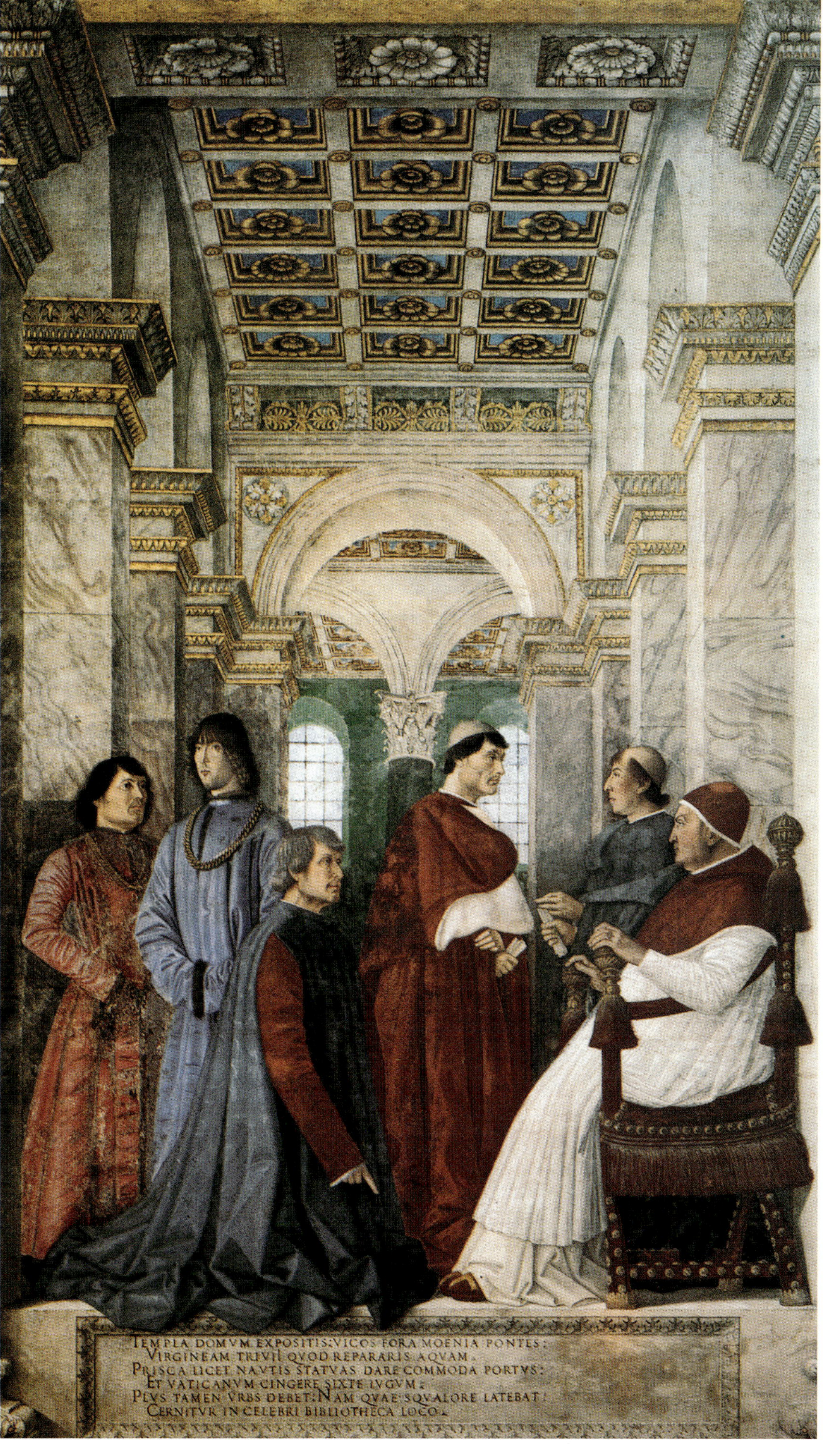

This fresco commemo-
rates the ceremony in
which Pope Sixtus IV
appointed the human-
ist Bartolomeo Platina,
shown kneeling before
him, prefect of the
Apostolic Library.
Witnessing the cere-
mony are, to the left,
Giovanni della Rovere
and Girolamo Riario,
and, to the right, the
cardinals Raffaele Riario
and Giuliano della
Rovere, all (except
Platina) members of
the pope's family. The
courtly scene is a quin-
tessential image of
fifteenth-century cul-
ture, including the
relationship between
the world of letters and
that of the arts by way
of the power of great
patrons. Behind the
perfect spatial represen-
tation are the theories
of perspective of Leon
Battista Alberti. The
solemnity of the epi-
sode is confirmed by
the long Latin epigraph
on the stone base
beneath the scene
("Rome, once full of
squalor, owes to you,
Sixtus, its temples,
foundling hospital,
street squares, walks,
bridges, the restoration
of the Acqua Vergine at
the Trevi Fountain, the
port for sailors, the
fortifications on the
Vatican Hill, and now
this celebrated library").
The composed gravity
of the poses closely
recalls the works of
Piero della Francesco.

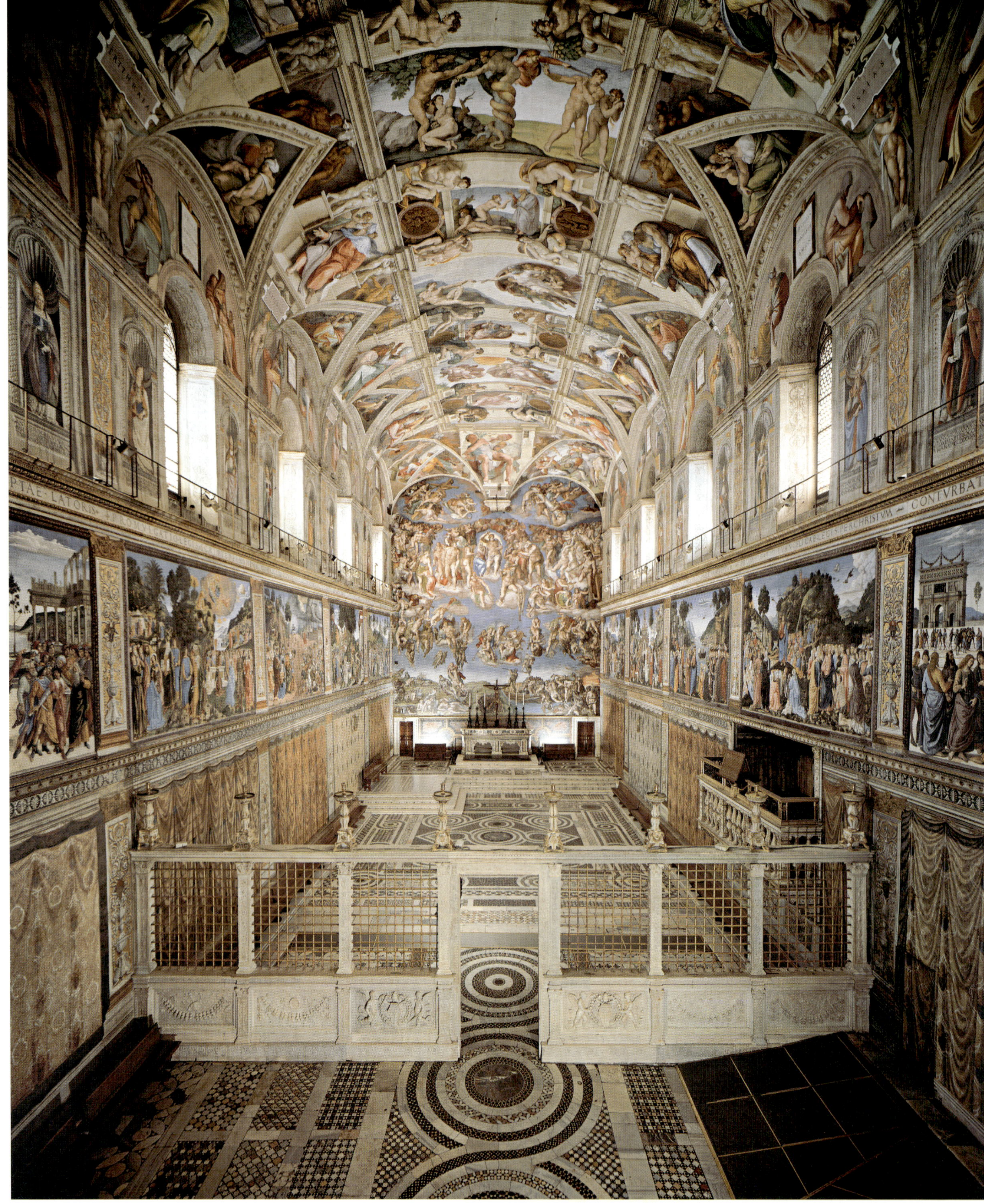

The rebirth of Rome

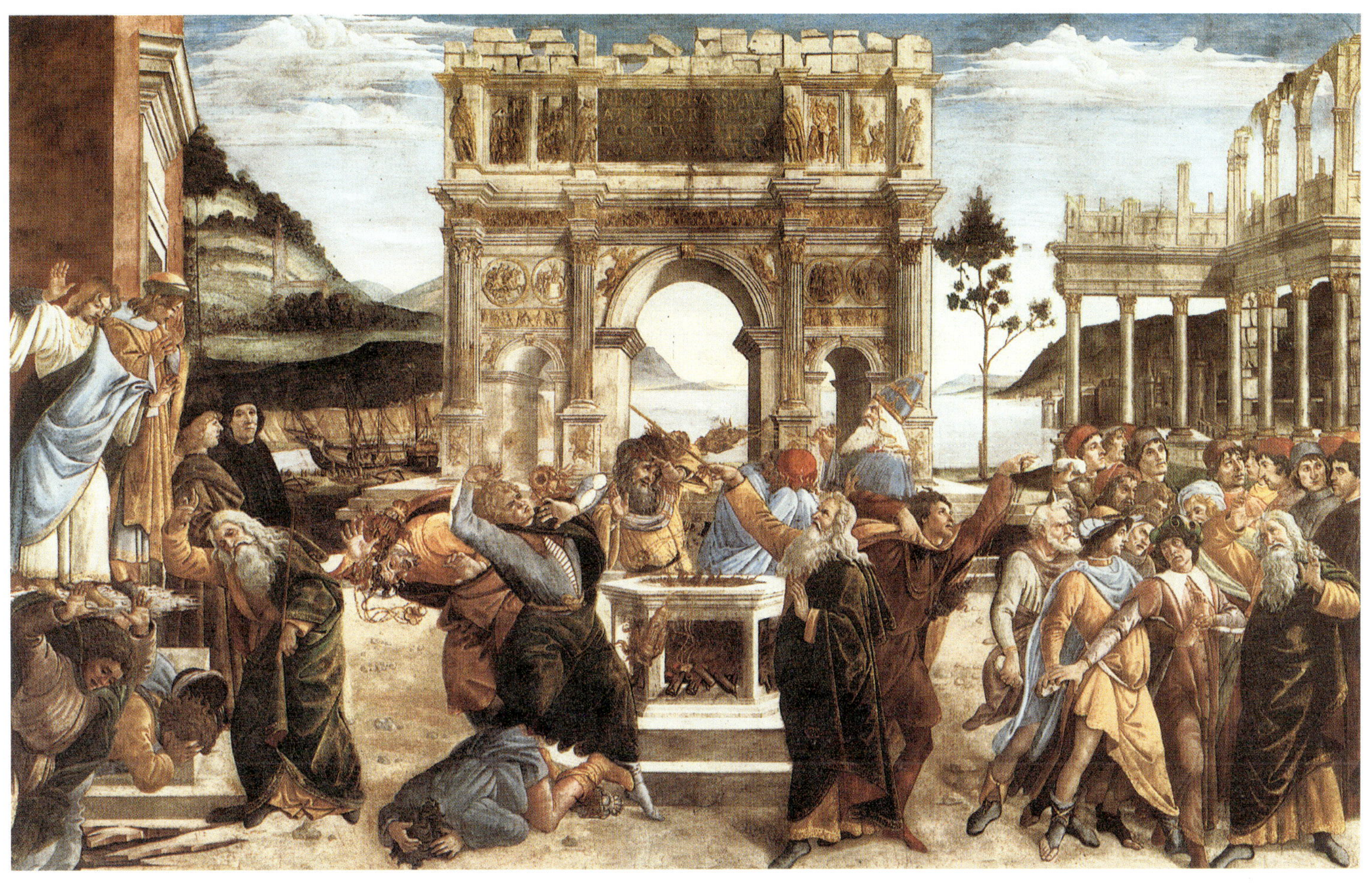

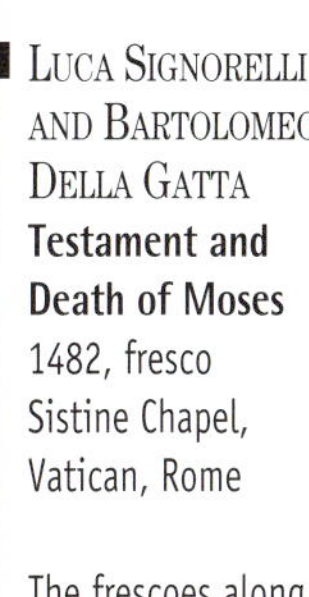

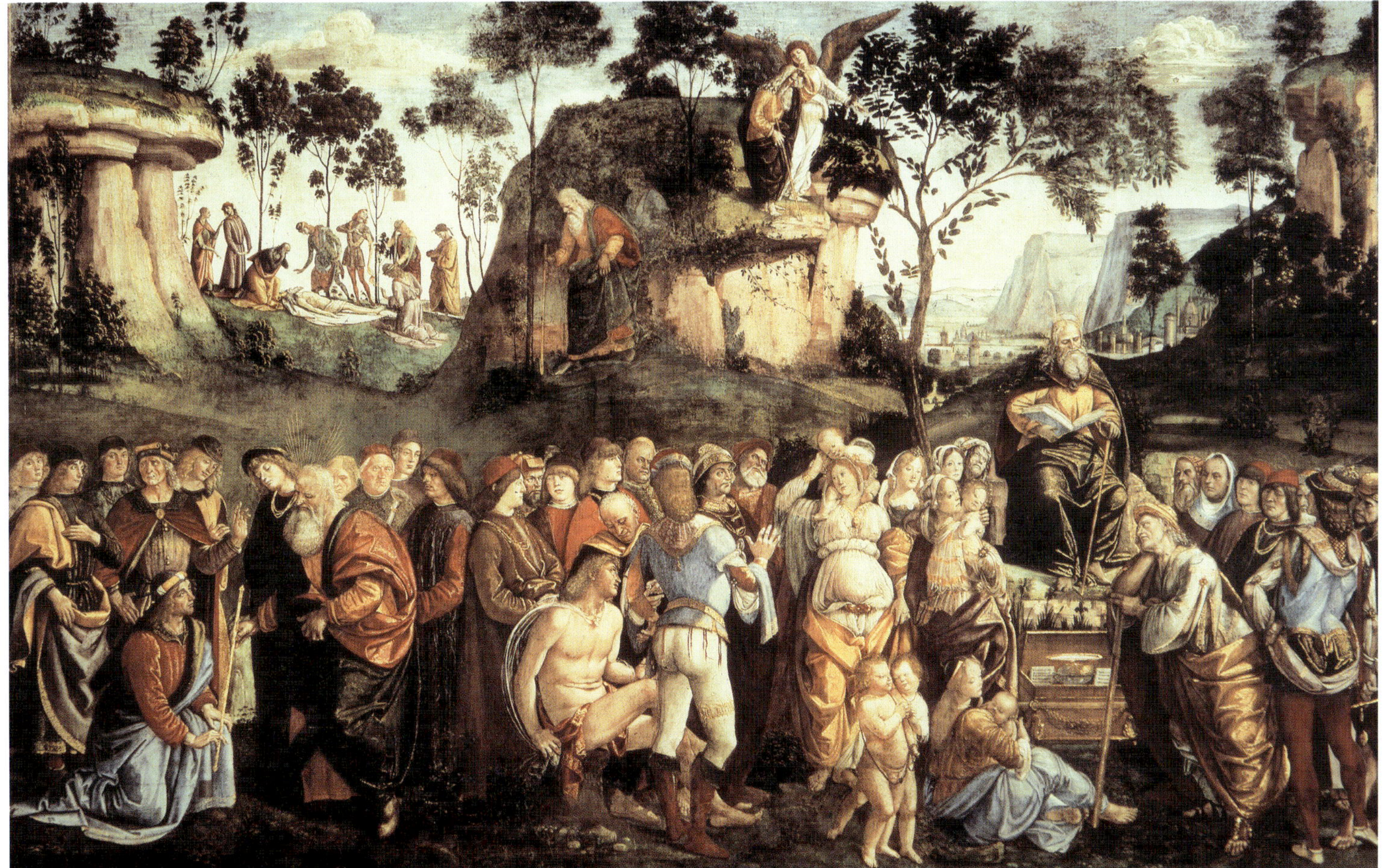

The rebirth of Rome

PERUGINO
Christ Consigns the Keys to St. Peter
1481–82, fresco,
340 x 550 cm
Sistine Chapel,
Vatican, Rome

Aside from the *Assumption,* made for the main altar and destroyed by Michelangelo to make room for his *Last Judgment,* and various portraits of popes in the upper strip, there are three paintings by Perugino in the Sistine Chapel: the *Baptism,* the *Journey of Moses,* and *Christ Consigns the Keys to St. Peter.* This scene can be taken as a synthesis of the ideological message of the entire cycle, directed at a celebration of the historical function of the church and the supremacy of the papacy by way of episodes from the stories of Christ and Moses, woven together with complex symbolic references and allusions to the present time, including the use of contemporary people. The composition, well balanced in every part, is dominated by the mole of the Temple of Solomon in Jerusalem, the octagonal structure of which alludes to the design of buildings with a central layout, a subject of great interest in the early Renaissance.

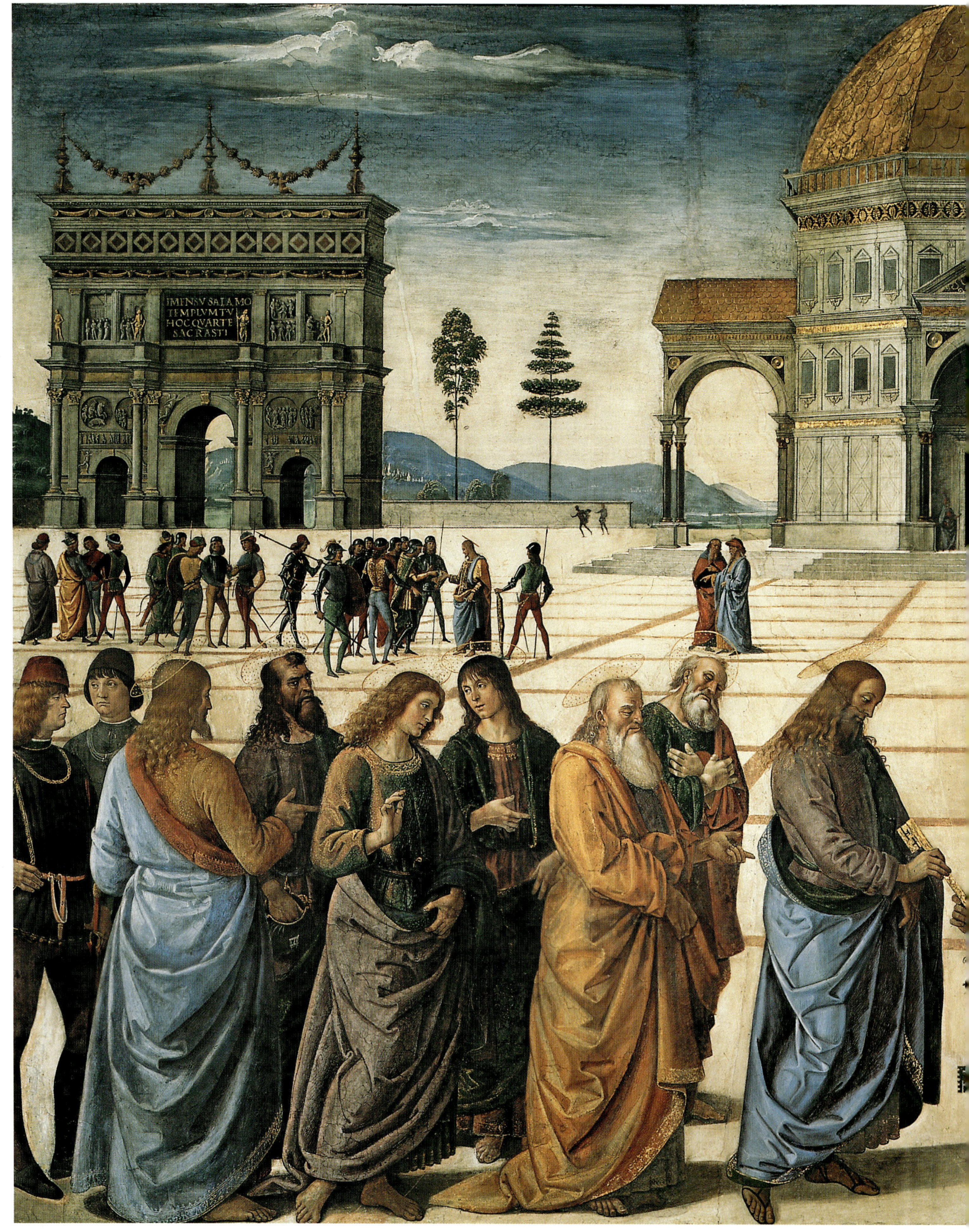

The rebirth of Rome

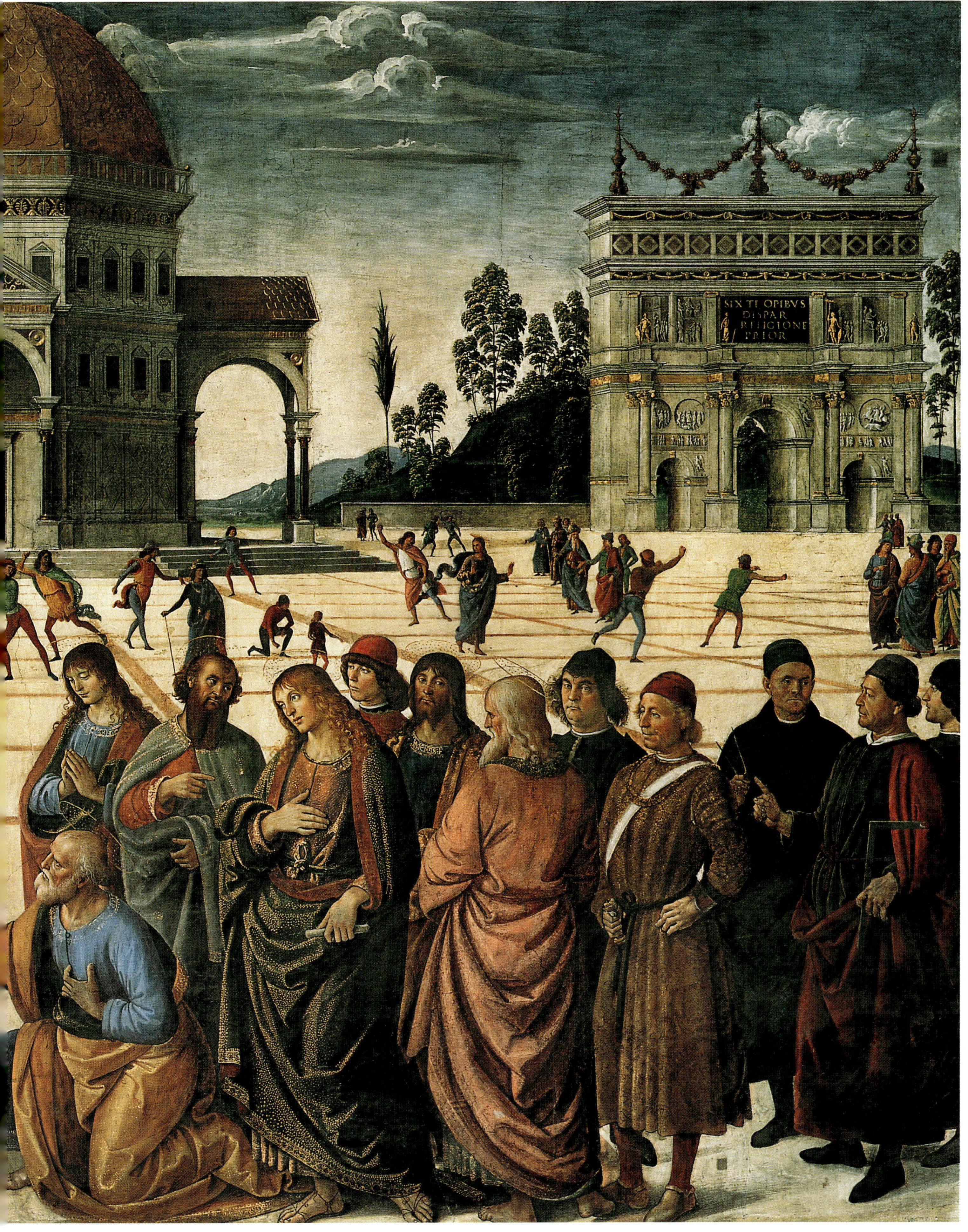

The rebirth of Rome

**Consignment of the
Keys and Healing
of the Cripple; Fall
of Simon Magus
and Dispute before
Nero; Martyrdom
of St. Peter**
1471–78; bas-reliefs
Treasury of St. Peter,
Vatican, Rome

These bas-reliefs, which
decorated the ciborium
of Sixtus IV, are distin-
guished by an anti-
quarian passion and
by true iconographic,
stylistic, and technical
citations of monuments
from the classical age,
most of all Trajan's
Column. Found in frag-
ments but substantially
reconstructible in its
figurative development,
the ciborium decorated
the main altar of the
basilica before the
demolition carried
out by Bramante in
preparation for the
Renaissance recon-
struction of the ancient
and tumbledown
building from the age
of Constantine. The
scenes, inspired by
the Acts of the
Apostles, celebrate
the figure of St. Peter.

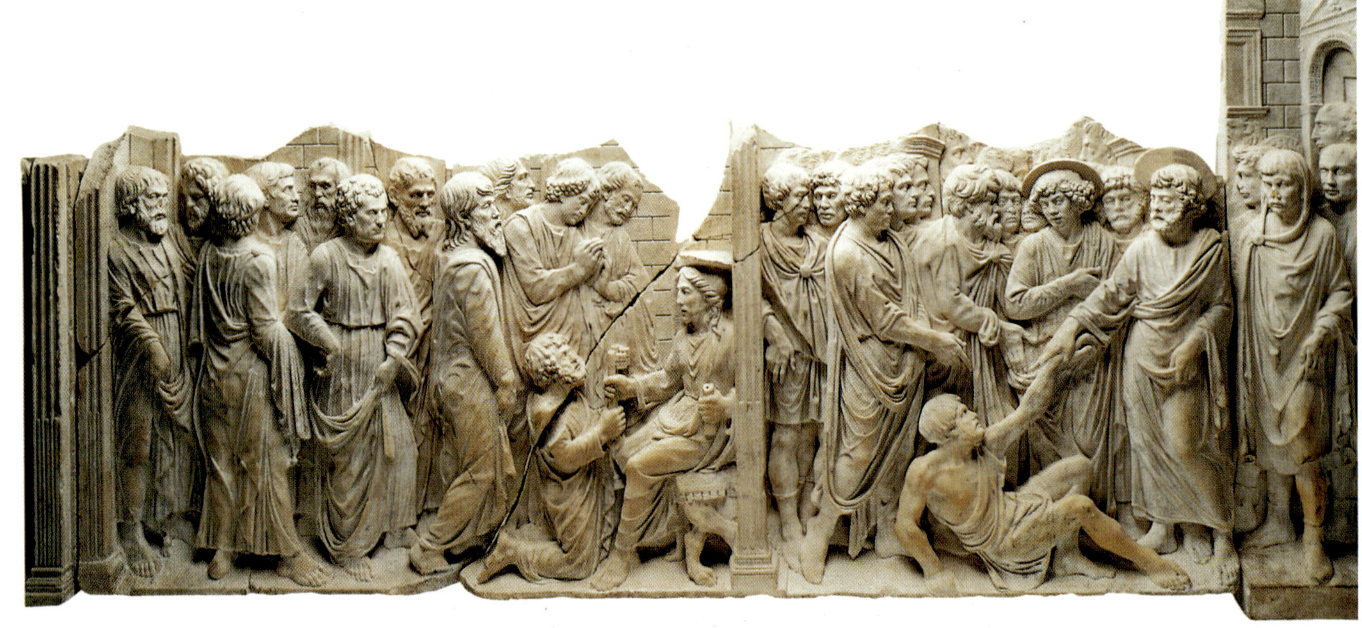

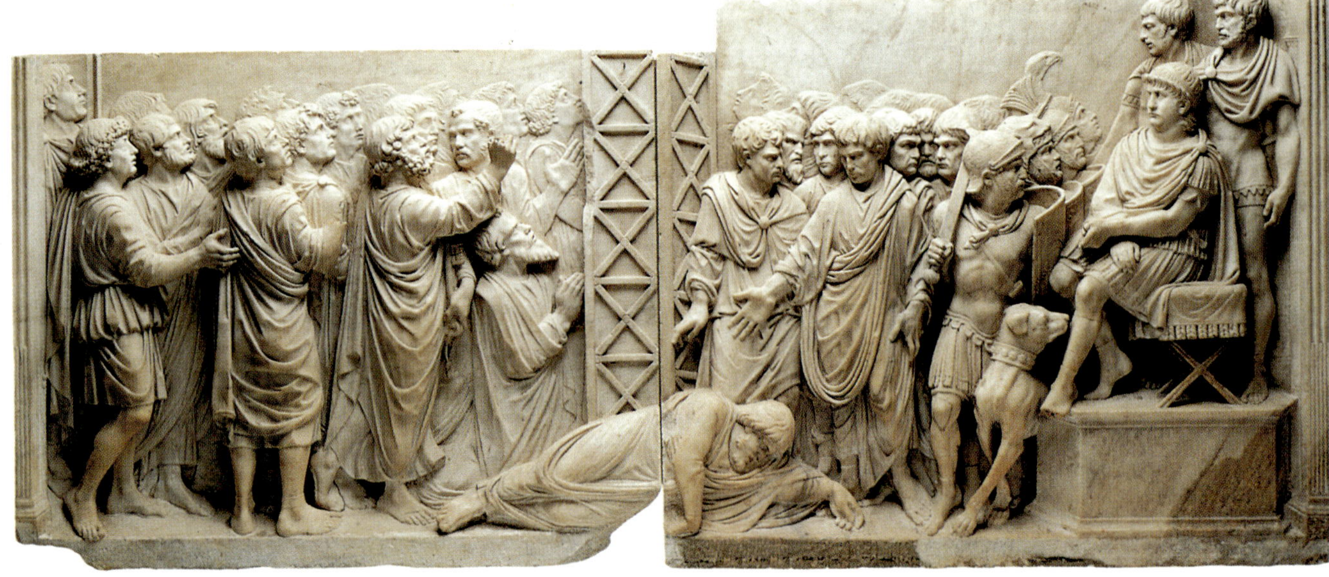

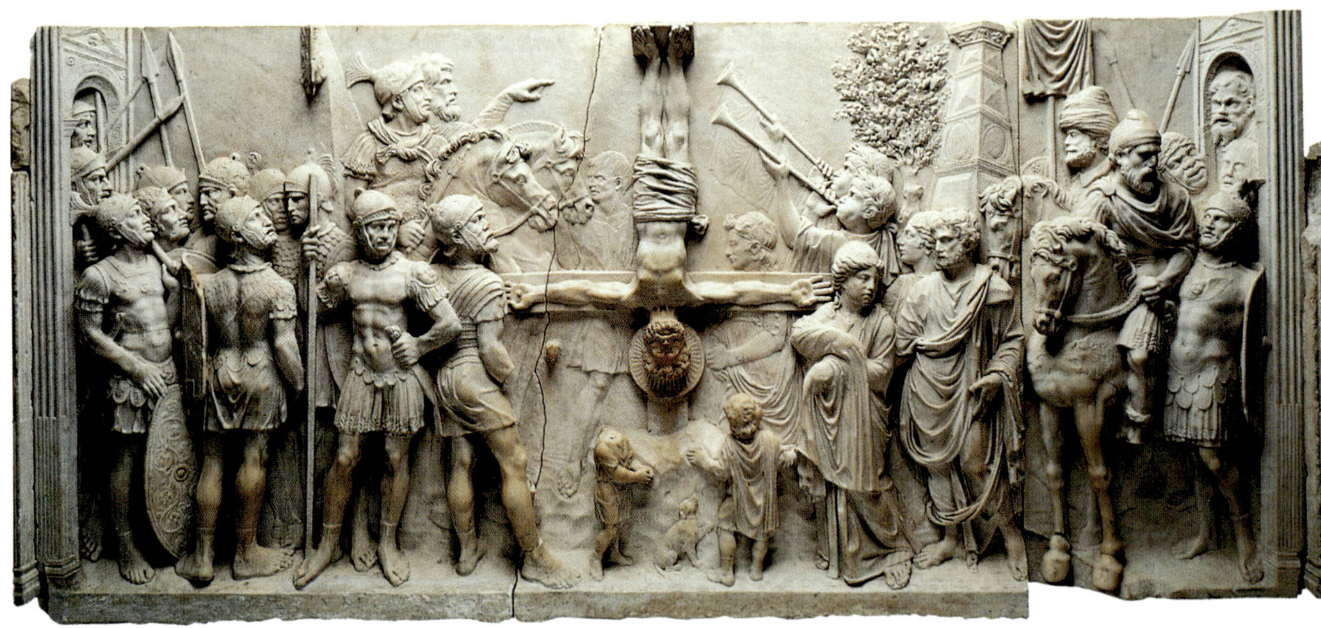

The rebirth of Rome

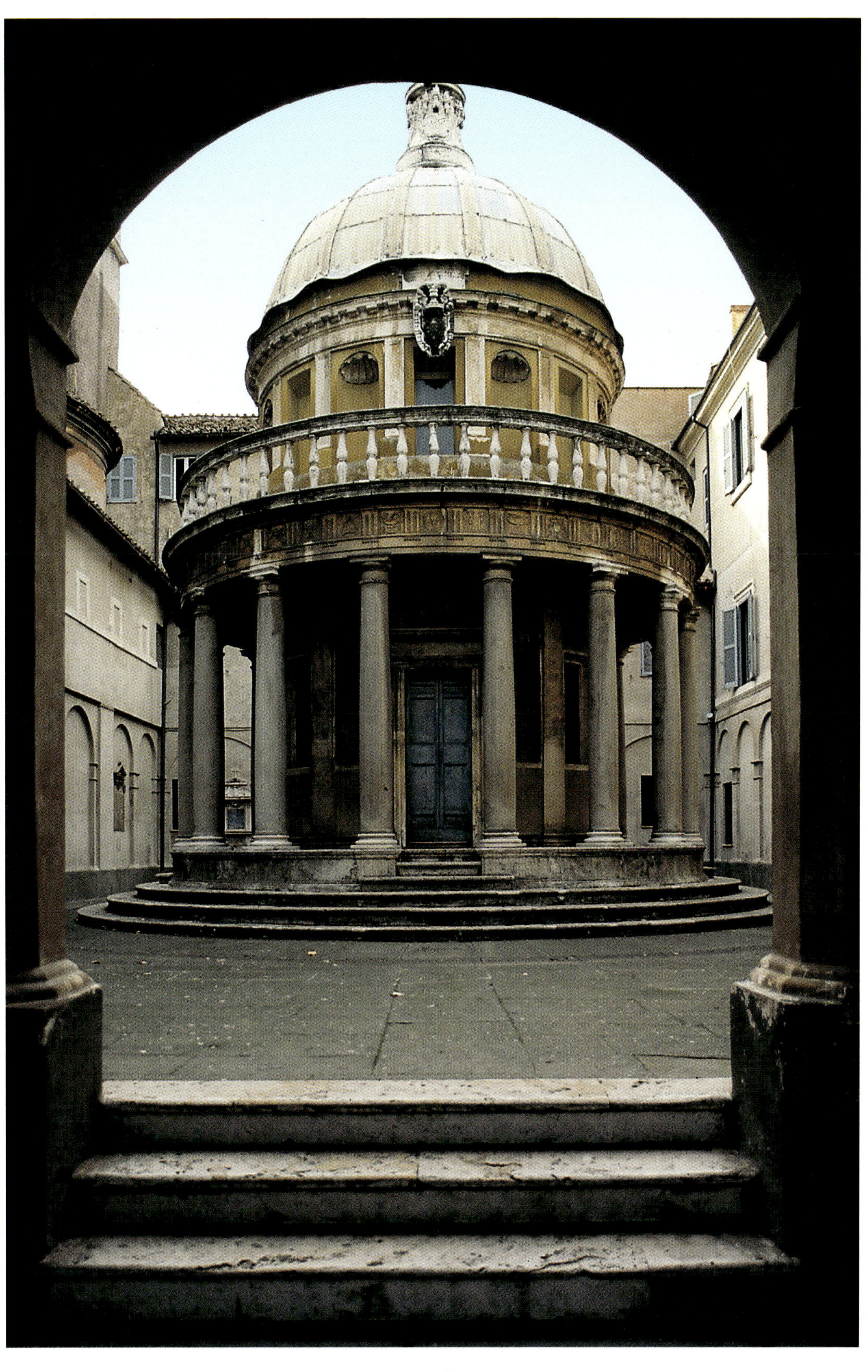

After two decades of intense activity in Lombardy, Bramante made a final departure from Milan for Rome, where Julius II made him general superintendent of the papal works. Located on the Janiculum, in a courtyard annexed to the church of San Pietro in Montorio, the little temple is one of the most precocious manifestations of the "modern" architecture. With a rigorous logic Bramante took elements from the lexicon of classical architecture and assembled them in a coherent way, making his building a true universal model, a paradigm for all sixteenth-century architecture. Inspired by the ancient theme of the circular temple with annular colonnade, the structure is based on the repetition of the geometry of the circle: it is in fact cylindrical, surrounded by sixteen Doric columns and, above the balustrade, is topped by a drum, also cylindrical, topped in turn by a dome. The motif of the circle is repeated even in the concentric steps that form the base.

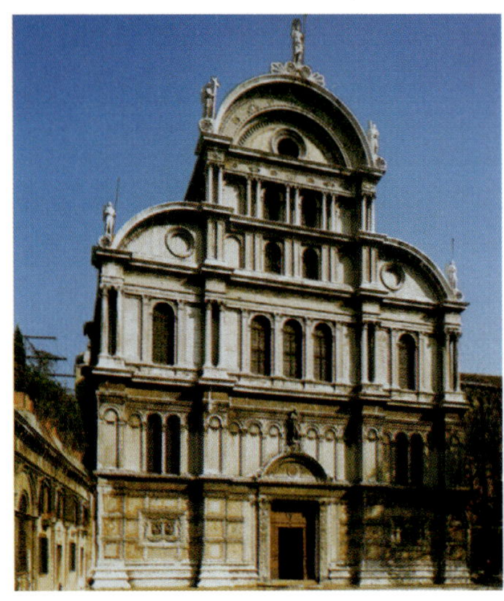

enice is the "unique city" par excellence. Its uniqueness has not gone unnoticed, or unchallenged, and in accordance with the sad realities that attend success many other cities have made claims to being its equal, dubbing themselves the Venice of the North or the South, not to mention the entire South American country of Venezuela, the name of which means "Little Venice." For many centuries Venice itself shied away from its own identity, preferring to present itself as the heir to other great capital cities of the past. Following the Fourth Crusade (which ended in the sack of Constantinople by the Venetians, with many precious objects, including the four famous bronze horses atop the basilica of St. Mark, finding their way to the lagoon), Venice assumed the role and image of "new Byzantium," choosing patently Oriental architectonic styles as though to emphasize the city's geographical and commercial eastward orientation. During the Renaissance, most of all after the conquest of large and important pieces of Italian territory by foreigners, Venice presented itself as the "capital" of traditional Italian culture and politics. By way of a well thought out operation of image control, which involved the construction of monumental buildings in the classical style, Venice was hailed as the "new Rome." Only at

Adda River. Until 1509 Venice also controlled the territory of Romagna. Along the costal arc of the Adriatic (renamed the "Gulf of Venice") the holdings of Venice included nearly all the coast, from Friuli to Istria and Dalmatia, with the islands of the intricate archipelago. Commercial ports of call and fortified coastal cities dotted the boundaries of the "state on the sea," including the islands of the Aegean and the eastern Mediterranean, along with Crete and Cyprus, the latter donated to Venice by Queen Caterina Cornaro. Venice was now one of the leading powers of the Mediterranean and a model of political and commercial organization, but until the middle of the fifteenth century Venetian artistic culture remained tied to models from the Byzantine tradition (maintained in the mammoth mosaic workshop of St

Venice, springtime

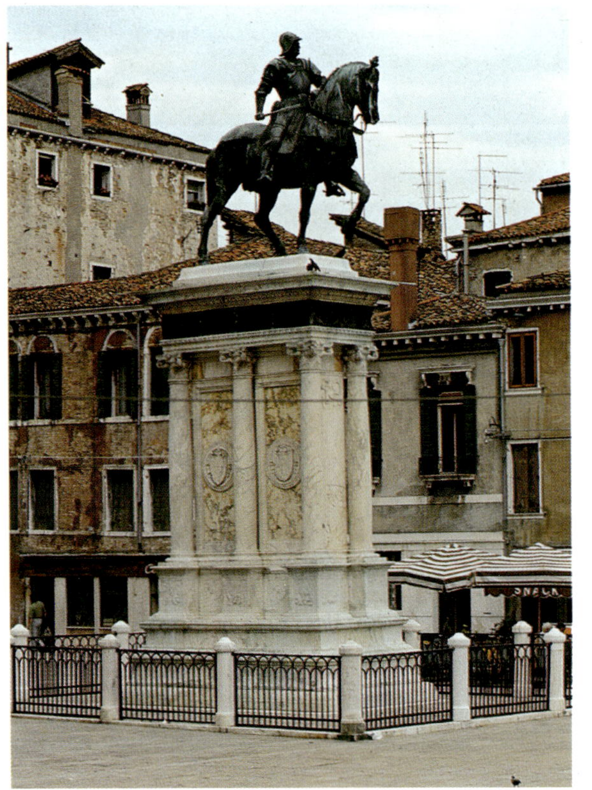

the end of the sixteenth century did Venice finally become aware of its own very special character—the first "tourist guide," published in 1571, was entitled *Venetia città nobilissima et singolare* ("Venice, most noble and singular city").

The winged lion, symbol of the evangelist Mark, patron of the city and unmistakable symbol of the Most Serene Republic of Venice, can still be seen atop columns, on walls, and over the doors to public buildings in many cities on the Adriatic and the eastern Mediterranean. It was in the thirteenth century that Venice's so-called empire began to take shape, and it reached the height of its territorial expansion in the fifteenth. Venice's "terra firma" holdings extended beyond the borders of today's Veneto region to include the Lombard provinces of Brescia and Bergamo, reaching all the way to the

Mark's) together with the fantastic and elaborate forms of the International Gothic, applied most of all to profane art and architecture, as in the city's characteristic image, the late Gothic palaces along the canals, with loggias and windows with unmistakable pointed arches.

After 1450, however, the presence in the city of Donatello and the growth of humanism in nearby Padua stimulated Venetian artists and patrons alike toward a major redirection. A key figure in this was Giovanni Bellini, for many years the official painter of the Venetian Republic. Son of an artist and son-in-law of Andrea Mantegna, Giovanni Bellini found a highly effective expressive solution in a combination of monumental composition and atmospheric light, thereby achieving results with great natural breadth. From Giovanni Bellini on, the Venetian painting school was characterized by the use of atmospheric effects, with light, colors, and landscape details fused, limiting the use of the sharp line in outlines. A further stimulus came with the 1475 arrival in Venice of Antonello da Messina, bearer of highly up-to-date information on Flemish painting and on Piero della Francesca. Thanks to the example of Antonello, the Venetian painters abandoned the old-fashioned polyptych layout and turned instead to large altarpieces arranged following Renaissance architectonic perspectives, as in the San Giobbe Altarpiece by Giovanni Bellini (1487). At the same time, Venetian architecture was also going through a period of profound change, thanks to Mauro Codussi (or Coducci) and a group of architect-sculptors of Lombard origin. Churches and palaces were designed as simple, linear architectonic structures, with prevalence given rounded lines (windows, pediments, loggias) and the abundant use of ornamental inserts with disks of colored stone, panels of streaked marble, and fine sculptures. In the period of a few decades the urban image of Venice changed profoundly, thanks to large-scale construction activity that extended to cover almost all the buildable

to a saint, and people associated through public-assistance services). These *scuole* promoted the development of Venetian painting through requests for cycles of large canvases on narrative subjects, usually scenes from the life of the saints to which the *scuole* were dedicated. Among the leading specialists in this specific genre were Vittore Carpaccio and Gentile Bellini, Giovanni's brother. The cycle of paintings on canvas replaced frescoes, which were poorly suited for use in Venice because of the damp climate and the salt air. This style, full of narrative details, with scenes set in sumptuous architectonic settings, was secondary to that of large sacred paintings and the nascent production aimed at private collectors. On the threshold of the year 1500, thanks to Giovanni Bellini and

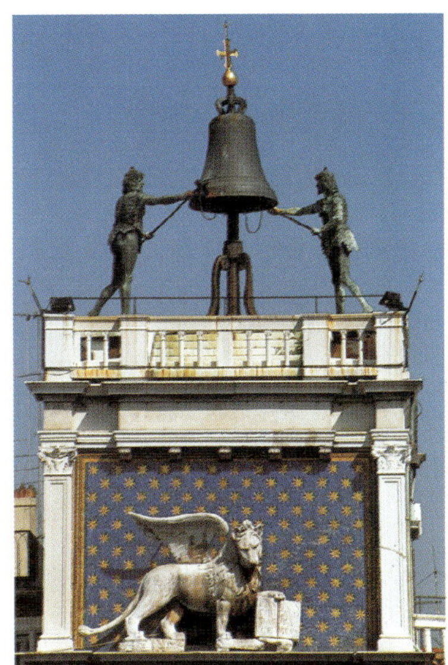

Clock tower, detail with the two statues and the lion of St. Mark, 1496–99; Venice

of the Renaissance

areas of the city. A significant role was played by the *scuole*, associations formed by groups of citizens (workers in the same art or craft, members of foreign communities resident in Venice, religious organizations dedicated

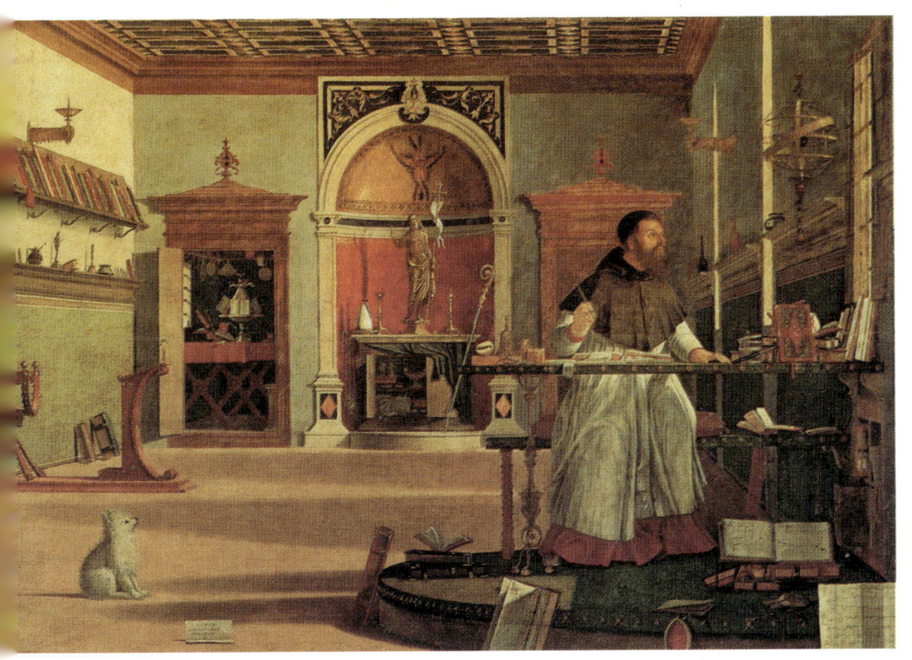

such promising young artists as Giorgione, Titian, and Sebastiano del Piombo, Venetian painting brought the stress on tonality to full realization, the painting technique based on the gradual application of paint in overlapping layers, with a soft effect of blending colors in natural atmosphere.

Giorgione was no mythical or fictional character, but an intellectual artist operating in an environment predisposed to codified languages and exotic symbols, with the exaltation of nature. Giorgione, in all probability a student of Giovanni Bellini, was able to quickly absorb the stimuli provided by the "foreigners" who passed through Venice, such as Leonardo da Vinci and Albrecht Dürer. His constant distinguishing trait is the use of a warm, embracing natural atmosphere. The outlines of the figures and the landscape appear slightly shaded, not defined with a clear graphic line, while the prevailing sense is of successive gradations of light and color. All of Giorgione's production belongs to the first decade of the sixteenth century. In 1510 the plague suddenly cut short his already brief career. Some works were left unfinished to be completed by his two most gifted students, Titian and Sebastiano del Piombo, and for Venetian painting the most "classical" and glorious phase of the Renaissance was about to begin.

Vittore Carpaccio, *Vision of St. Augustine*, 1502–04; Scuola di San Giorgio degli Schiavoni, Venice

The unmistakable face assumed by Venice between the end of the fifteenth and the beginning of the sixteenth century was the fruit of the local interpretation of the architectonic lines of the early Renaissance. Gothic pointed arches and intertwined decorations gave way to a repertory of classical inspiration with a quiet rhythm, although it was no less ornate than the Gothic, and the quality of the materials was equally precious. The taste for lacy decoration was replaced by broad curvilinear motifs in the pediments that close the façades of churches, in the loggias and arched windows of palaces. The colors of the buildings were given much care, the chromatic effect entrusted to elegant intarsias and marble panels. Introduced by Mauro Codussi and by Pietro Lombardo and his sons, this was the predominant building style on the Venetian lagoon until 1520. The harmonious decoration of the façade of the Scuola di San Marco, a powerful public-assistance institution, was the work of Pietro Lombardo, while the lunette of the cornice was by Mauro Codussi, who worked on the building around 1490, during the final phases of the project.

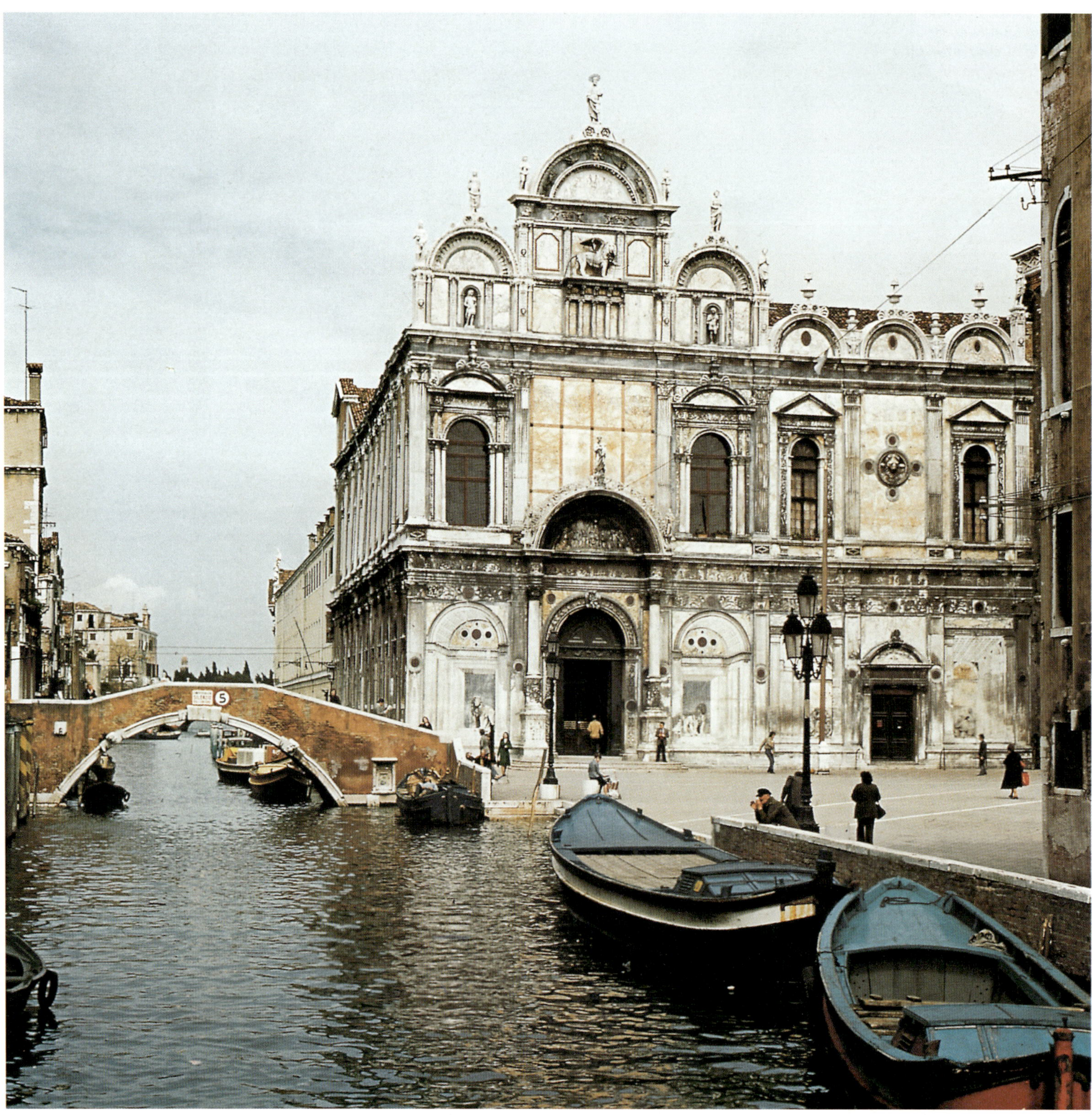

Venice, springtime of the Renaissance

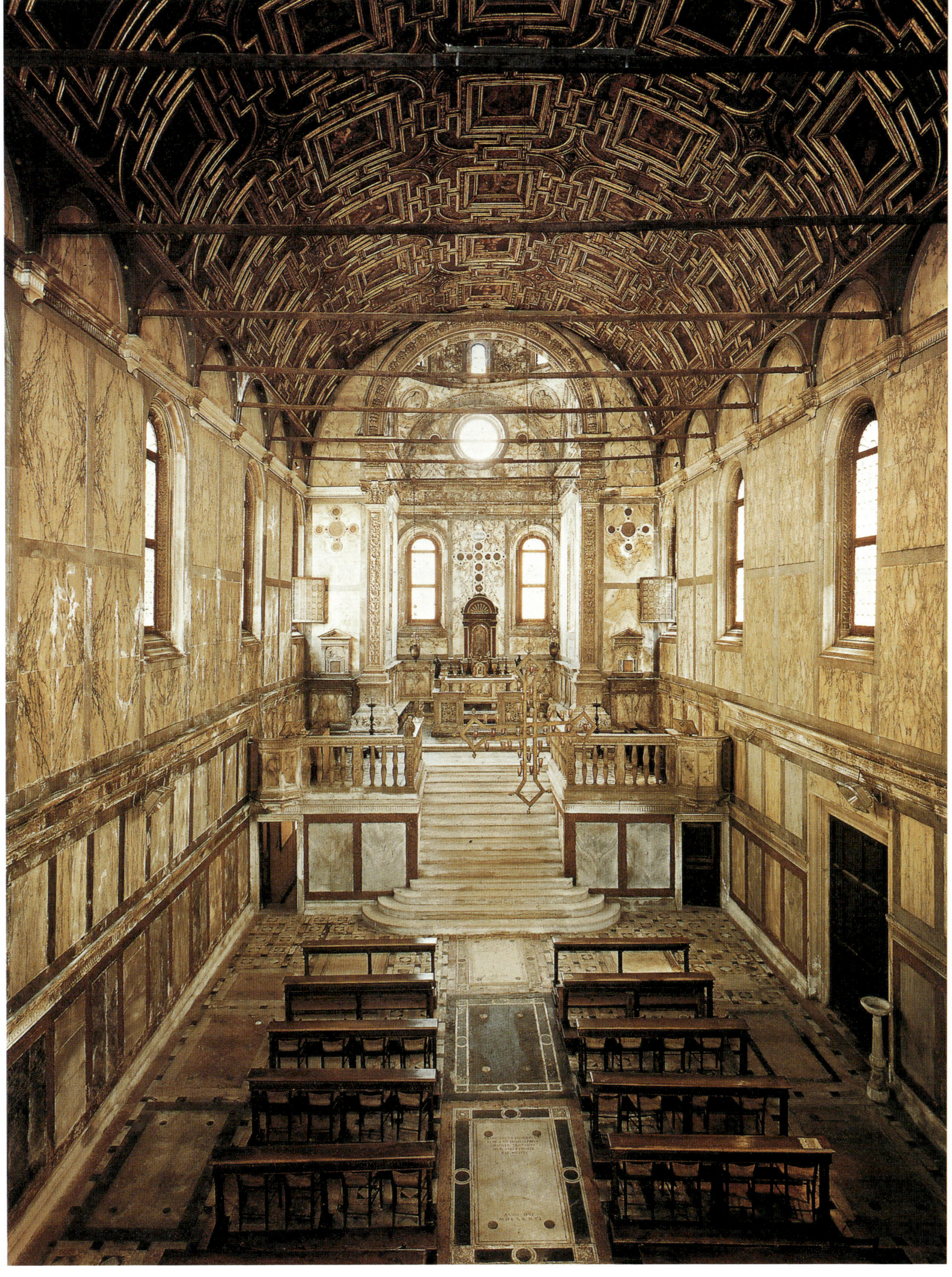

Venice, springtime of the Renaissance

One of the peculiar phenomena of Venetian culture are the *scuole*—associations of citizens for public devotion and the protection of trade guilds or communities of foreigners in Venice—which often commissioned for their buildings narrative cycles of paintings, usually with episodes of the life of the patron saint of the *scuola*. Canvas was the usual support for such works, being more suitable than the frescoes used elsewhere in Italy because better able to resist the damp of the lagoon. Among the leading specialists in this painting genre was Gentile Bellini, who showed particular skill at presenting the city in great detail and with topographical precision. Perhaps no other city in the world can boast such a rich and detailed figurative documentation from the same date, and not only in terms of the city's urban layout but also in its economic, social, and civil aspects.

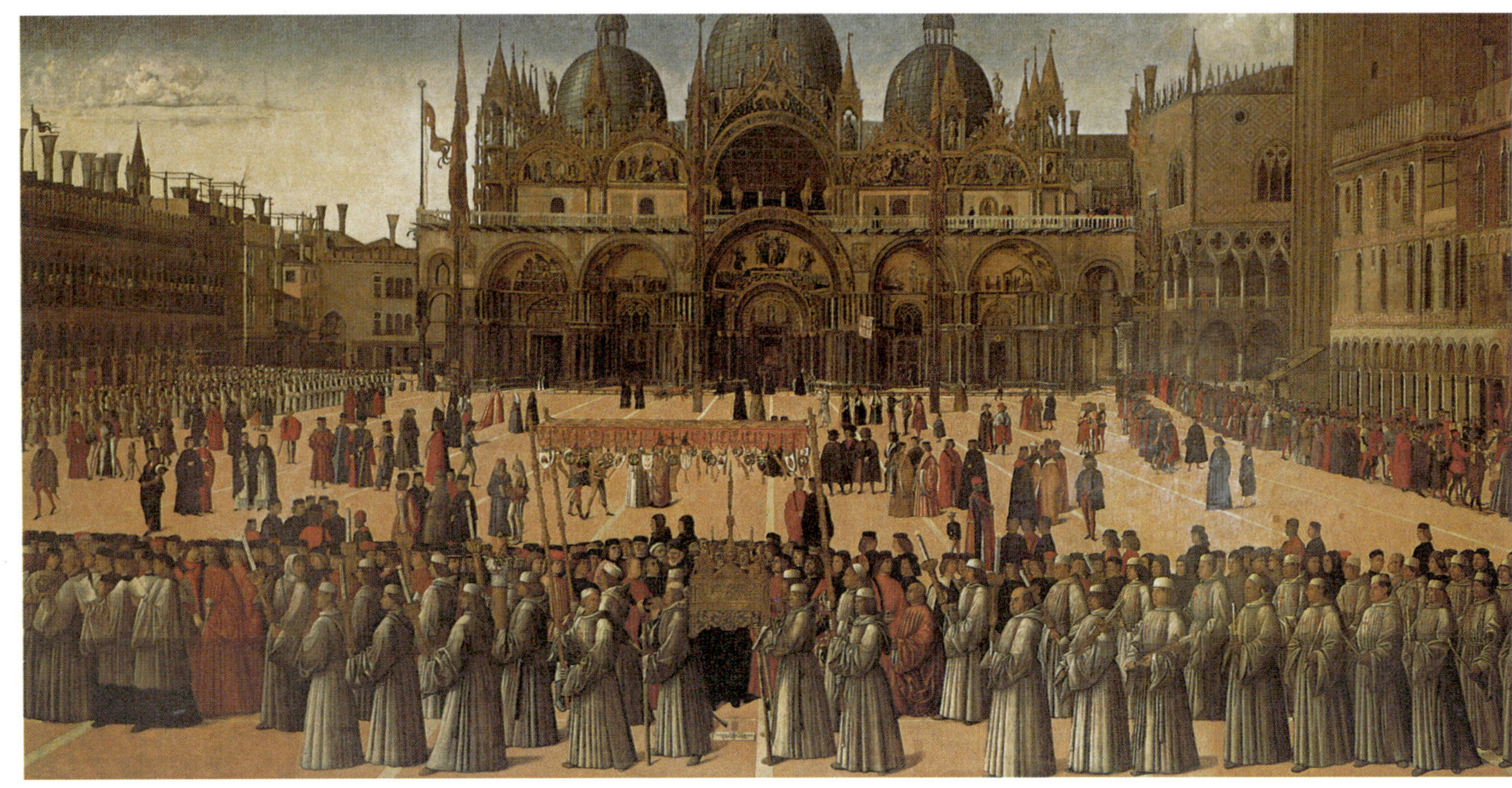

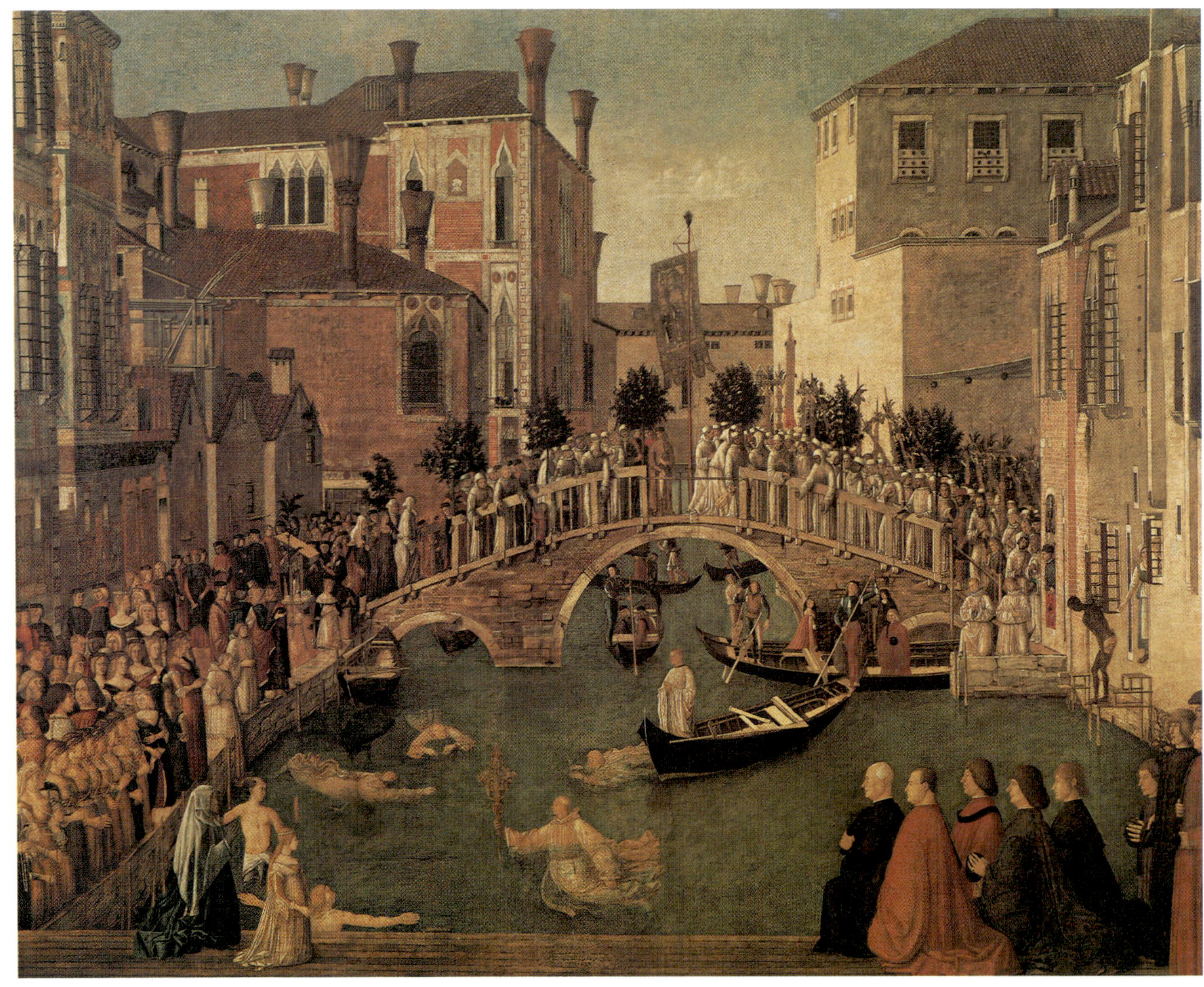

Venice, springtime of the Renaissance

■ VITTORE CARPACCIO
Miracle of the Relic of the True Cross at Rialto
1494, oil on canvas,
365 x 389 cm
Gallerie dell'Accademia,
Venice

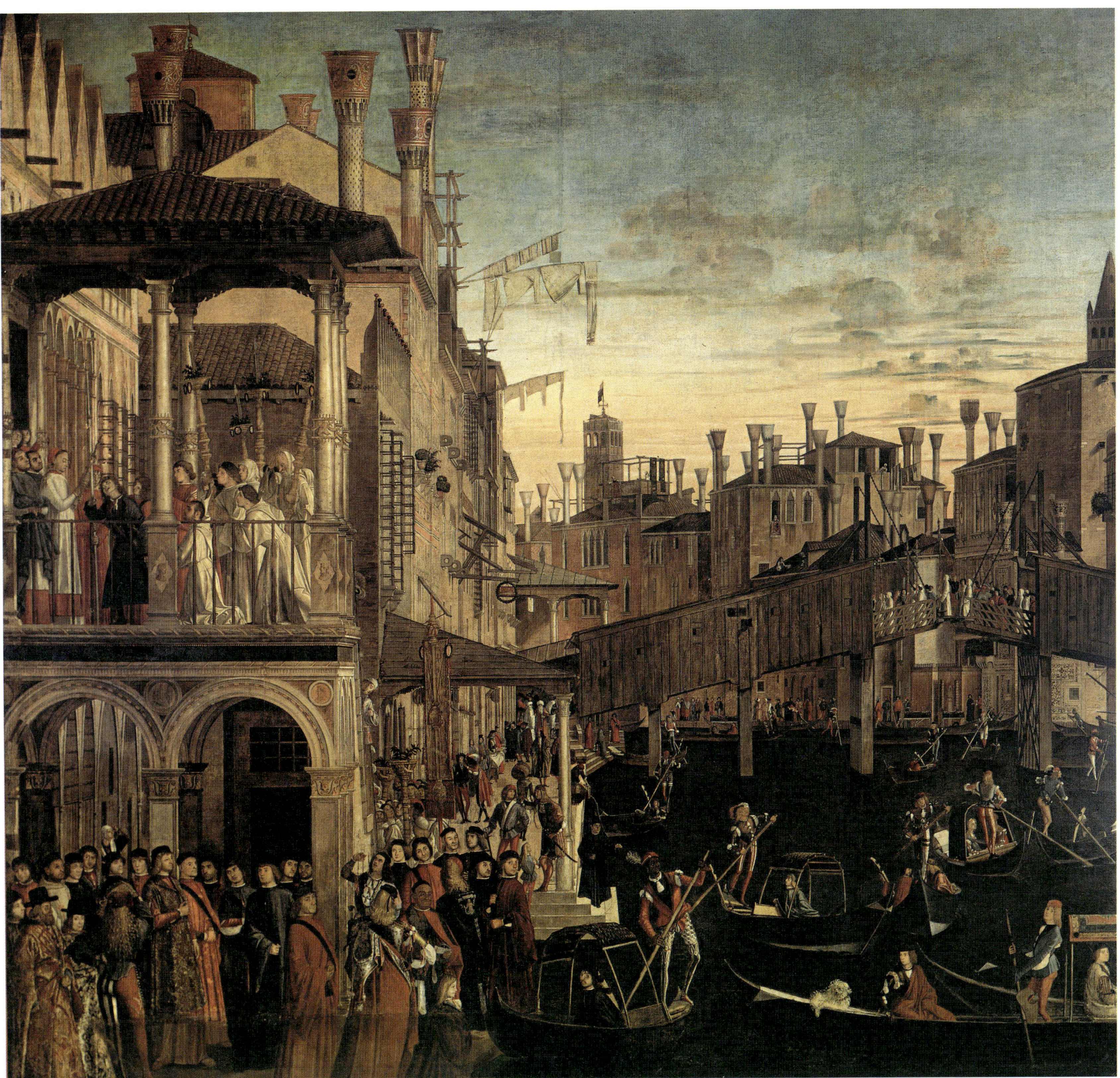

This is another work from within the cycle of canvases made for the Scuola Grande di San Giovanni Evangelista. This painting presents the healing of a possessed man by being shown the reliquary of the cross, once preserved in the *scuola* itself. The miracle takes place in an isolated corner of the painting, confined to the roof terrace at the far left. Most of the painting is dedicated to a presentation of the urban setting, in this case the area near the Rialto bridge, at that time still made of wood. The painting is thus an historical document of exceptional value as well as a magnificent work of art. One by one all the palaces in the area are perfectly identifiable in their appearance at the end of the fifteenth century. A crowd of figures, among whom the figure of a Moorish gondolier stands out, gives the scene an air of lively festivity.

Venice, springtime of the Renaissance

This spectacular altar-
piece is in an excellent
state of preservation,
including the original
frame with small scenes
dedicated to saints;
the scene of the cyma,
the panel painting that
once topped the work,
an *Embalming of Christ*,
is today in the Pina-
coteca Vaticana. This
work marked Giovanni
Bellini's debut in the
creation of enormous
altarpieces laid out fol-
lowing the dictates of
perspective and propor-
tion. The main scene
has a stately grandios-
ity, thanks to its
impeccable geometric
arrangement (visible in
the design of the floor
and the structure of
the throne). The land-
scape visible behind
the group of figures is
a real setting, a stretch
of hilly coastline
between the Marches
and Romagna, with the
Rocca, or fortress, of
Gradara. Aside from the
work's qualities, the
geographic proximity
of Pesaro to Urbino
suggests comparison
with the works of Piero
della Francesca.

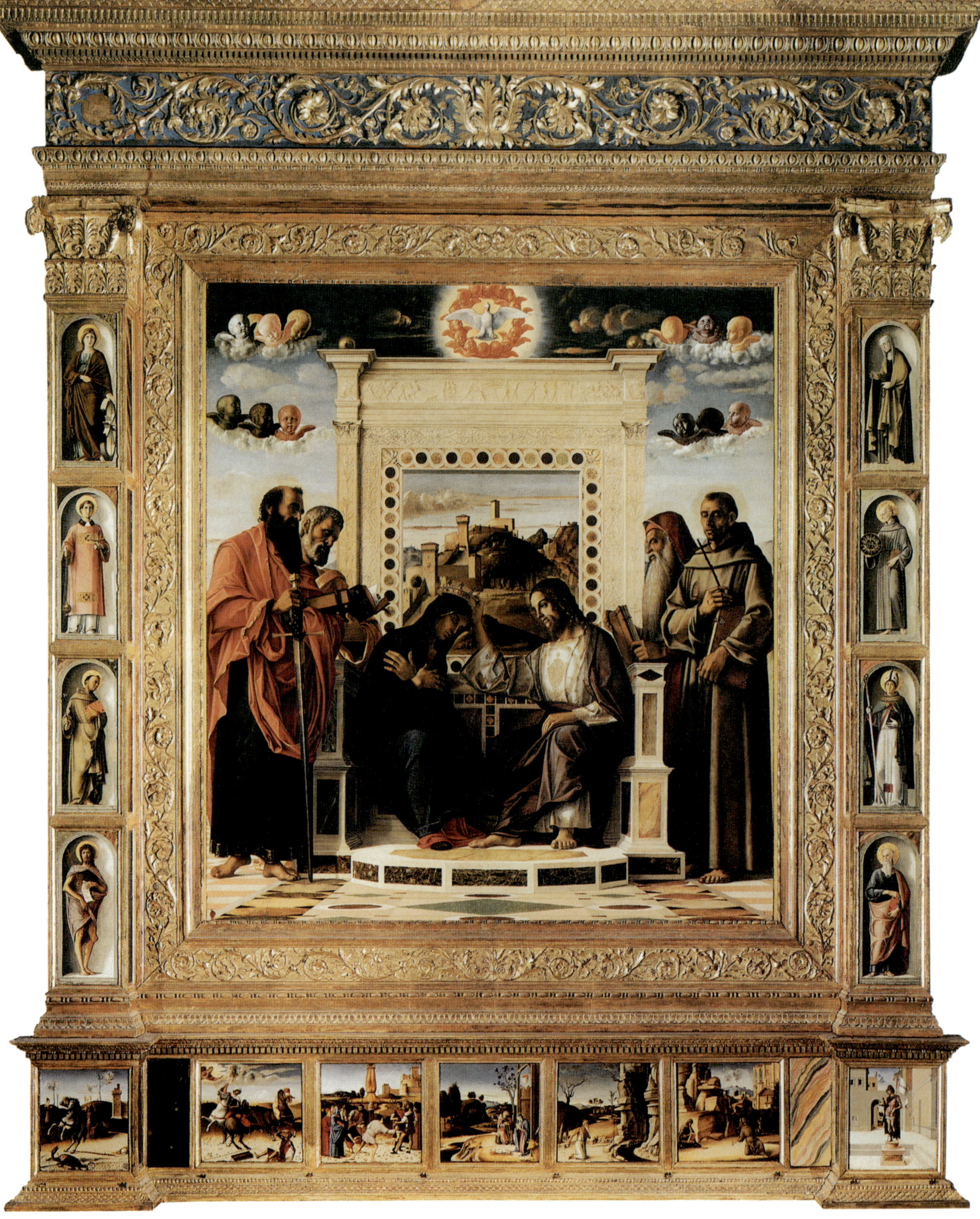

Venice, springtime of the Renaissance

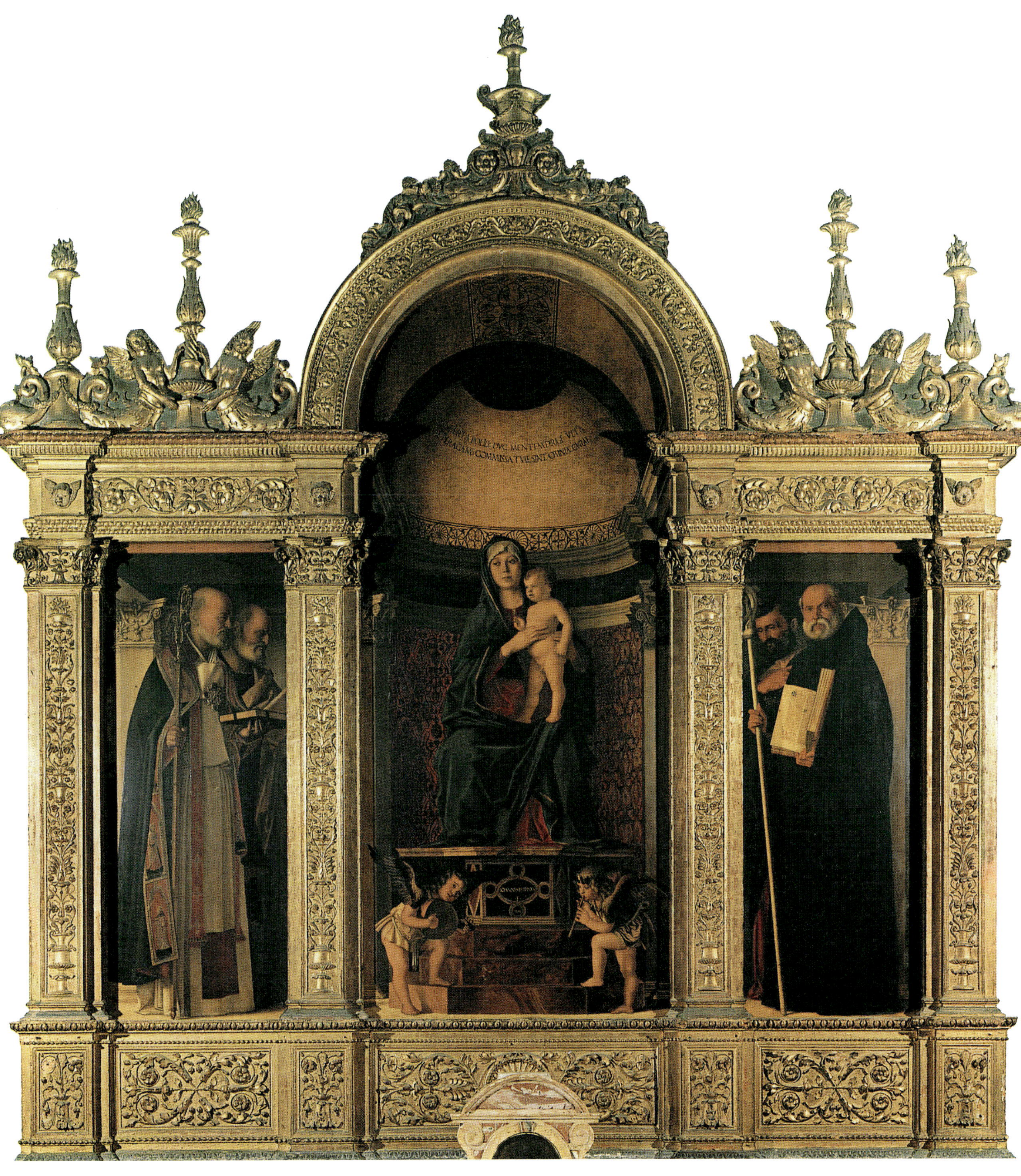

GIOVANNI BELLINI
Frari Triptych
1488, oil on panel,
central panel 184 x
79 cm, side panels
115 x 46 cm
Santa Maria Gloriosa
dei Frari,
Venice

Splendidly preserved,
this triptych is still
in its original frame,
designed by Giovanni
Bellini himself: the
actual architectonic
elements of the wooden
structure perfectly
match the painted
elements in the back-
ground of the triptych.
Bellini here repeats his
personal interpretation
of the art of Piero della
Francesca, distinguished
by a poetic definition
of moving light. The
perfectly symmetrical
arrangement of the
figures and the archi-
tecture is "warmed" by
the diffuse luminosity
and by the soft glow of
the apse, with its simu-
lated background of a
golden mosaic.

Venice, springtime of the Renaissance

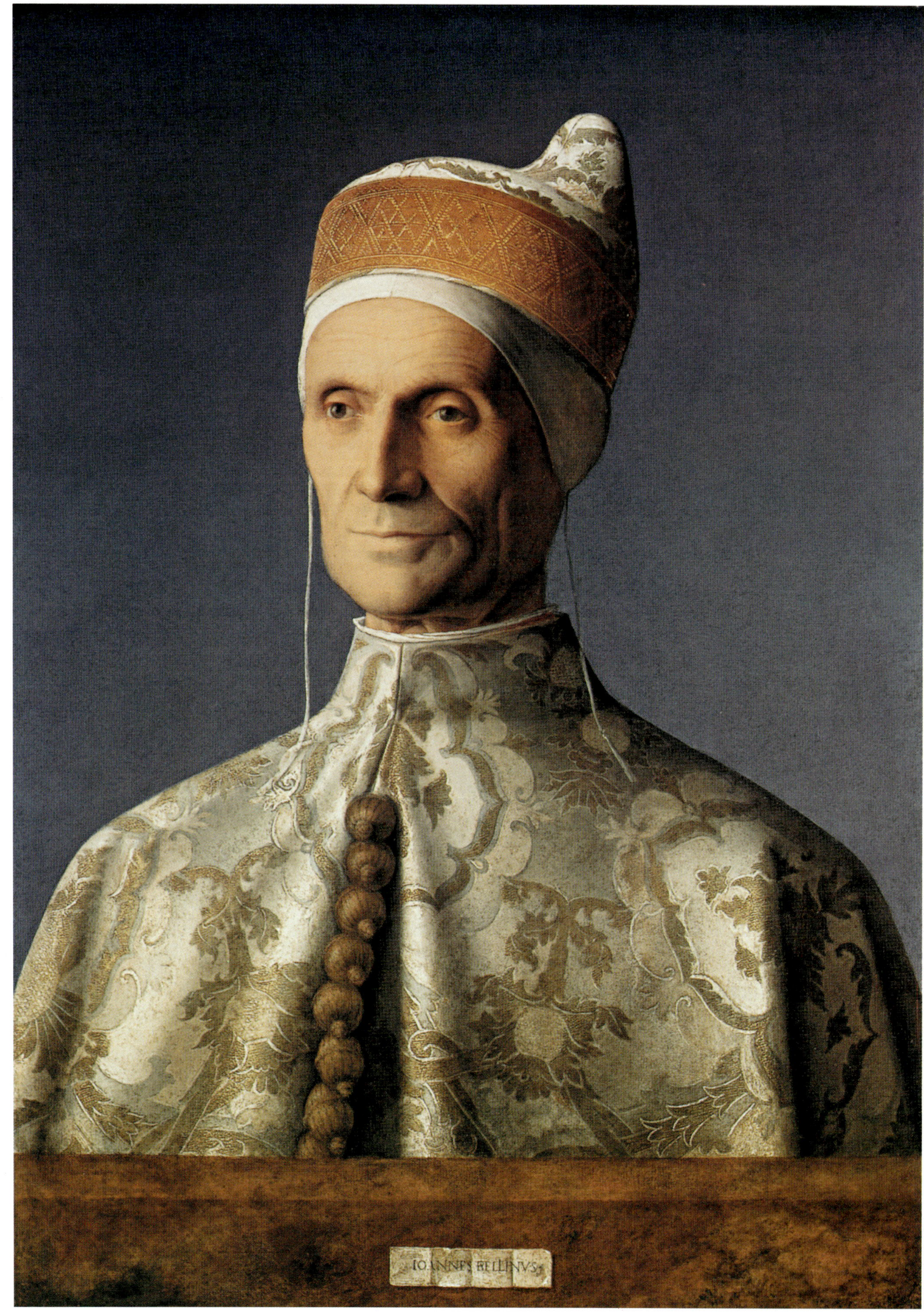

Venice, springtime of the Renaissance

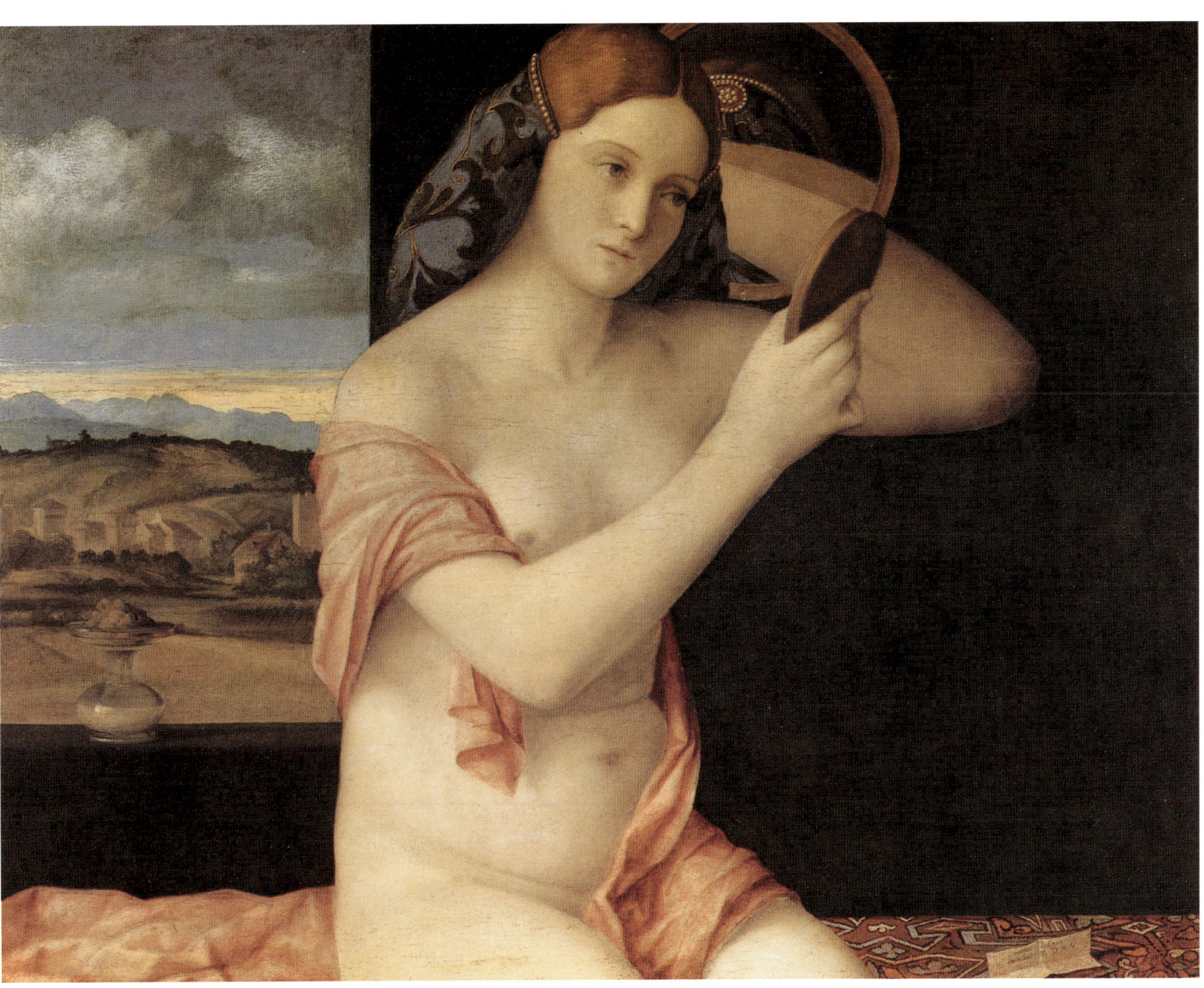

Venice, springtime of the Renaissance

JACOPO DE'BARBARI
Perspective
Map of Venice
1500, engraving
Museo Correr, Venice

Without doubt, the century of splendor, the most dazzling epoch in the history of Venetian art, was the sixteenth. All the world looked upon Venice, called "the most triumphant city in the universe," with an admiration that often grew into envy. Strengthened by the perfection of its commercial, administrative, and political organizations, Venice succeeded in not being overcome by the great and dramatic events then troubling all of Europe. In 1500 the painter and engraver Jacopo de' Barbi (up to date in terms of the evolution of techniques of printing thanks to visits to Germany) published this spectacular bird's-eye view of the city. The urban image, densely packed, full of solid ranks of buildings out of which emerge the masses of larger landmarks, has remained substantially intact to today.

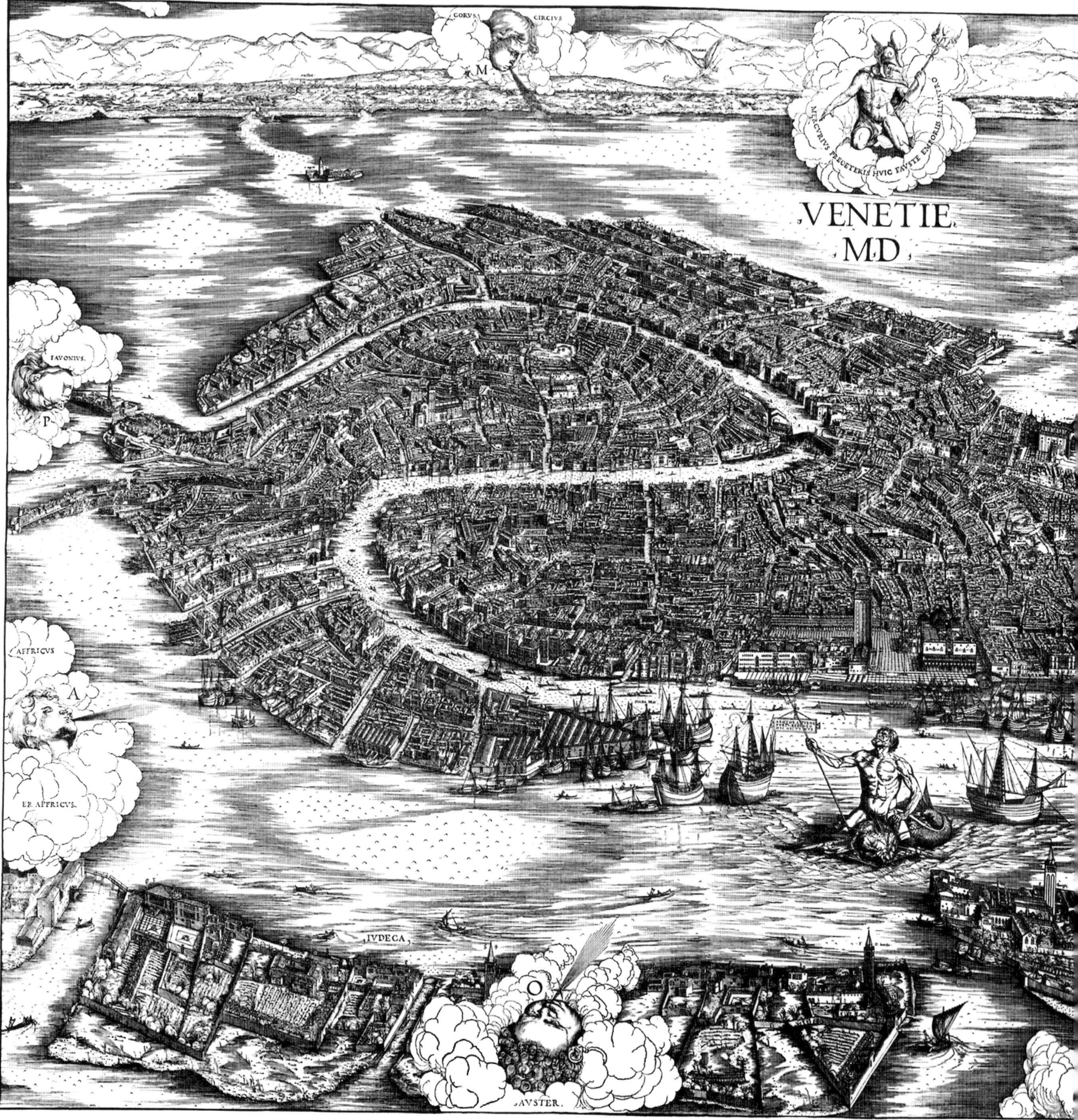

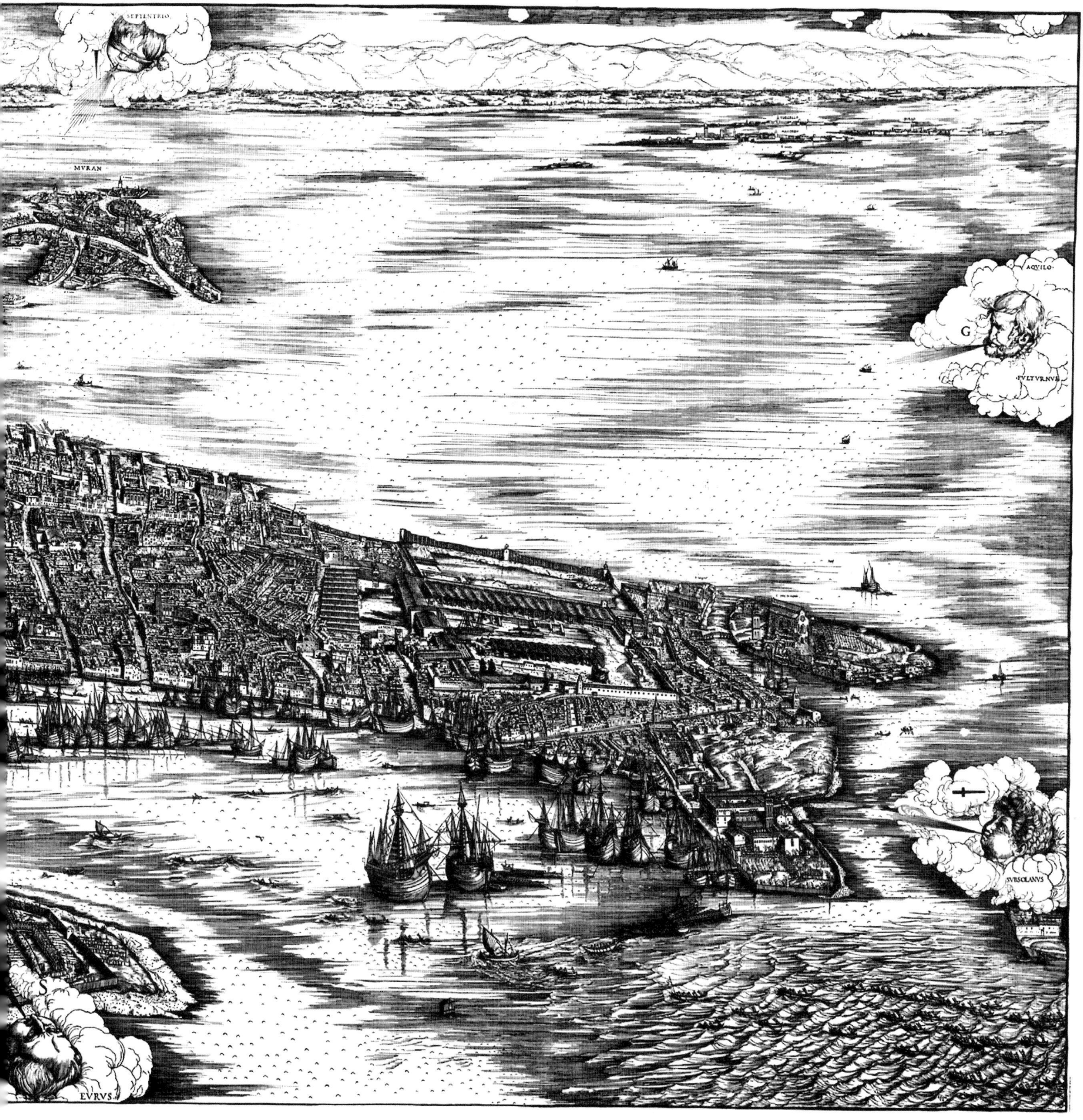

Venice, springtime of the Renaissance

Originally made for the small Scuola di Sant'Orsola, all of the paintings in the cycle are today located in a special hall of the Gallerie dell'Accademia. With subtle ambiguity, Carpaccio maintains a fine balance between reality and fantasy; alternating outdoor scenes with images of interiors, he creates a fabulous Venice that is the setting for events in the story of two betrothed youths, the princess Ursula and the prince who hopes to marry her. The spectacular image of an official chancellery (above right) is made with great attention to the use of light, giving it an almost Flemish feel. Below right, the ambassadors' galley docks, to the left, at a wharf that closely resembles that of the Arsenal of Venice. The motions of the messengers, and their ritual kneeling, are observed (or not observed) by a crowd of onlookers. The empty space near the lower middle of the painting was created when a doorway was opened in the wall, probably around 1647.

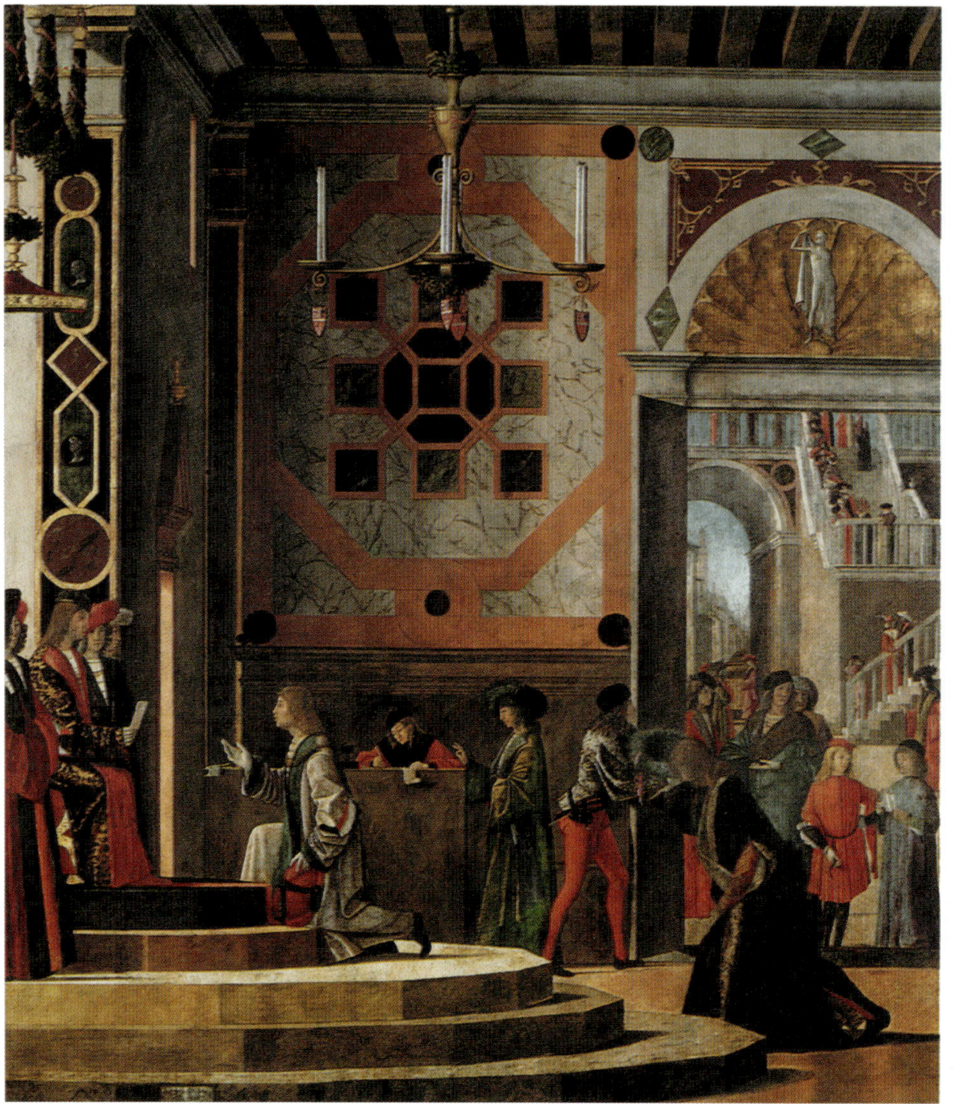

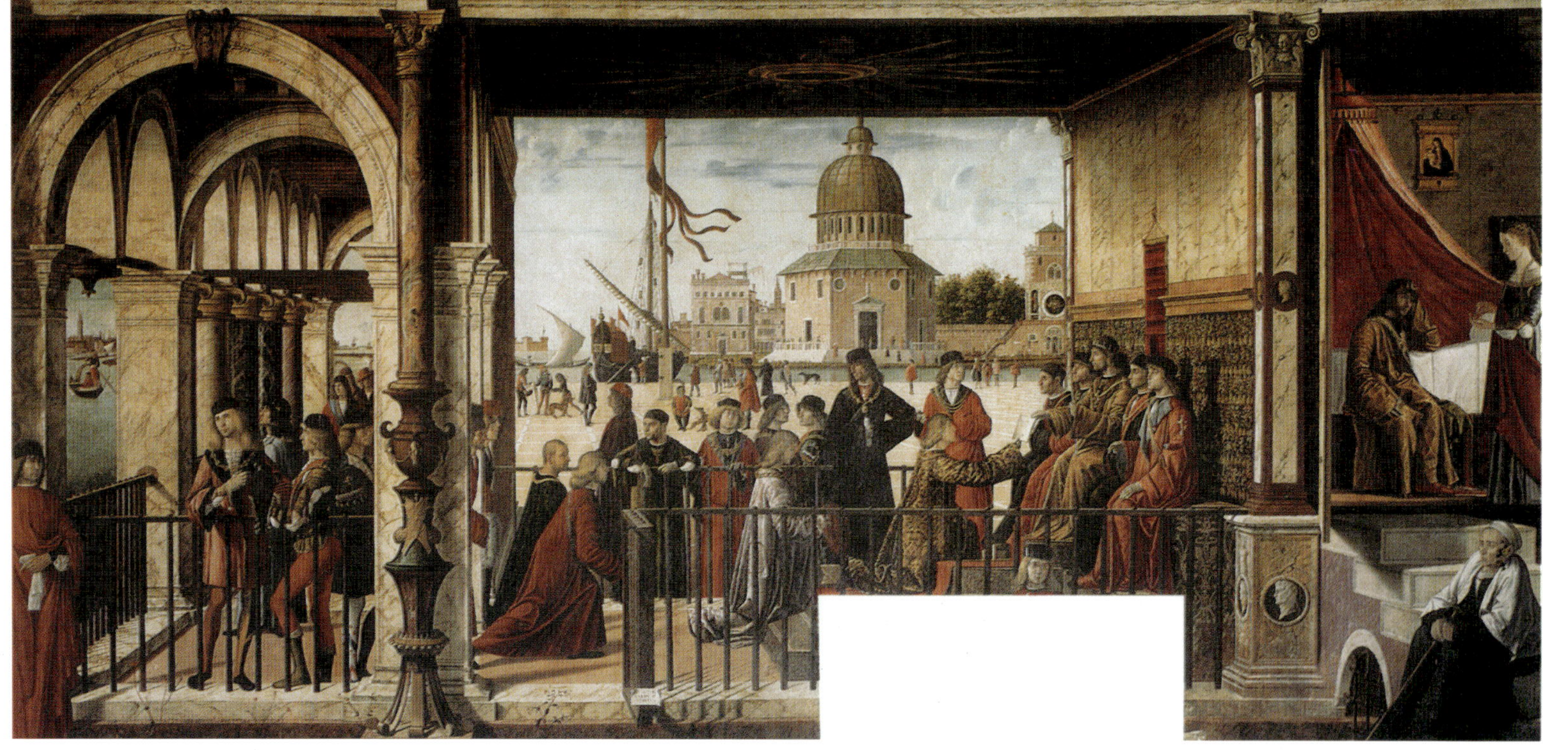

Venice, springtime of the Renaissance

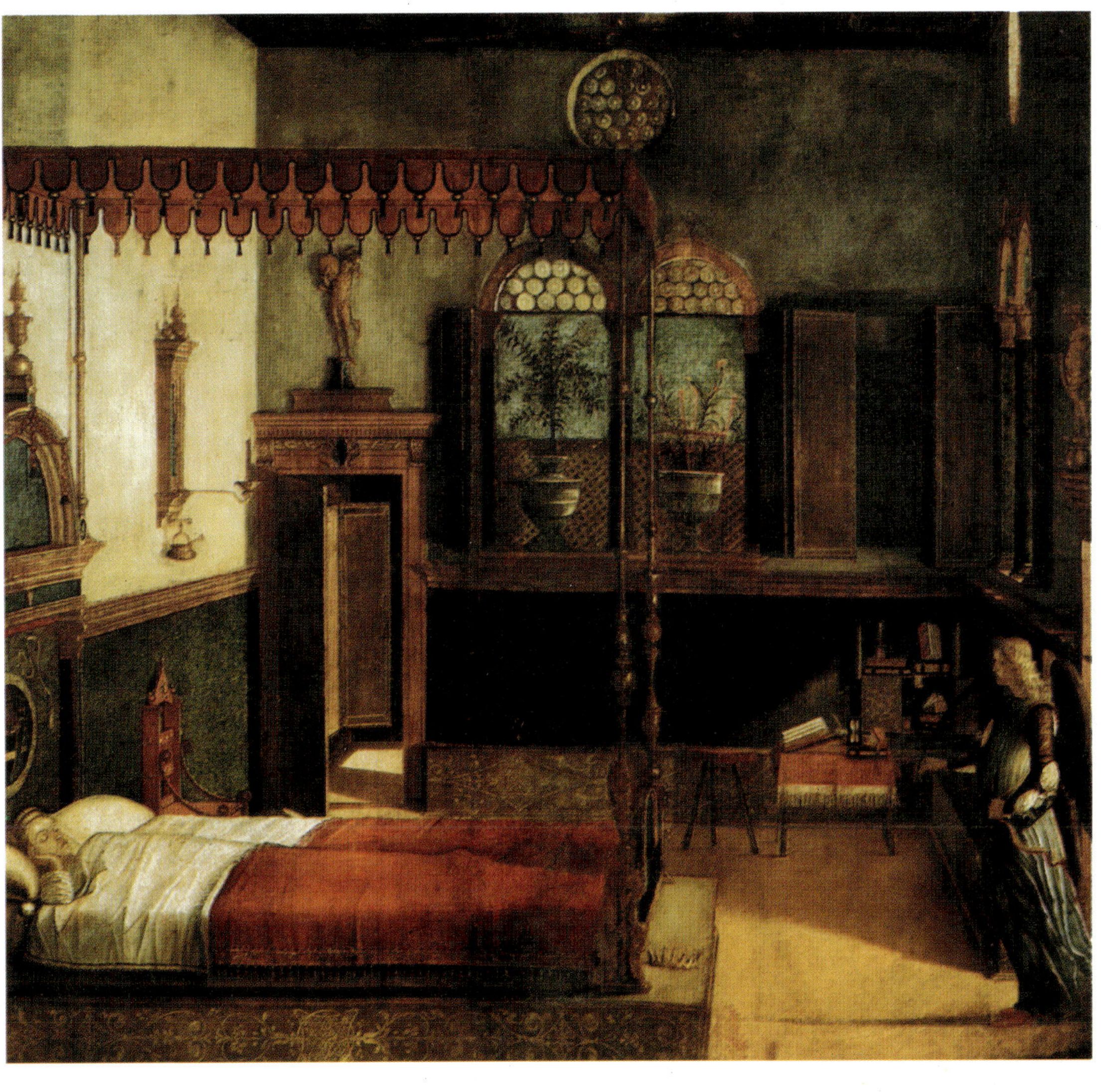

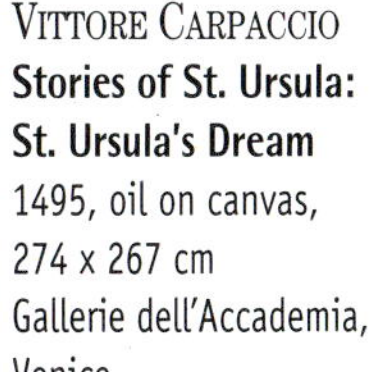

VITTORE CARPACCIO
Stories of St. Ursula:
St. Ursula's Dream
1495, oil on canvas,
274 x 267 cm
Gallerie dell'Accademia,
Venice

This famous painting
demonstrates Carpac-
cio's ability to move
from courtly episodes
to scenes of touching
intimacy. Bearing the
palm of the martyr, the
angel silently enters
the room in which
Ursula sleeps. Legible
on the pillow is the
word Infantia, as
though to emphasize
the innocence of the
princess's sleep. The
objects and furnishings
are meticulously ren-
dered, with delicate
care given even the
smallest, and together
they compose the most
faithful reproduction
of the interior of a
well-to-do Venetian
home of the late
fifteenth century.

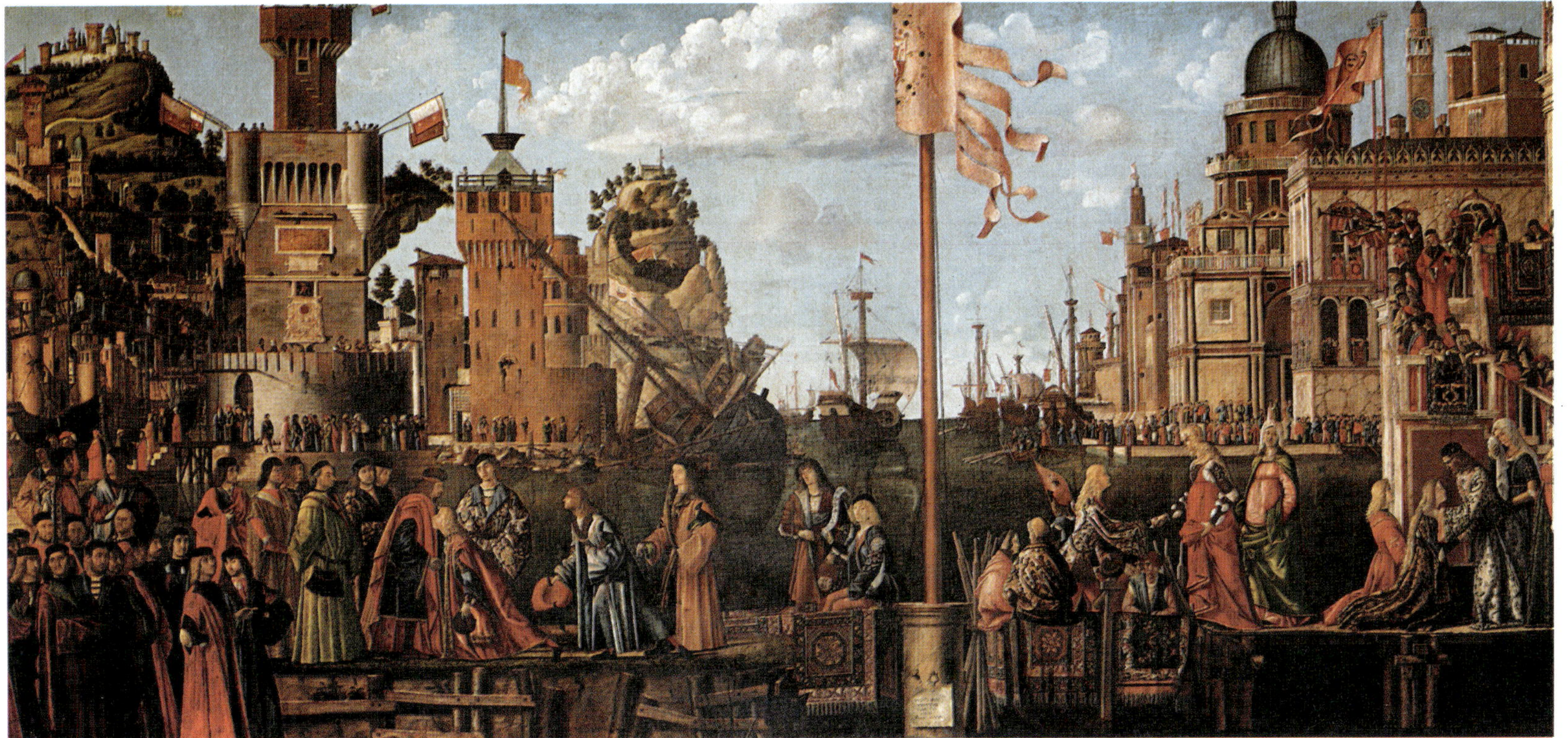

VITTORE CARPACCIO
Stories of St. Ursula:
The Meeting of the
Betrothed Couple
and The Departure
of the Pilgrims
1495, oil on canvas,
280 x 611 cm
Gallerie dell'Accademia

This, the largest of the
canvases in the cycle, is
divided in half by the
standard at the center.
With the slow move-
ments of a gondola
moving along a canal,
Carpaccio's painting
followed its special
route over the decades,
moving into the
labyrinth of the soul.
It is not clear whether
his images come from
reality or arise from
some golden dream of
a Venice-Atlantis.

Venice, springtime of the Renaissance

Destined for the Scuola Grande di San Marco in Venice, this is perhaps the highest point in the genre of narrative canvases. Begun by Gentile Bellini in 1504, it was completed after his death (1506) by his brother, Giovanni, who simplified the background wall of buildings and made it more monumental, thus favoring the orientation of the light and emphasizing the figure of St. Mark, who, from the top of a bridge-shaped podium, preaches to a crowd of people, at the center of which stands out a group of Arabs veiled in white. Despite the many exotic details, the superbly scenographic setting irresistibly recalls the background of St. Mark's Square, while the noble composure of the Oriental dignitaries is almost an involuntary admission of the power of the Ottomans, whom Gentile Bellini had met during a diplomatic journey to Constantinople.

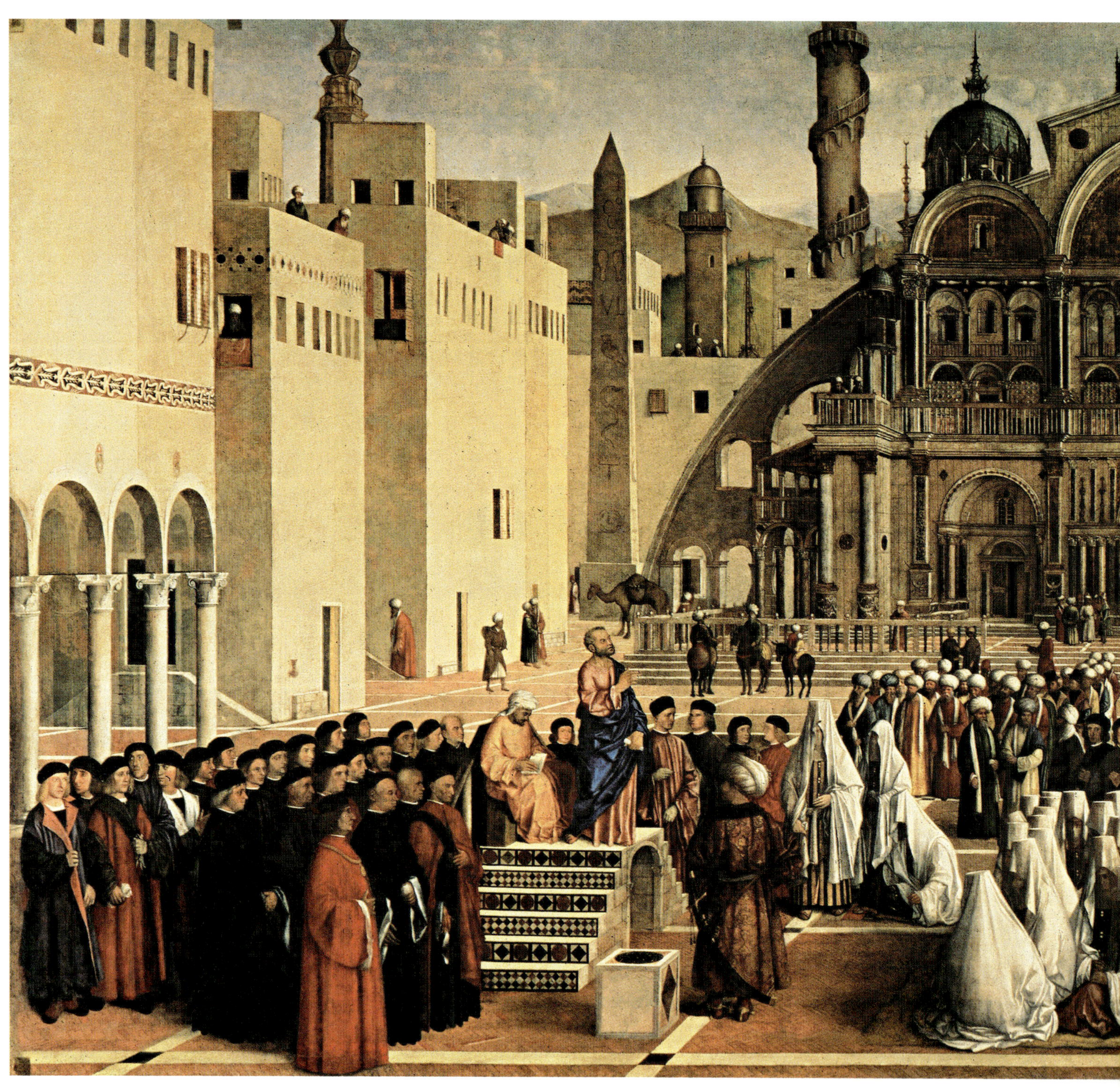

Venice, springtime of the Renaissance

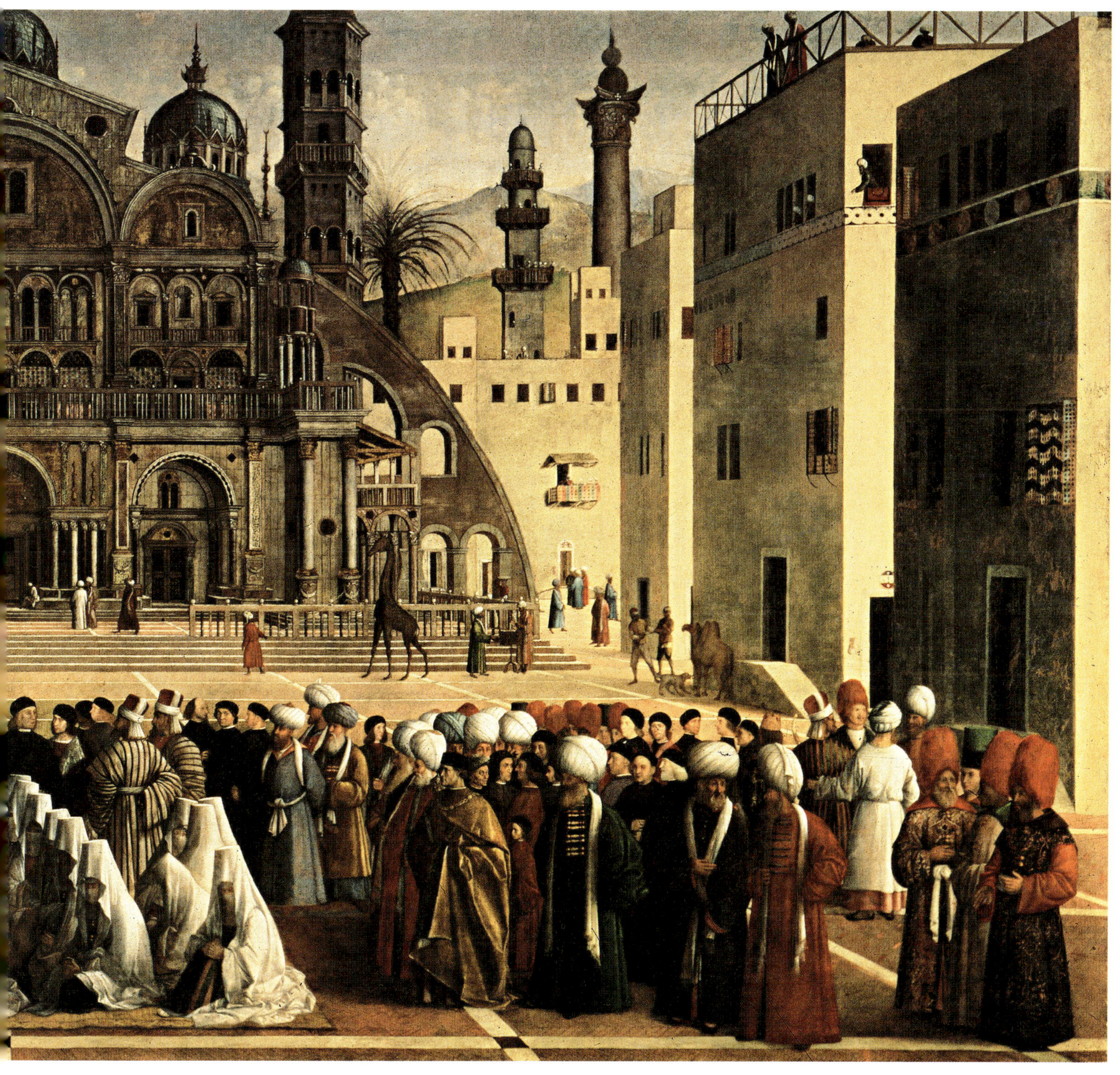

Venice, springtime of the Renaissance

This is among the few paintings by Giorgione documented by sources. A great many efforts have been made to determine its subject; the most recent theories see the two figures as Adam and Eve, cast out of Eden. Beyond such hypotheses, however, the unquestioned protagonist of the painting is the landscape. In the architecture in the background and the lush vegetation, Giorgione abandoned the minute definition of details that he had applied in his early paintings to achieve a richer and more modulated chromatic impasto. The branches of the trees, with their overlaid light and dark tones, are a particularly fine detail for an appreciation of the patient, fine luministic weaving that gives the painting its extraordinary and novel evocative powers.

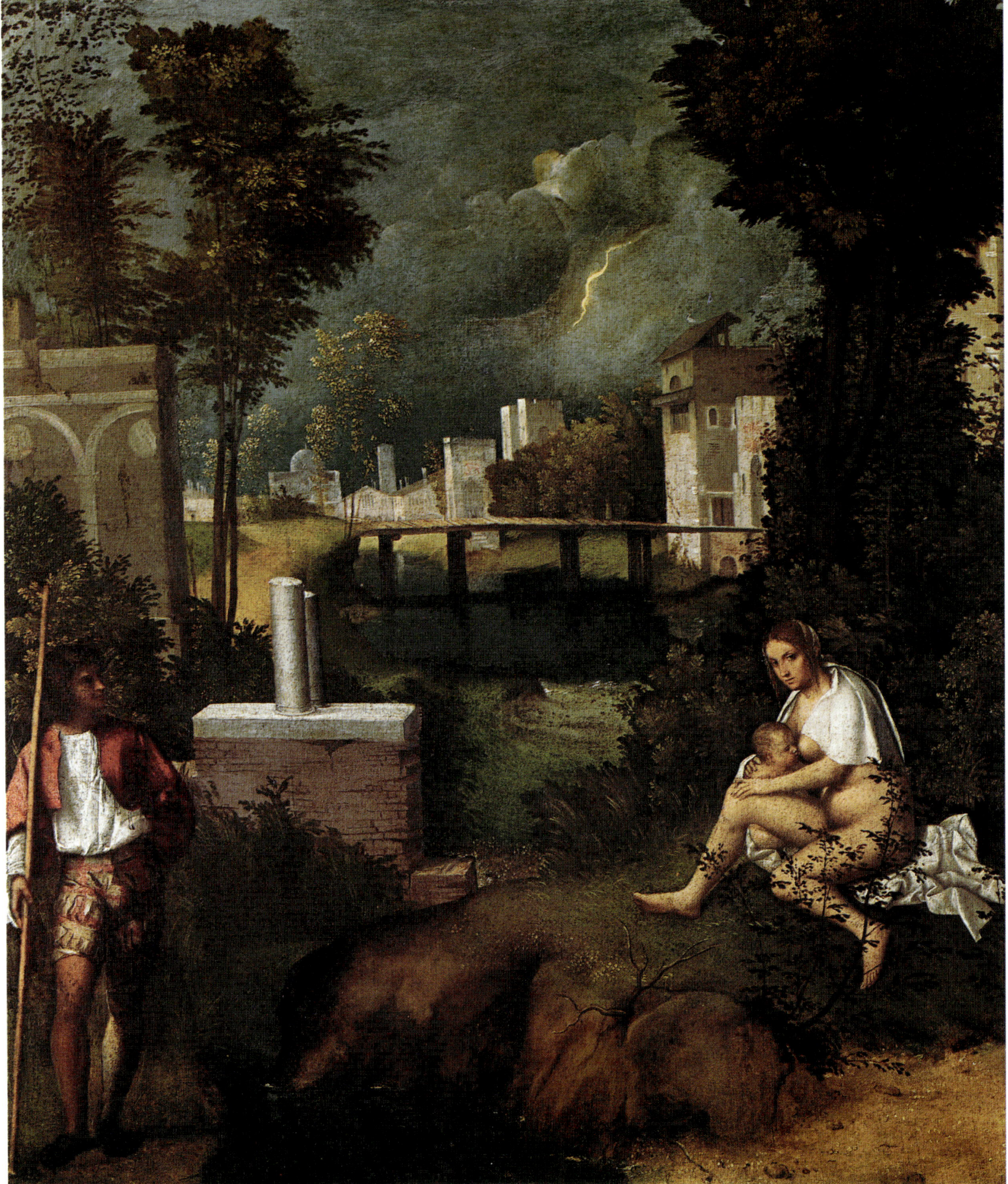

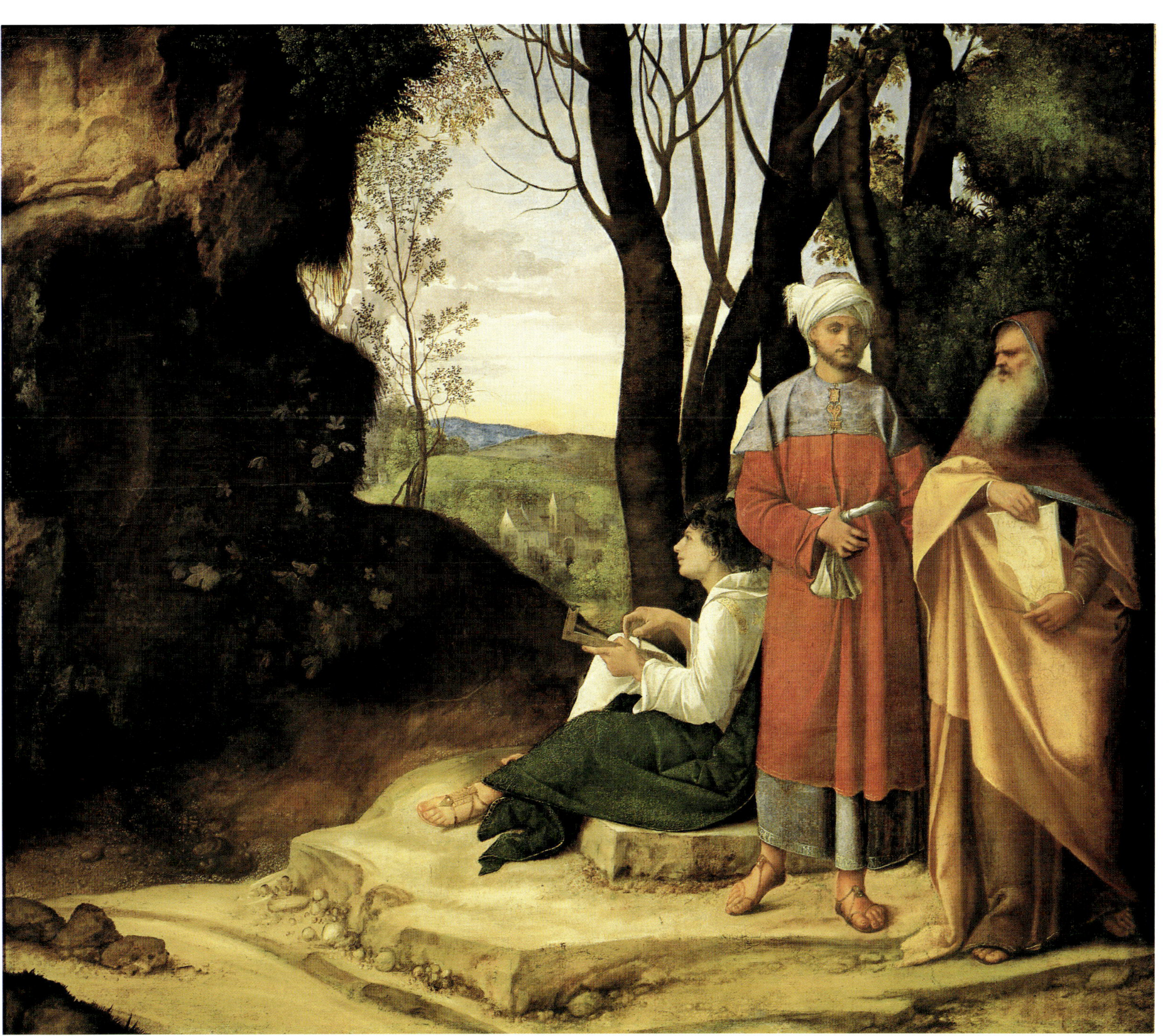

One of the most fascinating paintings of the Renaissance, this work presents three figures (sometimes interpreted as an allegory of the "three ages of man") on the edge of a wood. The three men differ in terms of age, dress, and national type. They are probably the Three Magi, having witnessed the first appearance of the star. The youngest stares at the landscape, as though awaiting a revelation, while the other two are in conversation. Looked at in this way, the painting becomes a profound reflection on the theme of the voyage: not only a dangerous adventure but also a meditation on the goal and on the signs that will help reach it. The Magi can thus be taken as symbolic of the three stages in the interior voyage undertaken by every human over the several ages of life. The work reveals a strong allegorical content but has no sense of being didactic thanks to the great peace that pervades the scenery and the quiet beauty of the light and colors, magisterially rendered by a painting style based on almost imperceptible shadings of tones.

Venice, springtime of the Renaissance

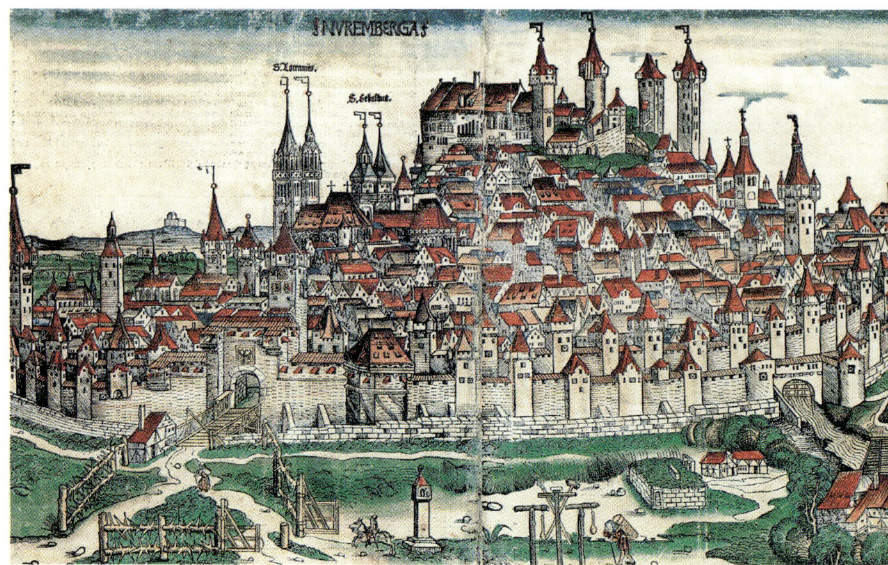

Hartmann Schedel, *Nuremberg,* woodcut from the *World Chronicle,* 1493; Nuremberg

ntil the beginning of the sixteenth century, the nations of Europe were still immersed in a fully Gothic universe. The International style, as elaborate in its forms as in the materials used, had successfully spread across all of Europe, with majestic structures and fanciful decorations that were substantially similar to the Mudéjar style of Spain and the Manueline of Portugal, up to the daring experimental solutions of the architect Benedikt Ried in the area of central Europe, between Prague and Budapest. The first decades of the sixteenth century were a busy and stimulating period for Europe: between the discovery of the New World (1492) and the beginning of the Protestant Reformation (1520) the Old World was going through a delicate period of redefinition, not only political and economic but also cultural. The concepts of Italian humanism were beginning to make themselves felt, being assimilated and reworked nation by nation as they spread. Most of all to the north of the Alps, the first decades of the sixteenth century constituted the time of a short Renaissance in which the last echoes of the refined Gothic confronted and blended with the new forms and the new ideals. During the first thirty years of the century this cultural activity was concentrated in several areas. The first of these was the Tyrol, where Emperor Maximilian I had a small but ambitious court. Learned, elegant, between the painting and the poetry of the time, intensely inspired by nature. The court poet Conrad Celtis, for example, sang of the landscape using expressions that could be taken as descriptions of the paintings of the masters of the Danubian school, the painting style of southern Germany distinguished by the passionate rendering of nature and the fascinating evocation of woods,

The age of Dürer

Albrecht Dürer, *Self-Portrait,* 1500, panel; Alte Pinakothek, Munich

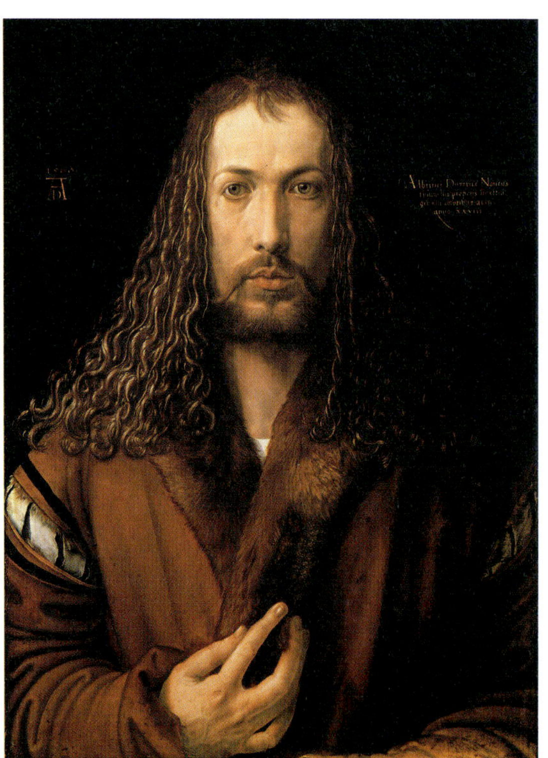

imbued with humanism, connected to Italy also by matrimonial ties (his second wife, Bianca Mary Sforza, was a niece of Ludovico il Moro), not at all intimidated by the growth of other European powers, Maximilian strove to give a new, courtly, and classical-style appearance to his Alpine empire, to which he added Gorizia and Trieste, tearing them away from Venice. In 1501 he founded the Collegium Poetarium et Mathematicorum and the University of Vienna—inviting many Italian intellectuals to come serve as teachers—and promoted innovative artistic undertakings, from a series of celebratory engravings to the cortège of colossal bronze statues made to flank his mausoleum. The best German artists of the period passed through the court at Innsbruck: Dürer, Altdorfer, Cranach, Burgkmair. There is an interesting consonance rocks, rivers. The death of the emperor, in 1519, marked the sudden decline of the Tyrol.

More enduring seemed to be the fortunes of the commercial cities, such as the Nuremberg of Dürer, the Regensburg of Altdorfer, the Augsburg of Burgkmair. These centers had solid economic foundations, specializing in the production of precious objects like goldwork, precision instruments, weapons, watches, mechanical automatons; they were also points of cultural diffusion thanks to the printing presses made possible by the introduction of movable type. Power was divided among a chessboard composed of these cities and the noble residences of the electors (such as that of Saxony, the patron of Cranach); there were also the duchies (such as that of William of Bavaria, patron of Altdorfer) and the seats of powerful cardinals (such as that of the archbishop of Mainz, Albert of Brandenburg, who invited Dürer and Grünewald to his lavish court).

There were also other important peripheral centers of culture, such as the cities of Alsace, distinguished by a brilliant pictorial tradition that passed from Schongauer to Grünewald and Baldung, and affluent Basel, where the Holbein dynasty of artists was active. The passage from the mentality of skilled artisans, as during the close of the Gothic, to a concept of the artist as "intellectual" interpreter of his times, in keeping with the Italian model that was becoming widespread throughout Europe, was perfectly synthesized in the activity of Albrecht Dürer (1471–1528). Dürer, who was born in Nuremberg and spent most of his life there, was the most important Renaissance artist from the northern side of the Alps. His powerful and varied pictorial production summarizes and elaborates various stimuli (from the German tradition to Flemish influences, but most of all the attentive study of Venetian art), achieving a supreme balance among impeccable graphics, a dazzling display of color, a brilliant sense of space and landscape, and the close characterization of figures. Always in the midst of every historical debate, friend to artists, thinkers, and sovereigns, a leading figure of his time, Dürer is a personage of inexhaustible fascination. Having finished his apprenticeship in Nuremberg at nineteen he set off on a series of study trips (to Basel, Strasbourg, Vienna, and Venice), enlarging his figurative culture such that it assumed a European perspective. At a time when German

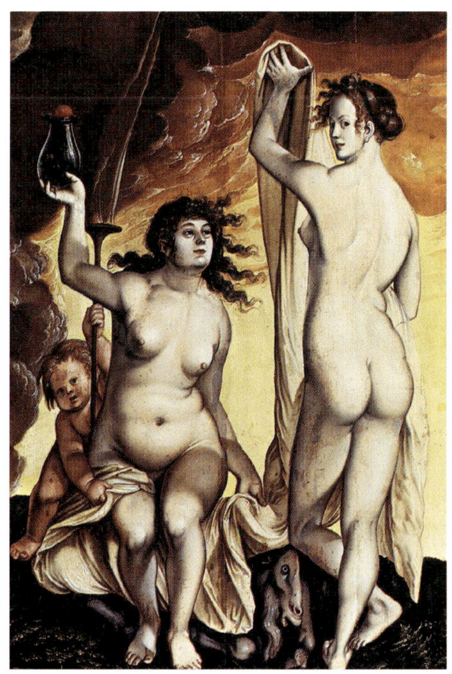

artists were still thought of as occupying the social rank of specialized artisans, Dürer saw himself as an *engagé* intellectual. He was helped in this by being gifted with magnetic beauty and by possessing a sharp sense of his self-worth. From 1505 to 1507 he returned to Italy. This was an encounter at the highest levels between the greatest German artist, at the moment of his full maturity, and the culture of the Italian Renaissance, at the apogee of its splendor. The result, halfway through the first decade of the sixteenth century, was one of the most stimulating pages in the history of European painting. The works of Dürer, which had always been distinguished by an sharp graphic sense, now took on a monumental stature. Dürer was driven by the desire to give life to a

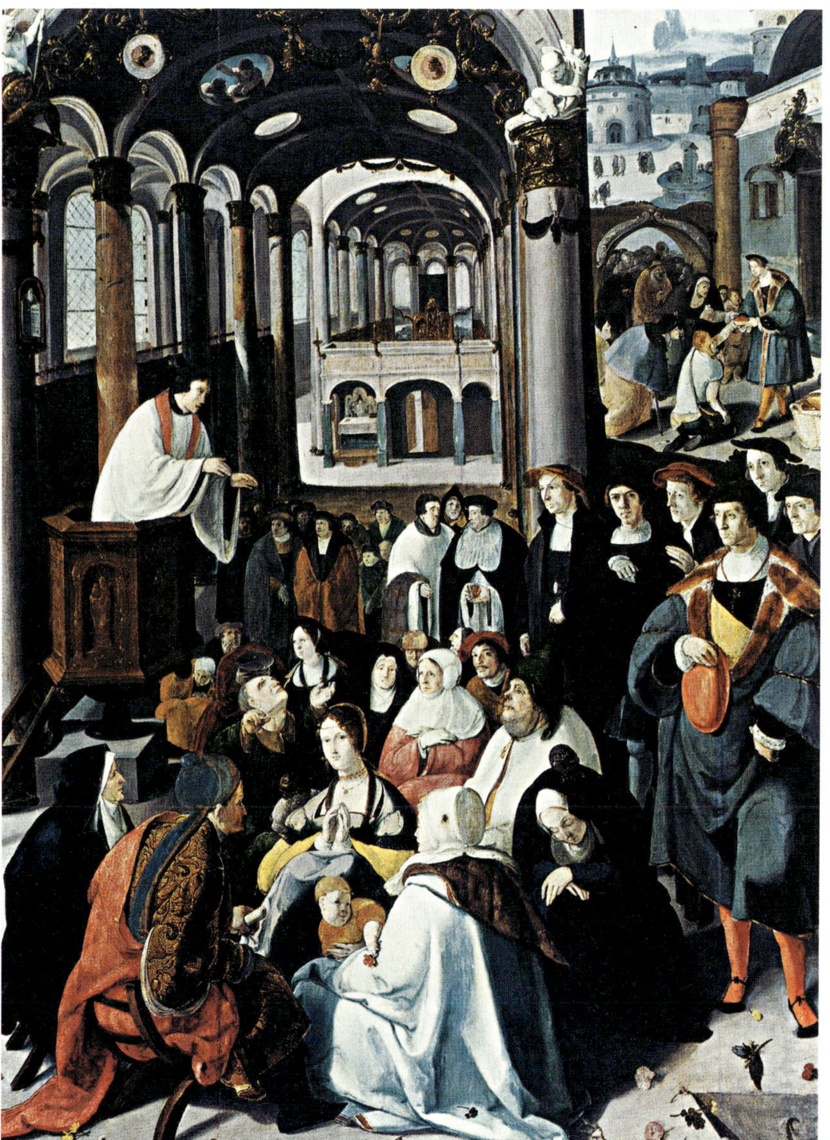

beauty that was both ideal and at the same time natural. In 1521 he again traveled, this time to Antwerp and the Low Countries, meeting with Quenten Metsys and Lucas van Leyden. When he returned home, the fifty-year-old painter seemed to be ill, and in fact the last years of his life were marked by declining health along with anguish over the dramatic events of the time.

This sense of anguish was related to the international panorama, with the initiatives of Luther, the election of Emperor Charles V, the spread of the Protestant Reformation. This genius's anger can be seen as symptom and symbol of a collective sentiment that shook the consciences of European intellectuals. Dürer had followed Martin Schongauer, studied the altarpieces of Michael Pacher and the engravings of Mantegna, he had met Giovanni Bellini and Leonardo, exchanged drawings with Raphael and Grünewald, influenced Pontormo and Lucas van Leyden, Gossart, and Lorenzo Lotto. On the threshold of history Dürer found himself beside his near contemporary Michelangelo, the two of them the most disappointed and disenchanted artistic consciences in Europe in the age of the Reformation.

The life of Albrecht
Dürer is a fascinating
mixture of highly suc-
cessful public activity
and enormous interior
torment. During many
periods of his life Dürer
seems to hover between
a pleased awareness of
his growing success,
outwardly expressed in
careful attention to his
dress, hair, and acces-
sories, and moments in
which he falls prey to
dark depression. This
ambiguity makes his
biography particularly
interesting and enriches
his self-portraits with
a profound sense of
introspection, a new
element in portraiture.
In this work from the
Prado, the twenty-
seven-year-old painter
clearly intends to ele-
vate himself above the
status of artisan and
celebrates his financial
and social success with
a pose and dress wor-
thy of a member of the
intellectual aristocracy
of the period.

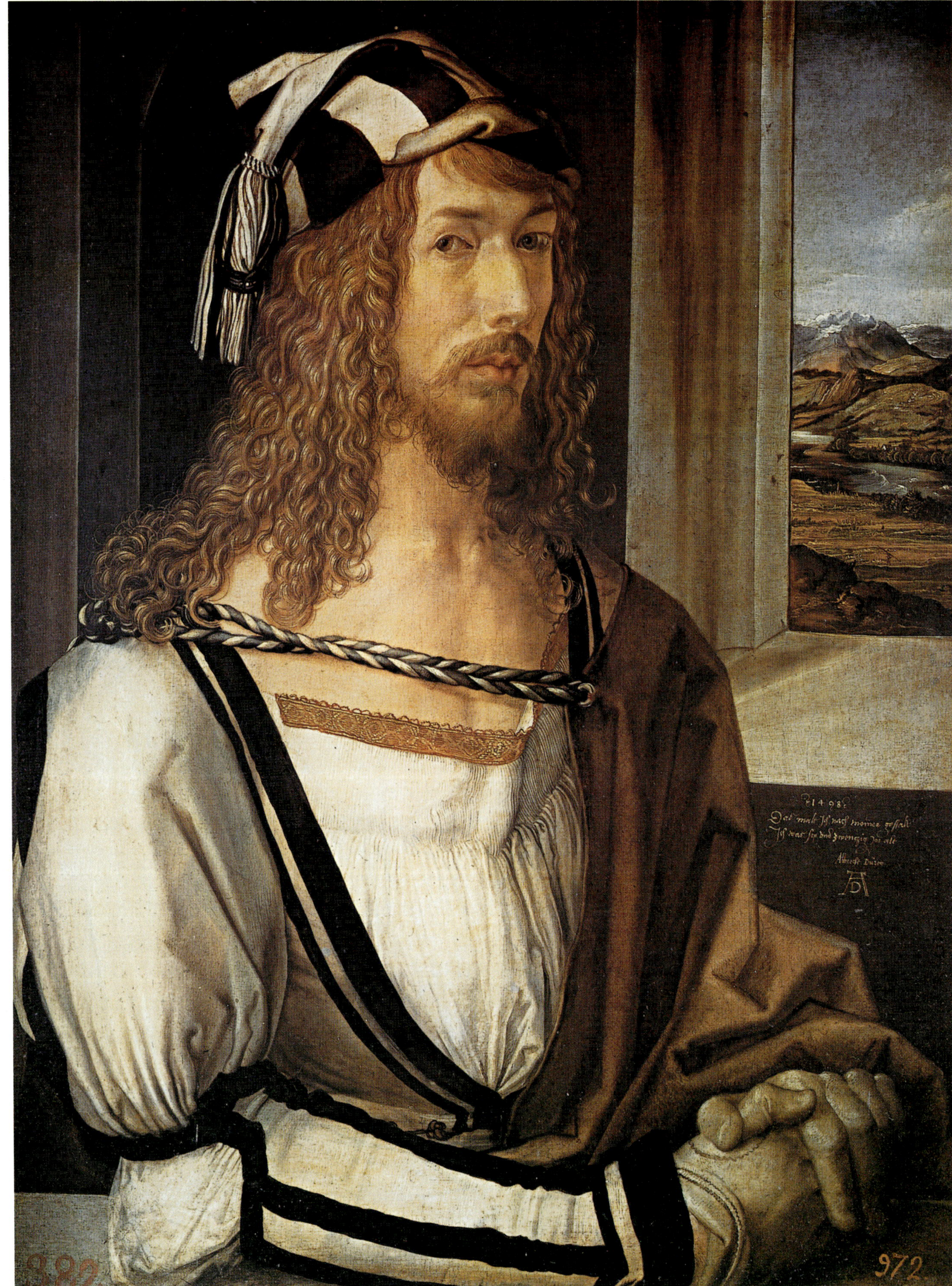

The age of Dürer

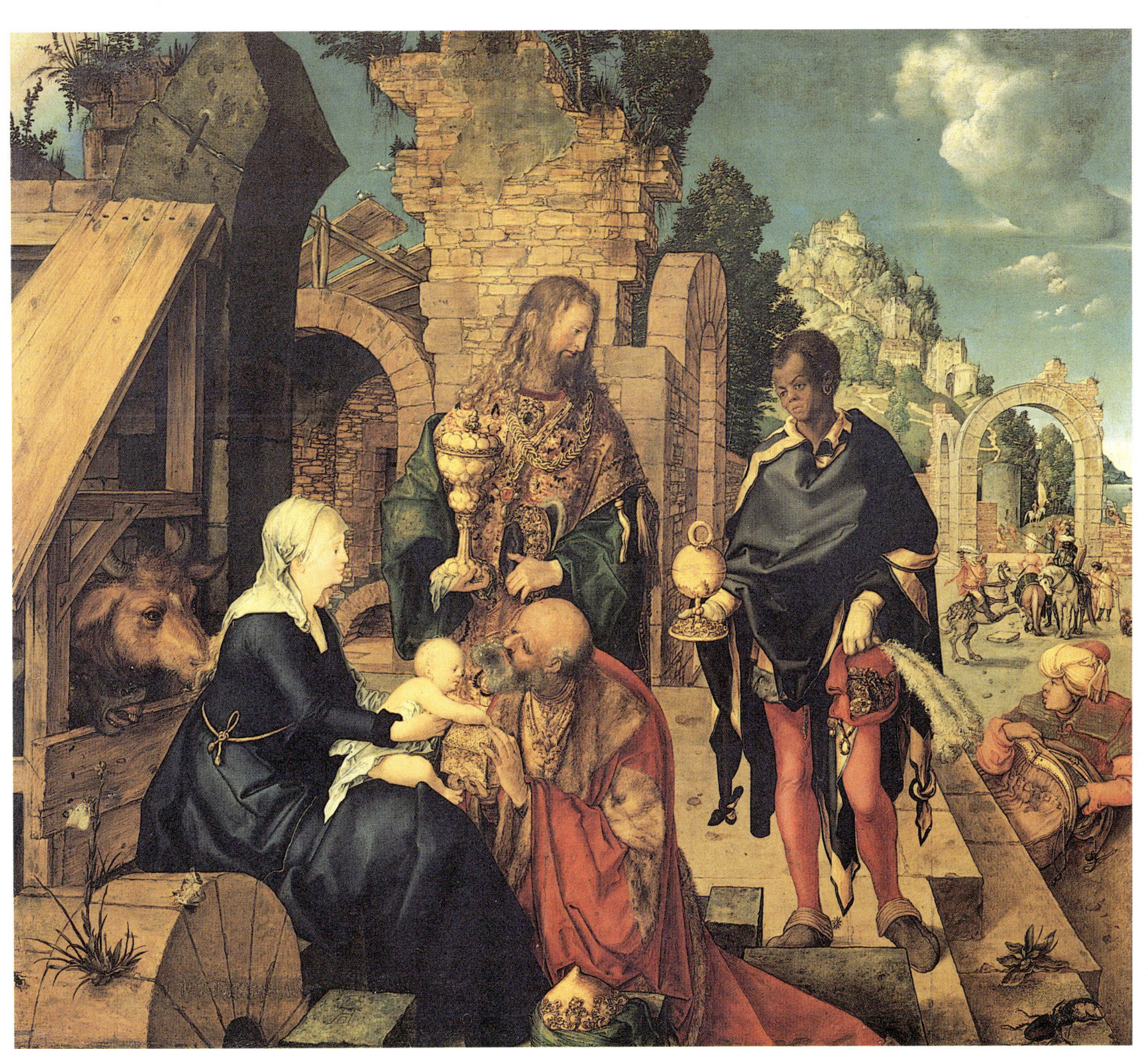

The age of Dürer

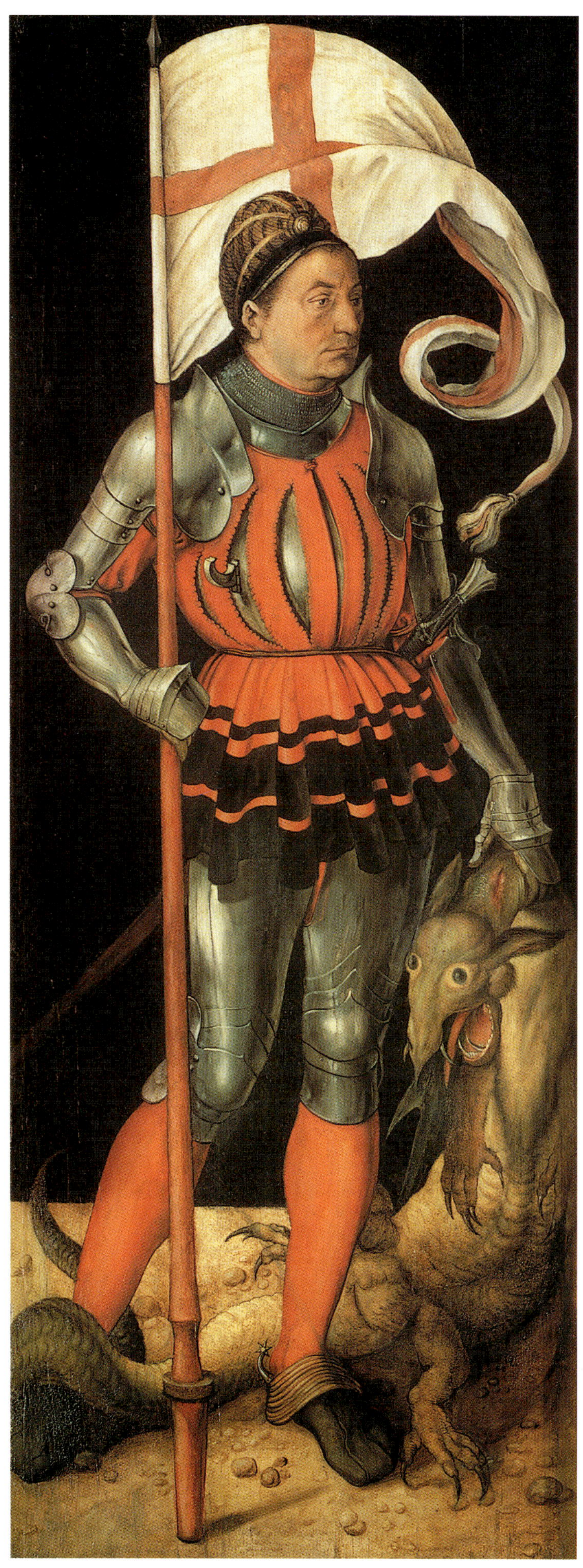
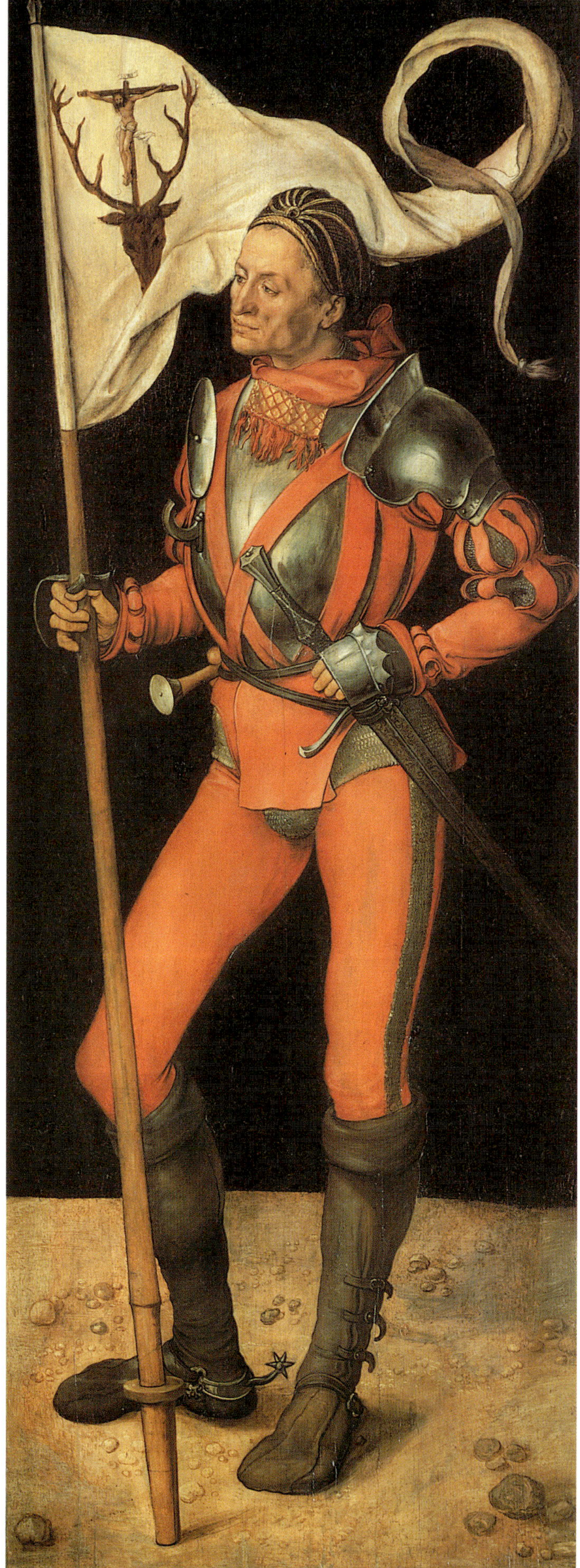

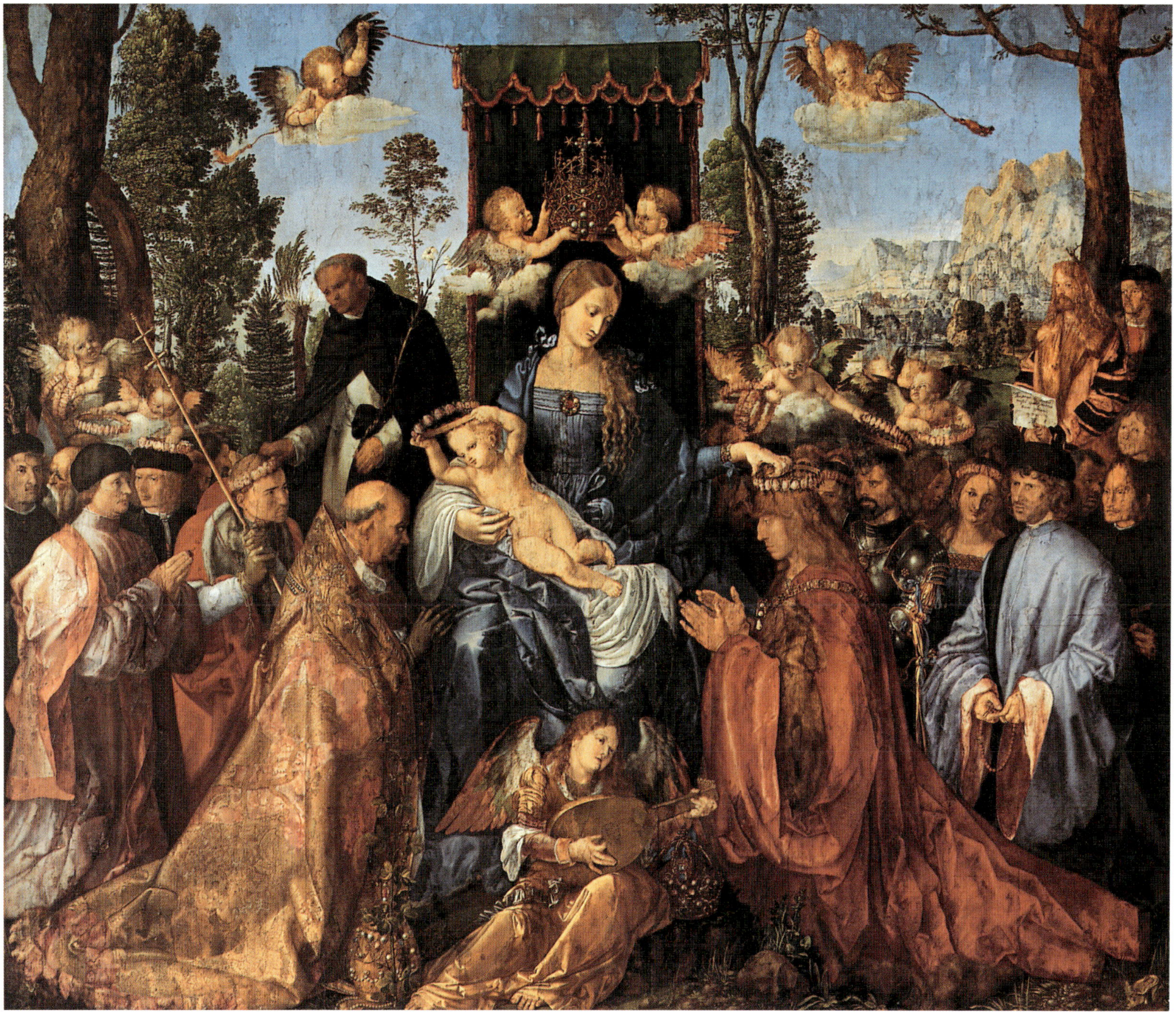

**The Feast of the
Rose Garlands**
1506, oil on panel,
162 x 194.5 cm
Národní Galerie, Prague

Made for the Confraternity of the Rosary
of San Bartolomeo, the
national church of the
Germans in Venice, this
altarpiece is one of the
great masterpieces of
Renaissance Europe,
a point of encounter
between northern and
Italian painting in
which the stupendous
descriptive details and
the penetrating portraits are joined to an
atmospheric setting
and a serene compositional structure. Many
leading figures of the
period are portrayed in
the work, among them
Jacob Fugger, Pope
Alexander VI, and
Emperor Maximilian I,
on whose head the
Madonna is placing a
crown of roses. Dürer
himself appears, off to
the right, holding up a
document with Latin
writing, including his
name, the date, and an
indication of the time
it took him to complete
the altarpiece (five
months of work).

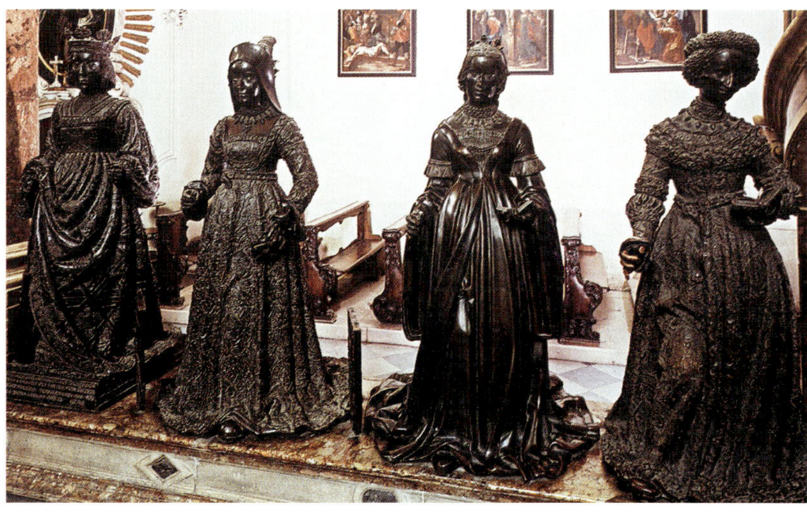

■ **Heroines of Antiquity
from the tomb of
Emperor Maximilian I**
1513–50, bronze
Hofkirche, Innsbruck

The marble tomb
presents a series of
bas-reliefs of the
principal events in
the life of the ruler.
To the sides, 28 bronze
statues of kings and
heroines of antiquity
form a sort of majestic
honor guard.

There are the first life-size nudes in German painting. Stimulated by the example of Italian art, during his second stay in Venice, Dürer dedicated himself to the theme of the human body. From this moment on, his activity had him performing two roles. On the one hand there was the intellectual in search of a utopian "canon of beauty," based on geometric relationships and the harmony of the parts of the human body; on the other there was the artist, capable of expressing emotions from the depths of the soul, fully prepared to flee any attempt at codification in his desire to record the reality of nature. Perhaps it was during these years that Dürer became aware of the insolvable contradiction that from then on would dominate his life: boundless love for the various aspects of creation (men and women first, but also animals, plants, rocks, landscapes, woods, cities) and the always frustrated desire to find general rules, objective and immutable, with which to define beauty.

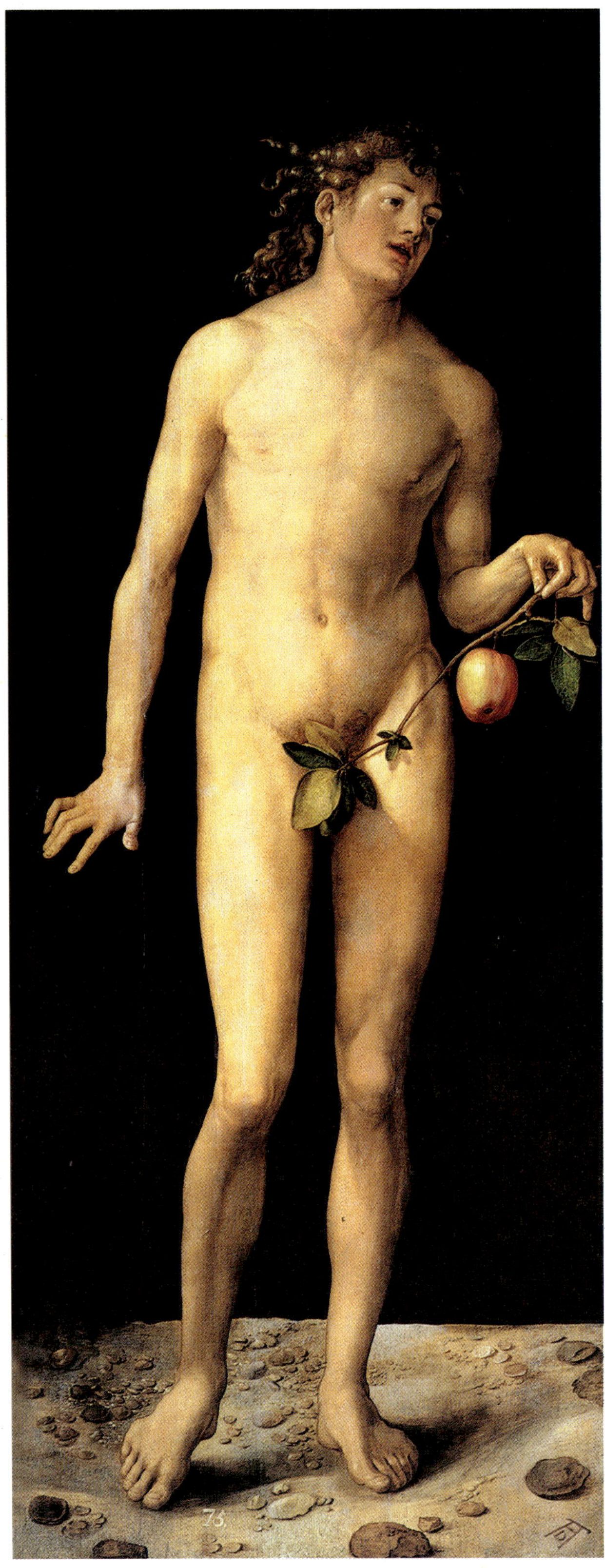

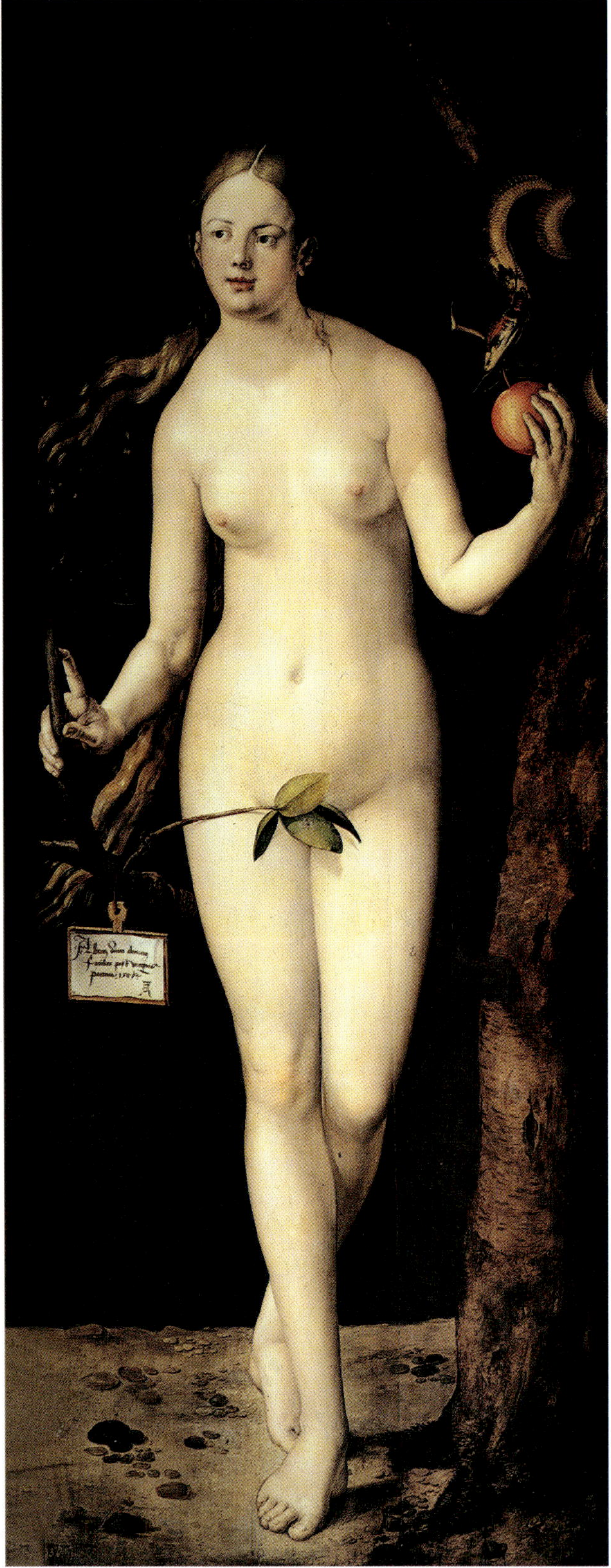

The age of Dürer

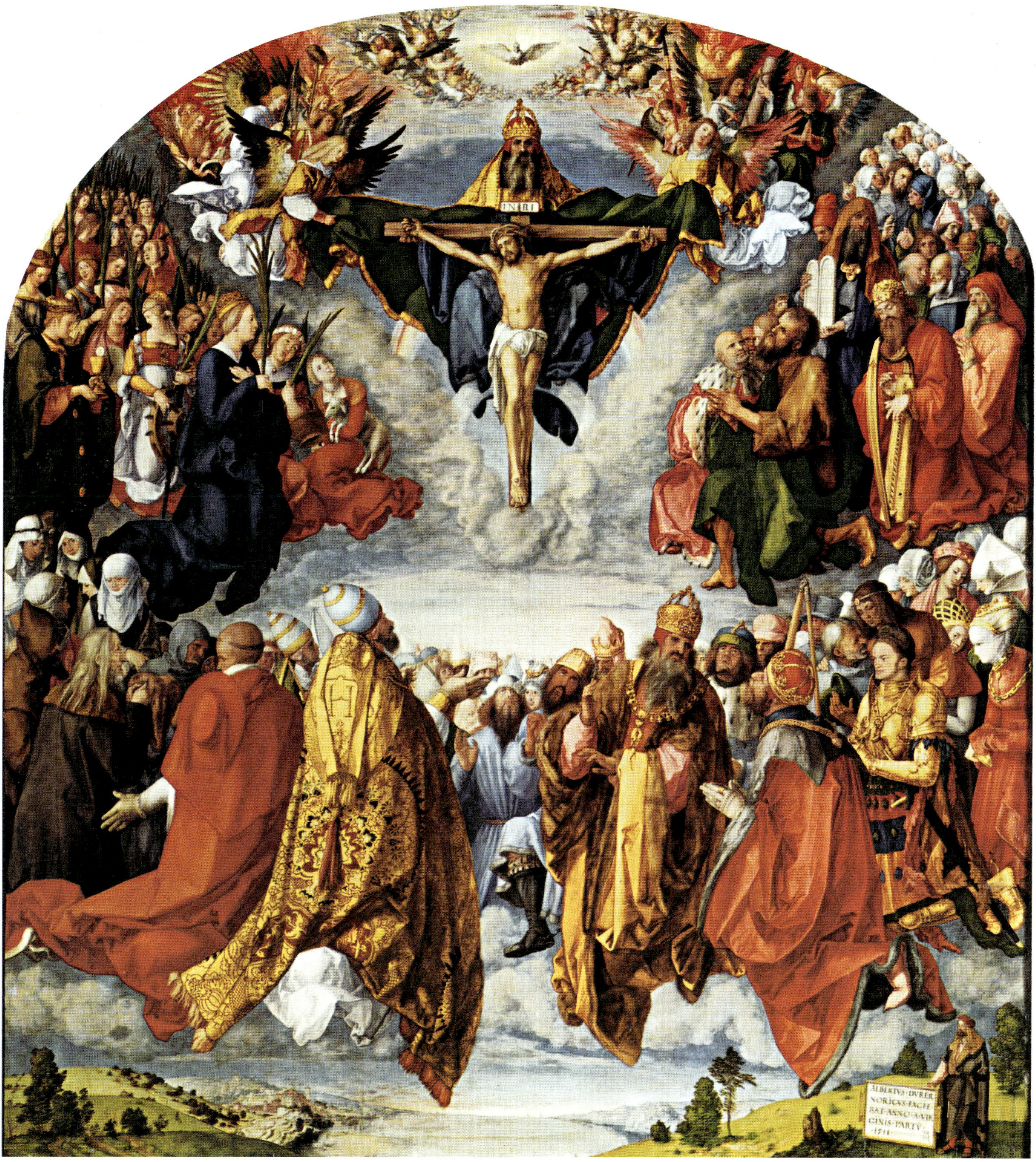

■ ALBRECHT DÜRER
**The Adoration
of the Trinity**
1511, oil on panel,
135 x 123.4 cm
Kunsthistorisches
Museum,
Vienna

This altarpiece was
commissioned by the
Nuremberg merchant
Matthäus Landauer for
the chapel of the Home
of the Twelve Brothers,
a shelter and clinic for
twelve aged and indi-
gent artisans. In the
extraordinary hemicycle
of saints suspended
in the air around the
Trinity Dürer makes full
use of the expressive
resources of the German
figurative culture, most
of all in the dazzling
colors, while at the
same time making use
of the most up-to-date
Italian models. For
example, the double
group of the saints
around the axis of the
Trinity can be compared
with the structure
Raphael adopted in
the *Dispute of the Holy
Sacrament* in the Stanze
del Vaticano (1511).
Despite the great
breadth of the land-
scape (inspired by Lake
Garda in northern Italy)
and the classical nobil-
ity of the composition,
the altarpiece reveals
many details of "north-
ern" customs, present-
ing a synthesis of art
from the north and
south of the Alps. In
the corner at bottom
right Dürer again pre-
sents himself, standing
beside a tablet inscribed
in Latin with his signa-
ture and the date.

The age of Dürer

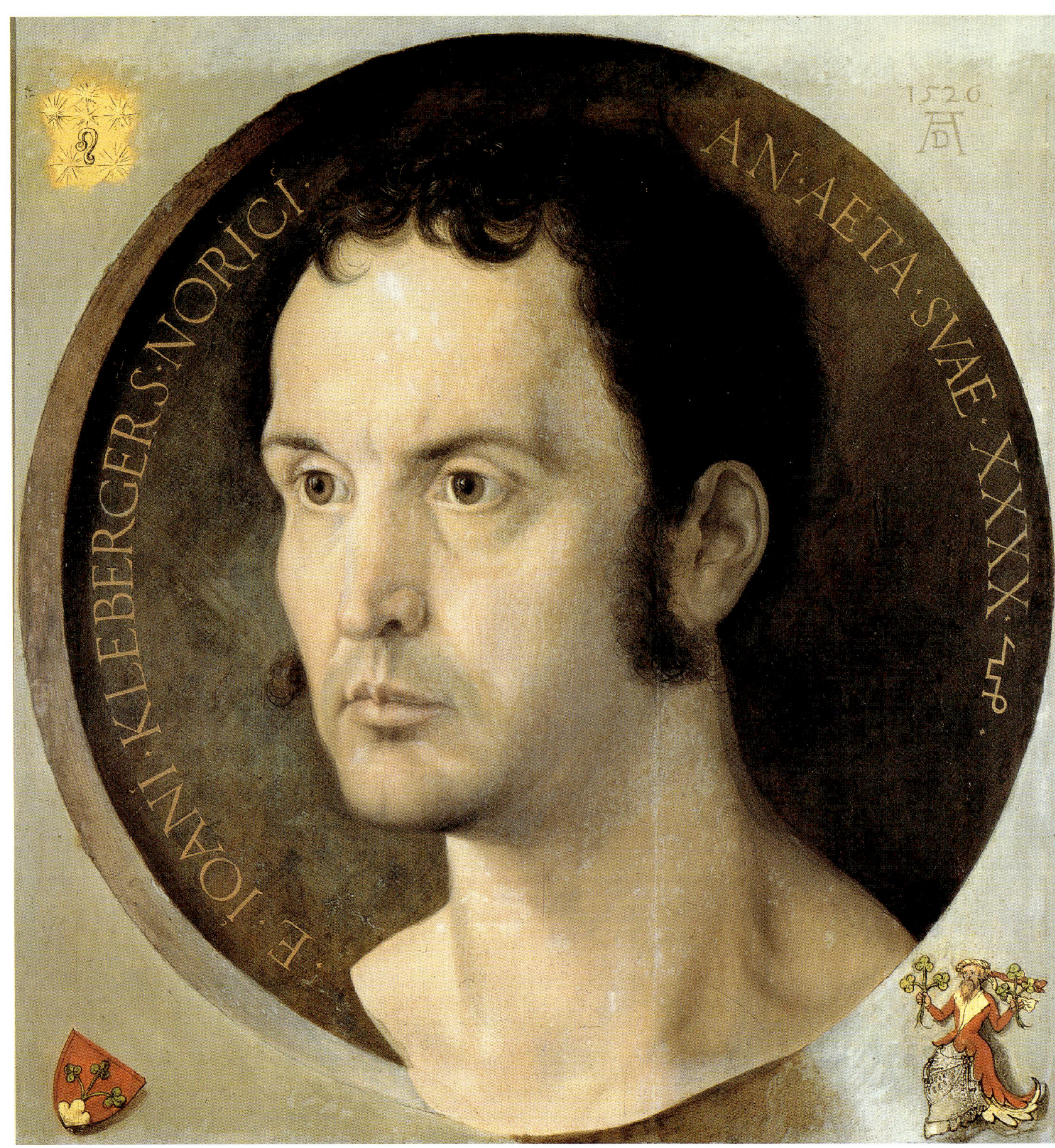

The age of Dürer

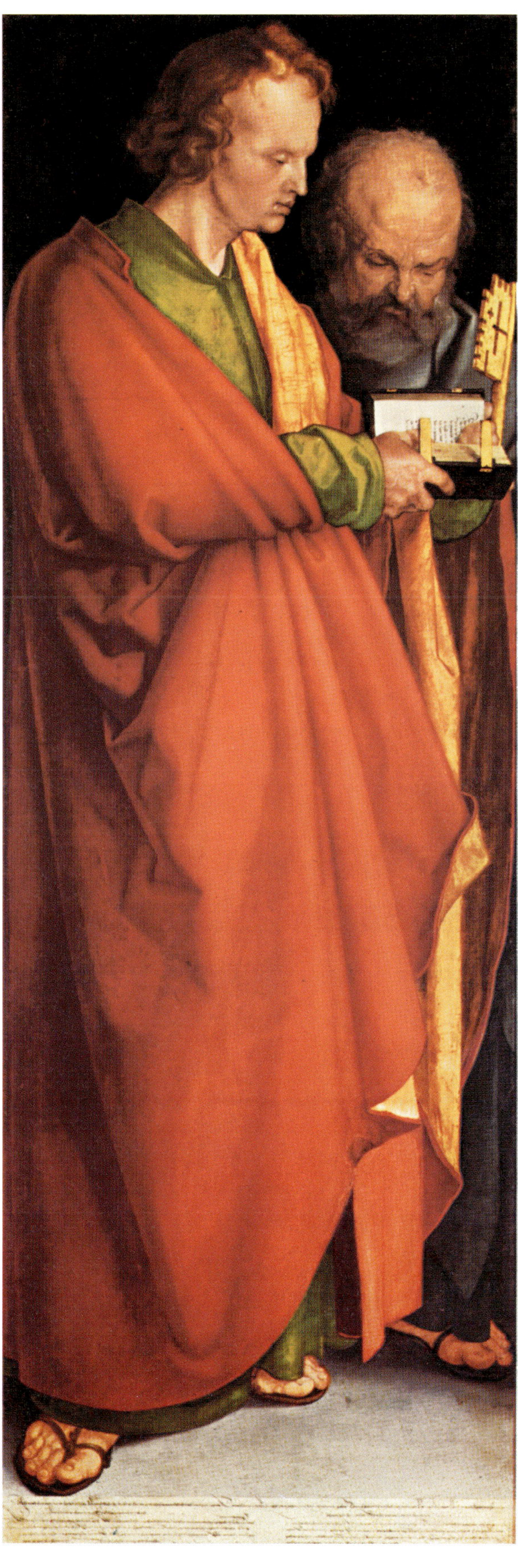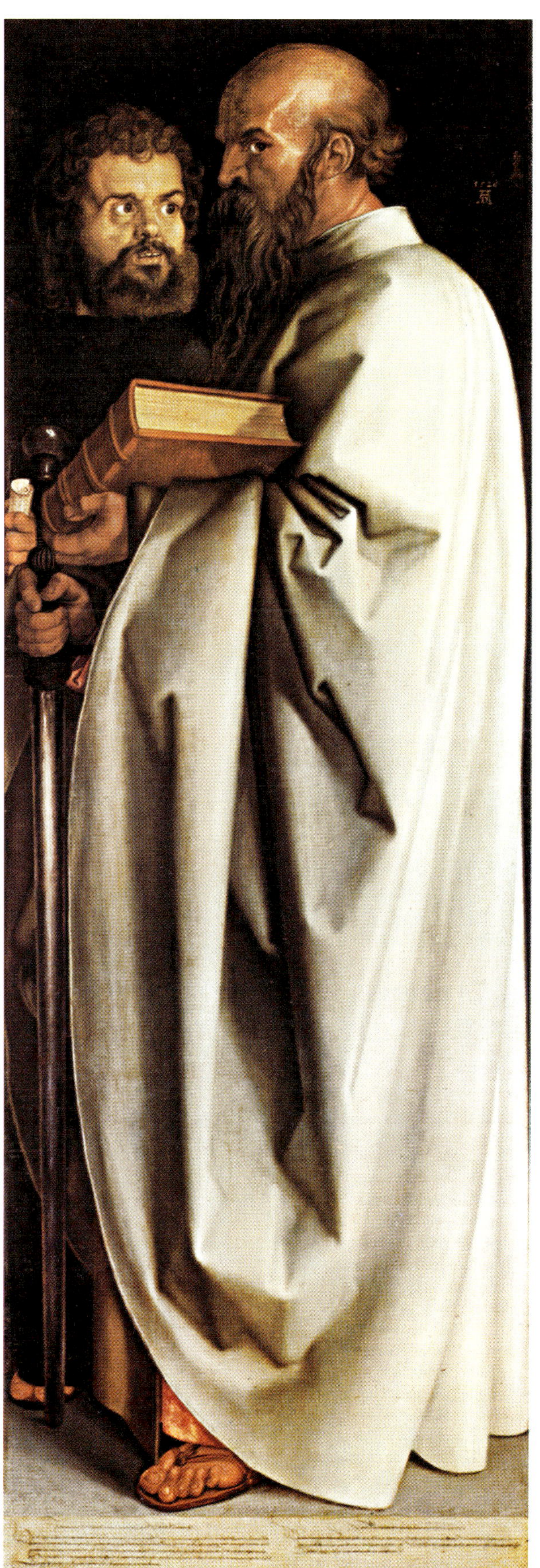

ALBRECHT DÜRER
The Four Apostles
1526, oil on panel,
215 x 76 cm each
Alte Pinakothek,
Munich

Donated by Dürer in
1526 to the city of
Nuremberg, these two
panels were a kind of
spiritual testament for
the painter. The four
faces correspond to the
theory of the four tem-
peraments, or humors.
The old and pale Peter
is the expression of the
"phlegmatic" tempera-
ment; to his side is the
"sanguine" John, rosy
and ardent. The austere
and introverted Paul
symbolizes the melan-
cholic, that being the
physical and mental
state with which Dürer
identified himself. Mark,
the choleric, bares his
teeth. The long inscrip-
tion at the bottom con-
demns excesses and
violence. The harsh
polemics, the icono-
clasm, and most of all
the bloody revolts of
the 1520s embittered
Dürer, who lamented
the loss of quiet dia-
logues. The artist must
have been greatly struck
by the decision of his
humanist friend Willi-
bald Pirkheimer who,
after having joined
the Reformation, had
returned to the Catholic
Church because of
Martin Luther's
aggressive tactics
and the excesses of
the Protestants.

ALBRECHT
ALTDORFER
**Martyrdom of
St. Florian**
1516–18, oil on
panel, 76 x 67 cm
Galleria degli
Uffizi, Florence

This painting is part of
a cycle of seven panels
(two of which are
today in Florence,
three in Nuremberg,
one in Prague, and one
in Berne) relating the
life and martyrdom of
St. Florian. The scene
of his martyrdom pre-
sents the saint about
to be thrown into the
Enns River with a mill-
stone around his neck.
The extraordinary view
of nature created by
Altdorfer is characteris-
tic of the so-called
Danubian school, in
the pictorial style of
which he was the lead-
ing practitioner.

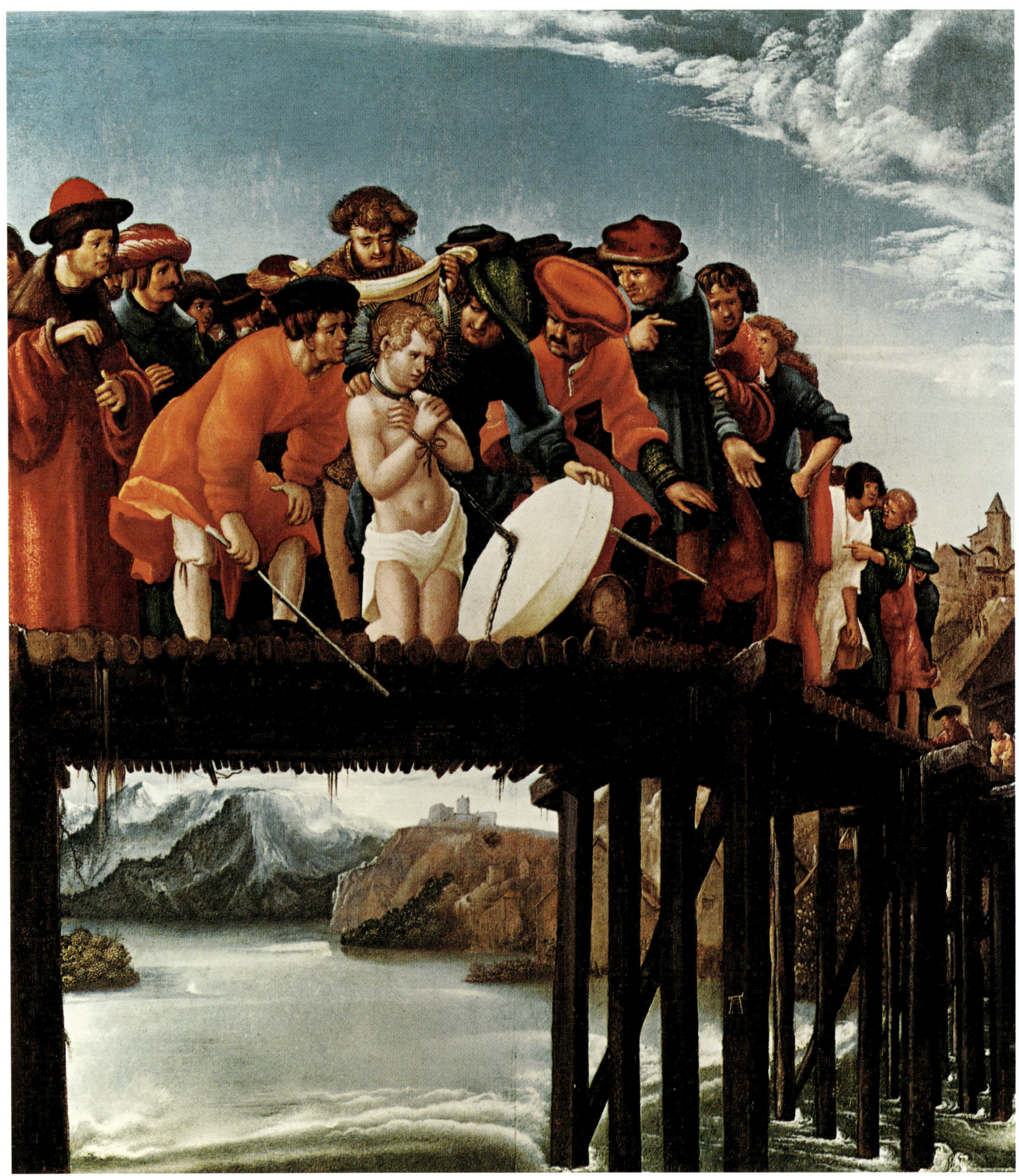

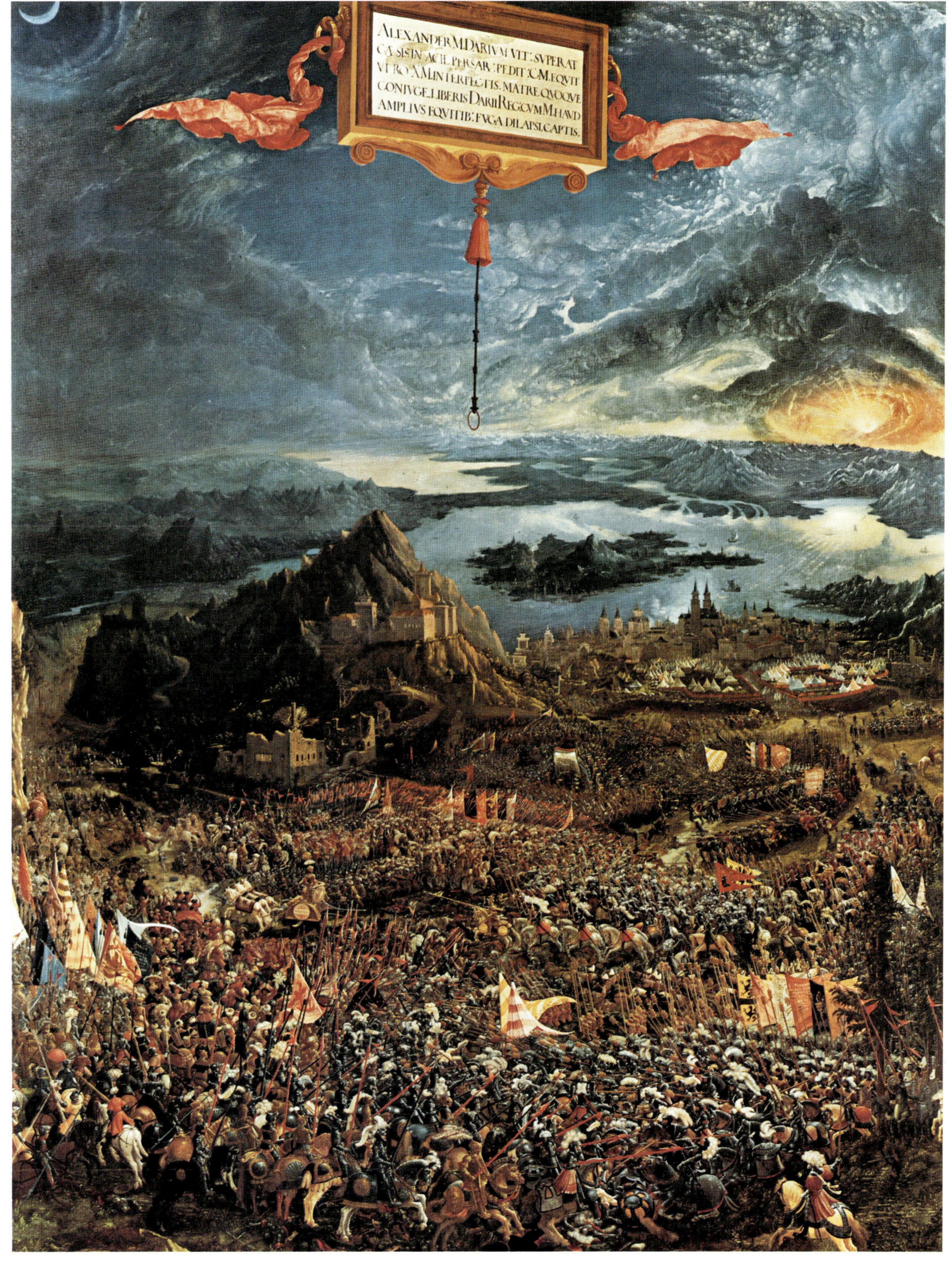

The Battle of Issus
1529, oil on panel,
158 x 120 cm
Alte Pinakothek,
Munich

In the desire to give his home a "classical" appearance, Duke William IV of Bavaria engaged a humanist and a series of painters in the illustration of historical episodes related to heroines and heroes of antiquity. This evocation of the battle of Issus (333 B.C.), with the victory of the "Greek" Alexander over the "Oriental" Darius, can also be seen as an allusion to the wars against the Turks. It is also likely that Altdorfer hoped to evoke recent battles, such as the battle of Pavia in 1525. Seen from an elevated point of view, the battle takes place on a cosmic landscape, indeed one of the most astonishing landscapes in all of art history, perhaps based on the area of Salzburg. In an atmosphere of mesmerizing fascination, the sun sets behind infinite chains of mountains, while a sickle moon already shines in the sky. Among the most direct precedents for the confused mass of men and horses are, perhaps, the graphic derivations based on the battle of Anghiari painted by Leonardo in Florence.

**Tomb Reliquary
of St. Sebaldus**
1515, bronze
Church of St. Sebaldus,
Nuremberg

The tomb reliquary
of St. Sebaldus is in
that saint's church in
Nuremberg. It is the
work of the brass-caster
and sculptor Peter
Vischer and his five
sons, who began work-
ing on it in 1508. More
exactly, it is a large
pierced tabernacle in
bronze that holds and
surrounds the old cas-
ket reliquary. This
monumental work of
goldworking confirms
the special role of the
city of Nuremberg
in the working of
precious metals.

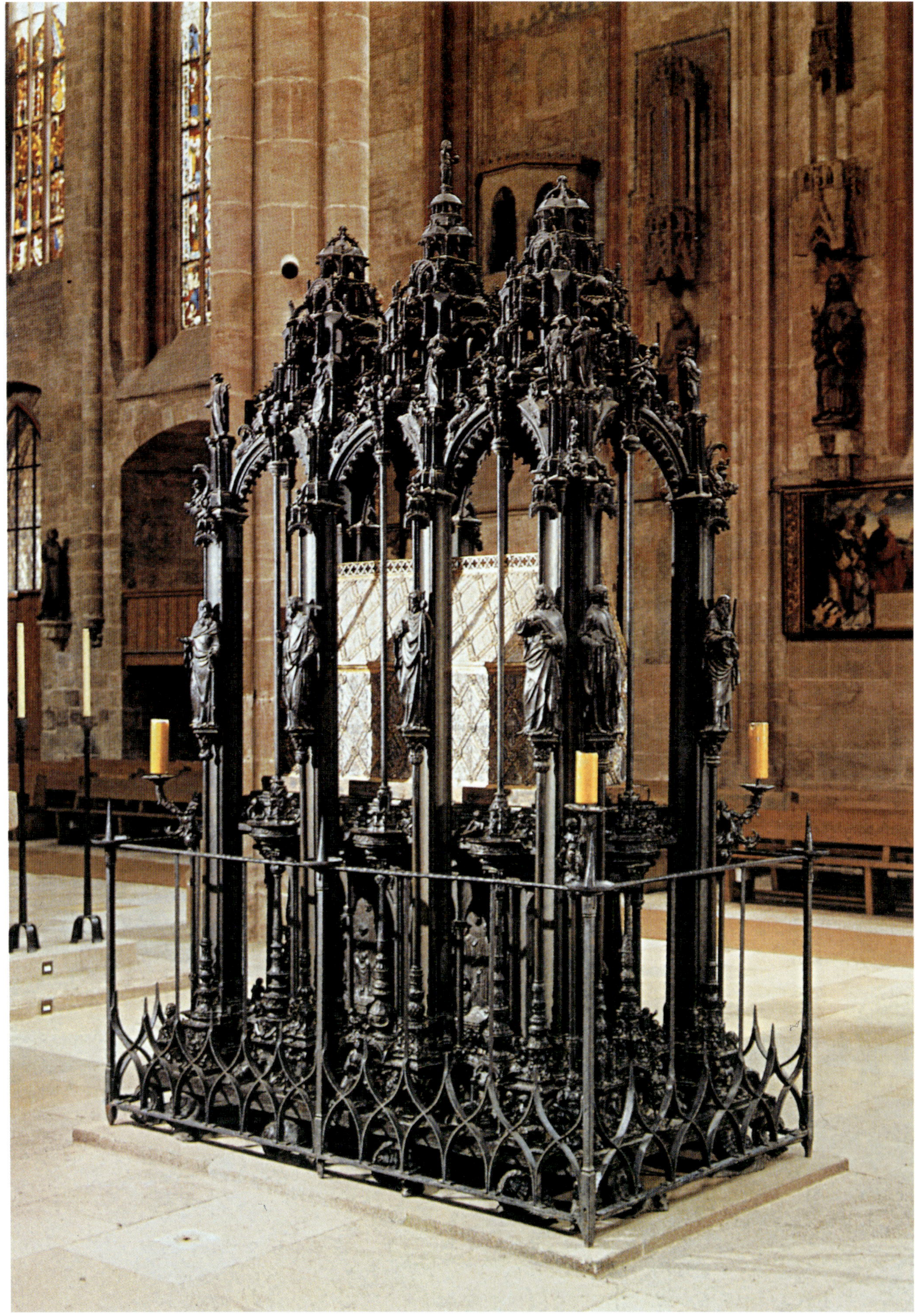

The age of Dürer

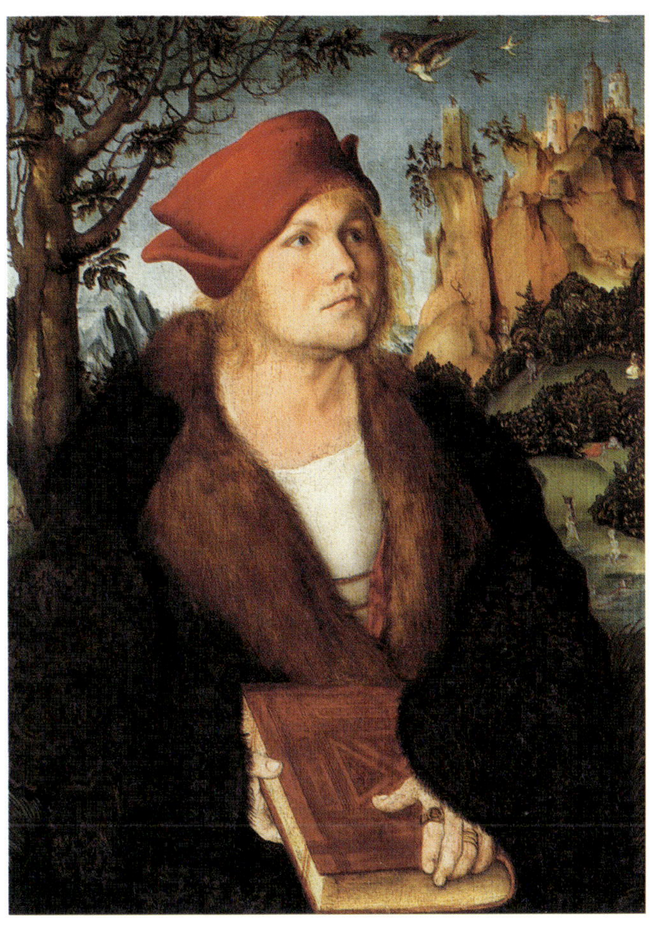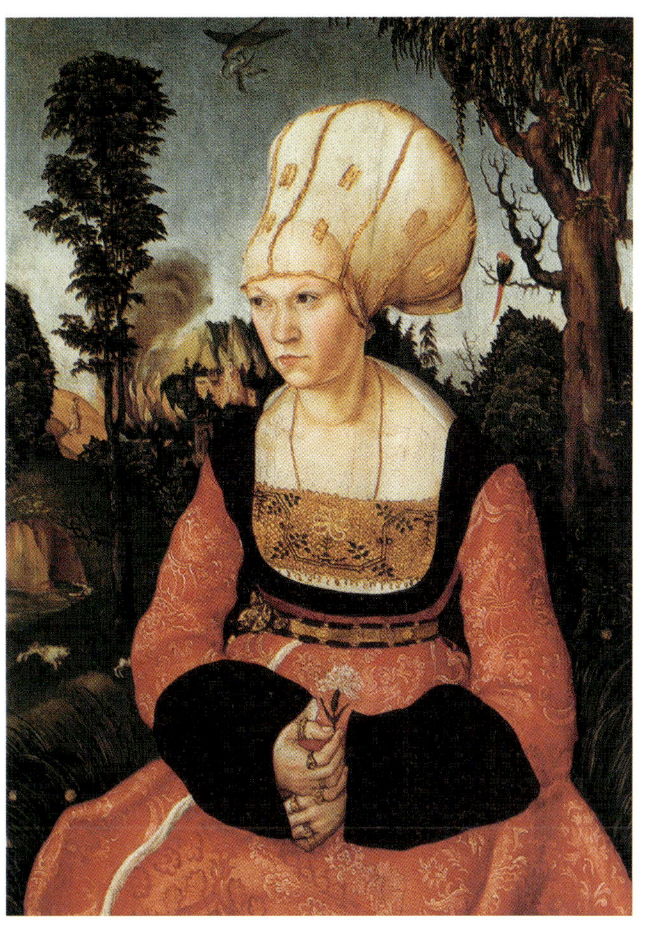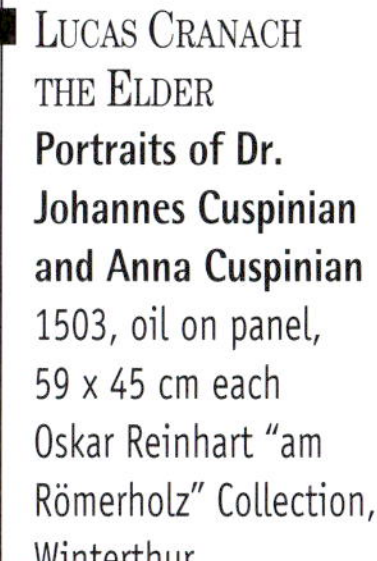

The Cuspinian portraits are the splendid proof of a young master who entered his early maturity already gifted with an important figurative culture. For the first time in German art, the portraits of the husband and wife are conceived as a pair, as in a diptych, with a landscape background that passes from one to the other: the reference to Italian Renaissance art is clear.

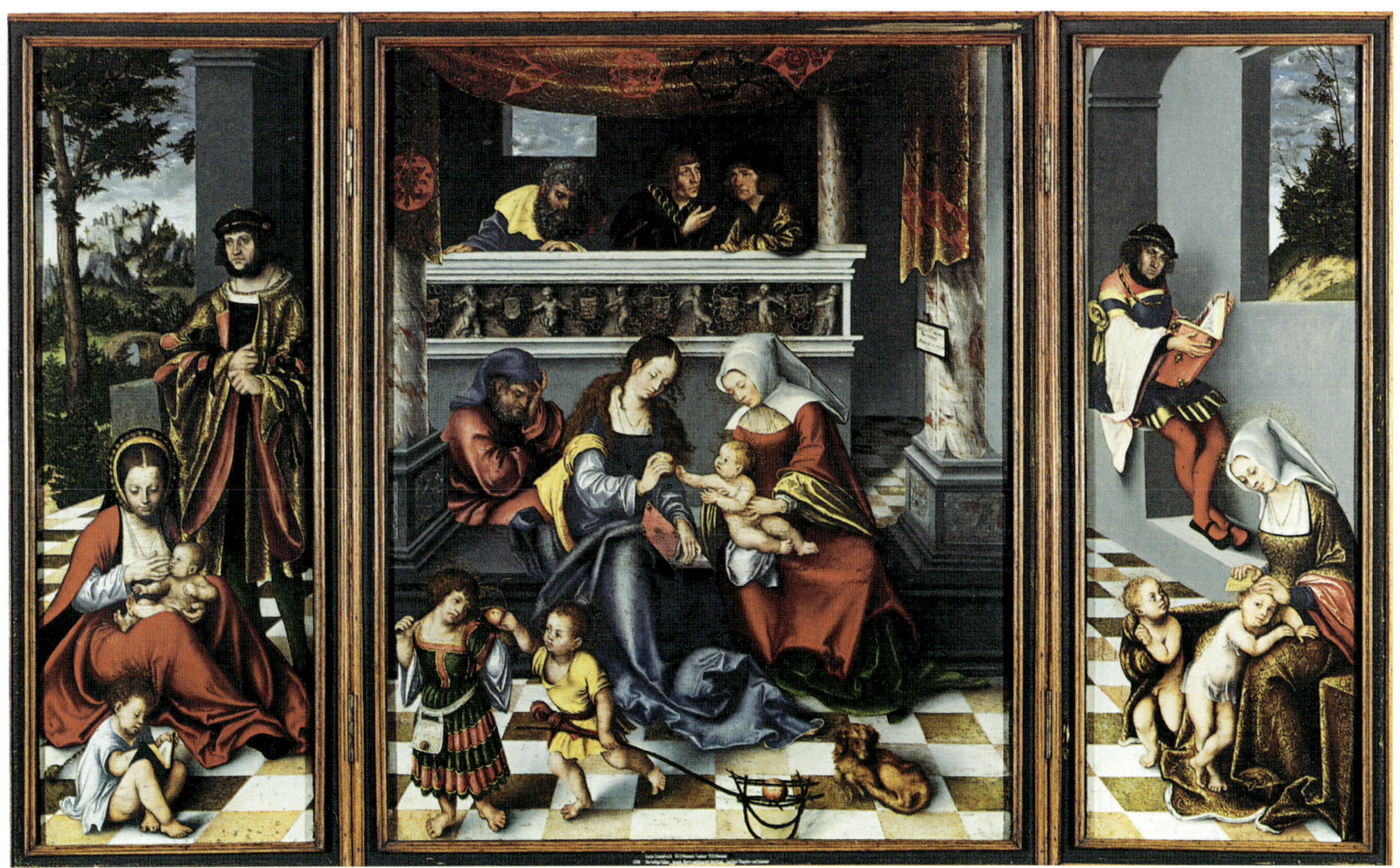

The triptych presents a rare and entertaining iconography. According to apocryphal tradition, St. Anne wed three husbands, from each of whom she had a daughter, all of them named Mary. From left to right, they are the Virgin Mary, mother of Jesus; Mary of Cleophas with four children; and Mary of Salome, wife of Zebedee, with two.

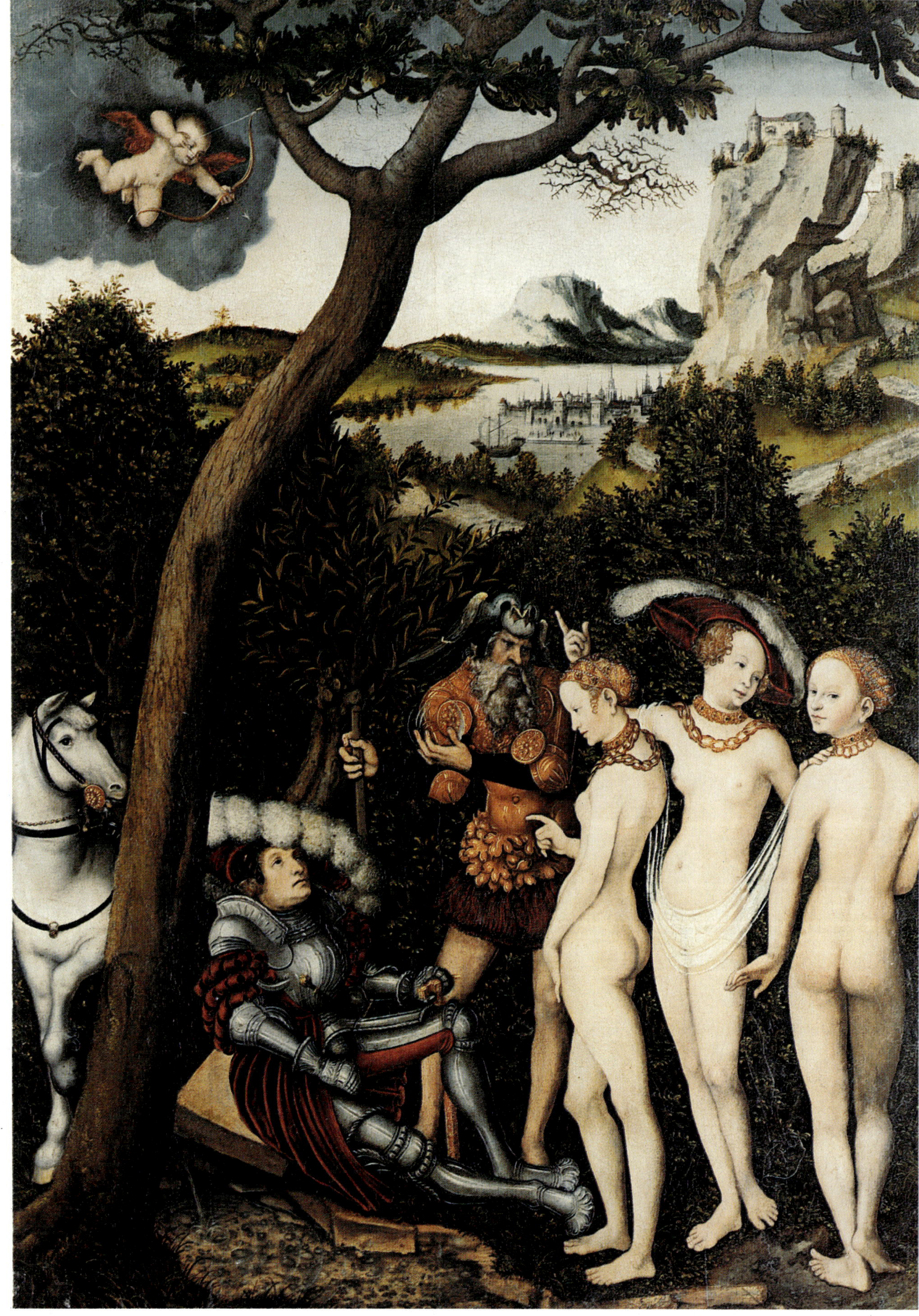

The age of Dürer

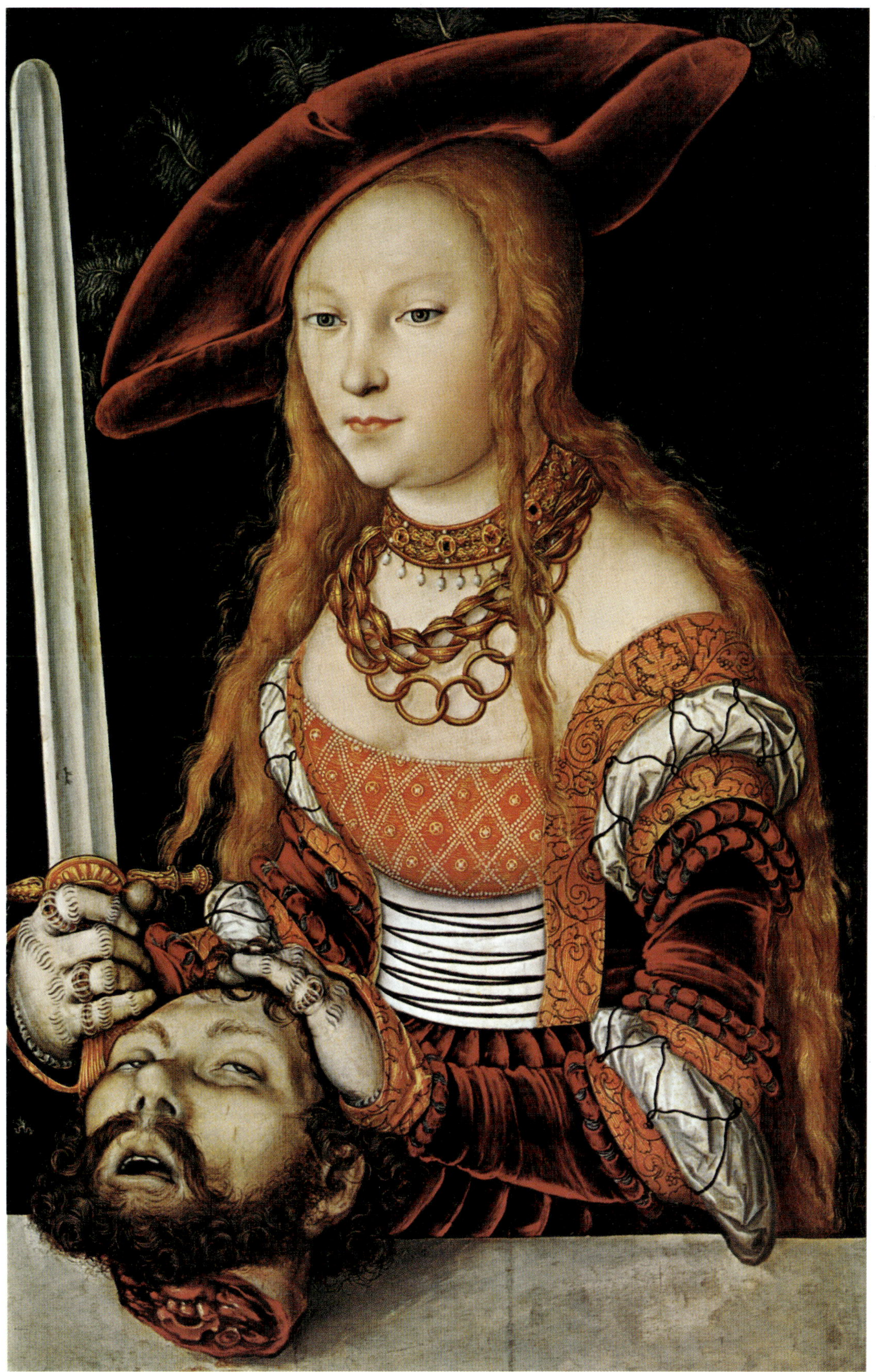

Cranach returns obsessively to the figure of Holofernes, perhaps in part projecting it onto the events of his own times. Like the devoted city of Bethulia besieged by the Assyrian nonbelievers, so too the cities of the German Protestant princes felt themselves threatened by the Catholic army of Charles V. The beautiful heroine can thus be symbolic of the independence of those who are faithful to the "true" God and of the divine protection conceded them. The work also reflects the period's reborn morality in terms of sexual habits—the Assyrian general's chopped-off head is a reminder not to be taken in by the enticements of lust. Beyond these possible meanings, there is the great fascination of the image, with its contrast between the horror of the neck of Holofernes and the exotic allure of Judith, whom Cranach often presents wearing sumptuous clothes and wide-brimmed hats that shadow and thus emphasize her long, almond-shaped eyes.

This is a delicate and magical image of the *Stille Nacht,* the silent night of Christmas, as is being announced to the shepherd with his flock visible through the doorway. The Child gives off the sweet light of all newborns, while even the ass and the ox seem to smile along with the small angels that assist Mary. Everything here is silence and shadows, sweetness and intimacy. The artist offers the viewer a sense of suspended enchantment, of an affectionate secret, the irresistible magic of a child that reaches his hands toward his mother. Faithful to her role of devout Virgin, Mary prays, but doing so she cannot hold back a smile, and her joined hands tremble. In a moment she will again caress the luminous, almost phosphorescent, little body, so defenseless before her.

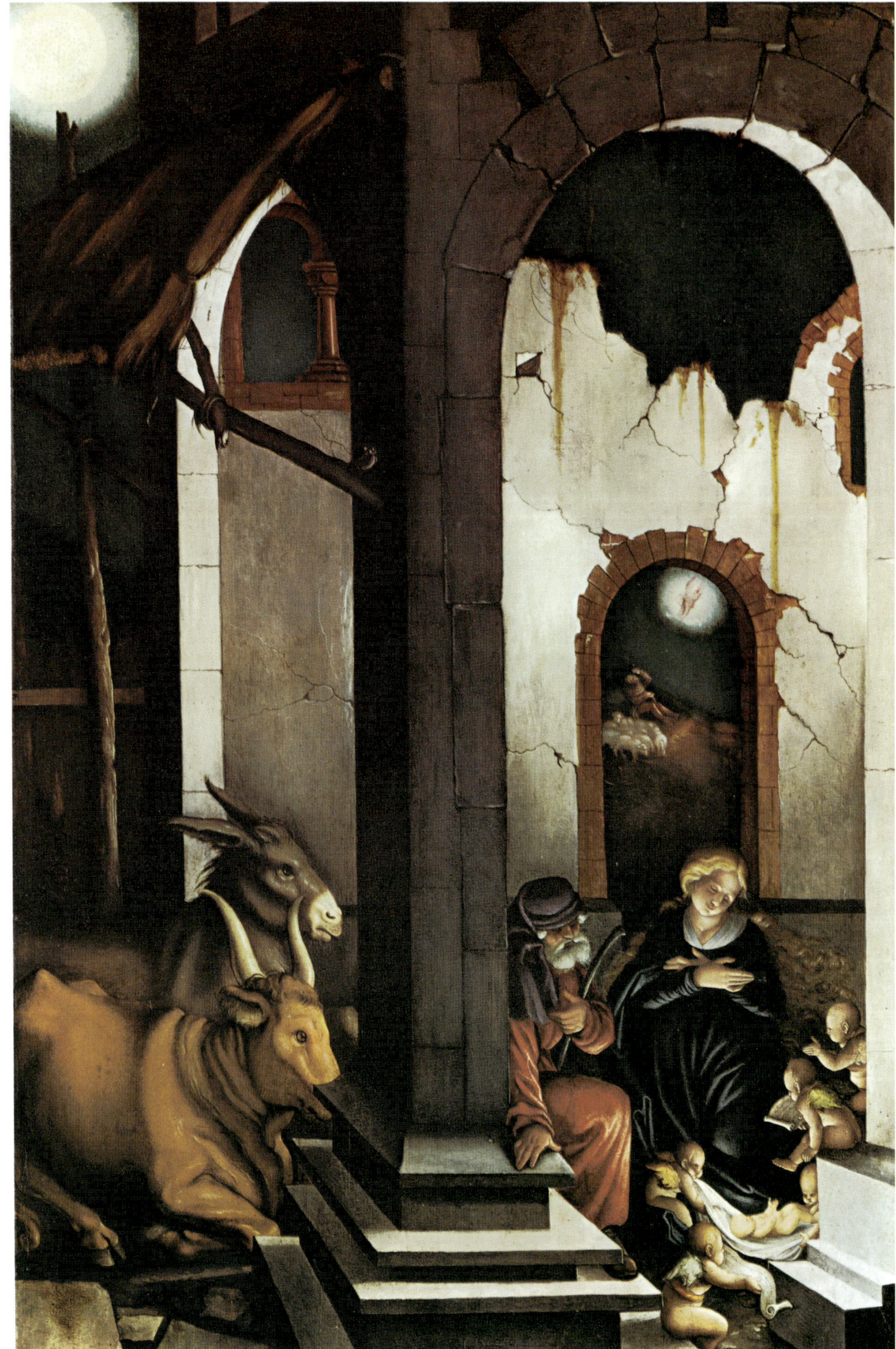

The age of Dürer

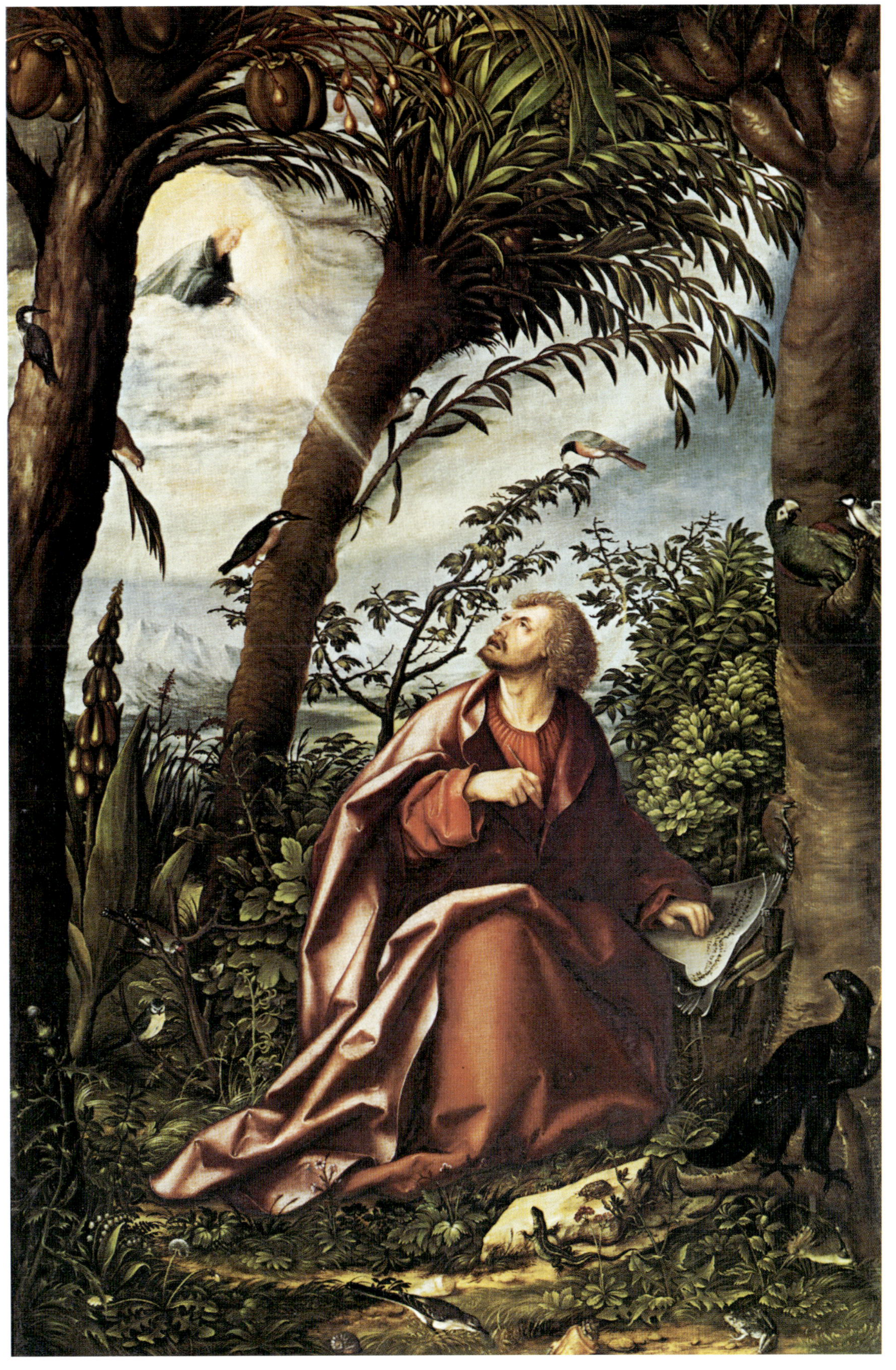

Hans Burgkmair
St. John on Patmos
1518, panel,
153 x 125 cm
Alte Pinakothek,
Munich

The central panel of a triptych altarpiece, this painting presents a subject dear to the culture of northern Europe, the evangelist having his vision of the Apocalypse on the island of Patmos. Comparison with the version by Baldung reveals Burgkmair's energetic, almost disheveled, vitality. The fascinating natural background, a predilection of the artists of the Danubian school, becomes the opportunity for the presentation of a detailed catalog of ornithological and botanical beings.

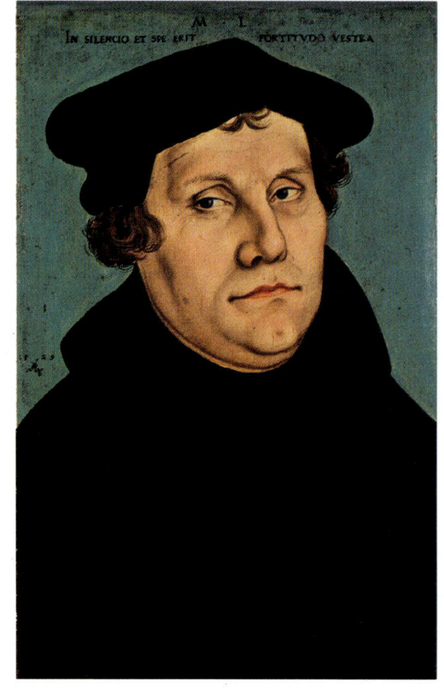

Workshop of Lucas
Cranach the Elder,
Martin Luther, sixteenth
century; Museo Poldi
Pezzoli, Milan

I n 1500 Erasmus, the greatest humanist of northern Europe, published his *Adagia,* a collection of Latin and Greek proverbs and other classical citations along with popular wisdom, tidbits of knowledge, and common sense. Bearers of truths held to be universal, proverbs synthesized the vision of the world of the lower classes. In the period between the fifteenth and sixteenth centuries, while the new concepts of humanism were being elaborated in Italy, northern Europe experienced a surge of interest in maxims, mottos, and sayings. Repeating the proverbs of antiquity, Erasmus's *Adagia* presented itself as a summation of ancient wisdom, and in the spirit of a return to original sources typical of the Renaissance age the work performed the role of link between "modern" ideas and the always lively interest in the popular forms of culture. This was precisely the same rich store of medieval legends and ideas about the realities of life on which Rabelais would draw for his *Gargantua* (1532) and *Pantagruel* (1533), and it is also the background to the art of Bosch and, after him, that of Pieter Bruegel the Elder

humanism, he undertakes a global reconsideration of history, morality, and religion, reaching bitter conclusions not unlike those expressed by the works of Bosch from the same period.

The learning of that painter (born around 1450 in the town of `s Hertogenbosch, from which took his surname) blended popular proverbs with humanistic ideas, ideas from other painters, peasant superstitions, magical alchemy, and science. In his art Bosch also made free use of an extremely eclectic array of literary sources. The breadth of the references reveals extensive learning, much of it still tinged with the medieval, but the open-minded use he made of such material makes his position indecipherable. Works of traditional iconography alternate with versions of religious themes that are so sacrilegious and diabolical that the suspicion arose that he had sympathies with heretical sects. These mixtures produced highly personal paintings, works that are closely related to their historical period while also interpreting moral values that are timelessly immutable.

Toward the Reformation:

The cultural world of northern Europe was in a lively ferment. Contacts with Italian humanism were multiplying, classical culture was spreading, but at the same time the drive to return to a more intense and direct form of religion was growing increasingly stronger. Just as they drew nearer "Latinness," the northern Europeans wanted to distance themselves from Rome, the popes, and the scandalous sale of indulgences.

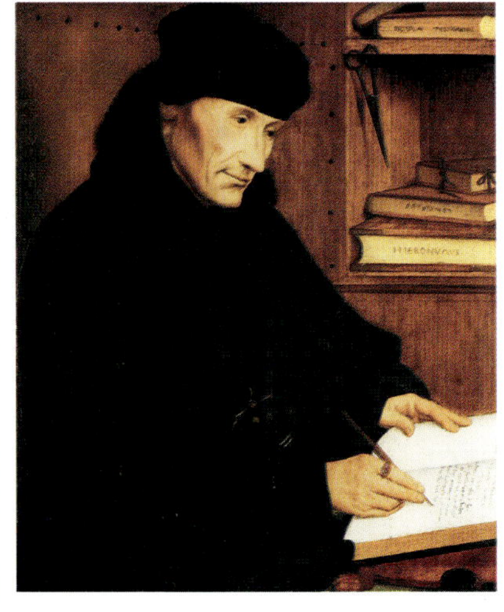

Quenten Metsys,
Erasmus, 1517; The
Royal Collection,
Hampton Court, London

In 1509, as a result in part of the great success of *The Ship of Fools,* the long poem written by the Alsatian Sebastian Brandt, Erasmus published his *Elogium insaniae (The Praise of Folly),* in which, calling into question the basic tenets of

Another important and dramatic interpreter of the religious and civil tensions of the period was Matthis Grünewald. He completed the Isenheim Altarpiece, his great masterpiece, in 1516, on the eve of the Lutheran crisis that was unleashed in 1517 by Martin Luther's posting of his 95 theses. The financier Jacob Fugger labored to organize a diet of conciliation in Augsburg, and Emperor Maximilian agreed to participate, but the undertaking failed. In 1520 Luther published three treatises in which he rejected the power of the pope, attacked the sale of indulgences, and affirmed that a Christian can achieve salvation only by means of divine grace. Pope Leo X, the son of Lorenzo the Magnificent, had until then dismissed the troubles as "quarreling among friars," but on July 2, 1520, he excommunicated Luther; Luther responded by publicly burning the papal document (December 10, 1520). The newly elected Emperor Charles V was forced to intervene and, with the Diet of Worms (1521), the debate on the Reformation moved from the purely religious plane to the political. Philip Melanchthon published the *Loci communes rerum theologicarum,* the most important doctrinal text of

Toward the Reformation: Bosch, Grünewald, Holbein

the Reformation, and Luther courageously repeated his stand. Proclaimed a heretic, he was in imminent danger of being captured and thrown on the pyre when Frederick III, elector of Saxony, intervened and took him into custody at the Wartburg castle. In the castle Luther was able to continue his studies and undertook the translation of the New Testament into German. Meanwhile the surge toward change was being transformed into dangerous anarchy. The knight Franz von Sickingen, member of the minor aristocracy, organized a band of "brigand knights" to battle the well-to-do and the upper middle class, the traditional aristocracy, and the ecclesiastical princes. This so-called Knights' War was bloodily put down in 1523. The worst was yet to come, however. One of the greatest tragedies in German history was the Peasants' War of 1524–26. There were also the related acts of the Anabaptists led by Thomas Müntzer. Gathering followers from the lowest classes, most of all peasants and weavers, Müntzer organized an army that attacked the soldiers of the nobles at Frankenhausen on May 15,

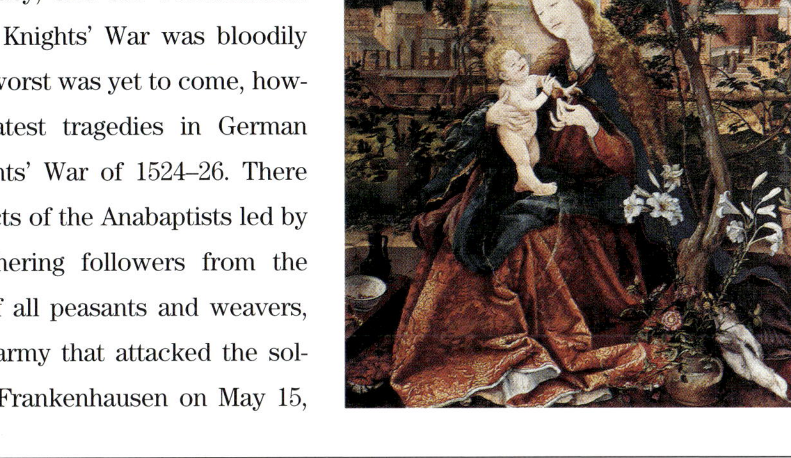

vast areas of Germany, closing monasteries and confiscating ecclesiastic goods. In 1526, following a literary dialogue with Erasmus, Luther published the two volumes of his *Catechism*. By then the Reformation was active in a large part of the nation. Although Luther banned the worship of devotional images, he should not be considered the promoter of the campaign of iconoclasm; he limited himself to saying, "tear the images from your heart, not from the altars." In reality, however, such statements only provoked the repudiation of religious painting and led to a sudden halt in German art. The *annus horribilis* for German painting was 1528, with the death of Dürer and Grünewald and Hans Holbein's departure for England, where he was to become the court portraitist of Henry VIII. After 1530 no more altarpieces were painted, nor were any wooden altars produced, even though Lucas Cranach worked to give a face and image to the protagonists and concepts of the Reformation. In Wittenberg, where he served under three successive electors, including Frederick III, Cranach was

Matthis Grünewald, *Virgin and Child*, 1517–19; Parish church, Stuppach (Würzburg)

Bosch, Grünewald, Holbein

1525. The result was a massacre, leaving 10,000 peasants dead on the field. Aside from killing ecclesiastics and sacking churches, the violent acts of this period included the destruction of many works of art. There were serious consequences for those artists who had shown sympathy for the peasants: Grünewald lost his employment with the archbishop of Mainz; Tilman Riemenschneider was tortured and thrown into prison.

Compared to such terrible events the organization of the elector princes obtained far greater success, carrying out the secularization of

among the first artists to embrace the Reformation, making popular portraits of Luther, Luther's wife, Katharina von Bora, and Philip Melanchthon (repeated in many versions). He also made vast religious scenes illustrating themes of Reform theology. Cranach's busy workshop turned out the woodcut illustrations for Luther's German translation of the Bible. Even so, German art would have to wait until the end of the sixteenth century and the important initiatives of Emperor Rudolf II for the creation of a true national school.

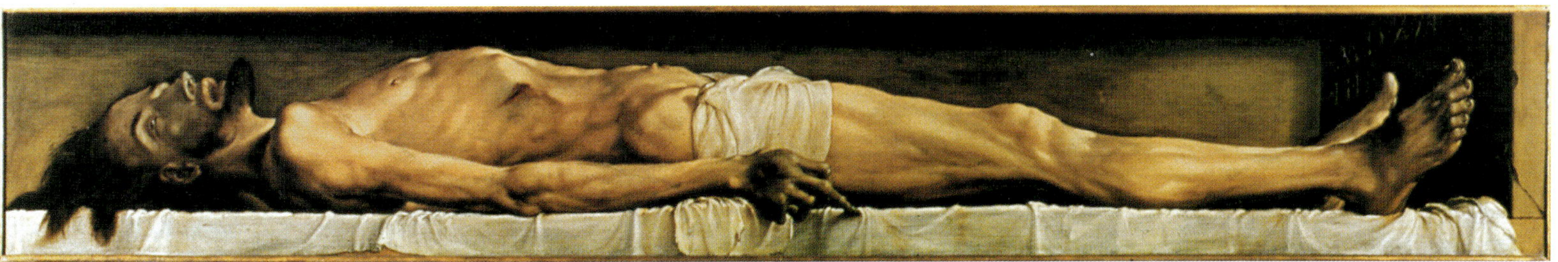

Hans Holbein the Younger, *Dead Christ*, 1521; Kunstmuseum, Basel

Toward the Reformation: Bosch, Grünewald, Holbein

This painting is based on one of the most popular books of the time, *The Ship of Fools*, a long poem by the Alsatian Sebastian Brandt published in several languages and illustrated by many woodcuts. At the end of the fifteenth century the border between madness and mental health was quite labile, and those considered fools were not confined or excluded; it was believed that God himself sometimes spoke through the mouths of "fools," who were left to roam the countryside and villages or were put aboard the so-called Blue Ship that sailed far and wide. Bosch loads the already crowded ship of fools with metaphors and allegories that shift between the obscene and the diabolical. The extraordinary pictorial result far outstrips, in terms of effectiveness and the figurative power of its images, Brandt's sometimes heavy-handed literary treatment.

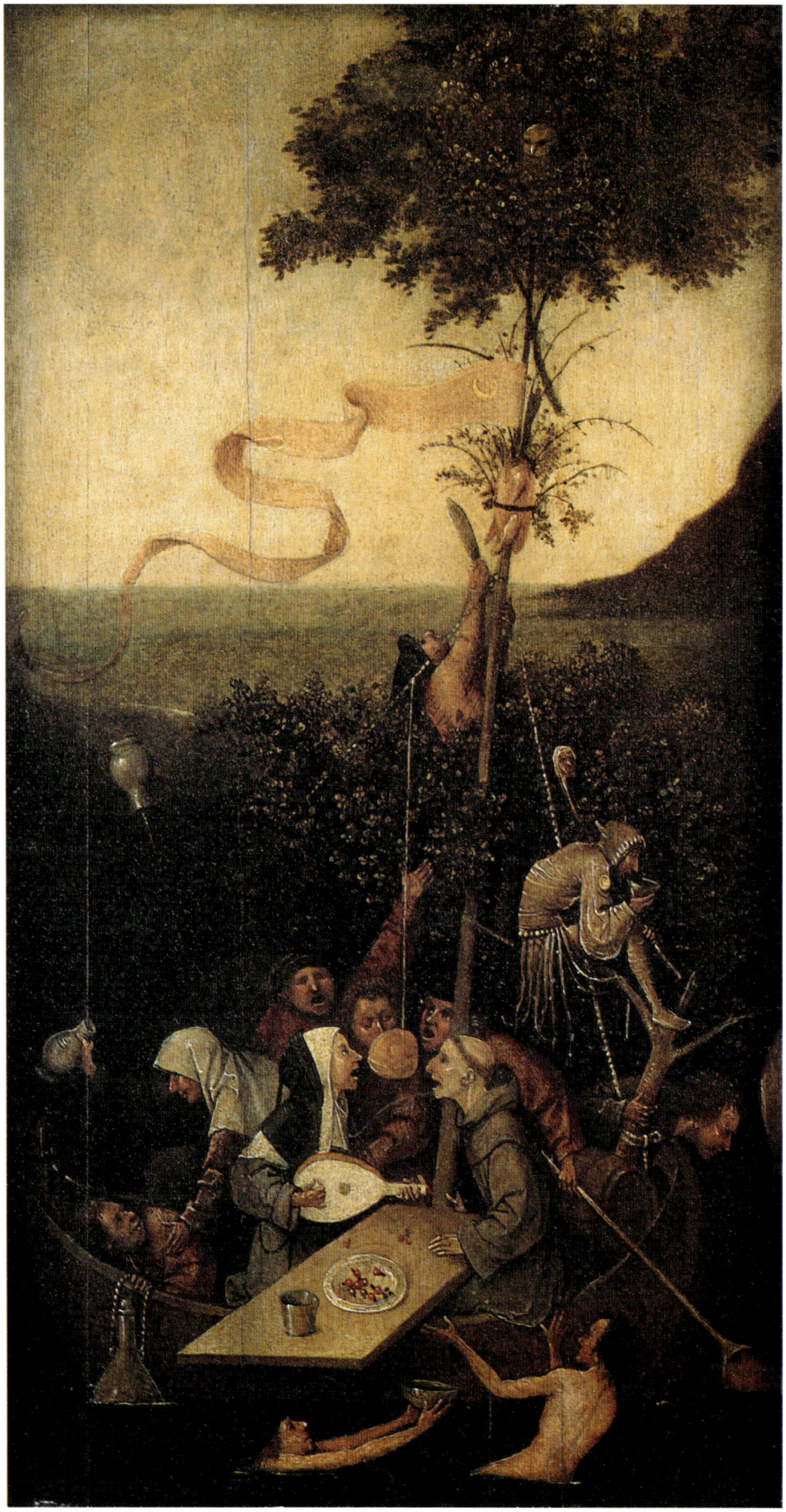

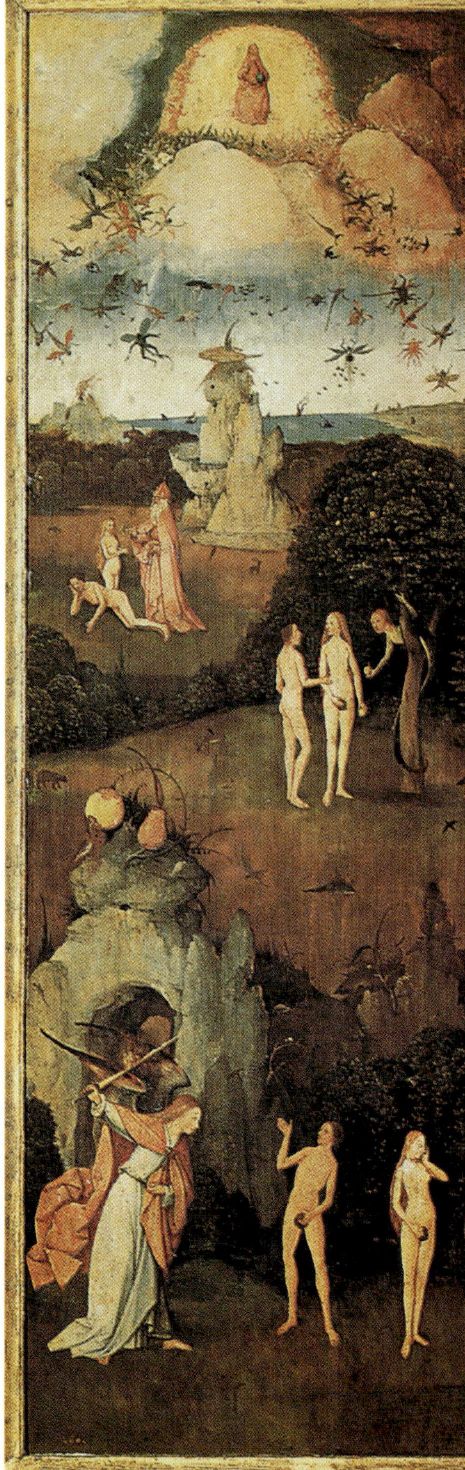

Toward the Reformation: Bosch, Grünewald, Holbein

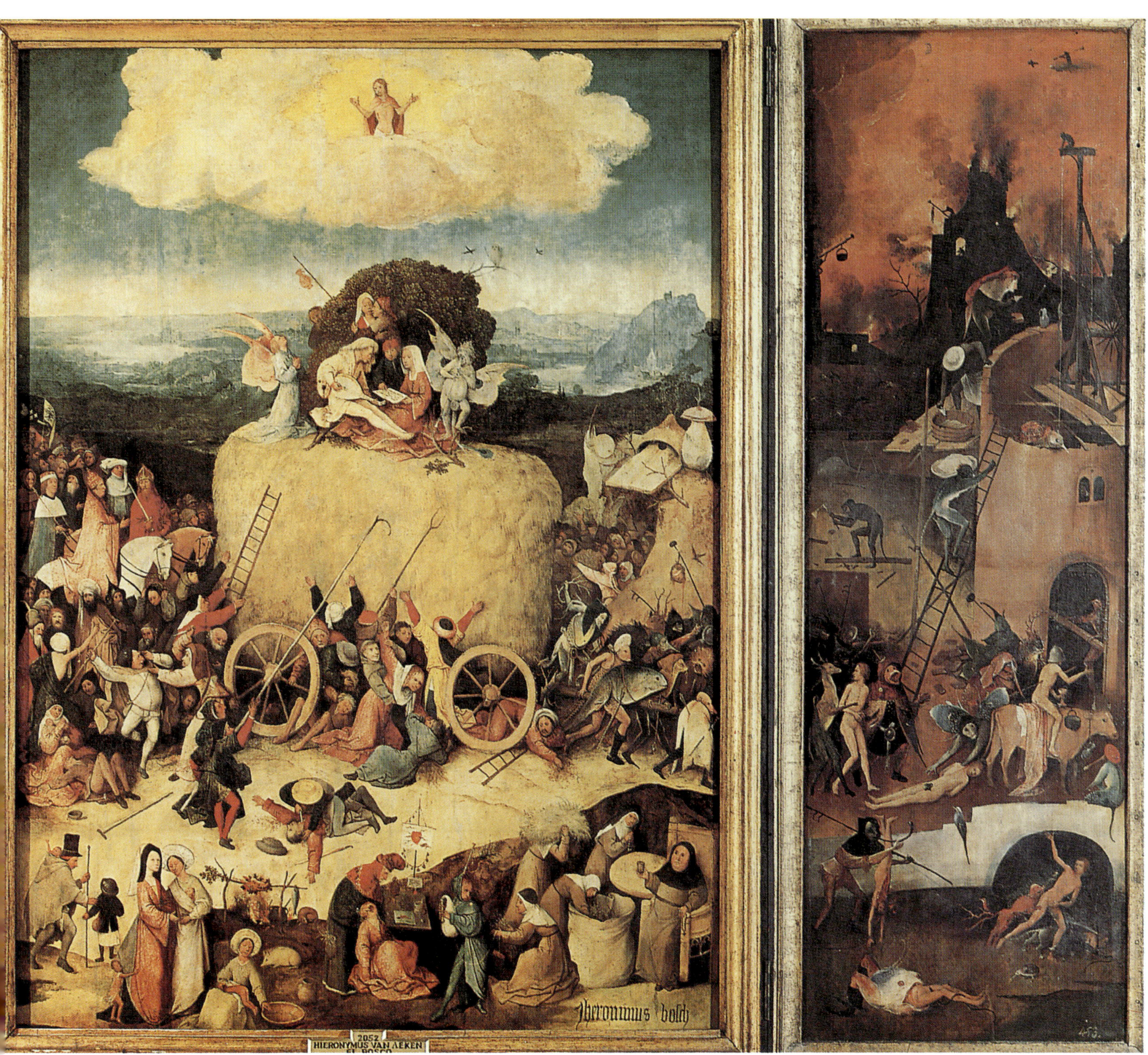

■ HIERONYMUS BOSCH
**Triptych of
the Haywain**
1500–02, oil on panel,
central panel 135 x
100 cm, side panels
135 x 45 cm
Museo del Prado,
Madrid

Humanity corrupted by
earthly pleasures, in
prey of folly, and inex-
orably heading fast to
eternal damnation—
Hieronymus Bosch's
favorite subject—is the
theme of the central
panel of the *Triptych
of the Haywain*, the
artist's first large-scale
satirical-moralistic allegory. An old Flemish
proverb holds that "the
world is a pile of hay:
everyone takes as much
as he can grab." Bosch
spent almost all of his
life in the town of his
birth, today in the
southern Netherlands,
and his learning was
a blend of popular
proverbs, humanistic
ideas, suggestions from
other painters, reli-
gious beliefs, peasant
superstitions, magical
alchemy, and science.
Bosch uses bitter humor
to ridicule the usual
human journey toward
rack and ruin, blinded
by the thirst for money,
possessions, and power.
In fact no one (not
even, at first, the
viewer) notices that
the wagon is being
drawn by demons,
its destination the
flames of hell.

Toward the Reformation: Bosch, Grünewald, Holbein

**The Extraction of the
Stone of Madness
(The Cure of Folly)**
1481, oil on panel,
48 x 35 cm
Museo del Prado,
Madrid

This small, delightful
painting initiated the
folk vein in Bosch's
production. At the
time, someone crazy
was said to "have a
rock in the head," and
the inscription relates
the afflicted man's
request: "Doctor,
remove my stone: my
name is Lubbert das"
(a play on words mean-
ing a simpleton). The
funnel worn by the
supposed surgeon is
a mocking allusion
to wisdom.

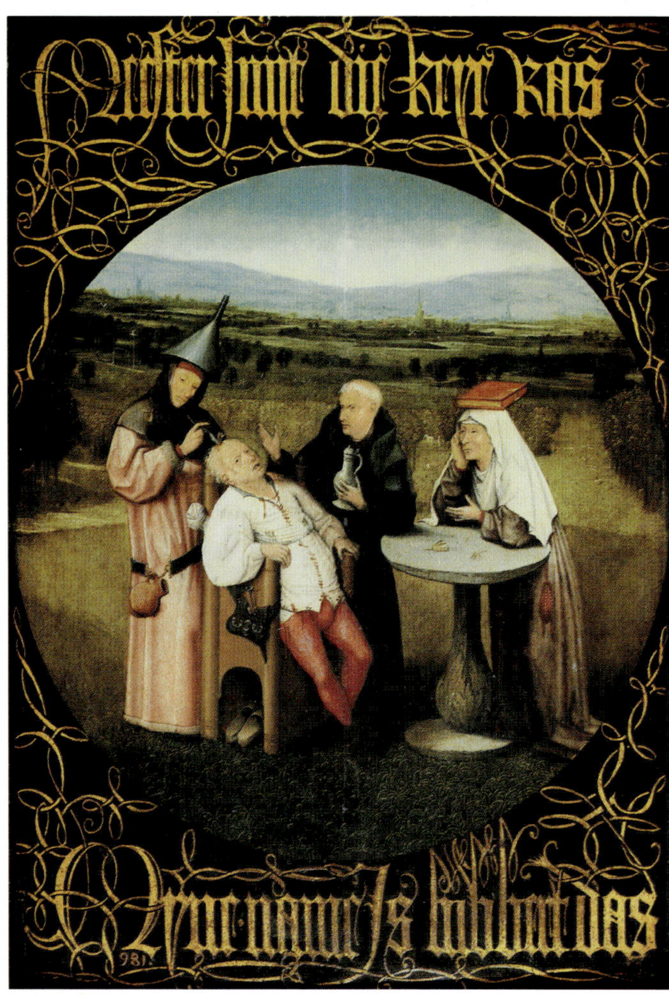

HIERONYMUS BOSCH
**Triptych of the
Temptation of
St. Anthony
(Flight and Fall of
St. Anthony, The
Temptation of St.
Anthony, Meditation
of St. Anthony)**
1505–06, oil on panel,
central panel 131.5 x
119 cm, side panels
131.5 x 53 cm
Museu Nacional de
Arte Antiga, Lisbon

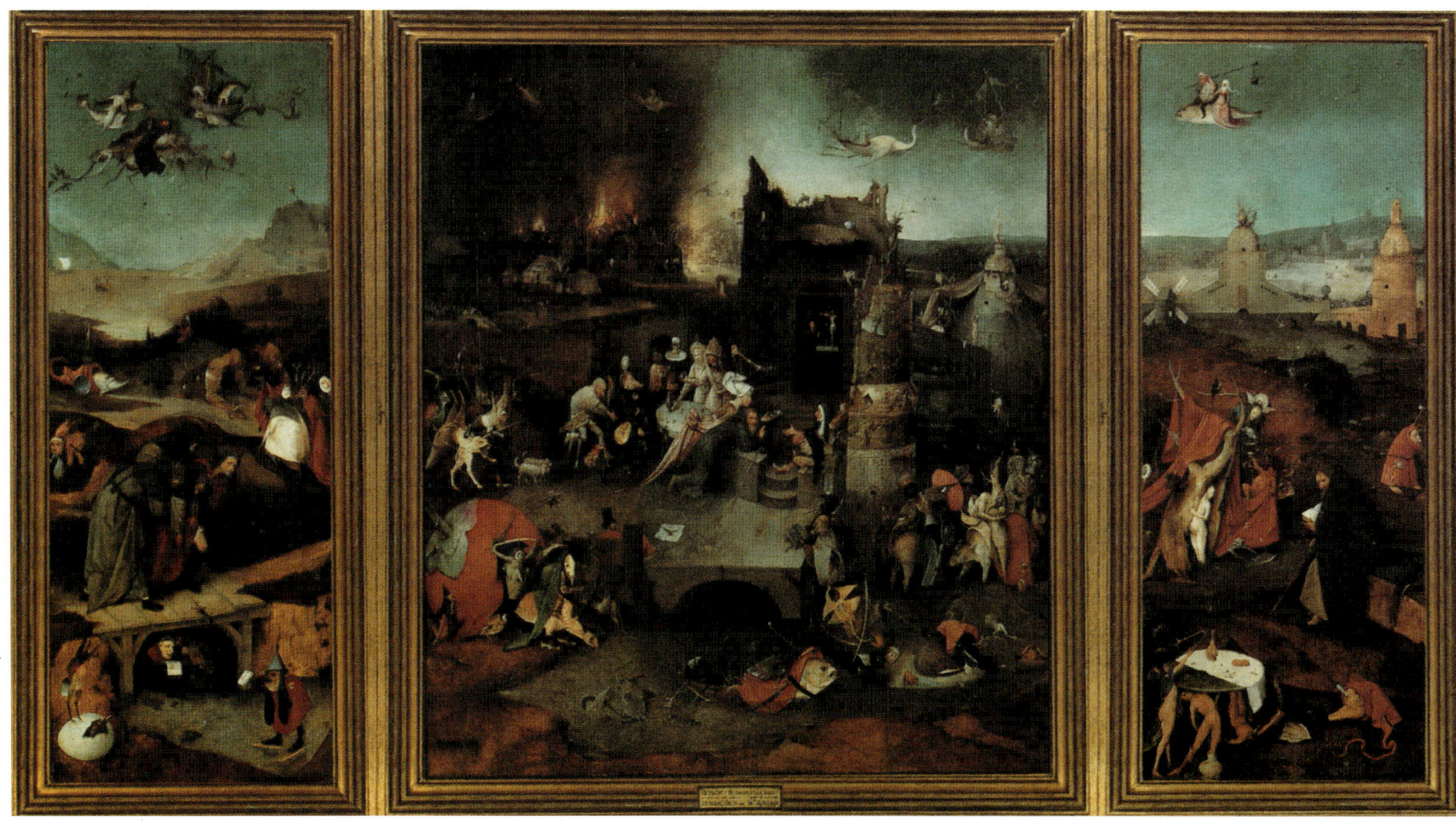

Toward the Reformation: Bosch, Grünewald, Holbein

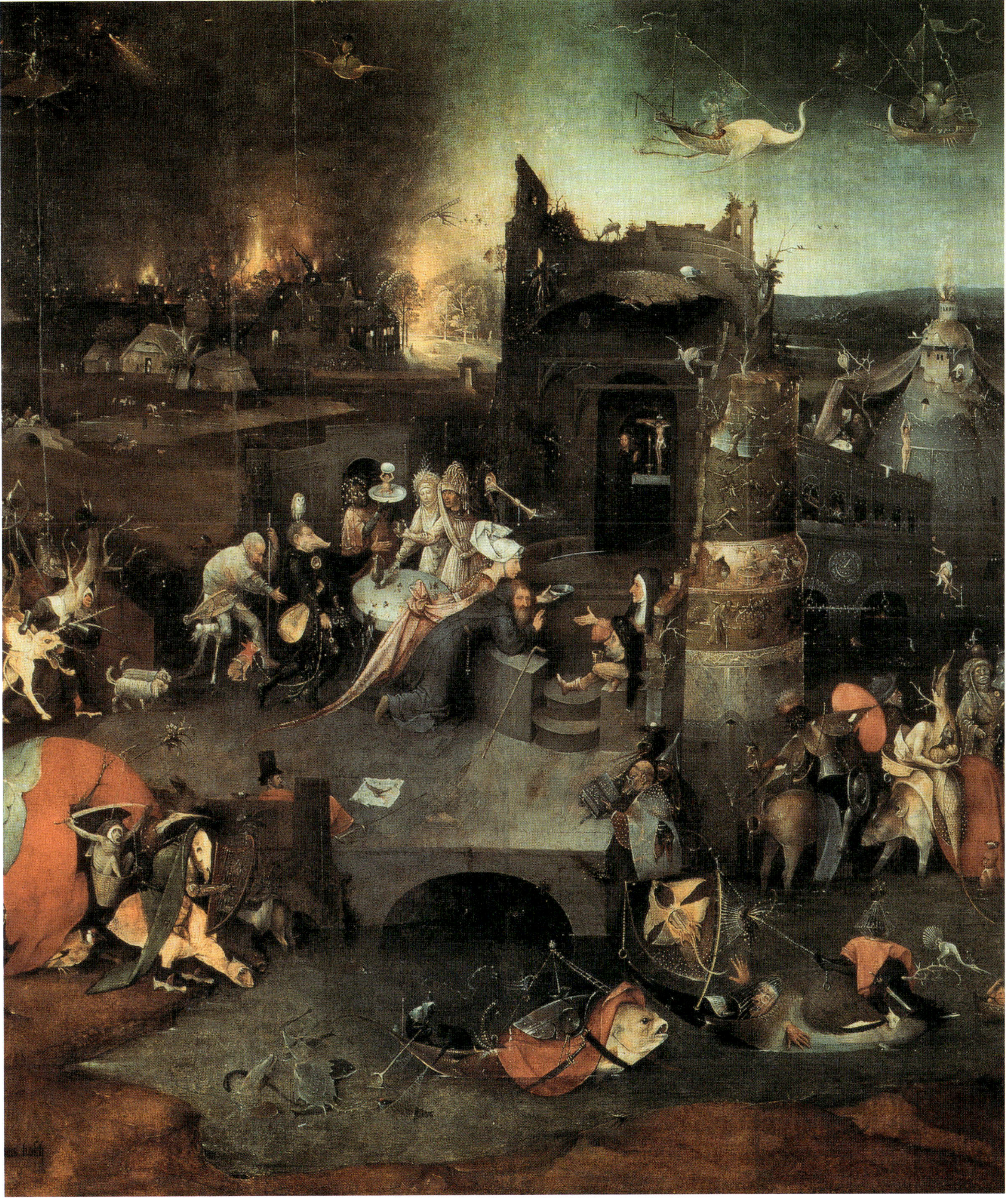

HIERONYMUS BOSCH
**The Temptation
of St. Anthony**
central panel of the
Triptych of the
Temptation of
St. Anthony
1505–06,
oil on panel,
131.5 x 119 cm
Museu Nacional de
Arte Antiga,
Lisbon

In 1478 the Dutch edition of the *Golden Legend*—the collection of lives of saints compiled by Jacobus da Varagine—made easily accessible also in northern Europe the story of the temptation of St. Anthony Abbot, the hermit in the desert put to the test by the devil with two types of torment: the aerial, with the saint carried into the sky by demons, and the terrestrial, involving seductive apparitions. Bosch and his workshop alone counted for fully eleven versions of this subject. This triptych is one of the painter's true masterpieces. In the central panel, elegantly dressed priestesses celebrate a sacrilegious mass while a crowd of heterogeneous figures gathers, all of them fruits of a truly fabulous imagination. Nothing seems real, beginning with the flying ships or the curious boats that navigate the lower areas of the painting.

Toward the Reformation: Bosch, Grünewald, Holbein

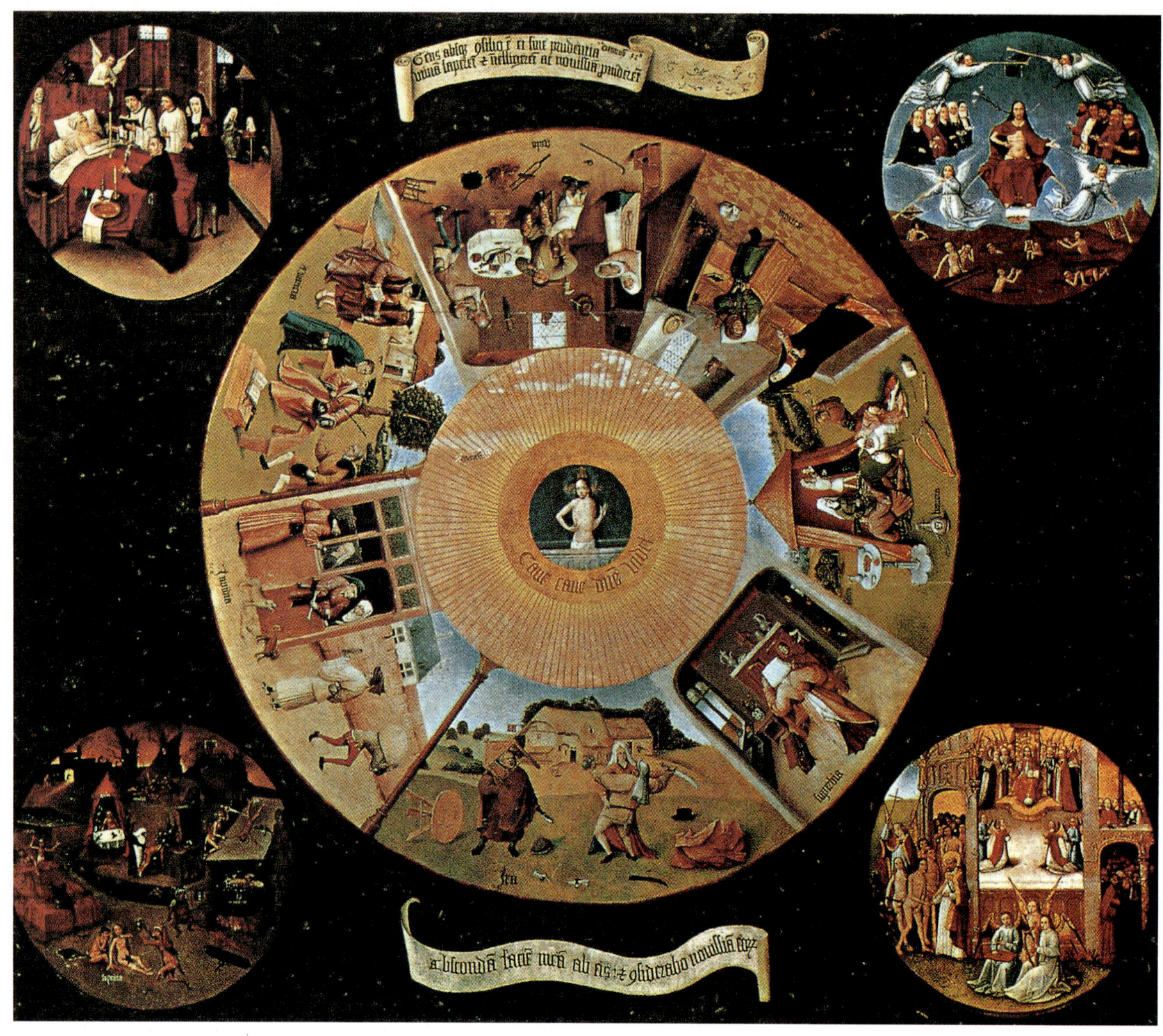

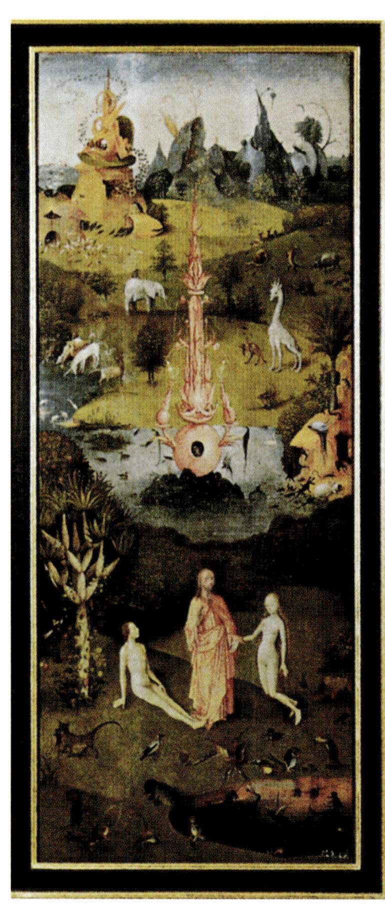
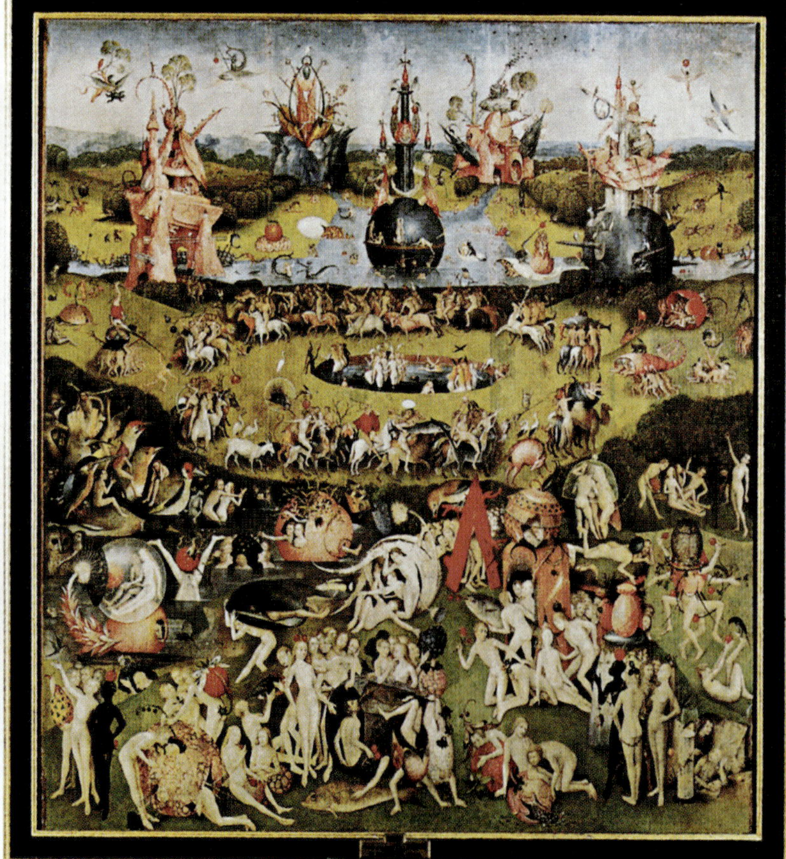
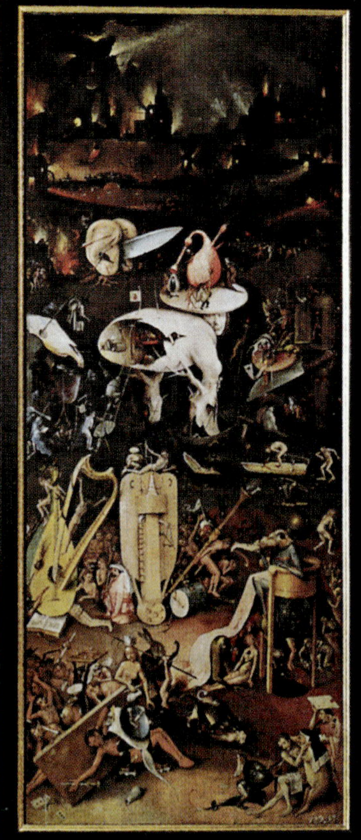

Toward the Reformation: Bosch, Grünewald, Holbein

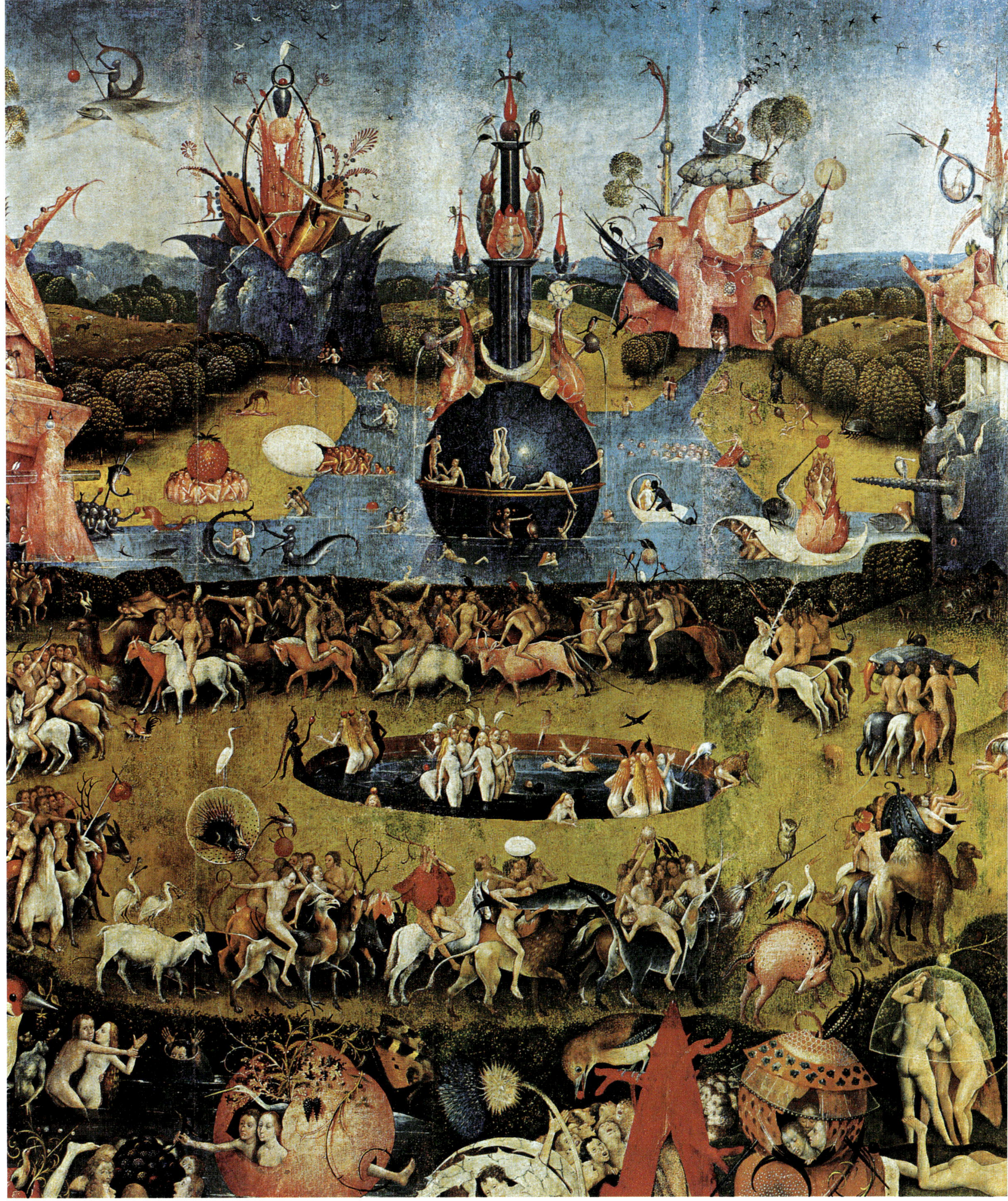

This triptych's side panels present the *Creation of Eve* and a terrifying vision of hell in which the tormented are punished by enormous musical instruments, and the exterior of the panels presents an evocative vision of the world during the creation. In the central panel, Bosch organizes the scene on four different levels with a circular progression populated by hundreds of naked human beings, monstrous creatures, animals, references to earthly possessions, and to alchemy. Many details, such as the berries and the birds around the lake in the second level, are dramatically out of scale, as though to emphasize their unnatural—excessive and sinful—condition. The "garden of the delights" is thus located during a phase of human history (understood as much as the overall destiny of mankind as the fate of each separate life) that is intermediate between the purity of divine creation and the punishment of eternal sin.

A throng of grotesque figures surrounds Christ: Evil has become incarnate in humanity. Demonic physiognomies, beaklike noses, sunken eyes, and toothless mouths emerge from the dark background, against which the bright colors of certain headwear stands out. Faces in profile alternate with heads presented frontally or in three-quarters, without leaving any space free, such that the nineteen figures begin a centrifugal movement along the diagonal of the cross, at the center of which is the serene face of Christ. To the upper right is the penitent thief, being harangued by a monk. His eyes too are half-closed, much like those of Jesus and, at the bottom end of this second diagonal line, those of Veronica. Only in that way can the Good isolate themselves from the disheartening spectacle offered by the incarnation of Evil. The unrepentant thief, below right, goes toward his fate with a sardonic grimace; Veronica has Christ's image on her cloth.

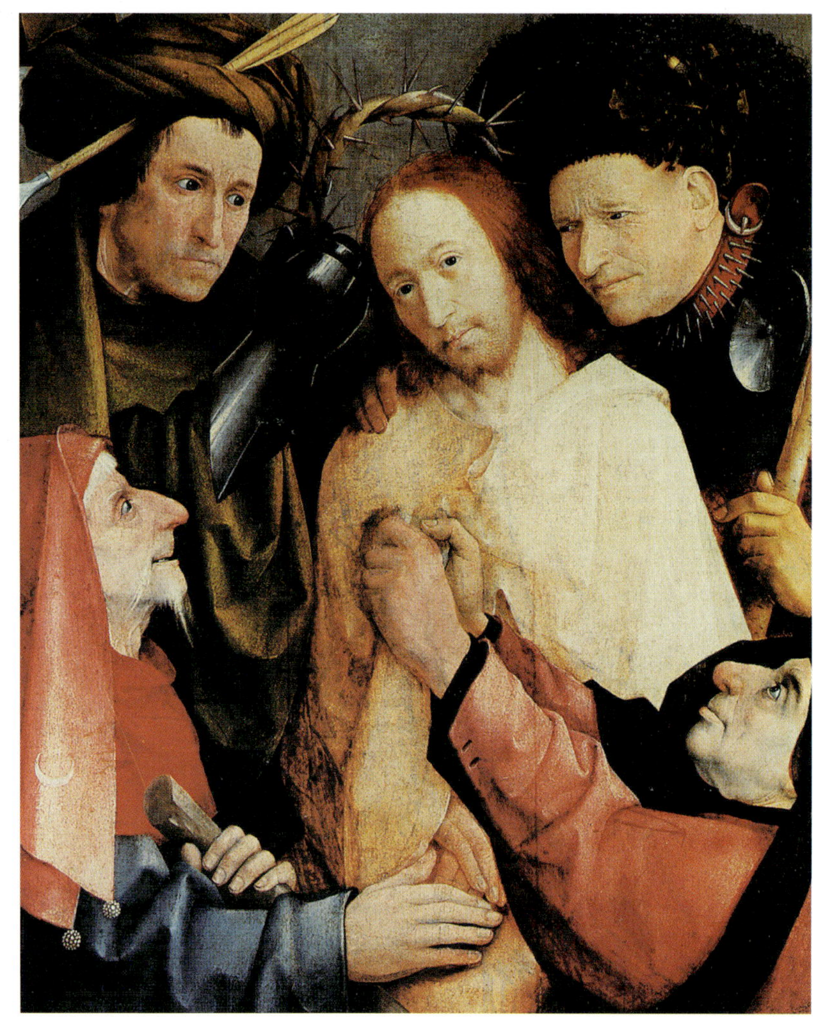

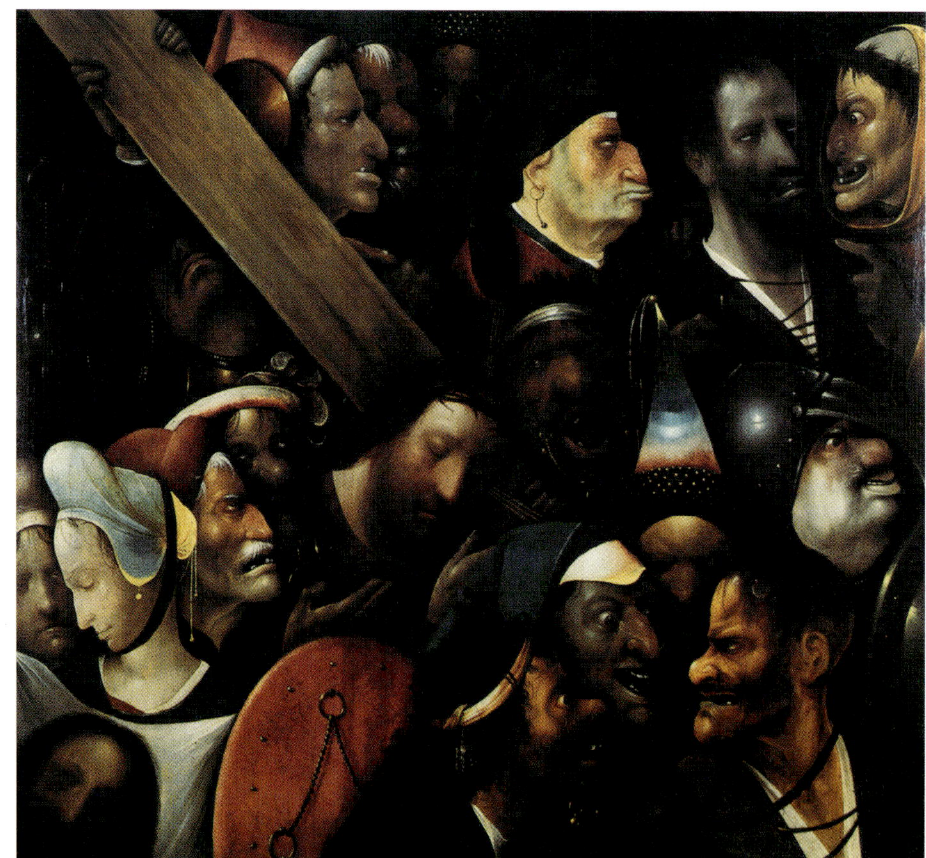

Toward the Reformation: Bosch, Grünewald, Holbein

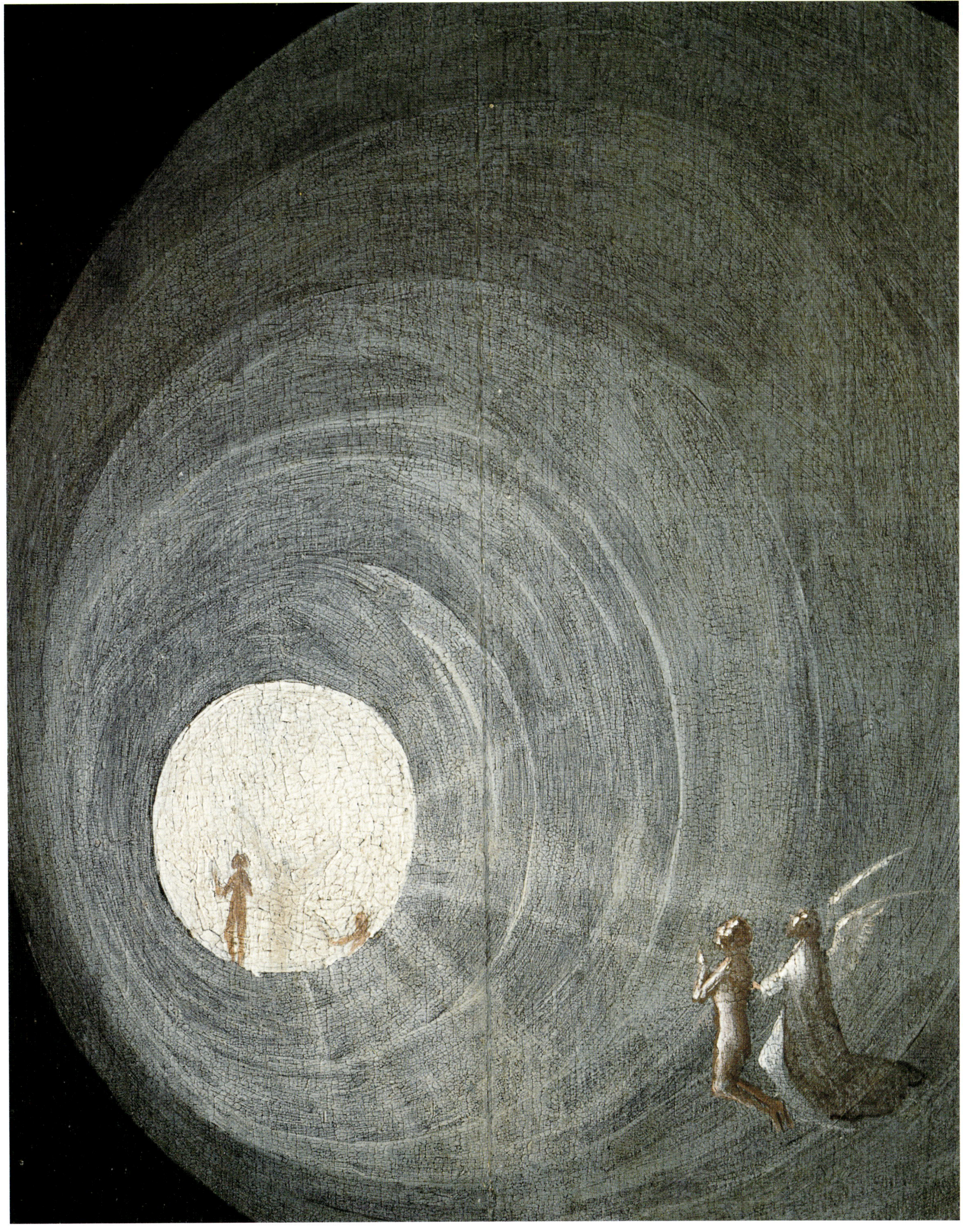

Toward the Reformation: Bosch, Grünewald, Holbein

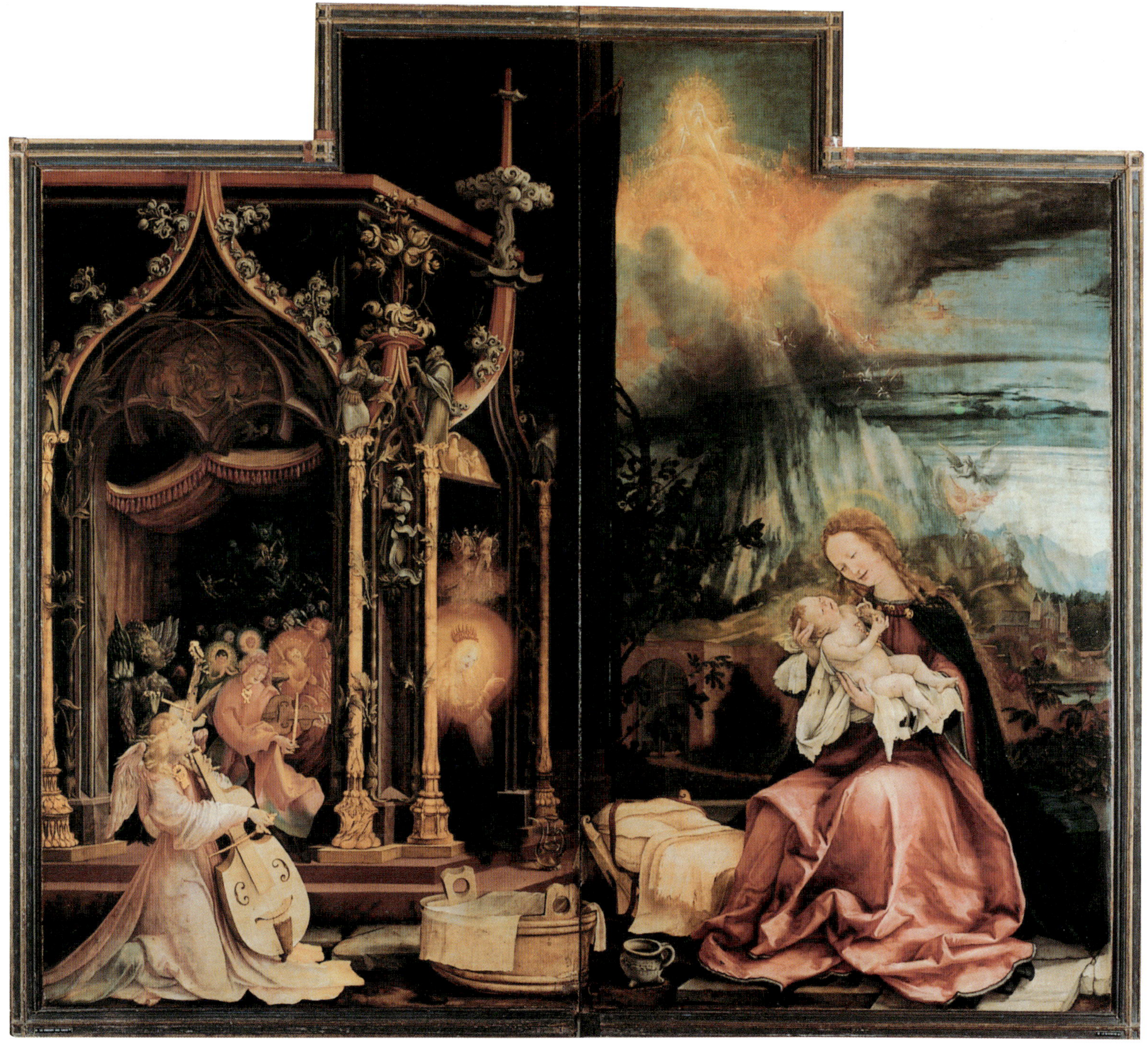

Toward the Reformation: Bosch, Grünewald, Holbein

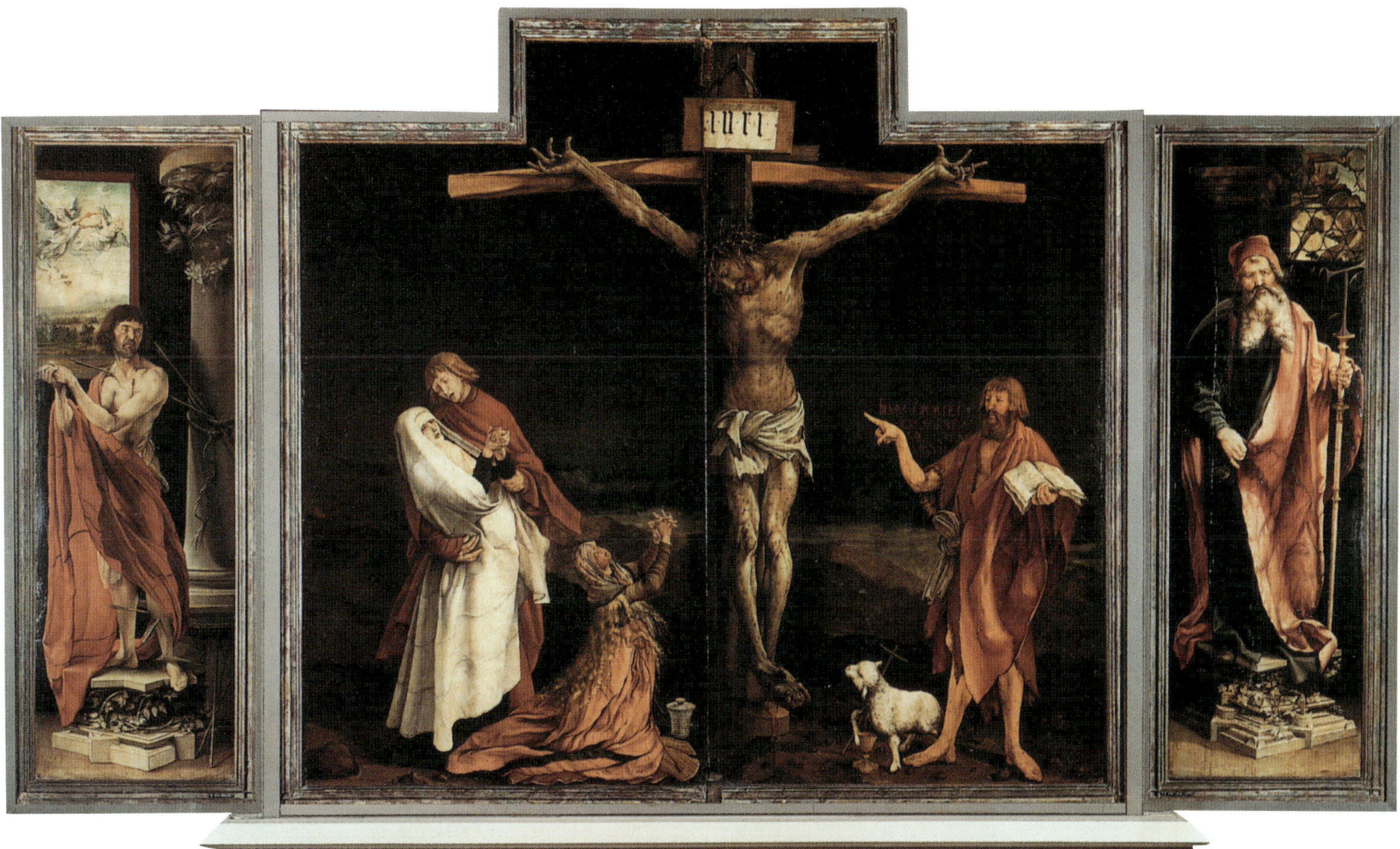

Toward the Reformation: Bosch, Grünewald, Holbein

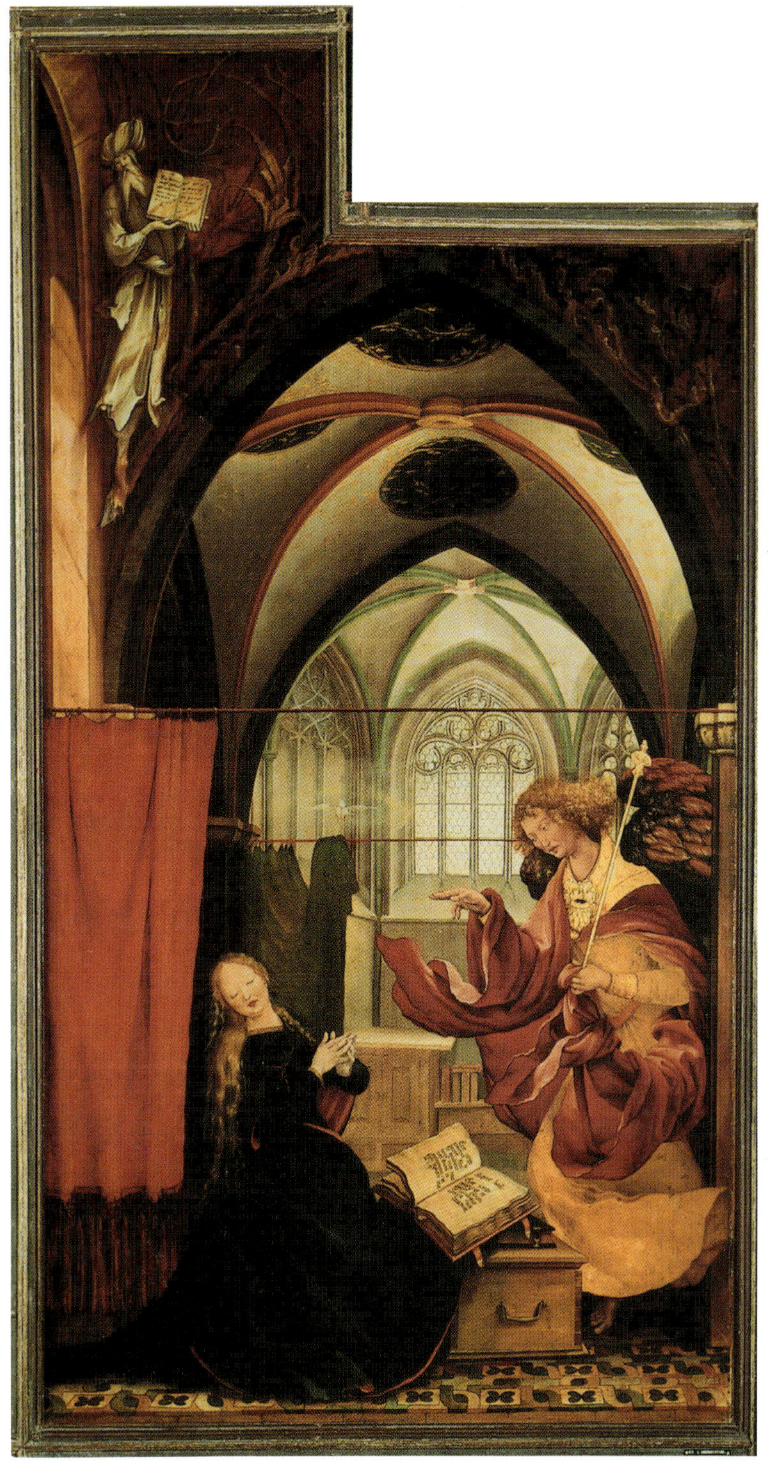

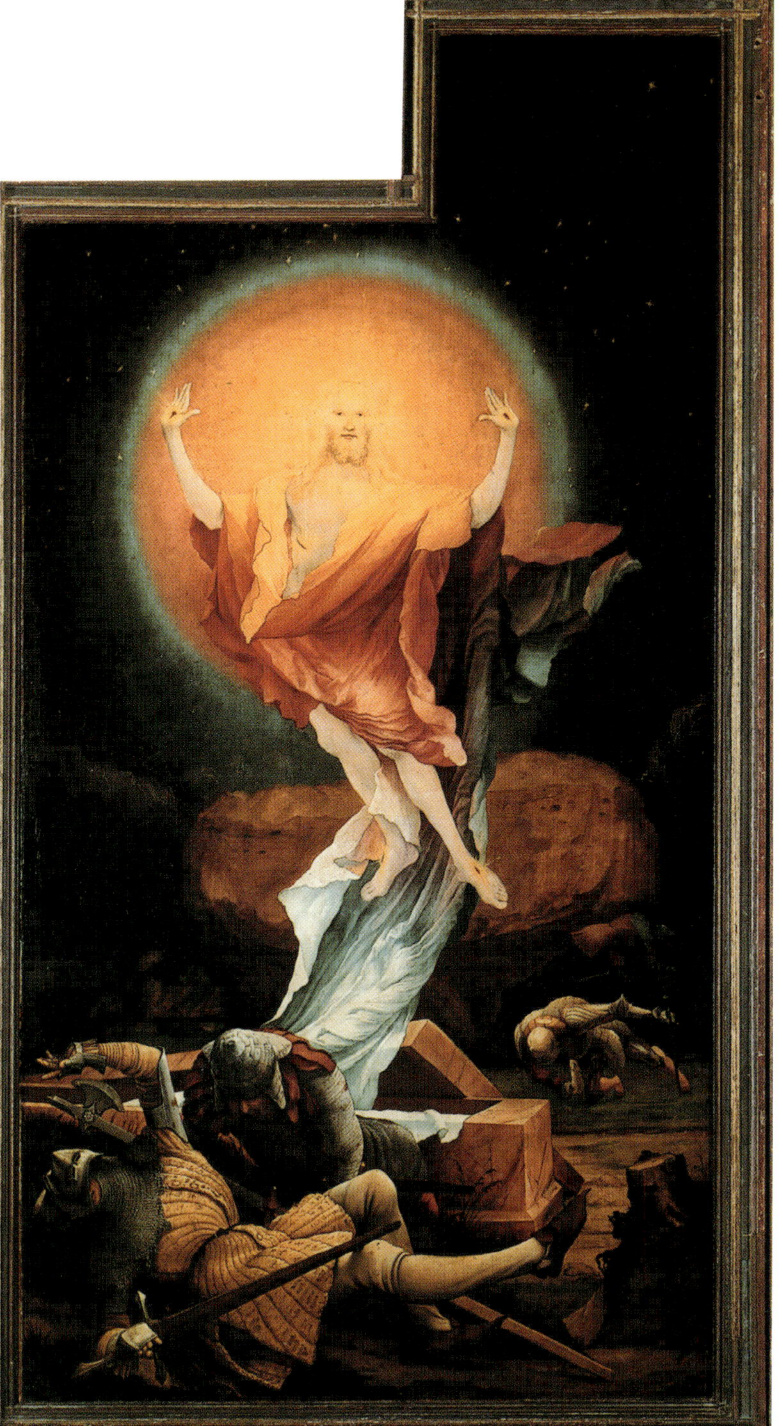

Toward the Reformation: Bosch, Grünewald, Holbein

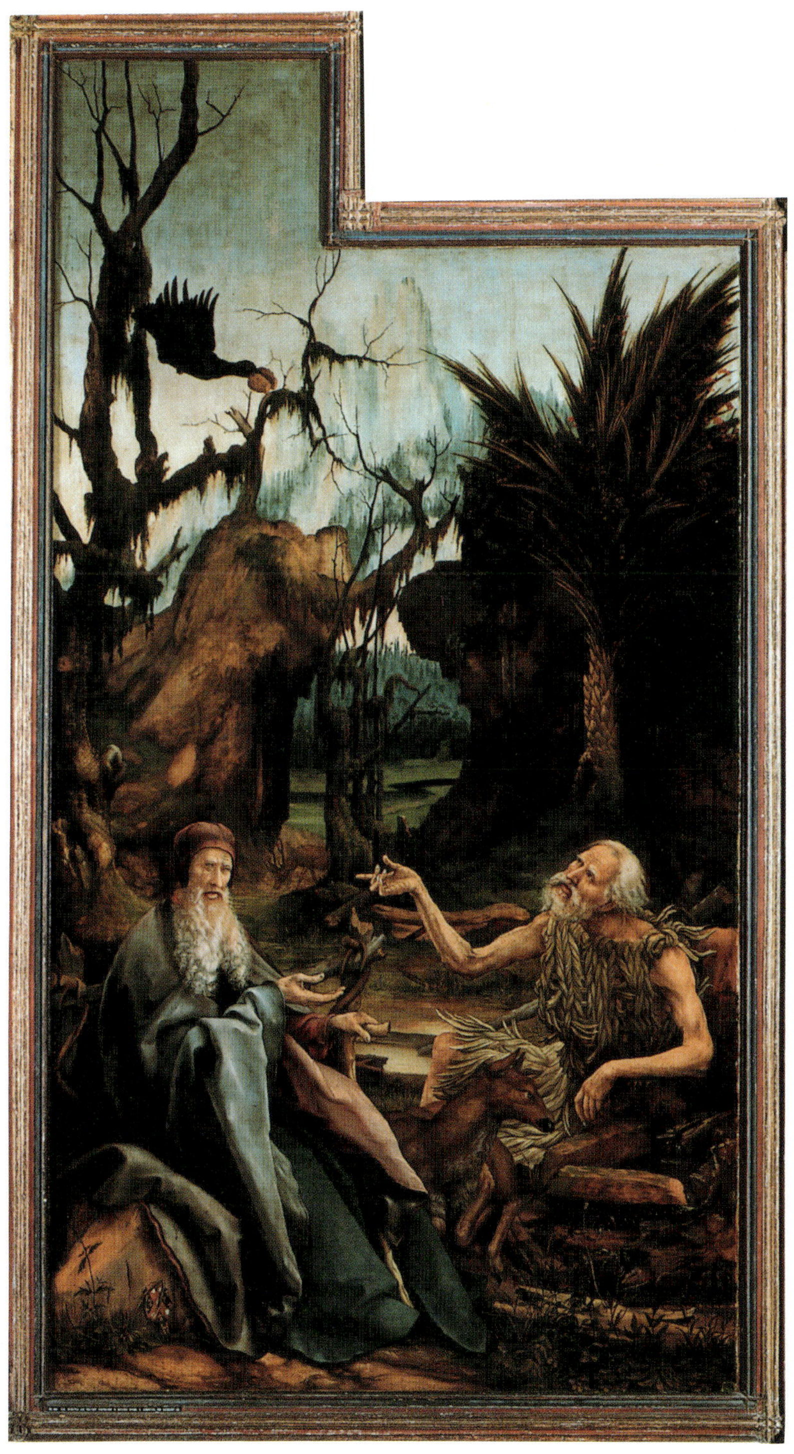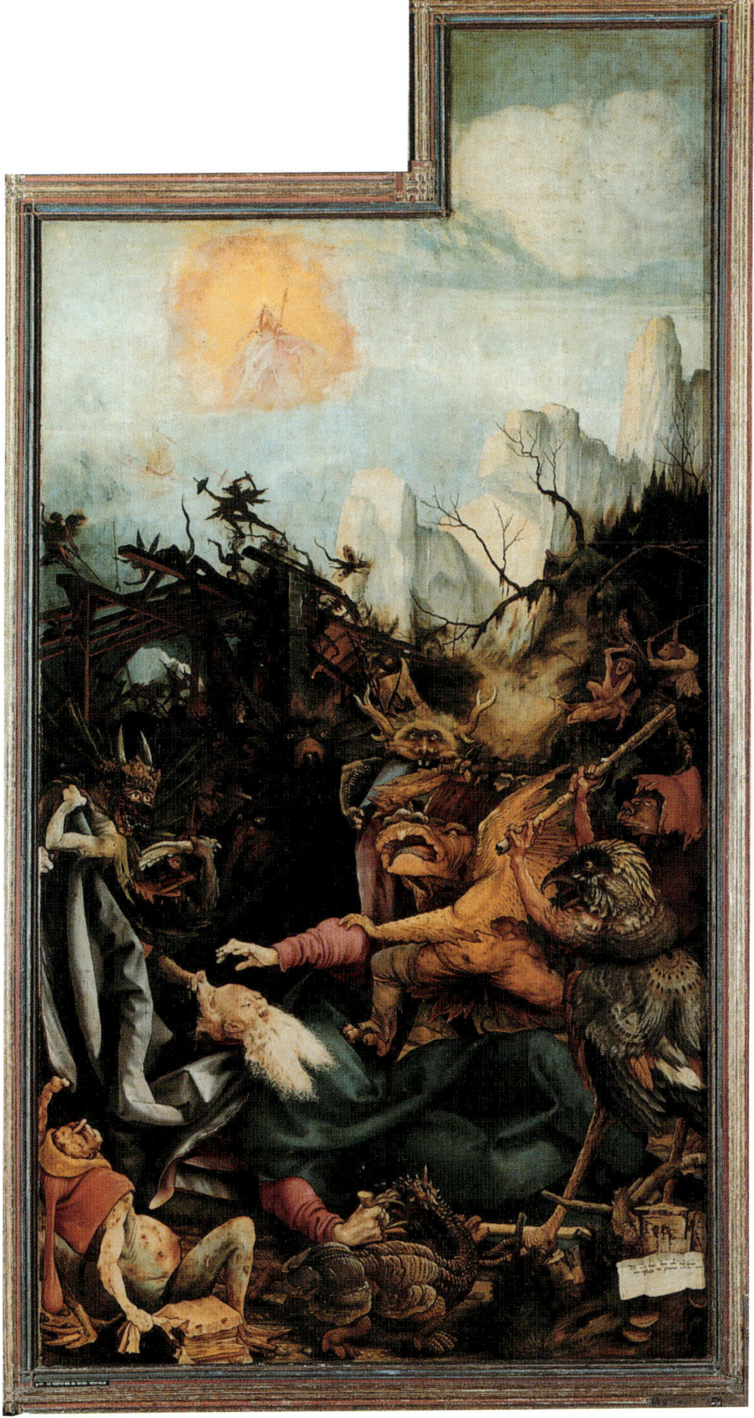

Toward the Reformation: Bosch, Grünewald, Holbein

Holbein makes the symbols of social rank of the nobles he presents plainly visible, but he does not stop at outward appearance. Because of his extraordinary awareness of the plastic masses, his psychological depth, and his realistic precision, Holbein is one of the most complete and ingenious portraitists of the European Renaissance. He demonstrates magnificent control of all aspects of painting: composition, light, color, and line in a perfect balance between physical verisimilitude, the evocation of the intellectual and spiritual reality of the figure, and care in the rendering of elegant details, although he never lets an overabundance of details detract from the figure. Holbein never allows any single element to prevail, nor does he seek "picturesque" effects, offering instead a kind of image that was to be the model for court portraiture for many years to come.

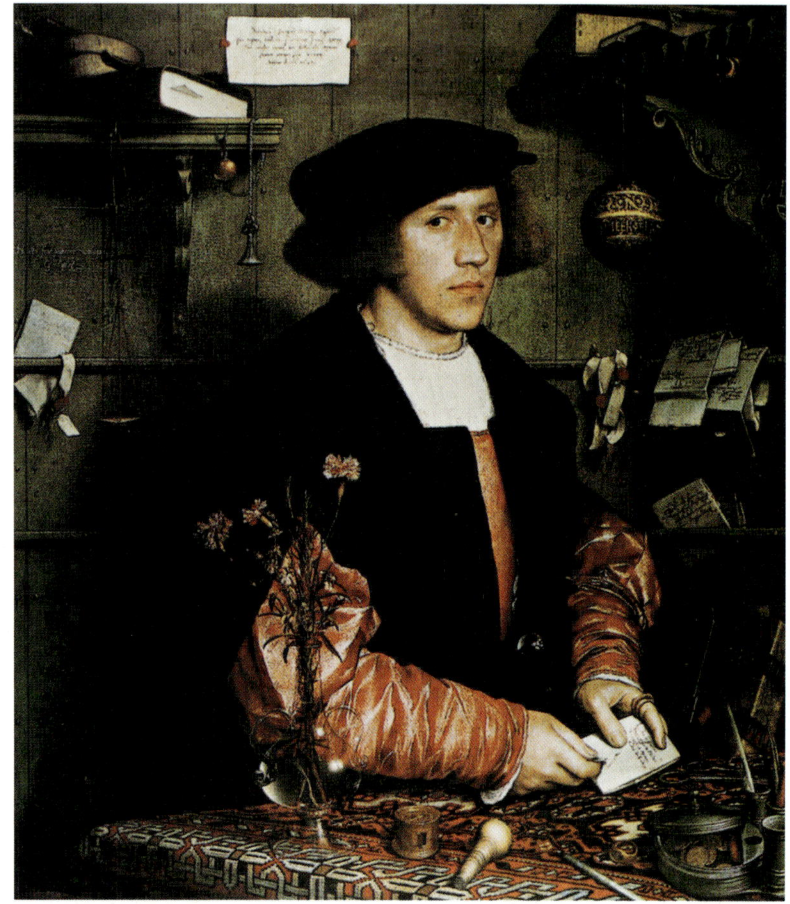

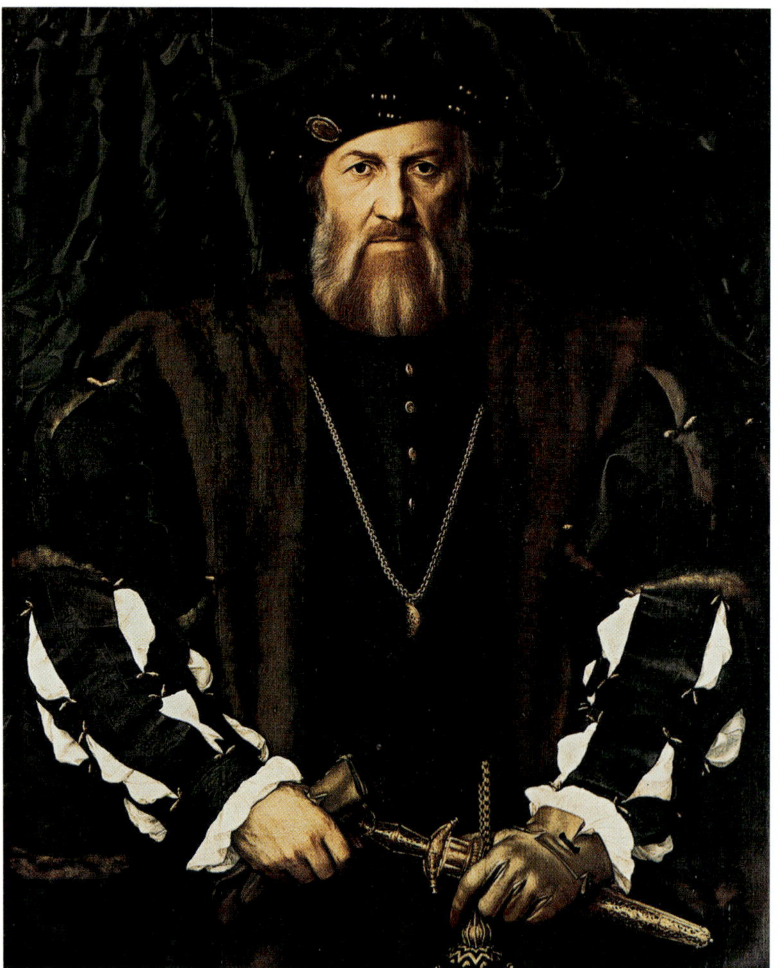

Toward the Reformation: Bosch, Grünewald, Holbein

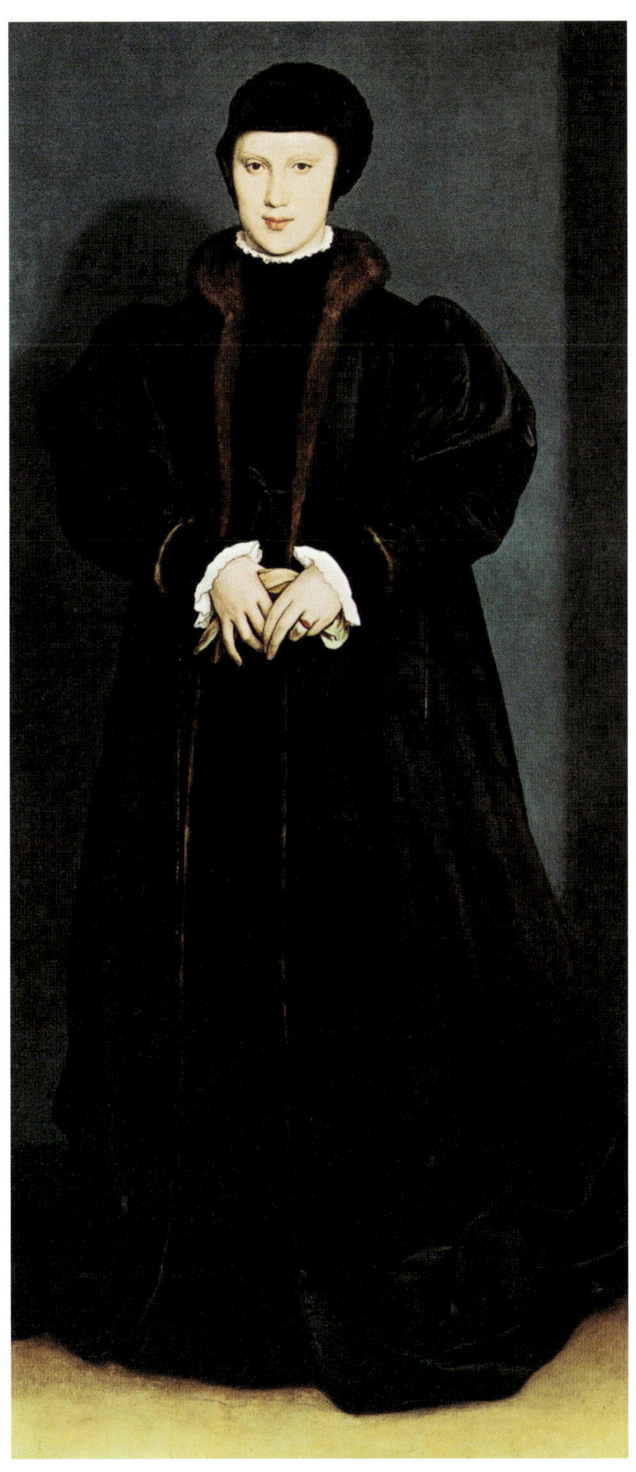

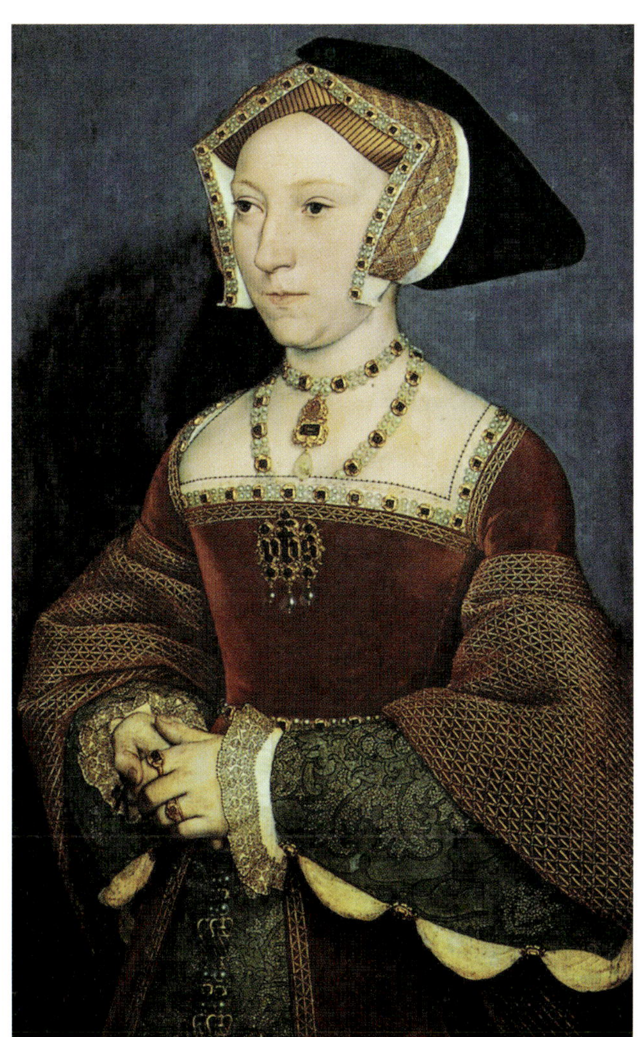

Toward the Reformation: Bosch, Grünewald, Holbein

HANS HOLBEIN
THE YOUNGER
The Ambassadors
1533, oil and
tempera on panel,
207 x 209.5 cm
National Gallery,
London

This panel, one of the
most complex and
interesting portraits of
the European Renais-
sance, was made on
the occasion of the
visit of Bishop Georges
de Selve (to the right)
to his friend Jean de
Dinteville, French
ambassador in London
(the floor of the paint-
ing reproduces that of
Westminster Abbey).
Both youths were fol-
lowing rapid and bril-
liant diplomatic careers.
But here too Holbein
goes beyond the out-
ward evocation of the
two figures. Both lean
against a piece of fur-
niture draped by an
Anatolian carpet with
geometric motifs; on its
shelves are books and
musical and scientific
instruments, arranged
in accordance with a
subtle scheme of sym-
bolic references. The
overall theme is a harsh
one: the transitory
nature of beauty, art,
and harmony. Yet a fur-
ther reference to this
allegory is made by the
mysterious object in the
foreground: a human
skull painted in the
optical deformation
achieved by an anamor-
phic lens.

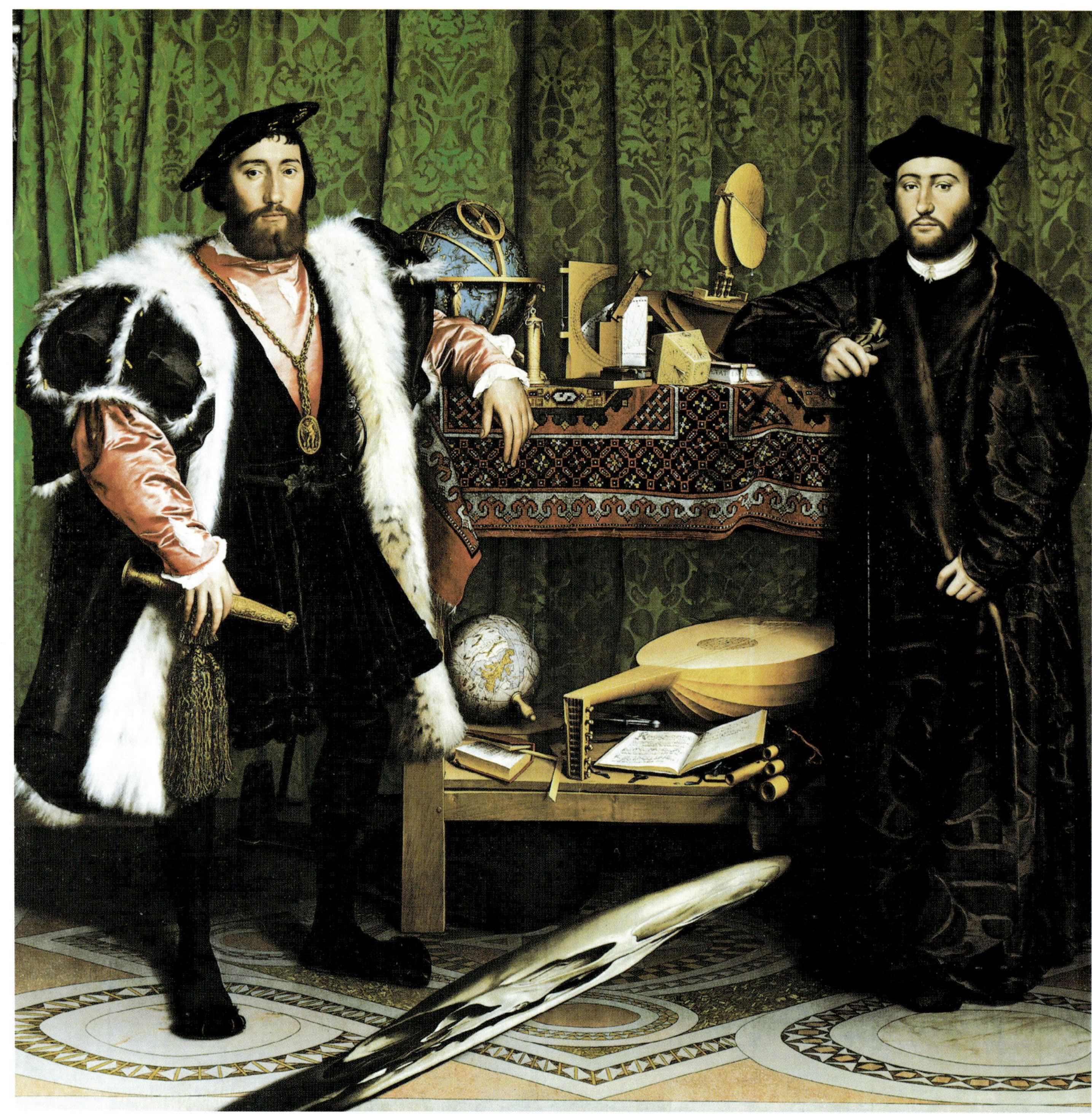

Toward the Reformation: Bosch, Grünewald, Holbein

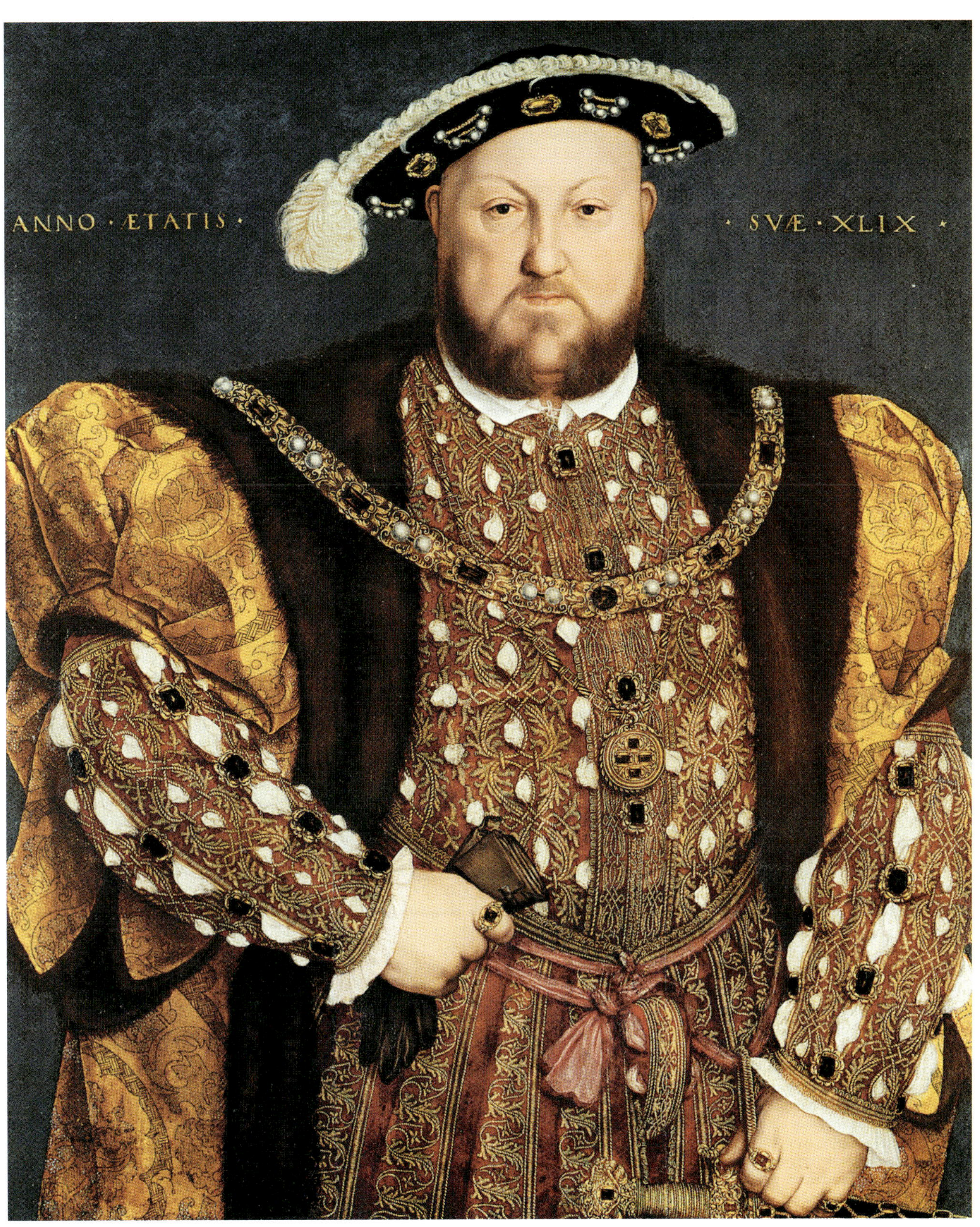

**Hans Holbein
the Younger**
Portrait of Henry VIII
1539–40,
tempera on panel,
88 x 75 cm
Galleria Nazionale di
Arte Antica, Rome

The king, age forty-
nine, is dressed in the
ornate costume pre-
pared for his fourth
wedding celebration,
that with Anne of
Cleves, on January 6,
1540, as soon as the
proposed marriage to
Christina of Denmark
failed. This may well be
the last portrait Holbein
made of the king, and
it has been the subject
of many replicas. Henry,
presented head-on
frontally, fully domi-
nates the image, his
shape expanding to the
point that he occupies
all the available surface;
in fact, he seems to
lift his right elbow
as though to make
more room.

Toward the Reformation: Bosch, Grünewald, Holbein

I n 1503, following the death of Alexander VI and the brief reign of Pius III, Giuliano della Rovere, a nephew of Sixtus IV, was elected pope and chose the name Julius II. In terms of military and financial affairs, the ten years of his pontificate (1503–13) proved disastrous. His attempts at conquest turned out to be sources of defeat, expense, and conflicts that shook the church. In terms of the arts it was another matter, for Julius II was also the pope who started the reconstruction of St. Peter's, who obliged Michelangelo to paint the ceiling of the Sistine Chapel, and who had Raphael decorate his private apartments in the Vatican, thereby wresting from Florence and giving to Rome primacy as the capital of the arts. Among his first actions was the nomination of Donato Bramante to superintendent general of papal buildings, with the task of upgrading existing structures to make them adequately stately and designing the new, monumental basilica of St. Peter. Bramante proposed a centrally planned structure, built around an immense dome about 40 meters in diameter, under which Julius II imagined placing his funerary monu-

ure displays its own individual personality, expressing with gestures and face the "movements of the soul."

In 1455, while Michelangelo was busy on the exhausting labor of the vault of the Sistine Chapel, Raphael began the pictorial cycle in the Stanza di Eliodoro. The decorative program exalts the political role of the pope and the church and their divine support against aggressors. Raphael, who had been able to study the large portion of the vault of the Sistine already completed by Michelangelo and who kept in touch with the Veneto painters in Rome (Lotto, Sebastiano del Piombo), left behind the quiet serenity of the Stanza della Segnatura to employ a style heavy in dramatic effects and tensions. Although they occupy similar spaces, the frescoes have a driving rhythm, emphasized by flashing light and looming architectonic structures.

In 1513, in the middle of Raphael's work on the Stanza di Eliodoro, Julius II died. In all probability, the fresco of the *Liberation of St. Peter,* a prodigy of luminous magic and silent, lunar emotion, recalls the death of the pope, his release from the "earthly prison." Leo X, the new pope, was Giovanni de' Medici, Lorenzo the Magnificent's son.

From Julius II to Leo X:

ment. With this in mind, he summoned Michelangelo to Rome in 1505. Thus began what Michelangelo's disciple and biographer, Ascanio Condivi, called the "tragedy of the tomb," an undertaking that would torment Michelangelo for nearly forty years. Meanwhile work had begun on the pope's new private apartments, on the second floor of the Vatican palaces, not far from the Sistine Chapel. The artists involved in this work came to include the Italians Perugino, Sodoma, Baldassarre Peruzzi, Bramantino, Lorenzo Lotto, and the German Johannes Ruysch. During the last months of 1508 Raphael joined the group. When Julius II realized the qualities possessed by this young man from Urbino, he ordered the destruction of what had just been made and asked Raphael to paint what is today called the Stanza della Segnatura. In this work Raphael took a decisive step away from the precedents he had at hand, even those prestigious, such as the Collegio del Cambio by Perugino. He did not limit himself to the presentation of a row of symbolic figures, but created narrative scenes within monumental architectonic or natural settings. Within each "story" each fig-

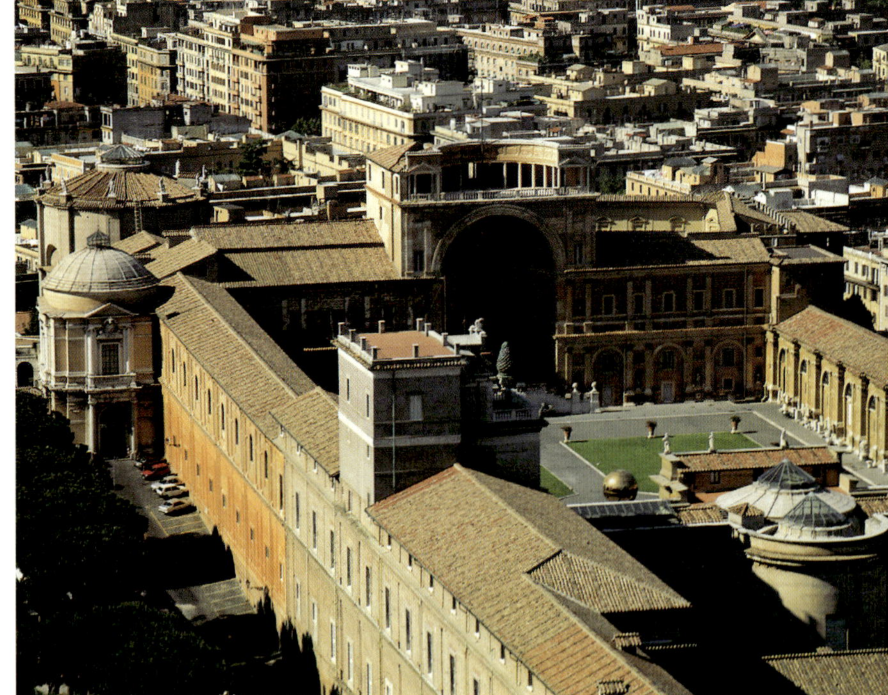

From Julius II to Leo X: the splendor of Rome

He and Raphael enjoyed a perfect harmony of ideals. When Bramante died, in 1514, Raphael was proclaimed architect of the building of St. Peter's. Also in 1514, in a letter addressed to the pope written together with Baldassare Castiglione, Raphael insisted on the importance of not destroying statues and classical ruins, but instead of preserving these "paragons of the ancients." This spirit is related to the third room in the Vatican, where Leo X wanted to recall historical episodes related to popes named Leo. The first fresco (summer 1514), based on the story of a fire *(incendio)* in the area of Rome known as the Borgo, gives the room its name, the Sala dell'Incendio. Raphael presented a further stylistic evolution: the features express emotions in a declamatory way, while the architecture has a strikingly theatrical tone.

After the popes, Raphael's major patron was the banker Agostino Chigi. In the work on La Farnesina, the villa on the Tiber River that Chigi had Baldassarre Peruzzi build for him, Peruzzi directed the decoration of the Sala delle Prospettive, Sodoma decorated Chigi's bedroom with *The Marriage of Alexander and Roxana* and *The Young Macedonian Taming Bucephalus*, and Sebastiano del Piombo made the lunettes with the *Loves of the Gods*. Raphael first frescoed the *Triumph of Galatea*, then, in 1517, he directed the team of artists in the frescoes of the entrance

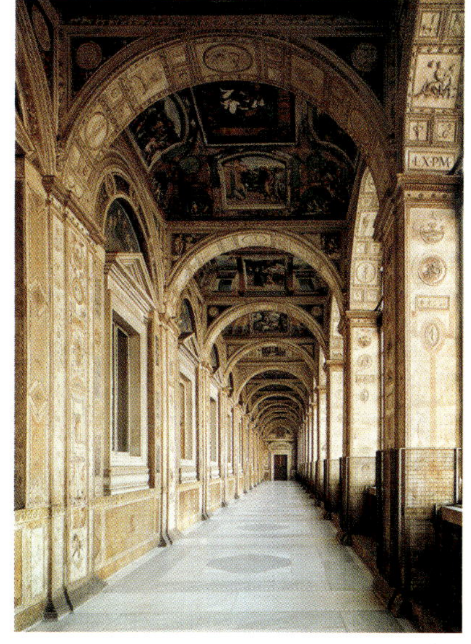

Raphael, Loggia of the Belvedere, 1516–19; Vatican, Rome

the four angular pendentives located near the entry and at the rear contain biblical stories, while the cells and the lunettes on the wall above the windows host the figures of the *Ancestors of Christ*. Despite the complexity, Michelangelo made some parts with impressive speed; each of the lunettes around the windows took him only three *giorante* (days of work). The middle of the vault nearest the entry was inaugurated on August 15, 1511; the completion of the whole took place fourteen months later, in October 1512. The next year, with the election of Leo X, Michelangelo returned to his work on the tomb of Julius II. He made the two *Slaves* in the Louvre and the *Moses*, the only statue put in place in its intended parietal position when the monument was finished, in 1545.

Before returning to Florence in 1516 Michelangelo established a working friendship with Sebastiano del Piombo. The final episode in

the splendor of Rome

loggia with scenes of Psyche and Cupid that were full of surprises and foretastes of the profane ornamentation of mannerism.

In 1508, Julius II had called Michelangelo to fresco the vault of the Sistine Chapel; the chapel itself was used for the most stately ceremonies of the papal curia. Michelangelo returned to Rome and on May 10, 1508, reluctantly put himself to work. With the exception of various assistants, who performed purely mechanical chores, he took on the immense ceiling alone. The thrones on which seven prophets and five sibyls sit are the fulcrum of an articulated architectonic structure of arches at the end of which, along the curve of the vault, open the nine *Stories from Genesis*. The panels alternate between those that are as large as the top of the vault and those that are smaller; the smaller ones are flanked by pairs of male nudes. Furthermore,

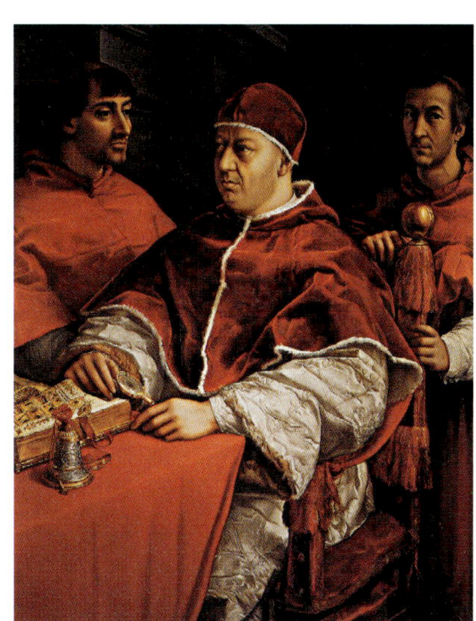

the competition between the style of Raphael and that of the Michelangelo-Sebastiano pair are the two large altarpieces commissioned in 1516 by Cardinal Giulio de' Medici (future Pope Clement VII) for his bishop's residence in Narbonne: the *Transfiguration* by Raphael, and the *Raising of Lazarus*, nominally by Sebastiano but in truth made "under the direction of Michelangelo, and in some parts from his design" (Vasari). The altarpiece by Sebastiano was finished in 1519; in April 1520, just as Raphael was about to finish his, he died, struck down by a fever. Raphael's premature death broke off the efforts to retrieve the ancient and to translate the classical tradition into a new civilization, and in that same year the Protestant Reformation initiated by Luther assumed the character of a major schism in Western Christianity.

Raphael, *Portrait of Leo X with Cardinals Giulio de' Medici and Luigi de' Rossi*, 1518–19; Galleria degli Uffizi, Florence

Thanks to the French cardinal Jean de Bilhères, the twenty-three-year-old Michelangelo received a very important commission, the *Pietà* to be located in the basilica of St. Peter. Michelangelo repeated a German stylistic and compositional scheme (the seated Madonna with the dead Christ across her lap), but took it to a new level with a fineness in the modeling, an absolute coherence in the relationship between the figures, and a softness in the folds of the drapery of extraordinary perfection. The crystalline purity of the marble, which the young sculptor had carefully selected in the quarries of the Apuan Alps, touches sublime heights. Michelangelo felt the need to proudly sign the sculpture along the ribbon that crosses the Virgin's chest, making the *Pietà* the only work he signed. Thanks to it, Michelangelo's artistic talents became known in many cities, and history began to lay claim to him. Around the year 1500 he began a long period of shuttling back and forth between Florence and Rome, responding to the requests and demands of popes and grand dukes, the Roman curia and the Florentine seignory.

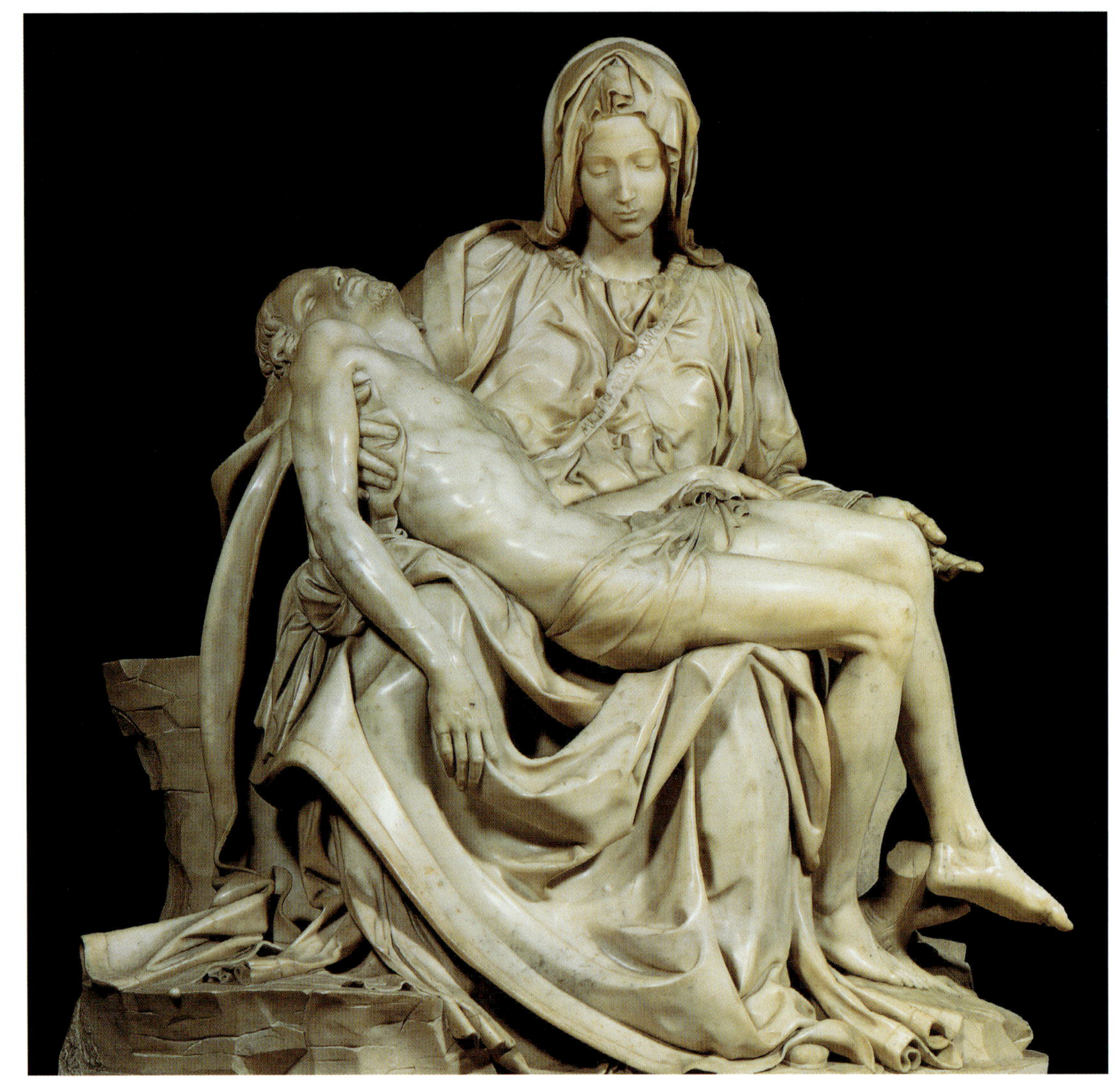

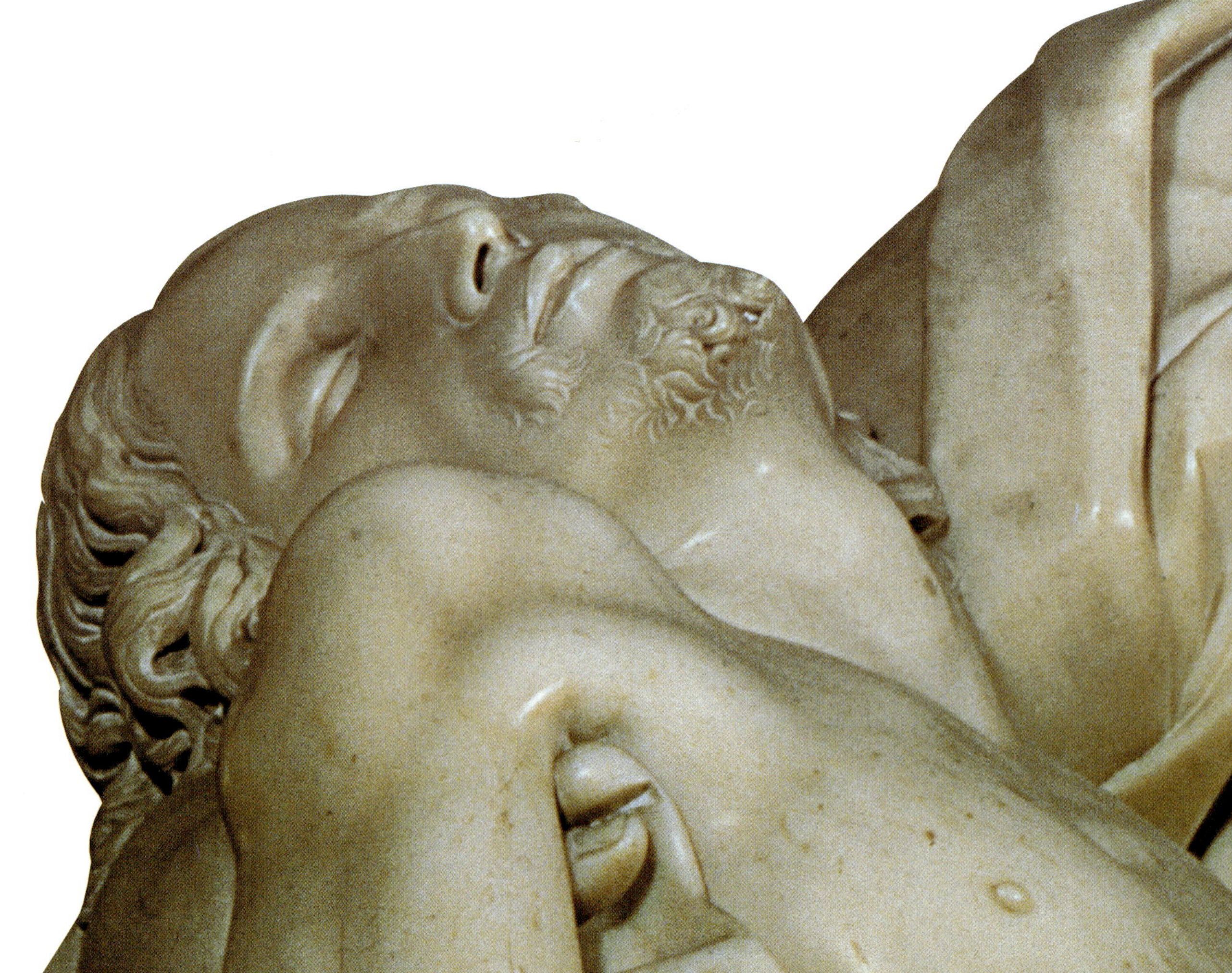

From Julius II to Leo X: the splendor of Rome

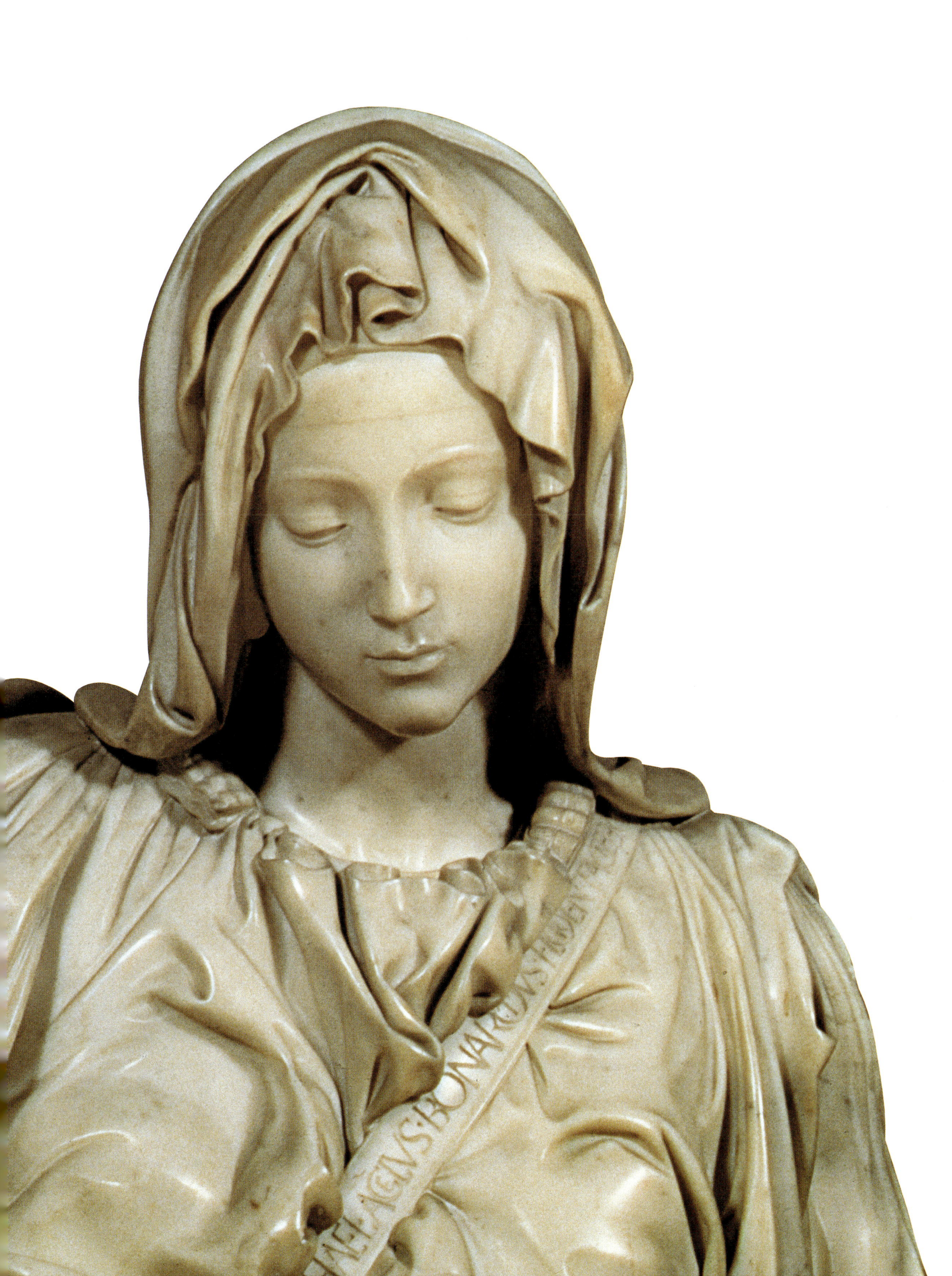

A leading figure, together with Michelangelo, on the artistic scene in Rome during the papacies of Julius II (1503–13) and Leo X (1513–21), Raphael was the leading promoter of the Renaissance dream of reviving the monumental and cultural greatness of Rome, and he sought to connect his art to the splendor of the ancient empire. To his career as a painter, occupied with making important fresco cycles, portraits, and altarpieces in which he achieved a fully classical expression, Raphael added activities as an architect (in 1514 he took over direction of the building of St. Peter's) and a scholar of archaeology. His position as superintendent of antiquities permitted him a privileged and close relationship with the great monuments of the past. In the architectonic and decorative solutions of his designs, from loggias in the Vatican to the Villa Madama, he revived the splendor of classical civilization.

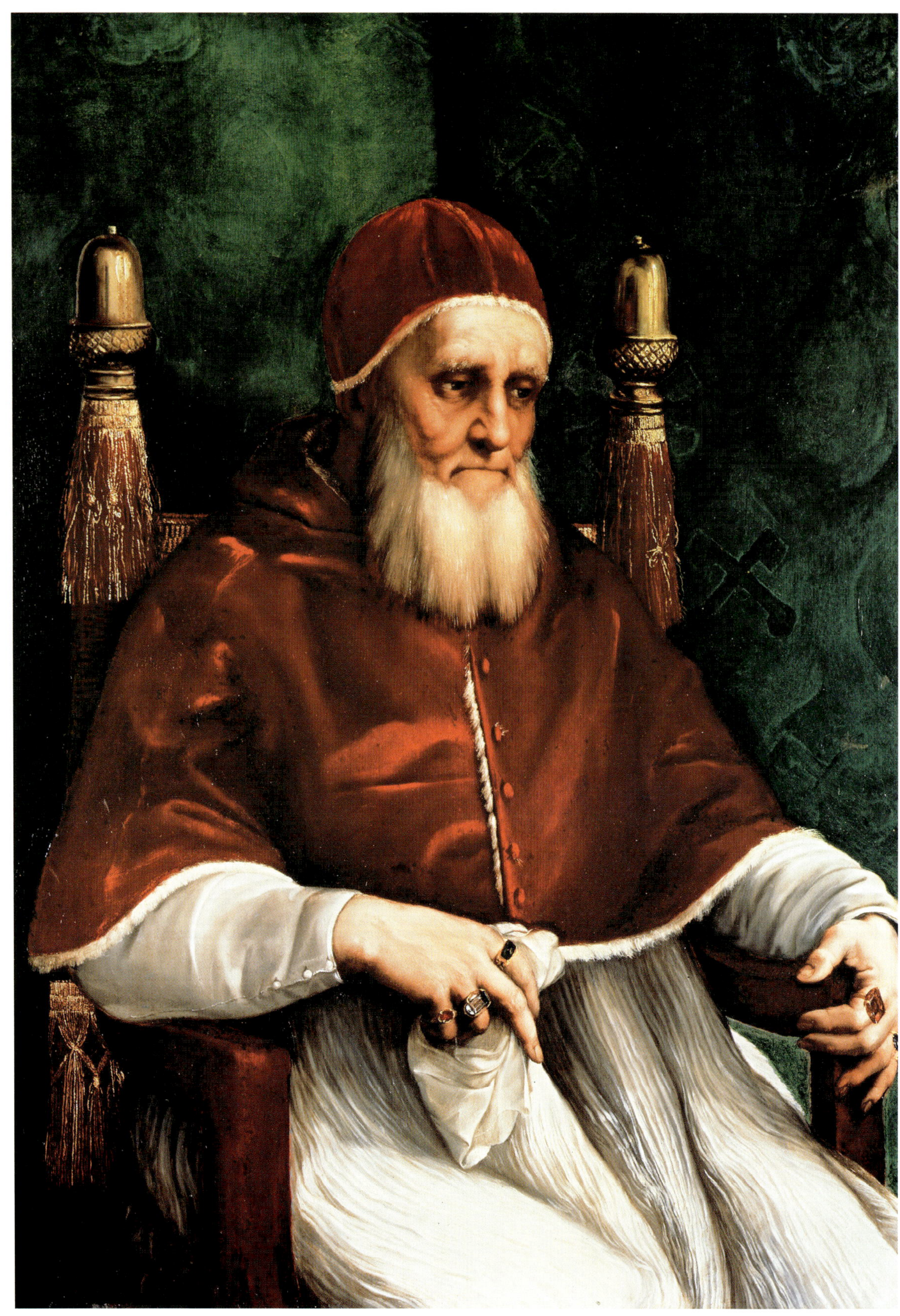

From Julius II to Leo X: the splendor of Rome

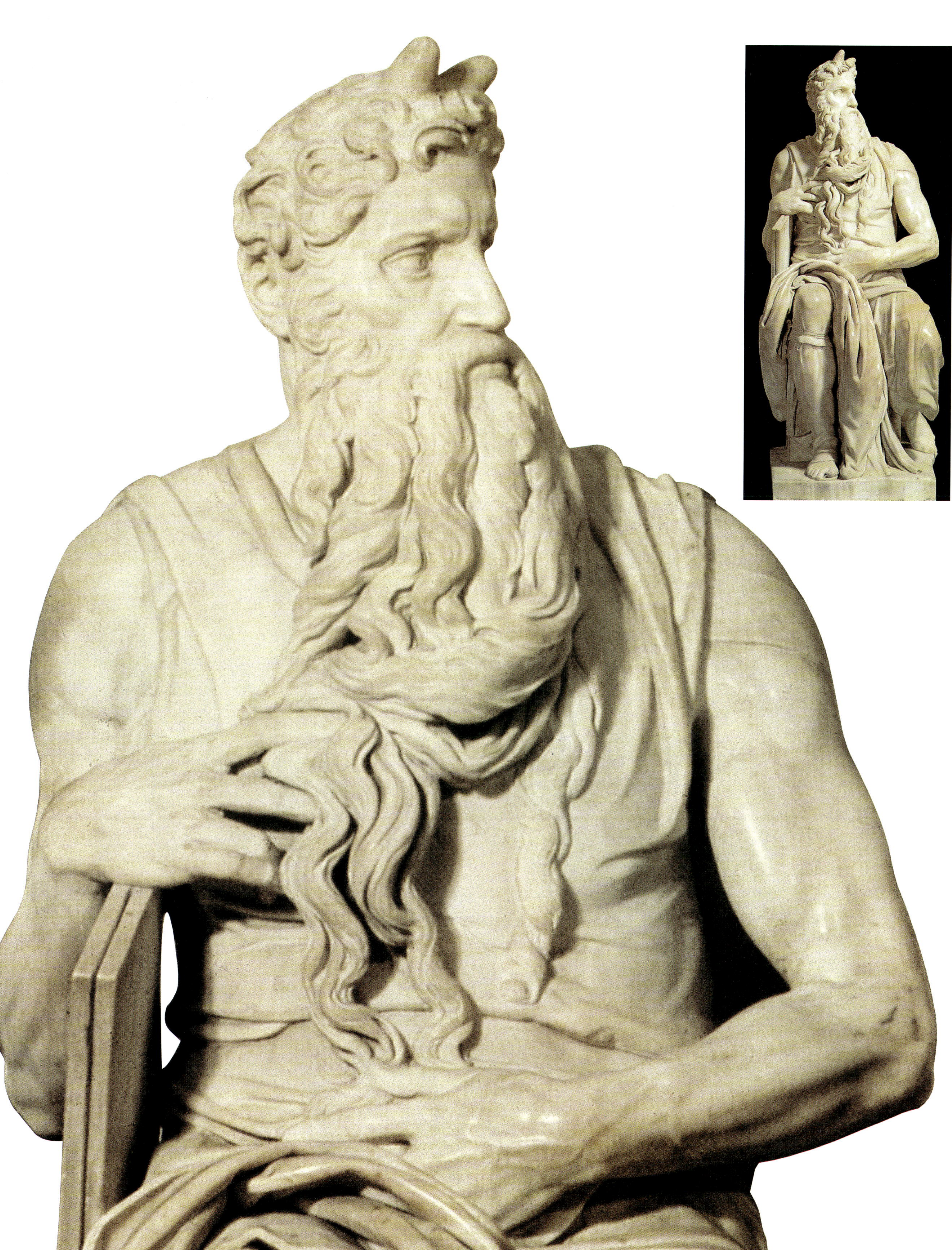

In 1505, as part of his campaign to make the papal see a center of artistic as well as spiritual primacy, Julius II called Michelangelo to Rome and entrusted him with the creation of an immense sepulchral monument to be located in the center of the new basilica of St. Peter, just begun by Bramante. Michelangelo's first design included forty marble statues, but he was gradually forced to modify and reduce his design as the exhausting labor dragged on, reaching completion after four decades of work. Following the death of Julius II, his heirs reduced the available funds; as changes were made to the design, Michelangelo became furious. Thus came into being the statue of Moses. The pose, expression, and treatment of the surfaces indicate a tense state of mind, concentrated. Moses seems to be using all his energies to hold back his feelings, which would otherwise explode in a blast of rage. This is clearly an autobiographical reflection, Michelangelo thus expressing his frustrations and unexpressed anger in his figures.

The Stanza della Segnatura, destined to house the private library of the pope in the new apartments chosen by Julius II, is frescoed with themes that recall the subjects dealt with by the volumes in an "ideal" library. In *Parnassus*, for example, the eternal value of poetry is celebrated by an assembly of ancient and modern poets, from Horace to Ludovico Ariosto, assembled around Apollo who plays his lyre accompanied by the Muses.

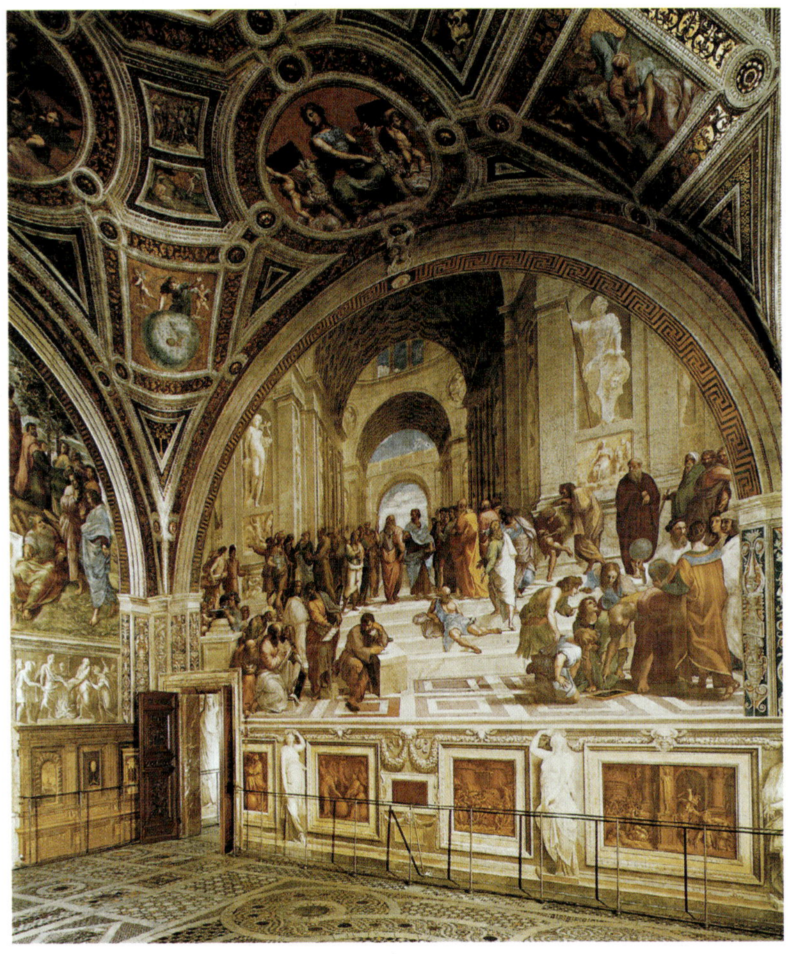

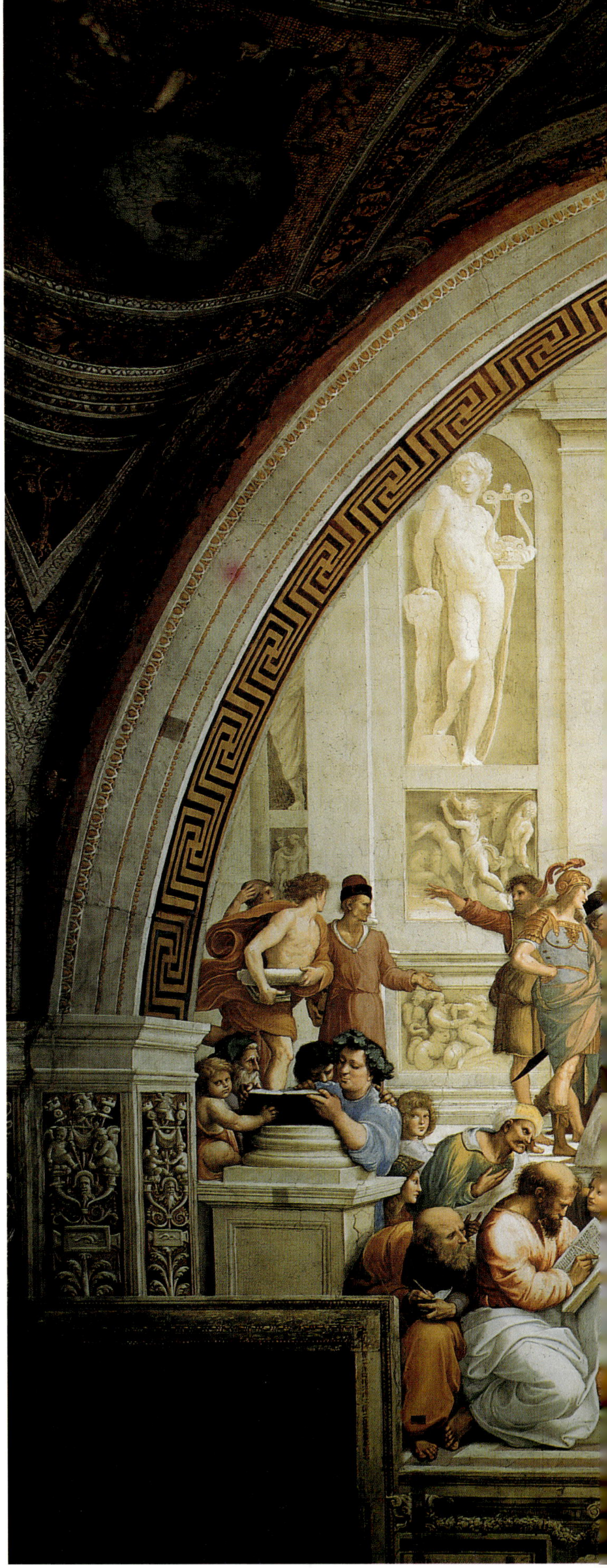

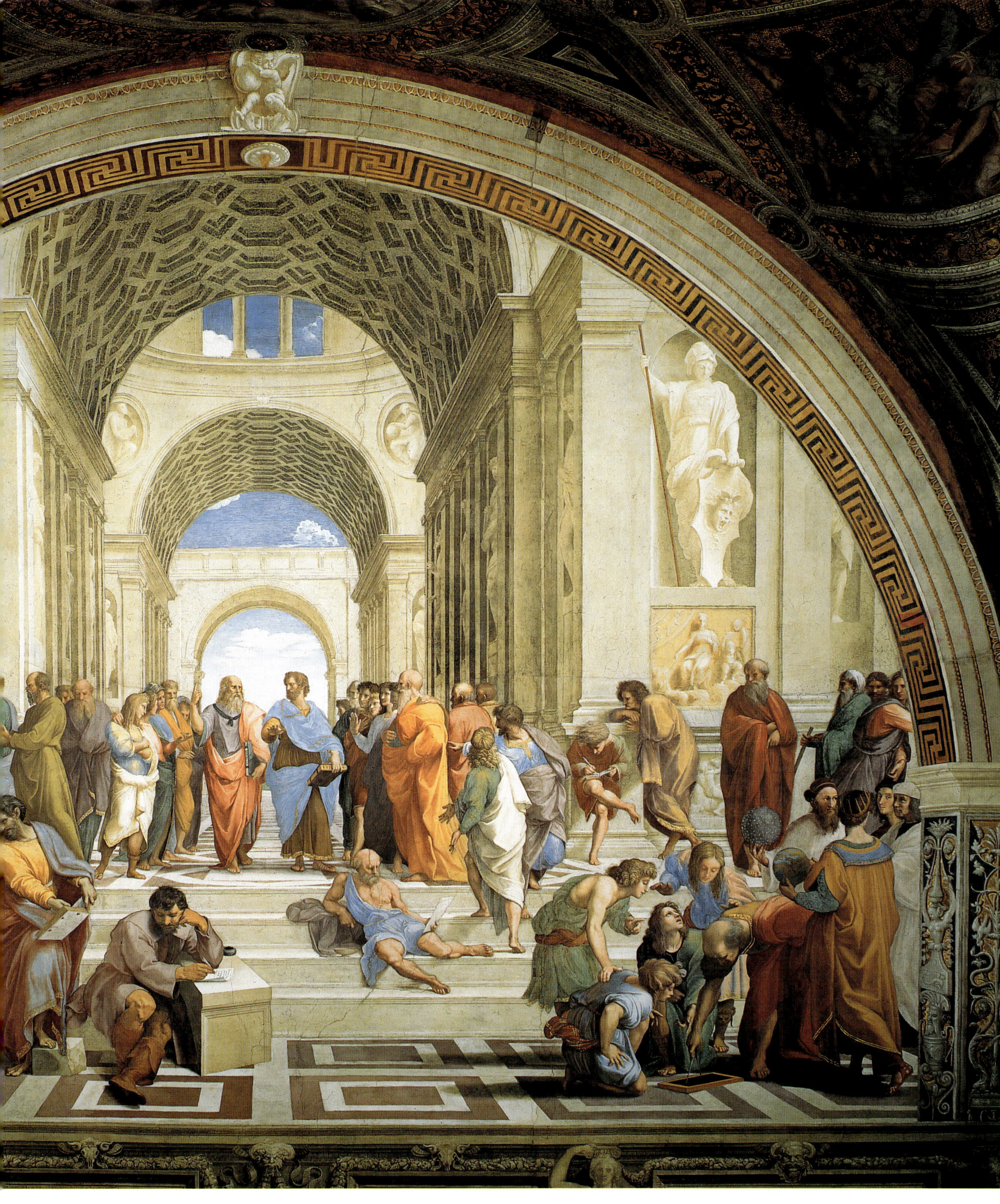

From Julius II to Leo X: the splendor of Rome

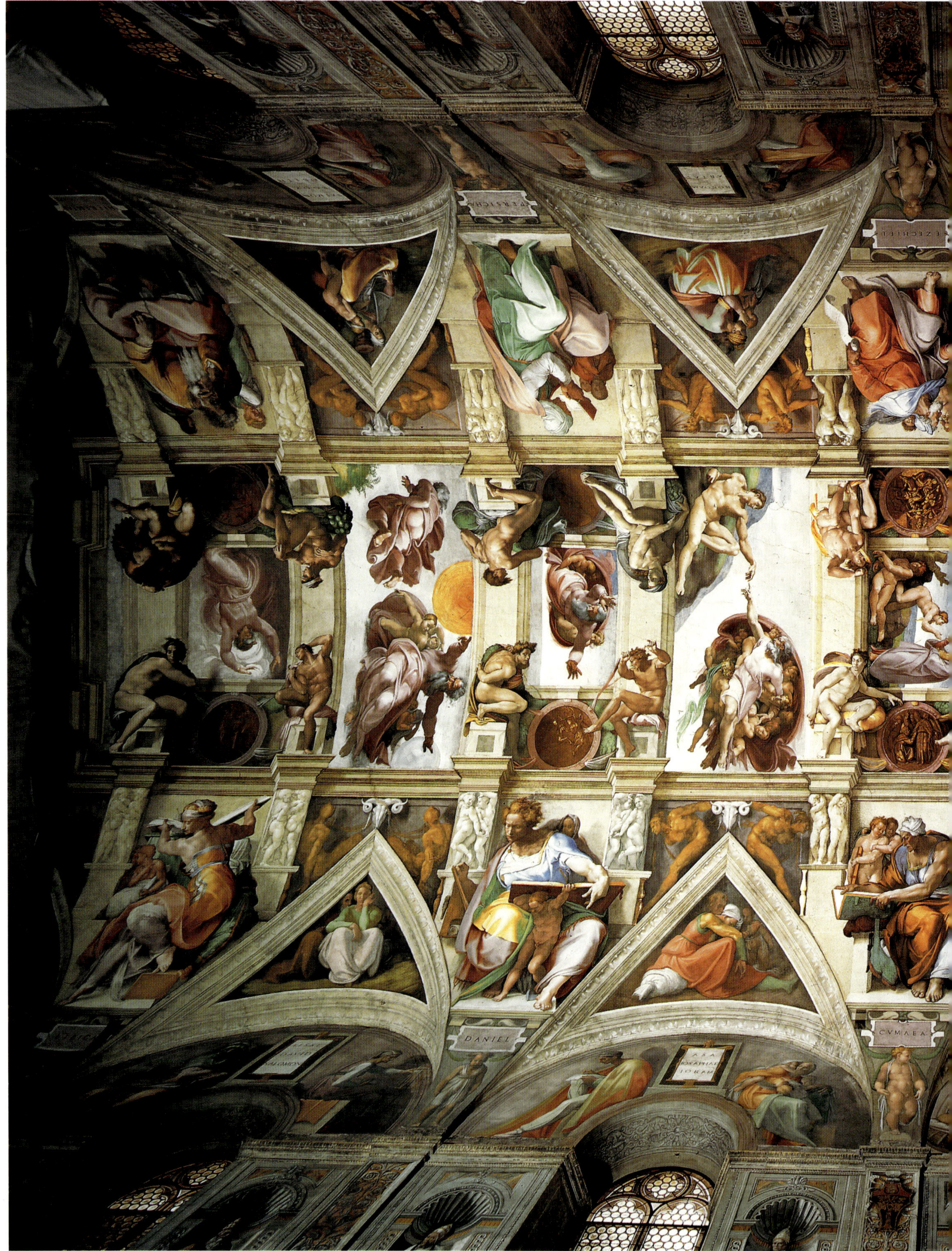

From Julius II to Leo X: the splendor of Rome

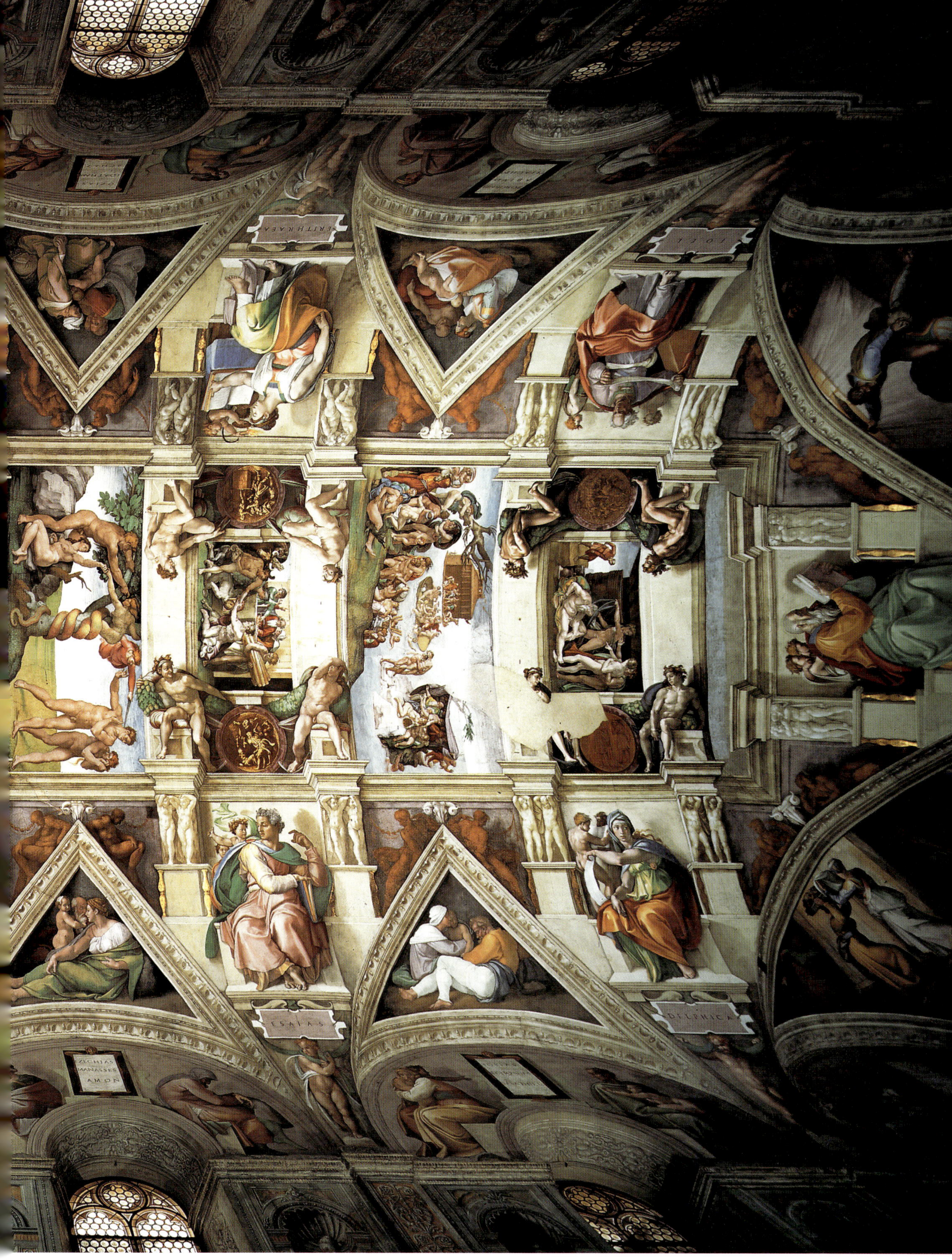

program included nine episodes from Genesis along the vault, from the Separation of the Light and Dark to the Drunkenness of Noah, alternating large pictures with those smaller in size. The Prophets and Sibyls were placed on monumental thrones along the sides, surmounted by the figures of *ignudi* ("nudes") to the sides of bronze medallions with biblical scenes. In the lunettes above the windows and the vault cells are painted the *Ancestors of Christ*. Inserted in a powerful architectonic frame, which connects the various episodes, at the same time dividing them into various registers of reading, the spectacular cycle constitutes a veritable apotheosis of Creation: Genesis, the condemnation of humanity following the original sin, the first salvation of mankind with the ark of Noah, constitute in fact the historical premises for the route to redemption.

From Julius II to Leo X: the splendor of Rome

In the vault of the
Sistine Michelangelo
constructed a spectacu-
lar structure of images
and false architecture,
a complex and organic
whole. Every figure was
studied with care in
preliminary studies and
drawings but without
losing sight of the effect
of the whole, which
remains the most glori-
ous aspect of the vault.
More than any other
element it is the clear
colors that bind the
work, and these power-
ful, enameled colors
have been brought back
to full life by recent
restoration work. In
the central part are the
scenes of Genesis. The
artist again uses images
with a spirit of "awe-
someness:" the power
and the will of God
dominate the vault.
The Creator passes by,
flying across the spaces
of the ceiling, each
of his gestures a com-
mand, each moment an
explosion of force that
reaches its height in the
scene of the *Creation
of Adam* in the cosmic
spark that crosses the
space, at once short
and incommensurable,
that separates the index
finger of God from that
of the first human.

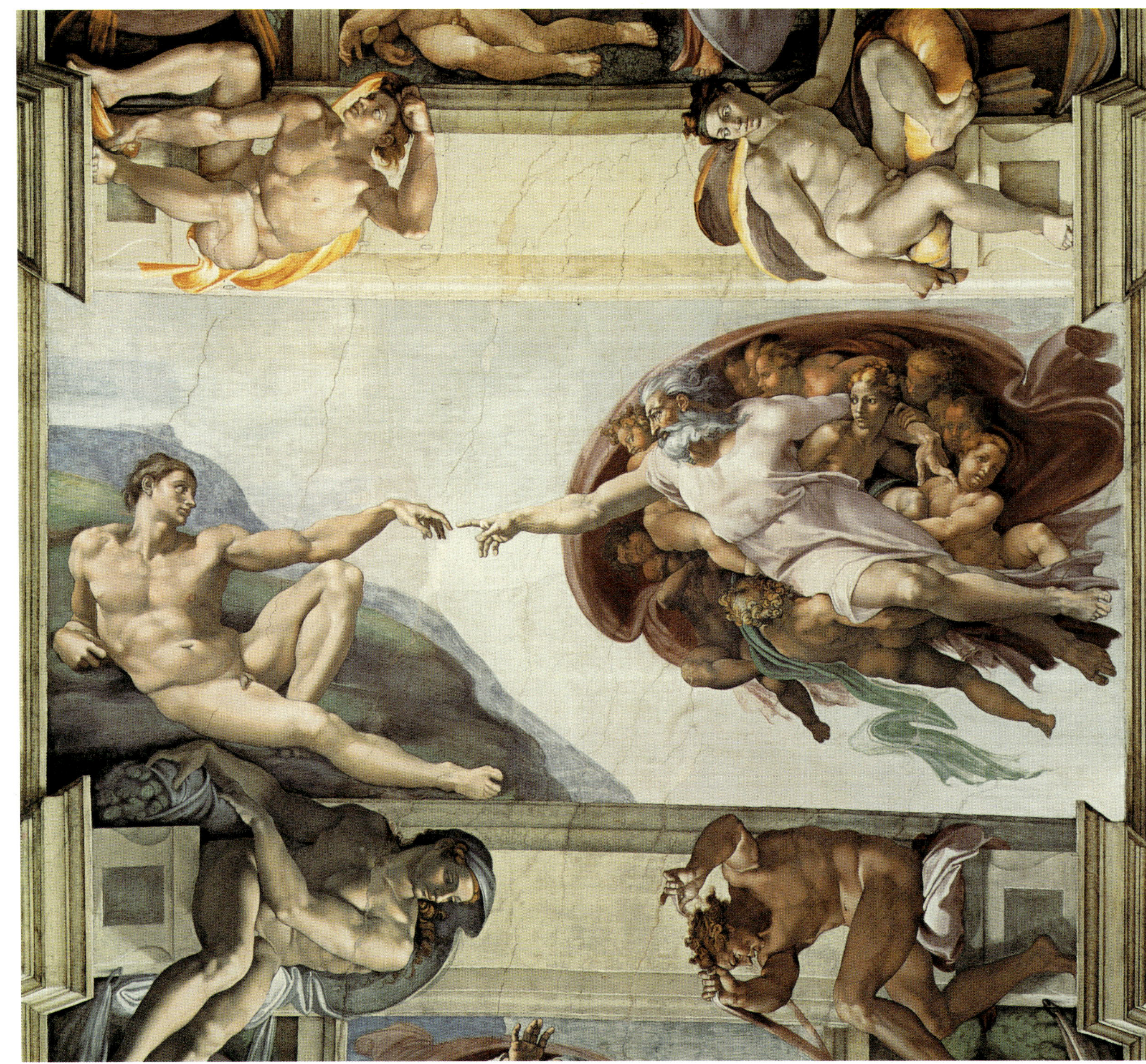

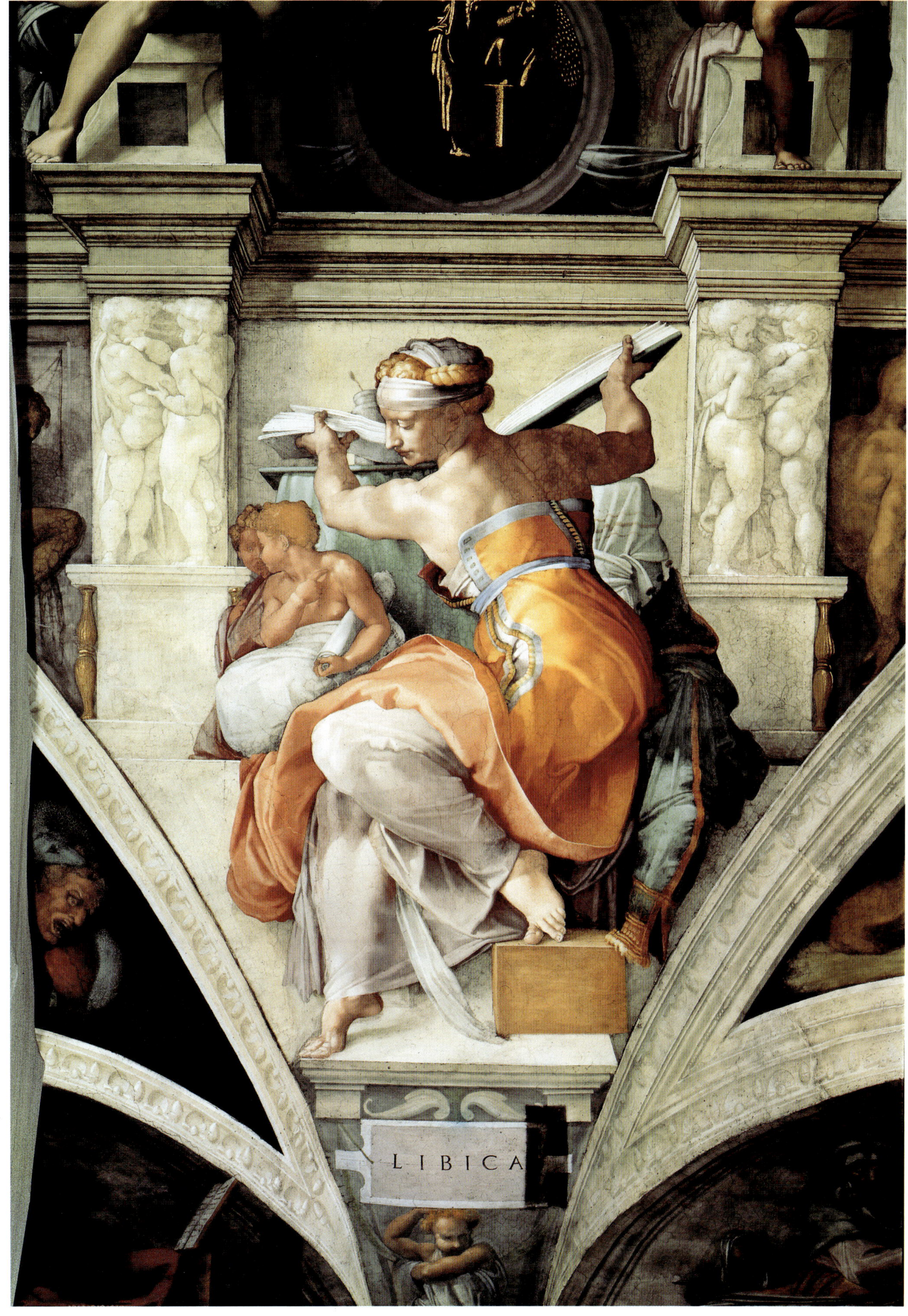

MICHELANGELO
The Libyan Sibyl
Detail of the vault
1508–12, fresco
Sistine Chapel, Vatican,
Rome

For four years and a half Michelangelo worked on the scaffolding in the Sistine, often on his back, giving his scoliosis, arthritis, cramps in his arms, and an eye infection from the paint dripping onto his face. He listed these woes in an apparently joking but in reality quite bitter sonnet, in the last line of which he says he is neither "in a good place, nor a painter." In open conflict with the pope, he had fired his two would-be collaborators, had no friends, no money, and found himself forced to seek financial help from his relatives. The result of all this suffering, of course, was a sublime work of art. The great figures of the prophets and the sibyls present an unforgettable gallery of physical types, feelings, actions, and emotions.

From Julius II to Leo X: the splendor of Rome

In 1513, while Raphael
was in the middle of
the work on the Stanza
di Eliodoro, Pope Julius
II died. The fresco of
*The Liberation of St.
Peter*, a wondrous work
of luminous magic and
silent, lunar emotion,
is almost certainly
meant to recall the
death of the pope, his
exit from the "earthly
prison." The features
of the aging St. Peter,
first sleepy and tired
in the central scene,
then stupefied as he
is accompanied by the
angel toward a new
existence, are similar
to those of Julius II.

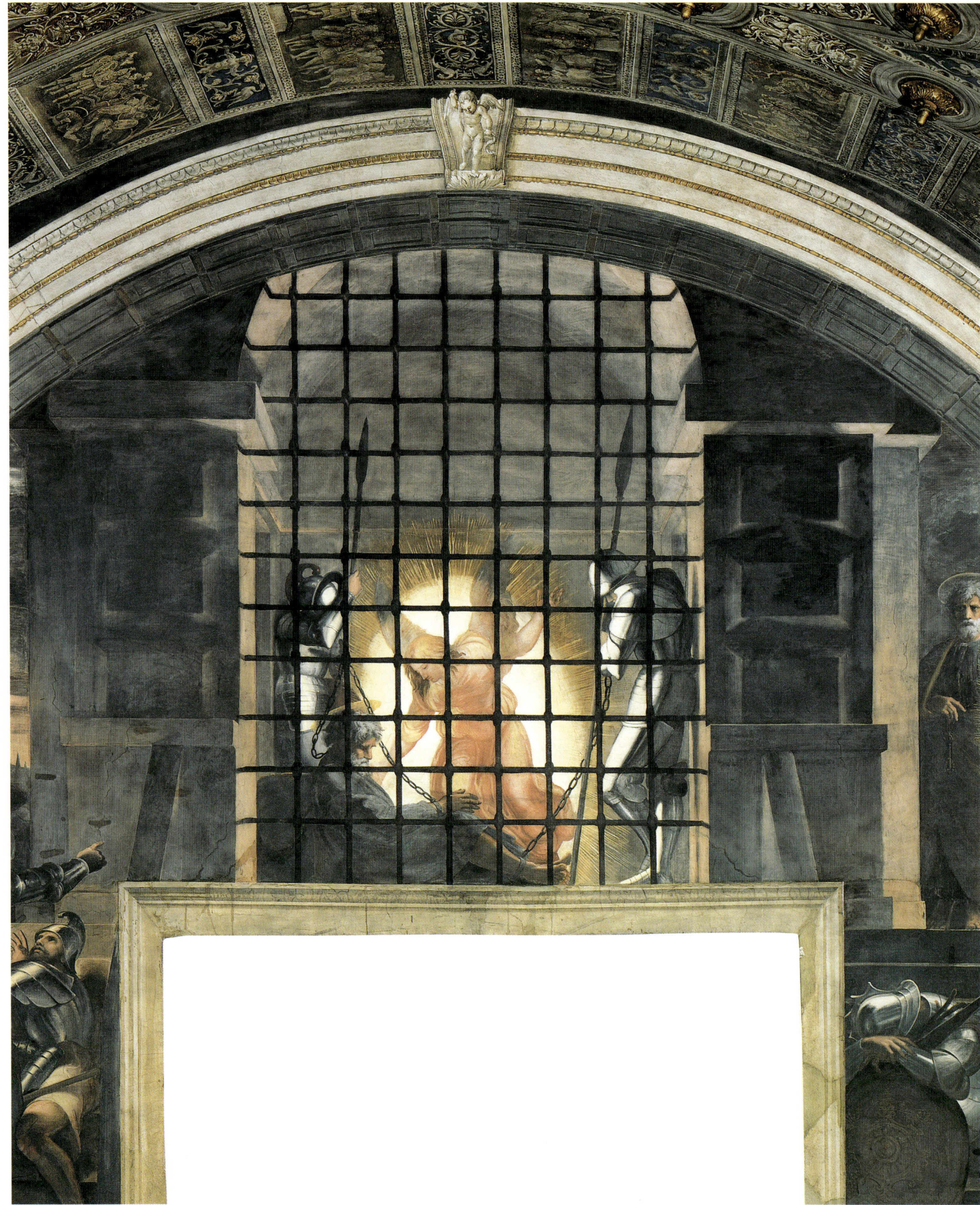

From Julius II to Leo X: the splendor of Rome

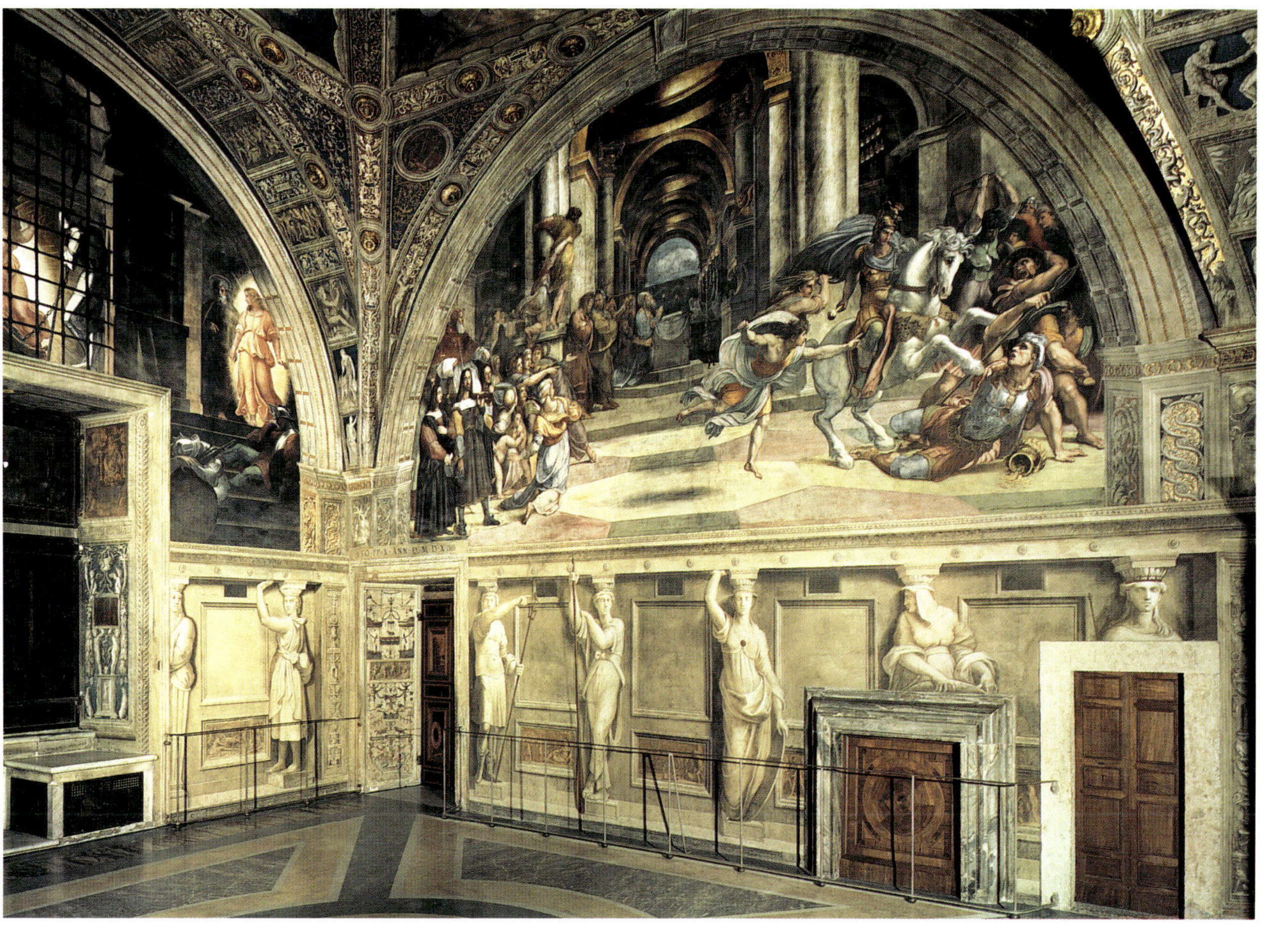

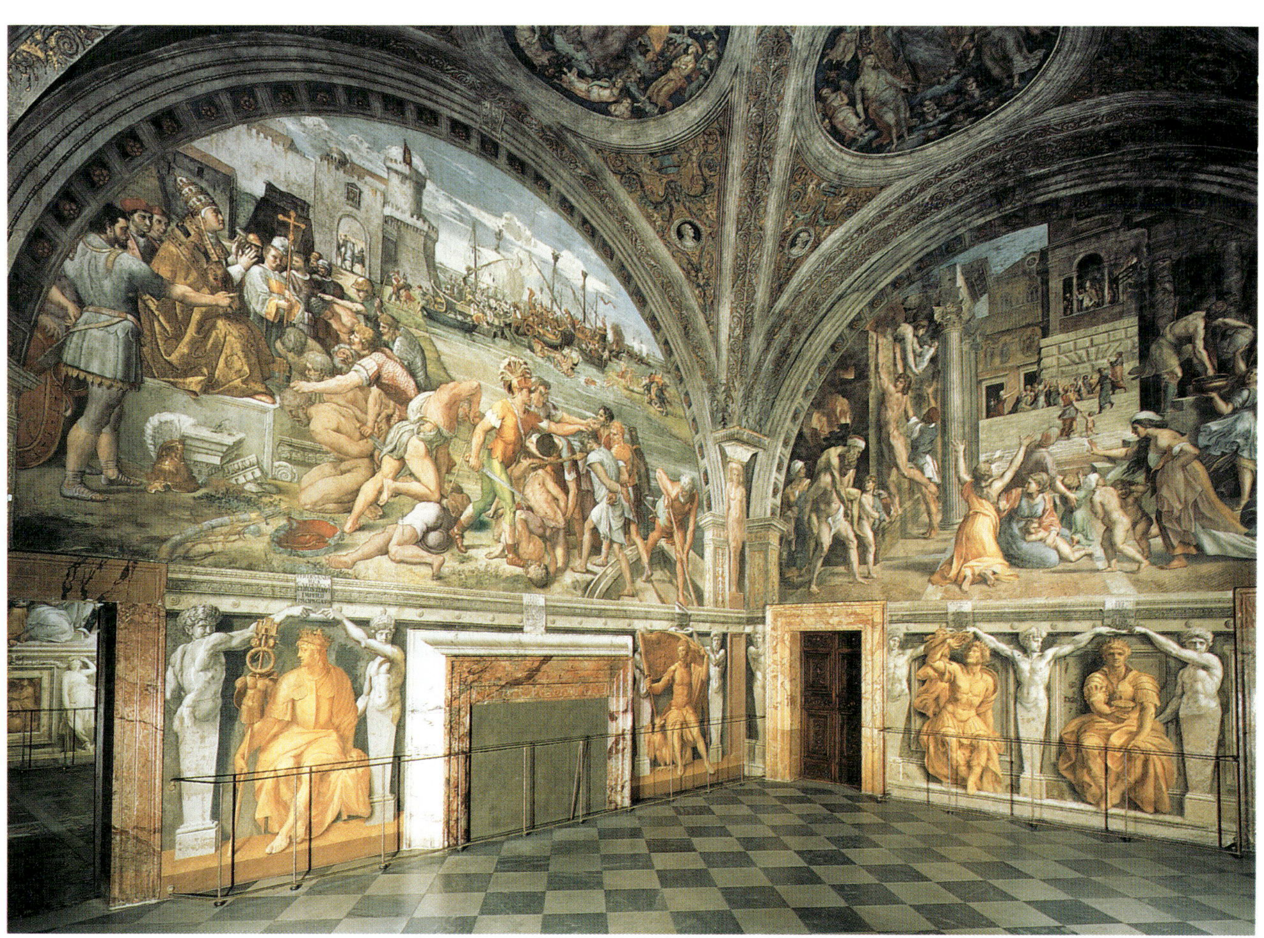

From Julius II to Leo X: the splendor of Rome

When he designed La
Farnesina (created as a
Renaissance "pleasure
palace" for Agostino
Chigi and later passed
to the Farnese family),
Peruzzi kept the sur-
rounding natural setting
very much in mind. The
southern face, arranged
on two floors divided
by horizontal frames
and by a double order
of pilasters, is related
to the typical designs
of city palaces; but this
façade, which over-
looks the garden, has a
U-shape, composed of
a loggia with five bays
enclosed between the
two projecting wings.
Raphael and his assis-
tants decorated this
garden loggia with
scenes of Psyche
and Cupid.

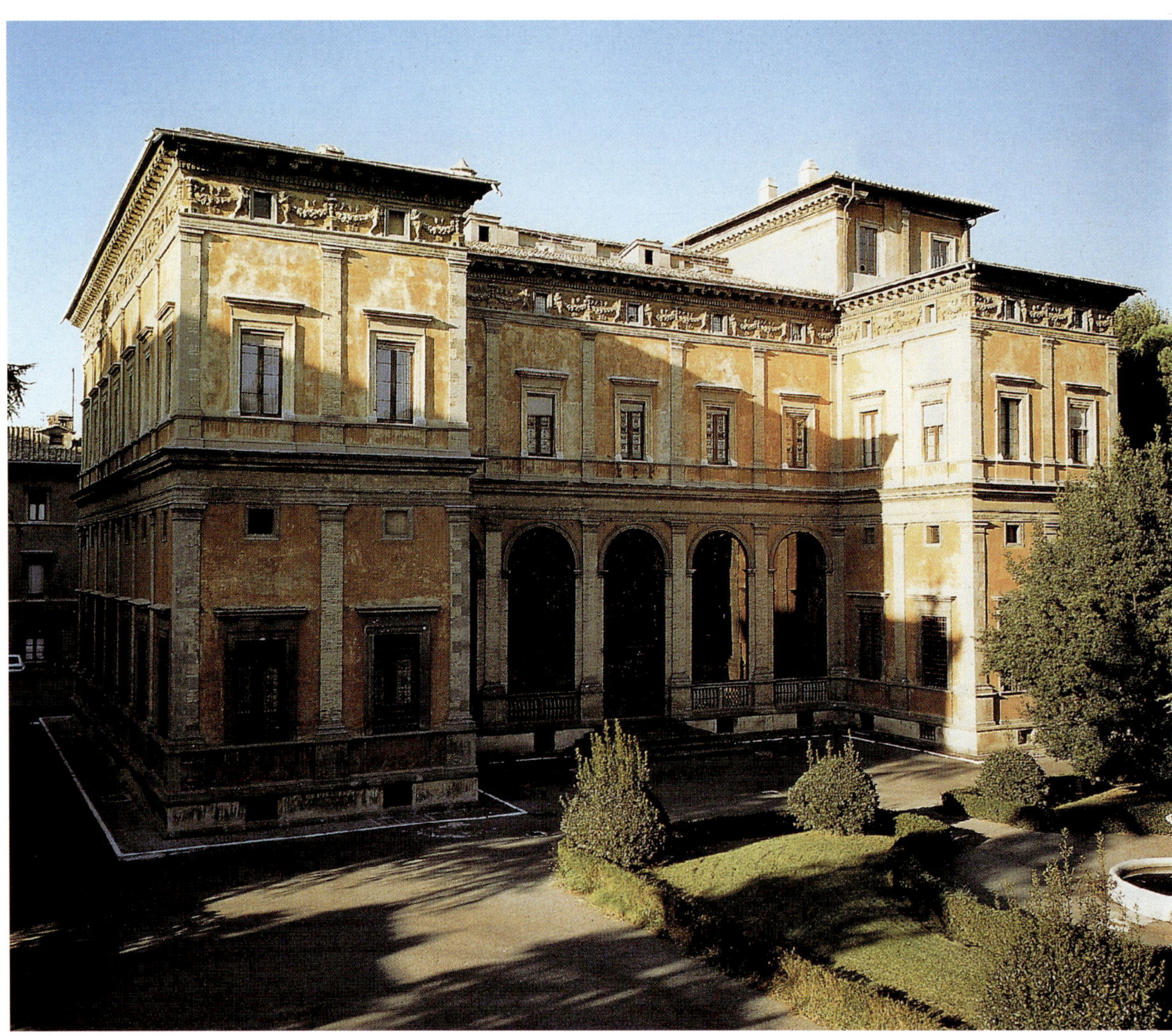

The large mythological
scene, inspired by clas-
sical sources and framed
within exuberant vege-
tal festoons, decorates
the center of the loggia.

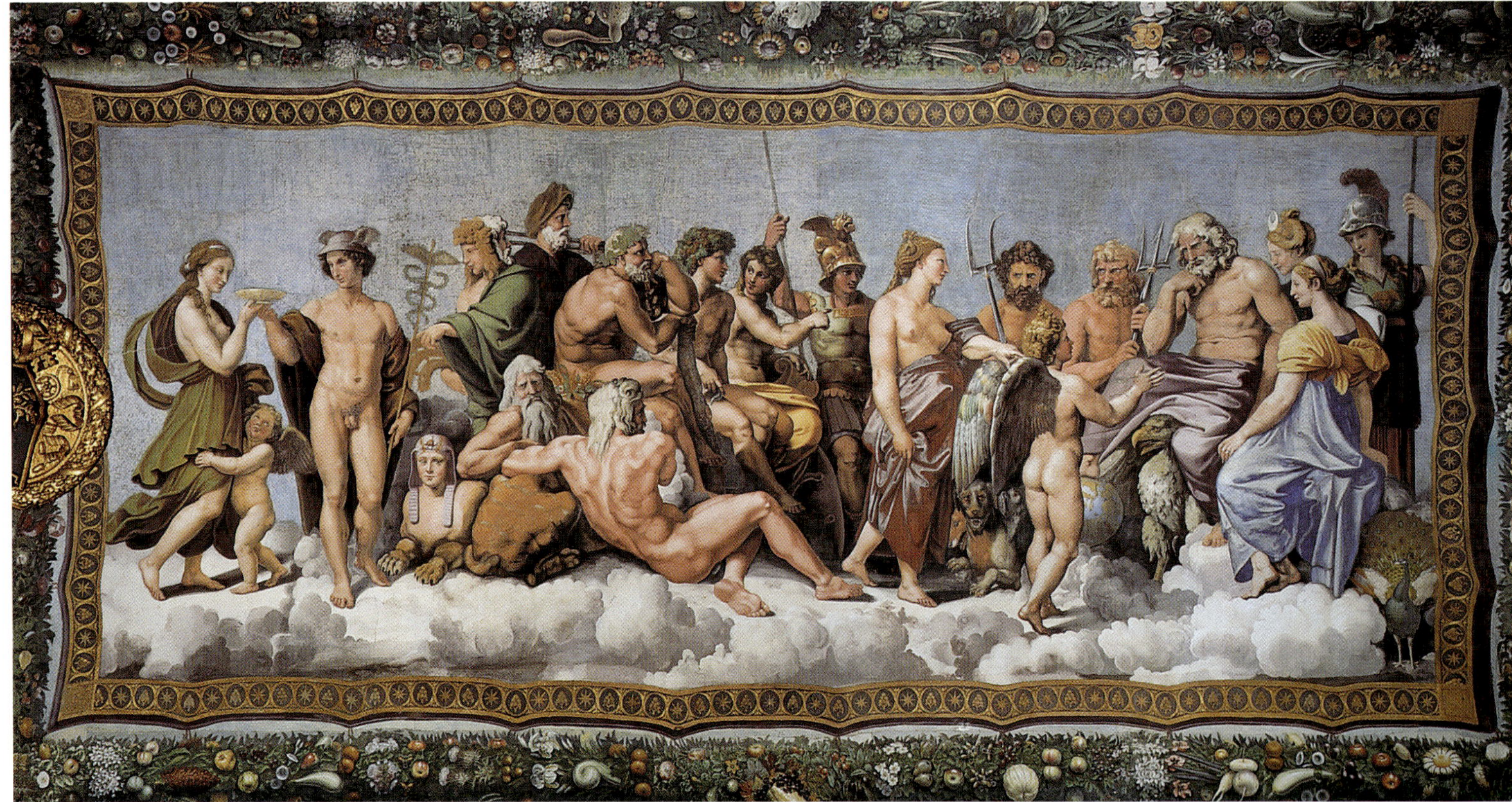

From Julius II to Leo X: the splendor of Rome

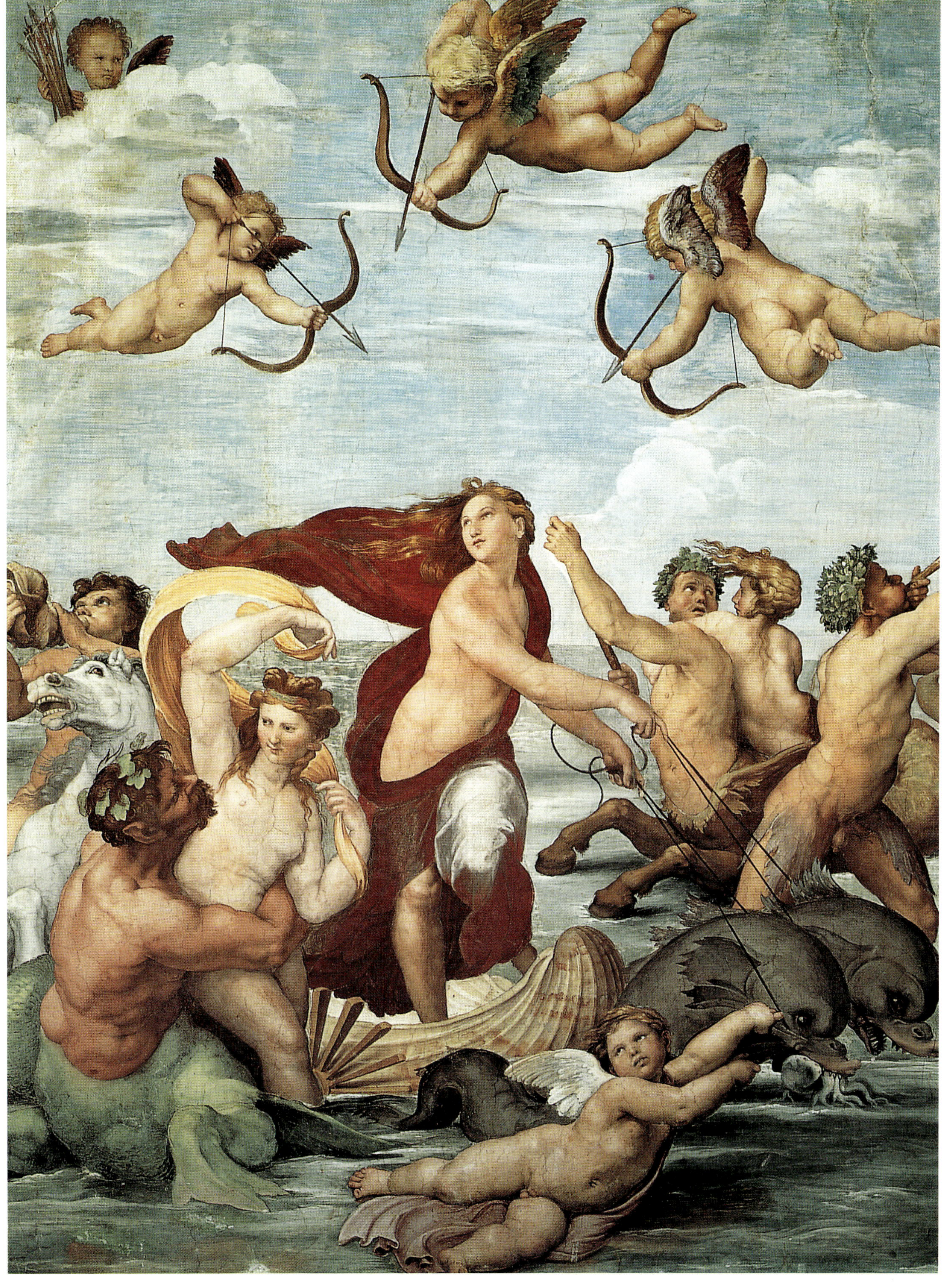

Raphael had a true gift for understanding classical culture and making it his own so as to revive ancient myths, as is made clear by this fresco with its profane subject taken from Ovid, showing the Triumph of Galatea. The protagonist of the scene, bursting with vitality, is the goddess with her wonderfully delicate beauty who crosses the sea atop a shell drawn by dolphins, with a cortège of tritons and nereids. The cloak of an intense "Pompeian" red that wraps the goddess and the rendering of the surface of the sea reveal close study of ancient Roman painting.

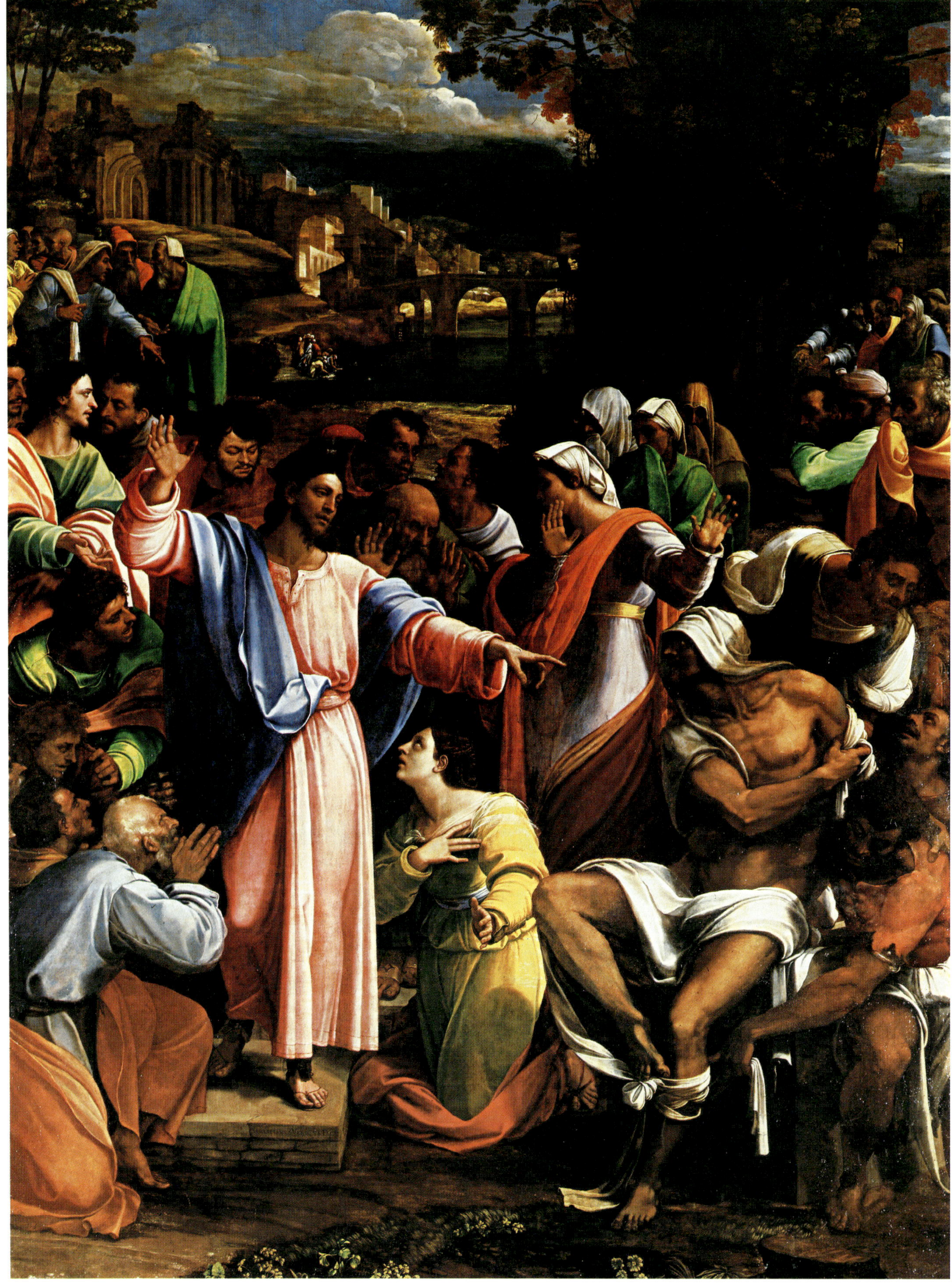

From Julius II to Leo X: the splendor of Rome

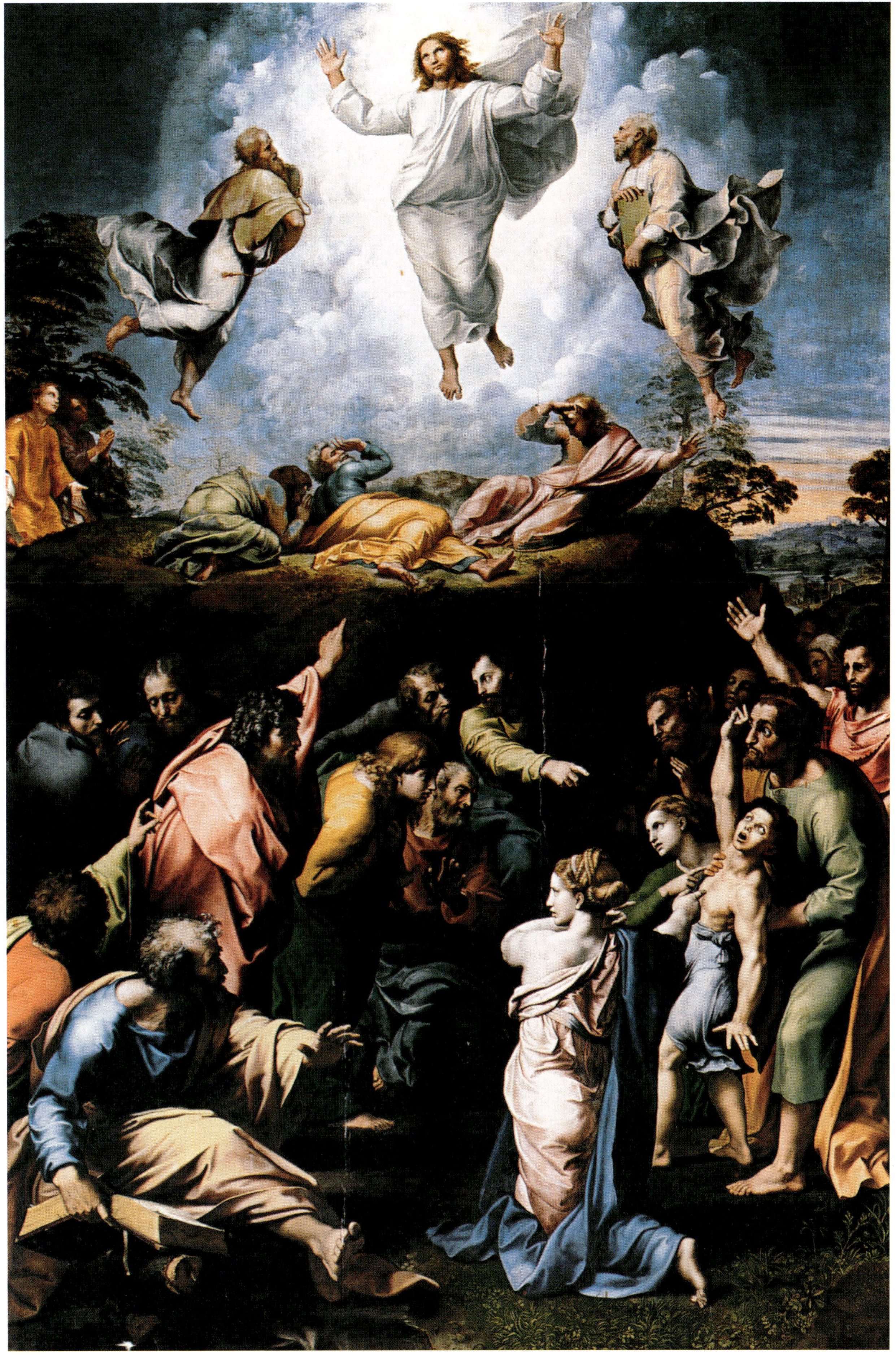

The Raising of Lazarus
is a highly rhetorical
work, with monumental
figures set against
the background of a
cloudy landscape. The
Sebastiano-Michelangelo
pair could not disguise
a certain excessive com-
plexity in the composi-
tion, which is perhaps
a little too crowded. On
the contrary, although
also making use of a
repertory of theatrical
gestures, Raphael suc-
ceeds in joining two
contrasting situations,
the silent mystical
scene of the Transfig-
uration and the agitated
commotion associated
with the healing of the
possessed boy. This
work is full of both
emotions and omens,
forming a ring joining
Leonardo to Caravaggio.

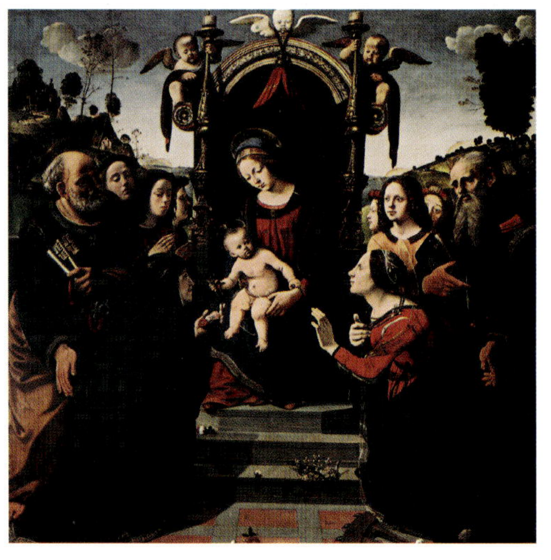

Piero di Cosimo, *Virgin and Child, Angels and Saints*, 1493; Museo dello Spedale degli Innocenti, Florence

hen the sixteenth century began, Florence was an oligarchic republic, its government modeled on the statutes of the administration of Venice. The government was led by Pier Soderini in the rank of Gonfalonier for life; as secretary he had Niccolò Machiavelli. The new Florentine republic entrusted its image to ambitious public and private patronage, sponsors of works of strong symbolic significance. The great Tuscan artists who had emigrated to other areas of Italy over the course of the preceding years now found themselves offered excellent opportunities. Over the period of a few years, Florentine painting underwent a radical renewal thanks to the presence in the city—and to the competition between them—of both Leonardo and Michelangelo, with the coming arrival of Raphael. The works made by these masters in Florence around 1505 seem to belong to a different world than the paintings by Botticelli and

pletion by the end of 1503 and placed in the Piazza della Signoria on January 25, 1504, the colossal work was a milestone in the kind of political images sought by Pier Soderini. Proud symbol of civic and republican virtues, the statue is an expression of the rule of reason over passion, of inner control over anger, carrying forward the premises established by Donatello with his *St. George* and *Judith and Holofernes* in bronze. The enormous popularity of the *David* made Michelangelo, not yet thirty, both the moral as well as the artistic model for Florence's civic pride: the rhythm of his commissions, both private and public, increased in a vertiginous way. The role of supporting actor on the Florentine stage at the beginning of the sixteenth century went to fifty-year-old Leonardo da Vinci, who returned to Florence in August 1500 after eighteen years spent working in Milan, with a few more months between Mantua and Venice. Leonardo presented the cartoon

The early sixteenth

Filippo Lippi that date to only a few years earlier. In Giorgio Vasari's interpretation of art history, it was precisely the years of Pier Soderini that witnessed the birth of a new and definitive "age" in art, the one destined to culminate with Michelangelo. After the death of Lorenzo the Magnificent (1492), the still young Michelangelo had moved to Rome for four years, making there his first monumental marble statues, the *Bacchus* in the Bargello and the *Pietà* in the Vatican, carved for the French cardinal Jean de Bilhères, works that exactly fit the model described by Vasari since they demonstrate attentive study of the rules of figurative models (Hellenistic sculpture in the case of the *Bacchus*, German carved-wood groups for the *Pietà*), reworked with an extraordinary attention to the imitation of nature in skin, features, and drapery, with effects of sensual softness. When Michelangelo returned to Florence in the spring of 1501, he was commissioned to sculpt a giant *David* in marble. Brought to near com-

of the *Virgin and Child with St. Anne*, to the enthusiastic admiration of artists and public alike. He began working on the panel, which is today in the Louvre, in 1501, but almost a decade was to pass before he completed it. The cartoon in London remains the main reference to an understanding of the novelties proposed by Leonardo in Florence. While forming a single block the figures also maintain their extraordinary psychological and personal intensity, almost echoing the apostles in the *Last Supper* in Santa Maria della Grazie in Milan; the graphic line perfectly renders the vibrations of the shaded atmosphere and the landscape grades from shadow to light without ever enclosing the figures within a closed design.

Michelangelo studied the cartoon of the *Virgin and Child with St. Anne*, but in place of Leonardo's all-embracing effects of atmosphere and movement he preferred concentrating on closed forms, stately and monumental. The *Doni Tondo*, the only well preserved panel painting unquestionably by Michelangelo, marks the conclusive step in his dialectical relationship with Leonardo's models. Painted probably in 1504, the tondo presents the Holy Family against a landscape; a low wall separates the three main figures from a young St. John the Baptist and a row of nude youths. The principal group has the power of a sculptural relief, emphasized by the arrangement of the figures, variously connected and separated by their positions and gestures, with areas of light and shadow clearly separated and the colors brightly illuminated, almost to the point of achieving the "overexposure" effect that would be adopted by the early mannerist painters. The value of the *Doni Tondo* in a comparison of Michelangelo to Leonardo is made abundantly clear by comparing it to the *Mona Lisa*, the portrait of the wife of Francesco del Giocondo, which Leonardo began in 1503. With this work, as with so many others by Leonardo, the execution stretched on over long years, with Leonardo bringing it with him to Milan and then to France to make a series of almost infinite retouches, rethinkings, veneers, reworkings. Even so, from its very beginning the portrait must have appeared an image at once seductive and unsettling, wrapped in the damp shimmer of the foggy landscape and just touched by that hint of a smile that makes the "movement of the soul" of the woman indecipherable.

In their goal of duplicating the institutions and settings of Venice, Soderini and Machiavelli had a new, grandiose hall built in Palazzo Vecchio for the meetings of the city council. Like the Sala del Maggior Consiglio in the Doge's Palace in Venice, the hall had an altar and, on the walls, painted depictions of glorious military episodes. In 1503 Michelangelo and Leonardo were commissioned to make wall paintings of battles for the two sides of the gonfalonier's bench. Neither artist succeeded in completing the battle scene assigned him (which were very different from each other). It is unlikely that Michelangelo managed to finish even the preparatory cartoon for his scene before being summoned to Rome in March 1505 to design the funeral monument for Pope Julius II.

It was a particularly tormented period. In April 1506, while the first stone of the new basilica of St. Peter's was being set in place, Michelangelo fled Rome to return to Florence. Seven months later, the pope forced him to go to Bologna to implore his pardon. Meanwhile Leonardo had already left for Milan. While the contest between Leonardo and Michelangelo grew hotter, Raphael had completed his youthful career and felt ready to leave the Umbro-Marches circuit and take part as an active player in the real world of painting.

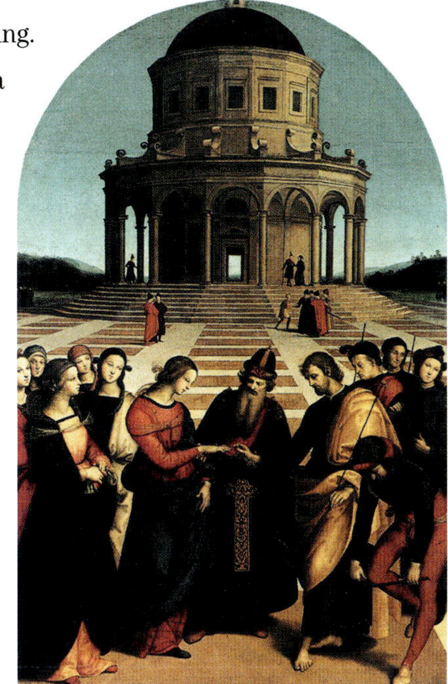

On October 1, 1504, Giovanna Feltria della Rovere, the duke of Urbino's sister-in-law, wrote to the Gonfalonier Pier Soderini, recommending the young painter to him. "For having good talent in his work he wants to spend some time in Florence to learn." With Raphael's arrival, even if only for the period of a few years, Florence could rival Venice in terms of artistic activity, and that even though the northern city then boasted, all at the same

century in Florence

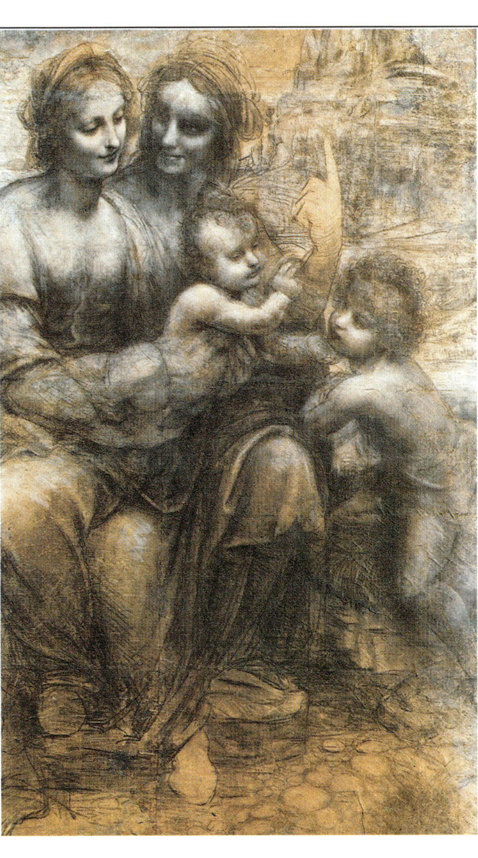

time, the presence of the elder Giovanni Bellini, Albrecht Dürer, during his second stay in the city, and the emerging Giorgione.

Born in Urbino in 1483, Raphael, when barely sixteen years old, was already being referred to as *magister* ("master") in documents and was directing his own workshop. In 1503 he made his first trip to Rome and witnessed the coronation of Pope Julius II; the works of this early period already display the theme of the intellectual awareness of the artist. At just twenty years of age, Raphael was already claiming a greater role as a painter, a position at the center of the cultural debate and not marginal status as a mere material executor (albeit highly gifted).

In 1504 Raphael returned to Città di Castello and painted the masterpiece that ended his youthful career. *The Marriage of the Virgin (The Sposalizio)*, today in the Pinacoteca di Brera in Milan, is an open homage to Perugino (who made a similar panel, today in the museum of Caen), but at the same time it demonstrates the overcoming of that master's models, which in comparison seem suddenly aged. It was at this point that Raphael decided he wanted to go to Florence. There, with lightning speed, Raphael absorbed the style of late fifteenth-century Florentine art, most of all that of Leonardo and Michelangelo. He also began a memorable series of variations on the theme of the group of the Virgin and Child, works that grew in complexity with the gradual addition of other figures, such as St. John the Baptist or Joseph. Comparison to Leonardo's cartoon for *The Virgin and Child with St. Anne* and to Michelangelo's *Doni Tondo* demonstrates Raphael's ability to find a mediation between the contrasting positions of Leonardo and Michelangelo. Knowledge of Leonardo's works is particularly clear in Raphael's portraits, especially those female, in which he pays homage to the compositional layout and the ineffable psychological insight of the *Mona Lisa*. There are also the eloquent wedding portraits of Agnolo Doni and Maddalena Strozzi (Galeria Palatina, Florence), the patrons of Michelangelo's *Doni Tondo*.

In 1508 Raphael was called to Rome, completing the triad of illustrious departures, following those of Leonardo and Michelangelo. The death of the aged Botticelli, in 1510, was the signal for a necessary change of generation. The political situation was uncertain. In 1512 Louis XII of France put the Medici back in power in Florence, but the discord lingered. Faced with a world in rapid change, artists sensed the urgent need for a radical rethinking of expressive forms and canons. Thus was born the new movement called mannerism, destined, over the course of the century, to become the predominant artistic style.

The figure that provides a link connecting the style of the great masters of the first decade to the beginning of the "modern manner" was Andrea del Sarto, dubbed by Vasari "the faultless painter." The most courageous innovators got their training in his school. He occupies an intermediate position between the by then eclipsed humanistic certainties and the trend toward the "manner," in which figures assume eloquent poses, but without even the slightest anatomical distortion, and the group structure freely reinvents the traditional triangular arrangement of the *sacre conversazioni* of the fifteenth century. The soft light, toned down colors, and slightly shaded outlines of his works reveal that Andrea del Sarto was up to date on artistic developments.

The early sixteenth century in Florence

Andrea del Sarto's students and assistants included Jacopo Carucci, called Pontormo after the name of his birthplace on the outskirts of Empoli. Pontormo made a great study of gestures and expressions; the application of color, which in the painting of Andrea del Sarto had already begun to move away from the fifteenth-century tradition, becomes in Pontormo deliberately cold and discordant. To emphasize the unnatural aspect of his compositions, Pontormo followed the precedent set by Michelangelo in both the *Doni Tondo* and the frescoes in the Sistine Chapel and began to load the expressions of his figures, moving away from the atmosphere of "indefinite psychology" of Botticelli and Perugino. Pontormo did not hesitate to make use of new figurative references, such as prints by Dürer, and to go beyond the experiments of his master, Andrea del Sarto.

Around 1520 Pontormo was the most interesting Tuscan artist. In the new emotional climate created by the Protestant Reformation Pontormo presented a version of religious painting that was far more intense, dramatic, and unsettling than it had ever before been in Italy. The *Lamentation* in Santa Felicita, one of the most innovative altarpieces of the Florentine sixteenth century, is the "manifesto" of nascent mannerism. The composition appears fragmented, ambiguous, lacking both architectonic and perspective points of reference. The figures, with their emotionally fraught gestures and features, seem to wander aimlessly.

The other great student of Andrea del Sarto was Rosso Fiorentino (Giovanni Battista di Jacopo Rosso), who made his debut together with his master and his contemporary Pontormo in the frescoes of the Santissima Annunziata. The event of the *Assumption* (1513–17), partially damaged by the artist himself, marks from the very beginning the controversial, polemical figure of Rosso. His figures often have bizarre faces (a "savage and desperate air," in the words of Vasari). His stylistic evolution was astonishingly rapid; in the span of only a few years, he went from the Florentine influence (in particular Pontormo and Andrea del Sarto) to the Roman of Michelangelo to finally take on that of Parmigianino. Rosso set himself up in Rome in 1523, and his paintings there assumed stately, controlled rhythms of smooth clarity. The *Dead Christ supported by Angels*, in perfect balance between Christian sentimentality and classical exaltation of the male nude, served as a fundamental model for Roman mannerism for a long time.

Rosso Fiorentino was among the many artists who fled Rome following the sack of the city in 1527. In fact, he took off on several trips, and

in his style sharp, almost demoniacal flashes alternate with a kind of increased sweetness, more in keeping with official patrons. In 1530 he moved to France, where he worked for King Francis I and made the spectacular gallery of the royal château of Fontainebleau (1532–37), a monument of fundamental importance to the diffusion of the mannerist aesthetic in Europe, as well as a prestigious point of reference for the laboratory of ideas and creations of the sixteenth-century French court.

Over the course of the 1520s, alongside the new ideas from Pontormo and Rosso Fiorentino, the Florentine scene was distinguished by the return of Michelangelo, then busy with the great Medici projects around the basilica of San Lorenzo: the Sagrestia Nuova with the tombs of the dukes Lorenzo and Giuliano, the façades for the Brunelleschi church (never made), and the Laurentian Library. All these works were given a special impulse in 1523 with the election to the papal throne of Giulio de' Medici, a nephew of Lorenzo the Magnificent and a cousin of the previous pope, Leo X . He took the name Clement VII. At the news of the Sack of Rome, the Medici were driven out of the city and the second Florentine republic was proclaimed. Michelangelo shared the fate of his fellow Florentine citizens in a city under siege by the imperial and papal army. The city capitulated on August 12, 1530, and only the intervention of Pope Clement VII saved Michelangelo from the reprisals of the pro-Medici party. From then on, Michelangelo made Rome his definitive home. The consequences of the siege of Florence had a powerful impact on the course of art history. The stage was suddenly swept bare: Michelangelo was in Rome, Rosso was in France, Pontormo closed in on himself in the solitary rage of a profoundly disturbed soul, and Andrea del Sarto died in 1531. In 1530, Charles V, following his sumptuous coronation as Holy Roman emperor in Bologna, reinstalled Medici power in the city. The Medici were made dukes of Tuscany; in 1537, with the murder of Alessandro in a plot, the main line of the family ended. Cosimo I, son of the heroic Giovanni dalle Bande Nere, took power. His long rule (1537–74) would mark the new course of Tuscan art.

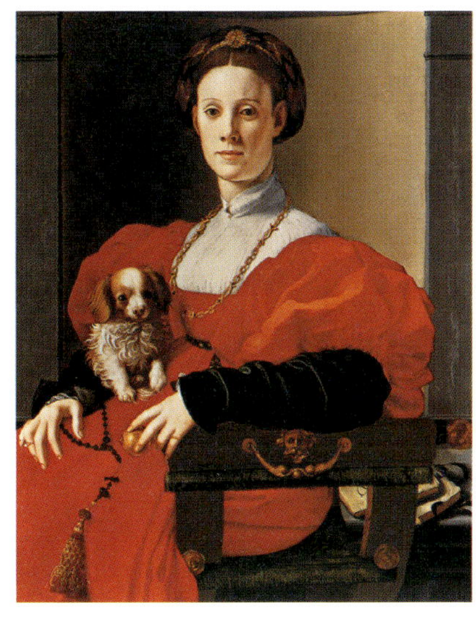

■ Michelangelo, *Sketch for the fortifications of Florence*, 1528–29; Casa Buonarroti, Florence

Michelangelo put to
use his virtuosic talent
as an imitator of
ancient art when he
moved to Rome for four
years, where he made
his first monumental
marbles, the Bacchus
in the Bargello and, for
the French cardinal
Jean de Bilhères, the
Pietà in the Vatican.
The works exactly fit
the model described
by Vasari since they
demonstrate attentive
study of the rules of
figurative models
(Hellenistic sculpture
in the case of the
Bacchus, German
carved-wood groups for
the Pietà), reworked
with an extraordinary
attention to the
imitation of nature in
skin, features, and
drapery, with effects
of sensual softness.

Michelangelo returned
to Florence from Rome
in the spring of 1501; in
August the directors of
the wool-workers' guild
and the Opera del Duomo
commissioned him to
sculpt a giant *David* in
marble. Brought sub-
stantially to completion
at the end of 1503, the
colossus was a milestone
in the politics of imagery
of Pier Soderini, and
following consultation
among the various
Florentine artists it was
decided to place it in
front of Palazzo Vecchio

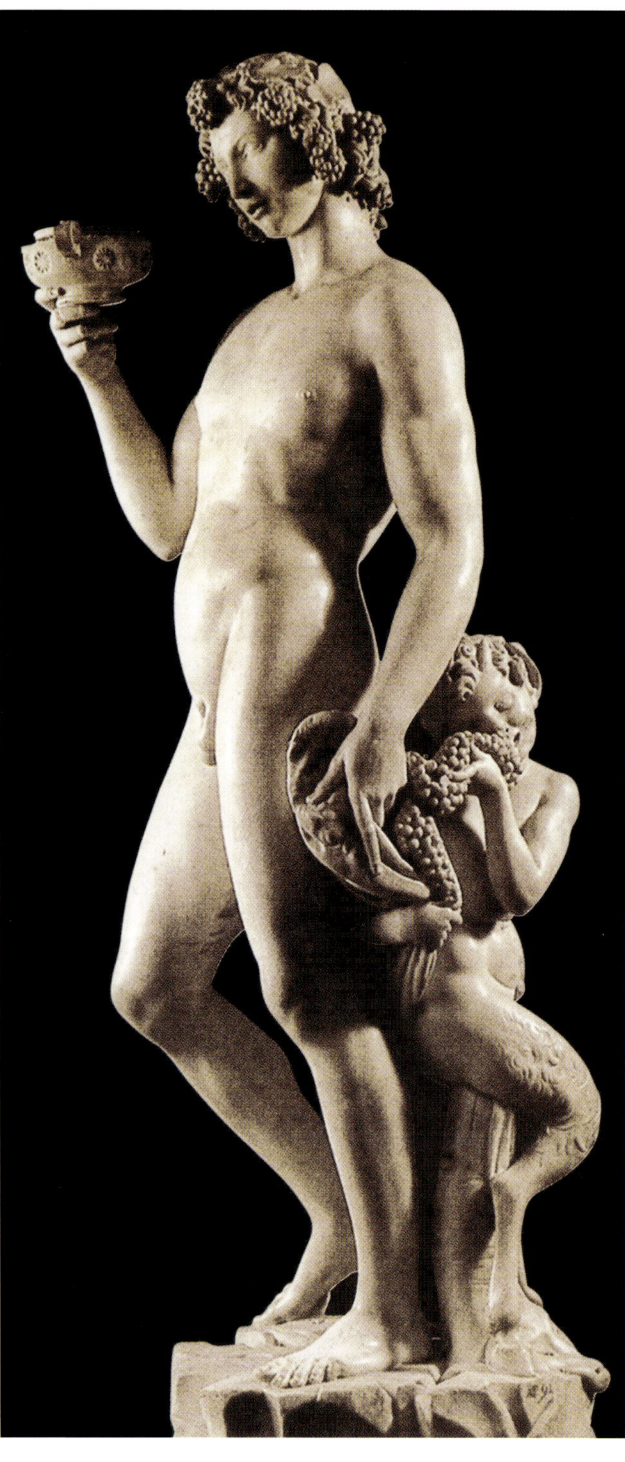

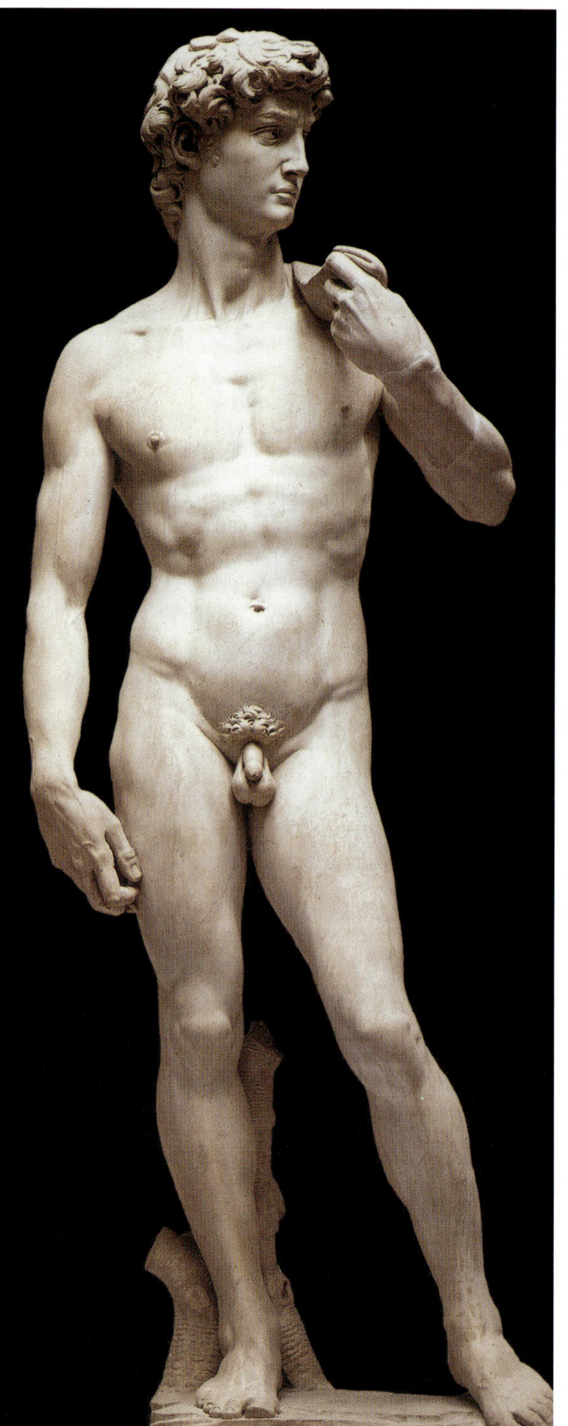

The early sixteenth century in Florence

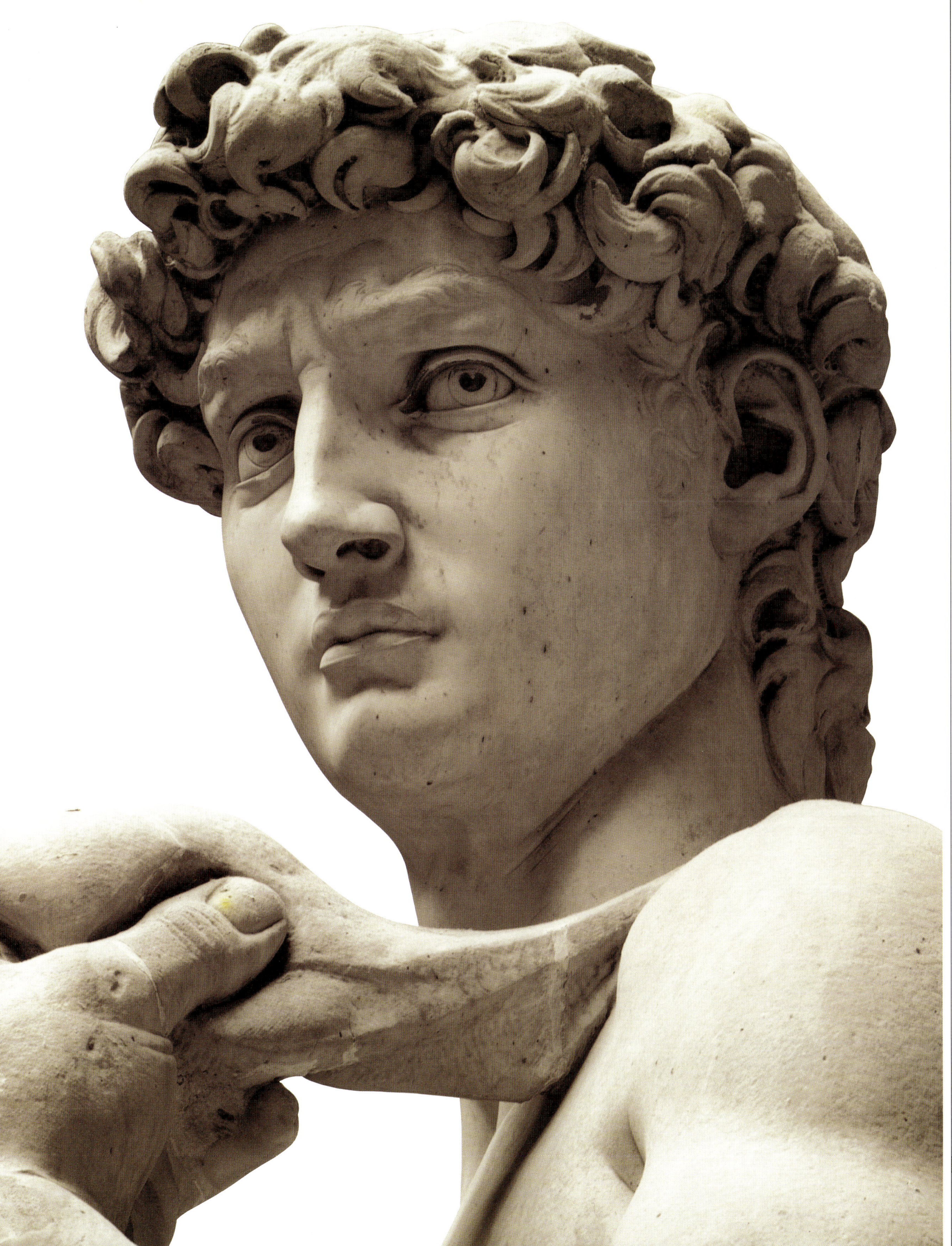

in Piazza della Signoria,
on January 15, 1504.
Proud symbol of civic
and republican virtues,
the statue is an
expression of the rule
of reason over passion,
of inner control over
anger, carrying forward
the premises established
by Donatello with his
St. George and *Judith* in
bronze. The enormous
popularity of the *David*
made Michelangelo,
not yet thirty, both
the moral as well as
the artistic model
for Florence's civic
pride. The rhythm of
Michelangelo's commis-
sions, both private and
public, increased in a
vertiginous way.

Co-protagonist on the Florentine art scene in the early sixteenth century was the fifty-year-old Leonardo, who returned to Florence in August of 1500 after eighteen years in Milan. The execution of this famous work stretched on over long years, with Leonardo bringing it back with him to Milan and then to France to make a series of almost infinite retouches, rethinkings, veneers, reworkings. Even so, from its very beginning the portrait must have appeared an image at once seductive and unsettling, wrapped in the damp shimmer of the foggy landscape and just touched by that hint of a smile that makes the "movement of the soul" of the woman indecipherable. The portrait makes full use of the studies and interests of the last years of the painter's life, most of all his work on expressing the relationship between a figure and a landscape, the rendering of foggy atmosphere, the design that shades into shadow. The final result is a cosmic image that is both climate and psychology, person and setting, subtle inner reality and religious pantheism.

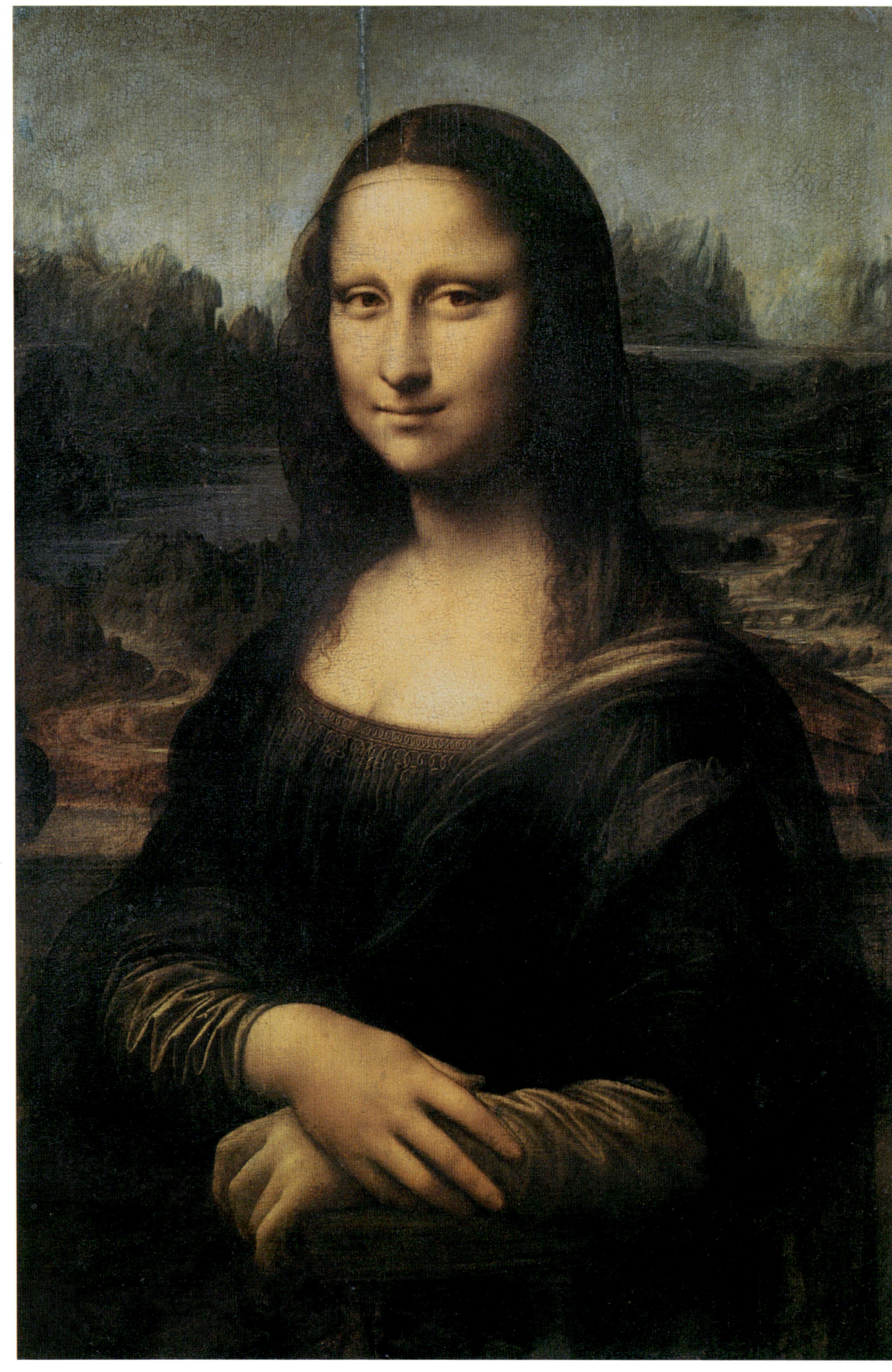

The early sixteenth century in Florence

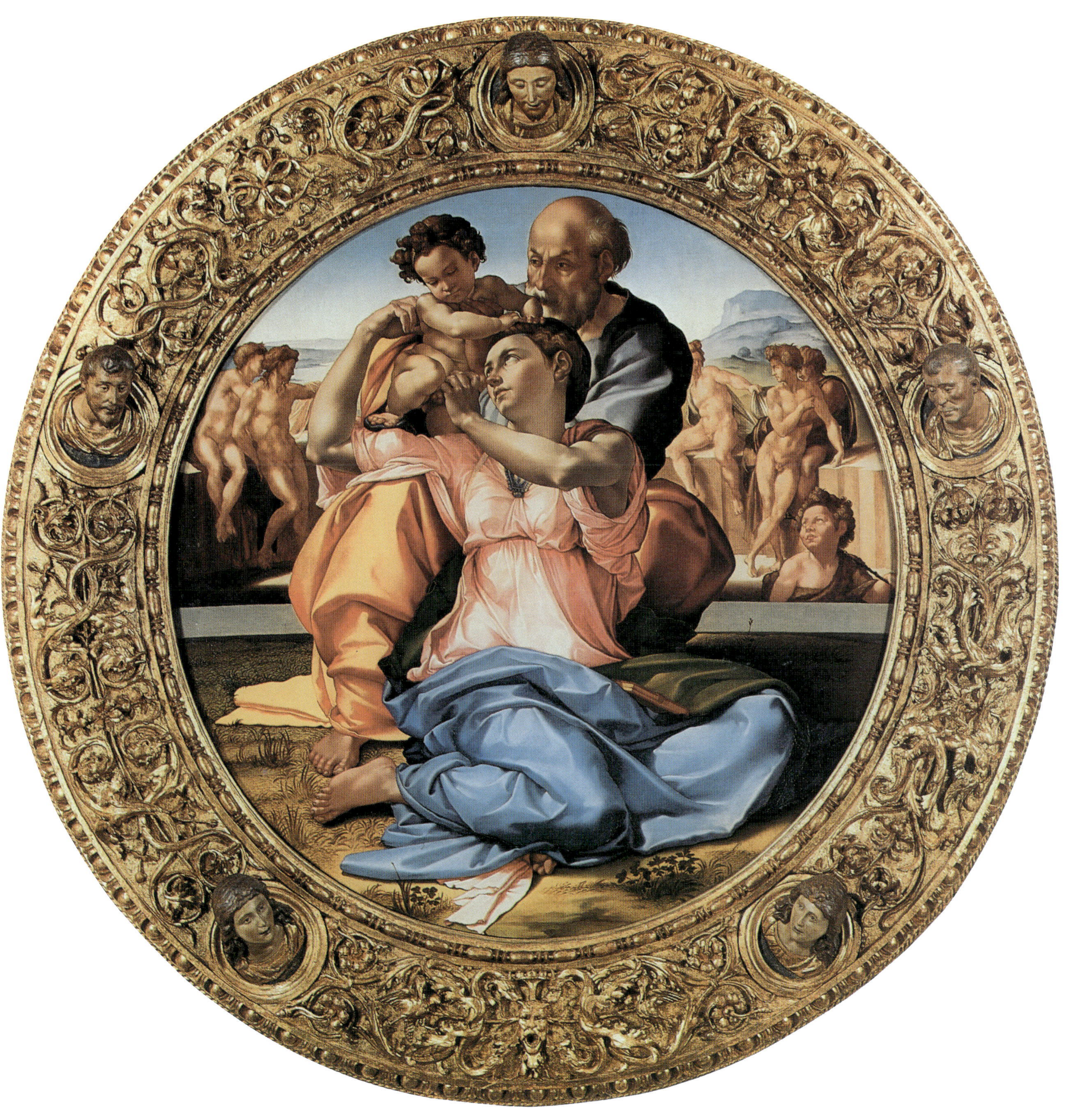

The early sixteenth century in Florence

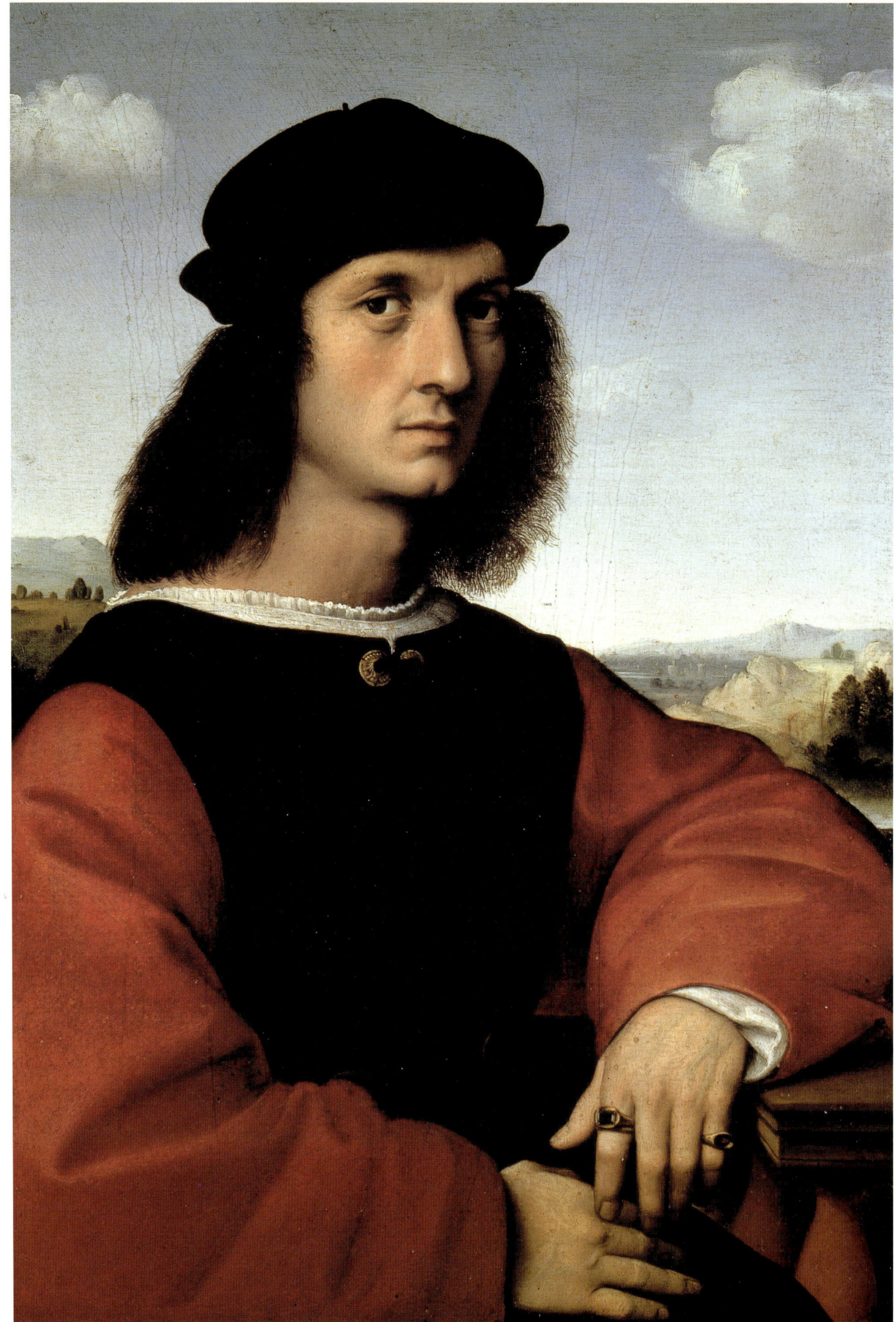

The early sixteenth century in Florence

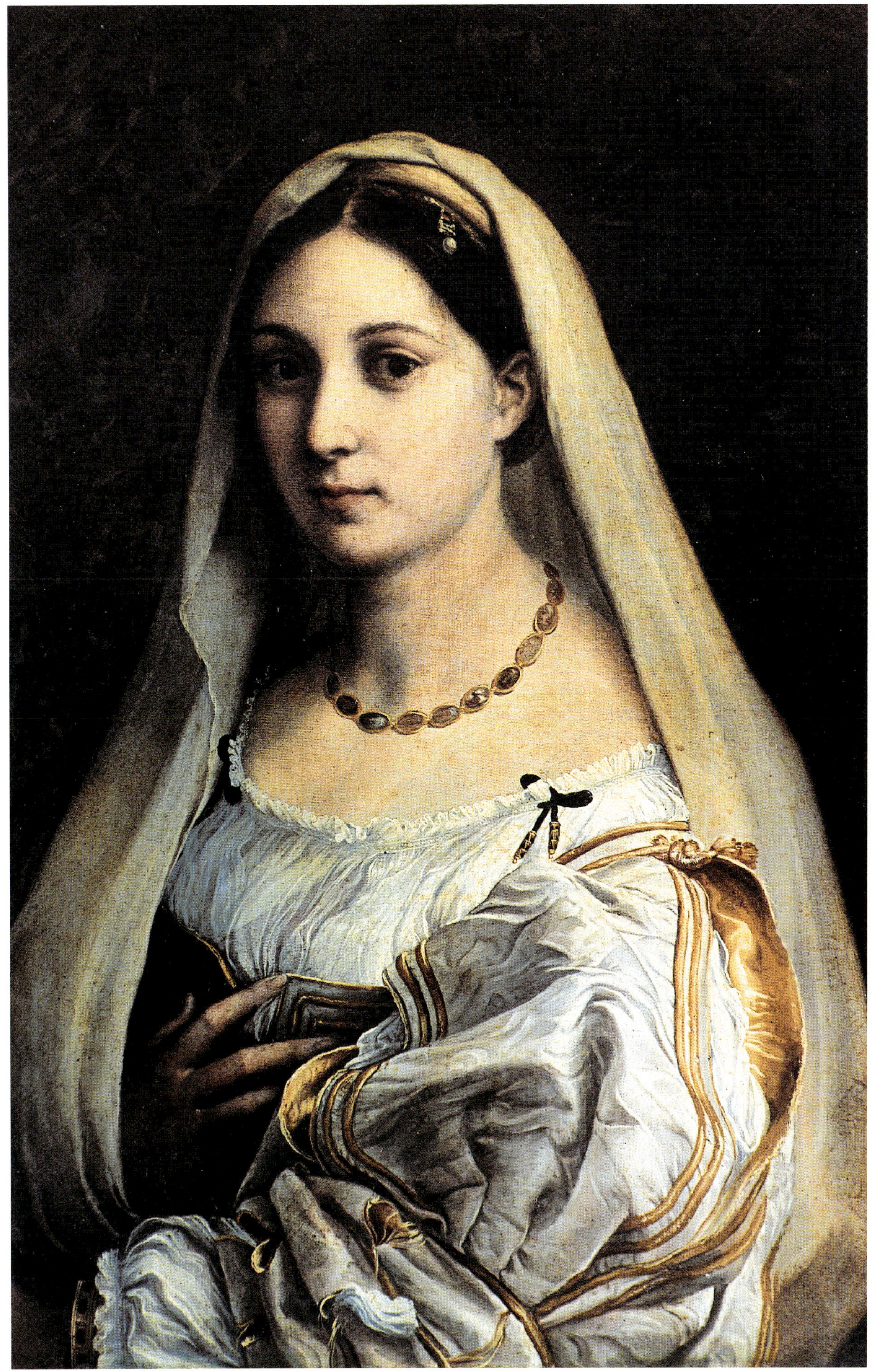

RAPHAEL
**Donna Velata
(Veiled Woman)**
1513, oil on panel,
85 x 64 cm
Galleria Palatina,
Palazzo Pitti,
Florence

Several female portraits have awakened imaginative and romantic hypotheses concerning Raphael's loves. The sitter here is Margherita Buti, daughter of a baker (*fornaio*) and thus known as the "Fornarina." The evocativeness of the marvelous painting, which Raphael made during his stay in Rome, has little to do with the hypothetical identification of the sitter and most of all with the application of the paint, and with the exceptional rendering of light on the folds of the sleeve in the foreground.

From the very beginning of his stay in Florence, Raphael began assimilating the stylistic traits of the last period of the Florentine fifteenth century, most of all those of Leonardo and Michelangelo. Thus was born a memorable sequence of increasingly complex variations on the theme of the group of the Virgin and Child. One after another, the pretty Madonnas by the master form an enchanting gallery of subtle gestures, hints of smiles, intimate tenderness; but these works are also proof of Raphael's skill at making modifications in attitudes, groupings, landscapes, light, and situations, the groups becoming more and more complicated with the addition of other figures, such as St. John the Baptist or Joseph. The stylistic experimentation in these works is obvious; there is the clear desire to try out new poses and compositional structures. But these never seem forced thanks to their marvelous naturalness, simplicity, and the apparent spontaneity of the feelings, the landscapes, and the rendering of light and colors.

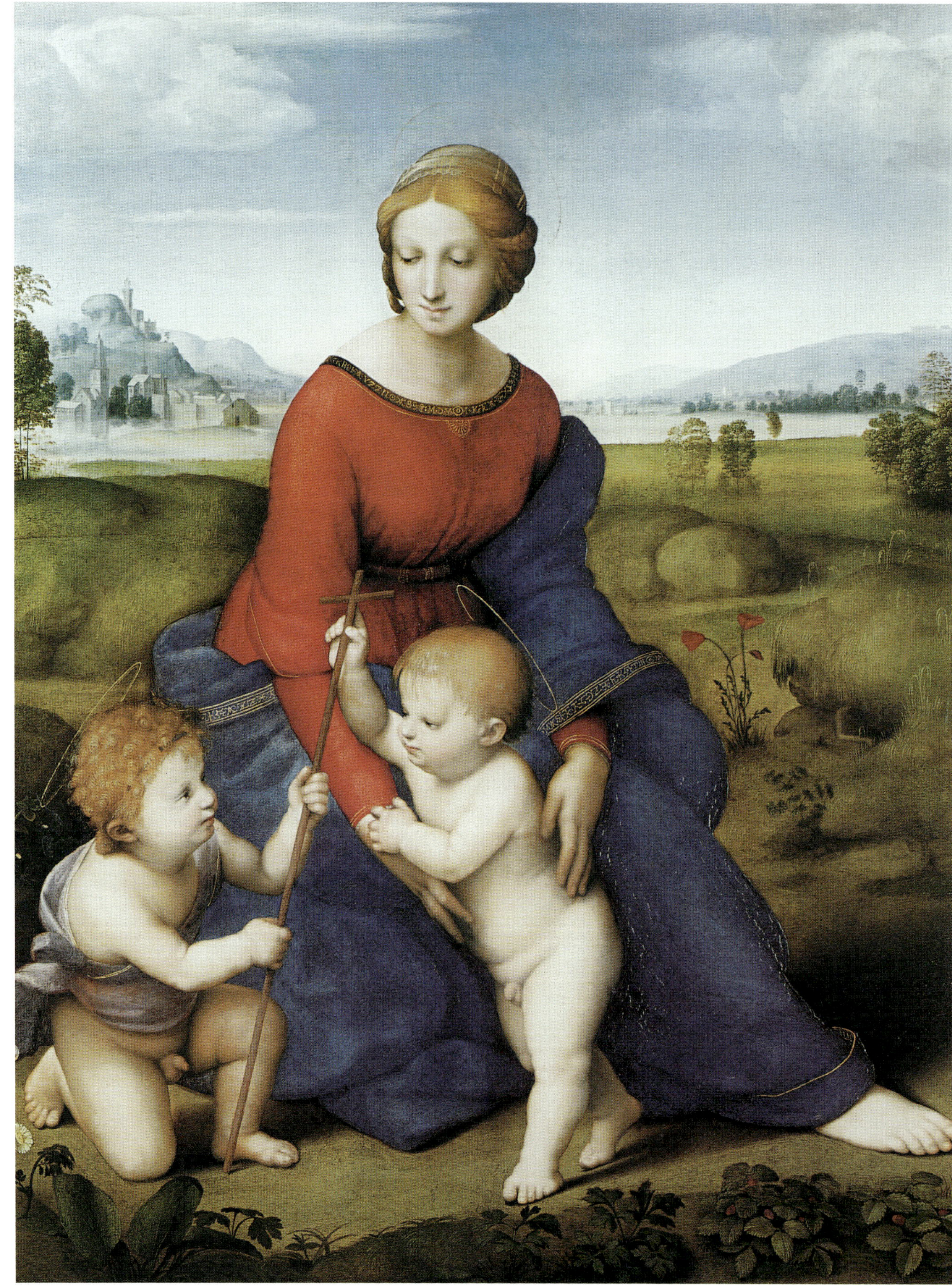

The early sixteenth century in Florence

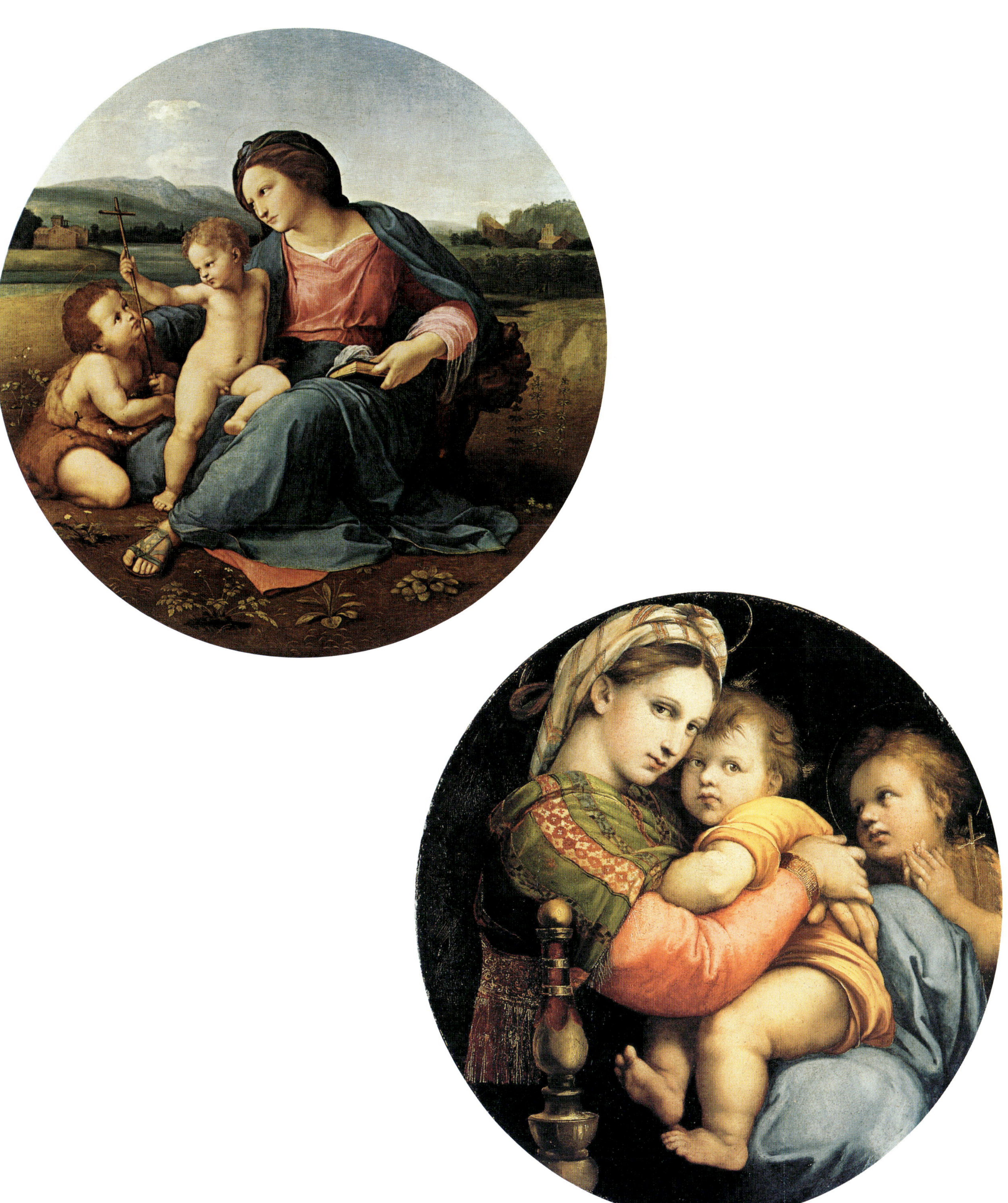

A fresco on the wall of a house is among the first known works by Raphael; the image is the profile of a very young Mary holding a sleeping Child. Thus did the painter begin his poetic career with the Virgin and Child, with each new image once again reviving the sweet and moving memory of the embrace of his lost mother, who died in 1491, when he was not yet nine years old. The *Madonna della Sedia* ("Madonna of the Chair") marks the culmination of this long process. Judged by way of the parameters traditionally used by critics, we can define it as a stupendous synthesis of Leonardo's *Mona Lisa* and Michelangelo's *Doni Tondo*. But this is a "different" painting. For once, it is not "we" who are looking at the Madonna but rather "she" who is looking at us, in doing so sweetly inviting us into a spiral of caresses and glances that may well have no equal in all of the history of art.

The early sixteenth century in Florence

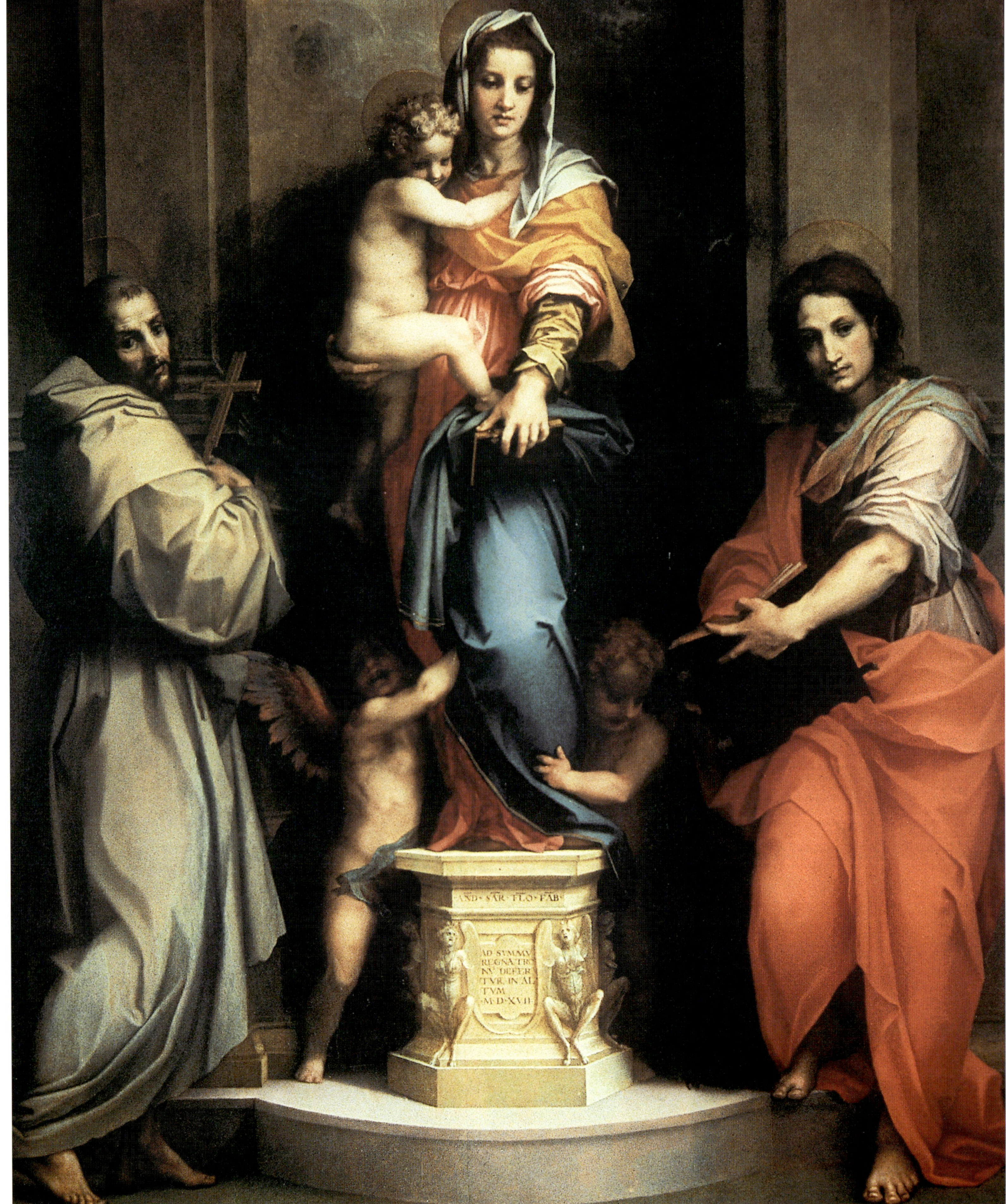

The early sixteenth century in Florence

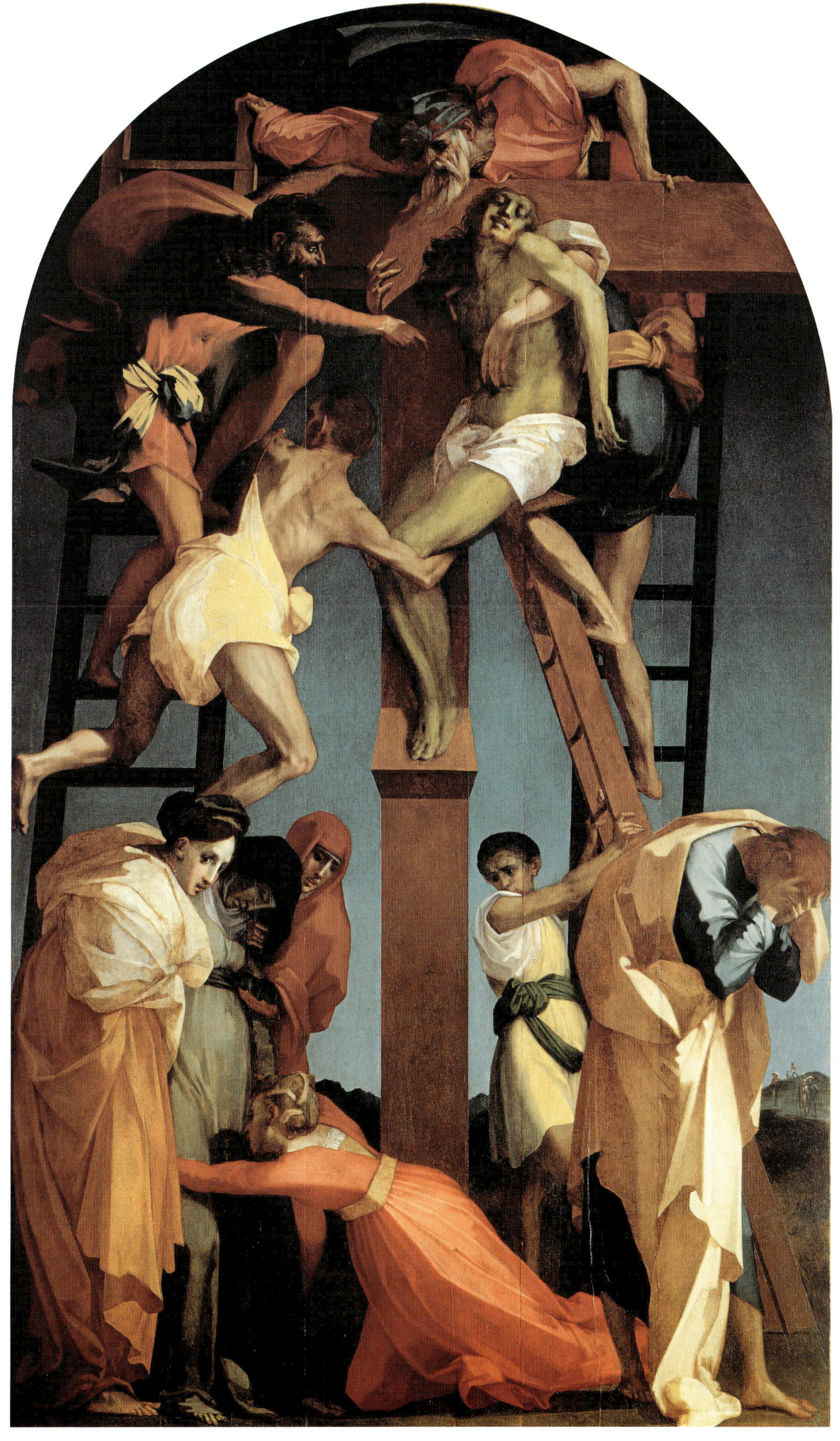

The early sixteenth century in Florence

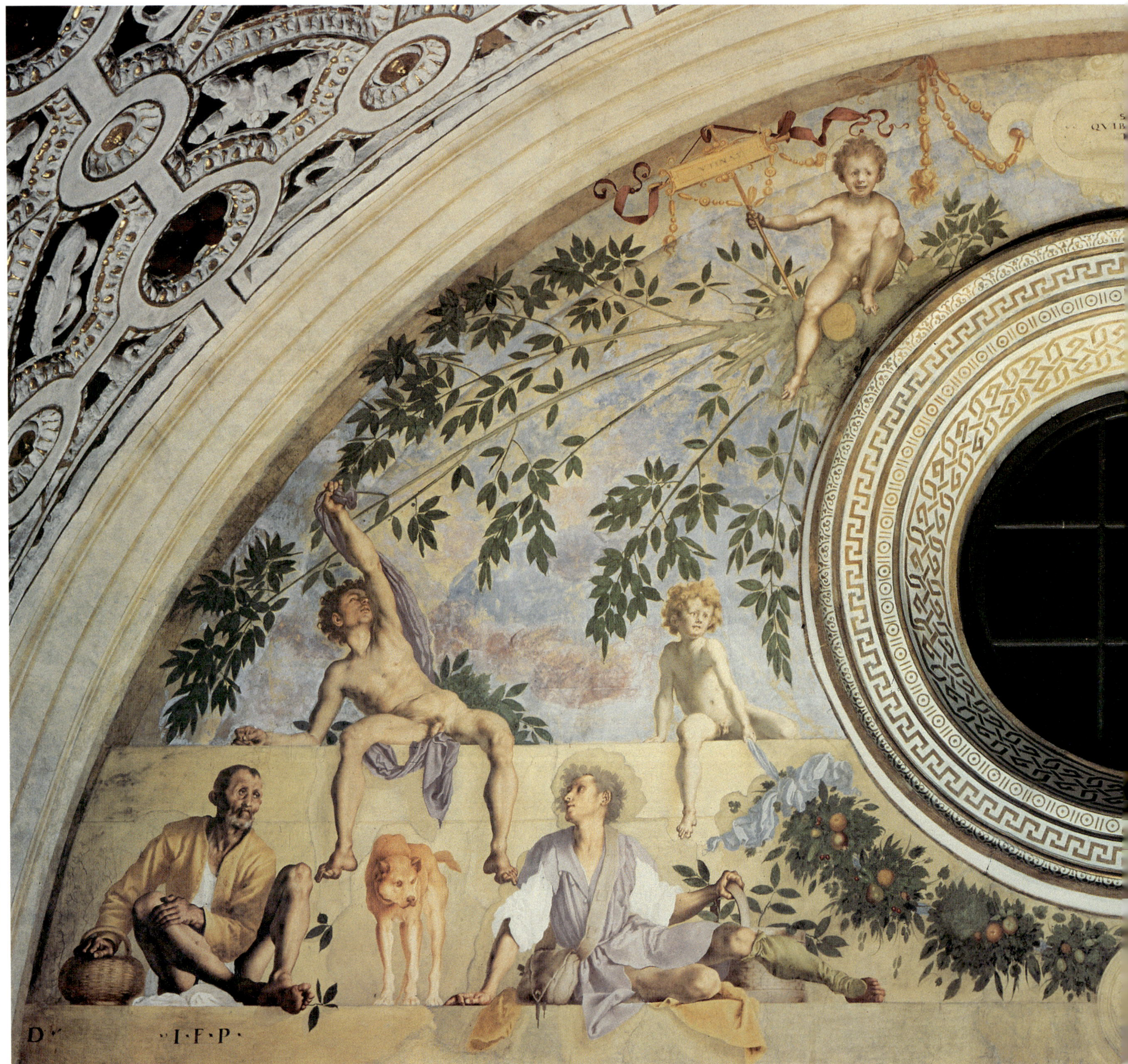

The early sixteenth century in Florence

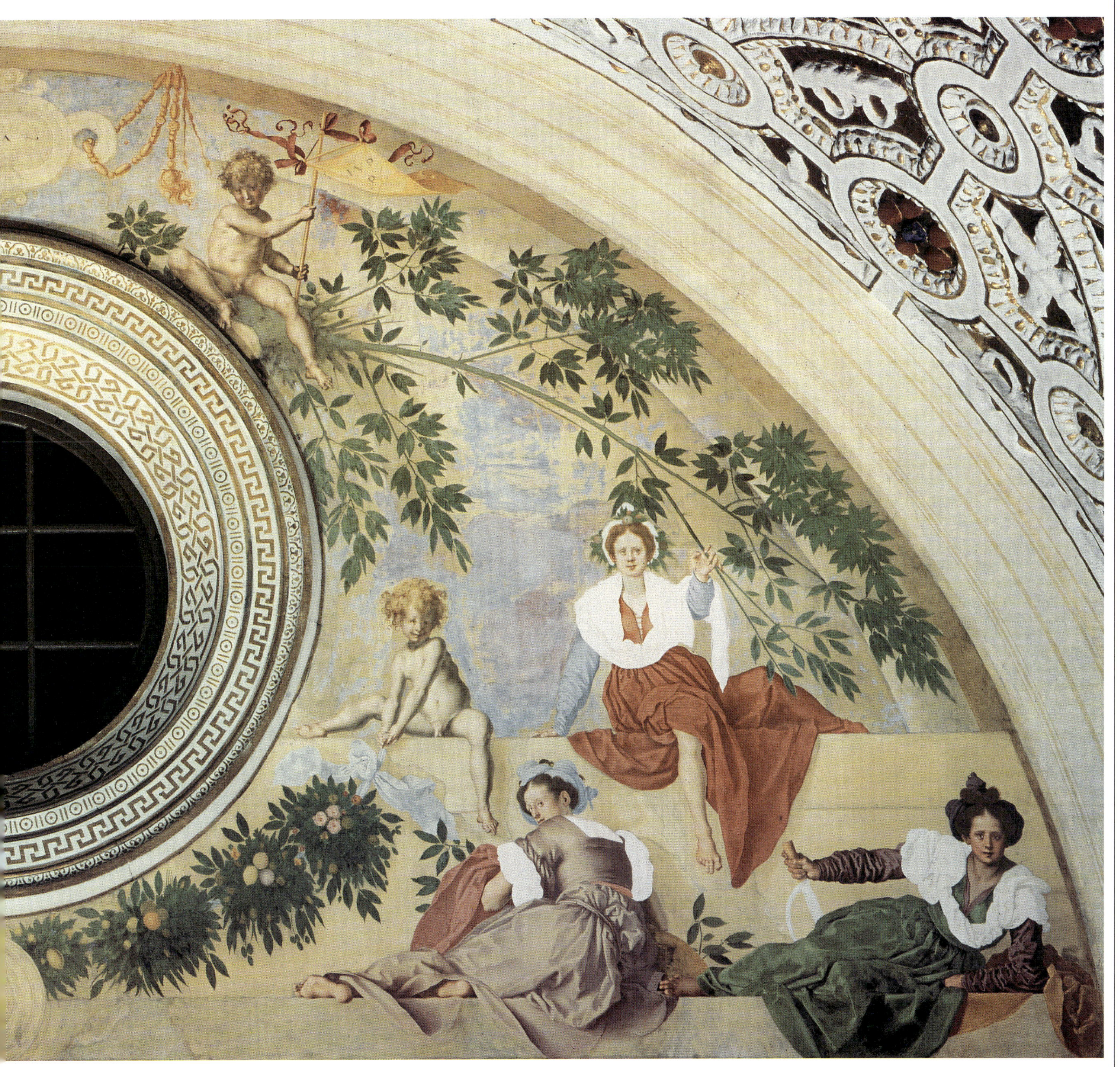

The early sixteenth century in Florence

In the new emotional
climate created by the
Protestant Reformation
Pontormo presented
sacred painting that
was far more intense,
dramatic, and unset-
tling than had ever
before been seen in
Italy. This *Lamentation*,
one of the most dis-
turbing altarpieces
of sixteenth-century
Florentine painting, is
a true "manifesto" of
mannerism. The regu-
lar, symmetrical struc-
ture of humanistic
painting is here frag-
mented in a composition
without stable points
of reference, neither
architectonic nor per-
spective. The figures,
with their emotionally
fraught gestures and
features, seem to wan-
der aimlessly.

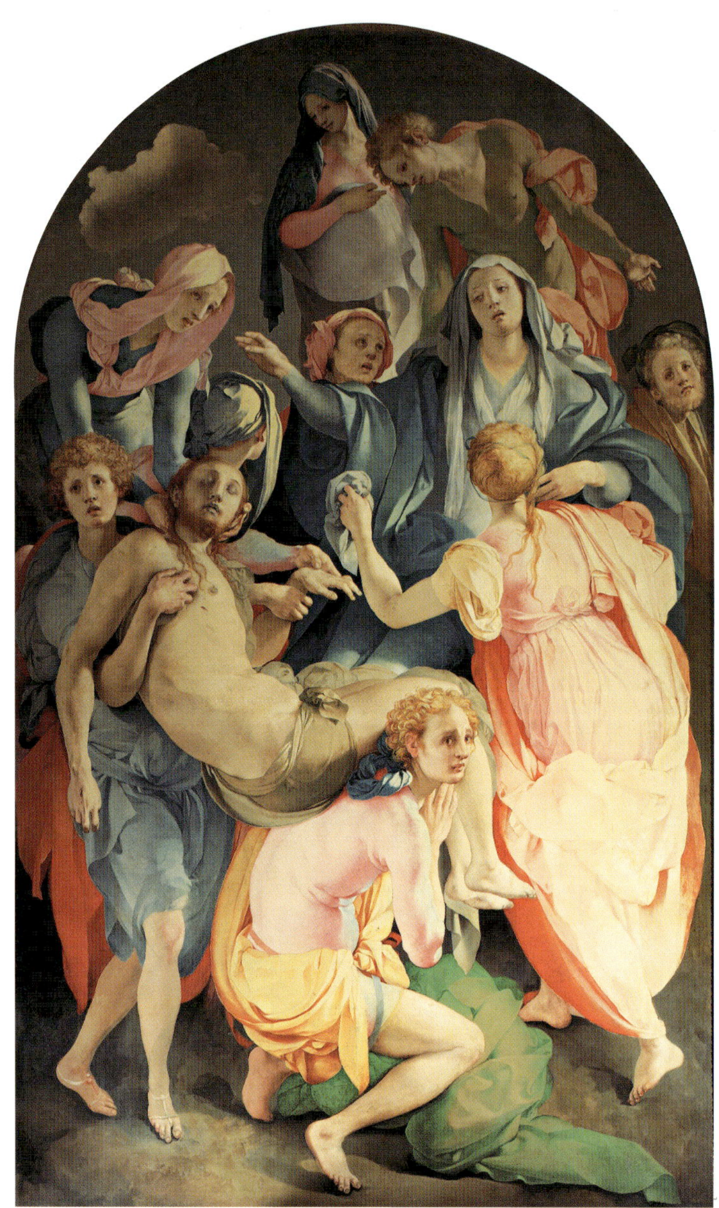

PONTORMO
Visitation
1528–29, oil on
panel, 202 x 156 cm
Parish Church of San
Michele, Carmignano
(Florence)

Paying no heed to all
previous iconography
for this scene, Pontormo
creates a hushed urban
setting, dark, almost
spectral. Filling up the
foreground, billowy and
stately, are Mary and
Elizabeth in profile;
behind them, as sort
of metaphysical "dou-
bles," the same two
women are presented
frontwise, turned to
the viewer.

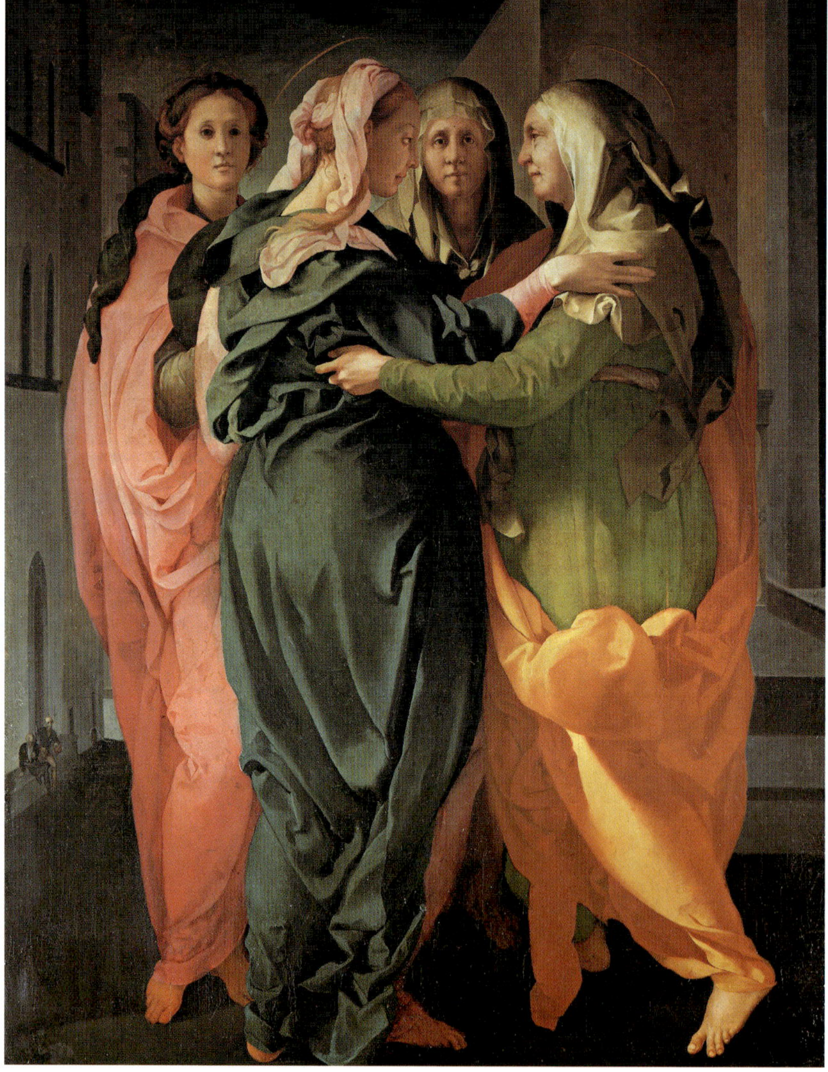

The early sixteenth century in Florence

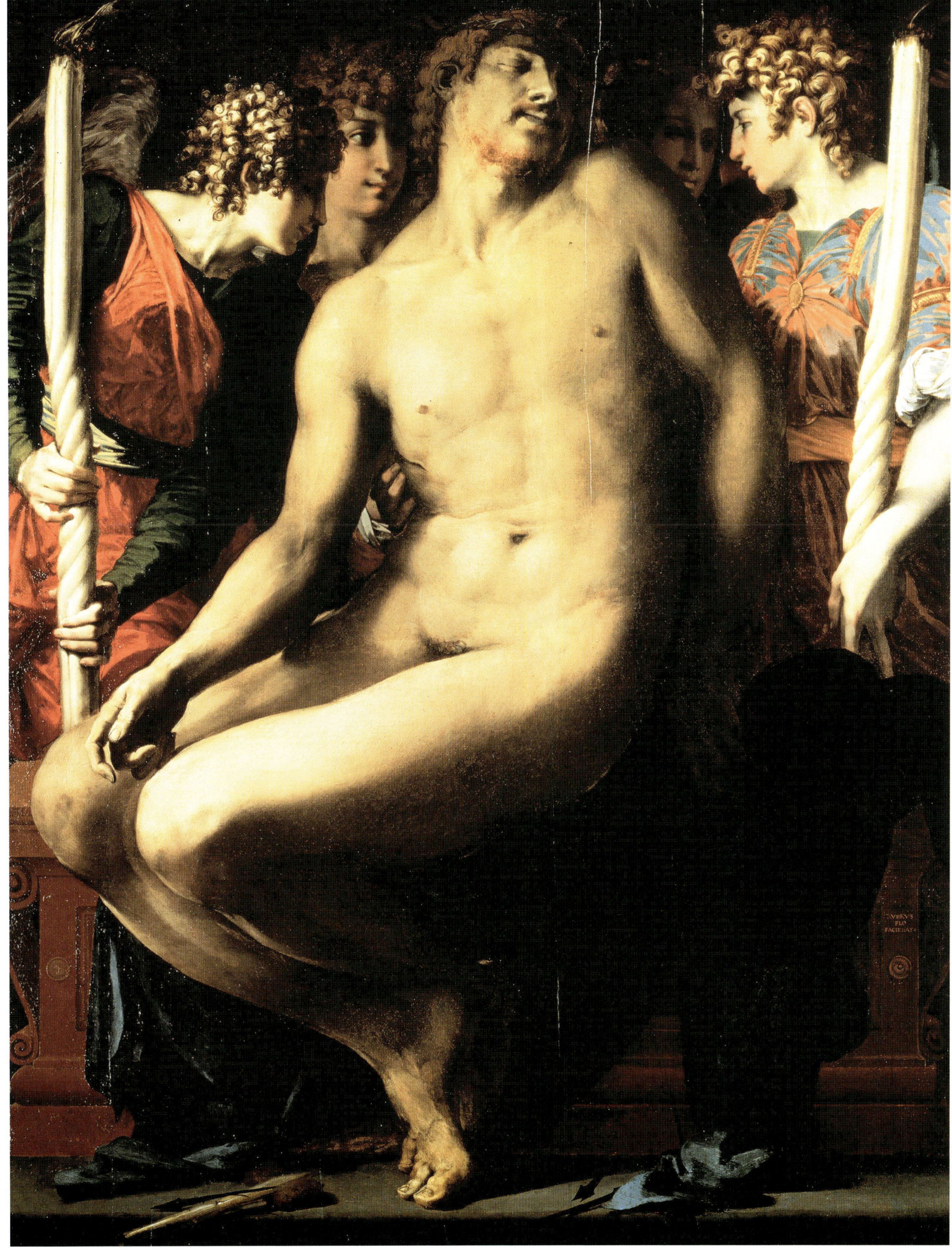

Rosso Fiorentino
**Dead Christ
and Angels**
1525–26, panel,
133.4 x 104.1 cm
Museum of Fine Arts,
Boston

Thanks to the arrival
in Rome of artists like
Parmigianino and
Rosso Fiorentino, the
so-called Clementine
age (the period of
Clement VII's pontifi-
cate before the cata-
strophic Sack of Rome
in 1527) was enriched
by sensual motifs and
refined languor. In this
composition, much
admired, imitated, and
copied in later decades,
Rosso Fiorentino draws
inspiration from the
nudes by Michelangelo
on the vault of the
Sistine Chapel, but
does without any sense
of dynamic and dra-
matic intensity in favor
of a satisfied, highly
elegant aestheticism.

The early sixteenth century in Florence

One of the most complex and important works by Michelangelo is the Sagrestia Nuova of the basilica of San Lorenzo in Florence, designed to hold the Medici tombs. Made in the course of the 1520s, it is a perfect blend of architecture and sculpture. The interior space, identical to that of the symmetrical Sagrestia Vecchia built by Filippo Brunelleschi almost a hundred years earlier, holds the vibrant tension between the white walls, the gray profiles in stone, and the refined decorative inserts. The two sarcophagi, located on the side walls, are perfectly inserted within the rhythm of the architecture. The portrait statues of the two members of the Medici family express two contrasting characters, one of contemplation the other of action. Resting

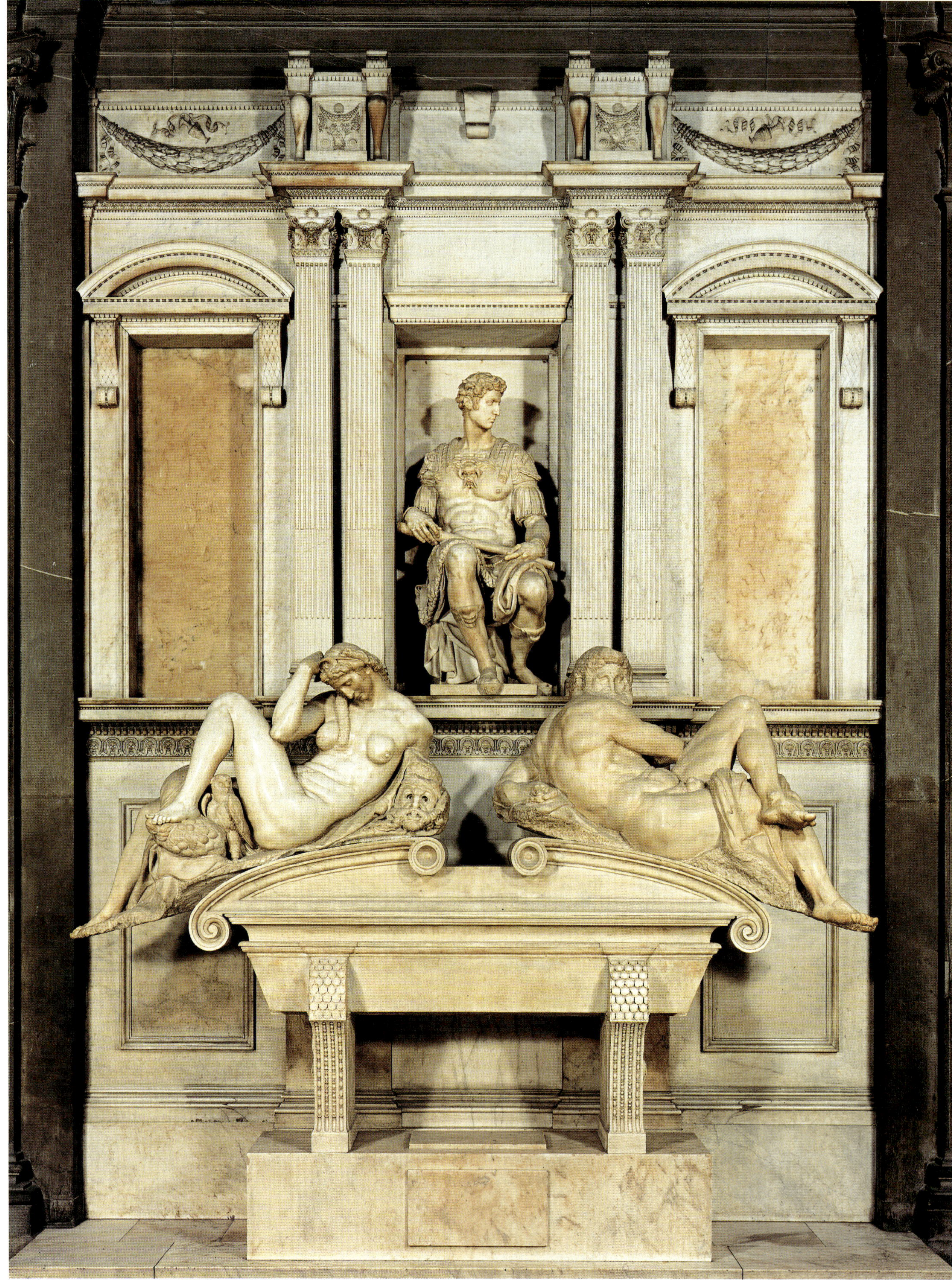

The early sixteenth century in Florence

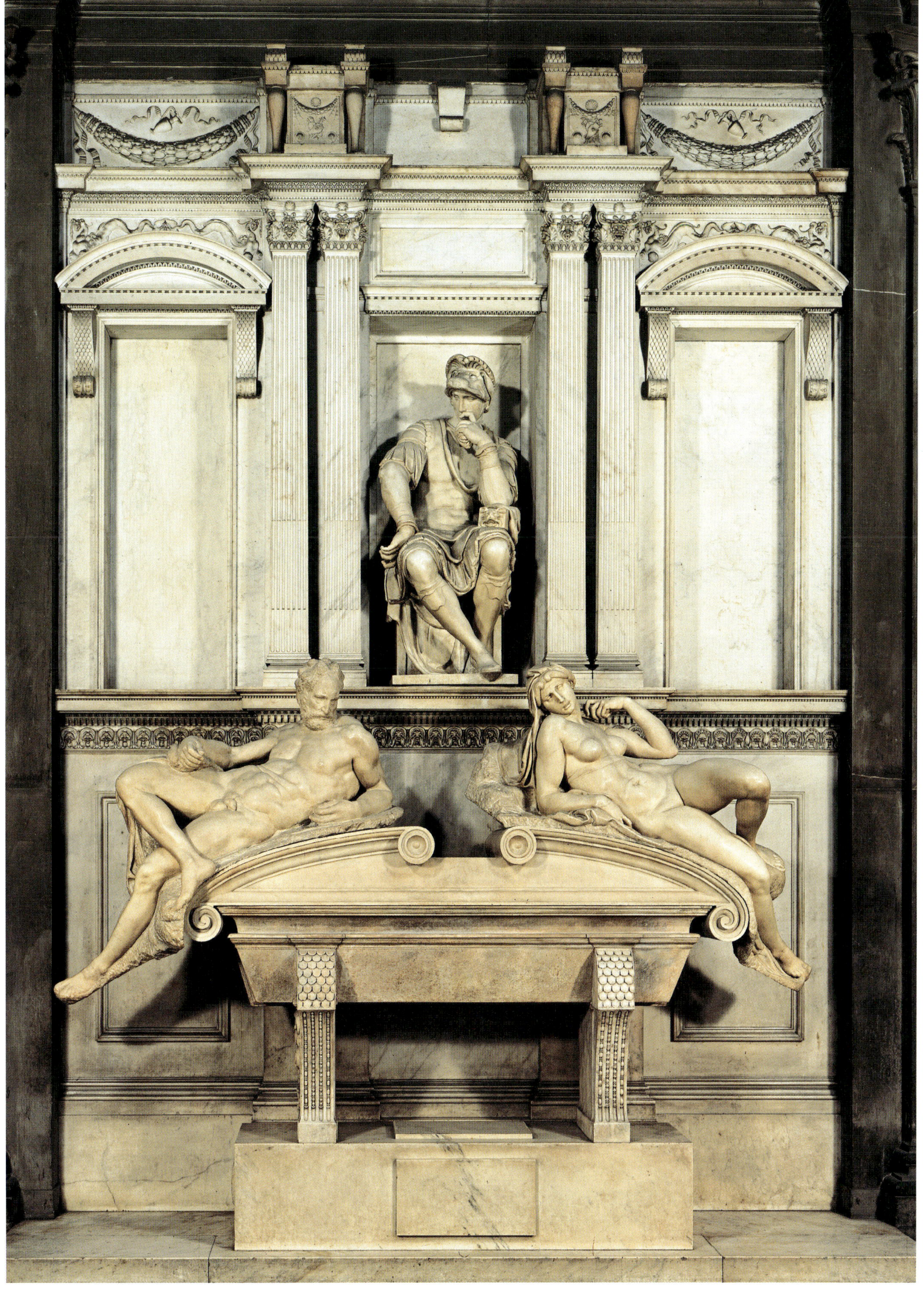

in pairs on top of the tombs are allegorical figures representing four times of the day: Dawn and Sunset, Day and Night. Each of these marvelous statues seems to be experiencing a different discomfort: Dawn stretches her limbs with a painful grimace, muscular Day reveals a misshapen face, almost that of a ghost; Sunset sinks down, opaque and tired. Only Night, sleeping, seems to forget the anguish of existence. This female figure was greatly admired by contemporaries for her naturalness; a man of letters sent Michelangelo a quatrain of praise in which he spoke of watching over Night in order to see her awaken. Michelangelo responded with a few, sharp lines in which he indicates that the abandonment of sleep is the reason for Night's serenity in comparison to the other allegories: "Dear to me is sleep, and even more being of stone, as long as injury and shame last. Not to see, not to hear, is a great advantage to me, so do not wake me and, please, speak softly."

The early sixteenth century in Florence

T itian's great power dominated entire centuries of the history of art. Perhaps no other painter has ever possessed his physical sense of color, translated into images of disconcerting energy. His long life can seem like a continuous series of successes and honors; in reality, however, it was an exemplary career of ongoing effort, of his tireless ability to put himself to the test and accept new challenges, competing with nature and with the tools of his art. For these reasons, reviewing Titian's artistic career means reviewing nearly an entire century of Renaissance painting, from the initial apogee of grace and harmony to the dramatic conclusion of the last works. One of the few things not certain in the long life of Titian is his date of birth, which is usually placed around 1488–90. For the rest, we know everything about this boy who came from the mountains to dominate not only the artistic scene in Venice but the entire course of European painting.

The first decade of the sixteenth century, distinguished by the arrival in Venice of such personalities as Bosch, Metsys, and most of all Dürer, saw a debate concerning compositional ideas, pictorial techniques, and figurative solutions. In 1508 Giorgione was called to fresco the façades of the Fondaco dei Tedeschi, the large building near the Rialto bridge

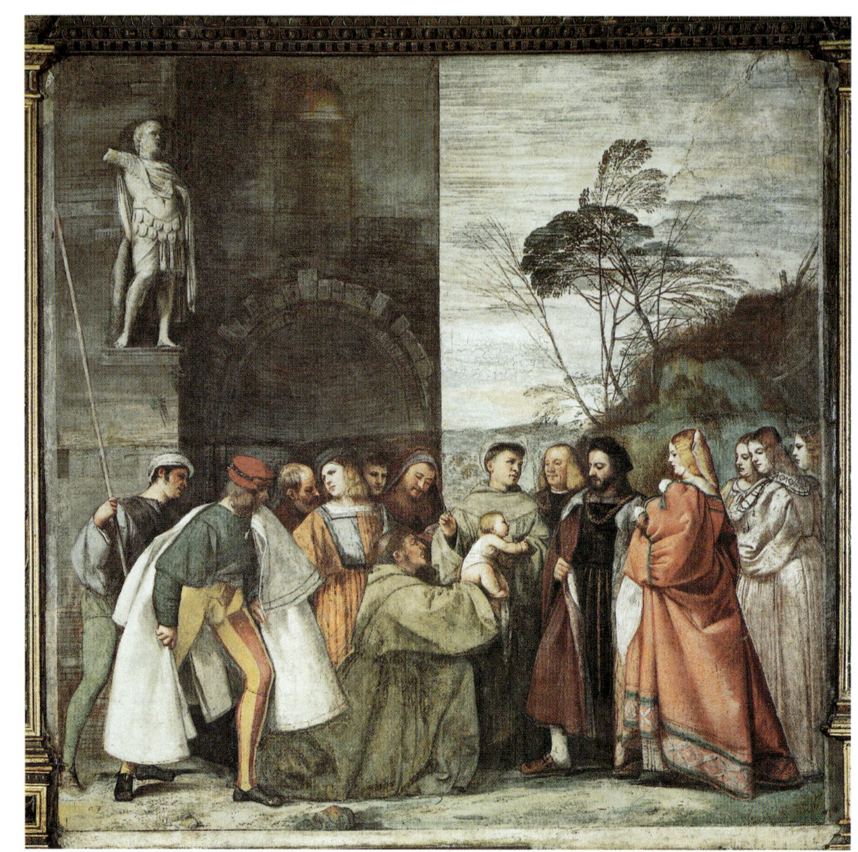

Titian, apotheosis

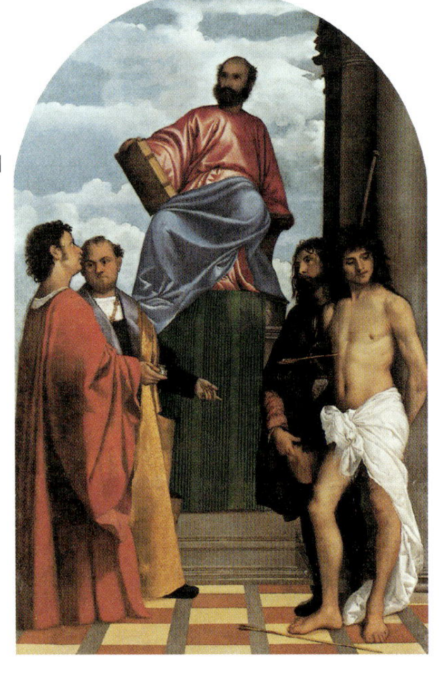

rebuilt after a ruinous fire. Reserving overall direction of the project and the execution of the part facing the Grand Canal, Giorgione entrusted to Titian the side facing the Mercerie. This was the beginning of an extraordinary career that, however, suffered a sudden setback in 1509 following the attack unleashed against the Venetian Republic by the allied powers of the League of Cambrai, namely the Holy Roman Empire, France, Spain, and the Papacy. The Peace of Noyon marked a drastic change in Venice's sphere of influence. The death of Giorgione, during the plague of 1510, further disturbed the situation. Titian moved to Padua, and in April 1511 began to fresco three episodes of the life of St. Anthony in the Scuola del Santo. With these paintings the artist, then

a little over twenty, affirmed his personality. The three scenes reveal a dramatic energy and a theatrical use of color unknown in Giorgione's patiently constructed harmonies. Titian began to assume the supremacy of Venetian painting, and in 1513 he received his first official commission for the Doge's Palace. Giovanni Bellini died in 1516, and in the span of a week Titan had become the city's new official painter, a position he would hold uninterruptedly for sixty years. In the same year, he received the request for an altarpiece for the main altar of the basilica of Santa Maria Gloriosa dei Frari. Thus came into being the *Assumption*, inaugurated on May 18, 1518. The initial reactions were a mixture of wonder and dismay. As Ludovico Dolce (1557) wrote, "The clumsy artists and the dimwit masses who had seen up till then nothing but the dead and cold creations of Giovanni Bellini, Gentile, and Vivarino—works which had no movement and no projection—grossly maligned this same picture. Later the envy cooled off, and in truth, little by little, opened people's eyes, so that they began to marvel at the new style opened up by Titian in Venice." Their marvel is understandable. The *Assumption* is without points of contact with

Titian, apotheosis and tragedy of a genius

the preceding Venetian painting, but is a point of departure for the "new style" that Dolce himself synthesized: "This panel has the grandness and the awesomeness of Michelangelo, the pleasing beauty of Raphael, and the colors of nature itself." In 1518 Titian began his international career. The first invitation came from Alfonso I d'Este, who called him to Ferrara to paint the three so-called bacchanals to put in the alabaster *camerino*, for which Giovanni Bellini had painted the *Feast of the Gods* and which would later be completed by the ceiling compartments by Dosso Dossi. With the unfortunate dismantling of this *studiolo*, following the relocation of the Este capital to Modena (1598), the paintings were moved first to Rome and then outside Italy. By 1520, alternating periods at the Este court with others spent in Venice, Titian greatly increased the amount of time he spent of his works, making them difficult

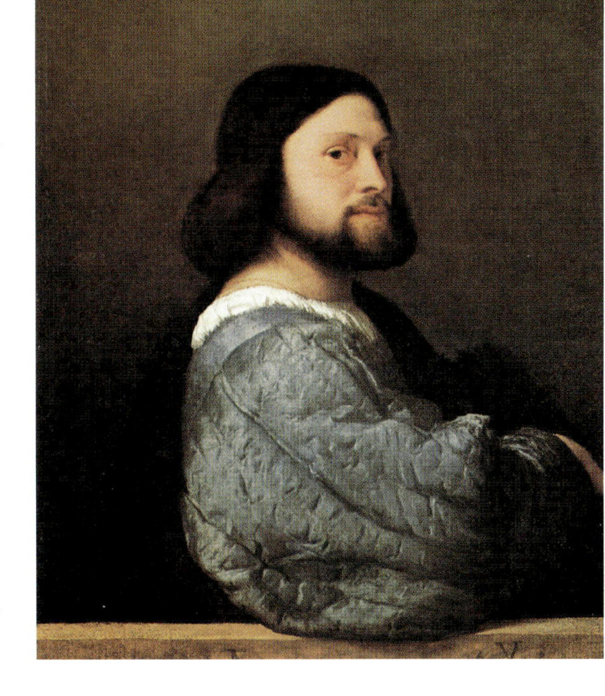

Titian, *Portrait of a Man,* 1511–12; National Gallery, London

with two large columns that extend beyond the edges of the frame. The colors are luminous, with a clear preference for pure tints and a substantial rejection of shaded half-tones. The inauguration of the Pesaro Altarpiece marks the full maturity of Titian, who by then was leading Venetian art toward a dynamic animation until then unknown, in keeping with the city's reestablished historical role. The project of making Venice into a "new Rome" started by Doge Andrea Gritti found a further impulse in 1527 when the Eternal City itself was sacked by the German and Spanish mercenaries of Charles V, the same emperor who, a few years later (1533), conferred on Titian the rank of Knight of the Golden Spur, gave him free access to the court, and nominated him *pintor primero*. Thus began a long a very fecund relationship between Titian and the Spanish court, beginning with the genre of portraits. In fact,

and tragedy of a genius

to acquire and thus expensive. In addition to the Estes his patrons now included the Gonzagas; in the span of a few years a great number of requests from various regions rained upon him.

In 1523 the greatly contested election of the ambitious Andrea Gritti as doge led to an acceleration in the culture and art of Venice. The new doge undertook a broad project to give the city a more dynamic image, adopting an up-to-date architectonic model. As official state painter, Titian was personally involved in the doge's undertakings. The key work of these years is the Pesaro Altarpiece in the basilica of the Frari. The long time he spent on it (commissioned in 1519, it was not completed until 1526) reflects the radical innovation in the compositional structure of the altarpiece. Taking into consideration the point of view from which the painting, located on a side altar to the left, would be seen, Titian moved the Madonna's seat from the center of the image to the right. He also turned the group of figures toward her, thereby revolutionizing the canonical triangular scheme of the *sacra conversazione*. The altarpiece's sense of novelty was accentuated by the articulation of the architectonic elements,

Titian initiated a new way of making official portraits, creating models that would be followed for several centuries by painters such as Velázquez, Rubens, Rembrandt, and Goya and, by way of them, would remain the preferred image for dictators up to the twentieth century. Titian chose dynamic moments and gestures and fluid expressions. Instead of a

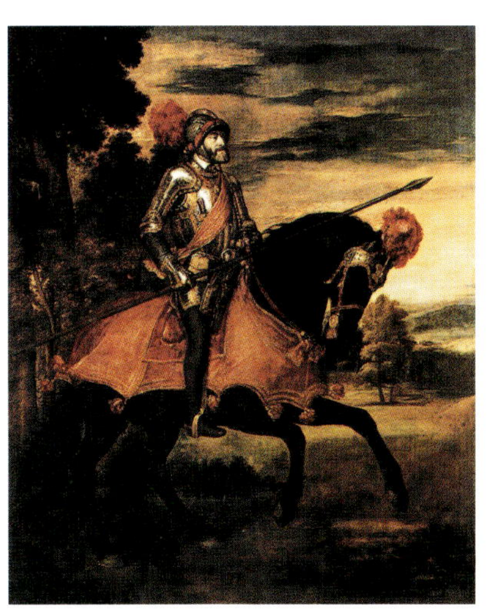

Titian, *Charles V at Mühlberg,* 1548; Museo del Prado, Madrid

rigorous but static presentation of physical features, what is exalted is the active nature of the illustrious man (emperor or pope, commander or doge), his dominant role, his presence on the scene of the world and history.

During the 1530s, thanks to the patronage of the Della Rovere family, with the seductive *Venus of Urbino* Titian undertook mythological painting, destined to become

Titian, apotheosis and tragedy of a genius

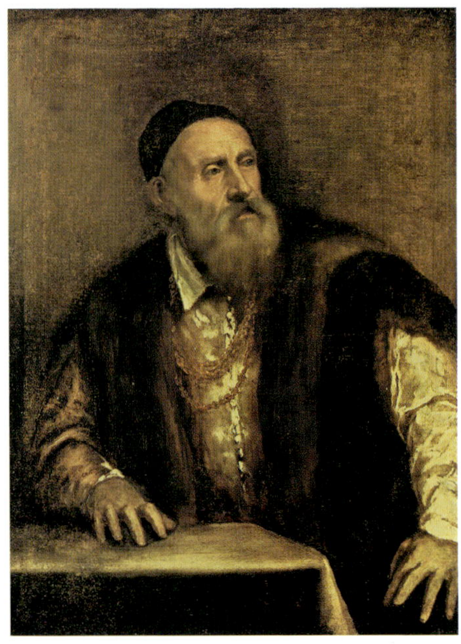

fundamental in the years of his old age. At the same time, in his position as leader of the Venetian painting school, he remained almost completely impervious to the stimuli coming from central Italy. The situation began to change with the arrival in Venice of Francesco Salviati (1539) and Giorgio Vasari (1541). The church of Santo Spirito in Isola, rebuilt by Sansovino, became the laboratory for the diffusion of the new style, and the writings of Pietro Aretino further aided its popularization. During his stays at the Gonzaga court in Mantua Titian had had ample opportunity to see the works of Giulio Romano; the circulation of prints and drawings made it possible to keep up to date on developments in the other schools. The favor met by mannerists in Venice stimulated him to seek direct experience and drove him to make his first trip to Rome. The mannerist moment of Titian culminated in the *Crown of Thorns* (1542–44), today in the Musée du Louvre but originally in the sanctuary of Santa Maria delle Grazie in Milan, an example of balance between ideas from central Italy, ties to the local tradition, and personal style. The action is given a high, monumental tone, a tragic sense that was destined to mark, a half century later, the formation of Caravaggio. In his small-size paintings Titian began to make use of a new method of applying paint, destined to become the expressive means of his later maturity. The first attempts at this "new nature" (as Pietro Aretino called it) show up in portraits of people very familiar to the artist. In the portrait of Pietro Aretino and in the posthumous portraits of Andrea Gritti the outlines are not defined with precision, the paint appears to have been applied in large strokes and is deliberately uneven. At the same time that Michelangelo was working toward his "unfinished" sculptures, Titian awakens an active and direct involvement of the viewer.

Accompanied by advice and letters from Pietro Aretino, escorted by the duke of Urbino, given hospitality by Pietro Bembo, introduced by Cardinal Alessandro Farnese (nephew of the current pope, Paul III), and feared by the entire local painting school, Titian arrived in Rome in October 1545. Giorgio Vasari guided him in the visit of the antique and modern monuments and recorded his more salient impressions. Vasari's biography of Titian also includes an episode set in the Vatican gardens. Michelangelo, observing Titian busy completing the splendid *Danaë*, after an initial expression of admiration (in Titian's presence), later made a negative comment about Titian's lack of skill in design, an observation that would become a commonplace for Tuscan culture.

When he returned to Venice in 1546, after a stop in Florence, Titian understood that his mannerist experience could consider itself over. From then on his efforts were to be dedicated to improving a technique for the dense and dramatic application of paint. As Aretino wrote in a letter to Charles V in October 1548, Titian sought "new forces of shadow and of light." At that time Venice was going through a period of dynamic construction, with nearly 180 new buildings going up between 1539 and 1550; to these must be added the villas being constructed on the mainland, which found in Andrea Palladio a designer of absolute genius. In a few years, a city palace and a country villa were of equal prestige. Titian, who continued in his role as official painter to the republic,

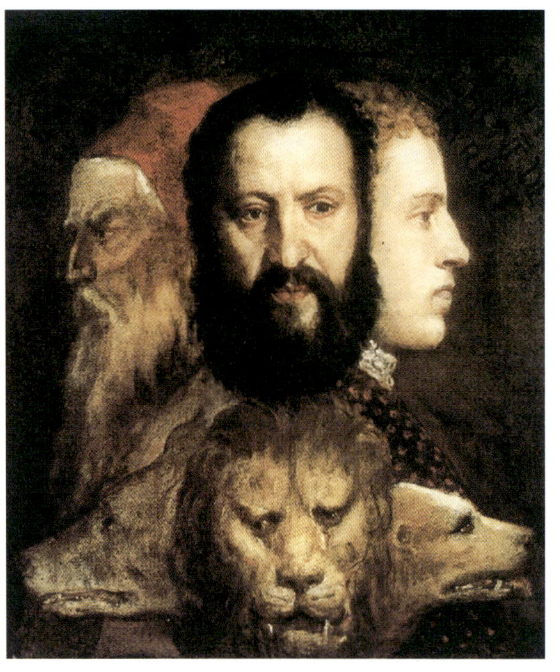

was very busy with works for Charles V and followed the emperor to Augsburg twice, in 1548 and 1551.

Around the middle of the century, the Venetian school reached another turning point. The consecration of Tintoretto occurred in 1548, when the thirty-year-old painter consigned to the Scuola Grande di San Marco the *St. Mark Rescuing the Slave*, today in the Gallerie dell'Accademia, of a richness of color at the height of the Venetian tradition, but in the service of a crowded, monumental composition, with gestures, expressions, torsions, musculature, and references to the "modern manner," in particular to Michelangelo. The affirmation of Tintoretto, followed a few years later by that of Paolo Veronese, the flow into the Venetian collections of canvases with pastoral themes by Jacopo Bassano, indeed the general request for "modern" paintings was accompanied by the death or departure from the scene of several old masters. Giovanni Girolamo Savoldo died amid general indifference; Lorenzo Lotto, at the limits of misery, took refuge in the Marches; Paris Bordone built himself a dignified career working most of all outside Venice, in Milan, for the Fugger bankers in Augsburg, and later in the French court.

Titian, apotheosis and tragedy of a genius

In 1551, with the Giustiniani Altarpiece for the church of San Francesco della Vigna, Paolo Veronese made his entrance into the world of Venetian painting. Veronese began with a rereading of the works of Titian of thirty years earlier; the group of figures clearly repeats the arrangement of the Pesaro Altarpiece in the Frari, and the lights and the colors recall the pure and dazzling tones of Titian's works from the 1520s. On the other hand, the young Veronese shows that he possessed an up-to-date repertory of models, in which the close study of mannerist art was expressed in forms of great breadth, in distended compositions, with grand, sweeping gestures.

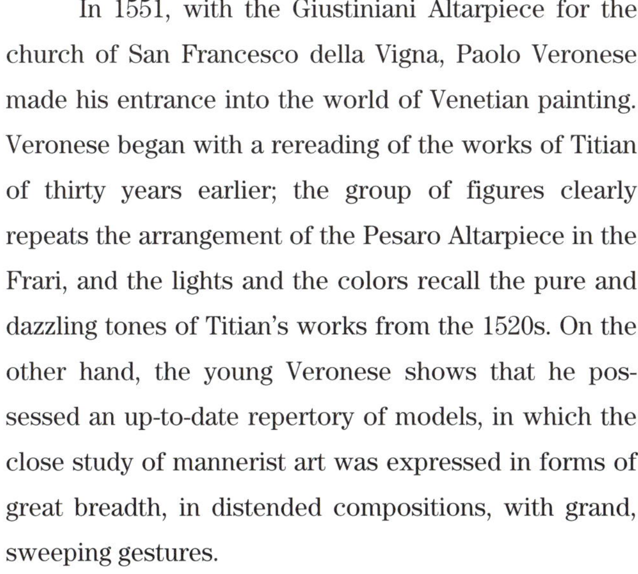

What distinguished the two emerging masters from each other was not so much differences in their technical methods as differences in their choice of subject. Tintoretto developed his figurative line with a spectacular theatricality, in narrative illustration, and with a great sensibility for spatial and dynamic values; Veronese distinguished himself as a highly promising interpreter of the celebratory and symbolic needs of the official settings of the government of the Most Serene Republic. His limpid and brilliant painting was patently reminiscent of the great teaching of the art of the young Titian; on the other hand, Veronese's clear and luminous images cannot escape being compared to the altarpiece on which Titian had been working by then for ten years, the *Martyrdom of St. Lawrence* for the church of the Crociferi (today Santa Maria Assunta dei Gesuiti). Completed in 1559, the great painting is the dramatic manifesto of the new phase in Titian's art. Every residue of humanistic conceptions has been abandoned for a free and independent layout. The composition has no true center, is avaricious of colors, and lives most of all in the extension of forms between deep shadow and spots of light. In this trembling context the architectonic elements fade away, and the outlines of the figures appear only to be lost, with a highly dramatic expressive dynamism.

From then on, Titian was projected into a different dimension compared to the other contemporary painters. Closed in a noble creative isolation, dedicated to exploring new expressive possibilities, he made a series of sacred and profane paintings for the Spanish court (among them the so-called *poesie*, mythological works for Philip II) and other patrons.

One of the most important works of this period is the large *Annunciation* for the church of San Salvatore in Venice (1566). Once again, Titian did not stop at a standard stylistic definition and instead reexamined the subject. Dense color, full and warm, overflows the outlines of the figures, and the painting has the feel of an iridescent impastoed stain.

After 1570, more than eighty years old, Titian entered a sphere of human and anguished meditation. The death of his friend Jacopo Sansovino in 1570 made his old age even more solitary. His last works dwell on the bitter theme of the torment of innocents. Whether the subject was religious, mythological, or historical, the type of poetic interpretation and the narrative technique were always similar. To represent the powerlessness and the suffering of the weak at the hands of the arrogant stronger, Titian pushed himself toward the farthest possibilities of technique. The outlines of objects dissolve, dramatic effect is obtained by way of a dense impasto of paint, brushstrokes are often replaced by streaks left by the fingers, with the pictorial substance left in lumps on the surface of the canvas.

Titian was the most famous victim of the plague that struck Venice in 1576. Until his last day, August 27, he stayed in the studio of Biri Grande, busy working on his last masterpiece, the *Pietà* for his own tomb, planned for the basilica of the Frari. In the city struck by the terrifying epidemic (about a quarter of the inhabitants died), the death of the great master increased the sense of discouragement: the death of Titian was the symbolic end of an epoch.

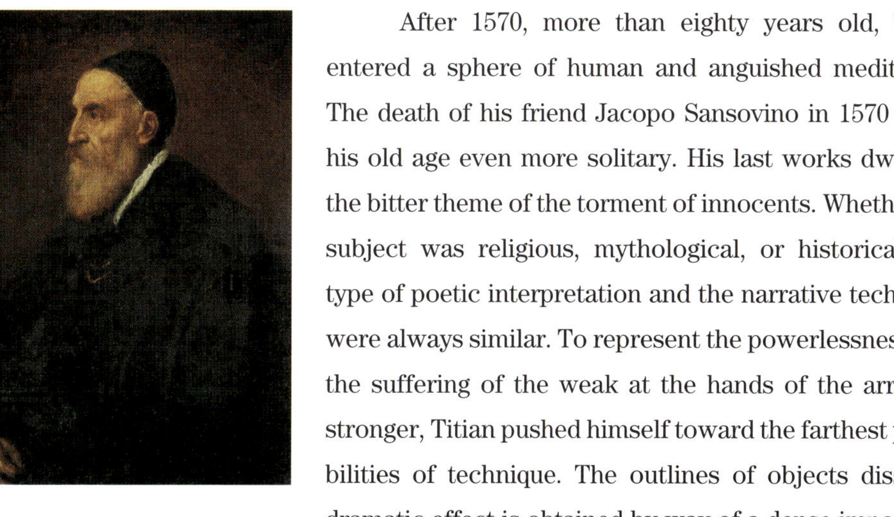

Titian, *Self-Portrait*, 1567–68; Museo del Prado, Madrid

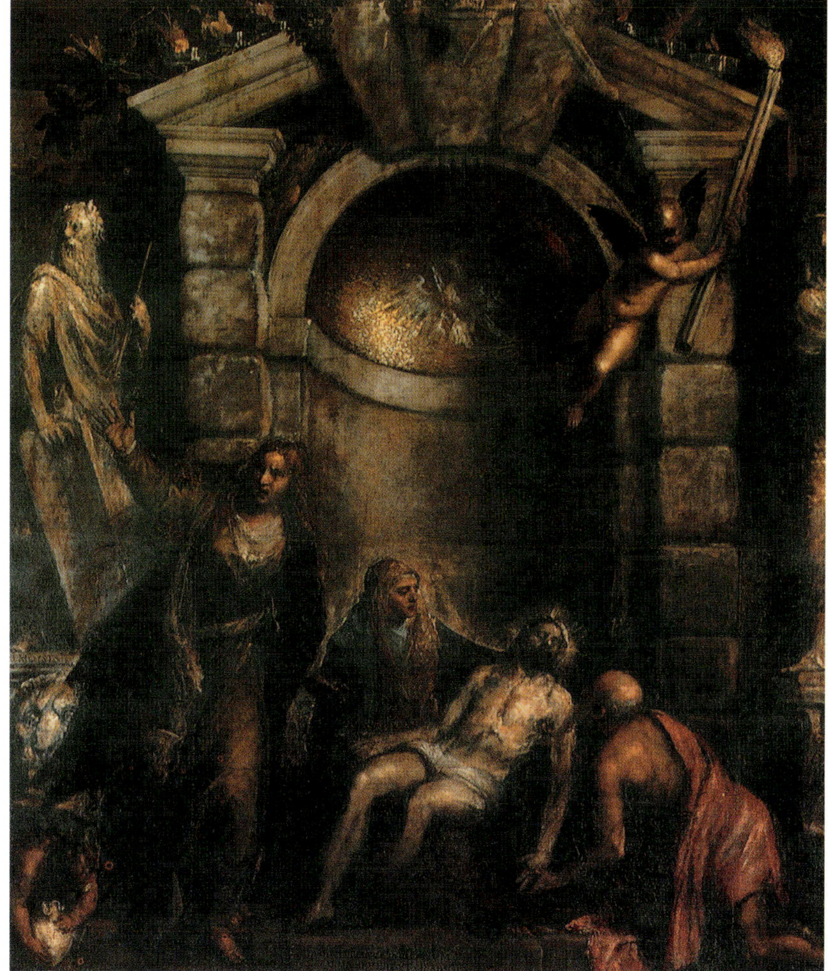

Titian, *Pietà*, 1576; Gallerie dell'Accademia, Venice

Titian, apotheosis and tragedy of a genius

Since the time of the
sixteenth-century writ-
ers on art, scholars
have often had to deal
with doubt concerning
the attribution of
several works, a few of
them quite famous, to
either Giorgione or to
Titian. In 1508 the two
artists worked together
on the frescoes on the
exterior of the Fondaco
dei Tedeschi, and cer-
tainly Titian integrated
Giorgione's style, which
he learned thoroughly
while studying with him.
This marvelous canvas
in the Louvre, a model
for Manet's *Déjeuner
sur l'Herbe* and in
general for the *en plein
air* painting of the
Impressionists, is one
of the most fascinating
of these questionable
works. Recent criticism
leans in favor of Titian.

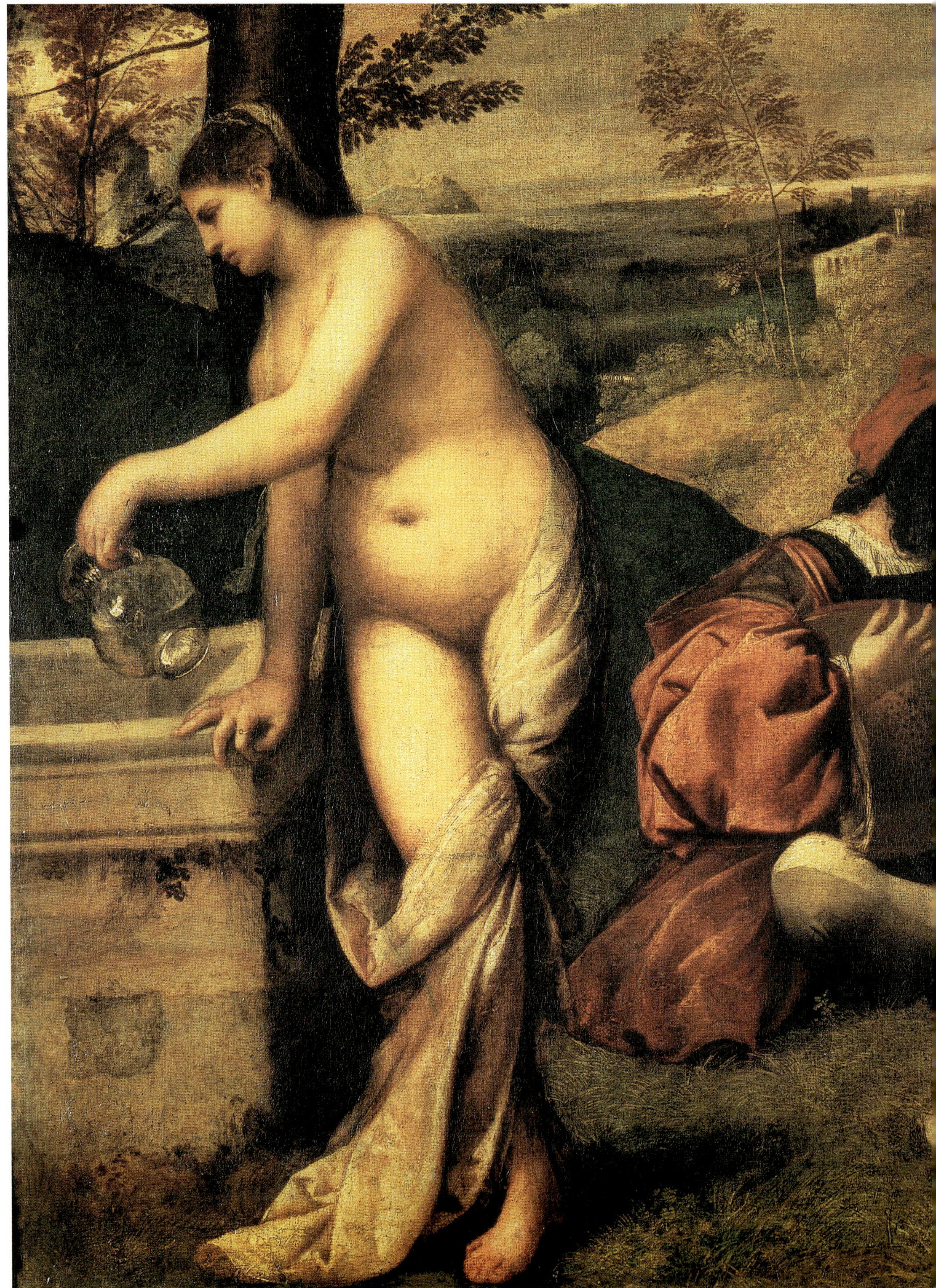

Titian, apotheosis and tragedy of a genius

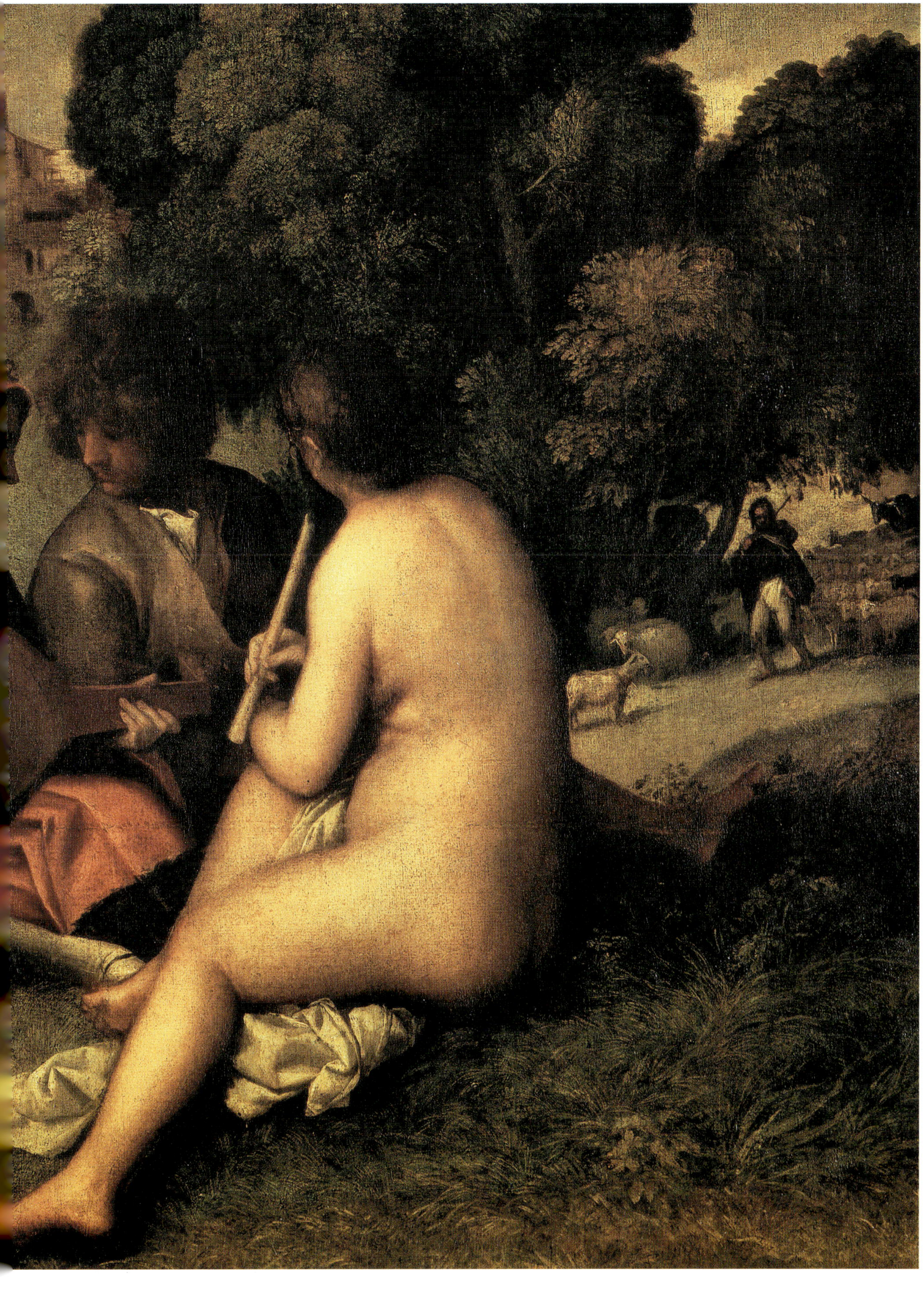

Titian, apotheosis and tragedy of a genius

**Sacred and
Profane Love**
1514, oil on canvas,
118 x 279 cm
Galleria Borghese,
Rome

Titian's vital and joyous interpretation of the classics is synthesized in this work, with its complex allegorical meanings that make it a manifesto of the artistic and cultural ideals of the High Renaissance. Christian and pagan elements blend together in this composition, in which all the elements are perfectly balanced, and with which the Veneto artist, influenced by Neoplatonic philosophy, presents earthly beauty as a reflection of divine perfection. Titian contrasts the bucolic serenity of a Giorgionesque landscape with a background full of action: clouds, wind, figures, branches, animals, and water participate in the active and inexhaustible rhythm of the universe. The two stupendous women, so similar they could pass for twins, are clothed in completely opposite ways: one is dressed sumptuously, the other is practically nude. Scholarly interpretations vary, but there is agreement on one point. According to

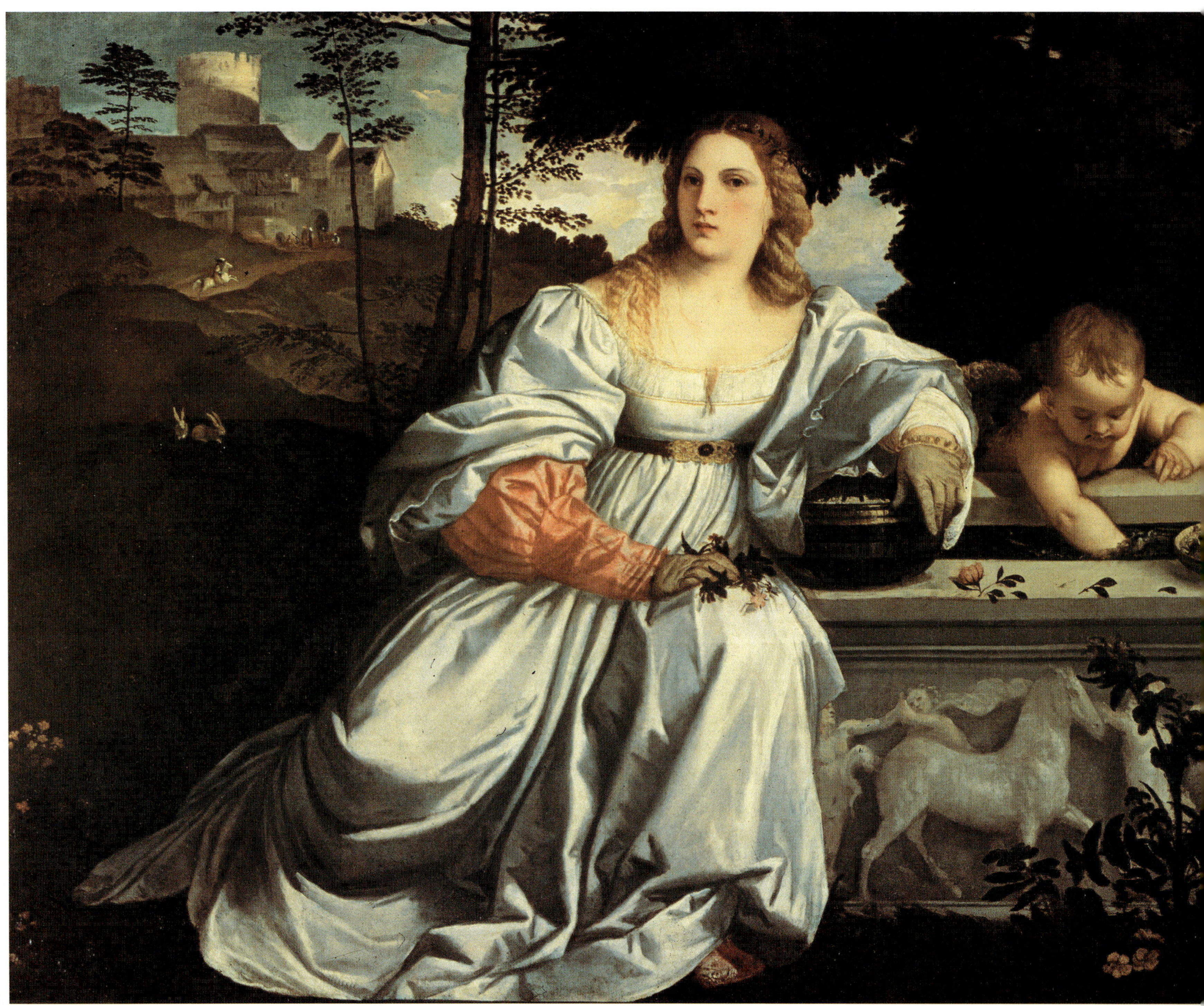

Titian, apotheosis and tragedy of a genius

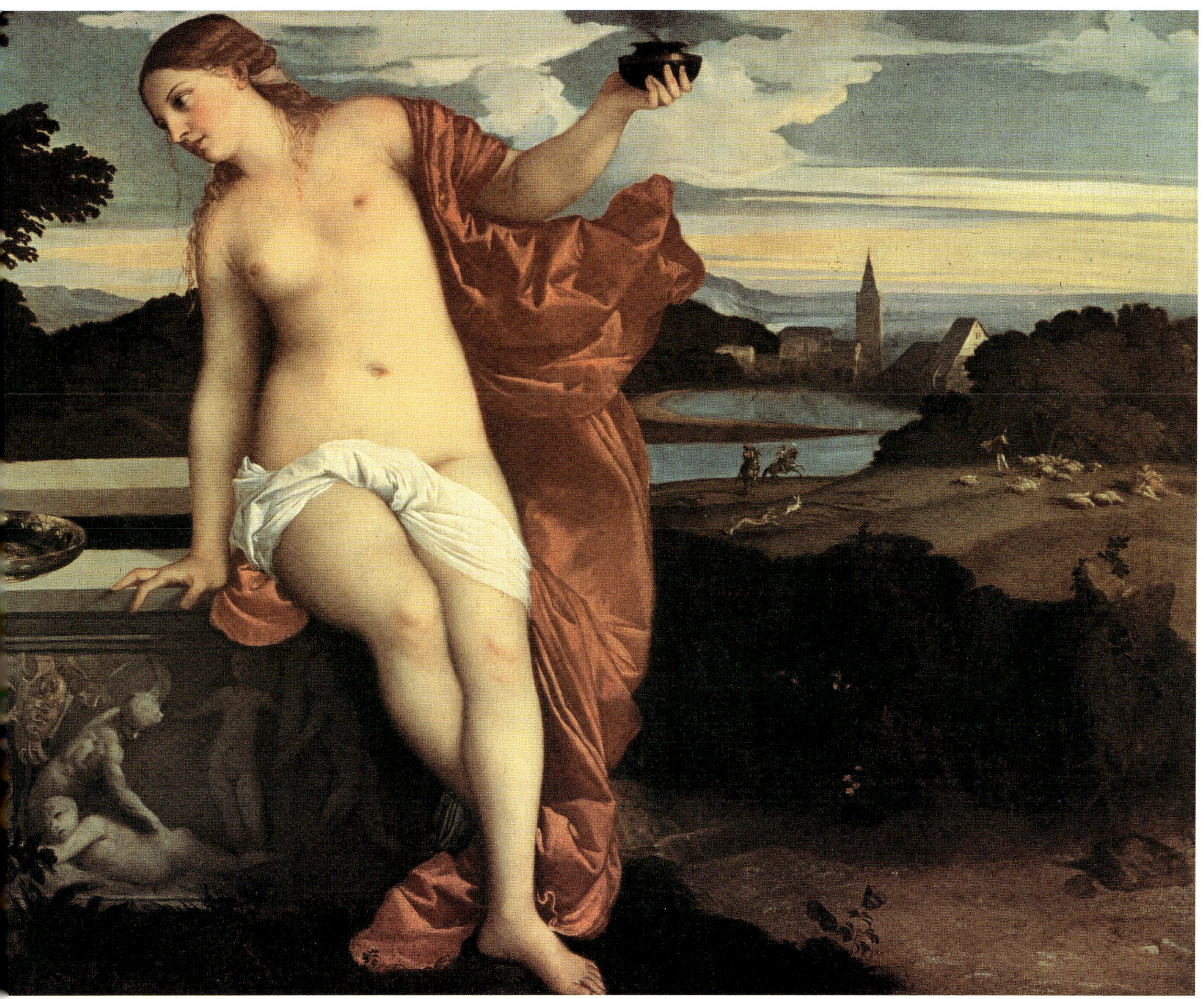

Titian, apotheosis and tragedy of a genius

classical and medieval iconography, the simultaneous presence of two figures, one nude and one dressed, does not signal an opposition (as the erroneous title given the work might indicate), but rather a state of complementarity. Unlike what one might first imagine, the clothed woman alludes to love in marriage, and the nude one raises that same love to a celestial, eternal plane, as is symbolized by the lamp. The painting is today understood to have been a magnificent wedding gift from the Venetian patrician Nicolò Aurelio to his bride. The canvas dates to an important moment in Venetian history. In 1514, a fire devastated the Rialto market, heart of the commercial activity of Venice. This event, which occurred during a period of serious tensions with Spain and her possessions and war against the Turks in Friuli and Dalmatia, was interpreted as being symbolic of the end of the old mercantile era and of the pressing need for change, change in the economic structures of the city, in its public buildings, and even in the habits of its citizens, the Venetians themselves.

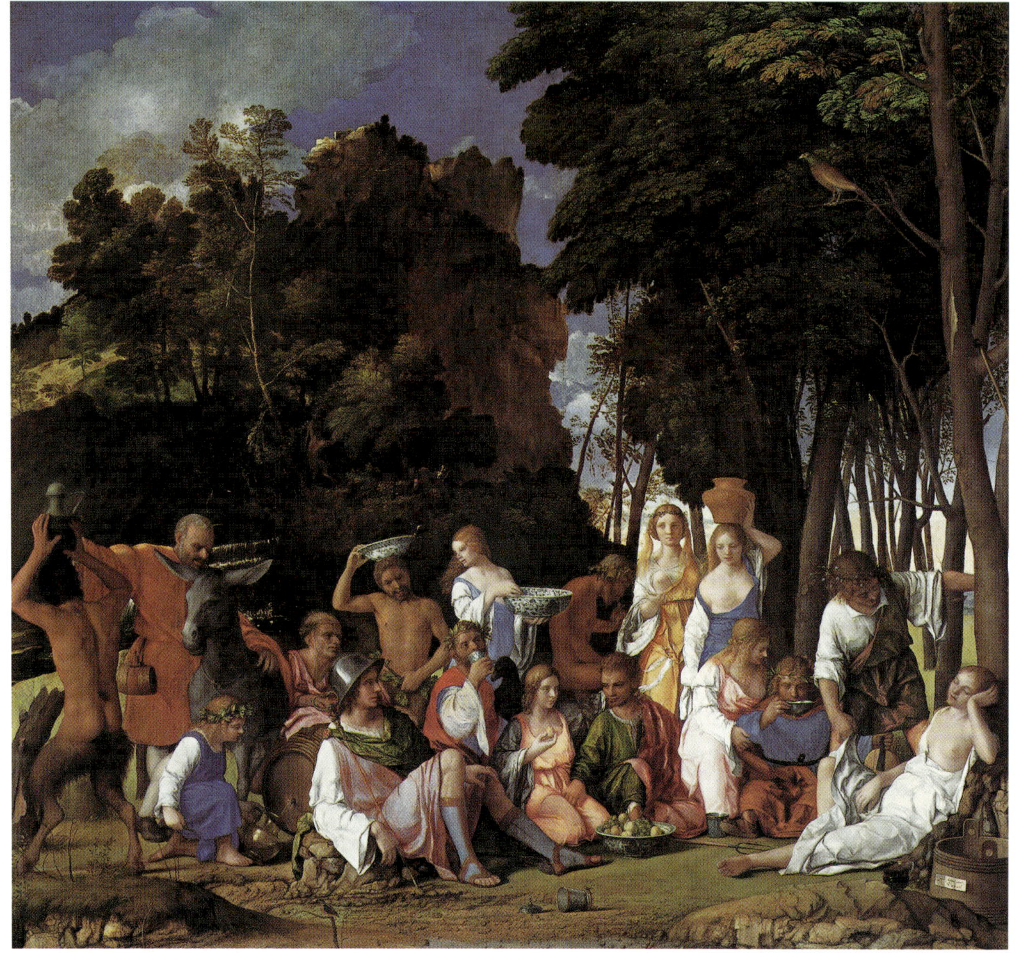

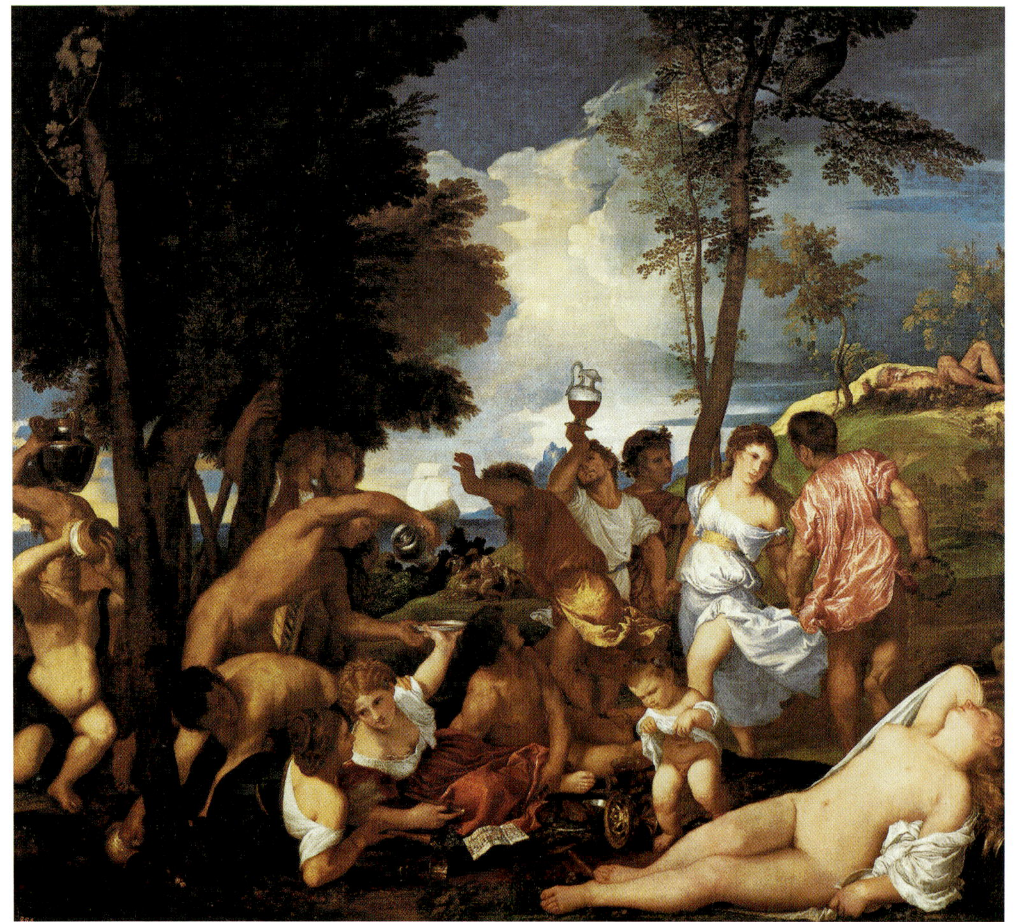

Titian, apotheosis and tragedy of a genius

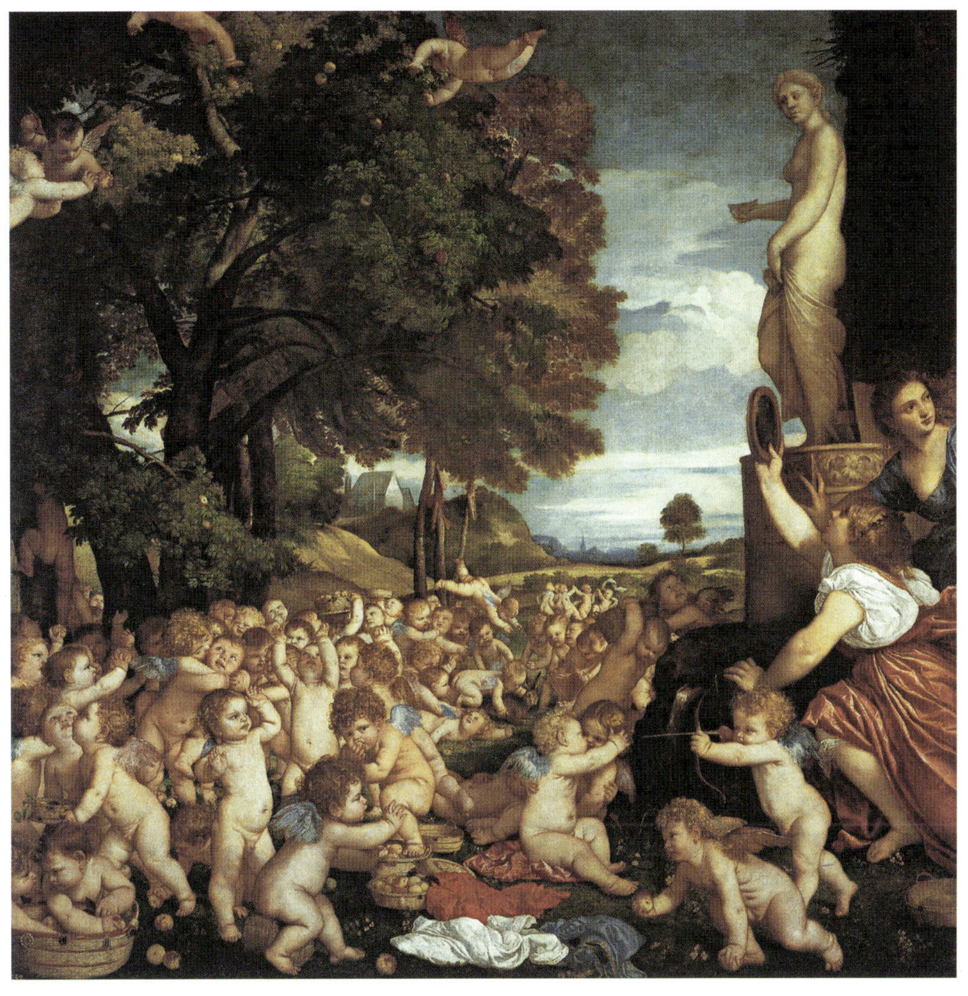

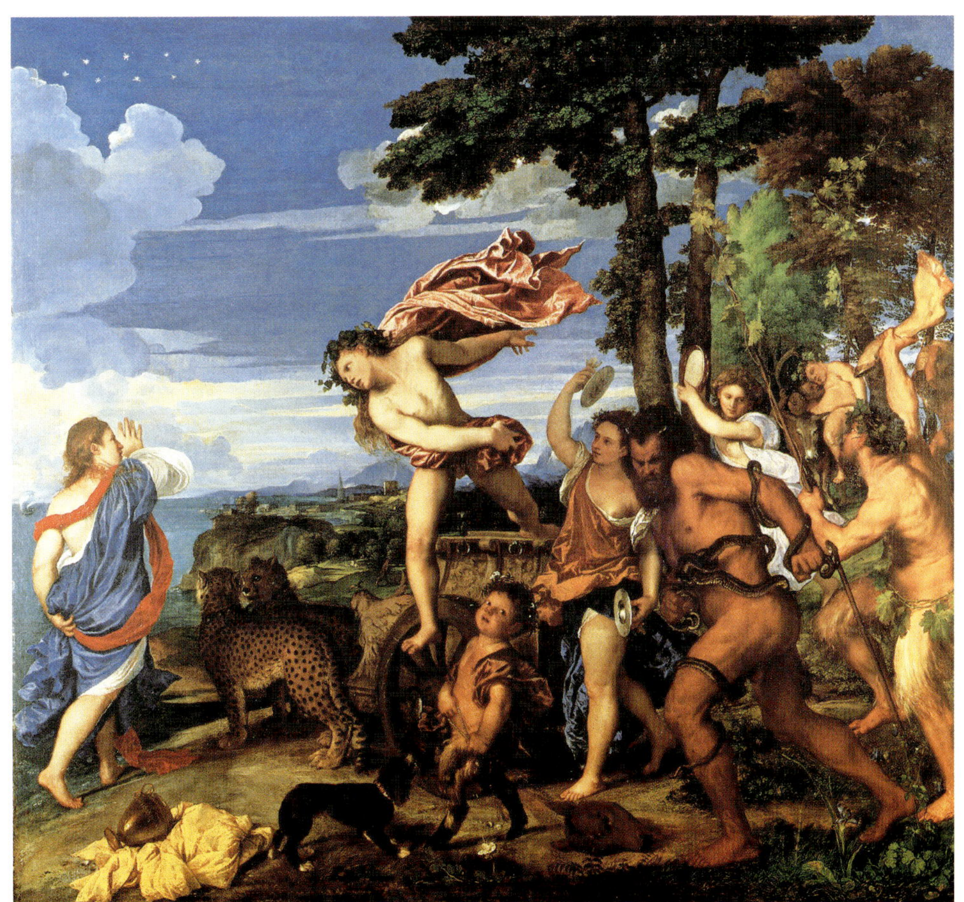

Titian, apotheosis and tragedy of a genius

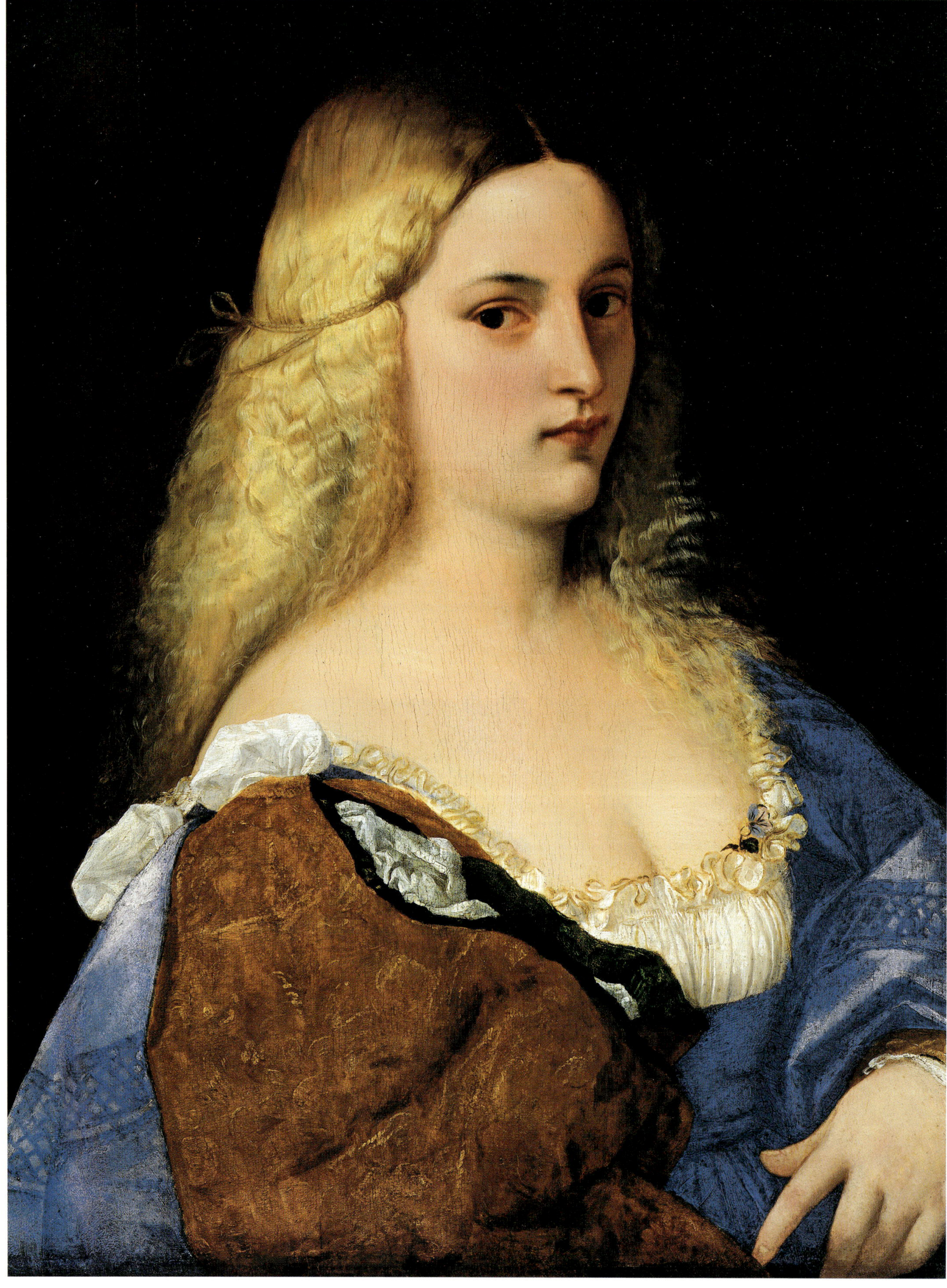

Titian, apotheosis and tragedy of a genius

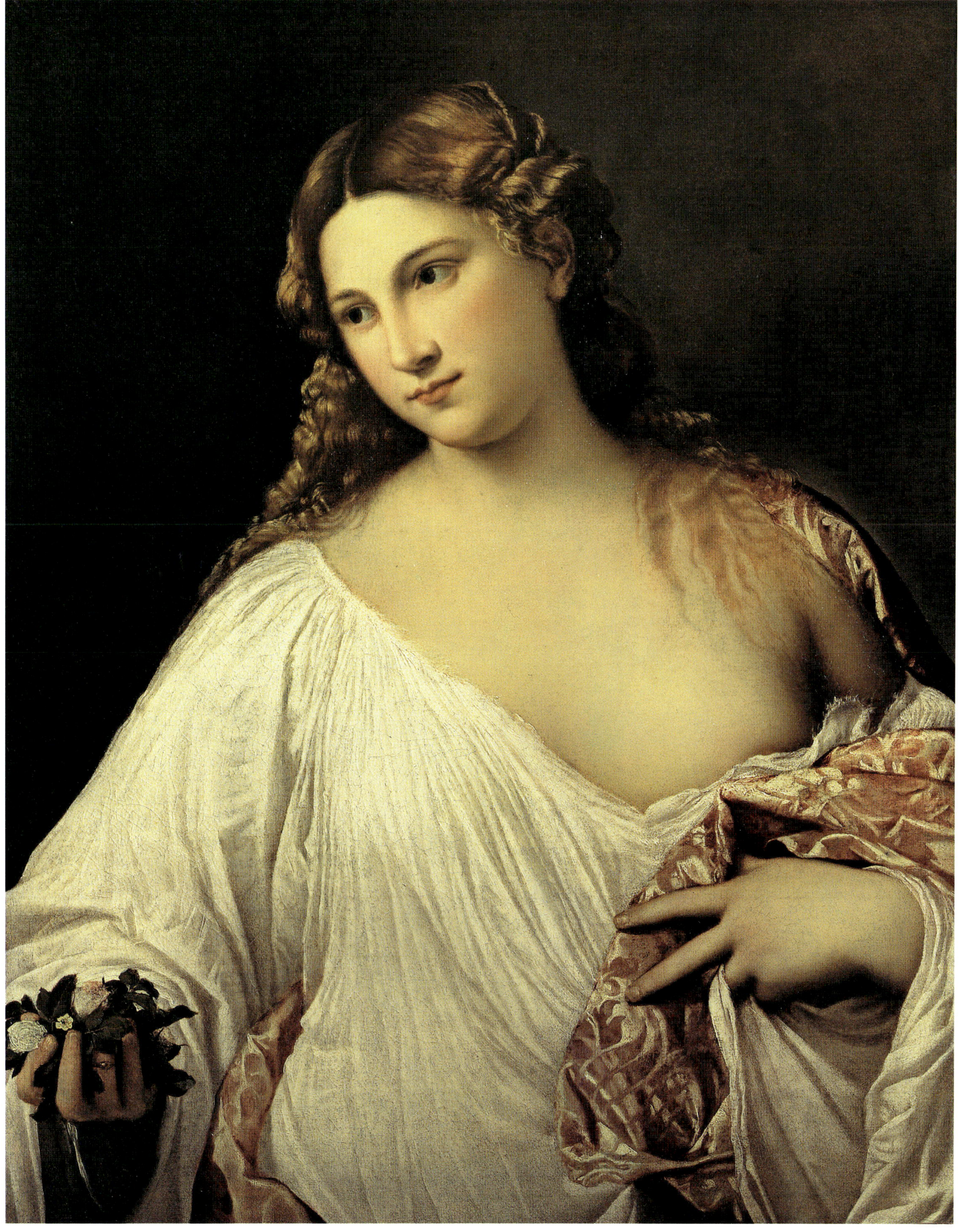

This is one of the most characteristic examples of the restricted genre of stupendous female figures in which Titian celebrated the generous ideal of Venetian beauty: blonde girls (or, more exactly, with hair of the auburn color today known as titian), with sweet expressions, rosy skin, and quite shapely bodies, following a model that would have a large following not only over the course of the Renaissance but also in baroque art. The vital immediacy and striking presence of these figures were repeatedly admired by men of letters during the sixteenth century. As the artist's first biographer, Ludovico Dolce, wrote, "Titian moves in step with nature."

This enormous altar-
piece, located on the
main altar of the Gothic
Franciscan basilica,
marks Titian's full con-
quest of the supremacy
of Venetian art. When
it was inaugurated, it
elicited opposing reac-
tions: popular enthusi-
asm was accompanied
by a note of perplex-
ity from the patrons
because of the impos-
ingness of the apostles.
There was also the
stupor of the other
Venetian painters, not
yet ready to receive
the novelty of the
orchestral "fortissimo"
of Titian's drums. Very
soon, the work became
a point of reference in
the area of the Veneto.
Ludovico Dolce saw in
it "the awesomeness of
Michelangelo, the pleas-
ing beauty of Raphael,"
but most of all the col-
ors of nature itself.

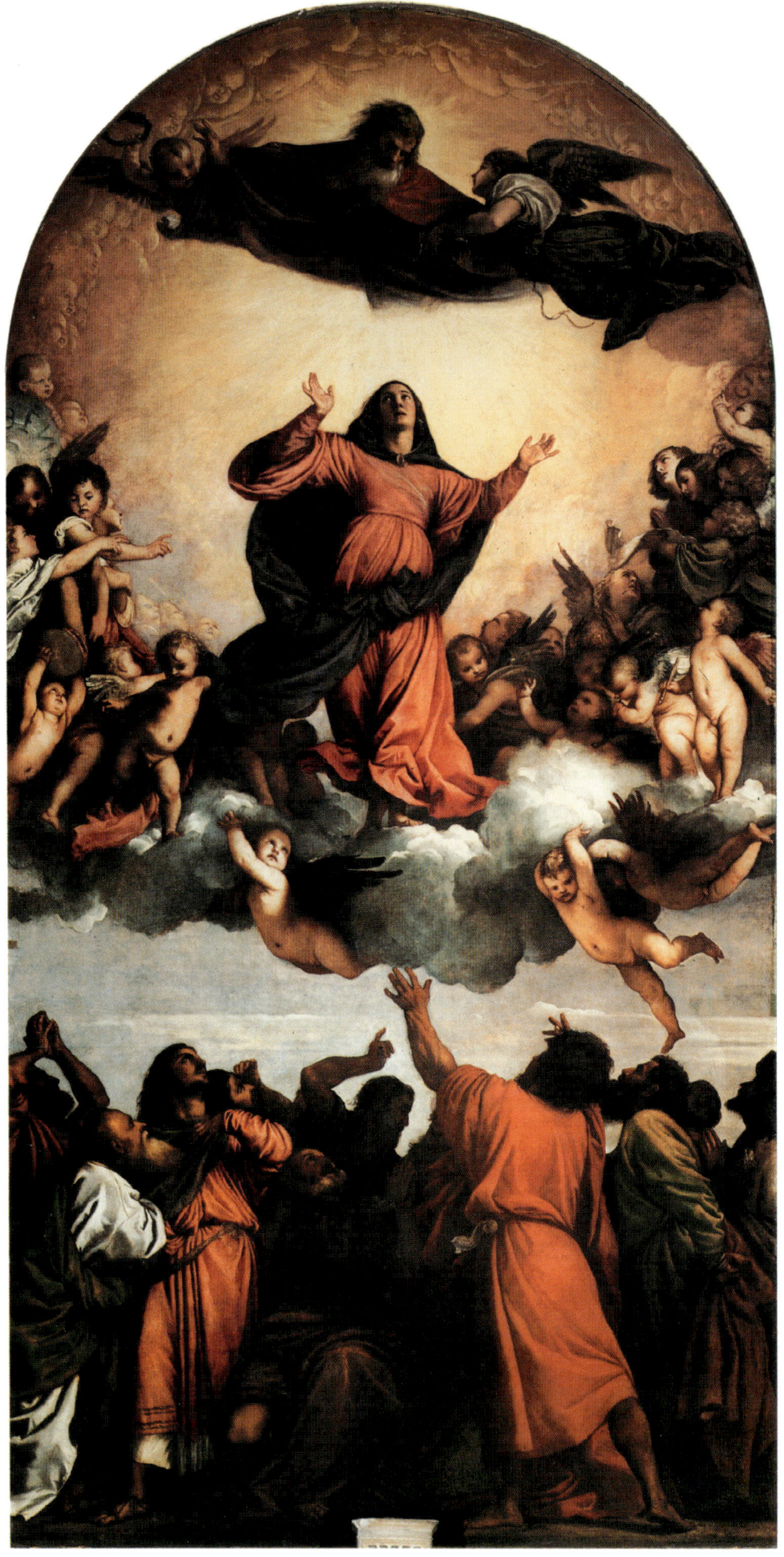

Titian, apotheosis and tragedy of a genius

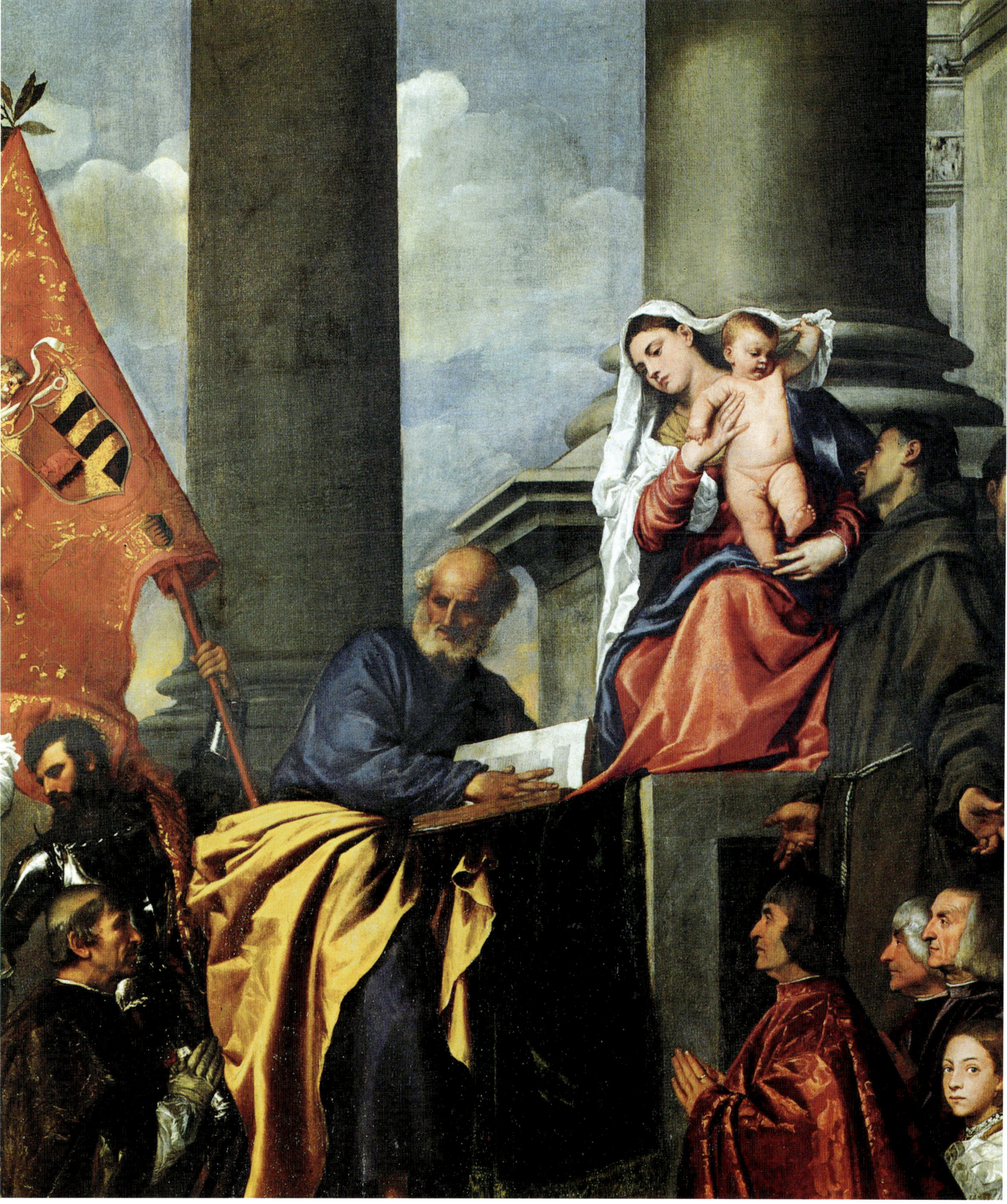

The compositional structure of this altarpiece marks the end of the geometric organization of the *sacre converzazioni* of the late fifteenth century. Taking into consideration the diagonal point of view of the altar, located along the left nave of the basilica of the Frari, Titian moved the seat of the Madonna from the center to the right, while the group of figures is directed toward the Virgin in a movement that revolutionizes the canonical triangular layout. The altarpiece's sense of novelty is increased by the articulation of the architectonic elements, with two enormous columns that extend beyond the frame. The colors are luminous, with a clear preference for pure tints and the rejection of shaded half-tones; the age of Giorgione, composed of tonal accords and foggy atmospheres, had come to a close. At thirty-five years of age, Titian had entered his artistic maturity and was directing Venetian art toward an expressive vitality and a dynamic anima-tion that until then had been unknown.

Titian, apotheosis and tragedy of a genius

**Presentation of the
Virgin in the Temple**
1538, oil on canvas,
345 x 775 cm
Gallerie dell'Accademia,
Venice

This is the only painting
by Titian of the narra-
tive genre, and it has
characteristics that dis-
tinguish it from all the
rest of his production.
For its broad action,
developed lengthwise,
Titian chose a strikingly
theatrical presentation,
and many of the
figures seem more like
actors posing than
actual personages.

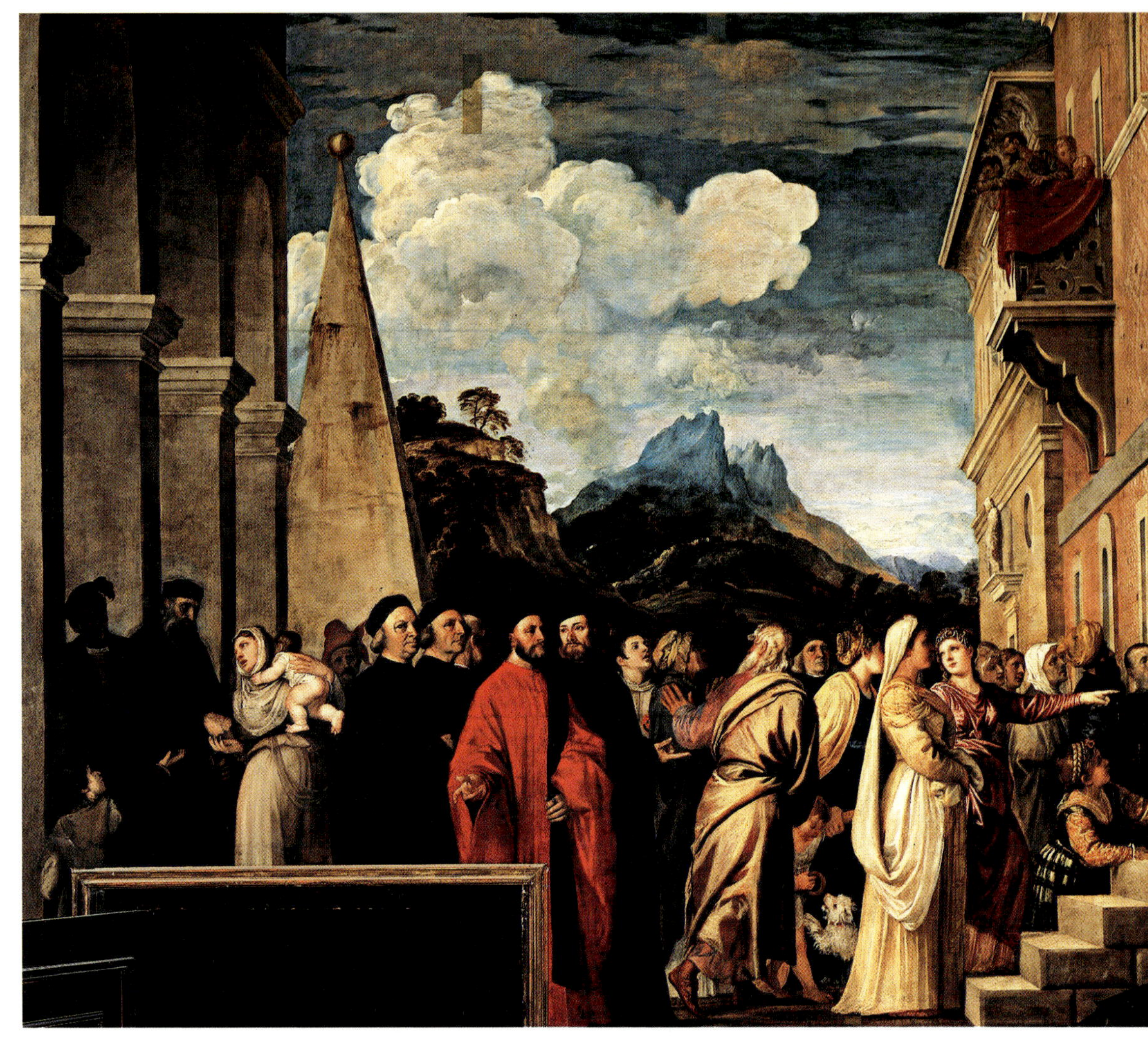

TITIAN

**Portrait of
Pietro Aretino**
1545, oil on canvas,
98 x 78 cm
Galleria Palatina,
Palazzo Pitti, Florence

This portrait is of such
a new style that even
Aretino, on first receiv-
ing it, thought it "more
just a sketch than not
finished." Titian was
experimenting with the
technique that would
be typical of the last
period of his career;
the outlines not are
well defined and the
large brushstrokes have
apparently been applied
quickly, almost as
though to indicate the
subject rather than to
describe it.

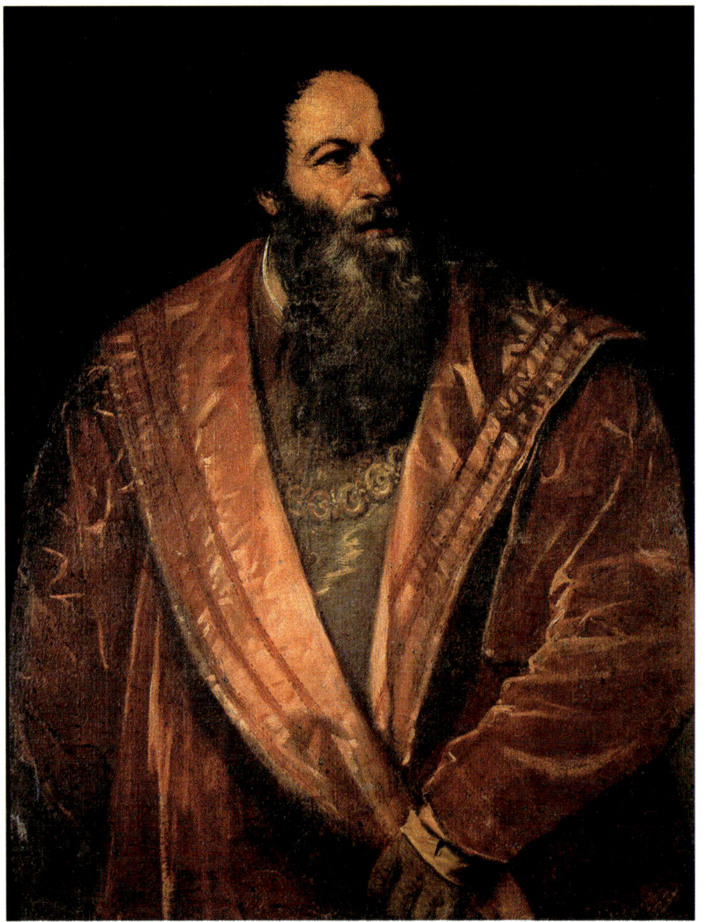

Titian, apotheosis and tragedy of a genius

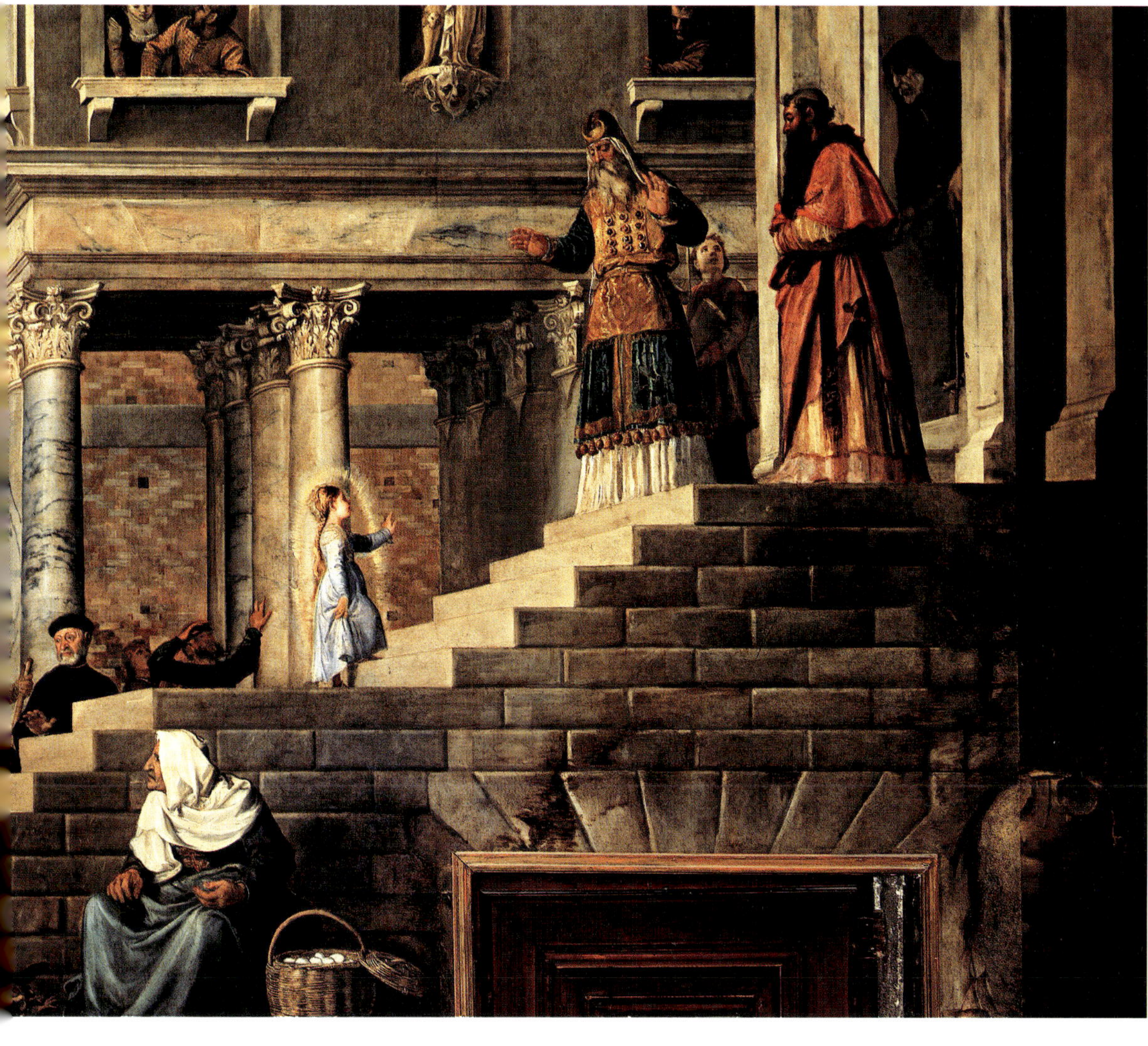

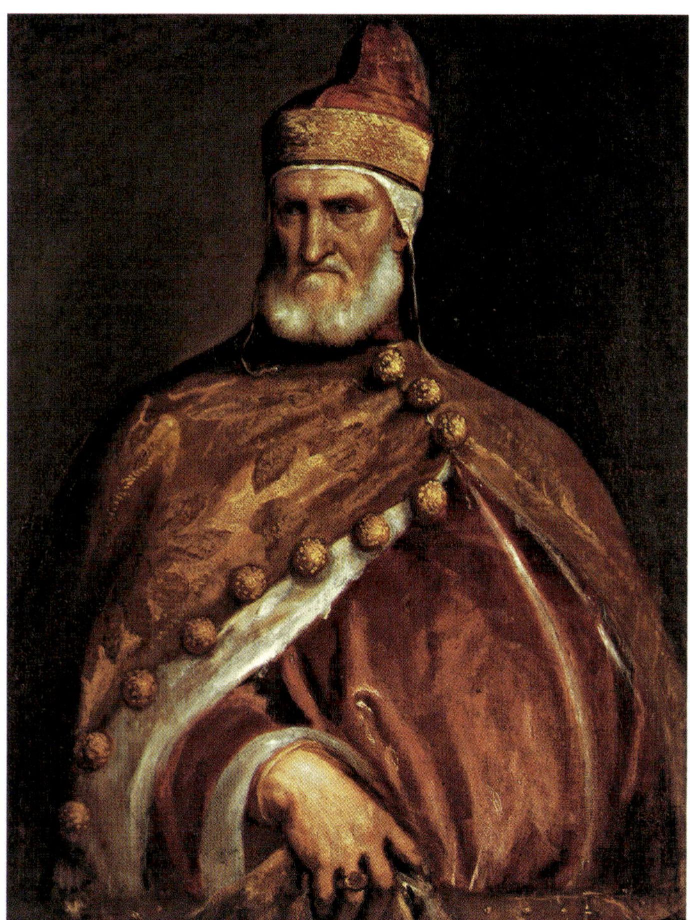

Titian, apotheosis and tragedy of a genius

This painting marks a decided evolution in the iconography of the reclining Venus. The serenity of the *Venus* attributed to Giorgione (Gemäldegalerie, Dresden) is here changed into tangible sensuality. The goddess is not asleep in a peaceful natural setting but instead is wide awake, staring out at the viewer with a touch of seduction, her body spread along the length of a bed made even more inviting by puffy cushions. The maidservants in the background and the little dog add a touch of daily routine that makes the seductive female seem even more alive and real.

This masterpiece (described by Monsignor Giovanni Della Casa as "a nude woman getting the devil to come to her") is mentioned in an episode in Vasari's *Lives*. Vasari claims to have gone with Michelangelo to visit Titian while he was at work on this painting. While in Titian's presence, Michelangelo praised his work but later, alone again with Vasari, he expressed a negative opinion, "saying that his coloring and his manner much pleased him, but that it was a pity that in Venice men did not learn to draw well."

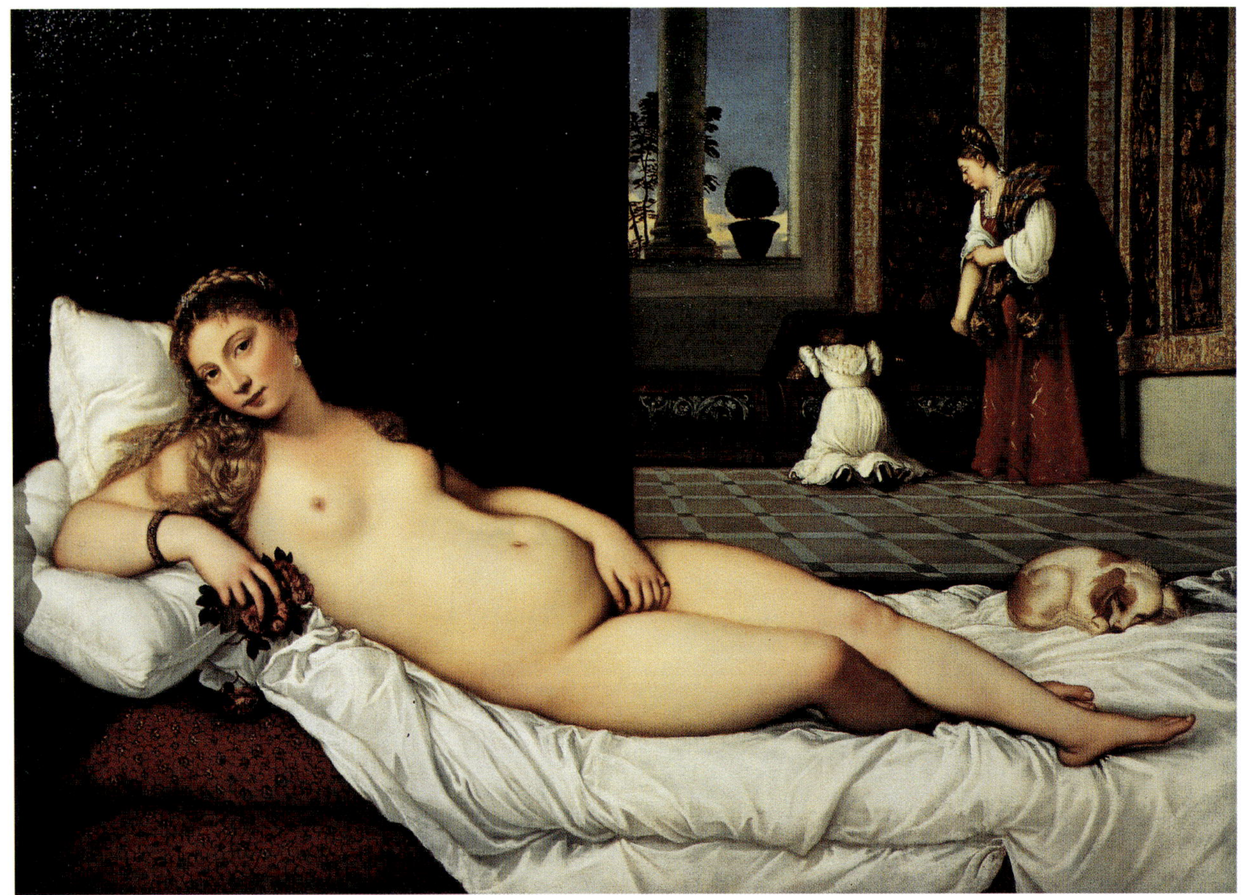

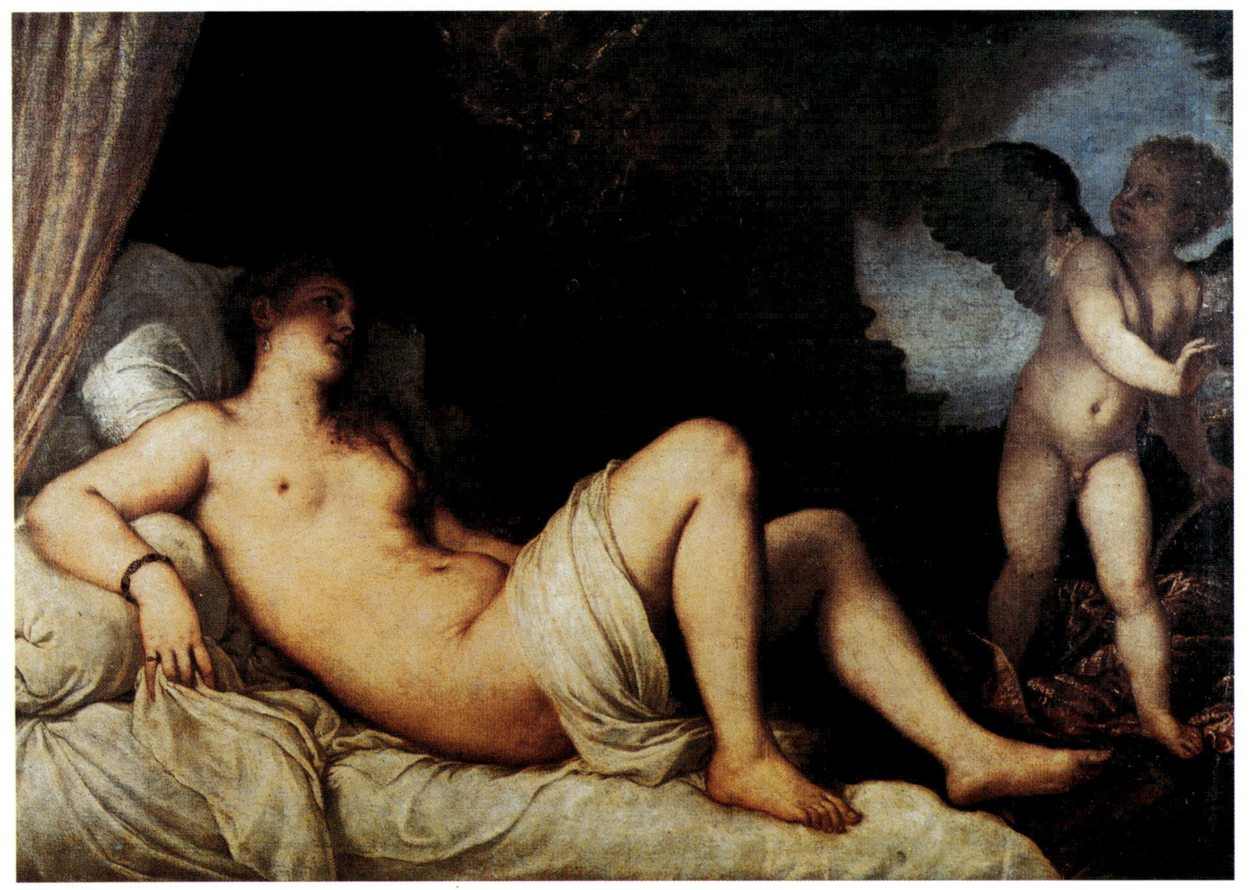

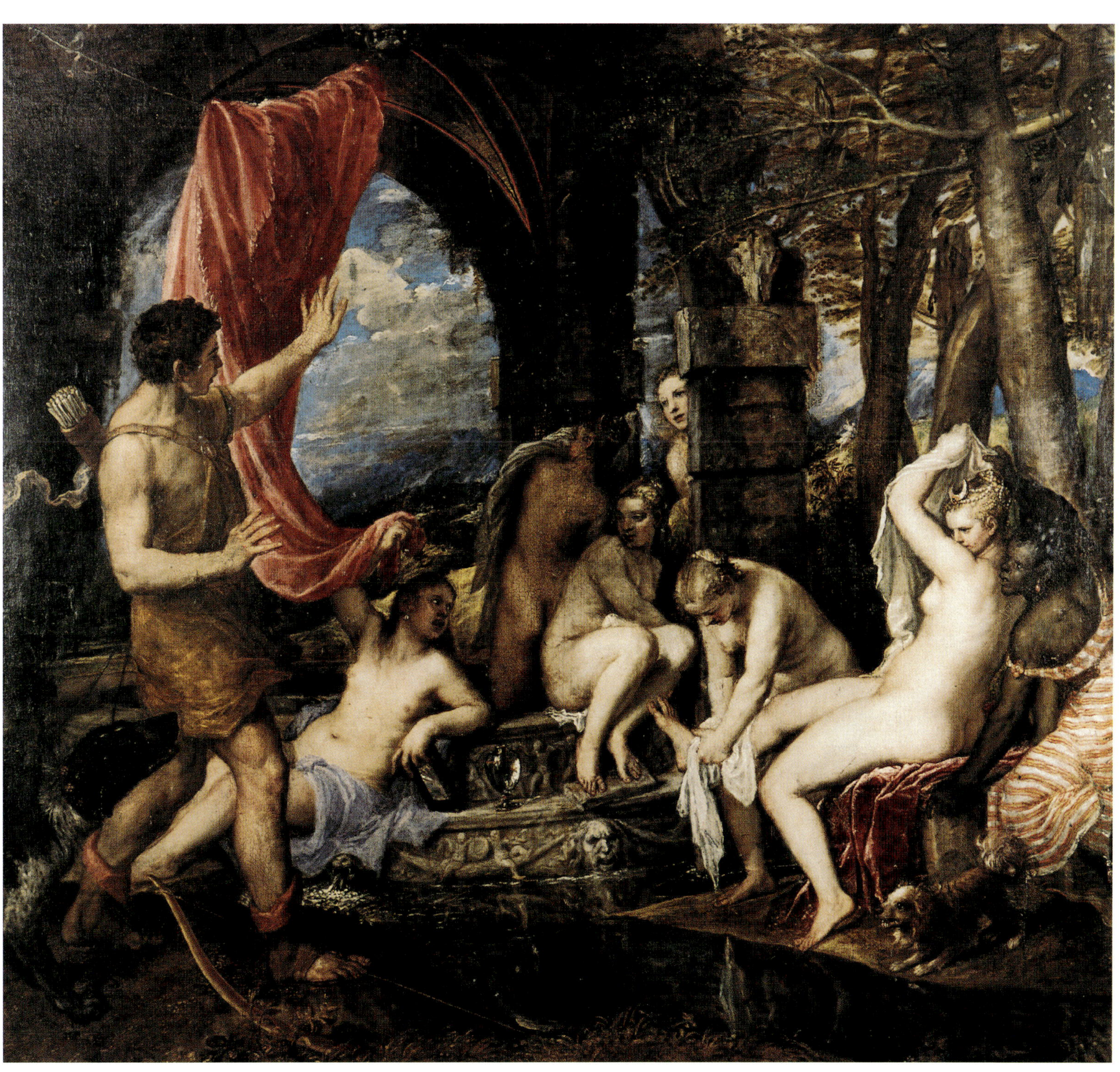

Titian, apotheosis and tragedy of a genius

TITIAN
**The Mocking
of Christ**
1570, oil on canvas,
280 x 182 cm
Alte Pinakothek,
Munich

Standing out among
the works of the last
period of Titian's life
is a group of paintings
that center on the
bitter theme of the
mistreatment of inno-
cents. To represent the
powerlessness and suf-
fering of the weaker
confronted by the arro-
gance and ferocity of
the stronger, the artist
pushed himself toward
the extreme limits of
technique. The outlines
of objects dissolve,
and dramatic effect is
obtained by means of
a highly dense impasto
of paint, with brush-
strokes often giving
way to strips of paint
left by the finger, such
that the pictorial sub-
stance remains to form
lumps on the canvas.
As Titian's contempo-
raries noted, no other
artist in Venice was able
to do the same, but
many also harbored the
suspicion that these
new techniques were
dictated by weakness
in his hands and eyes.
The truth was just the
opposite, the elderly
master was in full pos-
session of his faculties.
Quite simply, he was
far ahead of his time.

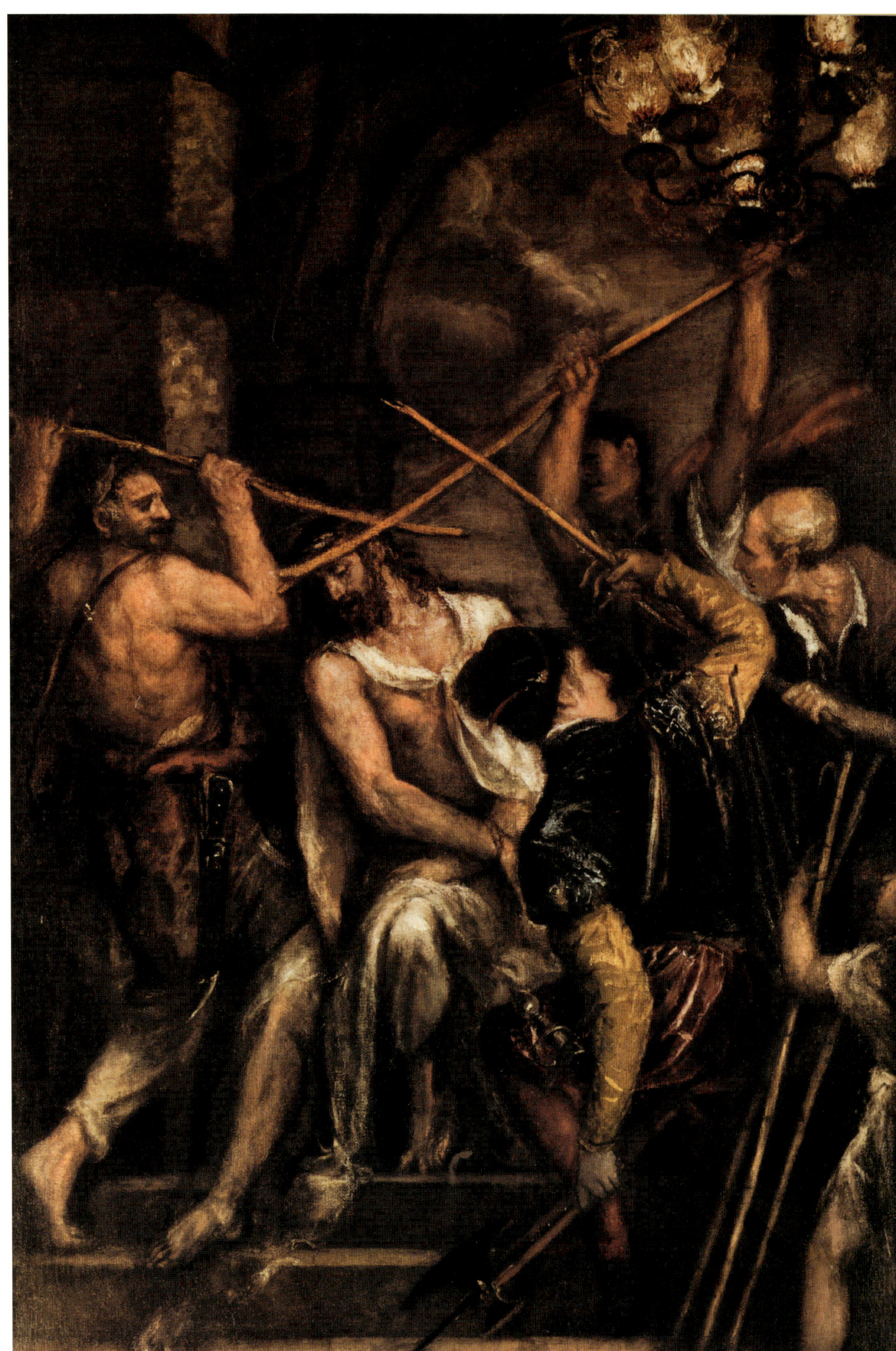

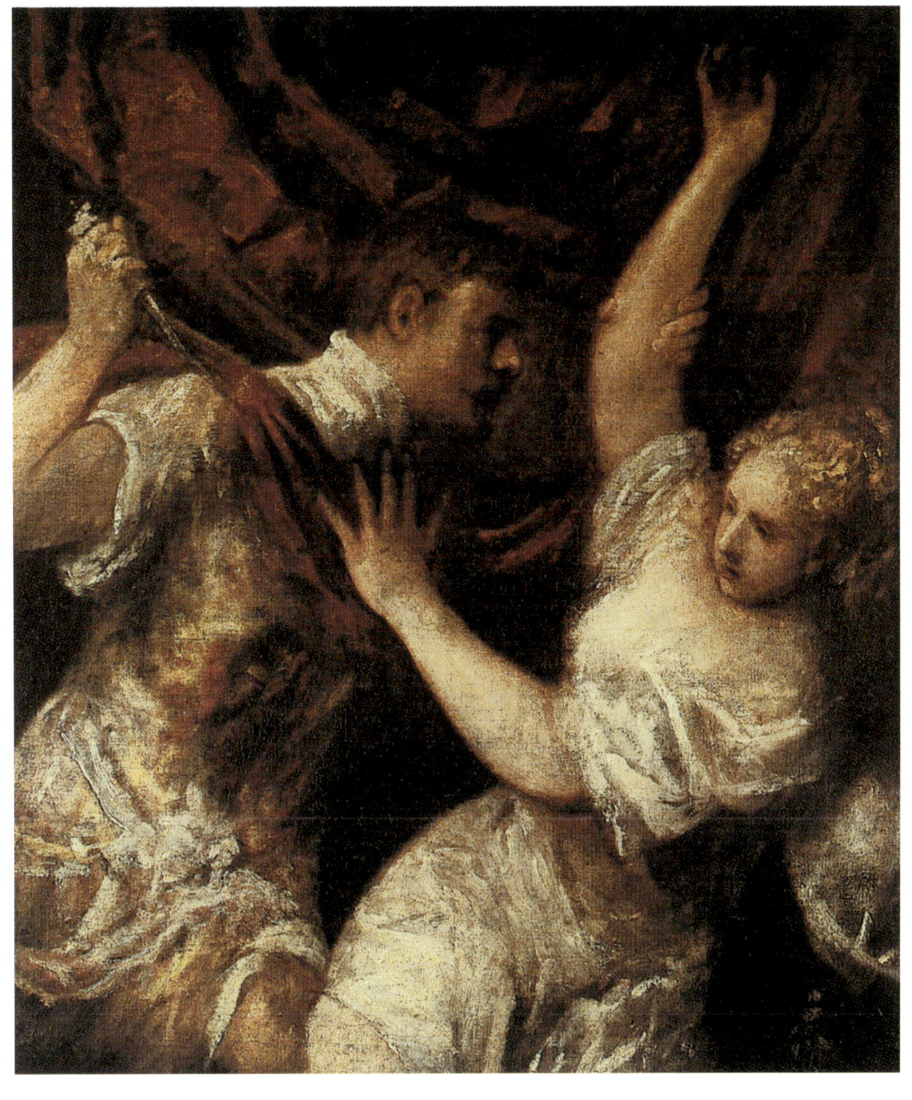

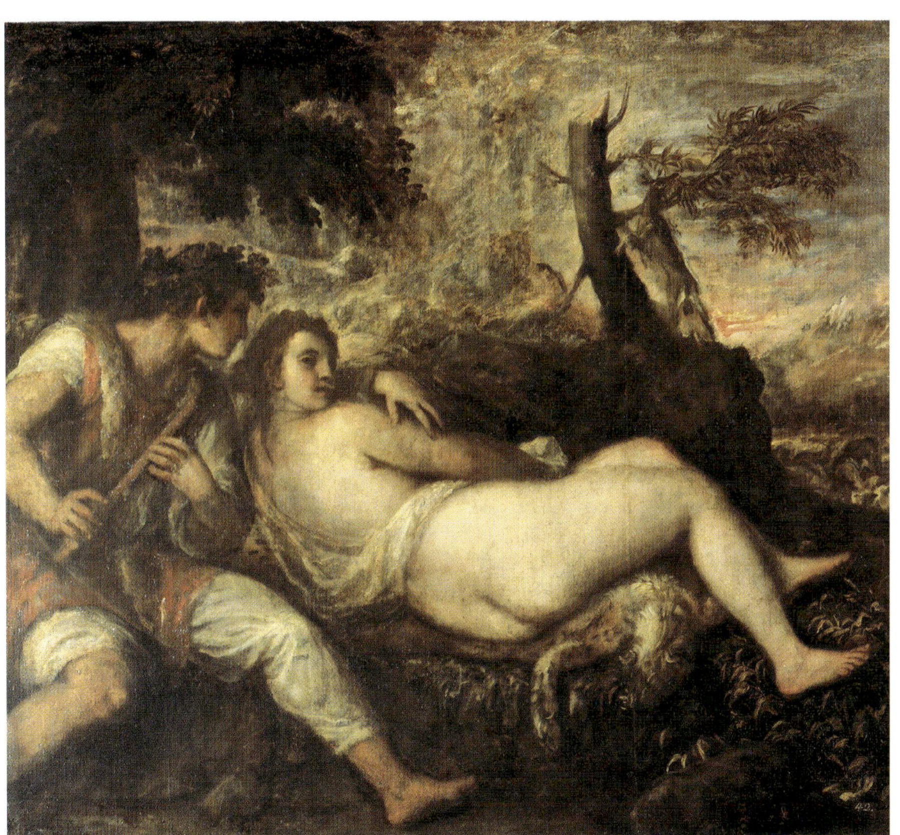

Titian, apotheosis and tragedy of a genius

The death of Raphael marked a turning point in the history of art. As had happened ten years earlier in Venice following the death of Giorgione, the painters in Rome in 1520 competed to take over the role of "heir" to the master. The first to make his move was Giulio Romano, in 1521 painting the great altarpiece with the *Martyrdom of St. Stephen* in the church of St. Stefano in Genoa, in which the open homage to Raphael is "corrected" by direct references to the muscular, heroic monumentality of Michelangelo.

Following the death of Leo X, in 1521, the leading artistic workshops in Rome stopped work, waiting to see what would happen. The new pope, the Netherlander Adrian VI of Utrecht, was a pious man, given to mysticism, and having been effected by the moralizing of the Reformation he looked askance at the worldly life he encountered in Rome. The extravagant Vatican curia was swept by a wind of austerity. Adrian VI went so far as to envision the destruction of Michelangelo's frescoes in the Sistine Chapel, and the Roman painters were

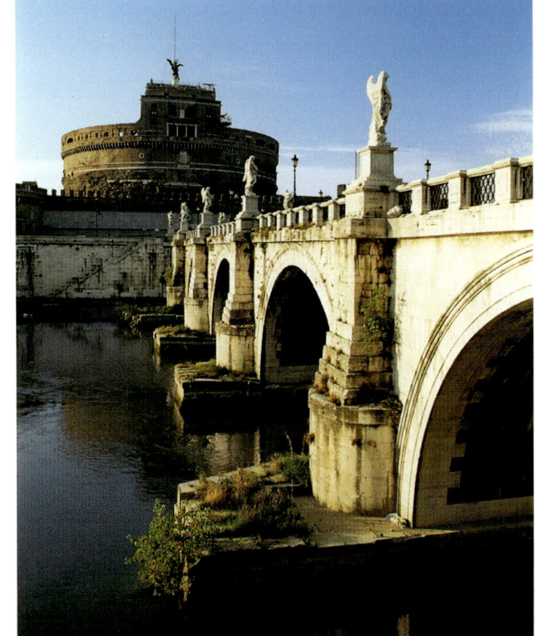

looming threat to the spiritual and temporal power of Rome. In 1524 Giulio Romano left Rome for Mantua, where he became the imaginative "director" of the undertakings of Federico II Gonzaga. His departure can be taken as the first step in the international diaspora of Raphael's students, each of whom contributed to the spread to diverse courts of the refined and vaguely nostalgic character of the decoration inspired by archaeological finds from the past. With the departure of Giulio Romano, a different orientation began to make itself felt in Rome. Artists from other regions of Italy were arriving in the city, such as Parmigianino and Rosso Fiorentino. Like those students of Raphael who chose to remain in Rome, such as Perin del Vaga and Polidoro Caldara da Caravaggio, these new arrivals shared a taste for lean shapes and tapering, elegant bodies, and not without a certain ambiguous sensuality. The subject of a work became substantially indifferent: both sacred themes and those mythological were presented with the same sense of sophisticated exoticism.

From the Sack of Rome

not pleased by his choice of the Dutch artist Jan van Scorel as successor to Raphael in the position of conservator of Vatican antiquities. The pontificate of Adrian VI lasted less than two years. He was succeeded, in November 1523, by Giulio de' Medici, who took the name of Clement VII. In selecting him the conclave had expressed the desire for a return to the status quo. Five years earlier Giulio had been portrayed by Raphael to the left of Leo X, his close relative, and he had been the instigator of the competition between Raphael and the Sebastiano del Piombo-Michelangelo pair. One of his first measures was the resumption of artistic activity. Raphael had left preliminary drawings for the decoration of the fourth and largest of the rooms, the one called the Sala di Constantino. Giulio Romano used the drawings by Raphael for the general organization of the room and for two large narrative scenes, but he accentuated the intellectual character of the whole with the insertion of archaeological citations made for a select group of "antiquarian" experts. The sense of the new times appears in the desire to accentuate the supremacy of the pope over the emperor, almost as though to exorcize the

This brief season was swept away by one of the most disastrous events of the Italian sixteenth century, the Sack of Rome perpetrated in 1527 by the mercenary army of Charles V. The massacre and systematic plundering of the city took place in two stages. The first wave, which lasted two months, began on May 6; the second began in September, and Rome was forced to submit to the damages and humiliation of six months of occupation. The pope was forced to abandon the Vatican Palaces and take refuge in Castel Sant'Angelo. The worksite of St. Peter's was devastated, the ancient treasury of the basilica despoiled. The sack caused thousands of deaths, the devasta-

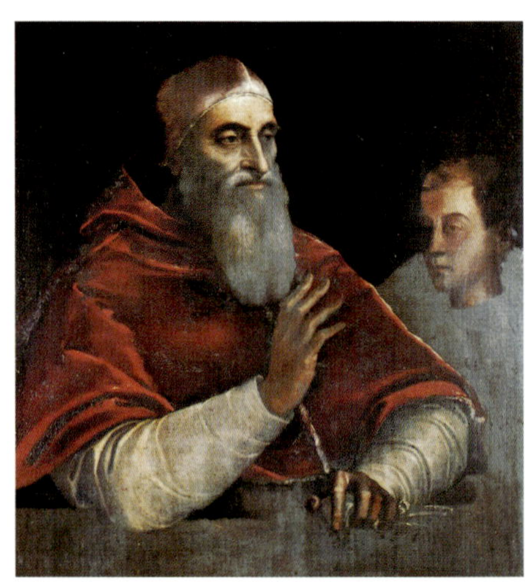

From the Sack of Rome to the *Last Judgment*

tion of churches, palaces, and incalculable art treasures. In a Christian Europe already shaken by the Reformation, the sack was interpreted as a terrible sign of the times. In the divergent opinions of contemporaries, some saw it as a dramatic but salutary penitential purification; others predicted catastrophe for the city and a coming era of sin. The event had enormous consequences for art. Only one leading artist stayed beside Clement VII, Sebastiano del Piombo, in return for which the pope heaped upon him so many lucrative tokens of his appreciation that his activity as a painter was greatly reduced. Otherwise, Rome was emptied of its principal artists.

Among those who fled Rome was Jacopo Sansovino, who initially was reluctant about going to Venice. His health was poor, and he thought it best to go to the French court at Fontainebleau, where King Francis I was having Italian artists build and decorate his palace. Doge Andrea Gritti, however, had no intention of letting a leading representative of classicism go and succeeded in getting Sansovino to Venice by calling attention to many prestigious commissions. Two years after his arrival, Sansovino was made "master builder," responsible for all public building in Venice, a position he held more than forty years and that gave a decisive role in fashioning the "new" face of Venice. The canons of classicism became the symbolic emblems of an architecture of power, in which

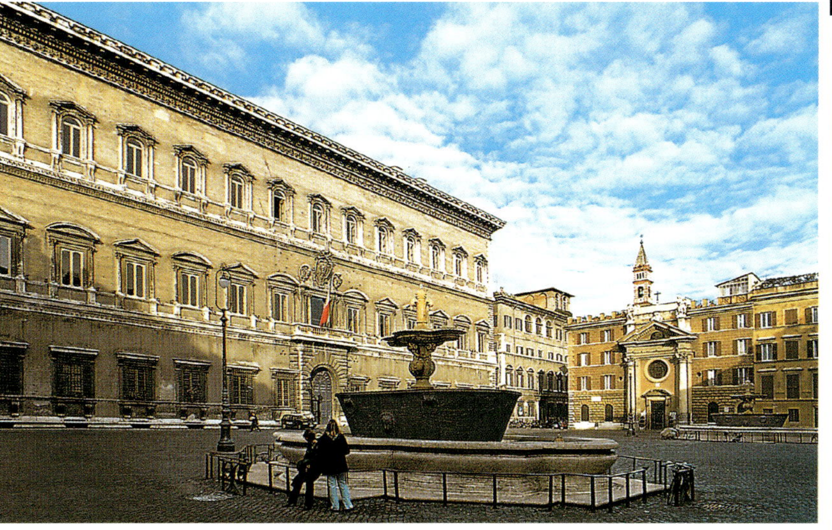

and Piacenza. Paul III entrusted to Antonio da Sangallo and then to Michelangelo the decisive phase in the construction of St. Peter's. He also formed a new school of painting by convincing some of the artists who had fled the city after the sack to return. In 1545 he convinced Titian to come to Rome. Even so, his pontificate is best known for Michelangelo's execution of the *Last Judgment*. Paul III gave Michelangelo great freedom, even allowing him to eliminate Perugino's frescoes. Michelangelo began work in

to the *Last Judgment*

authority was expressed by means of explicit references to antique monumental buildings. The decision to go to Venice proved beneficial to Sansovino—until 1570 he led an energetic and active life.

Late in his pontificate, Clement VII launched several large-scale projects. Baldassarre Peruzzi, having returned to Rome, dedicated himself to the work on St. Peter's; the pope supported Michelangelo, offering him sanctuary following the siege of Florence of 1529–30. Disturbed by the new politico-religious climate, the pope decided to modify the short walls of the Sistine Chapel. In 1533 Michelangelo began to study the composition of the rear wall, behind the altar of the chapel, until then decorated by delicate frescoes by Perugino. Clement VII died in 1534. Pope Paul III's pontificate lasted from 1534 to 1549. In it he laid the basis for the renewal of Catholic doctrine and art, while also enriching his family with the duchy of Parma

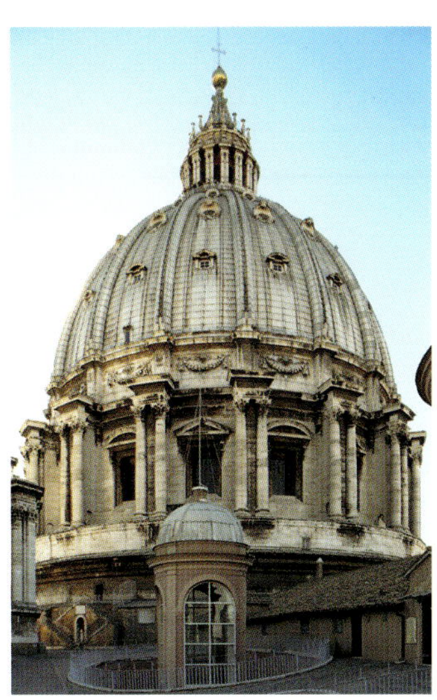

1535. He was sixty-two years old; an entire lifetime separated this disenchanted, bitter, aging man from the brazen youth who had taken on the decoration of the vault. The walls, inaugurated on October 31, 1541, immediately became one of the most astonishing and controversial works in the history of art. The *Dies Irae* is almost the opposite of the scenes of the *Creation* frescoed on the vault of the chapel; together with the body, the *Last Judgment* also tramples the soul. The man who had won dominion over nature with his intelligence, who had fashioned justice and beauty into ideals for which to labor and in which to believe, that man made strong and sure of himself by humanism, by the beliefs of the early Renaissance, the man whom Michelangelo had himself exalted in the *ignudi* of the Sistine Chapel vault, that Renaissance man had now been crushed. The time of illusions had ended.

The death of Leo X was
followed by a letup in
all the major artistic
workshops of Rome.
The new pope, the
Netherlander Adrian VI
of Utrecht, was a pious
man, given to mysti-
cism, and having been
effected by the moral-
izing of the Reformation
he looked askance at
the worldly life he
encountered in Rome.
He went so far as to
envision the destruc-
tion of Michelangelo's
frescoes in the Sistine
Chapel; according to
Vasari, he declared the
chapel "a bathroom full
of nude figures." His
pontificate, however,
lasted less than two
years. In November
1523, Giulio de' Medici
was elected pope with
the name Clement VII.
Five years earlier he
had been portrayed by
Raphael to the left of
Leo X, his close relative,
and he also had been
the instigator of the
competition between
Raphael and the pair of
Sebastiano del Piombo-
Michelangelo. One of
his first moves was to
have artistic activity in
the city resume.

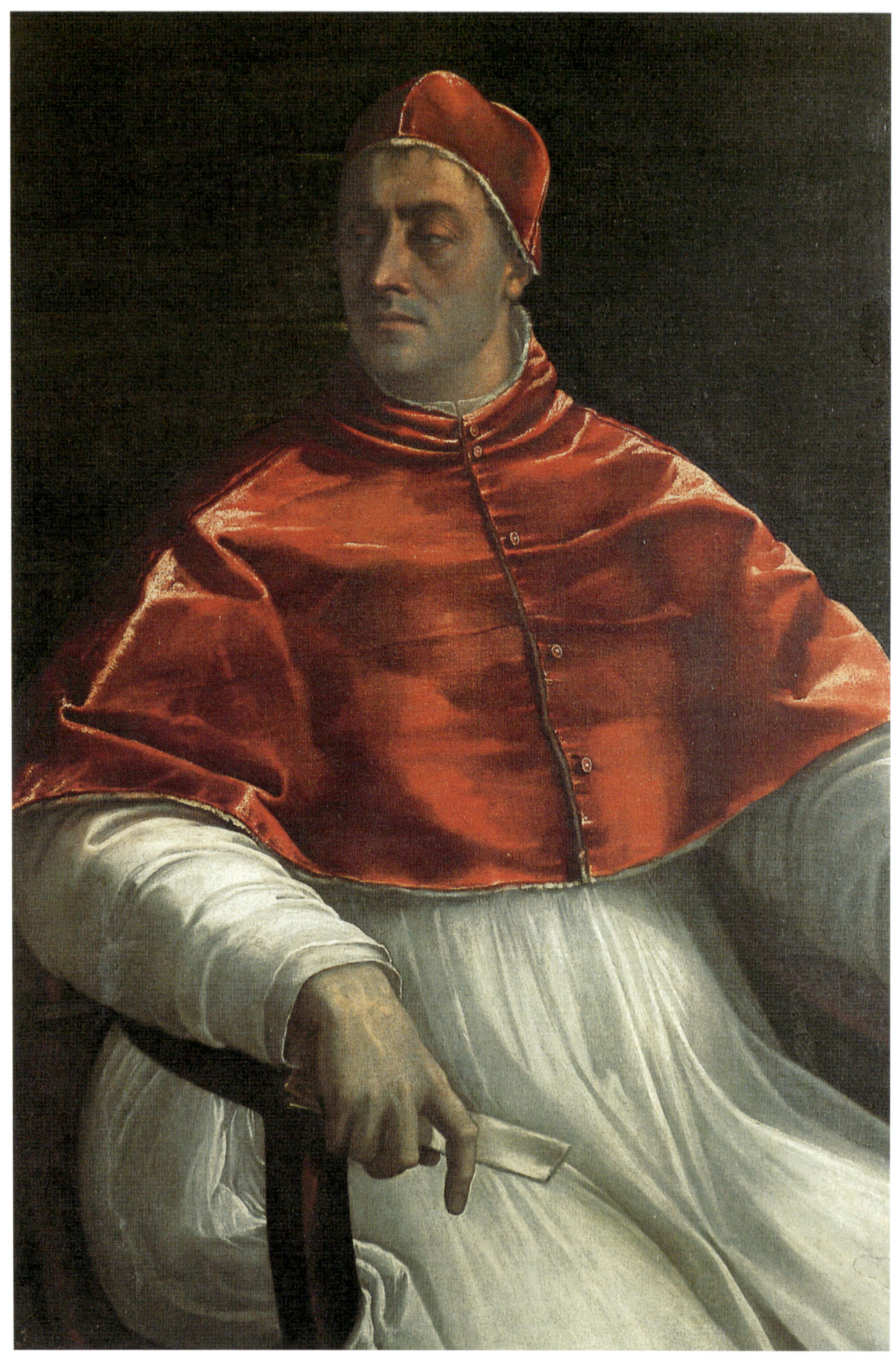

From the Sack of Rome to the *Last Judgment*

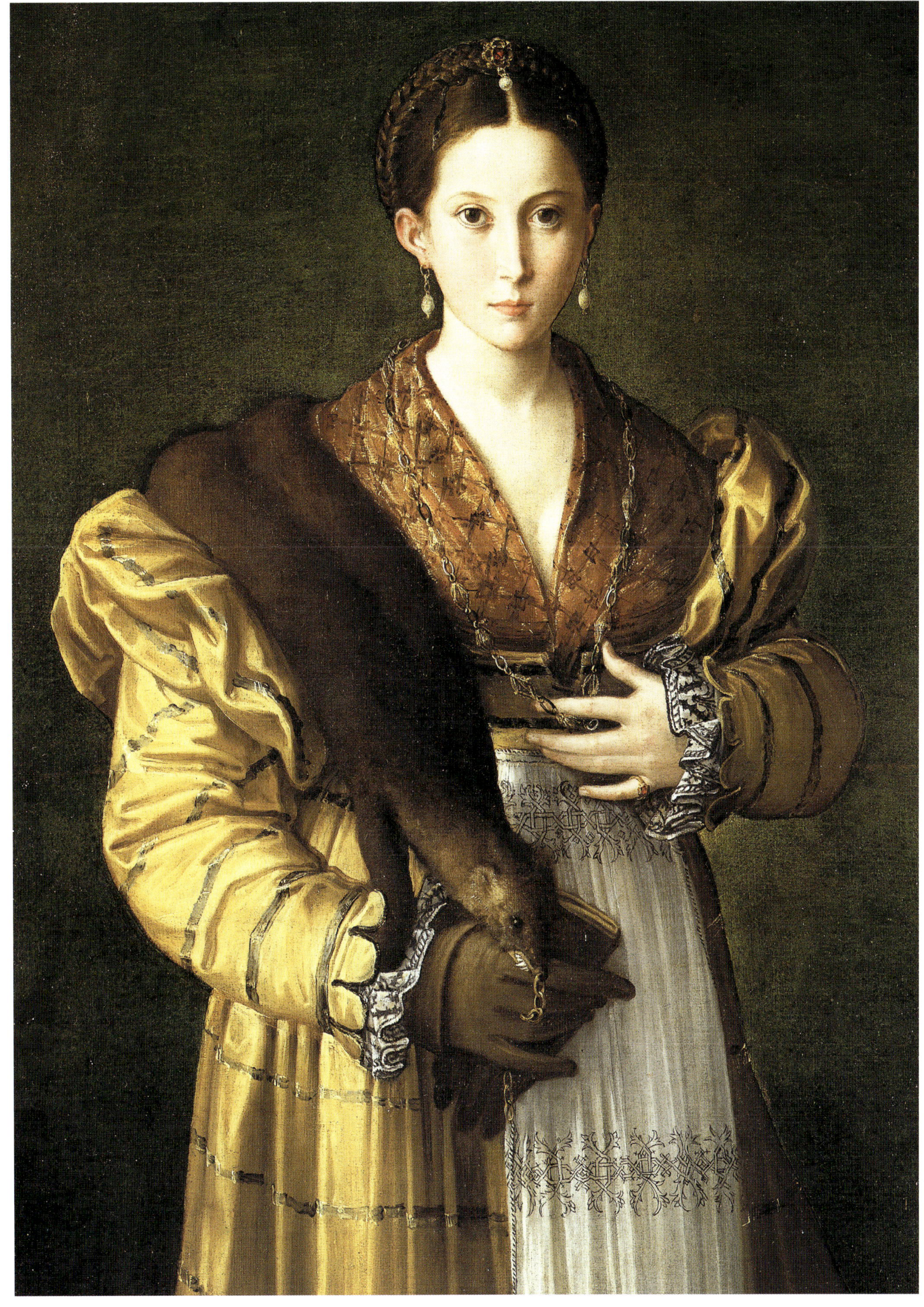

PARMIGIANINO
Antea (Portrait of a Young Woman)
1535–37, oil
on canvas, 135 x 88 cm
Museo di Capodimonte,
Naples

Restless, genial, still
in search of a personal
style, Parmigianino was
among the outstanding
group of artists that
came to Rome over the
course of the 1520s,
attracted by the climate
of renewed activity dur-
ing the age of Clement
VII. The extreme refine-
ment of his method,
with effects of an
almost magical hyper-
realism, made him an
excellent and fascinat-
ing portraitist. The
faces of his sitters
often express doubt
or tension, some
repressed emotion that
is barely perceptible
beneath a rigorous and
glacial immobility.

Villa Madama—the culmination of the theoretical reflections and first architectonic experiments of the Renaissance on the theme of the Roman villa—became the model for this type of building throughout the entire sixteenth century. Planned by Raphael, it stands in a splendid natural setting, an elevated position on the slopes of Monte Mario, and Raphael fully exploited this pleasant site, making the integration between the building and the surrounding landscape one of the cardinal points of the entire complex. Following Raphael's death, direction of the work went to Antonio da Sangallo the Younger, while Giulio Romano and Giovanni da Udine took charge of the execution of the internal decorations. In this section of the loggia, decorated by elegant pilasters and light "antique-style" stuccowork, the hand of Giulio Romano is clear, most of all in the plastic vigor of the figures of the small stucco panels that decorate the inside of the vault.

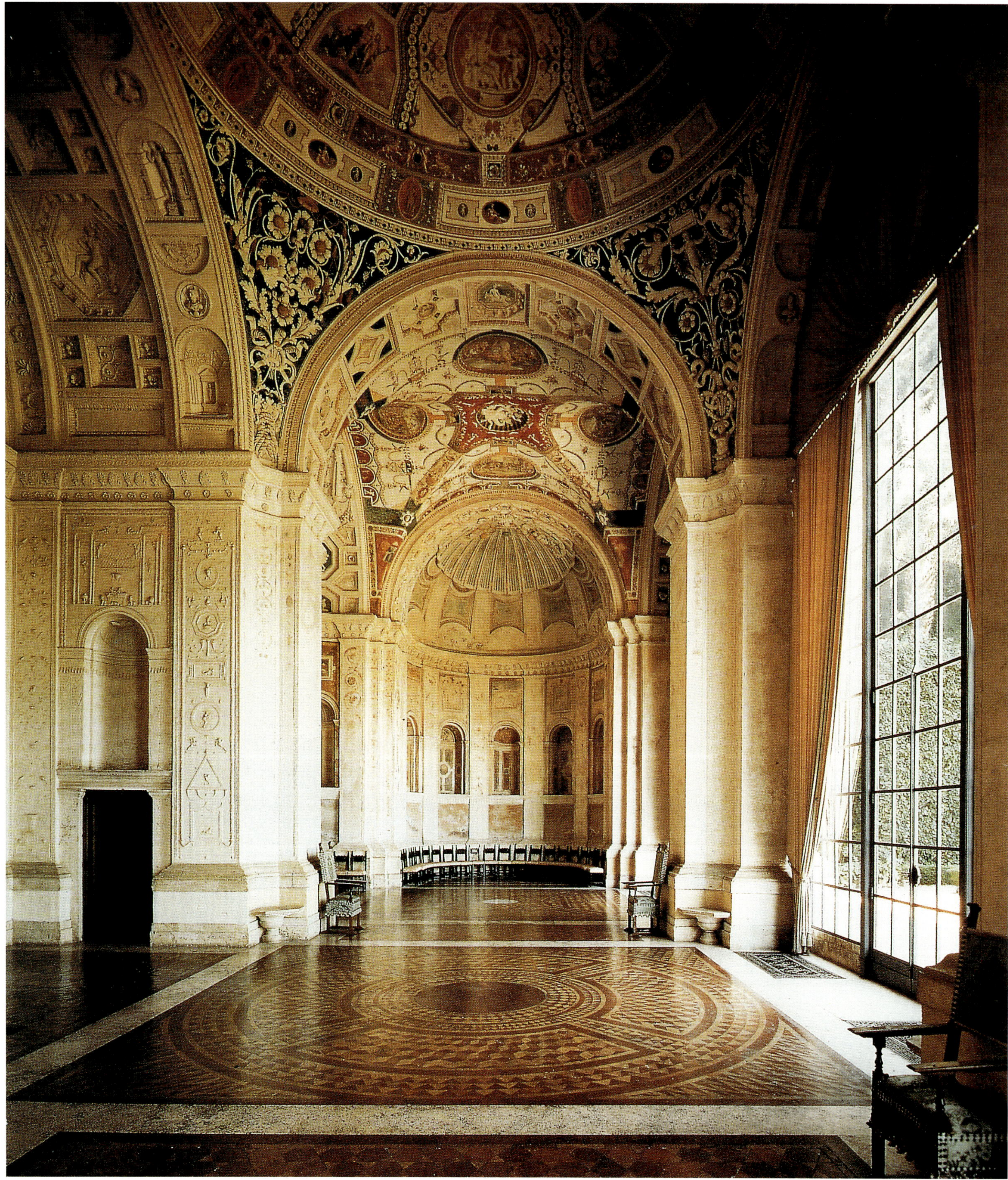

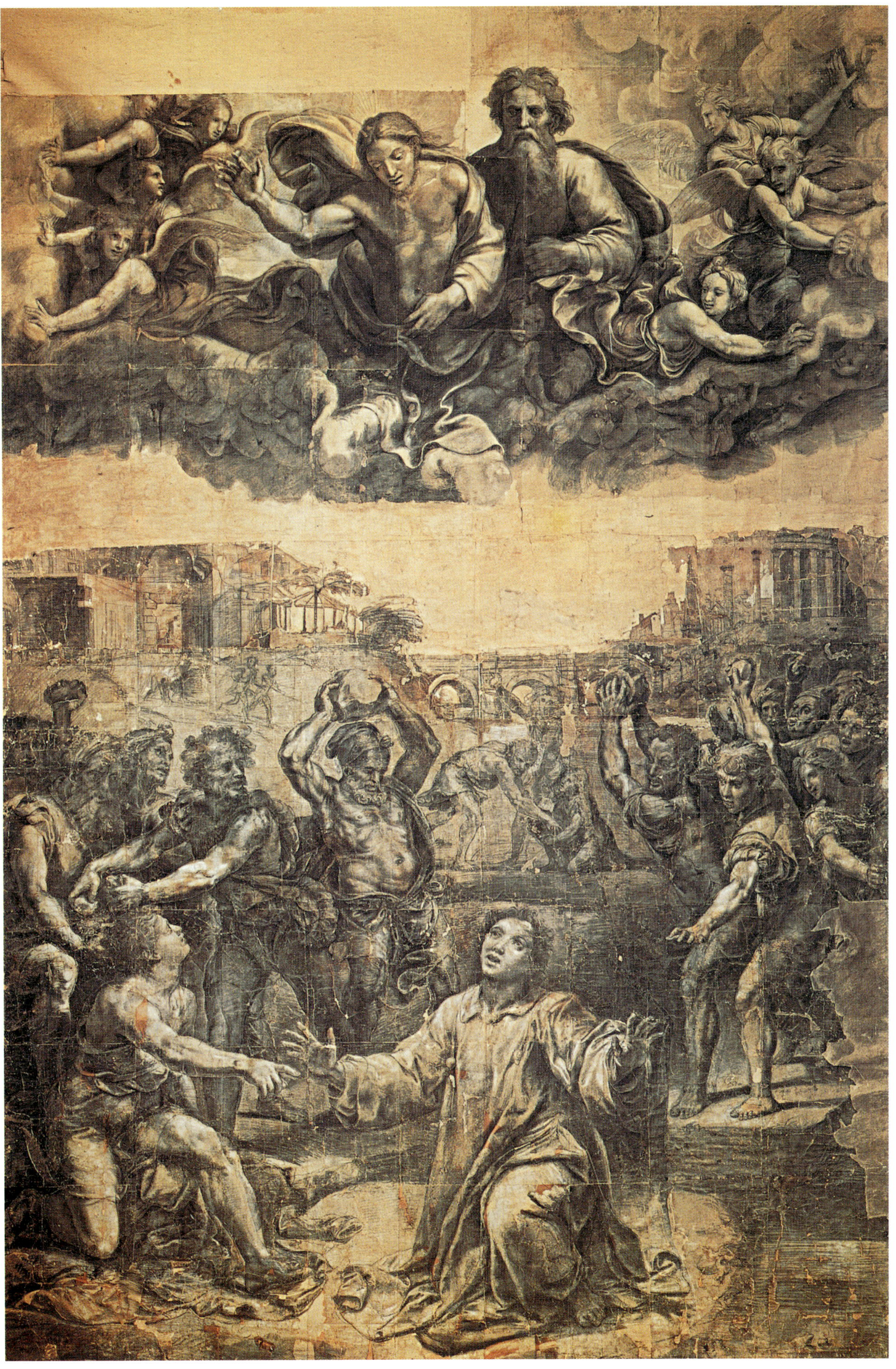

Giulio Romano succeeded in presenting himself as the true "heir" to Raphael. He was responsible for making the fresco cycle in the Stanze del Vaticano, with the completion of the Stanza dell'Incendio di Borgo and, on his own, the Sala di Constantino, for which Raphael had furnished only a few preliminary sketches. Giulio proved himself particularly capable at directing and coordinating the efforts of teams of artists, including architects, painters, stuccoists, and decorators, a talent that he made full use of in his work in Mantua. As a painter he attempted to achieve an ambitious equilibrium between Raphael and Michelangelo. The altarpiece of the *Stoning of St. Stephen,* preserved in the church of St. Stephen in Genoa and preceded by this important cartoon in the Vatican, was meant to occupy a "middle ground" between the great works of Raphael (*Transfiguration*) and those of Sebastiano del Piombo-Michelangelo (*Raising of Lazarus*) made a few years earlier.

From the Sack of Rome to the *Last Judgment*

PERIN DEL VAGA
Visitation
1538, fresco
Trinità dei Monti,
Rome

Perin del Vaga was a
student of Raphael and
a leading artist in the
Rome of the Clementine
age. His works reveal
his Tuscan training and
the influence of the
style of Rosso Fioren-
tino, especially in the
use of a changing
chromatic range. The
typical mannerist style
of achieving tension
and dynamic effects
through the theatrical
poses of figures is
abundantly evident in
the group of onlookers
to the left.

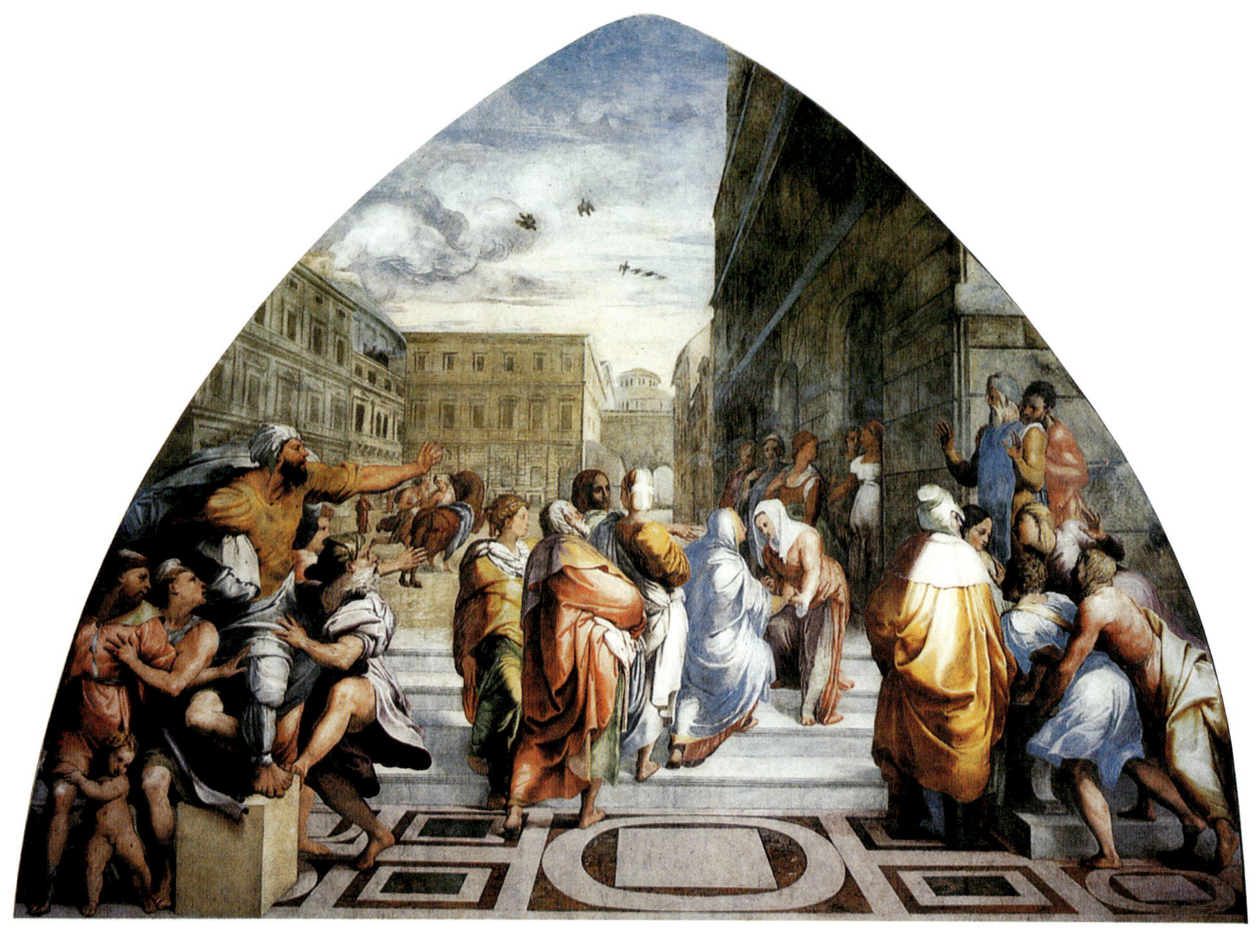

FRANCESCO SALVIATI
Visitation
1538, fresco
Oratory of San Giovanni
Decollato, Rome

Salviati's first works in
Rome show clear evi-
dence of his close study
of Raphael; the layout
of this scene, for exam-
ple, was inspired by
the architectonic back-
ground in Raphael's
Fire in the Borgo, and
the handmaiden to the
left repeats graceful
Raphaelesque move-
ments; other figures,
however, such as the
elderly man with the
staff to the right, reveal
the Tuscan painter's
bent for the irrational
and fantastic.

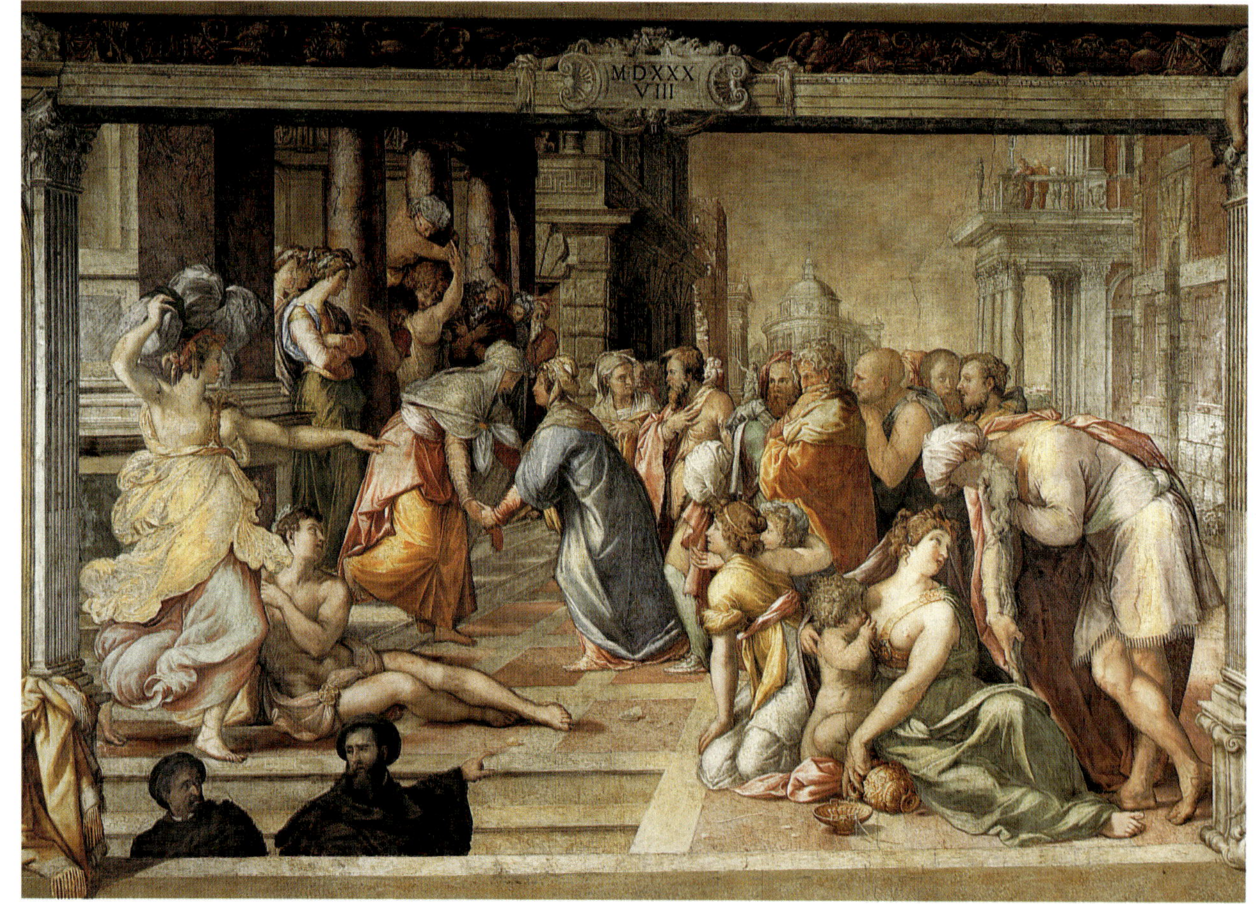

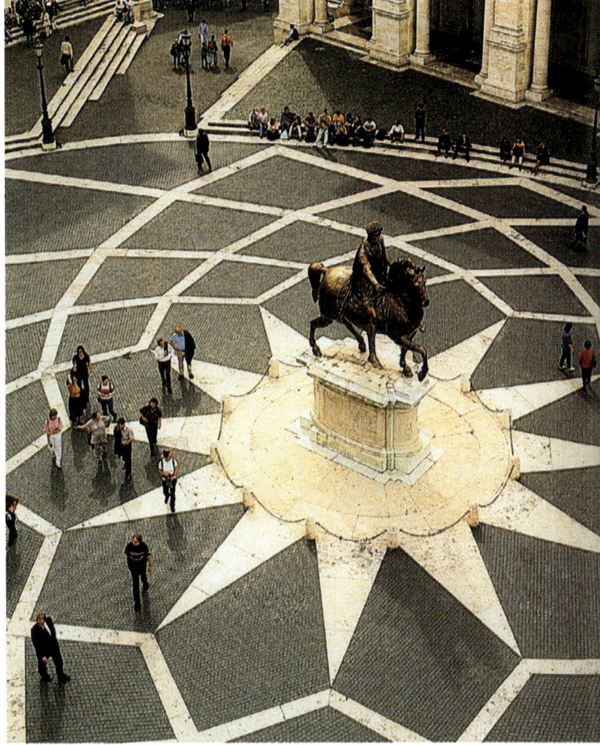

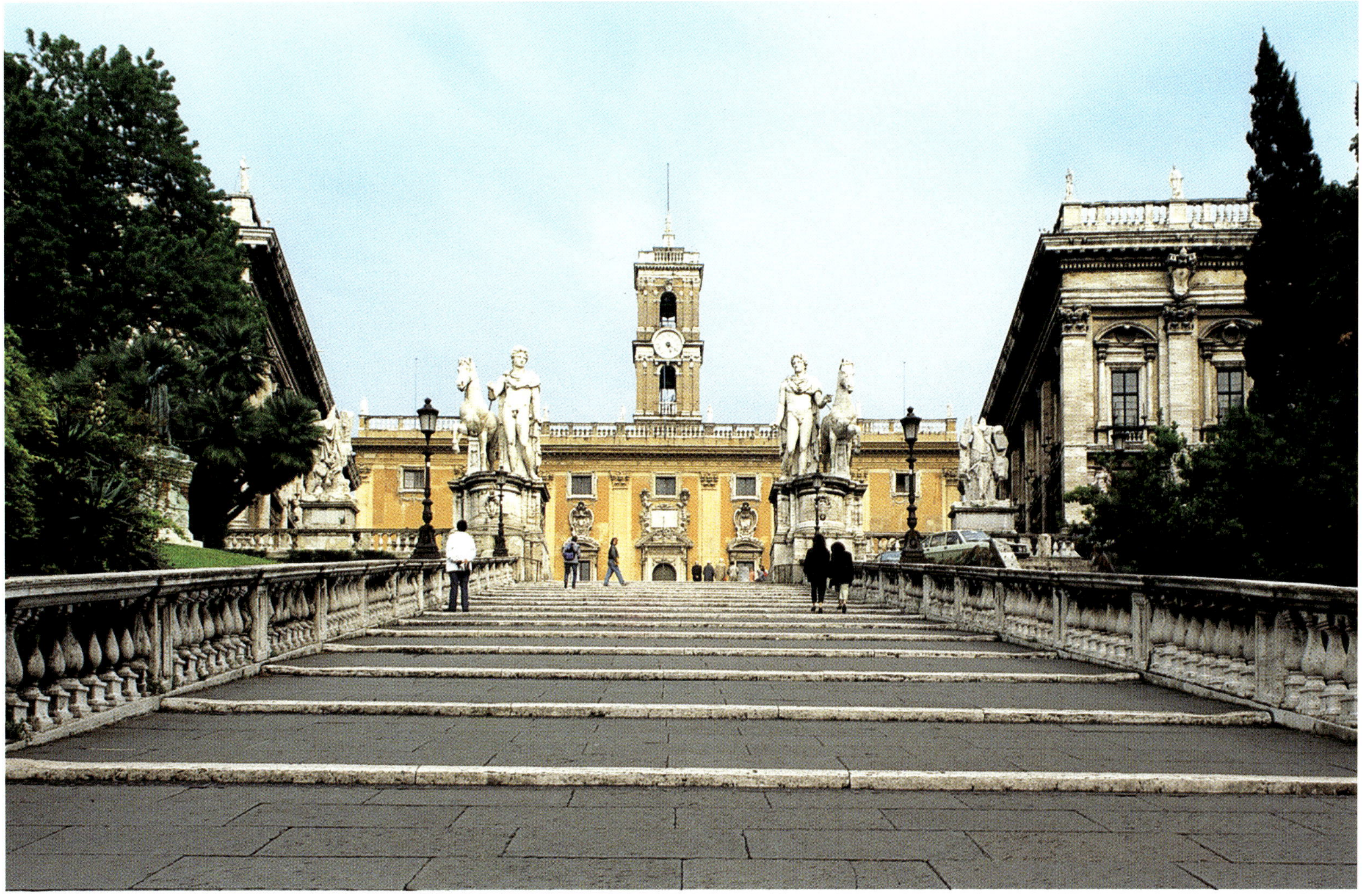

Michelangelo's Campidoglio, inspired by the concept of a defined urban space, is one of the greatest urban creations of the High Renaissance. It is based on the idea of a closed forum and of an ideal city above Rome, and it opens up before anyone who climbs its stately ramp. The arrangement by Michelangelo, which respected the preexisting plaza and created solutions in keeping with the site's high dignity, transformed the Campidoglio into an authentic terrace marked off by a balustrade overlooking the city on one side and the Roman Forum on the other. Even the theatrical ramp that leads up to the plaza was part of Michelangelo's design, which included a majestic accessway, worthy of one of the most important gathering places in all of Rome. The statues of Castor and Pollux standing beside their horses were set in place at the far end of the ramp, at the end of the balustrade that runs around the plaza, in 1583.

From the Sack of Rome to the *Last Judgment*

The great Venetian painter's stay in Rome in 1545–46 was a memorable page in the High Renaissance because of the encounter-clash of the uncontested ruler of the Venetian artistic scene with a completely different, in fact somewhat hostile, setting. Taking his idea from the portrait of Leo X painted by Raphael, Titian represents the pope with his nephews Alessandro and Ottavio. The aged pontiff, bony and hunchbacked, throws a shrewd look toward Ottavio, who is in the process of making a courtly bow. The rapid technique, a sketch that leaves some details incomplete, creates a sense of intrigue in a suffocating atmosphere. Titian's colors were then becoming richer, pasty, with a predominant tone of red; according to a maxim Titian was fond of repeating, anyone wanting to become a painter had to know three colors, white, red, and black "and have them in hand."

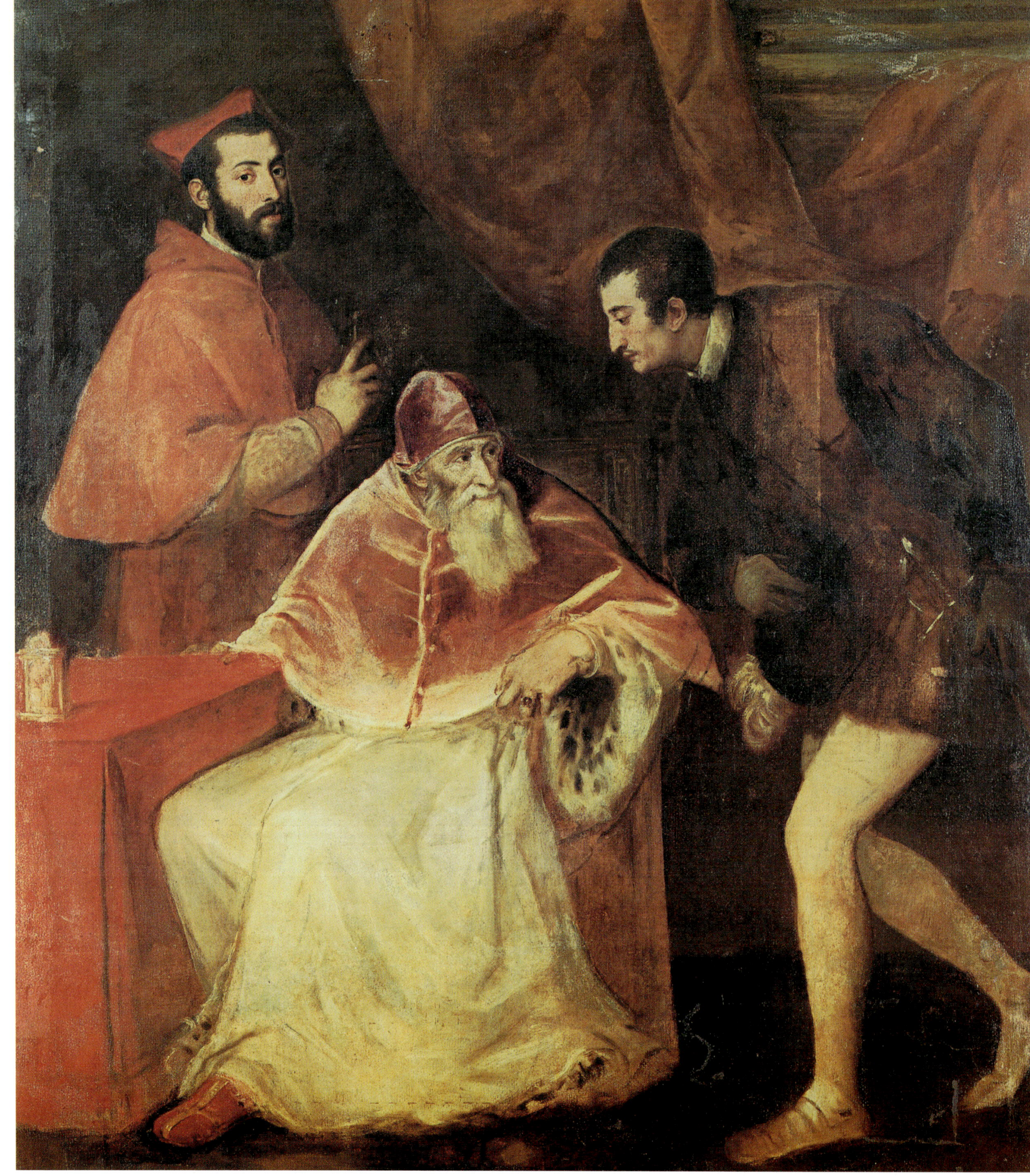

From the Sack of Rome to the *Last Judgment*

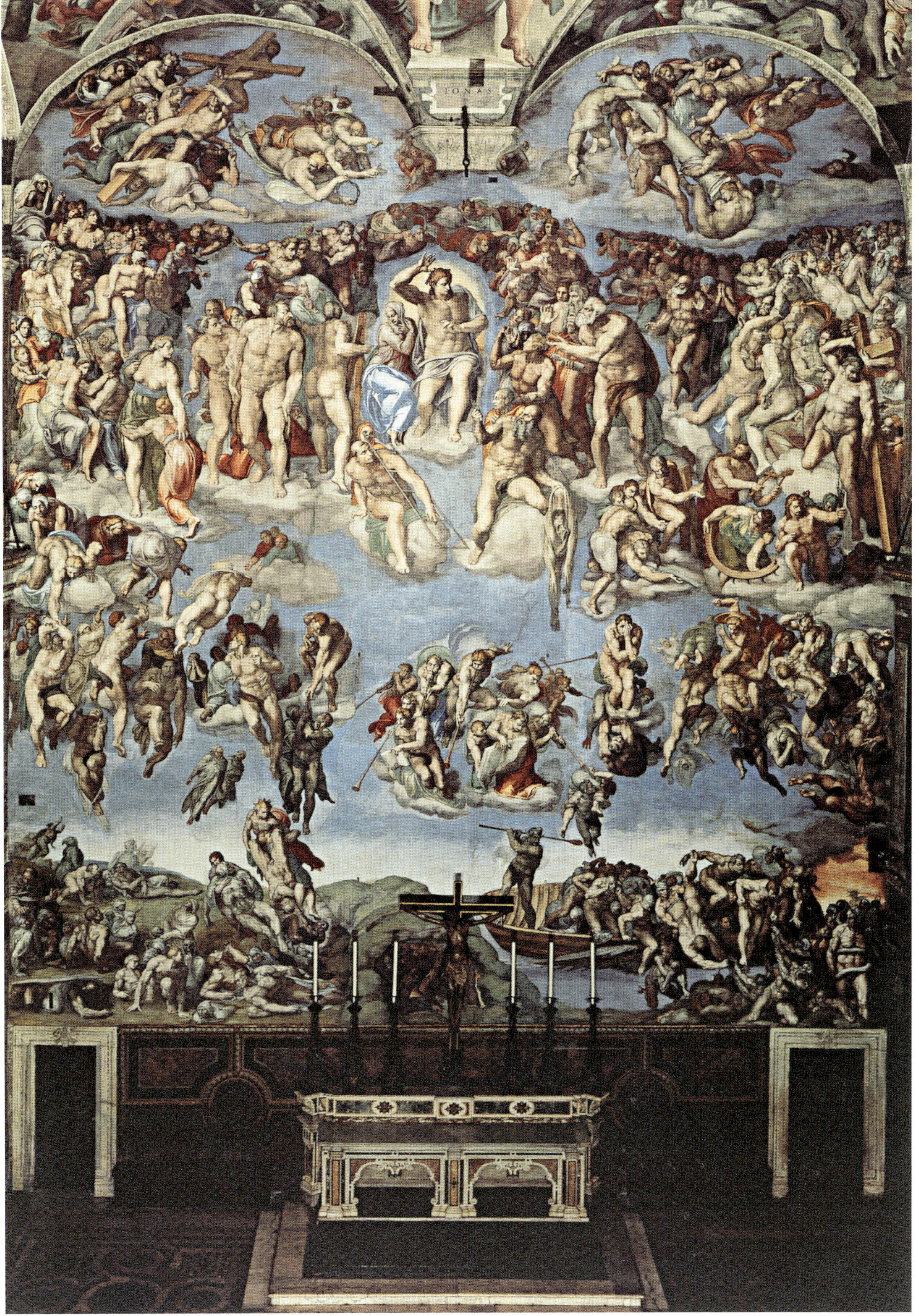

MICHELANGELO
Last Judgment
1537–41, fresco,
1,370 x 1,220 cm
Sistine Chapel, Vatican,
Rome

When it was inaugurated, on October 31, 1541, the great wall immediately became one of the most disturbing and controversial works in the history of art. The gesture of Christ the Judge who divides the chosen from the damned (similar to that of God the Father who, on the vault, separates the earth from the waters) becomes the motor for a scene animated by more than four hundred figures. A mass of bodies, almost all nude, is suspended between hell and paradise. There is nothing heroic about these nudes; they are only the physical shells of terrified humans. The man who had won dominion over nature with his intelligence, who had fashioned justice and beauty into ideals for which to labor and in which to believe, that man made strong and sure by humanism, by the beliefs of the early Renaissance, the man whom Michelangelo had himself exalted in the *ignudi* of the vault, that Renaissance man had now been crushed. The time of illusions had ended.

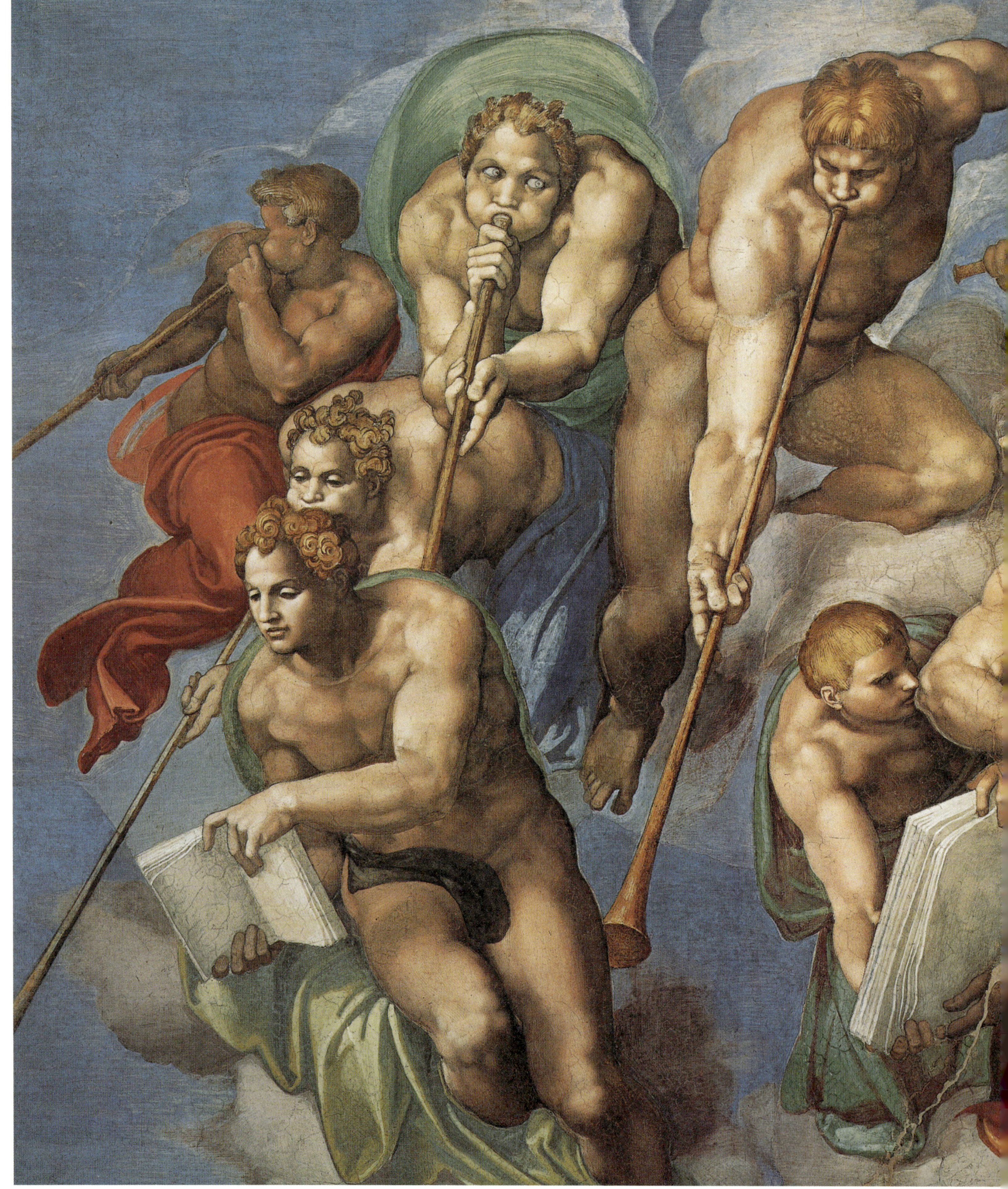

From the Sack of Rome to the *Last Judgment*

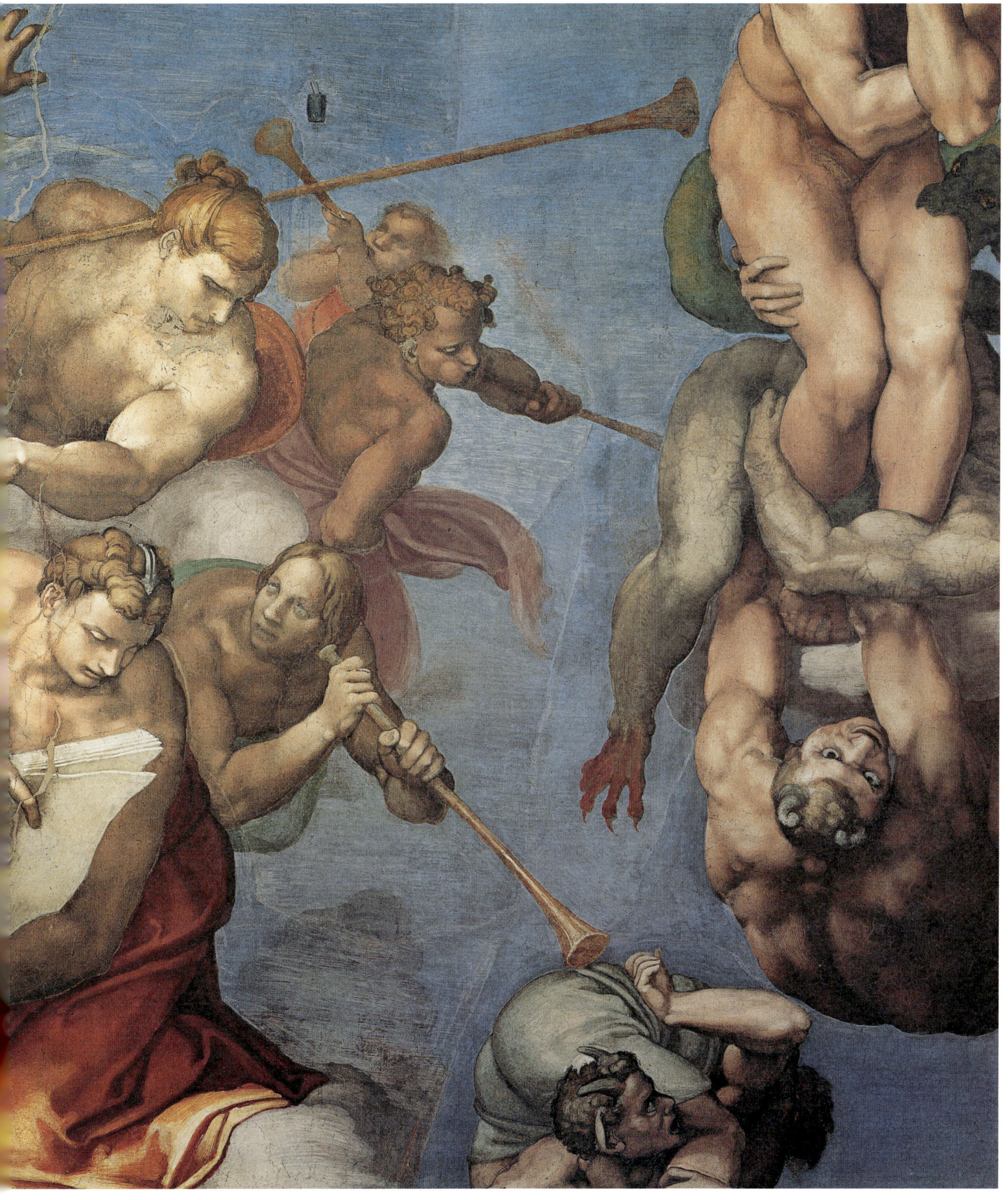

From the Sack of Rome to the *Last Judgment*

MICHELANGELO
**Basilica of St. Peter,
interior with dome**
1546
Vatican, Rome

The structure on which
Michelangelo concen-
trated his architectonic
efforts for the building
of St. Peter's is the
dome, final element of
the organism that was
to join, both on the
inside and on the out-
side, the volumes
beneath it. The artist
presents in a simplified
and concentrated form
Bramante's original
proposal for a "simple,
plain, luminous, and
isolated" dome, making
use of a Greek cross
inscribed in a square,
surrounded by an ambu-
latory and finished off
by a large dome. The
concept is also appar-
ent inside the basilica
where, at the end of

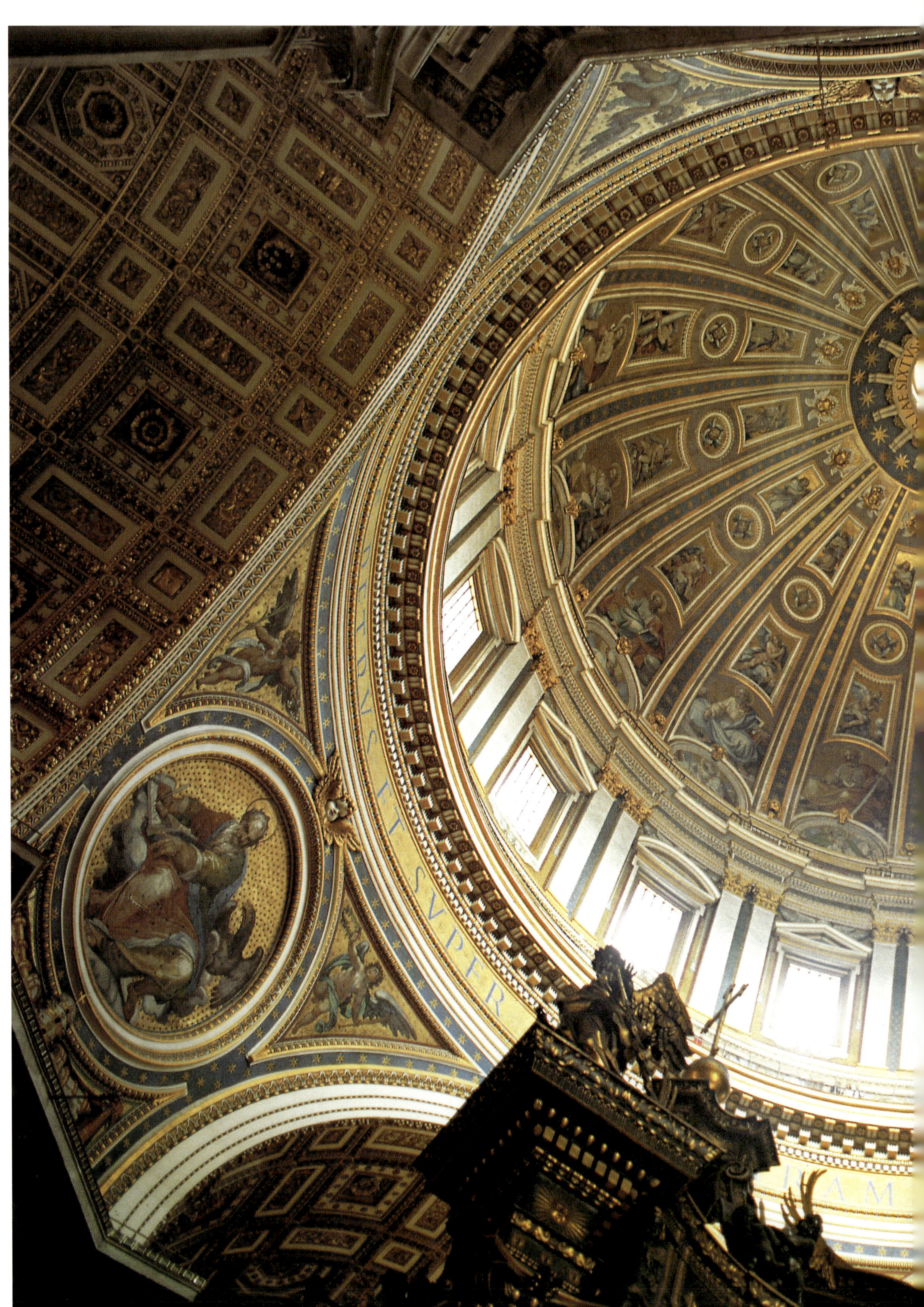

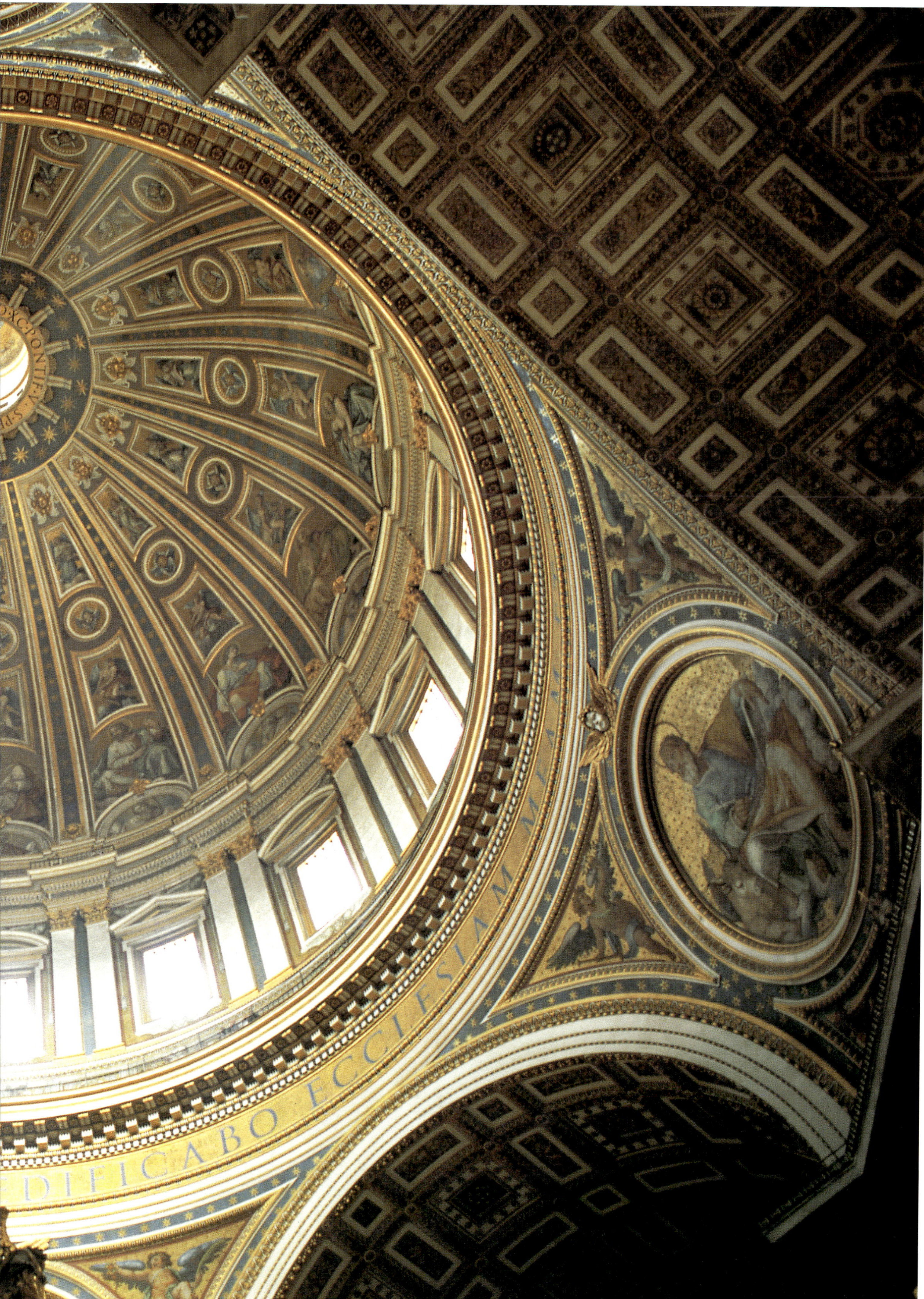

the central nave, with its serried play of spaces that expand and contract, the space opens to take in the majestic structure, flooded with light. Set on four immense arched barrel vaults, it presents a drum opened by windows separated by pairs of pilasters that support the cornice of the dome. The large mosaic tondos in the pendentives (which measure almost eight meters in diameter), the work of Giovanni de Vecchi and Cesare Nebbia, present the evangelists, while the mosaics on the inside of the dome, made on cartoons by Cavalier d'Arpino, present, on different levels, popes, doctors of the church, saints, apostles, and angels, ending with a blessing Eternal Father in the clerestory.

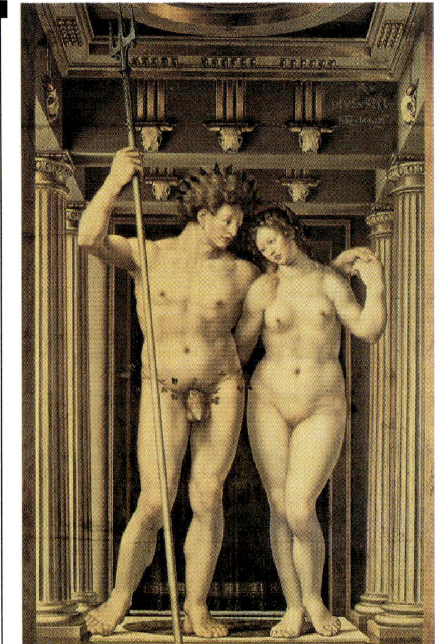

During the first two decades of the sixteenth century, Netherlandish art reached an epochal turning point. What was happening there was not unlike what was happening during the same years in Italy and Germany, and in fact the various centers of artistic activity were in contact with one another. In the Flemish-Dutch region, the waning of the last generation of great masters of the fifteenth-century tradition made way for a movement toward a decisive change, one based primarily on the interpretation of the new artistic ideas from Italy, encountered directly by way of trips to the south. It was a local interpretation, however, displaying the decorative exuberance and taste for descriptive details that were distinctive aspects of the Flemish matrix. While the old commercial centers of Bruges and Ghent were rapidly losing their luster, the star of Antwerp was rising higher and brighter. The large port at

ently crazy works, in which, alongside the unbridled fantasy, one can make out a perfectly straightforward adherence to the truth, a heartfelt attention to the most humble contexts of ordinary life. In the course of a trip to Flanders in 1522, Dürer had an affectionate meeting with Lucas van Leyden, an event that calls to light the important connections between Flanders and Germany and, most of all, the developments that were then taking place in the art of engraving.

These same years presented an apparently exceptional opportunity for Netherlandish artists. At the death of Leo X, the Netherlander Adrian VI was elected pope; more than half a millennium would pass before the election of another non-Italian as pope: John Paul II. Adrian VI's pontificate lasted just twenty months, far too short to have much influence on the arts, although he did name another Netherlander, Jan van Scorel, to serve in the prestigious post of superintendent of Vatican antiquities, previously held by Raphael, and even though Scorel saw the need of contact with the Roman scene. The art of the Low Countries began moving toward its own local version of mannerism, of which Lucas van Leyden was one of the leading and most interesting interpreters.

The rise
new capital of

the mouth of the Scheldt River was becoming the principal city of culture and economy along the North Sea coast.

Bosch, Metsys, Gossart, and Van Scorel made trips to study in Venice and Rome, acquiring the monumental sense of Italian linear perspective but also meeting other leaders of the world of international art of the period. For example, it is not at all improbable that between Venice and Milan Bosch and Metsys came in contact not only with Leonardo and Giovanni Bellini but also with Dürer.

The city of Antwerp, steadily affirming itself as the artistic capital of Flanders, presented a compact and recognizable artistic style, clearly distinguished by the reproduction of Italian models. The city was a continuous forge of new artistic ideas and artistic situations, working at overlapping contrasting artistic styles, such as the strong movements toward the irrational (Bosch, Patinir, the first works of Bruegel) and the constant demand for realism. An important example is offered by Bosch's most bizarre and appar-

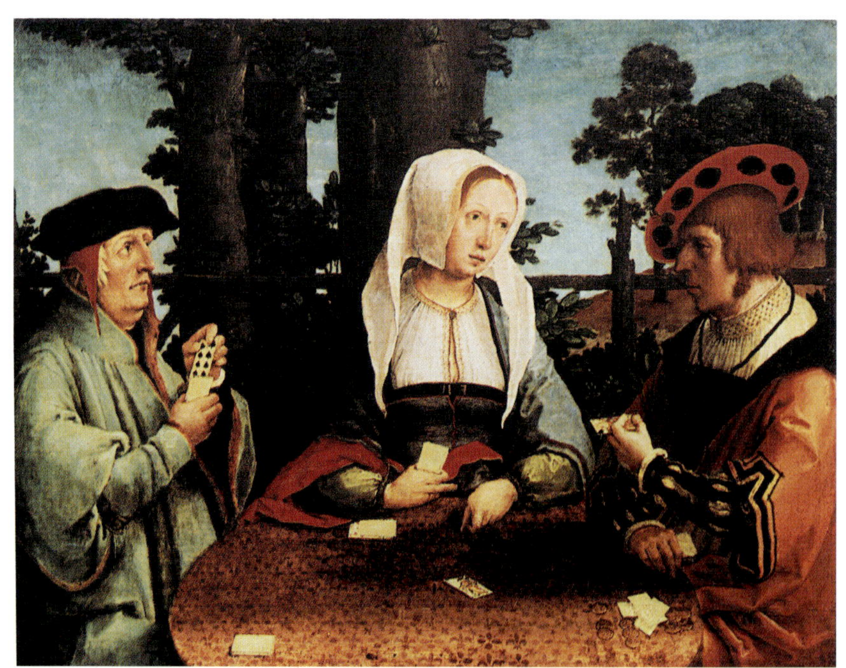

The rise of Antwerp, new capital of northern art

Around the middle of the sixteenth century, as a consequence of the new situation created by the religious wars, Flemish-Dutch painting went through a major evolution. After several decades of knowledgeable and often brilliant interpretation of the novelties of Italian art there was a return to traditional themes, characters, and scenes. This was by no means a rejection of the dialogue with mannerism and with the developments of the High and Late Renaissance. Pieter Bruegel the Elder made a memorable trip from the Alps to Naples; Maarten van Heemskerck made precise and invaluable drawings of the archaeological ruins and monuments of Rome; Aertsen and Beuckelaer, precursors of the still life, found enlightened patrons among the Italian aristocracy. On the other hand, there was the clear desire to present landscapes, subjects, and narrative situations based on the rapidly changing historical and social reality. A case in point is that of Bruegel the Elder, who created credible images of the peasant world, most often by way of an allegory, proverb, or satire on contemporary customs. Bruegel's education, like that of his "spiritual master" Hieronymus Bosch, was based in large part on popular traditions, proverbs, ways of speaking. Although his art works on several levels, including that of the moral or religious admonition, the prevalent atti-

proved the most ready and efficient to handle the enormous resources required for overseas commerce. In the sixteenth and early seventeenth centuries, the city of Antwerp was probably the wealthiest and most envied city in Europe; without doubt, the port docks on the Scheldt offered an international and cosmopolitan spectacle of nonstop exotic activity. Even more than the Spanish ports, Antwerp was the site of the distribution and sale of merchandise from Europe's far-flung colonies. Many of the city's inhabitants got rich from this lucrative business, forming the nucleus for the solid middle class that became the major buyers of art in the seventeenth century. An international city, sophisticated, open, and tolerant, with a well-merited fame for its polyglot printing, Antwerp stayed faithful to Catholicism and became an outpost of the Counter-Reformation in the face of the rebellious United Provinces, which embraced Calvinism. Even so, the city was swept by two successive waves of iconoclasm (1566–67

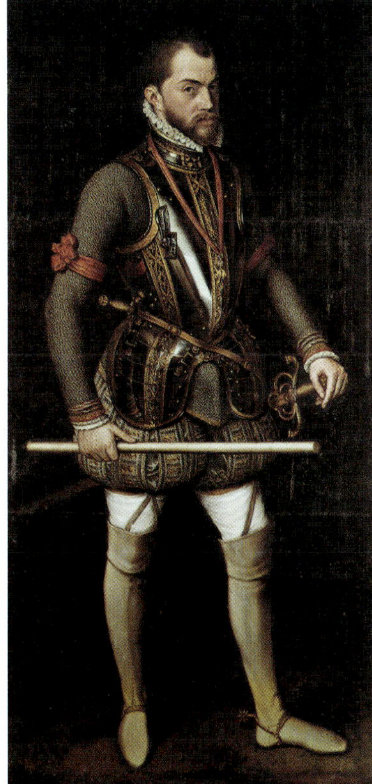

# of Antwerp, northern art

tude is that of an amused and disenchanted observer.

Under Spanish domination of the Low Countries, Flanders and the northern provinces (which later formed the Netherlands) were repeatedly the site of bloody wars, rebellions, and movements for independence from Spanish domination. Cruel and dramatic events led to terrible repression under the duke of Alba, sent by Philip II of Spain to turn the Low Countries into a Spanish province. The public beheading of the counts Egmont and Hoorn in the Grand-Place of Brussels, an act of terror perpetrated by the duke of Alba, and the assassination at Delft of William the Silent, the principal founder of Dutch independence, are among the period's notorious and terrible events. Such scenes took place against a background of burgeoning economic affairs. Thanks to excellent organization and the use of advanced nautical-commercial technology, the ports along the North Sea

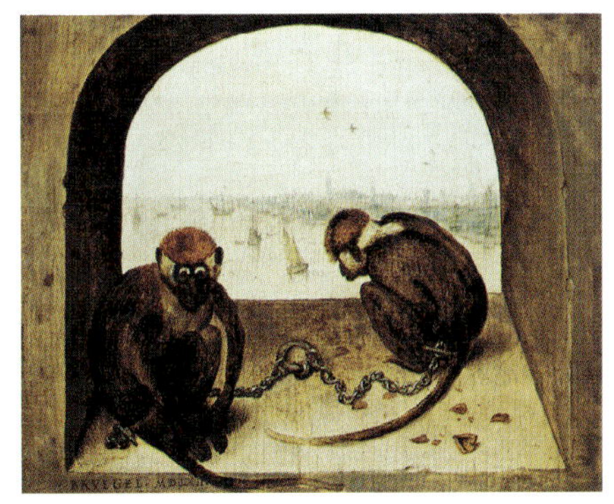

and 1581) during which many churches, including the cathedral, were wrecked; paintings, sculptures, and sacred furnishings, in many cases of great historical and artistic importance, were destroyed. In the 1580s the military situation settled down. Antwerp remained tied to Flanders, while the northern United Provinces continued to battle for their independence. Like many other families, that of the Rubenses, driven from the city for religious reasons, was rehabilitated, and young Peter Paul, born in exile, was able to return to his homeland. Around the stupendous late Gothic mass of Antwerp's cathedral, crowned by the tower by Rombout Keldermans II, arose the buildings housing several religious orders, including the Jesuits, who began the work of reaffirming Catholicism, one aspect of which was the large-scale patronage of works of art related to the themes and needs of the propaganda of the Counter-Reformation.

Signed and dated, this famous panel was imitated and replicated many times during the sixteenth century. In open homage to the tradition of the Flemish "primitives," the work repeats the layout and analytical accuracy of the *St. Eligius* by Petrus Christus. Metsys does away with the religious subject of the prototype and instead, with striking vivacity, presents a credible and direct scene. The quiet and intense image is imbued with great inner spirituality and a profound sense of participation in the dynamics of a society in rapid change. The painting has been copied and also abused; almost all of the later imitations and reproductions, even those by the painter himself, give the scene a grotesque, caricatured tone, sometimes viciously racist.

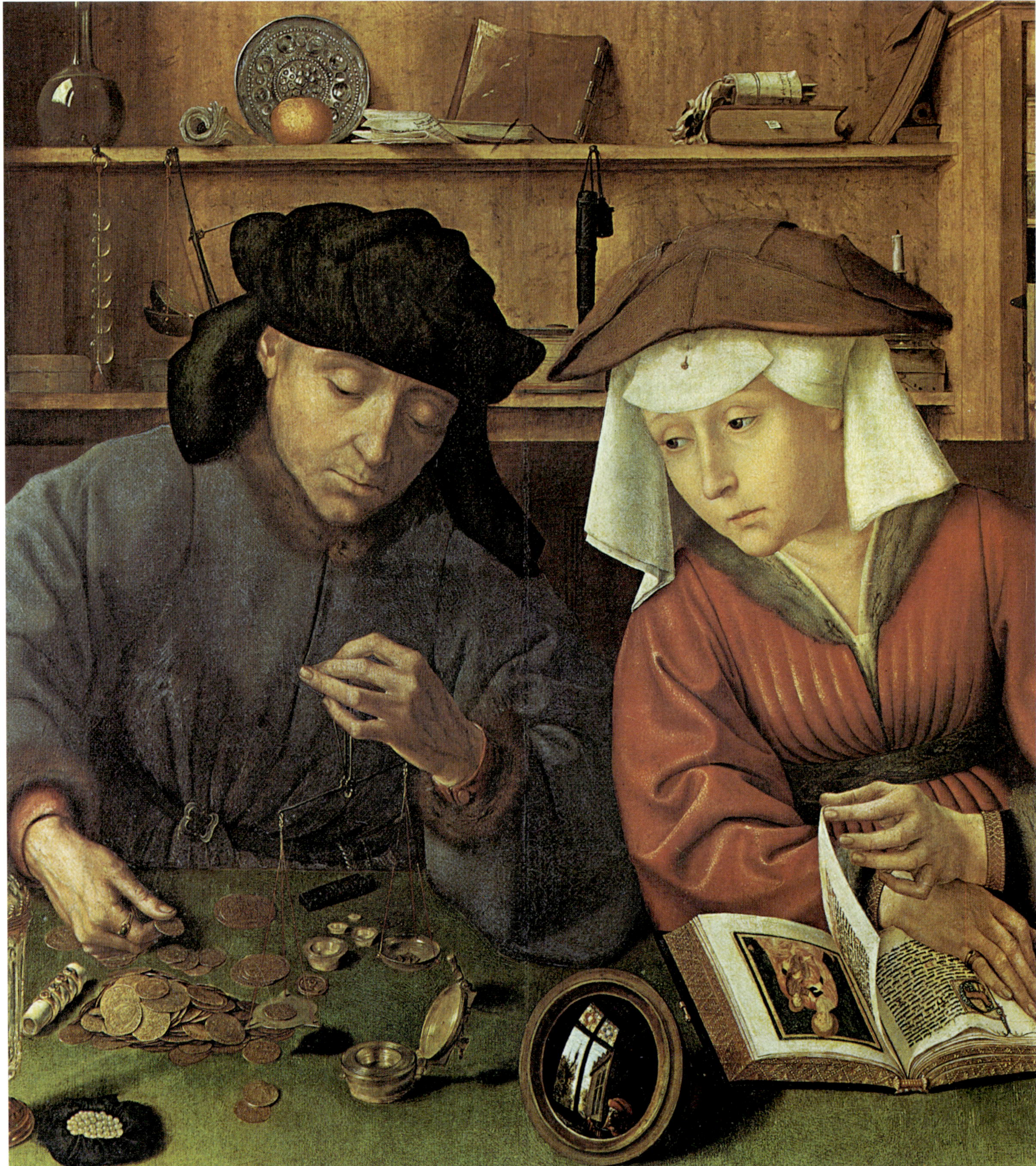

The rise of Antwerp, new capital of northern art

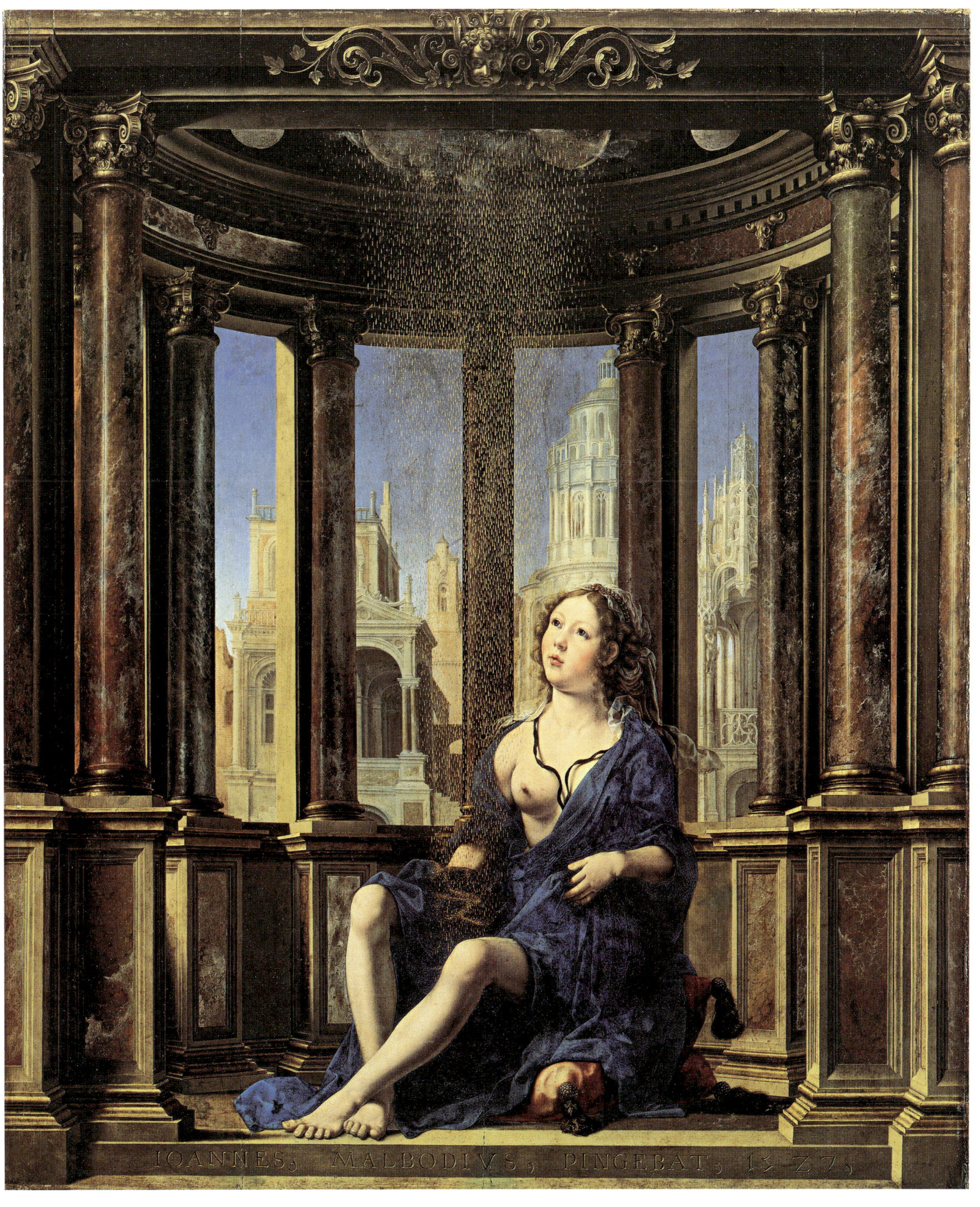

■ JAN GOSSART
Danaë
1527, oil on canvas,
113.5 x 95 cm
Alte Pinakothek,
Munich

In this oil panting, one of the first explicit homages to classical culture made north of the Alps, Gossart included many characteristics of his peculiar style. Having been in Rome during the period when Raphael and Michelangelo had just begun their work in the Vatican, in the fervor of new, sensational archaeological discoveries, Gossart can be considered the precursor of "Antwerp Romanism," a particular style that does not completely abandon the fifteenth-century Flemish tradition, with its rich attention to detail and its meticulous presentation of the real world, but that is also aware of the "modern" Italian style, not only in the rendering of perspective and the architectonic layout, but also in the monumental sense of the figures, in the use of light, in the relationship between people and their surrounding context, and the reference to antique models.

The rise of Antwerp, new capital of northern art

The only Dutch artist to profit in any way from the brief and austere pontificate of Adrian VI was Jan van Scorel, whom the pope made conservator of the Vatican antiquities, a highly prestigious position previously held by Raphael. Putting aside any questions of possible favoritism on the part of the pope in selecting a fellow countryman for the important post, the fact that a painter from the Low Countries could be considered qualified to perform the task of overseeing works from antiquity is highly significant and reflects the fact that the process of updating the Flemish-Dutch school, along with its integration within the figurative culture of Italy, was by then an accomplished fact. Van Scorel merited the papal faith. While not very abundant, his production was always of the highest quality, demonstrating great formal control, although sometimes at the loss of spontaneity.

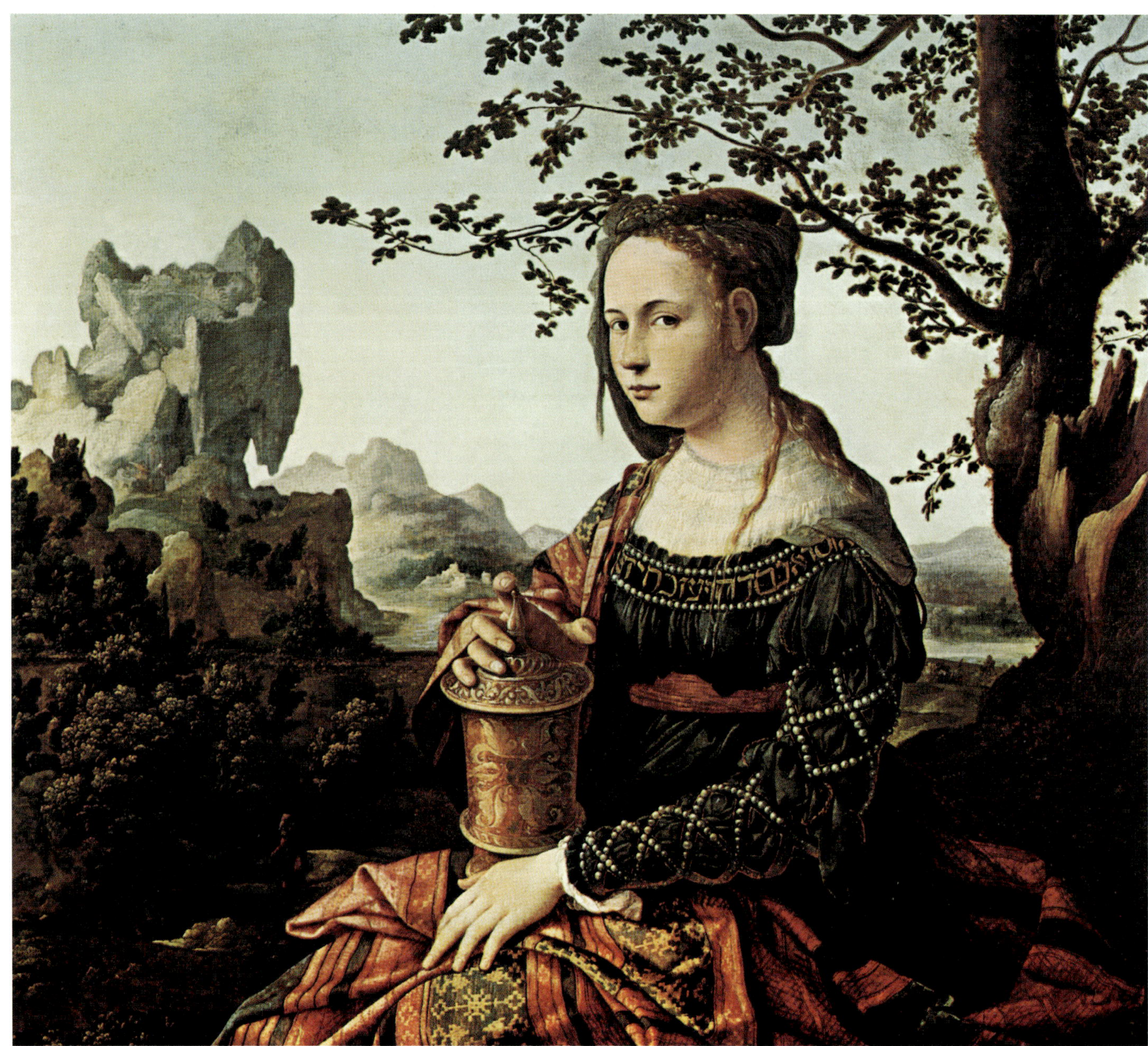

The rise of Antwerp, new capital of northern art

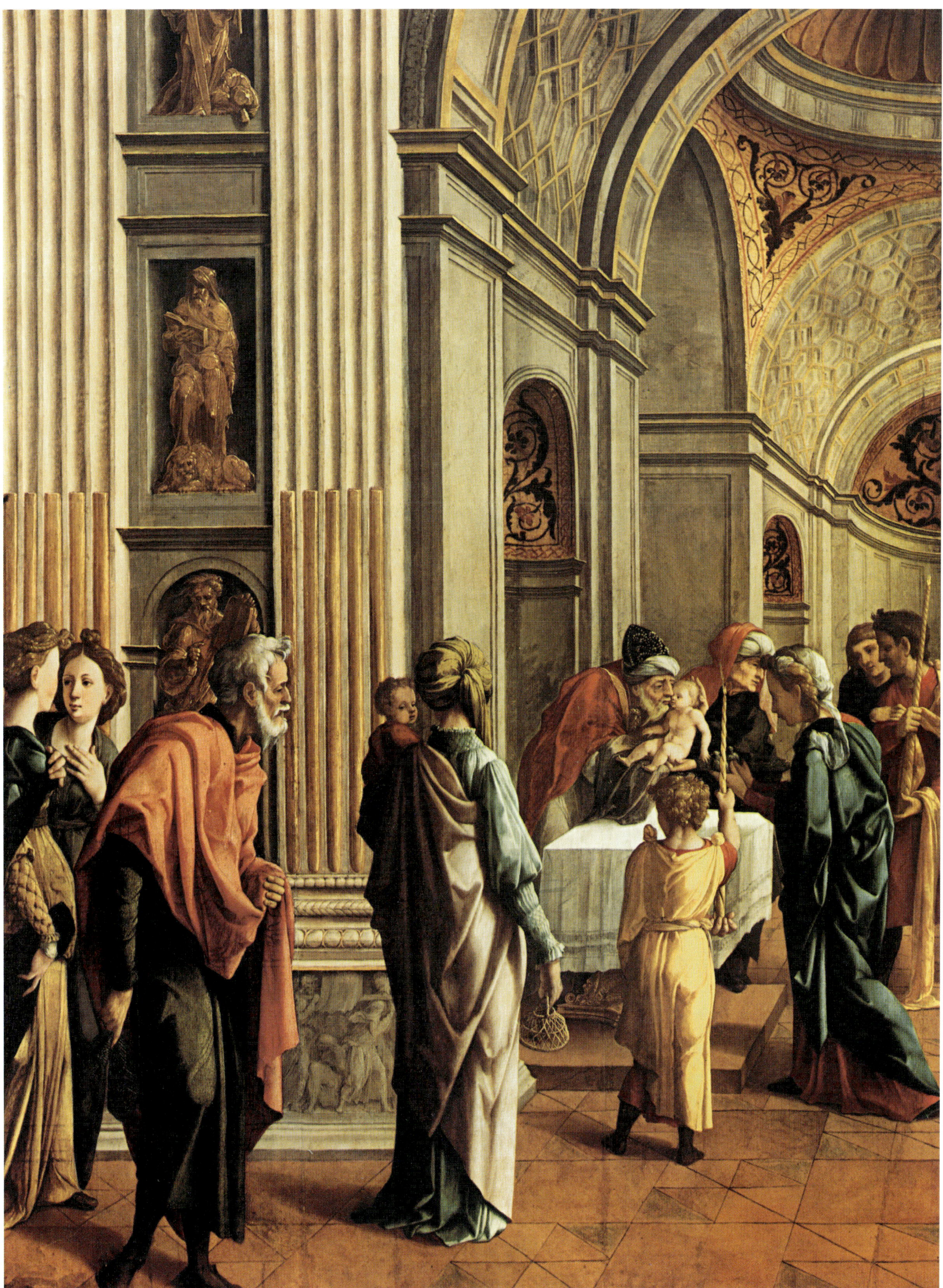

JAN VAN SCOREL
Presentation
in the Temple
1524, oil on panel,
114 x 85 cm
Kunsthistorisches
Museum,
Vienna

Unquestionably a result
of the painter's stay in
Rome, this painting is
a sort of compendium
of Italian Renaissance
motifs. The figures
have the statuesque
monumentality of the
engravings of Andrea
Mantegna, the colors
are similar to those of
Venetian painting, and
the architectonic set-
ting is an undisguised
homage to the recent
Roman works of
Bramante (the foun-
dations and his design
for the basilica of St.
Peter) and Raphael
(the loggia with stuc-
cos in Villa Madama).

Joachim Patinir and
Quenten Metsys
**The Temptation
of St. Anthony**
1515, oil on panel,
155 x 173 cm
Museo del Prado,
Madrid

A singular work of col-
laboration between two
of the greatest members
of Antwerp's guild of
painters, this painting
was laid out by Patinir
with a panoramic land-
scape view full of refer-
ences to Leonardo. The
figures of the hermit,
the three seductive
girls, and the laughing
shrew are the work of
Metsys. Patinir's vast
views presented a new
image of the landscape
and are related to the
overseas discoveries
and conquests of the
age, which had greatly
expanded the world
vision of Europeans.

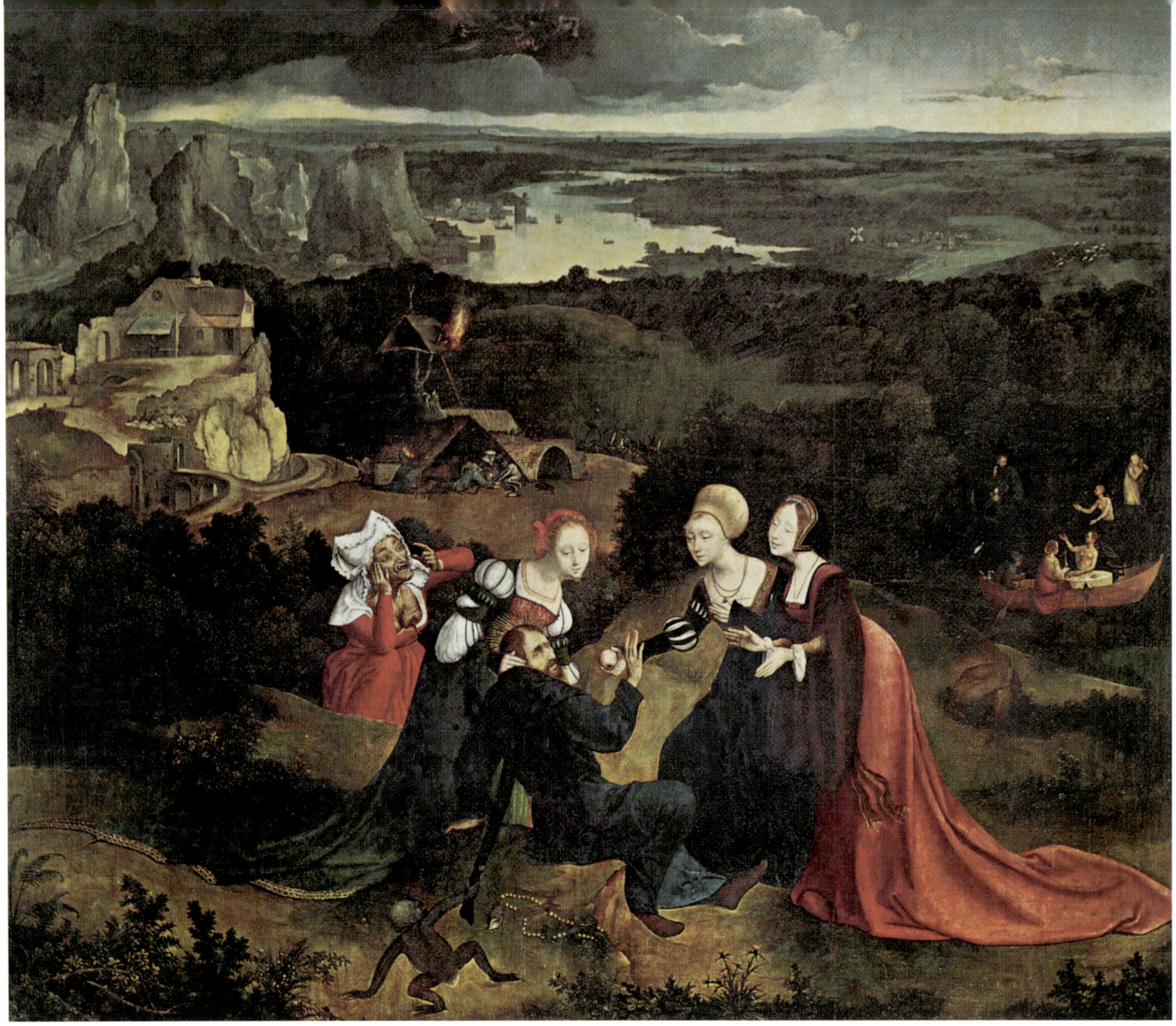

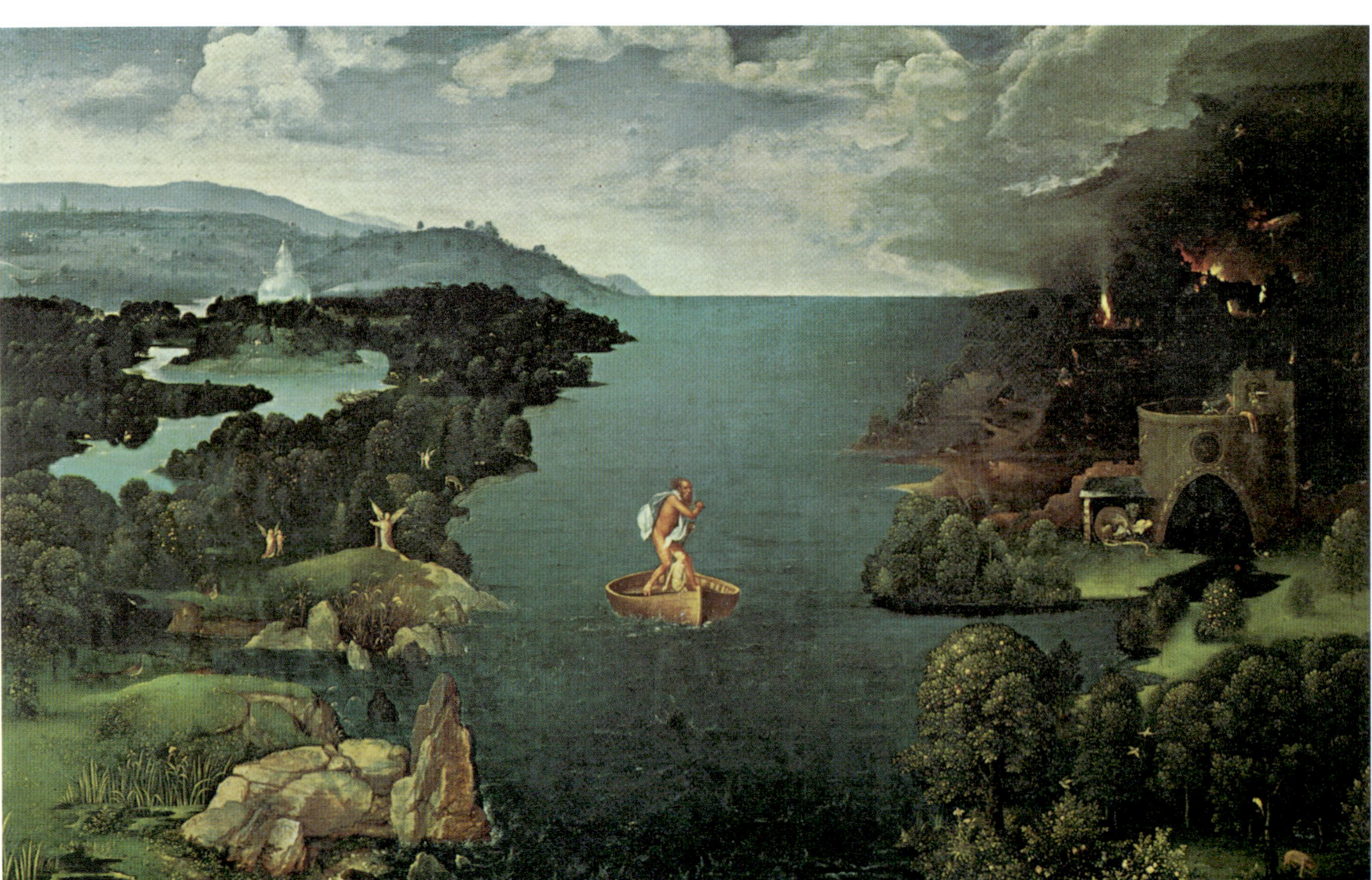

Joachim Patinir
**Charon Crossing
the River Styx**
1520, oil on panel,
64 x 103 cm
Museo del Prado,
Madrid

Charon ferries a pas-
senger toward flaming
Hades, to the right,
site of the guard dog
Cerberus, while to the
left can be seen the
Garden of Eden. The
panorama is truly extra-
ordinary, a fabulous
evocation of infinite
space that becomes
the soul itself of the
painting. The way
the colors of the work
all seem to shade
off toward blue is
an aspect of
Patinir's poetry.

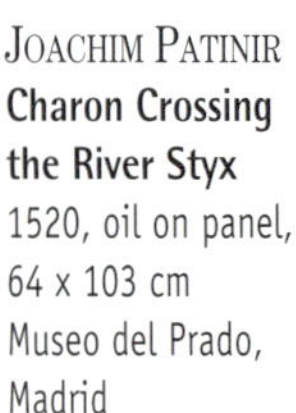

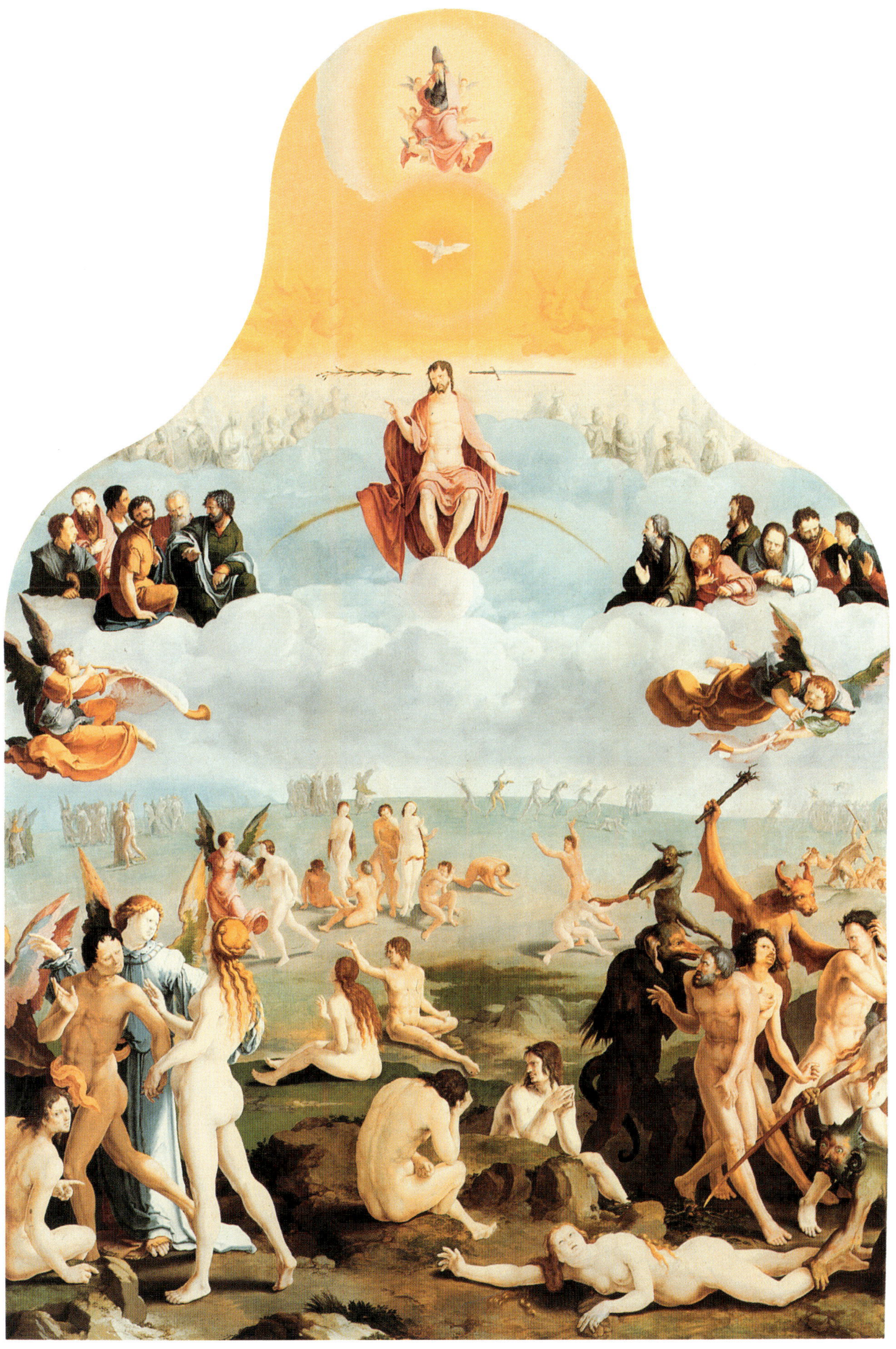

This triptych is certainly the most complex and significant of the few works by Lucas van Leyden that have remained in his city of origin. Completely different from Bosch's paintings of the same subject, which positively swarm with figures, this is a work of great compositional ingenuity and most of all expressive synthesis. The logic of the composition and the definition of the nudes justify the high opinion of Lucas held by Vasari and by sixteenth-century Italian culture in general. Discussing the realistic character of the works by the Dutch artist and comparing them to Dürer, Vasari says, "The scenes of Lucas are very happy in composition, being executed with such clearness and so free from confusion, that it seems certain that the action represented could not have taken place in any other way; and they are arranged more in accordance with the rules of art that those of Albrecht [Dürer]."

The rise of Antwerp, new capital of northern art

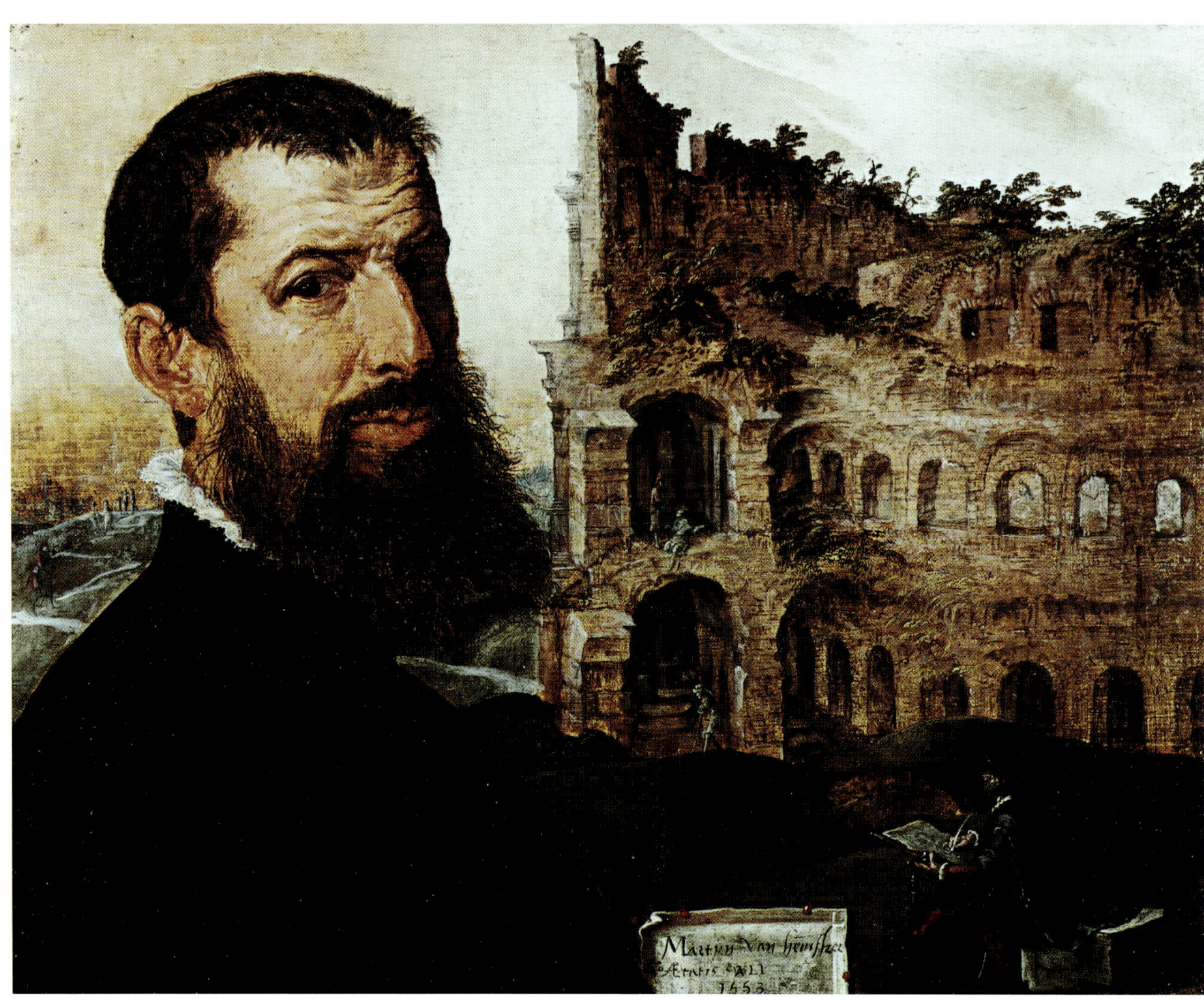

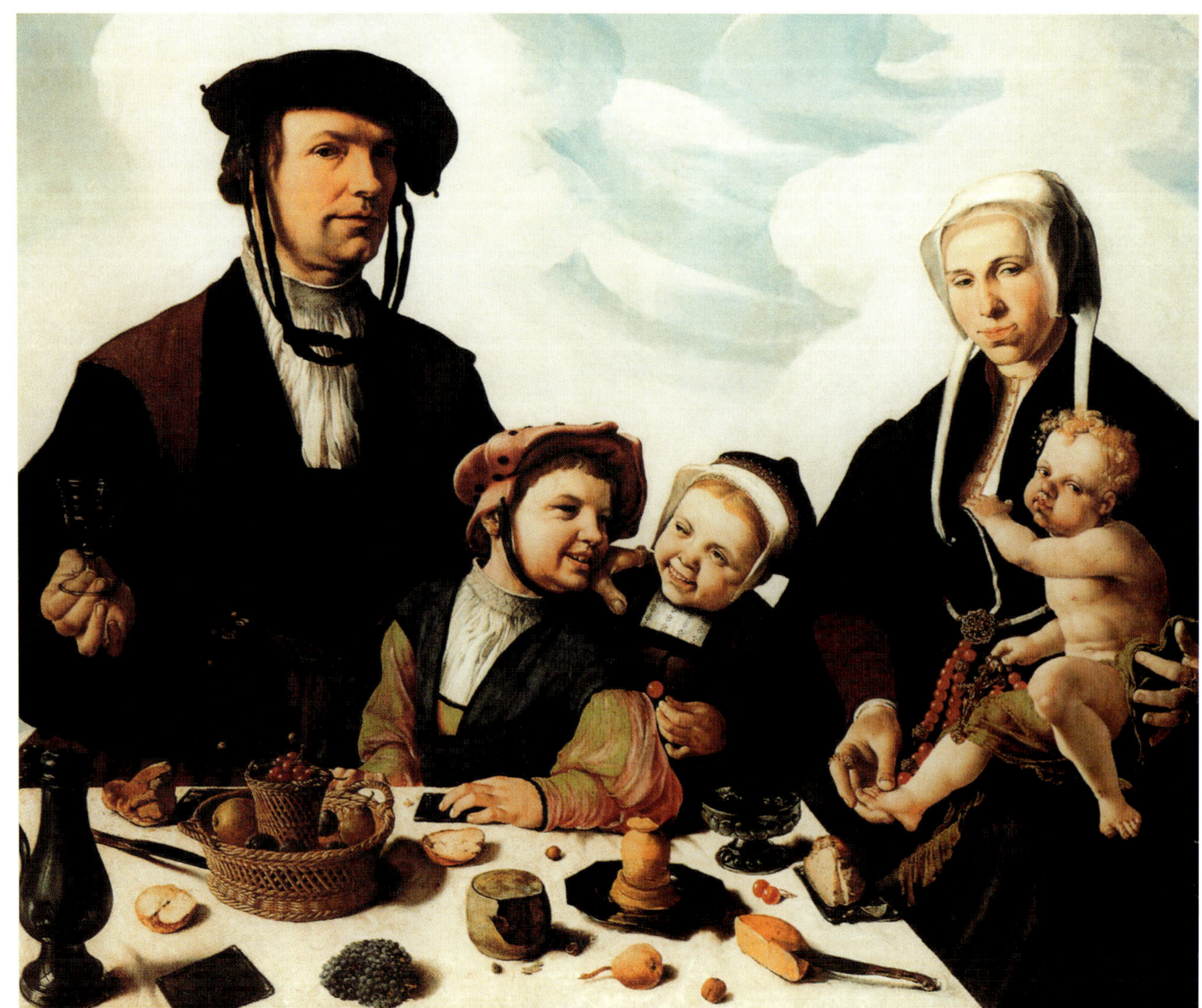

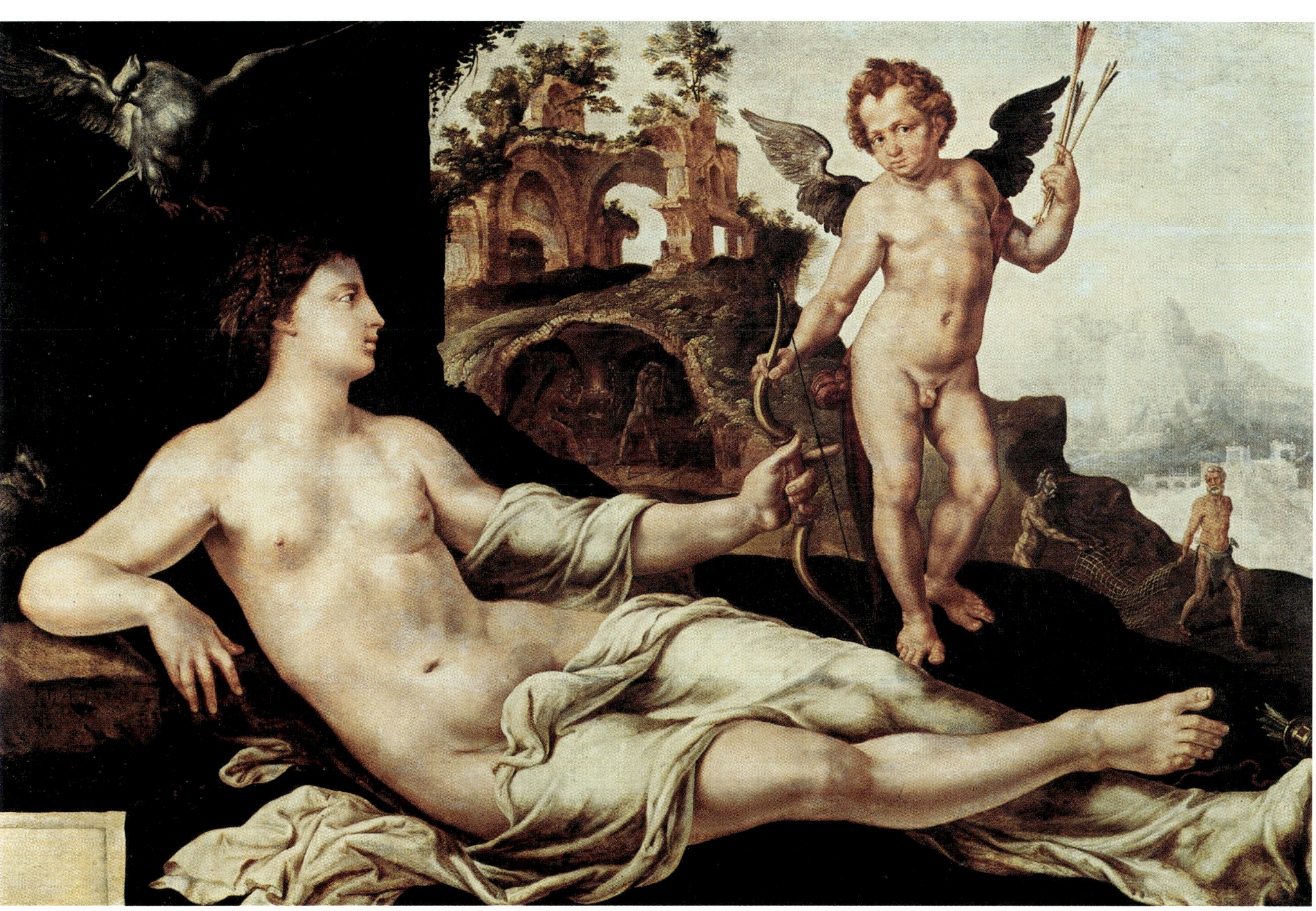

The rise of Antwerp, new capital of northern art

PIETER BRUEGEL
THE ELDER
The Tower of Babel
1563, oil on panel,
114 x 155 cm
Kunsthistorisches
Museum, Vienna

Bruegel's paintings can
be looked at in several
different ways. At first
glance, one admires
the vast spatial layout
of his panels, balanced
by the swarming activ-
ity of numerous figures;
the sheer wealth of
realistic details offers
endless subjects for
observation. Then, con-
sidering the dates of
the works and the gen-
eral developments in
the history of painting,
one must emphasize the
innovative breadth of
the landscapes, the
choice of particular
points of view, the abil-
ity to evoke spectacu-
lar atmospheric and
meteorological scenes.
Finally, there is the
wise play of metaphors
and allusions used to
illuminate some aspect
of human folly, most
often the futile attempt
to evade the simple,
eternal laws of nature.
During a period of dra-
matic doubts, changes,
and battles, Bruegel
delivers a profoundly
moral message. The
Tower of Babel, millen-
nial symbol of divisive-
ness and vanities, thus
assumes a strong char-
acter of concrete actu-
ality in Europe of the
second half of the six-
teenth century.

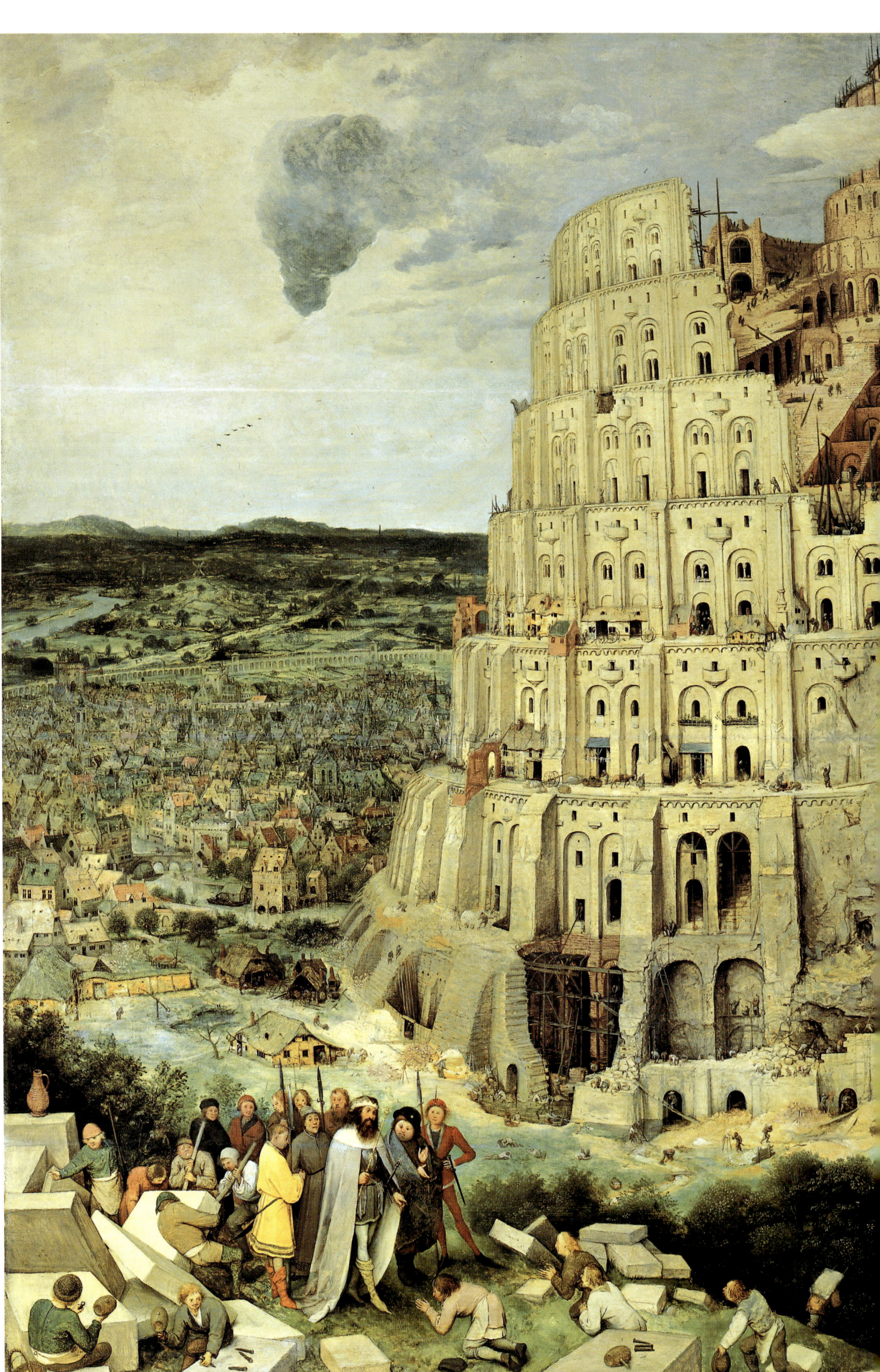

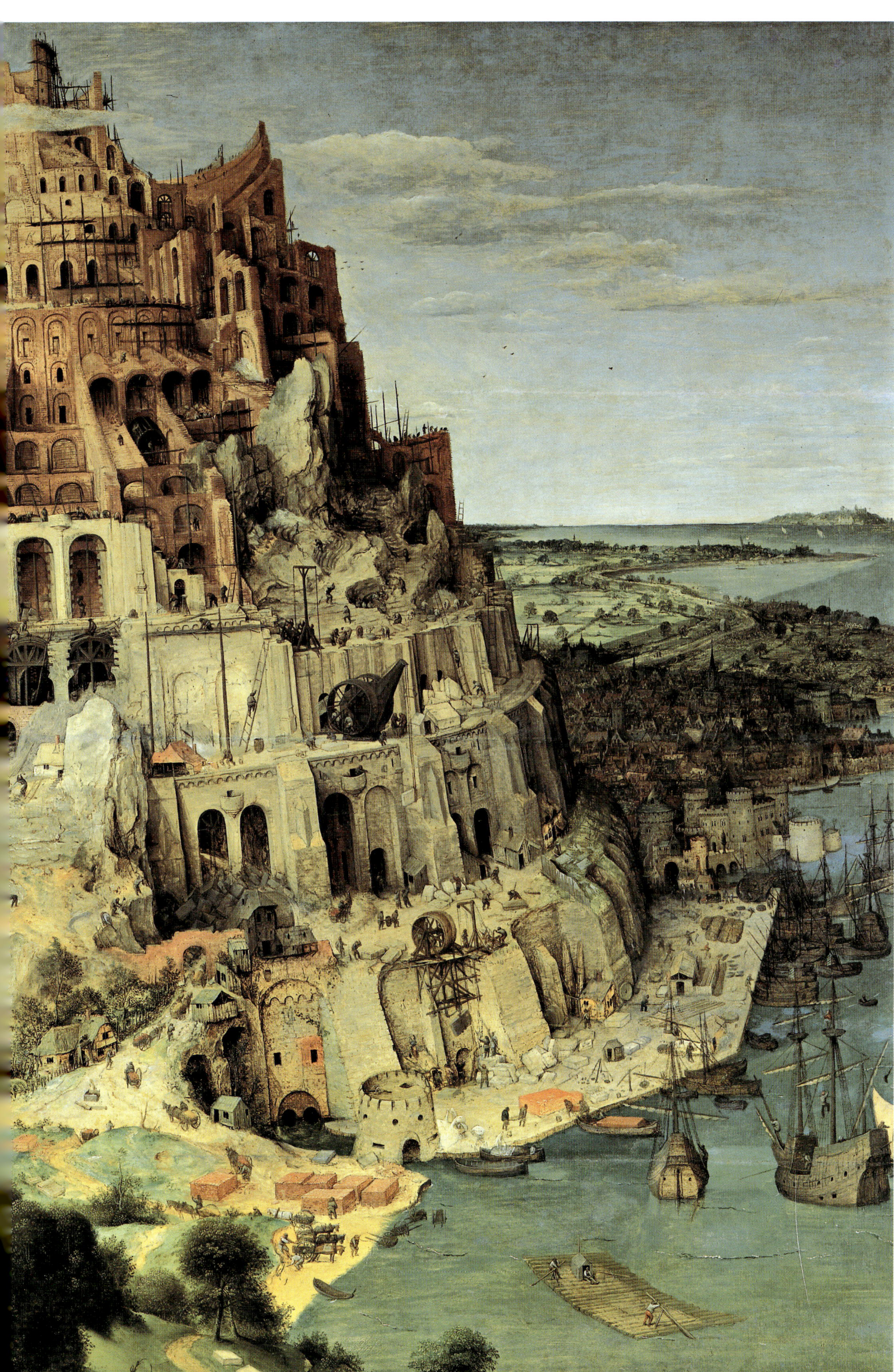

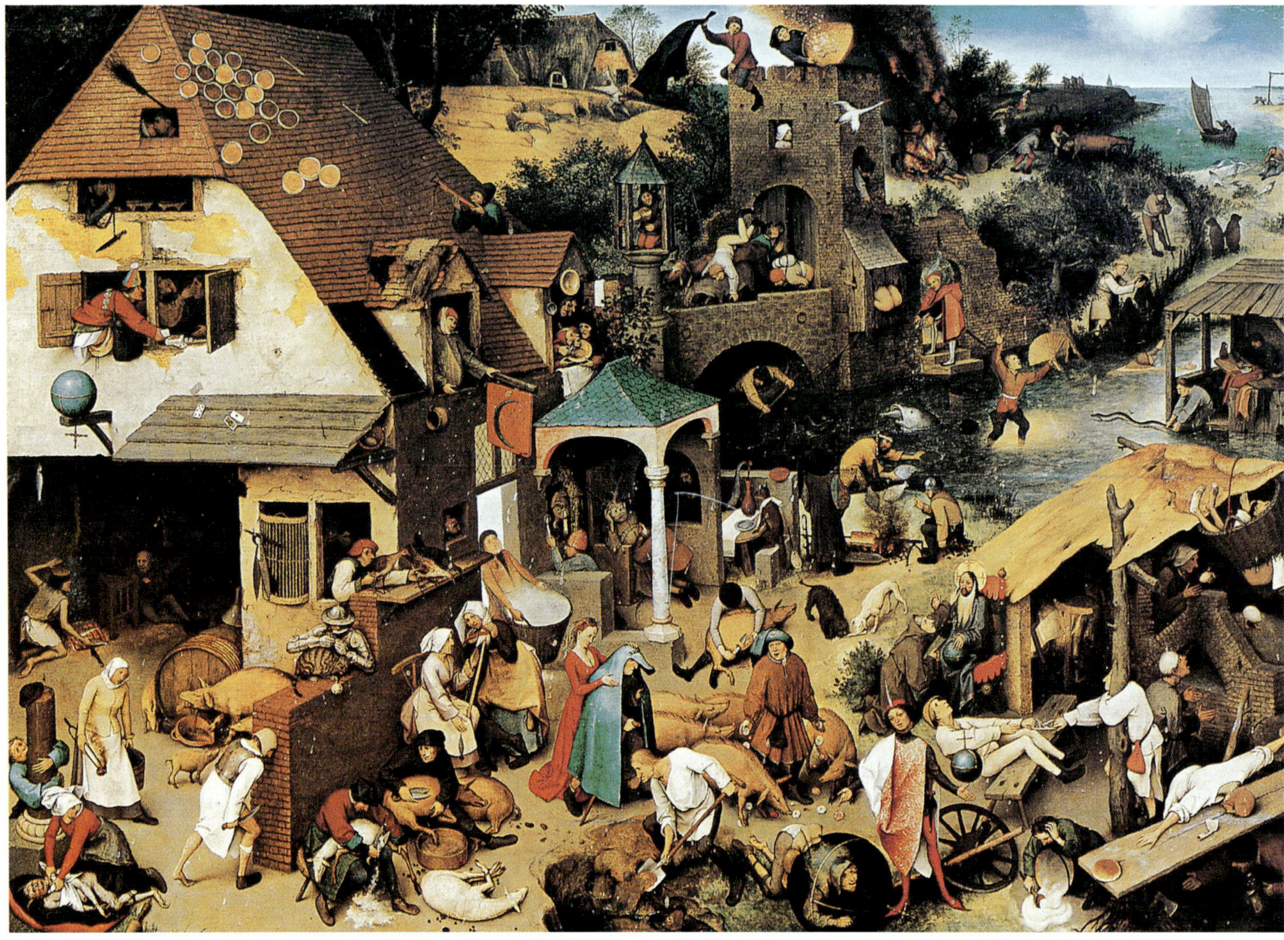

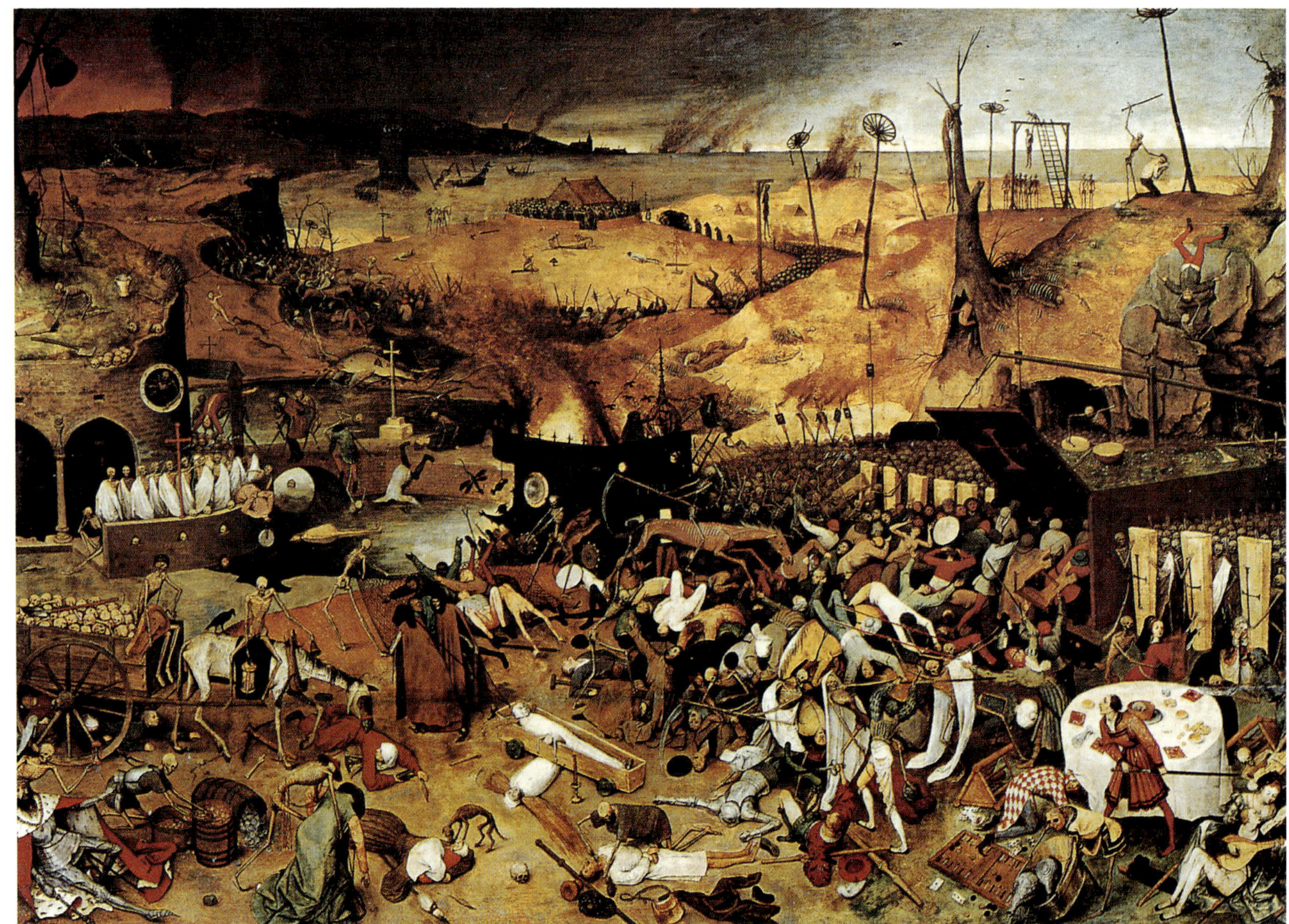

The rise of Antwerp, new capital of northern art

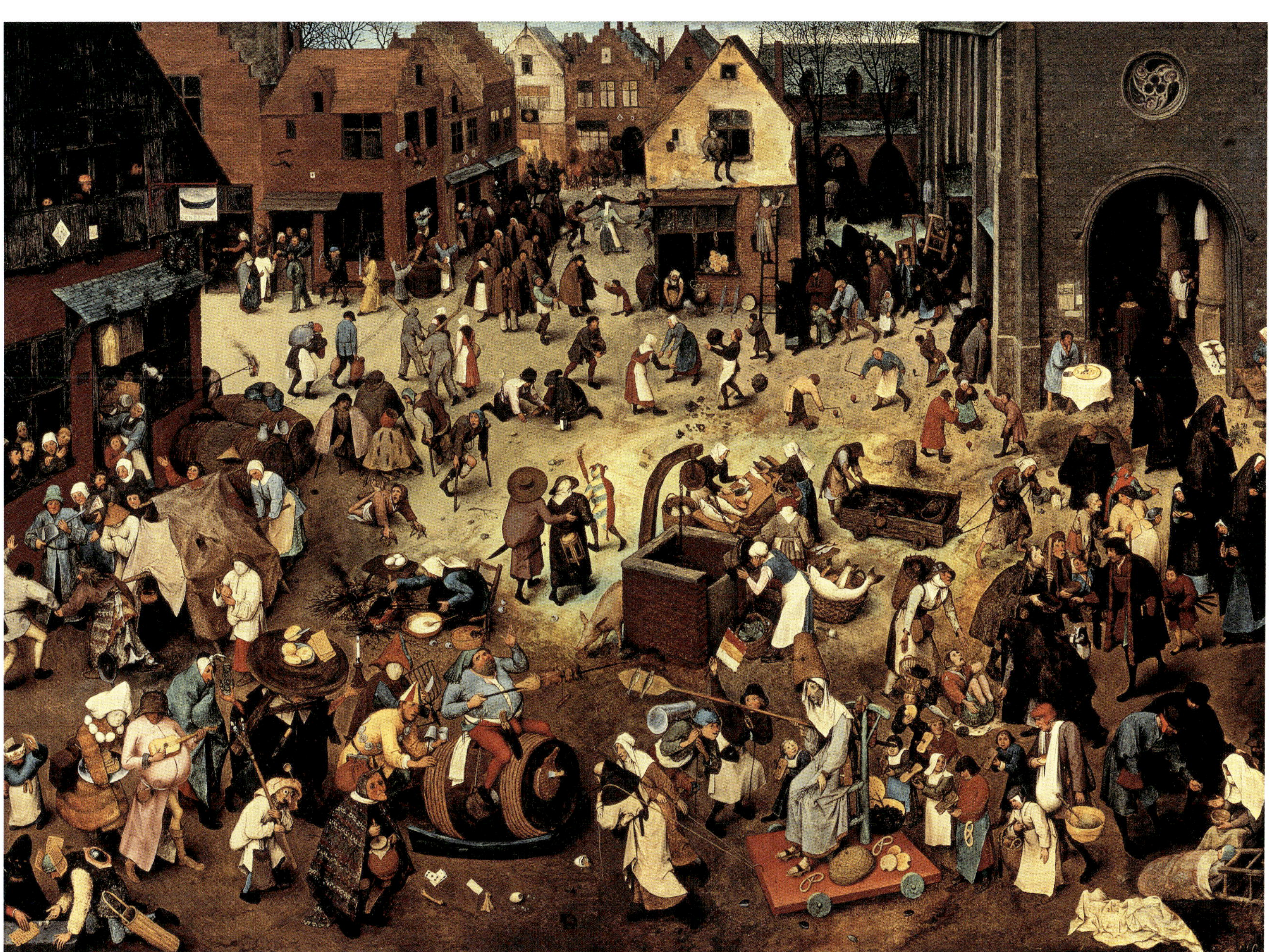

The rise of Antwerp, new capital of northern art

Bruegel presents the scene from a point of view much higher than the immediate foreground and concentrates on the contrast between the white of the snow and the dark shapes of the hunters and their hounds, the trees, and the buildings. Originally from the flat land of Flanders, Bruegel had been impressed by the Alps during his trip to Italy. The memory of snowy mountaintops and rocky peaks helps form an image in which reality and fantasy combine in an extremely evocative way. Few other works succeed in communicating a similar sense of cold air and imminent snow. The skeletal bare branches of the trees project a black pattern against the compact background of the sky. In the valley below, the tiny town seems literally huddled against the foot of the giant mountains. The children playing on the frozen lake are a delightful note of happiness that animates the entire scene with the pulse of life.

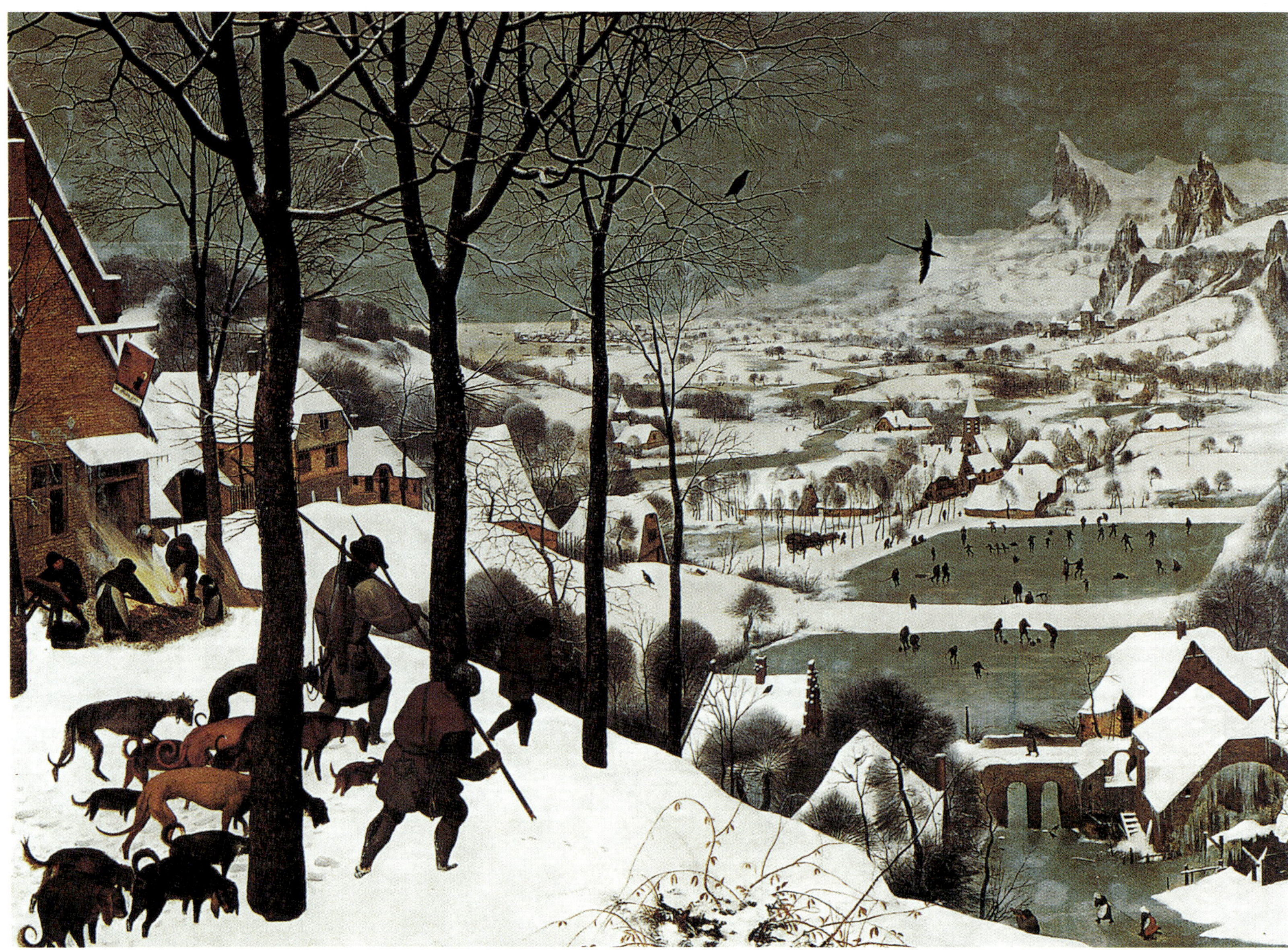

The rise of Antwerp, new capital of northern art

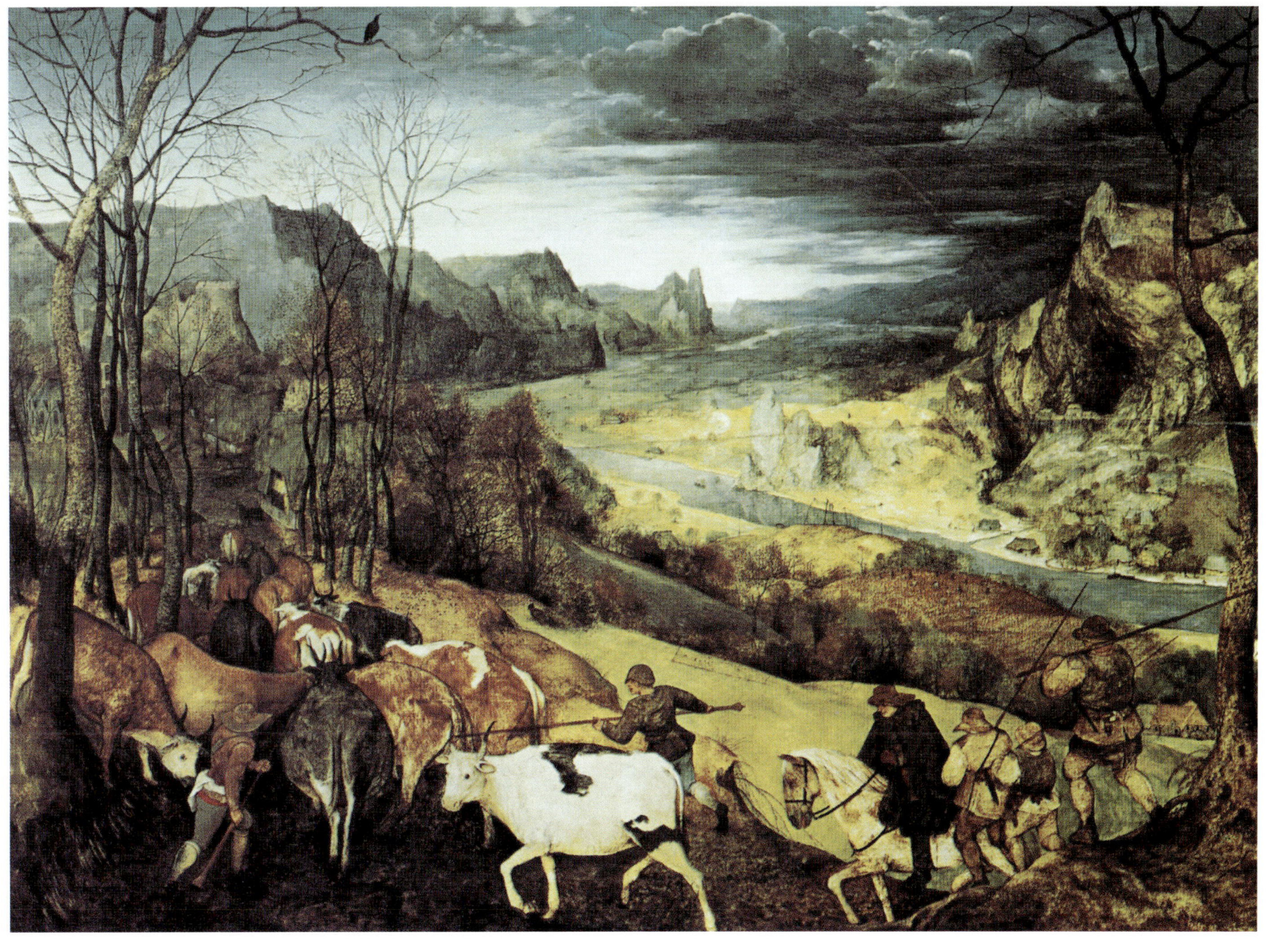

The cycle of *The Seasons*, the most organic and important works of the mature production of Bruegel the Elder, was probably composed of six panels. Only five have survived, among them the three in the Kunsthistorisches Museum in Vienna: *The Gloomy Day*, *Hunters in the Snow*, and this robust *Return of the Herd*. All of them are striking for the exceptional development of the landscape, with broad, harmonious views presented from the same elevated point of view.

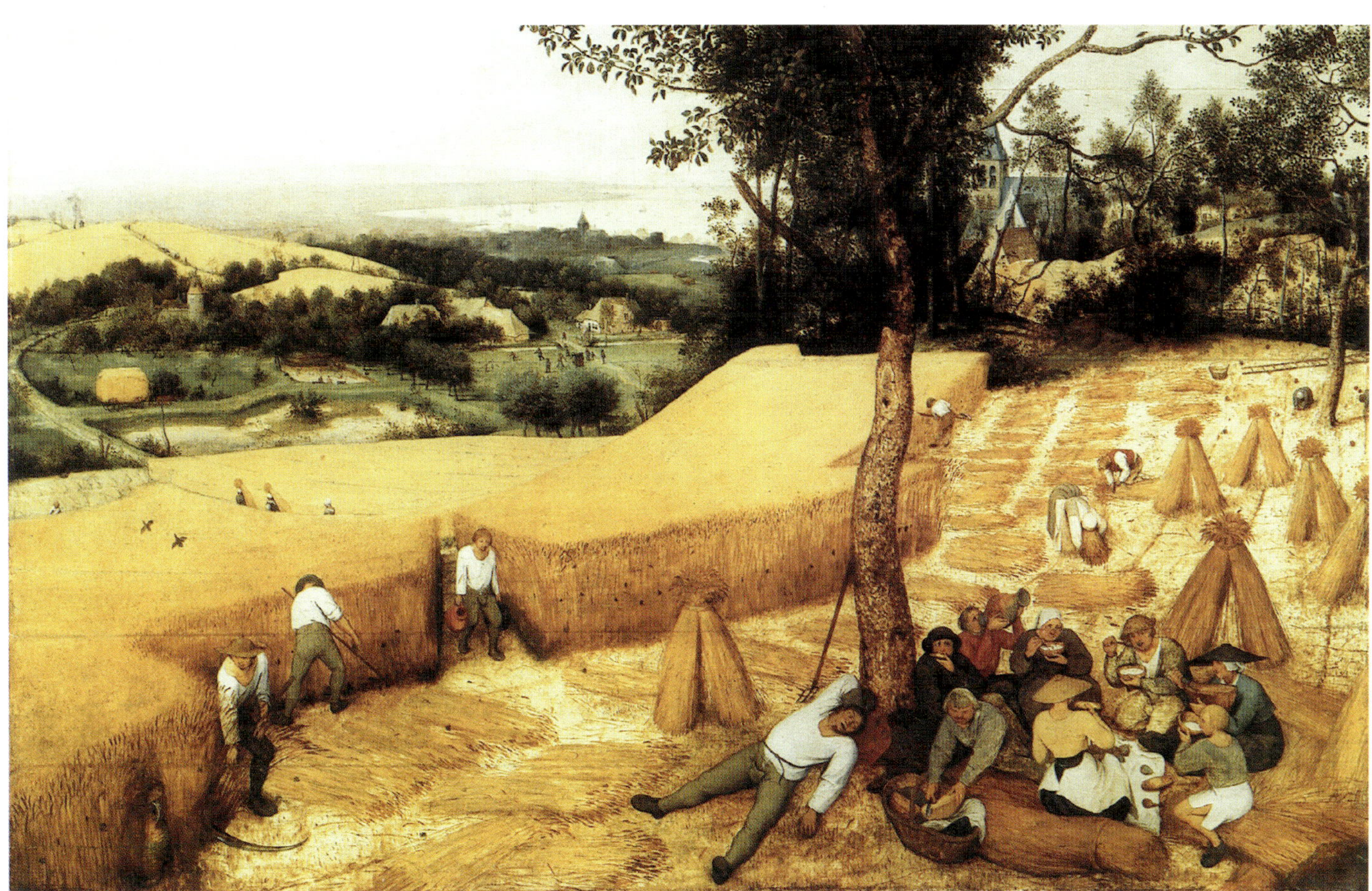

This famous image, dominated by the warm color of the mature grain, is the summer image from the cycle of *The Seasons*, more properly called *The Months*, made for Emperor Rudolf II. The sense of sultry heat, of the weariness and thirst of the resting peasants, contrasts with the golden glow of the crops, while the eye moves farther and farther into a panoramic view of dramatic depth.

The rise of Antwerp, new capital of northern art

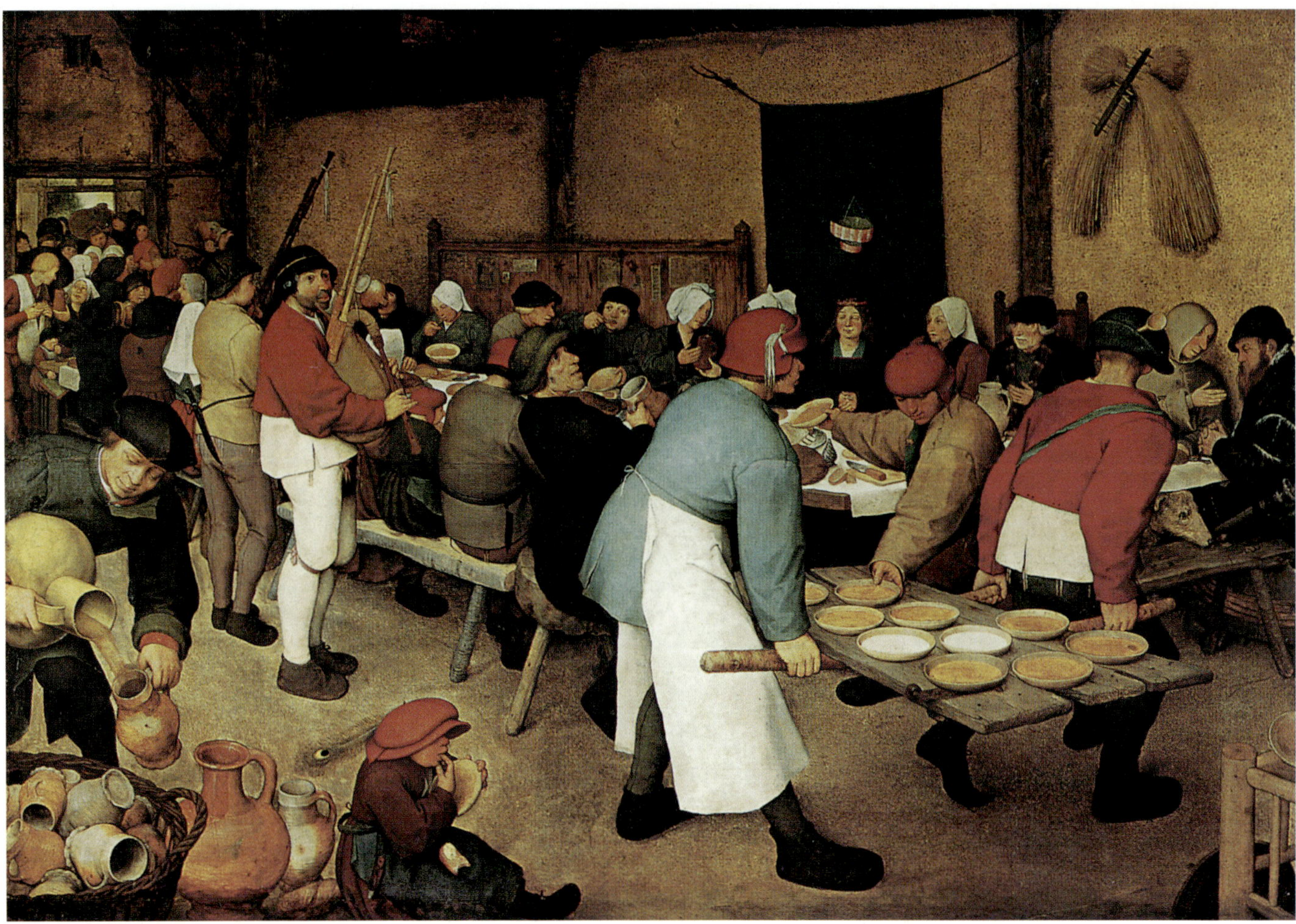

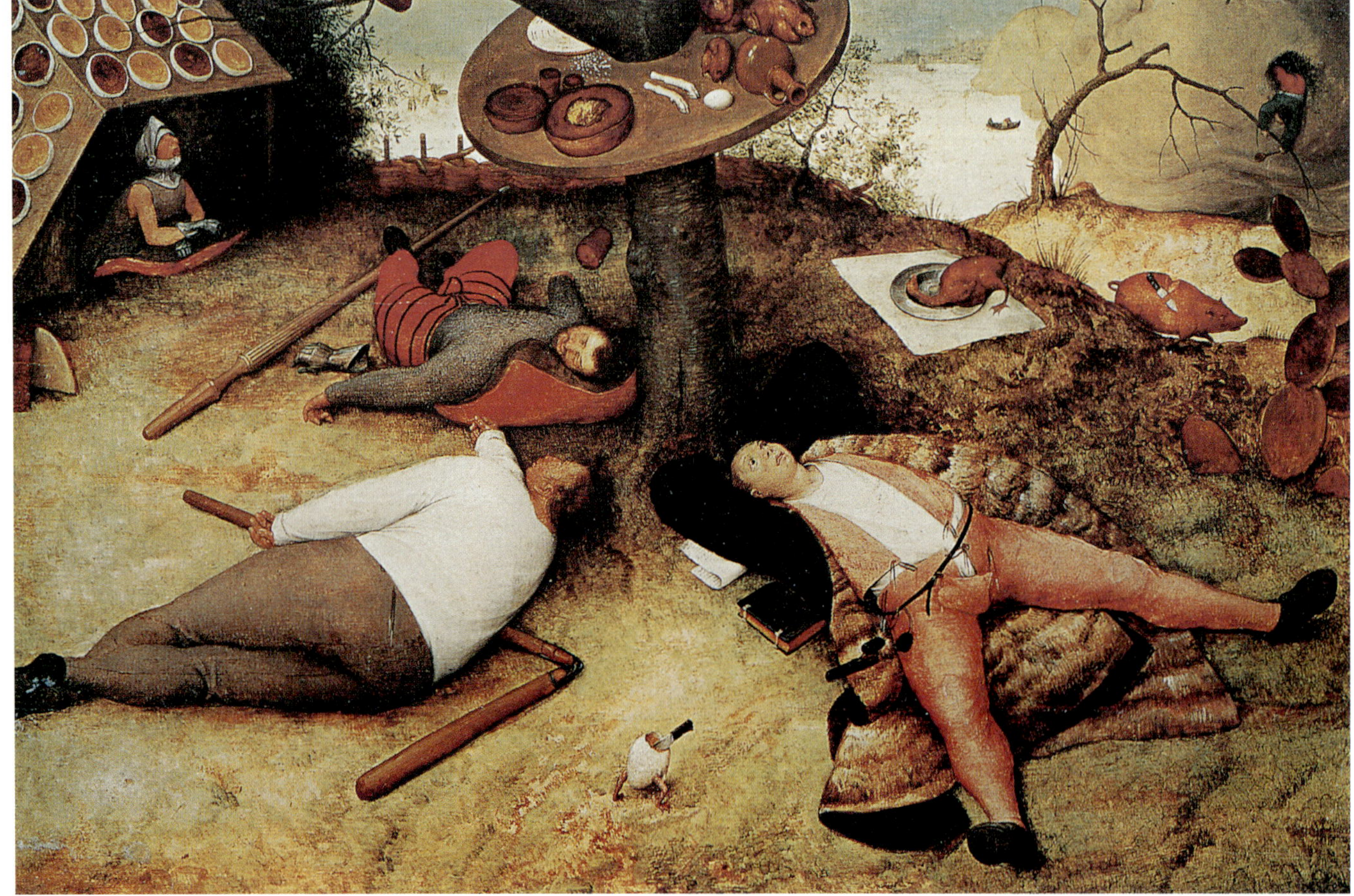

The rise of Antwerp, new capital of northern art

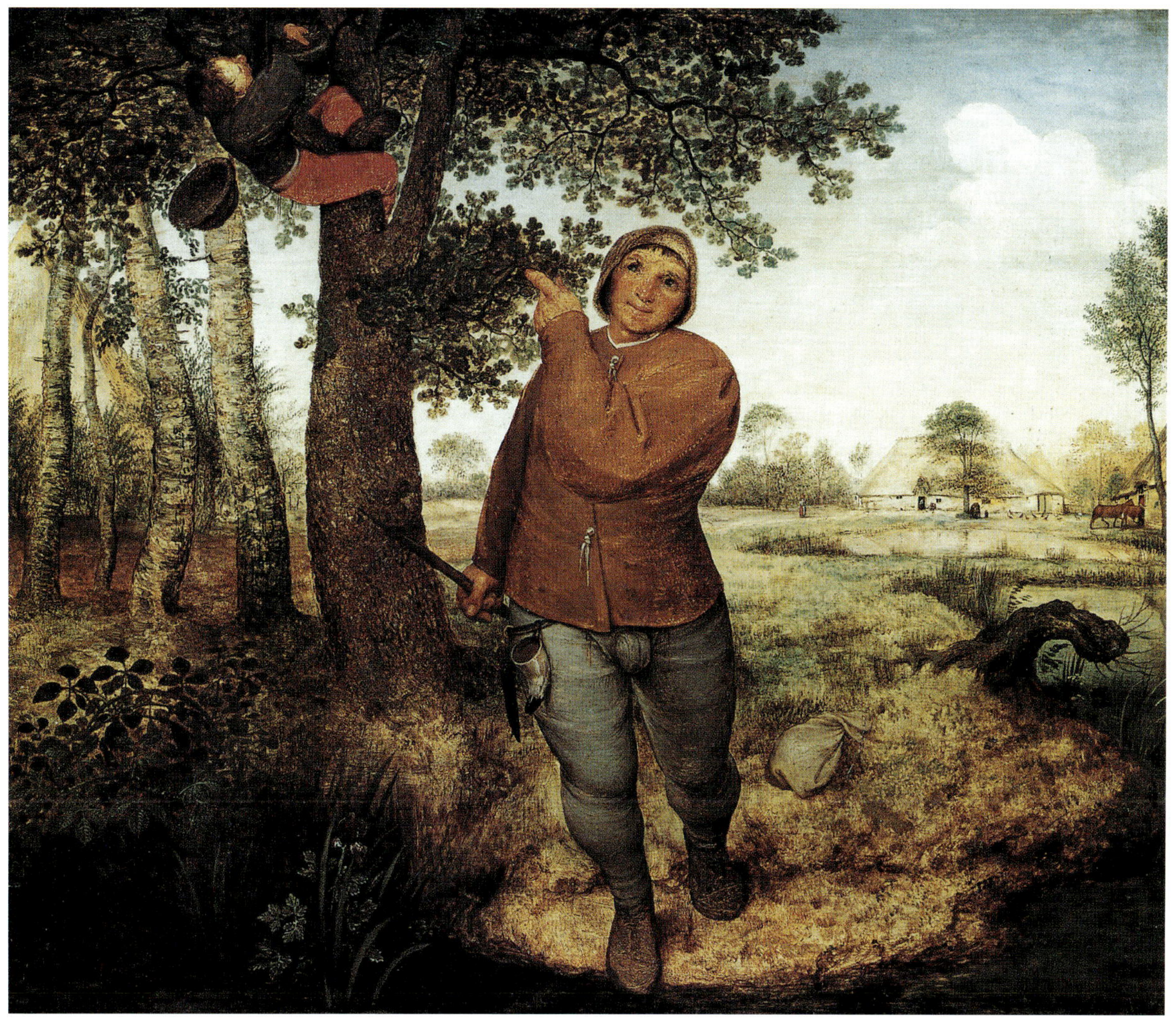

PIETER BRUEGEL
THE ELDER
Peasant and the Birdnester
1568, oil on panel,
59 x 68 cm
Kunsthistorisches
Museum, Vienna

Like many other works by Bruegel, this painting is based on an idiomatic expression from the peasant world. The boy climbing the tree to get at nests is risking a ruinous fall. The simplicity of the story, presented against an agrarian background, hides some important aspects of artistic culture. Bruegel, confirming his position as one of the most innovative landscape painters of the European Renaissance, matches all the colors to the full range of browns, obtaining an effect of light that freely circulates in the painting. The massive figure of the peasant walking toward the viewer is a sort of rustic and affable take on the majestic Michelangelesque models, almost a parody of classical models observed while bored or distracted during a trip to Italy.

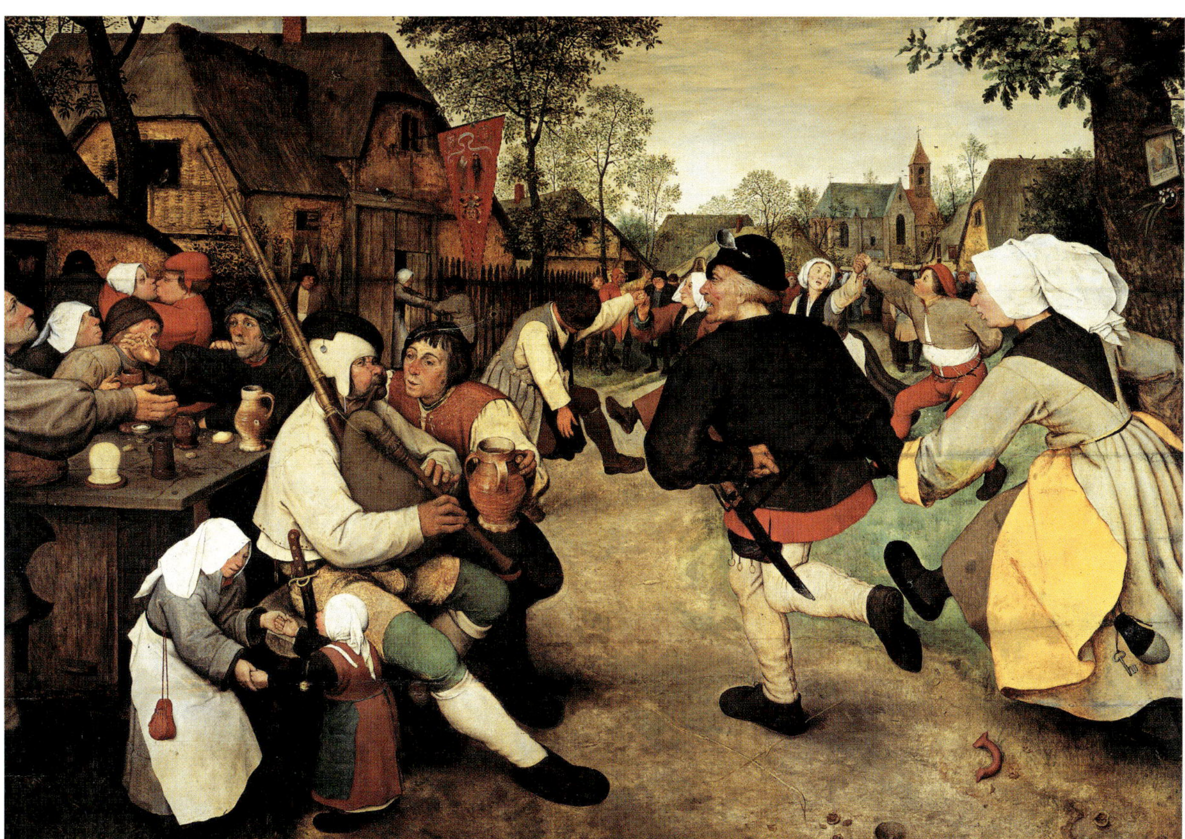

PIETER BRUEGEL
THE ELDER
Peasant Dance
circa 1568,
oil on panel,
114 x 164 cm
Kunsthistorisches
Museum, Vienna

The rise of Antwerp, new capital of northern art

The scenes of heaped-up abundance presented to the viewer by Dutch painters can be interpreted as metaphorical images of the exceptional growth of Europe's most advanced agricultural economy. Precisely in the second half of the sixteenth century the agrarian technique of triennial crop rotation was introduced to the fields of Holland and Flanders, with immediate results on the production of foodstuffs and, indirectly, on the raising of livestock. There is also a moral aspect to such scenes. Faced with such an overabundance of every kind of food the viewer is amazed, struck dumb, almost embarrassed. There is

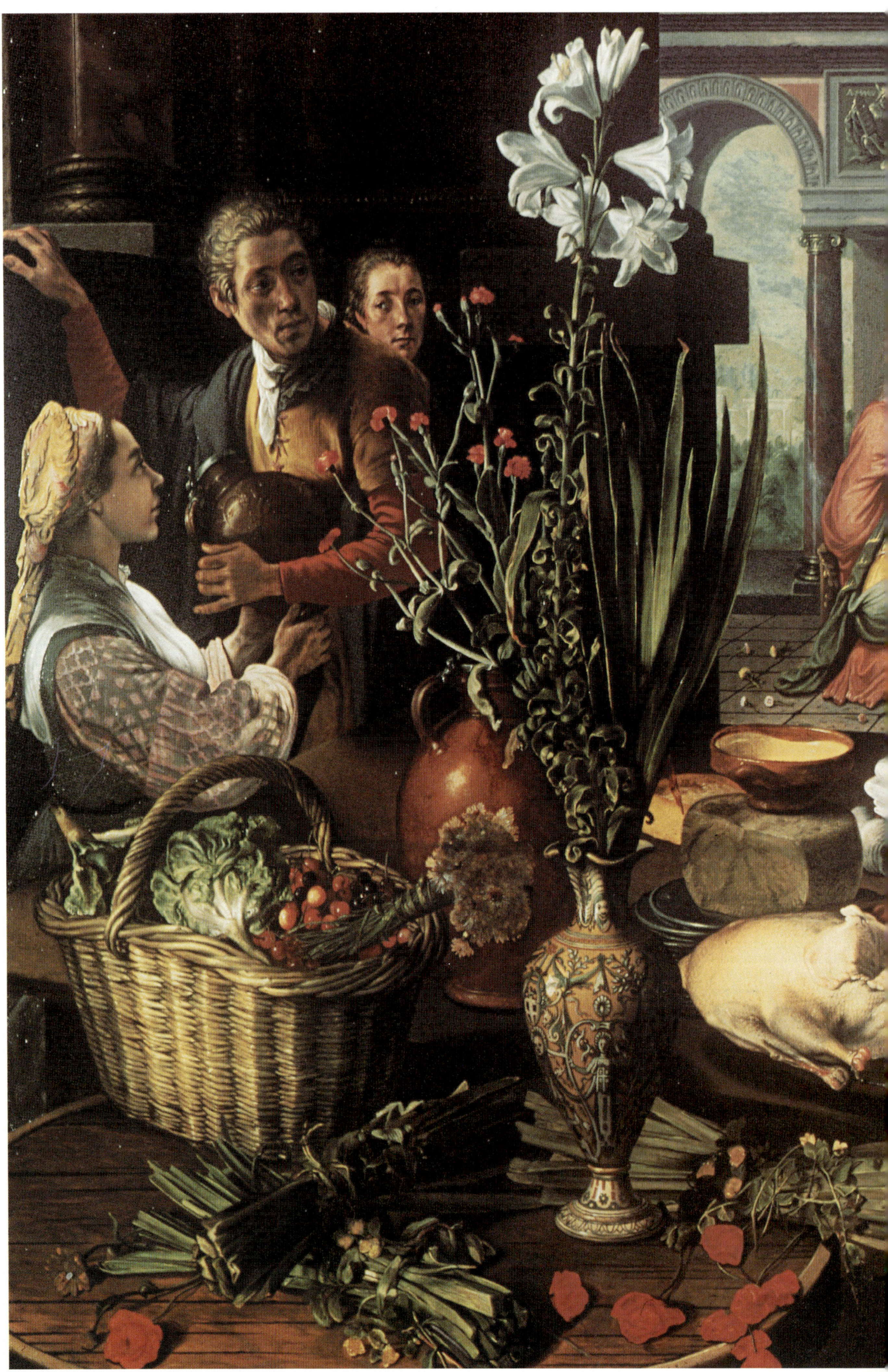

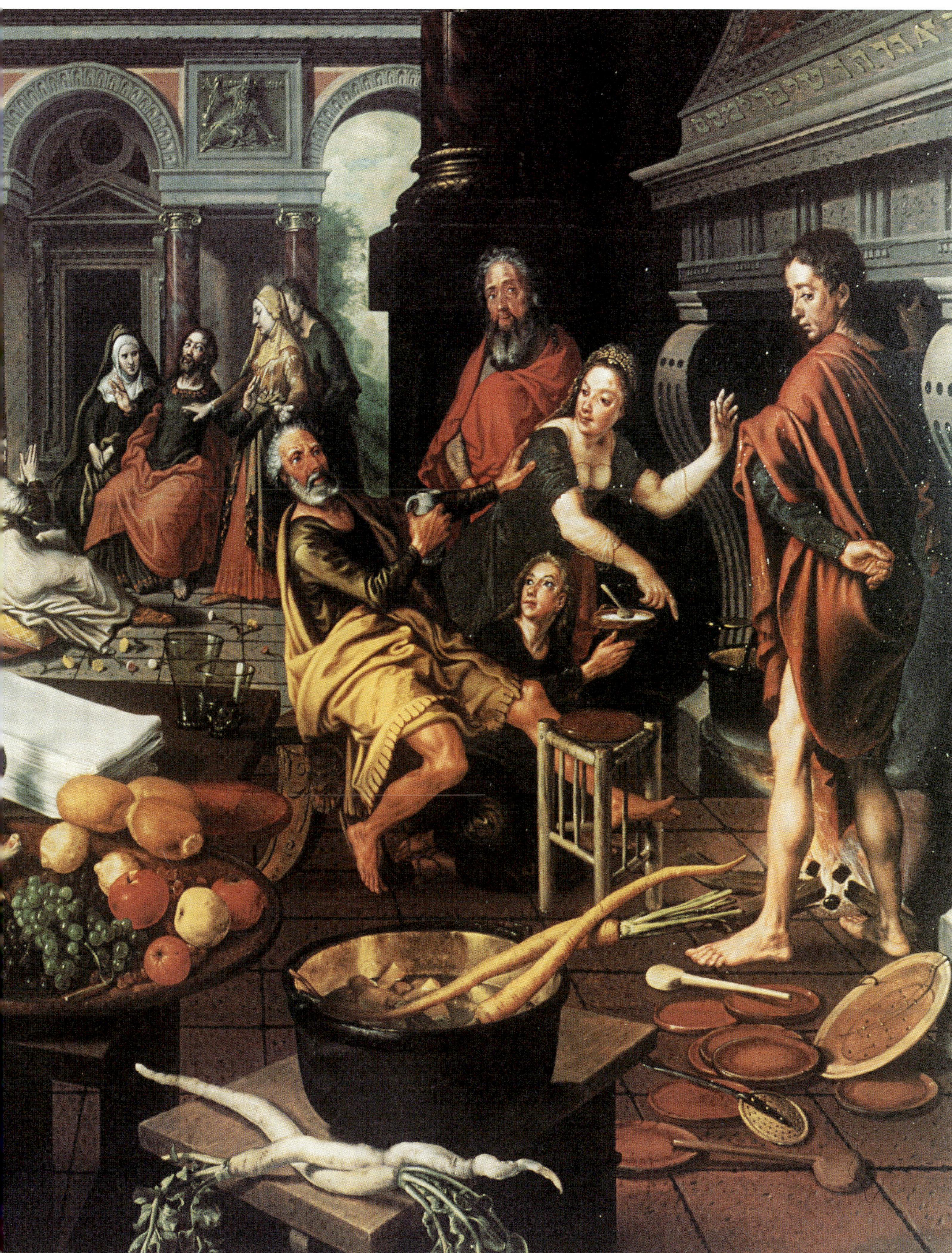

the hint of a sense of guilt, or at least of moral danger, hidden in the possession or in the desire to possess an exaggerated quantity of earthly goods, according to both Catholic doctrine and the principles of austerity of the Calvinists, although the latter looked with kindness on those who achieved prosperity. One can almost hear the echo of the contemporary and extraordinary works by François Rabelais, *Gargantua* and *Pantagruel*, when facing these overflowing displays of every kind of delicacy, always illustrated at the moment of their optimum perfection: perfectly mature fruit, fresh and colorful vegetables, spectacular fish, perfect slices of meat, whole fowls. The echo of such compositions would resonate for many years through the school of Antwerp, right up to Rubens and Jordaens.

he historical situation in the early sixteenth century, with the fall of the duchy of Milan and the turbulent political and military events in northern Italy, strongly effected the artistic scene in Lombardy, eastern Piedmont, and Emilia, leading these northern areas in the direction of an original version of mainland Venetian art combined with local traditions, a painting style notable for its intense emotions, innovative methods, and in some cases physical realism. This began a period of dynamic and profound change, with the rise of an independent, broadly speaking "Lombard" "third way," an alternative to both the developments in the "modern manner" of central Italy and the exaltation of color promoted in Venice by Titian. All during the same period, Lorenzo Lotto in Bergamo, Gaudenzio Ferrari in Varallo, Correggio in Parma, and a group of Brescian masters proposed a certain style of painting, and while it did not lead to the creation of a unitary "school" it nevertheless, over the period of a couple of generations, provided the invaluable material for the profound renewal of the figurative arts that occurred at the end of the sixteenth century.

As always during this period, the figure of Leonardo da Vinci was there in the background, looming over everyone. But while Leonardo's example inhibited the masters of the Milan area, who dared not take a step

angels in the Santo Spirito Altarpiece (1521) has an explicit relationship to Correggio, while the San Bernardino in Pignolo Altarpiece of the same period fashions the group of figures into a dynamic scene of striking imme-

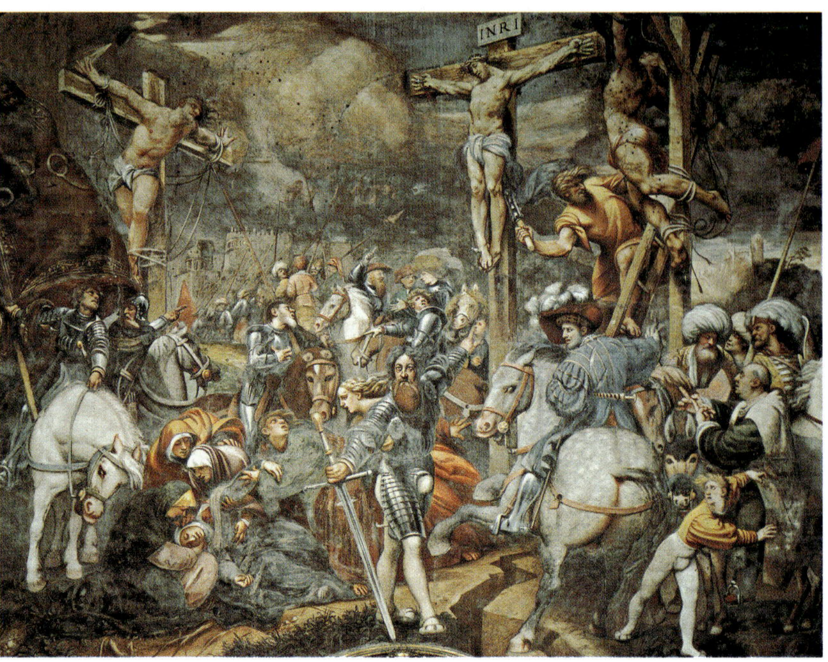

The "other Renaissance"

beyond faithful imitation, it proved extremely stimulating and dialectical for the leading artists of the broader area of the Po valley. Lorenzo Lotto spent the central part of his career, from 1513 to 1526, in Bergamo, and that chronological arc is marked by a series of memorable works, of great expressive liberty, full of original solutions.

The commission that originally brought Lotto to Bergamo was the great Martinengo Altarpiece, today in the church of San Bartolommeo, commissioned in 1513 and completed in 1516, an example of wonderful compositional power, strong originality in the play of light, the symbolic references, and the use of perspective. Lotto's later Bergamo altarpieces confirm both his eccentricity compared to the leading Italian art centers and his ability to absorb and interpret new stimuli. The flight of multicolor

diacy. In parallel, Lotto developed his own ability as a portraitist, seeking to bring to light the interior image of his figures, making for a subtle interpretation of character that involves the painter and the viewer in a shared experience. Even in the absence of supporting documents, it seems practically certain that Lotto had some contact with Holbein. In the frescoes he made in 1524 in the oratory of the Villa Suardi in Trescore Balneario, in the Bergamo region, Lotto used ingenious expressive devices to create a unity of reading among the episodes in a complex iconographic program. In the *Stories of St. Barbara* from that series, the row of separate buildings, snatches of landscape, and urban settings—all presented with striking realism—irresistibly recall the itinerary suggested by the Sacro Monte ("holy mountain") of Varallo, which in

The "other Renaissance" in northern Italy

those same years was receiving its decisive impulse thanks to Gaudenzio Ferrari.

Gaudenzio was certainly one of the most interesting and most innovative figures of the sixteenth century in northern Italy. Far from closing himself in a marginal dimension, he set off from Valduggia and opened himself to a wide-ranging apprenticeship, combining experiences in various artistic settings in Milan during the closing years of the fifteenth century, motifs derived from Albrecht Dürer and the Danubian painters, and the important results of a trip to central Italy and Rome, perhaps taken in the company of Bramantino, in 1508–09. The stay in Rome shows up in the precocious introduction in his works of references to Perugino and Raphael, during the period when they were beginning work on the Stanza della Segnatura; these references are intelligently and originally integrated with a strong interest in the problems of linear perspective as well as in the new images of classical art provided by the most recent archaeological discoveries. A few years later, beginning in 1517, Gaudenzio took over direction of the work on the

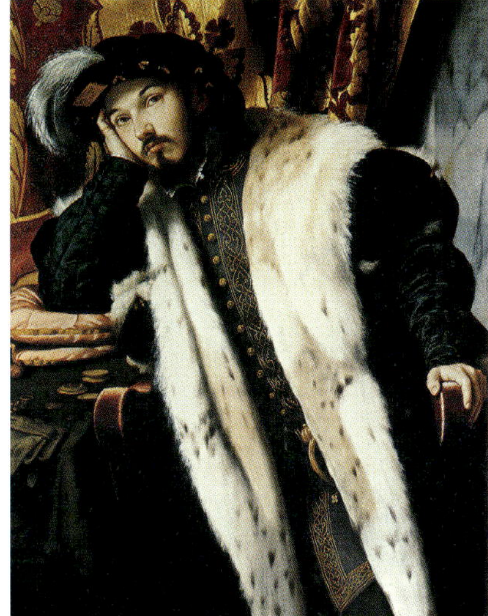

In those same years three artists of almost the same age emerged from the Brescian school. Although their careers followed different routes they had in common a certain realistic interpretation of the Venetian style: Girolamo Romani, called Romanino; Alessandro Bonvicino, known as Moretto (da Brescia); and Giovanni Girolamo Savoldo. Romanino's complex youthful experiences put him in contact with the art of Cremona and Ferrara; most of all, he was one of the first painters to intuit the formidable message of Titian, whose Paduan frescoes he admired. His Santa Giustina Altarpiece (Museo Civico, Padua), of 1513, is an explicit homage to Titian, although it also includes memories of the Lombard figurative culture, especially in the Bramante-style architecture of the barrel vault above the figures. After taking part, around 1520, in the decoration of the central nave of the cathedral of Cremona with moving scenes of the *Passion*, Romanino turned his activity to Brescia and the small towns in the surrounding valleys, where he left panels and frescoes of great expressive power with an antiaristocratic tone and a blunt sense

Moretto, *Portrait of a Youth (Count Sciarra Martinengo Cesaresco)*, 1530–40; National Gallery, London

in northern Italy

Sacro Monte in Varallo. The Sacro Monte rises on the summit of the wooded cliff that towers over Varallo; for at least a century and a half it was the model for a series of similar complexes in Piedmont and Lombardy in which architecture, painting, and sculpture are blended within a natural setting in an equilibrium between sincerely expressed pathos at a popular level and elegantly expressive art. From the very beginning, the buildings of the Sacro Monte hosted wooden statues, sometimes accompanied by scenes frescoed on the surrounding walls. Gaudenzio further developed this arrangement using his own ideas to give the whole a spectacular theatrical impact, drawing the pilgrims into a sort of sacred mystery, thanks to the forceful drama generated by the complementary action of the protagonists (the sculptures) and the "choir" of the bystanders (the figures frescoed on the walls), a drama in which the visitor soon becomes personally involved. Between 1520 and circa 1528 Gaudenzio completed the two chapels of the *Journey of the Magi* and the *Calvary*, in which the movements and gestures of the painted and carved figures guide the visitor on a visual and emotional route in a thoroughly innovative way.

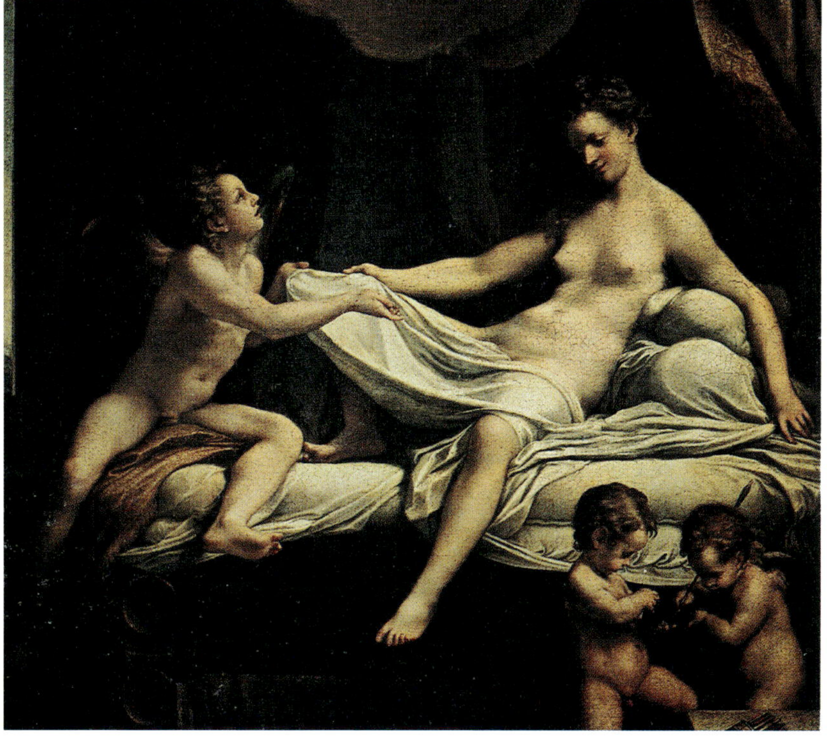

Correggio, *Danaë*, 1531–32; Galleria Borghese, Rome

The "other Renaissance" in northern Italy

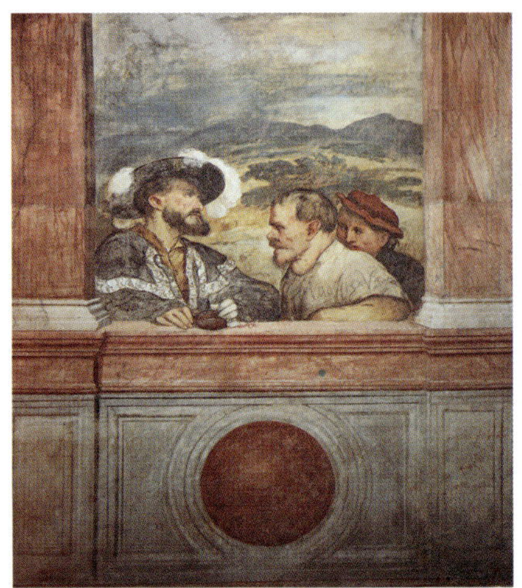

Girolamo Romanino, *Payment of the Workers*, 1532; Buonconsiglio Castle, Trent

of reality in the gestures, dress, and physical types. There was then the prestigious commission from Bishop Bernardino Clesio, who called him to Trent, where, just after 1530, he made the fresco decoration in Buonconsiglio Castle, together with the Ferraraese artist Dosso Dossi, presenting unusual versions of the classical themes of the great Renaissance aristocratic decoration.

Moretto worked primarily in Brescia, presenting himself as the heir to the tradition of Vincenzo Foppa, updated with learning from Titan and Lorenzo Lotto. While also making a name for himself as an incisive portraitist (Giovanni Battista Moroni trained in his school), Moretto was a prolific and at times brilliant creator of sacred iconography and, in the later period of his career, one of the first artists to provide the new interpretation of religious imagery called for as a figurative response to the Protestant Reformation. Author with Romanino of the cycle of Eucharistic canvases of the chapel of the Sacramento in San Giovanni Evangelista (1521–24), Moretto worked in a calm style in which the typically "Lombard" references to natural reality are mitigated by a formal elegance combining Venetian elements, Flemish notions, and even references to Raphael, encountered by way of the engravings by Marcantonio Raimondi. In the Brescian altarpieces, however, it is the reference to Titian that prevails.

Around 1520 Giovanni Girolamo Savoldo set himself up in Venice, and it was there that he spent the rest of his life, although he stayed in touch with his Brescian and Lombard patrons. While taking an active part in the artistic scene of the lagoon, Savoldo nonetheless continued to give preference to Lombard-style naturalism, which he combined to a personal way with northern-style luministic and atmospheric effects. The results were paintings of great contemplative suggestion in which one senses the memory of Giorgione and, at the same time, a preview of Caravaggio. This is especially true in the medium-size canvases, those Savoldo made for private collectors.

Despite its physical proximity to Brescia, the city of Mantua occupies a completely singular place in terms of art. While Brescia developed a religiously renewed art directed at the real world, Mantua, the noble city of the Gonzagas, carried on the fascinating and sophisticated style of a High Renaissance court. The director of the artistic scene in Mantua in the early sixteenth century was the marchesa Isabella d'Este, whose correspondence with various painters offers one of the most interesting glimpses of the relationship between patrons and artists during the High Renaissance. In her *studiolo*, decorated over a span of more than three decades, Isabella assembled a collection of paintings of mythological and allegorical subjects (today in the Louvre), including works by Mantegna, Perugino, Lorenzo Costa, and finally Correggio, whose training took place in Mantua. Like her brother Alfonso d'Este, duke of Ferrara, Isabella was a sensitive patron of Titian, who visited Mantua many times between the third and fourth decades of the sixteenth century, leaving various portraits of members of the court as well as the lost cycle of the "Twelve Caesars," idealized portraits of Roman emperors, imitated many times by many artists throughout the entire sixteenth century.

Beginning in 1520, Isabella's artistic activity was joined by that of her son, the ambitious Federico. Having received a classical-oriented cultural education in Rome, Federico Gonzaga intended to bring the court's art around to the "modern" style. In 1524 Giulio Romano, direct heir to the workshop and style of Raphael, arrived in Mantua and began what Vasari called "various, rich, and copious" activity. For more than twenty years Giulio Romano built or adjusted the most important aristocratic or religious buildings in Mantua and its territory, decorating them with stuccos and frescoes of wonderful inventiveness. His most complete and famous undertaking was Palazzo Te (1527–34), Federico Gonzaga's "pleasure palace," built on the edge of the historical city and endowed with outstanding characteristics, both from the architectonic point of view and from that of its pictorial decoration. By giving each of the spaces and rooms of the complex a different theme, Romano turned a stroll through the palace into a series of wonderful surprises in which the profane decoration was opened to the most audacious devices of perspective and light, with thrilling combinations of stuccos and frescoes.

Mantua was also the departure point of another great painter, Correggio (born Antonio Allegri but known by the name of his birthplace, the town of Correggio in Emilia), who before establishing his activity in Parma got his training in the

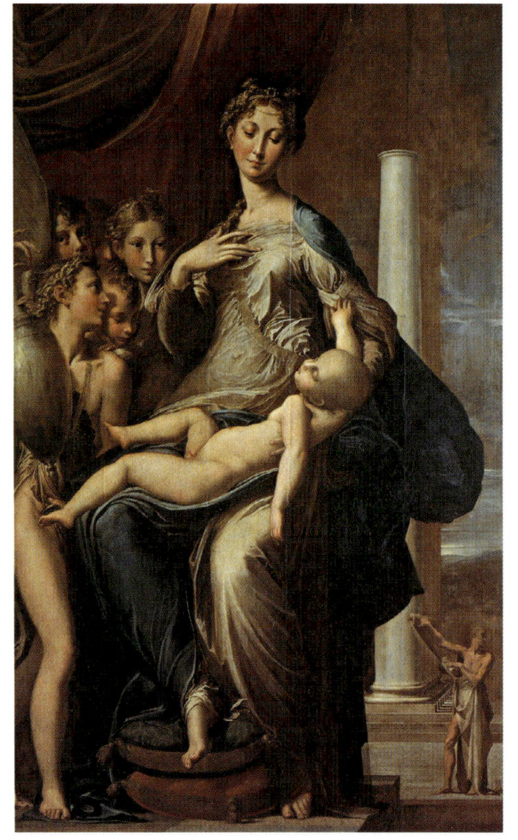

Parmigianino, *Madonna of the Long Neck*, 1534–40; Galleria degli Uffizi, Florence

The "other Renaissance" in northern Italy

Po valley region at the close of the sixteenth century. After early apprenticeship in Emilia he moved to Mantua, where he was among the last pupils of the aging Mantegna; he then developed, in the second decade of the sixteenth century, a free interpretation of the works of Leonardo. Knowledge of Raphael led him to a classical "modern"-style, with narrative fluidity, which was mediated by Leonardesque shading, the perfect control of perspective, and a mellow sense of light and color. Correggio's activity in Parma is marked by three successive fresco cycles, those in the Camera di San Paolo, the private room of the abbess of the convent of San Paolo (1518); the decoration of the church of San Giovanni Evangelista (1520–23); and the *Assumption of the Virgin* in the dome of the cathedral (1526–30). The artist distanced himself from fifteenth-century models with growing determination, thus laying the basis for the development of the great baroque decoration. In the Camera di San Paolo he repeated a motif used by Leonardo and Mantegna, that of an arbor painted on a ceiling, but Correggio took the theme further, inserting leafy oculi in the ceiling from which smiling putti look down, with glimpses of sky behind them. Beneath them he created monochrome lunettes that imitate delicate ancient bas-reliefs, in that way offering a quiet symbiosis between nature and classical myths, in particular, the myth of Diana the Huntress. The decorative program in San Giovanni Evangelista seems like an even greater undertaking, and this despite reworkings and gaps (*The Coronation of the Virgin* from the apse is today in the Pinacoteca Nazionale of Parma; what remains in the church is the figure of the *St. John the Evangelist* in the left transept and, most important of all, the *Vision of St. John the Evangelist on Patmos* in the dome). Correggio entrusted the side parts of this decoration to a group of assistants that included the emerging personality of Parmigianino. In the main scene the painter experimented with a trompe-l'oeil perspective opening in the dome to the open sky, against which the figures stand out. The source of this device can be recognized as the vault of the Camera degli Sposi in Mantua, with the famous oculus by Andrea Mantegna, but the result is completely different. Free of every concern of geometric measurements, the monumental figures of the apostles follow the perimeter of the dome, while the figure of Christ is suspended in the air, at the center, in an unusual chromatic and luminous opening. The frescoes that decorate the pendentives and the dome of the cathedral of Parma became fundamental models for the painting of the seventeenth century and for baroque ceilings. The scene of the *Assumption of the Virgin* takes place in a joyful and festive confusion of angels that spiral upward toward a cloudy sky; the separate figures lose their individuality to participate together in the choral decoration.

Parmigianino shared with Correggio certain contacts in Parma, but his career and his works were very different. As a student of Correggio, he revealed his abundance of gifts in the frescoes of San Giovanni Evangelistsa; in particular, he showed a precocious skill as a draftsman with an interest in visual effects. Like his teacher he was in search of a "new nature" and developed a subtly moralistic and allusive style, replacing Correggio's soft and luminous definition with a sharply graphic definition of forms. The mature work of Parmigianino is distinguished by smooth, tapering, almost unreal forms. In 1524 he decided to move to Rome and make contact with Raphael's former workshop. The date coincides with Giulio Romano's move to Mantua, and the coincidence is important, almost a signal of the beginning of the "northern" version of mannerism. In the artistic setting of the court of Clement VII, he made portraits of refined, clear immobility, and religious paintings of strong mannerist experimentation. After the Sack of Rome in 1527 he spent a few years in Bologna, returning to Parma in 1531 to renew his competition with Correggio. In that city he made the frescoes in the church of Santa Maria della Steccata, based on a stylized classicism. A characteristic feature of his works during these years is the unnatural elongation of figures, which assume almost serpentine poses. During the last years of his short life Parmigianino closed in on himself, dedicating himself to alchemical experiments to the point of fixation and mental disturbance.

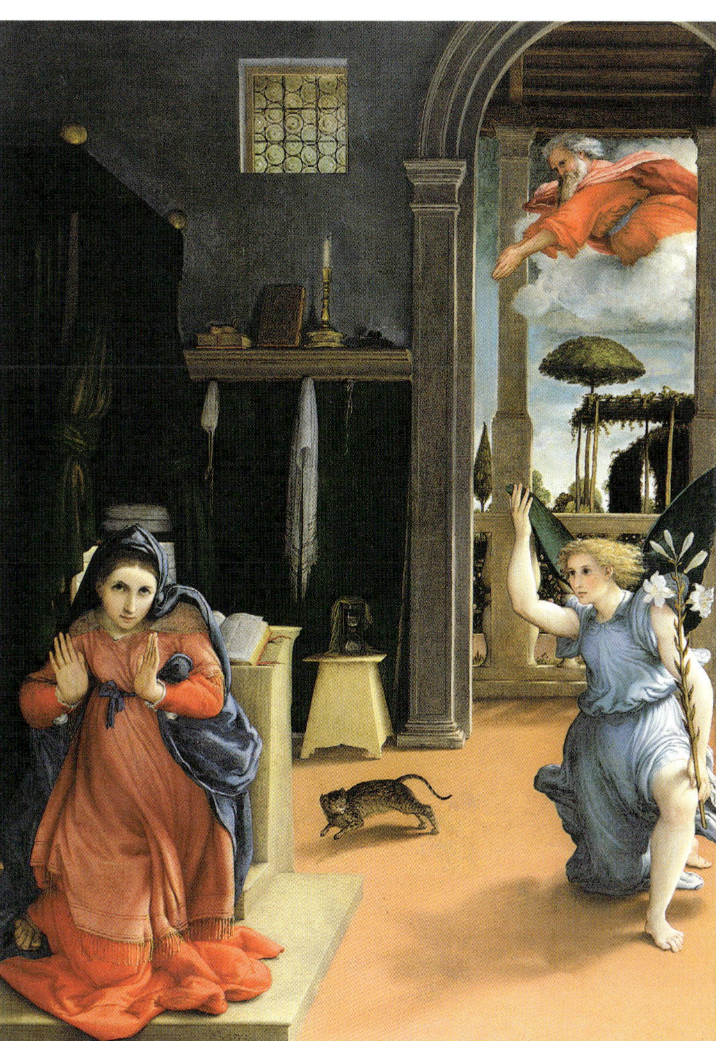

Lorenzo Lotto, *Annunciation,* circa 1527; Pinacoteca Comunale, Recanti

The "other Renaissance" in northern Italy

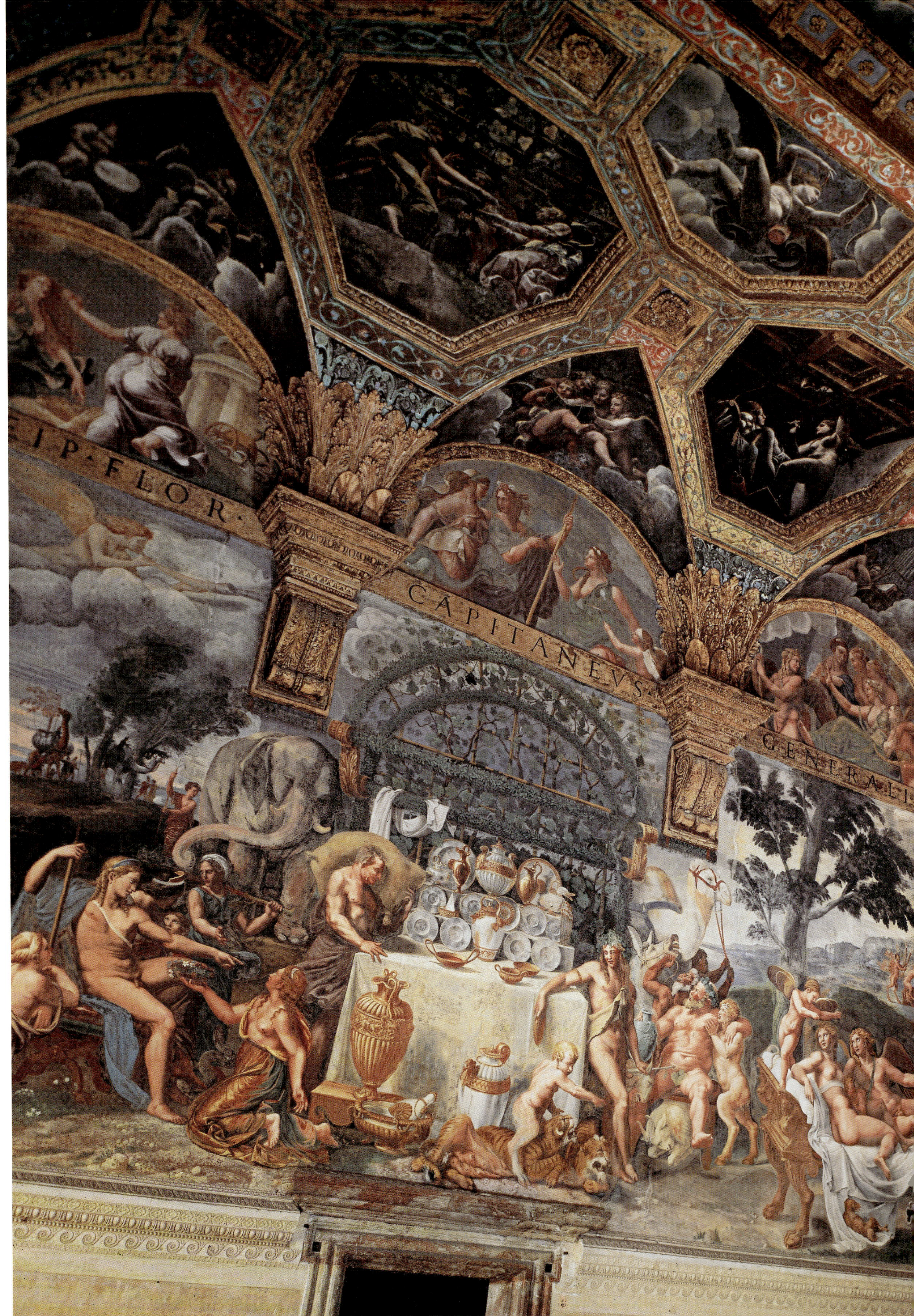

GIULIO ROMANO
**Sala of Cupid
and Psyche**
Overall view
1526–28, fresco
Palazzo Te, Mantua

Built as an amusement place for the court of Federico Gonzaga in a swampy area outside the center of Mantua, Palazzo Te is one of the first large complexes of European mannerism. Work on both the architecture and the pictorial decoration began in 1526, and the palace stands as one of the most fascinating testimonies of Giulio Romano's relationship of with classical architecture, which he employed and "reinvented" as though it were a living language, such that the schemes can be suddenly varied, as in the triglyphs in the courtyard that tend to slip downward, giving the static frieze a new dynamism. The same inventive talent that distinguishes the architectonic appearance of the building is found in the genial solutions adopted in the building's internal decoration, which presents a series of mythological themes,

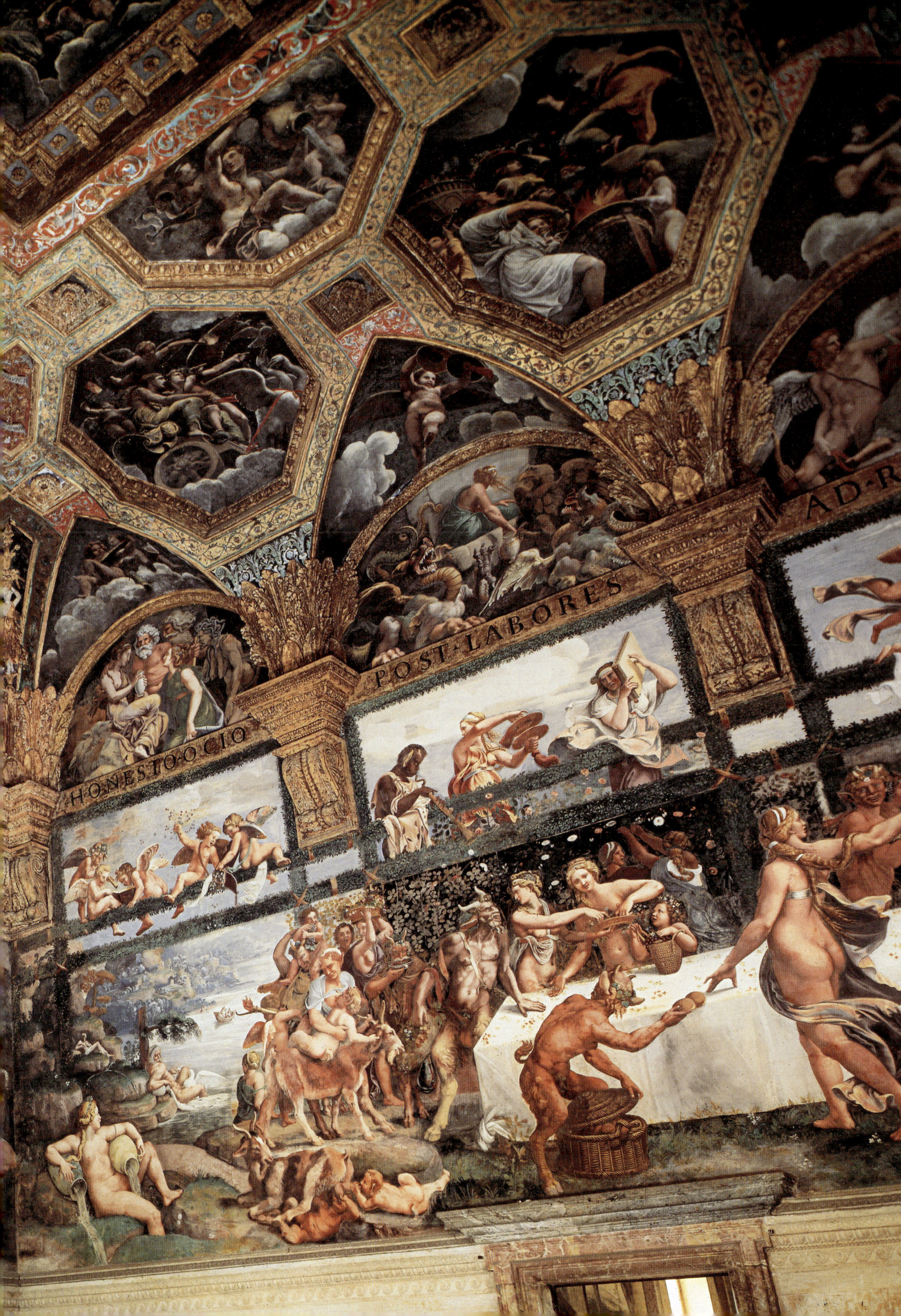

allegorical subjects, and fabulous episodes in which Romano unleashed his tireless imagination, turning every room into a surprise. The Sala of Cupid and Psyche, a pictorial rendition of the text by Apuleius, is one of the richest and important. The fluid sequence of the classical scenes along the walls is contrasted by the ceiling, which is divided into painted compartments loaded with perspective and luministic inventions and refined literary citations. In making the frescoes Romano had the help of a host of assistants and students, who transformed his designs into paintings. In fact, he was the single planner and director of the grand operation. Like Andrea Mantegna, who had served as court painter to the Gonzagas before him, Romano brought the ancient world back to life, but he loaded the gods and heroes with a vitality and passion, a dynamism and an emotional charge, that cannot be found in the more meditative and intellectual images made by his predecessor.

The subject of this portrait is probably the young Trevisan canon Broccardo Malchiostro, future patron of Titian. Lotto alludes to the canon's name by way of a play on words, painting behind him a curtain of "brocade" with thistles (*cardo* in Italian). Secretary of the willful and powerful bishop of Treviso Bernardino de' Rossi, Malchiostro had successfully escaped an attempt on his life, which may explain his somewhat absorbed or worried expression, as though suddenly made aware of the very real dangers in life. The small lamp that gives its name to this painting, visible at the far upper right, a symbol of the fragility of human fate, is probably a further reference to the dramatic event.

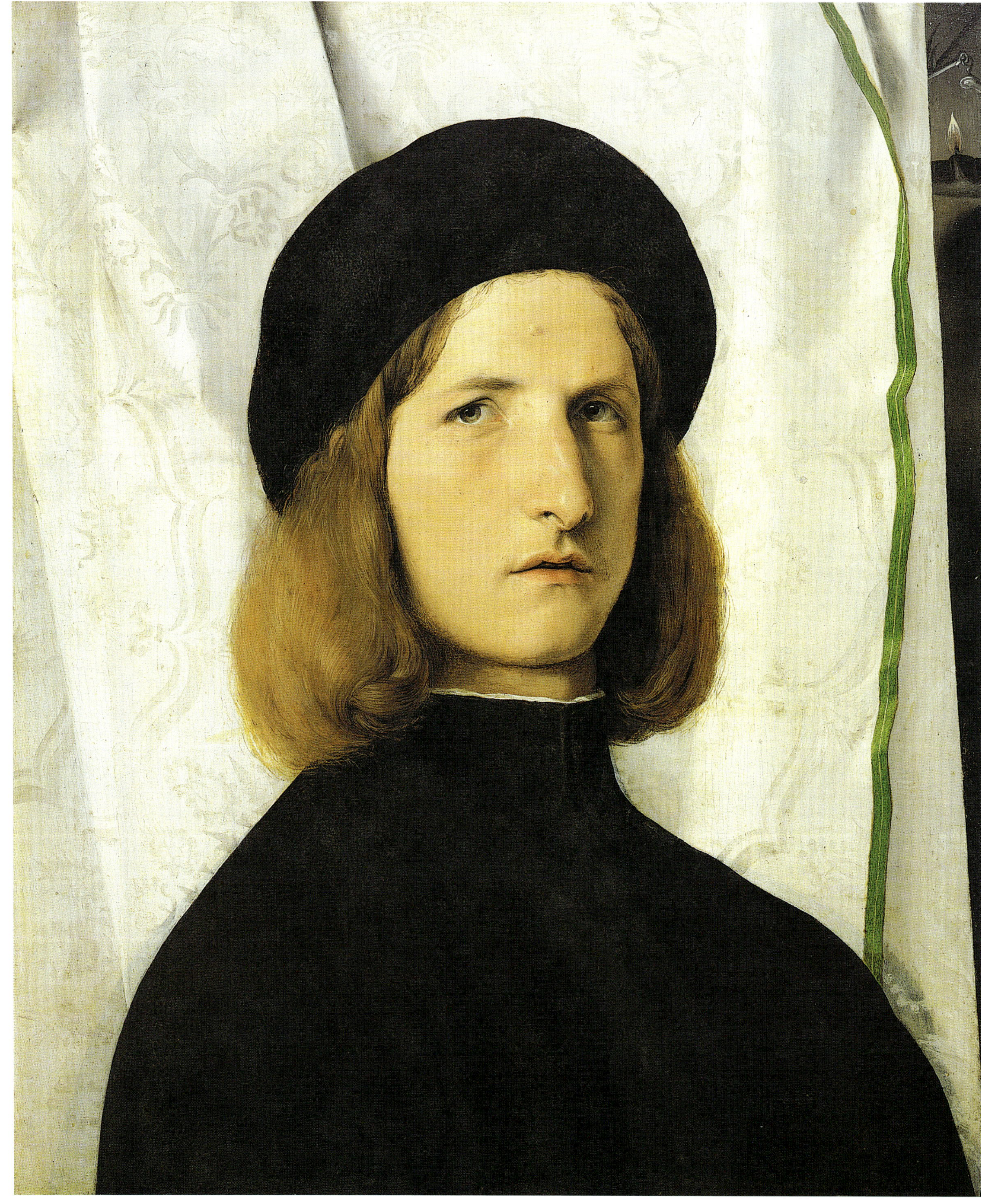

The "other Renaissance" in northern Italy

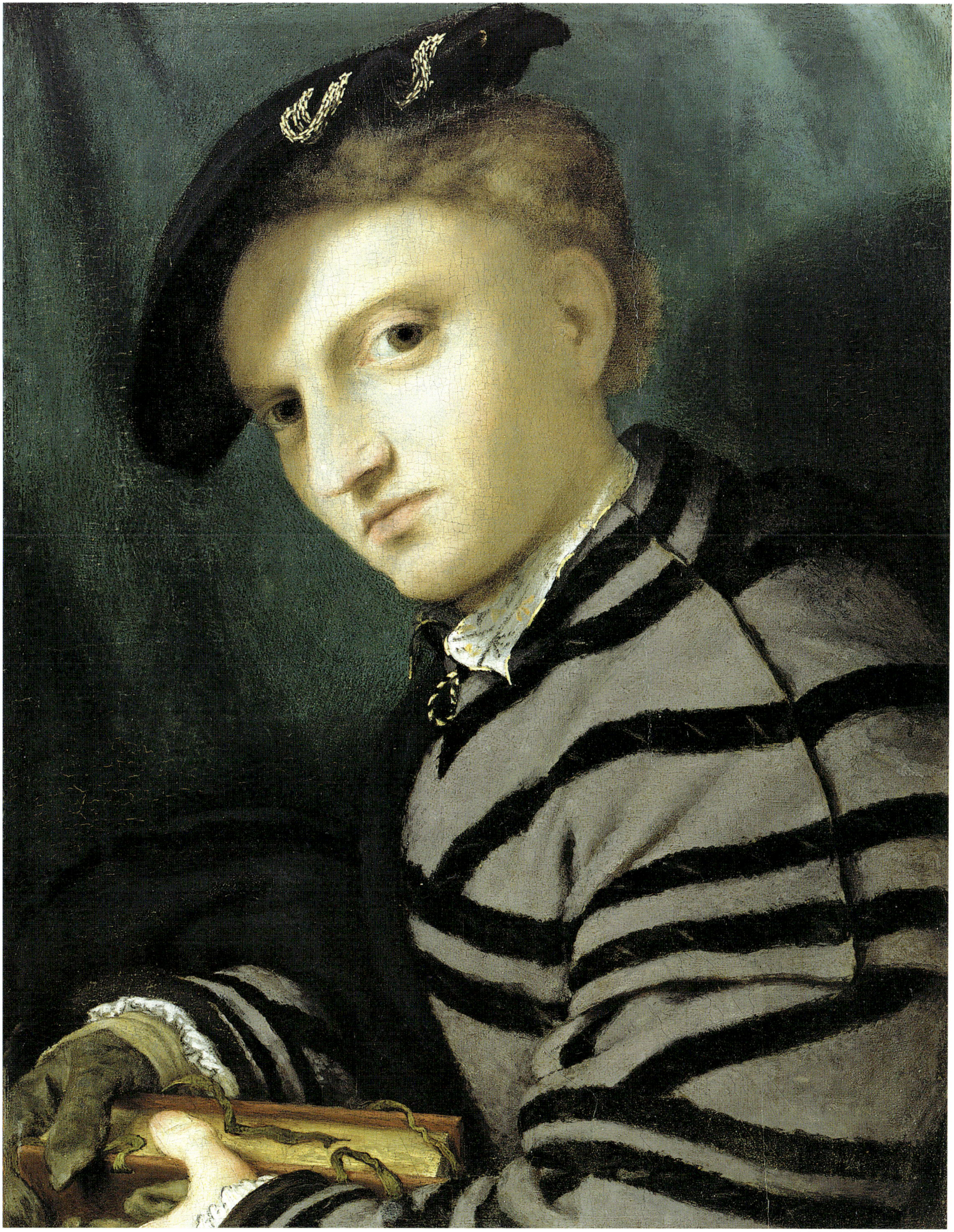

The "other Renaissance" in northern Italy

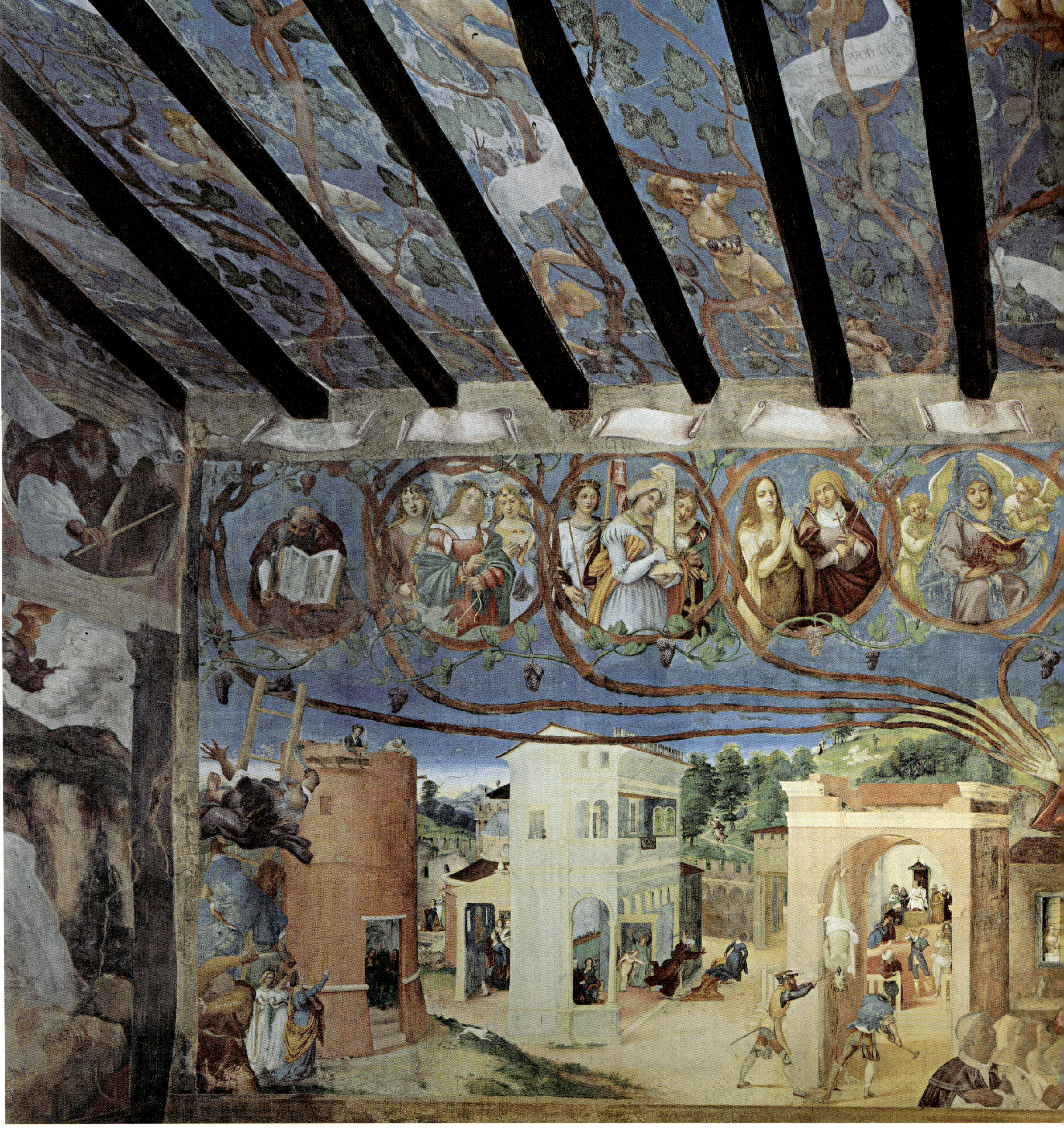

The "other Renaissance" in northern Italy

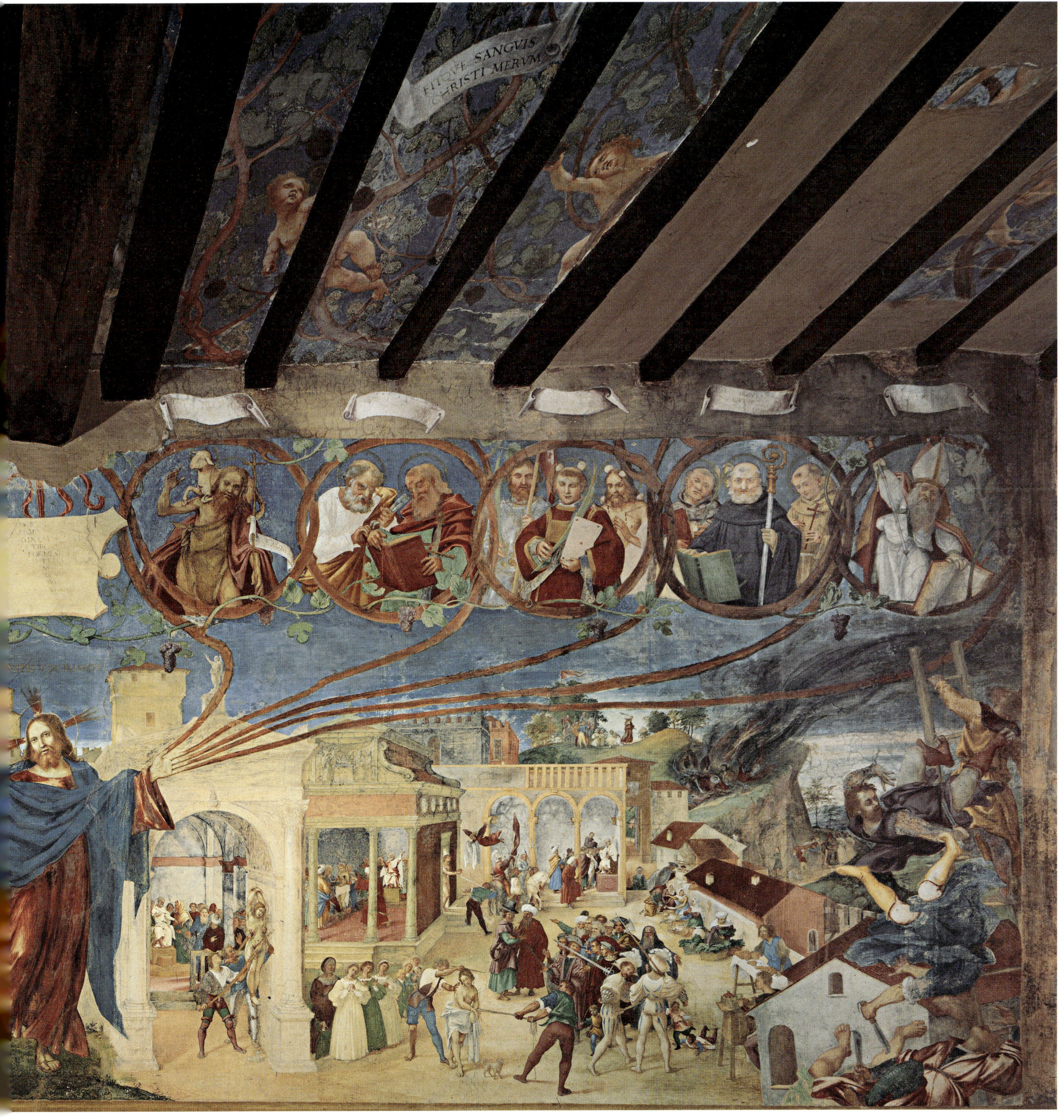

cartoon. At the far left can be seen the cylindrical tower in which saint was imprisoned by her father; then St. Barbara is seen praying in the open; there is then the outrage of a pagan idol and, under a portico, the attempt to explain to her father (recognizable by the turban) her conversion. Her attempt is useless: the furious father throws himself at her, wielding a scimitar. The chase (during which Barbara loses her yellow cloak) continues beyond the city walls, up to the top of a hill, where a shepherd indicates to the father the wood in which the saint is hidden. The next scene brings us back to the foreground, with the beginning of Barbara's long and bloody martyrdom; it ends in the lively scene in the marketplace, between the vendors of fruits and vegetables. Lotto locates each episode in a particular place, but does so without ever losing sight of the overall effect. This type of narrative has been compared to the system of chapels of the Sacro Monte of Varallo.

The "other Renaissance" in northern Italy

This extraordinary setting, a perfect example of Renaissance taste, was a secret for many centuries, having been walled up and abandoned. It was in fact thought to be quite unseemly that an abbess in a convent (the learned Giovanna da Piacenza) received guests and carried on literary conversations in such an overtly profane setting, dominated by the figure of Diana (above the fireplace) and magically transformed into an arbor thanks to the illusionistic frescoes of the umbrella vault, which continues an idea from Leonardo da Vinci and Andrea Mantegna. The monochromes that run along the top of the walls are both marvelous and unsettling: inside simulated lunettes are classical sculptures caressed by the light and supported by fake capitals of ram's heads, between which the painter created lengths of cloth holding up ritual objects in a wonderful effect of trompe l'oeil.

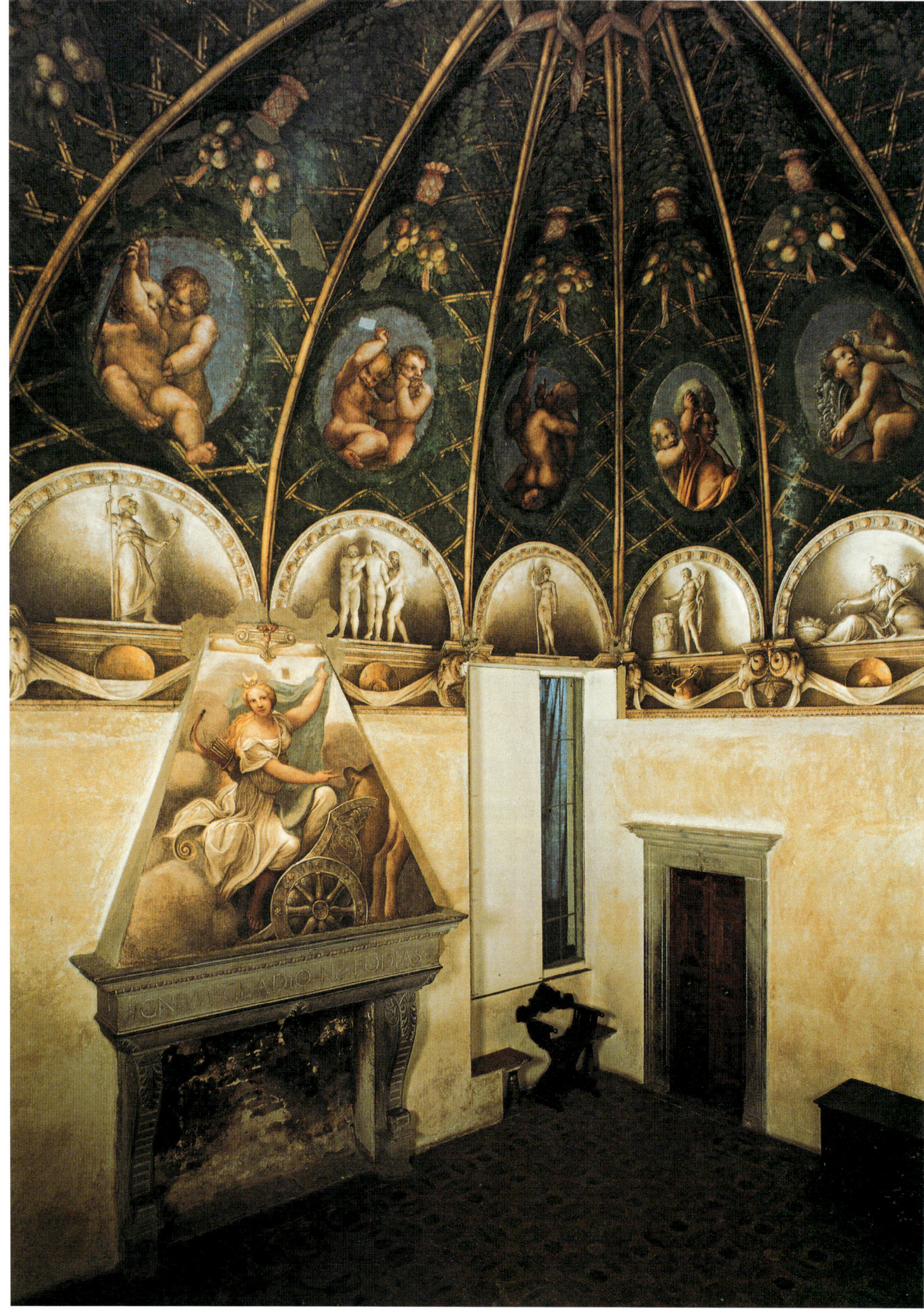

The "other Renaissance" in northern Italy

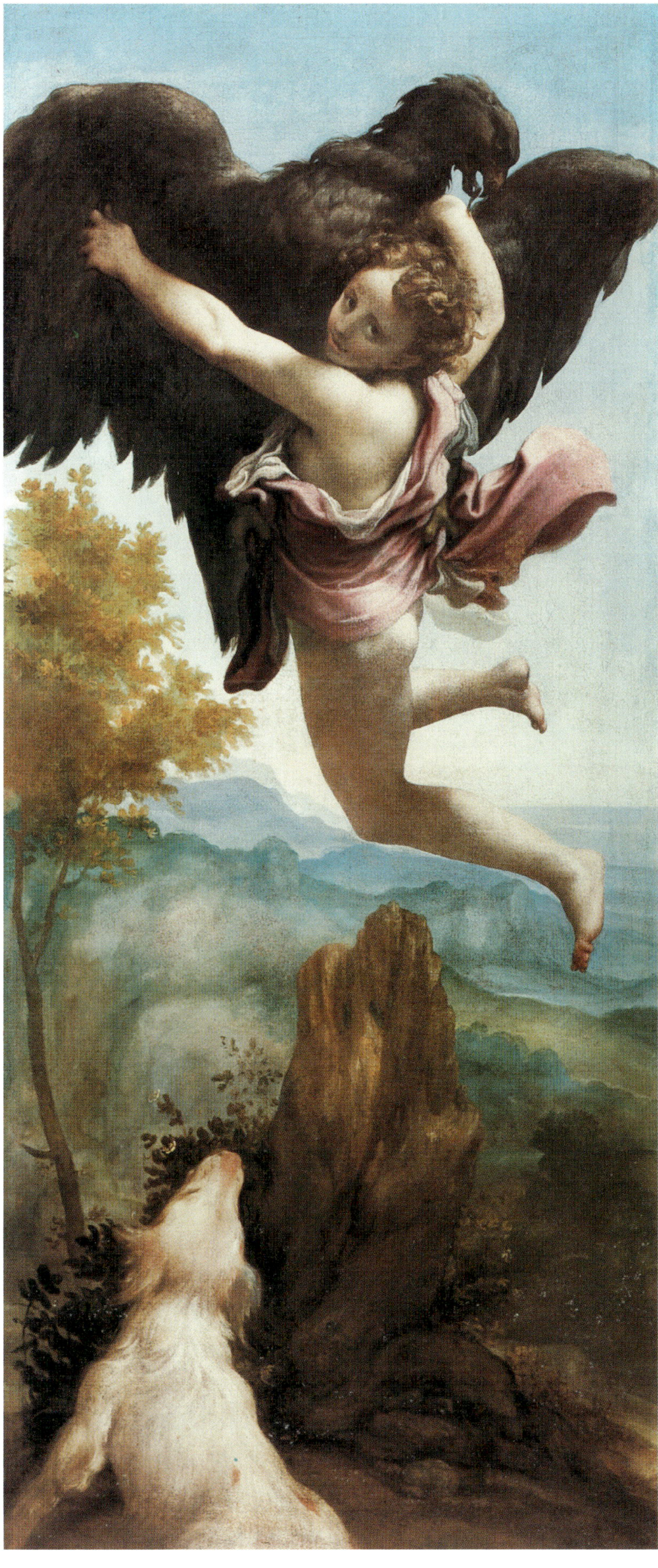

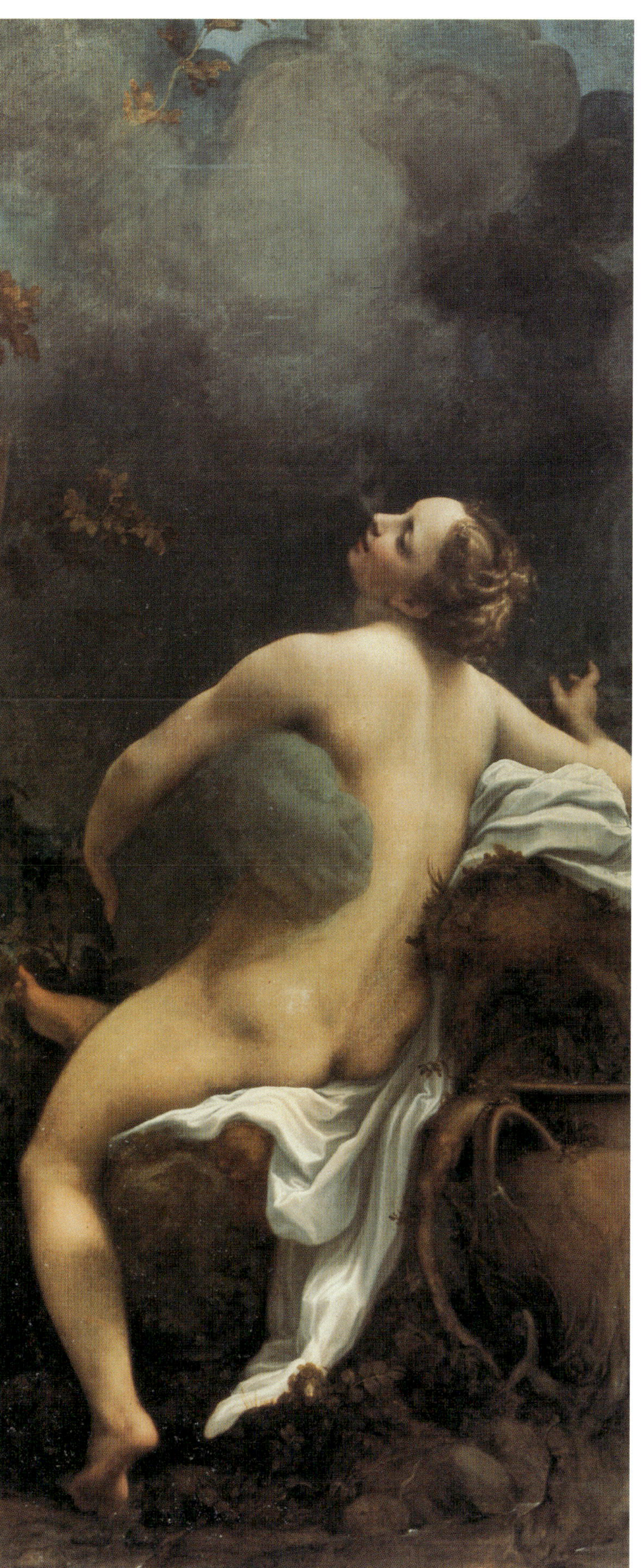

These two paintings are part of the exceptional cycle of the *Loves of Jupiter,* which also includes the *Danaë* in the Galleria Borghese in Rome and the *Leda and the Swan* in the Gemäldegalerie in Berlin. Taken together, the cycle stands at the pinnacle of the mythological-sensual paintings of the Renaissance, with passages of sweeping amorous abandon. In this sense, the scene in which Jupiter, in the shape of a cloud, embraces the nymph Io, kissing her and making her swoon, is a true prodigy. The puffy divine cloud truly seems capable of grasping the girl's smooth body, holding her in a soft yet irresistible embrace. The elegance, charm, and delight of Correggio's rendering always succeeds in keeping such scenes well away from the threshold of coarse eroticism.

The "other Renaissance" in northern Italy

GAUDENZIO FERRARI
The Last Supper
1541–42, panel,
330 x 232 cm
Santa Maria della
Passione, Milan

With its dazzling color,
this is the most impor-
tant work Gaudenzio
Ferrari made in Milan,
and it is still in its
original frame. The
panel, an unorthodox
response to the famous
Last Supper by Leonardo,
shook Lombard paint-
ing. For almost fifty
years, in fact, the exam-
ple of Leonardo had
become, in practice,
the only possible way
of painting the Last
Supper. Beginning with
his memory of a print
by Dürer, Gaudenzio
located the figures
around a square table,
with movements, ges-
tures, and expressions
of great dramatic effect.
It should be noted that
the Christ repeats almost
exactly Leonardo's ver-
sion in Santa Maria
delle Grazie, as though
to call further attention
to the changes made,
beginning from an
identical initial theme.

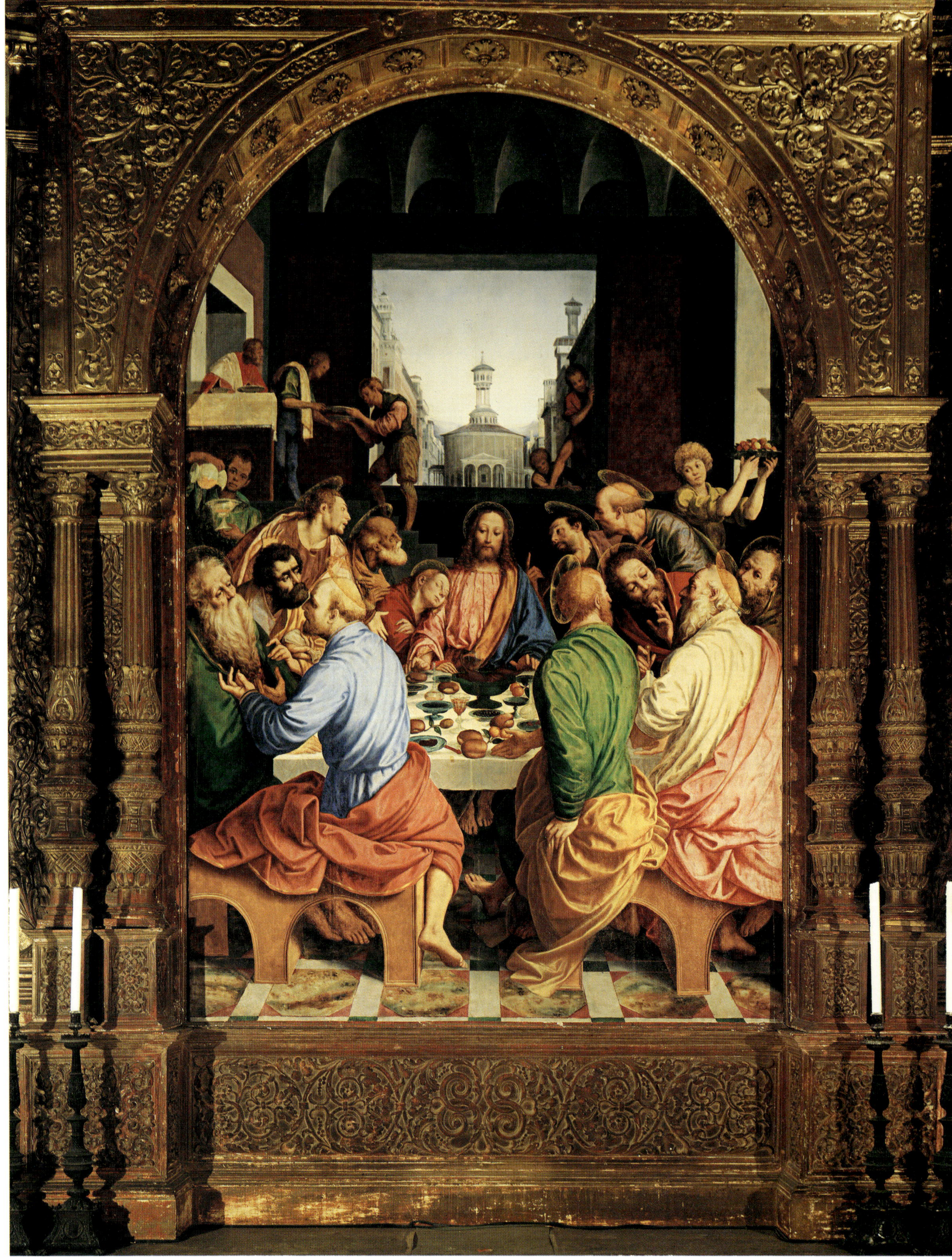

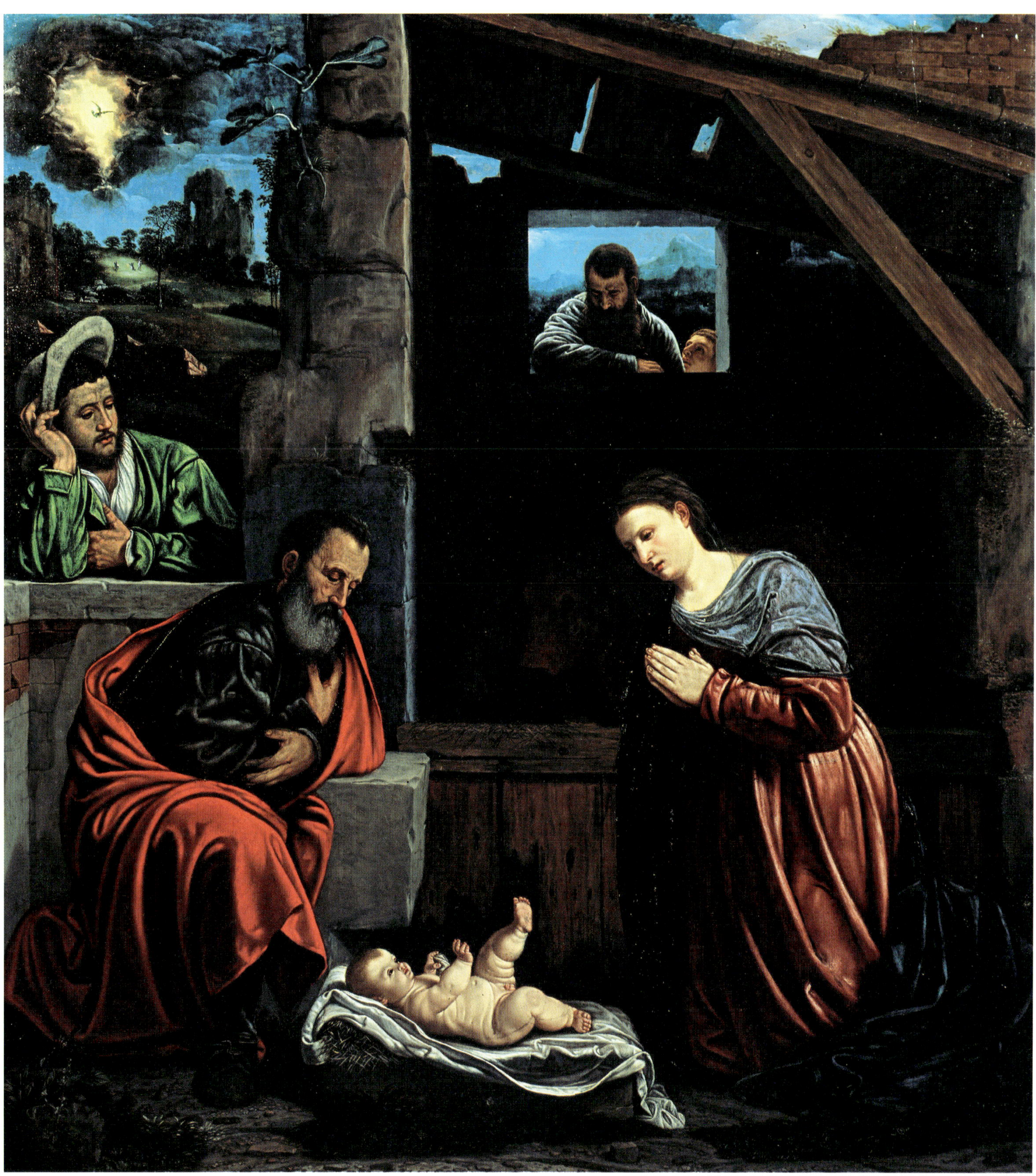

The "other Renaissance" in northern Italy

This is one of the most
important episodes in
the cycle of the Cappella
del Sacramento, which
Romanino began in col-
laboration with Moretto
around 1521, a true
milestone in the history
of the Brescian paint-
ing school. Romanino
uses expressive force to
emphasize the feelings
of the figures, as indi-
cated, for example, by
the theatrical gesture
of humiliation and pen-
itence of Magdalene,
wrapped in the lumi-
nous folds of a silken
mantle, an effect that
was repeated by both
Moretto and Savoldo.
There is also the beau-
tiful touch of the still
life created by the
objects on the table.

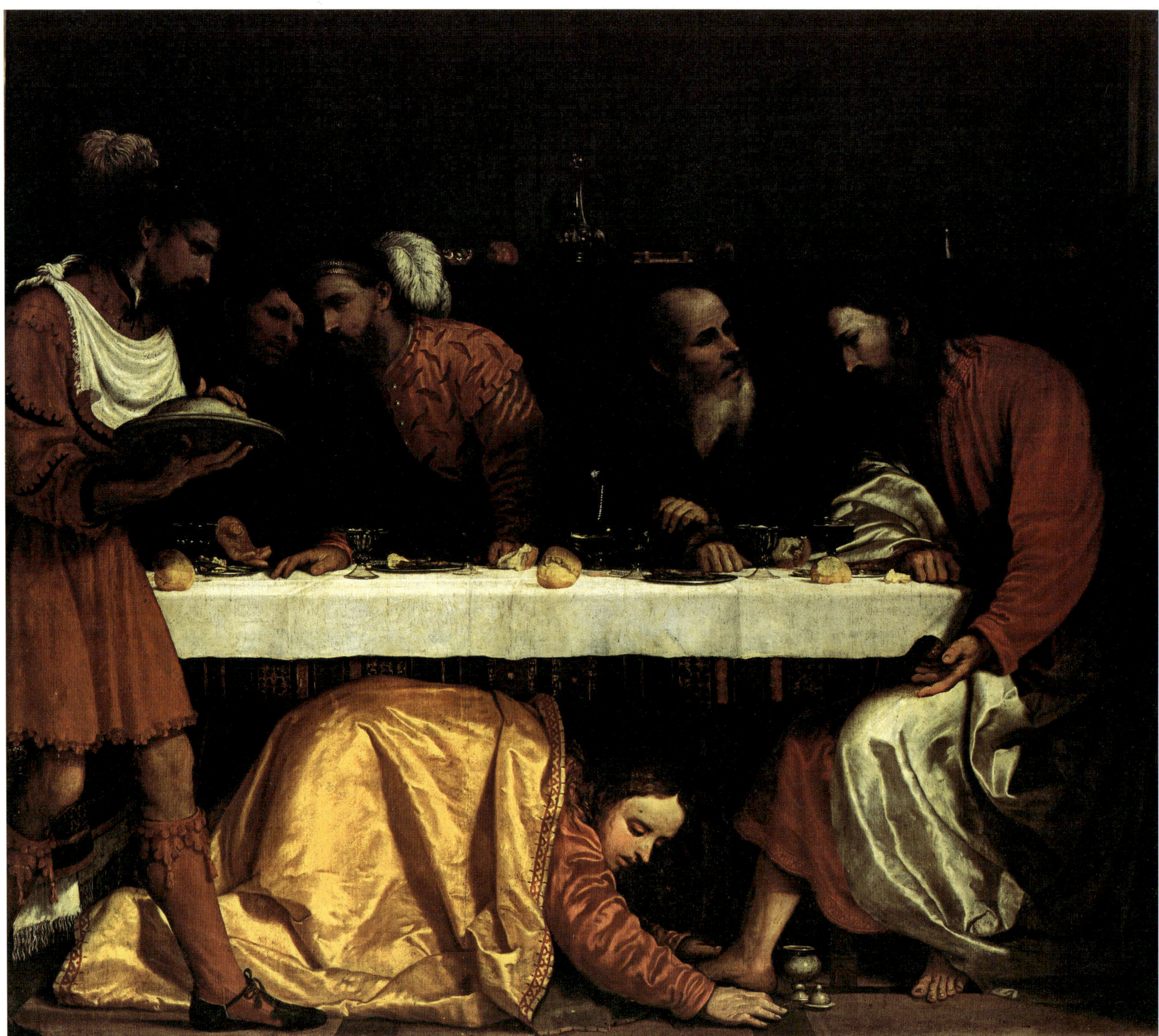

The "other Renaissance" in northern Italy

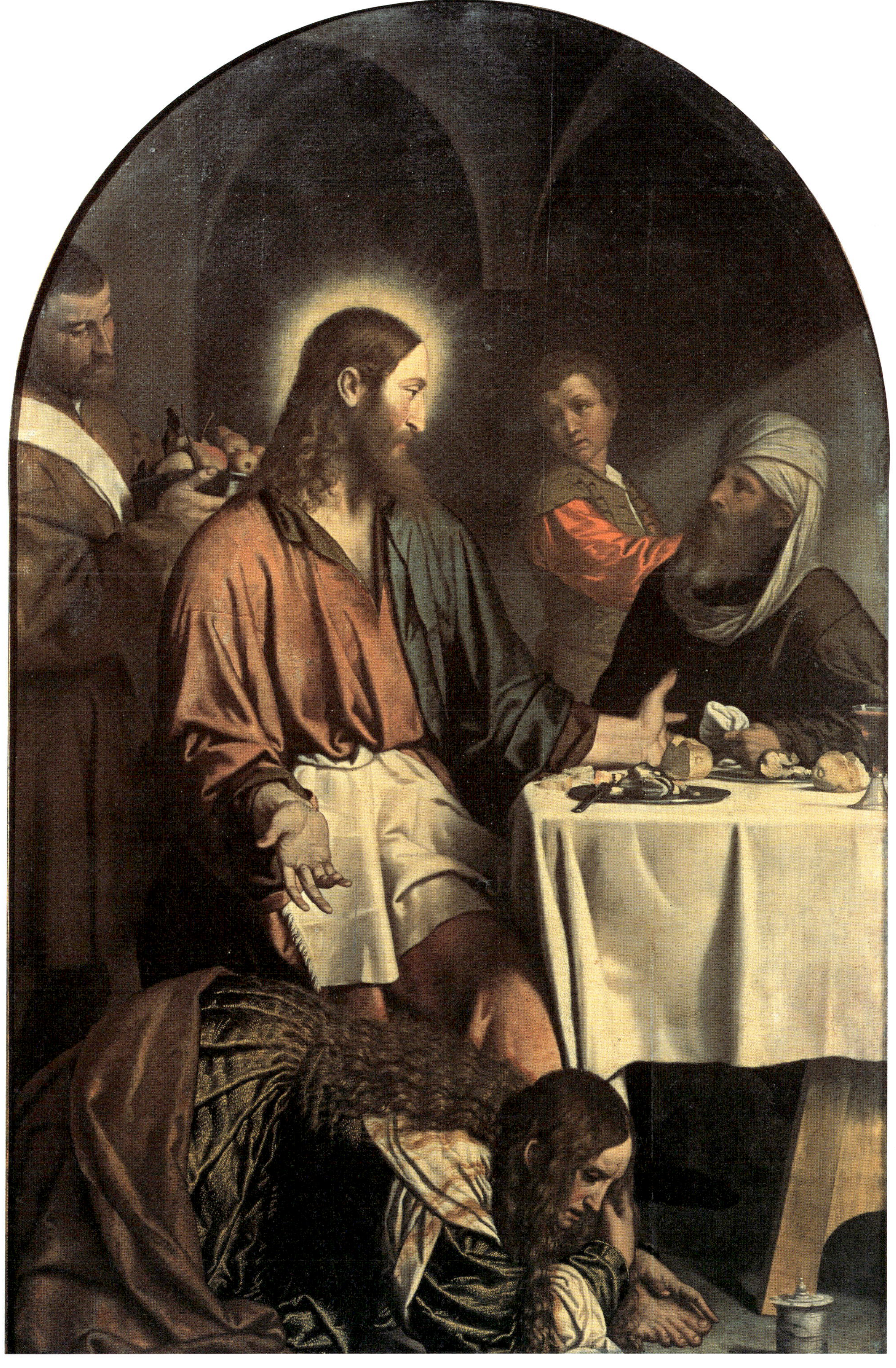

■ MORETTO
**Supper in the
House of Simon
the Pharisee**
1550–54, canvas
Santa Maria Calchera,
Brescia

The penitent Magda-
lene's gesture was
taken directly from the
similar subject dealt
with thirty years earlier
by Romanino in San
Giovanni Evangelista;
Moretto, however,
chooses a quieter and
more serene, almost
humble, setting; the
realistic detail of the
napkin on Christ's lap
is quite eloquent. The
soberness of the com-
position, the way the
light falls from the
right, and the detail
of the still life (fish,
bread, bowls of fruit
accurately presented by
the light but not shown
off as mere demonstra-
tions of skill) have
been seen as important
precedents of the sen-
sibility of Caravaggio.

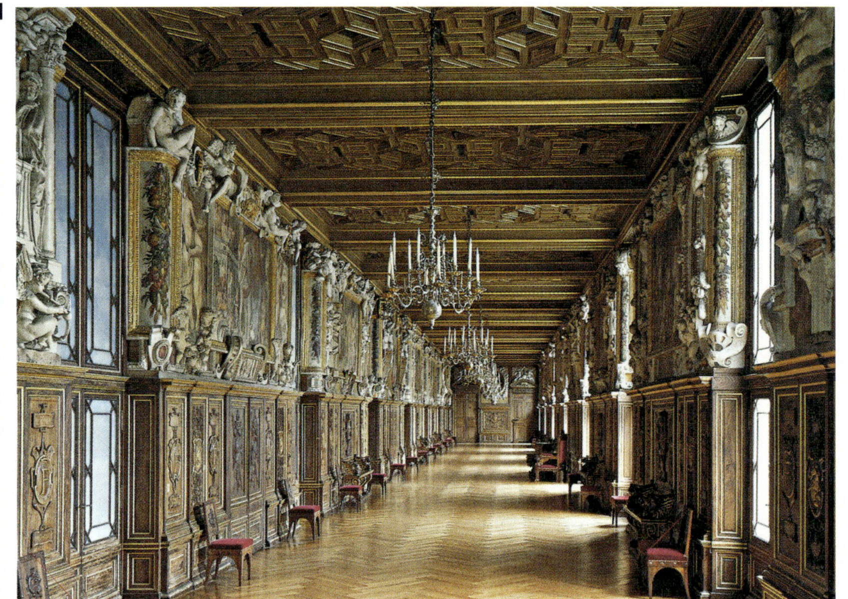

Rosso Fiorentino,
Gallery of Francis I,
1533–40; château of
Fontainebleau

Against a political backdrop in which great nation states were being created and smaller local powers were being absorbed, European art was rapidly making its way toward its own kind of "globalization," with similar manifestations of the same art in every country. The Sack of Rome in 1527 was of fundamental importance to this movement because of the many artists who left the city. Even after the death of their master, the students and collaborators of Raphael had stayed together and continued to form a compact school—but not so after the sack. Like so many other artists, they fled the city and dispersed among the many noble courts of Europe, both large and small. Because of the unquestioned authority of Raphael, Michelangelo, and their styles, because of the travels made by Italian artists, and because of the circulation of Classical-style models made available by the spread of printing, the stylistic phenomenon of mannerism had reached an international level by the second quarter of the sixteenth century. From the premises laid in Florence in the second decade of the century it spread across the continent, becoming a kind of artistic lingua franca in European courts at the end of the Renaissance. More than one nation passed almost directly from the late Gothic to mannerism without experiencing even a limited Renaissance stage. The first ruler of a large European state to promote mannerism was France's Francis I, who had hosted the aging Leonardo da Vinci at Amboise. In the first decades of the sixteenth century the French kings Louis XII and Francis I made repeated attempts to conquer northern Italy, in particular the former duchy of Milan. A quarter of a century of warfare led to the Spanish victory in the decisive battle of Pavia (1525). This setback was one more manifestation of a reality in the history and politics of Europe, namely, the difficulties France experienced in its efforts to become a continental "superpower." One result of the military campaigns in Italy, which took place at the same time that Leonardo was a guest of Francis I in the château of Amboise, was the final overcoming of the Gothic models of art and architecture and the acceptance in their place of the forms of the Italian High Renaissance. Defeated on the field of battle, the king of France sought and found revenge in the rapid elaboration of a celebratory model through architecture and images, making use in this campaign, at least initially, of Italian artists. Further dramatic events on Italian soil, most of all, of course, the Sack of Rome, helped Francis I attract to France entire squadrons of Italian painters, stuccoists, sculptors, and architects to whom he gave prestigious, large-scale commissions. Particularly important was the arrival of Rosso Fiorentino, who with

Mannerism in the

Philibert de l'Orme and Pierre Bontemps, Tomb of Francis I, 1548; Saint-Denis, Paris

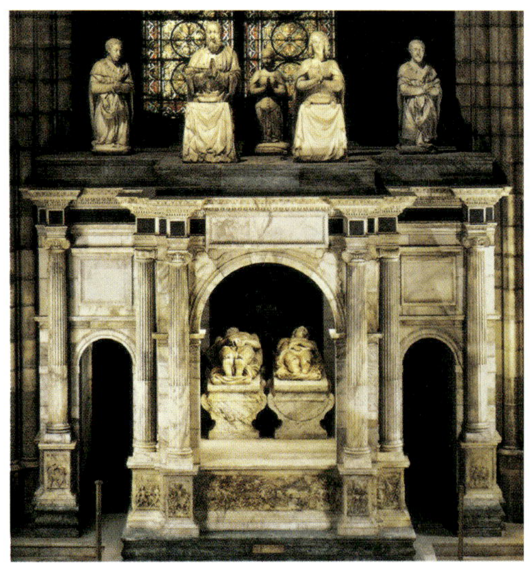

Francesco Primaticcio (author of the stuccos), frescoed the spectacular Gallery of Francis I in the château of Fontainebleau. Other specialists followed, such as the architect Sebastiano Serlio, the painter Niccolò dall'Abate, and the great sculptor Benvenuto Cellini. Thanks to their presence, a rich school of French masters began taking shape, standing out among them the portraitist François Clouet and the highly elegant sculptors Germain Pilion and Jean Goujon.

At the same time that all this progress was being made in mannerist painting and monumental sculpture, goldworking, tapestry making, and the other "artisan" and luxury crafts whose products had distinguished the Gothic courts began to fall into eclipse. The châteaux of the Loire, most of all the royal château of Fontainebleau, became important international laboratories of the new "modern

Mannerism in the courts of Europe

manner." Born in Florence as the *di fronda* ("leafy") style, the *maniera* ("manner"), as Vasari called it, was progressively transformed until, around 1540, it had become an art "of regime," a sort of obligatory formal code shared by the rulers of all Europe to express, most of all through portraits, their "modern" taste and to visually project the solid and untouchable image of absolute power. Aristocratic ideals, courtly etiquette, and the solid unflinching glare of power were expressed through a standardized, almost crystallized style of art. This style was composed of explicit or understood references to formal classical models, such as ancient statues or prints based on works by Raphael, that could be understood only by persons of refined and up-to-date figurative learning, and it therefore became a sort of cipher language accessible only to members of the elite. The situation in France made this clear. The taste for the "modern manner" (in France often called simply *Renaissance*) was expressed primarily in works commissioned directly by the court, such as the sixteenth-century wing of the Cour Carrée of the Louvre, the new royal tombs in Saint-Denis, or ornamental fountains and sculpture. In 1539, on the occasion of Cosimo I's marriage to Eleonora of Toledo, Agnolo Bronzino became the Medici's favorite painter. His rigorous, precise art, of impressive executive refinement,

and by the end of the century that city had become the most brilliant center of artistic creativity in central Europe. It was also a city of science as well as the city of the famous Rabbi Judah Löw, creator of the legendary *golem*. Driven by a mania for collecting just short of the pathological, Rudolf II amassed fabulous treasures, amazing objects, exquisite works of art, curiosities of natural history, masterpieces of goldworking, of woodworking, of intaglio, astonishing and exotic products of all kinds. A school took shape around Rudolf's court, its products easily recognizable despite the eclectic provenance of its members. Artists from various nations were included, such as Joseph Heintz from Basel, the German Hans von Aachen, the Italian Giuseppe Arcimboldo, and Bartholomäus Spranger from Antwerp. They had in common their Italian training, the abundance of openly erotic subjects they dealt with, and a certain fascinating and sensual taste that continued even after the emperor's death and came to an end in 1618 with the outbreak of the Thirty Years' War, which began with a famous event named for the city—the Defenestration of Prague—and which included, during its last year, the sack of part of the city by Swedes and the dispersal of the collections.

courts of Europe

seemed suitable to the presentation of the court's official image. The restless style of the Florentine painters of two decades earlier had been transformed into an ornate expression of power. The sense of this motionless, timeless refinement is particularly notable in the portraits of the Medici family. Projected outside time, with no apparent vitality, the figures are expressions of a mental "idea," the symbol of rule. It is a sophisticated presentation, a cultural operation directed at a select public, capable of appreciating the cold fascination of images "outside time," in which the recording of physical features was given second place to the need to present courtly, idealized models.

In the second half of the sixteenth century the stylistic phenomena of mannerism reached the international level, becoming the common language of courtly art at the end of the Renaissance. For painting, sculpture, and garden architecture the models of central Italian mannerism were used in courts throughout Europe. German nobles willingly adopted the style, which they found learned, artificial, and aristocratic. In 1583 Rudolf II, in an unforeseen decision, relocated the Holy Roman Empire's capital from Vienna to Prague,

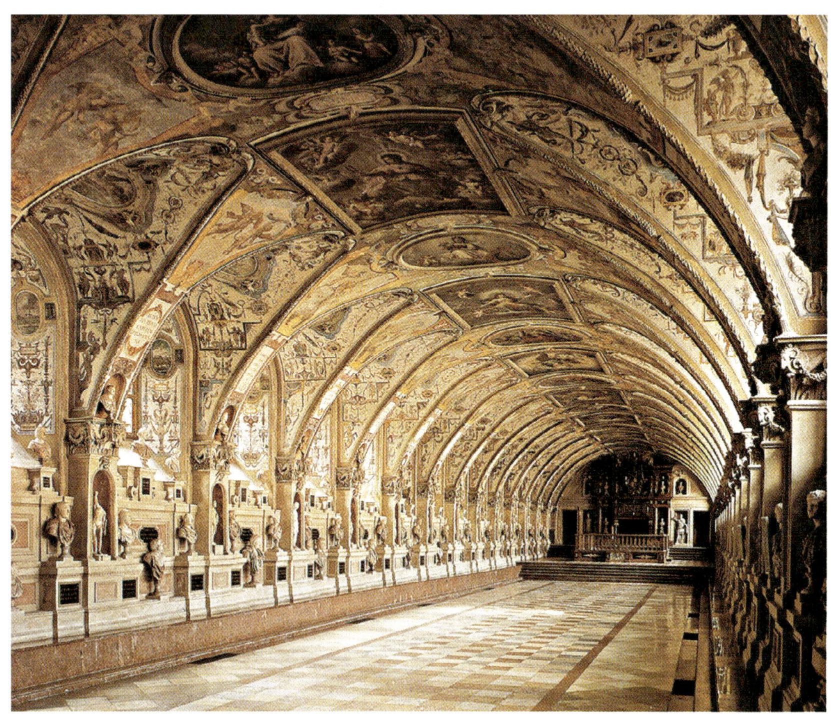

Appreciated for his literary talents as well as those artistic, Agnolo Bronzino assumed a highly important role within the Medici court. Aside from the execution of increasingly smooth and crystallized portraits and of elaborate allegorical works, he was also kept busy directing large-scale decorative works. A quintessential example of the intellectual culture of international mannerism, with its overt sensuality, this allegory delivers a potent moral message. The masks to the far right are the key to its meaning, the necessity of revealing what lies behind appearances. Behind the three main figures—Venus, Cupid, and the smiling putto who represents Folly— can be seen their "contraries"; behind Cupid is the furious Jealousy, the monster Fraud is behind Folly, while Truth and Time are about to draw a veil over the beauty of Venus. The intricate subject is presented with great formality, its colors enameled, adamantine, incorruptible.

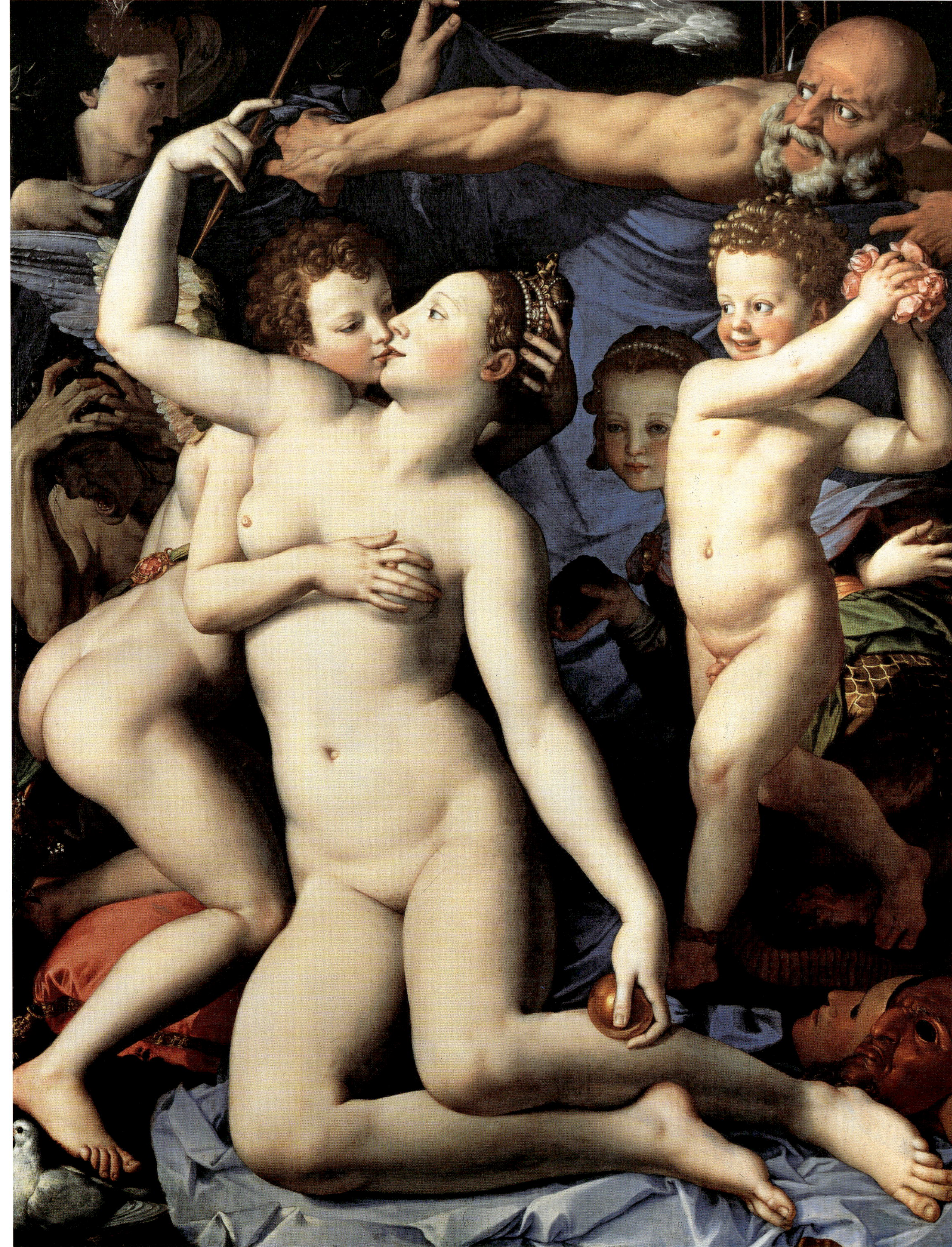

Mannerism in the courts of Europe

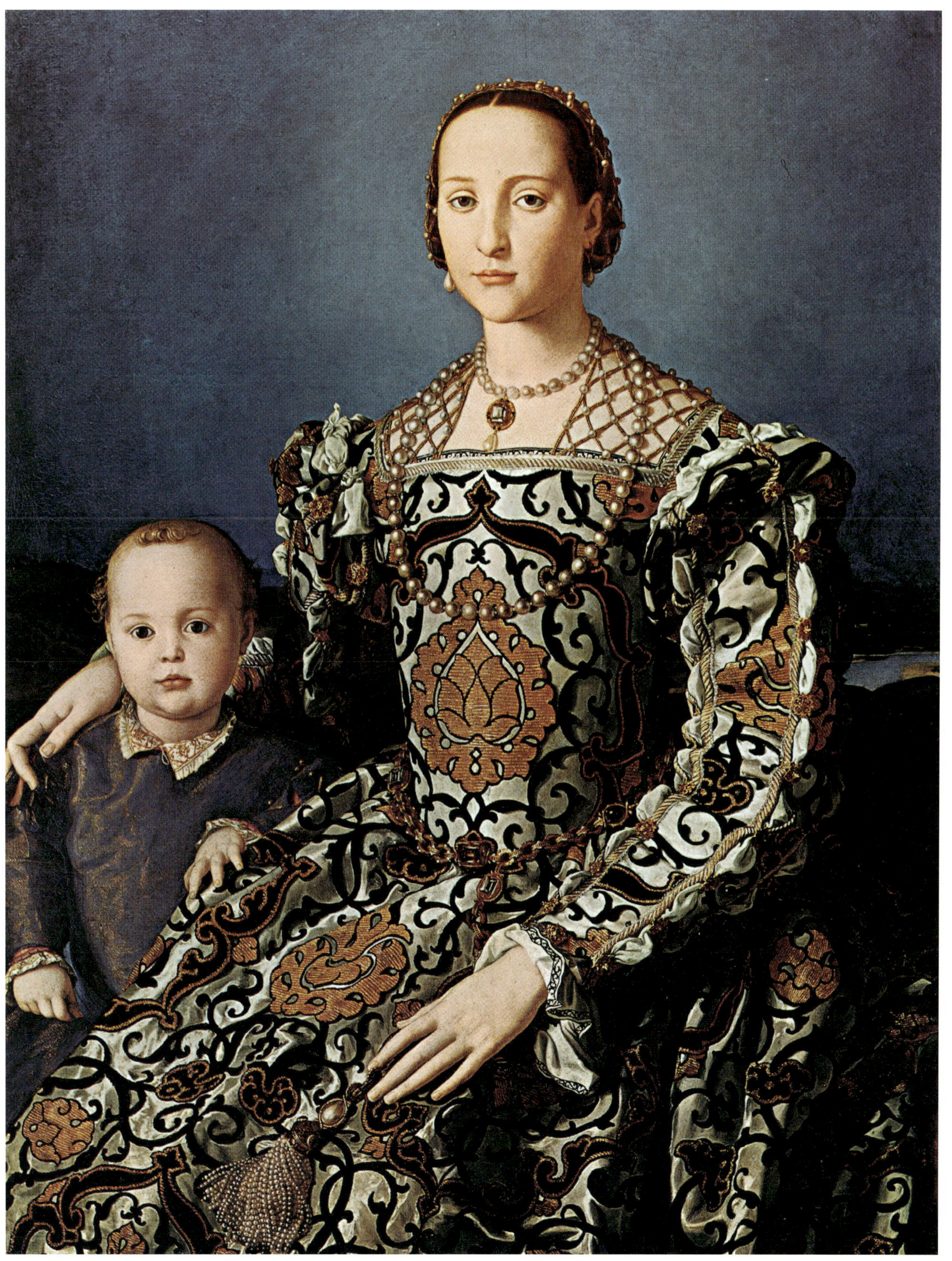

Mannerism in the courts of Europe

This enormously famous and elaborate salt cellar is emblematic of the most refined art of the European courts of the High Renaissance. Made by a Florentine artist in the Fontainebleau of the French king Francis I, donated to the court of the Hapsburgs of Austria, it is a virtuosic, sublime masterpiece of goldwork. Even though it was made with exquisite care in the details, it is the fruit of a monumental conception of the work of art. Dominating the entire work are allegorical figures of Earth and Sea, flanked respectively by a little temple and by a seashell made to hold pepper and salt. As Cellini himself wrote in his famous autobiography, the two figures were seated "with their legs interlaced, suggesting those lengthier branches of the sea which run up in to the continents." He concludes, "In that way I gave them grace."

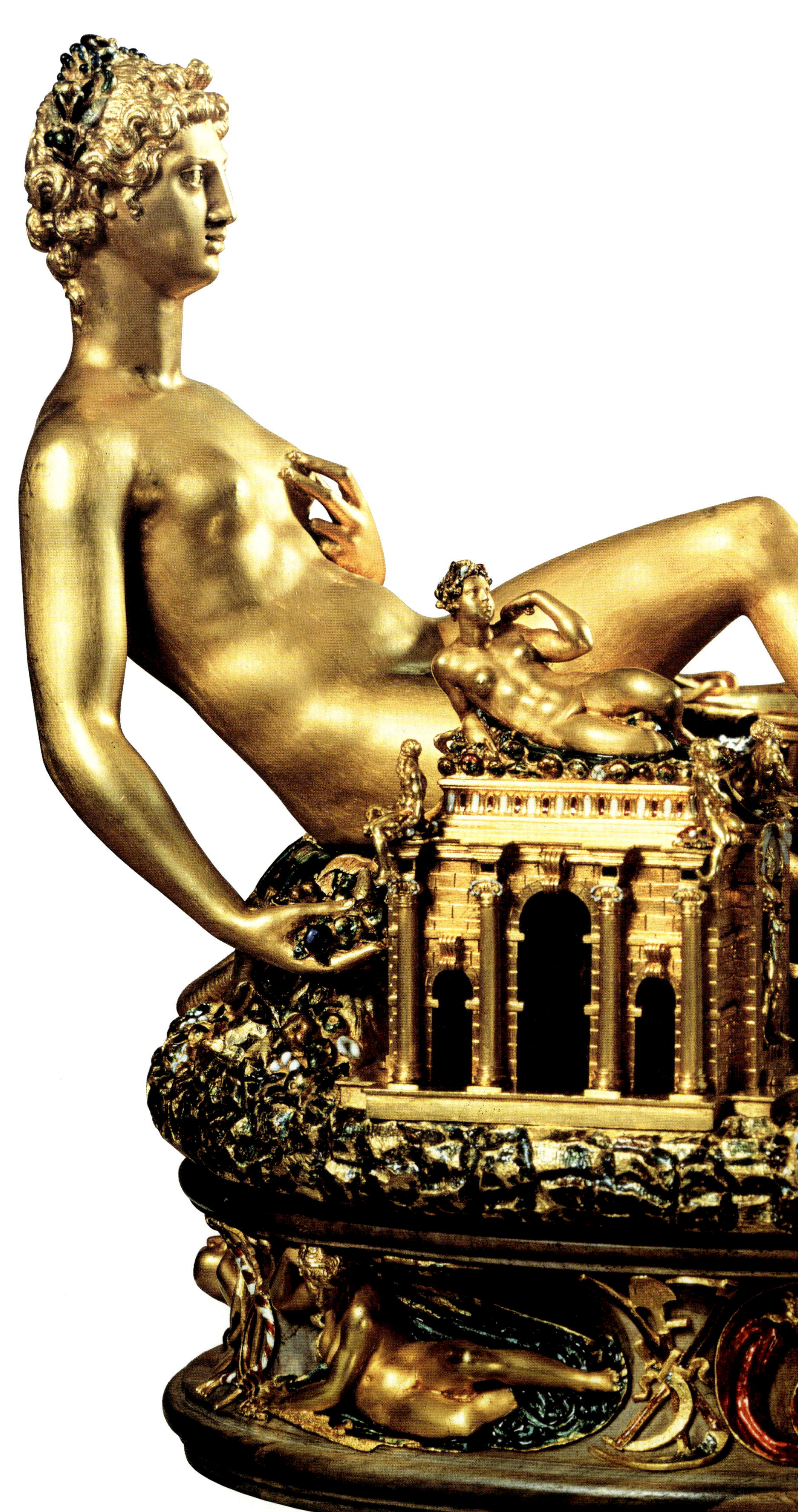

Mannerism in the courts of Europe

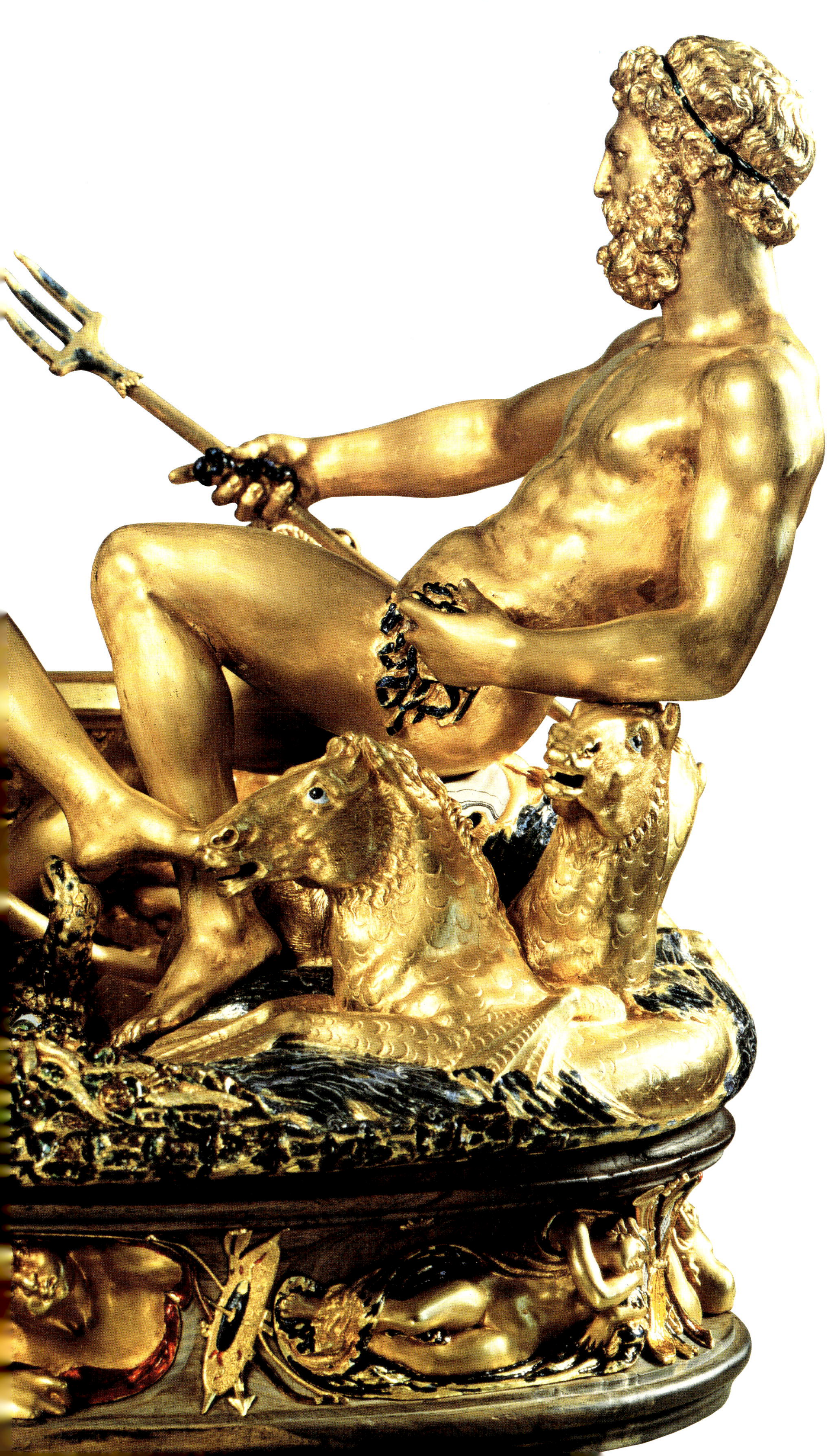

High Renaissance
French art is summa-
rized in the so-called
Fontainebleau school,
formed by a group of
artists who gravitated
around the court of
Francis I and his suc-
cessors from the 1530s
on. It was a very spe-
cial period in the arts,
with on the one hand
a reprise of classical
models in architecture
and in the poses of fig-
ures and an exhibition
of refined artisan tech-
niques brought to their
highest expressive and
creative levels; on the
other hand, there was
a patent and almost
obsessive desire for
visual seduction by
way of female nudes,
flowers, and other
meticulously repro-
duced objects.

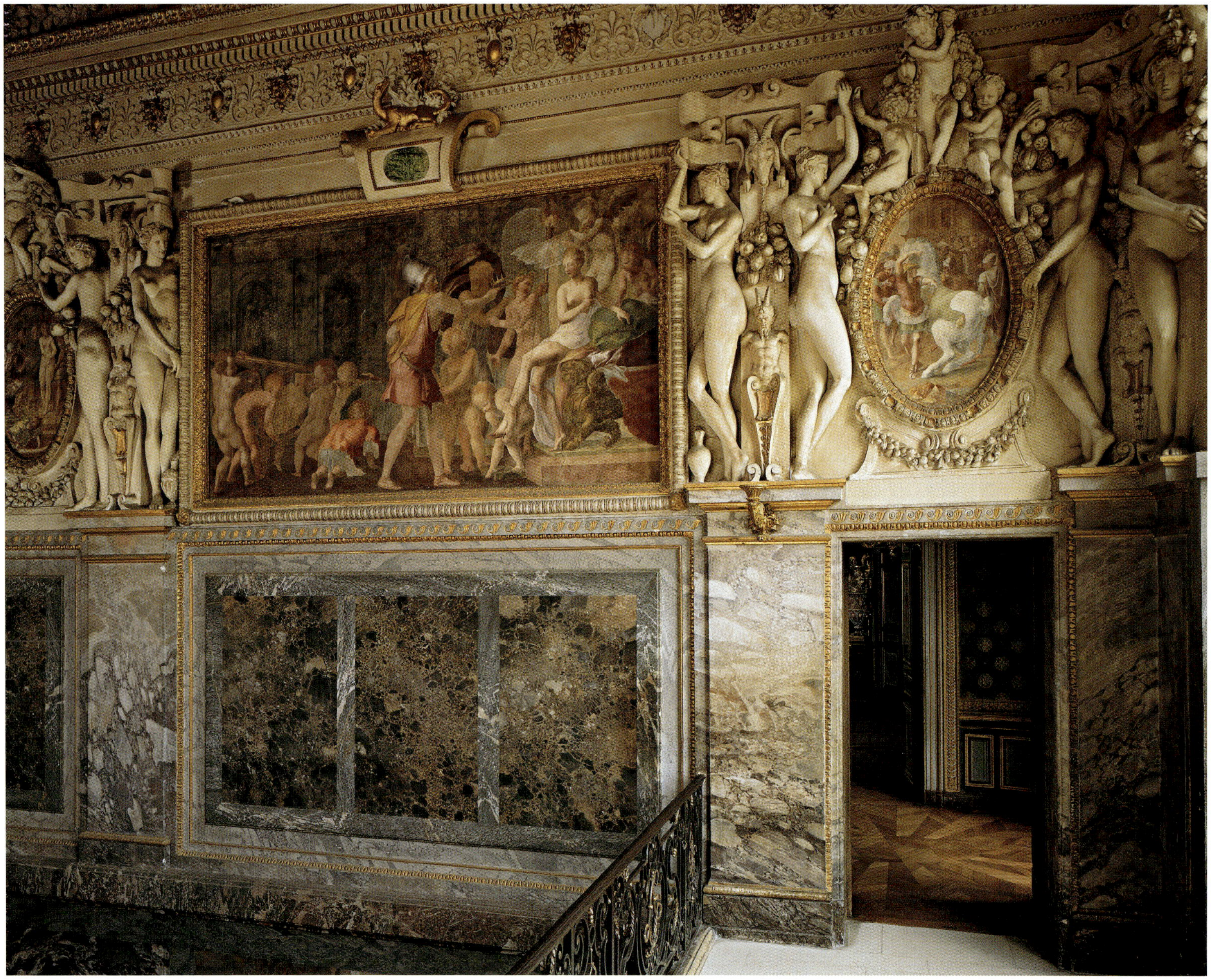

Primaticcio played an
important role among
the Italian artists
active in France at
Fontainebleau. Thanks
to his earlier experience
working with Giulio
Romano, he presented
precious models of
"combined" decoration,
meaning the perfect
integration of archi-
tectonic structure,
painting, and sculpture.

Mannerism in the courts of Europe

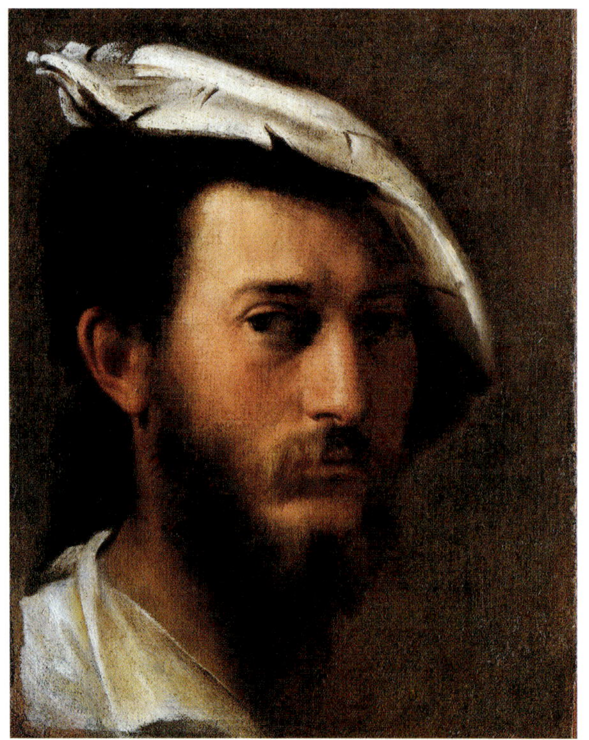

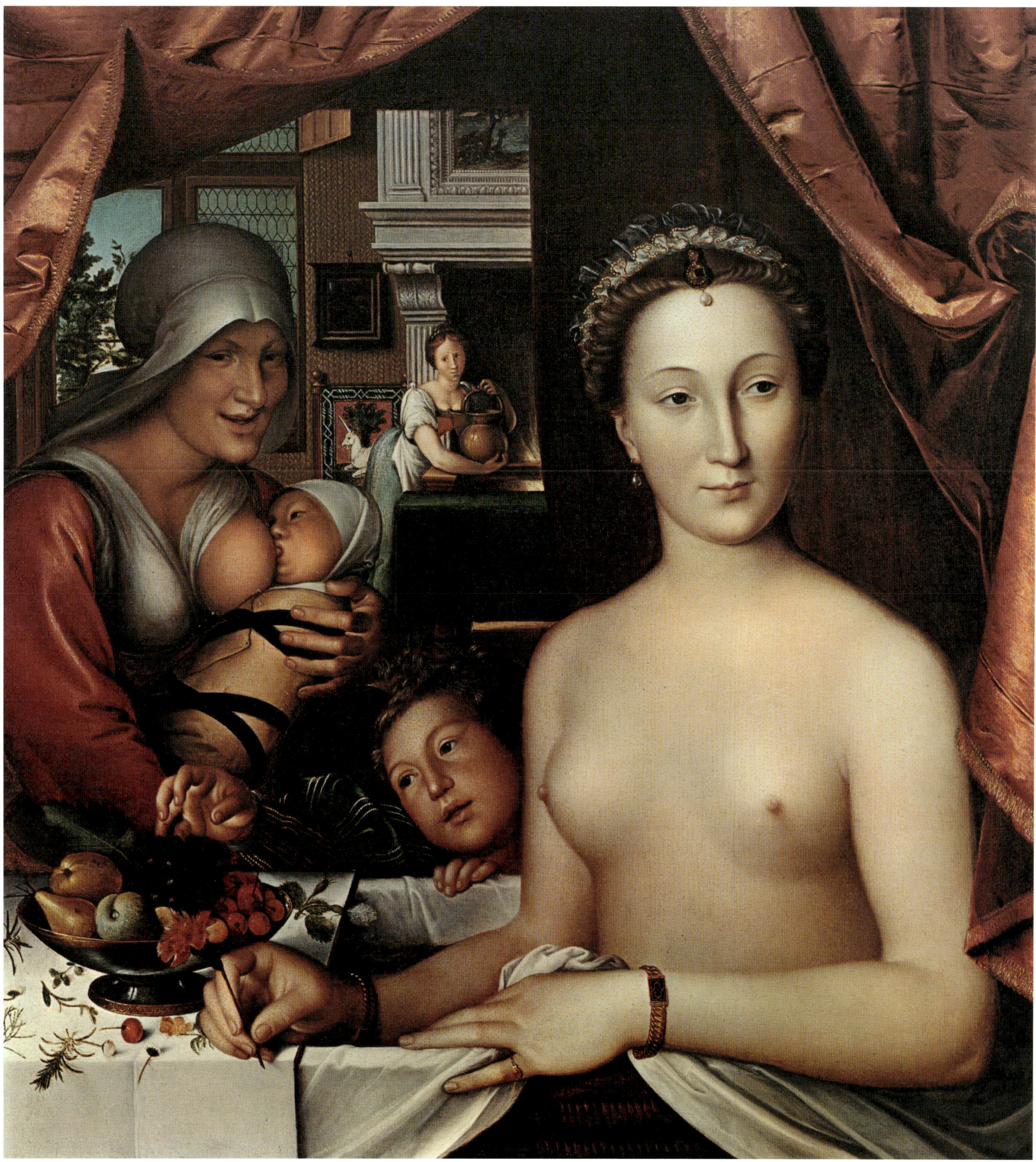

FRANÇOIS CLOUET
Lady in Her Bath
1570, oil on panel,
92 x 81 cm
National Gallery of
Art, Washington, D.C.

A masterpiece by the principal northern master of the sixteenth century, and a work that is emblematic of the French High Renaissance, this painting presents a complex in-depth articulation of space, marking off three different moments of a theatrical action. Heavy drapes have been drawn aside to reveal a nude woman in the foreground, languidly posed in a bathtub; to her right, in open contrast, is the simple but not graceless figure of a wet nurse, nursing a baby, while at the center, a boy reaches for a basket of fruit; past a second curtain appears an maidservant, based on a famous precedent in the *Venus of Urbino* by Titian, and a window that offers a view into a garden. The way the figures are arranged calls attention to the woman in the foreground, the idealization of whom is emphasized by the Flemish-style realistic vigor of the other elements of the scene.

The works created by
the Fontainebleau
painters are so close
in terms of character-
istics, subjects, and
styles that identifying
the personalities of
the various masters is
sometimes difficult,
with several works
remaining anonymous.
This anonymous replica
of Clouet's painting
demonstrates the
immediate celebrity
of that work, which
became a favored point
of formal and icono-
graphic reference for
the Fontainebleau
school. In this version,
however, the prevailing
sense is the desire to
describe objects with
meticulous accuracy:
the jewel box in the
foreground, the pre-
ciousness of the orna-
ments, the affected
grace of the gesture,
the fixed stare on the
woman's face all detract
from the fresh spon-
taneity of the model.

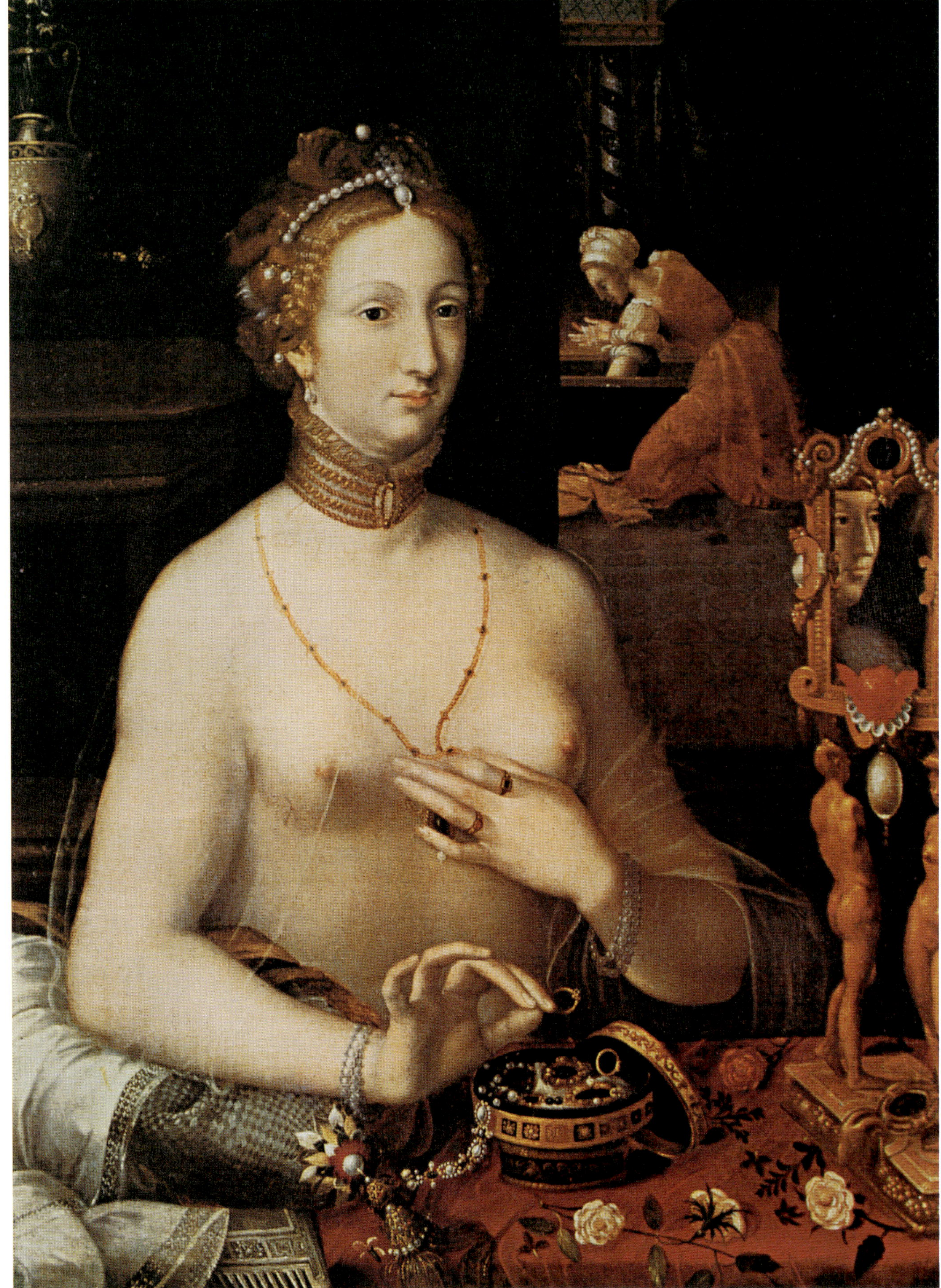

Mannerism in the courts of Europe

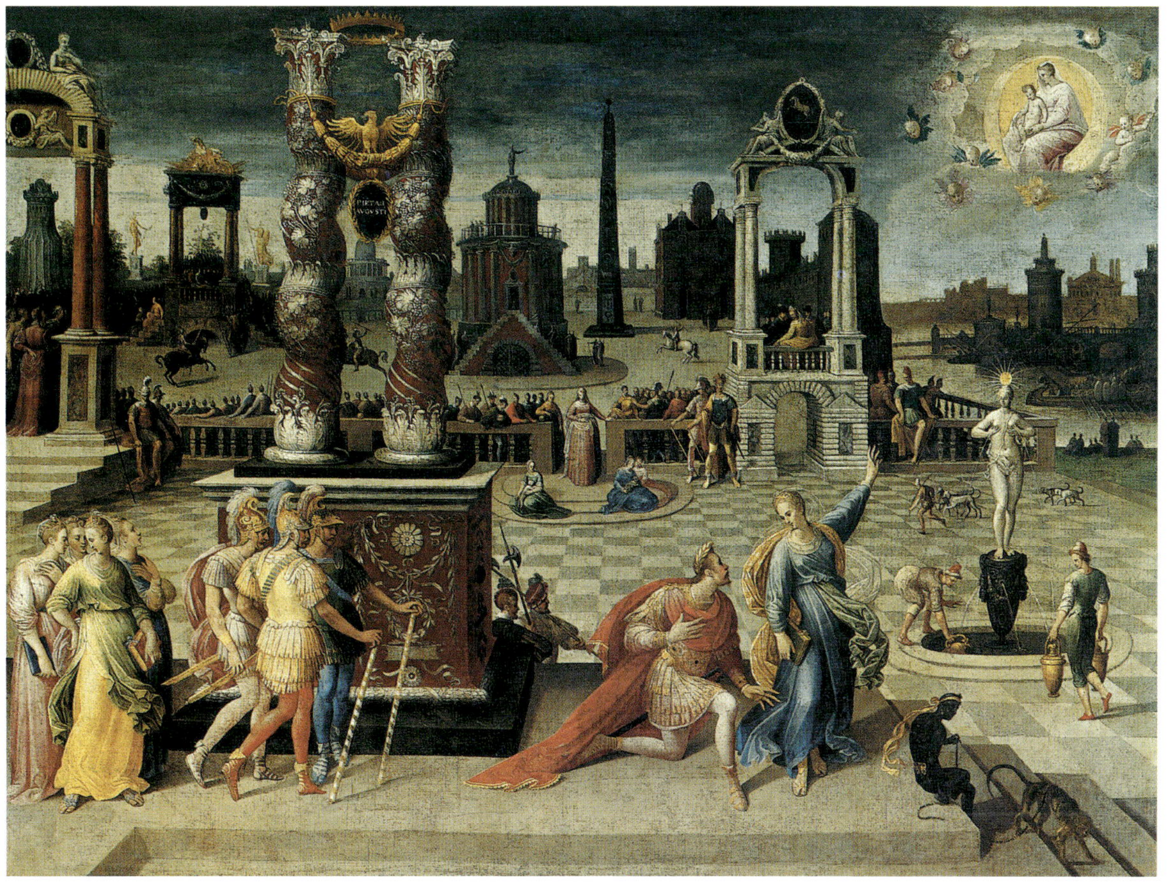

ANTOINE CARON
**Augustus and the
Sibyl of Tivoli**
1571, oil on canvas,
125 x 170 cm
Musée du Louvre,
Paris

Antoine Caron, formerly
assistant to Primaticcio
at Fontainebleau,
adopted the wide-
spread antique style,
but with a touch of
characterization in his
perspective views of
buildings. This scene is
located in an unreal
space where isolated
figures and large groups
cluster or wander amid
extravagant architec-
ture. The splendid
range of colors and the
studied grace of the
gestures are typical
of the artificial aspects
of mannerism.

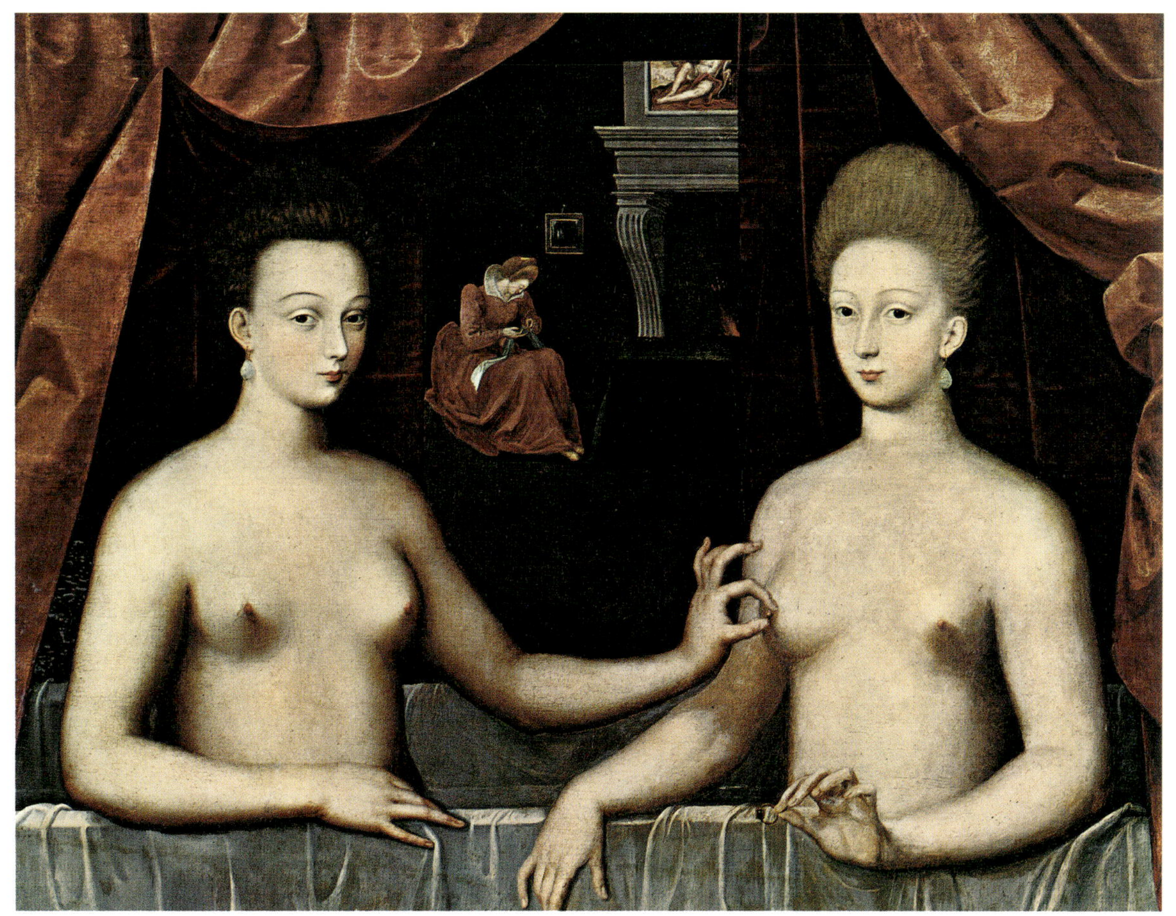

ANONYMOUS FRENCH
PAINTER OF THE
FONTAINEBLEAU
SCHOOL
**Two Women
in a Bath**
1594, oil on panel,
96 x 125 cm
Musée du Louvre, Paris

This problematic paint-
ing, related to the
Fontainebleau school
although its artist has
remained anonymous
(it is the work of a
painter from the period
of Henry IV), is thought
to be a portrait of
Gabrielle d'Estrées and
her sister. The precise
meaning of the iconog-
raphy is unknown, but
once again the basis for
the work is the paint-
ing by François Clouet,
now in Washington,
D.C., this time con-
strued into two nude
women in a bathtub
presented in an
ambiguous pose.

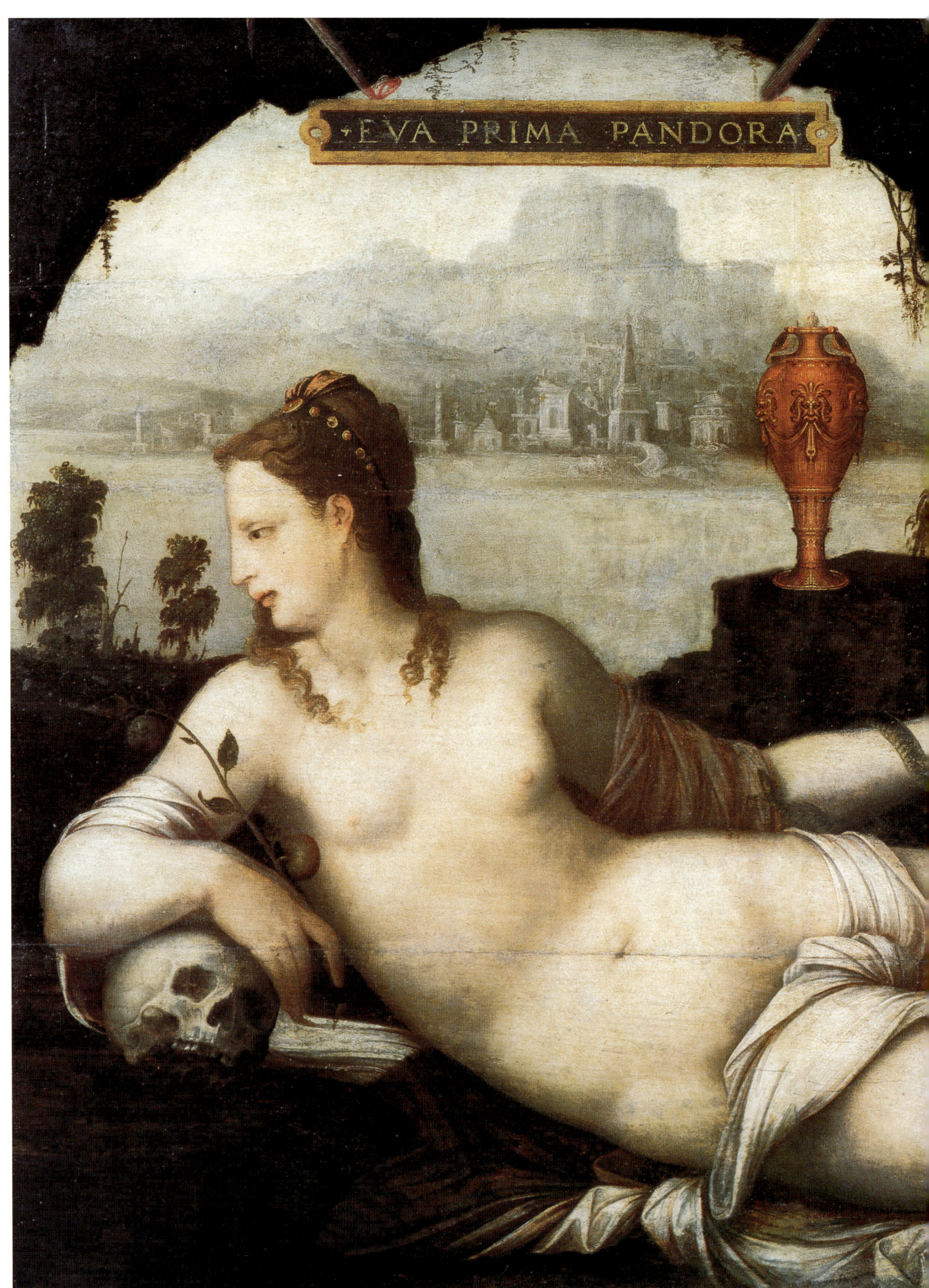

Jean Cousin
Eva Prima Pandora
1559, oil on panel,
97.5 x 150 cm
Musée du Louvre,
Paris

Painter, engraver, and essayist, Cousin *père* is one of the most interesting figures of the world of French art at the middle of the sixteenth century. This famous panel testifies to the intellectual but at times also morbidly erotic style that characterized the art of the European courts during the mannerist period. The label giving the title to the work calls attention to the audacious syncretism, blending classical and religious motifs, that was another characteristic trait of the later Renaissance.

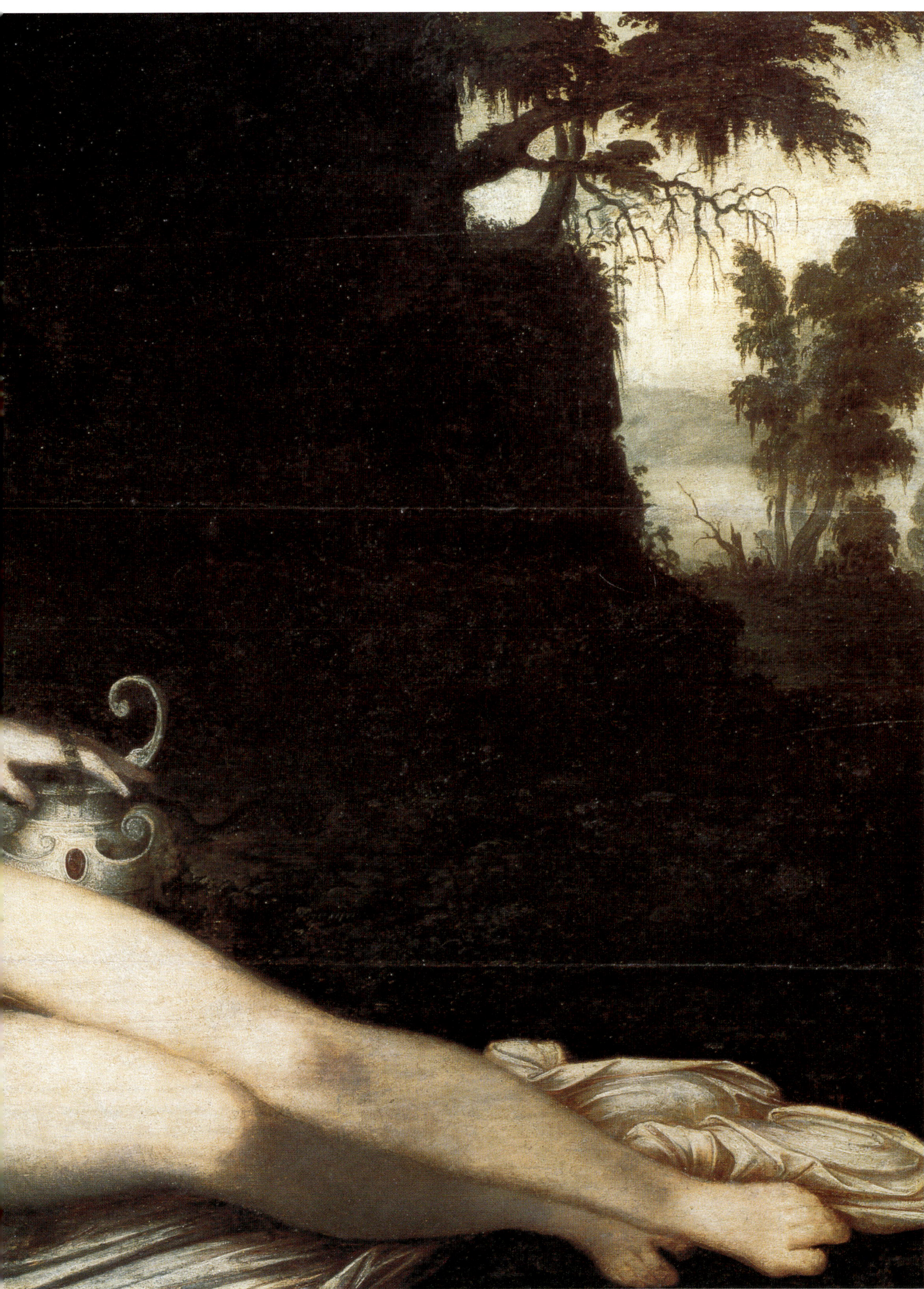

Comparison of the fluid "courtly" elegance of the bas-relief by Jean Goujon with the statue by Ligier Richier makes clear Richier's complex personality. His was a highly particular style in which a still Gothic virtuosic skill blended with domination of the materials and most of all with an energetic sense of a very troubled present, the late sixteenth century in which Europe awakened from the splendid dream of the Renaissance to find itself bloodied, crossed by the opposing armies of Catholics and Reformers. The macabre skeleton, stripped of flesh, that grasps its heart from its chest is a terrible work in which the nightmares of the medieval *danses macabres* are revived along with anticipations of the bizarre Triumphs of Death created by Bernini on the papal tombs of baroque Rome.

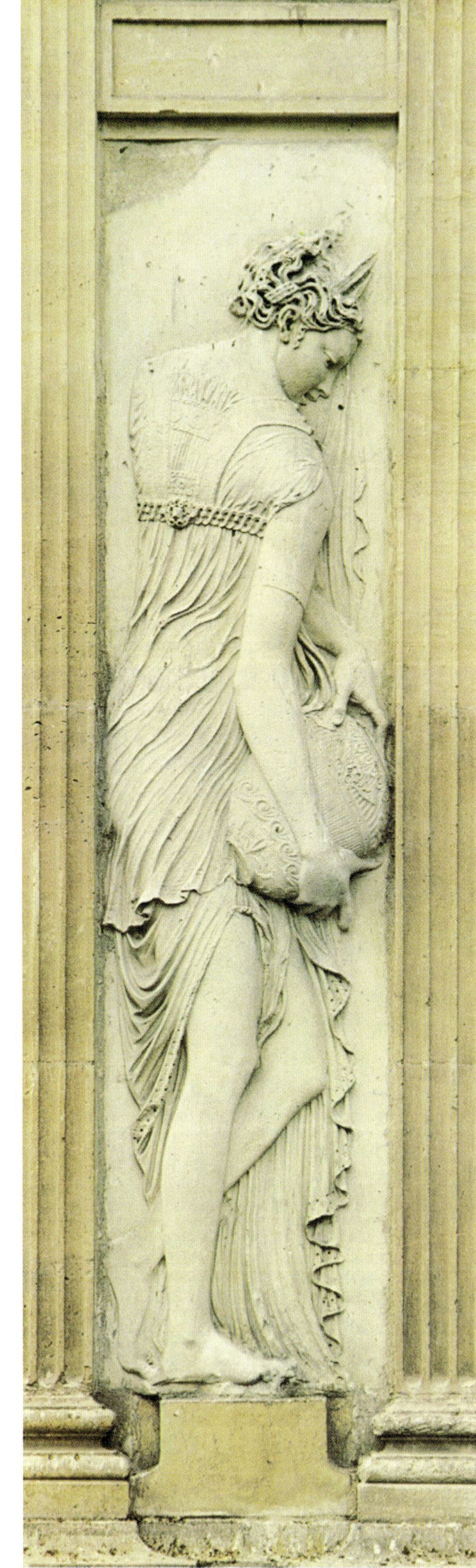

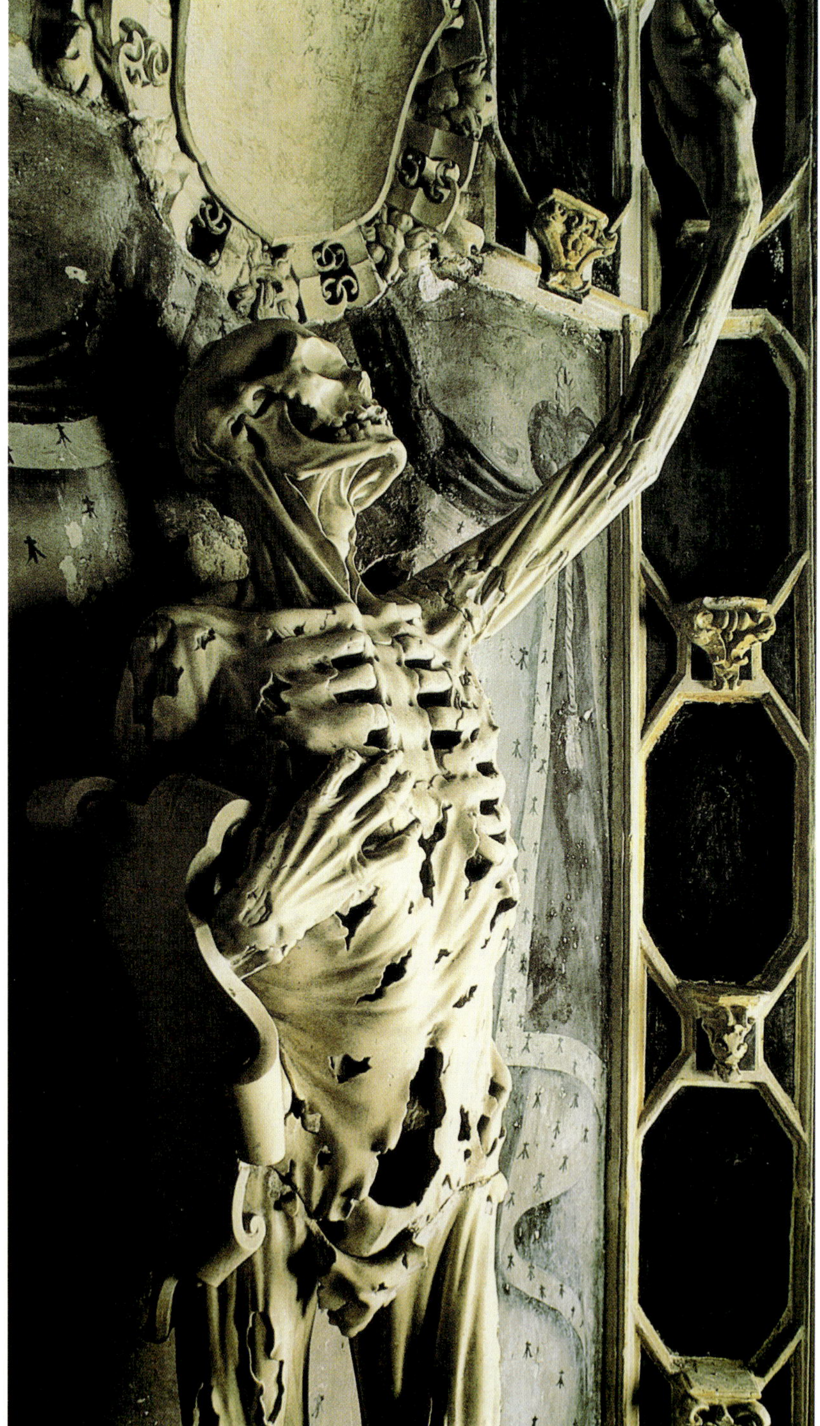

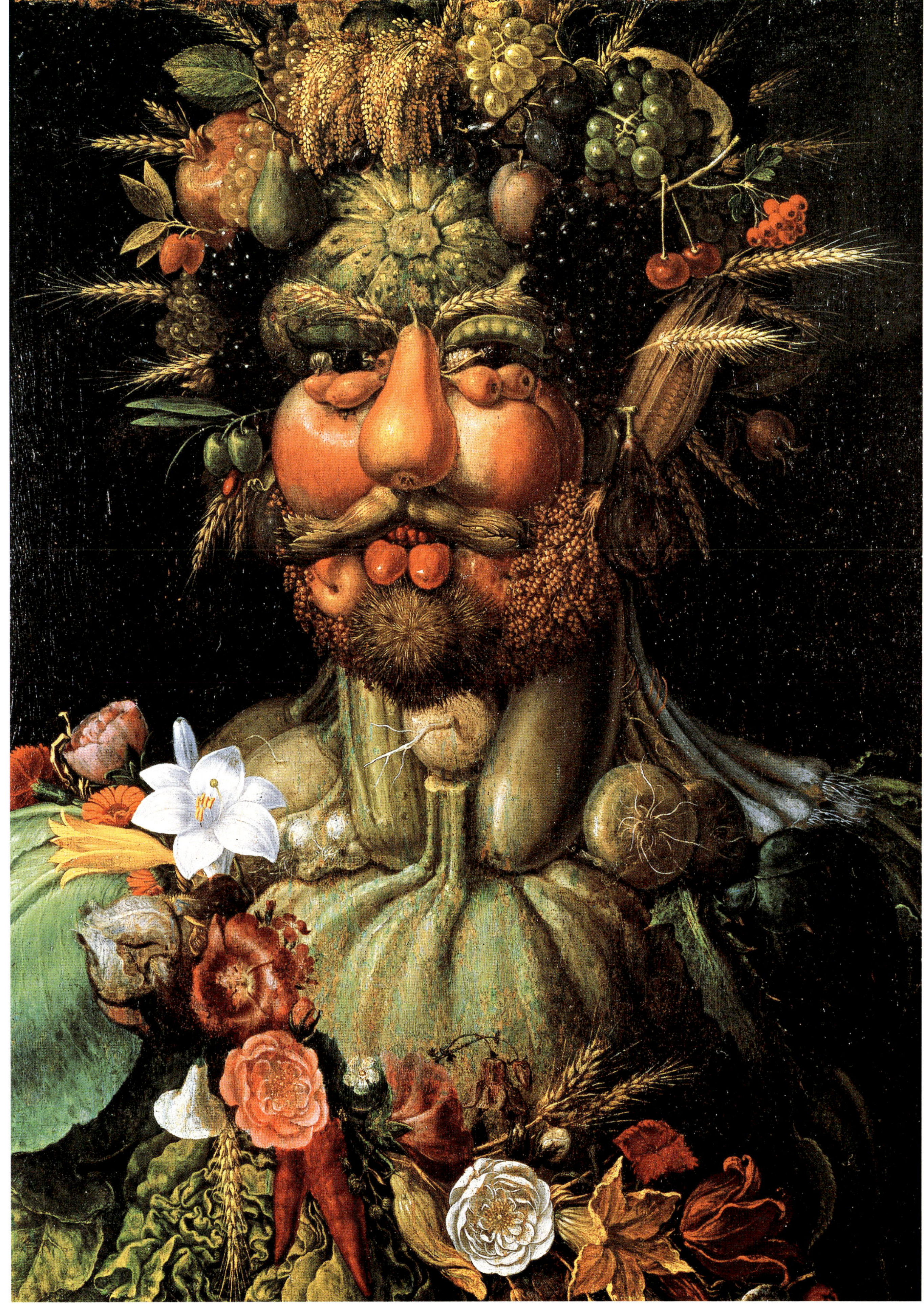

Mannerism in the courts of Europe

BARTHOLOMÄUS
SPRANGER
**Hermaphroditus
and Salmacis**
1582, canvas
Kunsthistorisches
Museum, Vienna

This is one of a series
of mythological can-
vases made for Rudolf
II inspired by the loves
of the gods as narrated
in Ovid's *Metamorphoses*.
In this scene, Hermaph-
roditus, son of Hermes
and Aphrodite, is about
to immerse himself in
the clear water of a
lake; Spranger concen-
trated most of all on
the figure of the nymph
Salmacis who, hidden,
is about to enter the
water and join with the
youth, whom she loved
so much she asked the
gods to let their bodies
be joined in a single
being. In the intense
but also calculated
sensuality of this
work there are clear
echoes of the painting
of Correggio and
Parmigianino. From
Parmigianino in partic-
ular Spranger derived
the soft sensuousness
of the elongated forms.
The use of colors and
the predilection for
multiple tonalities are
typical of the style of
late Italian mannerism.

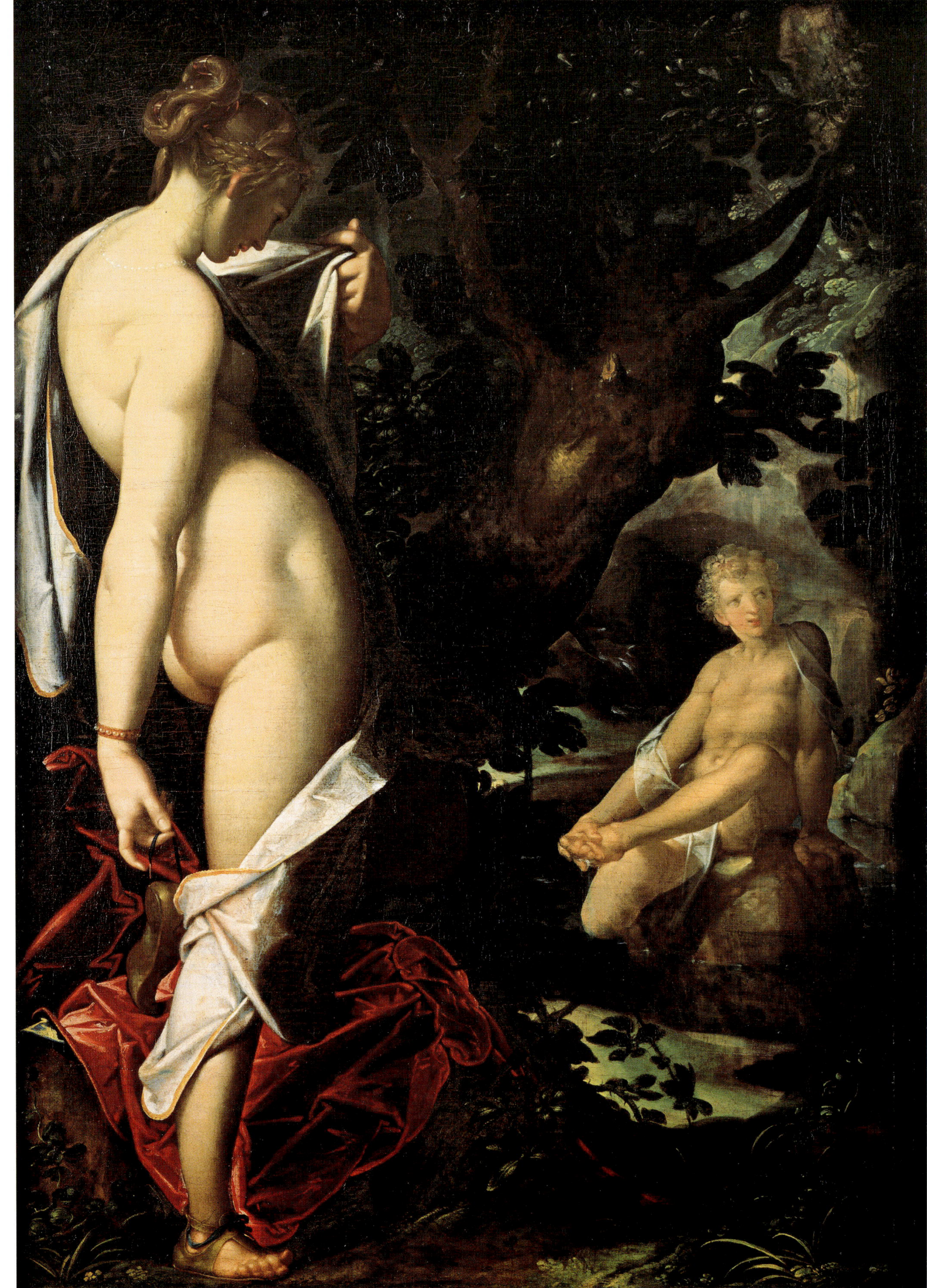

Mannerism in the courts of Europe

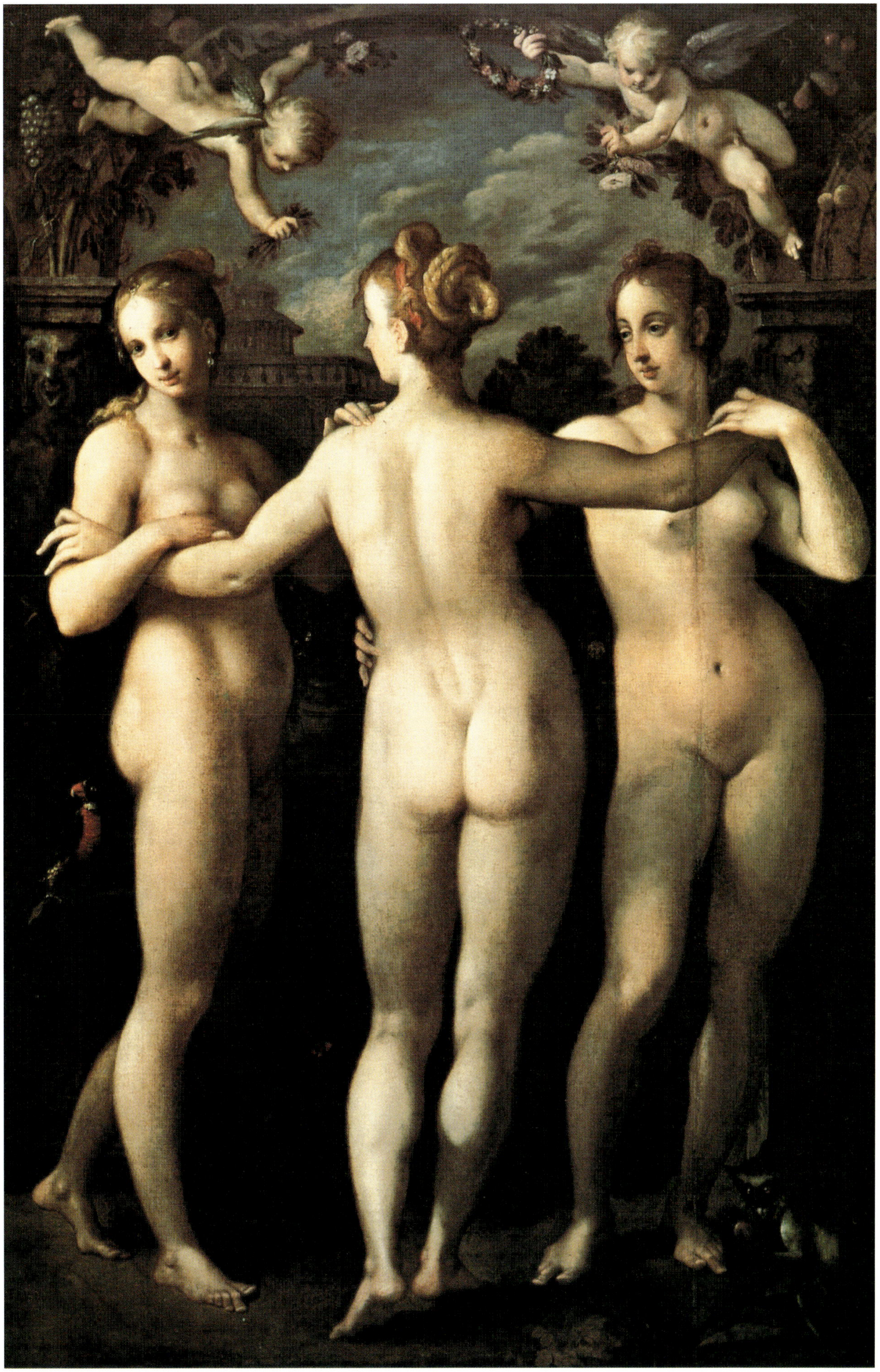

Thanks to the taste and
patronage of Rudolf II,
after the long period of
pause caused by the
religious wars, the
dialogue was resumed
between Germany and
Italian art, which was
looked upon as an
inexhaustible source of
"classical" and also
openly erotic models.
In this canvas, the
theme of the Three
Graces, inspired by a
famous Hellenistic
sculptural group and
repeated many times
over the course of the
Renaissance, becomes
the pretext for a triple
evocation of large-
scale female nudity.

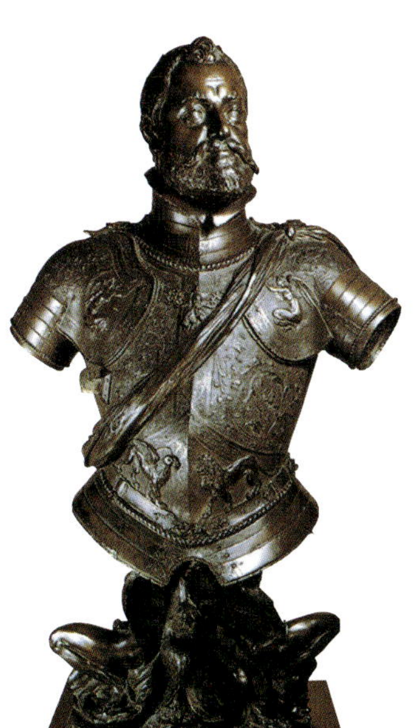

ADRIAEN DE VRIES
**Bust of the
Emperor Rudolf II**
1603, bronze
Kunsthistorisches
Museum, Vienna

The Dutch artist De
Vries, who made this
official portrait of
Rudolf II, was among
the leading interpreters
of the technique of
monumental bronze
sculpture at the end
of the Renaissance.

Mannerism in the courts of Europe

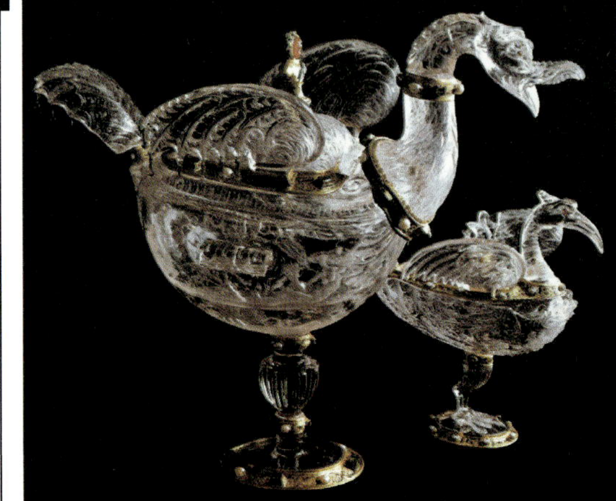

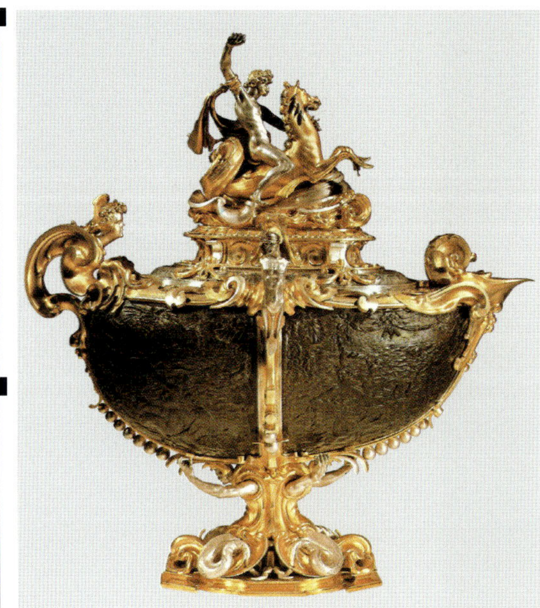

Spanischer Saal
end of sixteenth century
Schloss Ambras,
Innsbruck

The rooms of the castle of Ambras include the partially reconstructed "room of wonders" (*Wunderkammer*), a surviving example of a late sixteenth-century museum, in which the eclectic collections included works made by humans (*artificialia*) that were compared with scientific curiosities (*naturalia*). Every natural object was mounted like a precious piece of jewelry: branches of coral became Sirens' hair, ostrich eggs were wrapped in gilt filigree, narwhal horns, coconuts, pieces of engraved rock crystal were shown off in a wealth of creative fantasy.

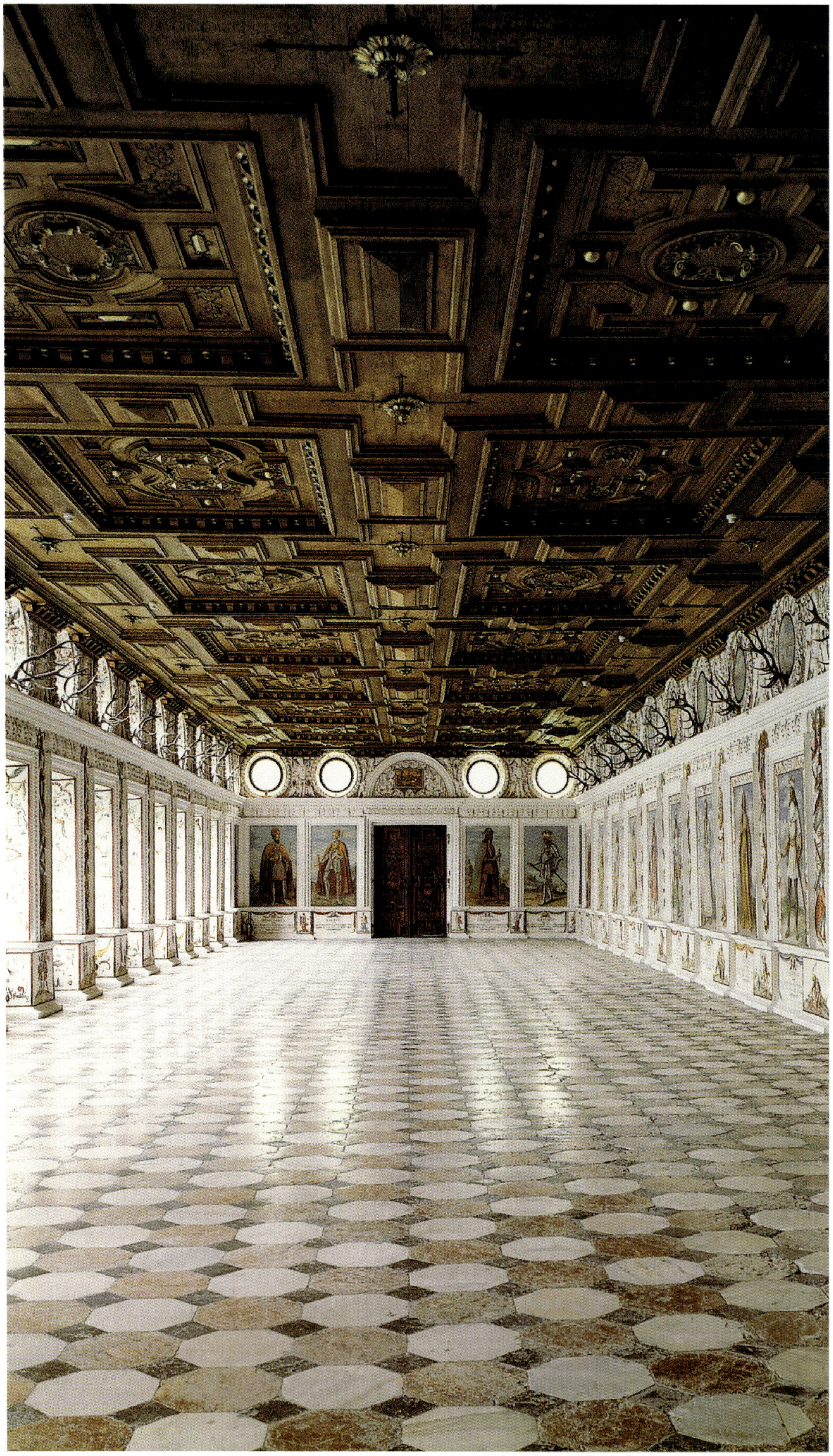

Mannerism in the courts of Europe

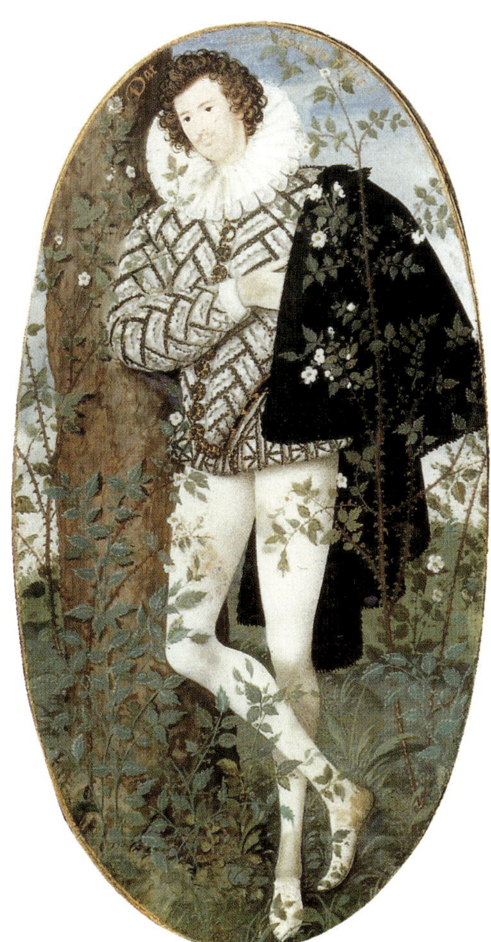

WORKSHOP OF NICHOLAS HILLIARD
Queen Elizabeth I
1599
Musée du Louvre, Paris

The highly refined miniaturistic portraits made in the circle of Nicholas Hilliard are a singular expression of English culture during the Tudor age. Although small in size, they succeed in evoking the Elizabethan atmosphere, with its blend of courtly etiquette and the "sporting" casualness of gentlemen, forming a human gallery that cannot help but call to mind the contemporary activity of William Shakespeare.

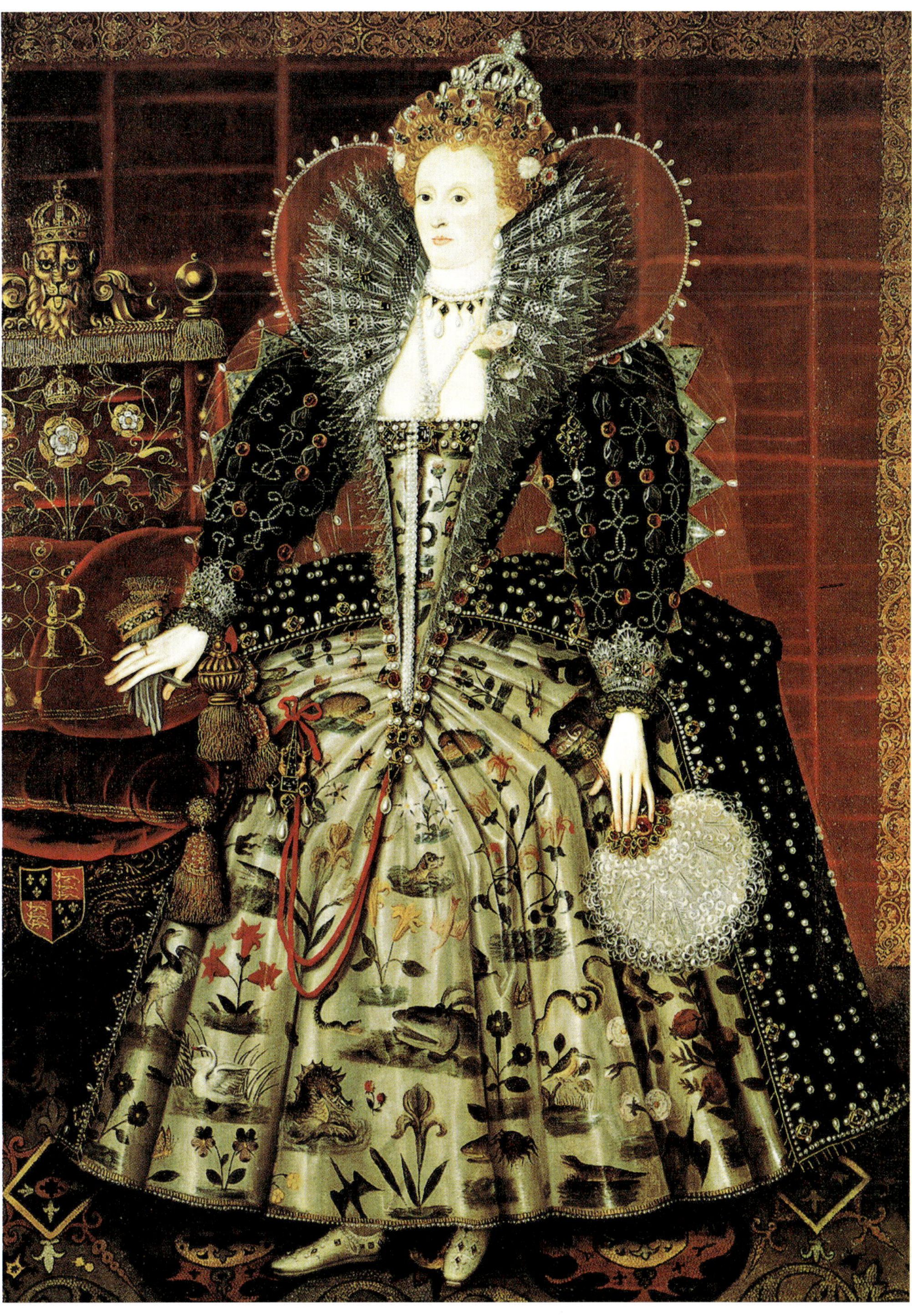

Mannerism in the courts of Europe

mperor Charles V's military campaigns against the Protestant princes of Germany ended with the Peace of Augsburg (1551), summarized in the formula (*cuius regio, eius religio*) by which each prince was granted the right to choose the religion of his region. Meanwhile, at the insistence of Pope Paul III, the upper hierarchy of the Catholic Church assembled in Trent to confront the delicate subjects of the internal reform of the Church and the beginning of a Counter-Reformation movement intended to bring Catholicism back to the regions and zones taken over by Protestantism. The Council of Trent continued until 1563, and aside from important decisions in the fields of liturgy, religious education, canon law, and the organization of the religious orders, the final documents contained precise guidelines to be followed in the creation of religious art. Around the middle of the sixteenth century the taste of the rulers of all Europe, thanks to the travels of artists and the circulation of works of art, was substantially similar. In painting, sculpture, and garden architecture the models

viewer could identity, and instruction in the articles of faith. It was strongly recommended that the figures and details be taken from daily life such that the action would appear to take place in actual reality, not in some uncertain past. One result of the Counter-Reformation was the birth and organization of new religious orders, destined to give an energetic impulse to the structure of the Catholic Church with an almost military spirit. Some of the new orders had strong educational and scholastic goals. One of the most well founded criticisms leveled against the Church by Protestants had been the Church's weak efforts against illiteracy, and an effort was now made to remedy that situation. Other orders were dedicated to missionary work in the recently discovered overseas lands, while also opposing the advance of the Protestant Reformation by adding new peoples to the Church. Still others, such as the Jesuits, underwent rapid expansion of their power, such that they became part of the Church's power structure and were involved in the spread of the faith.

The needs and ideas of the new religious orders led to new architectonic solutions and new figurative models that became some of the most important sources of baroque art. The construction of the Church of Gesù—an innovative work by Jacopo Vignola—and the first phase of its decoration, which was closely related to the religious attitudes of Ignatius of Loyola, led

The Counter-Reformation

of central Italian mannerism had spread to almost all the courts of Europe. It was an intellectual art, extremely elegant, full of literary references and symbols, designed for the enjoyment of a select public. Much different was the art of ordinary people. The cardinals of the Council of Trent (among them Charles Borromeo) wanted art to be capable of "speaking" to everyone. The Counter-Reformation proposed making the places and personages of the faith visible and recognizable. Great churches and sanctuaries arose along the entire pre-Alpine zone, most of them out of proportion to the small towns nearby but clear visual signs of the presence of the Catholic Church. In contrast to the Protestant rejection of the cult of saints, devotion for the more popular figures was emphasized, with their lives and martyrdoms illustrated in spectacular ways in statues, paintings, and frescoes. As for the field of painting, the guidelines from the council marked a change that is at the base of the passage from the Renaissance to the baroque. Sacred images were to be readily understandable and to contain didactic aspects, indicating examples of Christian virtues with which the

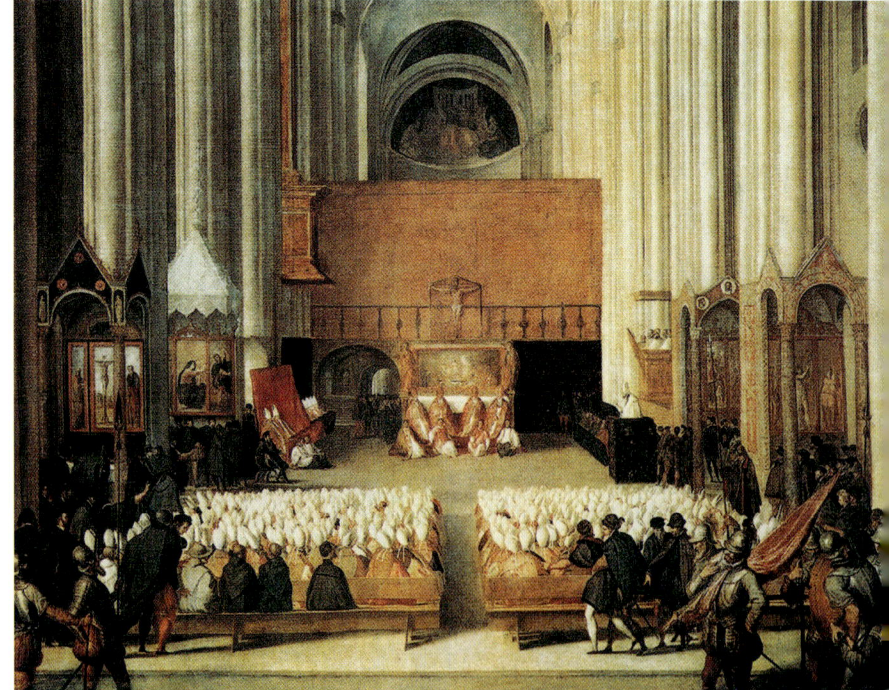

The Counter-Reformation and the question of art

during the 1580s to the formation of a school of architecture and painting in which sacred art was made extremely simple, austere, even severe, swept free of every trace of intellectual eccentricity in order to make immediate contact between the faithful and the religious image. The artists active in this sphere included, for example, Scipione Pulzone, creator of highly precise portraits, most of all of ecclesiastics. This artist's works are the extreme opposites of the portraits by Titian, which were little valued in clerical Rome. Whereas portraits by Titian are vibrant and forceful, quickly expressing the attitudes and gestures of character, those by Pulzone present a motionless calm, they have the crystallized purity of "timeless" images. The circle of painters related to the Jesuits presents a precise and relatively brief phase in the history of art, one that ended by closing in on itself, leaving no further development after the end of the century. Federico Barocci, born in Urbino, was instead the

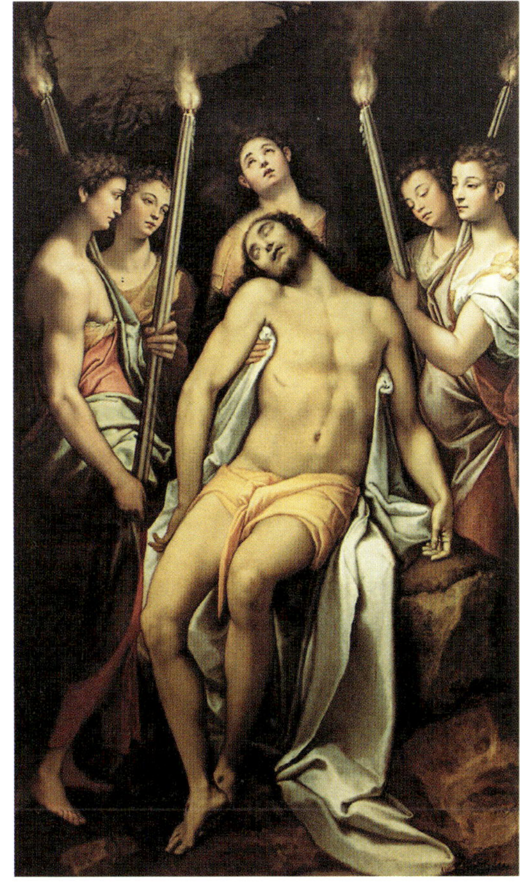

Federico Zuccari, *Pietà*, 1567; Galleria Borghese, Rome

Daniele da Volterra (from then on nicknamed *Il Braghettone*—"The Breeches Maker") early in 1564, only a few weeks before the death of Michelangelo.

Once again the great Tuscan artist was confirmed as the central figure of the High Renaissance, and in fact it is in that role that he appears in the most important book on Renaissance art, the *Lives of the Artists* by Giorgio Vasari. The first edition appeared in 1550, the second, enlarged and enriched after Michelangelo's death, in 1568. Vasari's work is sometimes referred to as the first manual of art history, whereas it is really a well organized series of biographies of painters, sculptors, and architects, from Cimabue and Giotto to Michelangelo. According to Vasari, art had followed an evolution, beginning from its lowest point in the Middle Ages to slowly rise, the steps of its progress marked off by conquests in the reproduction of nature, linear perspective, and the human

and the question of art

link between the sixteenth-century masters and those of the nascent seventeenth, from Carracci to Peter Paul Rubens. Trained in the artistic heredity of Urbino and Raphael, Barocci presented in his youthful works the grace of Correggio enriched with the warm colors typical of Venetian art. His visit to Rome, during which he took part in the decoration of the Casina of Pius IV in the gardens of the Vatican, ended with his return to Urbino (1565), where he made ambitious compositions and sent them off to various centers.

A typical outcome of the debate about religious painting was the decision to cover over the areas judged most "obscene" in Michelangelo's *Last Judgment* in the Sistine Chapel. The undertaking (which was limited in scope) was performed by

body. This evolution had approached its end during the period of Leonardo and Raphael to then reach its peak with Michelangelo, after whom there could be nothing but decline. No one would ever be able to outdo the sublime style of the master, most especially in terms of the representation of the highest subject, the human body, which Michelangelo had perfected. The particular vision of art history presented by Vasari, its marked preference for Tuscan masters, and its various inexact anecdotes and details have not obscured the fundamental importance of *The Lives*, which is an invaluable source of information about many artists as well as a significant expression of the taste and culture of the Renaissance, which had reached full maturity when Vasari's book was written, by which time there were signs of a coming crisis.

Domestic altar, 1580–90; Schatzkammer, Munich Residenz, Munich

The Counter-Reformation and the question of art

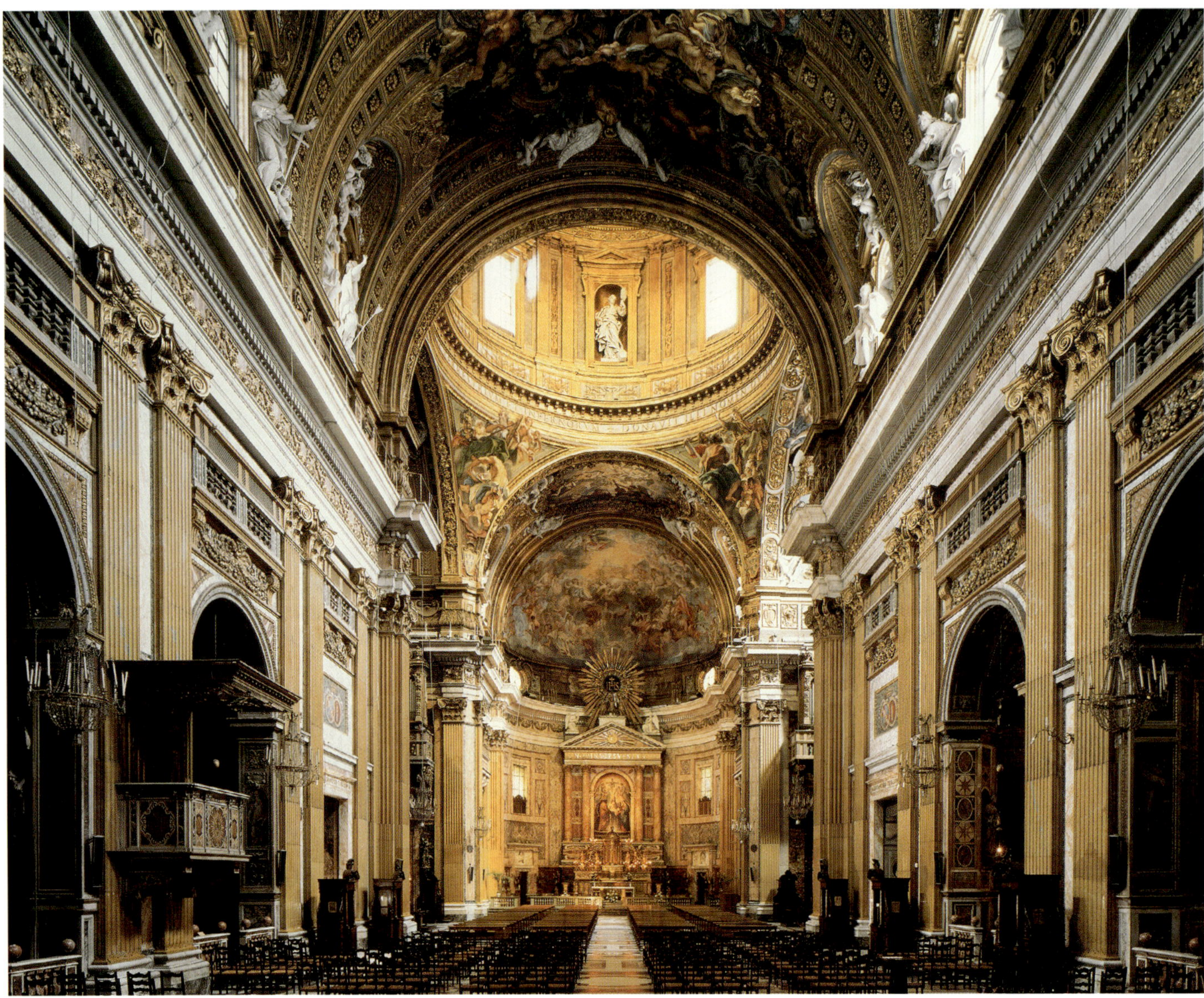

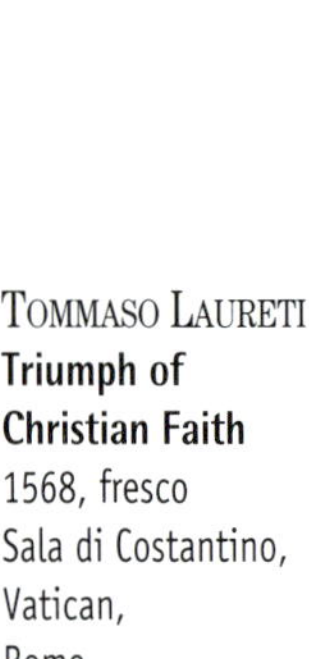

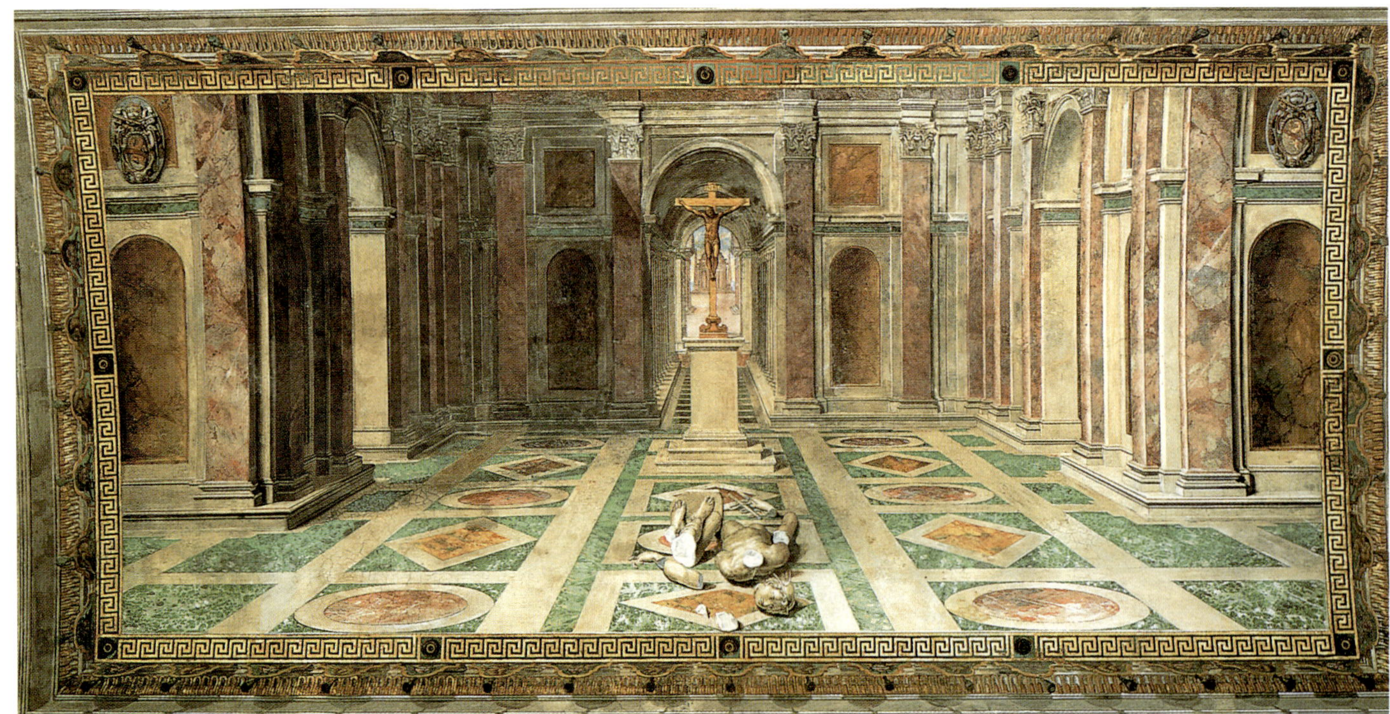

The Counter-Reformation and the question of art

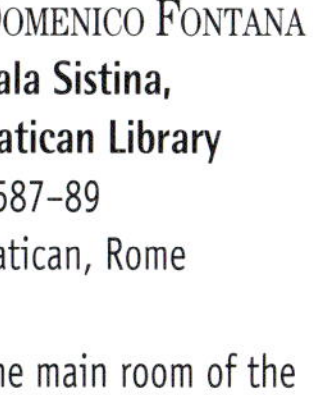

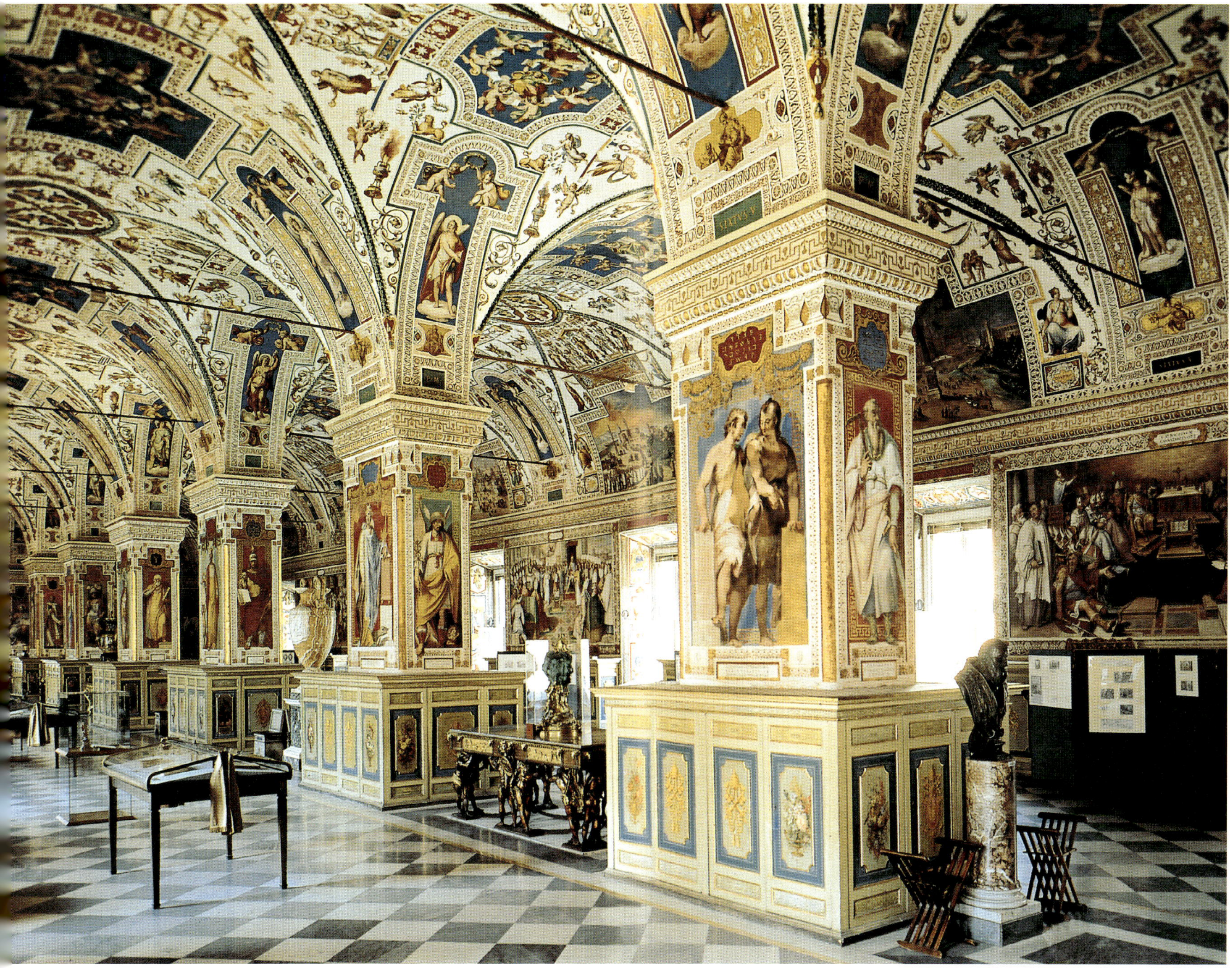

The main room of the new library by Domenico Fontana, the great Sala Sistina, is divided in three naves by massive piers, the surfaces of which, like all the rest of the room, are covered in frescoes. The team of painters that worked in the library was led by Cesare Nebbia and Giovanni Guerra, both of whom were primary artists in other Sistine works. Nebbia was originally from Orvieto and was related to the Tuscan-Roman and Lombard culture, while Guerra, from Modena, had a more refined and elegant style that mitigated some of Nebbia's severity. Among the artists working on the project was the painter and writer Giovanni Baglione, who recorded a large number of artists involved, including Paul Bril, Giambattista Pozzo, Paris Nogari, Andrea (Giovanni) Lilli, and Orazio Gentileschi. The cycle deals with four great themes: the great libraries of the ancient world, the ecumenical councils, the inventors of alphabets, and the works of Sixtus V. The vaults are decorated with grotesque motifs of Renaissance inspiration.

The Counter-Reformation and the question of art

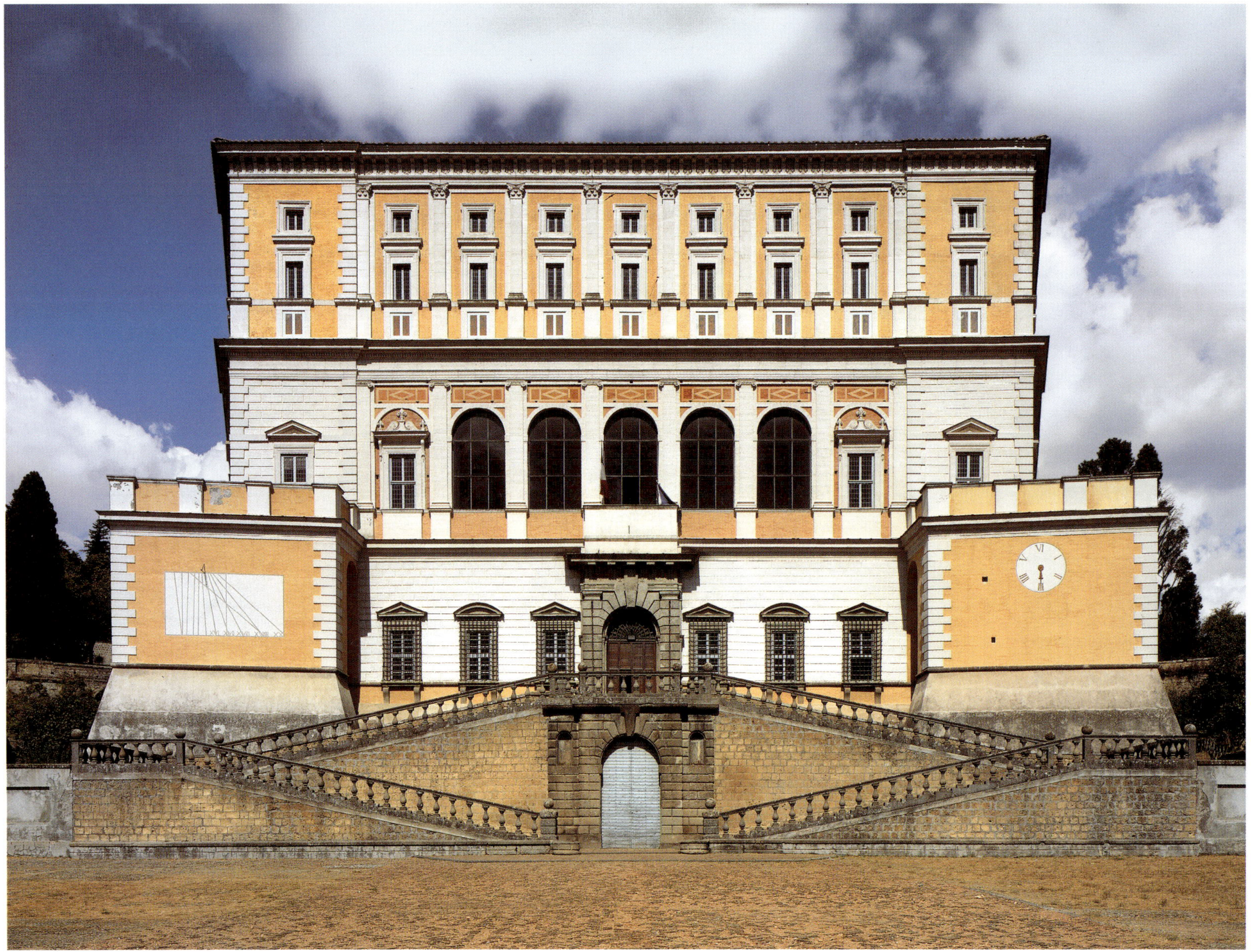

The Counter-Reformation and the question of art

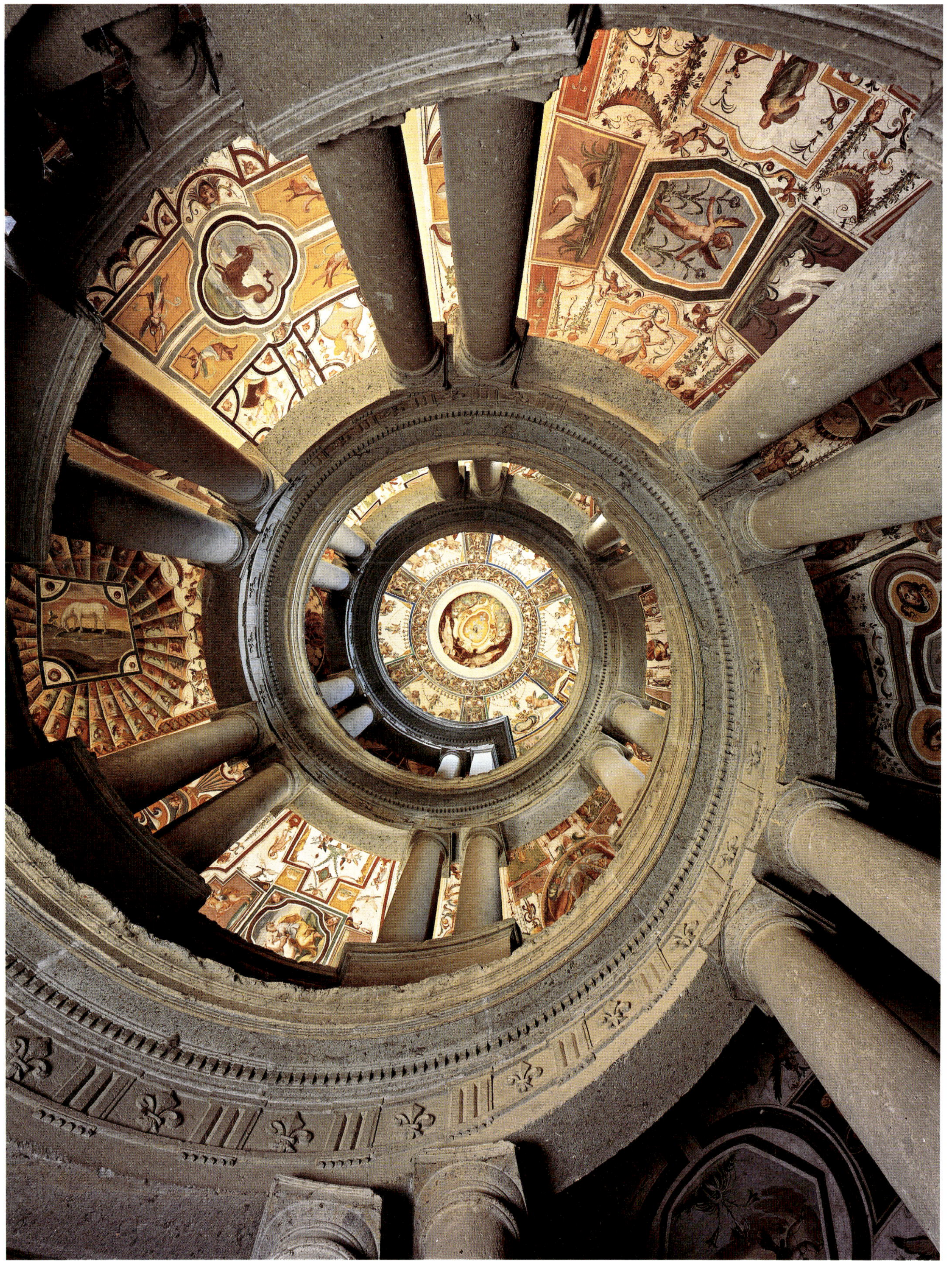

The Counter-Reformation and the question of art

The Most Serene
Republic of Venice
enjoyed well-merited
fame for its tolerance
and open-mindedness.
That was before the
tense atmosphere fol-
lowing the Council of
Trent and the worries
that arose about com-
ing wars against the
Turks, a situation in
which the Inquisition
began to reach even
as far as the lagoon.
Paolo Veronese, one
of the most radiant
painters of the late
Renaissance, the cre-
ator of joyful, straight-
forward works as far
removed as possible
from the palest shadow
of heresy, was nonethe-
less fated to experience
the Inquisition person-
ally. One of his paint-
ings, delivered to the
refectory of San
Zanipolo in 1573 to
replace a work by
Titian that had been
lost in a fire, awakened
the suspicions of the
Dominican inquisitors.
Summoned to appear
before the inquisitors
Veronese found himself
forced to defend him-
self against the serious
accusation of heresy.
A transcript of the
interrogation has been
preserved. He was
reproached for the pro-
fane tone of the vast
canvas (a *Last Supper*)
and for the fact that so

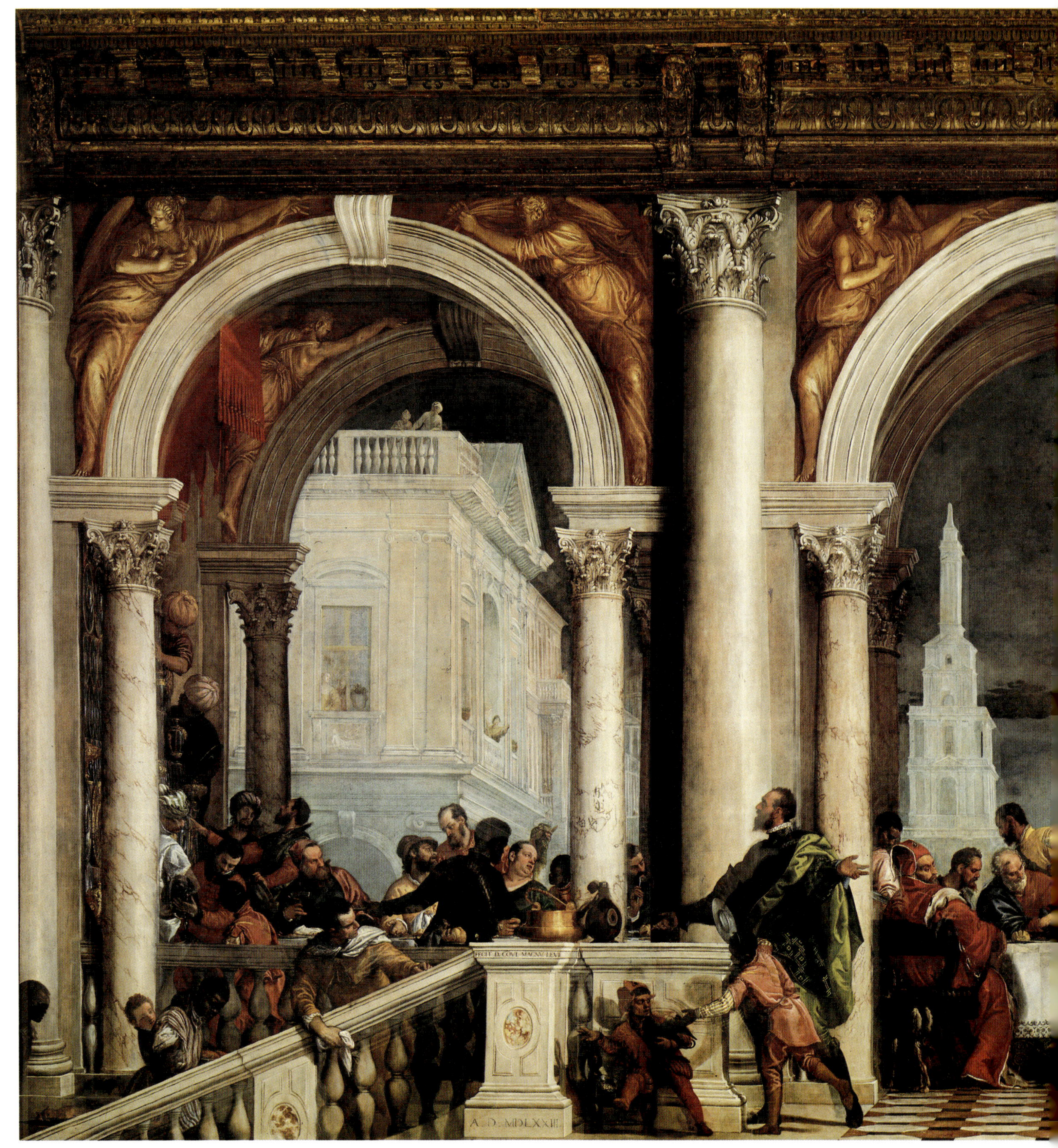

The Counter-Reformation and the question of art

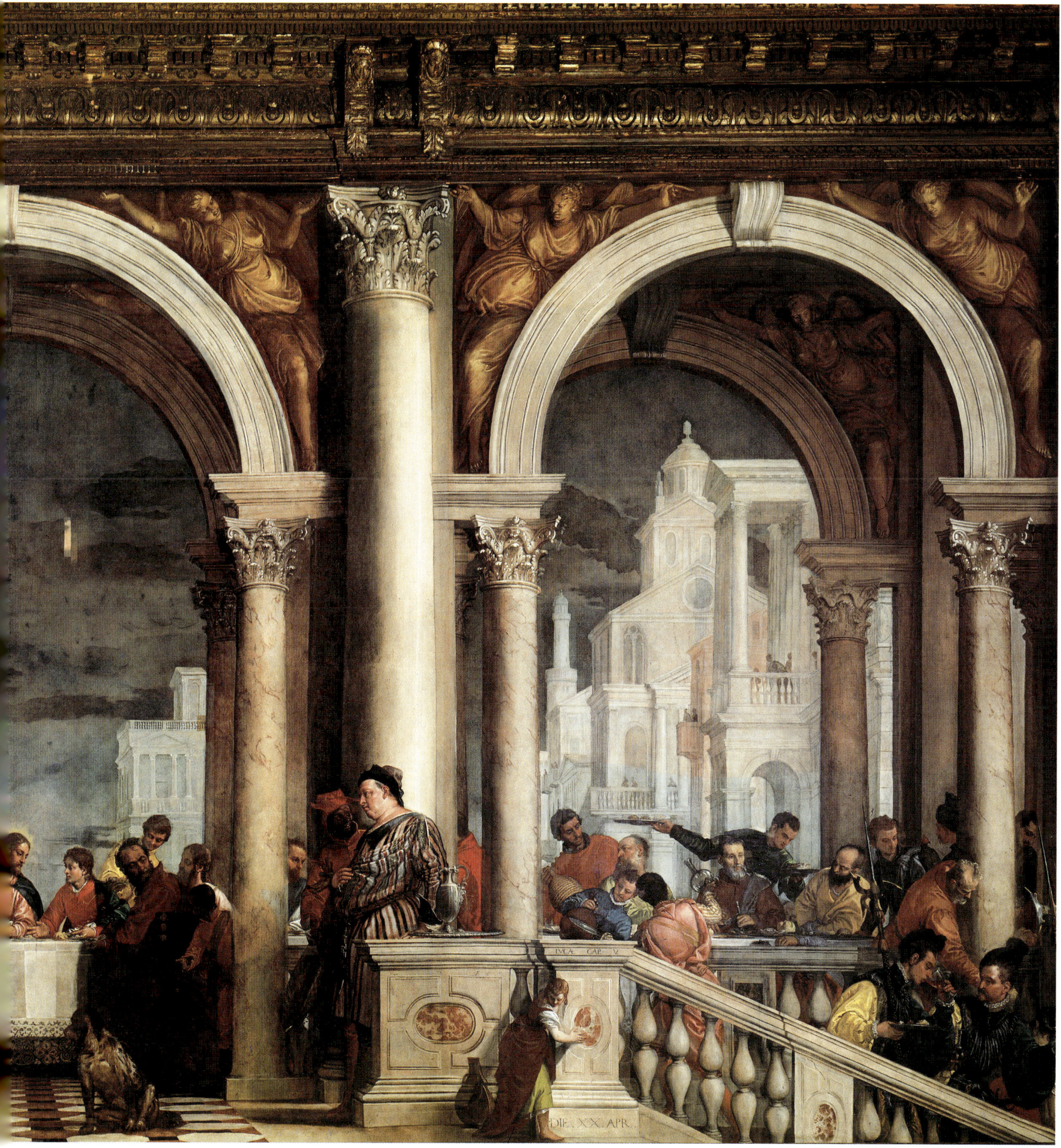

many figures appear in it. The painter defended himself with alacrity in the face of questions, the disarming simplicity of his responses turning away the malicious suspicions. For example, asked why he had painted so many figures (including, his accusers complained, "buffoons, drunkards, armed Germans, and dwarfs") the artist explained that "It—the picture—is large, and it seemed to me it could hold many figures." In one place, with a burst of pride, he states, "We painters take the same license as poets and madmen." This is a vindication of creative freedom, an exaltation of the "artistic license" that can disregard all canons, dictates, and rules. It is precisely by this measurement, the distance between norms and inventiveness, that much of the art and music of the baroque was to be judged. In the end, Veronese was given three months to improve or change the painting so that the passage in the Gospels being presented would be clear. Veronese left the painting alone and merely changed its title, adding an inscription (on the end posts of the stairway) to explain that it presents a *Feast in the House of Levi*. Under that name, the painting is today displayed in Venice in the main hall of the Galleria dell'Accademia.

The Counter-Reformation and the question of art

The works by Pieter
Aertsen and his nephew
Joachim Beuckelaer,
overflowing with food,
fruits, and flowers, had
an interesting continu-
ation in Italian figura-
tive culture up to the
1570s. The merit for
creating the mediation
between the Low
Countries and Italy
goes to Vincenzo
Campi. He was active in
Cremona, a provincial
city, but at the time
full of artistic activity
and open to all kinds

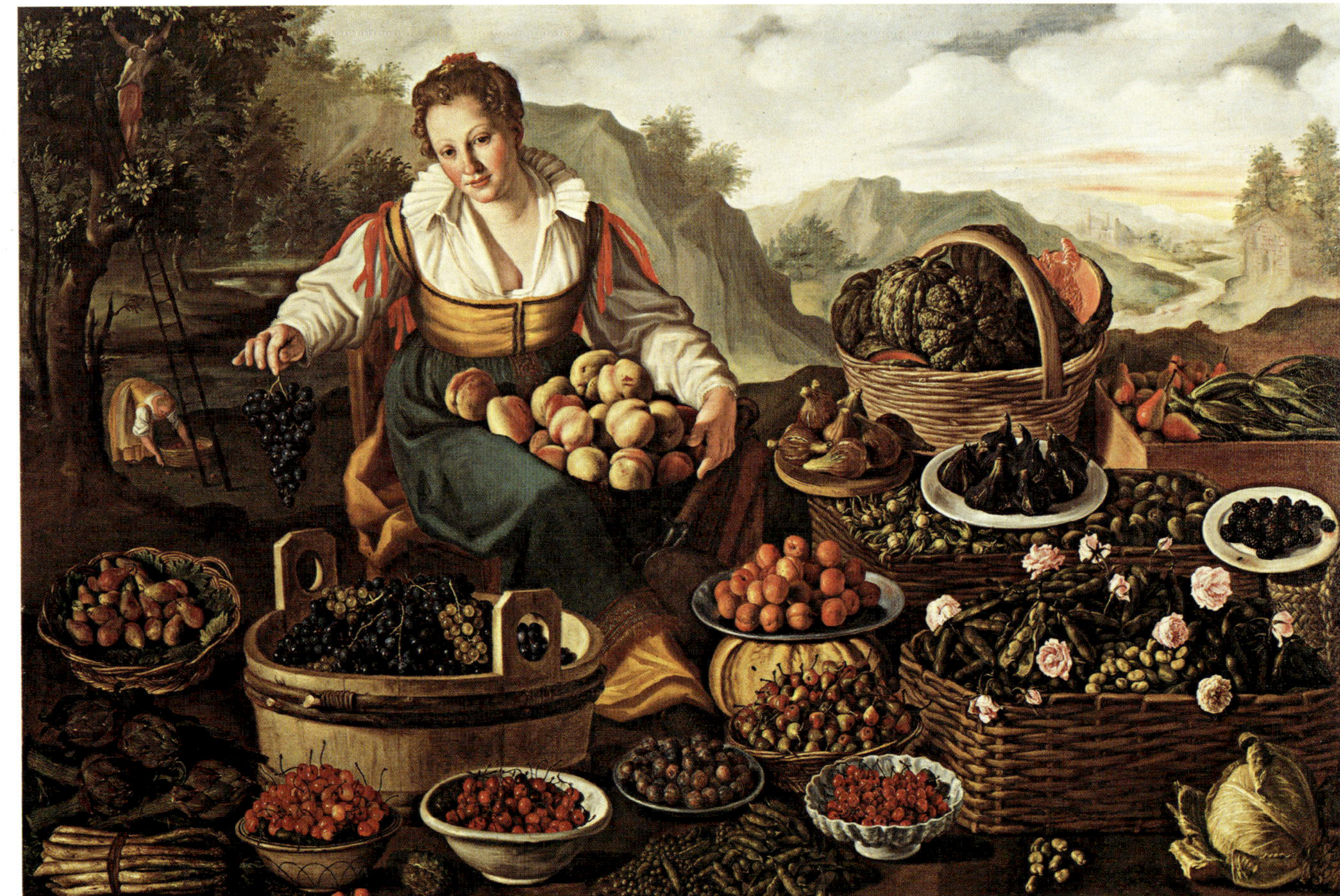

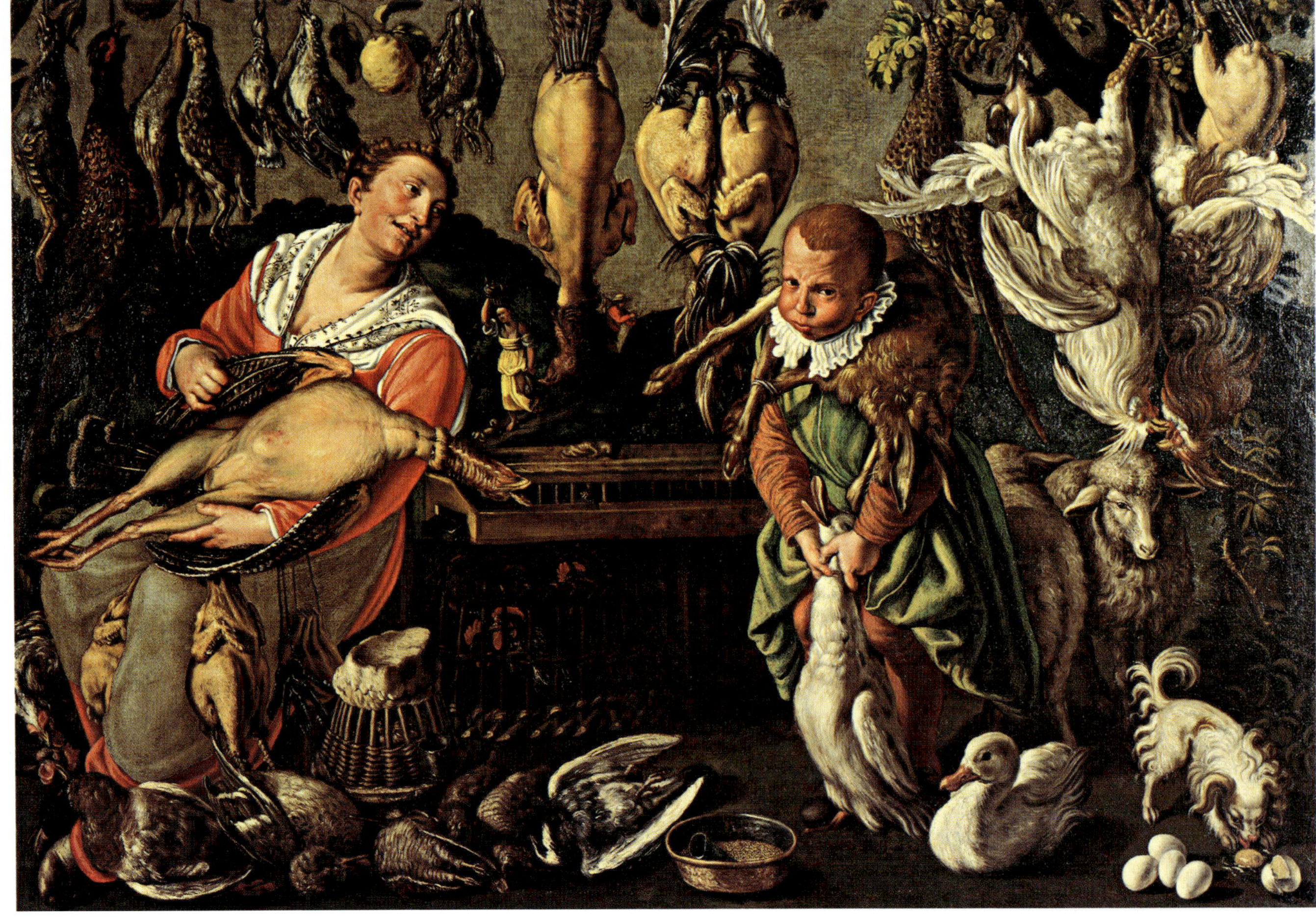

The Counter-Reformation and the question of art

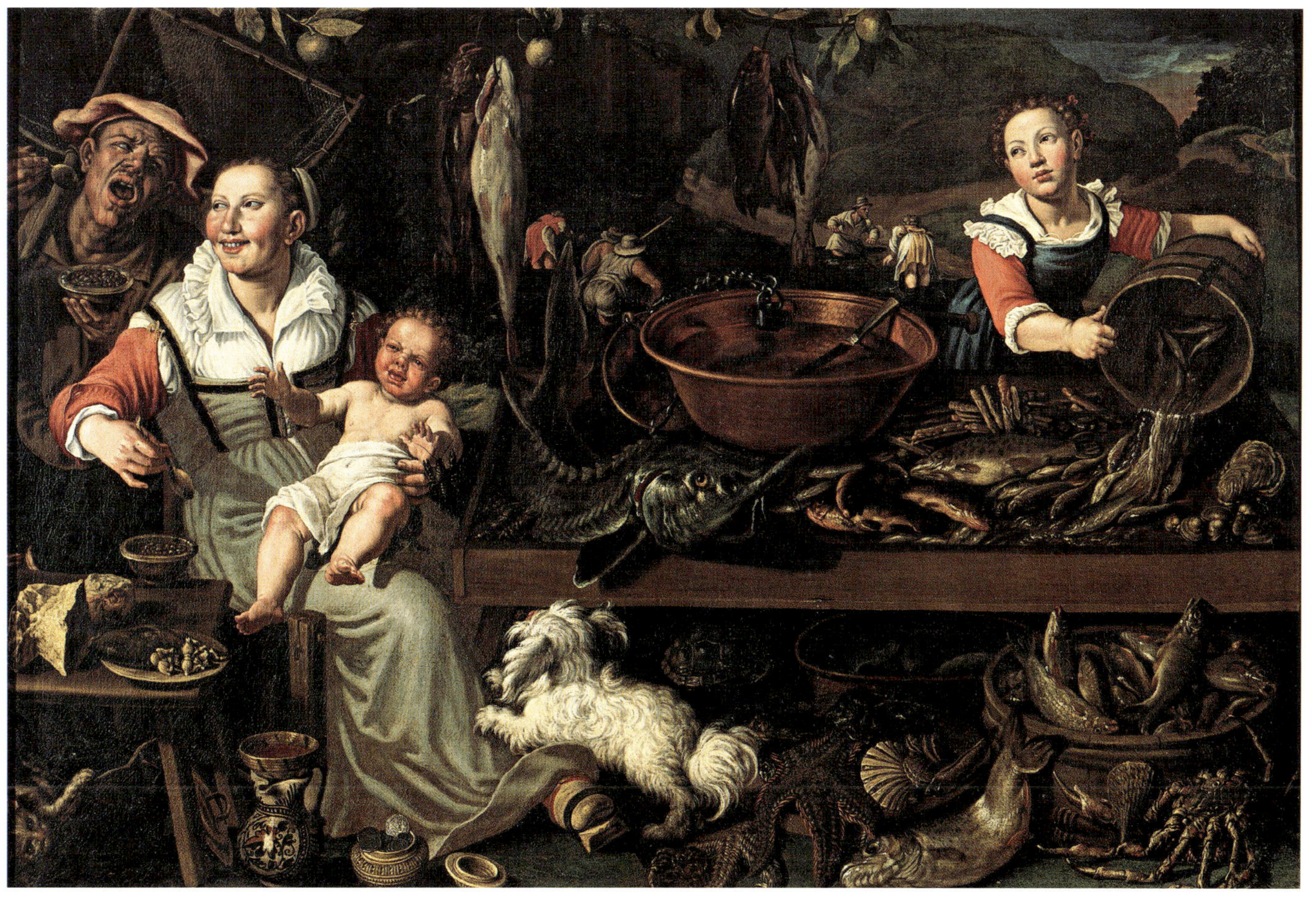

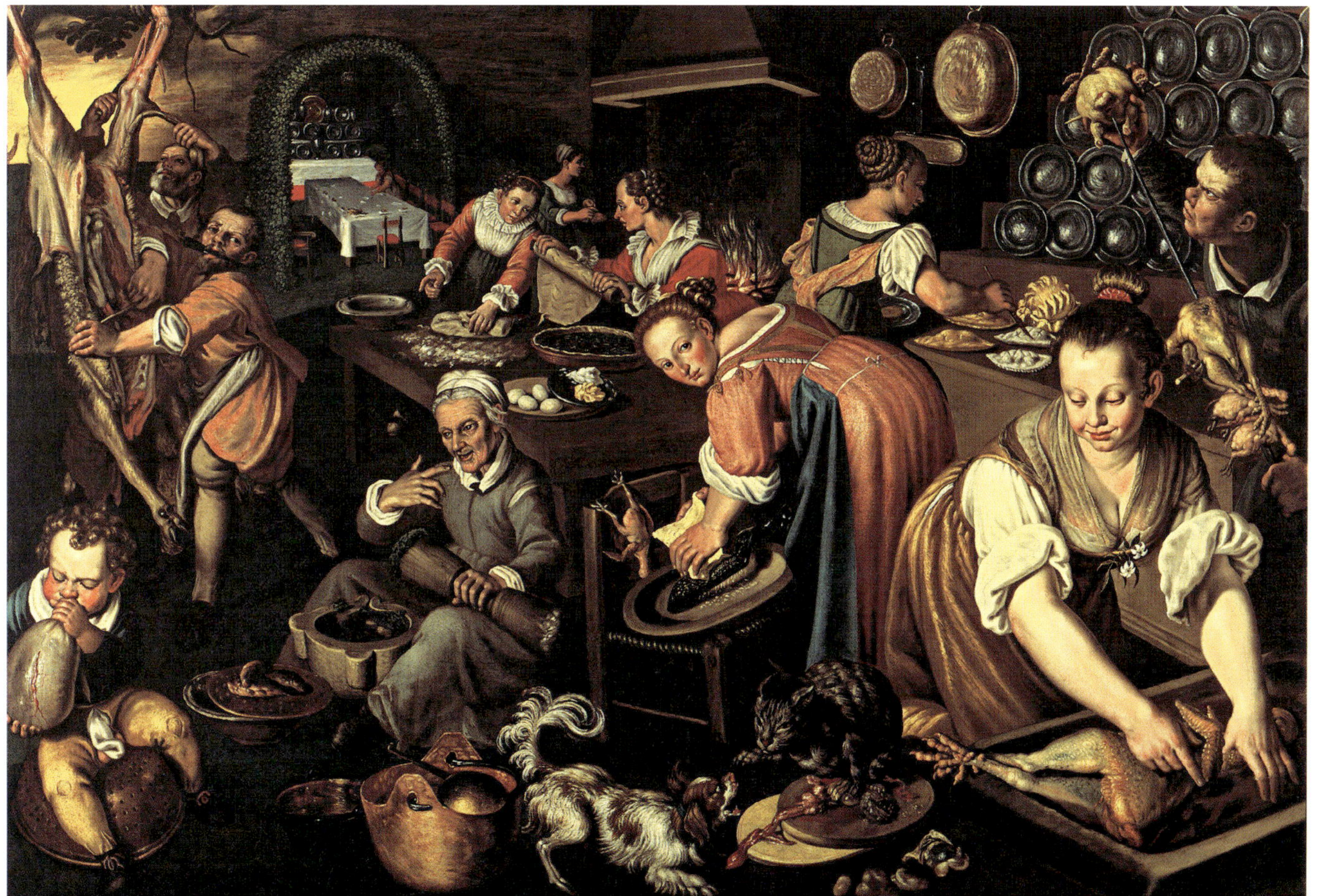

of stimuli, a city capable of finding a middle course between the extreme elegance of mannerism and the concrete reality of the Lombard tradition. Campi composed, and then replicated many times over, images full of a love for nature in which spectacular displays of fruit, game, birds, and fish become motifs of bursting pictorial exuberance. He never slips into the merely "picturesque." His scenes, like the four memorable canvases in the Brera shown here, are always regulated by a precise composition, by a vigorous, even severe, distribution of elements. It is the methodical "seriousness" of his paintings that places Campi among the precursors of a great change, a revolution, in fact, in the very concept of a work of art. Without doubt, this attitude of direction participation of the viewer with the image belongs to the same cultural background that produced Caravaggio and, in the same way, the reference to "natural" painting of the Carracci family in Bologna.

The Counter-Reformation and the question of art

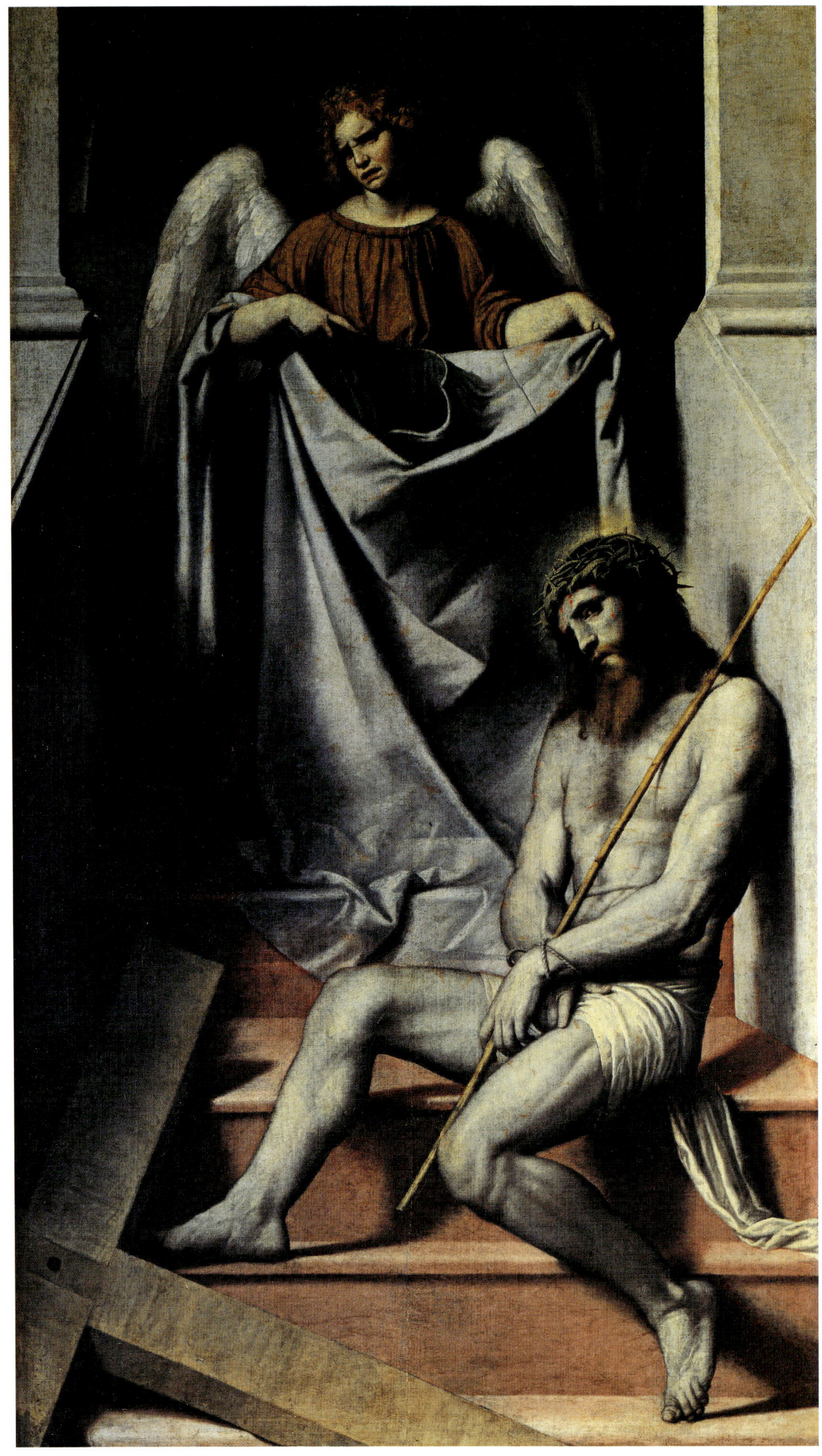

The Counter-Reformation and the question of art

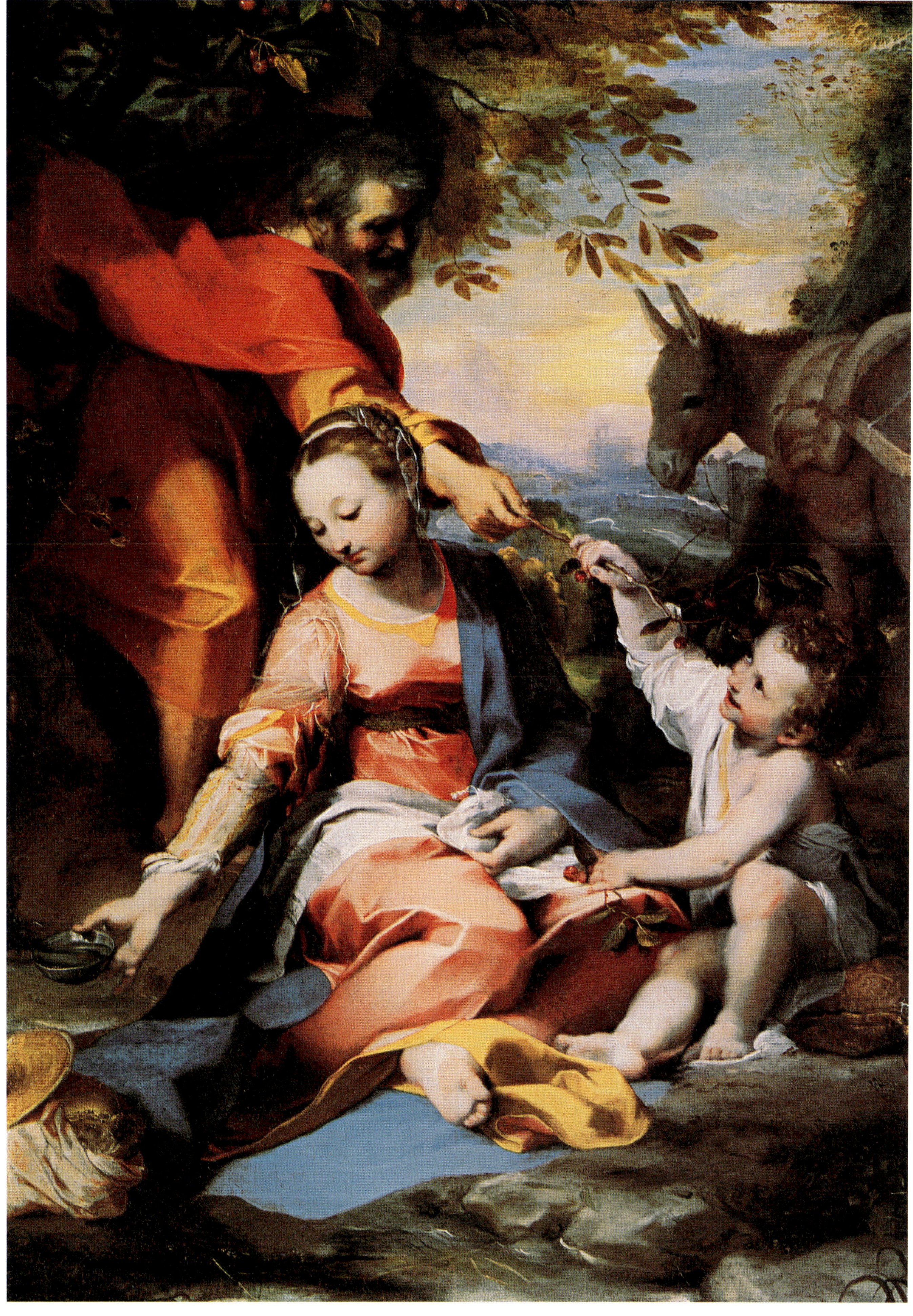

During his stay in Rome, Barocci met with particular favor from the religious orders and confraternities then promoting a radical renewal of the Catholic Church. The narrative clarity and the sentimental tone of his works are perfectly in line with the guidelines for religious art proposed by the Council of Trent. The sweetness of the expressions and the concatenation of the glances and gestures that affectionately unite the various figures in this work reveal a tight compositional study. The painter transformed the sacred episode into a scene of delicate family intimacy, thanks also to the use of soft light and a range of toned down colors that gradually shade into pale pinks.

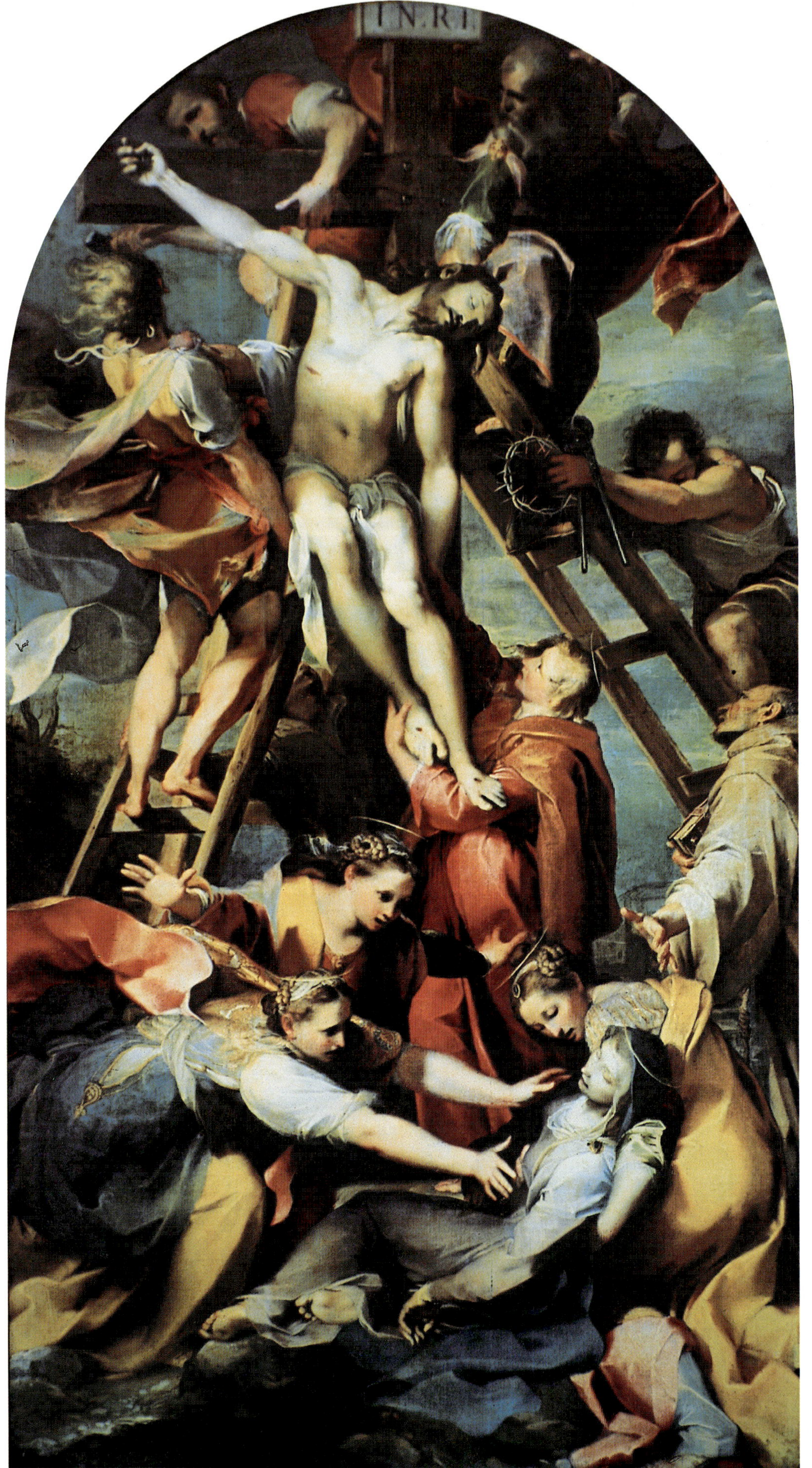

The Counter-Reformation and the question of art

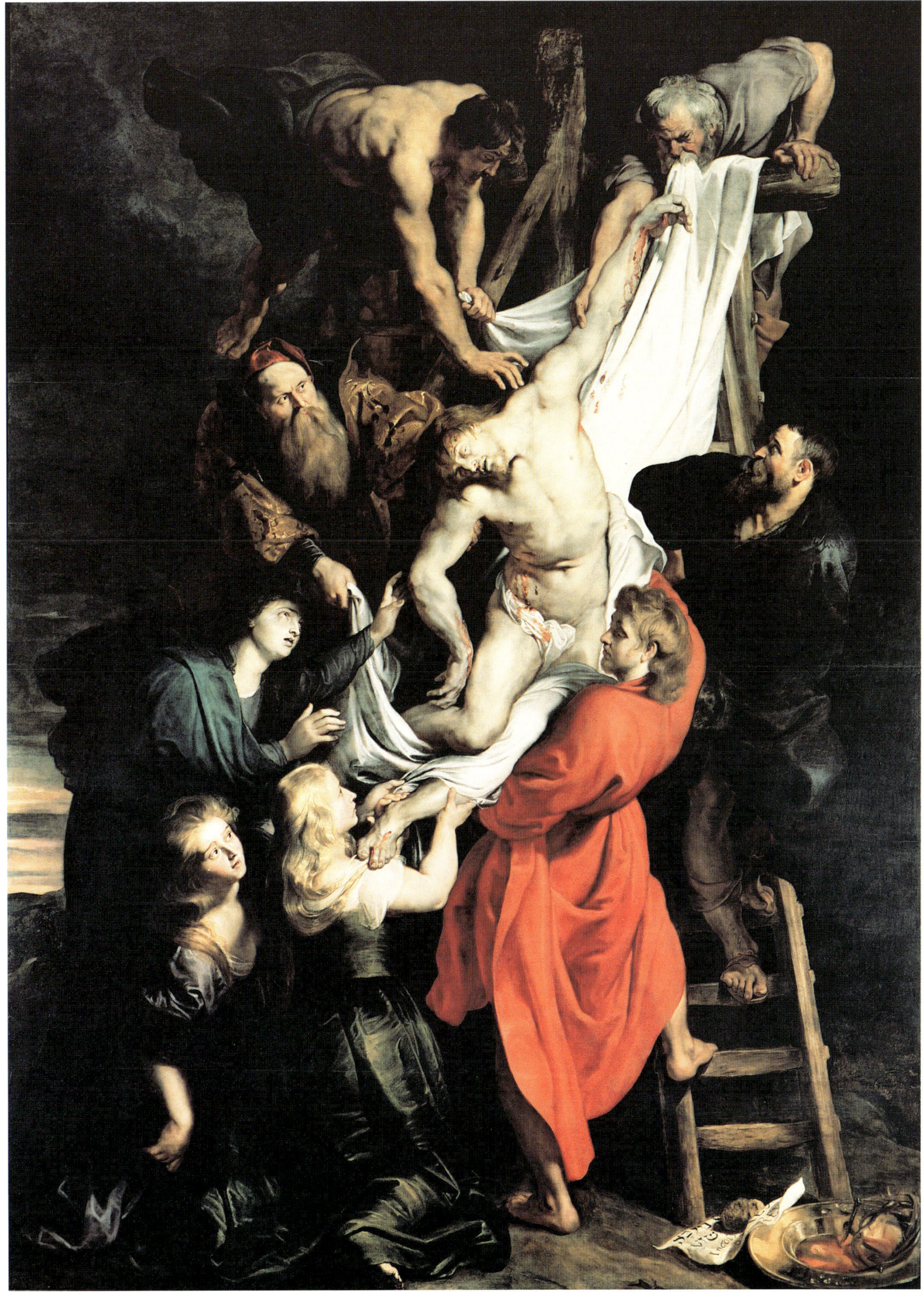

In his first great masterpiece, a symbolic work that confirms his role as the leader of European baroque painting, Rubens repeats observations made during his long stay in Italy and further develops them in an absolutely original manner. Comparison of this spectacular altarpiece in Antwerp with earlier iconographies of the same subject (Rosso Fiorentino, Barocci) offers a clear and useful sense of the stylistic evolution from early mannerism to the Counter-Reformation to the triumph of the baroque. It should be borne in mind that in the course of the religious wars of the sixteenth century Antwerp and Flanders remained Catholic, while nearby Holland became in large part Calvinist.

The Counter-Reformation and the question of art

O ver the course of the 1560s, the population of Venice rose to more than 170,000, a number never to be repeated, not even today, when the city's population is less than half that. The figure of the seventy-year-old Titian loomed over the background of local art, while Tintoretto and Veronese divided the patrons.

At the request of the noble and influential Barbaro family Veronese undertook the decorations of the villa built by Palladio at Maser, near Treviso. The iconographic program called for an exaltation of the nature and opulence of the fields, in the form of classical citations and references to the Olympian gods. The artist used this as the opportunity to offer the most complete proof of his skill at transforming elaborate intellectual allegories into lively, pulsating images set in radiant compositions.

For his part, Tintoretto had taken the road toward a

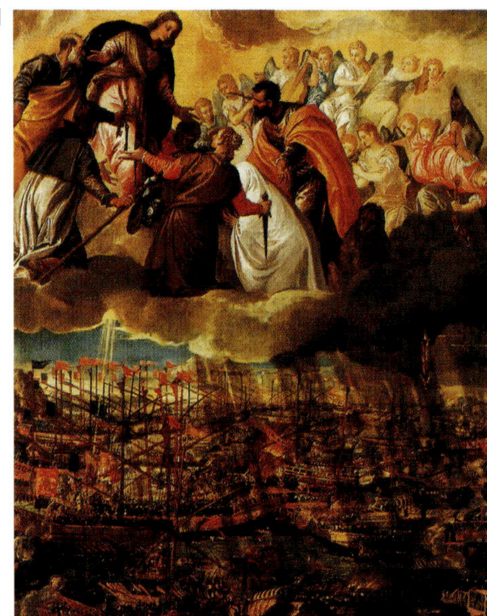

Paolo Veronese, *The Battle of Lepanto*, 1573; Gallerie dell' Accademia, Venice

aggressors. The result was a naval war of European proportion, the decisive encounter of which took place in 1571 in the waters off Lepanto, Greece. The Christian fleet, commanded by Don John of Austria and the Venetian admiral Sebastian Venier won a memorable victory, although its primary importance was symbolic and psychological. In fact, the separate peace signed by the Venetian senate in 1574 confirmed the loss of Cyprus. The enthusiasm over the victory at Lepanto gave way to a widespread sense of dread and a climate of unusual austerity. The taste of Venice's art patrons veered toward a far stronger religious enthusiasm than in the preceding decade.

In 1573 Veronese completed one of his largest and most successful canvases, a *Last Supper* for the refectory of the convent of Saints Giovanni e Paolo, in which he laid out the scene beneath three large Palladian-style arches, giving it the spirit of a theatrical performance. Aside from Christ and the apostles, a crowd of figures fills the scene, dressed in contemporary clothes and caught in relaxed poses. The tribunal of the Inquisition, convoked by the Dominican friars, judged this composition unacceptable and accused the painter of lacking in adhesion to the dictates of Catholic iconography. The transcript of the proceeding reveals that Veronese, faced with the questions

The waning of century on the

dark luminism in which the poses of the figures and the perspective structure suggest expressive forms different from the tradition of symmetry and control. In 1564, thanks to what Vasari considered an illegal act (Tintoretto had completed his painting while his competitors were still preparing theirs and had managed to have it installed, thus giving himself an edge), he was judged the victor in the competition for the decoration of the Scuola Grande di San Rocco. Thus began a cycle of paintings that would absorb his best creative energies for more than twenty years. In 1570 the Ottoman empire again attacked Venetian holdings in the Aegean and eastern Mediterranean. Venice made an alliance with Pope Pius V and Philip II of Spain to repulse the

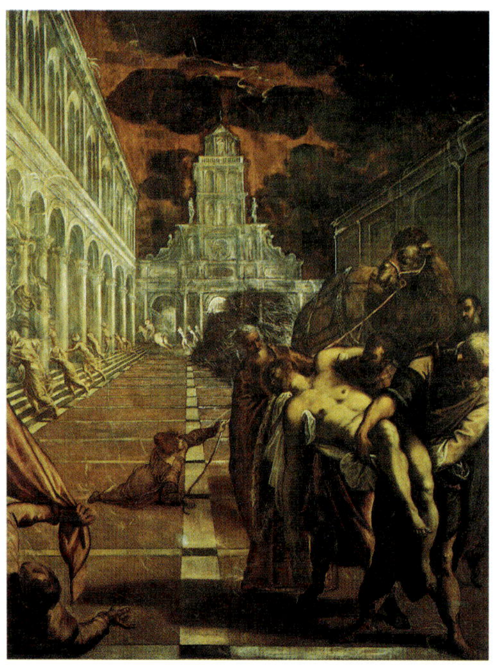

Tintoretto, *The Removal of the Body of St. Mark*, 1562–66; Gallerie dell'Accademia, Venice

of the judges, who insisted on proper respect in the image and on the recognizability of the subject, defended his artistic freedom. In the inquisitors' demand that the participants in the scene should be easy to identity one can make out an echo of the guidelines on religious art proposed by the Council of Trent, the sessions of which had ended ten years earlier. From then on, a change came over Veronese's art. He reserved his decorative colors, bright lights, and crowded scenes almost exclusively for paintings of allegorical or mythological subjects, showing restrained caution and greater doctrinal orthodoxy in his religious works.

In 1576 southern Europe was struck by a tragic plague that soon raged through Venice, car-

The waning of the sixteenth century on the Venetian lagoon

rying off the great Titian. The panorama of Venetian art following the plague seemed impoverished not only by the loss of the master by also by the departure of Domenikos Theotokopulos (El Greco) for Spain. Then, during the first days of 1577, a catastrophic fire devastated the Doge's Palace. An entire wing of the building was burned to the ground, and the Sala del Maggior Consiglio, symbol of the government, was completely ruined. The flames destroyed many works of art, including masterpieces by Titian and Giovanni Bellini. Palladio proposed rebuilding the palace in a new form. The proposal that was accepted, however, called for maintaining the image of the palace and replacing the lost decorations with completely modern versions. It was decided therefore to re-create the Gothic structure of the exterior while at the same time carrying out a complete redecoration of the interior. Within a few months, the building had been raised, and by 1578 work was going ahead on the new decorations for the

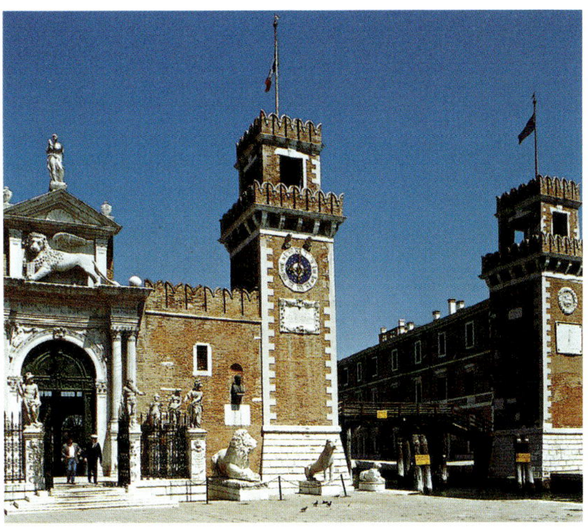

success on the market. However, the subtle aristocratic melancholy that every so often veiled those paintings became an intense and heartfelt interpretation of the mysteries of Christianity in his late religious works. He died in 1588 and was buried in his beloved church of San Sebastiano.

Tintoretto divided his activity between the worksite of the Doge's Palace and the Scuola di San Rocco. When he completed the cycle of paintings in the Salone Maggiore of the *scuola*, he moved on to the paintings between the windows on the ground floor. This series of canvases, dated to between 1582 and 1587, marks a change in Venetian art at the end of the Renaissance. Tintoretto sought and found a new expressive dimension: a refined, at times unreal luminism supported meditative compositions absorbed in the contemplation of the landscape.

The last canvases of the Scuola di San Rocco were the prelude to the painter's last phase. In the works dated to around 1590, mysterious

the sixteenth Venetian lagoon

rooms. The rooms were given gilt-wood ceilings in which were inserted canvases on celebratory subjects. All the best talents in Venetian painting were put to work. The necessity of getting this group of artists to work in coordination gave life to a new "school," meaning a compact group of artists with similar stylistic traits.

The direction of the works and their stylistic orientation were tacitly entrusted to Tintoretto, beginning with the paintings of mythological subjects now on the walls of the Sala dell'Anticollegio. His supremacy was confirmed ten years later, in 1588, with the enormous canvas of *Paradise* (22 meters by 9), which he made for the rear wall of the Sala del Maggior Consiglio.

While Tintoretto's style became a sort of obligatory standard for Venetian painters, Veronese was going through a very interesting phase, during which his expressive language appeared more sumptuous than ever. His profane works, packed with alluring figures in luxurious costumes, often just touched with a hint of seductive sensuality, met with constant

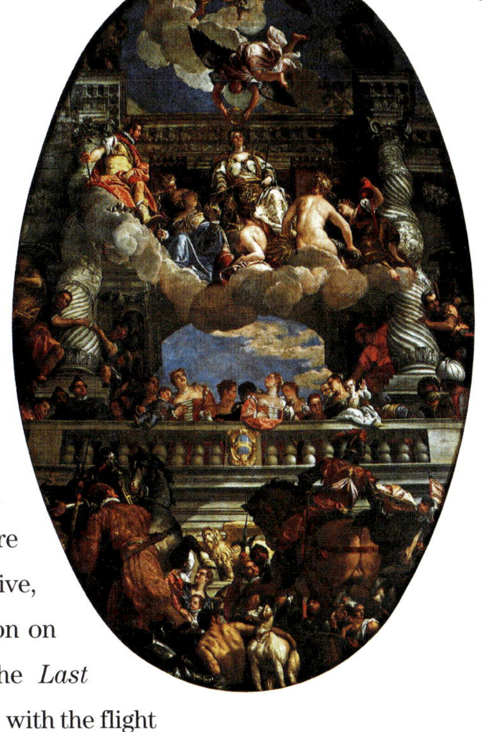

presences hover, suspended between the level of the earth and an ineffable celestial world, while the compositional structure of the paintings becomes elusive, subject to unpredictable rotation on the perspective axis, as in the *Last Supper* in San Giorgio Maggiore, with the flight of spectral shadows over the Eucharistic table illuminated by the radiant figure of Jesus Christ. The thoughtful and intimist approach of the last ten years of Tintoretto finds in Venice a single opposite, the work of Jacopo Palma, called Palma Giovane, the forerunner of the new generation. It was clear, however, that Venetian art was gasping for breath, and with the deaths of Veronese (1588), Jacopo Bassano (1592), and Tintoretto (1594), the most glorious epoch of Venetian painting had truly come to an end.

**Statues of Mars
and Neptune on the
Scala dei Giganti**
1554
Cortile d'Onore, Doge's
Palace, Venice

Throughout the second
half of the sixteenth
century the Doge's
Palace, supreme symbol
of the republic of St.
Mark, was the subject
of prestigious decora-
tive works and restruc-
turing. The giant stat-
ues to the side of the
stairway leading to the
main floor were made
by Jacopo Sansovino
and represent the tute-
lary divinities of Venice
and her independence.
It is interesting to note
that Neptune, god of
the sea, is here pre-
sented alongside Mars,
god of war. On the map
of the city engraved by
Jacopo de' Barbari at
the beginning of the
century (pages 210-
11), Neptune appears
in the company of
Mercury, the peaceful
god of commerce. What
is apparently a minor
change reflects the
far larger change in
Venice's political situa-
tion, at the time facing
serious military threats.

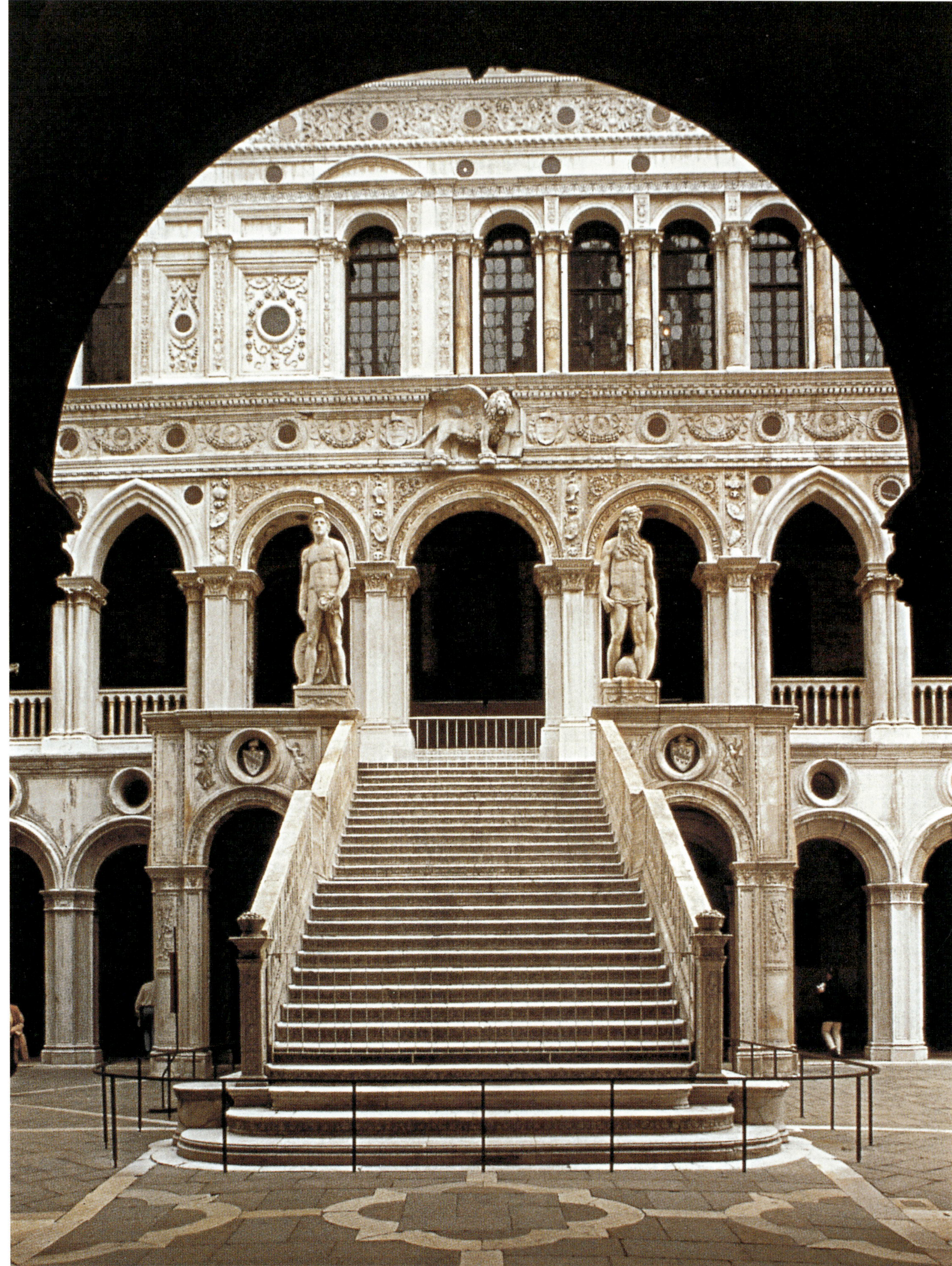

The waning of the sixteenth century on the Venetian lagoon

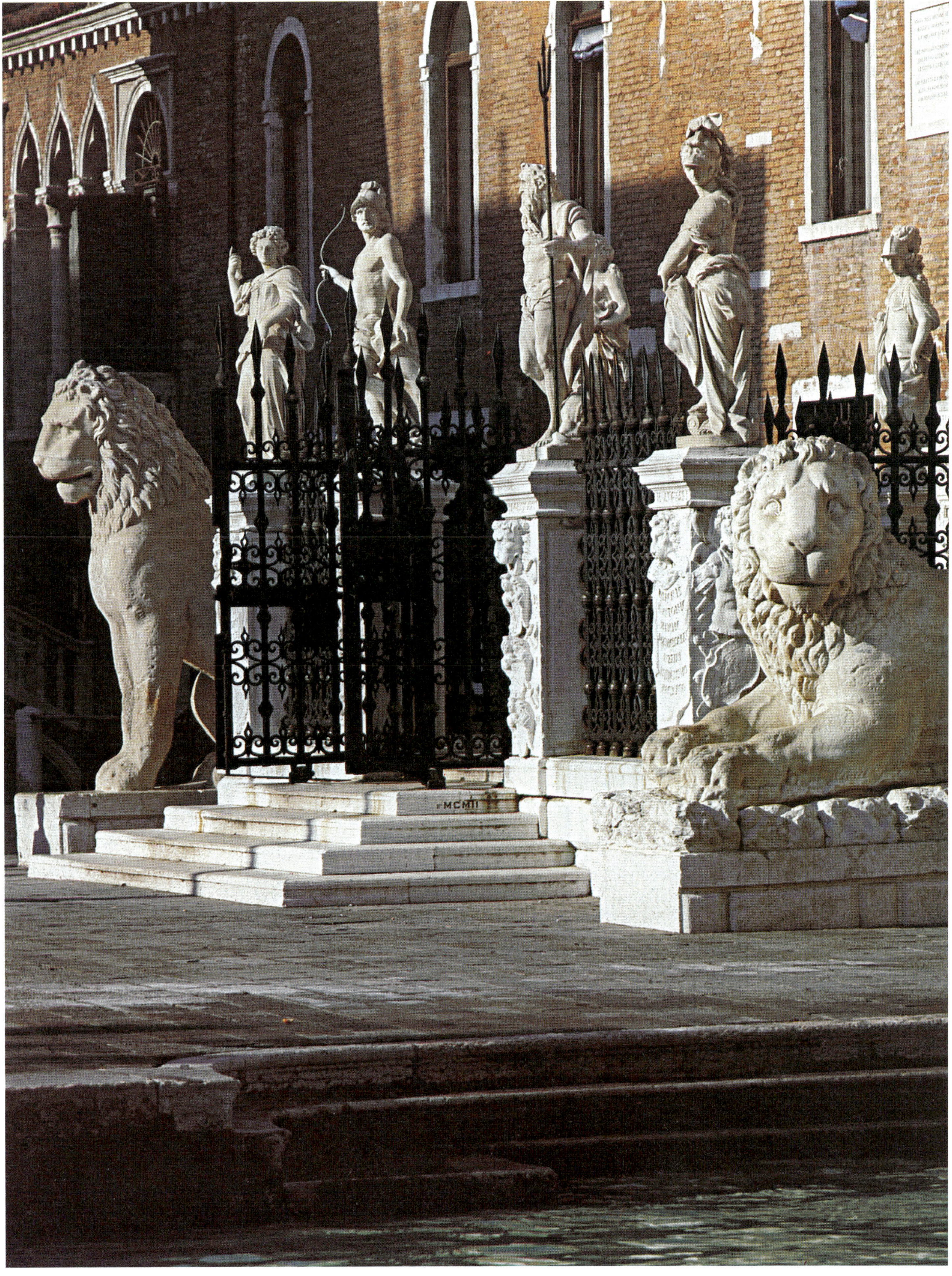

For a long period of time, from at least the fourteenth to the eighteenth century, the Venetian Arsenal was the largest concentration of workers in Europe, a factory with thousands of employees and an exceptionally productive organization. On the occasion of the battle of Lepanto, the Arsenal succeeded in producing, in the space of a few months, about a hundred fully equipped war galleys. This extraordinary effort was at the base of the victory over the Turks and was celebrated with large-scale additions to the land-side entrance to the complex. The bas-reliefs with the lion and the statue of St. Justina were added in 1571. The bridge that led to the Arsenal was further transformed by a parade of statues during the last decade of the seventeenth century. Aside from the baroque statues of the Olympian gods, two lions of Greek origin were placed beside the portal. The one lying down, which comes from the port of Piraeus, bears writing that has been recognized as the work of Viking mercenaries.

The waning of the sixteenth century on the Venetian lagoon

Paolo Veronese
Juno Bestowing Gifts upon Venice
1553–54, oil on canvas,
365 x 147 cm
Sala del Consiglio dei
Dieci, Doge's Palace,
Venice

In 1553, as assistant to
the mediocre Giovanni
Battista Ponchino,
Veronese too, twenty-
five years old, made
some canvases for the
ceilings of the Sala del
Consiglio dei Dieci in
the Doge's Palace. He
was soon made director
of the undertaking.

Paolo Veronese
**Arachne or
the Dialectic**
1575–77, oil on canvas,
150 x 220 cm
Sala del Collegio
Doge's Palace, Venice

The ceiling of the Sala
del Collegio is among
the most elaborate in
the palace. The can-
vases by Veronese are
arranged within sump-
tuous gilt-wood frames.
The artist created deli-
cious female figures
alluding to various
virtues or liberal arts,
inserted within the
shapes of the frames
with solutions of
great grace and
sharp chromatics.

Paolo Veronese
**Venice Enthroned
with Justice and
Peace**
1575–77, oil on canvas,
250 x 180 cm
Sala del Collegio,
Doge's
Palace, Venice

In this important
canvas, located in
the central part of the
ceiling, the steep set
of semicircular stairs
becomes a brilliant
perspective device.

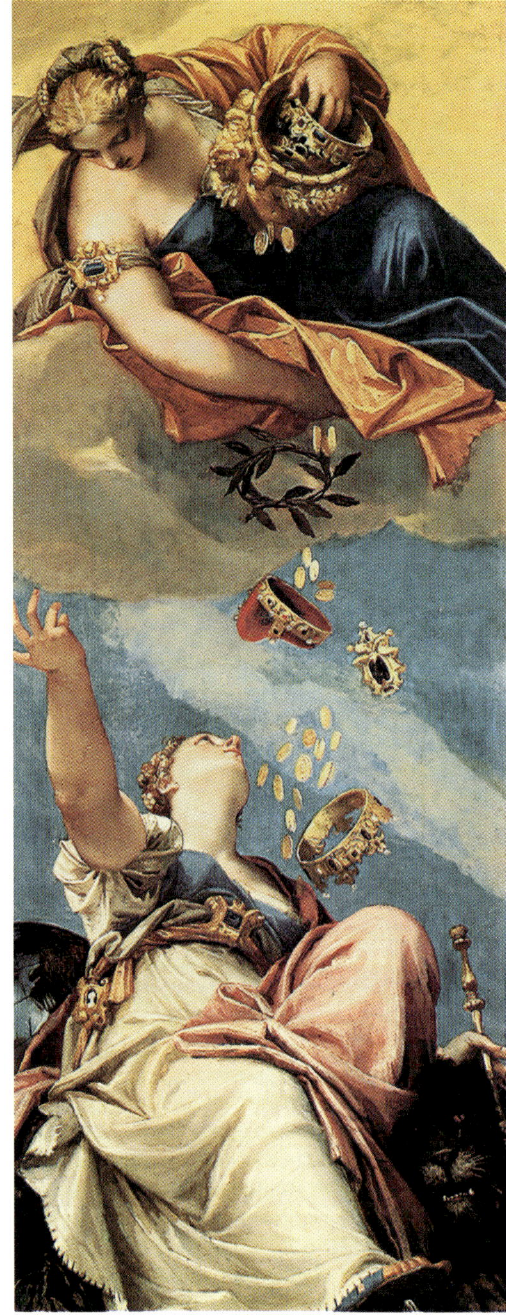

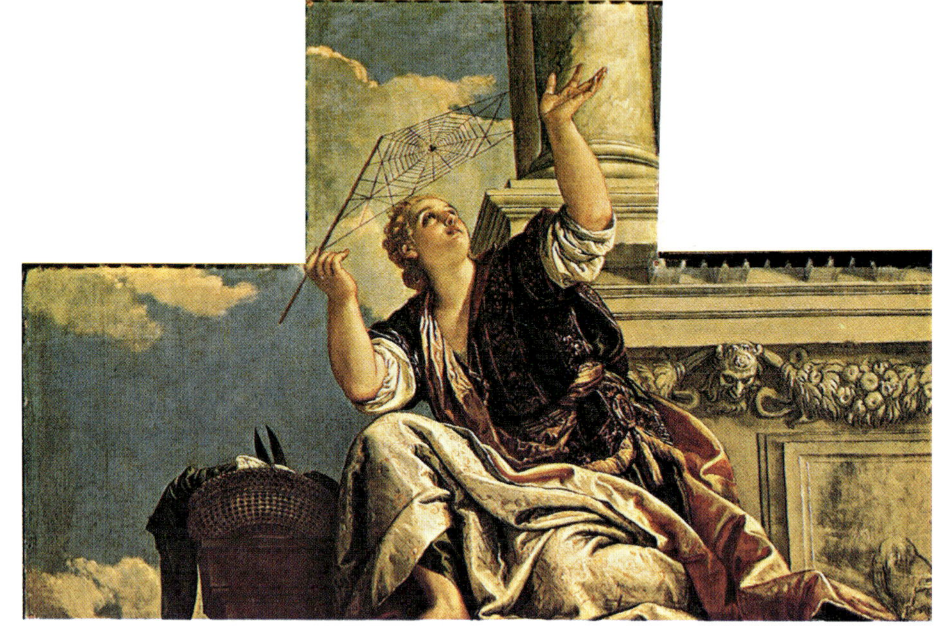

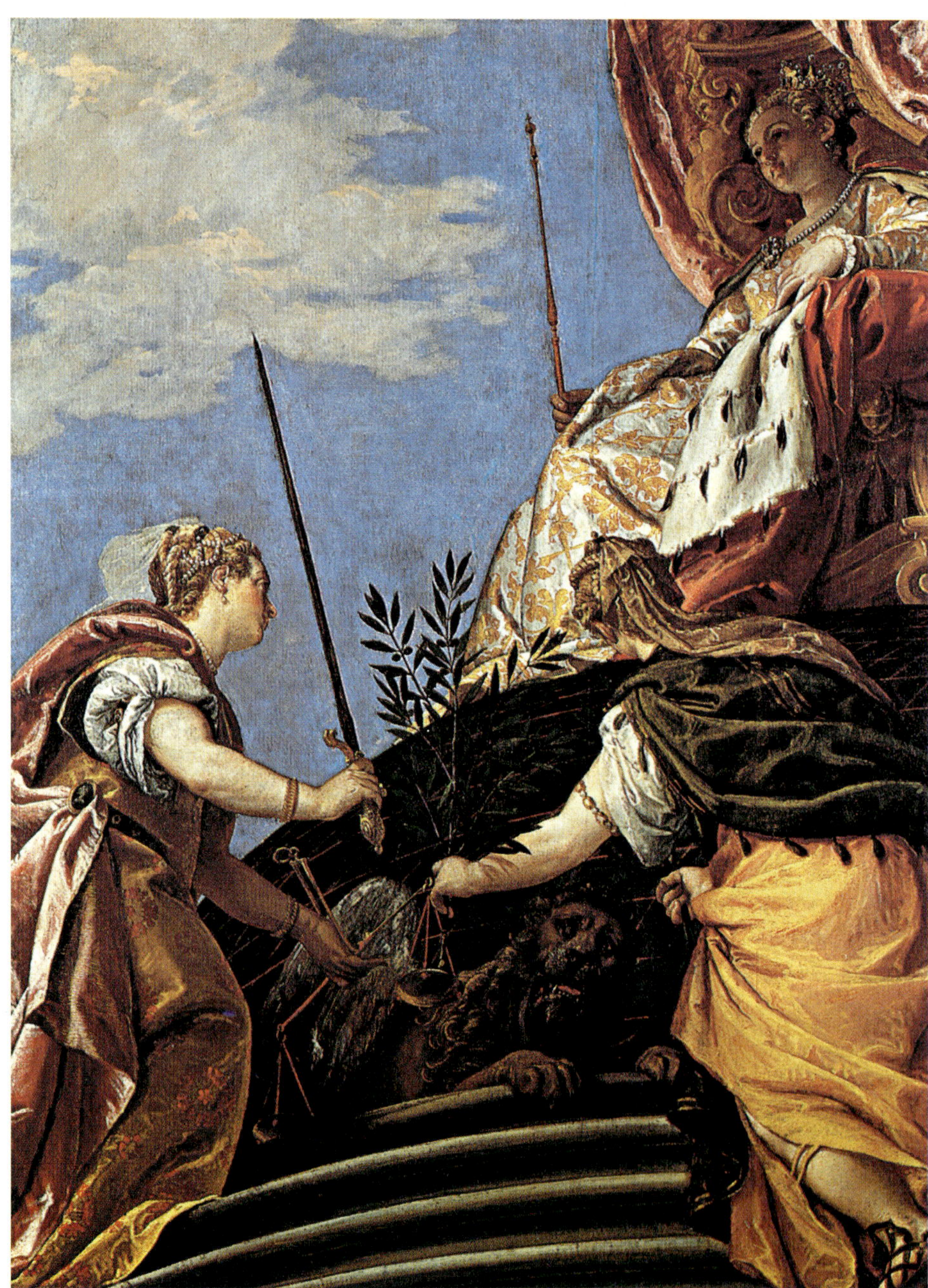

The waning of the sixteenth century on the Venetian lagoon

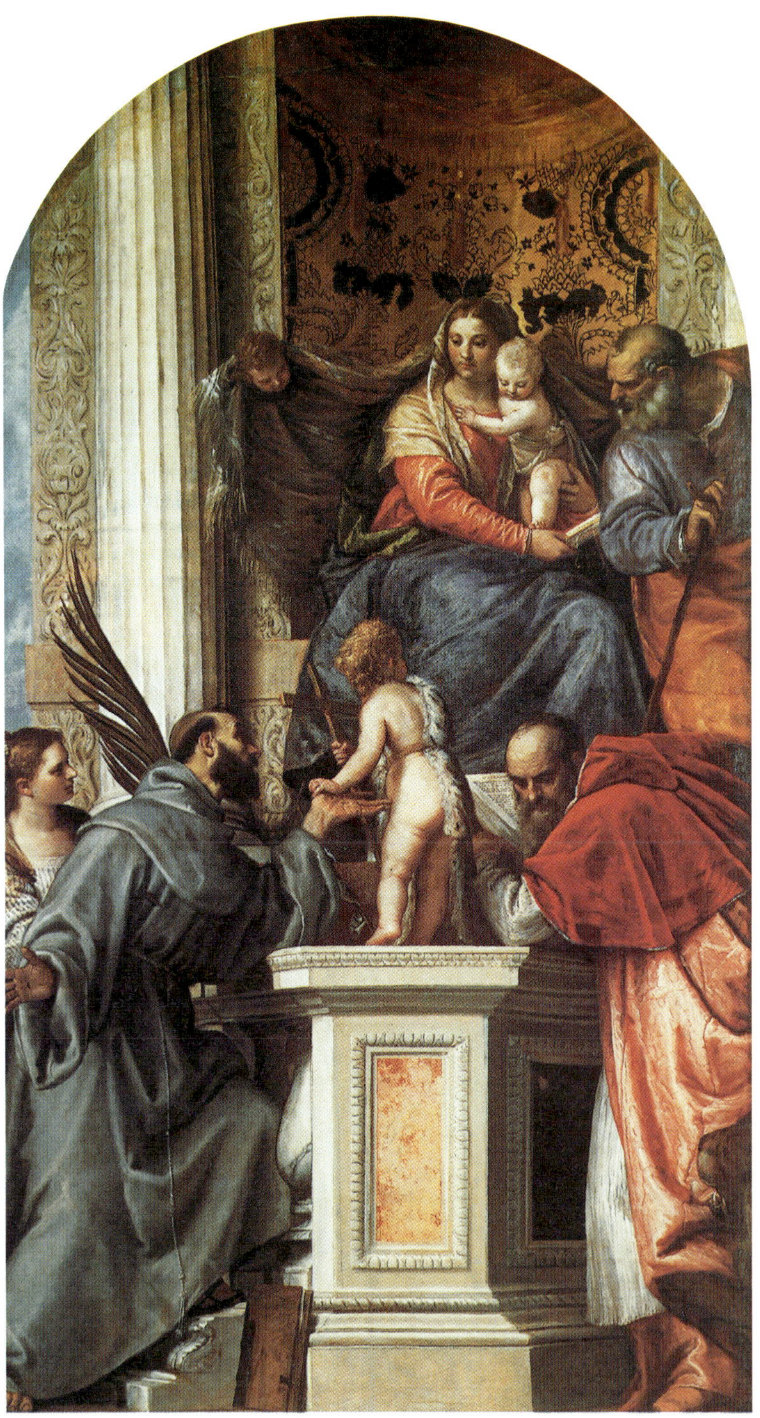

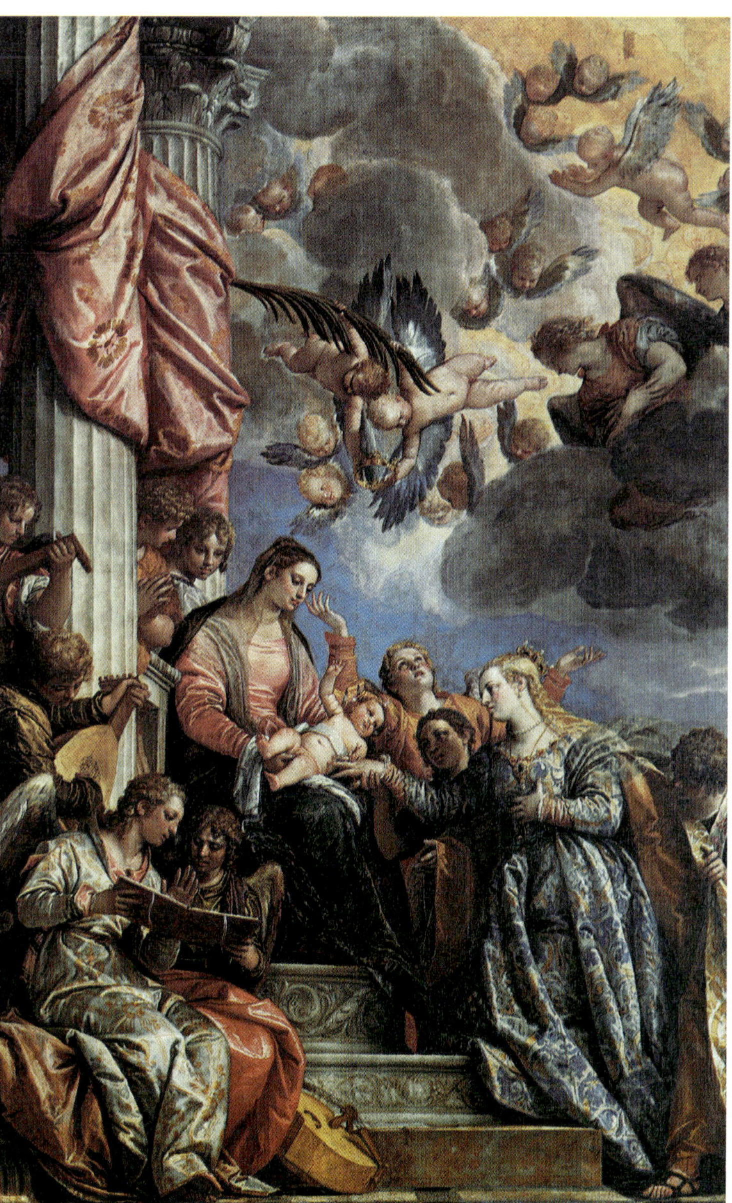

Veronese's habitual taste for exceptionally rich colors, lit by dazzling effects of light, reaches truly opulent effects in this canvas, which was celebrated in period commentaries. The imaginative art writer Marco Boschini, author of a 681-page poem on Venetian art entitled *La Carta del Navigar Pittoresco* ("Map to Pictorial Navigation"), published in 1660 and written in the Venetian dialect, celebrated the effects of this painting, imagining that Veronese had "worked into it gold, pearls, and rubies, and emeralds and sapphires, more than fine, and the most pure and perfect diamonds."

The waning of the sixteenth century on the Venetian lagoon

The waning of the sixteenth century on the Venetian lagoon

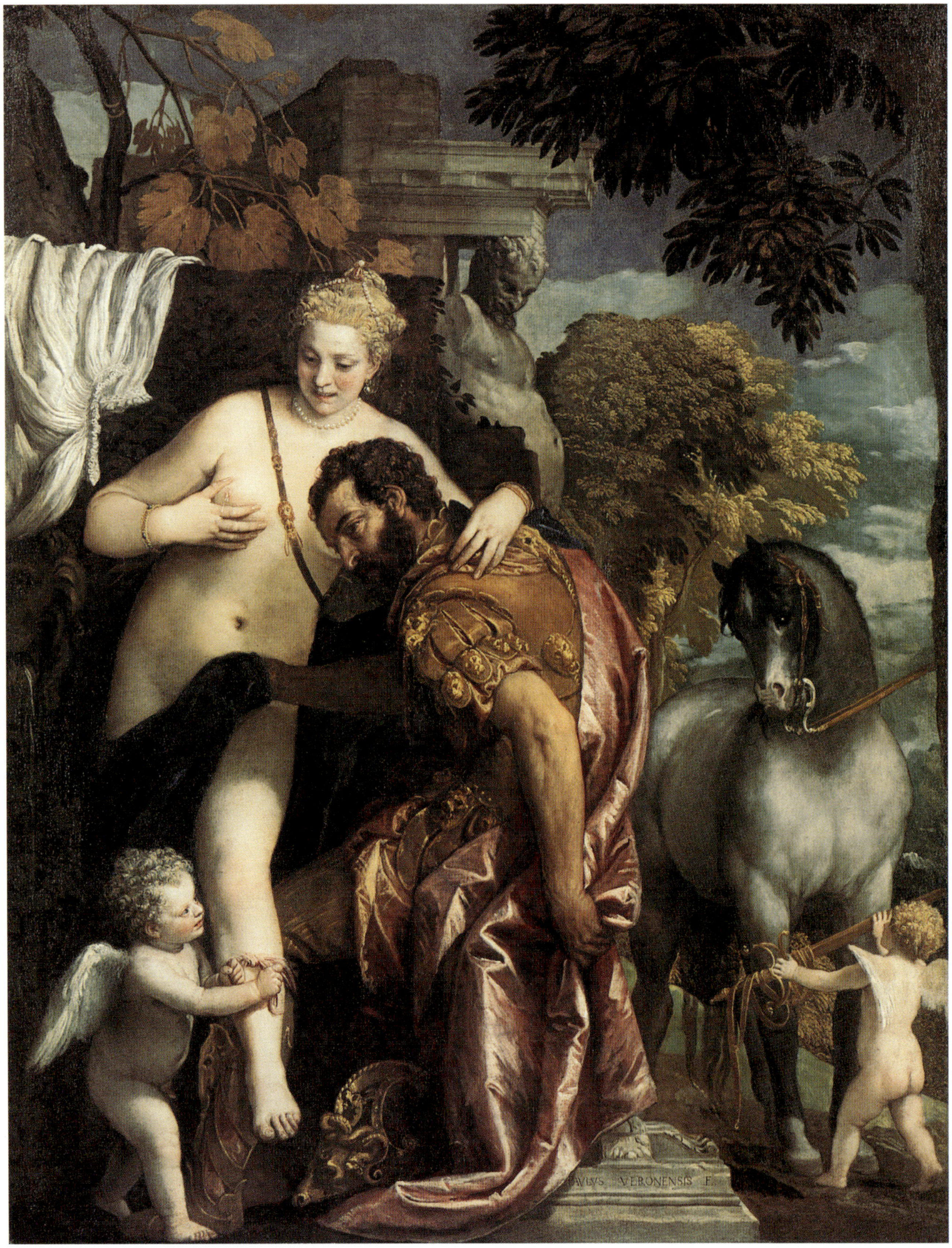

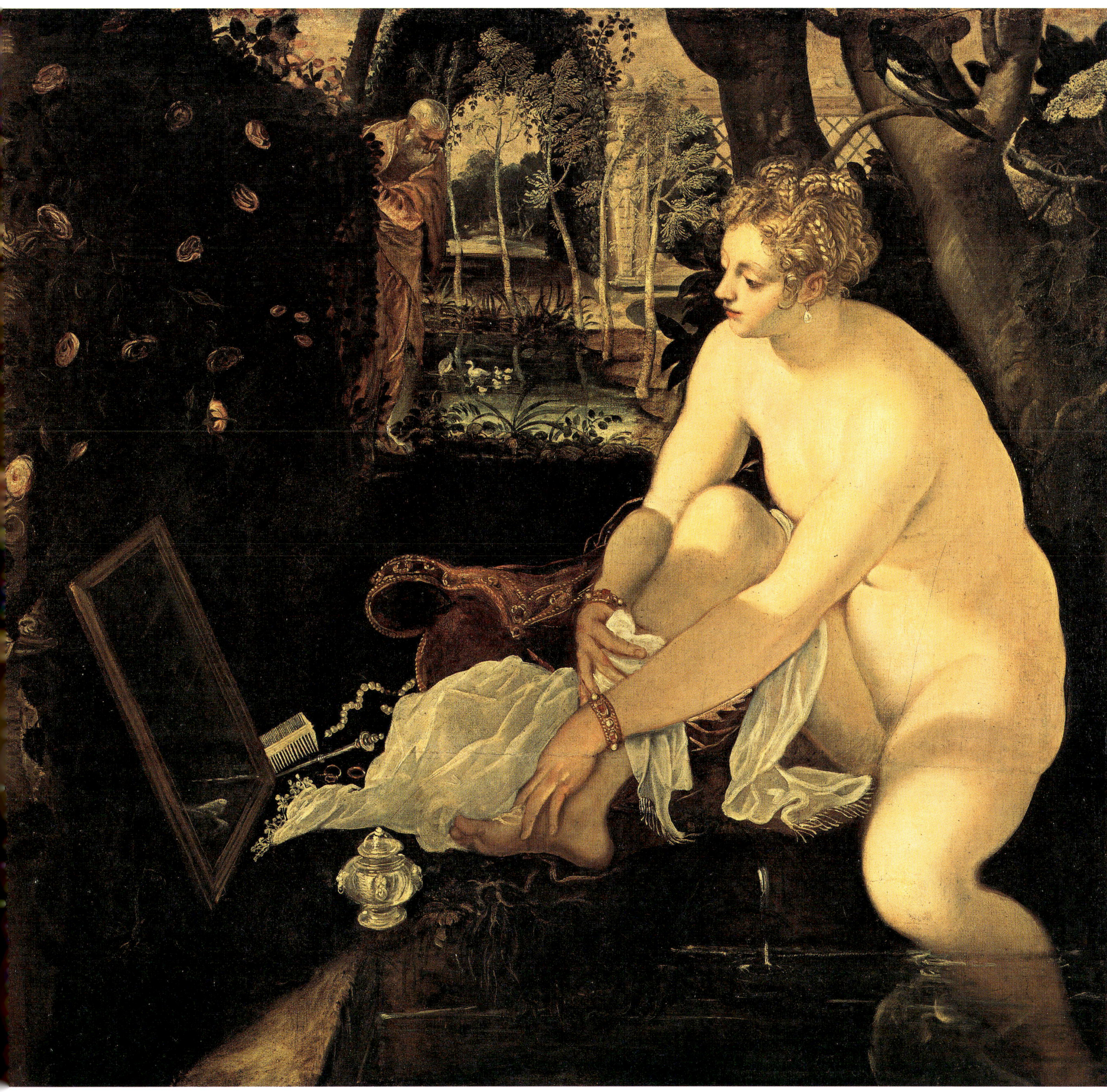

This work of stupendous beauty belongs to the most luminous and elegant period of Tintoretto's painting. He interprets the biblical tale in a delicately elegiac way. The viewer's attention is most certainly not directed to the two elders, who peek in from the far ends of the flowering hedge to the left, and is drawn instead to the luminous body of the youthful Susanna, near the bubbling fountain. Her toilette articles are spread across the grass in capricious disorder. The natural light that filters through the green of the garden increases the fascination of this masterpiece.

The waning of the sixteenth century on the Venetian lagoon

In 1564 the Scuola
Grande di San Rocco,
a well-to-do public-
assistance institution
with a superb Ren-
aissance building
beside the Venetian
church of the Frari,
held a competition
for the decoration of
its reception hall.
Tintoretto was judged
the victor, winning out
against not only the
other competitors but
also a certain hesita-
tion about him on the
part of the directors of
the *scuola*. The *Stories
of the Passion of Christ*
in the Sala dell'Albergo,
in particular the giant
Crucifixion (circa 1565),
began a cycle of paint-
ings that in various
stages was to absorb
the artist's best cre-
ative energies for more
than twenty years. The
decorations of the ceil-
ing and the walls of
the upper room date to
1576–81, while the ten
canvases on the ground
floor date to 1583–87.
This long series of works
records the gradual
passage in Tintoretto's
style from the strong
descriptive realism
characteristic of
the beginning to the
visionary sense of his
later phases.

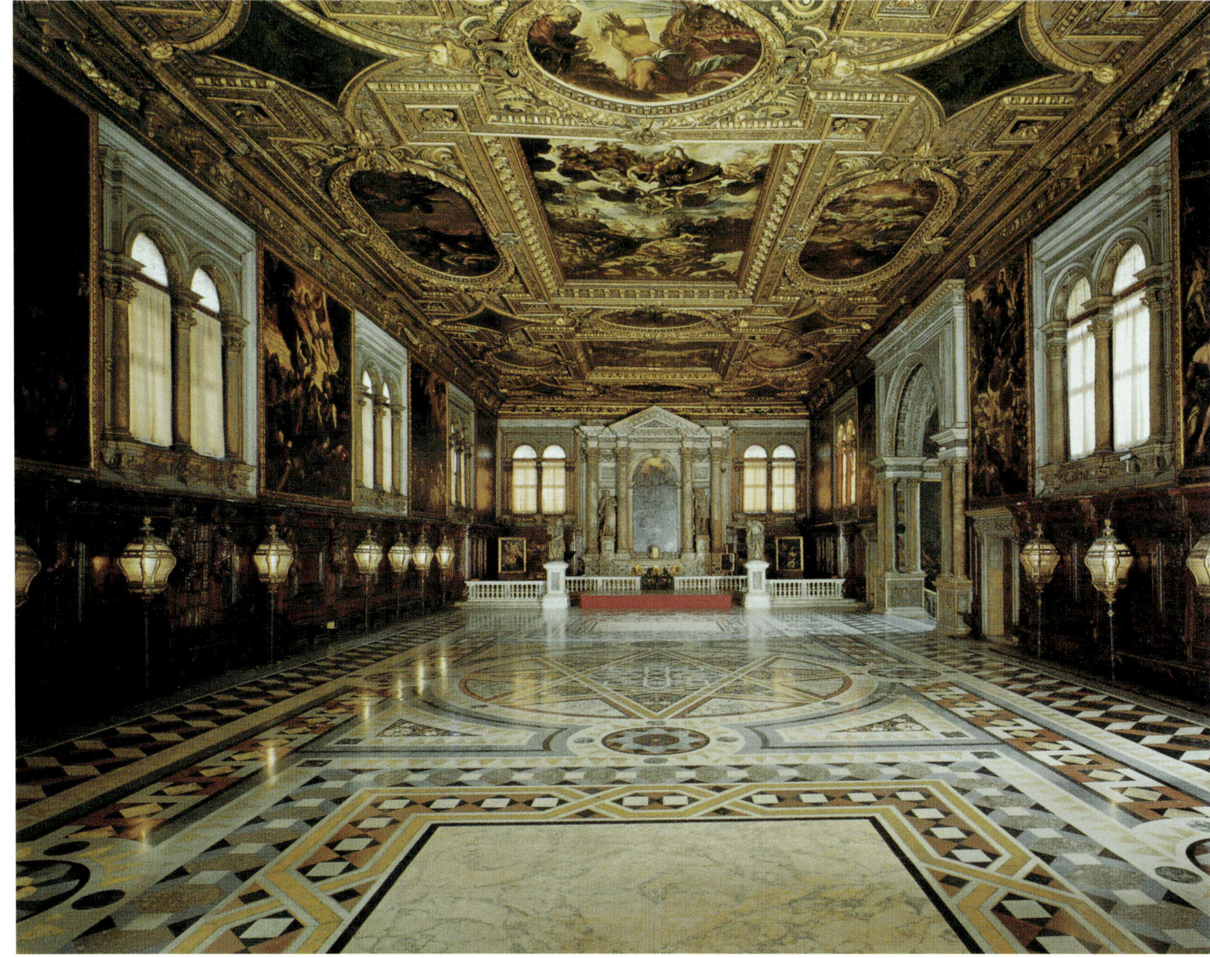

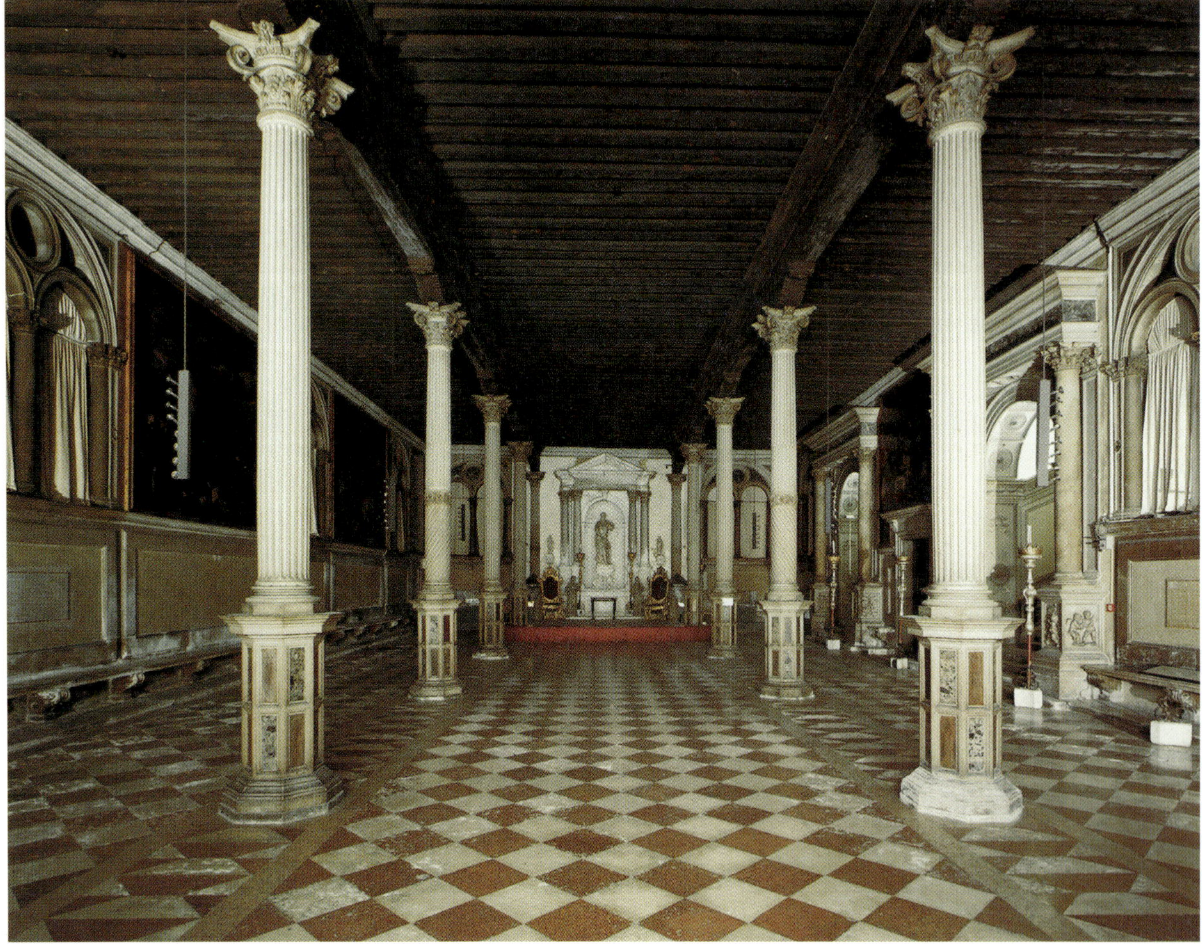

The waning of the sixteenth century on the Venetian lagoon

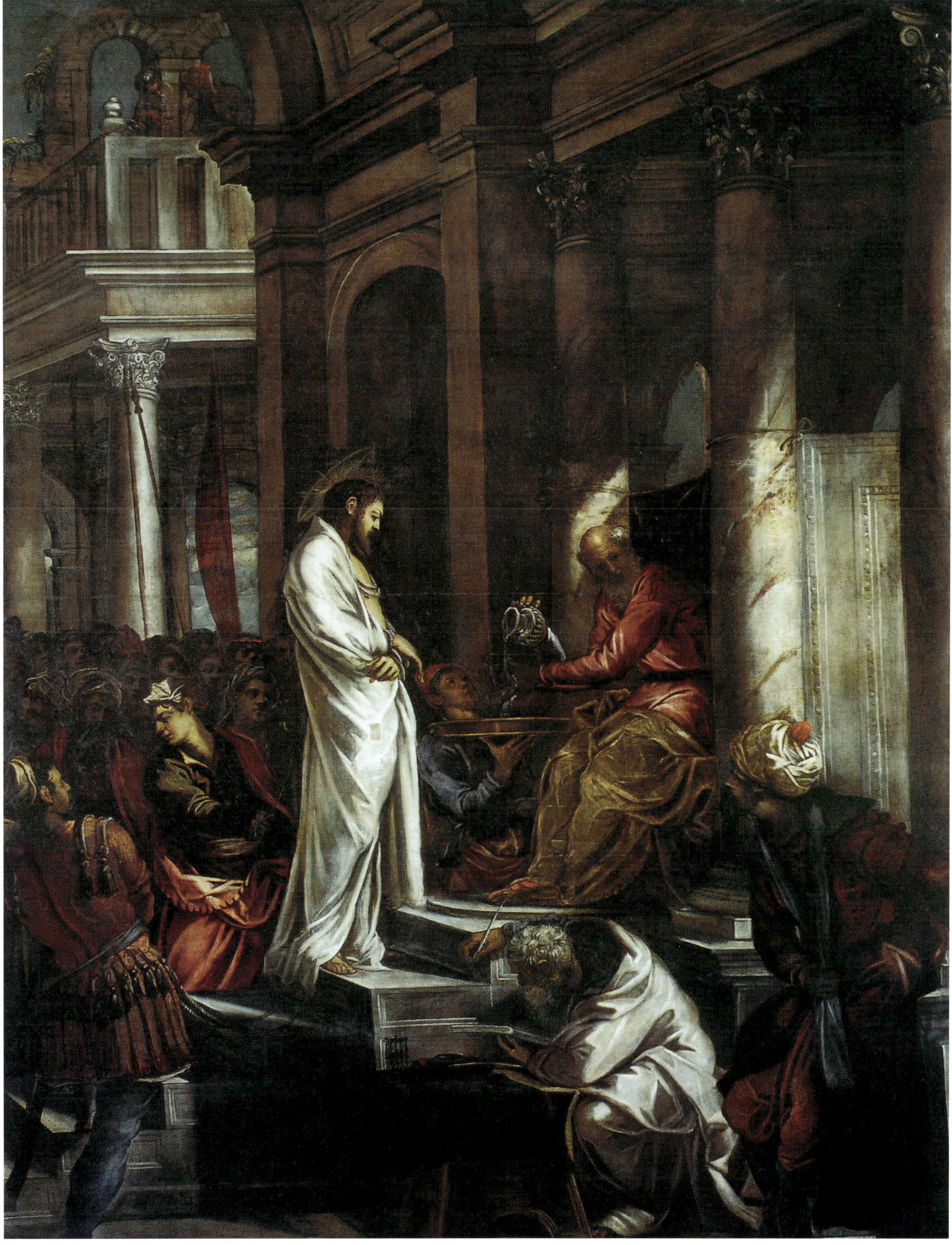

The waning of the sixteenth century on the Venetian lagoon

The spectacular upper
room of the Scuola di
San Rocco is one of the
most impressive interi-
ors in Venice. The sim-
ple structure, measured
off by Renaissance mul-
lioned windows, has
a gilt-wood ceiling in
which the artist set vir-
tuosic canvases with
themes of the Old Testa-
ment; along the walls,
between the windows,
are vast episodes of
the gospels. Tintoretto
made the entire cycle,
which numbers thirty
canvases in all, between
1576 and 1581, at
the same time that he
was beginning work on
the redecoration of
the Doge's Palace. The
*Adoration of the Shep-
herds* is one of the
most famous evangeli-
cal scenes on the walls.
Thanks to a truly inno-
vative iconographic
invention, making use
of his open-minded
sense of perspective
and points of view,
Tintoretto gave the
manger two levels,
with the shepherds
arriving below and
the Holy Family above,
while a supernaturally
golden light pours in
between the beams
of the ceiling.

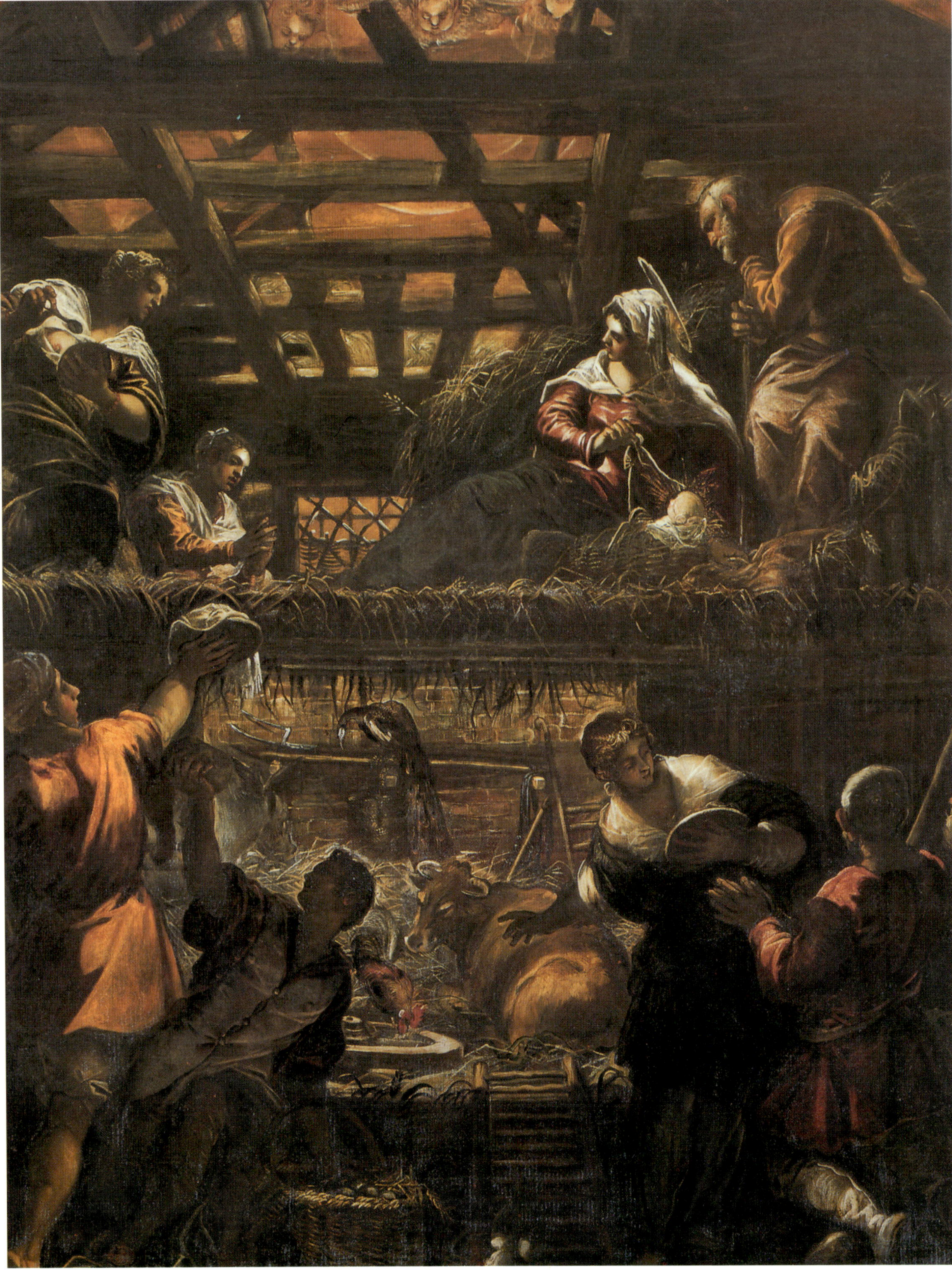

The waning of the sixteenth century on the Venetian lagoon

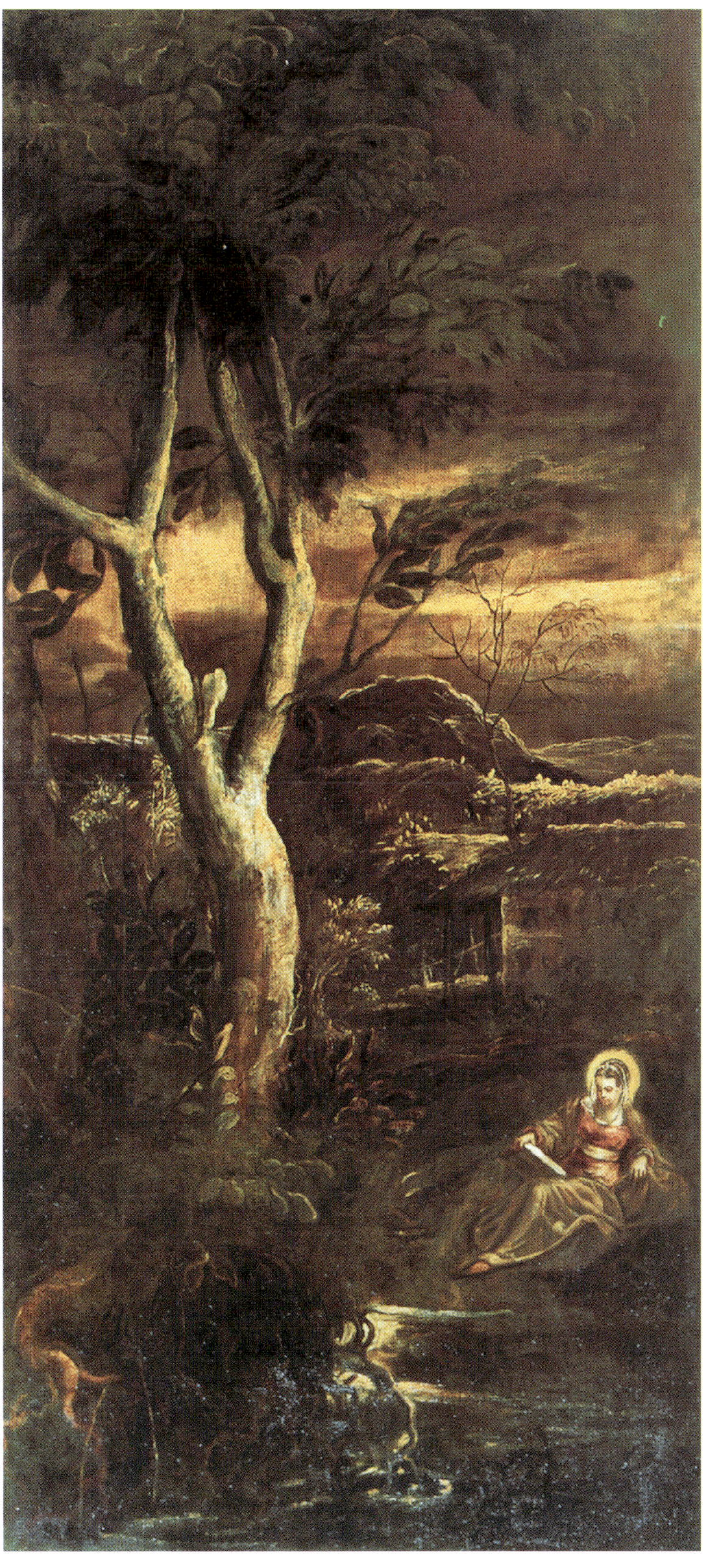

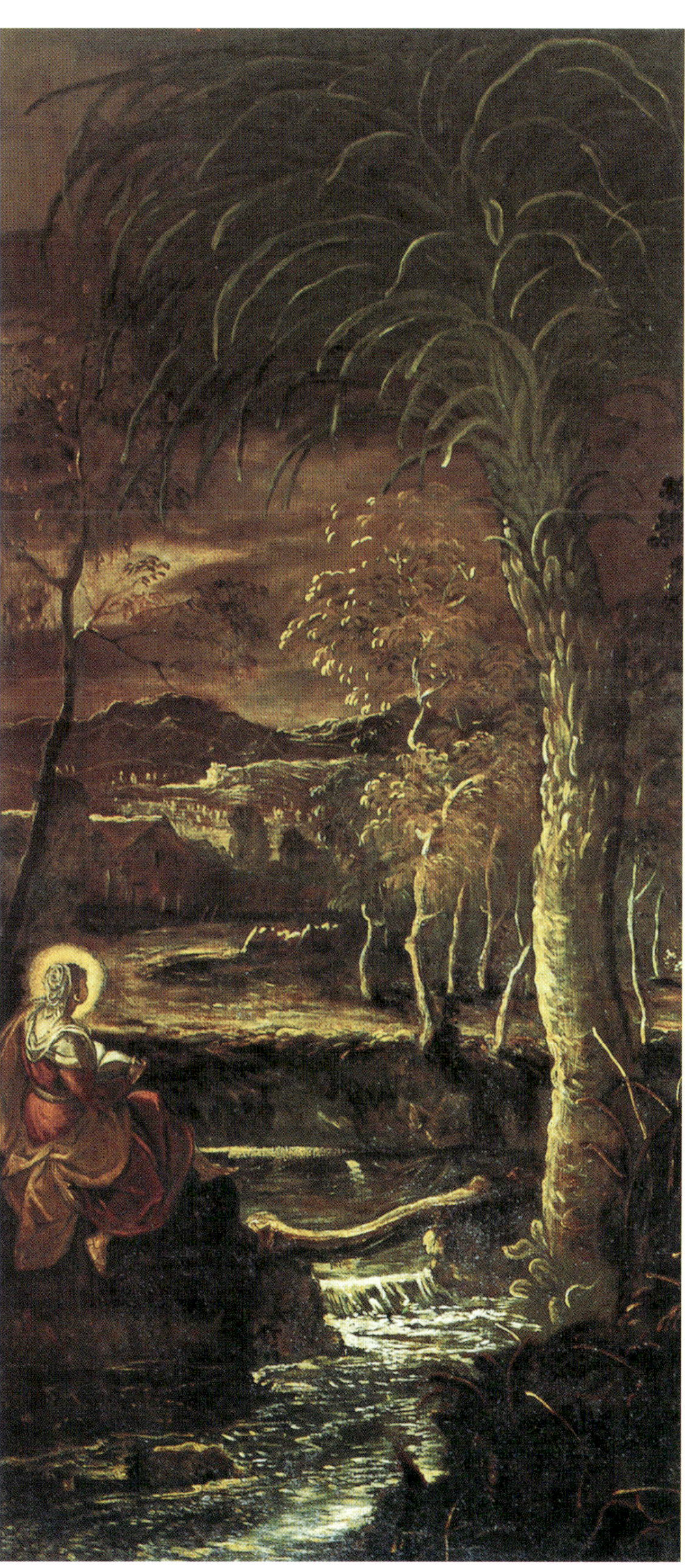

From July 1583 to August 1587 Tintoretto, by then nearly seventy years old, returned to work in the Scuola di San Rocco. This time he worked on the eight large canvases along the walls of the ground-floor room, the space of which is divided into three naves by narrow columns. By then, the impetuous raging and luministic ardor that animate the scenes in the Salone Maggior had calmed. Here the artist demonstrated a more contemplative mood, a sincere and poetic spirituality. The relationship between the figures and nature becomes particularly intense in these scenes of saints immersed in the landscape. In enormous natural settings of vast panoramas, seen at the hour of sunset, the saints are alone. Quivering leaves, reflections across water, views that grade off into the distance are illuminated by a mysterious light that protects their fascinating serenity.

The waning of the sixteenth century on the Venetian lagoon

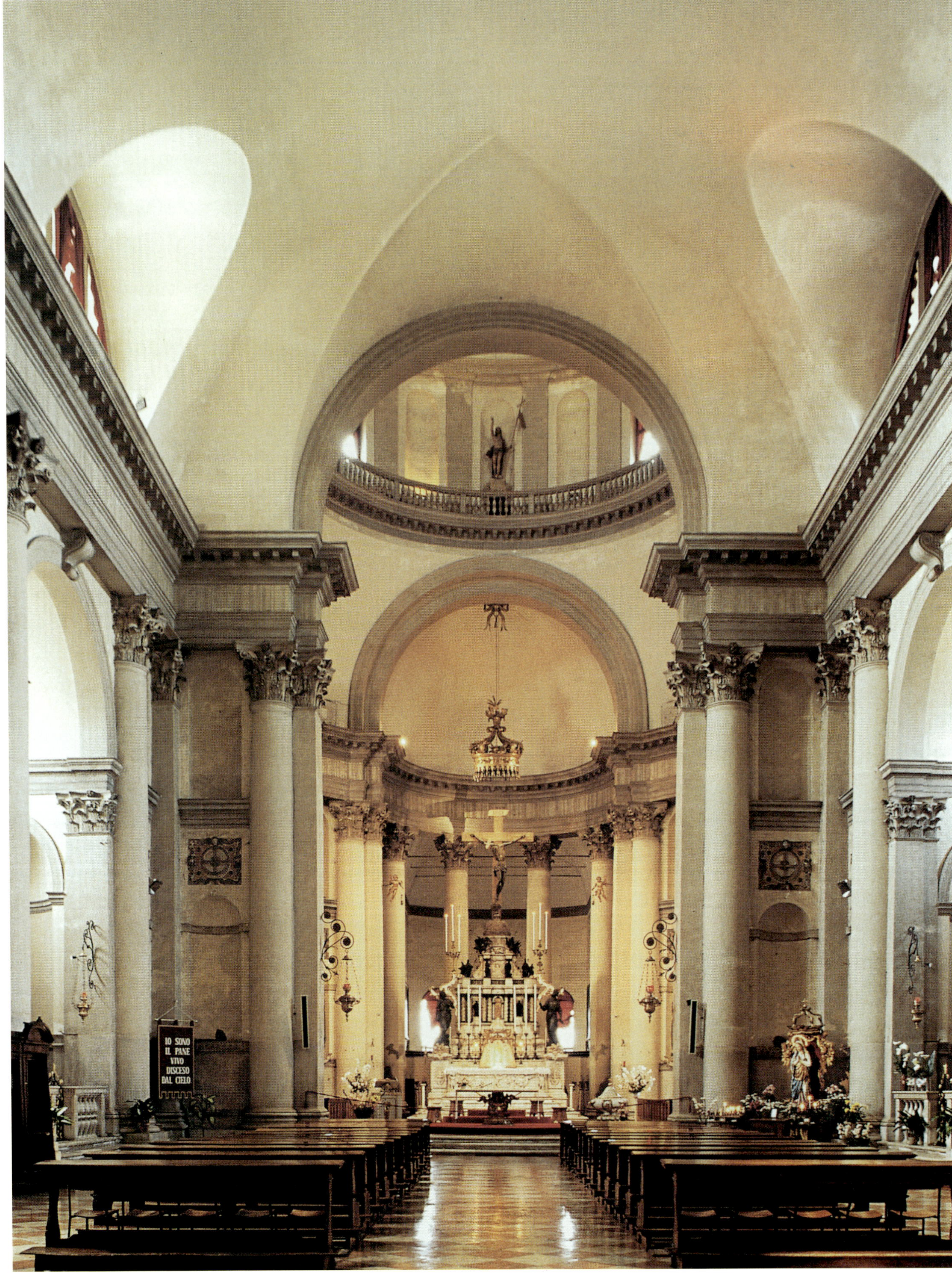

The waning of the sixteenth century on the Venetian lagoon

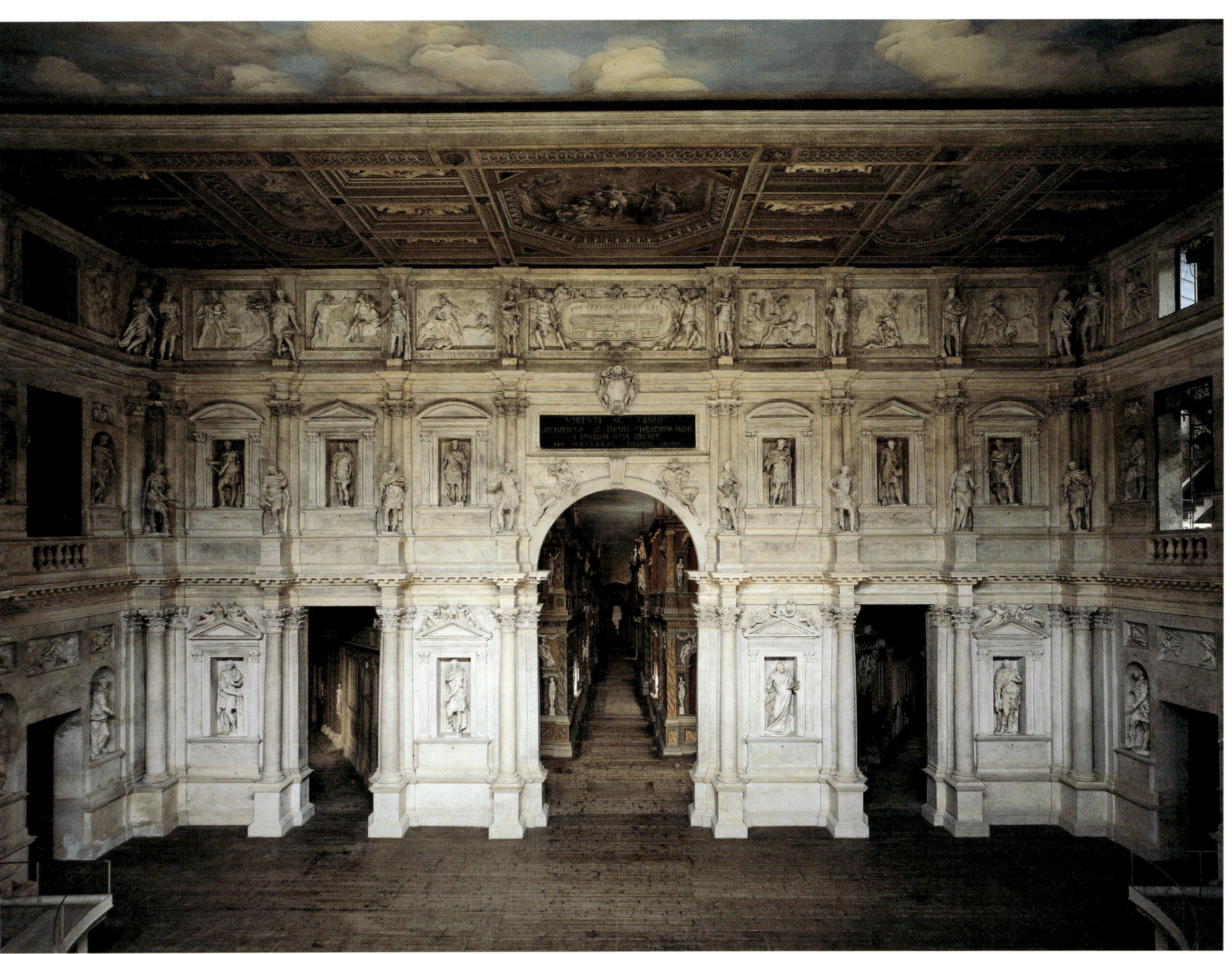

In 1570 Palladio assumed the role of official architect of Venice and moved there, where he published his *Four Books of Architecture*, texts that proved fundamental to the spread of Palladianism. In truth, Palladio met a certain amount of resistance in Venice. He busied himself with public works, but his projects were not built. Such was the case with his three-arched design for the Rialto bridge and most of all with his "modern" reconstruction of the Doge's Palace, which had been devastated by fire in 1577. Even so, Palladio continued to design buildings, some for his favorite city, Vicenza. His last work was this small theater in masonry for performances at the Accademia Olimpica, which marks the return to European architecture of the fixed-scene theater, which had been abandoned by the time of the fall of the Roman empire. The work was still in progress when Palladio died, on August 19, 1580. Completed by Vincenzo Scamozzi, the theater opened five years later with a memorable performance of *Oedipus Rex*.

The waning of the sixteenth century on the Venetian lagoon

TINTORETTO
Last Supper
1592–94,
oil on canvas,
365 x 568 cm
San Giorgio Maggiore,
Venice

The cycle of canvases for the Palladian basilica of San Giorgio Maggiore was Tintoretto's last work, by then having reached the end of an enormous career of nearly fifty years of tireless effort. In the *Last Supper* (his final version of a theme he had presented many times), mysterious mystical presences fly around, suspended between the solid earthly plane and an ineffable celestial world, while the compositional structure becomes elusive, subject to unpredictable rotations on the axis of its perspective. A flight of angels, similar to spectral shadows, spreads across the Eucharistic table, illuminated by the radiant figure of Christ. The ambiguous relationship between reality and miracle reaches moments of intense poetry in profound mysticism, especially in the evanescent figures of the angels in the darkness behind the table. Tintoretto died shortly after completing this canvas. He was buried in his favorite church, Madonna dell'Orto, and together with him an entire epoch came to an end.

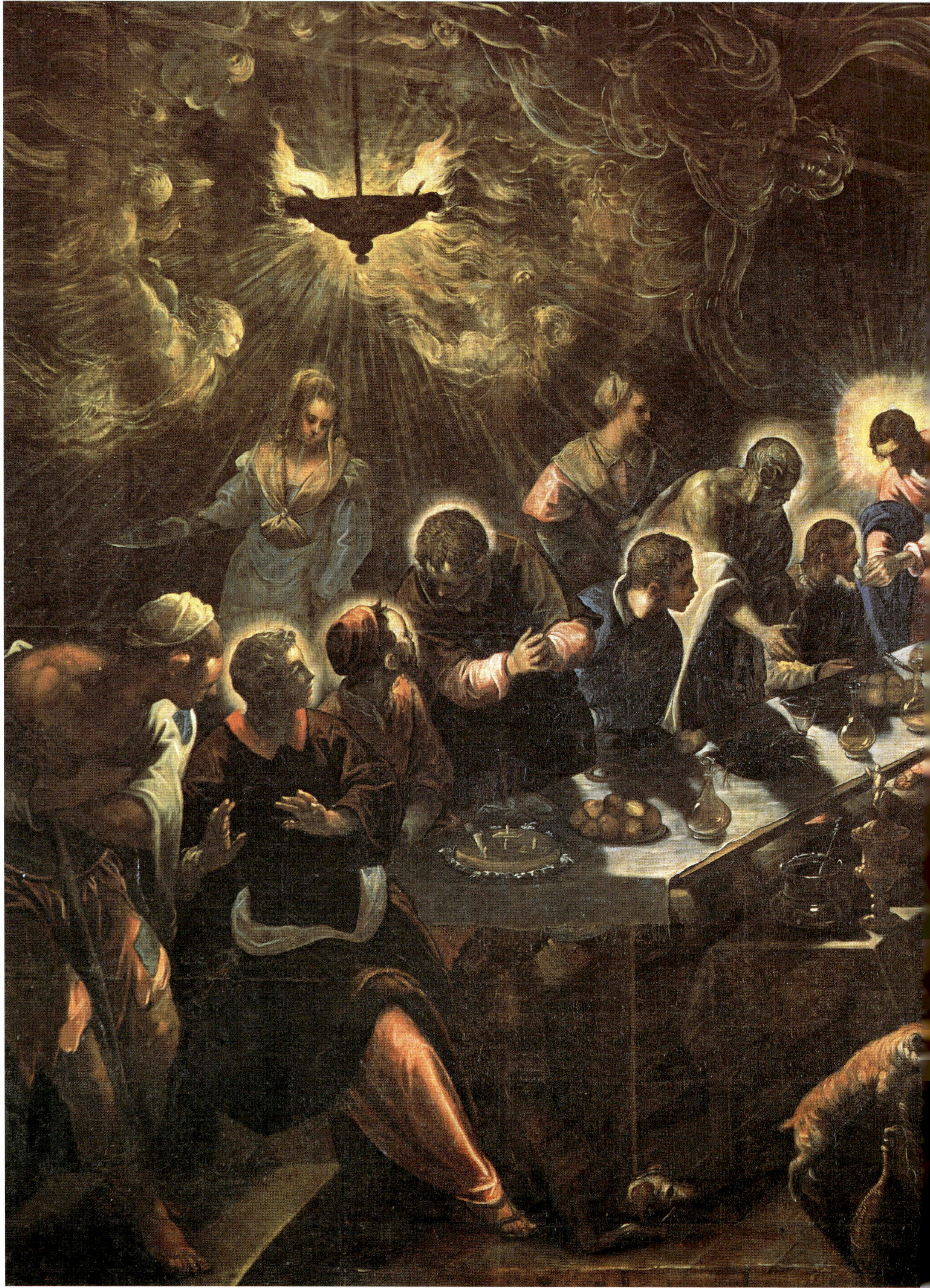

The waning of the sixteenth century on the Venetian lagoon

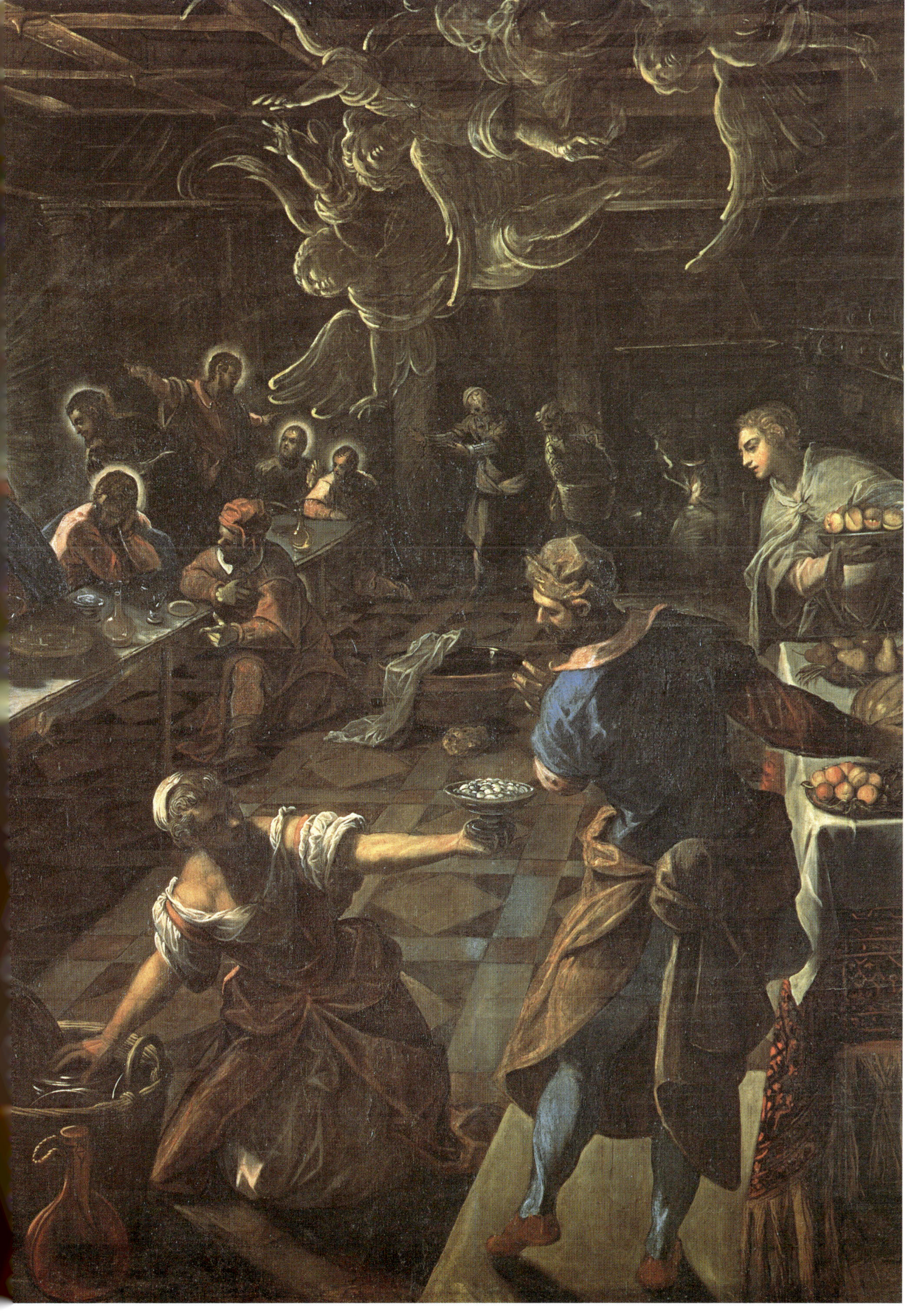

The waning of the sixteenth century on the Venetian lagoon

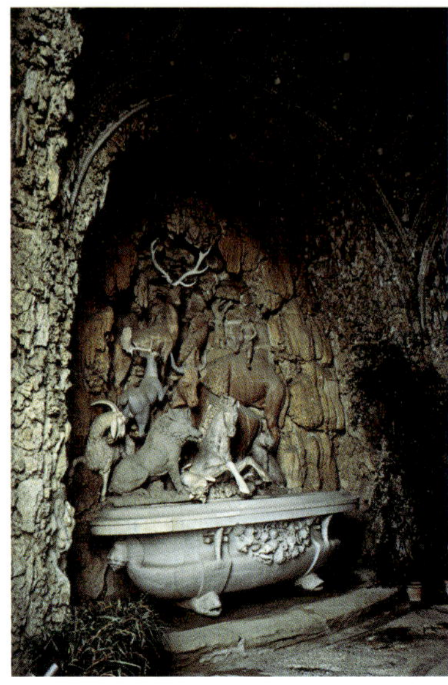

Bernardo Buontalenti
and assistants, Villa
Medici, interior of the
Grotta degli Animali,
circa 1585; Villa di
Castello, Florence

Exhausted by the enormous and relentless psychological and physical strain of more than thirty years spent ruling over territories where "the sun never set," Charles V decided to abdicate, which he did formally in 1558, having previously divided up the empire, so that once again it was split between Austria and Spain. The "Austrian" part he entrusted to his younger brother Ferdinand I, and the "Spanish" part (including the Italian colonies of Naples and Milan, along with the territories in the New World) went to his son Philip II. It was under Philip II (who died in 1598) that Spain's progressive loss of power began, with the growth of an enormous bureaucratic structure, increasingly isolated yet endowed with absolute administrative power over a vast world empire. There were centuries to come before the end, which arrived with the revolutions in the countries of South America, but the break-up of the Spanish empire began in the second half of the sixteenth century. The greatest masters of Spanish art, from El Greco to Velázquez, and the great writers of the late sixteenth and seventeenth centuries (Cervantes, Góngora, Tirso de Molina, Quevedo) masterfully presented this period of sumptuous decline. It is interesting to compare the construction of the Escorial, the somber, gigantic sanctuary-palace-museum-cemetery built by Philip II, and the total failure of the most important military undertaking of his reign, the would-be invasion of

fortunes, Iberian culture moved into its so-called Golden Age.

In the field of painting, the change was due principally to the extraordinary creativity of a bizarre and ingenious master, Domenikos Theotokopulos, known as El Greco. Born on the island of Crete (at the time a Venetian possession), he arrived in Toledo at the age of thirty-six, already in possession of broad artistic training that he had matured in Venice and Rome in contact with the great masters of the Italian High Renaissance (Titian, Michelangelo, Tintoretto). However, the paintings he made in Italy had given only small hints of the fire of passions, feelings, and violent emotions that flared from El Greco's works after his arrival in Spain. His case presents a perfect congruence between the mystical and intense temperament of a painter and the historical-cultural setting in which he found himself. The "extreme" and intense emotions he expressed were projected onto the scenario of

Dreams and visions at the

Leone Leoni, *Charles V
and Fury Restrained*,
1551; Museo del
Prado, Madrid

England led by the Invincible Armada, the monster fleet defeated by the English in 1588.

With this victory Queen Elizabeth I of England rose to become one of the dominant figures of European history and culture of the late sixteenth century. On the other hand, for the first time since the heroic age of Ferdinand the Catholic and his wars against the Moors of Granada, proud Spain suffered a drastic military defeat. Since its moment of glory at the battle of Lepanto, the Spanish war machine had experienced great difficulties in putting down the independence movements in the northern Low Countries, and it now received a mortal blow. Spain began to close in on itself and its American colonies. It gave Catholicism a passionate voice, the mystical drive and the organizational talents of such people as Ignatius of Loyola and Theresa of Ávila, and it began a wonderful period in literature and art. In stark contrast with its declining political and military

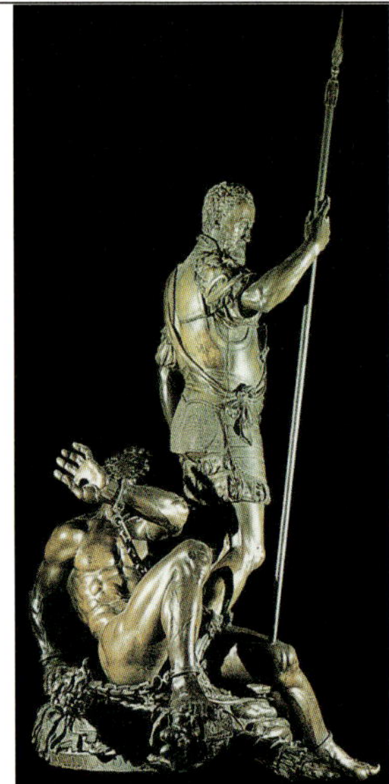

Castile and reverberated even stronger and more violently than they would have elsewhere. Hoping to become a painter-courtier El Greco offered his services to Philip II and tried to enter in the artistic workshop of the Escorial, but the response from the king was chilly, and the painter remained on the outside. His art was made most of all for the churches of Toledo, for which he made enormous and marvelous paintings in which the memory of the Italian masters slowly waned, giving way to an astonishing, dazzling, fantastic creativity.

During the second half of the sixteenth century a new artistic genre found rapid favor across all of Europe; apparently a radical alternative to the grim rigors of the Spanish court it was in fact a result of the same climate of a search for a "refuge" from reality. The genre was that of garden architecture, in particular the "intellectual" garden, full of surprises, pavilions, sculptures, fountains, fake grottoes. In a hypothetical "continuum" between nature

Dreams and visions at the close of the Renaissance

and art, between literary references and technical devices, splendid sculptures and esoteric labyrinths, fake stalactites and shell incrustations, the garden of the declining Renaissance is an enchanted and secret place. The highly difficult preservation of the artistic creations, the life cycle of the species of plants, and changes in taste and ownership have drastically reduced the number of aristocratic gardens that still bear the memory of the their original form. The few that remain, however, possess an unequaled fascination. The point of departure is the Palazzo Te in Mantua, where Giulio Romano created a "secret" garden for Federico Gonzaga, a place separate from the rest of the building and the surrounding green areas, with stone mosaics, a false grotto, and frescoes based on themes from Ovid's *Metamorphoses*. From there the style spread across Europe. There were the fabulous (and sadly almost totally lost) ceramic creations made by the French glass painter and potter Bernard Palissy for the "grottoes" in the Tuileries gardens in Paris, the grotto of Orpheus made for Henry IV in Saint-Germain-en-Laye, the Grottenhof in the residence of the princes of Bavaria at Munich, the Hortus Palatinus in Heidelberg, the playful water fountains in the villa of the bishop Markus Sitticus at the gates Salzburg, the fountain of Pirro Visconti in his villa in Lainate near Milan, and that of the Villa d'Este on Lake Como. The most important of these cre-

presents a truly astonishing itinerary between small "impossible" buildings and gigantic sculptural groups of dragons and monstrous animals immersed and sometimes almost hidden by the dense vegetation.

The Sacro Bosco remains an isolated example, however. Far more complex and important, also in terms of their immediate international fame, were the parks made in the Medici residence in Florence and the environs, beginning with the vast green space of the Boboli Gardens of Florence, planned by Niccolò Tribolo with the help of Bartolomeo Ammanati and

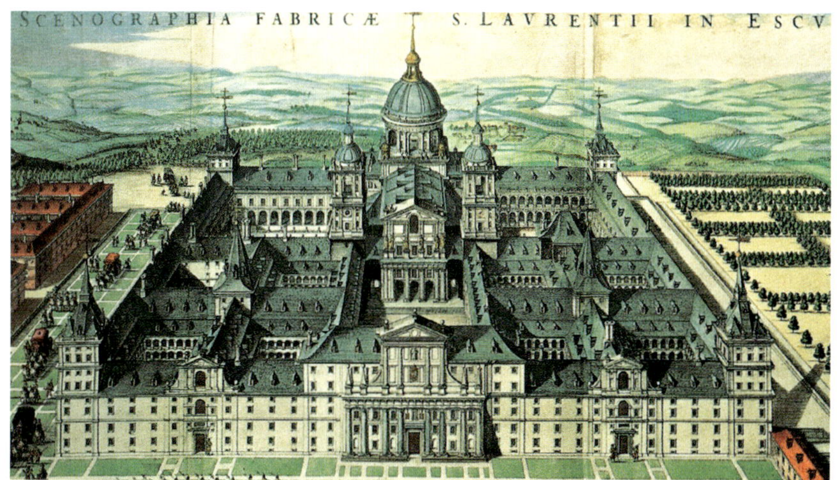

Juan Bautista de Toledo and Juan de Herrera, design for the Escorial, circa 1559; Royal Geographic Society, London

close of the Renaissance

ations were in central Italy and were part of the special architectonic form known as the "Italian garden." There is even an example in the heart of the Vatican gardens, where the architect Pirro Ligorio made the Casina for Pope Pius IV (1559–65). The very elegant pavilion, preceded and completed by the ingenious landscaping of the surrounding area, with benches and fountains, presents a perfect model of the ornamental use of stuccos to give a building an "antique" look. In Latium there are the gardens of the majestic aristocratic villas, such as the impressive Villa Farnese, built by Jacopo Vignola at Caprarola, and the Sacro Bosco of Bomarzo (in the area of Viterbo, 1550–53), certainly the most extravagant of the mannerist gardens. Made on the large estate of Villa Orsini, the wood

located in the new grand duke residence of Palazzo Pitti and extending to the bastions of the Forte de Belvedere. The "great grotto" made by Bernardo Buontalenti in the Boboli Gardens (1583–88) is the most famous example of ambiguity between a work of nature and a sculptor's creation. In the first room, which serves as vestibule, the walls drip with an infinity of rocky concretions that at times take on the strange and frightening appearance of rock-men, while in the four corners Buontalenti placed the four unfinished *Slaves* by Michelangelo (today replaced by copies), as if they were struggling to free themselves from the living rock. From this extraordinary locale one enters a series of internal rooms made with the collaboration of Giambologna, always full of the sense of surprise.

Jacques Fouquier, *View of the Hortus Palatinus of Heidelberg Castle*, circa 1600; Kurpfälzisches Museum, Heidelberg

Dreams and visions at the close of the Renaissance

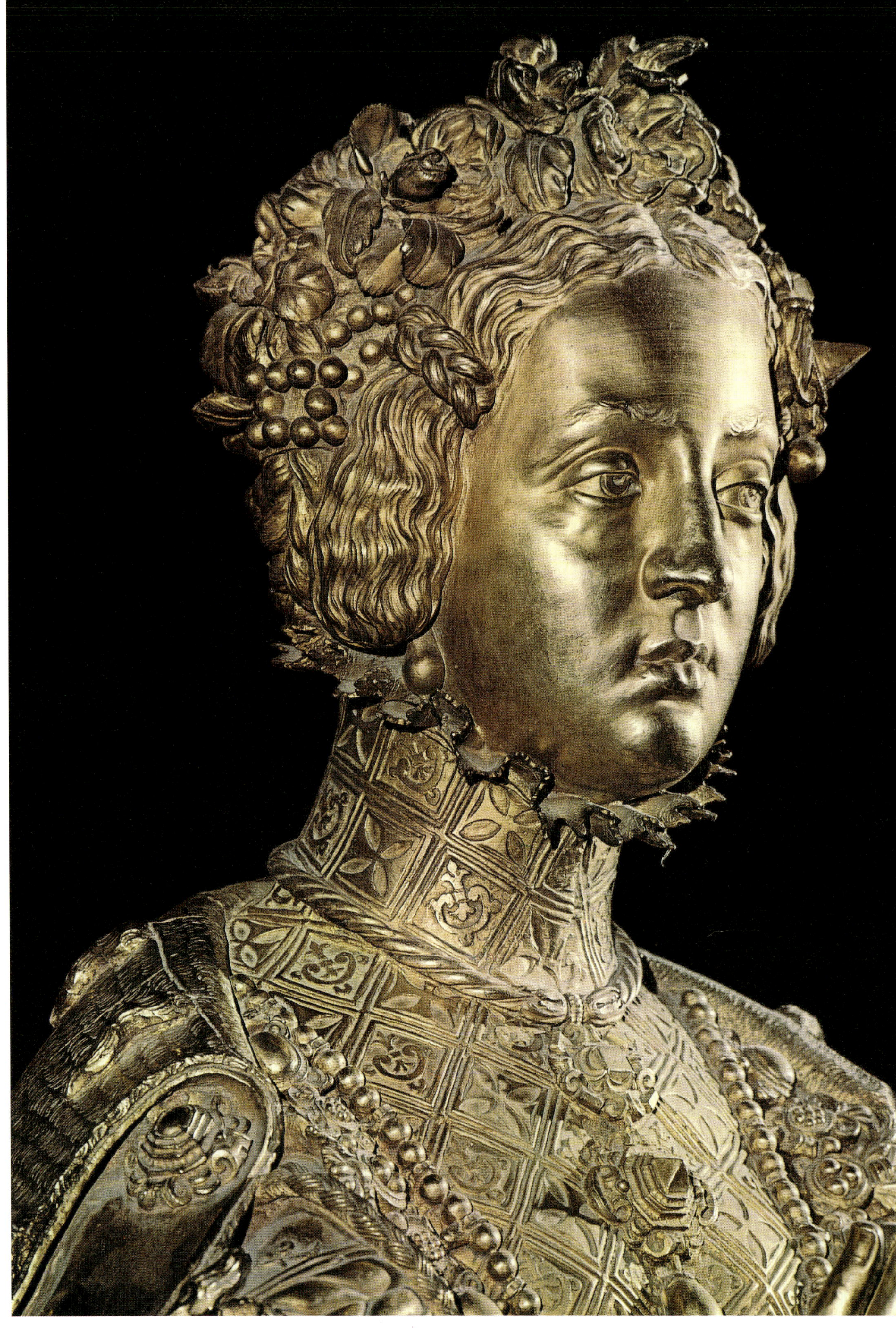

Dreams and visions at the close of the Renaissance

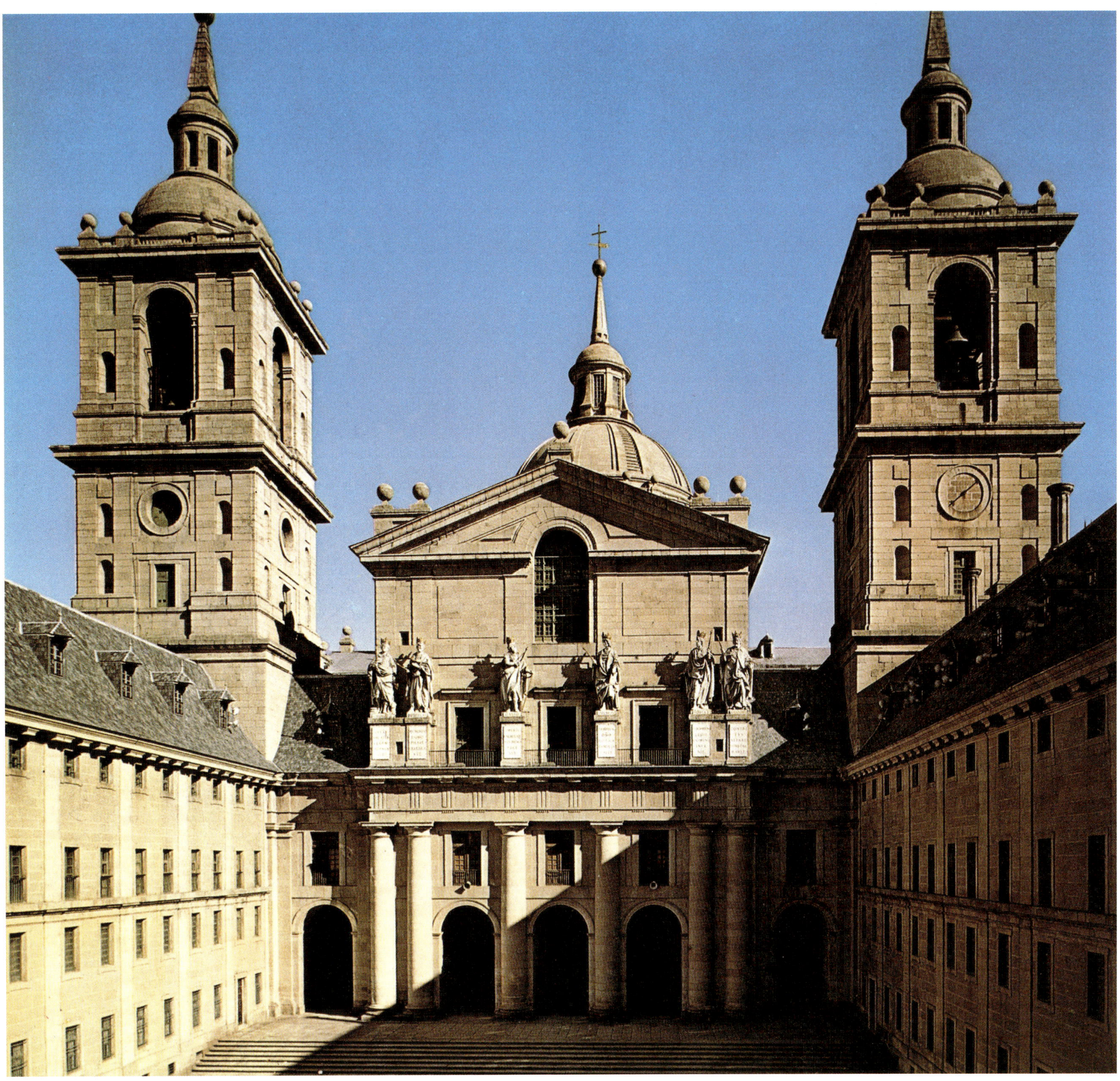

In celebration of the Spanish victory over the French in the battle of Saint-Quentin, fought on the feast day of St. Lawrence, Philip II ordered the construction of a monastery as a votive offering. In 1563 the first stone of the Escorial was put in place, and the enormous and somewhat gloomy building was laid out in the form of a gridiron, in memory of the one of which St. Lawrence was martyred. The severe mole, substantially completed by 1585 but enriched in later centuries, is in large part the work of Juan de Herrera. An exemplary monument of the Counter-Reformation, the Escorial includes a vast series of rooms around the church. Among the most important of these, aside from the king's Spartan apartments, are the grand library and the lugubrious pantheon with the tombs of the kings of Spain. Italian artists made many important contributions during the late sixteenth century.

Dreams and visions at the close of the Renaissance

The presentation of the dead Christ supported by the Father is a theme of medieval origin (known as the "Throne of Grace" or the "Imago Trinitatis") that was brought back during the period of the Counter-Reformation. In this key painting from El Greco's early maturity, the expressive force and the tendency toward the imaginative are balanced by a powerful rendering of anatomy, in a broad and abundant wave of color.

This stupendous canvas, which opens the period of El Greco's activity in Toledo, marks not only a turn in the painter's career but also a precise turning point for the Spanish art of later centuries, from Goya all the way to Picasso. The expressive distortions of the faces, the compressed, suffocating composition, the violence of the colors form a figurative score on which appear alternatively images of great naturalism and visionary figures.

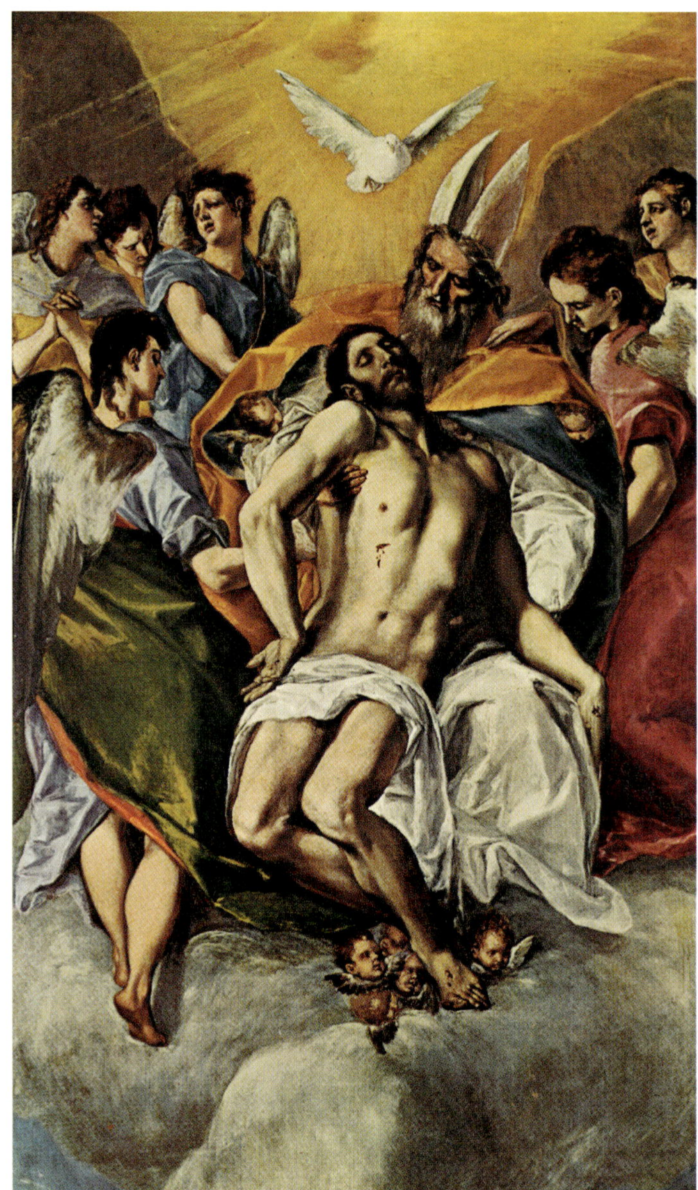

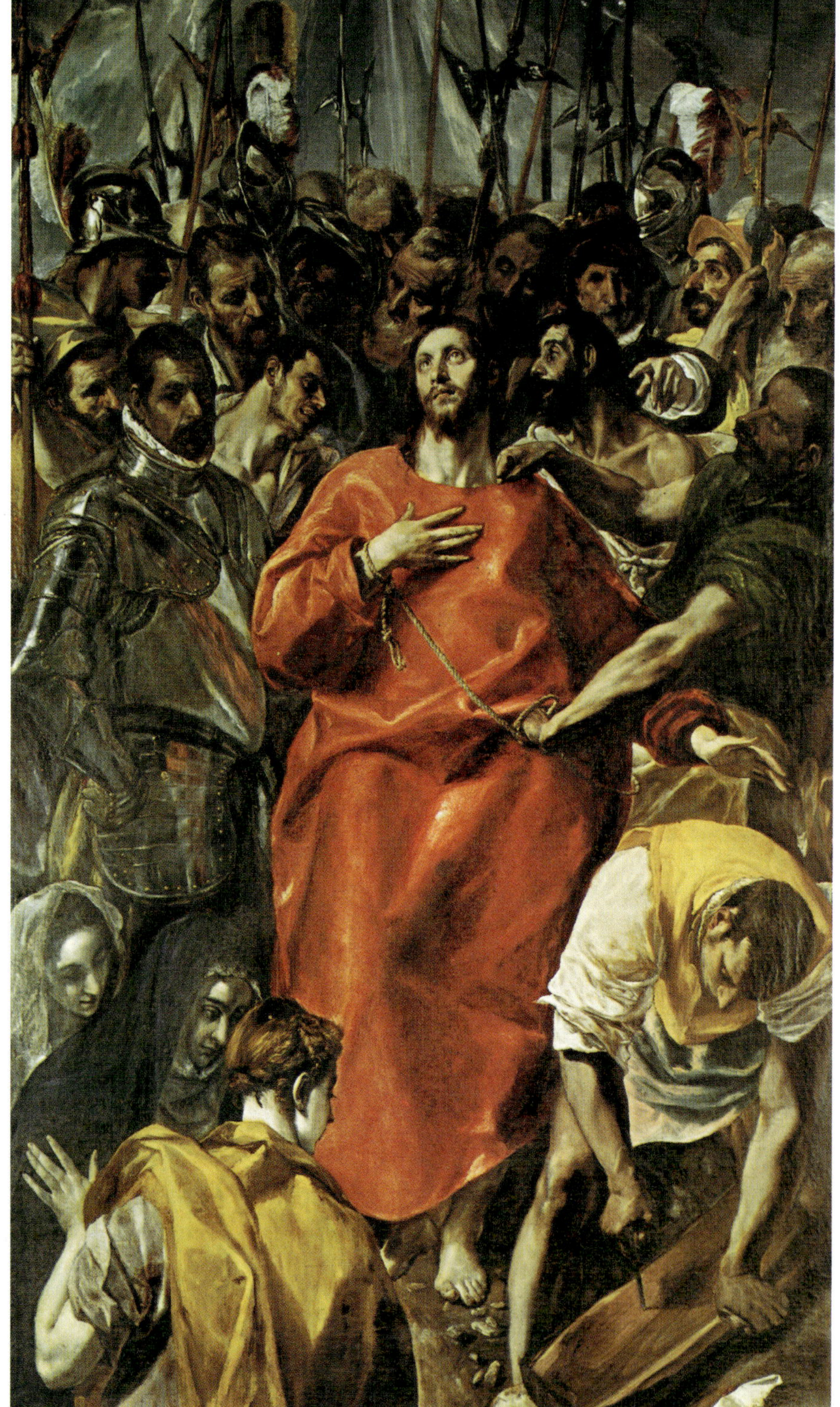

Dreams and visions at the close of the Renaissance

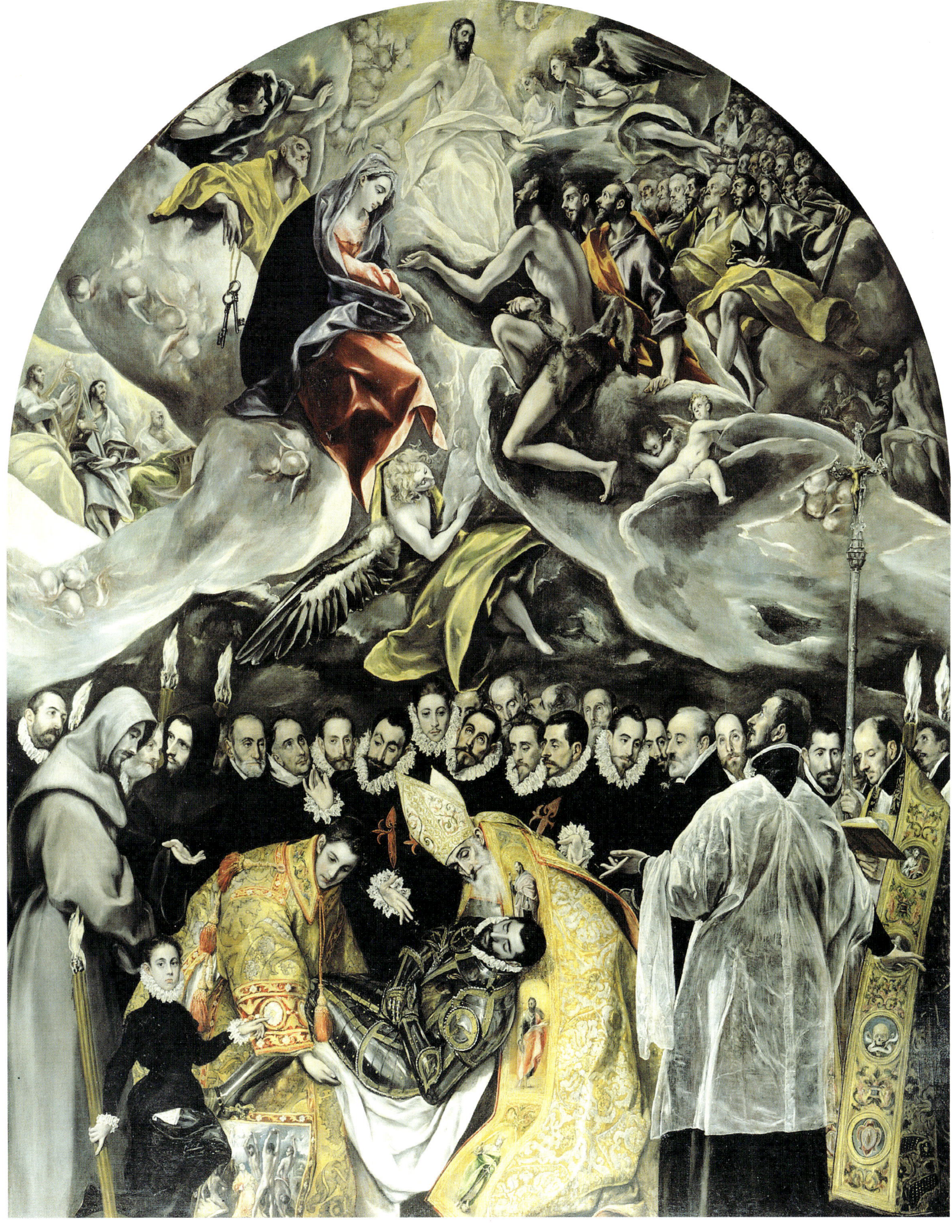

Dreams and visions at the close of the Renaissance

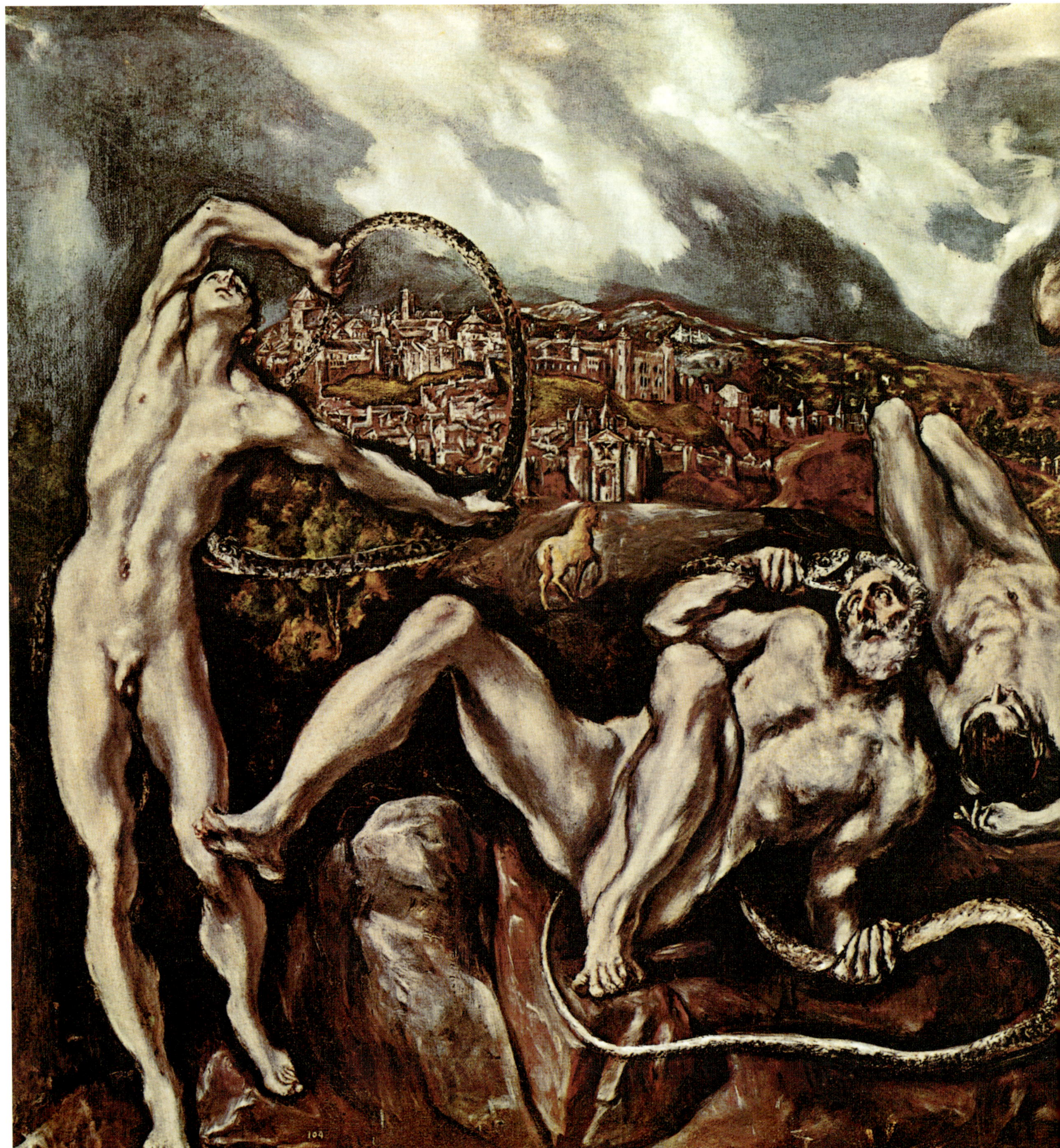

Dreams and visions at the close of the Renaissance

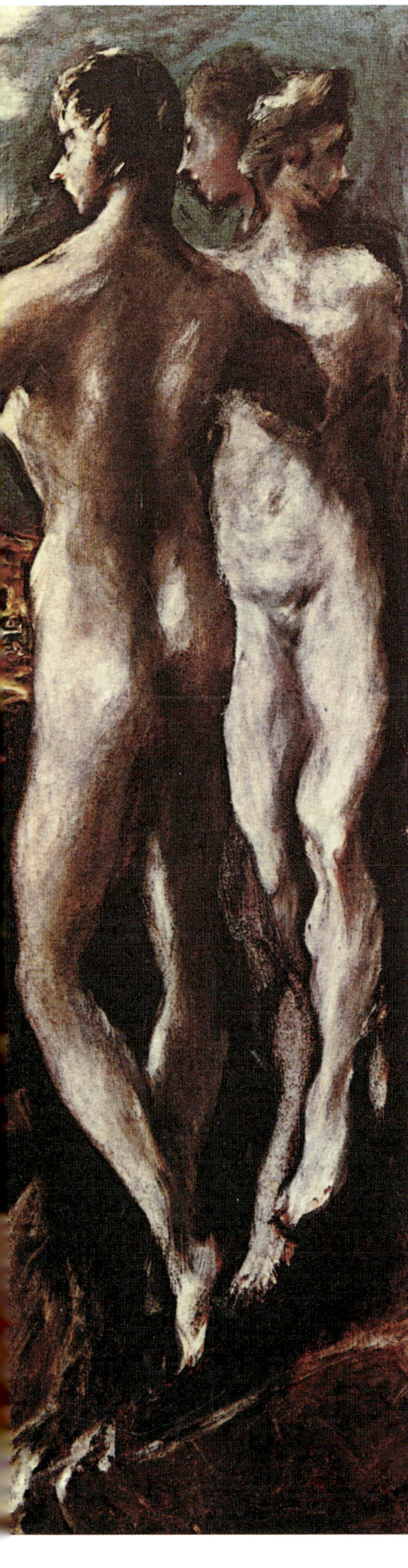

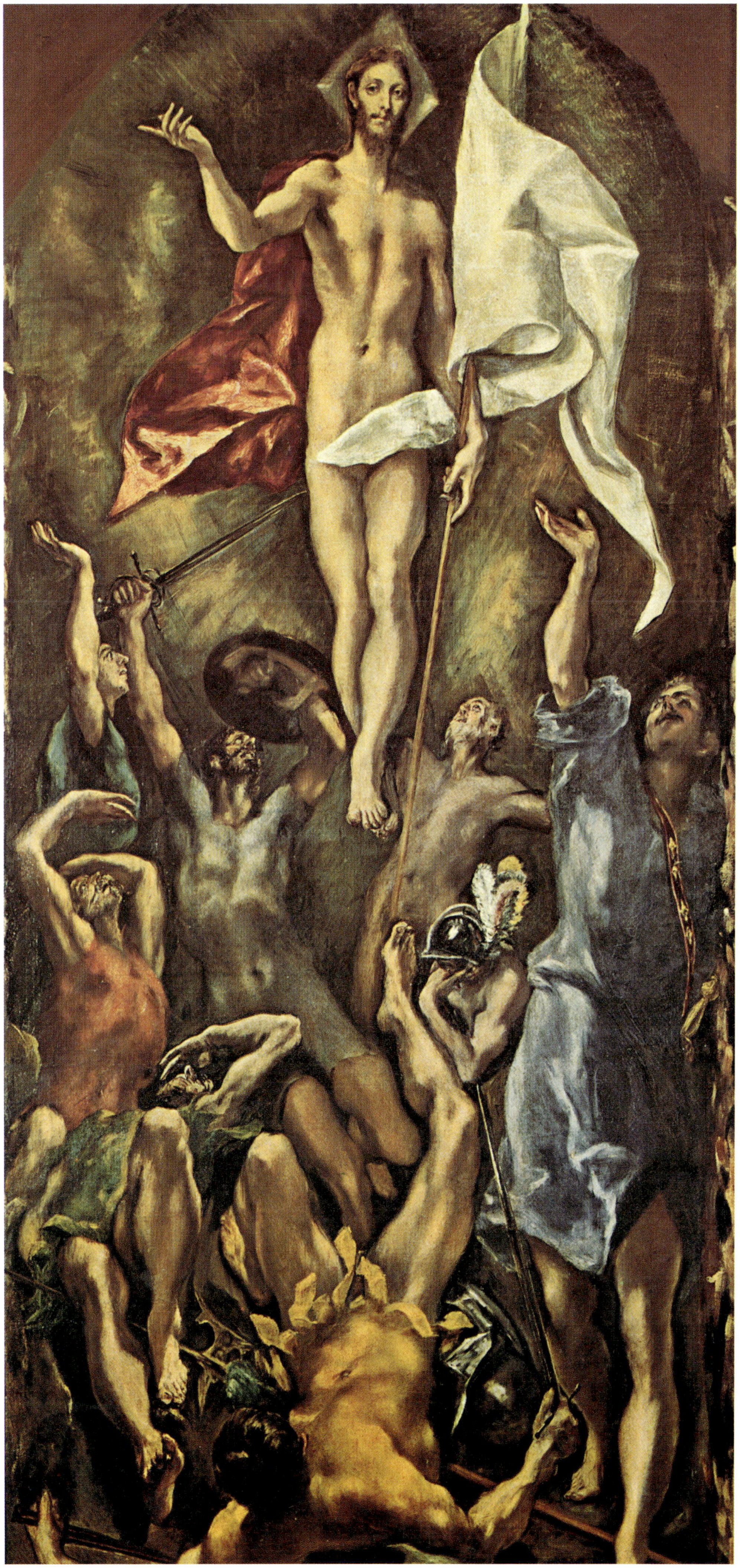

The altarpieces El Greco made can be used to reconstruct the highly intense creative route of his renewal of sacred art, in particular his profound reworking of iconography that until then had seemed untouchable and inalterably established. El Greco took the dictates of the Catholic Counter-Reformation and gave them his own completely original interpretation. Once again, one must recall the decisive moment in the Italian artistic culture of the 1570s, in the middle of the terse debate on the development of paintings with religious subjects. The involvement of the faithful, so often emphasized as the indispensable goal of devotional paintings, could be achieved in many different ways, as shown by the versions created by Annibale Carracci and Caravaggio during the last years of the sixteenth century. For his part, El Greco chose the route of the visionary, with compelling images that are both unreal and distorted.

Group masterpiece of Florentine art of the later mannerism, this small private room has niches that hold elegant statues by such sculptors as Ammanati, Giambologna, Bandini, and Vincenzo de' Rossi and 34 wonderful paintings made by a group of painters, chief among them Joannes Stradanus, Alessandro Allori, Maso da San Friano, Santi di Tito, Girolamo Macchietti, Mirabello Cavalori, and Jacopo Zucchi. The *studiolo* reflects the taste and the spirit of Francesco I, an eccentric character who was a collector and a scholar of chemistry, alchemy, and the natural sciences. Many of the panels are based on a sophisticated interweaving of mythology and science, hermetism and research. In this way the mannerist style began to become the visual translation of the melancholies, manias, and neuroses of the great collectors at the end of the century. Francesco I de' Medici, who became grand duke of Tuscany in 1574, had a close equivalent in Emperor Rudolf II.

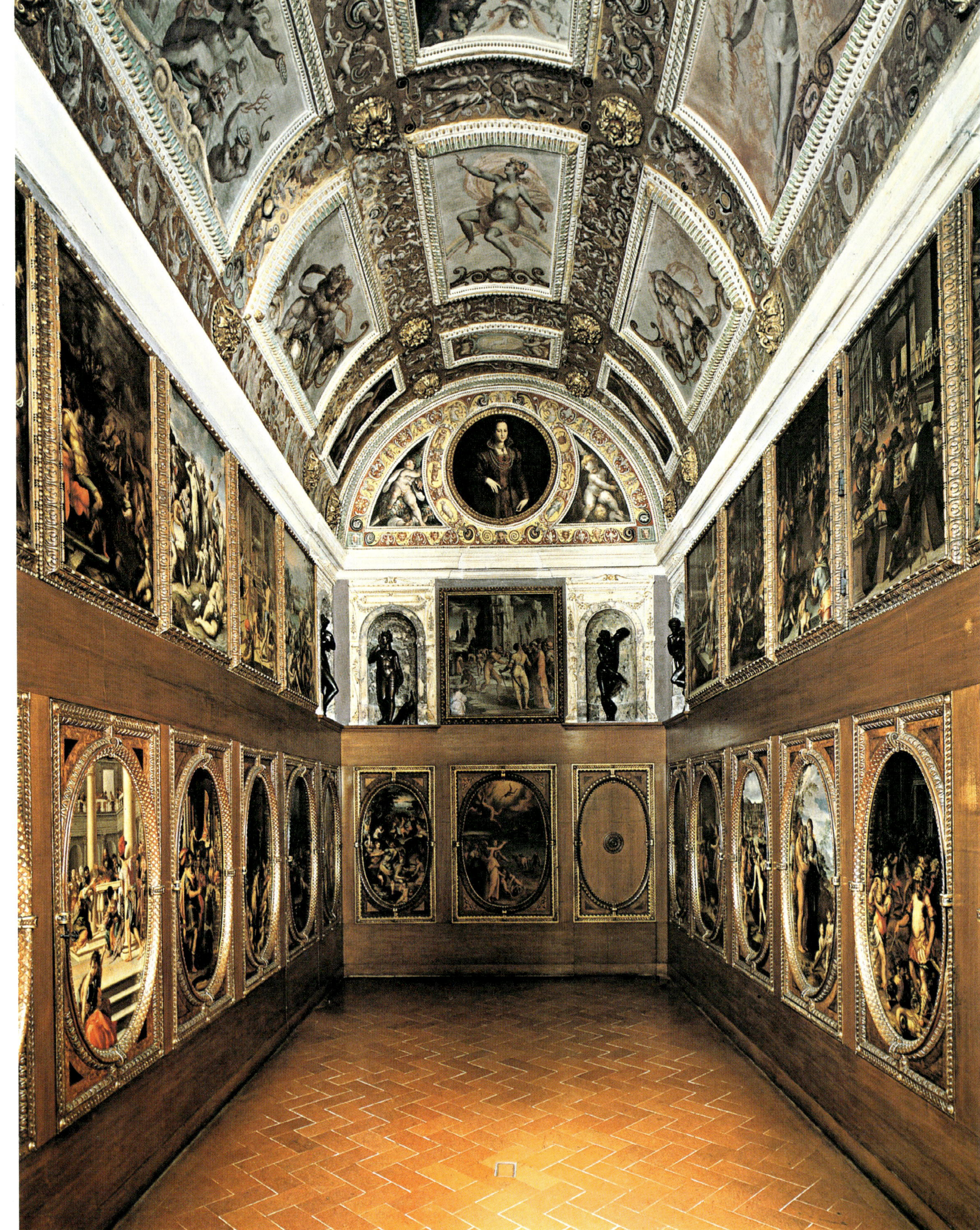

Dreams and visions at the close of the Renaissance

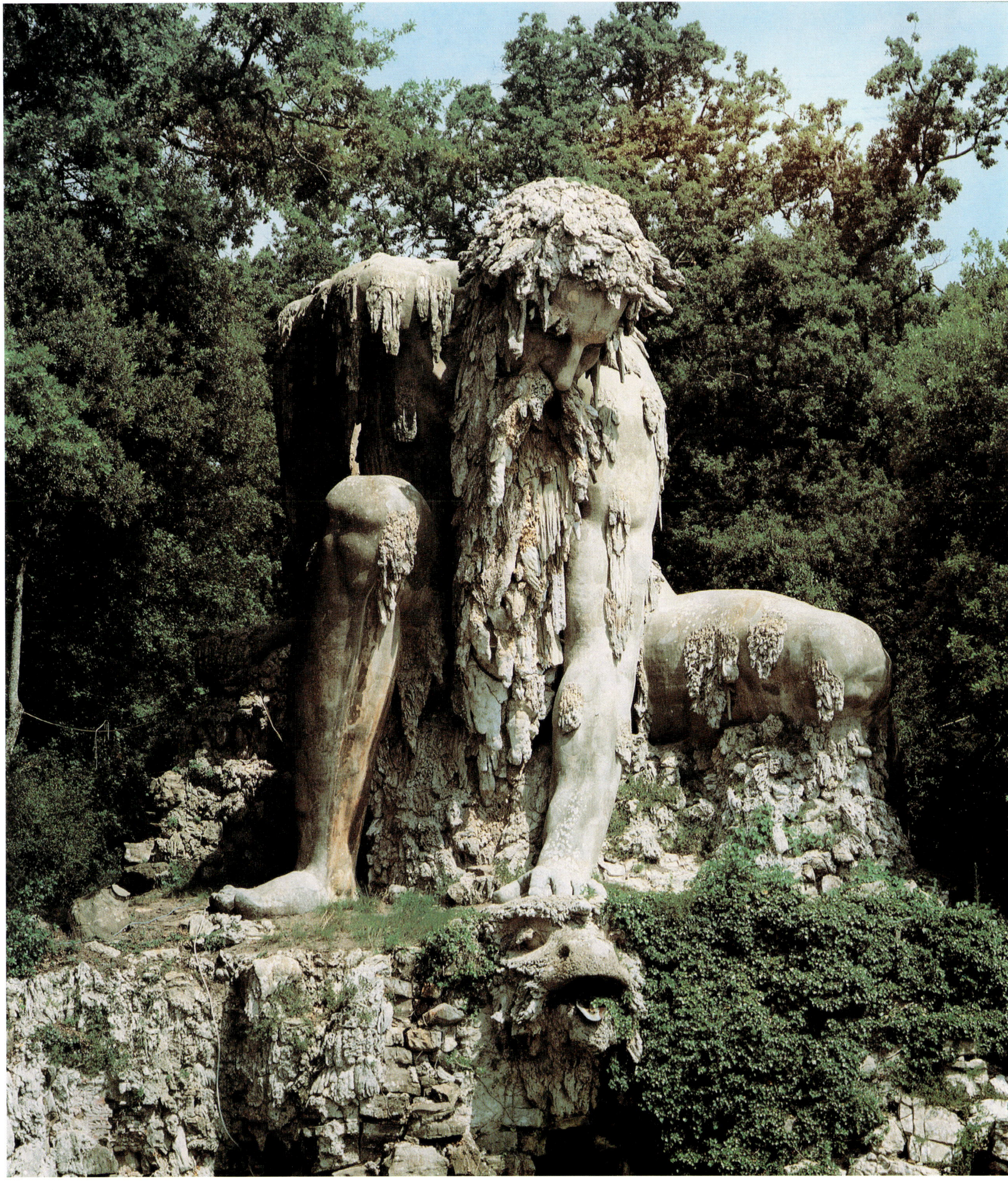

Dreams and visions at the close of the Renaissance

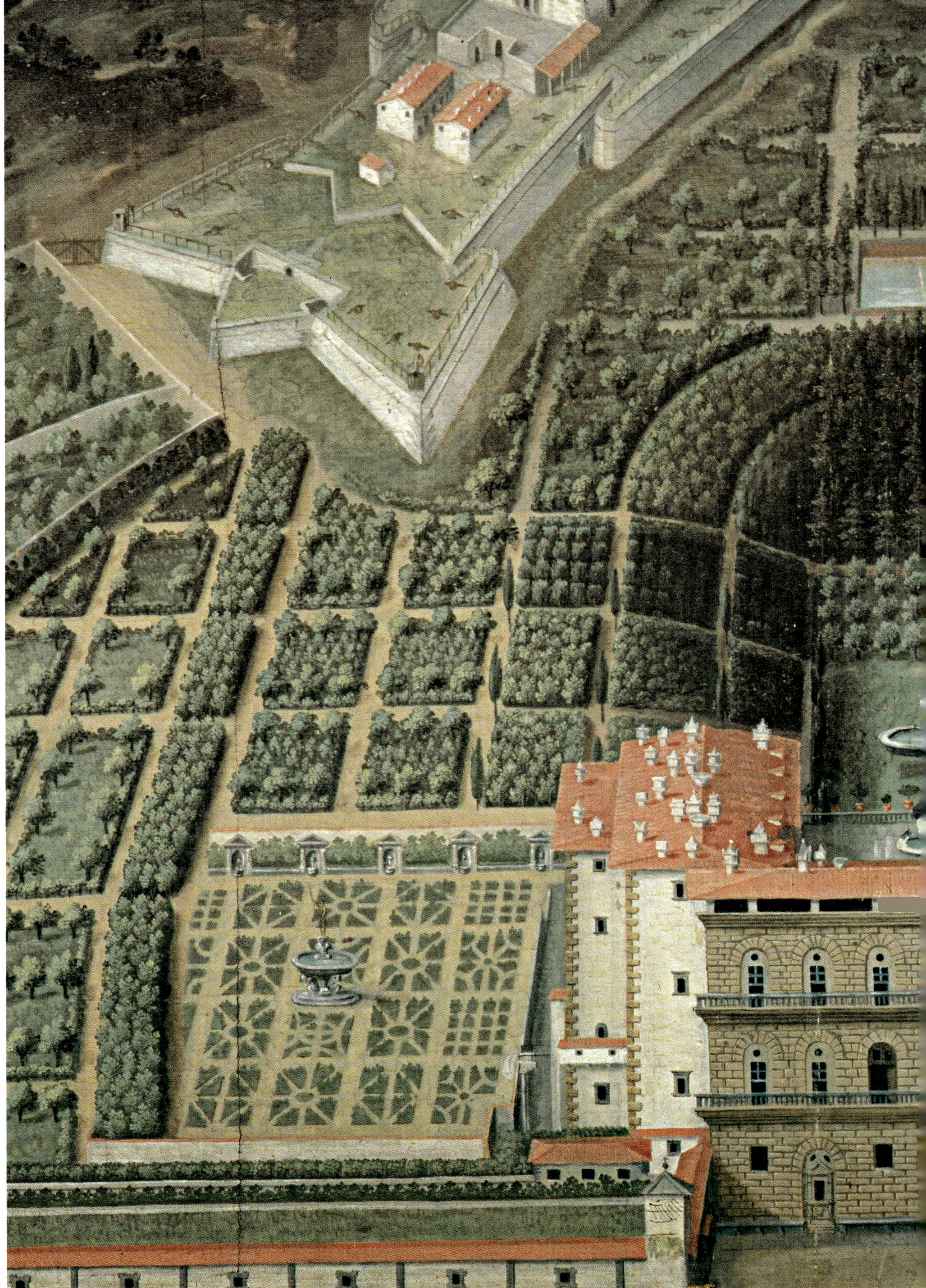

GIUSTO UTENS
**Palazzo Pitti with
Boboli Gardens**
Detail
Painted lunette
circa 1590
Museo di Firenze
com'era,
Florence

A very effective image
of the Medici residences
and their gardens in
Florence and the envi-
rons at the end of the
sixteenth century is
offered by the series of
lunettes "as the bird
flies" by Giusto Utens.
With meticulous preci-
sion but at the same
time with a subtle
intellectual sense of
the melancholy flight
from time and reality,
the painter succeeds
in communicating the
magic of settings that
are at once natural
and artificial.

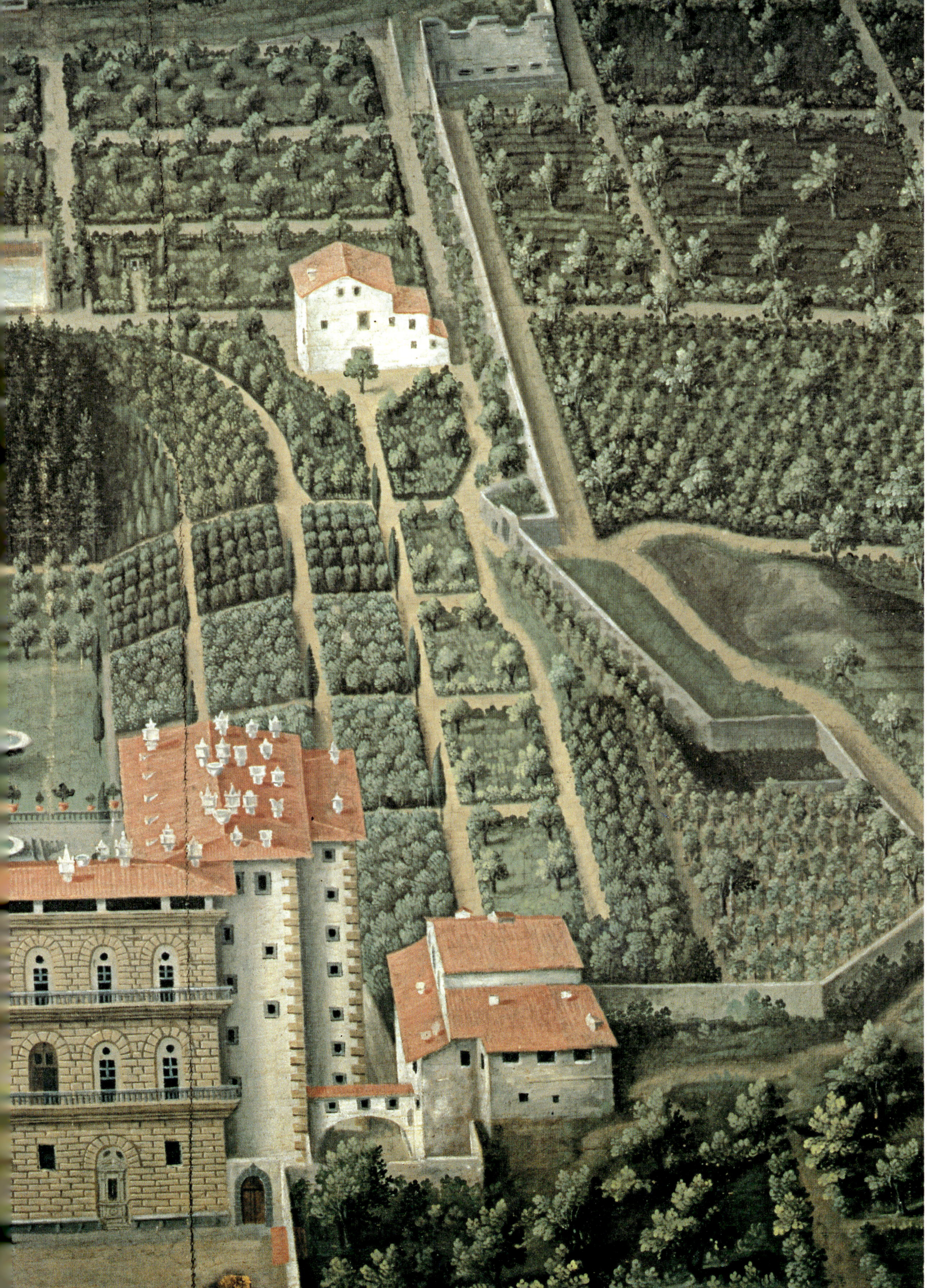

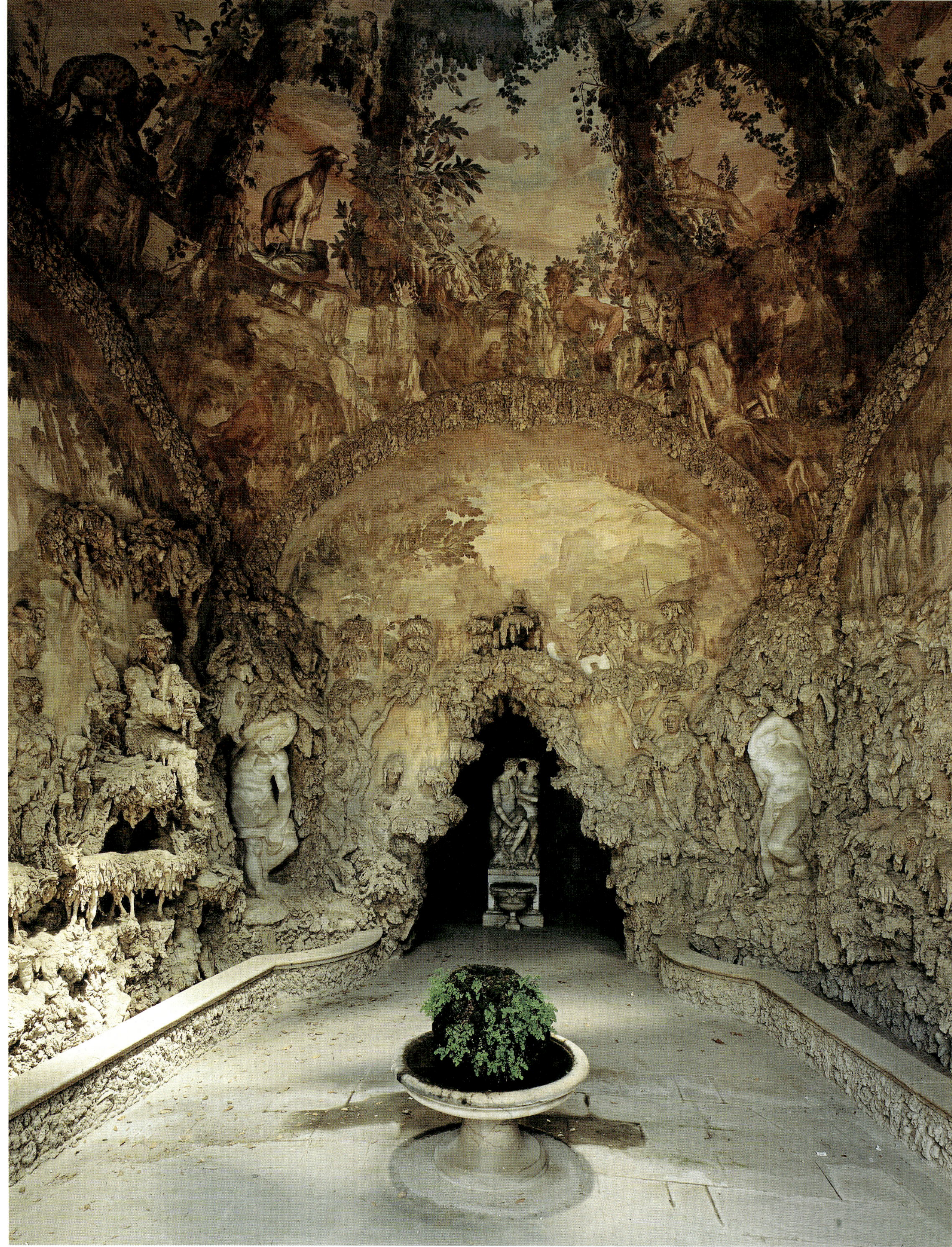

Dreams and visions at the close of the Renaissance

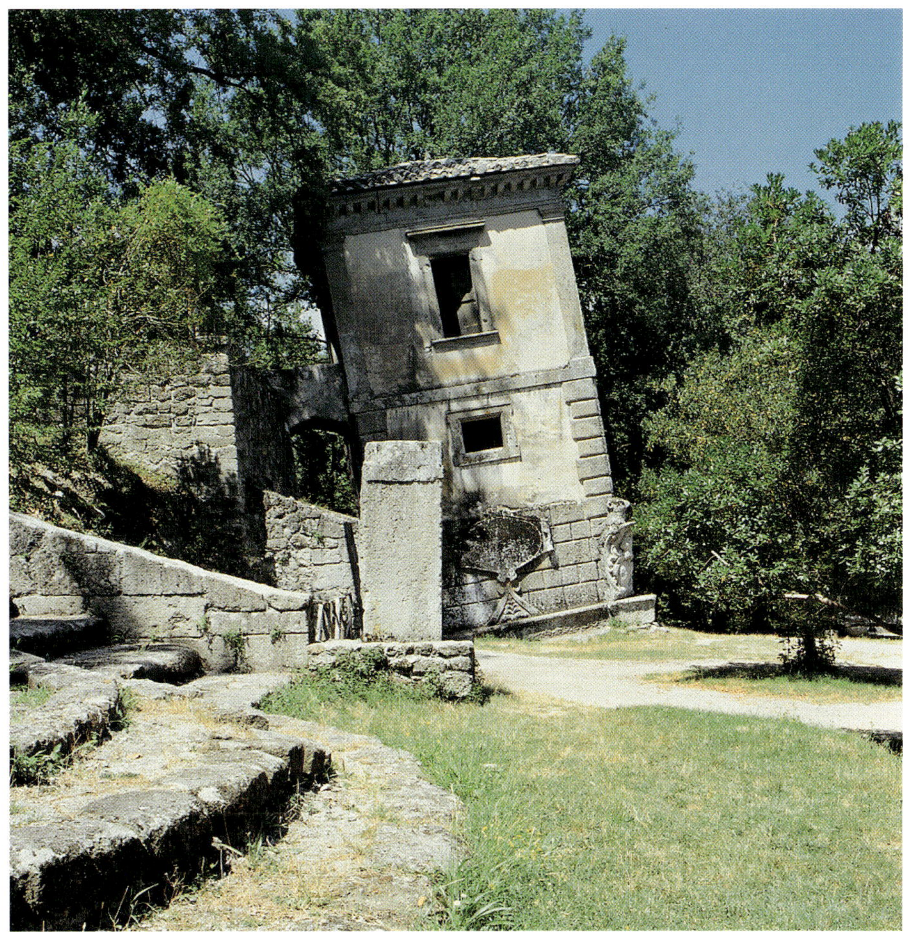

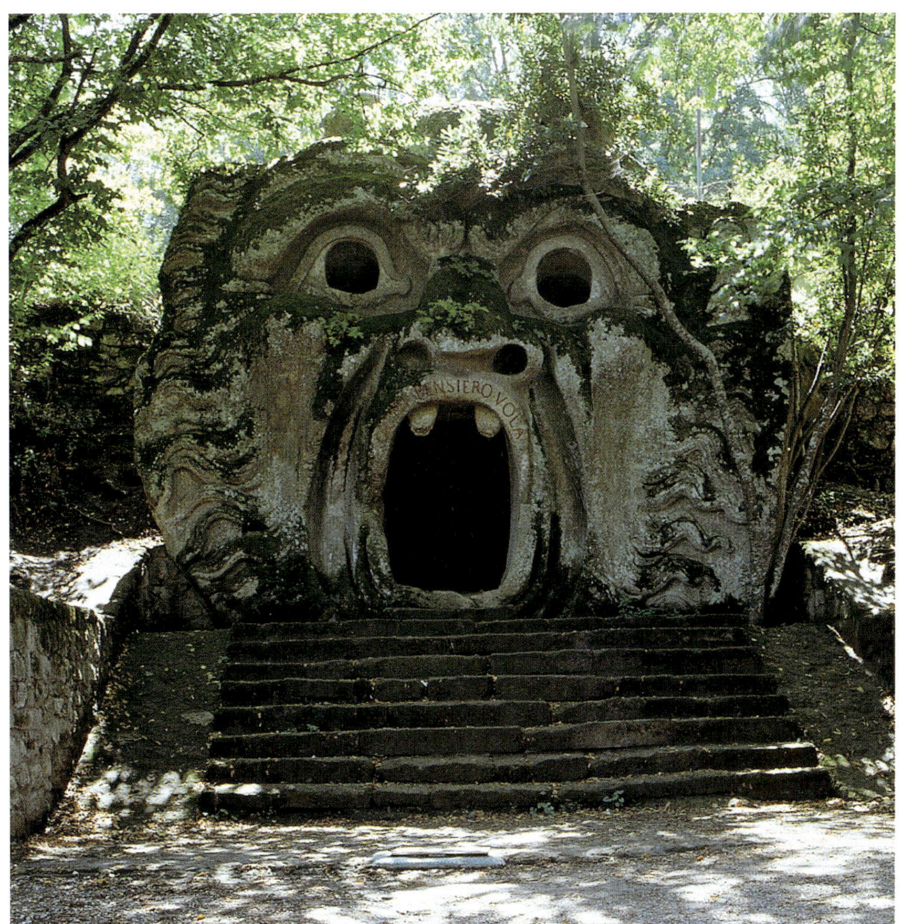

Dreams and visions at the close of the Renaissance

Federico Zuccari,
detail of the façade
of Palazzo Zuccari,
1592; Rome

T he end of the Council of Trent (1563) and the vast generational change that took place among artists during the last quarter of the sixteenth century accelerated the reflections on the moral and pedagogical meaning of works of art and in particular of religious painting and the earliest versions of genre painting. According to Gabriele Paleotti, the cardinal of Bologna, art must "illuminate the intellect, excite devotion, and touch the heart" through order and clarity, simplicity, control of form, rejection of the strange forms of mannerism.

These same years also saw the "reform" of the Carracci family of painters, founders of an academy of painting in Bologna. In explicit opposition to the composed and substantially cold style of the Catholic Counter-Reformation, the cousins Ludovico and Annibale Carracci proposed a series of radical novelties. Happy to work together but also capable of manifesting their respective and increasingly different

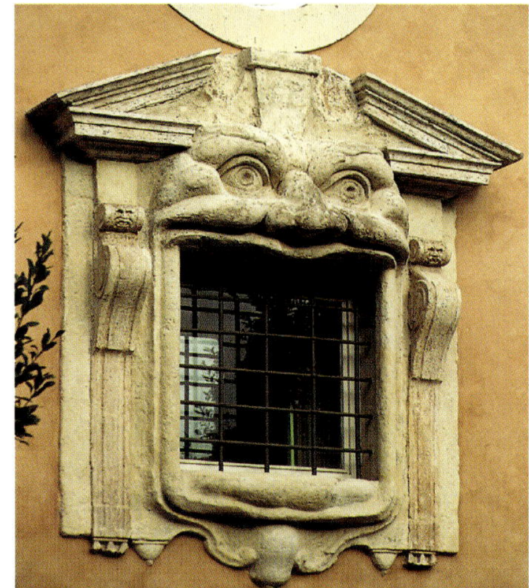

Europe had entered a period of profound political, social, and cultural change, between the crisis of the traditional powers (from the Spanish empire to the small Italian states) to the appearance of new nations against a background that by then embraced a span of oceans and far-distant continents. The coming seventeenth century promised to be full of surprises and paradoxes. The arts were to produce their most fanciful style during the same years that the sciences were working out the rules and methods of modern research; the economy was to see the birth of middle-class entrepreneurial capitalism precisely while rulers had themselves built palaces of incredible size; Italian culture and taste would spread across Europe while Italy itself would be shoved to the outer edge of international commerce. The circulation of ideas and artists reached a new intensity; yet at the same time that new national schools were taking shape (as in the Flanders of Rubens, the Holland of Rembrandt, the Spain of Velázquez, the France of Poussin), a style with more

Annibale Carracci,
The Bean Eater, 1584;
Galleria Colonna, Rome

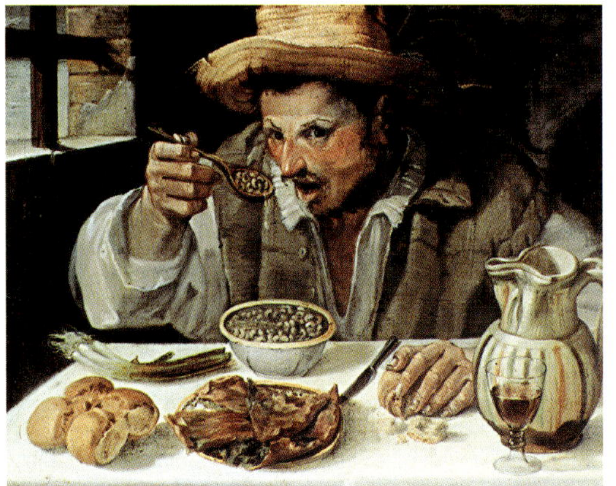

On the threshold all roads

styles, Ludovico and Annibale authoritatively presented the sense of natural truth, of real light, of life that is passing. The two artists drew on numerous sources for inspiration, the undeniable "Lombard" substratum, the memory of Correggio, the knowledge of Venetian painting, and attention to the delicacies of Federico Barocci. The works of Annibale became increasingly rich and complex, especially in relation to his direct experience of sixteenth-century Venetian art with the growth of a figurative and humanistic culture directly translated in pictorial forms and in academic teaching. The movement to Rome of the academy of the Carracci during the last decade of the sixteenth century was the physical response to a process of artistic renewal that had reached maturity. Thus Rome once again took its place as the international center for the most modern trends in art. A new page in painting opened with the extraordinary undertaking of the decorations of the gallery in the Farnese Palace by Agostino and Annibale.

or less homogeneous characteristics began to take hold all across Europe.

In the period of passage from the Renaissance to the baroque, Rome was the heart and soul of the entire system of the arts. At the end of the sixteenth century, under the brief heading Eternal City was summarized a vast quantity of projects, masterpieces, princely collections, international artists, currents in which the baroque art of all of Europe was being conceived, articulated, and distributed. The five intense years of the pontificate of Sixtus V (1585–90) were full of undertakings to rebuild and embellish. It was all light and shadows. Rome was both display window and workshop, showroom and back alley, glory and misery. Ranks of artists from every far corner of Europe set themselves up in the city. All came to learn, only a few arrived with contracts or with precise prestigious commissions. To find work, most of them put their faith in the support of the various national communities long rooted in the city (the Lombards, the Ticinese, the Emilians, French, Flemish-Dutch, Germans, and so on); a few were adventurers in search of fortune. This

On the threshold of the baroque, all roads lead to Rome

chaotic and multilayered human panorama, with all its chance encounters, exchanges of opinion, and parallel developments in style, has no comparison in history, especially if one projects this exciting situation against the monumental backdrop of the city's great classical ruins and the masterpieces of Raphael and Michelangelo.

Between the last years of the sixteenth century and the first half of the seventeenth (speaking in terms strictly artistic, from the arrival of Caravaggio to Velázquez's second stay in Rome), the city of Rome was the scene of an intense debate, with continuous variations in the influence and the prevalence of styles and trends, the exchange and discussion of specialized treatises, and, of course, the creation of great masterpieces. From a generalized formulation, three main trends can be made out, which alternated in a sort of ideal relay race of prevalent styles: the naturalism of Caravaggio, the classicism

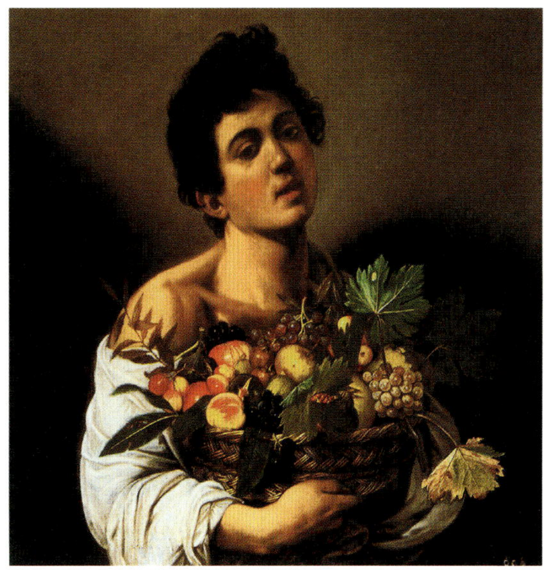

Caravaggio, *Boy with Basket of Fruit*, 1594; Galleria Borghese, Rome

observed the life of the streets and the *osterie* and reproduced it with a profound sense of participation. His first works were inspired by daily reality, with a few figures on a pale background crossed by a ray of diagonal light. This was not an absolute novelty (the current of realism, as we have seen, has firm roots in sixteenth-century European painting), but the spirit with which he painted his works was highly innovative. Soon enough it became clear that the great "revolution" of Caravaggio involved most of all the role of the viewer looking at the work, who can no longer remain a passive spectator, but instead becomes an active eye-witness, directly involved in an event that is taking place *hic et nunc*, here and now. The year 1600, with the execution of the canvases in the church of San Luigi dei Francesi, marks a clear liberation in his style, applied now to large scenes of religious themes, with many figures and primarily dark backgrounds. In the scene of the *Calling of*

of the baroque, lead to Rome

of Guido Reni and the Emilian school, and the baroque properly called inaugurated by Rubens and developed by Bernini and Pietro da Cortona. These three different figurative models constitute the support columns for all of seventeenth-century Europe.

Shortly after reaching the age of eighteen, Caravaggio left Milan for Rome, never to return to the city of his birth. Quarrelsome and violent, he soon enough found himself in trouble with the law; looking for work, he offered himself as assistant to various masters; he ended up in the hospital from an attack of malaria. He finally landed a steady job with Giuseppe Cesari (called Cavaliere d'Arpino). By then twenty, Caravaggio's chore was to insert details of flowers and fruit in the master's paintings. This was the beginning of his Roman career and also a signal of his coming predilection for the creations of nature, to which Caravaggio conferred an autonomous dignity. In the span of a few short years, this attitude had made him one of the pioneers of the still life. Caravaggio did not draw inspiration from courtly models. He

St. Matthew, the saint is seated at a table; to the right, in part covered by the figure of St. Peter, appears Christ. One look is enough, along with a finger raised with the decisiveness of the frescoes of Michelangelo in the Sistine Chapel. St. Matthew, like an apostle in Leonardo's *Last Supper*, responds with a gesture indicating himself. The *Martyrdom* instead is painted like a brutal execution, with a killer that breaks into the church to pierce St. Matthew, making him roll down the steps of the altar during the Mass. From that moment on, new vistas were opened for the history of art, entire universes of emotions and passions all yet to be explored.

Stefano Maderno, *St. Cecilia*, 1600; Santa Cecilia in Trastevere, Rome

On the threshold of the baroque, all roads lead to Rome

The vital rediscovery of classical works and the free evocation of the ancient by way of the study of the great masters of the Renaissance are at the base of the extraordinary illusionistic pictorial space designed for the Farnese Gallery. Summoned by Cardinal Odoardo Farnese, in 1595, Annibale Carracci left Bologna to move to Rome. In search of a beauty that is both ideal and at the same time natural, he freely drew on tradition and succeeded in creating the grace and joyful vitality of the ancient mythological fables. Some of these episodes are set in faux gilt and stucco frames; others are bordered by enormous telamons that simulate ancient stone statues or by young nudes wearing large medallions and garlands. At the center of the barrel vault, in a sunny and radiant world, a frolicsome cortege of maenad bacchantes, satyrs, and nymphs accompanies the *Triumph of Bacchus and Ariadne*, an exaltation of love and sensual beauty.

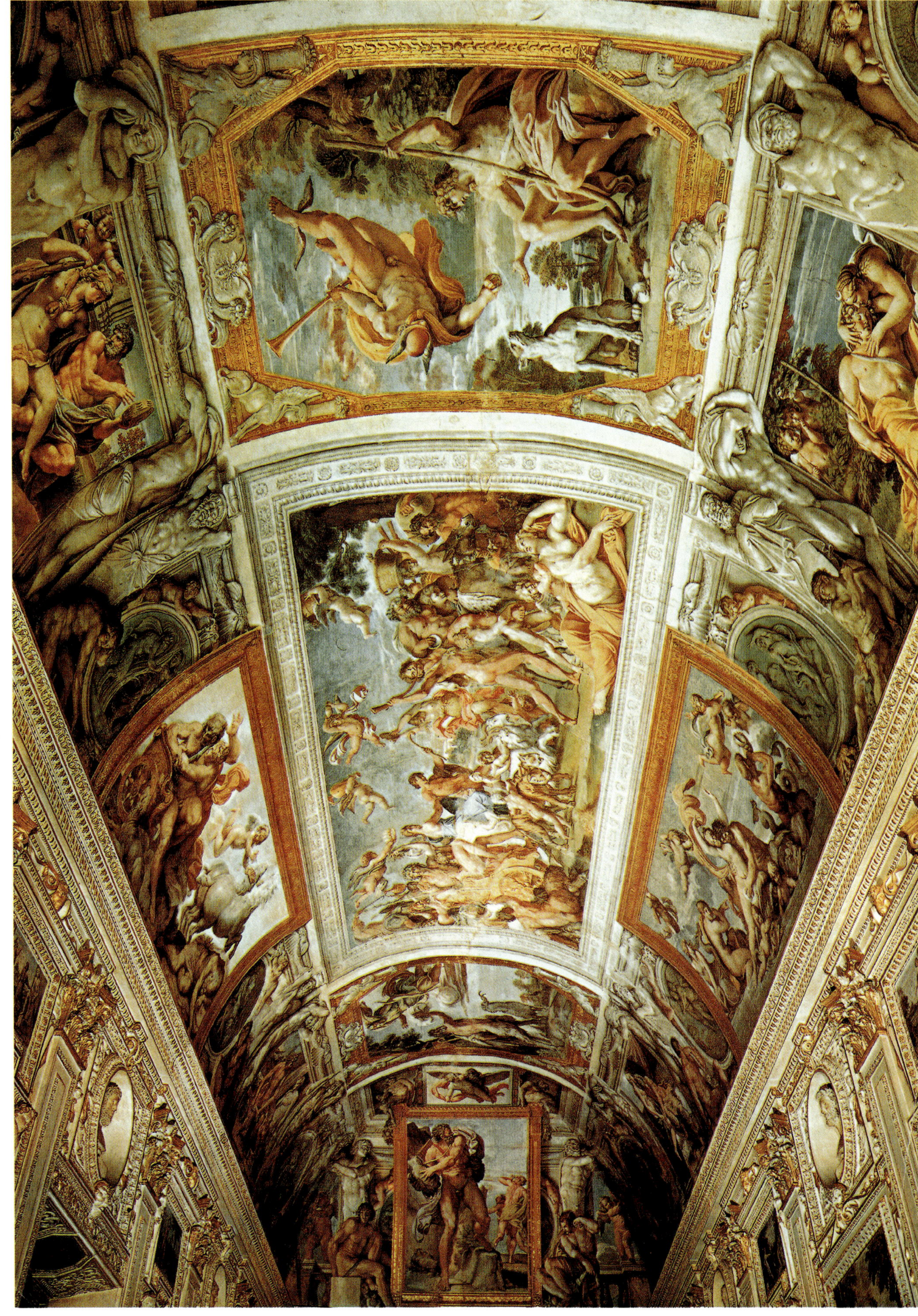

On the threshold of the baroque, all roads lead to Rome

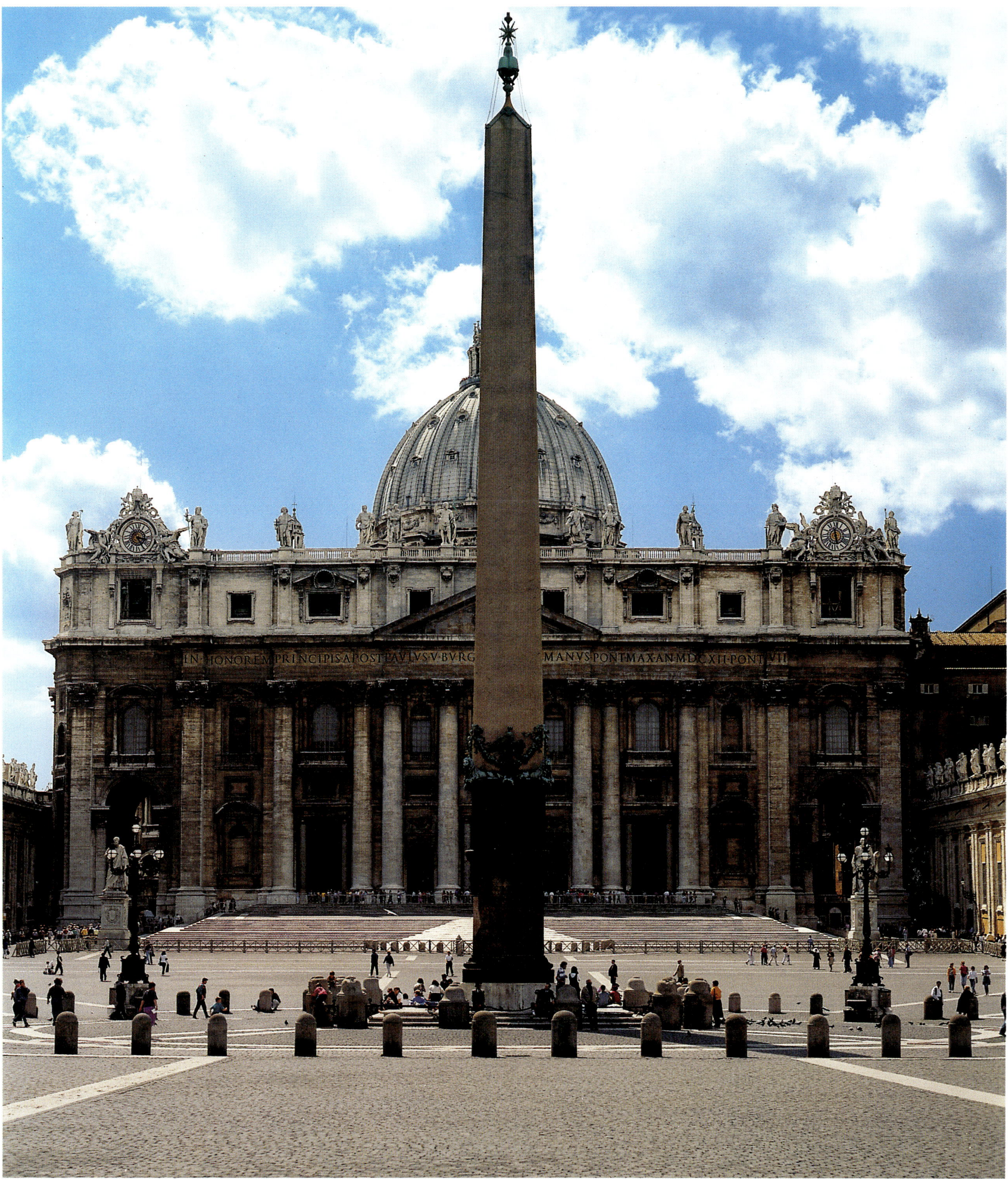

The Ticinese Carlo
Maderno continued
in the tradition of mas-
ter builders from the
region of the Lombard
lakes. He set up frag-
ments of Roman antiq-
uity and turned them
into focal points in the
new wave of building
and urban renewal pro-
moted by the popes, in
an ideal continuity
between the classical
world and the Christian
world. Maderno per-
formed the arduous
chore of modifying and
enlarging Michelangelo's
plans, with the creation
of the nave and façade
of St. Peter's.

On the threshold of the baroque, all roads lead to Rome

PETER PAUL RUBENS
The Four Philosophers
1611–12, oil on panel, 167 x 143 cm
Galleria Palatina, Palazzo Pitti, Florence

Early in the seventeenth century, when he was at the outset of his career, Rubens was without doubt one of the most enthusiastic exponents of Roman artistic culture. This self-portrait together with another three figures was made sometime after his return to Antwerp (1608) following nine years in Italy. With its references to antiquity, lively conversation, and the constant presence of beauty, this work can be seen as an evocation of the intellectual climate the painter had entered.

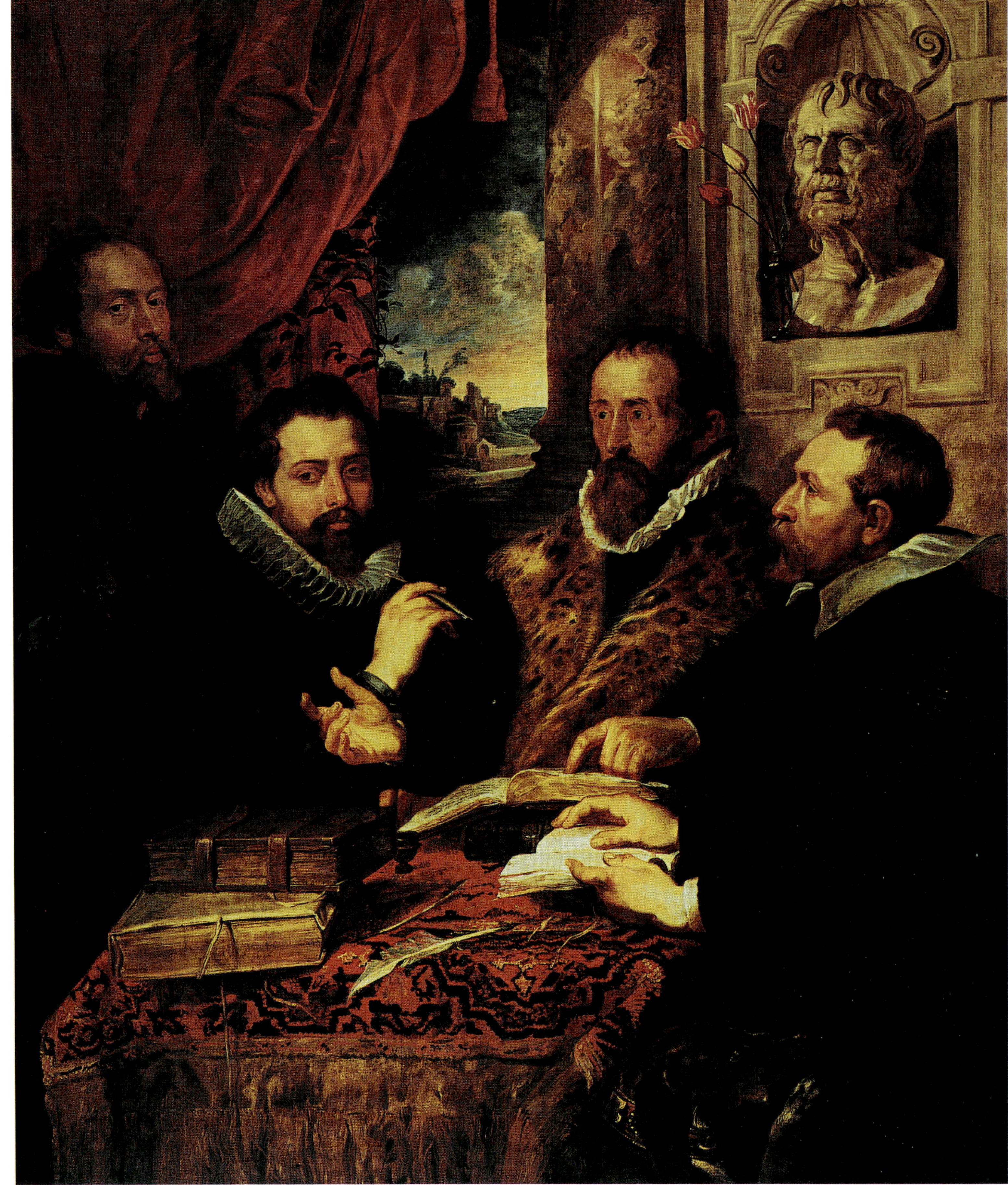

On the threshold of the baroque, all roads lead to Rome

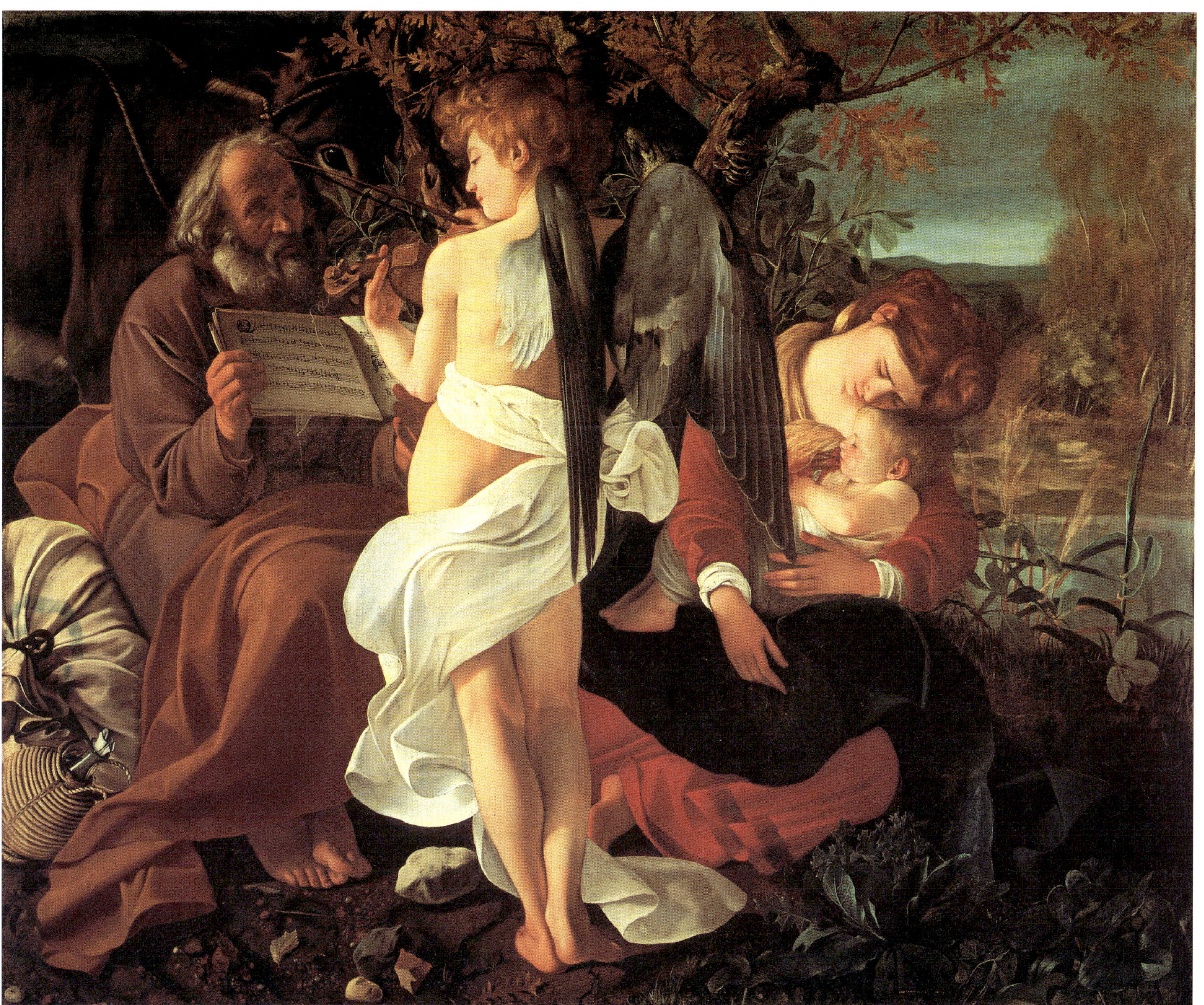

On the threshold of the baroque, all roads lead to Rome

Caravaggio
The Cardsharps
1594–95,
oil on canvas,
94.2 x 130.9 cm
Kimbell Art Museum,
Fort Worth

A youth, attracted by
the easy earnings of
gambling, is tricked by
a pair of cardsharps.
The older makes a sign
to his accomplice,
who draws a card from
behind his back. The
canvas is an outstanding
example of Caravaggio's
powers of observation,
capable of presenting
the immediacy of a
scene, the gestures,
the narrative flavor of
the details of clothes
and the card table. The
subject of card players
was to become one
of the most popular
themes in seventeenth-
century genre painting.

Valentin de Boulogne
Cheats
circa 1616, oil on
canvas, 95 x 137 cm
Gemäldegalerie,
Dresden

Among the many French
"pensioners" in Rome
(artists with a means
of support, however
precarious), Valentin
de Boulogne is today
perhaps the most
admired of all. The
Carravaggioesque real-
ism, passionately
studied but never
banally imitated, is
transformed in his
hand into a darkly
dynamic and often
grim current event,
painted with
unusual energy.

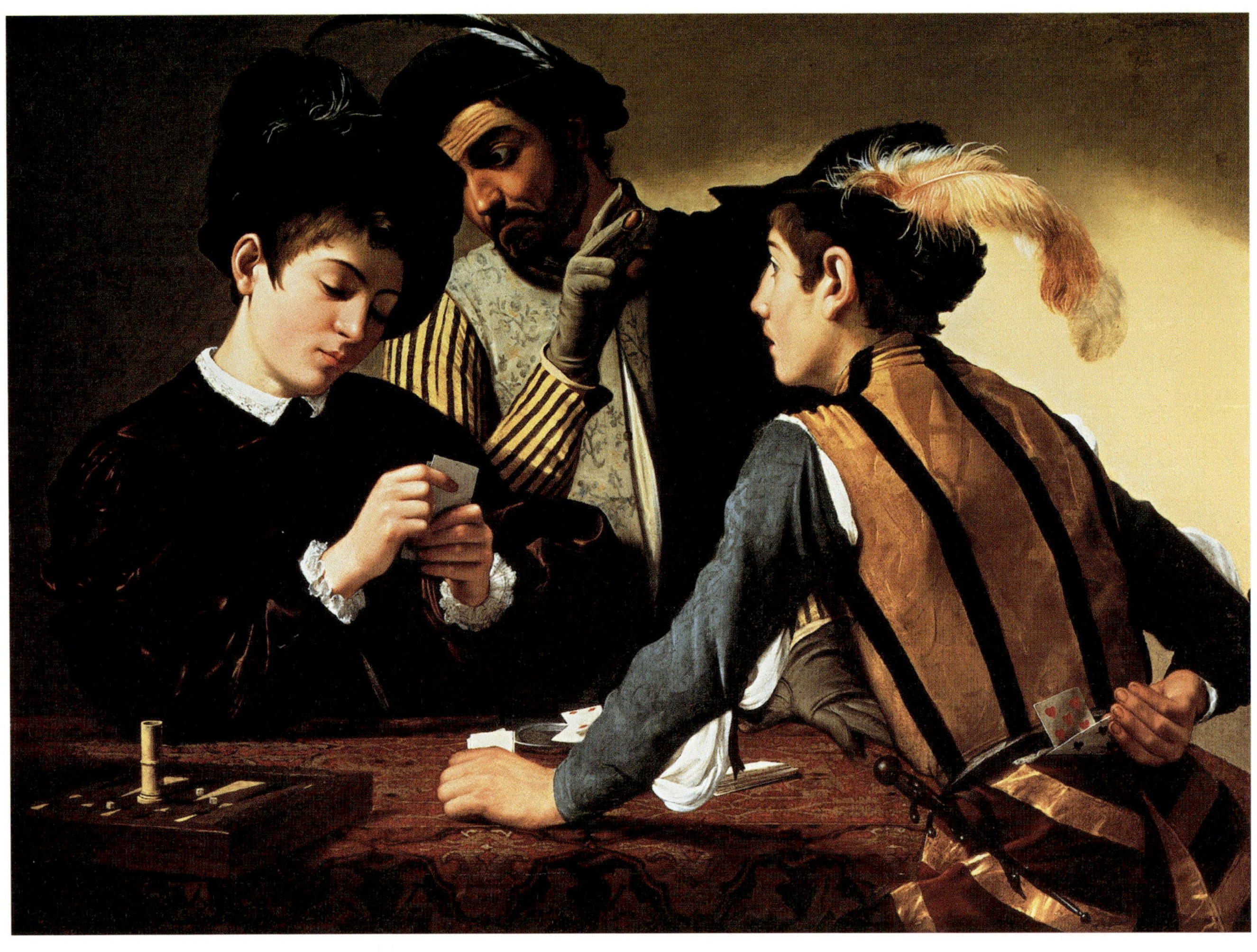

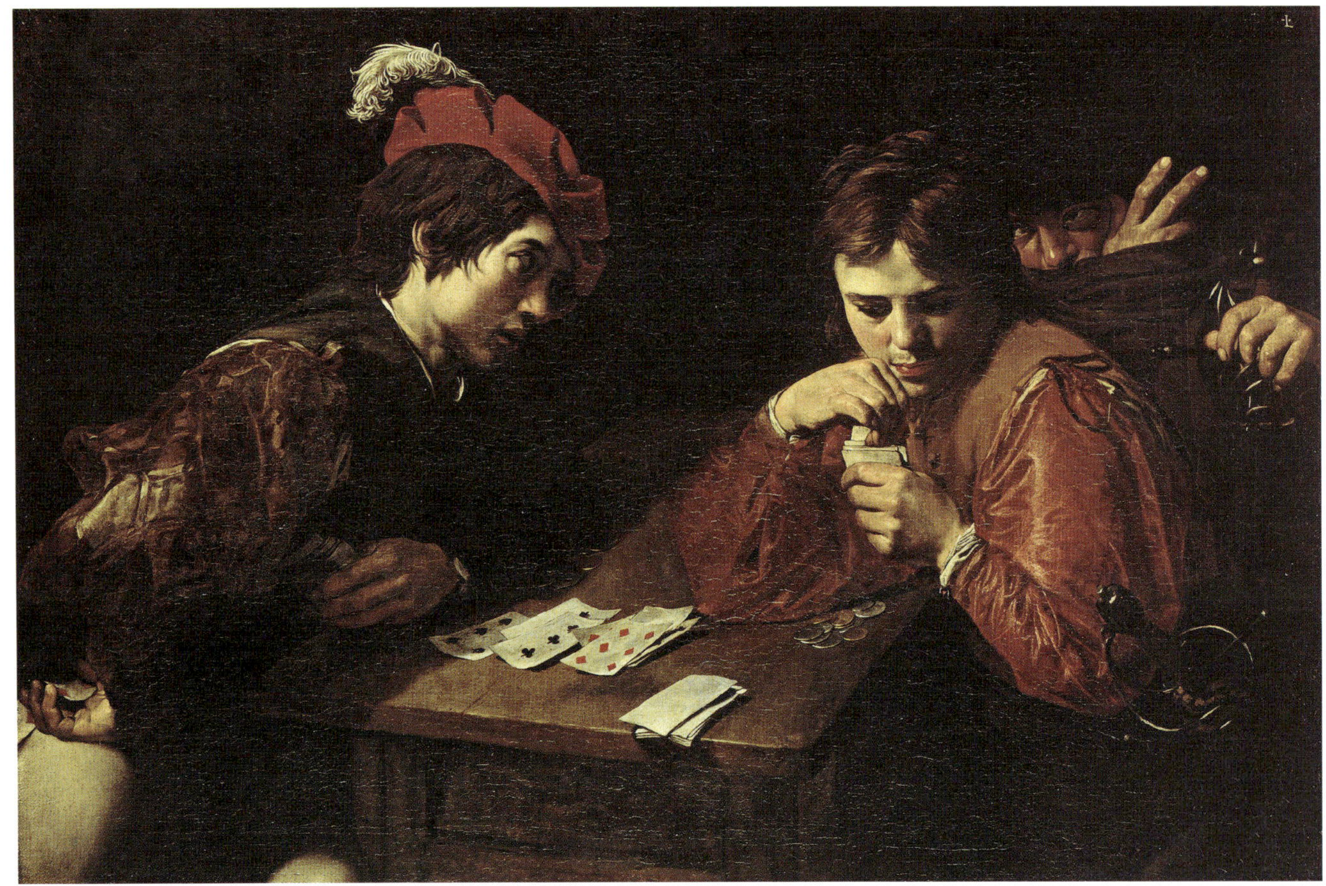

On the threshold of the baroque, all roads lead to Rome

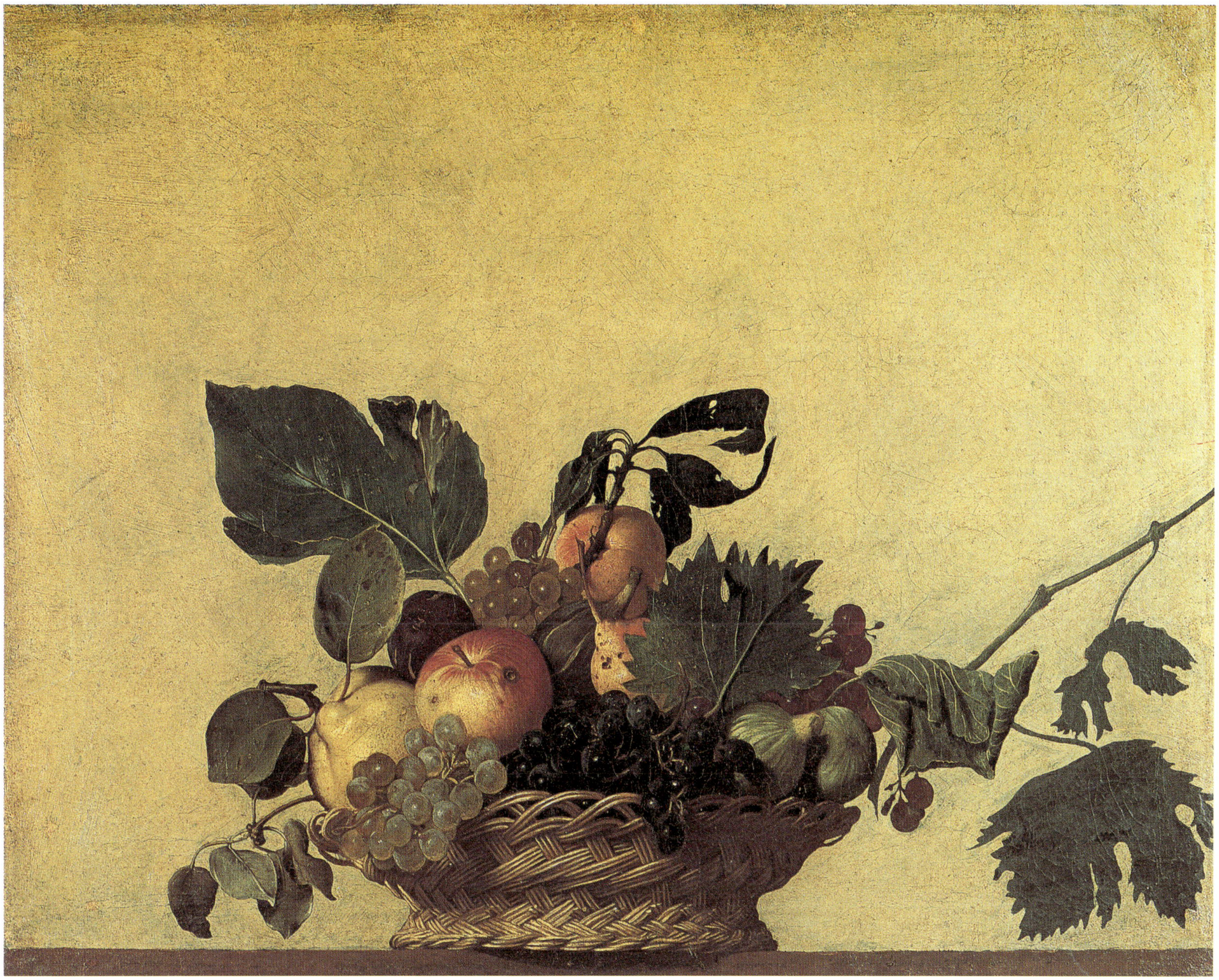

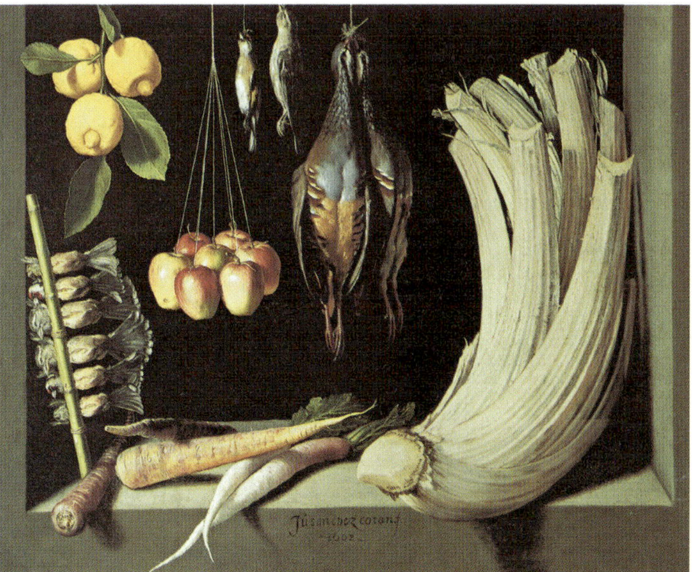

On the threshold of the baroque, all roads lead to Rome

The cycle Caravaggio made between 1599 and 1602 for the Contarelli Chapel in San Luigi dei Francesi constitutes the painter's first important public commission. Thanks to the efforts of Cardinal Del Monte, the artist received the prestigious commission to complete the decoration of the chapel, acquired by Cardinal Mathieu Contarel in 1565. Because of the success of his first canvases (the *Calling* and the *Martyrdom of St. Matthew*), he was also entrusted with the creation of the altarpiece. This is the second version of the subject: the first was rejected because the poses of the saint and the angel were judged unbecoming. In this new work, which the patron approved, the evangelist, whose attitude is still loose and unconventional, receives inspiration from the flying angel sent by God.

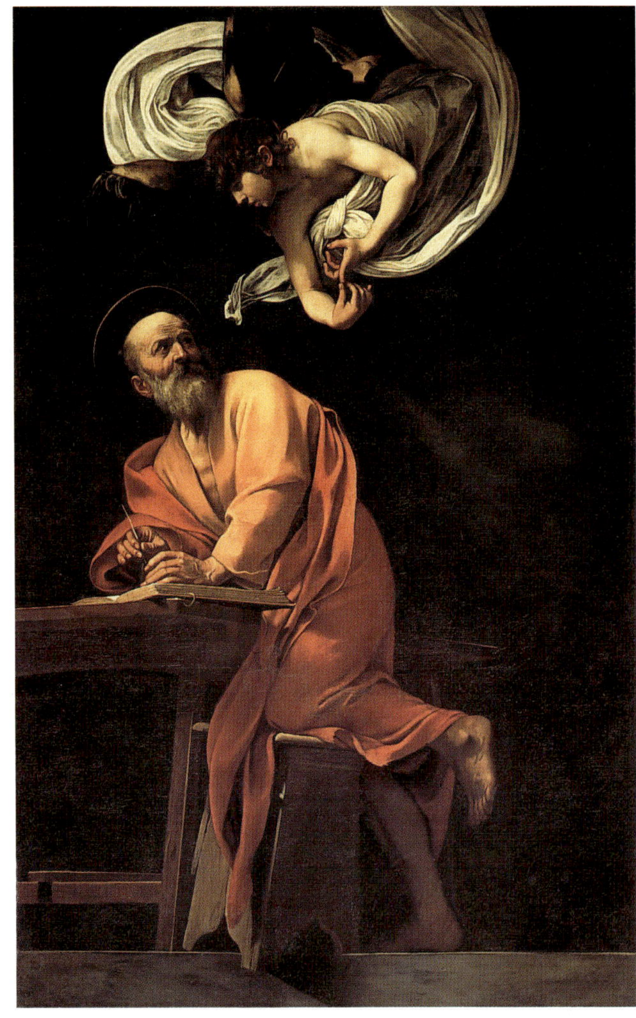

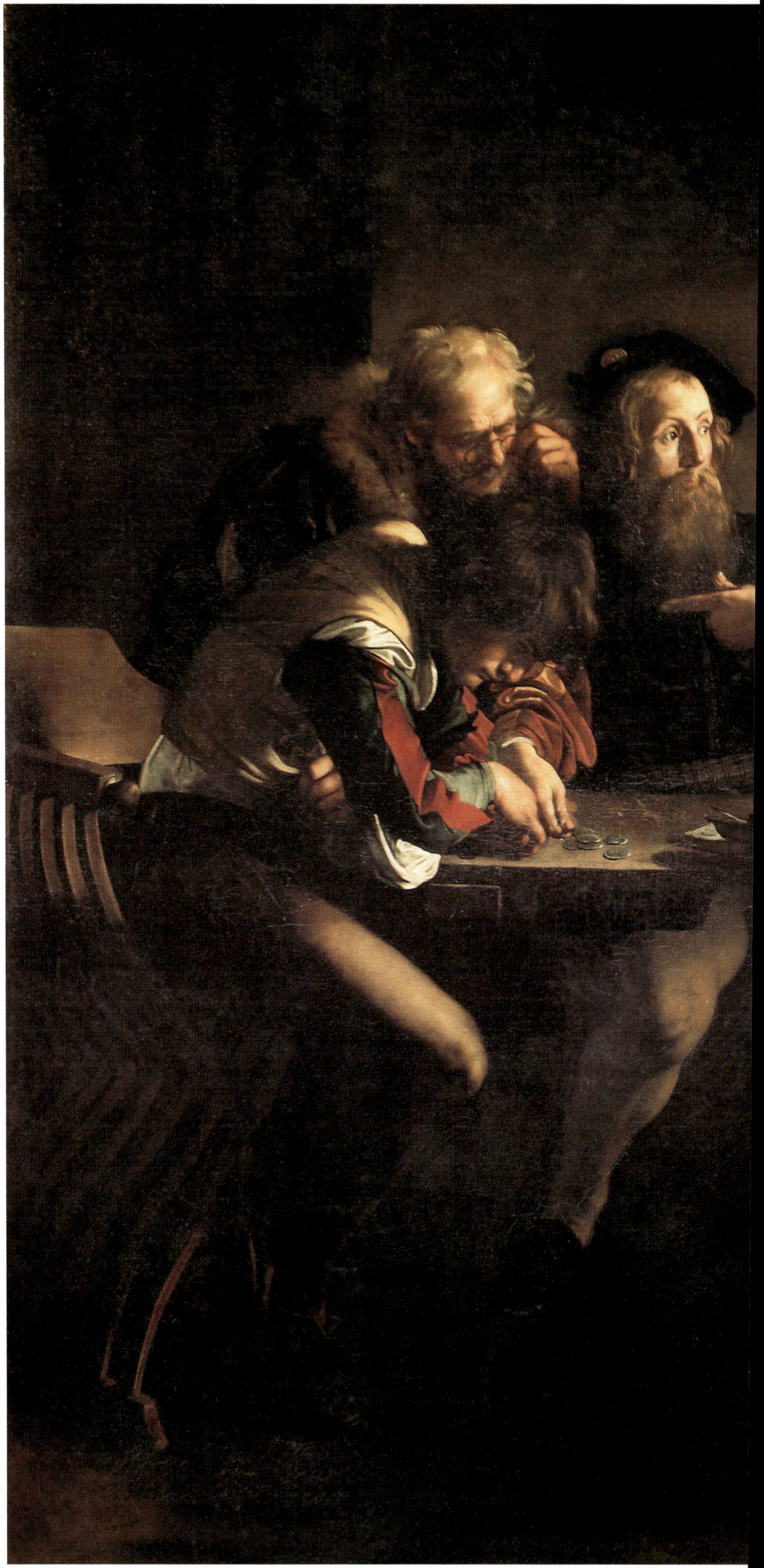

On the threshold of the baroque, all roads lead to Rome

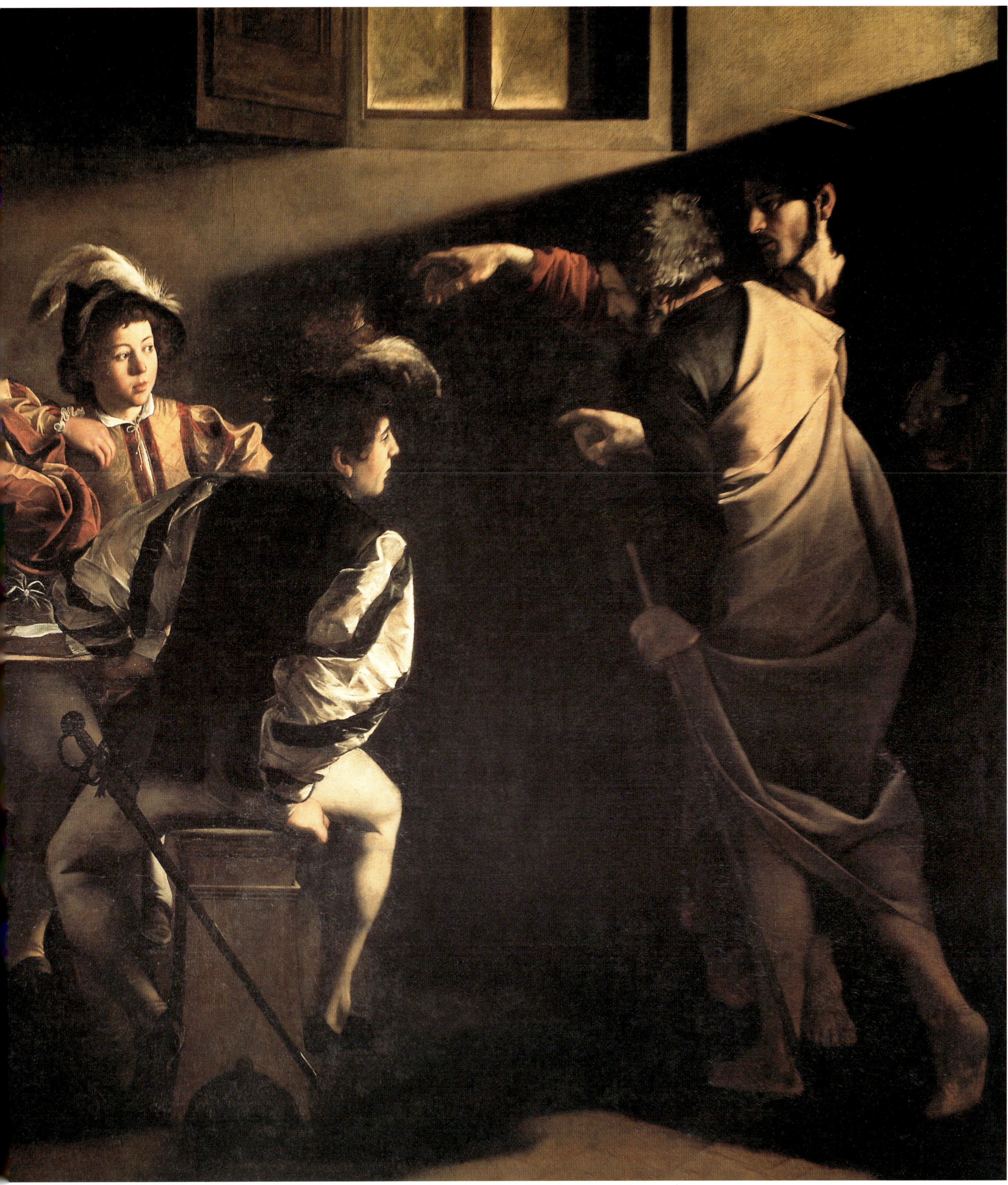

■ CARAVAGGIO
**The Calling of
St. Matthew**
1599–1600,
oil on canvas,
322 x 340 cm
Contarelli Chapel, San
Luigi dei Francesi,
Rome

The *Calling of St.
Matthew* illustrates the
moment in which the
tax collector, seated
with companions at a
table in the simple
guardroom, is surprised
by Christ's invitation to
follow his calling. The
carefully constructed
luminist layout, ori-
ented with great pre-
cision, indicates the
key to the reading the
work: a beam of light
comes from the right
and is projected onto
the chipped wall and
the dusty window, indi-
cating the direction
that the eyes of the
spectator should
follow, moving from
Christ's eloquent
gesture of invitation
to the questioning,
amazed gesture of
Matthew, who responds
to the call. In this
sense the light also
assumes a symbolic
value, an allusion to
the divine grace that
moves naturally into
the sphere of daily life,
bringing salvation.

During the second half
of the sixteenth cen-
tury, literature and art
faced the great ques-
tion of the relationship
between human beings
and nature. On the
threshold of the seven-
teenth century, the
culture of Europe
sensed the obvious
need to use new means
to confront the great,
eternal questions: is it
permissible (and in
what way) to explore
the mysteries of life,
of the cosmos, of the
"functioning" of the
universe and the posi-
tion of humanity within
it? Protected by Grand
Duke Cosimo II with the
title "court philoso-
pher," Galileo published
his *Sidereus Nuncius*
("The Starry Messenger")
in 1610, the first essay
of great scientific
importance by the
famous scholar, who
in that same period
was perfecting
the telescope.

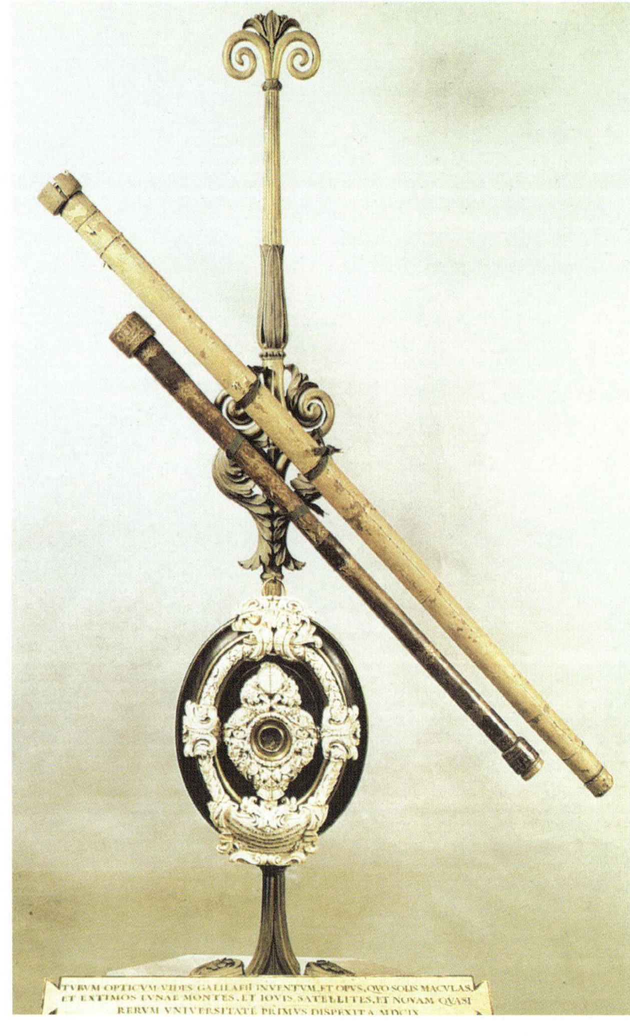

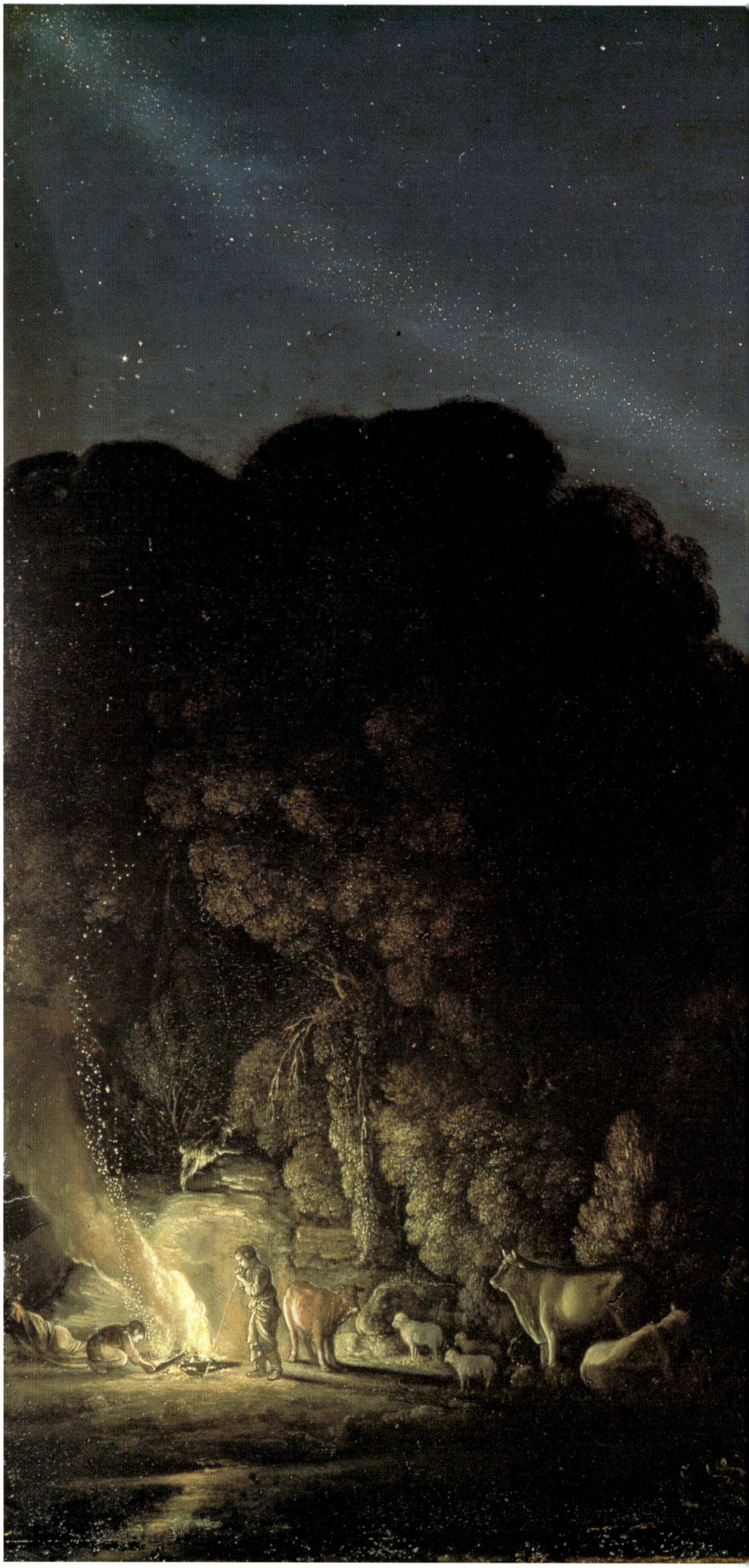

On the threshold of the baroque, all roads lead to Rome

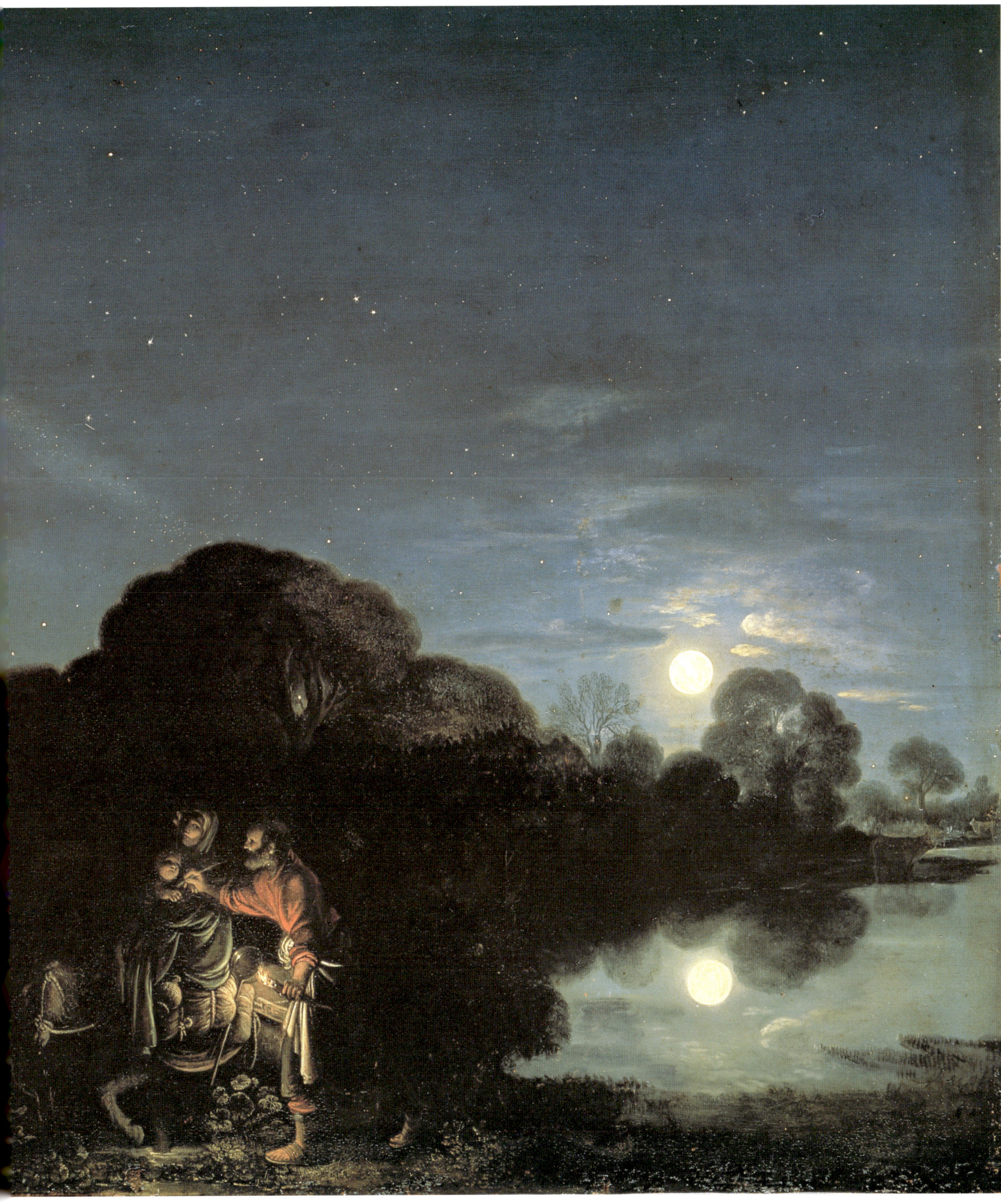

■ ADAM ELSHEIMER
Flight into Egypt
1609, oil on copper,
31 x 41 cm
Alte Pinakothek,
Munich

This enchanting nocturnal elegy is without doubt the best known work from the short life of Elsheimer. Despite its small size, it is often considered one of the most fascinating paintings of the early seventeenth century, and also a true milestone in the history of landscape painting. Painted a year before Galileo published his observations, this is the earliest known landscape painting to include the Milky Way. The perfect presentation of the celestial vault, with the Milky Way and the constellations shining from a sky illuminated by a full moon, indicates Elsheimer's powers of observation and his attention to the scientific world.

1400–99: Events,

1400

1400. An anonymous Parisian miniaturist begins the *Boucicaut Hours*

1401. Competition in Florence for the execution of the second door of the Baptistery: the winner is Lorenzo Ghiberti

1402. Brunelleschi and Donatello go to Rome to study classical antiquity, a trip that will prove decisive to the beginning of humanism

1404. Death of Philip the Bold, activist ruler of the duchy of Burgundy

1410

1410. The Limbourg brothers begin the miniatures for the *Très Riches Heures* of the Duke of Berry

1414/17. Council of Constance The schism in the Church, with the popes in Avignon, ends

1420

1423. Gentile da Fabriano paints the *Adoration of the Magi* in Florence

1424. Masolino and Masaccio begin the frescoes in the Brancacci Chapel in Florence

1430

1430. Fra Angelico paints the *Annunciation* in Cortona

1431. The Council of Basel begins discussion of the role of the pope and the question of the schism. Joan of Arc, heroine of the Hundred Years' War is executed in Rouen

1432. Pisanello makes the fresco of *St. George and the Princess of Trebizond* in Verona

1434. In Florence the rule of the Medici is affirmed; the dome of the Duomo, a work by Brunelleschi, is completed
Jan Van Eyck makes the portraits of the *Arnolfini Couple*, today in London

1440

1442. Alfonso V of Aragon conquers Naples

1443. Barthélemy d'Eyck paints the *Annunciation* in Aix-en-Provence

1444. Rogier van der Weyden paints the polyptych of the *Last Judgment* in Beaune
Konrad Witz paints the Geneva Altarpiece

1450

1450. Artists of many nations converge on Rome for the Jubilee
Jean Fouquet paints the Mélun Diptych
Francesco Sforza conquers the duchy of Milan

1451. Stephan Lochner, leading exponent of the Rhine painting school, dies

1452. Piero della Francesca begins the *Legend of the True Cross* in Arezzo Birth of Leonardo da Vinci

1453. Constantinople falls to the Ottoman Turks, ending the Eastern Roman Empire
Enguerrand Quarton paints the *Coronation of the Virgin* for the charterhouse of Villeneuve-lès-Avignon

1460

1460. Nuño Gonçalves paints the polyptych of Lisbon, masterpiece of Portuguese painting

1470

1470. Building of the Ducal Palace in Urbino

1471. Michael Pacher sculpts and paints the altar of St. Wolfgang Albrecht Dürer is born in Nuremberg

1472. Piero della Francesca paints the Montefeltro Altarpiece, today in Milan

1473. Martin Schongauer paints the *Virgin of the Rose Bower*, in Colmar

1474. Bartolomé Bermejo paints the altarpiece of San Domenico di Silos, today in Madrid
Leonardo paints his first personal work, the *Annunciation* in Florence

1480

1480. Pope Sixtus IV summons the best painters of central Italy to Rome to fresco the walls of the Sistine Chapel

1481. In Florence Leonardo paints the unfinished altarpiece of the *Adoration of the Magi*

1482. Leonardo da Vinci moves to Milan and the court of Duke Ludovico il Moro

1483. Raphael Sanzio is born in Urbino

1490

1492. Christopher Columbus discovers America
Lorenzo the Magnificent dies; Florence becomes a republic
Battle of Granada ends the Spanish war against the Moors

1494/99. The states of Naples and Milan are conquered by foreign armies, France and Spain begin wars for control of Italy

1400–99: Events, artists, works

1400

1405. Claus Sluter dies in Dijon, leaving the tomb of Philip the Bold unfinished

1406. In Lucca, Jacopo della Quercia carves the tomb of Ilaria del Carretto, prototype of fifteenth-century funerary sculpture

1408. Nanni di Bando and Donatello sculpt statues of the *Evangelists* for the Duomo of Florence

1410

1417. Donatello carves the *St. George* for the church of Orsanmichele in Florence

1418. Brunelleschi's design for the dome of the Duomo of Florence is approved

1420

1426. Hubert and Jan van Eyck begin work on the Ghent Altarpiece

1427. Robert Campin (known as the Flémalle Master) paints the Mérode Triptych, today in New York
Hans Multscher carves the *Man of Sorrows* for the cathedral of Ulm

1429. Around this year Paolo Uccello begins work on the frescoes in the Chiostro Verde of Santa Maria Novella, Florence, making clear his use of perspective

1430

1435. Rogier van der Weyden paints the *Deposition from the Cross*, today in Madrid

1436. Leon Battista Alberti writes his treatise *On Painting* in which he presents the scientific theory of perspective representation

1440

1446. Death of Filippo Brunelleschi

1447. Johann Gutenberg invents printing with movable type in Mainz

1448. Stained glass of the *Annunciation* in the cathedral of Bourges, probably a work by Jacob de Littemont

artists, works

1450

1454. Peace of Lodi and state of balance among the Italian states

1458. Mantegna paints the triptych in the basilica of San Zeno, Verona

1459. Benozzo Gozzoli frescoes the *Procession of the Magi* in the Medici Chapel in Palazzo Medici, Florence

1460

1465. Mantegna begins the decoration of the Camera degli Sposi in Mantua

1466. Death of Donatello
Memling begins the triptych with the *Last Judgment*, today in Gdansk

1469. Wedding of Ferdinand of Aragon and Isabella of Castile, the "Catholic kings"

1470

1475. In Venice, Antonello da Messina paints *St. Jerome in His Study*, today in London
Michelangelo Buonarroti is born

1476. Nicolas Froment paints the triptych with the *Burning Bush* in Aix-en-Provence
Pedro Berruguete paints the portrait of *Federico da Montefeltro with His Son Guidobaldo*

1477. Marriage of Maximilian I and Mary of Burgundy
Botticelli begins painting secular allegories
Veit Stoss begins the St. Mary Altarpiece in Cracow

1478. Hugo van der Goes paints the Portinari Triptych, today in Florence

1480

1485. Beginning of the Tudor dynasty in England

1488. In Venice Giovanni Bellini paints the Frari Triptych

1490

1495. With the acquisition of Cyprus, Venice reaches the height of its territorial expansion

1497. Leonardo completes the *Last Supper*

1498. Girolamo Savonarola is executed and burned in Florence
The Portuguese navigator Vasco da Gama rounds the Cape of Good Hope

1499. Luca Signorelli begins frescoes with scenes of the end of the world in the cathedral of Orvieto
Tilman Riemenschneider begins the *Holy Blood* altarpiece in Rothenburg-ob-der-Tauber

1400–99: Events, artists, works

1500. In Rome Michelangelo finishes the *Pietà* in St. Peter's; the next year, in Florence, he begins the *David*
Dürer celebrates his social success with the *Self-Portrait,* today in Munich

1502. In Florence, Leonardo and Michelangelo will decorate the Salone dei Cinquecento with two battles; Leonardo begins the *Mona Lisa*
In Venice, Carpaccio begins the paintings for San Giorgio degli Schiavoni

1503. Alexander VI dies and Julius II is elected pope
Around this date Bosch paints the *Garden of Earthly Delights*

1504. In Rome Bramante begins construction of the Cortile del Belvedere in the Vatican

1510. Deaths of Giorgione in Venice and Sandro Botticelli in Florence

1511. In Rome, having completed the Stanza della Segnatura, Raphael begins the Stanza di Eliodoro

1512. In Rome Michelangelo finishes the vault of the Sistine and works on the tomb of Julius II
With help from the French king Louis XII, the Medici return to power in Florence

1513. Julius II dies and the son of Lorenzo the Magnificent is elected pope as Leo X

1514. Giovanni Bellini: *The Feast of the Gods* for Alfonso d'Este, duke of Ferrara
Bramante dies in Rome
Quenten Metsys, of the Antwerp school, paints the *Moneychanger and His Wife*, today in Paris

1520. In Rome Raphael dies, leaving his *Transfiguration* unfinished
Pope Leo X excommunicates Luther

1521. Rosso Fiorentino paints the *Deposition* in Volterra
The Spaniard Hernán Cortez conquers the Aztec empire

1522. François Rabelais publishes *Gargantua et Pantagruel*

1523. Hans Holbein the Younger paints the portrait of *Erasmus*, today in Paris

1530. Coronation of Charles V in Bologna
Siege and capitulation of Florence

1531. Formation of the Schmalkaldic League of German princes supporting the Reformation

1532. Beginning of the Gallery of Francis I at Fontainebleau
Giulio Romano builds and decorates the Palazzo Te in Mantua

1533. Francisco Pizarro conquers the Inca empire in Peru

1534. Henry VIII proclaims himself head of the Church of England, beginning the Anglican schism
Ignatius of Loyola founds the Jesuit order

1540/43. Benvenuto Cellini makes the *Salt Cellar* for Francis I of France, today in Vienna

1541. Michelangelo completes the *Last Judgment* in the Sistine Chapel

1500–99: Events,

1550. In Constantinople the architect Sinan builds the mosque of Suleiman I, a refined evolution of Moslem architecture

1551. Peace of Augsburg between Charles V and the German Protestant princes
The most dramatic period of the religious wars in Europe ends

1553. Paolo Veronese moves to Venice and begins work on the Ducal Palace

1554. The Bolognese Ulisse Aldrovandi begins collecting objects and natural curiosities, forming the prototype of the *Wunderkammer*, the eclectic collection of the late Renaissance

1560–63. Paolo Veronese paints the *Marriage of Cana,* today in Paris

1563. Conclusion of the Council of Trent
Construction of the Escorial begins

1564. Death of Michelangelo
In Venice Tintoretto begins the decoration of the Scuola di San Rocco

1571. Battle of Lepanto: the Holy League (Spain, Venice, and the Papacy) defeats the Turks; Antoine Caron paints *Augustus and the Sibyl of Tivoli*, one of the most important works of French mannerism, today in Paris

1572. St. Bartholomew's Day Massacre of French Huguenots

1573. Bernardo Buontalenti creates the grotto in the Boboli Gardens of Florence

1580. Death of Andrea Palladio

1583. Emperor Rudolf II moves the imperial court from Vienna to Prague

1584. Reunification of the kingdoms of Spain and Portugal
Assassination of William of Orange, hero of Dutch independence
Sir Walter Raleigh founds the first English colony in America at Roanoke

1592. The young Caravaggio moves from Milan to Rome

1594. Death of Jacopo Tintoretto

artists, works

1505. Giorgione paints the Castelfranco Altarpiece

1506. During his second trip to Italy Dürer paints the *Feast of the Rose Garlands*
    Andrea Mantegna dies in Mantua
    The marble group of the *Laocoön* is found in Rome

1508. The Holy League successfully attacks Venetian lands
    In Rome Michelangelo is commissioned to fresco the vault of the Sistine Chapel; Raphael begins frescoes in the Stanza della Segnatura

1509. Erasmus publishes the *Elogium insaniae* ("The Praise of Folly")

1515. The sculptor Anton Pilgram make the pulpit for the cathedral of St. Stephen in Vienna

1516. Matthis Grünewald paints the Isenheim Altarpiece
    Treaty of Noyon between Maximilian and the Venetian Republic
    Death of Giovanni Bellini; Titian is made official painter of Venice

1517. Martin Luther nails up his 95 Theses in Wittenberg
    The Protestant Schism begins
    In Florence Andrea del Sarto paints the *Madonna of the Harpies*

1518. In Venice presentation of the *Assumption* by Titian
1518–19. In Parma Correggio frescoes the Camera di San Paolo

1519. Charles I of Spain is elected Emperor Charles V of the Holy Roman Empire
    In Cloux, near Amboise, Leonardo da Vinci dies

1525. Peasants' War begins in Germany
    Battle of Pavia: the Spanish defeat the French in their struggle for Italy

1526. Lucas von Leyden paints the triptych with the *Last Judgment*

1527. Sack of Rome, international diaspora of artists, leading to development of the worksite of the royal château of Fontainebleau

1528. Death of Albrecht Dürer

1529. Albrecht Altdorfer paints the *Battle of Issus*, today in Munich

1535. Dutch painter Maarten van Heemskerck travels to Rome; the Italian style is embraced in Antwerp

1536. Michelangelo begins the *Last Judgment* in the Sistine Chapel

1537. Cosimo I de' Medici takes power; period of the grand dukes begins in Florence

1538. Titian paints the *Venus of Urbino*, today in Florence

1539. Hans Holbein paints the *Portrait of Henry VIII*, today in Rome

1545. Beginning of the Council of Trent, fundamental debate within the Catholic Church

1547. In Paris Jean Goujon carves the Fountain of the Innocents

1548. Charles V defeats the Protestant prices at Mühlberg: the victory is celebrated by an equestrian portrait by Titian, today in Madrid
    In Venice Tintoretto makes his name with the *St. Mark Rescuing the Slave*

1549. The architect and sculptor Philibert de l'Orme builds the château of Anet for Diane de Poitiers

1500 · 1510 · 1520 · 1530 · 1540

1555. In Moscow construction of the cathedral of St. Basil begins

1556. Charles V abdicates and divides the empire of the Hapsburgs between his son Philip II (Spain and the overseas territories) and his brother Ferdinand I (the "Austrian" part)

1557. In Rome construction begins on the Gesù, mother church of the Jesuits

1558. Elizabeth I, daughter of Henry VIII and Anne Boleyn, takes the throne of England

1559. France, Spain, and England sign the Treaty of Cateau-Cambrésis, ending the wars in Italy

1565. Pieter Bruegel paints the cycle of the *Seasons*

1566. Revolt against Spanish domination begins in the Low Countries, eventually leading to independence of the United Provinces (Holland)

1568. Giorgio Vasari publishes the second edition of his *Lives*, an important source of information on the artists from the fourteenth to the sixteenth centuries

1575. Torquato Tasso completes *Jerusalem Delivered*

1576. In Venice Titian dies of plague, leaving his *Pietà* unfinished

1577. In Venice a fire destroys the Doge's Palace; the redecoration of the rooms is entrusted to Tintoretto and Veronese
    In Toledo El Greco paints the *Christ Disrobed*

1578. Acting as governor of the Netherlands, Alessandro Farnese defeats rebels against Spanish rule

1585. Sixtus V is elected pope and promotes important urban works in Rome

1586. In Toledo El Greco paints the *Burial of Count of Orgaz*

1588. Defeat of the Spanish Armada marks the waning of Spanish power and the rise of England

1595. First complete edition of Montaigne's *Essays*

1596. Caravaggio paints the *Basket of Fruit*, today in Milan, reference point in the birth of the still life

1597. In Rome Annibale Carracci frescoes the gallery of Palazzo Farnese

1598. Edict of Nantes: the king of France Henry IV grants freedom of worship to Protestants

1599. In Rome Caravaggio begins painting the canvases in San Luigi dei Francesi

1550 · 1560 · 1570 · 1580 · 1590

References

Biographies

•

Bibliography

•

Index of names and places

•

Photographic references

Biographies

HANS VON AACHEN
(Cologne 1552–Prague 1615)

Exponent of the Prague mannerist school, this German painter's training included a long period spent in Italy, between Venice, Rome, and in particular Florence. The result was a refined, elaborate style, perfectly up to date on the most sophisticated developments of the mannerism, which he applied primarily to mythological subjects. Hans von Aachen moved to the Prague court of Rudolf II, where he became a member of Bartholomäus Spranger's entourage and was active as a portraitist.

PIETER AERTSEN
(Amsterdam, ca. 1508–1575)

Although he was born and died in Amsterdam, Aertsen spent much of his career in Antwerp, where he is recorded from 1535 to 1560 and where he formed an interesting school in which his nephew and continuator, Joachim Beuckelaer, trained. Aertsen did not join in the widespread taste of the Antwerp "Romanists" and instead introduced popular themes and a physical, solid realism to his works, such that he can be considered a precursor of Pieter Bruegel as well as a pioneer of the still life. When Aertsen presents traditional subjects or episodes from the Bible, such as the *Ecce Homo*, Jesus's encounter with the adulterous woman, or his visit to the home of Martha and Mary, he pushes the narrative scene to the background and dedicates most of his effort to the creation of food markets or well-stocked kitchens. The references to figures and scenes from the Gospels gradually disappeared as his style progressed, but he simply replaced them with similar narrative pretexts, using scenes from daily life, much like *bodegones* of the young Velázquez or similar scenes from the early works of Vermeer. Around 1560 Aertsen returned to Amsterdam, adding a dose of dense realism to the development of the local school.

JORGE AFONSO
(Lisbon, documented from 1504 to 1540)

An outstanding figure in Portuguese painting at the end of the Manueline age, Afonso was involved in all the major painting undertakings in Portugal at the beginning of the sixteenth century. His style was still related to the late fifteenth-century Flemish tradition in its precise description of details and adherence to realism, which is evident most of all in the landscape backgrounds and the accurate description of buildings. Thanks to the assistance of a large workshop, Afonso was able to make vast pictorial works, such as the panels of the *Passion of Christ* for the convent of Tomar and the enormous retable for the Church of Gesù in Setúbal.

AGOSTINO DI DUCCIO
(Florence 1418–Perugia ca. 1481)

Extremely refined sculptor of the mid-fifteenth century, Agostino had a somewhat unusual career, marked in 1441 by his expulsion from Florence (where he had begun to sketch a giant statue for the cathedral; Michelangelo later used the marble for his *David*) following an accusation of theft. For this reason, Agostino found himself forced to seek professional opportunities elsewhere, accepting works in which he achieved elegant compromises between his humanistic-perspective training and late Gothic elegance. After periods in Modena and Venice (1446), he spent the main years of his activity in Rimini, where he made the exceptional decoration of the Tempio Malatestiano (1449–55). His style was unmistakable, based on barely indicated reliefs and characterized by the supple waves of his line. A fine example is the façade of the oratory of San Bernardino in Perugia, completed in 1461.

MASTER OF THE AIX ANNUNCIATION (Barthélemy d'Eyck)
(active in France from 1447 to 1470)

Active in the court of René of Anjou in Angers, in Naples, and then for a long time in Provence, as indicated from documents relating to the years between 1447 and 1470, this artist is referred to by contemporary biographers as one of the greatest artists of his time. Although there is no mention of any of his works, critics tend to identify Barthélemy d'Eyck with the Master of the Aix Annunciation and also with the Master of the Coeur, author of the *Livre du Coeur d'Amour Epris*, among the marvels of European miniatures of the fifteenth century. Perhaps the brother of Han and Hubert van Eyck, this artist was distinguished by the plastic vigor of his modeling, which reveals the influence of the sculptural works of Claus Sluter, and also by the function given light, used to unify space and join figures, following modalities that would become common to the Avignon school.

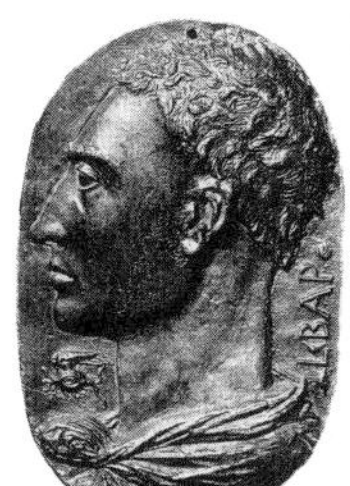

LEON BATTISTA ALBERTI
(Genoa 1404– Rome 1472)

Eclectic and rich personality, a writer and architect, Alberti is emblematic of the artist-intellectual of fifteenth-century humanism. After early studies at the universities of Padua and Bologna, he moved to Rome in 1432. Passionate scholar of antiquity, he studied the architectonic typologies of the classical world and undertook their "updating" to a modern level. He did this through the treatises he wrote, the buildings he designed and built, and the monuments he restored and integrated. In Florence he designed Palazzo Rucellai, a historical prototype of the noble residence of the Renaissance period; in the Tempietto of Santo Sepolcro annexed to the palace he presented a jewel of measurement and decoration. Even more complex is his design (left partially unfinished) for the Tempio Malatestiano in Rimini (1450), a combination of classical architectonic motifs applied freely to a sacred structure. In 1459 he moved to the Gonzaga court in Mantua, where he built the church of San Sebastiano.

ALBRECHT ALTDORFER
(Regensburg or Altdorf ca. 1480–Regensburg 1538)

Son of the painter Ulrich, Altdorfer trained with his father and acquired an almost miniaturistic taste for detail. It is possible that while young he made a trip to northern Italy; he may also have come in contact with Michael Pacher. He moved to Regensburg in 1505, becoming a public figure, highly active in the city administration. In 1509 he began the execution of his most complex work, the altar for the Austrian abbey of St. Florian, completed in 1516 and unfortunately dismembered. Altdorfer became an important painter in the "Danubian school," the pictorial current in southern Germany distinguished by its passionate rendering of nature. In 1513 he was called by Emperor Maximilian to Innsbruck to execute various court commissions. He was later further involved in public life, first becoming a city councilor and then serving as city architect for Regensburg. In 1528 he was offered the post of burgomaster. In the course of the 1520s, he was primarily involved in public buildings, and his painting activity slowed. In 1528 he made the celebrated *Battle of Issus* for Duke William IV of Bavaria. The works of his later years reveal his inner turmoil, most of all the terrible division between Catholic tradition and the Lutheran Reformation.

BARTOLOMEO AMMANATI
(Settignano, Florence, 1511– Florence 1592)

A leading architect and sculptor of Florentine mannerism, Ammanati worked in and further developed the stylistic themes of the late Renaissance and then, having grown particularly pious in his later life, in part as a result of contact with the Jesuits, he ended his career with a "recantation" of the most declaredly secular and intellectual of his works. He got his training around 1540 as a collaborator of Jacopo Sansovino in Venice, had an important stay in Rome (1550–55), during which he worked on marble monuments and the arrangement of the grotto of Villa Giulia, a prototype of the mannerist garden. He returned to Florence and worked on the completion of various important Renaissance buildings, such as the Laurentian Library, the Salone dei Cinquecento in Palazzo Vecchio, and, most of all, Palazzo Pitti, for which he designed the majestic courtyard facing the Boboli Gardens. A symbol of his art is in Piazza della Signoria with the enormous and complex Fountain of Neptune (1563–77), in which elegant parts, agile and leaping, alternate with areas that are serious and rhetorical.

FRA ANGELICO (Beato Angelico; Fra Giovanni da Fiesole; Guido di Pietro)
(Vicchio di Mugello ca. 1395– Rome 1455)

After training as a painter and miniaturist in Florence during the 1520s, he was soon collaborating with the most advanced artists of the period, as with Lorenzo Ghiberti, for example, on the Linaiuoli Triptych (1433; Museo di San Marco, Florence). He became a Dominican friar and was very active in that order's monasteries. He concentrated on such subjects as the *Madonna Enthroned* and the *Annunciation*, elaborating on his own a series of "variations" of each theme. The vast series of frescoes in the convent of San Marco in Florence dates to between 1439 and 1442 and was made with the assistance of a school that brought to light Benozzo Gozzoli. In 1446 he was called to Rome by Pope Nicholas V to fresco the chapel dedicated to Saints Stephen and Lawrence. The next year he was in Orvieto, where he began work on the decoration of the chapel of San Brizio in the cathedral; he worked on only one part of the vault, leaving the frescoes unfinished (they were completed fifty years later by Luca Signorelli). Around 1450 he was back in Florence, busy on various works for the convent of San Marco. In 1453 he was summoned back to Rome, and he died there in 1455 and was buried in the church of Santa Maria sopra Minerva.

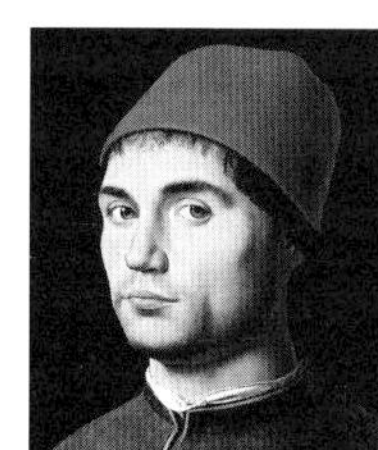

ANTONELLO DA MESSINA
(Messina ca. 1435–1479)

Antonello moved from Sicily to Naples around 1450 and studied Flemish and Provençal painting in the important collections of the Neapolitan Angevin kings, concentrating most of all on two themes that he repeatedly returned to in later years, the *Crucifixion* and half-bust male portraits on dark backgrounds. The dialogue between Antonello and northern European painting, in particular Petrus Christus and Hans Memling, took place in installments based on the Antonello's geographical itinerary. In fact, he divided his time between stays in Sicily and a progressive advance up the Italian peninsula. He visited

Rome and studied the works of Piero della Francesca between Tuscany and the Marches, in that way coming to apply solid monumentality in his groups of figures and learning to organize his images on the basis of the rules of linear perspective. Even more important, however, was his stay in Venice (1475–76), where he painted his main works, such as the San Cassiano Altarpiece, the surviving parts of which are in Vienna, and the *St. Sebastian*, today in Dresden, and where he increased his taste for color and light, opening the way for the tonalism of Giovanni Bellini. In the last years of life Antonello returned to Sicily.

GIUSEPPE ARCIMBOLDO
(Milan 1527–1593)

The youthful production of cartoons for the stained-glass windows of Milan's cathedral, of tapestries for the cathedral of Como, and of frescoes for that of Monza gave no hint of this artist's highly original evolution. Called in 1562 to the Hapsburg court in Prague, Arcimboldo unleashed a completely new and paradoxical fantasy, making paintings that assemble objects—most often vegetables and flowers and domestic items—to form portraits and allegories. Arcimboldo's style, sometimes interpreted as an progenitor of modern surrealism, is best seen as an aspect of the final phase of the Renaissance, when a new attention was directed on the natural world (visible in that period's passions for collecting and for scientific studies). The Milanese painter designed costumes, theatrical staging, and decorations for the Prague court; aside from commissioning many paintings from him, Emperor Rudolf II used him as his agent in acquiring works of art and naturalistic curiosities. In 1587 Arcimboldo returned to Milan, although he did not lose contact with the emperor.

HANS BALDUNG
(Schwäbisch Gmünd 1484/85–Strasbourg 1545)

Baldung arrived in Strasbourg as a child and got his training in that city, which remained his preferred residence. In 1503 he went to Nuremberg and the workshop of Albrecht Dürer, where he came in contact with the avant-garde of the international Renaissance. On his return to Strasbourg he demonstrated surprising versatility, making devotional illustrations for treatises on the Madonna and painting nude women being seduced by Death (as in *Death and the Maiden*); he presented fabled knights galloping through woods and images of Christ on his tomb. In 1510 he began to dedicate himself to themes related to the image of the female body, from the monstrous and seductive figures of witches to allegorical figures. In 1512, while Grünewald was working in nearby Isenheim, he started the execution of the polyptych for the high altar of the cathedral of Freiburg, one of the most important works of the German Renaissance. The year after finishing work on that polyptych (1516) he returned to Strasbourg, and a little later he was among the first artists to respond to the words of Martin Luther. From then on, his works with religious subjects were few and smaller; in their place he made allegories, moral subjects, book illustrations, and further excursions into his favored theme of witches.

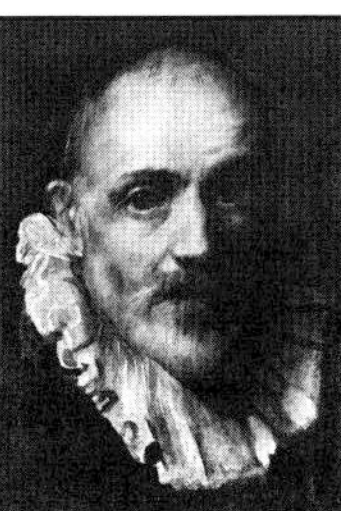

FEDERICO BAROCCI
(Urbino 1535–1612)

This painter from the Marches served as a connection between the great sixteenth-century masters and the new artists of the nascent seventeenth century, from the Carracci to Rubens. Trained in the extraordinary artistic legacy of Urbino, and most of all Raphael, Barocci showed even in his earliest works the gentle grace of Correggio, enriched with the warm taste of Veneto colors. An unhappy stay in Rome ended with his permanent return to Urbino (1565). This marginal location did not prevent him from exercising a decisive influence on the world of art, thanks also to his perfect adhesion to the guidelines on sacred art produced by the Council of Trent. His compositions are simple and direct, with touching details drawn from the realities of ordinary life. In his most ambitious works (the *Deposition* in the cathedral of Perugia, 1569; the *Madonna del Popolo*, Uffizi, Florence, 1576–79; *Martyrdom of St. Vitale*, Brera, Milan, 1583) one notes the increasing suggestion of space, while in his later maturity the spiritual aspects of contemplation are emphasized, anticipating baroque art.

FRA BARTOLOMMEO
(Bartolomeo di Paolo del Fattorino)
(Savignano, Prato, 1472–Florence 1517)

A student together with Piero di Cosimo under Cosimo Rosselli, Fra Bartolommeo began his career working with Mariotto Albertinelli, but following the preaching of Savonarola he experienced a profound mystical crisis, and in 1500 he abandoned painting to take Dominican vows. He returned to art in 1504, opening a workshop inside the convent of San Marco. Beginning with his *Vision of St. Bernard* (Uffizi, Florence) he demonstrated a perfectly up-to-date artistic awareness, making use of the delicate atmospheric rendering of Leonardo. He went to Venice in 1508, and following that trip his colors assumed warmer, more physical tones, as indicated in the two altarpieces he made in Lucca. In his later works, the mystical monumentality of the divine figures increased within a more sensitive rendering of nature and landscapes.

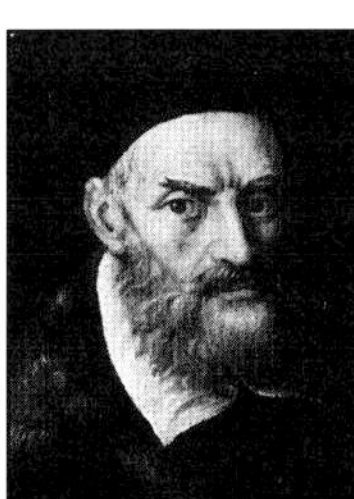

JACOPO BASSANO
(Da Ponte)
(Bassano del Grappa ca. 1510–1592)

Central figure of a thriving family of artists, Jacopo did his apprenticeship in Bassano del Grappa with his father, Francesco da Ponte. Around 1535, after a stay in Venice, his style revealed contact with Bonifacio de' Pitati and Titian. Without ever abandoning a provincial-type solid narrative sense, he absorbed a vast quantity of cultural references, such that in his works notions from prints and drawings by northern artists and artists of the Roman Renaissance overlap with those from Parmigianino, Salviati, and mannerism in general. Although he did all his work in the provinces, he possessed a figurative culture comparable to that of Veronese and Tintoretto. His rustic scenes and figures alternate with studies on color and light, illuminated by an electric brilliance. By the 1570s he seems to have concluded his mannerist style and returned to Titian, showing a preference for "genre" paintings, in which he was often assisted by his sons.

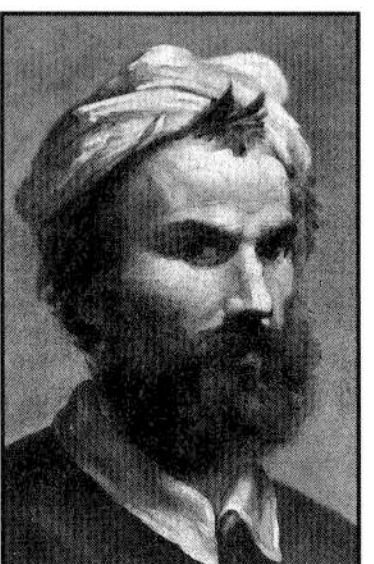

DOMENICO BECCAFUMI
(Domenico di Giacomo di Pace)
(Montaperti, Siena, ca. 1486– Siena 1551)

Principal figure of Sienese art of the first half of the sixteenth century, Beccafumi worked in his city for forty years, changing a sleepy antique capital into an experimental laboratory of effects of light, color, and expression. Well up to date on the works of Leonardo and the frescoes by Raphael and Michelangelo in the Vatican, Beccafumi began his career with the Triptych of the Trinity (1513; Pinacoteca Nazionale, Siena), followed, also in Siena, by the robust *St. Paul* in the Museo dell'Opera and the frescoes in the oratory of San Bernardino (1518). In 1519 he began furnishing cartoons of scenes from the Old Testament for the pavement decorations in the cathedral of

Siena, an activity that went on for roughly thirty years. A variety of influences can be recognized over the course of his artistic career, but his works were always based on a search for magical, visionary effects, with flat light and mutable colors on spectacular compositions. The panels in the cathedral of Pisa date to 1536, and they were followed by the frescoes in the choir of the cathedral of Siena, for which Beccafumi also made eight bronze angels.

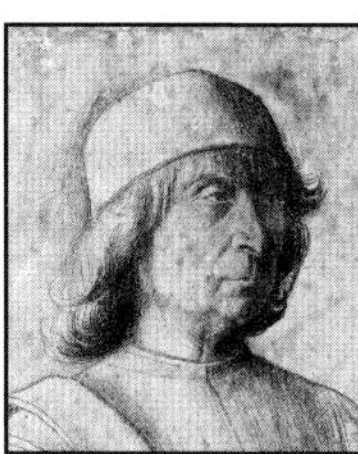

GENTILE BELLINI
(Venice ca. 1429–1507)

Typical example of a specialized painter, Gentile Bellini was a "portraitist" of people and cities, creating what are perhaps the first true views of Venice, and at the moment of its greatest splendor. For a long time he studied and collaborated with his father, Jacopo (along with his brother Giovanni); he started his independent career in the course of the 1460s, obtaining official commissions from the Republic of Venice as early as 1466. In 1479 he was sent to Constantinople on an artistic and diplomatic mission (*Portrait of the Sultan Mehmed II*, National Gallery, London). In 1496 he began the execution of the cycle of canvases with narrative scenes for the Scuola di San Giovanni Evangelista, today in the Gallerie dell'Accademia, with accurate and lively scenes of the city. For the Scuola di San Marco he began work on the vast *St. Mark's Sermon in Alexandria* (Pinacoteca di Brera, Milan), left unfinished at his death and completed by his brother Giovanni.

GIOVANNI BELLINI
(Venice ca. 1430–1516)

Member of an illustrious family of painters, Giovanni trained in the workshop of his father, Jacopo, alongside his brother Gentile; he must have received a touch of humanistic thinking from the marriage of his sister Nicolosia to Andrea Mantegna (1451), but unlike his brother-in-law, Giovanni showed a greater attention to color than to graphics. From his first independent works, in the 1460s, Giovanni sought to render natural atmospheres, an aspect of his work that would become a characteristic trait. The monumental *Coronation of the Virgin* in Pesaro (1471–74) indicates the similarity of his style to the works of Piero della Francesca, although he followed it with an independent interpretation of the novelties proposed by Antonello da Messina, who was in Venice in 1475. In 1483 Giovanni was made official painter of Venice, a post he held until his death, 33 years later. Giovanni Bellini led an important workshop in which painters like Lotto, Giorgione, and Titian trained. He continued in his efforts to create atmospheric visions, which he also applied to large-scale altarpieces. The final surprise, a confirmation of his exceptional creative vitality, was the creation of paintings on secular subjects near the end of his life.

AMBROGIO BERGOGNONE
(Ambrogio da Fossano)
(Milan 1453?–1523)

The training of this leader of Lombard painting at the end of

fifteenth century took place through contact with Vincenzo Foppa, to which was added an acute interest in Flemish art, which shows up most of all in the use of light and the highly detailed rendering of descriptive details. The Foppa influence appears dominant until 1488, when Bergognone began to paint altarpieces and frescoes for the charterhouse of Pavia, and activity that kept him busy until 1494. In these years Bergognone reached his full stylistic maturity, acquiring a monumentality and an attention to perspective derived from Bramante. In 1495 he was active in Milan, working on the execution of the frescoes in the church of Santa Maria presso San Satiro (now in the Brera); a few years later he was documented in Lodi, where he made four panels for the main chapel of the church of the Incoronata. In the following years he divided his activity among Milan (numerous works, among them the frescoes of San Simpliciano and Santa Maria della Passione), Bergamo, and, again, the charterhouse of Pavia.

BARTOLOMÉ BERMEJO
(Bartolomé de Cárdenas)
(Cordova ca. 1440–Barcelona ca. 1500)

This talented and restless artist got his training in the Low Countries and lived in Daroca in Aragon between 1474 and 1476, painting the retable of *St. Domingo de Silos* for that saint's church in Daroca, begun in 1474 and completed in 1477 by his follower Martín Bernat, and the retable of Santa Grazia, since dismembered, of which the *Crucifixion* (now in

Biographies

the collegiate church of Daroca) is
one of the outstanding fragments.
He moved to Saragossa, where he
lived from 1477 to 1481, and then
in Valencia, where he lived until
1486. It is also possible that he
visited Italy, which would explain
the presence of one of his works
in the cathedral of Acqui. He then
shows up in Barcelona, which was
probably the end of his incessant
traveling and where he made one
of the most important works of
Spanish painting, the *Pietà*,
commissioned by the canon
Desplá in 1490. Aside from clear
references to Van Eyck, this
paintings shows evidence of
Venetian tonal painting and the
broad style of Lombard painting.
After 1498 there are no further
indications of his activity.

PEDRO BERRUGUETE
(Paredes de Nava, Palencia,
ca. 1450–Ávila ca. 1504)

Despite Berruguete's early training
in the circle of Fernando Gallego,
even his earliest works display
clear Flemish influence, in
particular that of Van Eyck. In
1474 he was in Urbino, where he
collaborated with Justus of Ghent
on the decoration of the palace of
duke Federico da Montefeltro, in
particular the *studiolo* and library.
In the *studiolo*, a gallery of
half-bust portraits of *Famous Men*
from the past and present was to
decorate the upper part, with the
full-figure portrait of the duke,
seated in profile at a reading
stand with his son Guidobaldo,
overlooking the entire group; in
the library, the liberal arts were
presented seated on sumptuous
thrones decorated with precious
stones. On his return to Spain in

1483 he returned to the use of gold
backgrounds and overwrought
decoration, aspects that are
clearly visible in such works
as the retable in the church of
St. Eulalia, made between 1490
and 1500 and dedicated to the life
of the Virgin. His last commission
was for the main retable in the
cathedral of Ávila, a work that was
left unfinished, to be completed by
Juan de Borgoña, and in which
Italian references appear, most of
all in terms of perspective and the
use of light.

MASTER BERTRAM
(Bertram von Minden)
(Minden ca. 1345–Hamburg 1415)

Outstanding figure in the art of the
Hanseatic area during the age of
the International Gothic, Bertram
was one of the most active creators
of large-scale carved and painted
altarpieces characterized by the
dense presence of numerous
narrative panels but also, in his
case, by the sharp characterization
of the figures and the settings.
Much of his life and activity took
place in Hamburg, where his
principal works remain, but his
presence in other cities indicates
a far greater renown. Following
a pilgrimage to Rome in 1390,
Bertram became associated with
the Bohemian court and adopted
various characteristics of the art
of the painters of Prague during
the period of Emperor Wencelas IV.

JOACHIM BEUCKELAER
(Antwerp ca. 1535–1574)

Student of his uncle Pieter Aertsen
and like him he specialized in the
production of spectacular market
and kitchen scenes, a precedent

for the birth of the still life. Even
more than Aertsen, Beuckelaer
reduced the narrative subjects of
his works to a mere pretext,
putting his attention into the
representation of inanimate
objects. Well represented in the
princely collections of the late
Renaissance, Beuckelaer's most
direct followers were artists in
northern Italy.

HIERONYMUS BOSCH
(Jeroen Van Aeken)
(`s-Hertogenbosch ca. 1450–1516)

Bosch lived and worked in the city
of his birth, where he inherited
the activity of his father and
grandfather, both of whom were
painters. His oldest works, satirical
scenes of human foolishness and
vices, date to the 1470s. In 1480, by
which time he was an independent
master, he entered in contact with
the Brotherhood of Our Lady,
annexed to the cathedral of
`s-Hertogenbosch, becoming a
member of the brotherhood in
1486–87. During the last decade
of the fifteenth century he created
the great triptychs of the *Haywain*
and the *Garden of Earthly Delights*.
Between 1500 and 1503 he took a
trip to Venice, where he left
important paintings. Through
contact with Italian painting and
with Dürer his style gained a
deeper awareness of layout, with
vast landscapes, and also came by
new chromatic effects. Proof of
this is the exceptional triptych of
the *Temptation of St. Anthony* in
Lisbon, which was followed, as a
further evolution, by the *Adoration
of the Magi* in the Prado in Madrid.
In 1503–04 he returned to his
birthplace as an artist famed
throughout Europe and alternated

small works for the Brotherhood
of Our Lady with commissions from
foreign collectors. A development
of his late activity are paintings
with half-figure busts.

SANDRO BOTTICELLI
(Alessandro di Mariano Filipepi)
(Florence 1445–1510)

The biographical and stylistic
career of Botticelli began in the
workshop of Filippo Lippi during
the 1460s; when Lippi moved to
Spoleto (1466), Botticelli became a
collaborator of Verrocchio, thus
coming in contact with other
young students, among them
Perugino and Leonardo. In 1472
he enrolled in the confraternity
of Florentine painters, where
Filippino Lippi was already active.
Following a series of portraits of
Medici family members he became
the preferred artist of the ruling
family. The so-called *Spring* was
the first of the cycle of mythological
allegories that he probably made
for a cousin of Lorenzo the
Magnificent. Botticelli was called
to Rome in 1482, becoming the
leader in the collective undertaking
of the wall decoration of the
Sistine Chapel. He returned to
Florence as the preferred painter
of Lorenzo the Magnificent and
made frescoes and altarpieces
along with religious and secular
paintings of a highly elegant linearism. Following the death of
Lorenzo, in 1492, and the emotional
turmoil caused by Girolamo
Savonarola, the style of Botticelli
went through a clearly evident
change. The artist's last
masterpieces, which can be seen
as foretastes of the imminent
mannerism, date to this period
of spiritual disturbance.

DIERIC BOUTS
(Haarlem ca. 1415–Louvain 1475)

Bouts's early years are wrapped in mystery, but his earliest known works, made around the 1450s, show the clear influence of Van der Weyden. The presence of Bouts in Louvain, a city then in rapid expansion, is documented beginning in 1457; in 1468 he was made the city's official painter. Standing out among his most important works are the two large winged altarpieces he made for Louvain, that of the *Holy Sacrament of the Eucharist (Last Supper)* in the collegiate church of St. Peter and the *Last Judgment*, commissioned by the town in competition with the masterly Beaune Polyptych by Van der Weyden. Along with official, large-scale works, Bouts also made many versions of the *Virgin and Child*. His precise and controlled spatial vision enabled him to create settings and landscapes of great precision and coherence in which the figures appear perfectly integrated, anticipating the solutions to be adopted by Gerard David.

DONATO BRAMANTE
(Donato di Pascuccio)
(Fermignano, Urbino, 1444– Rome 1514)

A great architect and artist, Bramante was a splendid interpreter of the classical in forms that grew increasingly monumental and audacious, from the Milan of the Sforzas to the Rome of Pope Julius II. Bramante reached Milan around 1480. Aside from important works of architecture (Santa Maria presso San Satiro, Santa Maria delle Grazie, the cloisters of Sant'Ambrogio) he made paintings with rigorously monumental figures in stately spatial settings that influenced the Lombard school. After the fall of Ludovico il Moro he left Milan and moved to Rome in 1499, where be began an extraordinary reworking of classical architecture (the Tempietto built beside San Pietro in Montorio left a profound impression on the artists of the period, among them Raphael), such that in the span of only a few years he became the most important architect at the papal court. For Julius II he designed the overall rearrangement of the Vatican palaces around the Cortile del Belvedere, and beginning in 1506 he laid the basis for the reconstruction of the basilica of St. Peter's, later carried forward by Michelangelo.

BRAMANTINO (Bartolomeo Suardi)
(Milan ca. 1465–1530)

Bartolomeo Suardi studied with Bramante and followed his master's style so faithfully that he became known as Bramantino ("little Bramante"). In a Milan dominated by the influence of Leonardo, he worked out a hard, incisive style, in some cases even violently deformed although always with full control of the architectonic and perspective contexts. Thanks to the example of Bramante, his compositions, full of intense symbolic allusions, achieved monumental proportions with a sorrowful expressiveness. During the first decade of the sixteenth century, in the general crisis of the ex-Sforza duchy, Bramantino emerged as the most important Milanese artist. While working for the governor Gian Giacomo Trivulzio, he made the cartoons for the twelve tapestries of *The Months* (Castello Sforzesco, Milan), a masterpiece of Italian textile art. A trip to Rome (1508) enlarged and updated his style, which he expressed in forms so frozen and austere they seem almost metaphysical. During the last years of his life he was primarily active as an architect and adviser on the reconstruction of the Duomo of Milan.

AGNOLO BRONZINO
(Agnolo di Cosimo di Mariano Tori)
(Florence 1503–1572)

Supreme interpreter of the demanding etiquette of the grand ducal court of Florence, Bronzino characterized the age of mannerism, accompanying the developments of that style, from its initial rebellion against traditional schemes up to its affirmation as "court art," an enigmatic style made for a restricted cultural elite. Student of Pontormo, and for a long time his collaborator, Bronzino worked with his master on important undertakings in Florence during the 1520s. Called to the Marches court of the Della Rovere family in 1530, Bronzino began painting portraits, elaborating a personal style distinguished from that of Pontormo by his use of paint, which he applied in a sharp, compact manner, with results close to enamel. By around 1540 he had become the preferred painter of the Medici court and the Florentine aristocracy, popular also because of his literary talents. Bronzino alternated the creation of increasingly smooth and crystalline portraits with the direction of memorable decorative works, including the frescoes in the Medici villas, the arrangement of the private apartments in Palazzo Vecchio, and the creation of cartoons for the grand duke's tapestry works.

PIETER BRUEGEL THE ELDER
(Breda? 1525/30–Brussels 1569)

The life and activity of Pieter Bruegel the Elder took place in important cultural centers during an historical period full of major events, yet little is known of his biography beyond a few scattered fragments. The first document to mention him is his enrolment in the Antwerp guild of artists (1551). For the most part unaffected by the classical-style of the Antwerp school of painters, and almost completely impervious to the products of the Italian Renaissance, despite a trip to Italy between 1552 and 1556, Bruegel directed his career along three parallel lines as a designer, engraver, and painter. Following his marriage he moved to Brussels, where his first son, known as Bruegel the Younger, was born in 1564. His second son, Jan, born in 1568, became an excellent painter of extremely smooth still lifes, coming to be known as Velvet Bruegel. The cycle of the *Seasons* dates to 1565, by which time the master was a well-known personality. His works gradually assumed a new monumental solidity, with the abandonment of the multitude of details typical of

Biographies

the preceding period. He died in Brussels on September 5, 1569.

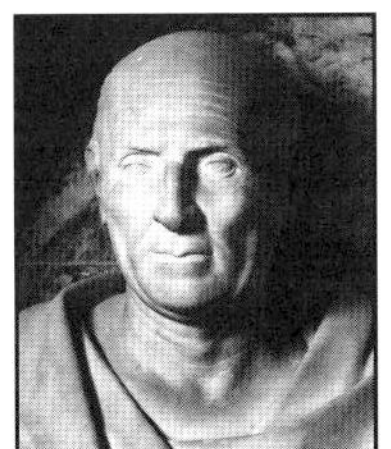

FILIPPO BRUNELLESCHI
(Florence 1377–1446)

Trained as a goldsmith and skilled in the techniques of working metals (altarpiece of St. Jacopo in the cathedral of Pistoia) and carving wood (*Crucifixion* in Santa Maria Novella, Florence), Filippo Brunelleschi "discovered" his true calling for architecture as the result of a series of trips to Rome, the first and most important of which he made in the company of Donatello (1402). A leader of Florentine cultural life, in 1409 he began his involvement on the worksite of the cathedral of Santa Maria del Fiore, and beginning in 1418 he undertook the creation of the cathedral's enormous dome, designed in accordance with absolutely new technical and aesthetic criteria. A scholar of applied mathematics, Brunelleschi inaugurated the period of "scientific" perspective in order to conceive and rationally construct measured spaces; it is with Brunelleschi that humanism in art comes into being. The buildings he made in Florence present a series of prestigious prototypes in a wide variety of styles, from majestic basilicas to centrally planned chapels, from private palaces to hospitals, from urban layouts to military and mechanical designs. Everything he did was dominated by the constant sense of a marvelous calculated rhythm, such that every part of a structure has a striking relationship to the proportions of the whole.

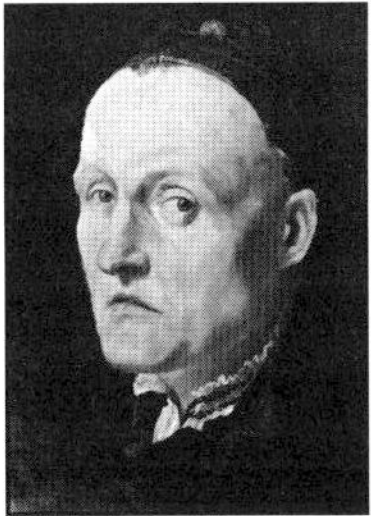

HANS BURGKMAIR
(Augsburg 1473–1531)

After training at Colmar with Martin Schongauer, Burgkmair enrolled in the artists' guild of Augsburg in 1498, alternating stays in his birthplace with important trips south. Involved in artistic undertakings for Emperor Maximilian, he worked with Altdorfer and Dürer on the various series of engravings celebrating imperial glories. He visited Italy several times, traveling to Venice in 1507 and to the Po valley around 1518. His patrons included Duke William of Bavaria and the Fugger bankers. With its impressive and dramatic monumentality, Burgkmair's style has greater severity than that of his colleagues in the Danubian school.

ROBERT CAMPIN (Master of Flémalle)
(Valenciennes? ca. 1378– Tournai 1444)

What little information exists about this artist indicates that he lived most of his life in Tournai in today's Belgium, where in 1423 a revolt led by representatives of the trade guilds weakened aristocratic power and enlarged the guilds' participation in city government. In this middle-class society Campin held prestigious posts, such as deacon of the corporation of goldsmiths and painters. He also directed a flourishing and well organized workshop in which both Rogier van der Weyden and Jacques Daret trained. When, toward the end of the 1430s, the city was swept by a movement toward restoration, Campin's fortunes too seemed to wane, and he found himself involved in a series of legal disputes. His solid realism had an extraordinary influence on artists of the next generation. Campin was a contemporary of Van Eyck, but his artistic language was less detached than that of the more famous artist. Influenced by the sculpture and painting of the Dijon school, Campin elaborated a style composed of tender, daily images and, in a thoroughly innovative way, he exalted the very human presence of his figures.

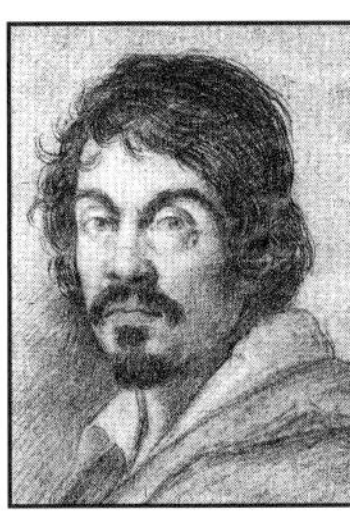

CARAVAGGIO (Michelangelo Merisi)
(Milan 1571–Porto Ercole 1610)

Most probably born in Milan, Caravaggio trained under Simone Peterzano, but more important to his artistic formation was his attentive study of the art of Leonardo, Titian, and the Brescian masters of the sixteenth century. The result was a strong drive toward reality through the expression of emotion and light. Around 1590 he moved to Rome and began a true revolution in art. Caravaggio brought to painting the world of the small alleys of Rome: cardsharps, gypsies, prostitutes, shady characters, laborers, wandering musicians. His first religious paintings still bore traces of the inspiration of Lombard naturalism, but the great religious canvases he painted in Rome between 1600 and 1606 were the cause of enormous controversy and debate. Some were rejected by the people who had commissioned them, scandalized by their brutal realism. In 1606, Caravaggio was found guilty of murder and condemned to death; he fled Rome. After a brief stay in Naples, he went to Malta, where he was admitted to the Knights of St. John, but the murder charge was soon revealed and he was imprisoned. He succeeded in fleeing to Sicily, and then (1609–10) he was again in Naples. With hopes of a papal dispensation, he prepared to return to Rome, but following a series of misadventures he died of malarial fever in the sunny port of Porto Ercole.

ANTOINE CARON
(Beauvais ca. 1527–Paris, 1599)

Active at Fontainebleau as assistant to Primaticcio, Caron adhered to the widespread classical style, and the works he made as court painter to Catherine de' Medici constitute the beginning of the second phase in the French mannerist school. His work presents an important testimony to the evolution of the Fontainebleau school. He uses a fantastic language to describe events of the period, taking refuge in an unreal world where, against a background of classical buildings, a confused crowd moves about, communicating the sense of uneasiness that is characteristic of the last period of the sixteenth century.

VITTORE CARPACCIO
(Venice 1460/65–Venice or Capodistria 1525/26)

Carpaccio's training and early activity have not yet been clearly established; he is known to have made his debut in 1499 with the beginning of the great cycle of canvases dedicated to St. Ursula (Gallerie dell'Accademia, Venice), which carried on through the last decade of the fifteenth century and remains the most complete proof of the balance he struck between narrative rhythm and the presentation of a myriad of details of architecture, costume, and physical features. His next cycle, the only one to have remained in its original site, was for the Scuola di San Giorgio degli Schiavoni (1502–07); the cycle he painted a little later for the Scuola degli Albanesi *(Stories of the Virgin)* and the one begun in 1514 for the Scuola di Santo Stefano *(Stories of St. Stephen)* have both been dismantled and dispersed. At the same time he was also making portraits and panels destined for devotion or for private collectors, all with a lucid, precise, and highly detailed style. Carpaccio remained substantially faithful to the fifteenth-century tradition, as is confirmed by the sacred works painted in Venice and its provinces. He ended his career in Istria.

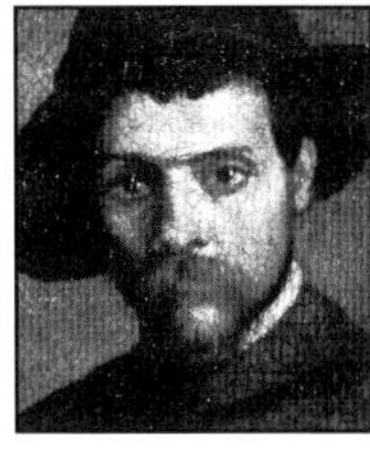

ANNIBALE CARRACCI
(Bologna 1560– Rome 1609)

Illustrious member of a family of painters, Annibale Carracci played a shaping role in the passage from late Renaissance to early baroque art. It is most likely that he got his training under his older cousin Ludovico (1555–1619), with whom he also collaborated on several youthful works. Annibale and Ludovico shared the desire for a return to "natural" painting, simple and direct, not wrapped in the intellectual folds of mannerism. Studies of Correggio and Titian led Annibale to enrich his palette and soften his outlines. The result was a supple, delicate art, both classical and up to date in terms of Renaissance developments. Around 1590 he moved to Rome, where his formalism was enriched by the enormous repertory of classical art. The culmination of his Roman activity was the vault of the gallery of Palazzo Farnese, with one of the greatest masterpieces of painting between the sixteenth and seventeenth centuries. Worn out by this work—and not only because of the physical demands but also because of the intellectual effort— Annibale grew weaker and died in 1609, one year before Caravaggio.

ANDREA DEL CASTAGNO
(Castagno nel Mugello 1421–Florence 1457)

Austere and sensitive personality of Florentine art in the humanistic period, Castagno stands out from among the other Tuscan painters of the fifteenth century because of the expressive force of his design and the plastic and realistic power of his modeling. In 1439 he was in Florence, working among the collaborators of Domenico Veneziano and alongside Piero della Francesca; in 1442 he was in Venice, where he frescoed the apse of the chapel of San Tarasio in San Zaccaria, courageously laid out in a humanistic perspective design, thus completely different from the context of contemporary Venetian painting. On his return to Florence, he participated in the stained-glass windows of Santa Maria del Fiore and stood out as one of the most brilliant artists of his generation. His most complex masterpiece was the decoration of the refectory of St. Apollonia, a large and impressive *Last Supper* (1445–50). Other important works by Castagno include frescoes on historical themes, such as the cycle of the *Famous Men*, today in the Uffizi, and the *Monument to Niccolò da Tolentino*, a monochrome fresco in Santa Maria del Fiore.

BENVENUTO CELLINI
(Florence 1500–1571)

Considered one of the greatest goldsmiths of all time, Cellini also proved himself an outstanding monumental sculptor in both bronze and marble as well as a brilliant writer: his autobiography is one of the more direct accounts of the life and thought of a late Renaissance artist. After early activity in Rome, he began a successful career and moved to the court of Francis I at Fontainebleau (1540–45); the works he made there include the famous gold and enamel salt cellar, and he soon became a leader in the sophisticated climate of courtly mannerism. On his return to Florence, he began the long and complex execution of the *Perseus* for the Loggia dei Lanzi, a work of extraordinary technical skill that was highly esteemed in the intellectual milieu at the time of Grand Duke Cosimo I. Because of his activity as a writer, and because of his lively temperament, Cellini stands as one of the essential reference points of international styles and techniques of the later sixteenth century.

PETRUS CHRISTUS
(Baerle-Duc ca. 1410–Bruges 1472/73)

Petrus Christus belongs to what is commonly called the second generation of fifteenth-century Netherlandish artists, the one that followed that of the "founding fathers" Van Eyck, Campin, and Van der Weyden. Little is known of his early activity, but he probably studied closely the works of the most renowned artists, most of all Van Eyck. In 1444 Christus moved to Bruges, remaining there the rest of his life. His highly personal pictorial language drew on Van Eyck's micrographic realism, but concentrated most of all on the rendering of space; in fact, he was the first northern Renaissance painter to use a rational construction of space based on a single vanishing point. The novelties of the work of Petrus Christus were by no means limited to the control of geometric space and also involved the rendering of a palpable reality.

CIMA DA CONEGLIANO
(Giovanni Battista Cima)
(Conegliano, Treviso, 1459/60– 1517/18)

Characteristic exponent of the painting of the Venetian mainland, Cima revealed an independent style even in his earliest works, the fruit of discerning meditation on a broad range of cultural references. He moved to Venice around 1490 and stayed there almost without interruption until 1516. Cima was primarily interested in the style of Antonello da Messina, which he viewed in terms of the works of Alvise

Vivarini. His best works are of a religious character, such as several Madonnas and the large, dazzling altarpieces. Aside from peaceful images of the countryside of the Veneto hills, these works are notable for the absolute clarity of their vision, with an almost "northern" light that investigates the details of objects and natural realities with great precision. Even after the arrival of Giorgione and the early works of Titian, Cima did not convert to tonal painting and remained faithful to clearly defined descriptive details, at the most opening himself slightly to secular subjects and perhaps putting a more rhythmic lilt in the composition of his beloved natural backgrounds.

JOOS VAN CLEVE (Joos van der Beke)
(Cleves or Antwerp ca. 1485–Antwerp 1540/41)

An important artist of the Antwerp school of the early sixteenth century, Van Cleve used an eclectic style that combined many of the figurative models of European art. The principal interest of his activity consists in the central role he performed, absorbing and distributing pictorial culture. An important factor in this was his willingness to travel, for he visited many different nations, although always returning to the city of Antwerp and the local painters' guild, in which he enrolled in 1511 and which he later served as dean (1515 and 1525). Over the course of later travels to Germany, Genoa, the court of Francis I of France, and England, his style was further enriched, including a sense of Leonardo, references to Patinir in terms of the vast horizons of his landscapes, and homage to Dürer in his refined portraits.

FRANÇOIS CLOUET
(Tours ca. 1515–Paris 1572)

Portraitist, creator of mythological paintings in the mannerist style of the Fontainebleau school and of gallant-style genre scenes, François Clouet replaced his father, Jean, as *peintre et valet de chambre* to Francis I in 1541. François did away with the traditional half-bust portrait and the cold chromatic tonalities of the northern style, preferring a new layout and a warmer range of colors, of which the equestrian portrait of Francis I is a fine example. His portraits were made in keeping with the "ancient" style that reached its peak during the reigns of Henry II (1547–59) and Charles IX (1560–74) and in which the model is inserted in a narrative context in an imaginary dimension.

JEAN CLOUET
(Brussels ca. 1485–Paris 1540)

This painter of Flemish origin became the court portraitist of France's Francis I; in 1533 he was granted the title of *peintre et valet de chambre* to the king. Aside from the two portraits of *Francis I* and *Guillaume Budé*, few painted works can be attributed to him with any certainty. On the other hand, there is an enormous number of small-format portraits of members of Francis I's court that he made with charcoal and touches of paint. Along with the influence of northern European art, his portraits show signs of the art of Leonardo, most of all in terms of the softness of the outlines and the use of chiaroscuro.

CORREGGIO (Antonio Allegri)
(Correggio ca. 1489–1534)

Correggio got his training in Mantua, between the last years of Mantegna's life and the early years of the spread of the sweeter Raphaelesque style. Atop this substratum Correggio added Leonardesque and Venetian stimuli. All these influences can be seen in his youthful works, up to his first large work in Parma, the Camera di San Paolo in the convent of San Paolo (1519). The originality of his iconographic and pictorial solutions, always tempered by refined taste for expressions and for color, anticipated the ingenious cycle of San Giovanni Evangelista, begun with the scene frescoed in the dome (1520–21) and then followed in other parts of that Parma church, in some cases with the help of assistants. In the 1520s he made a series of altarpieces of spectacular conception with linked gestures, smiling expressions, and alluring colors. The overall masterpiece was the *Assumption of the Virgin* in the dome of the cathedral of Parma, a work of wondrous perspective. During the last years of his life he returned to work for the Gonzagas, with two canvases for Isabella's *studiolo* (now in the Louvre) and the cycle of the *Loves of Jupiter*, today divided among Vienna, Berlin, and the Galleria Borghese in Rome.

FRANCESCO DEL COSSA
(Ferrara ca. 1436–1477/78)

Collaborator and companion of Cosimo Tura at the center of the active and extravagant Ferrara school, Cossa mitigated the harshness of his older colleague with painting of broad narrative breadth. A masterpiece in that sense was the execution of the months of *March* and *April* in the hall of Palazzo Schifanoia in Ferrara (ca. 1470), with an ingenious three-level combination of mythological scenes, astrological references, and contemporary elements drawn from the duke's life or from the court, city, or countryside. Not satisfied with his financial treatment, Cossa left Ferrara and, sometime after 1470, moved to Bologna. There he painted important altarpieces and, for the basilica of San Petronio, the ambitious Griffoni Polyptych, today divided among various museums. The plastic energy of Cossa's figures is projected against landscapes or architectonic backgrounds full of rich detail presented with great care.

LUCAS CRANACH THE ELDER
(Kronach, Upper Franconia, 1472–Weimar 1553)

Son of a painter, Cranach got his training and did his earliest work in Bavaria. In 1498 he began traveling between southern Germany and Austria, becoming one of the leaders of the of the *Donauschule* ("Danube school") because of the magical vitality, fabulous nature, and incisive force of his figures. In 1505 he was invited to Wittenberg by the elector prince of Saxony Frederick III (called Frederick the Wise), who was also a patron of Dürer and who supported a refined style of humanism. Until his death, almost fifty years later, Cranach worked at the Saxon court, becoming one of the most long-lived and active creators of images in the German Renaissance, with a stylistic arc that evolved almost imperceptibly from the legendary expressionism of his early years to the intellectual, decorative, almost abstract graphic style of his last works. In addition to engraving, he was active in a wide variety of media and subjects, from altarpieces to classical nudes, from portraits to allegories, from hunting scenes to Lutheran propaganda. Cranach was in fact one of the first artists to embrace the Reformation, creating portraits of Luther, Luther's wife, Katharina von Bora, and Melanchthon and creating religious paintings illustrating themes of Reform theology.

CARLO CRIVELLI
(Venice ca. 1430/35–Marches 1494/95)

Trained first in the workshop of the Vivarini in Venice, then in the lively humanistic setting of Padua at mid-century, Crivelli experienced a series of misadventures that led him first to Istria (1459) and then to the Marches, where he remained from 1468 until his death. He found an agreeable setting in that provincial area, eventually becoming one of the most singular Italian artists of the second half of the fifteenth century. His works reveal that he was quite knowledgeable concerning the most advanced rules of visual perspective and classical monumentality, which he wrapped in a gaudy, exuberantly decorative style that at times included the use of antiquated gold backgrounds. With the help of a well equipped workshop, Crivelli left polyptychs and altarpieces in numerous cities and towns in the Marches, some large, others small or even tiny.

GERARD DAVID
(Oudewater ca. 1455–Bruges 1523)

The last great artist active in Bruges in the fifteenth century was born in the north of the Low Countries in the province of Holland. He probably got his training in his father's workshop before taking a trip that took him first to Haarlem and then southward. In 1484 he set himself up in Bruges, where his style underwent a substantial change. Perhaps influenced by the sober and detached language of Memling, David gave all his compositions a quieter and more composed sensibility that met with immediate public favor. Toward the end of the century, as contact between Flanders and Italy intensified, he was among the first artists to introduce Renaissance characteristics to his works. Even so, the most innovative aspect of his works was the importance he gave the landscape, which he presented as a tangible and vibrant essence, in that way anticipating the extraordinary works of Joachim Patinir.

DOMENICO VENEZIANO
(Domenico di Bartolomeo)
(Venice ca. 1405–Florence 1461)

Domenico got complex training in his art in Rome and Florence in the course of the 1420s, working alongside Gentile da Fabriano, Masolino, Pisanello, and Masaccio; the result was a composite but also highly personal style that he used to become one of the busiest painters during the period of the affirmation of humanistic Florentine art. Among his most precocious

works is the tondo of the *Adoration of the Magi* (Gemäldegalerie, Berlin), which he made only a short time before beginning work on the frescoes (almost completely destroyed) in the church of St. Egidio in Florence, made with the collaboration of Andrea del Castagno and Piero della Francesca. He completed his masterpiece, the St. Lucy Altarpiece (main panel, Uffizi, Florence), in 1447; that work indicates his final overcoming of the use of the polyptych for altarpiece paintings.

DONATELLO (Donato di Niccolò Bardi)
(Florence 1386–1466)

Donatello was in his eighties and still working when he died, and his long activity represents an epochal turning point in the history of art. During the steps of his career, which he spent almost entirely in Florence (the major exception being a long and productive stay in Padua), Donatello expressed himself in the most varied dimensions, from gigantic equestrian monuments to small "table" bronzes, and he showed equal ease in the handling of the most varied materials (marble, bronze, terracotta, mixed media), presenting an almost inexhaustible variety of creations. He was just over twenty when he produced his first work, working alongside Nanni di Banco in the worksite of the cathedral of Santa Maria del Fiore, and he soon attracted attention because of his powerful large-size sculptures. He was commissioned to make the *St. George* for Orsanmichele in 1416; later, in the course of the 1420s, he worked together with Michelozzo on the creation of works combining

sculpture and architecture in Florence, Prato, Rome, and Naples. During the same period he participated in the group undertaking of the decoration of the baptismal font in gilt bronze of Siena, and in 1433 he competed with Luca della Robbia in the execution of a marble choir gallery for the Duomo of Florence. In 1443 he moved to Padua, eventually staying there about a decade. This is the period of the great bronzes, the equestrian statue of Gattamelata, and the stately figures of the altarpiece in the church of Sant'Antonio. The experience in casting large bronze statues that he got in Padua he later applied to works in Florence, such as the *Judith* today in Palazzo Vecchio and the pulpits in San Lorenzo, made with the involvement of a new generation of Tuscan sculptors.

DOSSO DOSSI
(Giovanni di Niccolò Luteri)
(between Mantua and Ferrara ca. 1490–Ferrara 1542)

Precisely when and where Dosso Dossi was born is not known, but today he is credited with being the leading artist of the Ferrara school of the early sixteenth century, in perfect chronological and ideal accord with Ludovico Ariosto, who was the Estes' court poet. Trained in the Giorgionesque circle, around 1510 Dosso was working in Mantua, and in 1514 he became the court painter in Ferrara and participated in the artistic undertakings of Alfonso d'Este alongside Giovanni Bellini and Titian. Thanks to frequent trips (to Venice, but also Florence and Rome) Dosso kept himself up to date on the world of art, most of

Biographies

all the evolution of sixteenth-century painting. During his long period working for the Este family, he alternated altarpieces with decorative cycles based on literary or mythological themes. The principal stylistic reference behind Dosso's art is Venetian art, but there are also references to the expressive tradition of the Ferrara school along with an independent narrative vein. The frescoes in the Villa Imperiale of Pesaro and the Buonconsiglio Castle in Trent, works that were made with the assistance of his brother Battista, date to around 1530.

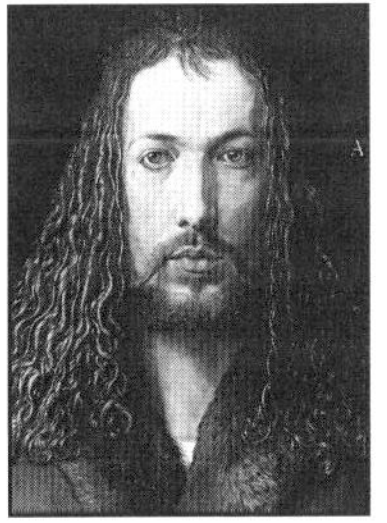

ALBRECHT DÜRER
(Nuremberg 1471–1528)

The greatest German artist of the Renaissance was a "universal" master, active in widely disparate formats, themes, and techniques and always involved in the progress of painting, through his own works and also by way treatises and technical works. He performed his apprenticeship first with his goldsmith father and then in the workshop of Michael Wolgemut; then, at the age of nineteen, Dürer set off on a long study trip, thanks to which his figurative culture expanded to a European perspective. He was away from Nuremberg for four years, from April 1490 to May 1494. A trip to Venice completed his training, after which he began important activity as a painter and engraver, including service to Maximilian I. From 1505 to 1507 he returned to Italy, spending a long period in Venice at the time when the local school was experiencing the stylistic passage from the Bellini tradition to the new generation of Giorgione and Titian. Dürer's later compositions, always distinguished by a precise graphic line, have an ample monumental and perspective breadth. A further trip, in 1521, took him to Antwerp and the Low Countries, where he met Quenten Metsys and Lucas van Leyden. In the last years of his life he sought in art and in moderation a balance between the tensions then shaking Germany.

ADAM ELSHEIMER
(Frankfurt am Main 1578–Rome 1610)

A great artist of the same generation as Caravaggio and Rubens, Elsheimer died when he was still very young, leaving unfinished the poetic discourse he had begun with such extreme delicacy and fascinating productions. From his youth he was attracted to Italian Renaissance art, and in 1598 he moved to Venice and studied painting with Tintoretto. In 1600 he moved to Rome, and there he spent the last ten years of his short life. Inserted in the lively ambience of the "Romanized" northern painters, Elsheimer modified his style, turning primarily to landscape painting. In this field he found an expressive vein of intense originality, both classical and romantic, idealized and scientific. An attentive scholar of the art movements of his time, he was aware of both the luminism of Caravaggio and the broad and peaceful layouts of the Roman countryside views begun by Annibale Carracci. Even so, his technique remained tied to his northern roots, with a fine and accurate execution of impeccable brilliance.

JAN VAN EYCK
(Maaseik ca. 1390–Bruges 1441)

Jan van Eyck, the great innovator of Flemish painting, received a very traditional type of training, so much so that his early works reveal a close relationship to miniatures; his paintings show the same kind of refined technique and attention to detail that is typical of illuminated manuscripts. From 1422 to 1424 he worked for the court of John of Holland at The Hague, and in fact all of Van Eyck's career was tied to the official powers in Flanders. In 1425 he was made court painter to Philip the Good, duke of Burgundy, and he served in that capacity until his death. In addition to his activity as an artist Van Eyck also served the Burgundian court in the role of diplomat, making international trips that contributed to the rapid spread of his fame and his style, which concentrated on the analytical rendering of reality, a style favored by the technique of painting in oil. The central work of his career was the enormous Ghent Altarpiece with its central *Polyptych of the Lamb*, made for the cathedral of Ghent (1426–32); he left this unfinished, and it was completed by his brother Hubert. Van Eyck is known for a wonderful series of other masterpieces, as much in the field of religious painting as in the special genre of the portrait, a field on which he had an enormous impact, originating the use of the slightly turned half-bust figure.

PEDRO FERNÁNDEZ
(documented in Gerona from 1519 to 1522)

Originally from Murcia, Pedro Fernández worked in Catalonia, a region where the Renaissance took hold very slowly because of the strong influence exercised by Jaume Huguet, who was active in Barcelona in the second half of the fifteenth century. Fernández set himself up in Gerona in 1519 and worked in the cathedral on the main retable, dedicated to *St. Helena*, the Renaissance architecture of which, enriched with up-to-date references to Leonardo, emphasizes the importance of his long stay in Italy, during which he was active from Lombardy to Naples and came in contact with various religious patrons and with members of avant-garde figurative movements. Only recently have his biography and career been reconstructed; for a long time he was known by the indicative name "Pseudo-Bramantino."

GAUDENZIO FERRARI
(Valduggia, Vercelli, 1475/80–Milan 1546)

Moved by a powerful and moving popular spirit, but at the same time highly attentive to the most up-to-date figurative stimuli, Gaudenzio was the creator of a particular genre of art, the *sacromonte* ("holy mountain"). The fusion of landscape, architecture, painting, and sculpture makes the Sacro Monte complex above the town of Varallo a "complete work of art" and also one of the most novel artistic creations of the sixteenth century. Gaudenzio's artistic training was in the Lombardy-Piedmont style, with the addition of elements from the style of Perugino; he entered his artistic maturity with the great partition wall of Santa Maria delle Grazie in Varallo (1513), a prelude to the two chapels of the Sacro Monte (*Adoration of the Shepherds* and *Calvary*), in which he made both the sculptures and the frescoes. This powerfully moving choral sentiment also shows up in his later works, the frescoes of the altarpiece in San Cristoforo in Vercelli (1529–34), the dome of the sanctuary of Santa Maria delle Grazie at Saronno, with *Angel Musicians* (1534–36), and the paintings in Milan from near the end of his career.

VINCENZO FOPPA
(Orzinuovi, Brescia, 1427/30–Brescia 1515/16)

After studying together with Andrea Mantegna in Padua, Foppa went on to become the most important painter of the early Renaissance in Lombardy. In a Milan dominated by the court's late Gothic taste, he painted the up-to-date fresco cycle in the Portinari Chapel in the church of St. Eustorgio (1468). His panel paintings and altarpieces show the acquisition of linear perspective, veined by a contemplative melancholy that is expressed through the delicate chiaroscuro of faces. In addition to Milan, Foppa was active in Pavia and Liguria, dictating the figurative style of the northwestern Lombardy area in terms of a quiet grace and a concrete adhesion to reality. One of the few Lombard artists not to be influenced by Leonardo, Foppa ended his long career in Brescia, becoming an example for the nascent local painting school.

JEAN FOUQUET
(Tours ca. 1420–1481)

The foremost representative of fifteenth-century French painting, Jean Fouquet trained in Paris in a workshop of miniaturists. He was heir to the great Gothic tradition, as is indicated by the bright chromatic tonalities of his works, but he distanced himself from the unreal fantasies of the later Middle Ages, formulating a new language in which the new concepts of perspective learned during a trip to Italy blend with the naturalistic discoveries of the Flemish. The trip to Italy, between 1445 and 1447, permitted him to learn not only the recent perspective formulations, but also a classical architectonic language that proved useful to him later in his career. Only two works are known from his activity prior to the visit to Italy, the *Portrait of Charles VII* and the Nouans *Pietà*, both of which are indebted to the teaching of Jan van Eyck and the sculpture of the Burgundian master Claus Sluter. During his stay in Rome Fouquet met Fra Angelico, at the time working in the Vatican, and the influence of his work is legible in the miniatures of the *Book of Hours of Étienne Chevalier*. Back in France in 1448 he was active in the court of Charles VII and then Louis XI, becoming the latter's official painter in 1475. His patrons included many high state officials, such as the chancellor of France Guillaume Juvénal des Ursins and the treasurer Étienne Chevalier.

FRANCESCO DI GIORGIO MARTINI
(Siena 1439–1501)

Architect, sculptor, military engineer, inventor, painter, and technologist, Martini played a central role in the development of art as well as in the figure of the artist-intellectual of the late fifteenth century. He got his training and made his debut as a painter, a student of Vecchietta and colleague of Neroccio. In 1477 he was called to Urbino to act as the principal architect in the court of Federico da Montefeltro. Aside from works in the Ducal Palace in Urbino, he designed and made important forts and fortifications. Other masterpieces of architecture, datable to the 1480s, include the church of Santa Maria del Calcinaio near Cortona and the Ducal Palace in Gubbio. In 1489 he returned to Siena to sculpt the bronze angels in the apse of the cathedral and to make a few paintings, but he left immediately first for Milan and then Naples, eventually returning to Siena, where he ended his eclectic career painting.

NICOLAS FROMENT
(Uzès ca. 1435–Avignon 1483)

Froment served his apprenticeship in northern France, and after 1468 was called by King René of Anjou to his court at Avignon, where the sovereign had created an artistic center of great vitality. Froment became an important figure among the artists of the Provençal school, which contributed to the creation of a new language in French fifteenth-century painting. The presence in the Uffizi of *The Resurrection of Lazarus*, his earliest known work, signed and dated 1461, has made some propose a stay in Florence, but this is belied by the form of the work, a winged triptych, and by its hard, contracted graphics and the throng of figures with contorted faces, all traits that suggest instead a Flemish influence. The triptych of the *Burning Bush*, the only other work unquestionably attributed to this artist and commissioned by King René (as perhaps was the diptych with the portraits of René d'Anjou and his wife, Jeanne Laval, today in the Louvre), has different tones but is also related to the Flemish tradition.

GEERTGEN TOT SINT JANS
(Haarlem? ca. 1450–ca. 1490)

Geertgen is an important representative of the painting of the northern Low Countries. His training took place in Haarlem, but a trip to Flanders put him in contact with the artistic center of Ghent and perhaps also of Bruges. He was given the name "tot Sint Jans" ("of St. John") because he lived in Haarlem near the Knights of St. John, where in fact he worked as both laborer and painter. He made his most important work for the order, a polyptych, the remaining parts of which are the *Lamentation on the Dead Christ* and the *Bones of St. John the Baptist*, both today in Vienna. His youthful works were still caught in a somewhat static arrangement, but he soon absorbed the echoes of the teaching of Hugo van der Goes, whose works he clearly studied. His images were enriched by a greater sense of space and movement, and their dramatic and narrative effects also increased.

GENTILE DA FABRIANO

(Fabriano 1370/80–Rome 1427)

The painting of Gentile da Fabriano is the most fascinating and conscious expression of the phase of transition between the highest developments of Gothic decorativism and the beginning of the early season of humanism. The Valleromita Polyptych (Brera, Milan) offers an assessment of the artist's youthful stylistic development, following his artistic apprenticeship in the Umbria-Marches area into which are blended influences from Rimini and Lombardy. In 1408 he completed frescoes (lost) in Doge's Palace in Venice that influenced Venetian art of the first half of the fifteenth century; he then spent a period in Lombardy before returning to the Marches. In 1419, Gentile moved his workshop to Florence. Without giving up on his style—indeed, he increased the fabulous aspect of the figures defined by sinuous lines and clothed in dazzling garments— he began a dialogue with nascent humanism and studied ancient sculpture. His most famous work, the *Adoration of the Magi* for the Strozzi Chapel in Santa Trinita, today in the Uffizi, dates to 1423. After stays in Siena and Orvieto, Gentile went to Rome early in 1427, where he began the decoration of the basilica of St. John Lateran. His death, in August of 1427, put an end to his work on the large project.

NICOLAUS GERHAERT

(Leiden ca. 1430–Vienna 1473)

This complex and appealing "wandering" sculptor can be generically included within the history of German art (he worked in Trier, Baden-Baden, and Constance), despite his Netherlandish origin and his activity over a broad geographical region. Unfortunately, many of his works have been lost or compromised. Such is the case with the sculptures he made for the cathedral of Strasbourg, of which only fragmentary heads remain, although these possess a wonderful psychological and emotional intensity. His works combine the memory of the dramatic power of Claus Sluter with a subtle skill at penetrating portraiture, as shown by the monumental tomb of Emperor Frederick III in the cathedral of Vienna, which he began work on in 1467 (at which time he had moved to the Austrian capital) and which was completed after his death by his students.

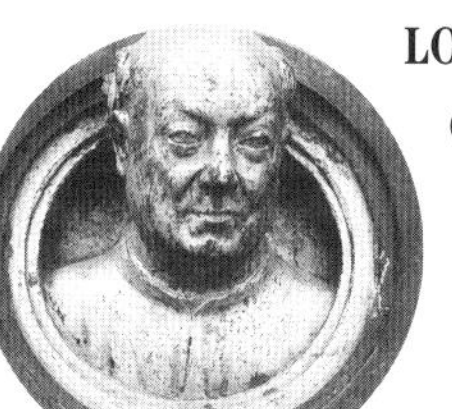

LORENZO GHIBERTI

(Florence 1378–1455)

An enormously important figure from the early fifteenth century in Florence, Ghiberti excelled most of all in works of goldworking and bronze sculpture, but he was also active in the field of monumental sculpture and in the writing of important treatises. He won the competition with Brunelleschi in 1401 for the execution of the second door of the Baptistery in Florence, which he completed only in 1423. During that period he also made statues for Orsanmichele and began the important baptismal font in Siena, with gilt bronze panels. After a stay in Venice, he began in work in 1425 on his masterpiece, the third door of the Baptistery (known as the *Gates of Paradise*). The ten panels, completed and mounted in 1452, present the stylistic passage of the age, with the adoption of increasingly complex structures in perspective and increasingly monumental and intimately "classical" layouts.

DOMENICO GHIRLANDAIO

(Domenico di Tommaso Bigordi)

(Florence 1449–1494)

Principal exponent of a numerous family of artists, Domenico found the best outlet for his creativity in the execution of large-scale fresco cycles, earning him Vasari's description as "quick, ready, and facile." With Ghirlandaio, fifteenth-century Florentine painting discovered a pleasantly narrative side, as indicated by his family nickname (*Ghirlandaio* from a kind of jewelry *garland* he invented). After serving his apprenticeship alongside Perugino and Botticelli in the workshop of Verrocchio, Domenico was able to begin independent activity early in the 1470s thanks to the support of the Vespucci family, for which he made several works in the Florentine church of Ognissanti and in the convent of which he frescoed the *Last Supper*. In 1475 he went to San Gimignano, where he frescoed the elegant *Stories of St. Fina* in the collegiate church. By then at the apex of the Florentine school, he went to Rome in 1481 to make two frescoes in the Sistine Chapel; the prestige of those works is reflected in the important commissions he received on his return to Florence: the decoration of the Sala dei Gigli in Palazzo Vecchio (1483) and the beginning of the frescoes in the large Tornabuoni Chapel, the main apse of Santa Maria Novella. This last work, completed in 1490, involved the participation of Ghirlandaio's large workshop, in which Michelangelo received early training.

GIAMBOLOGNA

(Jean de Boulogne)

(Douai 1529–Florence 1608)

Key sculptor in the second half of the sixteenth century, Giambologna is a point of reference for the mannerist style, most of all in terms of the layout of gardens and large-scale urban embellishments (fountains, celebratory monuments). A Fleming by birth, he trained in France, at Mons, under the sculptor Jacques Dubroeucq; in 1550 he went to Rome. The experience was to prove a shaping event in his career, for after his visit to Rome he sought a mediation between the power of Michelangelo and the elegance of Hellenism. He entered the service of Cosimo I de' Medici, and throughout the second half of the sixteenth century he played a central role on the Florentine artistic scene, making numerous works in the gardens, villas, and many homes of the Medici family as well as large sculptural groups in marble and bronze for Piazza della Signoria. Imitated and admired in the European courts, he made spectacular works in other cities, such as the fountain of Neptune in Bologna's Piazza Maggiore.

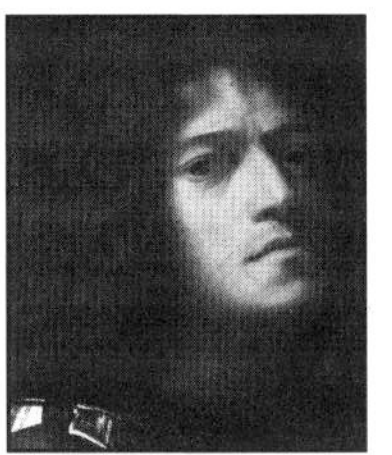

GIORGIONE
(Castelfranco Veneto 1478– Venice 1510)

Only scant biographical information is available for Giorgione, and very few works can be attributed to him with any certainty. All of his artistic career dates to the first decade of the sixteenth century, and although it has been painstakingly reconstructed by scholars, many questions remain unresolved. Giorgione made many of his early works in collaboration with other artists, and from his first paintings he showed a particular skill at landscapes. Around 1505, in keeping with developments in the painting of Giovanni Bellini, Giorgione set his Castelfranco Altarpiece in the open air, thus marking the affirmation of tonalism. This work was followed by such masterpieces as *The Tempest* and the *Three Philosophers*, in which the delicate chiaroscuro relationships among the figures suggest a possible contact with Leonardo. In 1508 he worked with Titian on the frescoes for the Fondaco dei Tedeschi, entering a period of more withdrawn melancholy. By then the master from Castelfranco was surrounded by a circle of collaborators and imitators, so much so that identifying the individual hands is sometimes extremely difficult. In the *Concert Champêtre* in the Louvre it is difficult for experts to tell Giorgione from Titian; the *Venus* in Dresden that is attributed to Giorgione may well have been his last work. He died of the plague in 1510.

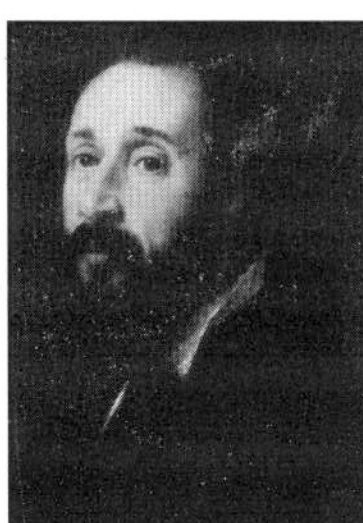

GIULIO ROMANO (Giulio Pippi)
(Rome 1492/99– Mantua 1546)

A prestigious architect and master at organizing and directing decorative undertakings, Giulio Romano got his training and was involved in his first artistic projects through the workshop of Raphael, becoming that artist's most trusted assistant in the creation of major cycles, such as the rooms and loggias in the Vatican, La Farnesina, and Villa Madama. At the death of Raphael (1520) he took over direction of the workshop, completing works of great importance (Sala di Constantino in the Vatican). In 1524 he moved to Mantua and became the director of the last great artistic season of an Italian Renaissance court. For the Gonzagas he designed cycles of frescoes and ambitious constructions (Palazzo Te, the cathedral of Mantua, the abbey of San Benedetto Po), and he also made cartoons for tapestries and designs for jewelry, taking care in all his works to give the public image of the court of Isabella and Federico Gonzaga the proper look. The dispersion and destruction of the Gonzaga residence caused the loss of much of these works. Giulio Romano's most complex operation remains the design and decoration of Palazzo Te, in which every room presents new and more exciting ornamental devices.

HUGO VAN DER GOES
(Ghent ca. 1440–Roode Kloster, Brussels, 1482)

Van der Goes's activity in Ghent dates to 1467, when he enrolled in that city's guild of painters. Most of his works have religious subjects, and around 1475, because of his profound faith, he became a lay brother the Augustinian monastery of Roode Kloster, where he lived until his death. His withdrawn life did not him prevent from working, and his fame attracted so many people to the monastery that the painter enjoyed special privileges to permit him to entertain illustrious guests. The creation of the Portinari Altarpiece, sent to Florence, marks the height of his career (1477). The artist's emotional difficulties increased; he seems to have been tormented by profound depression. It is unclear how much effect these personal problems had on his artistic vision, but he worked in a nervous and deeply felt style. Artificial and discontinuous spatial presentations prevail in his later works, calling into attention the dichotomy between the real image and the painted image.

HENDRICK GOLTZIUS
(Mühlbrecht 1558– Haarlem 1617)

As painter and most of all as engraver, Goltzius was a major force in the spread of the motifs of international mannerism, especially by way of his friendship and collaboration with Bartholomäus Spranger, beginning in 1583. After a trip to Italy in 1590 he founded an academy of design and painting in Haarlem, with Karel van Mander and Cornelisz van Haarlem, moving from the technique of engraving to work in painting.

JAN GOSSART (Mabuse)
(Maubeuge ca. 1478–Middelburg ca 1532)

Gossart has also been known as Mabuse, a name based on an ancient version of the name of his birthplace. He enrolled in Antwerp's guild of painters in 1503, and in 1508 accompanied the duke of Burgundy to Rome. The result of this was a very particular style in which the fifteenth-century Flemish tradition, with its meticulous rendition of the real world, was not yet fully abandoned but appears alongside a sense of the "modern style" from Italy, and not only in the rendering of perspective and the use of architectonic layouts but also in the monumental breadth of the figures and the setting. Along with Lucas van Leyden, Gossart took a memorable trip in 1527. The pair of artists visited the principal cities of Flanders, the Brabant, and Zeeland, taking a boat along the navigable canals and rivers. With his presence sought by the courts of Burgundy and Denmark and the Flemish line of the Hapsburgs, Gossart alternated complex works with penetrating portraits. During his maturity, Gossart painted forceful portraits distinguished by sharp chiaroscuro contrasts and impressive realism.

JEAN GOUJON
(Paris? ca. 1510–Bologna ca. 1566)

Highly refined, meticulous sculptor of the High Renaissance, Goujon is a perfect example of the taste of the French court of Francis I. First involved in one of the last worksites of the Parisian Gothic

Biographies

(Saint-Germain-l'Auxerrois), in the 1540s Goujon began to approach the Italianist taste of the court of Francis I, such that he was officially nominated royal sculptor. His activity was concentrated on ornamental works and those with secular subjects, inspired by models by Primaticcio and Cellini, in the castles of Écouen and Anet but most of all in the palace of the Louvre, always the most important court residence in Paris. Goujon's works include the monumental caryatids in Louvre, but preference usually goes to the delicate bas-relief panels of the dismembered Fountain of the Innocents. Goujon was a Huguenot, and his career ended traumatically in 1562 when he was forced to flee France.

BENOZZO GOZZOLI (Benozzo di Lese)
(Florence ca. 1420–Pistoia 1497)

Student and then collaborator of Fra Angelico in the convent of San Marco in Florence and in later works in Rome and Orvieto, Benozzo entered the Florentine artistic school in the course of the 1440s, working alongside Ghiberti on his *Gates of Paradise.* In 1450 he was in Montefalco, Umbria, where he left important frescoes in the churches of San Fortunato and San Francesco. Following a trip to Rome and various works in Latium and Umbria, in 1458 he received the most important commission of his career, the decoration of the private chapel in Palazzo Medici in Florence with the sumptuous *Journey of the Magi*, in which he portrayed various members of the ruling family. Between 1464 and 1466 he lived in San Gimignano, making frescoes in the collegiate church and in the

church of St. Agostino. Another important step was the commission for the *Stories of the Old Testament* in the Camposanto of Pisa (1468–84), unfortunately in large part lost. After a series of jobs in Florence and smaller towns in Tuscany, he died in Pistoia during the 1497 outbreak of plague.

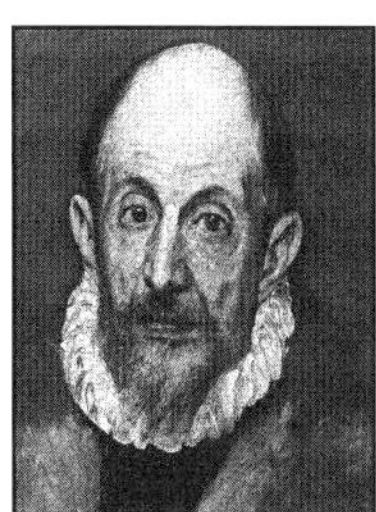

EL GRECO
(Domenikos Theotokopoulos)
(Crete 1541– Toledo 1614)

After training under the Cretan icon painter Michele Damaskinos, he was already being called a master painter in his homeland in 1560. Shortly after that, he moved to Venice (Crete was then a possession of Venice) and came in contact with some of the leading artists of the High Renaissance, most of all Titian, Tintoretto, and Jacopo Bassano. Around 1572 the still young painter was in Rome, where he studied the works of Michelangelo and enrolled in the Accademia di St. Luca. In 1577 he was in Toledo, the city that became his adopted home; his name was replaced by the nickname that made him famous. El Greco took part in the enormous swirl of religious art created by the Counter-Reformation. Alternating altarpieces, medium-size devotional paintings, and intense portraits, he marked a drastic change in Spanish art, making himself the keystone in the arch between the Renaissance and the baroque. Indeed, El Greco performed a role of central importance in Spanish painting. With him the repetitive, weary adoption of

aged models ended and a new era of courageous innovation began. Even so, despite the well equipped workshop he established in Toledo, El Greco's style had no followers, making his career unique on the panorama of European art on the threshold of the baroque.

MATTHIS GRÜNEWALD
(Mathis Neithardt Gothardt)
(Würzburg ca. 1480–Halle 1528)

In 1505, "Meister Matthis" was commissioned to paint an epitaph in Aschaffenburg; nothing is known of his life or career before that date. Beginning in 1510 Grünewald worked between Mainz and Frankfurt, alternating paintings with activity as a hydraulic engineer. These multifaceted talents earned him the post, beginning in 1511, of court artist to the archbishop of Mainz, Uriel von Gemmingen. The next year he began the execution of the large Isenheim Altarpiece (today in Colmar), completed in 1516, the year in which Grünewald entered the service of Cardinal Albert of Brandenburg, archbishop of Mainz, and patron of Dürer, Cranach, and Holbein. His contacts with the other great artists of the German Renaissance increased; in 1520 Grünewald witnessed the coronation of Emperor Charles V at Aachen, alongside Dürer. The repressions following the defeat of the followers of Thomas Müntzer affected Grünewald, who was forced to leave Mainz and move to Frankfurt, where he substantially quit painting to dedicate himself to selling paint and the production of a soap with pharmaceutical properties. In 1527 he was in Halle, where he took commissions as a

hydraulic engineer. He died the next year.

MAARTEN VAN HEEMSKERCK
(Heemskerck, Alkmaar, 1498–Haarlem 1574)

Student and then rival of Jan van Scorel, Van Heemskerck is one of the most interesting but also elusive Dutch masters of the sixteenth century. The first period of his career, in Van Scorel's workshop in Haarlem, involved primarily portraits. His rapid affirmation as an artist stirred his teacher's jealousy, leading Van Heemskerck to set off for Rome (1532). The four years he spent in the Eternal City, taking notes on works of art both antique and modern, turned him into one of the most up-to-date and original masters of northern Europe, capable of overcoming the generic Raphaelism of the Antwerp "Romanists" with the plastic and dramatic force of both classical sculpture and Michelangelo. Indeed, on his return to his homeland, Van Heemskerck gave life to a particular form of mannerism, one distinguished by a nervous graphic line revealing memories of Pontormo and Parmigianino.

JOSEPH HEINTZ THE ELDER
(Basel 1564–Prague 1609)

Heintz trained in Basel and while still young began following the tradition tied to Hans Holbein the Younger. At twenty, stimulated by the widespread references to Italy in the figurative culture of southern Germany, he decided to move to Rome. In 1591 he moved to Prague, where he spent most of the rest of his life, soon becoming, together with Bartholomäus Spranger and Hans von Aachen, one of the major figures in the eclectic period under Emperor Rudolf II. Typical of the emperor's sensual and intellectual taste are Heintz's paintings on copper of mythological scenes, which have abundant nude female figures. Heintz's works suffered the same fate as those of many other Prague artists and collectors, being sacked and in large part dispersed during the conquest of Prague by the Swedish army during the Thirty Years' War. In addition to his activity as a painter, Heintz made works of architecture and ornamentation, most often together with Elias Holl.

JUAN DE HERRERA
(Mobellán ca. 1530–Madrid 1597)

Military engineer under Emperor Charles V, Herrera was chosen in 1569 by Philip II to take over construction of the monastery of the Escorial after the death of the first designer, Juan Bautista de Toledo. Laid out with a severe, monumental style, up-to-date in terms of Michelangelo's constructions in Rome, and also in keeping with the guidelines of the Council of Trent on religious art, the Escorial became the symbolic monument of its period. After the construction of the church (completed in 1582), Herrera worked on other official buildings in Seville (the palace of Lonja) and Valladolid (cathedral).

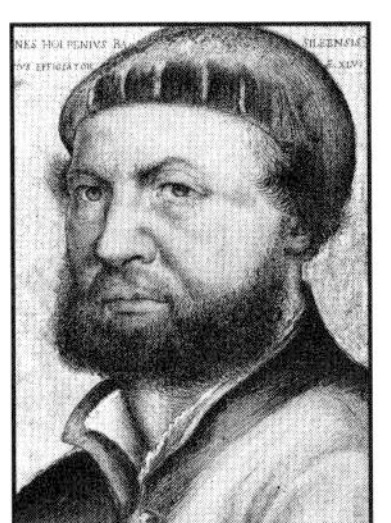

HANS HOLBEIN THE YOUNGER
(Augsburg 1497/98– London 1543)

Son and student of Hans the Elder, Holbein trained in the city of his birth, one of the main Renaissance art centers of southern Germany. In 1516 he began his own activity together with his brother Ambrosius, first in Basel and then in Lucerne (1517–19). The effects of a study trip to Lombardy are recognizable in his works and confirmed by the half-figure females based on Leonardo and his first portraits, which already stand apart because of the force of their psychological penetration and the sharp rendering of the physical reality of the figures. Most of the works Holbein painted during the 1520s are of a religious character; he also made cartoons for stained-glass windows and engravings. His first visit to England took place in 1526–28, favored by the support of the humanist Thomas More. It was followed by new frescoes in Basel and a trip to Italy, during which Holbein saw portraits by Lotto. The effects of the Reformation and the almost complete disappearance of patronage for religious art in the German lands convinced Holbein to move to London, which he did in 1531. In 1536 (year of Henry VIII's marriage to Jane Seymour) he became the favorite portraitist of the king and his court and the English intellectual aristocracy. He died in 1543 of the plague.

JAUME HUGUET
(Valls, Tarragona, 1414– Barcelona 1492)

Sharp observer of reality, Huguet refused to adopt the Flemish style and insisted on the use of the old technique of tempera with gilt backgrounds. His first work probably took take place in the province in the city of his birth, one of the main Renaissance art centers of southern Germany. Aragon and most of all Saragossa; in 1448 he moved to Barcelona, where he married in 1454 and was active until 1487. The retable of *Saints Abdon and Sennen* (Santa Maria, Terrassa), made between 1458 and 1461, is the best of what remains of the artist, with a fine melancholy expressed in the subtle figures of the titular saints. His later works show the increasing participation of assistants. The shiny brocades and jewels, the heavy gold backgrounds, and the gleaming scrolls and gemmed borders are prime examples of the tendency to overwrought decoration typical of the Aragon court. Huguet's style became widespread in the vast Aragonese dominion, in Catalonia, and even in Corsica and Sardinia. Even so, after reaching this level the Barcelona school fell into a long period of obscurity and silence.

JACOMART (JAIME BAÇO)
(Valencia 1410–1461)

Favorite painter of Alfonso V of Aragon, who called him *"el nostro leal maestro Jacomart,"* he worked in Valencia until 1442, when he left for Naples, where he exercised a notable influence on the painters of the time, among them Colantonio. He returned to Valencia in 1445, but in 1446, called by Alfonso (who was on a military campaign), he returned to Italy, this time to Rome. Despite his relationships with Italy, his training remained tied to the Flemish tradition. His only documented work is the retable for the parish church of Catí, which he was commissioned to make in 1460, one year before his death, and which he made with the important collaboration of his follower Juan Rexach; the works usually attributed to him, such as the St. Ann Retable in the collegiate church of Játiva, and the panels in the cathedral of Valencia with *St. Benedict* and *St. Ildefonsus,* denote a fine sensibility and a very personal interpretation of Flemish formulas.

JACOPO DELLA QUERCIA
(Siena ca. 1371–1438)

Son of a goldsmith, the great sculptor Jacopo della Quercia had a rebellious temperament and led a disordered life. In 1401 he took part in the competition for the Baptistery doors in Florence, but soon found himself out of sorts in the Florentine environment. He therefore became active over a wide range of central Italy, working in Lucca, Siena, Ferrara, and Bologna, his work presenting an elegant middle ground between the refined drapery surfaces of the late Gothic and the monumental synthetic sense typical of humanistic culture. His last works, the powerful relief panels for the portals of San Petronio in Bologna, have often been interpreted as anticipating the style of Michelangelo.

JUAN DE FLANDES
(Ghent? ca. 1450–Palencia 1519)

This artist of south Netherlandish origin arrived in Spain by way of Italy, where he presumably had gone in the retinue of Justus of Ghent. In 1496 he entered the service of Isabella the Catholic, a great patron and promoter of Flemish art. He made a retable with scenes of the life of Christ

Biographies

for her, known as the *Oratorio de la Reina Católica*. This polyptych, today dismembered, was composed of forty-six panels, twenty-seven of which have survived. With the queen's death in 1504, Juan de Flandes, spent a short time in Salamanca, where he made the St. Michael Altarpiece in the cloister of the old cathedral and the main altar in the chapel of the university. He then moved to Palencia, where he was active until 1519. His paintings are distinguished by the analytical meticulousness typical of the Flemish tradition and have a delicate luminist and chromatic sensibility.

JUSTUS OF GHENT
(Joost van Wassenhove)
(documented from 1460 to 1475)

The scarcity of biographical information does nothing to diminish the importance of this artist, who was a direct link between the Flemish school and the international setting of Urbino, with an important branch in the direction of Spain by way of Pedro Berruguete. Originally from Antwerp, Justus spent the years of his training and early activity in Ghent (triptych of the *Crucifixion* in the cathedral), working alongside Hugo van der Goes and taking his name from the city. In 1471, in the service of Duke Federico da Montefeltro, he was involved in the decoration of the Ducal Palace in Urbino. Applying experimentally Piero della Francesca's rules of perspective, Justus made the great panel of the *Communion of the Apostles* (for which Paolo Uccello made the predella), and, together with Berruguete, made the sequence of busts of *Famous Men* for the duke's *studiolo*.

ADAM KRAFT
(Nuremberg 1455/60–1508/09)

During the period in which German wood sculpture saw its greatest flowering, Adam Kraft stands out as a sculptor in stone and marble. Active in the city of Nuremberg, the true cultural capital of the German Renaissance, Kraft revealed knowledge of the daringly virtuosic language of the late Gothic, as displayed in the excellent and capricious ciborium in the church of St. Lawrence. However, the works he made after 1500 show a tendency toward a more majestic and concentrated compositional rhythm: typical, in that sense, are the great panels with high-relief scenes of the *Seven Stations of the Cross*, made for the church of St. Sebaldus.

FRANCESCO LAURANA
(Zara ca. 1430–Avignon? ca. 1502)

Probably originally from La Vrana near Zara (hence his name), Laurana was the principal sculptor active in southern Italy in the fifteenth century. Trained in the sphere of the Adriatic culture (perhaps in the circle of Giorgio Orsini da Sebenico), he stood out as the leader in the decoration of the Arch of Triumph in the Castel Nuovo in Naples (1453–58), a large-scale group effort made with Aragon patronage and still insertible in the tradition of the taste of the Gothic court. After a long stay in France (1461–66), during which he seems to have worked primarily as a medalist, he moved to Sicily. He worked in a characteristic style, composed of simple, smooth volumes of great purity, best suited perhaps to idealized female portraits. He returned to Naples and stayed there until 1477, ending his career in Provence, where his undertakings included the ancient cathedral of Marseilles and a dramatic marble altarpiece with *Christ Carrying the Cross* that is today in the church of Saint-Didier in Avignon.

LUCIANO LAURANA
(Zara ca. 1420–Pesaro 1479)

Example of a late fifteenth-century Italian "court" architect, Luciano Laurana was probably in Naples at the end of the 1450s; in 1465 he was in Mantua, where he came in contact with Leon Battista Alberti. His absorption of central Italian humanistic culture showed up the next year, when he moved to Urbino. Luciano Laurana became the principal designer of the Ducal Palace, where he worked until 1472, following the instructions of his patron, Federico da Montefeltro, while developing his own independent and ingenious style based on the application of mathematical ideas introduced by Piero della Francesca.

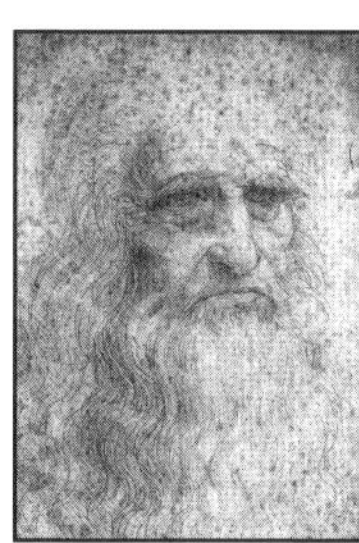

LEONARDO DA VINCI
(Vinci, Florence, 1452–Cloux, Amboise, 1519)

Leonardo's artistic training took place in Florence, in the multifaceted workshop of Verrocchio; this youthful experience would help determine his many interests in various artistic and technical applications, each of which involved the necessary exercise of design. After his debut as a collaborator of Verrocchio, Leonardo began his own independent activity, early on showing his predisposition for portraiture and the investigation of nature. At thirty, in 1482, he left Florence for the court of Ludovico il Moro in Milan, where he spent much of his career. Painting and writing notebooks (the "codices") were two different but complementary aspects of Leonardo's creativity, for he was open to the most diverse fields of interest. The *Virgin of the Rocks* (begun in 1483, today in the Louvre) and the *Last Supper* (1494–98) date to his early period in Milan. With the arrival of French soldiers, he left Milan for Mantua and then Venice. On his return to Florence he began work on the *Mona Lisa* and continued the technological, geographical, and scientific studies he had started in Milan. He returned to Milan in 1506 and completed the *Virgin and Child with St. Anne*, today in the Louvre. Finally, in 1513 he accepted the invitation of the French king Francis I and moved to Amboise, bringing with him several paintings, thousands of pages of drawings and notes, and a crowd of students.

POL, HERMANN, AND JEAN DE LIMBOURG
(Nijmegen, end of fourteenth cent.–Dijon 1416)

Active in France in the early fifteenth century, the Limbourg brothers brought about a true revolution in the field of manuscript illumination. Trained in Paris in the workshop of a goldsmith and under the tutelage of their uncle, the well established painter Jean Malouel, around 1402 they were working in the service of Philip the Bold, duke of Burgundy, and after his death they were active in the court of Jean, duke of Berry. The most talented was probably Pol, who became close to the duke of Berry and in 1413 was named his *valet de chambre*. As early as their first works, a Bible illuminated in 1402 for Philip the Bold and the *Belles Heures*, the Limbourg brothers demonstrated a firm knowledge of the most modern Flemish and Italian artistic concepts, although also tied to the meticulous aesthetics of the French tradition. With the great full-page miniatures of the *Très Riches Heures*, begun in 1413, they left the most conspicuous document of their extraordinary talent, particularly reflected in the pages of the *Months*, where the casually posed figures of peasants and the rigid poses of courtly nobles animate landscapes that were at that time the vastest created in miniatures. All three brothers probably died in the plague that struck Dijon in 1416.

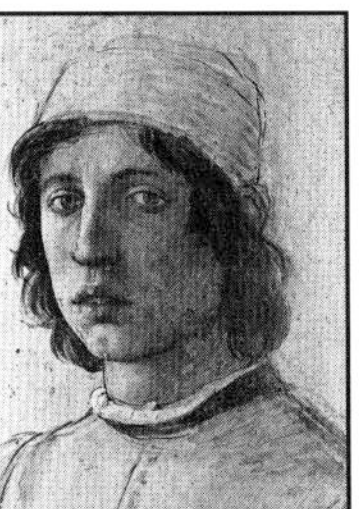

FILIPPINO LIPPI
(Prato ca. 1457–Florence 1504)

Son of Filippo Lippi and Sister Lucrezia Buti, Filippino was an authentic *enfant prodige*; assistant to his father from an early age, he was hardly over twelve years of age when his father died, but was already competent enough to complete the frescoes in the cathedral of Spoleto and then to begin working with Botticelli, beginning a long and fruitful period of collaboration. The first certain works by Filippino are distinguished by a sweet restlessness of the line, which uses sinuous rhythms to create firmly controlled designs. The early years of the 1480s were of great importance to Filippino's independent career, for it was in that period that he made highly important works in Florence, including the completion of the frescoes by Massaccio and Masolino in the Brancacci Chapel (ca. 1485). In 1488, through the intervention of Lorenzo the Magnificent, he was called to Rome to fresco the Carafa Chapel in Santa Maria sopra Minerva. On his return to Florence, he saw with great clarity the crisis in humanism caused by the death of Lorenzo the Magnificent (1492) and the preaching of Savonarola. His painting became bizarre, fantastic, increasingly tense and hallucinatory.

FILIPPO LIPPI
(Florence ca. 1406–Spoleto 1469)

A link between Masaccio and Botticelli, Filippo Lippi entered the Florentine scene early in the 1430s. Among his first works are the frescoes in the convent of Santa Maria del Carmine, where he had taken his vows a few years earlier. In 1434 Filippo enlarged and sweetened his artistic culture with a stay in Padua and perhaps a trip to Flanders. Having become a stable point of reference in Florentine culture, Filippo began in 1441 the monumental *Coronation of the Virgin* (today in the Uffizi), followed by numerous altarpieces made in keeping with the perspec-tive canons of Domenico Veneziano but also distinguished by a delicate realism in the details and expressions that had an effect even on Leonardo. With his well organized workshop he moved in 1452 to Prato, where he made the frescoes in the cathedral choir and other works. The long stay in Prato is related to the scandal caused by his relationship with the nun Lucrezia Buti, mother of his son, Filippino. When he returned to Florence he obtained prestigious commissions such as the *Nativity* for the Medici chapel in Palazzo Medici, today in Berlin. It was on a commission from the Medici that he began what would prove to be his last work, the frescoes in the Spoleto cathedral choir.

FERNANDO LLANOS
(active in Spain from 1506 to 1525)

Along with Fernando Yáñez, Llanos was the most important exponent of Renaissance trends in Valencia. He came in contact with the work of Leonardo da Vinci, very probably during a trip to Italy before 1506, the year in which he worked with Yáñez in the cathedral of Valencia, beginning a long artistic association that lasted until 1515. Between 1506 and 1507 the two artists made for the cathedral the retable of *Saints Cosmas and Damian* and the doors of the main retable, repeating stylistic and compositional traits from Leonardo and the serene balance of Raphael. Yáñez's works have more spectacular architecture that do those of Llanos, and his elegant figures are more serene, whereas Llanos is more nervous, his figures are more expressive, presented in everyday relationships. After 1515 Llanos continued to work in the cathedral of Valencia on works of less quality. His activity is known until 1525, when he is mentioned for the last time, working in the service of the cathedral of Murcia.

STEFAN LOCHNER
(Meersburg ca. 1410–Cologne 1451)

Stefan Lochner is the most representative figure of the lively artistic climate in Cologne at the middle of the fifteenth century, when the cultural horizon of Germany began to open to Flemish and Italian innovations. Born and trained on Lake Constance, he undertook a youthful trip to the Low Countries, where saw the works of Jan van Eyck and Robert Campin. He moved to Cologne around 1437 and became the central figure in the local, flourishing painting school. In 1447 he joined the town council, the most prestigious and representative organism of Cologne. Lochner followed the tradition of the "soft" style in the typology of his Madonnas, with thin, oval faces and elegant, well measured gestures. In his masterpiece, the *Patron Saints of Cologne* altarpiece in the cathedral of Cologne, the use of a gold background and the minutely detailed presentation of the fabrics and jewels reflect the aristocratic status of his patron. Lochner, however, joined these traditional elements to a sympathetic description of the figures and a Flemish-style attention to natural reality, creating a harmonious and personal style that was highly esteemed by Albrecht Dürer.

Biographies

PHILIBERT DE L'ORME (Delorme)
(Lyon ca. 1510–Paris 1570)

French architect of the High Renaissance, leader during the central phase of the sixteenth century and the period of the "castles of the Loire," Philibert de l'Orme had an important period of training in Rome between 1533 and 1536. He thus acquired a solid sense of classical proportions, but he did not give up on a subtle, elegantly decorative vein, which he expressed most of all during the years of the reign of Henry II (1547–59). He worked on the châteaux of Anet, Chenonceaux, and Fontainebleau, and designed the monumental tomb of Francis I in Saint-Denis. During the 1560s he wrote treatises that served as true manuals during the long period of classical French architecture.

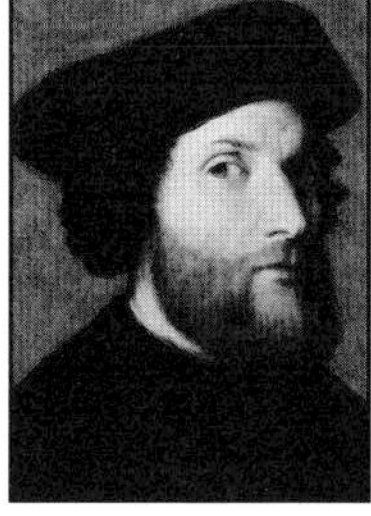

LORENZO LOTTO
(Venice ca. 1480–Loreto 1556)

After apprenticeship, probably with Giovanni Bellini, Lorenzo Lotto soon revealed a personal and independent vein, in which references to northern painting and homage to the pre-Giorgione Veneto tradition flow together. After an initial stay in the Marches, he was called to Rome to paint the Stanze Vaticane with Raphael. Lotto was deeply troubled by this experience of contact with the great masters of the mature Renaissance. He returned to the Marches and then found himself welcomed in the area around Bergamo. He remained in Bergamo from 1513 to 1525, painting several altarpieces, portraits, and fresco cycles (including those in the oratory of the Villa Suardi in Trescore from 1524). He also provided the cartoons for the intarsia panels of Santa Maria Maggiore. During these years Lotto elaborated a highly personal style, blending a diverse range of cultural elements (Gaudenzio Ferrari, Correggio, Pordenone). In 1525 he returned to Venice and made stupendous portraits, but he found little opportunity in terms of patrons for religious paintings. In the 1540s he returned to the Marches and found peace in the solitude of the Loreto sanctuary.

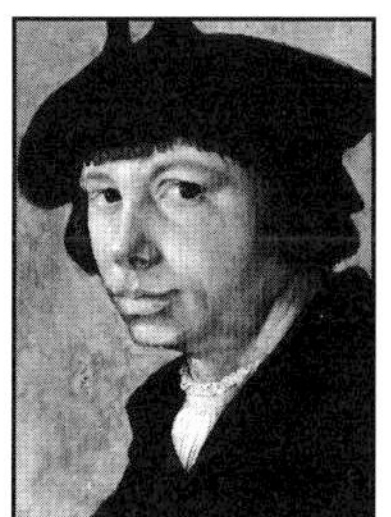

LUCAS VAN LEYDEN (Lucas Hugenszoon)
(Leiden 1489/94–1533)

Gifted with an extraordinary natural talent for drawing, Lucas trained in the Dutch city of Leiden in the workshop of Cornelis Engebrechtsz, the best local artist at the end of the fifteenth century. Lucas was not yet twenty when he made his debut as an engraver, and his work immediately put him on a level of technical skill, inventive power, and graphic sureness that could be compared only to Albrecht Dürer. Along with prints of biblical subjects Lucas also made early "genre" subjects, scenes of people and situations drawn from the daily life of peasants. This double aspect of Lucas's art also appears in his pictorial work, which combined the ability to rework the iconographic tradition along with the desire to introduce themes that anticipate seventeenth-century realism by almost a century. His style shows something of the Romanist style of nearby Antwerp but is more strongly related to the German Renaissance and the limpid, rich humanism of Dürer, with whom Lucas established a firm friendship. The great triptychs that he made during the later phase of his career, such as the *Worship of the Golden Calf* in Amsterdam and the *Last Judgment* in Leiden, are particularly eloquent. In 1527, in the company of Jan Gossart, he embarked on a ship for a trip along the regions of Flanders, Zeeland, and Brabant. He returned to Leiden seriously ill and was bedridden for much of the last six years of his life, afflicted with tuberculosis.

BERNARDINO LUINI
(Luino, Varese, ca. 1485–Milan 1532)

The origins of this leader of the Lombard Renaissance art of the early sixteenth century are still wrapped in uncertainty. The first certain news of the artist dates to 1512, when Bernardino Luini made a *Virgin and Child Enthroned with Two Angels* for the abbey of Chiaravalle. The painting denotes a pictorial language already consolidated and mature, inspired by the physiognomic solutions of Leonardo, but already diluted by a classical perfection in the forms, a calibrated balance of the proportions, and a gamut of colors in somber and restful tonalities. Aside from exquisite devotional works on panel, the art of Luini was fully displayed in the many commissions he received from churches in Milan and Lombardy in general. He also made a notable production of frescoes in patrician villas, works that gave him the opportunity for pleasant periods of rural life.

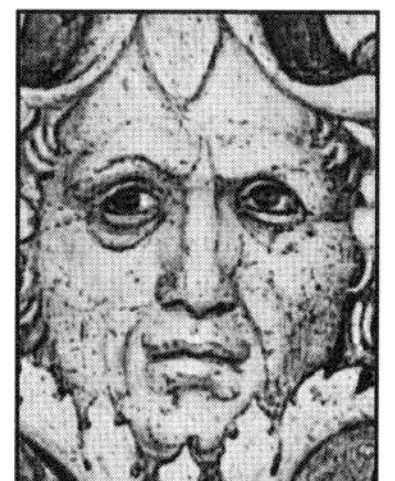

ANDREA MANTEGNA
(Isola di Cartura, Padua, 1431–Mantua 1506)

Mantegna had the great fortune to enter the eclectic workshop of Francesco Squarcione in Padua in the same years when such masters as Donatello and Paolo Uccello were also in the city. His career moved ahead rapidly, helped by his attraction to certain aspects of humanism, most of all linear perspective and interest in archaeology. The frescoes in the Ovetari Chapel of Padua were followed, in 1451, by his marriage to Nicolosia, Giovanni Bellini's sister, a relationship that involved him with the principal family of Venetian artists. The altarpiece in the basilica of San Zeno in Verona (1457–59) marks the end of his youthful period; in 1460 he moved to Mantua to assume the position of court painter. He spent the rest of his life living and working in the city of the Gonzaga court, the only exception being a brief stay in Rome (1489–90) for study. The Camera degli Sposi is the most striking and complete image of his style, supported by an analytic ability and skilled draftsmanship. Even in advanced age and despite his relationships with Giovanni Bellini and, later, with Leonardo, he never adopted the techniques of tonal coloring and shading, preferring until the end a lucid, infallible visual precision.

MASACCIO
(Tommaso di Giovanni Cassai)
*(San Giovanni Valdarno,
Florence, 1401–Rome 1428)*

In all the history of art, no other artist who died at the age of only twenty-seven has had as profound effect on art as Masaccio. He began his career in the provinces, with the triptych of the church of San Giovenale a Cascia di Reggello (1422), and went on to Florence, where he was in close contact with Masolino. The two painters made together the altarpiece of the *Virgin and Child with St. Anne* in the Uffizi (1424) and began a cycle of frescoes destined to change the course of the history of painting: the Brancacci Chapel in Santa Maria del Carmine. Masaccio concentrated on the expressive force of the figures, solidly placed in urban or landscape settings. Masaccio confirmed these gifts also in the works he did alone, such as the great polyptych with gold background for the Church of the Carmine in Pisa (1426; the panels are dispersed among various museums) and the impressive fresco of the *Trinity* in the basilica of Santa Maria Novella in Florence (1427). At the end of 1427 Masolino and Masaccio rejoined to take on a series of commissions in Rome; shortly afterward, in circumstances not clear, Masaccio died.

MASOLINO (DA PANCIALE)
(Tommaso di Cristofano Fini)
*(Panciale in Valdelsa
1383–Florence 1440)*

Student of Ghiberti, master of Masaccio, creator of important works from Florence to Lombardy and from Umbria to Rome, Masolino appeared on the scene of Tuscan painting early in the 1420s with works in Florence and Empoli. In 1424 he began his artistic association with Masaccio, the culminating episode of which was the Brancacci Chapel in Santa Maria del Carmine. In 1425 he interrupted his work in Florence to leave for Hungary, in the retinue of Cardinal Branda Castiglione, who then invited him to Rome in 1428 to fresco his private chapel in the basilica of San Clemente with the *Stories of St. Catherine of Alexandria*. Several important panel paintings date to these Roman years, while the wonderful fresco of the *Virgin and Child* in the church of San Fortunato in Todi dates to 1432. In 1435, once again called by Cardinal Branda Castiglione, Masolino went to Lombardy, to Castiglione Olona, where he frescoed the choir of the collegiate church, various rooms in the cardinal's palace, and the spectacular room of the baptistery.

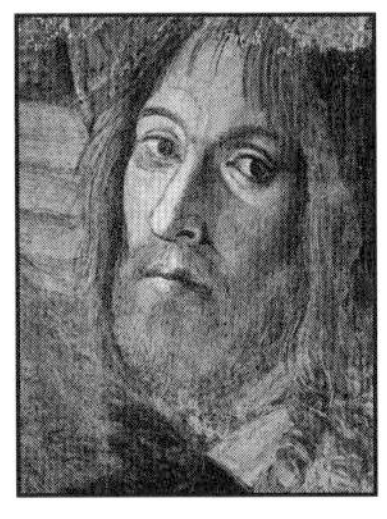

MELOZZO DA FORLÌ (Melozzo di Giuliano degli Ambrogi)
(Forlì 1438–1494)

The activity of Melozzo took place first in Forlì, under the primary influence of Piero della Francesca. In 1469 he was in Rome, where he made a banner that is still preserved in the basilica of St. Mark's; in the 1470s he was busy in the cosmopolitan court of Urbino. In 1475 he returned to Rome, this time with highly prestigious commissions. Between 1475 and 1477, having been named by Sixtus IV to the position of *pictor papalis*, he painted the fresco decoration of the Biblioteca Apostolica; all that remains is the noble celebratory scene, today in the Pinacoteca Vaticana. Giuliano Della Rovere (future pope Julius II) involved him in the reworking of the basilica of the Santi Apostoli, of which he frescoed the apse with the *Christ Blessing*; fragments of this majestic composition remain in the Quirinale and in the Pinacoteca Vaticana. Around 1484, by then supported by an efficient workshop, Melozzo frescoed the chapel of the treasury of the sanctuary of Loreto. He was later active between Forlì, Rome, and Ancona, but not a trace of these works remains, and the frescoes he made in the Forlì church of San Biagio were destroyed in 1944.

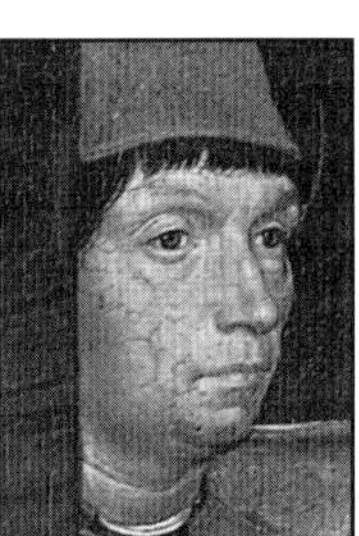

HANS MEMLING
(Seligenstadt ca. 1440–Bruges 1494)

Originally from Germany, having been born in a small town near Mainz, Memling, during his youth, studied the works of the school of Cologne, known for an elegant interpretation of reality. He moved to Flanders and served a period of apprenticeship in the workshop of Rogier van der Weyden. After Van der Weyden's death, in 1464, he moved to the wealthy city of Bruges. While the star of Petrus Christus was setting, Hans Memling filled an important empty space, creating a series of impressive of devotional paintings and portraits. His met with immediate success with works that reflect a sophisticated and idealized cul-ture. He reworked the basic elements of the great Flemish tradition that had preceded him, creating a harmonious and measured language in which all sense of tension or excess is replaced by an imperturbable formal perfection.

QUENTEN METSYS
(Quinten Metsijs)
(Louvain 1466–Antwerp 1530)

Metsys got his artistic training in his birthplace and made his debut as a painter at a relatively late age, but spent his youth in the climate of the last season of the Flemish "primitives." He joined Antwerp's guild of painters in 1491 and in a short time became the leading member of the local school. He received many commissions from the artisan guilds of Antwerp and Louvain. At some point during the first decade of the sixteenth century he took a trip to Italy, during the course of which he must have visited Milan and Venice and seen some of the works of Leonardo. This contact with humanistic culture also led to his increased intellectual involvement. In 1517 he met Erasmus and Thomas More, and he had more intense contacts with Holbein, Lucas van Leyden, and Dürer, aside from a friendship with Patinir.

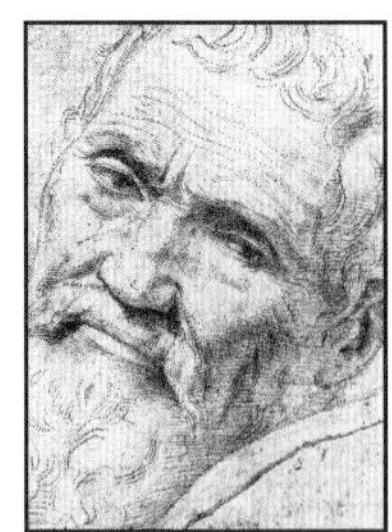

MICHELANGELO BUONARROTI
(Caprese, Arezzo, 1475–Rome 1564)

The greatest marble sculptor of all time, as well as a painter and an architect,

Michelangelo was the critical conscience of the Renaissance at the moment of its apogee and was thus an attentive witness of its crisis; he dominated the sixteenth century in Europe and has become its emblematic figure. Involved from his youth in the exciting artistic climate in Florence during the period of Lorenzo the Magnificent, with the rediscovery of the classical past, Michelangelo created the *Pietà* in St. Peter's in Rome before the year 1500, and shortly after made the *David* in the Accademia in Florence. During the first decade of the sixteenth century he dedicated himself repeatedly to painting, first in Florence, where he competed with Leonardo in the decoration (lost) of Palazzo Vecchio and made the *Doni Tondo*, and then in Rome, where at the request of Pope Julius II he began the undertaking of the vault of the Sistine Chapel, a dramatic synthesis of the history of man and also a celebration of the beauty and wonder of creation. After this undertaking, which he worked on almost without interruption from 1508 to 1512, Michelangelo abandoned painting for more than twenty years, dedicating himself to sculpture and architecture (Sagrestia Nuova of San Lorenzo in Florence, then in Rome with the dome of St. Peter's and the plaza of the Campidoglio). He returned to his brushes in the 1530s for the long creation of the *Last Judgment* in the Sistine Chapel. In his old age he followed this "awesome" masterpiece with two more marble versions of the *Pietà* (Museo dell'Opera del Duomo, Florence, and Castello Sforzesco, Milan).

ANTONIS (VAN DASHORST) MOR
(Utrecht ca. 1520–Antwerp 1576)

Also known by the name of Antonio Moro, which he used most of all in his intense relationships with the Spanish crown, Mor was one of the most famous northern European portraitists of the late sixteenth century. The cold self-possession of his figures made him an ideal interpreter of the suspicious arrogance of the international elite aristocracy. Student of Van Scorel, and directed toward the Italian style from the beginning of his training, Mor enrolled in the Antwerp painters' guild in 1547. A born traveler, he moved often among the courts of Madrid, Lisbon, and London, inheriting the role of Holbein and competing with the uninterrupted success of Titian's portraits in Spain. He was in Rome in 1550–51, adding further to the wide range of his cultural learning. He spent the latter part of his life more stably in his homeland, alternating stays in Utrecht and Antwerp and specializing in the genre of the portrait, with a characteristic cold manner, impersonal, of extreme nobility.

LUIS DE MORALES
(Badajoz ca. 1510–1586)

The art of the most influential Spanish painter of the High Renaissance was strongly marked by Italian, in particular Lombard, elements; in fact, his soft rendering of chiaroscuro is so reminiscent of Leonardo that some critics posit a short visit by the artist to Italy. Flemish influences were also decisive to his artistic formation, as indicated by the way he accentuates the expressions of pathos in his versions of the *Ecce Homo* and his Virgin and Childs, so much so that he anticipated the mystical exaltations of seventeenth-century Spanish art. He was summoned to the court of Philip II but spent only a very short time there, perhaps because his popular taste did not satisfy the king's refined sensibilities. Although he was highly esteemed, ranked among the leading artists of his day, and called *el divino* because of the mystical idealization of his works, Luis de Morales died poor. The enormous popularity of his works spread his form of iconography over a wide range, such that it had large echo in Spanish religious painting of the seventeenth century.

MORETTO (DA BRESCIA)
(Alessandro Bonvicino)
(Brescia ca. 1490–1554)

In the absence of confirmed information concerning Moretto's date of birth or training, his biography begins in 1515 with works that reveal a certain dependence on the style of Romanino. In paintings dating to the 1520s, however, Moretto already demonstrates that he had shifted his attention toward Titian and Lorenzo Lotto. His later production takes shape around an increasingly erudite and classical-minded style, and because of this his style clearly set him apart from the other leaders of the Brescian school. He showed a progressive tendency toward realism, and he translated models based on Titian's Pesaro Altarpiece in the pleasant key of daily domestic reality. Moretto reached the height of his production in his last works, which are large-scale religious paintings already in keeping with the guidelines for religious art presented by the Council of Trent.

GIOVANNI BATTISTA MORONI
(Albino, Bergamo, 1520/24–1578)

Moroni was one of the greatest and also timid portraitists of the sixteenth century. He trained in Brescia under Moretto and then spent nearly his entire career in the area of Bergamo, becoming heir to the Lotto tradition. During that time he did make two visits to Trent (1548 and 1551), during the period of the religious council, to paint various works, and he was in contact with the Madruzzo family and with Titian.

MASTER OF MOULINS
(probably Jean Hey or Jean Prévost)
(active in Moulins from 1475 to 1500)

The identification of the creator of a group of works (*Triptych of the Virgin in Glory* in the Moulins Cathedral, a *Nativity* in Autun, and several portraits) is still the subject of controversy, and he is known simply as the Master of Moulins. He was active at the court of Peter II, duke of Bourbon, in the last quarter of the fifteenth century; the most widely accepted theory today is that he was Jean Hey. His works show the influence of Fouquet in the plastic vigor with which the figures are inserted in space; but the perfect elegance, lightness of clothes, and graceful poses of the orderly rows of angels to the sides of the Virgin recall the medieval tradition. The Master of Moulins was also a sensitive and up-to-date portraitist.

HANS MULTSCHER
(Reichenhofen ca. 1400– Ulm 1467)

Painter and sculptor of southern Germany, he was the link between the solemn season of the Burgundian sculpture of Claus Sluter and the age of the wonderful wooden German altarpieces. His *Christus Patiens (Schmerzensmann*, 1430) in the cathedral of Ulm, is based on models from Sluter, but is at the same time charged with a new realistic pathos. The same cathedral held other works by Multscher, but they were seriously compromised by the wave of Protestant iconoclasm. His most complex work, also in terms of its combination of painting and sculpture, was almost certainly the winged altarpiece in the parish church of Vipiteno in the South Tyrol (1458), broken up into several fragments, of which the painted wings remain in the city.

NICCOLÒ DELL'ARCA
(Niccolò d'Antonio d'Apulia)
(Bari 1435/40–Bologna 1494)

This Puglia-born artist was named for his most prestigious work, the decoration of the ark, or tomb, of St. Dominic in the church in Bologna of that name, an extraordinary sculptural complex begun by Nicola Pisano to which other artists contributed, including even the young Michelangelo. A marble sculptor but most of all a sculptor in terracotta, Niccolò was active exclusively in Bologna, putting together widely different stylistic ideas, from Jacopo della Quercia to Claus Sluter and demonstrating an impressive albeit eclectic figurative culture that embraced the late Gothic as much as Tuscan humanism. His activity can be divided into two distinct stylistic categories: there are the controlled and refined classical-style cadences that prevail in the statues for the tomb in St. Dominic (1469–73), but then there is the dramatic realism of the group of terracotta statues of the *Pietà* (Santa Maria della Vita, Bologna), a work on which he unleashed an expressive violence that has few equals in European art of the late fifteenth century.

MICHAEL PACHER
(Brunico ca. 1435–Salzburg 1498)

The most original and atypical figure of German art in the late fifteenth century, Pacher was born in the Tyrol, a region on the border of the Holy Roman Empire that was an important crossroads between the east and the west, the north and the south of the Alps. Pacher was probably born in Brunico, in the Val Pusteria, and like many other artists of his generation he was both painter and sculptor, a double talent that found its full expression in impressive winged altarpieces. The Tyrolean artist's pictorial production was rooted in the northern European tradition, blending Rhenish and Flemish examples, and Pacher's youthful trips for artistic training probably took him as far as Flanders. Even so, he was particularly attentive to the profound changes taking place in the world of art and early on in his career he had come into contact with Italian art. Sometime around 1460 he was in Padua, where he admired the works of Donatello, Andrea Mantegna, and Paolo Uccello. The multiplicity of these stimuli produced an extraordinary effect: the northern elements blended with a distinctly Italian sense of perspective and volumes, resulting in a style that is as unmistakable as it is isolated.

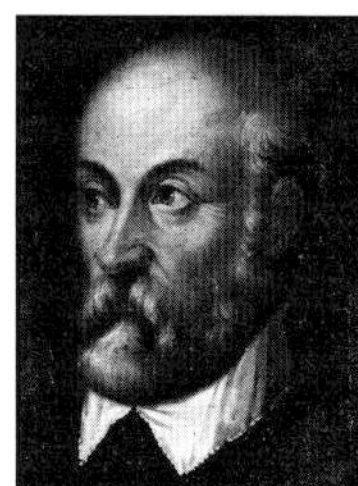

ANDREA PALLADIO
(Andrea di Pietro della Gondola)
(Padua 1508– Maser 1580)

After learning the rudiments of sculpture in Padua, in 1523 Andrea moved to Vicenza, which became his adopted city. In 1537, nearly thirty years old, he was noted by Giangiorgio Trissino, an alert intellectual, very much aware of current literary, philological, and architectural matters, who gave him the classical-style name Palladio and opened the way for his astonishing career. Between 1538 and 1543 Trissino and Palladio took part in archeological campaigns, first in the Veneto and then in Rome, on the Latian hills, in the Phlegraean Fields. The most typical period of Palladio's production began in 1542–43 with the solid Villa Godi-Malinverni at Lonedo di Lugo, north of Vicenza. Palladio became the symbolic architect of the Vicenzan aristocracy, the absolute leader of the renewal of the city in its private palaces and public buildings, including, beginning in 1546, the reworking of the façade of the basilica. In 1556 he took part in the foundation of the Accademia Olimpica in Vicenza, and in the same period on the outskirts of the city he designed Villa Almerico-Valmarana, the much imitated "Villa Rotonda," followed by, among others, the Villa Pisani of Mira and the Villa Barbaro in Maser. In 1570, at the death of Jacopo Sansovino, Palladio assumed the role of official architect for Venice and moved to that city. In November of that same year he published his *Four Books of Architecture*, the fundamental text for the spread of Palladianism. In Venice he was kept busy primarily with church architecture (San Giorgio Maggiore, Il Redentore). His last work was the Teatro Olimpico in Vicenza. The work was still in progress when Palladio died, on August 19, 1580; the theater opened five years later thanks to the efforts of Vincenzo Scamozzi.

PALMA GIOVANE (Jacopo Negretti)
(Venice 1544–1628)

Left as the sole heir to the great Venetian Renaissance, Palma Giovane maintained the characteristics of its style for a long time, becoming the most popular painter in Venice. His complex training included a prolonged stay in Rome (1567–74) and attendance in Titian's workshop, whose unfinished *Pietà* he completed. After his involvement in the decoration of the Doge's Palace with Veronese and Tintoretto, Palma immersed himself in Venetian tradition, painting between 1580 and 1590 cycles of canvases for the *scuole* or for religious sites (the sacristies of San Giacomo in Orio and of the Gesuiti, the Scuola di San Giovanni Evangelista, the oratory of the Crociferi). Because of their intelligent comprehension of Tintoretto and their fluid narrative vein, these were his best works. He then returned to his official commissions in the Doge's Palace,

Biographies

assembling around himself a vast workshop, thanks to which he produced an enormous and somewhat monotonous series of religious and allegorical paintings that were distributed throughout the territory of Venice.

PALMA VECCHIO (Jacopo Negretti)
(Serina, Bergamo, ca. 1480–Venice 1528)

Typical exponent of the charming artistic current of masters from the Venetian mainland, Palma represented the version "moderated" by the rapid evolution of painting in Venice. Born near Bergamo, he moved to Venice in 1510 and went into two distinct areas of production, making altarpieces for the churches of Venice and the Veneto region and canvases distinguished by seductive female figures for the art market. The recurrent traits of Palma Vecchio's painting include diffuse light, serene compositions, clear and sonorous colors, and atmospheres of calm splendor. The sweetness of his half-figure females and his secular paintings in general made its way into his religious works, which are often distinguished by the presence of appealing female figures.

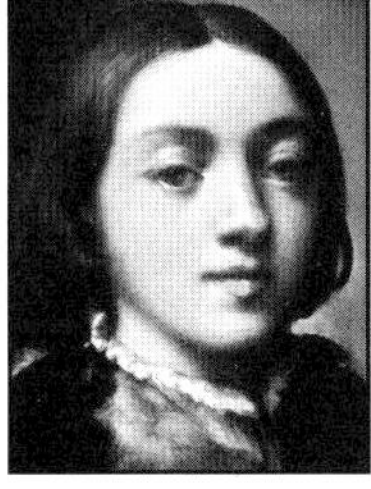

PARMIGIANINO (Francesco Mazzola)
(Parma 1503–Casalmaggiore 1540)

Intense, icy, and intellectual, Parmigianino created a stylistic counterpoint to Correggio, such that during the 1520s and 1530s he turned the city of Parma into one of the most advanced laboratories of sixteenth-century art. Gifted with precocious talent, Parmigianino immediately compared himself to Correggio, offering an up-to-date style based on nascent mannerism. He was only twenty when he painted his first important work, the frescoes of *Diana and Actaeon* in the Rocca Sanvitale of Fontanellato. In 1524 he went to Rome and became involved in the swirling artistic milieu of the papal court of Clement VII. The results of this trip include portraits of a sharp, refined clarity and religious paintings with a strong mannerist influence. Following the Sack of Rome he spent several years in Bologna, returning to Parma in 1531. He then made the frescoes in the church of Santa Maria della Steccata, which are inspired by a stylized and sophisticated classicism. A typical expression of this period is the unnatural elongation of the figures, which assume serpentine poses. In the last years of his short life Parmigianino closed in on himself, thoroughly dedicated to alchemical experiments.

JOACHIM PATINIR
(Bouvignes or Dinant ca. 1485–Antwerp 1524)

Dürer, who knew him well, called Patinir *ein gut Landschaftmaler* ("a good landscape painter"). Extraordinary views over panoramas that open out toward far distant horizons, with fantastic combinations of twisting rocks and stretches of water constitute the most dramatic aspect of the production of Joachim Patinir, truly an authoritative representative of the Antwerp school.

Originally from the French-speaking area of Belgium, Patinir may have received his artistic training in Bruges, under Gerard David, and he arrived in Antwerp in 1515. At some point in his early career he undoubtedly had the chance to see and admire the work of Bosch, whose visionary style he repeated along with the ability to create absolutely fantastic scenes making use of thoroughly realistic details. Patinir soon rose to the top of the Antwerp guild of painters and formed close ties with the leading Antwerp masters, in particular with Quenten Metsys, sometimes asking him to paint the figures in his works, an aspect that he found less important, if not irrelevant. Patinir's works, so advanced and courageous in terms of their landscapes, are in fact mediocre in terms of the figures, which appear for the most part simple pretexts to justify the spectacular panoramic scenes, played out in dense tones of blue and green.

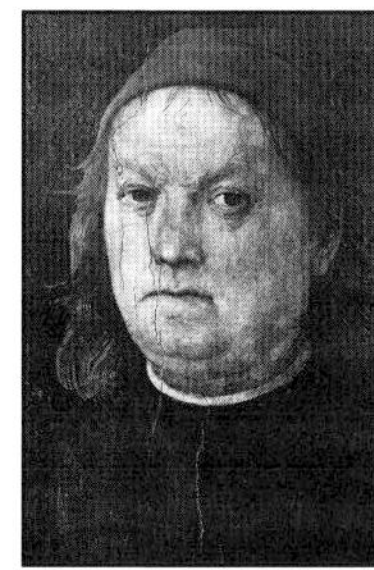

PERUGINO (Pietro Vannucci)
(Città della Pieve ca. 1450–Fontignano 1523)

Perugino trained in Florence, first as a student of Verrocchio and then under Botticelli and finally Leonardo. Early on he stood out for his sweet and elegant style, always controlled, without forced expressions. In 1481 Pope Sixtus IV called him to Rome to participate in the decoration of the Sistine Chapel; he then worked on various Florentine commissions, making altarpieces, frescoes, and portraits. Soon he assembled a repertory of gestures, expressions, and costumes that he reused repeatedly for his entire career, his style undergoing no substantial evolution. During the last decade of the fifteenth century the very youth Raphael was a member of Perugino's workshop; the principal undertaking of those years was the decoration of the Collegio del Cambio in Perugia, made between 1496 and 1502. After 1500, Perugino's painting began to move out of the center of the artistic debate, and the painter wisely chose to limit his activity to work in the provinces.

PIERO DELLA FRANCESCA
(Sansepolcro, Arezzo, 1416/17–1492)

Piero occupies a central position in fifteenth-century Italian and European art. A member of the second generation of humanistic painters, he achieved full concordance between art and geometry, between the calculated application of the rules of perspective and poetic expression. Piero's training took place in Florence. In 1439 he worked alongside Domenico Veneziano on a cycle of frescoes (almost completely lost). Except for this youthful period, almost all of Piero's activity took place in the "provinces" (Sansepolcro, Arezzo, Rimini, Ferrara, Urbino, Perugia), not in Florence. During the 1440s he alternated periods of work in Sansepolcro with stays in other cities, among them Rome; in Ferrara he came in contact with Leon Battista Alberti and perhaps also with the Netherlandish artist Van der Weyden. In 1452 he began work on what would prove to be the most important undertaking of his career, the frescoes with the *Legend of the True Cross* in the church of San Francesco in Arezzo. Most of his work in the 1460s took place in Urbino, at the court of Duke Federico da Montefeltro. Aside from some memorable works, the period in Urbino was important because of the close contact it offered to international artists and with the development of his studies on geometry, perspective, and algebra, gathered in important treatises. Around the middle of the 1470s, Piero was forced to quit painting because of eye problems. He returned to Sansepolcro and dedicated himself to mathematical studies and the completion of his treatises. By a curious coincidence, the artist most emblematic of the intellectual world of the fifteenth century died on October 12, 1492, the day that Columbus stepped ashore in the New World.

PIERO DI COSIMO
(Florence 1461/62–1521)

A singular personality in the Florentine school during the period of transition between the fifteenth and sixteenth centuries, Piero di Cosimo adopted the name of his master, Cosimo Rosselli, under whom he got his training and who involved him at an early age in the decoration of the Sistine Chapel (1482). Piero followed this prestigious debut with a quietly successful career, full of important works marked by heterogeneous cultural references: the clear light of the Dutch, the expressive charge of Leonardo, the nervous instability

of Filippino Lippi. Very few of Piero di Cosimo's paintings have remained in Italy; most are today in international museums, such as the interesting cycle of historical and mythological scenes of the life of primitive humanity, painted for the Dal Pugliese family during the last decade of the fifteenth century and dispersed among various museums. At the beginning of the sixteenth century Piero di Cosimo increased his style's eccentricity, further distancing himself from the contemporary artistic scene while making evocative compositions that are "outside time."

FRANZ ANTON PILGRAM
(Brno 1460–Vienna after 1515)

Pilgram made the last, imaginative, and virtuosic works of the final stage of Gothic, after the year 1500, between Austria and his native Moravia. After early activity in southern Germany as an architect and sculptor of church furnishings, Pilgram spent a long time in Brno, where he built and decorated churches and monumental portals. In 1511 he moved to Vienna, where he was put in charge of the building of St. Stephen's Cathedral. Here, in addition to presenting himself, compass in hand, in two carved self-portraits, he made his two most famous works: the organ loft in the left nave and the pulpit with the effigies of the evangelists (completed in 1515).

GERMAIN PILON
(Paris 1528–1590)

The son of an artist, Pilon got his early training from his father, André, and became one of the out-

standing sculptors of the French Renaissance. Like almost all the master artists of mannerism in the age of Francis I, he dedicated much of his career to working in Fontainebleau, where he was active alongside Primaticcio. As the royal sculptor, he made official works in marble and bronze (and some in wood, today lost), including the tomb of Henry II in Saint-Denis (finished in 1570) and the urn for the king's heart, today in the Louvre. Aside from architectonic decorations (reminiscent of the style of Primaticcio) and monumental groups made with finely finished surfaces, Pilon was also the creator of incisive portrait busts.

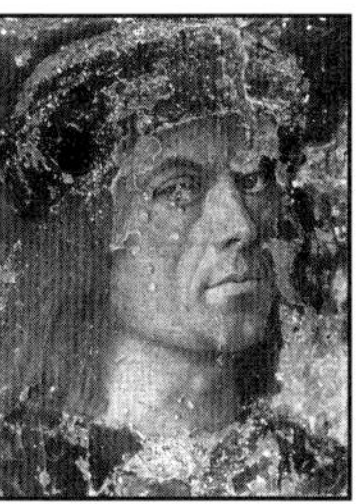

BERNARDINO PINTURICCHIO (Bernardino di Betto)
(Perugia ca. 1454–Siena 1513)

Fascinating master of large-scale decoration, Pinturicchio created some of the most pleasant ornamental solutions of the Renaissance in Umbria and Rome. Trained in the lively artistic school of Perugia in the mid-fifteenth century, he soon entered the workshop of Perugino, becoming his principal collaborator, first in the *Miracles of St. Bernardino of Siena* (1473; Galleria Nazionale dell'Umbria, Perugia) and then in the prestigious undertaking of the Sistine Chapel (1481). He then began his independent career, which was divided between Perugia and Rome, where he left his most important works, such as the frescoes in Santa Maria d'Aracoeli and Santa Maria del

Popolo and, most of all, the papal apartment of Alexander VI in the Vatican (1492–95). All these works reveal his interpretation of the Roman wall decorations found during the archaeological excavations of the period. On his return to Umbria, Pinturicchio painted altarpieces and frescoes, among which stand out those of the Baglioni Chapel in Spello (1501). Pinturicchio's masterpiece was the splendid fresco decoration of the Libreria Piccolomini, annexed to the cathedral of Siena (1505).

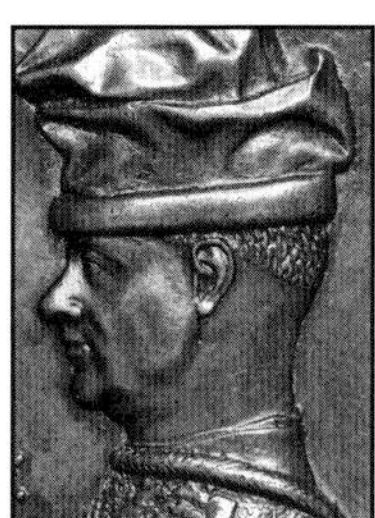

PISANELLO (Antonio Pisano)
(Verona ca. 1395–Mantua 1455)

With all probability born in Verona, son of a merchant from Pisa (hence his name), Pisanello trained in the Veneto, first in Verona and then in Venice, soon coming in contact with Gentile da Fabriano, who became his close collaborator in the period 1418–20. Still associated with Gentile, Pisanello was in Florence in 1423. Reflections of this experience, although projected onto a late Gothic stylistic current, can be seen in Pisanello's first known works, in Verona. Following the death of Gentile (1427), Pisanello was called to Rome to complete the frescoes left unfinished by that master in St. John Lateran. On his return north, he began a successful career among the aristocratic courts, alternating pictorial cycles with the creation of medallions and other activities typical of a court painter. Aside from the frescoes on chivalric subjects in the Ducal Palace of Mantua, Pisanello also made portraits during his stay in Ferrara. The most important surviving work by Pisanello is the great scene of *St George and the Princess of Trebizond* (1436–38) in the Verona church of Sant'Anastasia. Following this masterpiece Pisanello seems to have substantially abandoned painting, occupying himself primarily with the creation of stupendous celebrative medallions for the Neapolitan court. After the middle of the fifteenth century his celebrity declined rapidly in the face of the spread of the figurative culture based on linear perspective. It seems most likely that Pisanello died in Mantua, where his position as court painter was a few years later taken by Andrea Mantegna.

ANTONIO DEL POLLAIUOLO
(Antonio Benci)
(Florence ca. 1431–Rome 1498)

Artist of notable technical and stylistic eclecticism, Antonio alternated activity as a sculptor in bronze and goldworking with engraving and painting, in each case, however, showing a preference for agitated and dramatic animation, which he expressed through a minute and energetic graphic line. Most of his work in Florence was as a goldworker and pungent painter, already open to the kind of secular and mythological subjects later to attract popularity; following his move to Rome he worked primarily as a monumental bronze sculpture. The tombs of popes Sixtus IV (1484–92) and Innocent VIII (1492–98) in St. Peter's were part of the large-scale program of artistic and cultural rebirth of the papal see. Antonio, known as "*del pollaiuolo*" ("of the poulterer") because of his father's modest occupation, was sometimes assisted by his less energetic brother Piero (Florence 1443–Rome 1496).

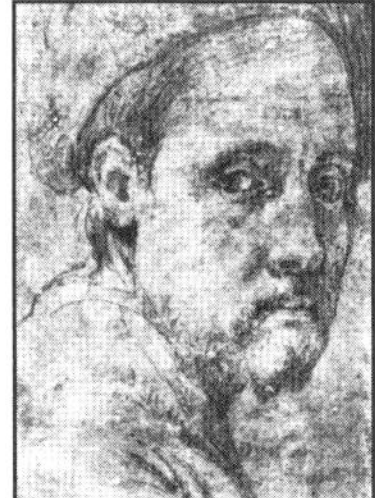

JACOPO DA PONTORMO
(Jacopo Carucci)
(Pontorme, Florence, 1494– Florence 1557)

An unusual and tormented artist, unsatisfied, truly ingenious and courageous but given to fits of anguish, Pontormo was the leader in the change in Florentine painting from the High Renaissance to the period of mannerism. After complex training that ended with experience under Andrea del Sarto, he made his debut with the frescoes in Santissima Annunziata, which already revealed hints of novelty. Soon attracted by Michelangelo and by the prints of northern artists, Pontormo achieved such great fame that around 1520 he was receiving official commissions. The frescoes of the charterhouse of Galluzzo (1523–25) and the decoration of the Capponi Chapel in Santa Felicita (1525–26) reveal his use of new expressive effects along with a great tension. After the siege of Florence (1529) Pontormo closed in on himself, and the last years of his life were occupied with dramatic and unfortunate undertakings (the frescoes in the choir of San Lorenzo, destroyed in 1762; the cartoons for tapestries rejected by the duke) that further aggravated his existential melancholy.

PORDENONE
(Giovanni Antonio de' Sacchis)
(Pordenone ca. 1483– Ferrara 1539)

Pordenone, the most important Friulian painter of the Renaissance, was active over a vast area of northeastern Italy. After training in the mainland Venetian tradition, he debuted around 1510 with works in Friuli; a trip to Rome gave him the opportunity to study the works of Michelangelo and Raphael, while the circulation of prints of Dürer gave him new compositional ideas. After the execution of the frescoes in the Malchiostro Chapel in the cathedral of Treviso, he took on the colossal commission of frescoing the central nave of the cathedral of Cremona (1520–22). The theatrical and virtuosic drama of the Cremona frescoes is repeated by his later works, both in Friuli (Spilimbergo, Pordenone) and in Venice, while around 1530 he returned to the Lombard area, working in Piacenza and Cortemaggiore. Reinforced by new stimuli drawn from Gaudenzio, Correggio, and Parmigianino, in the last years of his life he openly rivaled Titian, with whom he competed for artistic supremacy in the Venetian territories. The contest ended suddenly with Pordenone's tragic and mysterious death during a trip to Ferrara early in 1539.

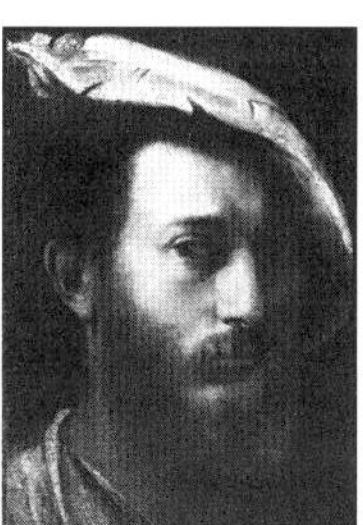

FRANCESCO PRIMATICCIO
(Bologna 1504– Paris 1570)

Involved in the workshop of Giulio Romano in Mantua, Prima-ticcio distinguished himself in the decorations of the Ducal Palace and Palazzo Te, revealing talents not so much as a painter as a highly original creator of friezes in stucco, and not only ornamental friezes but also those with a narrative development, complementing the frescoes. In 1532 he moved to Fontainebleau and entered the service of Francis I. Together with Rosso Fiorentino he designed and decorated the gallery of the château, a work of up-to-date intellectualism. At the death of Rosso Fiorentino (1540) he was made general director of the artistic works. With the exception of two brief returns to Italy, he spent the rest of his career and life in France. He suffered a period of eclipse during the reign of Henry II (1547–59), but later returned to favor and fame, replacing Philibert de l'Orme in the official post of royal architect.

ENGUERRAND QUARTON
(also called Enguerrand Charonton)
(Laon ca. 1415–Avignon ca. 1466)

Active in the south of France (Aix, Arles, and Avignon) between 1444 and 1466, Quarton played a decisive role in the rebirth of Provençal art. His authorship of the *Coronation of the Virgin by the Holy Trinity* and the *Madonna of Mercy* (Musée Condé, Chantilly) is unquestioned; uncertainties surround the attribution of the *Pietà* of Avignon. Characteristics of this artist are the rigor of the construction based on a tripartite scheme, the sobriety of the style, and the monumental treatment of the figures, qualities not unlike those of the outstanding Italian models, from Fra Angelico to Piero della Francesca. The stylization of forms, reduced to essential volumes, the balance of volumes, and the violent light that highlights the cheekbones of faces make Quarton an ingenious creator who was working in advance of his time, in some ways anticipating the art of Cézanne.

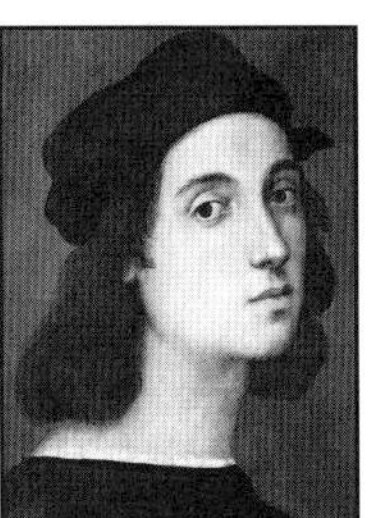

RAPHAEL
(Raffaello Sanzio)
*(Urbino 1483–
Rome 1520)*

Raphael, son of the portraitist and painter Giovanni Santi, while still an adolescent drew attention to his father's workshop because of his talents; at sixteen he was already an independent master. He began his career in the artistic culture of Urbino in the wake of Piero della Francesca, and around 1500 he joined Perugino in a close and critical collaboration. His Florentine period (1504–08) was also distinguished by his ability to absorb and rework ideas from other artists. In dialogue with Michelangelo and Leonardo, the still young artist achieved a supreme balance between the correct application of the rules of Renaissance art, the imitation of nature, and the sweetness of expression. In 1508 Pope Julius II called him to Rome and entrusted him with the fresco decoration of the rooms of his private apartment in the Vatican. The cycle began with the Stanza della Segnatura (1508–11) and continued with that of Eliodoro (1511–13), with a progressive passage from harmonically imposed scenes within symmetrical backgrounds to more dramatic episodes, with plays of evocative light. Raphael also made altarpieces, portraits, and frescoes. During the papacy of Leo X he was kept busy with decorative works (the loggias in the Vatican, La Farnesina), and he once again changed his style, anticipating the themes and solutions of coming mannerism.

LIGIER RICHIER
*(Saint-Mihiel ca. 1500–
Lausanne 1567)*

The essential background to the career of this great and tormented Lorraine-born sculptor was his long apprenticeship in Rome, from 1515 to 1520, during which he studied Michelangelo. On his return to the area of his birth he began working for increasingly demanding and important patrons. In 1531 and in 1540 he made two dramatic monumental groups of the *Deposition from the Cross* for the churches of Saint-Mihiel (the first in the abbey church, the second, more complex, for the church of St. Stephen), in which a still Gothic skill is blended with a total domination of the material and most of all with the energetic sense of a tormented present. Around 1544 Ligier made his best known work, the tomb of René de Châlons, Prince of Orange, with the decomposing corpse that grips the heart torn from its chest, today in the church of St. Peter in Bar-le-Duc, a work that marked the point of contact between the medieval *danses macabres* and the coming baroque Triumphs of Death. A few years later Richier sculpted in white and black marble the tomb of Philippa of Guelders, second wife of René II, duke of Lorraine, preserved in the church of the Cordeliers in Nancy. After carving the great altar in Bar-le-Duc, Richier embraced the Protestant Reformation. He practically quit work and, in 1564, he moved to Lausanne, where he died three years later.

TILMAN RIEMENSCHNEIDER
*(Osterode ca. 1460–
Würzburg 1531)*

A versatile and dynamic artist, Riemenschneider is considered the greatest German wood sculptor of the Renaissance. He came away from his apprenticeship, spent in both Saxony and Bavaria (Erfurt, Ulm), with equal skills in working stone, marble, and wood. In his production, he was able to easily alternate materials, sometimes with extraordinary results, as in the alabaster monument of Emperor Henry II, in the cathedral of Bamberg, and in the spectacular wooden altars of Rothenburg and Creglingen. Characteristic of the style of the sculptor is the exaltation of the tactile and chromatic values of the materials, left in evidence in their natural colors, without recourse to the usual gilding or polychromy. Riemenschneider's career was uneven, with periods of great fame (marked by the success of his large workshop in Würzburg and official commissions) alternating with periods of obscurity. Involved in the popular movement of the Reformation, he was arrested and forced to stop working.

LUCA DELLA ROBBIA
(Florence ca. 1400–1482)

Founder of a large family of sculptors and decorators, in the middle of the artistic world of Florentine during the first half of fifteenth century, Luca della Robbia chose the route of a noble and quiet classicism, which he first revealed around 1440 in the highly successful genre of polychrome glazed terracotta. The conventional image of his work as serene white-and-blue Madonnas is misleading. Luca della Robbia was an up-to-date and powerful sculptor, in constant dialogue with Ghiberti and Donatello. With the marble choir gallery for the Duomo of Florence, begun in 1433, Luca revealed his efforts to achieve a sensitive, elegant balance. For the worksite of the same cathedral he made panels for the bell tower and for the bronze doors of the sacristy, surmounted by lunettes in glazed terracotta. He applied this highly refined and innovative technique (handed on to later generations of followers) not only in a series of splendid Madonnas but also to monumental groups.

GIROLAMO ROMANINO
(Gerolamo Romani)
(Brescia ca. 1484/87–1562)

Leader of the Brescian Renaissance, Romanino got his training in both the Milanese and the Veneto artistic cultures. The influence of Titian is apparent in the large altarpiece he made in Padua (1513), and it reappears in the no less spectacular *Virgin and Child Enthroned with Saints* in the church of San Francesco in Brescia (1517). From 1517 to 1519 he worked on the decoration of the cathedral of Cremona, later being replaced by Pordenone. Between 1521 and 1524 he made the cycle of canvases

Biographies

in the chapel of the Santissimo Sacramento for the church of San Giovanni Evangelista in Brescia, marked by a solid, human, at times even coarse realism. This was followed by a series of altarpieces and frescoes in Brescia and the surrounding area, always centered on the direct presentation of reality. In 1531 he went to Trent to makes frescoes in the Buonconsiglio Castle. He followed this prestigious undertaking with another group of frescoes, these in Valcamonica, which have an expressive force that reaches levels of caricature.

ROSSO FIORENTINO
(Giovan Battista di Jacopo)
(Florence 1495– Fontainebleau 1540)

Leader of the first and fundamental period of Florentine mannerism, Rosso trained together with Pontormo in the workshop of Andrea del Sarto and made his debut with them in the frescoes of the choir of the Servites in Santissima Annunziata. His sketches often had bizarre, even diabolical features ("a sort of savage and desperate air," in the words of Vasari) that perplexed patrons. The *Deposition from the Cross* (1521) that he painted in Volterra is emblematic in this sense, with the violent deformity of the figures and the colors, almost disconcertingly aggressive. Rosso's style went through a rapid evolution, moving in the span of a few years and by way of several important works from the original Florentine influence (Pontormo and Andrea del Sarto) to the Roman of Michelangelo, and he then competed with Parmigianino. After the Sack of

Rome (1527) his style mixed flashes of bitterness with a certain increased sweetness that was more pleasing to his official patrons. In 1530 he moved to Paris; for Francis I he made the spectacular gallery in the royal château at Fontainebleau (1532–37), a work of fundamental importance to the spread of mannerism in Europe.

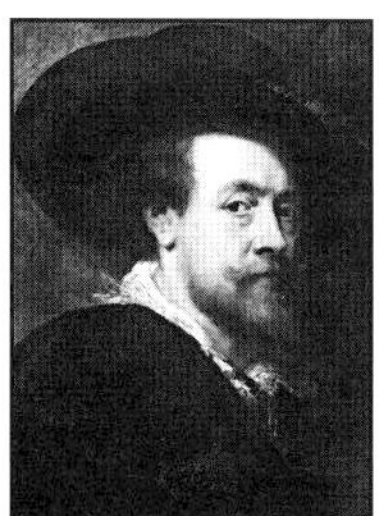

PETER PAUL RUBENS
(Siegen 1577– Antwerp 1640)

Rubens learned the rudiments of art in Cologne, but his true training took place in Antwerp. In 1598, at nineteen, he enrolled in the Guild of St. Luke, and two years later he left for Italy. He absorbed much about the history of art, copying ancient masters to imitate their style; there were also Holbein, Lucas van Leyden, and Dürer, the inevitable points of reference for a northern artist. To them he added Raphael, Michelangelo, Correggio, Tintoretto, Leonardo and, most important of all, the great Titian. Rubens studied classical antiquity and moved toward the style of Caravaggio. On a salary from the duke of Mantua, Rubens stayed in Italy until 1608, often traveling between Genoa and Rome. He returned to Antwerp and conquered the heights of the local school with the marvelous works he made for the cathedral. After his marriage to Isabelle Brandt, Rubens enlarged his pretty house in Antwerp, transforming it into a palace-atelier. Rubens's workshop became the great forge of the baroque, through which all the

most important Flemish artists of the seventeenth century passed. In 1620 he began traveling among the great capitals of Europe (Paris, Amsterdam, Madrid, London), and by then he was without doubt one of the most celebrated men in Europe. During the last years of his life, always distinguished by a constant stream of paintings, Rubens enjoyed the economic fruits of his career as a major artist, dividing his time between his splendid home in Antwerp and the castle of Steen.

MASTER OF THE SAINT BARTHOLOMEW ALTAR
(documented in Cologne from ca. 1470 to ca. 1510)

This highly original artist was among the outstanding artistic personalities in Cologne at the end of the fifteenth century, but little is known of his life and career—he is named for a masterpiece from his maturity, today preserved in Munich—leaving much to be clarified. He was probably born in the Low Countries (there are clear ties to the art of Arnhem and Utrecht) and went to Cologne around 1470. He kept in contact with the artistic scene in Flanders, aware most of all of the works of Hugo van der Goes. He had such a fecund relationship with the charterhouse of Cologne that some believe he may himself have been a Carthusian friar. Using a moving and vigorous style he expressed his desire to create works of great breadth, with a monumental layout that completely surpasses the courtly tradition of the preceding generation. The minute description of details and of precious fabrics is

joined to a profound and sympathetic religious sensibility that gives religious scenes an extraordinary immediacy, further helped by a skillful use of perspective, unknown to his predecessors.

MASTER OF SAINT VERONICA
(active in Cologne from 1395 to ca. 1425)

As is the case with many German masters of the fifteenth century, the identity of this painter is unknown. His conventional name derives from that of his best known work, a painting of St. Veronica today in Munich. He moved to Cologne, perhaps around 1400, after a period of apprenticeship in Dortmund in the workshop of Conrad von Soest. Putting together stimuli from Franco-Flemish painting, he worked out a personal language that interpreted sacred subjects with great freedom and religious sensibility. His skillful use of color, formal skills, and the subtle modeling of his figures make his paintings among the most important of the period.

FRANCESCO SALVIATI
(Francesco de' Rossi)
(Florence ca. 1510–Rome 1563)

Trained in Florence but almost always active in Rome, Salviati was the champion of the second generation of mannerism, when the style, having lost the subversive force of its first interpreters, became the official style of central Italian painting. Salviati took mannerist decoration to levels of supreme elegance, with a meticulous attention to classical citations in secondary friezes and in human anatomy inspired by Michelangelo. His cold, sharp light exalted outline designs, achieving results of sophisticated abstraction and great virtuosic skill. Salviati took part in all the laboratories of mannerist decoration in Rome, such as the oratories of the Gonfalone and San Giovanni Decollato, the convent of San Salvatore al Lauro, and Palazzo Sacchetti. His trips to Venice (1539–41) and France (1555–57) were of great importance to the diffusion of mannerism, as was his long stay in Florence (1543–49), during which he frescoed the Sala d'Udienza in Palazzo Vecchio.

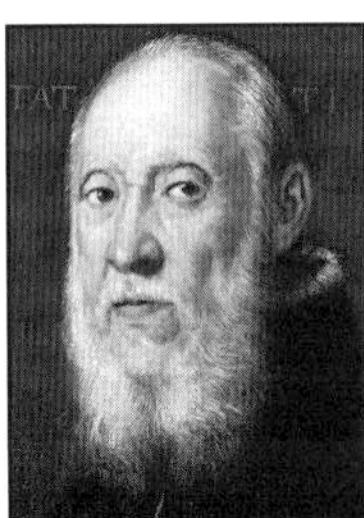

JACOPO SANSOVINO (Jacopo Tatti)
(Florence 1486– Venice 1570)

One of the leaders in sculpture and architecture in Venice for many decades, Sansovino was among the greatest interpreters of the broad, serene, and solid classicism of the High Renaissance. Most of his early works in Florence were marble sculptures, comparable to the model of Andrea Sansovino, from whom he took his name, and related to the youthful works of Michelangelo. It was during the course of a long stay in Rome (1516–27) that he moved more decidedly toward architecture. He fled Rome after the sack of that city in 1527, planning to go to France, but almost by accident he stopped in Venice, which became his adopted city. Involved in the renovation of the city promoted by Doge Gritti, he soon became the city's official architect and as such

the author of buildings of great symbolic value, in the most important sites of the city (Procuratie, Loggetta del Campanile, Libreria Marciana, the interior of the Doge's Palace, the Mint). Although most of his activity was as a designer, Sansovino also worked as a sculptor in Venice, showing a preference for bronze with creations anticipating themeticulous works of mannerism.

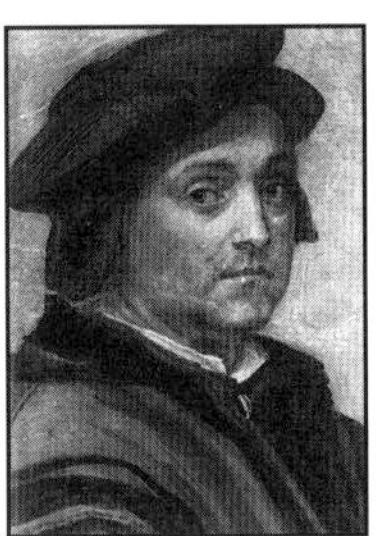

ANDREA DEL SARTO (Andrea d'Agnolo)
(Florence 1486–1530)

Faithful heir of the great Florentine tradition of the late fifteenth century, Andrea del Sarto updated it in a pleasing way and with great breadth, but without moving on to the audacious polemics of the early mannerists, many of whom were in fact his students. After training with Piero di Cosimo, Andrea opened his own independent workshop in Florence in 1508 and immediately found activity in the cycle of frescoes in the cloister of the Servites in Santissima Annunziata. After a trip to Rome, where he met Raphael and saw the works of Michelangelo and Sansovino, he began the highly original monochrome decoration of the cloister of the Scalzo, a fundamental text for the development of Florentine design in the early sixteenth century. The *Madonna of the Harpies* (Uffizi, Florence), from 1517, preceded a brief stay in France, in the wake of Leonardo and in advance of Rosso Fiorentino. His style became increasingly devotional over the course of the 1520s,

with important experiments in color; the masterpiece of this period is the *Last Supper* in the Convent of San Salvi in Florence.

GIOVANNI GIROLAMO SAVOLDO
(Brescia 1480/85–ca. 1548)

The most sophisticated sixteenth-century Brescian painter, known for his skilled use of light and reflections, Savoldo has been justly called the direct predecessor to the painting of Caravaggio. Although Savoldo spent almost all life in Venice, it is best to see him as a member of the Brescian school, both because of his relationship with patrons in that city and because of his unquestionable relationship to the realism and delicate psychological interpretations of the Renaissance in Brescia (Romanino, Moretto) and Bergamo (Lotto and later Moroni). Savoldo began working in the Veneto around 1520, but his earliest works are uncertain. His production included altarpieces, portraits, and paintings of religious subjects made for private patrons; these he sometimes repeated in several versions. In this period the painting of Savoldo was illuminated by flashes of light, vivid colors, and silvery effects. This luminosity tended to diminish over the course of the 1530s, as Savoldo worked to achieve more delicate landscapes imbued with an intimate and melancholy poetry.

MARTIN SCHONGAUER
(Colmar ca. 1450–Breisach 1491)

Born in Alsace to a family of goldsmiths and artists, Schongauer

completed his training in contact with the art of the Low Countries. During a stay in Cologne he saw the Columba Triptych by Van der Weyden, and after studies at the university of Leipzig he took a trip to Burgundy. He thus came to abandon the gestural sense of the late Gothic in favor of a classical serenity, making essential compositions in which the human and poetic element rises to the fore. Despite Schongauer's importance as a painter, his fame is tied to his activity as an engraver. With artisan skills and extraordinary manual dexterity he created works in which the broken and moving line transmits a strong sense of solidity with a three-dimensional effect. His engravings spread immediately and formed a repertory of motifs and models on which many artists drew inspiration, including Michelangelo. Even Dürer, who was destined to take the technique of engraving t o its greatest heights, felt himself indebted to the older Schongauer. In 1492 Dürer began a trip to Alsace to visit Schongauer, but when he reached Colmar the master was already dead, leaving unfinished the cycle of frescoes with the *Last Judgment*.

JAN VAN SCOREL
(Schoorl, Alkmaar, 1495– Utrecht 1562)

Named for the town in which he was born, Van Scorel trained in nearby Alkmaar and completed his youthful training with stays in Amsterdam and Utrecht (1517–19), where he studied painting with Jan Gossart. Before setting himself up in Haarlem, he traveled through

Europe, his lengthy itinerary eventually spanning four years and taking him all the way to Palestine. Important stops were in Nuremberg, where he met Dürer; Venice; and most of all Rome, where he arrived during the pontificate of the Dutch pope, Adrian VI. In Rome Van Scorel absorbed motifs from Raphael and Michelangelo and served the pope as director of Vatican antiquities. Back in Holland, he made use of his cultural experience to create a painting style in keeping with the nascent mannerism. In this sense it is interesting to note that Venetian elements (from Giorgione and Titian) appear in his works in place of the fantasy settings of Patinir and Bosch.

SEBASTIANO DEL PIOMBO
(Sebastiano Luciani)
(Venice ca. 1485–Rome 1547)

A figure of enormous interest and a leading artist in two European capitals (Venice and Rome), Sebastiano was in touch with all the leading artists of the first half of the sixteenth century (Giorgione, Titian, Raphael, Michelangelo), creating a personal style of robust appeal. His first works date to around 1510, the period of transition between the warm harmony of Giorgione and the aggressiveness of Titian. It was Titian's success that induced him to move to Rome in 1511, where he became involved alongside Raphael in the frescoes in La Farnesina. In that way he began his role as mediator between the color of the Venetian style and the expressive style of the Roman school, most of all Michelangelo,

of whom Sebastiano del Piombo became the trusted friend, even using a drawing by Michelangelo in the large altarpiece with the *Raising of Lazarus* (1519; National Gallery, London), painted in competition with the *Transfiguration* by Raphael. Sebastiano stayed in Rome after the sack (1527), for which (in 1531) he was given the post of Keeper of the Papal Seals, known as the *Piombo* ("lead"), hence the nickname by which he is today known. This highly remunerative position had an effect on his activity as a painter, which seems to have diminished.

LUCA SIGNORELLI
(Cortona ca. 1445–1523)

Student of Piero della Francesca in Arezzo and then a follower in Florence of Pollaiuolo, Luca Signorelli completed his training with a stay in Urbino. In 1482 he was in Rome, collaborating with Perugino on the frescoes in the Sistine Chapel, and contact with Perugino led him to soften his style. He then moved to Florence, becoming a leader in the cultural setting around Lorenzo the Magnificent. After Lorenzo's death, Signorelli left Florence to take on two large and memorable fresco cycles, the *Legend of St. Benedict* in the cloister of the monastery of Monte Oliveto Maggiore, near Siena (1496–98), and the fearsome *End of the World* in the San Brizio Chapelin the cathedral of Orvieto (1499–1504). Signorelli spent the last two decades of his career almost entirely in the provinces, between Cortona and Città di Castello.

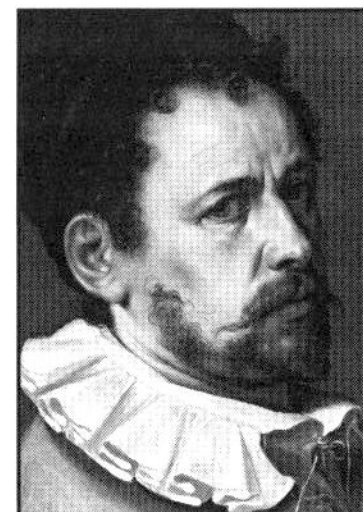

BARTHOLOMÄUS SPRANGER
(Antwerp 1546–Prague 1611)

Spranger received his initial training in Antwerp, a city permeated by the Italian-style taste of the High Renaissance. In 1565 he took a trip to Italy, along the way encountering the mannerist school of Fontainebleau; in Italy, he visited Milan, Parma, and Rome. He absorbed stimuli from the Lombard artistic culture, saw the art of Correggio and Parmigianino, and was offered prestigious commissions from the Farnese family, thus immersing himself in the meticulous style of Roman mannerism. He did this so well that in 1570 he was named official painter to the pope. Spranger showed a preference for themes from mythology and literature, using a style of learned sophistication in which intellectuals could take delight in deciphering the many artistic and literary references; in these works he also succeeded in transmitting a sort of frigid sensuality, as apparently detached as it was provocative. He entered the service of Emperor Rudolf II, working first in Vienna and then, beginning in 1581, in Prague. Other artists there included Arcimboldo, Joseph Heintz, and Hans von Aachen, aside from Milanese masters of intaglio and goldworking. Made popular as engravings, Spranger's paintings with erotic and mythological backgrounds became famous throughout Europe, contributing to the international status of the mannerist style.

VEIT STOSS
(Nuremberg? 1437/47–Nuremberg 1533)

A product of the brilliant artistic life of Nuremberg, Stoss specialized in the execution of large wooden altarpieces. When still young he was accused of forgery, branded on both cheeks, and expelled from the city. In Cracow in 1477 he began work on the immense altarpiece with the *Death of the Virgin* for the church of St. Mary. It took him twelve years to complete the work. Using the preferred limewood, Stoss laid out the most colossal version of the fifteenth-century *Theatrum Sacrum*. After other works in wood and marble in Cracow (tomb of Casimir IV Jagellon in the cathedral), in 1496 he was pardoned and returned to Nuremberg, where he made important sculptures in a moving and expressive style. In a climate effected by the presence of Dürer, Stoss put a partial brake on his habitual whimsy and also took up painting. Working for Italian patrons, he sent important wooden sculptures to Florence. His last winged altarpiece, dedicated to the life of the Virgin (1518), is in the cathedral of Bamberg.

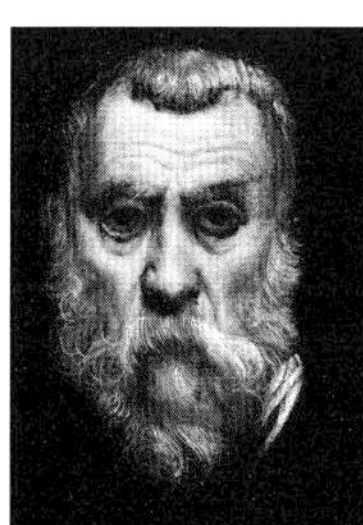

TINTORETTO
(Jacopo Robusti)
(Venice 1519–1594)

The spectacular *St. Mark Rescuing the Slave* (1548, Gallerie dell'Accademia, Venice) marks Tintoretto's eruption onto the artistic scene of Venice, which saw him become an alternative to the great Titian. While maintaining the traditional Venetian taste for color and light, Tintoretto introduced grand gestures, muscular bodies, and daring perspective views of the mannerist type. Not intimidated by even the most colossal of undertakings, he began in 1564 the decoration of the Scuola di San Rocco, a work that he returned to repeatedly over the years, thus revealing the evolution of his style. From crowded, magniloquent scenes he passed to compositions with an intense expressiveness, finally arriving at the late, astonishing visionary scenes on the ground floor. In 1577, as the director of an efficient workshop, Tintoretto took over direction of the work redecorating the Doge's Palace, an undertaking that ended in the enormous canvas of the *Paradise* for the Sala del Maggior Consiglio. After the deaths of Titian and Veronese, the elderly Tintoretto wrapped his last works, such as the *Last Supper* in San Giorgio Maggiore, in mystery and magic.

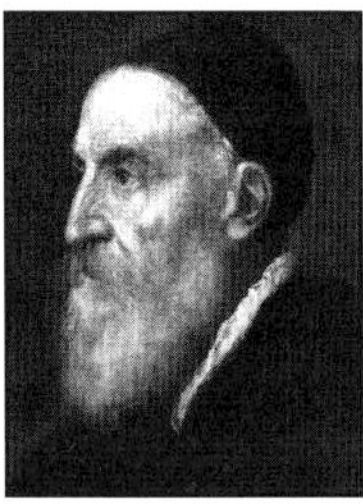

TITIAN
(Tiziano Vecellio)
(Pieve di Cadore, Belluno, 1488/90–Venice 1576)

Student of Bellini and involved from an early age in Giorgione's workshop, Titian quickly took over leadership of the Venetian school thanks to the formidable richness of the colors and the dynamism of his compositions. In 1516 he became the republic's official painter, a position he held until his death, sixty years later. In 1518, with the bacchanals for Alfonso d'Este, duke of Ferrara, he began his activity for the noble courts. This was soon followed by works for the Gonzaga court and, later, for the Della Rovere and Farnese families. In 1530 Titian came in contact with Emperor Charles V, who became his most prestigious patron. Titian's palpable dynamism went through a brief pause around 1540, when he faced the works of the mannerists. A trip to Rome (1545–46) to update his art culminated in a meeting, not without polemics, with Michelangelo. He took two trips to Germany in the retinue of Charles V. Titian's production after 1551 can be divided in two categories, the last awe-inspiring altarpieces in Venice and the mythological paintings, interpreted as tragic mirrors of the human condition.

COSIMO TURA
(Ferrara ca. 1430–1495)

Principal exponent of the Ferrara school, he led the city of the Este court into an absolutely original artistic season in which late Gothic experiences and the celebratory needs of the court were brought up to date with references to Flemish painting, Piero della Francesca, and Leon Battista Alberti. A stay in Padua during the 1450s put the young Tura in contact with the environment of Squarcione and Mantegna, then at the outset of his career. On his return to Ferrara Tura became the court painter of Ercole and Borso d'Este and never again left the city. His major works include the organ doors in the cathedral (1469; Museo del Duomo, Ferrara), the enormous Roverella Polyptych (1470–74; disassembled and held in various museums in Italy and elsewhere), and the late, dramatic *St. Anthony of Padua* (Galleria Estense, Modena). Tura was also director of the decorative works in the various Este residences, including the frescoes in the Salone dei Mesi in Palazzo Schifanoia.

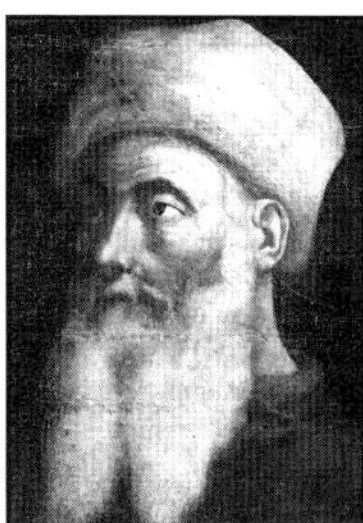

PAOLO UCCELLO
(Paolo di Dono)
(Florence 1397–1475)

Paolo Uccello belongs to the same generation as Masaccio and Fra Angelico, and like them he began his career during the 1420s in the Florentine artistic scene dominated by Gentile da Fabriano on one side and the new humanistic theories of Brunelleschi, Donatello, and Lorenzo Ghiberti on the other. In 1425, after his first works in Florence (frescoes in the Chiostro Verde of Santa Maria Novella), Paolo Uccello took an important trip to Venice, including visits to both Padua and Bologna. On his return to Florence he became one of the leading painters in the city. In 1436 he made the commemorative fresco of *Sir John Hawkwood* in Santa Maria del Fiore; his other works in the cathedral include the frescoes around the clock and cartoons for the stained-glass windows. His most famous work is the decoration of a room in Palazzo Medici with three panels presenting the *Battle of San Romano*, today divided among the Uffizi, the Louvre, and the National Gallery in London. In 1465 Paolo Uccello was working for Federico da Montefeltro in Urbino, and it was there that he made the *Stories of the Profanation of the Host*, the predella to the large altarpiece by Justus of Ghent.

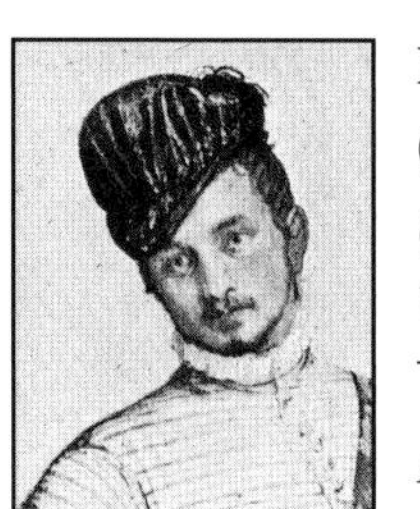

PAOLO VERONESE
(Paolo Caliari)
(Verona 1528–Venice 1588)

After completing his apprenticeship in his birthplace, Veronese took part in various team efforts, and with such success that in 1553 he was working in the Doge's Palace in Venice (Sala del Consiglio dei Dieci). From then on Veronese became one of the principal "public" painters in Venice. His large-scale paintings, laid out in accordance with classical symmetry using bright, dazzling colors, won him prestigious patrons. It was during this period of his career that he worked with Andrea Palladio on the masterpiece of the Villa Barbaro in Maser. Throughout the 1570s he made an uninterrupted series of sparkling paintings for the churches of Venice. Being called before the Inquisition to explain his *Supper in the House of Levi* (1573; Gallerie dell'Accademia, Venice) seems to have put a brake on his creative exuberance. His religious paintings became more reflective, leading to the intimist effects of his last years. At the same time, however, his participation in state works increased, in particular the reconstruction and decoration of the Doge's Palace.

Biographies

ANDREA DEL VERROCCHIO
(Andrea di Francesco di Cione)
(Florence 1435–Venice 1488)

Andrea del Verrocchio—goldsmith, painter, sculptor, expert architect when necessary, armor maker, and furniture decorator—is a prime example of the multi-talented artists of the fifteenth century. The students in his large workshop in Florence, including Leonardo and Perugino, were made to learn a wide variety of arts, manual techniques, and styles, so that they obtained incomparable levels of mastery. Despite his important activity as a painter, Andrea del Verrocchio is best known today as a sculptor, beginning with the Medici tomb in porphyry and bronze in the Sagrestia Vecchia of San Lorenzo in Florence. The elegant works he made in marble and bronze include portraits and statues for fountains; he took part in the execution of the altar in San Giovanni in silver (Museo dell'Opera del Duomo, Florence) and even made large-scale groups, such as the *Incredulity of St. Thomas* for Orsanmichele (1483) and the famous equestrian monument of Bartolomeo Colleoni, which stands in front of the church of Saints Giovanni e Paolo in Venice (1488).

PETER VISCHER THE ELDER
(Nuremberg ca. 1460–1529)

Founder of a famous family of sixteenth-century artists, Vischer was the greatest bronze sculptor of the High Renaissance in Germany. He carried on a profitable reciprocal dialogue with his fellow citizen Albrecht Dürer, sharing at least in part his stylistic evolution and also certain aspects of his career, such as serving Maximilian I, which Vischer did in 1513 (he designed some of the spectacular bronze statues that crown the emperor's tomb in the Hofkirche of Innsbruck). Vischer began within the Gothic artisan tradition of artists, but thanks to contact with the Italian artistic culture he progressively assumed an "intellectual" awareness of his activity, which was crowned by his overall masterpiece, the tomb-reliquary in St. Sebaldus, Nuremberg, completed in 1519.

ALVISE VIVARINI
(Venice 1442/53–1503/05)

Son of Antonio and for a long time collaborator of his uncle Bartolomeo, Alvise saw the need to renew the family tradition through a more attentive consideration of the novelties proposed by Giovanni Bellini and Antonello da Messina. The graphic clarity and steady illumination of works from the Vivarini workshop were thus joined by a monumental vision and perspective to form a unitary concept of space. The success of Alvise's cultural operation is proved by the numerous Bellini-style Madonnas and altarpieces he made in Venice, aside from the interesting male portraits that reveal his great admiration for Antonello.

ANTONIO VIVARINI
(Murano ca. 1418–1476/84)

Head of a family of artists of fundamental importance to the passage from the late Gothic to the Renaissance, Antonio Vivarini is best known for enormous, highly ornate polyptychs in flamboyant gilt frames, often made together with his brother-in-law, the German painter known as Giovanni d'Alemagna, and with the collaboration of highly skilled woodworking masters. Having been trained in a tradition still tied to Byzantine models but open to the fabulous decoration typical of the late Gothic, Antonio opened an independent workshop in Venice in the 1440s, immediately obtaining important commissions. The Vivarinis' Murano school competed with that of the Bellini family but also was in dialogue with it, and the Vivarinis' fame soon extended beyond the borders of the Veneto region to take on new competitors. In 1447 Antonio and Giovanni d'Alemagna enrolled together in Padua's guild of painters; the two then undertook the decoration of the Ovetari Chapel in the Eremitani, left unfinished when Giovanni d'Alemagna died (1450) and later finished by Mantegna at the beginning of his career. Antonio seems to have withdrawn from the scene in the 1460s, giving way to his brother Bartolomeo and, later, his son Alvise.

BARTOLOMEO VIVARINI
(Murano ca. 1430–after 1491)

Younger brother of Antonio, Bartolomeo spent a long time working in the family workshop. During the 1460s, as Antonio gradually withdrew from the scene, Antonio was able to display his own style, composed of static, statuesque poses, clear colors, and graphic outlines of impeccable purity. He made a long series of altarpieces and polyptychs for Venetian churches. With the affirmation of Giovanni Bellini at the height of Venetian painting (1483) the style of Bartolomeo Vivarini appeared suddenly old. He found new success working in the provinces, and he painted many works for Bergamo and the Venetian mainland.

ADRIAEN DE VRIES
(The Hague ca. 1546– Prague 1626)

An exemplary mannerist sculptor, De Vries took the art of monumental bronzes to the extreme heights of refinement and elegance. A student of Giambologna in Florence, he enjoyed a constantly successful career, with prestigious commissions from ambitious cities and refined noble courts, from Turin to Scandinavia, from Bavaria to Prague. The "civic" series of three great fountains along the main street of Augsburg (ca. 1590), with mythological figures in which the spiraling line triumphs, are majestic works masterfully presented. His period of service with the emperor in Prague was particularly long and also full of important work. He was made portraitist to Rudolf II and offered a sophisticated sculptural version of the long, tapering, sensual forms preferred by the court taste.

ROGIER VAN DER WEYDEN
(Tournai ca. 1399–Brussels 1464)

This artist, whose original name was Rogier de la Pasture, was born in Tournai and got his early training in that city in the flourishing workshop of Robert Campin, becoming an independent master only in 1432. In 1435 he moved to Brussels, where he was appointed official painter to the city. His style took as starting points those of the two most illustrious painters of the time, Jan van Eyck and Robert Campin. Of the first he admired the extraordinary technique and the analytical rendering of detail; of the second he took the sense of three-dimensional volumes and space. The artist reworked these models by way of his dynamic language, and his realism acquired a human and deeply felt tone, capable of transmitting a vast range of sentiments, measured within the limits of a composed dignity. The trip he made to Rome for the 1450 Jubilee, with stops in Milan, Ferrara, and Florence, is famous for its profound consequences on the development of Italian art.

KONRAD WITZ

(Rottweil ca. 1400–Geneva or Basel ca. 1445/46)

Konrad Witz, one of the great innovators in northern European painting, sharply distanced himself from the languid tones and the lyricism of the preceding generation of German painters. Originally from a small town in Swabia, in 1434 he became a member of the painters' guild of Basel and the next year he was given citizenship. In that city's cosmopolitan climate, site of the council called to heal the schism in Catholicism, Witz affirmed his original personality, supported by a vigorous talent and by an earthy vision of reality. Although influenced by the works of his Flemish contemporaries, his figures have a powerful corporeal reality that reveals knowledge of Burgundian sculpture in general and Claus Sluter in particular.

FERNANDO YÁÑEZ

(Fernando Yáñez de la Almedina)
(known from 1506 to 1531)

This Castilian artist collaborated with Fernando Llanos on the retable of *Saints Cosmas and Damian* in the cathedral of Valencia (of which only the predella with the *Pietà*, attributed to Yáñez, remains) and on the wings of the retable of the main altar with scenes from the *Life of the Virgin*. The coherence of the spatial layout and the monumental balance of these works suggests assimilation of the Italian Renaissance, most of all the works of Leonardo da Vinci, whom the artist must have met during a stay in Italy early in the sixteenth century. Yáñez's production is difficult to distinguish from that of Llanos, both of them sharing the influence of Leonardo; even so, the hand of Yáñez is recognizable for its greater sense of monumentality and balance, with massive architecture or imposing ruins in the backgrounds of scenes full of figures delineated with exquisite skill. He left Valencia in 1515 and was active until 1531, first in Barcelona and then in Cuenca, where he made several works for the local cathedral.

Biographies

Bibliography

The Renaissance has been the subject of a vast number of books over a period of nearly five hundred years. Most of the following books are recent publications that should be easy to find in a library or bookstore; also included are some of the books referred to in this text.

Benzi, Fabio and Caroline Vincenti Montanaro. *Palaces of Rome*. New York: Rizzoli International Publications, 1997.

Bologna, Giulia. *Illuminated Manuscripts*. New York: Weidenfeld & Nicolson, 1988.

Brown, Patricia Fortini. *The Renaissance in Venice*. London: Weidenfeld & Nicholson, 1997.

Camusso, Lorenzo. *Travel Guide to Europe 1492*. New York: Henry Holt, 1992.

Cardini, Franco. *Europe 1492*. New York: Facts On File, 1989.

Chastel, André. *The Sack of Rome, 1527*. Trans. by Beth Archer. Princeton, N.J.: Princeton University Press, 1983.

Franklin, David. *Painting in Renaissance Florence, 1500–1550*. New Haven: Yale University Press, 2002.

Goffen, Rona. *Giovanni Bellini*. New Haven: Yale University Press, 1989.

Goffen, Rona. *Renaissance Rivals: Michelangelo, Leonardo, Raphael, Titian*. New Haven: Yale University Press, 2002.

Gombrich, Ernst Hans. *The Heritage of Apelles: Studies in the Art of the Renaissance*. Ithaca, N.Y.: Cornell University Press, 1976.

Gombrich, Ernst Hans. *The Story of Art*. London: Phaidon Press, 1995.

Hale, John. *The Civilization of Europe in the Renaissance*. New York: Simon and Schuster, 1995.

Hale, John, ed. *Encyclopedia of the Italian Renaissance*. London: Thames and Hudson, 1989.

Huizinga, J. *The Waning of the Middle Ages*. New York: St. Martin's Press, 1949.

Joannides, Paul. *Masaccio and Masolino: A Complete Catalogue*. New York: Harry N. Abrams, 1993.

Joannides, Paul. *Titian to 1518: The Assumption of Genius*. New Haven: Yale University Press, 2001.

Martineau, Jane; Boorsch, Suzanne; et al. *Andrea Mantegna*. New York: Metropolitan Museum of Art, 1992.

Panofsky, Erwin. *The Life and Art of Albrecht Dürer*. Princeton: Princeton University Press, 1955.

Partridge, Loren. *The Art of Renaissance Rome 1400–1600*. New York: Harry N. Abrams, 1996.

Pilliod, Elizabeth. *Pontormo, Bronzino, Allori: A Genealogy of Florentine Art*. New Haven: Yale University Press, 2001.

Rasmo, Nicolò. *Michael Pacher*. Trans by Philip Waley. London: Phaidon, 1971.

Rearick, William R. *The Art of Paolo Veronese, 1528–1588*. Washington, D.C.: National Gallery of Art, 1988.

Richter, Irma A. *The Notebooks of Leonardo da Vinci*. Oxford, New York: Oxford University Press, 1952.

Rowlands, John. *The Age of Dürer and Holbein*. Cambridge, New York: Cambridge University Press, 1988.

Sgarbi, Vittorio. *Carpaccio*. New York: Abbeville Press, 1998.

Steer, John. *Venetian Painting*. London: Thames and Hudson, 1970.

Tempestini, Anchise. *Giovanni Bellini*. New York: Abbeville Press, 1999.

Vasari, Giorgio. *Lives of the Painters, Sculptors and Architects*. Trans. by Gaston du C. de Vere. New York: Alfred A. Knopf, 1996.

Welch, Evelyn. *Art and Society in Italy 1350–1500*. Oxford, New York: Oxford University Press, 1997.

Zeri, Federico and Elizabeth E. Gardner. *Italian Paintings, Florentine School: A Catalogue of the Collection of the Metropolitan Museum of Art*. New York: New York Graphic Society, 1971.

Zeri, Federico and Elizabeth E. Gardner. *Italian Paintings, Venetian School; A Catalogue of the Collection of the Metropolitan Museum of Art*. New York: New York Graphic Society, 1973.

Zuffi, Stefano, ed. *Art in Venice*. New York: Harry N. Abrams, 1999.

Numbers in *italic* refer to captions

Aachen 455
Aachen, Hans von 363, *377,* 441, 456, 469
Acqui 445
Adrian VI 312, *314,* 326, *329,* 469
Aertsen, Pieter 327, *344, 388,* 441, 445
Afonso, Jorge 441
Agostino di Duccio 441
Aix Annunciation, Master of the 90, *92,* 441
Alberti, Leon Battista 16, 45, 47, 61, *193,* 442, 457, 463, 470
Albertinelli, Mariotto 443
Albert of Brandenburg 219, 455
Albert of Saxony *221,* 237
Alexander VI 189, *223,* 254, 464
Alfonso V of Aragon, *109,* 456
Alkmaar 470
Allegri, Antonio 348, 449
Allori, Alessandro *418*
Altdorfer, Albrecht 22, 218, 219, *228, 229, 442,* 447
Altdorfer, Ulrich 442
Amboise 362, 457
Ammanati, Bartolomeo 411, *418, 419,* 442
Amsterdam 441, 458, 467
Ancona 460
André d'Ypres. *See* Dreux-Budé Master of
Andrea d'Agnolo. *See* Sarto, Andrea del
Andrea Pisano *48*
Angelico, Fra 45, *45, 58,* 61, 77, 122, *171, 173, 184,* 188, *192,* 442, 452, 455, 465, 470
Angers 459
Anne of Beaujeu *130*
Antonello da Messina 61, 90, 91, *96, 97, 98,* 188, 201, 442, 443, 444, 448, 471
Antwerp 20, 60, 91, 153, 219, 326, 327, *329, 332, 336, 345, 393, 428,* 441, 446, 451, 454, 458, 460, 461, 463, 467, 468, 469, 470
Apuleius, Lucius *351*
Arcimboldo, Giuseppe 363, *375,* 443, 469
Aretino, Pietro 294, *306*
Arezzo 122, *124,* 463, 468
Ariosto, Ludovico *111, 260,* 450
Aristotle *261*
Arles 465
Arnhem 459
Arnolfini family 168
Arnolfo di Cambio 44, *46*
Aschaffenburg 455
Athens *51*
Augsburg 20, 218, 236, 294, 295, 380, 447, 472
Avalos, Iñigo de *109*

Averulino, Antonio 188
Avicenna *36*
Avignon 28, 90, 93, 122, 188, 190, 452, 456, 459, 465
Ávila *101,* 445

Baço, Jaime. *See* Jacomart
Baden-Baden 453
Baerze, Jacques de *40*
Baglione, Giovanni, *383*
Baldung, Hans 219, *219, 234,* 235, 443
Bamberg 139, *146,* 466, 469
Bandini, Giovanni *418*
Barbari, Jacopo de' *210, 396*
Barbaro family 394
Barcelona *102,* 445, 451, 456, 472
Barocci, Federico 381, *391, 392, 393,* 424, 443
Barozzi, Jacopo. *See* Vignola, Jacopo
Bartolommeo, Fra 443
Basel 20, 76, 77, *86,* 219, 455, 472
Bassano, Jacopo 294, 395, *415,* 443, 455
Bataille, Nicolas *34*
Beaune 446
Beccafumi, Domenico 444
Belbello da Pavia *36*
Bellini, Gentile 201, *204, 214,* 444
Bellini, Giovanni 91, *97,* 200, 201, *206, 207, 208, 209, 214,* 219, 273, 293, *300,* 395, 443, 444, 450, 454, 459, 471
Bellini, Jacopo 105, 444
Bellini, Nicolosia 444, 459
Bembo, Pietro 294
Benci, Piero 465
Benecke, Paul *162*
Bergamo 200, 346, 444, 458, 461, 467, 471
Bergognone, Ambrogio 444
Berlin 449, 457
Bermejo, Bartolomé 90, *102,* 444, 445
Bernardino di Betto. *See* Pinturicchio
Bernat, Martin 444
Bernini, Gianlorenzo *191, 374,* 425
Bernard of Gordon *36*
Berruguete, Pedro 90, *91, 100, 101,* 105, 122, *159,* 445, 457
Bertram, Master *28,* 445
Bertram von Minden. *See* Bertram, Master
Beuckelaer, Joachim 327, *388,* 441, 445
Bilhères, Jean de *256,* 272, 276
Boiardo, Matteo Maria *111*
Bologna 273, 275, 349, *389,* 424, *426,* 441, 449, 450, 453, 462, 463, 469
Bolzano 123
Bomarzo 411, *423*
Bontemps, Pierre *362*
Bonvicino, Alessandro. *See* Moretto da Brescia

Bora, Katharina von 237, 450
Bordone, Paris 294
Borromeo, Carlo 380
Borromeo, Federico *431*
Bosch, Hieronymus 21, 236, *238, 239, 240, 241, 242, 243, 244, 245,* 292, 326, 327, *333,* 445, 463
Boschini, Marco 399
Botticelli, Sandro 20, 168, 169, *174, 175, 176, 178, 179, 181,* 189, *194, 195,* 272, 274, 275, 445, 453, 458, 463
Boulogne, Valentin de 430
Bourges 126
Bouts, Dieric *84,* 153, 445, 446
Bramante, Donato *17,* 105, 189, *190, 191, 198, 199,* 254, 255, *261, 324, 331,* 444, 446
Bramantino 254, 347, 446
Brancacci, Felice *54*
Branda da Castiglione 188, 460
Brandt, Isabelle 467
Brandt, Sebastian 236, *238*
Breisach *150*
Brera 274, 444
Brescia 200, 347, 348, 452, 461, 466, 467
Bressanone 123, *134*
Bril, Paul *383*
Brno 464
Broederlam, Melchior *40*
Bronzino, Agnolo 363, *364, 365,* 446
Bruegel, Jan 446
Bruegel, Pieter the Younger 446
Bruegel, Pieter the Elder 236, 326, 327, *327, 336, 338, 339, 340, 341, 342, 343,* 441, 446, 447
Bruges 17, 20, 26, 60, 152, 153, *154, 156, 160, 161, 162,* 326, 448, 449, 452, 460, 463
Brunelleschi, Filippo 44, *44, 45, 46, 47, 48, 49, 52, 53, 57, 85, 290,* 447, 453, 470
Brunico 122, 462
Brussels 60, 61, 152, 153, 251, 327, 446, 470
Budapest 218
Buon family, *39*
Buontalenti, Bernardo *410,* 411, 419, *422*
Burgkmair, Hans 218, *235,* 447
Buti, Lucrezia 458
Buti, Margherita *281*

Cabral, Pedro Alvares 18, 91
Caliari, Paolo. *See* Veronese, Paolo
Campi, Vincenzo *388, 389*
Campin, Robert 61, *62, 63, 70, 73, 155,* 447, 448, 458, 472
Cangrande I Della Scala *37*
Capra, Almerico 462

Caprarola *384*, 411

Caravaggio, Michelangelo Merisi da 23, *271*, 348, *389*, *417*, 425, *425*, 429, *430*, *431*, *432*, *433*, 447, 448, 451, 467, 468

Caron, Antoine *371*, 447

Carpaccio, Vittore 201, *201*, *212*, *213*, 447, 448

Carracci, Annibale *417*, 424, *424*, *426*, 448, 451

Carracci, Ludovico 424, 448

Carracci family 381, *389*, 424, 443

Carucci, Jacopo. *See* Pontormo, Jacopo da

Casimir IV Jagellon 139, 469

Castagno, Andrea del *184*, 448, 450

Castiglione, Baldassare 255

Castiglione Olona 460

Cavaliere d'Arpino *325*, 425

Cavalori, Mirabello *418*

Cellini, Benvenuto 362, *366*, 448, 455

Celtis, Conrad 218

Cervantes Saavedra, Miguel de 410

Cesari, Giuseppe. *See* Cavaliere d'Arpino

Cézanne, Paul 466

Champmol, charterhouse of *40, 41*

Charlemagne *76*

Charles the Bold *61, 69*, 152

Charles VII of France *126*, 452

Charles VIII of France *117*, 168

Charles IX of France 449

Charles IV (Holy Roman Emperor) *32 33*, 445

Charles V (Holy Roman Emperor) 21, 22, 23, 219, *233*, 236, 275, 293, 294, 312, 380, 410, *412*, 455, 456, 470

Charonton, Enguerrand. See Quarton, Enguerrand

Chevalier, Etienne *128*, 452

Chigi, Agostino *255, 268*

Christina of Denmark, *251, 253*

Christus, Petrus *154, 155, 328*, 442, 448, 460

Cima da Conegliano 448, 449

Cimabue 16, 381

Città di Castello 273, 468

Clement VII 255, *270*, 275, *289*, 312, 313, *314, 315*, 349, 463

Clesio, Bernardino 348

Cleve, Joos van 449

Cleves, Anne of *253*

Clouet, François 362, *369, 370, 371*, 449

Clouet, Jean 21, *449*

Coducci. *See* Codussi

Codussi, Mauro *200*, 201, 202

Coeur, Jacques *126*

Colantonio, Niccolò *90*, 91, 456

Colmar 20, 122, 447, 468

Cologne 29, 76, 77, 152, *161*, 457, 458, 459, 460, 467, 468

Como 442

Columbus, Christopher 18, 21, 168

Condivi, Ascanio 254

Conrad von Soest *81*, 467

Contarel, Mathieu 432

Cornaro, Caterina 200

Cornelisz van Haarlem 454

Correggio *119*, 346, *347*, 348, 349, *356, 357, 376*, 381, 424, 443, 448, 449, 459, 463, 465, 467, 469

Cortona 58, 460, 468

Cossa, Francesco del 105, *110*, 449

Costa, Lorenzo 348

Constantinople 200, *214*, 444

Constance 76, 188, 453, 458

Cousin, Jean *372*

Cracow 139, *144*, 468

Cranach, Lucas 22, 218, 219, *231*, 232, *233, 236*, 237, 449, 450, 455

Creglingen-am-Tauber 139, *148*, 466

Cremona 347, 465, 466

Crete 200, 455

Crivelli, Carlo 105, 450

Cronaca, il. *See* Pollaiuolo, Simone del

Cuenca 474

Cyprus 200, 394

Damaskinos, Michele 455

Daniele da Volterra *322*, 381

Dante Alighieri 17, 23, *37*, 165

Danzig. *See* Gdansk

Daret, Jacques 447

David, Gerard 26, *132*, 153, *153, 164, 165, 166*, 446, 450, 463

Delft 327

Della Casa, Giovanni *308*

Della Gatta, Bartolomeo 195

Della Rovere, Giuliano. *See* Julius II

Della Rovere family 293, 446, 469

Del Monte, Antonio *431*, 432

De' Rossi, Francesco. *See* Salviati, Francesco

De' Rossi, Vincenzo *418*

Desiderio da Settignano *52*

Desplà, Lluis *102*, 445

Dijon *25, 41*, 447, 457

Dinteville, Jean de *252*

Dolce, Ludovico 292, *303, 304*

Domenico di Bartolomeo. *See* Domenico Veneziano

Domenico Veneziano 122, 450, 457, 463

Donatello 44, 45, *50, 51, 53*, 104, 122, 123, *134*, 168, *168, 182*, 200, 272, 447, 450, 459, 462, 466, 470

Dortmund *81*, 459

Dossi, Dosso, 293, 348, 450, 451

Dresden 442

Dreux-Budé, Master of *127*

Dubroeucq, Jacques 453

Dürer, Albrecht *8-9*, 20, *20*, 76, 123, 139, 150, 201, 208, 218, *218*, 219, *219, 220, 221, 222, 223, 224, 225, 226, 227*, 237, 273, 275, 293, 326, *333*, 347, 358, 443, 445, 447, 449, 451, 455, 458, 459, 460, 463, 467, 468, 469, 471

Edward the Confessor *30*

Eleonora of Toledo 363, *365*

Elizabeth I of England, *379*, 410

Elsheimer, Adam *435*, 451

Empoli 275, 460

Engebrechtsz, Cornelis 458

Erasmus *150*, 236, *237*, 460

Erfurt 466

Este, Alfonso d' 293, *300, 301*, 348, 450, 470

Este, Borso d' 469

Este, Ercole d' 105, 469

Este, Isabella d' *120*, 348

Este, Lionello d' 105

Este family 105, *110*, 293, 451

Eyck, Barthélemy d' 90, *90, 92*, 441

Eyck, Hubert van *2-3, 64, 65*, 90, 441, 451

Eyck, Jan van *2–3, 16, 41, 43*, 60, 61, *62, 63, 64, 65, 66, 67, 68, 69, 73, 74*, 90, *98, 129*, 153, *155, 157*, 168, 441, 445, 448, 451, 452, 458, 472

Fabriano 42

Farnese, Alessandro 294

Farnese family *384*, 469

Ferdinand II of Spain 19, 90, 410

Fernández, Pedro 451

Ferrara 61, 104, 105, *109, 110, 111*, 122, 293, *300, 301*, 348, 449, 450, 451, 463, 465, 469, 470

Ferrari, Gaudenzio 346, 347, *358*, 451, 452, 459

Ficino, Marsilio *175*

Filarete. *See* Averulino Antonio

Flémalle, Master of. *See* Campin, Robert

Florence 17, 19, 20, 23, *43*, 44, 45, *50, 51, 53, 57*, 61, 104, 122, *156, 162*, 168, 169, *170, 179, 182*, 189, 254, 255, *256*, 272, 273, 274, 275, *278, 282, 290*, 294, 313, 362, 411, *420*, 441, 442, 443, 444, 445, 446, 447, 448, 450, 451, 452, 453, 454, 455, 456, 457, 461, 463, 464, 465, 467, 468, 469, 470, 471, 472

Fontainebleau 22, 275, 313, 362, *368, 370, 371*, 447, 448, 450, 464, 465, 467, 468

Fontana, Domenico *191, 383*

Foppa, Vincenzo, 105, 444, 452

Forlì 460

Fornovo *117*

Fouquet, Jean 122, *128, 129*, 188, 452, 461

Fouquier, Jacques *411*

Francesco di Giorgio Martini *104, 105, 112*, 452, 460

Francis I of France 20, 22, 275, 313, 362, *366, 368, 418*, 448, 449, 454, 455, 457, 459, 464, 465, 467

Francke, Master *76*

Frankfurt 455

Frankfurt Garden of Paradise, Master of the *78*

Frankenhausen 237

Frederick of Saxony 449

Frederick III (Holy Roman Emperor) 453

Frederick the Wise 237

Freiburg 443

Froment, Nicolas *93*, 452

Fugger, Jacob *223*, 236

Fugger family 295, 447

Gabrielle d'Estrées *371*

Galen 36

Galileo *434*

Gama, Vasco da 18, 91

Gdansk 152, *162*

Geertgen tot Sint Jans 153, *167*, 452

Gemmingen, Uriel von 455

Genoa 312, *317*, 467, 469

Gentile da Fabriano *42, 43*, 45, *170*, 188, 450, 453, 464, 470

Gentileschi, Orazio *383*

Gerhaert, Nicolaus *85*, 453

Gerona 451

Ghent 21, 60, 61, 152, 153, 326, 452

Ghiberti, Lorenzo *44, 45, 45*, 48, *49, 53*, 442, 453, 455, 460, 466, 470

Ghirlandaio, Domenico 19, 168, *179, 181, 183, 184*, 189, 453

Giambologna 411, *419, 422*, 453, 471

Giorgione 201, *216, 217*, 273, 292, *296, 298, 305*, 312, 348, 444, 449, 451, 454, 469, 470

Giotto 16, 17, 23, 28, 44, 45, 381

Giovannetti, Matteo 28

Giovanni da Fiesole. *See* Fra Angelico

Giovanni d'Alemagna 471

Giovanni dalle Bande Nere 275

Giovanni da Udine 316

Giuliano da Maiano *52, 114*

Giulio Romano *267*, 294, 312, *316, 317*, 348, 349, *350, 351, 368*, 411, 454, 465

Goering, Hermann *162*

Goes, Hugo van der *131, 132*, 153, *156, 157, 158*, 168, 452, 454, 457, 467

Goethe, Johann Wolfgang *80*

Goltzius, Hendrick 454

Gonçalves, Nuño *99*, 123

Góngora, Luis de 410

Gonzaga, Cecilia *109*

Gonzaga, Federico 348, 454
Gonzaga, Federico II 312, *350*
Gonzaga, Isabella 449, 454
Gonzaga family 105, *117, 118,* 293, 294,
348, *350, 351,* 441, 449, 454, 459, 469
Gorizia 218
Gossart, Jan 20, 219, *326,* 326, *329,* 454,
459, 470
Goujon, Jean 362, *374,* 454, 455
Goya y Lucientes, Francisco 293, *307,* 414
Gozzoli, Benozzo *170, 171, 192,* 442, 455
Granada 410
Greco, El *10–11, 22,* 395, 410, *414, 415,
416, 417,* 455
Gregory XI 1990
Grimani, Domenico 26
Gritti, Andrea 293, 294, *307,* 313, 467
Grünewald, Matthis 20, 21, 123, 219, 236,
237, *237,* 246, 247, *248, 249,* 443, 455
Guerra, Giovanni *383*
Guido di Pietro. *See* Fra Angelico

Haarlem 153, 449, 452, 454, 470
Halle 455
Hamburg 445
Hapsburg 458
Heemskerck, Maarten van 327, *334, 335,*
455, 470
Heidelberg 411
Heintz, Joseph the Elder 363, 455, 456, 469
Hennequin de Bruges *34*
Henry II of France 449, 459, 464, 465, 466
Henry IV of France 23, 411
Henry VIII of England 20, 237, *251, 253,*
456
Herrera, Juan de *411, 413,* 456
Hey, Jean 461
Hilliard, Nicholas *379*
Hippocrates *36*
Hohenfurth, Master of *33*
Holbein, Ambrosius 456
Holbein, Hans the Younger 20, *21,* 237, *237,
250,* 251, *252, 253,* 455, 456, 460, 461,
467
Holbein, Hans the Elder 455, 456
Holbein family 219, 346
Holl, Elias 456
Horace *260*
Huguet, Jaume 451, 456
Huizinga, J. *26*
Huss, John *33*

Ignatius of Loyola 380, 410
Innocent VIII *190,* 465
Innsbruck 123, 218, 441, 471
Isabella I of Spain 90, 456, 457
Isenheim 123, 236, *249,* 443

Jacobus da Varagine *241*
Jacomart 90, 456
Jacopo della Quercia *48,* 456, 462
Jamnitzer, Wenzel *363*
Jean de Boulogne. *See* Giambologna
John VIII Palaeologus *108*
John of Holland 451
Jordaens, Jacob *345*
Juan de Flandes 456, 457
Julius II 20, 189, *193, 199,* 254, 255, *258,
259, 260, 262, 266, 267,* 273, 446, 460,
461, 466
Justus of Ghent *100,* 105, 122, *159,* 445,
456, 457, 470

Karlstejn Castle *32*
Keldermans II, Rombout 327
Kleberger, Johann *226*
Kloster, Roode 470
Kraft, Adam 457

Lainate 411
Lama, Giovanni del *178*
Landauer, Matthäus *225*
Lanzi 448
Laurana, Francesco *104,* 457
Laurana, Luciano *112,* 457
Laureti, Tommaso *382*
Lausanne 466
La Vrana 456
Leiden 458
Leipzig 468
Leo X 236, 254, 255, *258, 267,* 275, 312,
314, 320, 326, 466
Leochares 254
Leonardo da Vinci 16, 19, *19,* 20, *53,* 61,
104, 105, *106, 121, 149,* 168, 169, *179,
180, 183, 186,* 201, 219, *229, 261, 271,*
272, 273, *273,* 274, *278, 284,* 326, 346,
349, *357, 358,* 362, 444, 445, 446, 447,
449, 451, 452, 454, 456, 457, 458, 459,
460, 461, 463, 464, 466, 467, 471, 472
Leoni, Leone *311, 410, 412*
Leoni, Pompeo *311, 412*
Leopardi, Alessandro *200*
Leuven. *See* Louvain
Lieferinxe, Josse *123*
Life of the Virgin, Master of the *84*
Ligorio, Pirrro *191,* 411
Lilli, Andrea (Giovanni) *383*
Limbourg, Pol, Hermann, Jean de *25, 26,
27,* 456, 457
Lippi, Filippino *54,* 168, 189, 272, *272,* 458,
464
Lippi, Filippo 45, 123, *134,* 168, 445, 458
Lisbon 123, 445, 461
Littemont, Jacob de 126

Llanos, Fernando 458, 472
Lochner, Stefan 76, 77, *77, 82, 83,* 152, 458
Lodi 168, 444
Lombardo, Antonio *203*
Lombardo, Pietro *202, 203*
Lombardo, Tullio *203*
London 20, 272, 455, 461, 467
Loredan, Leonardo *208*
Lorenzo di Credi 169
Lorenzo the Magnificent. *See* Medici,
Lorenzo di Piero de'
Loreto 458, 460
L'Orme, Philibert de, 362, *459,* 465
Lotto, Lorenzo 219, 254, 294, 346, 348,
349, 352, 353, 354, 355, 444, 456, 459,
461, 468
Louis I, duke of Anjou *34*
Louis XI of France *130,* 152, 452
Louis XII of France 274, 362
Louvain 60, 72, 153, 446, 461
Loyet, Gerard *61*
Lucas van Leyden 219, *219,* 326, *326, 333,*
451, 454, 459, 460, 467
Lucca 450, 452
Lucerne 455
Luciani, Sebastiano. *See* Sebastiano del
Piombo
Ludovico il Moro. *See* Sforza, Ludovico
Luini, Bernardino 459
Luther, Martin 20, 22, *150,* 219, *227,* 236,
237, 255, 443, 450

Mabuse. *See* Gossart, Jan
Macchietti, Girolamo *418*
Macchiavelli, Niccolò 272, 273
Maderno, Carlo *427*
Maderno, Stefano *425*
Madrid 445, 461, 467
Madruzzo family 461
Magellan, Ferdinand 18, 21, 91
Mainz 219, 237, 455, 460
Malouel, Jean *25,* 458
Malta 447
Mander, Karel van 454
Manet, Edouuard 296
Mantegna, Andrea *4-5, 18,* 105, *117, 118,
119, 120,* 122, 123, *134,* 200, 219, *301,
331,* 348, 349, *351, 357,* 444, 449, 459,
462, 465, 470, 471
Mantua 20, 104, 105, 169, 272, 294, *301,*
312, 348, 349, 441, 449, 451, 454, 456,
457, 459, 464, 465, 467
Manuel I of Portugal 91
Mary of Burgundy 138, 152
Marseilles 456
Martin V 188
Martini, Simone 28

Masaccio *43,* 45, *54, 55, 56, 57, 58,* 61, *65,
125,* 168, 188, 450, 459, 460, 470
Maschio Angioino *91*
Maser 394
Maso da San Friano *418*
Masolino *43,* 45, *54, 55, 56, 57,* 188, 450,
458, 460
Master H. L. *150*
Maximilian I (Holy Roman Emperor) 20,
138, 152, 218, 223, 236, 442, 447, 451,
471
Mazzola, Francesco. *See* Parmigianino
Medici, Caterina de' 447
Medici, Cosimo di Ferdinando de' (Cosimo II)
434
Medici, Cosimo di Giovanni de' *171, 178*
Medici, Cosimo di Giovanni de' (Cosimo I)
275, 363, *365,* 448, 453
Medici, Giovanni de' 254
Medici, Giulio. *See* Clement VII
Medici, Lorenzo di Pierfrancesco de' *175*
Medici, Lorenzo di Piero de' (Lorenzo the
Magnificent) 19, *156,* 168, *175,* 189,
236, 254, 272, 275, 445, 458, 461,
468
Medici, Piero de' 168
Medici family *156, 162, 170, 171, 176, 178,
286, 290*
Melanchthon, Philip *150,* 236, 237, 449
Melozzo da Forlì *100,* 188, *188, 193,* 460
Memling, Hans 26, *98, 132,* 152, *152,* 153,
153, 160, 161, 162, 163, 168, *339,* 442,
450, 460
Merisi, Michelangelo. *See* Caravaggio
Metsys, Quenten 20, 219, *236,* 292, 326,
328, 332, 451, 460, 463
Michelangelo Buonarroti 16, 20, 23, 44, 45,
51, 53, 123, 168, *173, 183,* 189, *194,
197,* 219, 254, 255, *256, 258, 259, 261,
262, 264, 265, 270, 271,* 272, 273, 274,
274, 275, *275, 276, 277, 279, 280, 282,
283, 289, 290, 291,* 293, 294, *304, 308,*
312, 313, *313, 314, 317, 319,* 321, 322,
324, 329, 362, 380, 381, 410, 411, *415,
422,* 425, *427,* 441, 444, 446, 453, 455,
456, 460, 461, 462, 465, 466, 467, 468,
469, 470
Michelozzo Michelozzi *59, 182,* 450
Mies, François de *86*
Milan 20, 29, 104, *121, 149,* 168, 169, *186,*
188, *199,* 272, 273, 274, *278,* 295, 326,
358, 362, 410, 411, *412,* 442, 443, 444,
446, 447, 451, 452, 456, 457, 460, 461,
468, 470
Modena 293, 441
Mons 453
Montefalco 454

Index of names and places

Photographic references

Archivio Electa, Milan
Photographic Archives of the Vatican
    Museums, Vatican City
Archivio Lessing/Contrasto, Milan
Artothek, Weilheim
Corbis/Grazia Neri, Milan
Diego Motto, Milan
© Photo RMN, Paris/C. Jean Gérard Blot;
    R. G. Ojeda
Arnaudet; J. Schormans; Hervé
    Lewandowski; Daniel Arnaudet
Scala Group, Antella, Florence
Sergio Anelli/Electa, Milan
The Bridgeman Art Library, London

The images furnished by the following
organizations appear courtesy of the Italian
Ministry of Monuments and
Fine Arts:
    Fine Arts Service of Mantua
    Fine Arts Service of Milan, Bergamo,
    Como, Lecco, Lodi, Pavia, Sondrio,
    Varese
    Fine Arts Service of Piedmont, Turin
    Special Service for the Polo Museale
    Veneziano, Venice

The editors regret any omissions and will
correct any improperly identified
photographs.

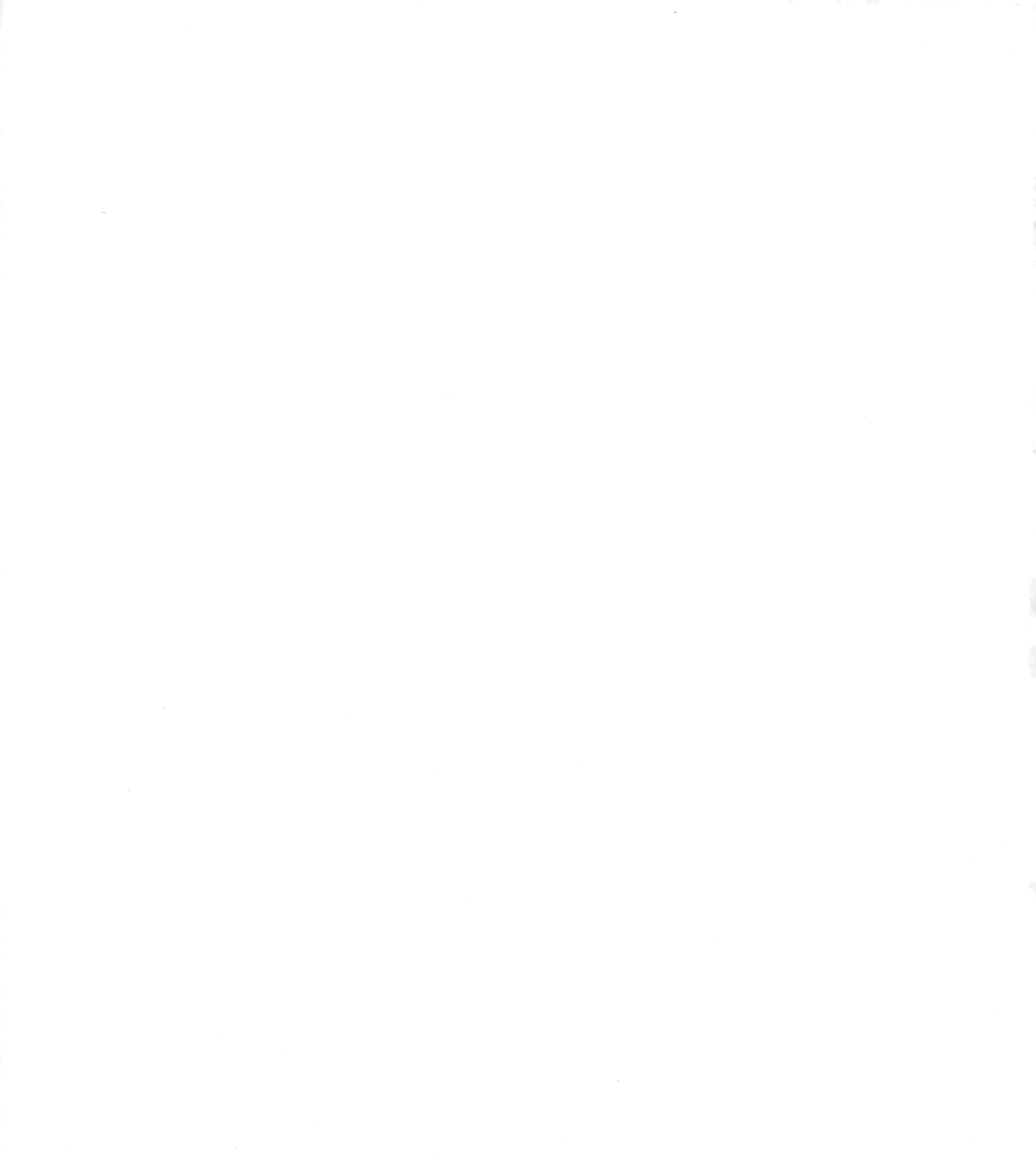